...Um... Yeah...
I can't think of anything to
write in the comments section
and that's why, right this
very moment, I'm going to just
scribble down the first thought
that comes to me while I sit here
at my desk staring outside...
*"These clouds are
pretty gray!!"*

岸本斉史

—Masashi Kishimoto, 2013

D1454931

Author/artist Masashi Kishimoto was born in 1974 in rural
Okayama Prefecture, Japan. After spending time in art college,
he won the Hop Step Award for new manga artists with his
manga **Karakuri** (Mechanism). Kishimoto decided to base his
next story on traditional Japanese culture. His first version of
Naruto, drawn in 1997, was a one-shot story about fox spirits;
his final version, which debuted in **Weekly Shonen Jump** in
1999, quickly became the most popular ninja manga in Japan.

NARUTO

3-in-1 Edition

Volume 22

SHONEN JUMP Manga Omnibus Edition

A compilation of the graphic novel volumes 64–66

STORY AND ART BY MASASHI KISHIMOTO

Translation/Mari Morimoto
Touch-up Art & Lettering/ John Hunt
Design/Sam Elzway (Original Series), Alice Lewis (Omnibus Edition)
Editor/Alexis Kirsch (Manga Edition)
Editor/Erica Yee (Omnibus Edition)

Printed in the U.S.A.

Published by VIZ Media, LLC
P.O. Box 77010
San Francisco, CA 94107

10 9 8 7 6 5 4 3 2
Omnibus edition first printing, April 2018
Second printing, April 2020

VIZ MEDIA
viz.com

ratings.viz.com

RATED T TEEN

PARENTAL ADVISORY
NARUTO is rated T for Teen and is recommended for ages 13 and up. This volume contains fantasy violence.

SHONEN JUMP
shonenjump.com

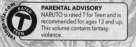

SHONEN JUMP MANGA EDITION

NARUTO

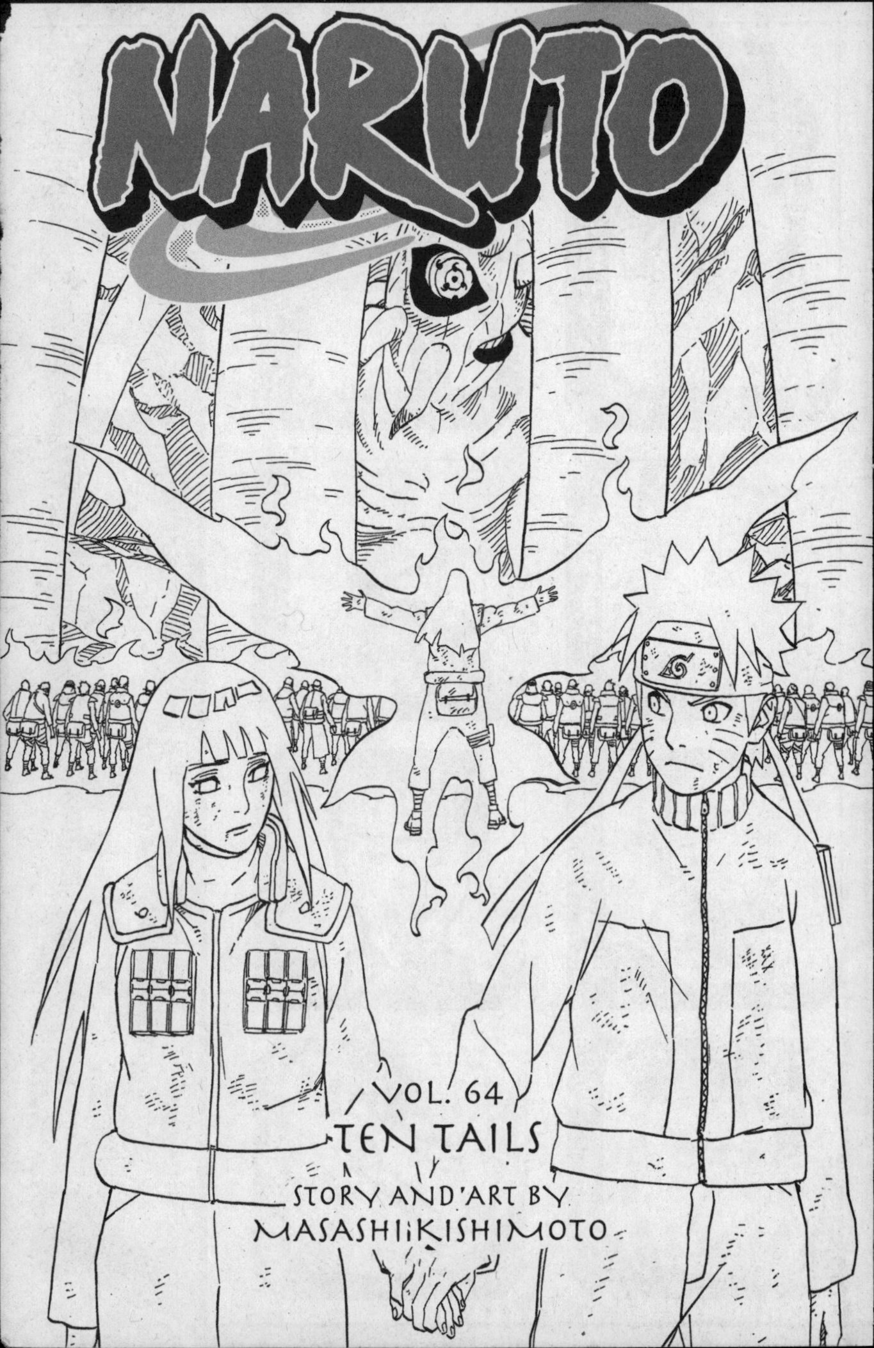

VOL. 64

TEN TAILS

STORY AND ART BY

MASASHI KISHIMOTO

CHARACTERS

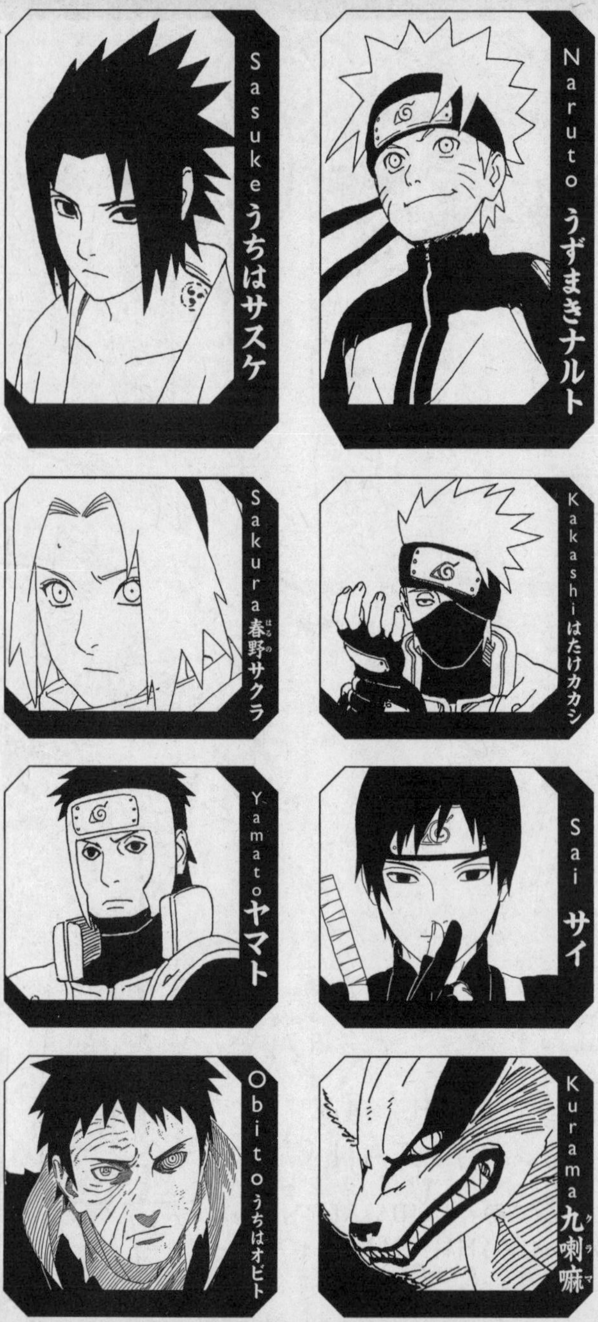
Naruto うずまきナルト
Sasuke うちはサスケ
Kakashi はたけカカシ
Sakura 春野サクラ
Sai サイ
Yamato ヤマト
Kurama 九喇嘛
Obito うちはオビト

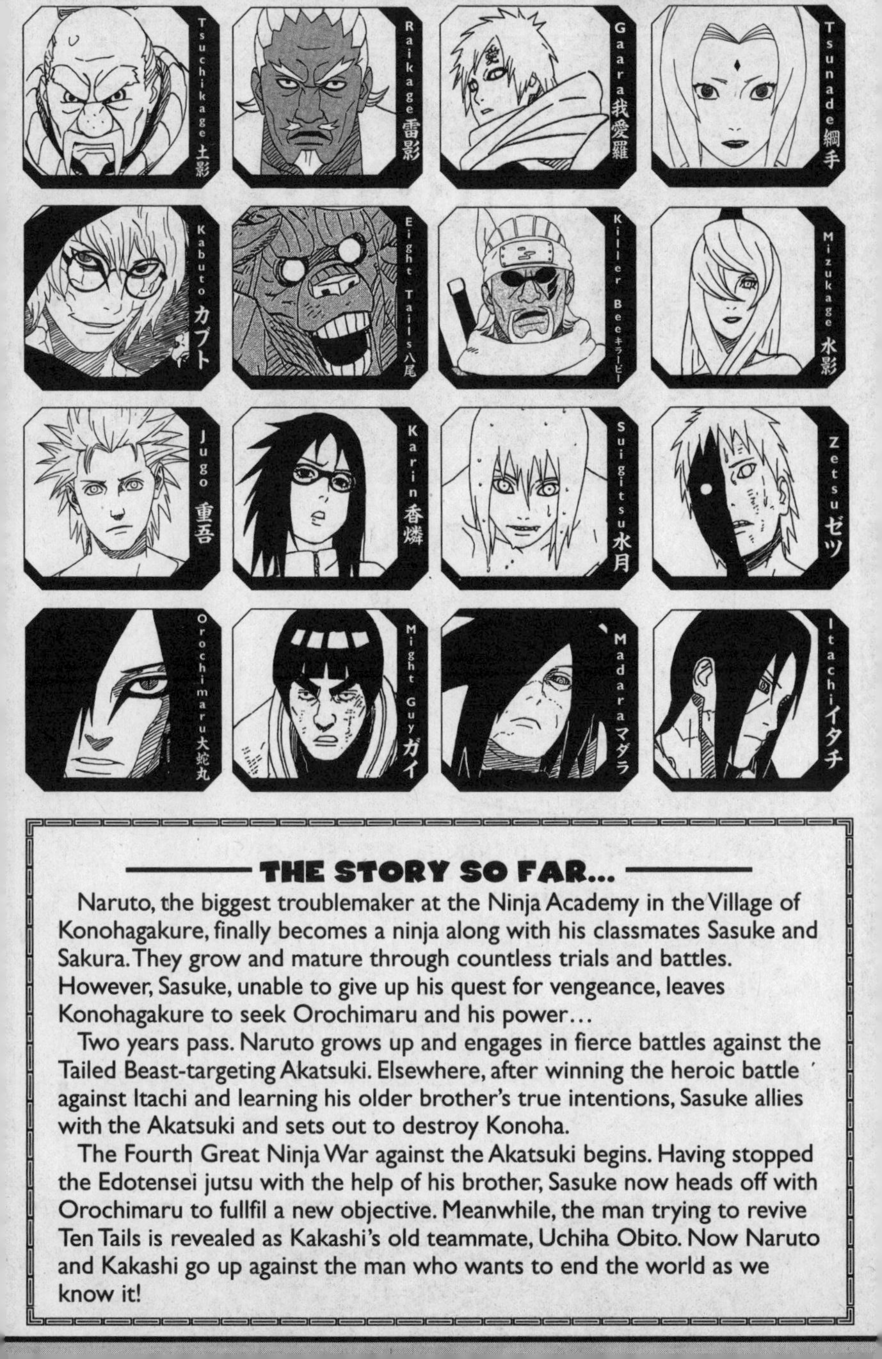
Tsunade 綱手
Gaara 我愛羅
Raikage 雷影
Tsuchikage 土影
Mizukage 水影
Killer Bee キラービー
Eight Tails 八尾
Kabuto カブト
Zetsu ゼツ
Suigitsu 水月
Karin 香燐
Jugo 重吾
Itachi イタチ
Madara マダラ
Might Guy ガイ
Orochimaru 大蛇丸

THE STORY SO FAR...

Naruto, the biggest troublemaker at the Ninja Academy in the Village of Konohagakure, finally becomes a ninja along with his classmates Sasuke and Sakura. They grow and mature through countless trials and battles. However, Sasuke, unable to give up his quest for vengeance, leaves Konohagakure to seek Orochimaru and his power…

Two years pass. Naruto grows up and engages in fierce battles against the Tailed Beast-targeting Akatsuki. Elsewhere, after winning the heroic battle against Itachi and learning his older brother's true intentions, Sasuke allies with the Akatsuki and sets out to destroy Konoha.

The Fourth Great Ninja War against the Akatsuki begins. Having stopped the Edotensei jutsu with the help of his brother, Sasuke now heads off with Orochimaru to fullfil a new objective. Meanwhile, the man trying to revive Ten Tails is revealed as Kakashi's old teammate, Uchiha Obito. Now Naruto and Kakashi go up against the man who wants to end the world as we know it!

NARUTO

VOL. 64
TEN TAILS

CONTENTS

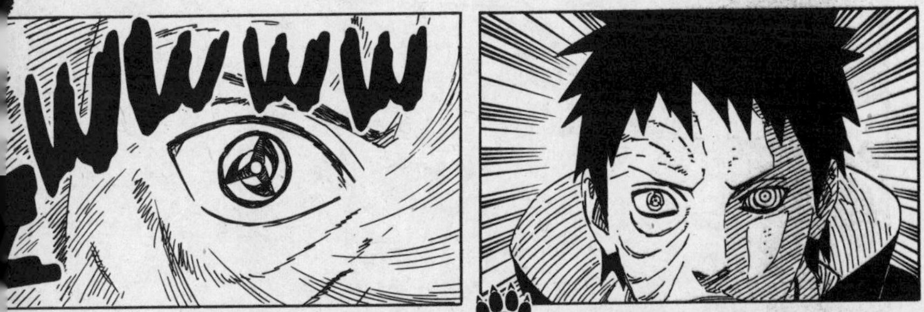

Number 608: Kakashi's Resolve

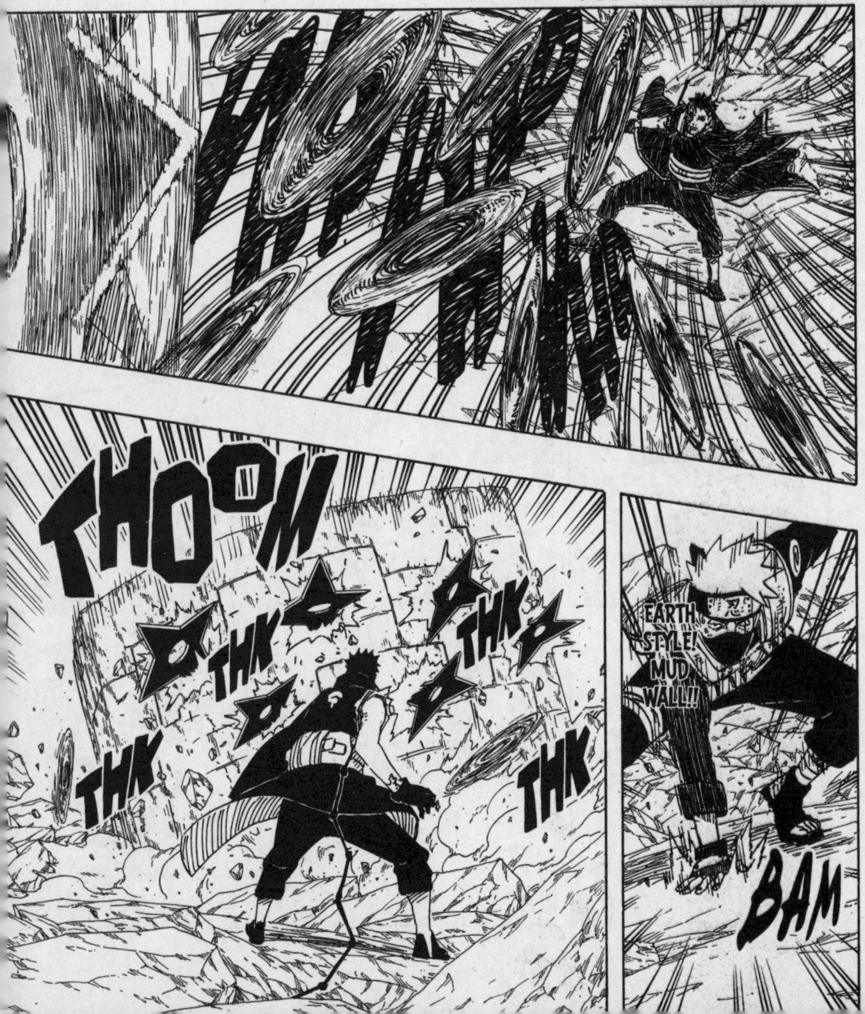
EARTH STYLE! MUD WALL!!
BAM
THOOM
THK
THK
THK
THK
THK

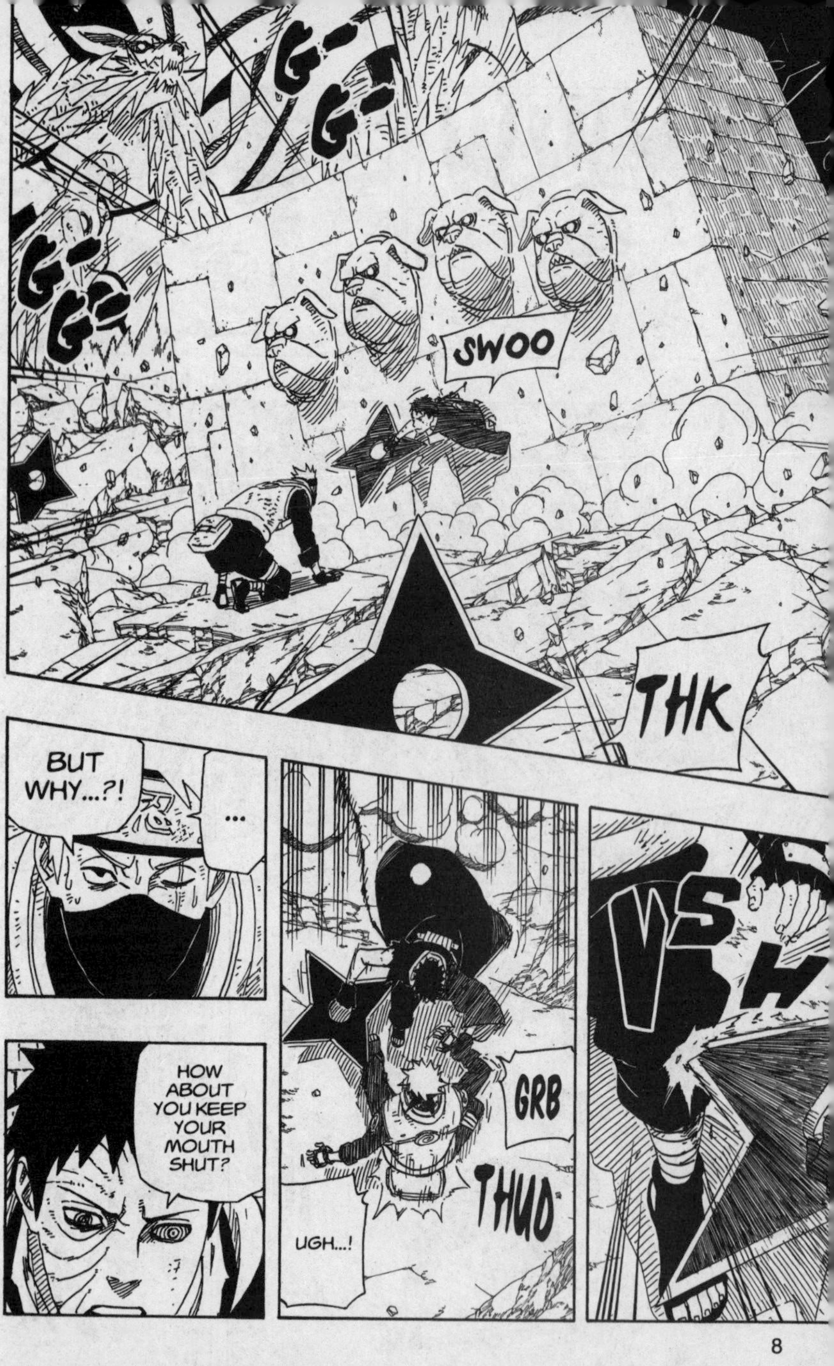

G-G-G
SWOO
G-G-G
THK
VSH
GRB
THUD
UGH...!
BUT WHY...?!
...
HOW ABOUT YOU KEEP YOUR MOUTH SHUT?

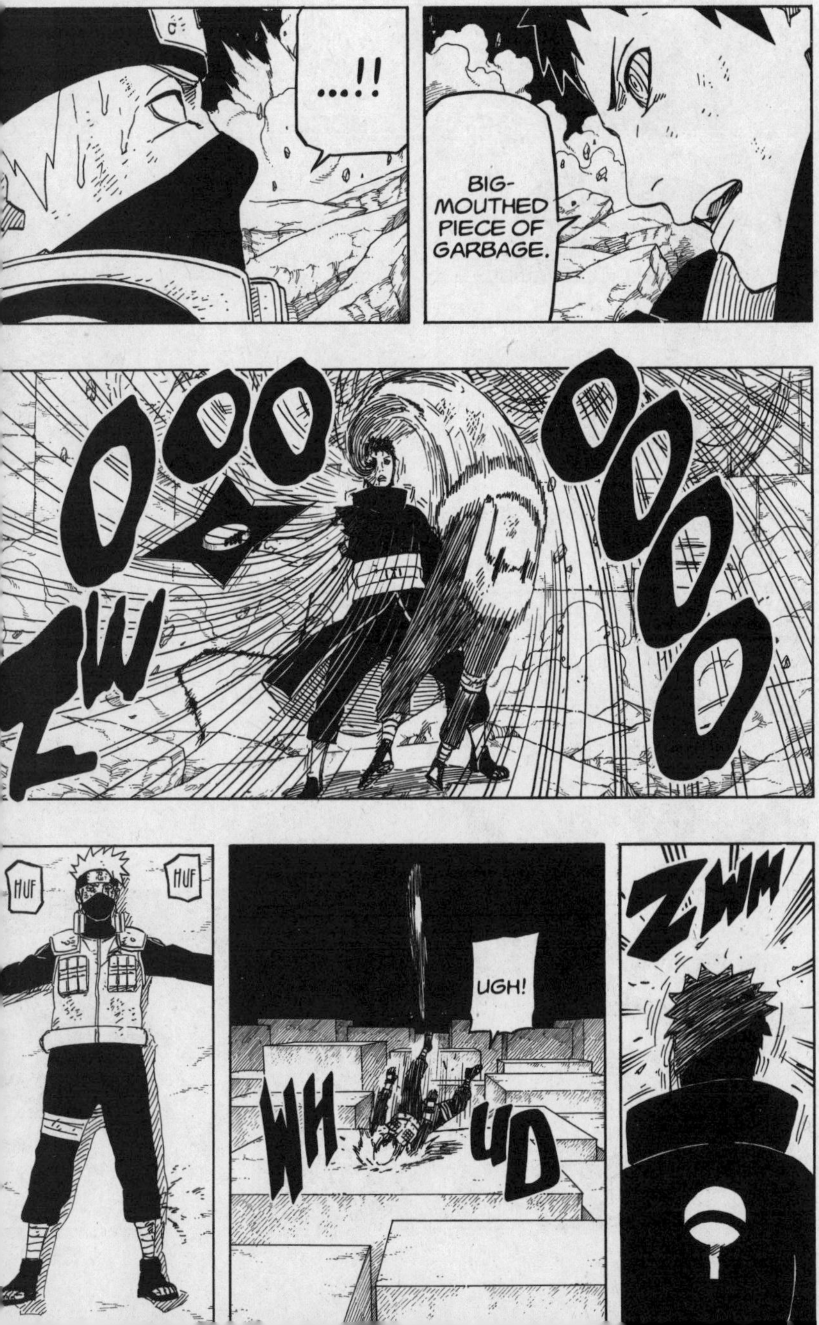
BIG-MOUTHED PIECE OF GARBAGE.
...!!
ZWOOO
OOOOO
ZWM
UGH!
WHUD
HUF
HUF

HOW-
EVER...

...OR, IN A
NINJA'S
WORLD,
THOSE WHO
VIOLATE
THE RULES
AND FAIL TO
FOLLOW
ORDERS
ARE LOWER
THAN
GARBAGE.

THAT'S
WHY THE
WHITE
FANG WAS
A TRUE
HERO.

PROBABLY
BECAUSE...
YOU LET
RIN DIE...

...THOSE
WHO DO
NOT CARE
FOR AND
SUPPORT
THEIR
FELLOWS
ARE EVEN
LOWER
THAN
THAT!

HUFF

BUT
OBITO...
YOU'VE
ALWAYS...

HUFF

KAMUI...

HUFF

HUFF

I AM
GARBAGE,
FOR
SURE...

DRIP
DRIP

10

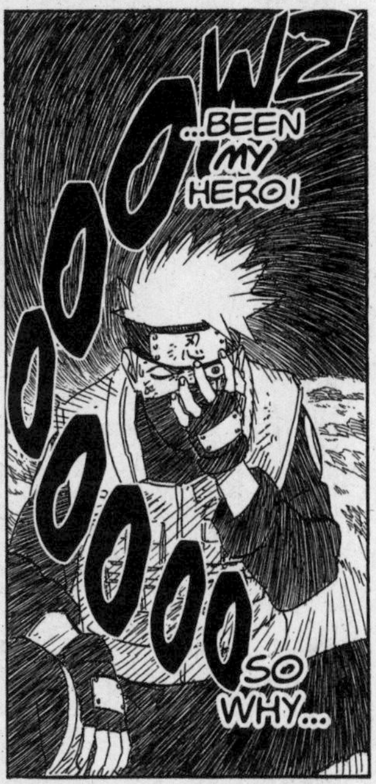
...BEEN MY HERO!
SO WHY...

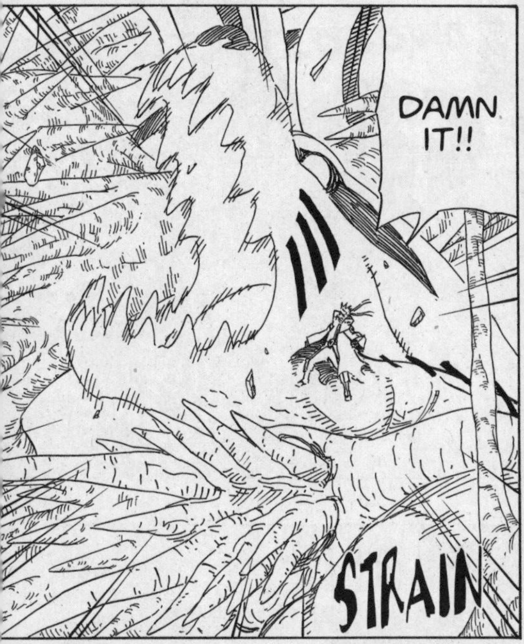
DAMN IT!!
STRAIN

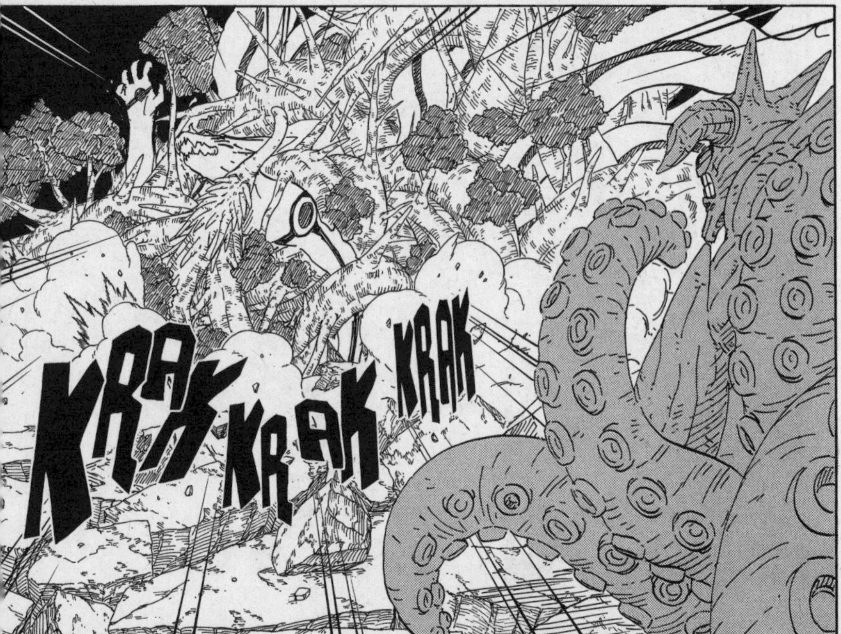
KRAK
KRAK
KRAK

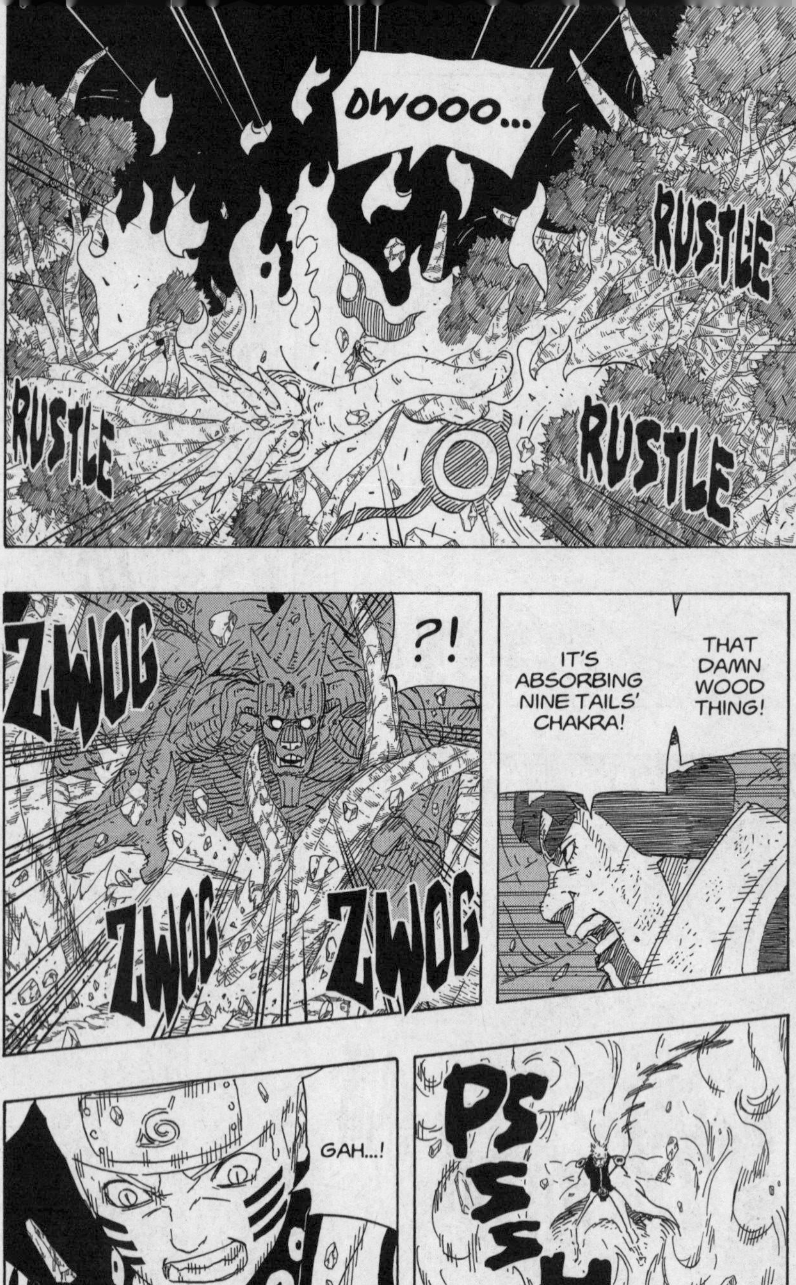
DWOOO...
RUSTLE
RUSTLE
RUSTLE
THAT DAMN WOOD THING!
IT'S ABSORBING NINE TAILS' CHAKRA!
?!
ZWOG
ZWOG
ZWOG
PSSSH...
GAH...!

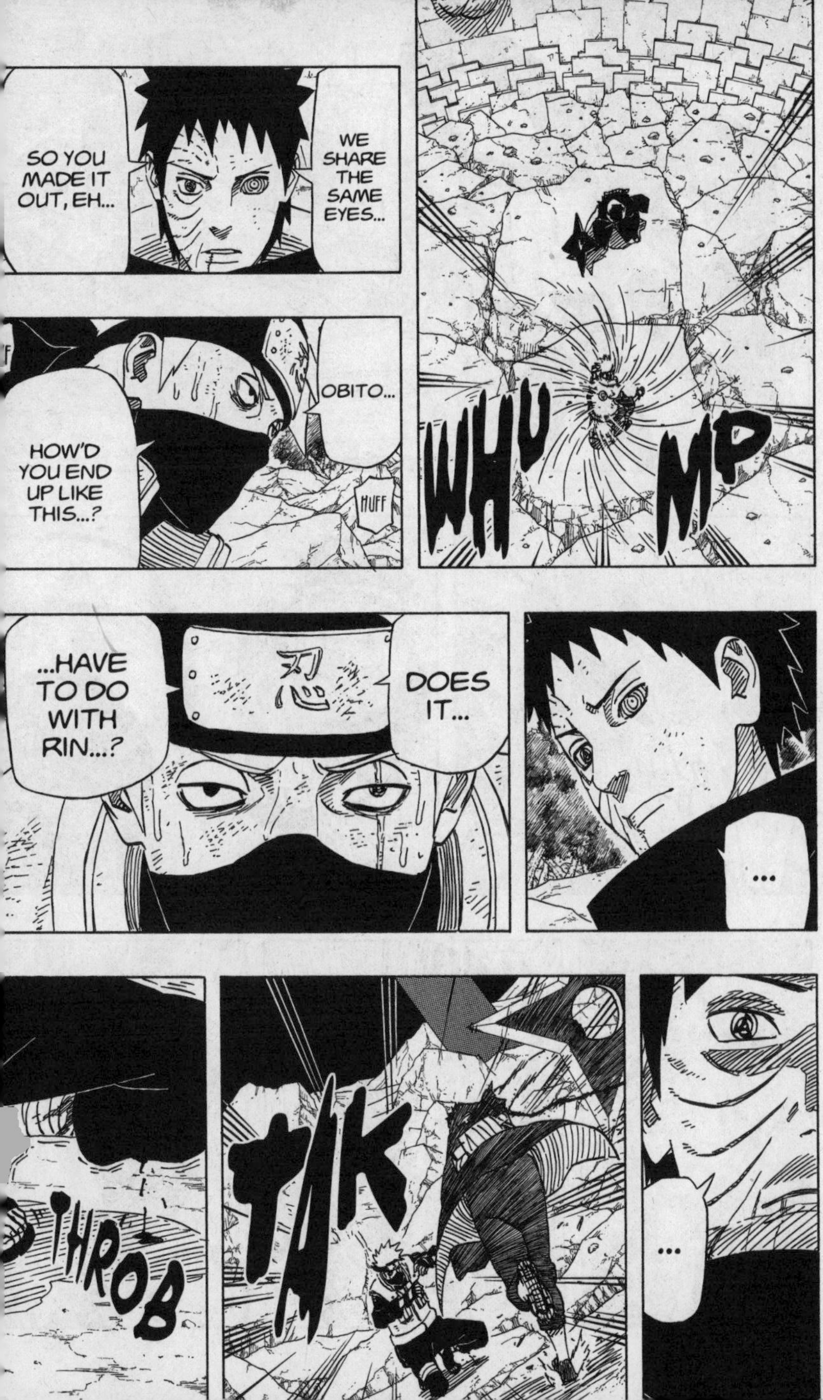
WHUMP
WE SHARE THE SAME EYES...
SO YOU MADE IT OUT, EH...
OBITO...
HUFF
HOW'D YOU END UP LIKE THIS...?
...
DOES IT...
...HAVE TO DO WITH RIN...?
...
TAK
THROB

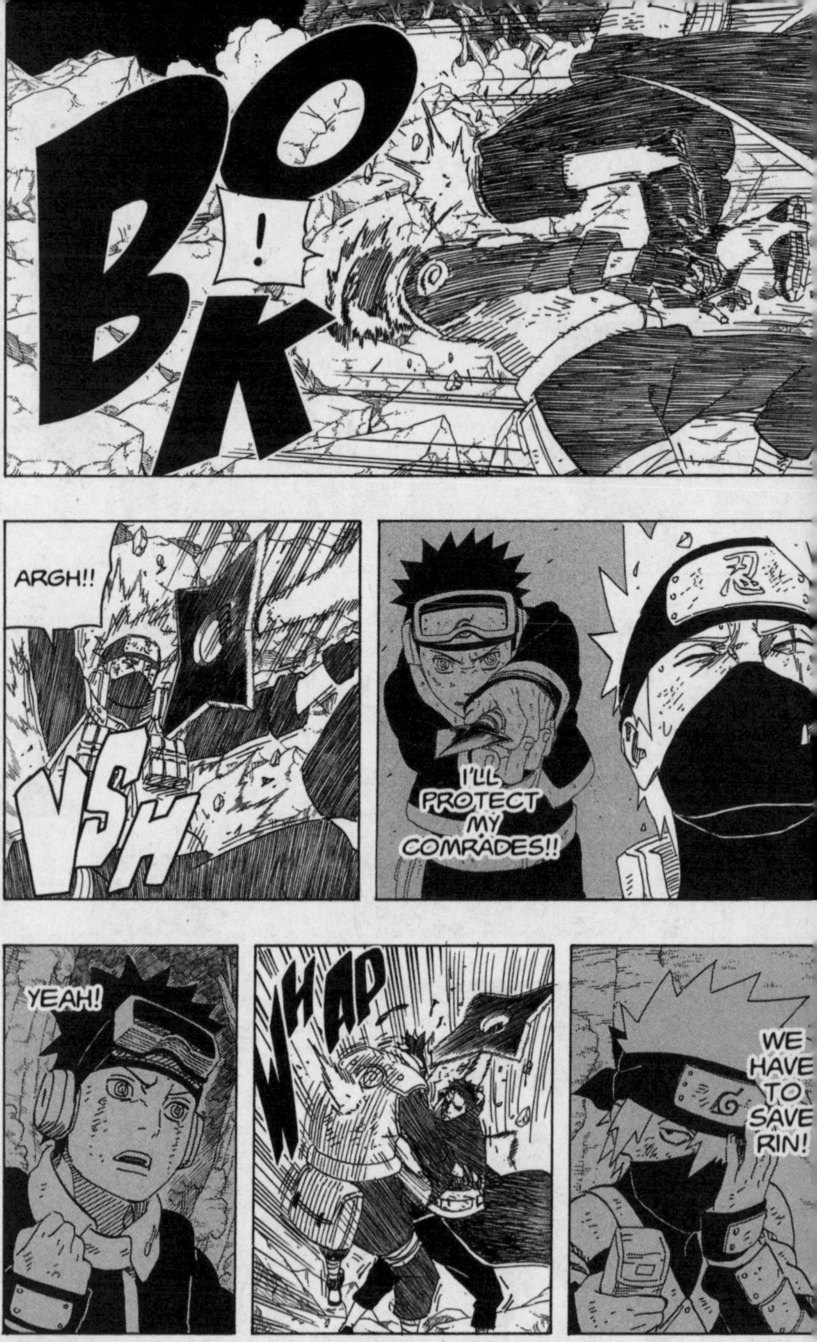
BOOK!
I'LL PROTECT MY COMRADES!!
ARGH!!
VSH
WE HAVE TO SAVE RIN!
WHAP
YEAH!

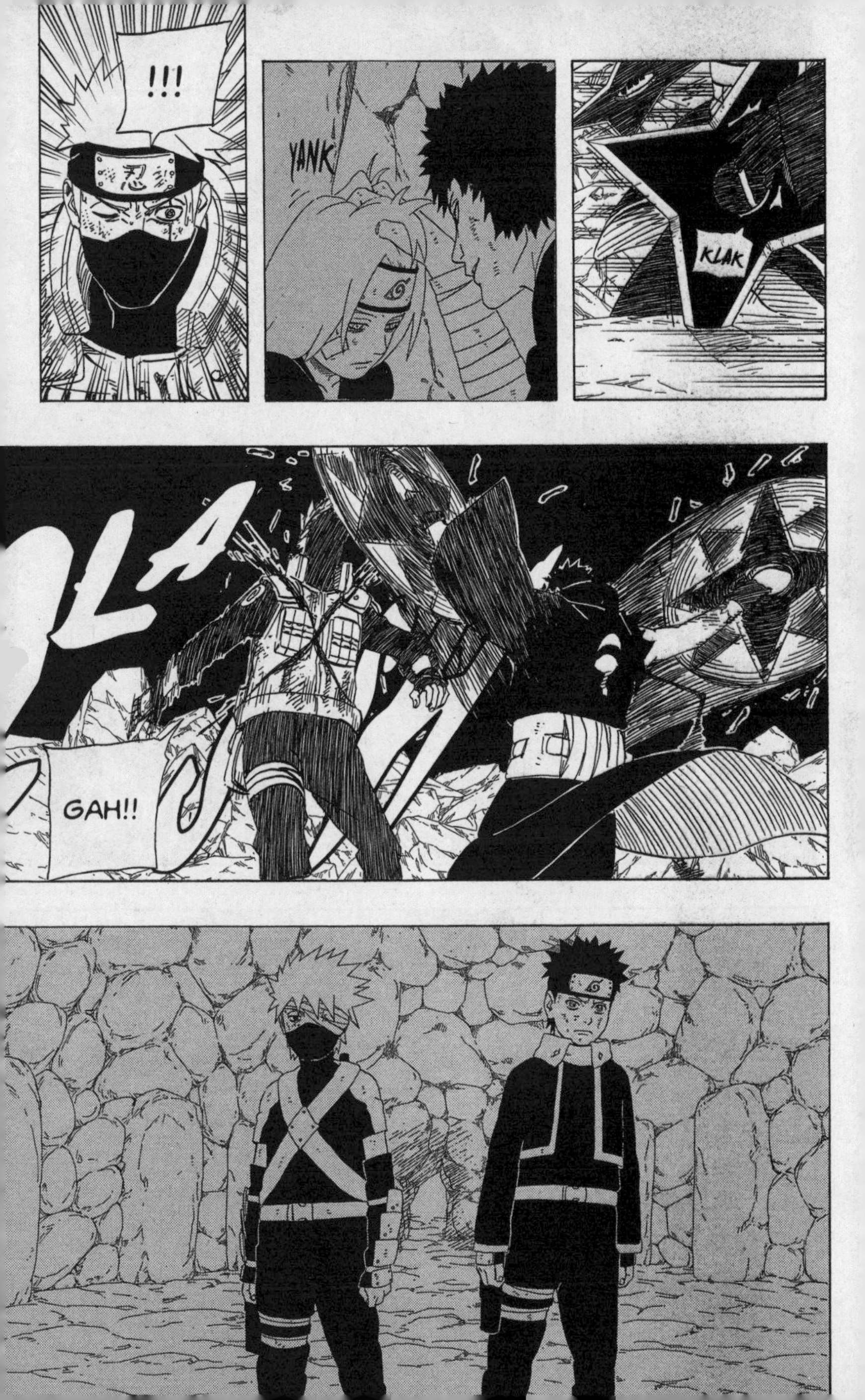
KLAK
YANK
!!!
GAH!!

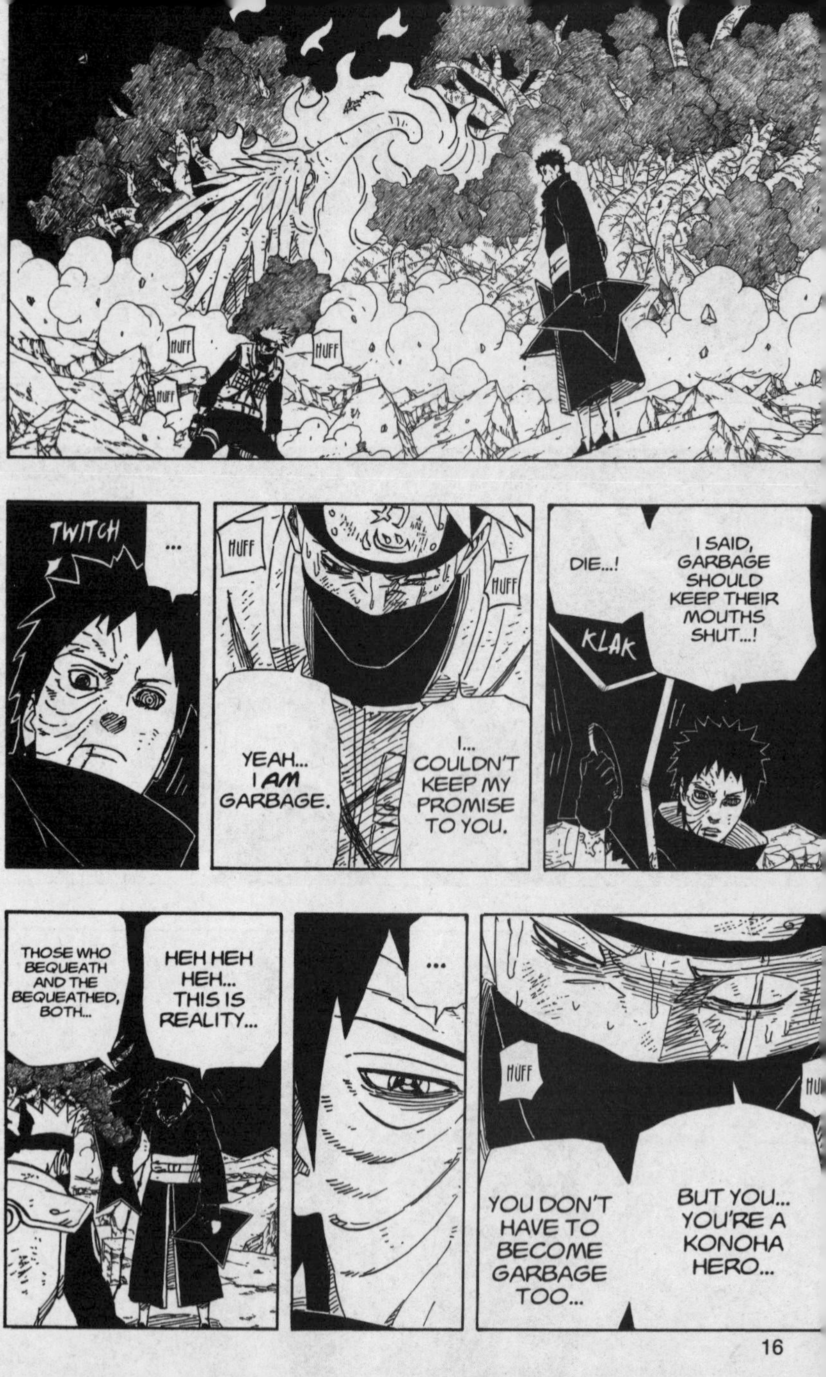
HUFF
HUFF
HUFF
I SAID, GARBAGE SHOULD KEEP THEIR MOUTHS SHUT...!
DIE...!
KLAK
HUFF
HUFF
I... COULDN'T KEEP MY PROMISE TO YOU.
YEAH... I AM GARBAGE.
...
TWITCH
BUT YOU... YOU'RE A KONOHA HERO...
HUFF
YOU DON'T HAVE TO BECOME GARBAGE TOO...
...
HEH HEH HEH... THIS IS REALITY...
THOSE WHO BEQUEATH AND THE BEQUEATHED, BOTH...

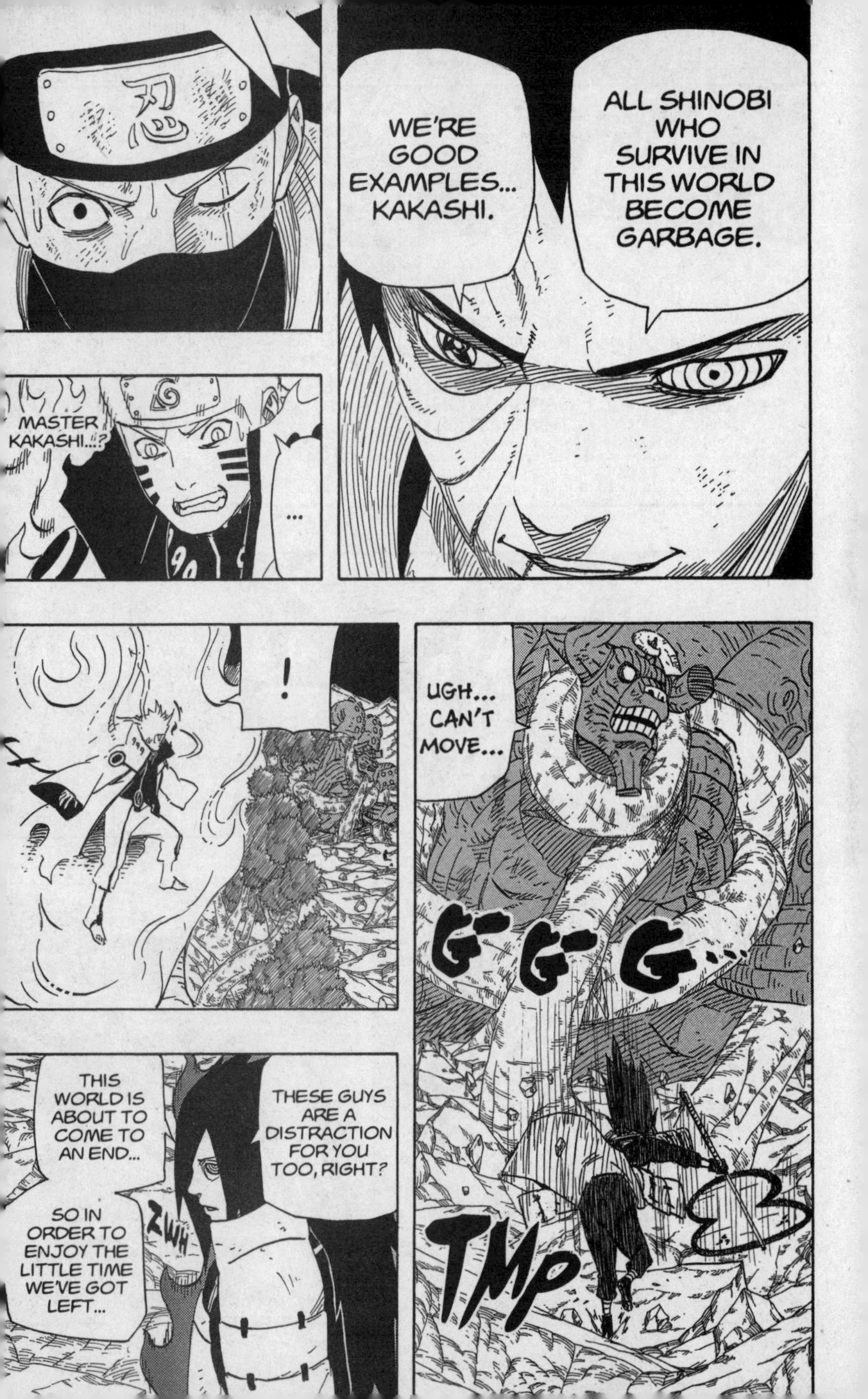
ALL SHINOBI WHO SURVIVE IN THIS WORLD BECOME GARBAGE.
WE'RE GOOD EXAMPLES... KAKASHI.
MASTER KAKASHI...?
...
UGH... CAN'T MOVE...
G-G-G...
TMP
!
THESE GUYS ARE A DISTRACTION FOR YOU TOO, RIGHT?
THIS WORLD IS ABOUT TO COME TO AN END...
SO IN ORDER TO ENJOY THE LITTLE TIME WE'VE GOT LEFT...
ZWH

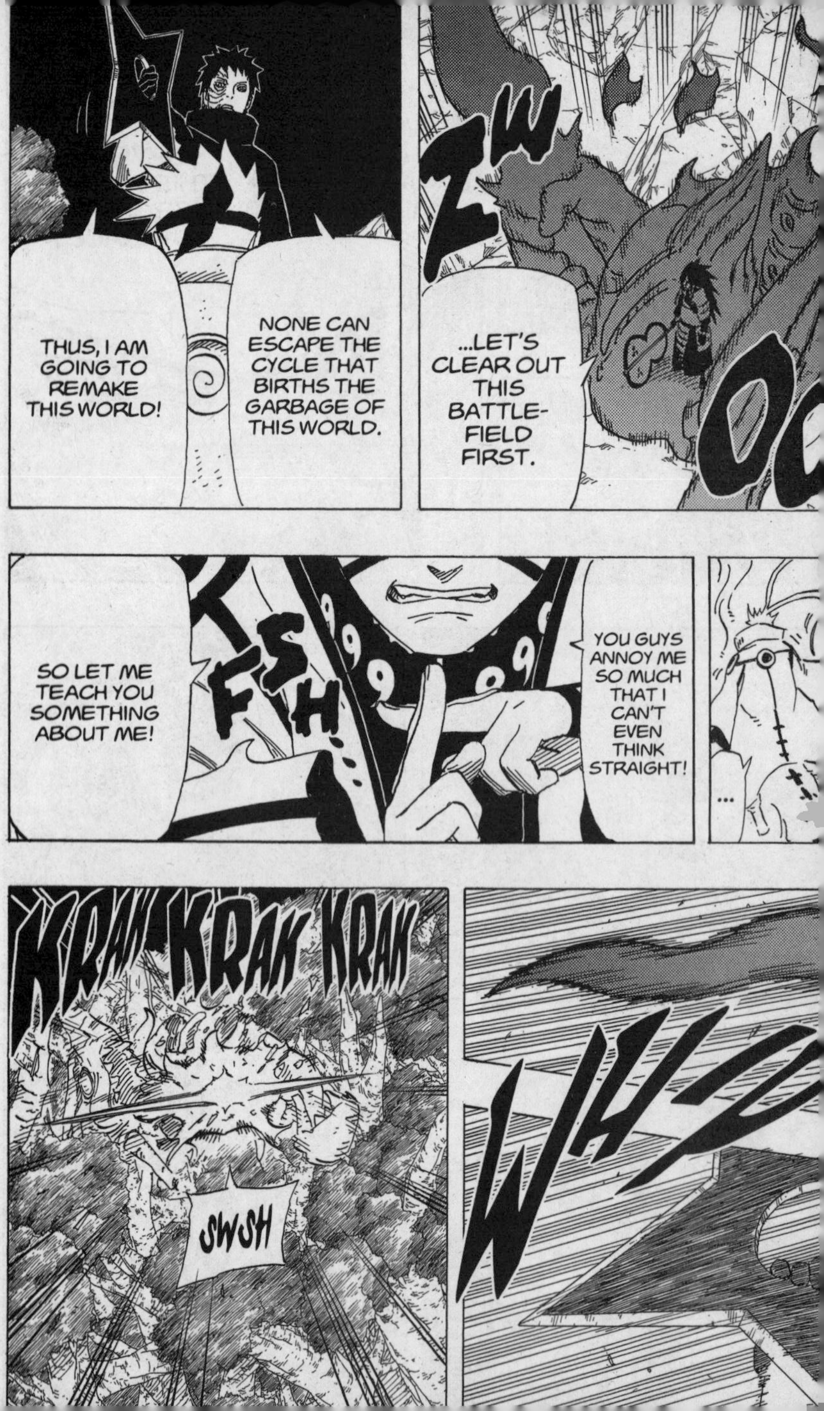

...LET'S CLEAR OUT THIS BATTLEFIELD FIRST.
NONE CAN ESCAPE THE CYCLE THAT BIRTHS THE GARBAGE OF THIS WORLD.
THUS, I AM GOING TO REMAKE THIS WORLD!
...
YOU GUYS ANNOY ME SO MUCH THAT I CAN'T EVEN THINK STRAIGHT!
FSH
SO LET ME TEACH YOU SOMETHING ABOUT ME!
KRAK KRAK KRAK
SWSH

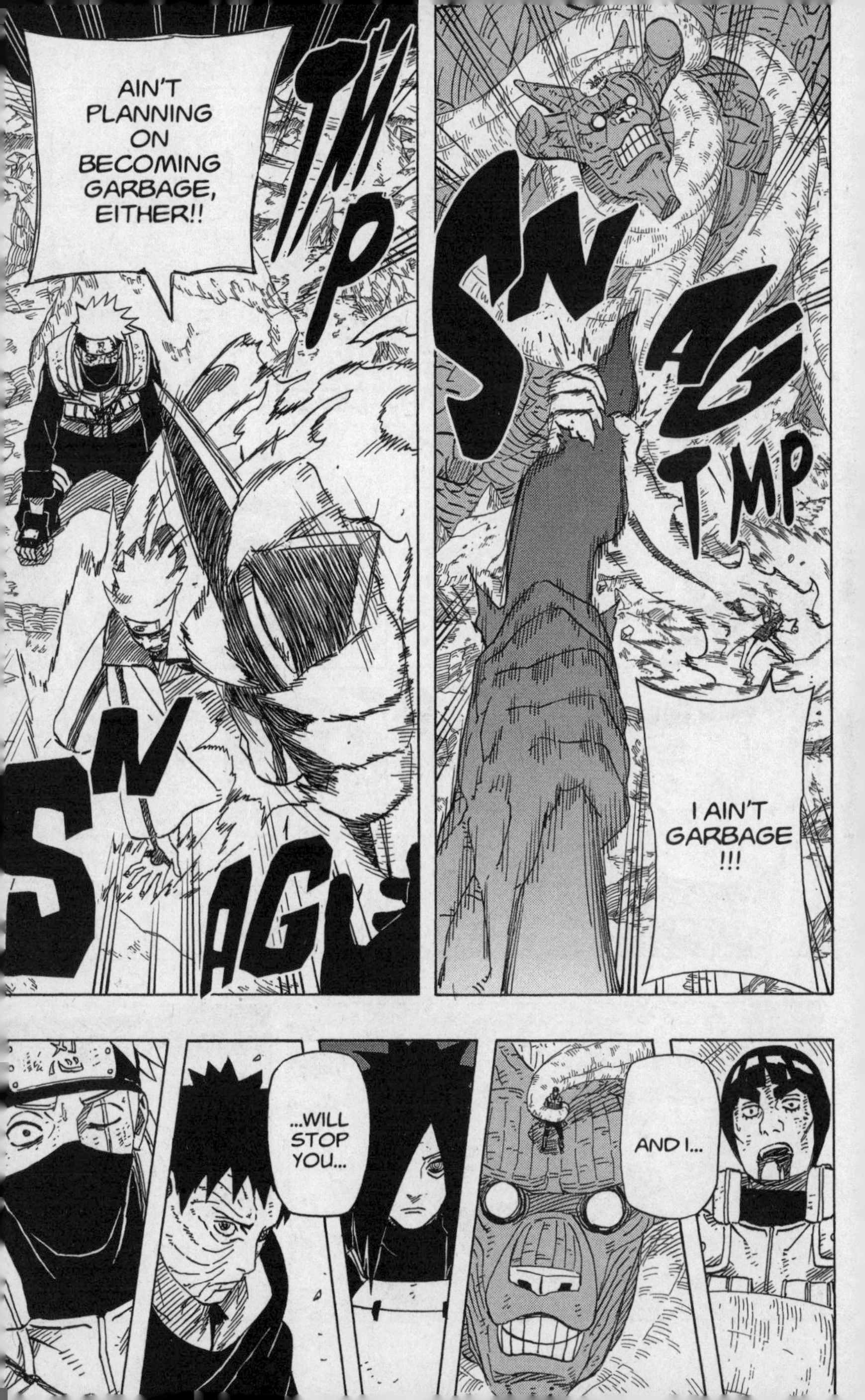
SNAG
TMP
I AIN'T GARBAGE!!!
AIN'T PLANNING ON BECOMING GARBAGE, EITHER!!
SNAG
AND I...
...WILL STOP YOU...

I'LL NEVER LET MY COMRADES DIE!!

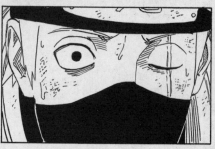

...NEVER LET MY COMRADES DIE!

I WILL...

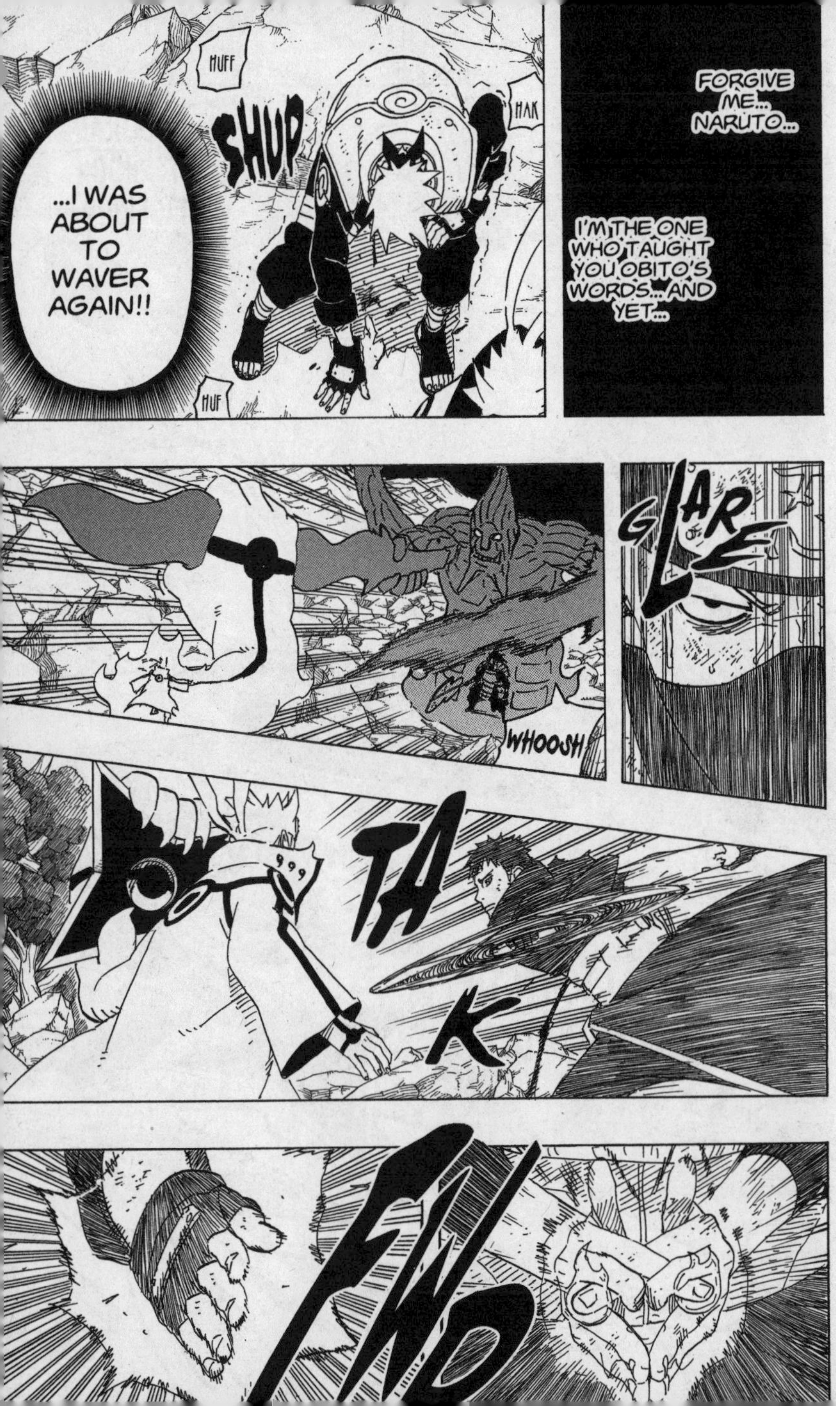
FORGIVE ME... NARUTO...
I'M THE ONE WHO TAUGHT YOU OBITO'S WORDS... AND YET...
HUFF
HAK
SHUP
...I WAS ABOUT TO WAVER AGAIN!!
HUF
GLARE
WHOOSH
TAK

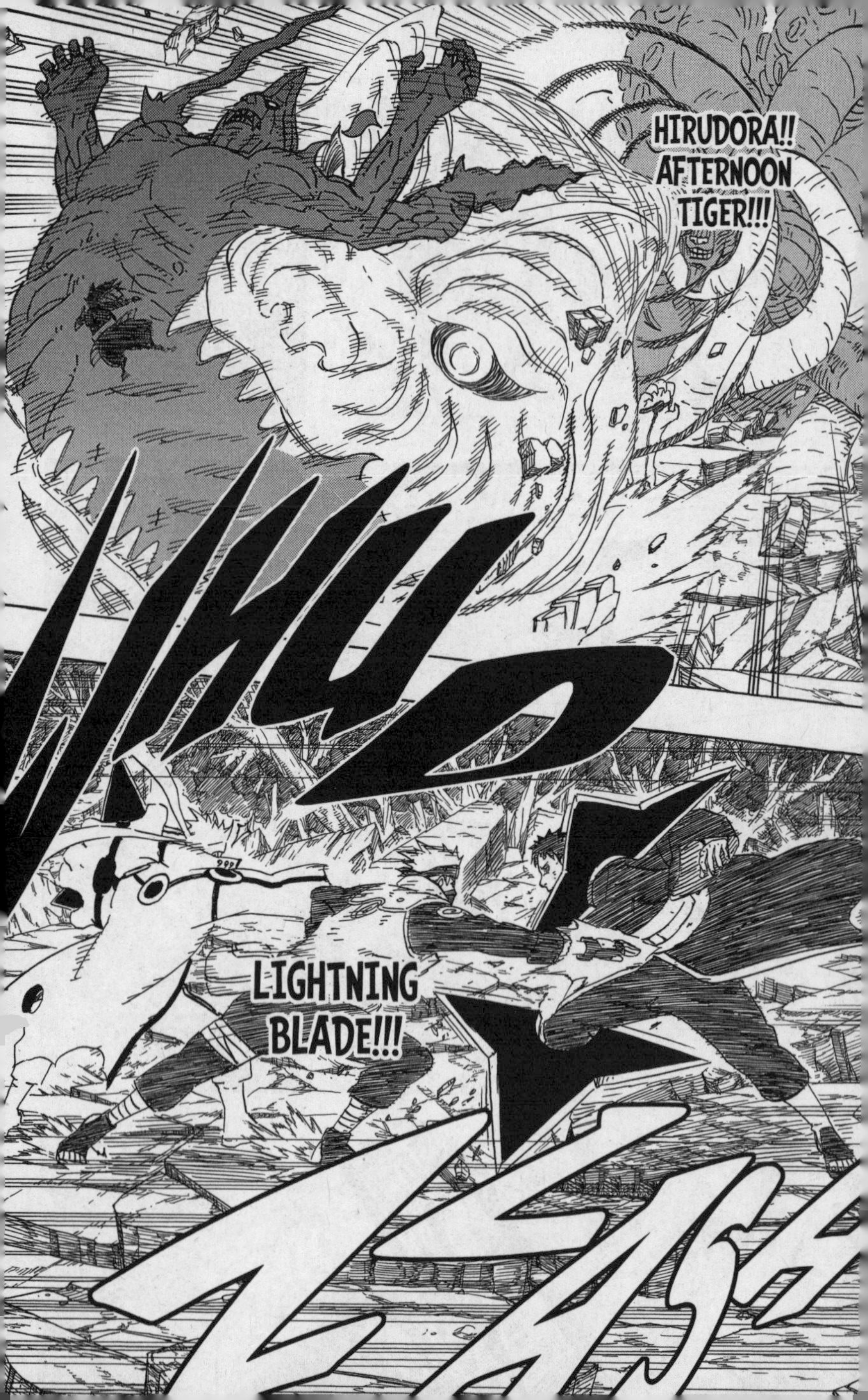
HIRUDORA!! AFTERNOON TIGER!!!
LIGHTNING BLADE!!!

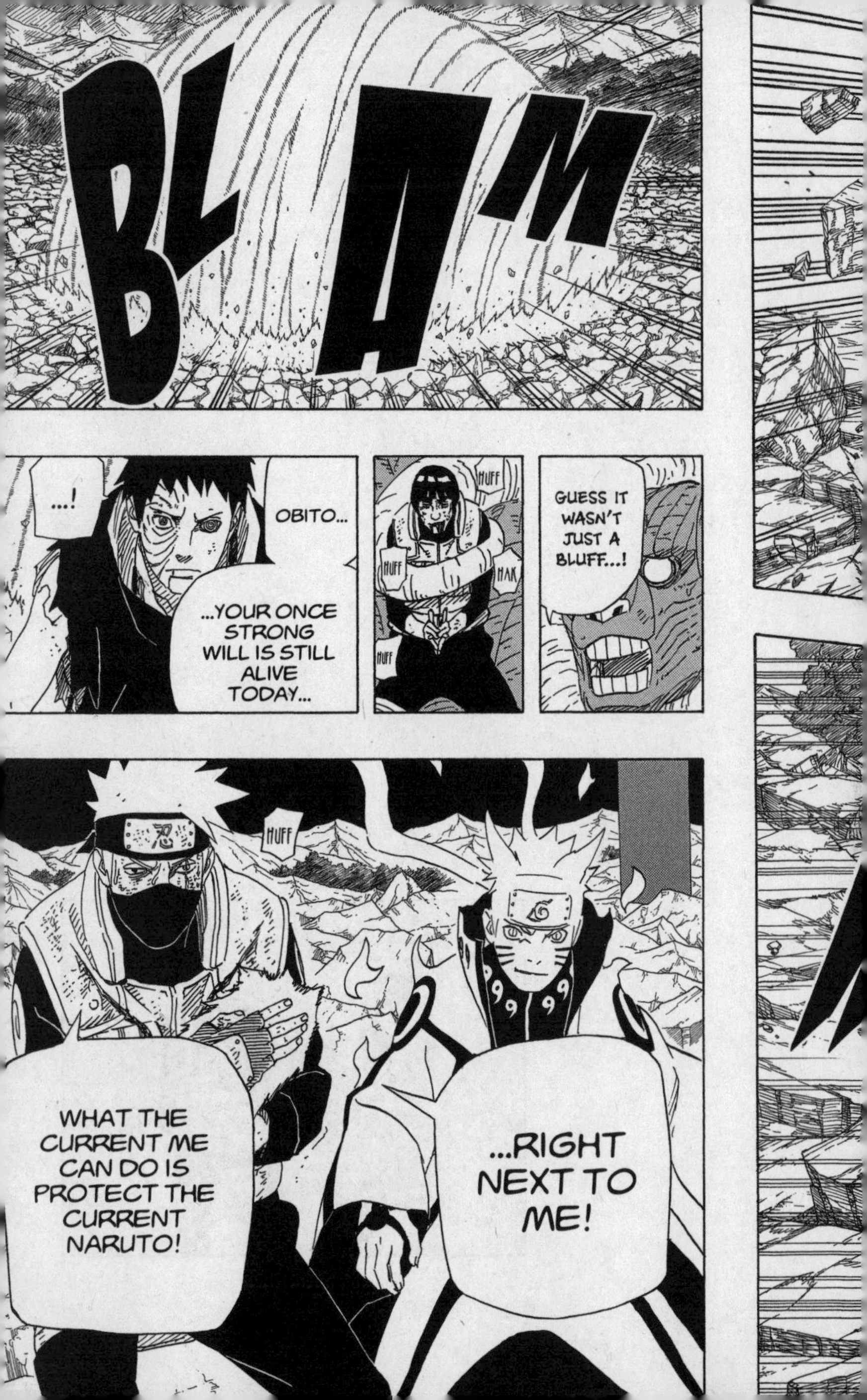
BLAM
GUESS IT WASN'T JUST A BLUFF...!
HUFF
HUFF
HAK
HUFF
...!
OBITO...
...YOUR ONCE STRONG WILL IS STILL ALIVE TODAY...
HUFF
...RIGHT NEXT TO ME!
WHAT THE CURRENT ME CAN DO IS PROTECT THE CURRENT NARUTO!

Number 609: The End

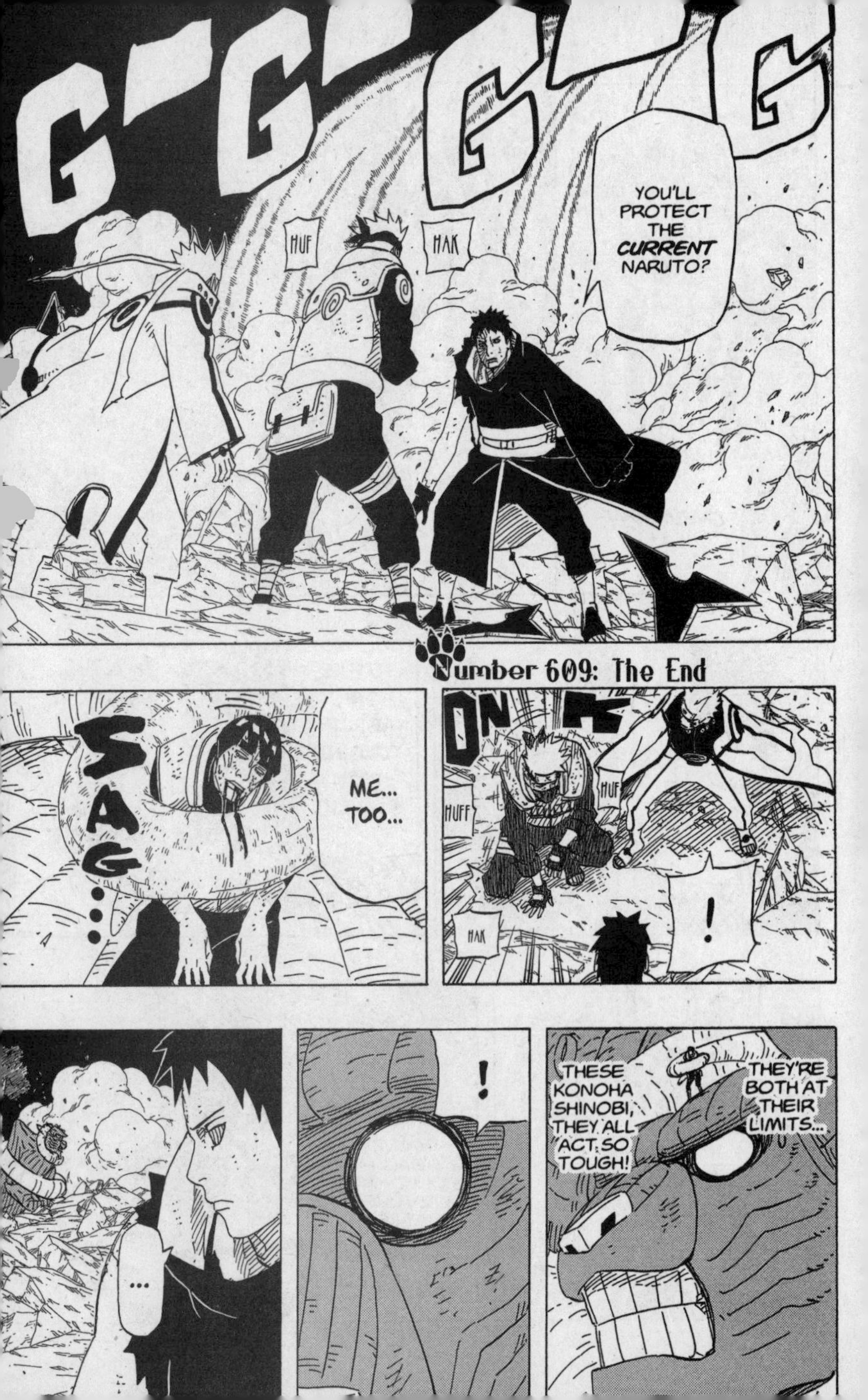
G'G'G'G
YOU'LL PROTECT THE CURRENT NARUTO?
HAK
HUF
ONK
HUF
HUFF
HAK
!
ME... TOO...
SAG...
THEY'RE BOTH AT THEIR LIMITS...
THESE KONOHA SHINOBI, THEY ALL ACT SO TOUGH!
!
...

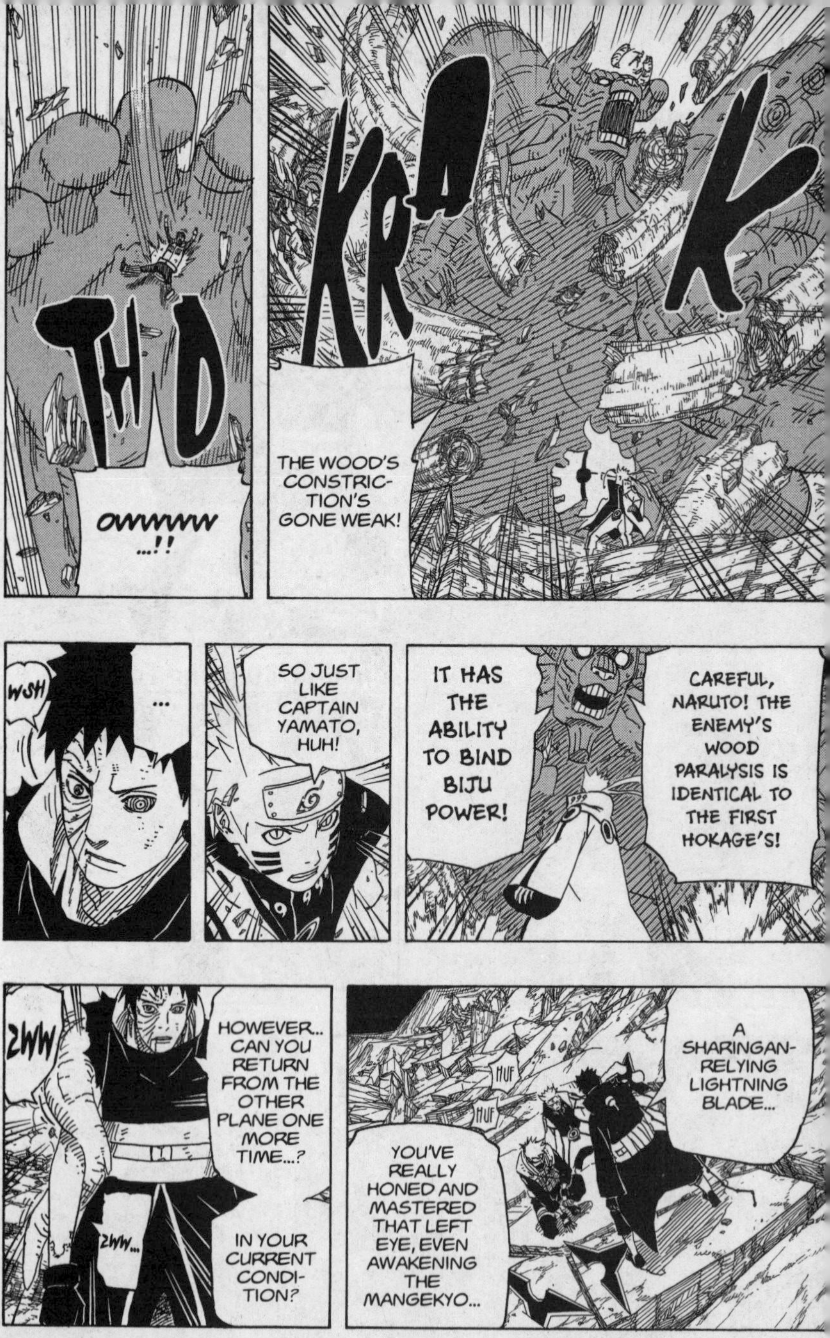
KRAK
THE WOOD'S CONSTRICTION'S GONE WEAK!
THD
OWWWWW ...!!
CAREFUL, NARUTO! THE ENEMY'S WOOD PARALYSIS IS IDENTICAL TO THE FIRST HOKAGE'S!
IT HAS THE ABILITY TO BIND BIJU POWER!
SO JUST LIKE CAPTAIN YAMATO, HUH!
WSH
...
A SHARINGAN-RELYING LIGHTNING BLADE...
HUF
HUF
YOU'VE REALLY HONED AND MASTERED THAT LEFT EYE, EVEN AWAKENING THE MANGEKYO...
ZWW
HOWEVER... CAN YOU RETURN FROM THE OTHER PLANE ONE MORE TIME...?
IN YOUR CURRENT CONDITION?
ZWW...

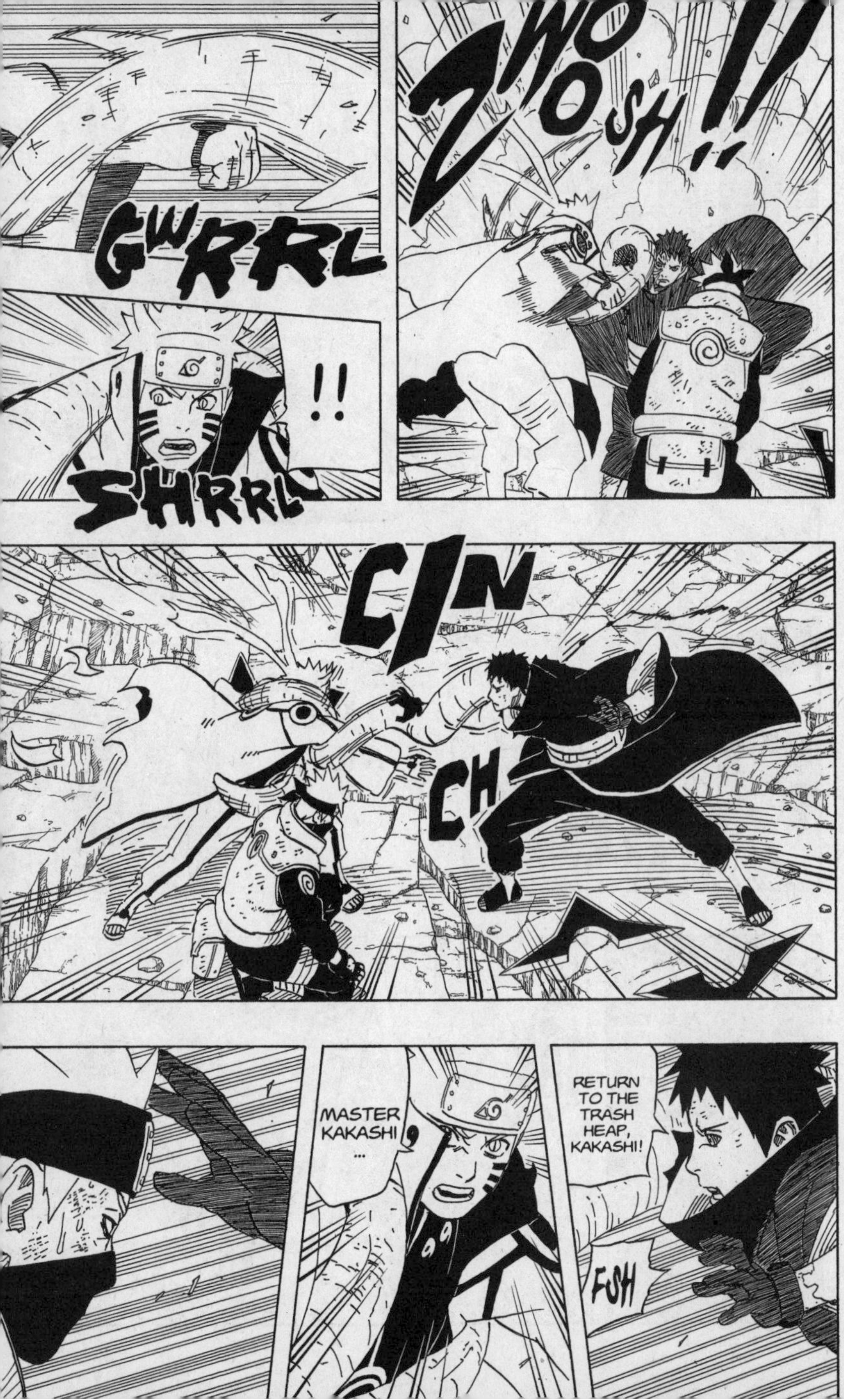

ZWOOSH!!
GWRRL
!!
SHRRL
CIN
CH
RETURN TO THE TRASH HEAP, KAKASHI!
FSH
MASTER KAKASHI...

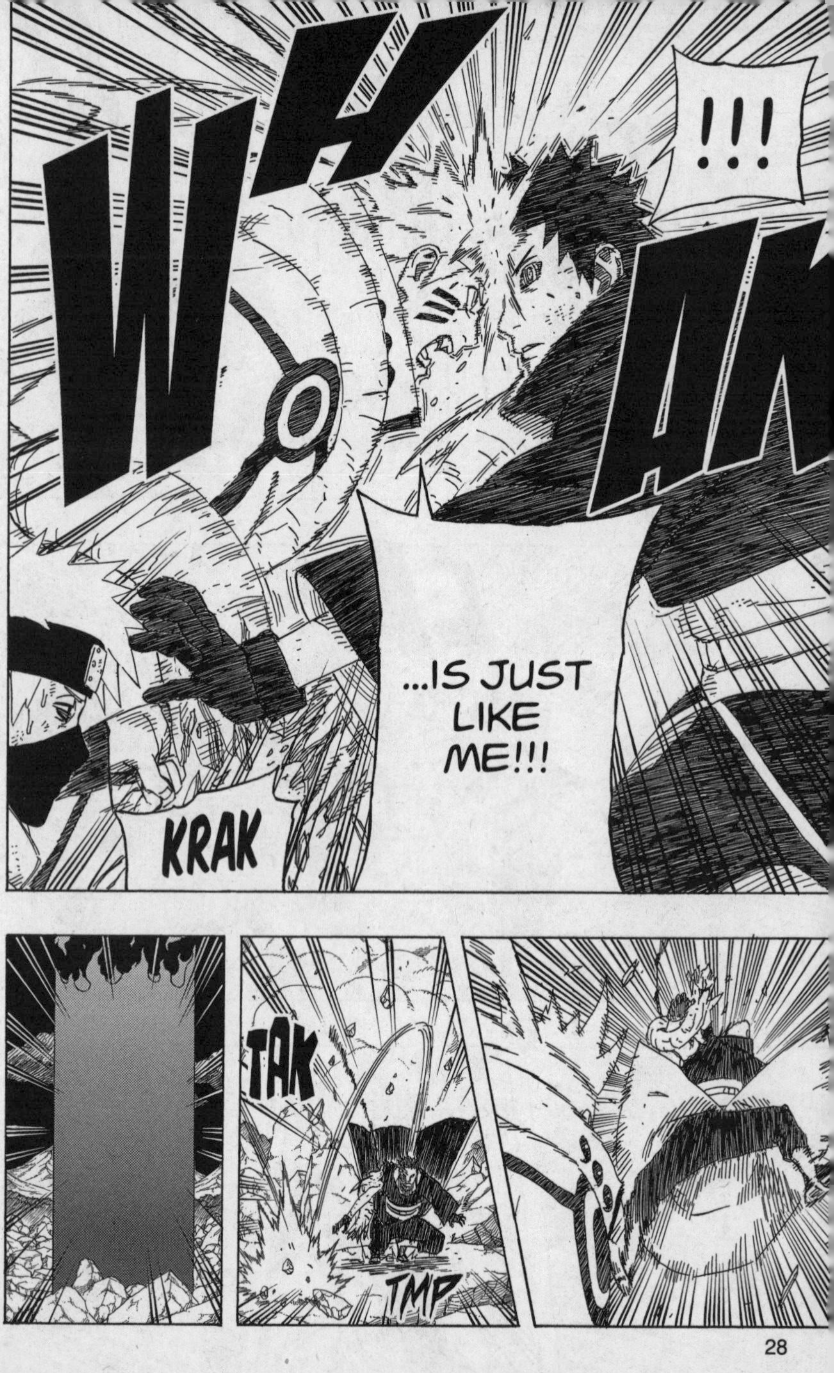
!!!
WHAM
...IS JUST LIKE ME!!!
KRAK
TAK
TMP

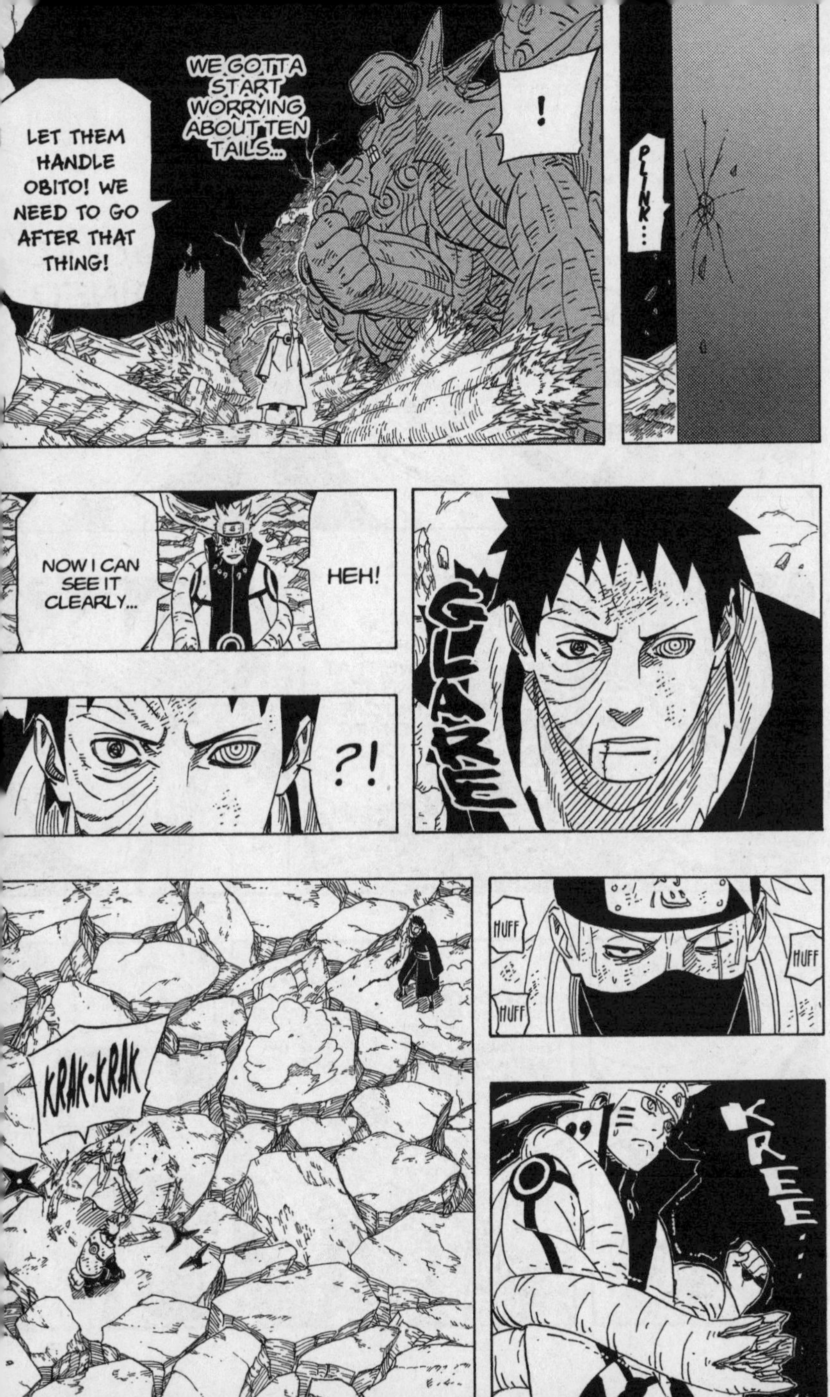
PLINK...
!
WE GOTTA START WORRYING ABOUT TEN TAILS...
LET THEM HANDLE OBITO! WE NEED TO GO AFTER THAT THING!
GLARE
HEH!
NOW I CAN SEE IT CLEARLY...
?!
HUFF
HUFF
HUFF
KREE...
KRAK-KRAK

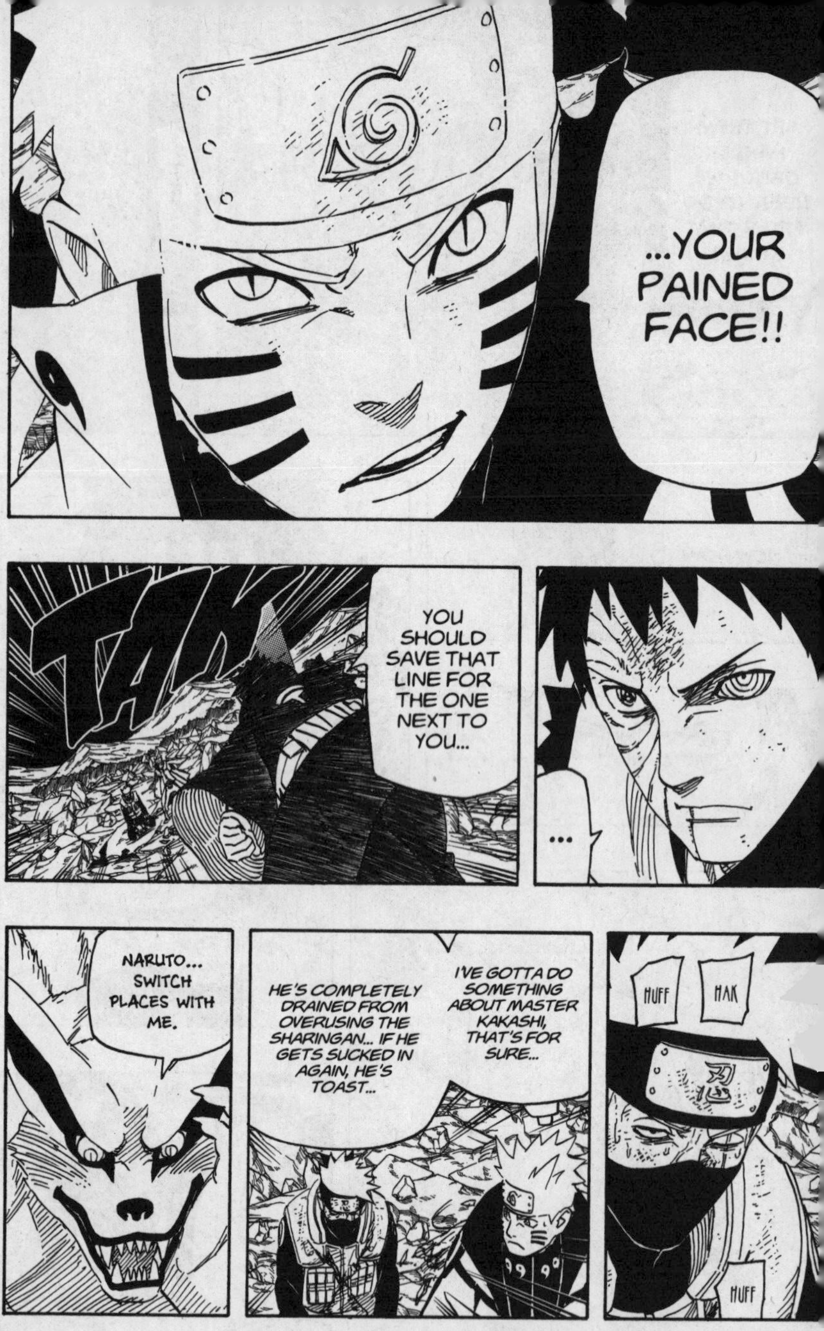
...YOUR PAINED FACE!!
...
YOU SHOULD SAVE THAT LINE FOR THE ONE NEXT TO YOU...
HAK
HUFF
HUFF
I'VE GOTTA DO SOMETHING ABOUT MASTER KAKASHI, THAT'S FOR SURE...
HE'S COMPLETELY DRAINED FROM OVERUSING THE SHARINGAN... IF HE GETS SUCKED IN AGAIN, HE'S TOAST...
NARUTO... SWITCH PLACES WITH ME.

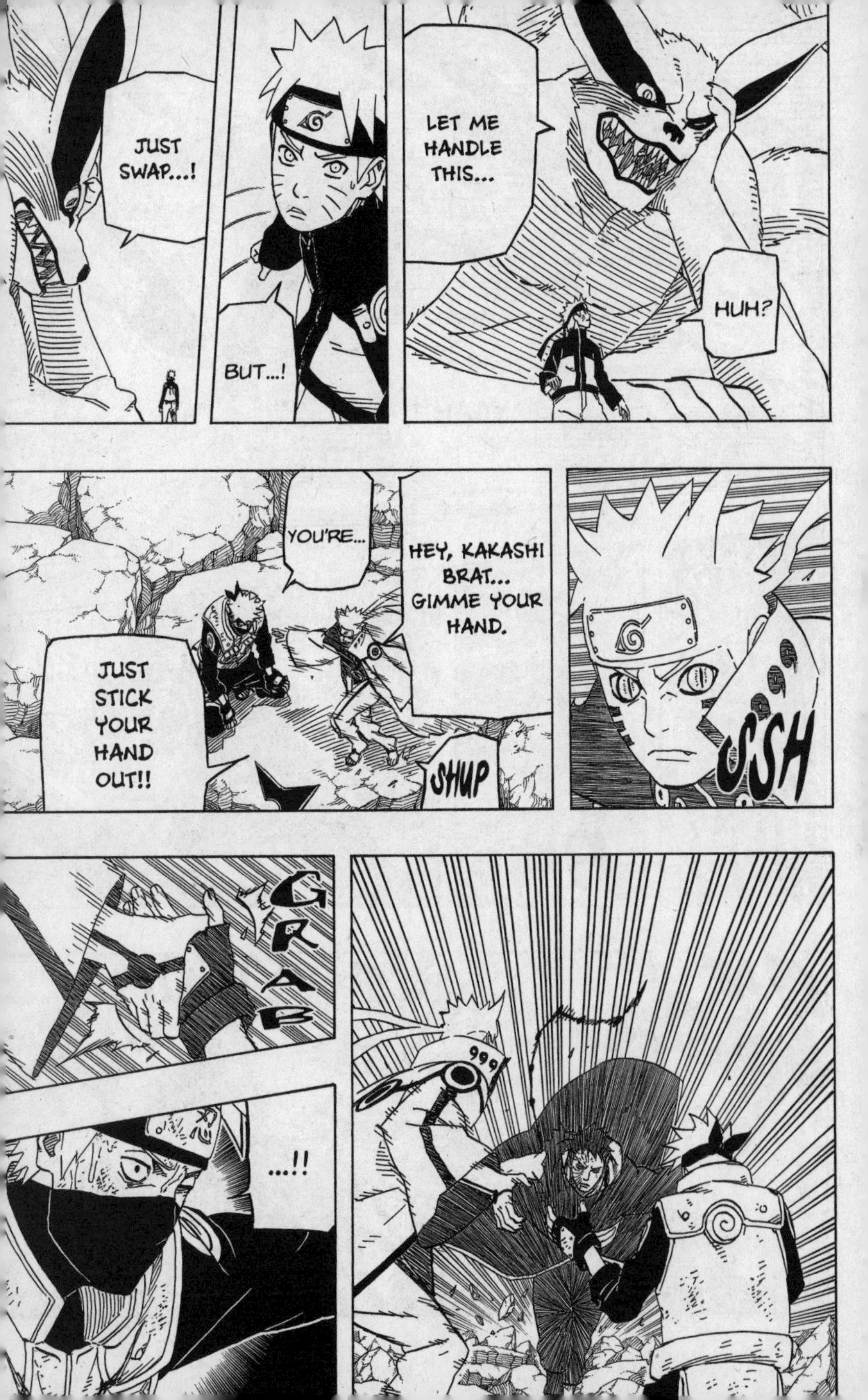
LET ME HANDLE THIS...
HUH?
BUT...!
JUST SWAP...!
SSH
HEY, KAKASHI BRAT... GIMME YOUR HAND.
YOU'RE...
JUST STICK YOUR HAND OUT!!
SHUP
GRAB
...!!

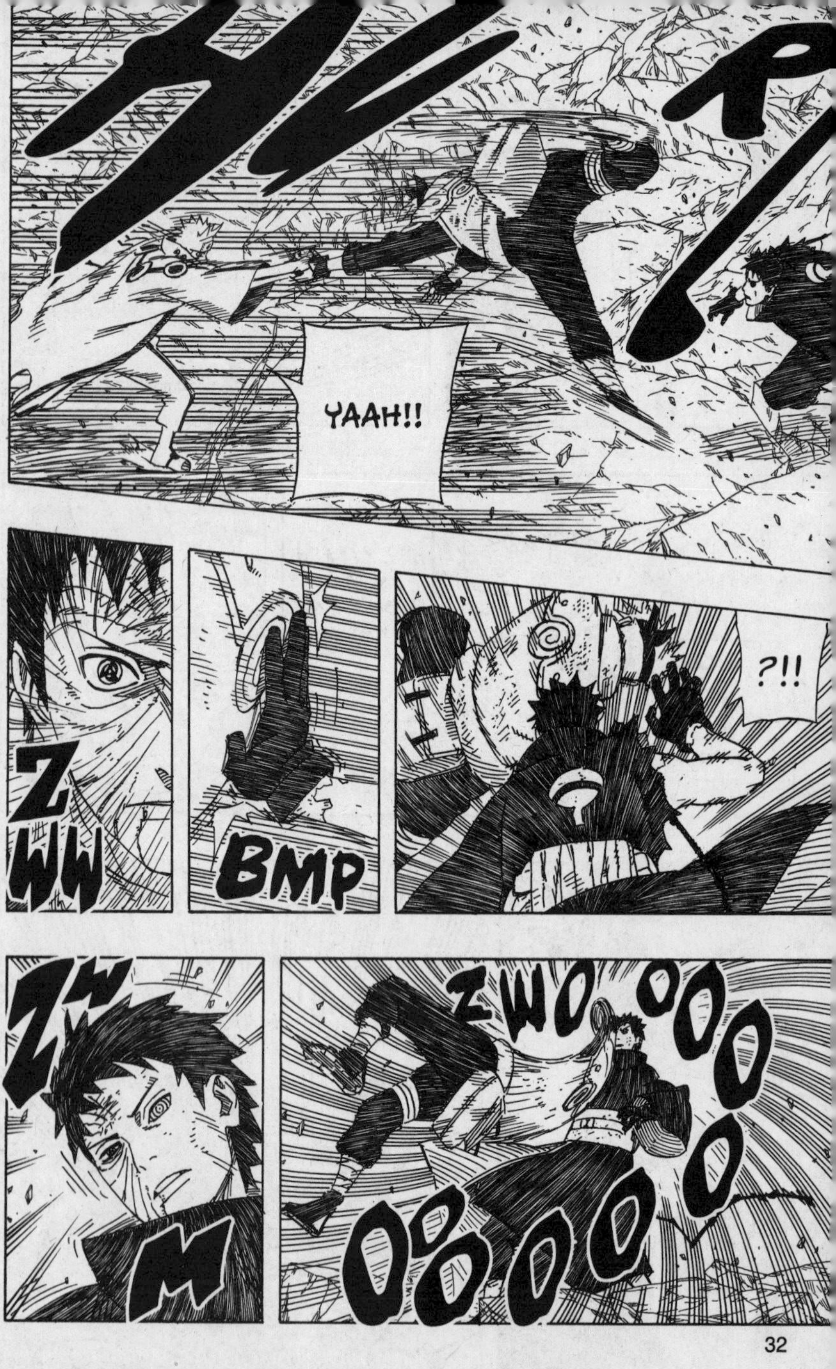
SHUR
YAAH!!
?!!
BMP
ZWW
ZWOOOOOOOOOOOO
ZWM

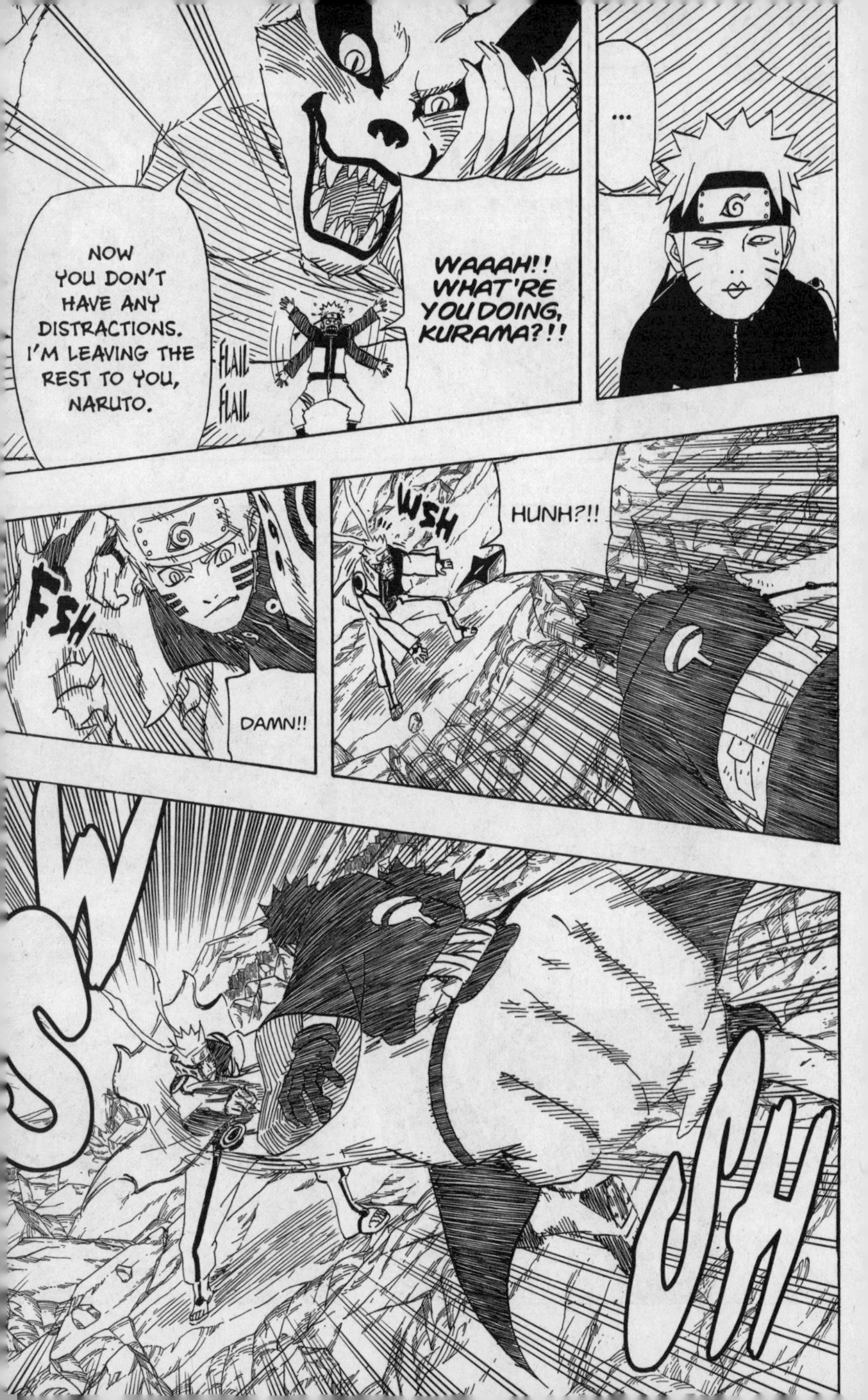
...
WAAAH!! WHAT'RE YOU DOING, KURAMA?!!
FLAIL FLAIL
NOW YOU DON'T HAVE ANY DISTRACTIONS. I'M LEAVING THE REST TO YOU, NARUTO.
HUNH?!!
WSH
FSH
DAMN!!

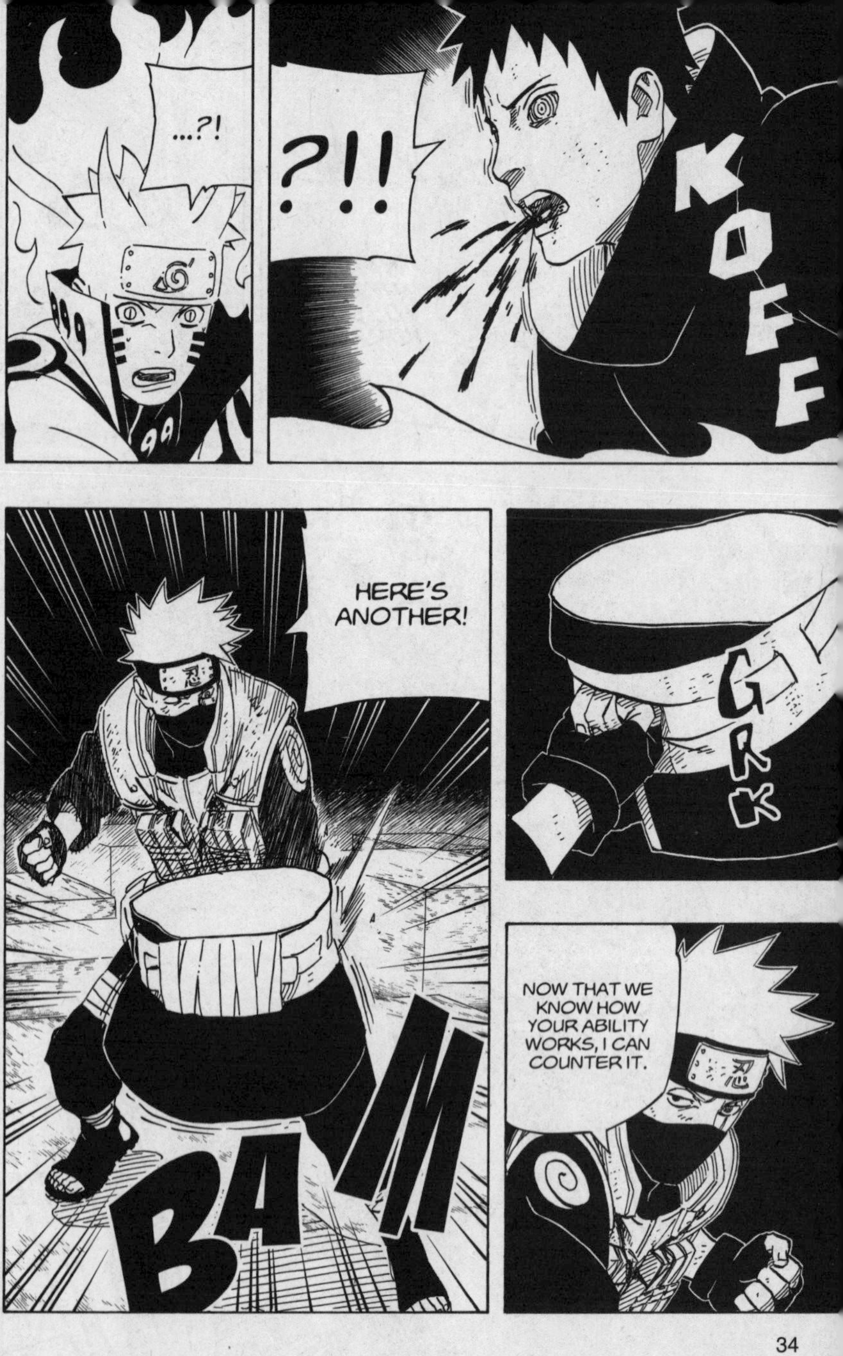
?!!
KOFF
...?!
GRK
NOW THAT WE KNOW HOW YOUR ABILITY WORKS, I CAN COUNTER IT.
HERE'S ANOTHER!
BAM

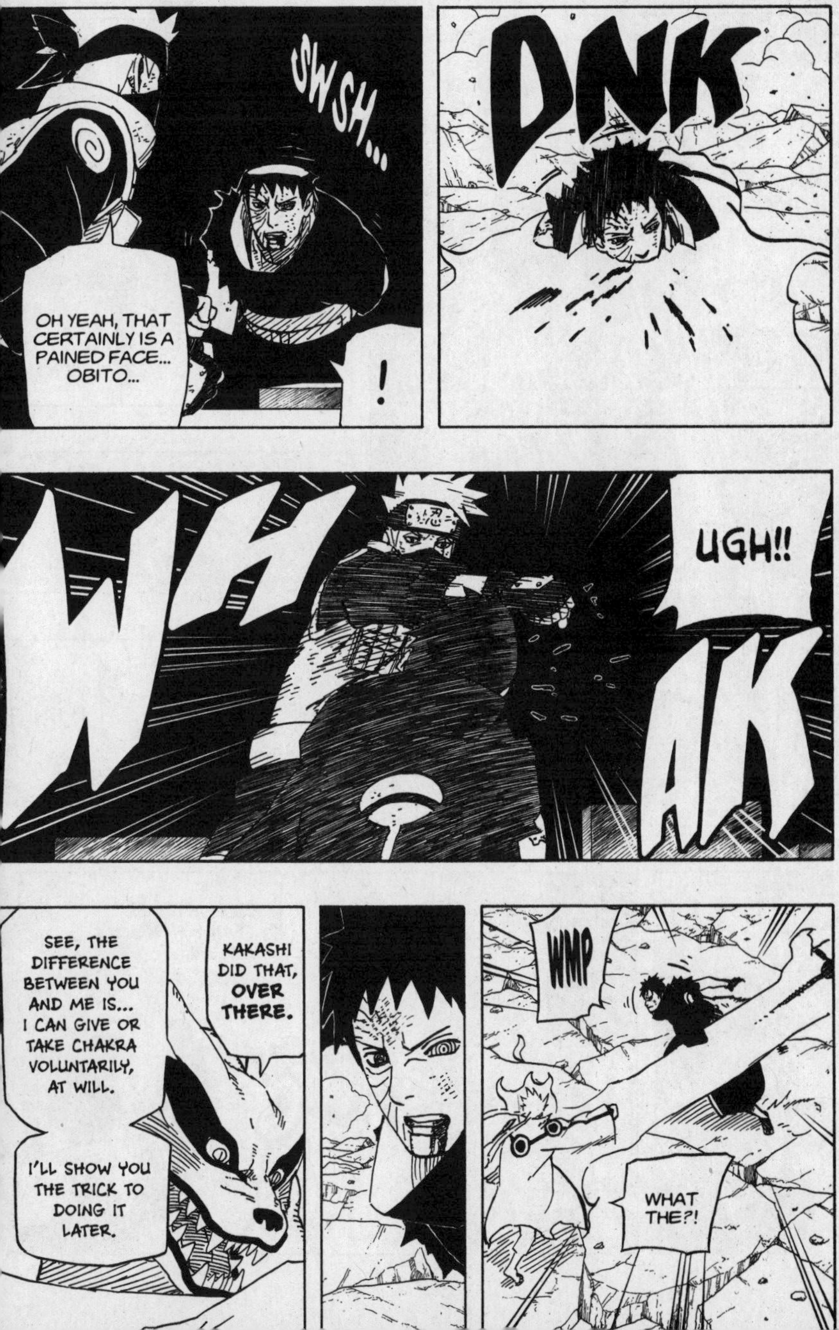
DNK
SWSH...
!
OH YEAH, THAT CERTAINLY IS A PAINED FACE... OBITO...
WHAK
UGH!!
WMP
WHAT THE?!
KAKASHI DID THAT, OVER THERE.
SEE, THE DIFFERENCE BETWEEN YOU AND ME IS... I CAN GIVE OR TAKE CHAKRA VOLUNTARILY, AT WILL.
I'LL SHOW YOU THE TRICK TO DOING IT LATER.

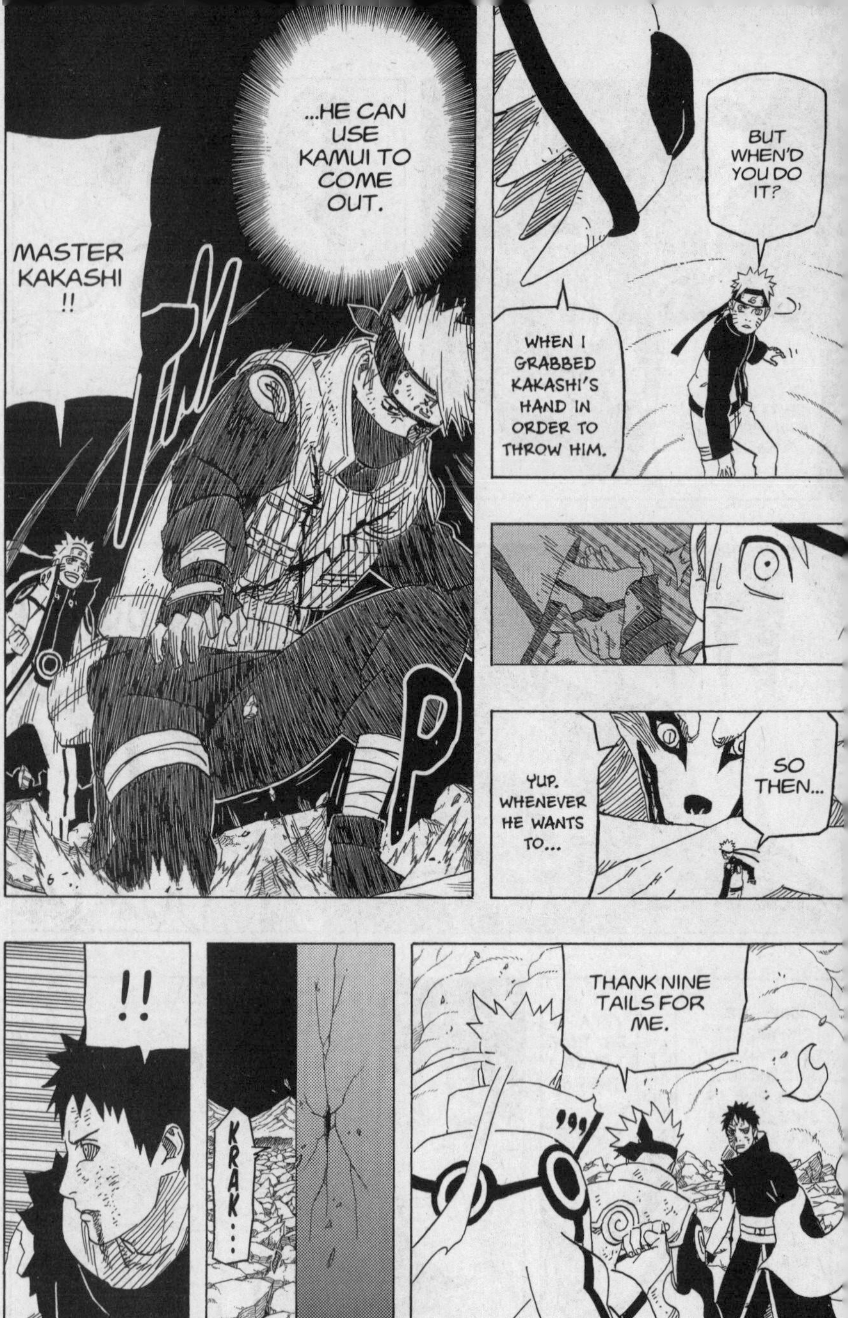
BUT WHEN'D YOU DO IT?
WHEN I GRABBED KAKASHI'S HAND IN ORDER TO THROW HIM.
SO THEN...
YUP. WHENEVER HE WANTS TO...
...HE CAN USE KAMUI TO COME OUT.
MASTER KAKASHI !!
THANK NINE TAILS FOR ME.
KRAK...
!!

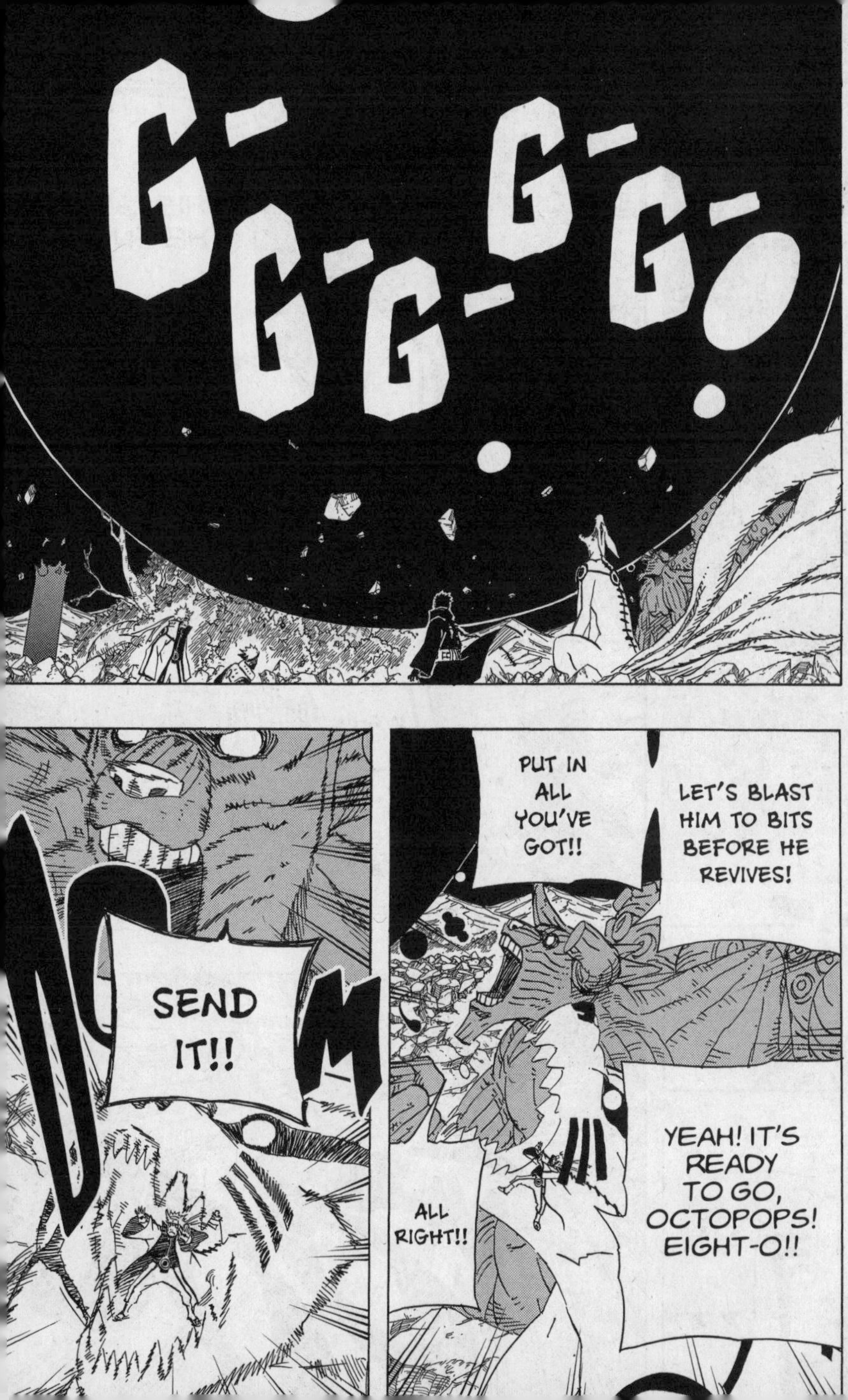
G-G-G-G-G-O
LET'S BLAST HIM TO BITS BEFORE HE REVIVES!
PUT IN ALL YOU'VE GOT!!
YEAH! IT'S READY TO GO, OCTOPOPS! EIGHT-O!!
ALL RIGHT!!
SEND IT!!

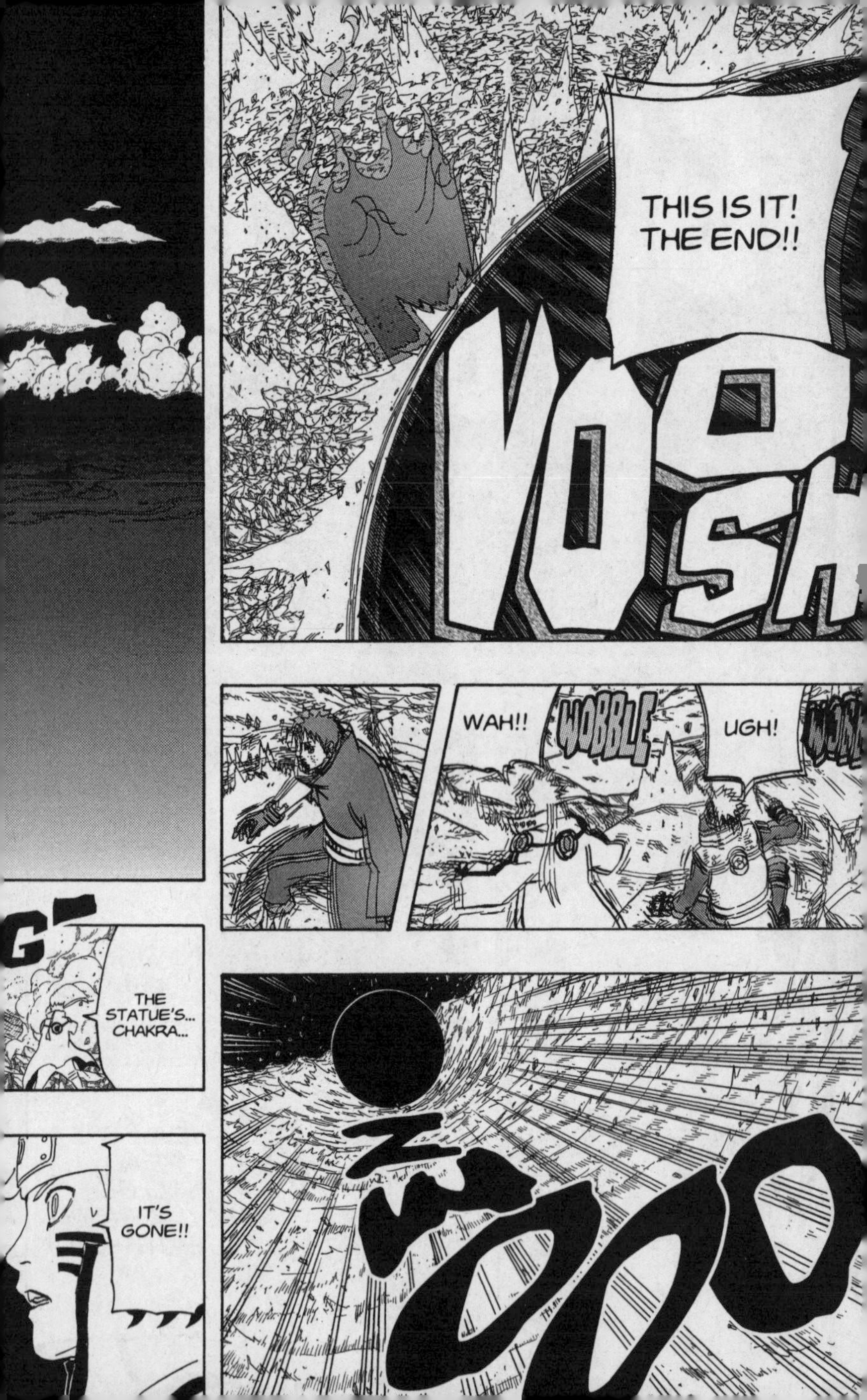
THIS IS IT! THE END!!
VOSH
UGH!
WOBBLE
WAH!!
THE STATUE'S... CHAKRA...
IT'S GONE!!

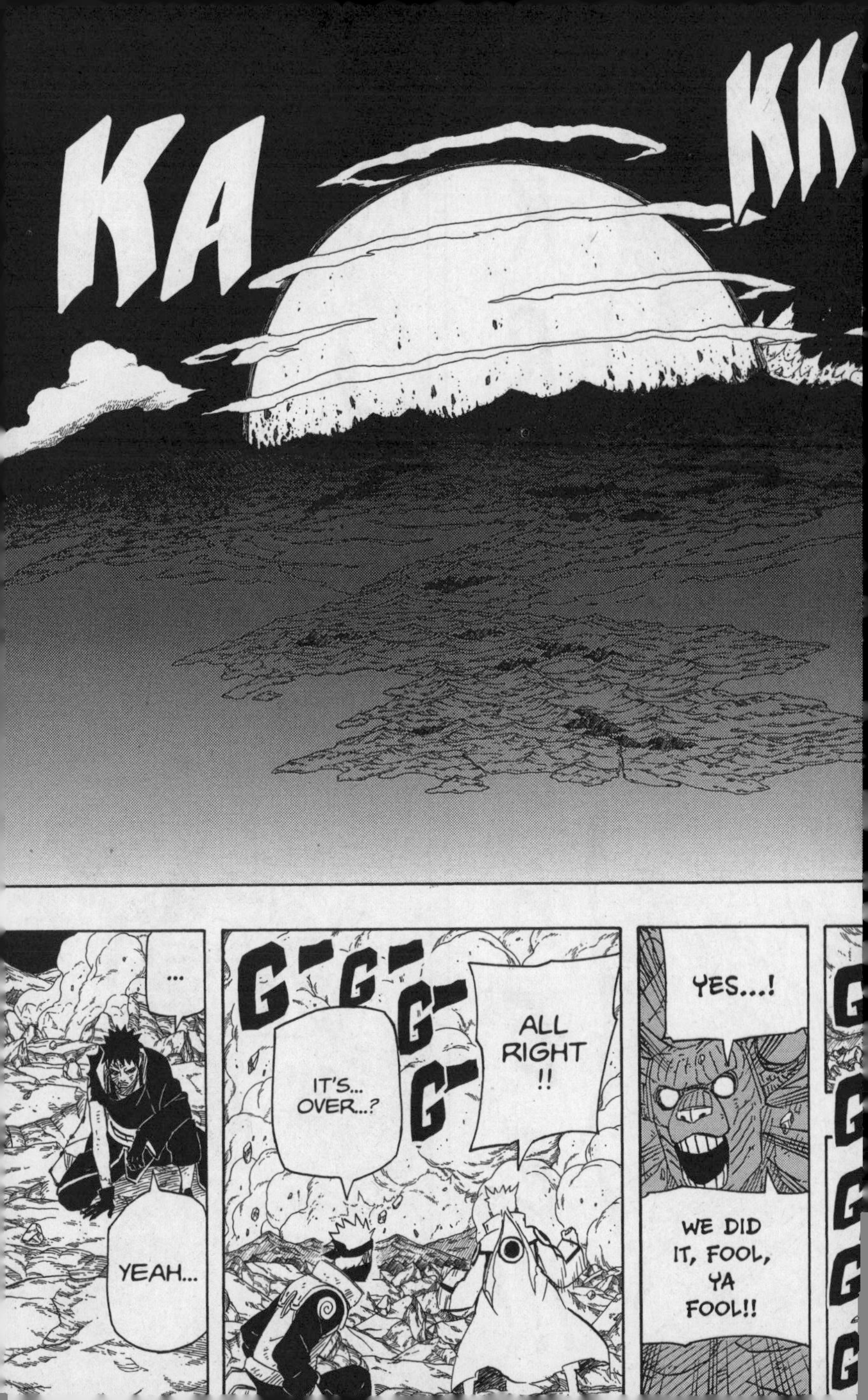
KA
KK
G
G
G
G
G
G
YES...!
WE DID IT, FOOL, YA FOOL!!
ALL RIGHT !!
G-G-G-G-
IT'S... OVER...?
...
YEAH...

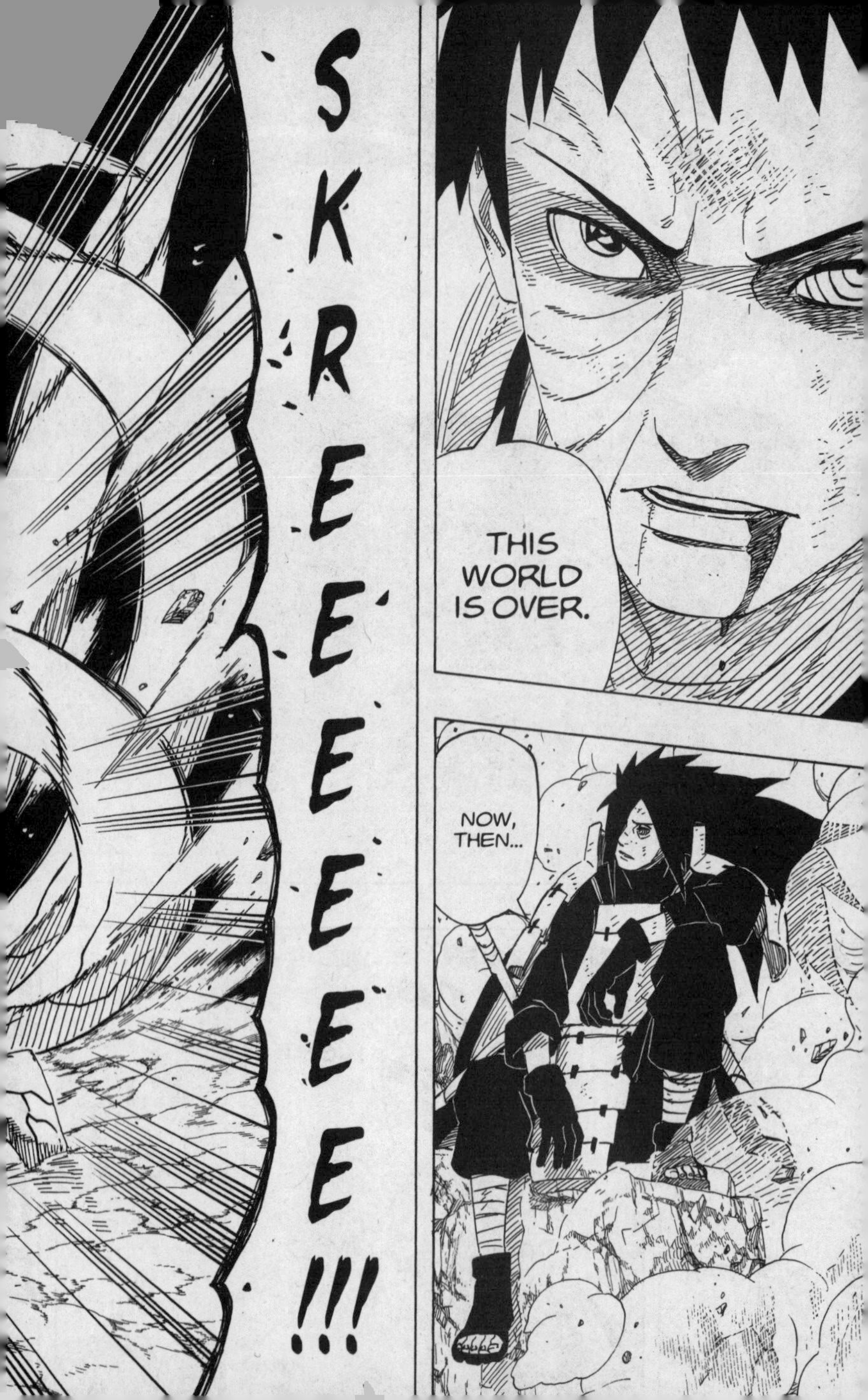
THIS WORLD IS OVER.
NOW, THEN...
SKREEEEEE!!!

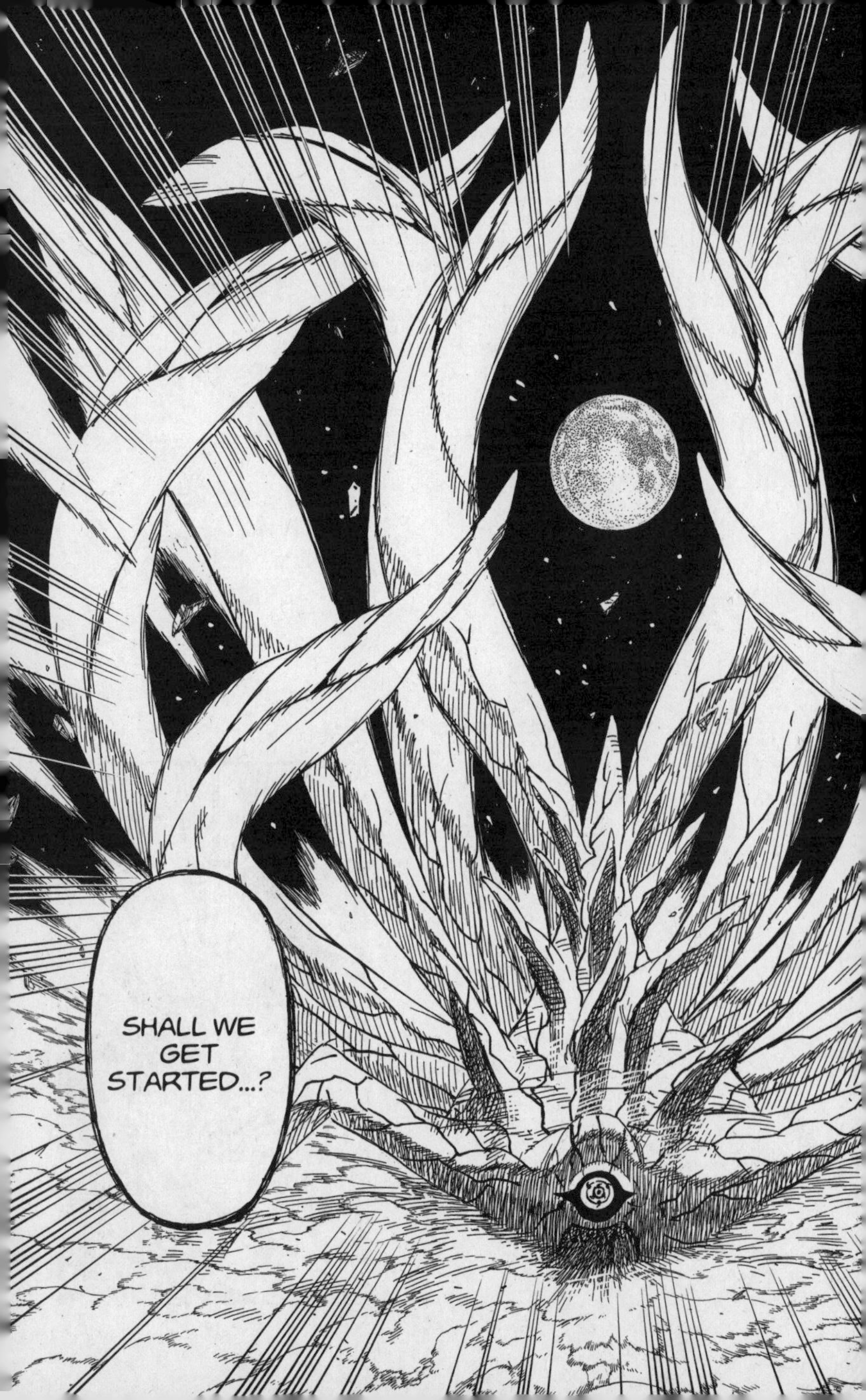
SHALL WE GET STARTED...?

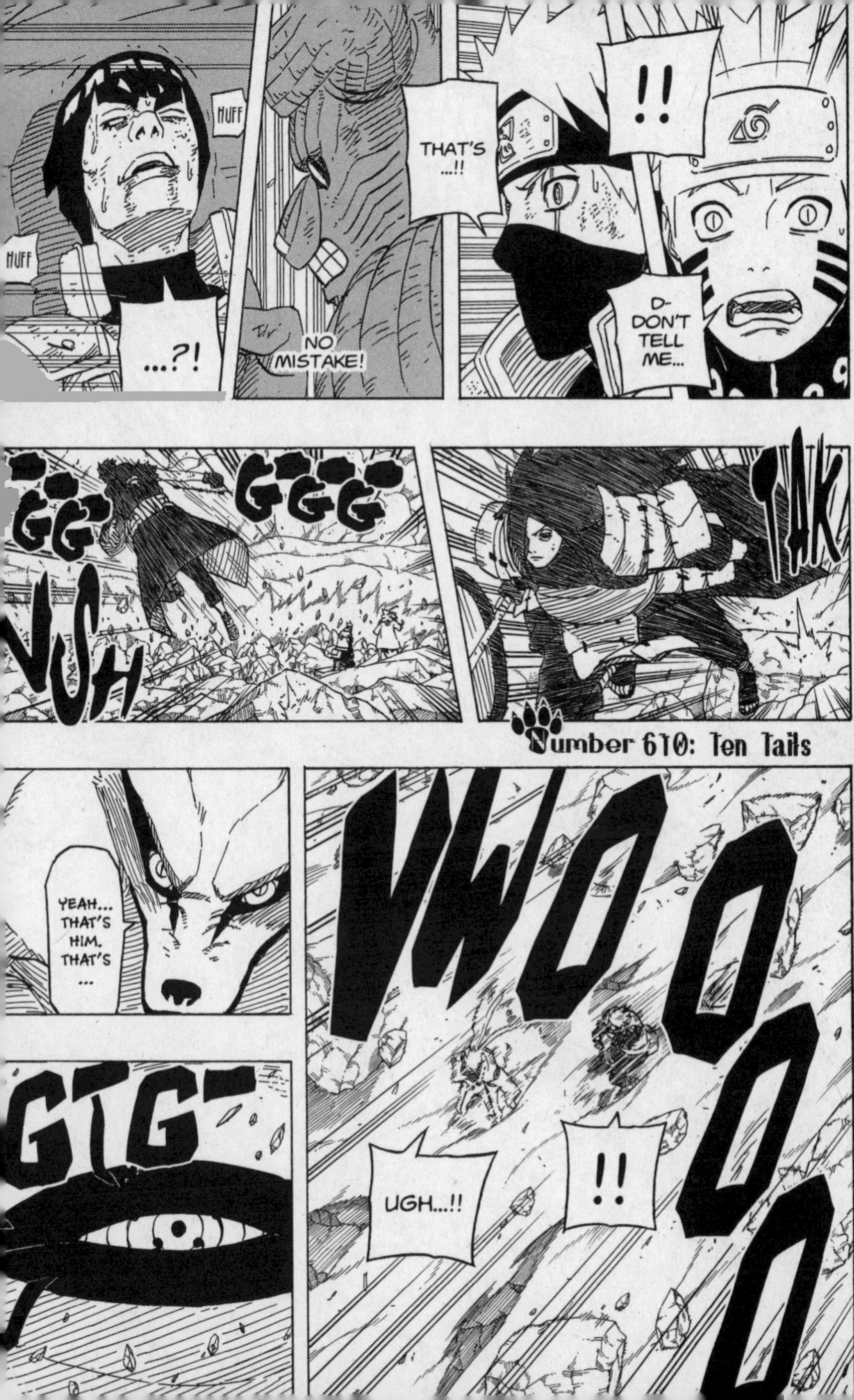
!!
THAT'S ...!!
D-DON'T TELL ME...
NO MISTAKE!
HUFF
HUFF
...?!
TAK
GGG
GG
VSH
Number 610: Ten Tails
VWOOOO
!!
UGH...!!
YEAH... THAT'S HIM. THAT'S ...
GIG

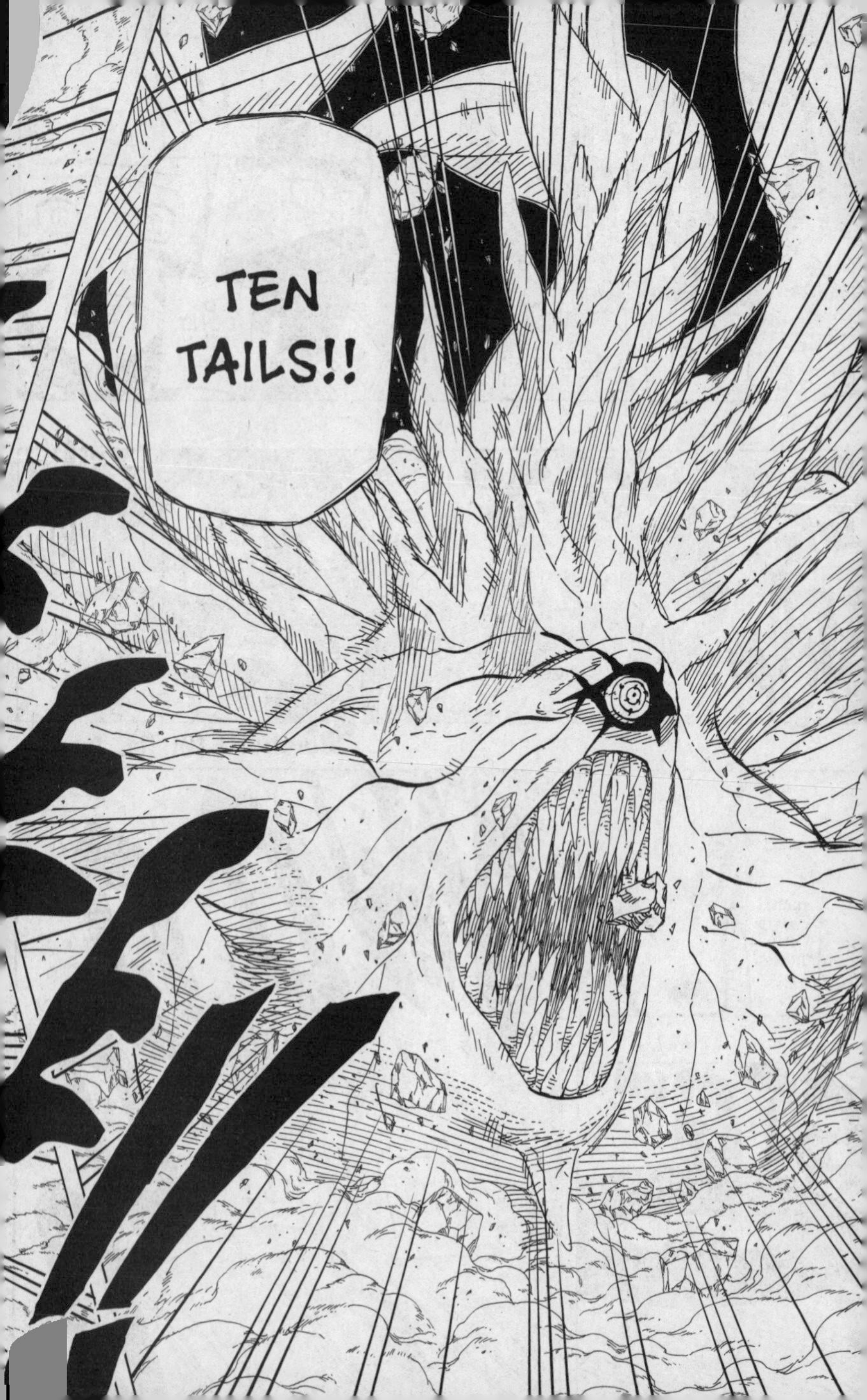
TEN TAILS!!

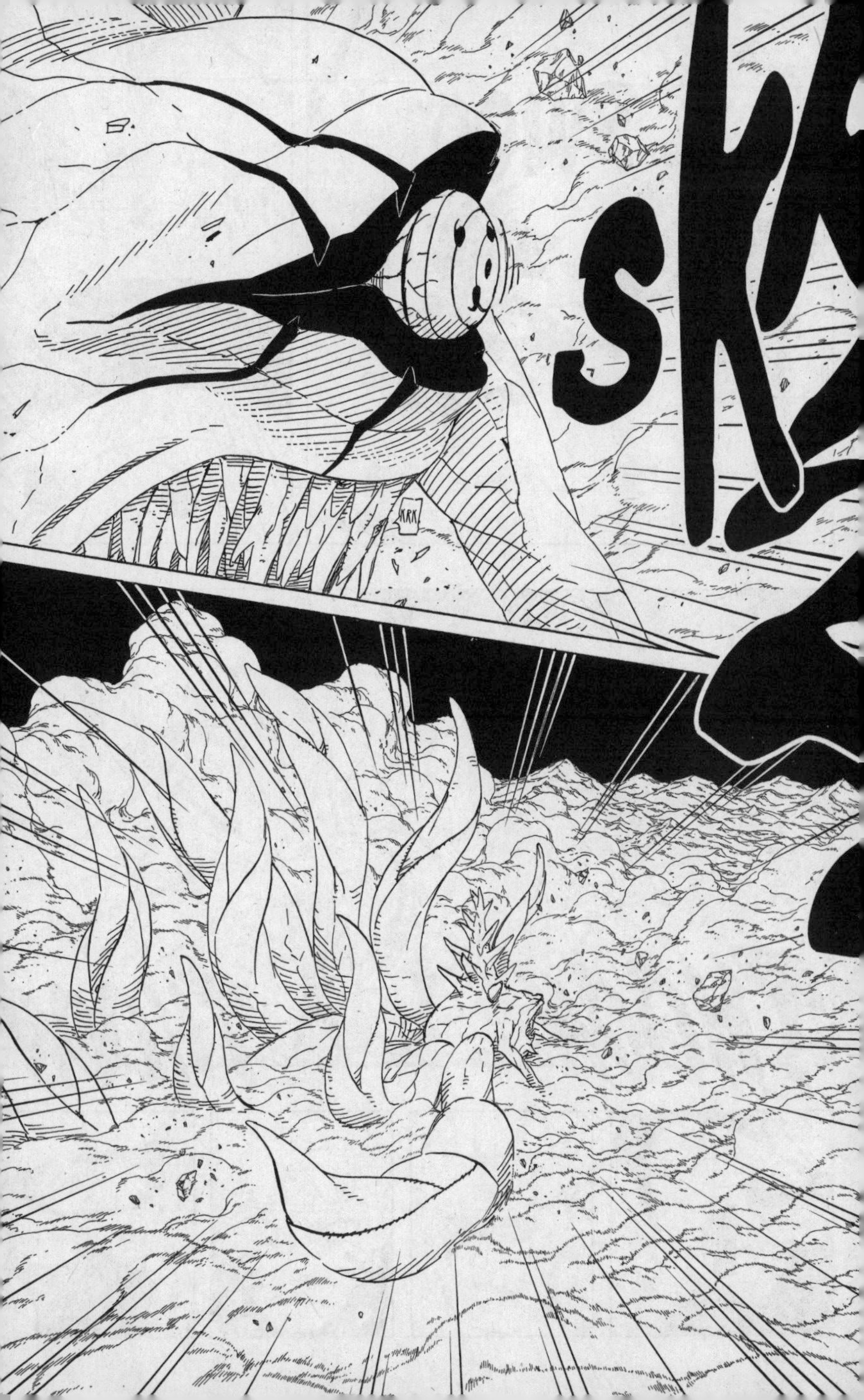
SK
KRK

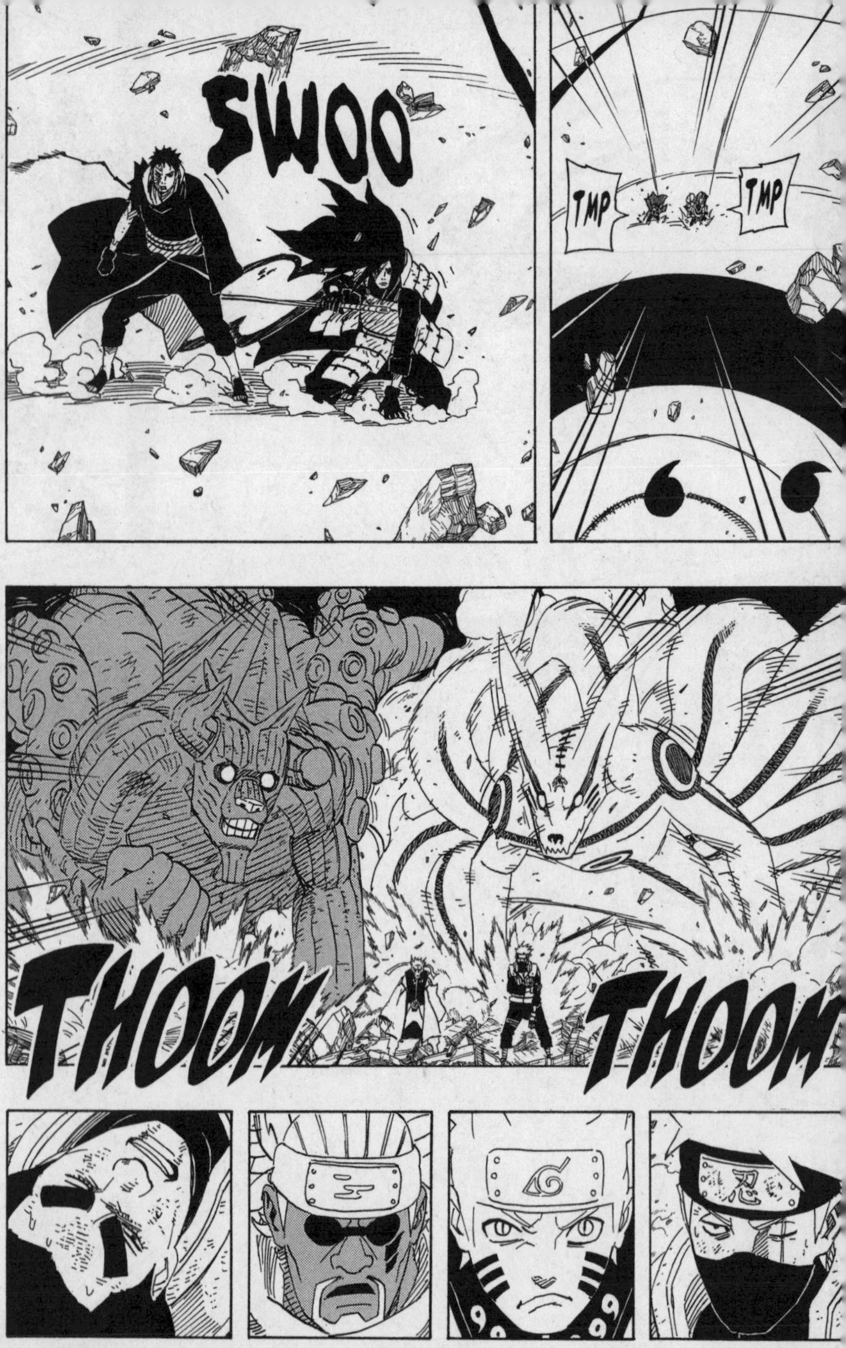
TMP
TMP
SWOO
THOOM
THOOM

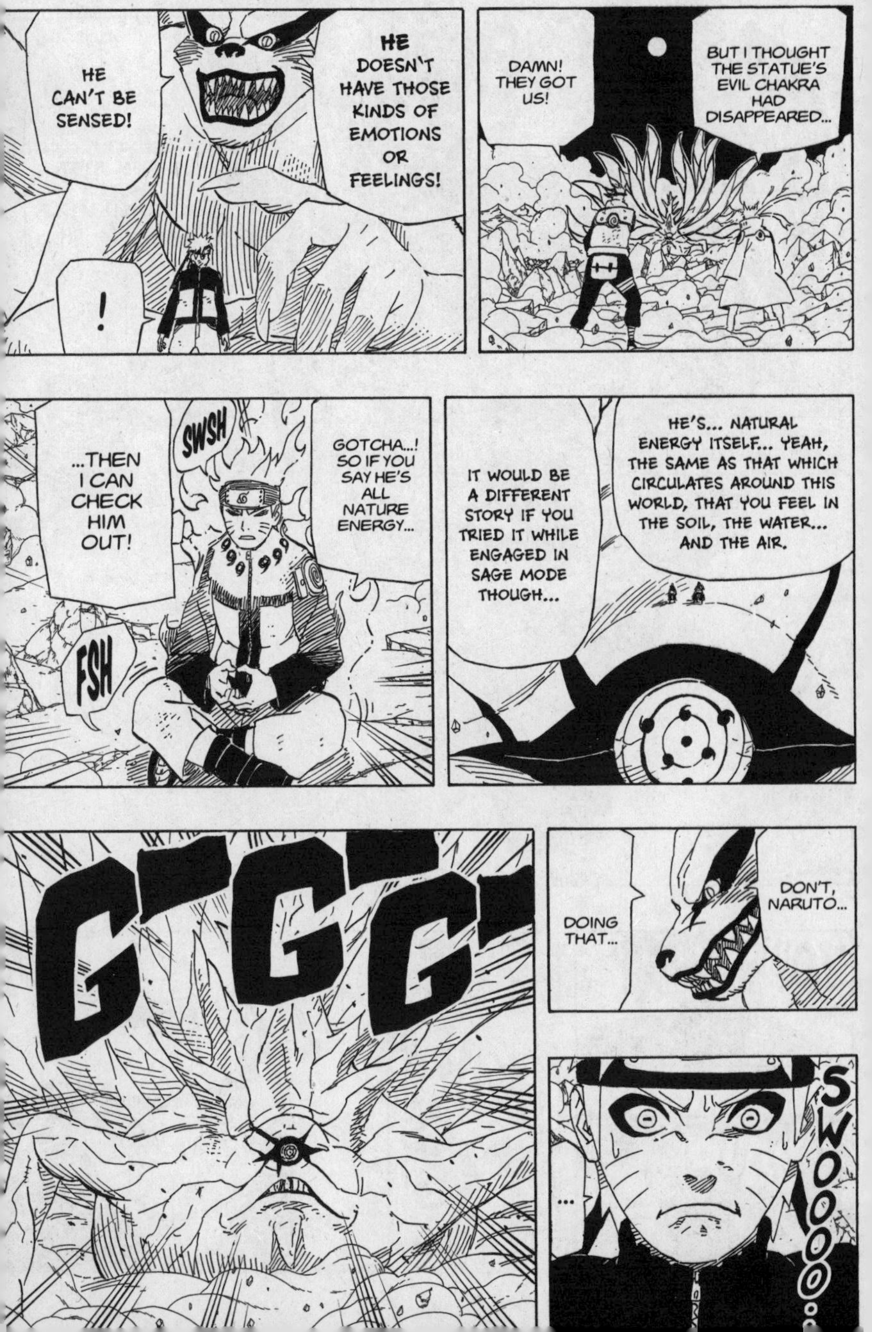
BUT I THOUGHT THE STATUE'S EVIL CHAKRA HAD DISAPPEARED...
DAMN! THEY GOT US!
HE DOESN'T HAVE THOSE KINDS OF EMOTIONS OR FEELINGS!
HE CAN'T BE SENSED!
!
HE'S... NATURAL ENERGY ITSELF... YEAH, THE SAME AS THAT WHICH CIRCULATES AROUND THIS WORLD, THAT YOU FEEL IN THE SOIL, THE WATER... AND THE AIR.
IT WOULD BE A DIFFERENT STORY IF YOU TRIED IT WHILE ENGAGED IN SAGE MODE THOUGH...
GOTCHA...! SO IF YOU SAY HE'S ALL NATURE ENERGY...
SWSH
...THEN I CAN CHECK HIM OUT!
FSH
DON'T, NARUTO...
DOING THAT...
SWOOOO...
...
GGG

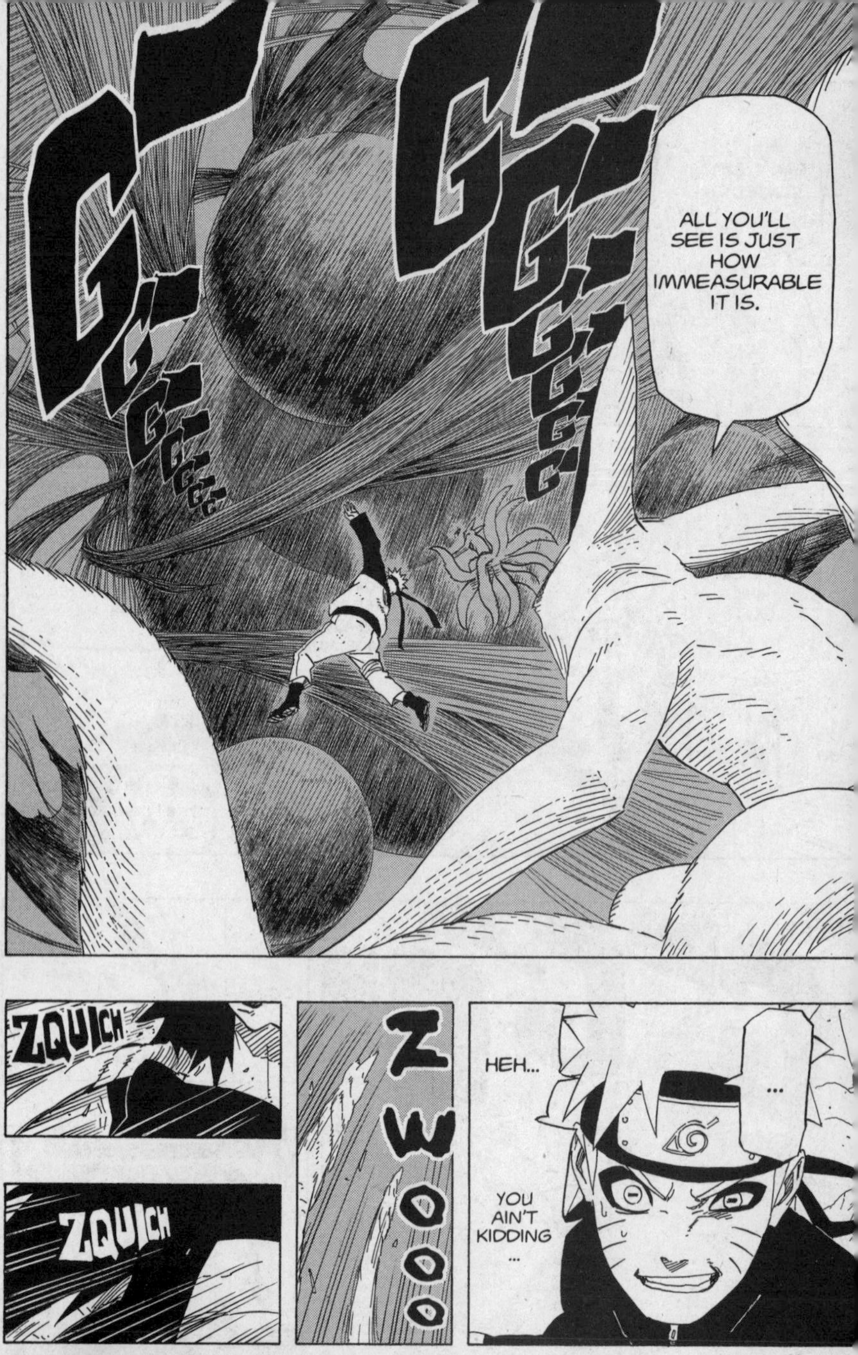
ALL YOU'LL SEE IS JUST HOW IMMEASURABLE IT IS.
GGGGGG
GGGGGG
...
HEH...
YOU AIN'T KIDDING ...
ZWOOO
ZQUICH
ZQUICH

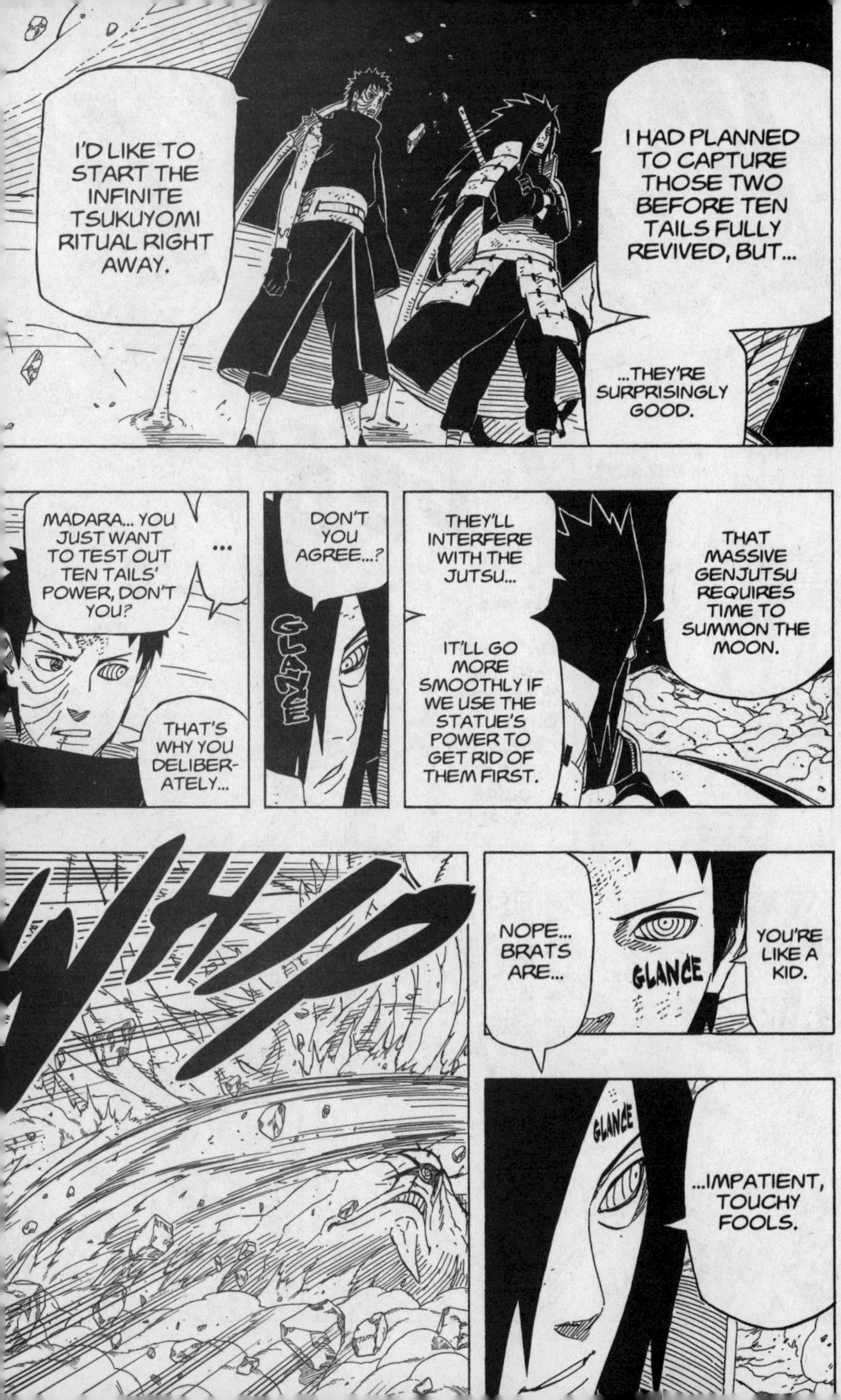
I HAD PLANNED TO CAPTURE THOSE TWO BEFORE TEN TAILS FULLY REVIVED, BUT...
...THEY'RE SURPRISINGLY GOOD.
I'D LIKE TO START THE INFINITE TSUKUYOMI RITUAL RIGHT AWAY.
THAT MASSIVE GENJUTSU REQUIRES TIME TO SUMMON THE MOON.
THEY'LL INTERFERE WITH THE JUTSU...
IT'LL GO MORE SMOOTHLY IF WE USE THE STATUE'S POWER TO GET RID OF THEM FIRST.
DON'T YOU AGREE...?
GLANCE
...
MADARA... YOU JUST WANT TO TEST OUT TEN TAILS' POWER, DON'T YOU?
THAT'S WHY YOU DELIBERATELY...
YOU'RE LIKE A KID.
GLANCE
NOPE... BRATS ARE...
...IMPATIENT, TOUCHY FOOLS.
GLANCE

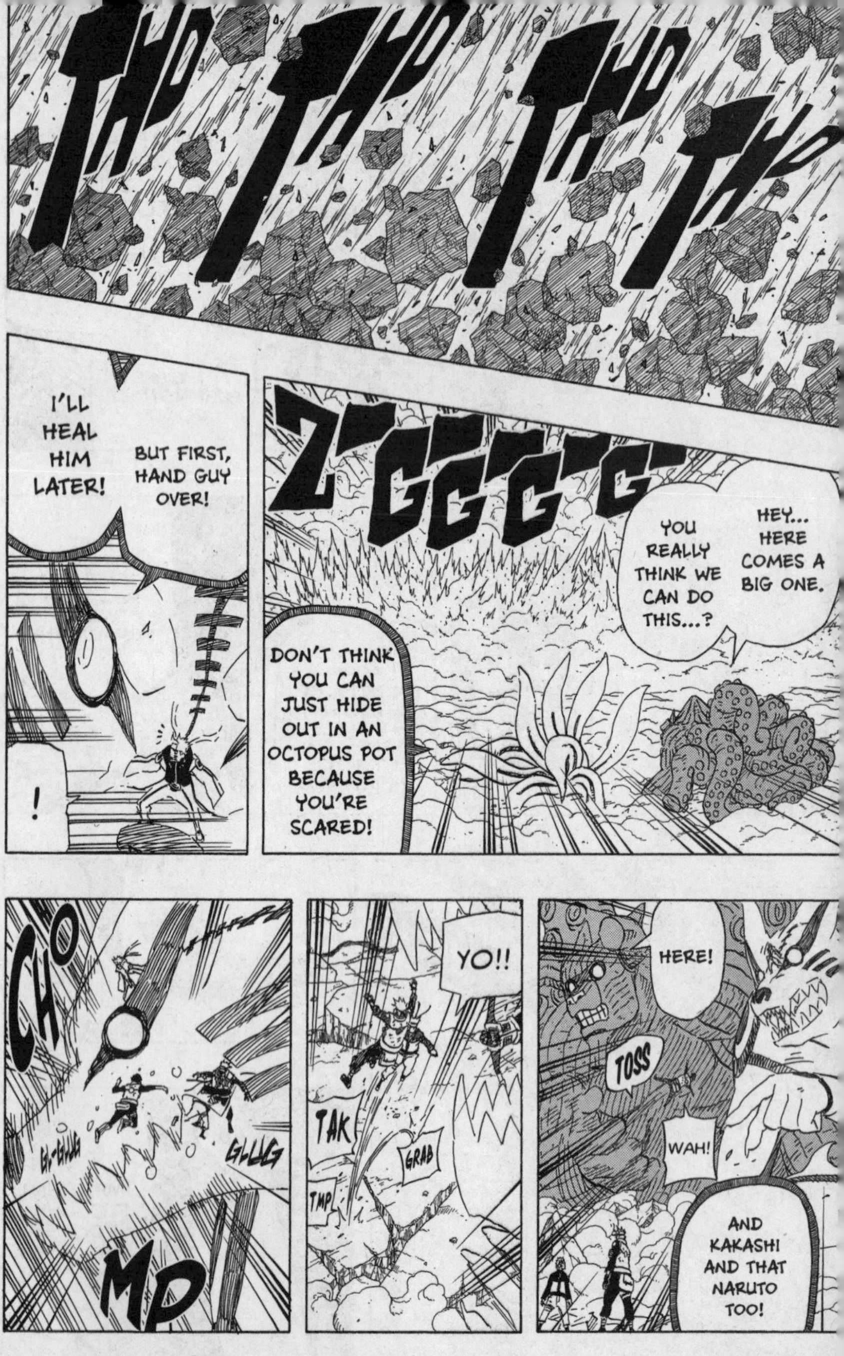
THD THD THD THD
HEY... HERE COMES A BIG ONE.
YOU REALLY THINK WE CAN DO THIS...?
ZGGGG
DON'T THINK YOU CAN JUST HIDE OUT IN AN OCTOPUS POT BECAUSE YOU'RE SCARED!
BUT FIRST, HAND GUY OVER!
I'LL HEAL HIM LATER!
!
HERE!
TOSS
WAH!
AND KAKASHI AND THAT NARUTO TOO!
YO!!
TAK
GRAB
TMP
CHO
GL-GLUG
GLUG
MP

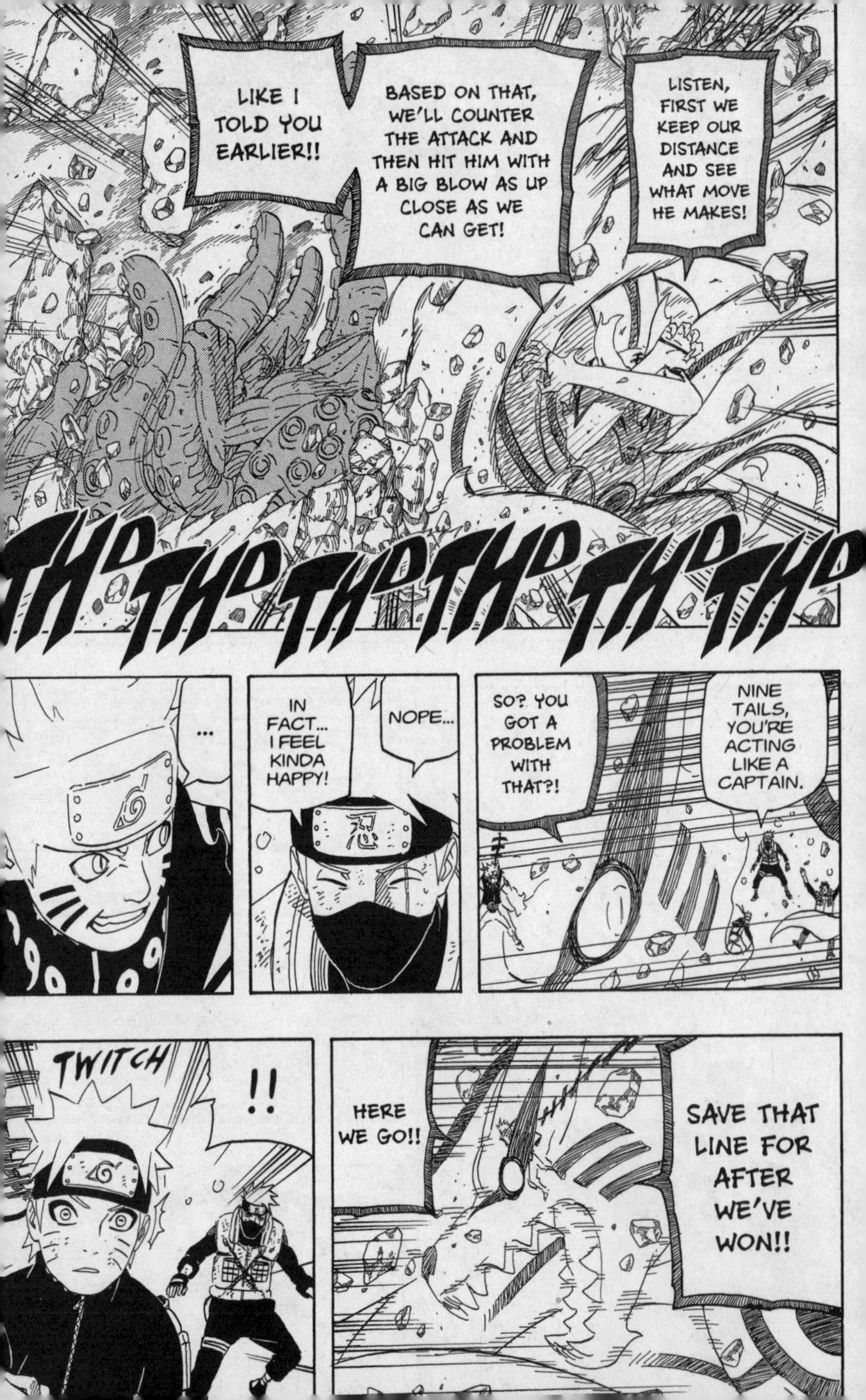
LISTEN, FIRST WE KEEP OUR DISTANCE AND SEE WHAT MOVE HE MAKES!
BASED ON THAT, WE'LL COUNTER THE ATTACK AND THEN HIT HIM WITH A BIG BLOW AS UP CLOSE AS WE CAN GET!
LIKE I TOLD YOU EARLIER!!
THP THP THP THP THP THP
NINE TAILS, YOU'RE ACTING LIKE A CAPTAIN.
SO? YOU GOT A PROBLEM WITH THAT?!
NOPE...
IN FACT... I FEEL KINDA HAPPY!
...
SAVE THAT LINE FOR AFTER WE'VE WON!!
HERE WE GO!!
!!
TWITCH

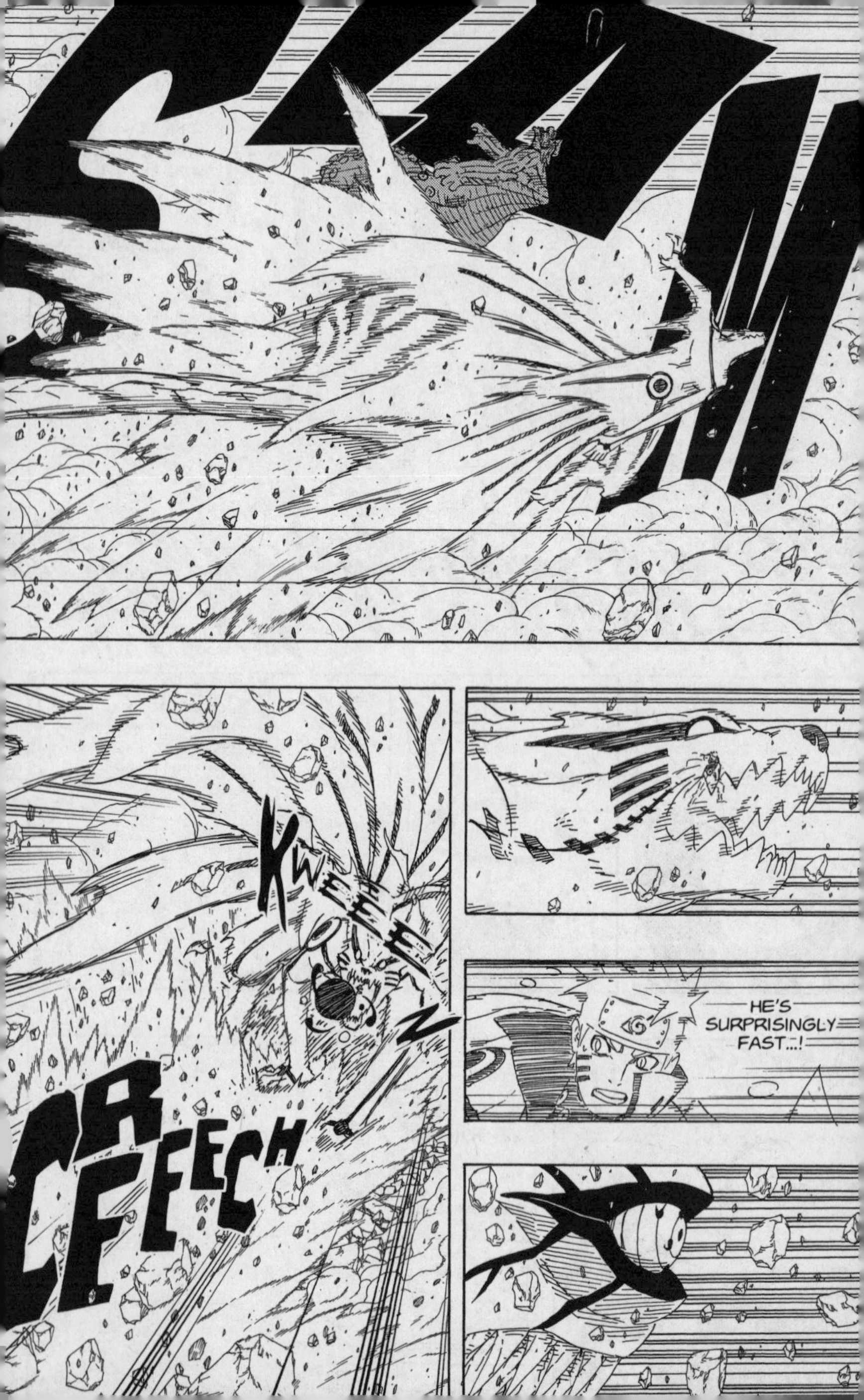
HE'S SURPRISINGLY FAST...!
KWEEEEN
CREEECH

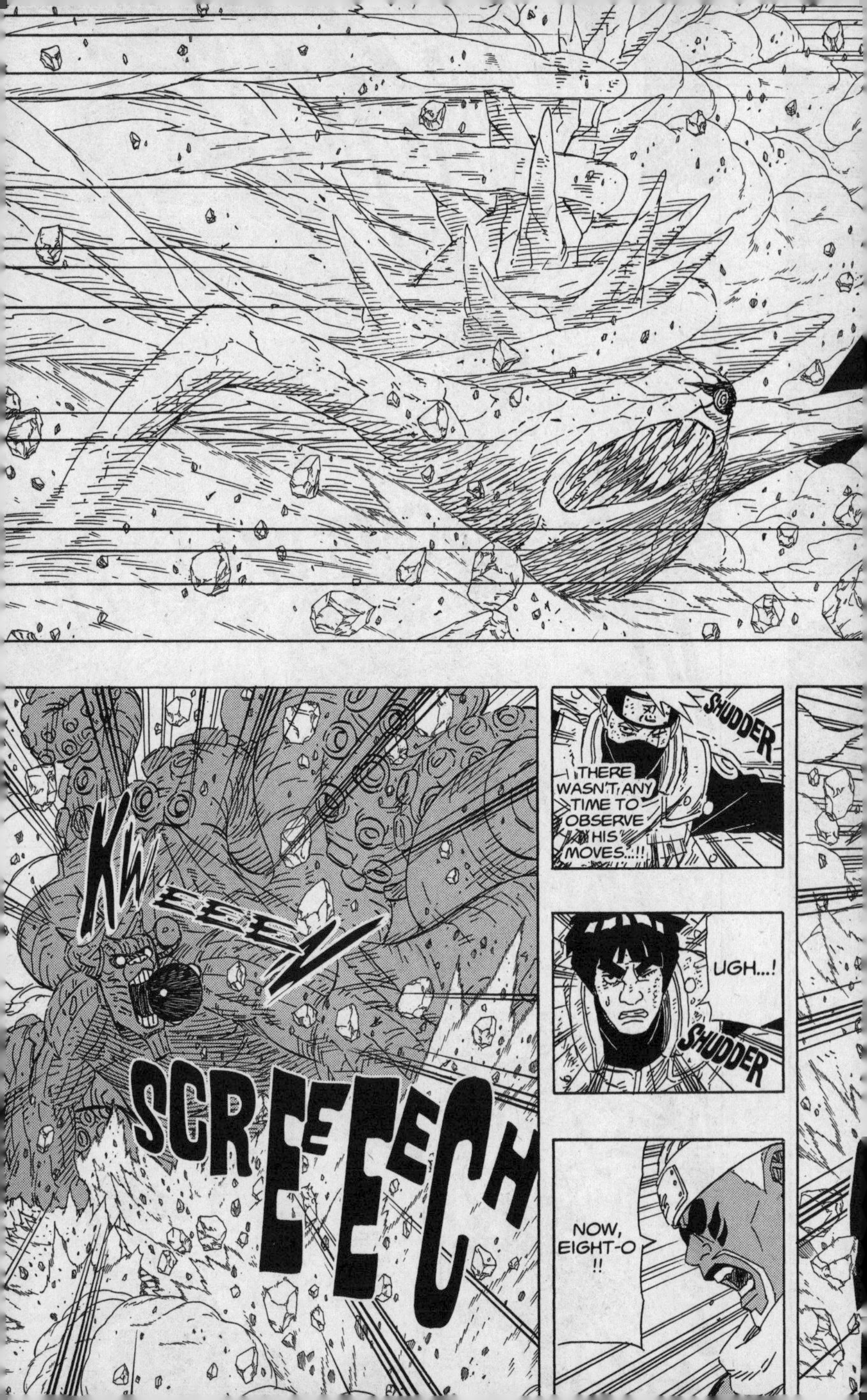
SHUDDER
THERE WASN'T ANY TIME TO OBSERVE HIS MOVES...!!
UGH...!
SHUDDER
NOW, EIGHT-O !!
KWEEEN
SCREEECH

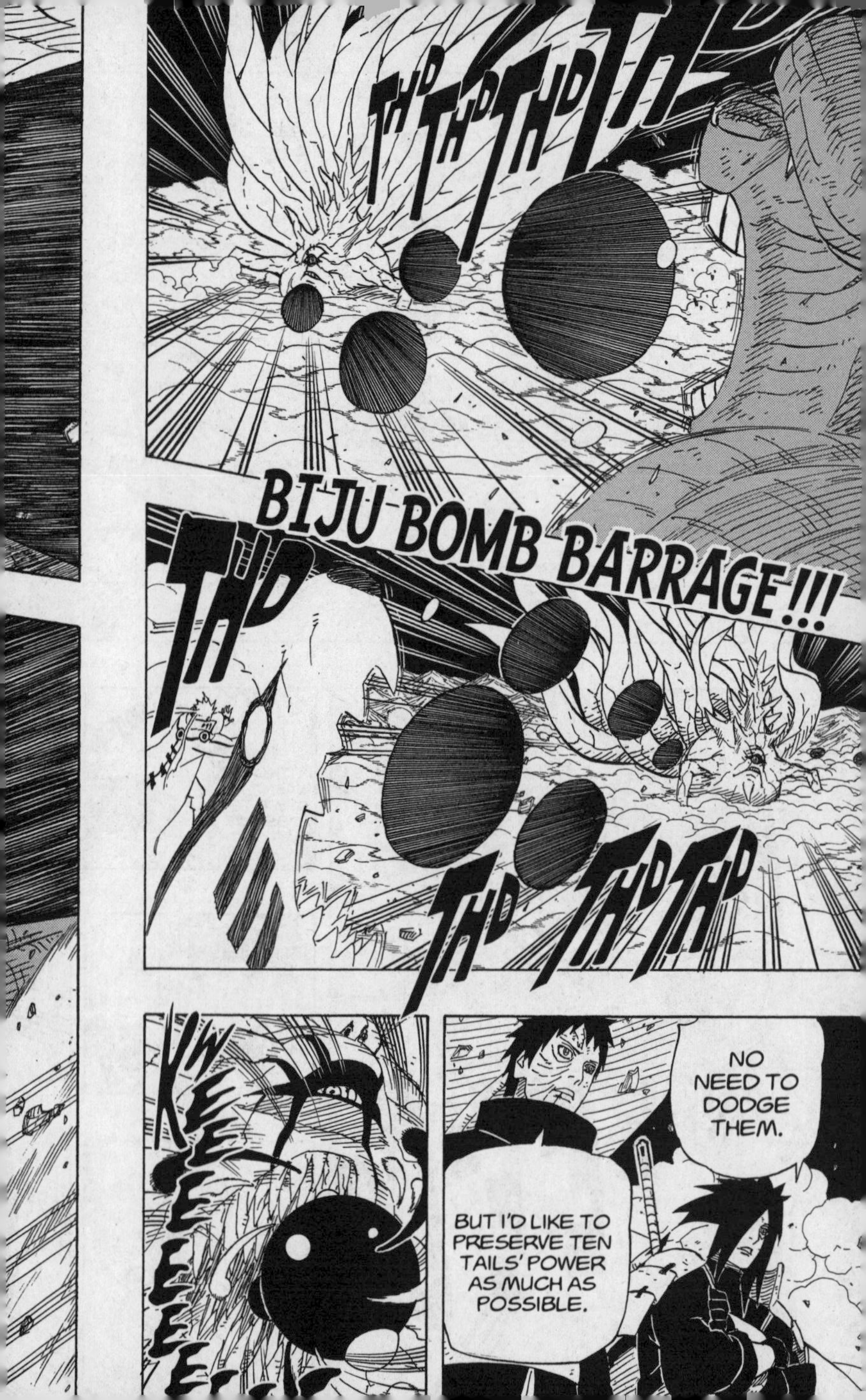
THD THD THD THD
BIJU BOMB BARRAGE!!!
THD
THD THD THD
NO NEED TO DODGE THEM.
BUT I'D LIKE TO PRESERVE TEN TAILS' POWER AS MUCH AS POSSIBLE.
KWEEEEEEE

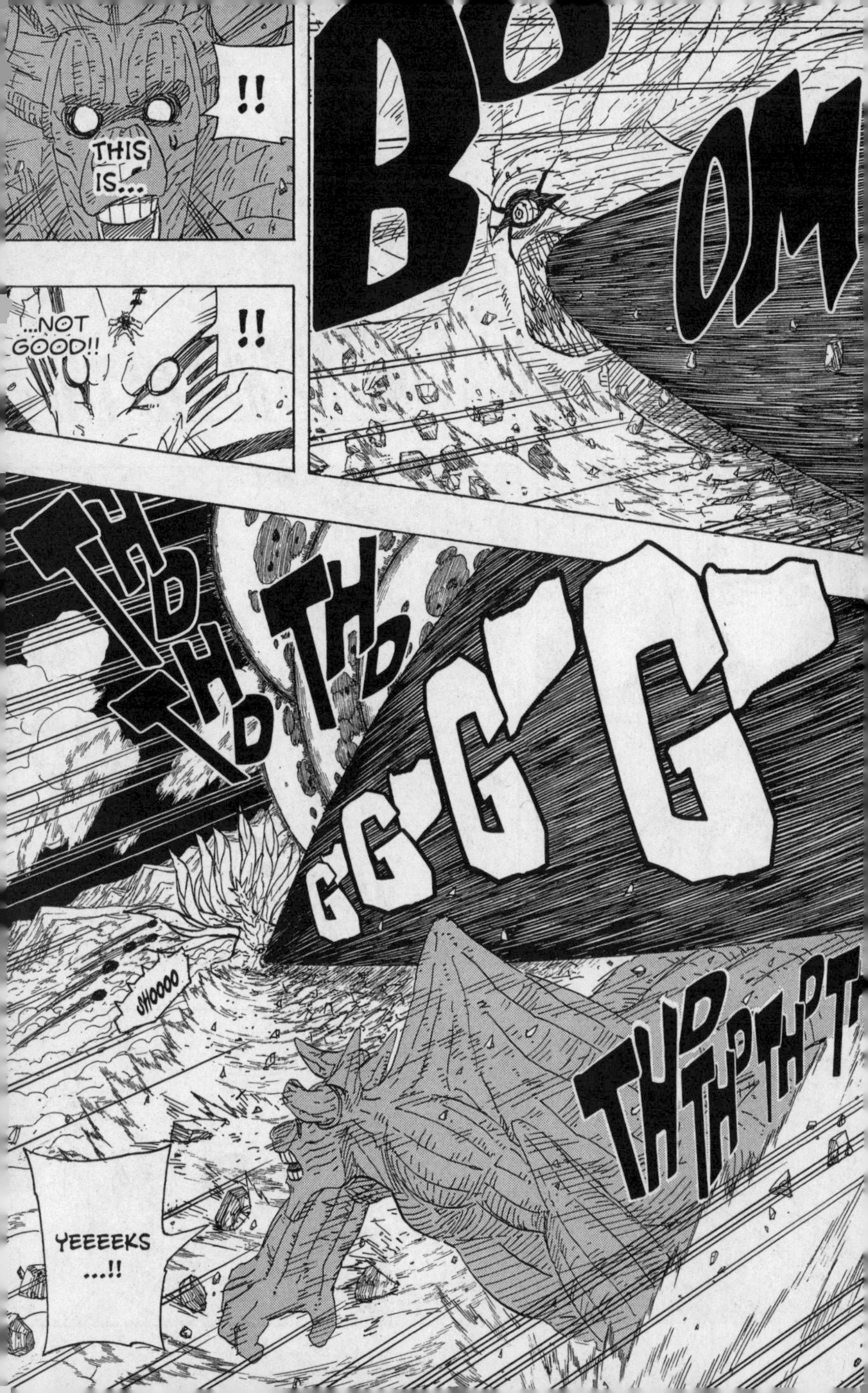
BOOM
!!
THIS IS...
!!
...NOT GOOD!!
GGGG
THDTHDTHDT
THD THD THD
SHOOOO
YEEEEKS ...!!

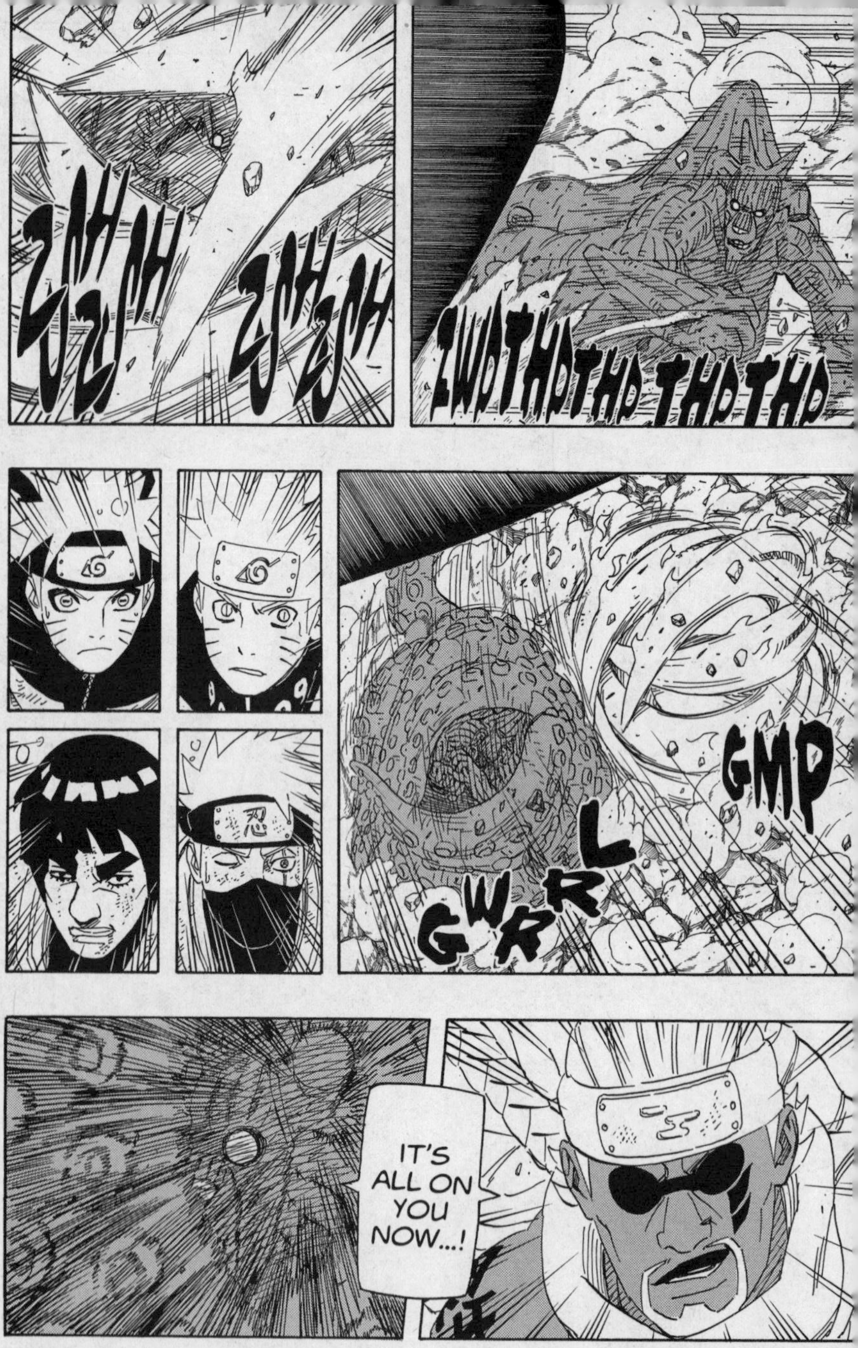
GMP
IT'S ALL ON YOU NOW...!

BOOF BOOF
BOOF BOOF

WHD

G'G'G'G'

ZWWW...

ZW...

TENA-
CIOUS
BUGGERS
...

HEY...
NARUTO,
DON'T TELL
ME...!!

!!

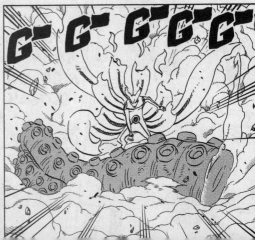

G'G'G'G'G'

NICE CONTROL, NARUTO!

DON'T WORRY... MASTER UBER-BROWS!

WE FOCUSED TOO MUCH ON TEN TAILS...!

BUT HERE WE GO!

I'M SORRY ABOUT THE ONE LEG

KAMUI!!

ZOO

YOU GOT THEM IN NICE AND CLOSE!!

LOOKS LIKE WE LEFT ONE OCTOPUS LEG BEHIND, BUT...

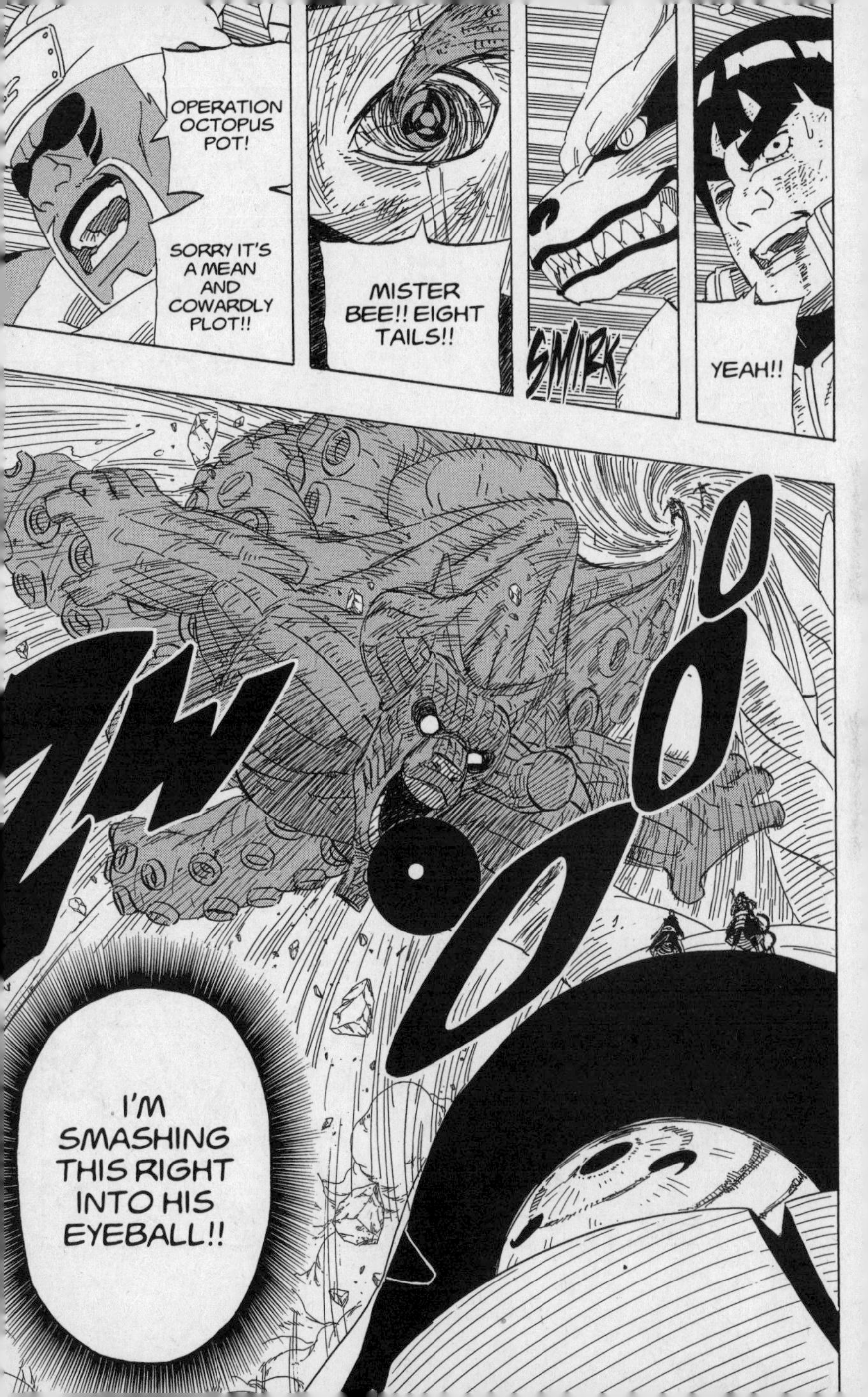
YEAH!!
SMIRK
MISTER BEE!! EIGHT TAILS!!
OPERATION OCTOPUS POT!
SORRY IT'S A MEAN AND COWARDLY PLOT!!
I'M SMASHING THIS RIGHT INTO HIS EYEBALL!!

Number 611: The Arrival

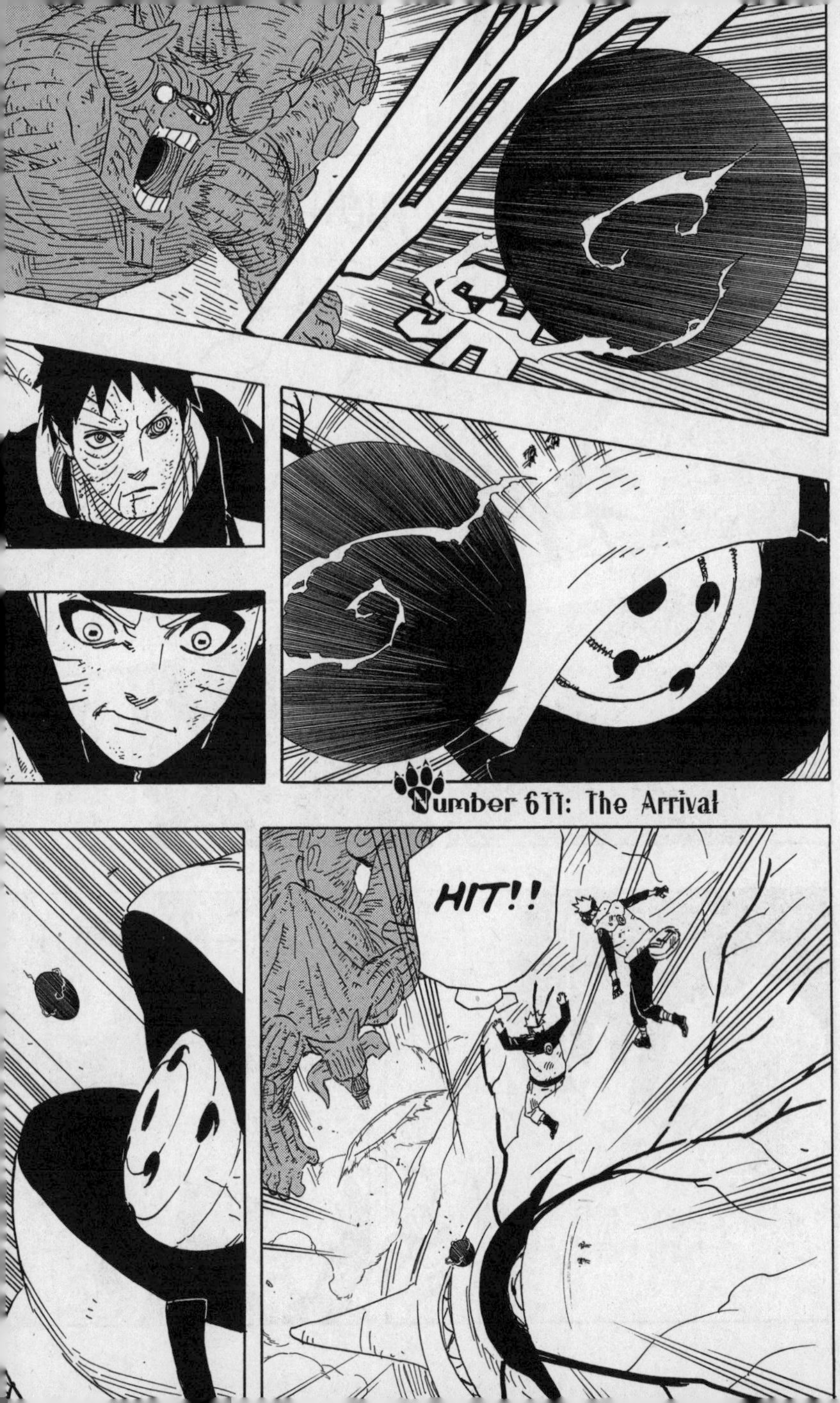
HIT!!

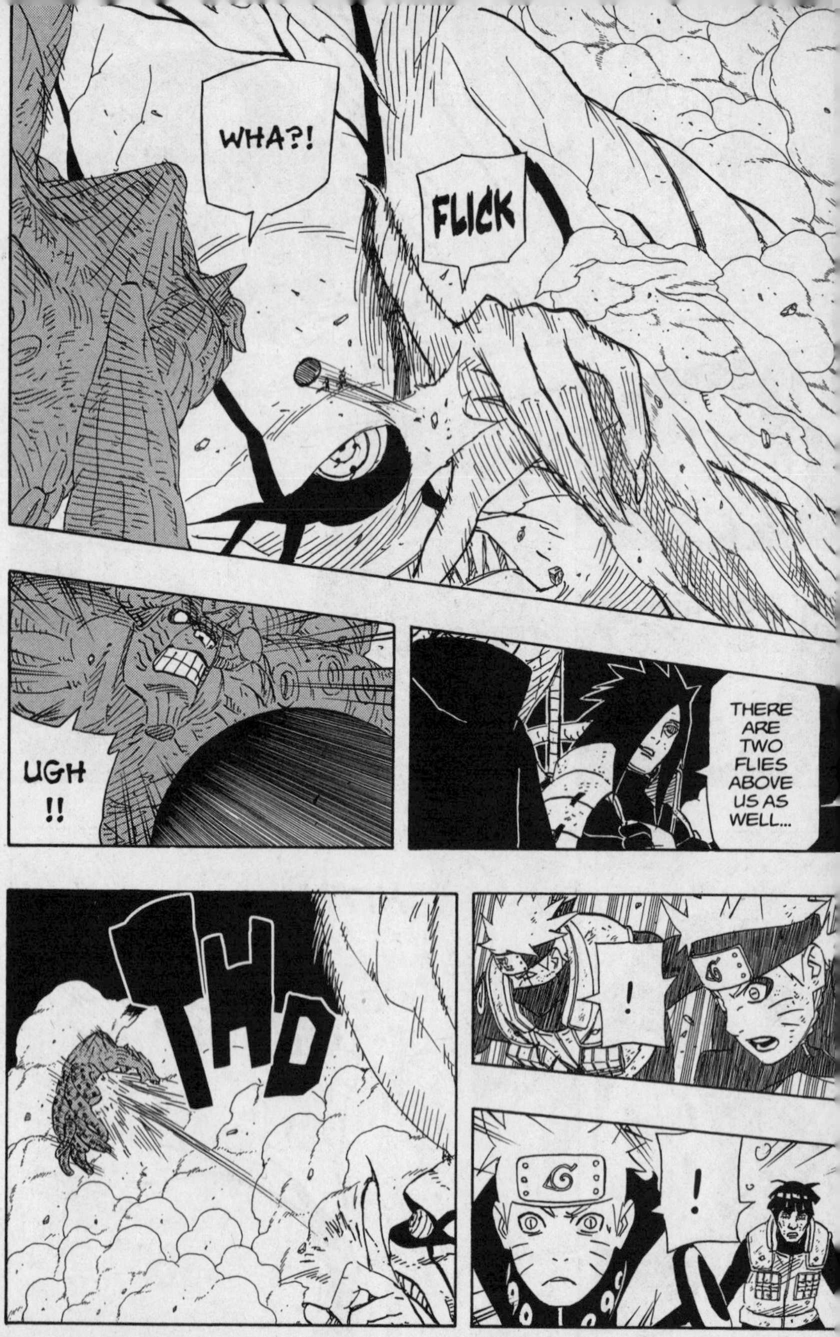
FLICK
WHA?!
THERE ARE TWO FLIES ABOVE US AS WELL...
UGH !!
!
!
THD

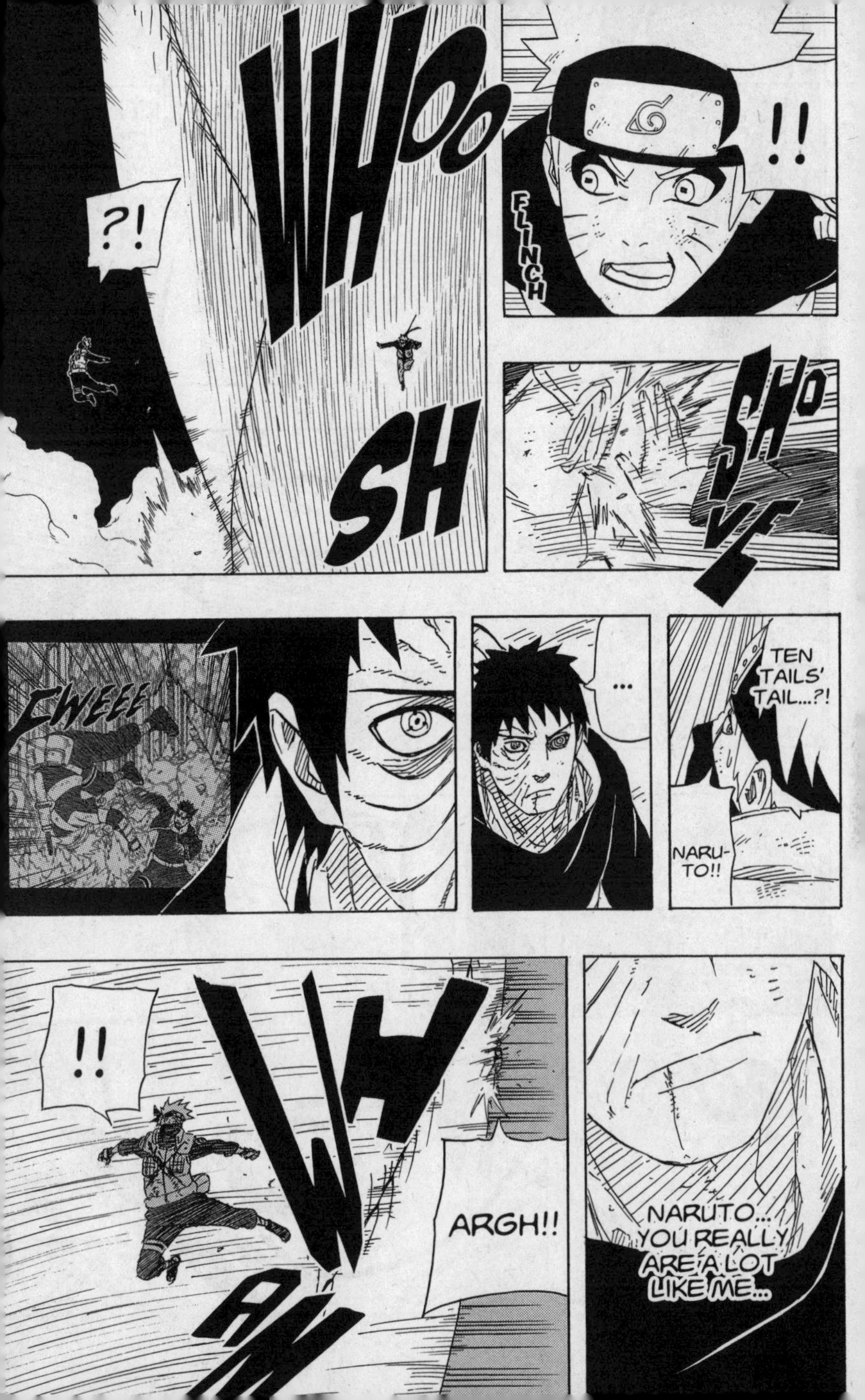
!!
FLINCH
SHOVE
WHOOSH
?!
TEN TAILS' TAIL...?!
NARUTO!!
...
CWEEE
NARUTO... YOU REALLY ARE A LOT LIKE ME...
ARGH!!
WHAM
!!

EVENTUALLY... THAT'S RIGHT... YOU'RE MERELY YOUNGER THAN ME.

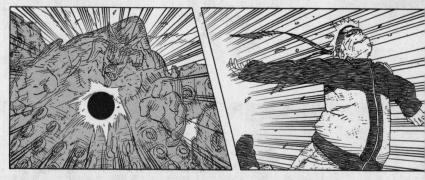

FORGIVE ME...

EIGHT-O AND OCTOPOPS!!

AARGH!!!

KAB

KOOM

BO

OF

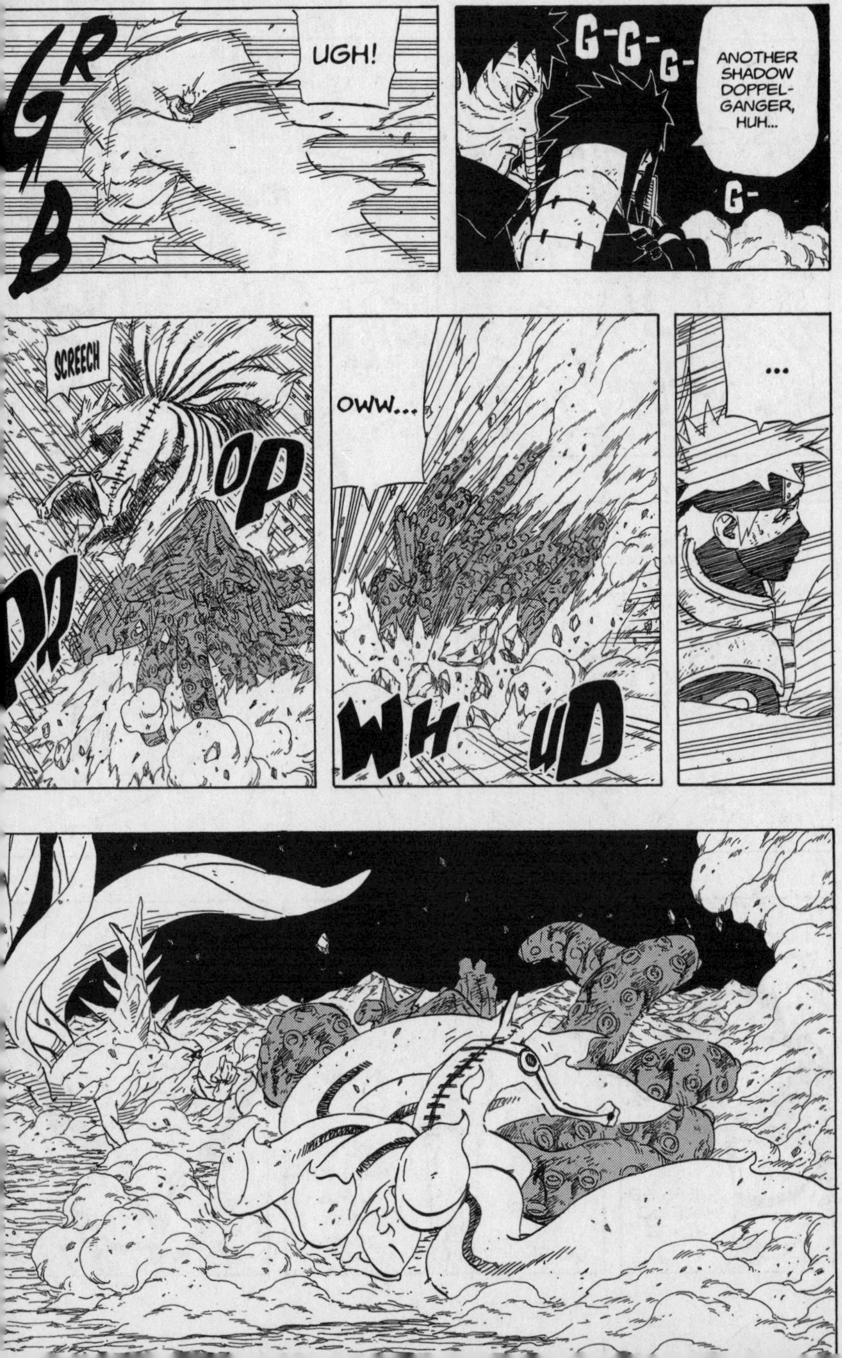
ANOTHER SHADOW DOPPEL-GANGER, HUH...
G-G-G-
G-
UGH!
...
OWW...
WHUD
SCREECH

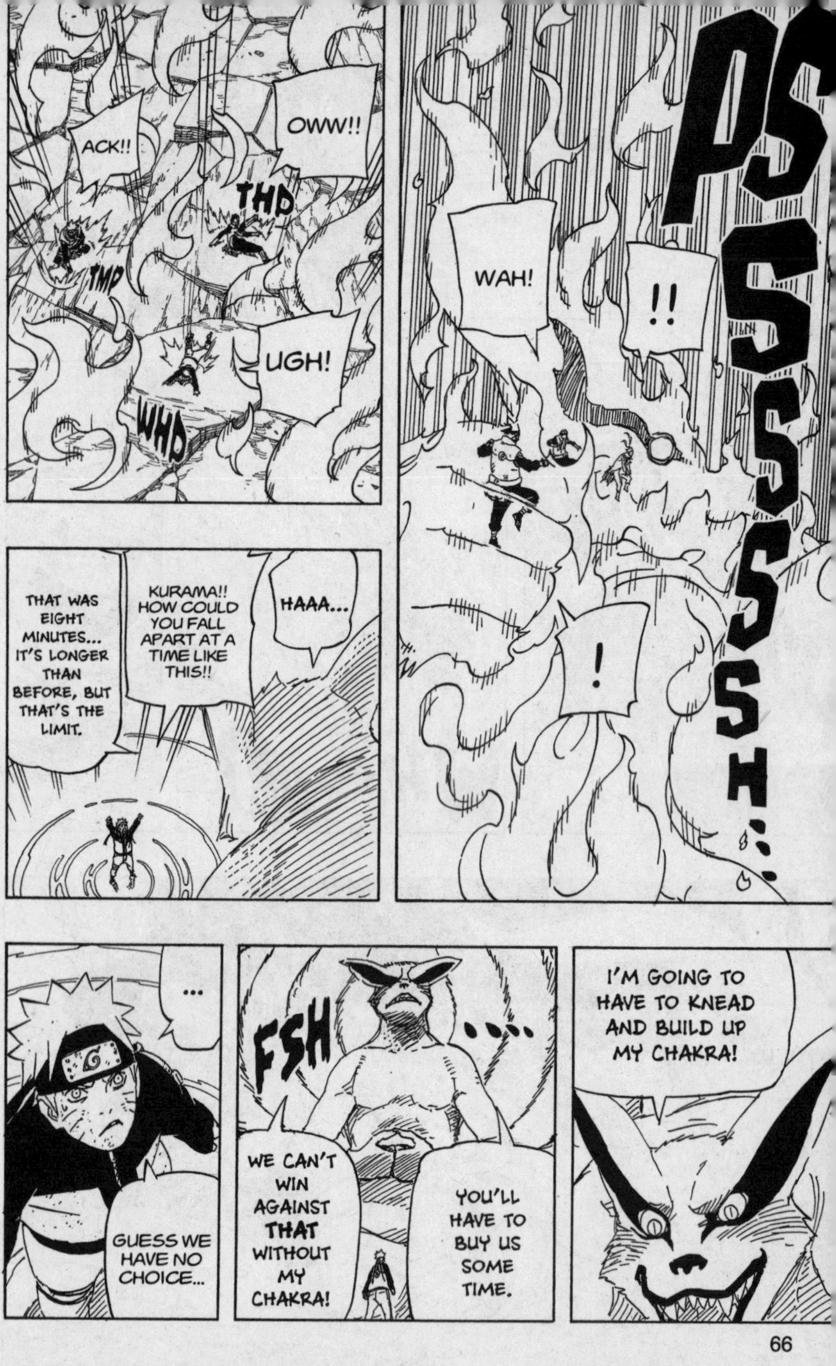
PSSSSH...
!!
WAH!
!
OWW!!
THD
ACK!!
TMP
UGH!
WHD
HAAA...
KURAMA!! HOW COULD YOU FALL APART AT A TIME LIKE THIS!!
THAT WAS EIGHT MINUTES... IT'S LONGER THAN BEFORE, BUT THAT'S THE LIMIT.
I'M GOING TO HAVE TO KNEAD AND BUILD UP MY CHAKRA!
....
FSH
WE CAN'T WIN AGAINST THAT WITHOUT MY CHAKRA!
YOU'LL HAVE TO BUY US SOME TIME.
...
GUESS WE HAVE NO CHOICE...

BEE! I'M GOING TO REST A BIT TOO... I'M ALSO AT MY LIMIT.

THAT HURT, FOOL, YA FOOL...!

ZWWW

ZWWW

I'M DRAINED ALREADY...

PULLING SOMETHING AS MASSIVE AS EIGHT TAILS IN AND OUT... SURE COMES WITH A CORRESPONDINGLY LARGE COST...

HAK

HUFF

I CAN'T... GET HEALED YET?

SEEMS EIGHT TAILS AND NINE TAILS HAVE TEMPORARILY RUN OUT OF CHAKRA...

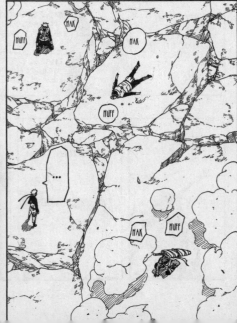

HAK

HUFF

HAK

HUFF

...

HAK

HUFF

GLANCE

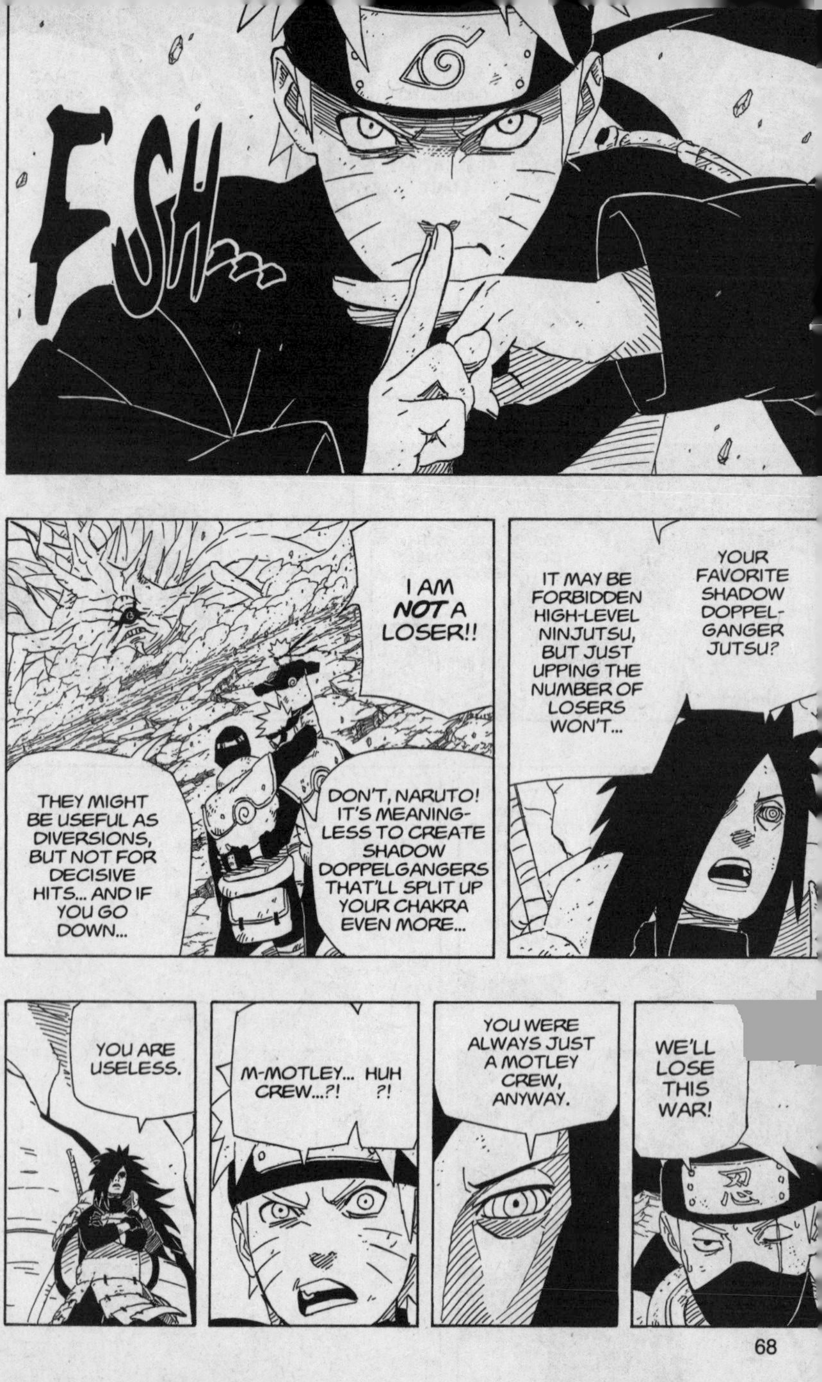
FSH
YOUR FAVORITE SHADOW DOPPEL-GANGER JUTSU?
IT MAY BE FORBIDDEN HIGH-LEVEL NINJUTSU, BUT JUST UPPING THE NUMBER OF LOSERS WON'T...
I AM *NOT* A LOSER!!
DON'T, NARUTO! IT'S MEANING-LESS TO CREATE SHADOW DOPPELGANGERS THAT'LL SPLIT UP YOUR CHAKRA EVEN MORE...
THEY MIGHT BE USEFUL AS DIVERSIONS, BUT NOT FOR DECISIVE HITS... AND IF YOU GO DOWN...
WE'LL LOSE THIS WAR!
YOU WERE ALWAYS JUST A MOTLEY CREW, ANYWAY.
HUH ?!
M-MOTLEY... CREW...?!
YOU ARE USELESS.

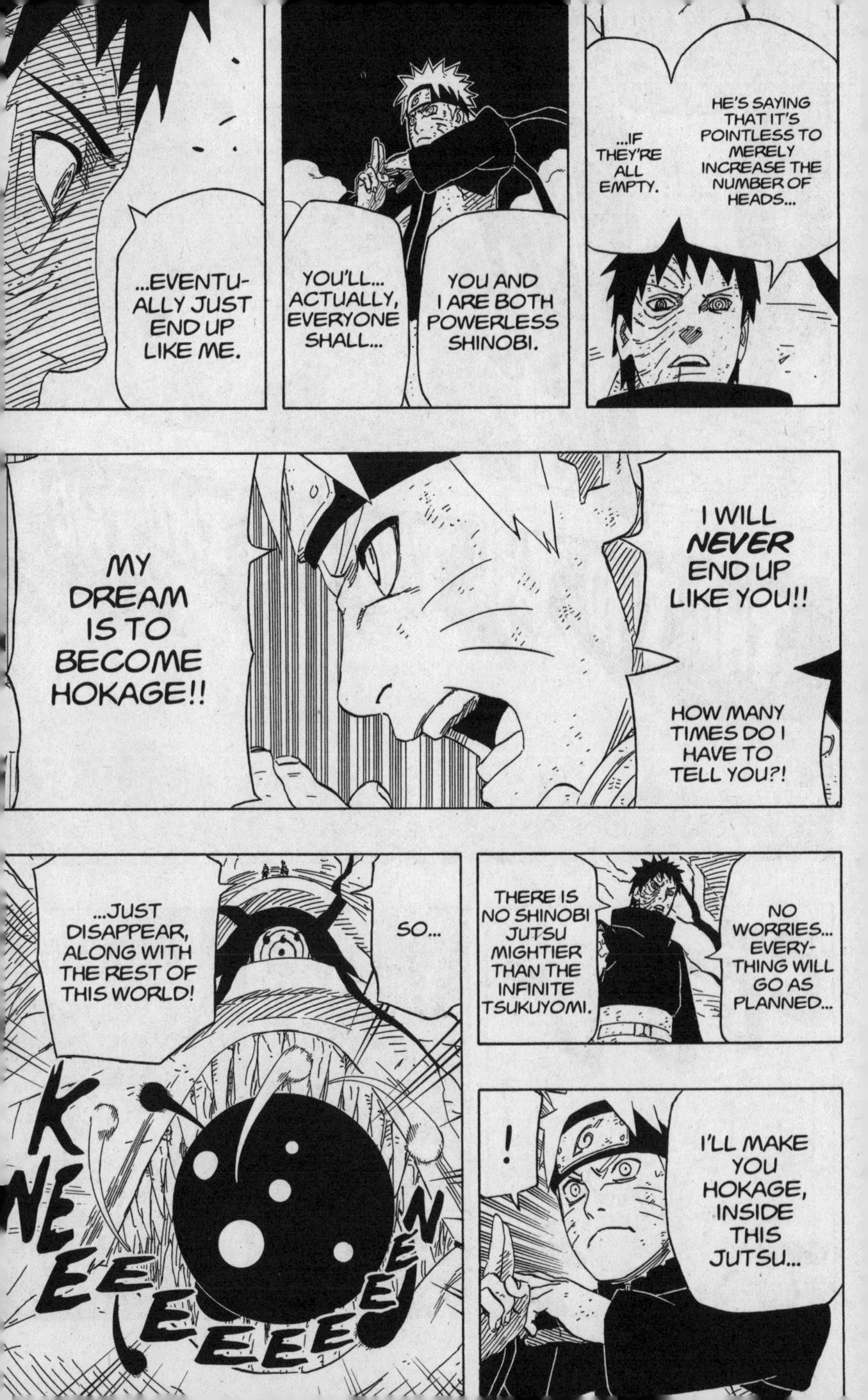
HE'S SAYING THAT IT'S POINTLESS TO MERELY INCREASE THE NUMBER OF HEADS...
...IF THEY'RE ALL EMPTY.
YOU AND I ARE BOTH POWERLESS SHINOBI.
YOU'LL... ACTUALLY, EVERYONE SHALL...
...EVENTU-ALLY JUST END UP LIKE ME.
I WILL **NEVER** END UP LIKE YOU!!
HOW MANY TIMES DO I HAVE TO TELL YOU?!
MY DREAM IS TO BECOME HOKAGE!!
NO WORRIES... EVERY-THING WILL GO AS PLANNED...
THERE IS NO SHINOBI JUTSU MIGHTIER THAN THE INFINITE TSUKUYOMI.
!
I'LL MAKE YOU HOKAGE, INSIDE THIS JUTSU...
SO...
...JUST DISAPPEAR, ALONG WITH THE REST OF THIS WORLD!
KNEEEEEEEEEEEN

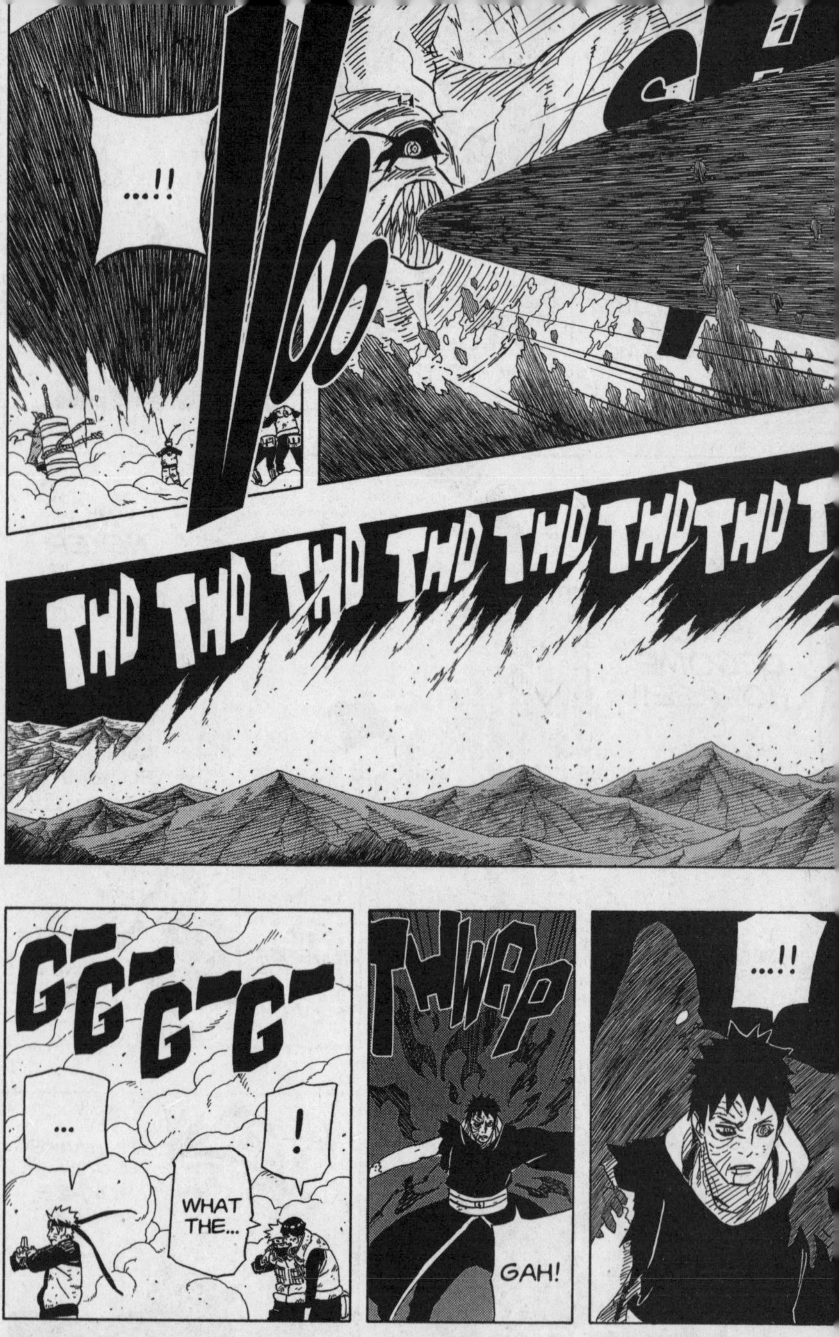
...!!
THD THD THD THD THD THD THD THD
...!!
THWAP
GAH!
G-G-G-G-
!
WHAT THE...
...

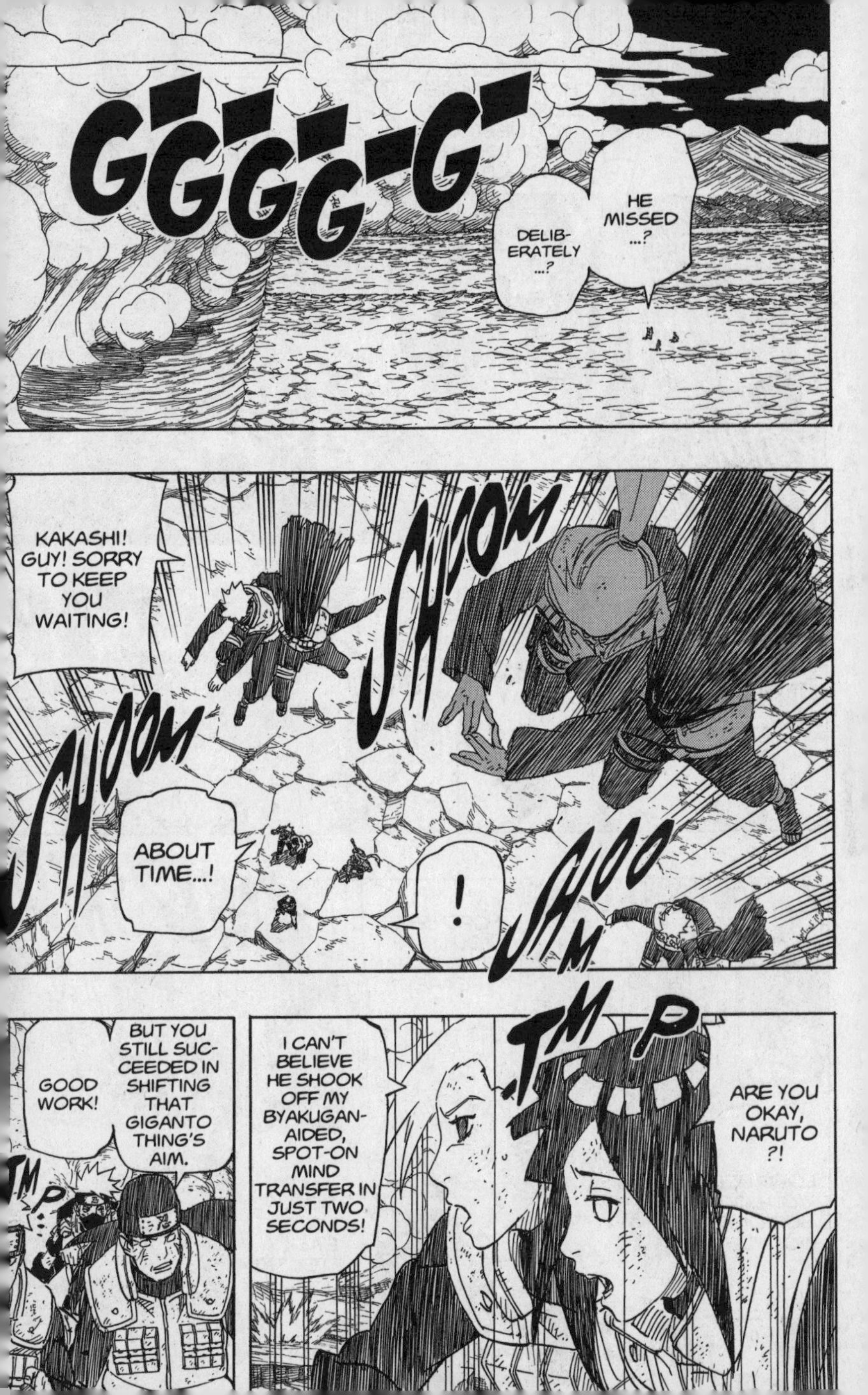
G-G-G-G-G
HE MISSED ...?
DELIB-ERATELY ...?
SHOOM
SHOOM
KAKASHI! GUY! SORRY TO KEEP YOU WAITING!
!
ABOUT TIME...!
SHOOM
TMP
ARE YOU OKAY, NARUTO?!
I CAN'T BELIEVE HE SHOOK OFF MY BYAKUGAN-AIDED, SPOT-ON MIND TRANSFER IN JUST TWO SECONDS!
BUT YOU STILL SUC-CEEDED IN SHIFTING THAT GIGANTO THING'S AIM.
GOOD WORK!
TMP

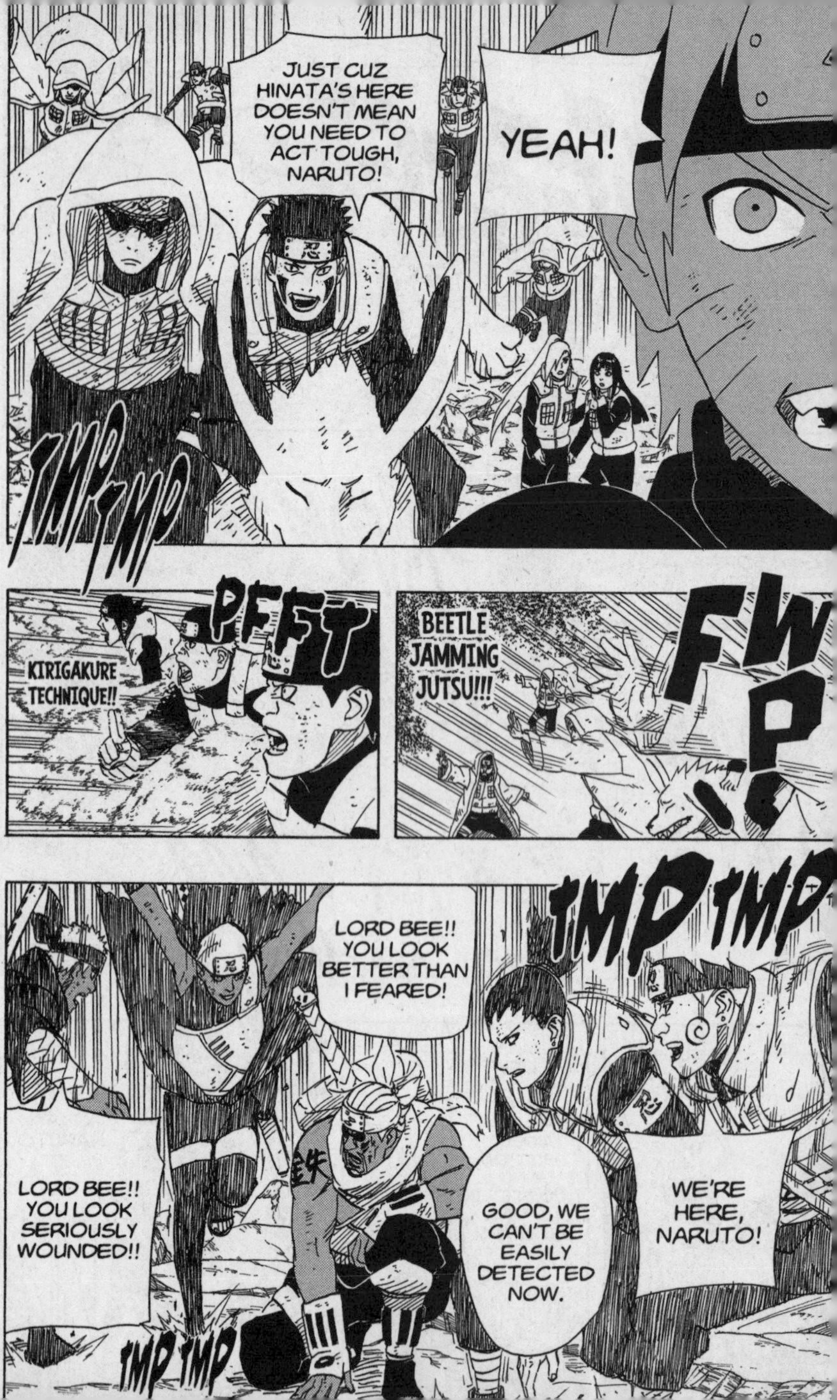
YEAH!
JUST CUZ HINATA'S HERE DOESN'T MEAN YOU NEED TO ACT TOUGH, NARUTO!
TMP TMP
FWP
BEETLE JAMMING JUTSU!!!
PFFT
KIRIGAKURE TECHNIQUE!!
TMP TMP
WE'RE HERE, NARUTO!
GOOD, WE CAN'T BE EASILY DETECTED NOW.
LORD BEE!! YOU LOOK BETTER THAN I FEARED!
LORD BEE!! YOU LOOK SERIOUSLY WOUNDED!!
TMP TMP

I'M SORRY WE'RE LATE, CAPTAIN KAKASHI.

!!

MASTER GUY, DON'T TELL ME YOU UNLEASHED THE HIRUDORA?!!

TMP TMP TMP

I KNOW!

SHUP....

SAKURA, FIRST OFF...!

INOICHI! AO! CONFIRM THE SITUATION!

BYON BYON

THE SENSORY WATER SPHERE JUST WON'T MAINTAIN ITS ORIGINAL SHAPE... WE BETTER...

OKAY!!

ROGER!!

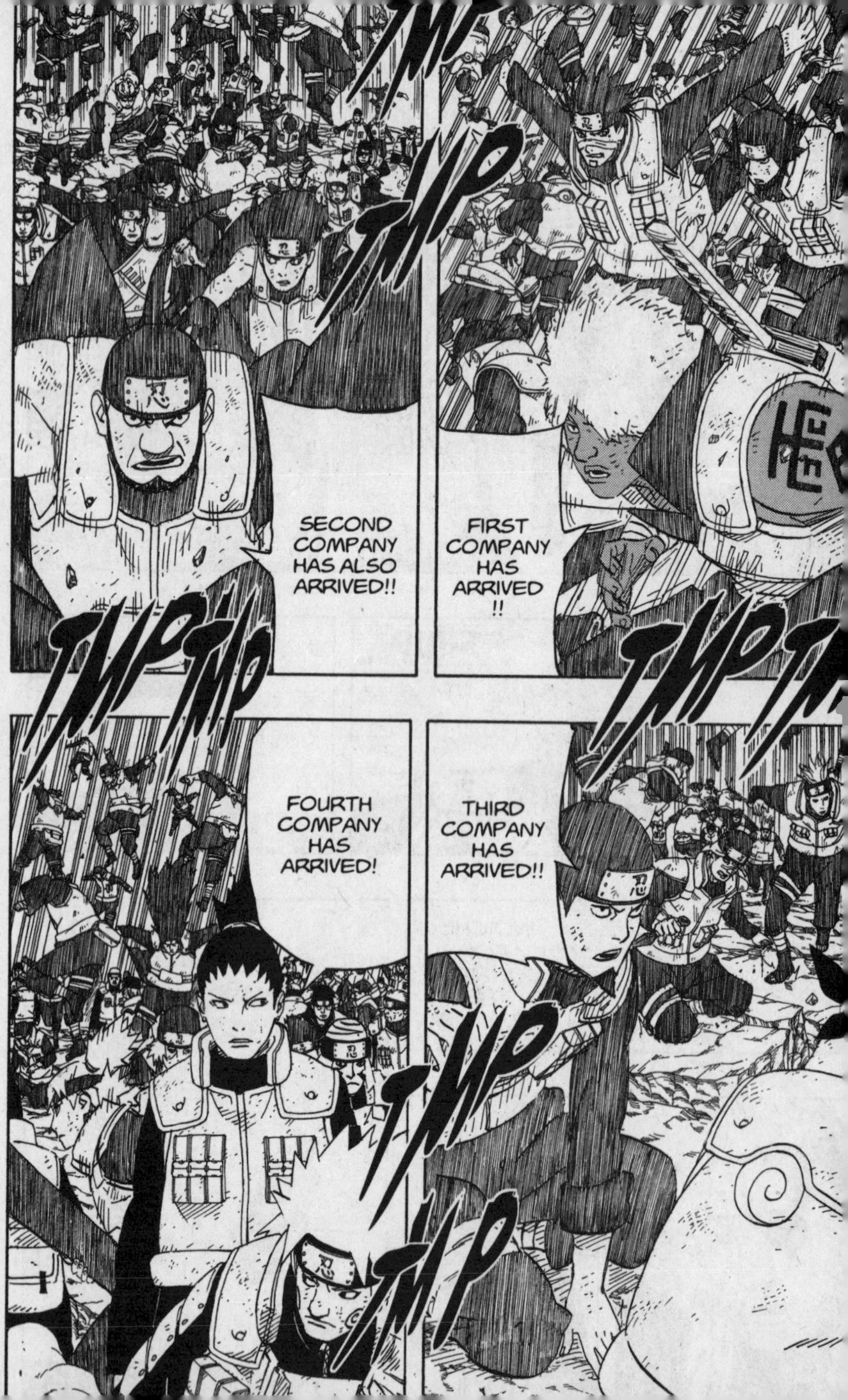
TMP
TMP
FIRST COMPANY HAS ARRIVED !!
SECOND COMPANY HAS ALSO ARRIVED!!
TMP TMP
THIRD COMPANY HAS ARRIVED!!
TMP
TMP
FOURTH COMPANY HAS ARRIVED!

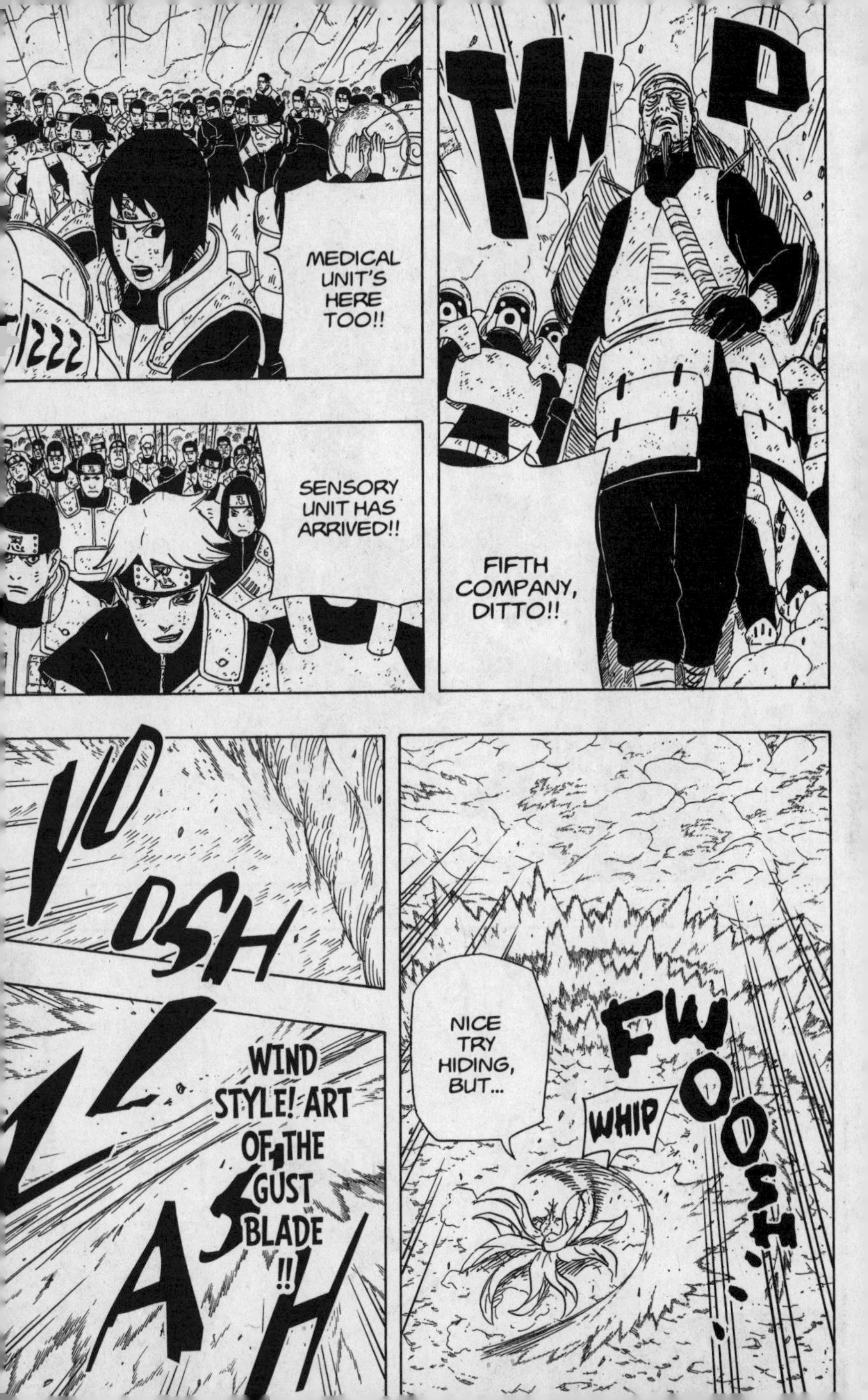
TMP
FIFTH COMPANY, DITTO!!
MEDICAL UNIT'S HERE TOO!!
SENSORY UNIT HAS ARRIVED!!
NICE TRY HIDING, BUT...
WHIP
FWOOSH
VOOSH
WIND STYLE! ART OF THE GUST BLADE!!

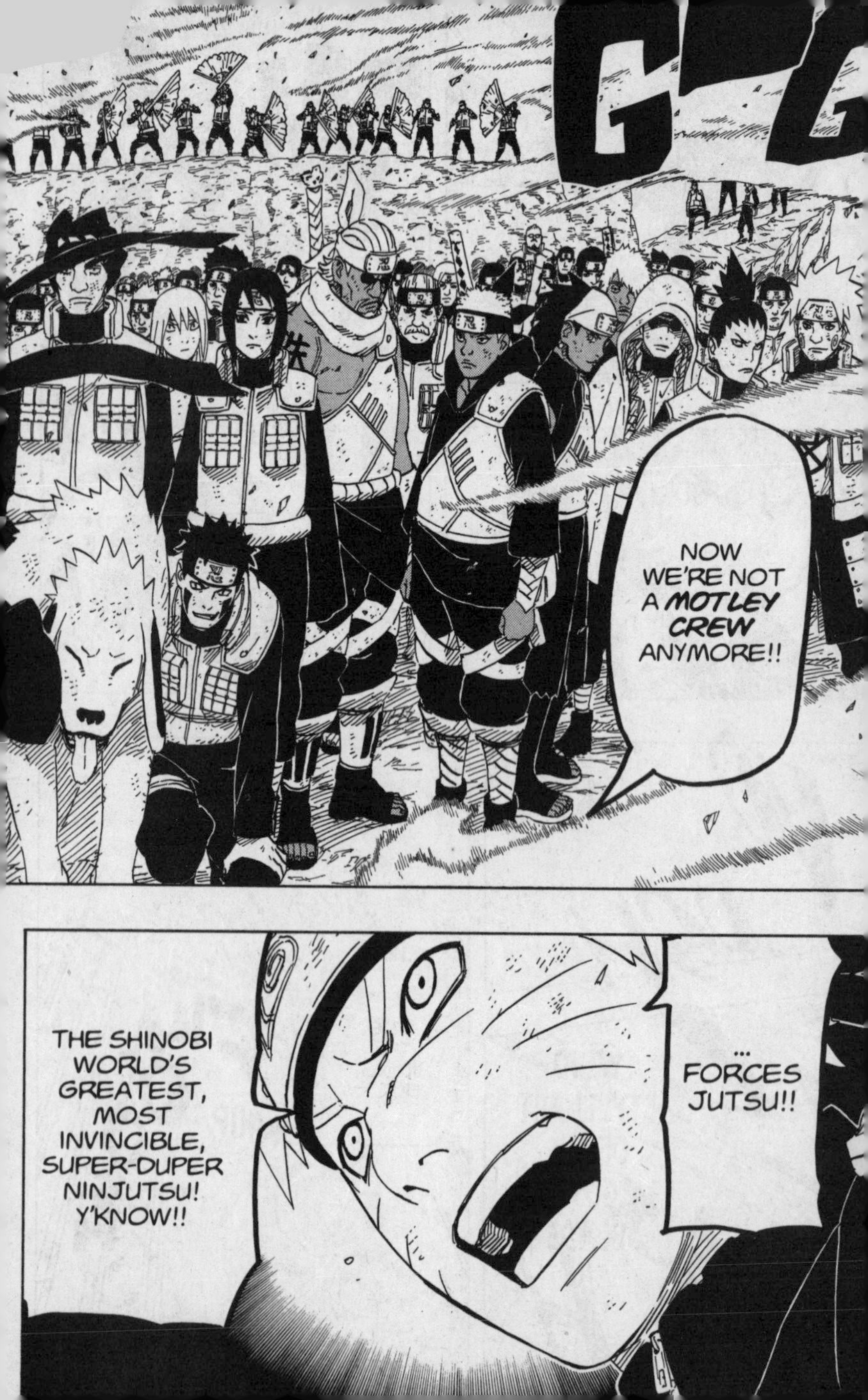
NOW WE'RE NOT A MOTLEY CREW ANYMORE!!
... FORCES JUTSU!!
THE SHINOBI WORLD'S GREATEST, MOST INVINCIBLE, SUPER-DUPER NINJUTSU! Y'KNOW!!

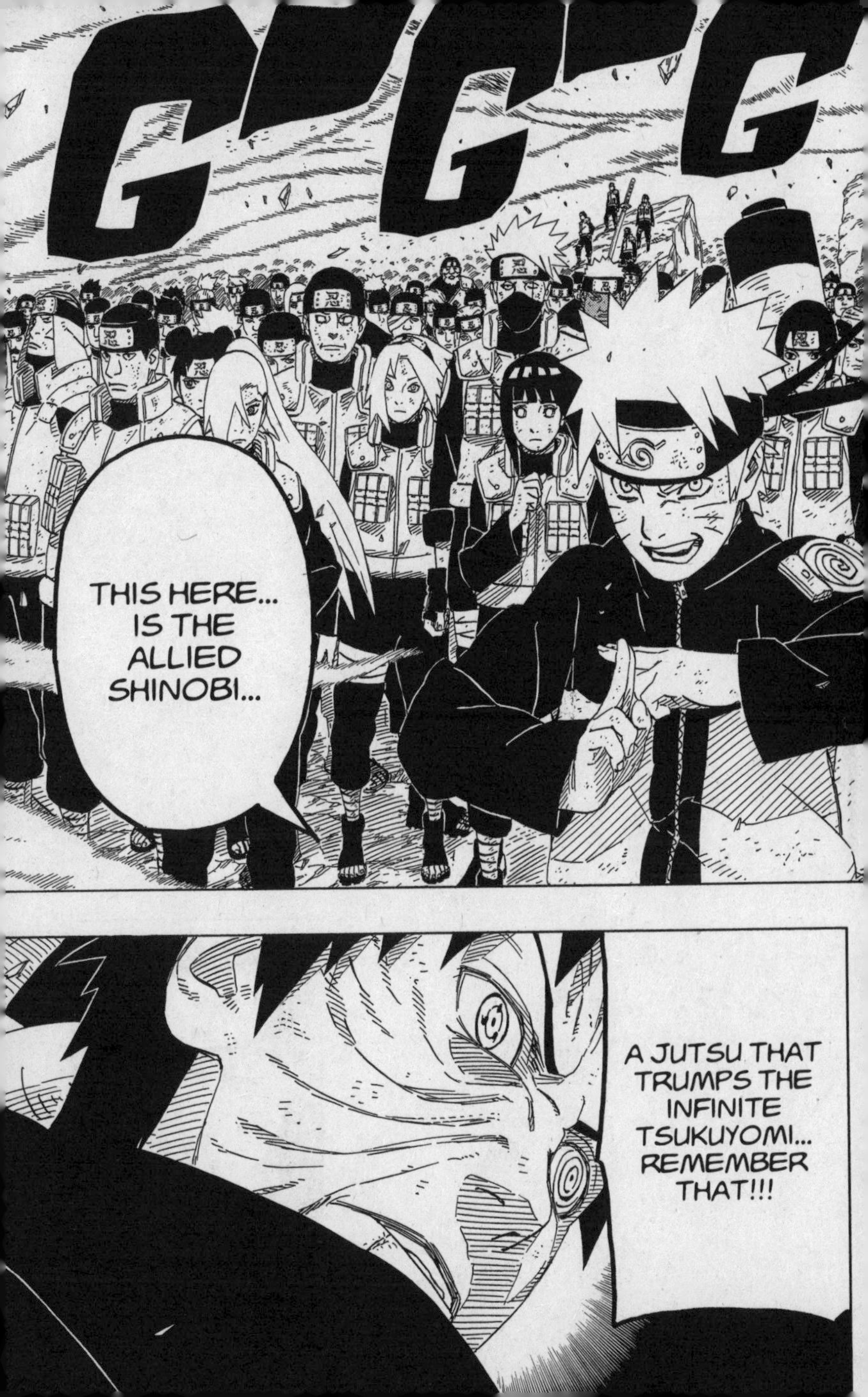
G-G-G
THIS HERE... IS THE ALLIED SHINOBI...
A JUTSU THAT TRUMPS THE INFINITE TSUKUYOMI... REMEMBER THAT!!!

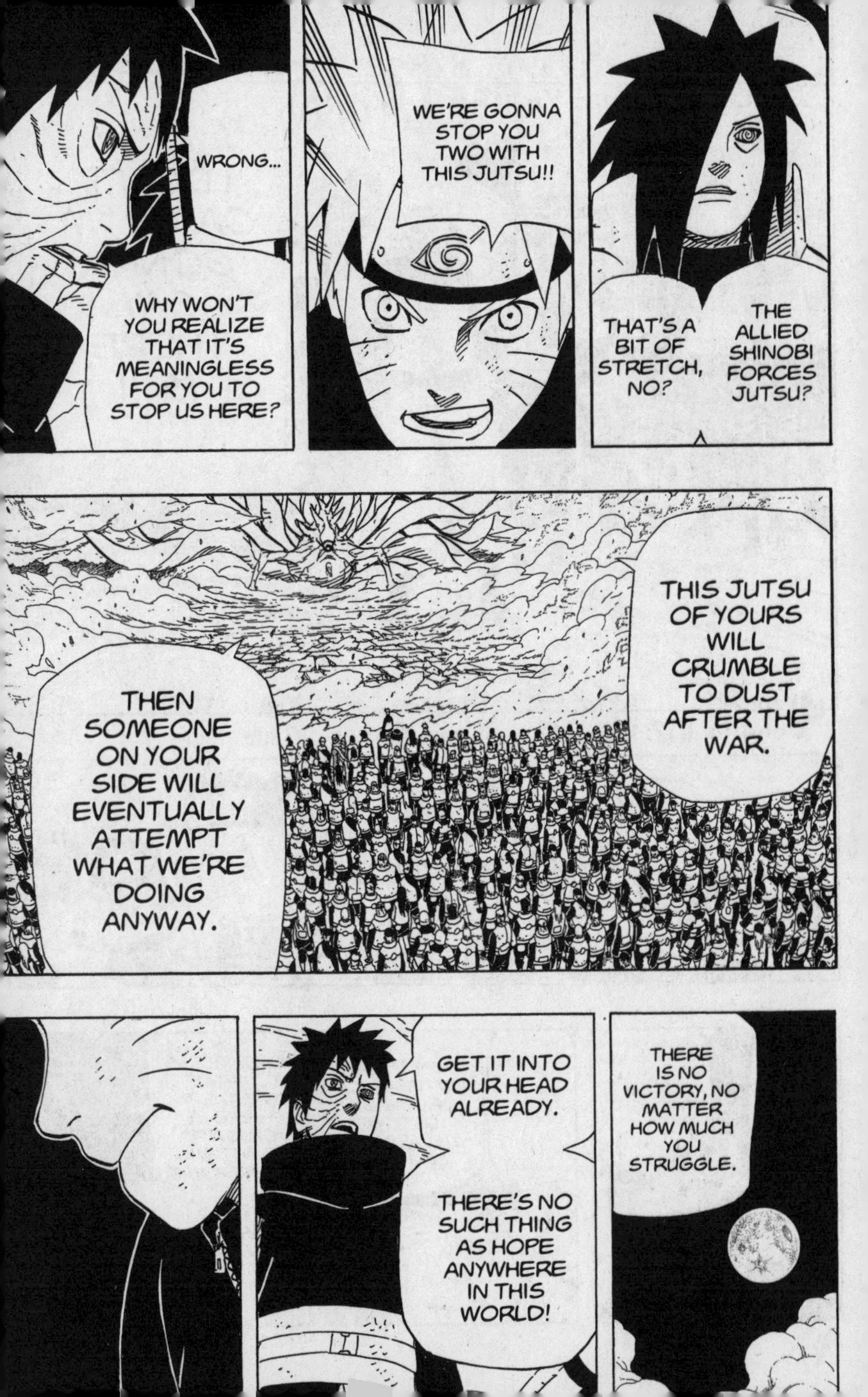
THE ALLIED SHINOBI FORCES JUTSU?
THAT'S A BIT OF STRETCH, NO?
WE'RE GONNA STOP YOU TWO WITH THIS JUTSU!!
WRONG...
WHY WON'T YOU REALIZE THAT IT'S MEANINGLESS FOR YOU TO STOP US HERE?
THIS JUTSU OF YOURS WILL CRUMBLE TO DUST AFTER THE WAR.
THEN SOMEONE ON YOUR SIDE WILL EVENTUALLY ATTEMPT WHAT WE'RE DOING ANYWAY.
THERE IS NO VICTORY, NO MATTER HOW MUCH YOU STRUGGLE.
GET IT INTO YOUR HEAD ALREADY.
THERE'S NO SUCH THING AS HOPE ANYWHERE IN THIS WORLD!

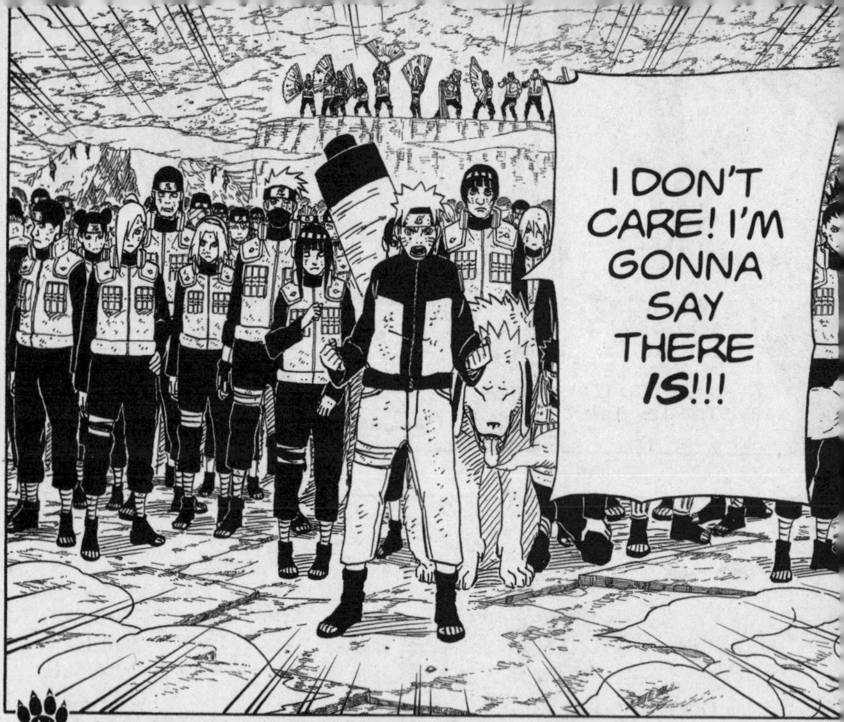
I DON'T CARE! I'M GONNA SAY THERE IS!!!

Number 612: The Allied Shinobi Forces Jutsu!!

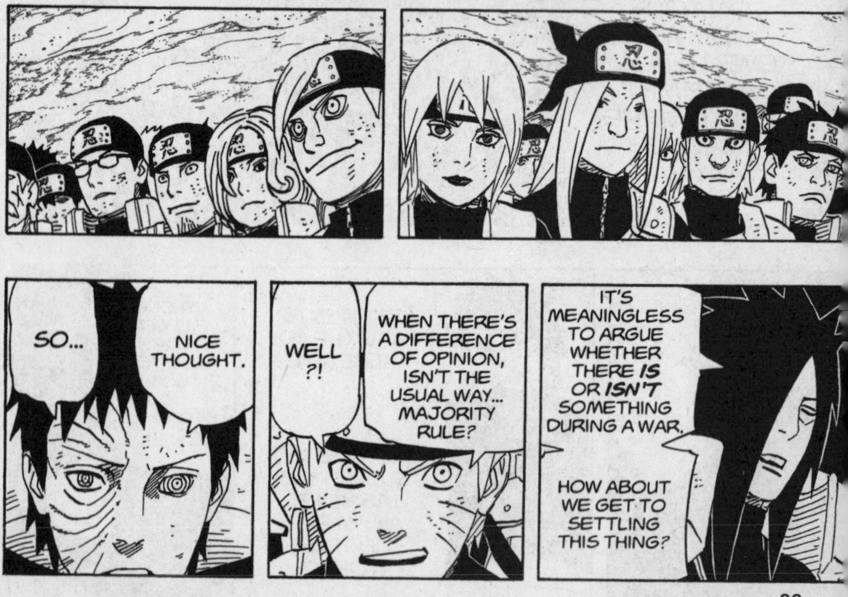
IT'S MEANINGLESS TO ARGUE WHETHER THERE IS OR ISN'T SOMETHING DURING A WAR.
HOW ABOUT WE GET TO SETTLING THIS THING?
WHEN THERE'S A DIFFERENCE OF OPINION, ISN'T THE USUAL WAY... MAJORITY RULE?
WELL ?!
NICE THOUGHT.
SO...

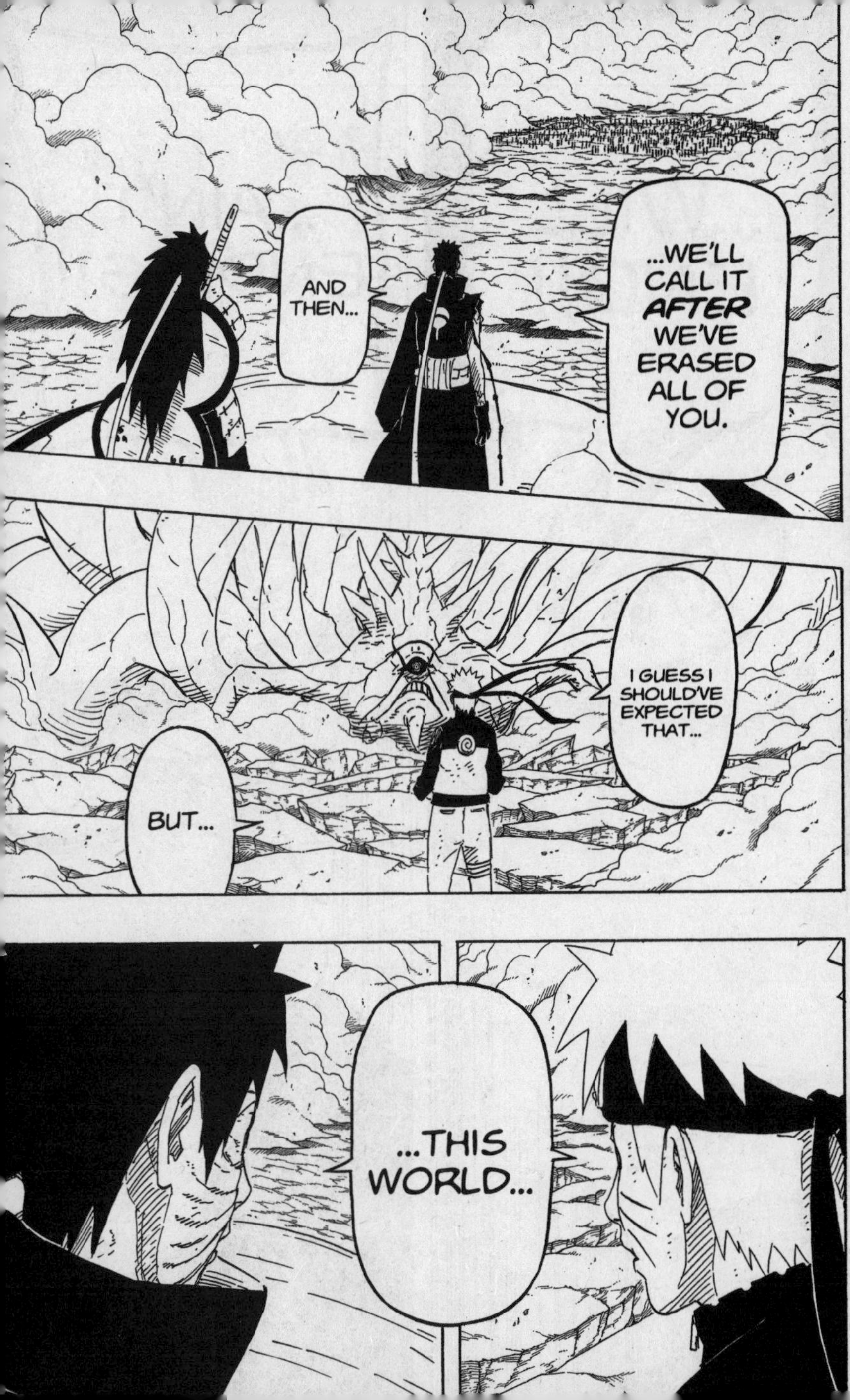
...WE'LL CALL IT *AFTER* WE'VE ERASED ALL OF YOU.
AND THEN...
I GUESS I SHOULD'VE EXPECTED THAT...
BUT...
...THIS WORLD...

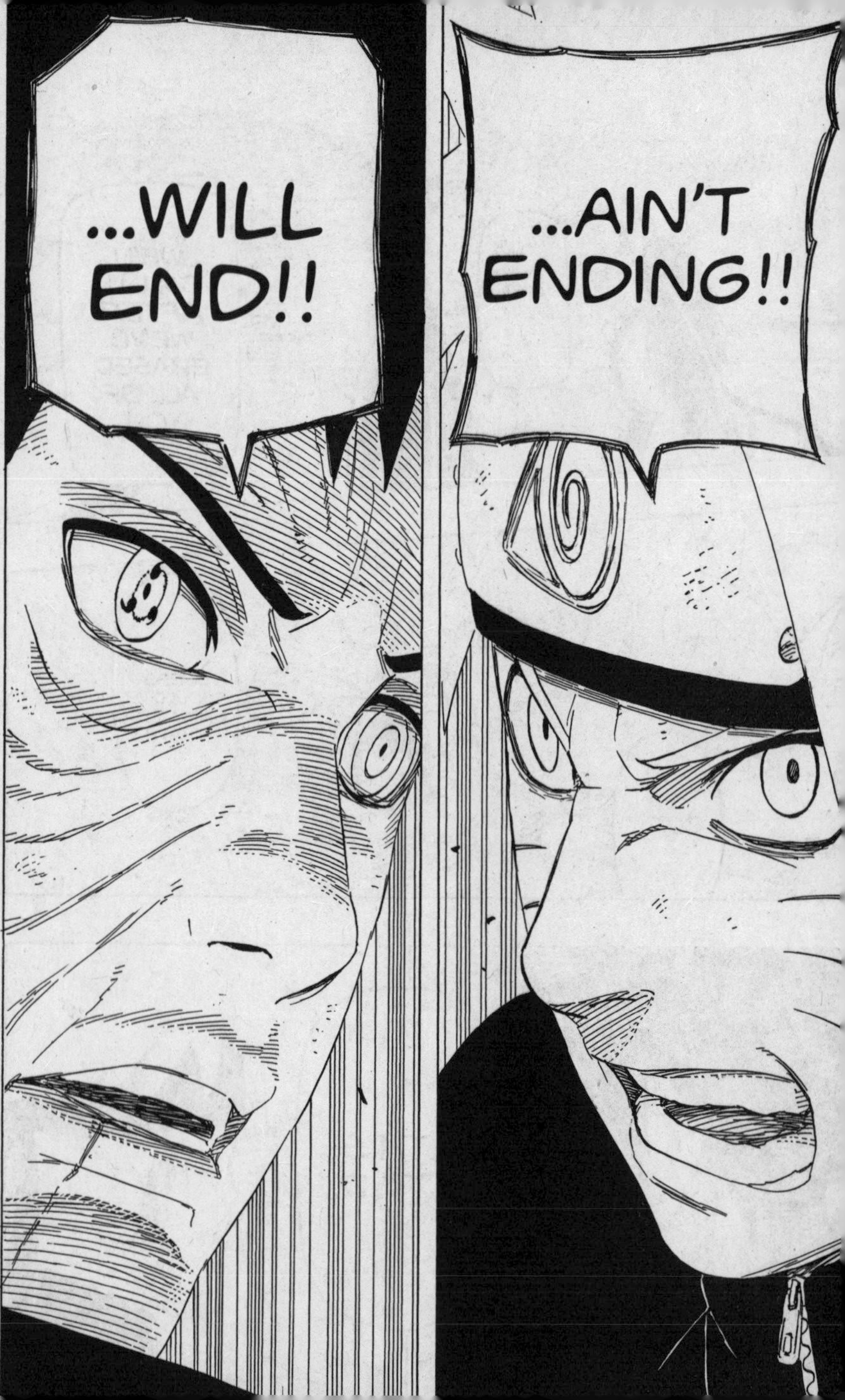
...AIN'T ENDING!!
...WILL END!!

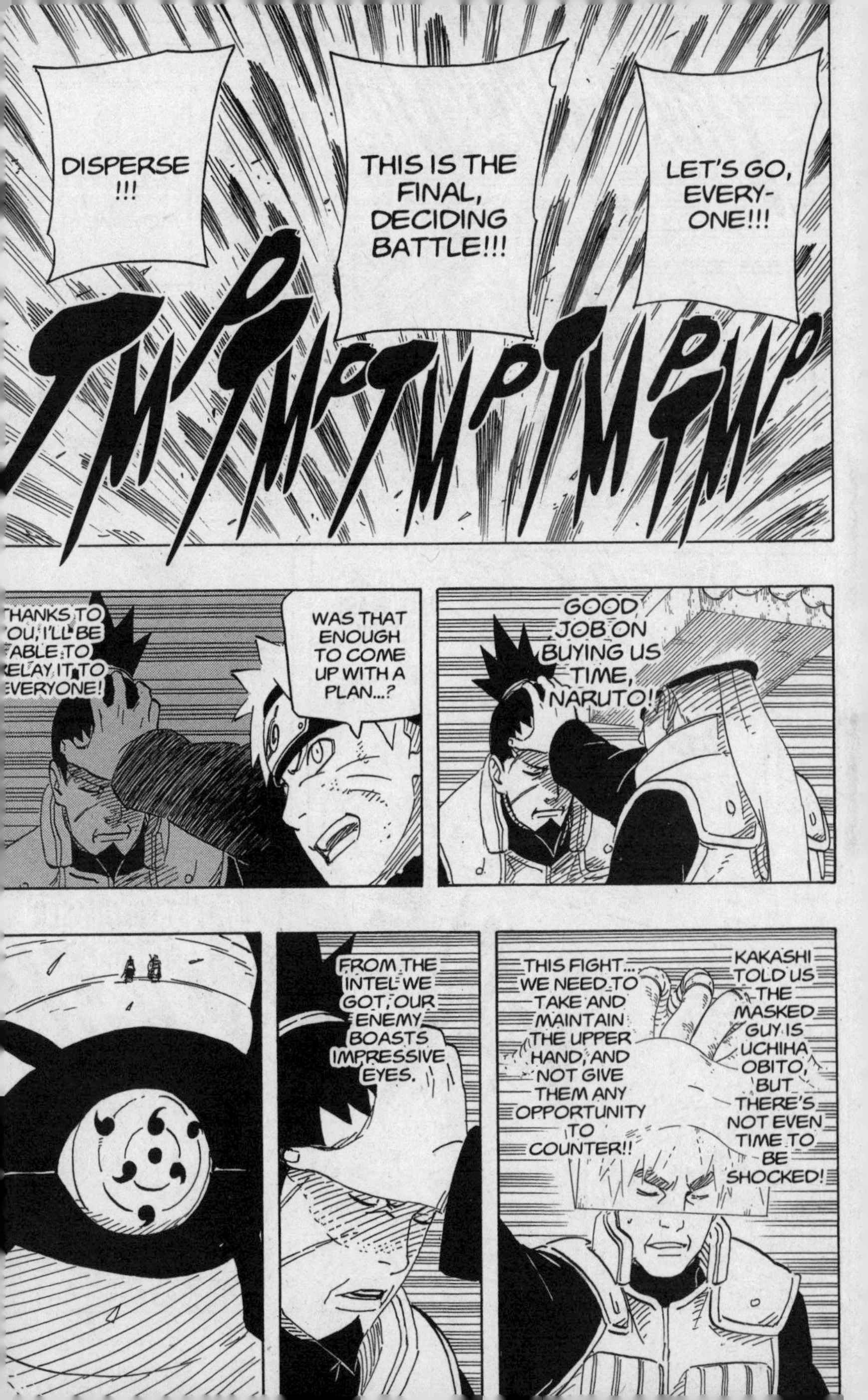

LET'S GO, EVERYONE!!!
THIS IS THE FINAL, DECIDING BATTLE!!!
DISPERSE!!!
GOOD JOB ON BUYING US TIME, NARUTO!
WAS THAT ENOUGH TO COME UP WITH A PLAN...?
THANKS TO OU, I'LL BE ABLE TO ELAY IT TO EVERYONE!
KAKASHI TOLD US THE MASKED GUY IS UCHIHA OBITO, BUT THERE'S NOT EVEN TIME TO BE SHOCKED!
THIS FIGHT... WE NEED TO TAKE AND MAINTAIN THE UPPER HAND, AND NOT GIVE THEM ANY OPPORTUNITY TO COUNTER!!
FROM THE INTEL WE GOT, OUR ENEMY BOASTS IMPRESSIVE EYES.

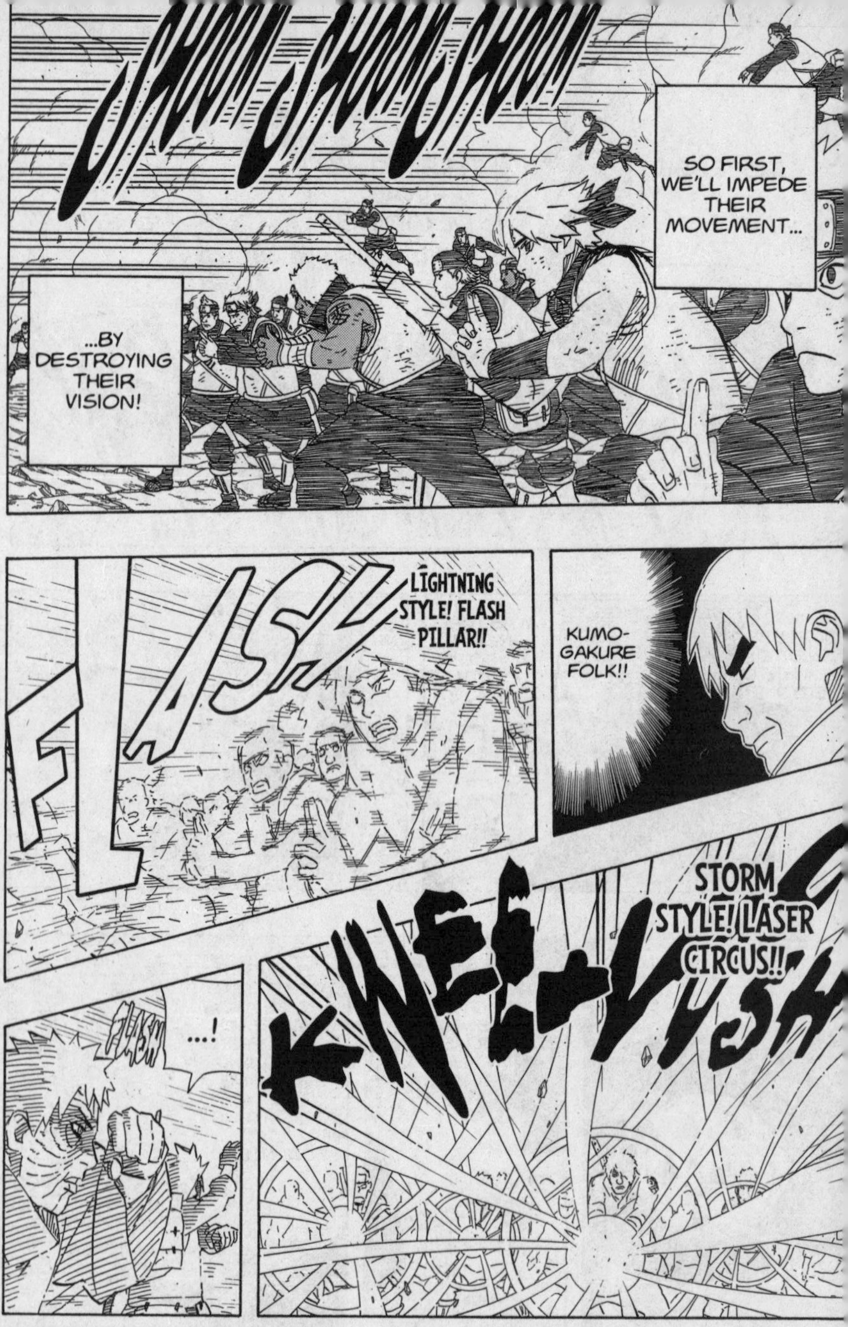
SO FIRST, WE'LL IMPEDE THEIR MOVEMENT...
...BY DESTROYING THEIR VISION!
KUMO-GAKURE FOLK!!
LIGHTNING STYLE! FLASH PILLAR!!
FLASH
STORM STYLE! LASER CIRCUS!!
...!

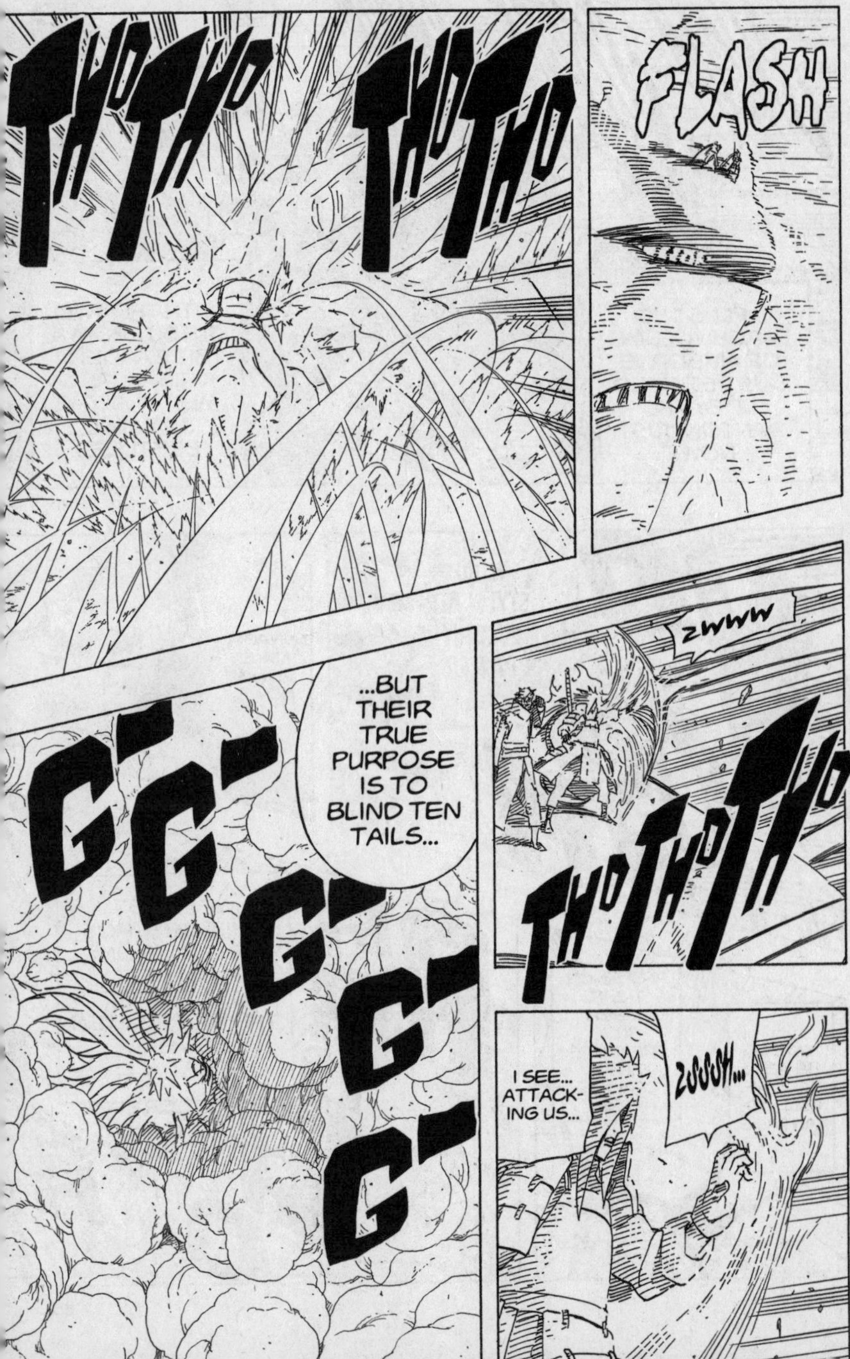
FLASH
THUD THUD THUD THUD
ZWWW
THUD THUD THUD
I SEE... ATTACKING US...
ZUSSSH...
...BUT THEIR TRUE PURPOSE IS TO BLIND TEN TAILS...
G-G-G-G-G-

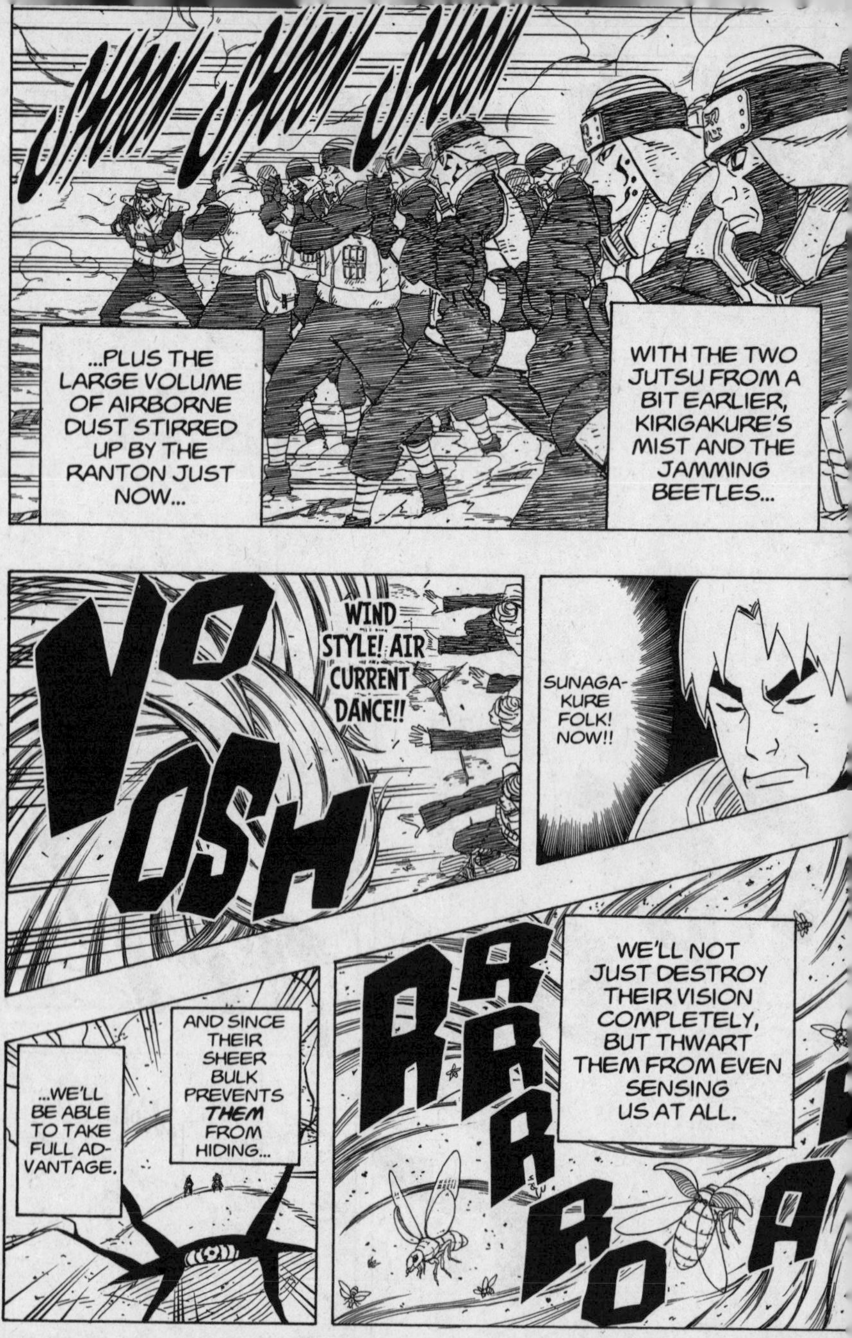
WITH THE TWO JUTSU FROM A BIT EARLIER, KIRIGAKURE'S MIST AND THE JAMMING BEETLES...
...PLUS THE LARGE VOLUME OF AIRBORNE DUST STIRRED UP BY THE RANTON JUST NOW...
SUNAGAKURE FOLK! NOW!!
WIND STYLE! AIR CURRENT DANCE!!
VOOSH
WE'LL NOT JUST DESTROY THEIR VISION COMPLETELY, BUT THWART THEM FROM EVEN SENSING US AT ALL.
AND SINCE THEIR SHEER BULK PREVENTS *THEM* FROM HIDING...
...WE'LL BE ABLE TO TAKE FULL ADVANTAGE.

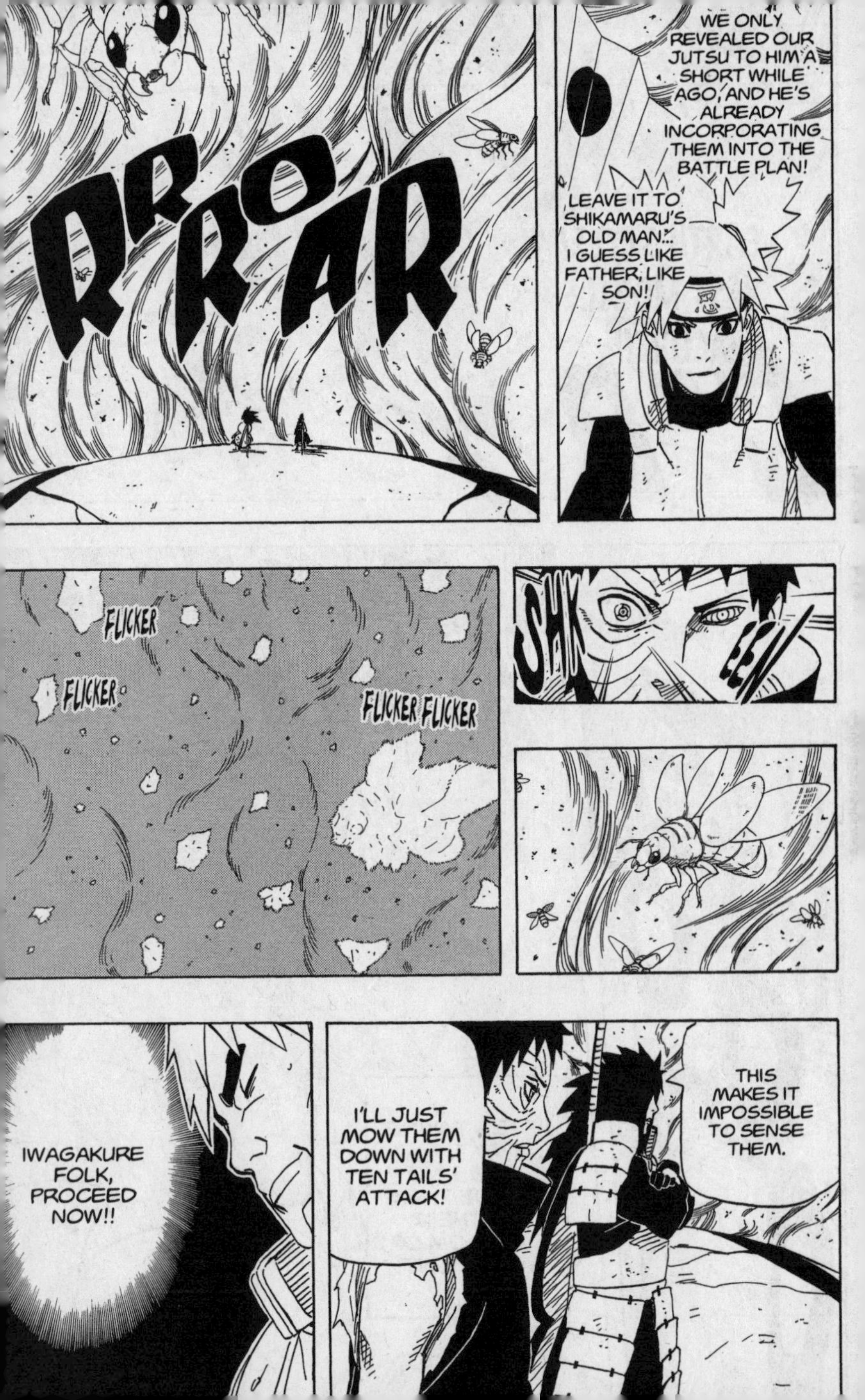
WE ONLY REVEALED OUR JUTSU TO HIM A SHORT WHILE AGO, AND HE'S ALREADY INCORPORATING THEM INTO THE BATTLE PLAN!
LEAVE IT TO SHIKAMARU'S OLD MAN!... I GUESS LIKE FATHER, LIKE SON!!
SHKEEN
FLICKER
FLICKER
FLICKER FLICKER
THIS MAKES IT IMPOSSIBLE TO SENSE THEM.
I'LL JUST MOW THEM DOWN WITH TEN TAILS' ATTACK!
IWAGAKURE FOLK, PROCEED NOW!!

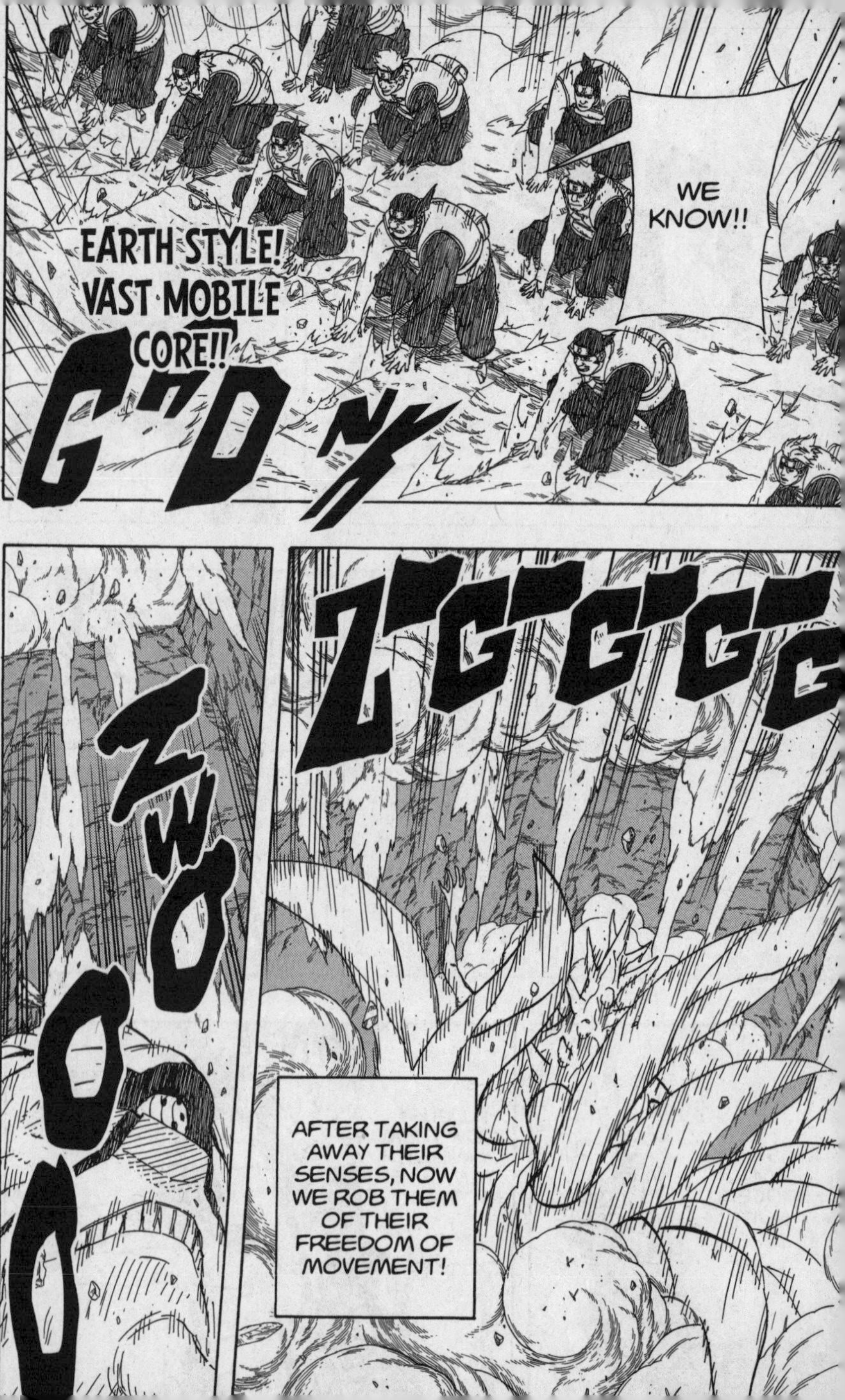
WE KNOW!!
EARTH STYLE! VAST MOBILE CORE!!
ZGGGG
AFTER TAKING AWAY THEIR SENSES, NOW WE ROB THEM OF THEIR FREEDOM OF MOVEMENT!

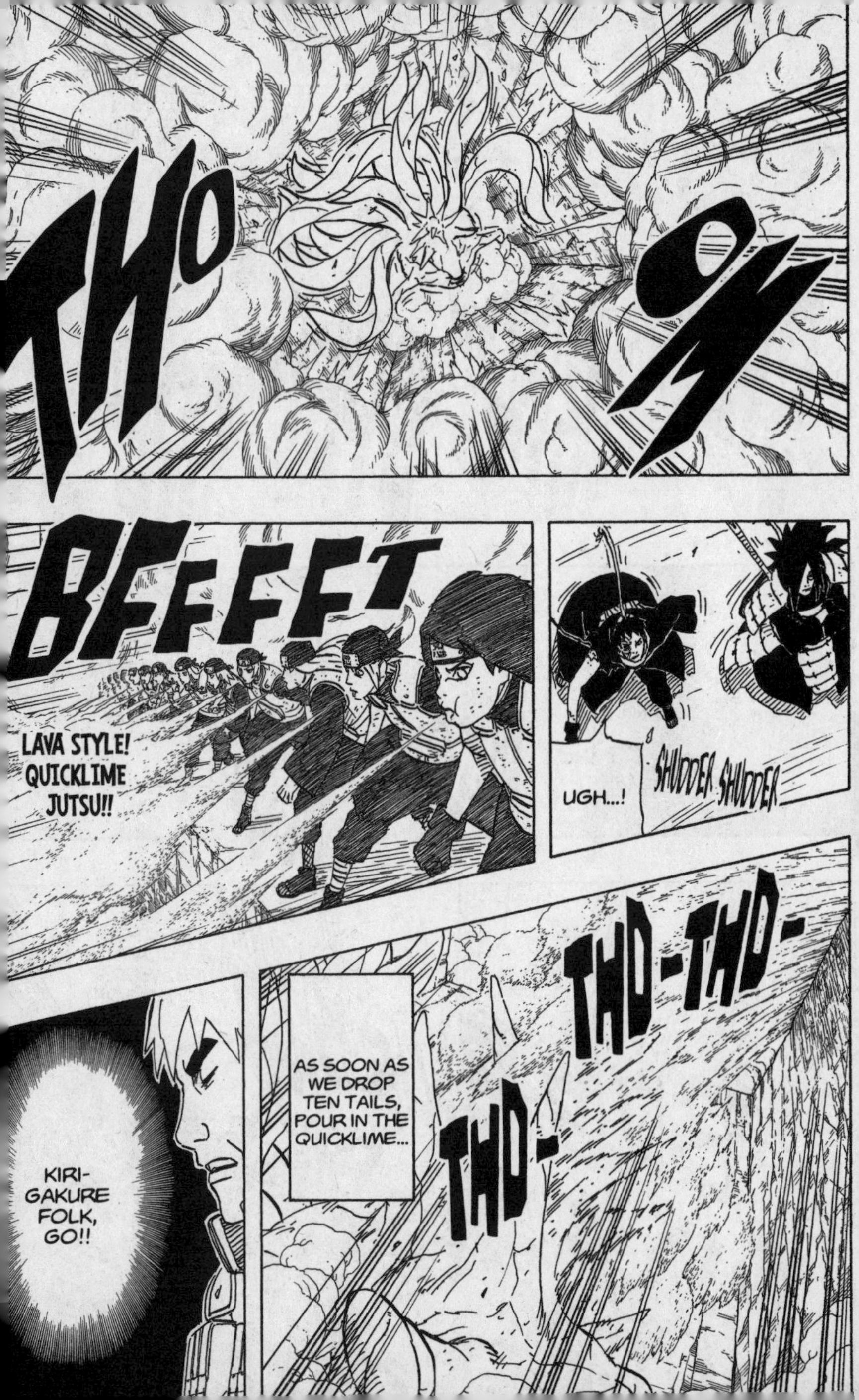
THOOM
UGH...!
SHUDDER SHUDDER
BFFFFT
LAVA STYLE! QUICKLIME JUTSU!!
THD-THD-
AS SOON AS WE DROP TEN TAILS, POUR IN THE QUICKLIME...
THD-
KIRI-GAKURE FOLK, GO!!

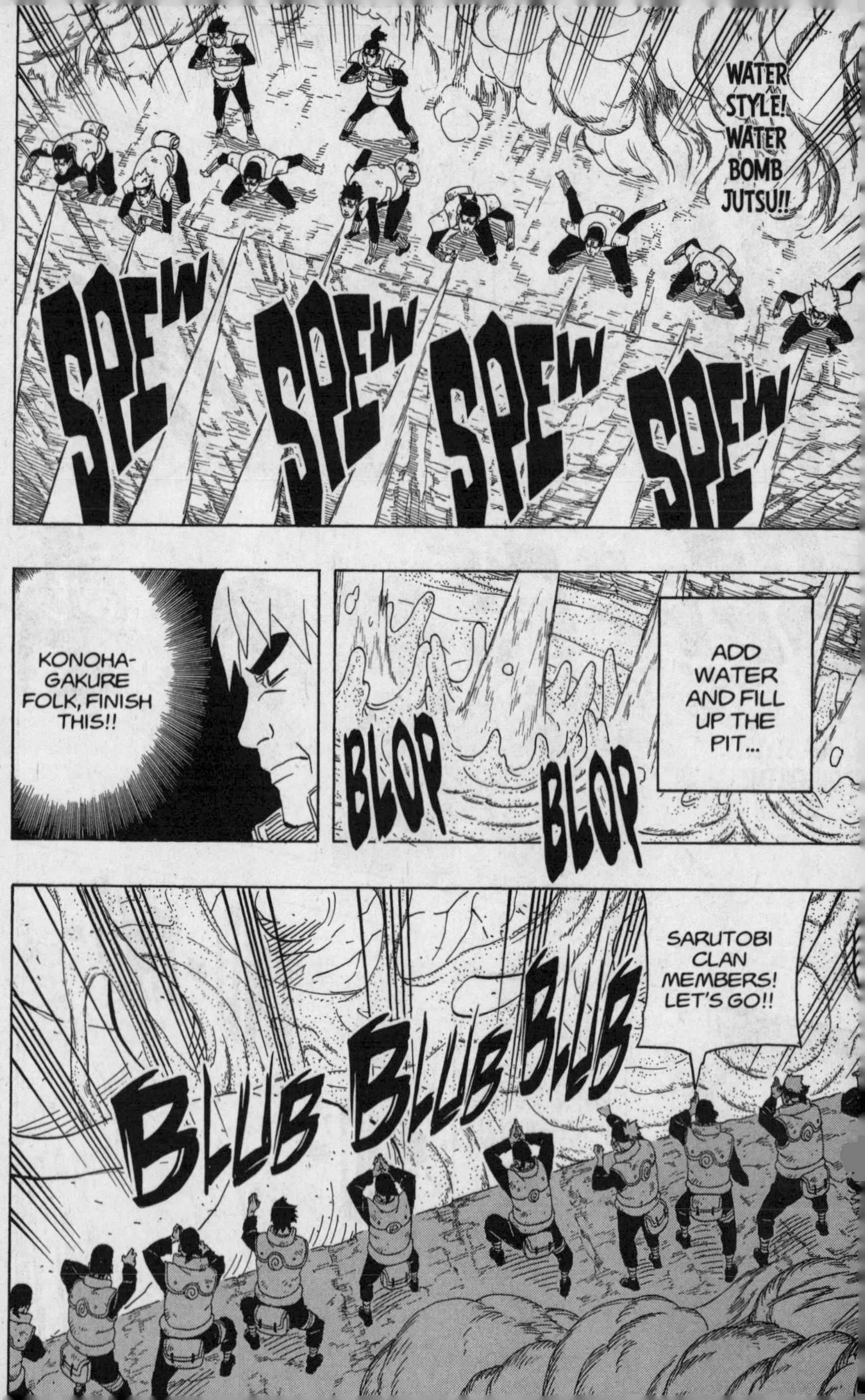
WATER STYLE! WATER BOMB JUTSU!!
SPEW
SPEW
SPEW
SPEW
ADD WATER AND FILL UP THE PIT...
BLOP
BLOP
KONOHA-GAKURE FOLK, FINISH THIS!!
SARUTOBI CLAN MEMBERS! LET'S GO!!
BLUB
BLUB
BLUB

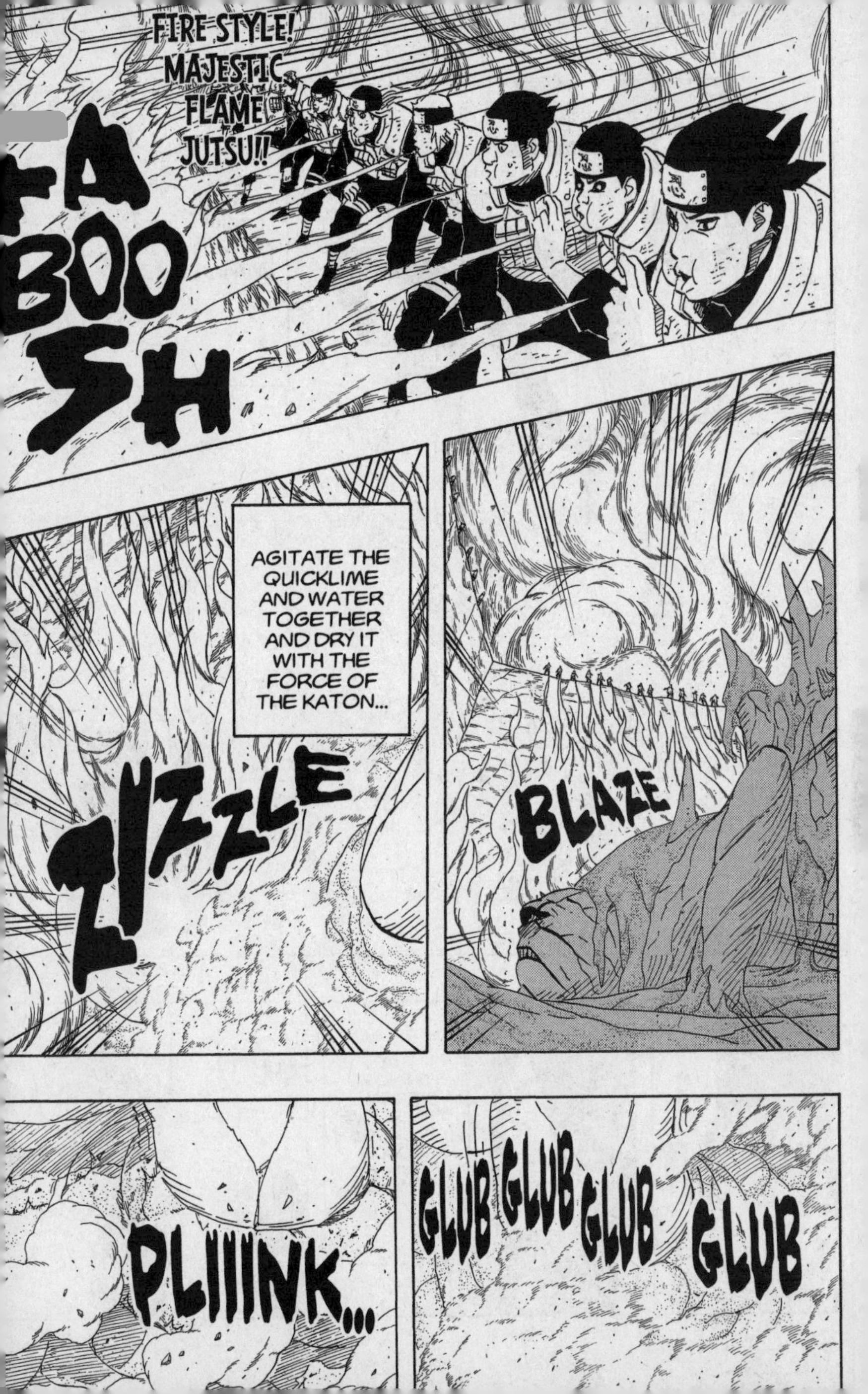
FIRE STYLE! MAJESTIC FLAME JUTSU!!
FABOOSH
BLAZE
AGITATE THE QUICKLIME AND WATER TOGETHER AND DRY IT WITH THE FORCE OF THE KATON...
ZIZZLE
GLUB GLUB GLUB GLUB
PLIIINK...

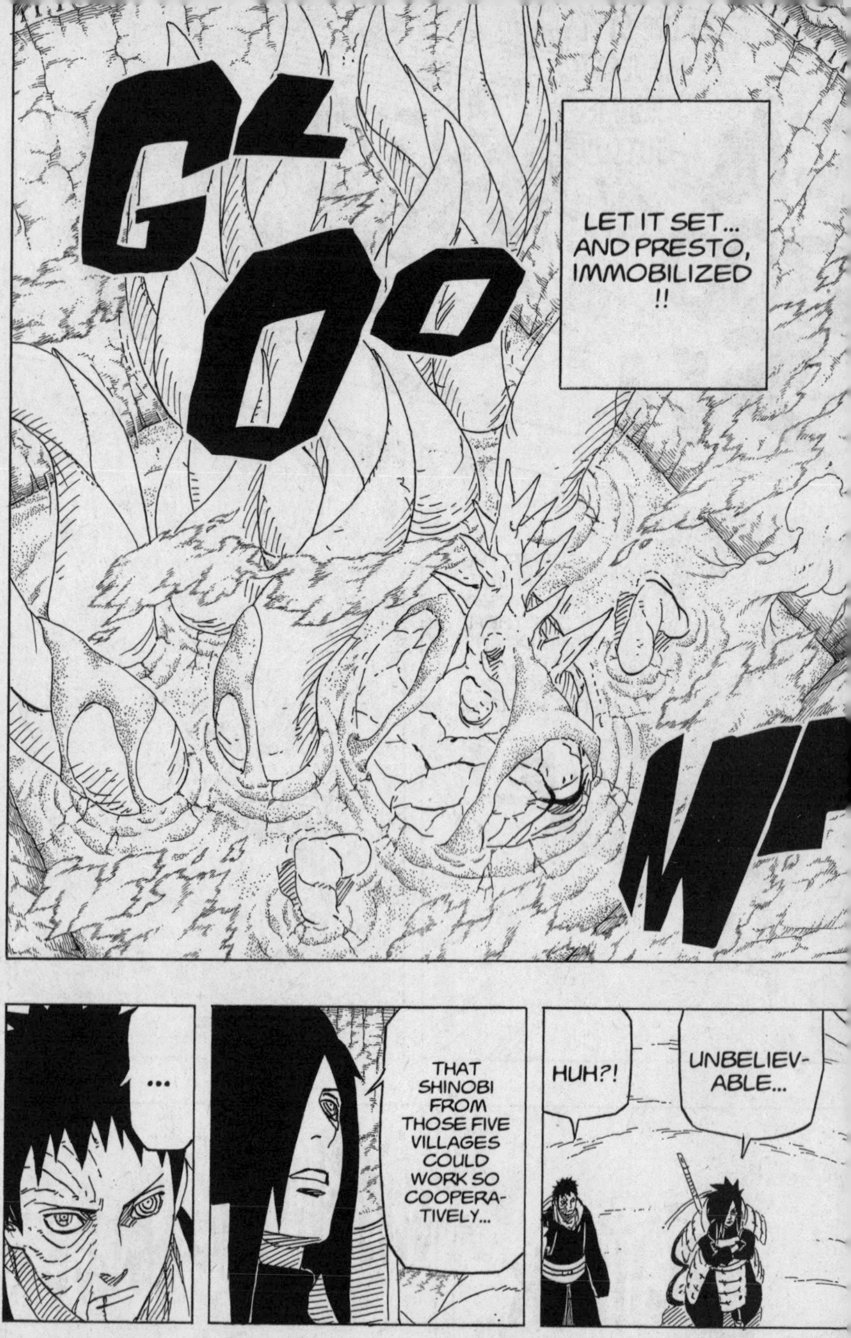

LET IT SET... AND PRESTO, IMMOBILIZED !!
GLOO
UNBELIEV-ABLE...
HUH?!
THAT SHINOBI FROM THOSE FIVE VILLAGES COULD WORK SO COOPERA-TIVELY...
...

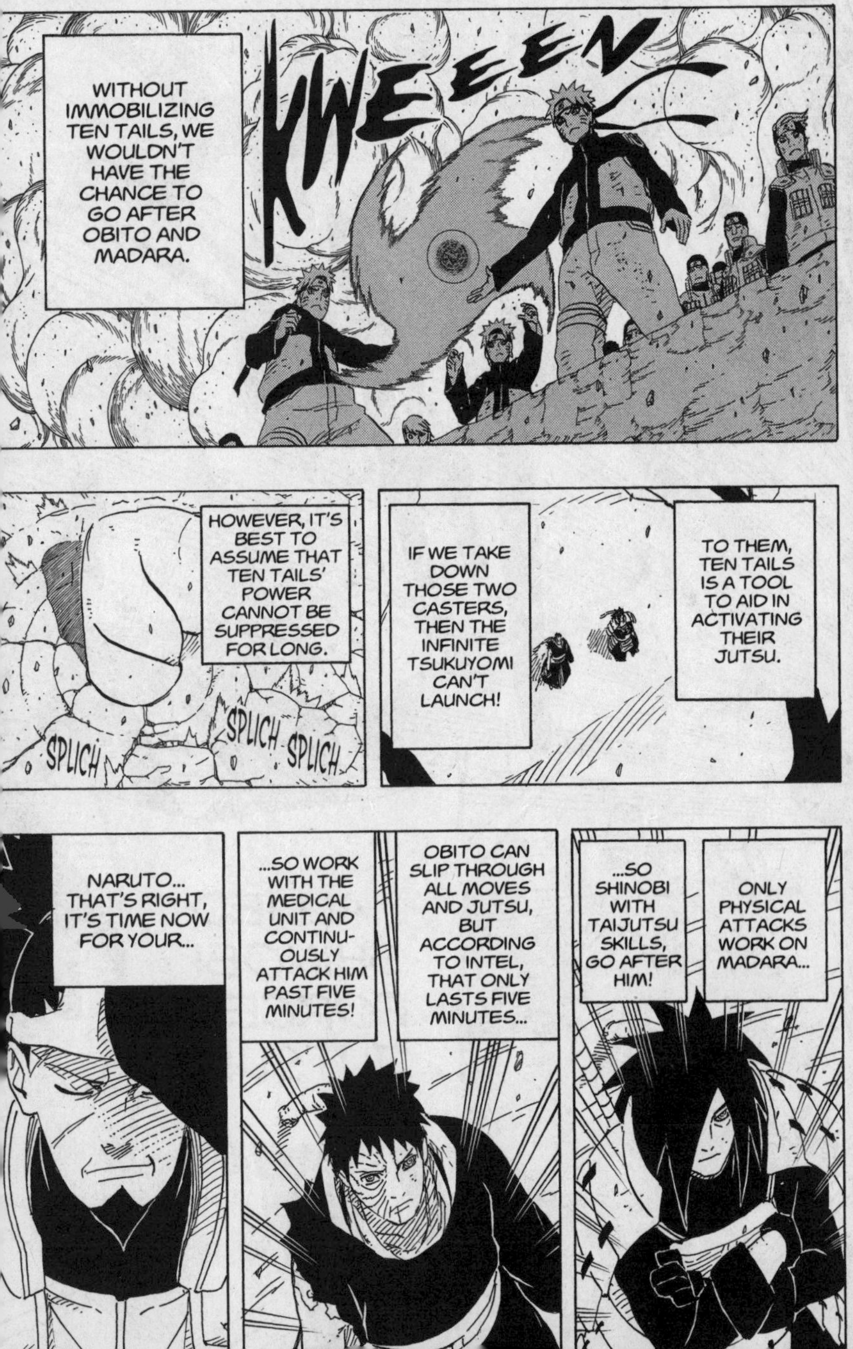
KWEEEN
WITHOUT IMMOBILIZING TEN TAILS, WE WOULDN'T HAVE THE CHANCE TO GO AFTER OBITO AND MADARA.
TO THEM, TEN TAILS IS A TOOL TO AID IN ACTIVATING THEIR JUTSU.
IF WE TAKE DOWN THOSE TWO CASTERS, THEN THE INFINITE TSUKUYOMI CAN'T LAUNCH!
HOWEVER, IT'S BEST TO ASSUME THAT TEN TAILS' POWER CANNOT BE SUPPRESSED FOR LONG.
SPLICH SPLICH
SPLICH
ONLY PHYSICAL ATTACKS WORK ON MADARA...
...SO SHINOBI WITH TAIJUTSU SKILLS, GO AFTER HIM!
OBITO CAN SLIP THROUGH ALL MOVES AND JUTSU, BUT ACCORDING TO INTEL, THAT ONLY LASTS FIVE MINUTES...
...SO WORK WITH THE MEDICAL UNIT AND CONTINU-OUSLY ATTACK HIM PAST FIVE MINUTES!
NARUTO... THAT'S RIGHT, IT'S TIME NOW FOR YOUR...

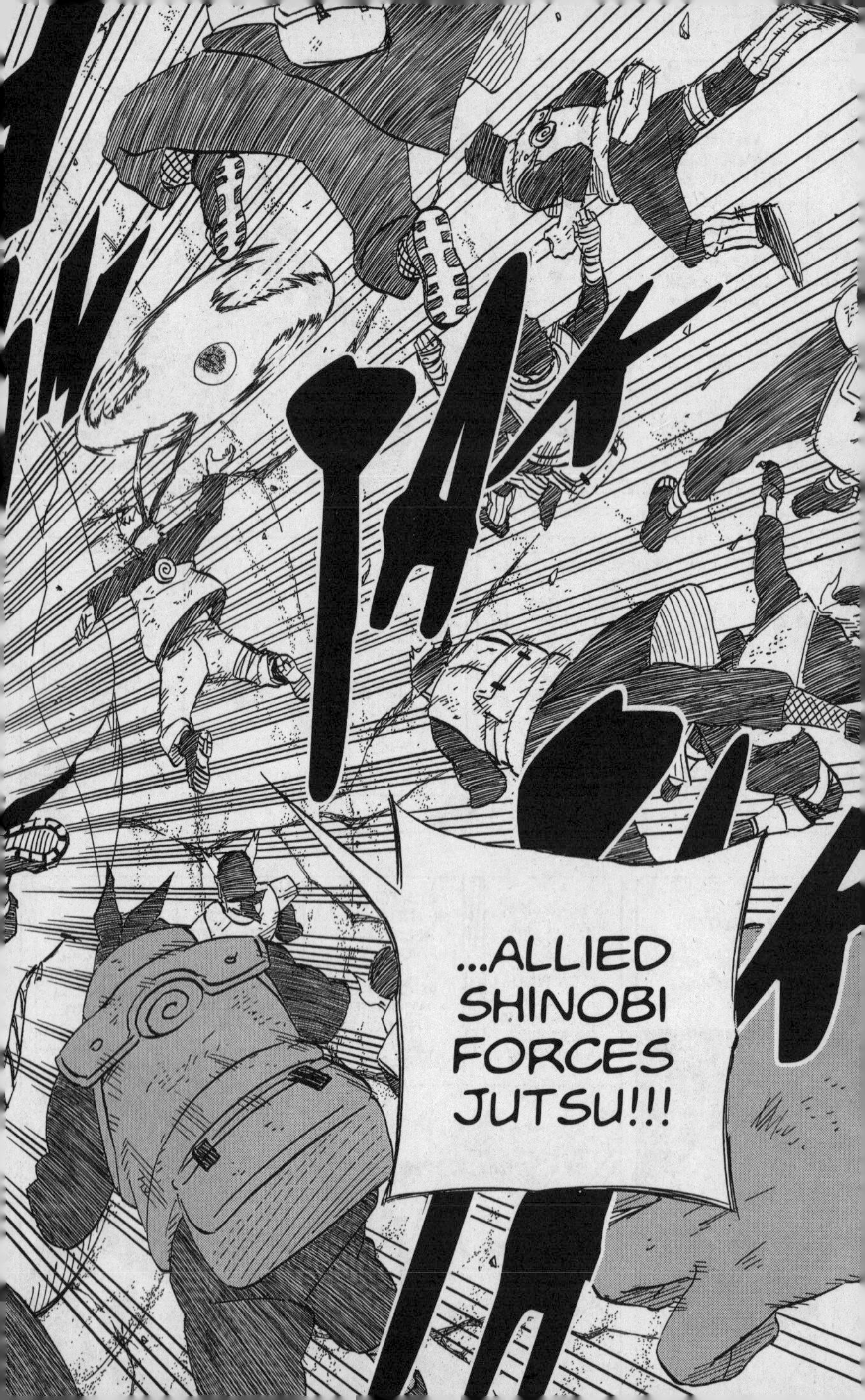
...ALLIED SHINOBI FORCES JUTSU!!!

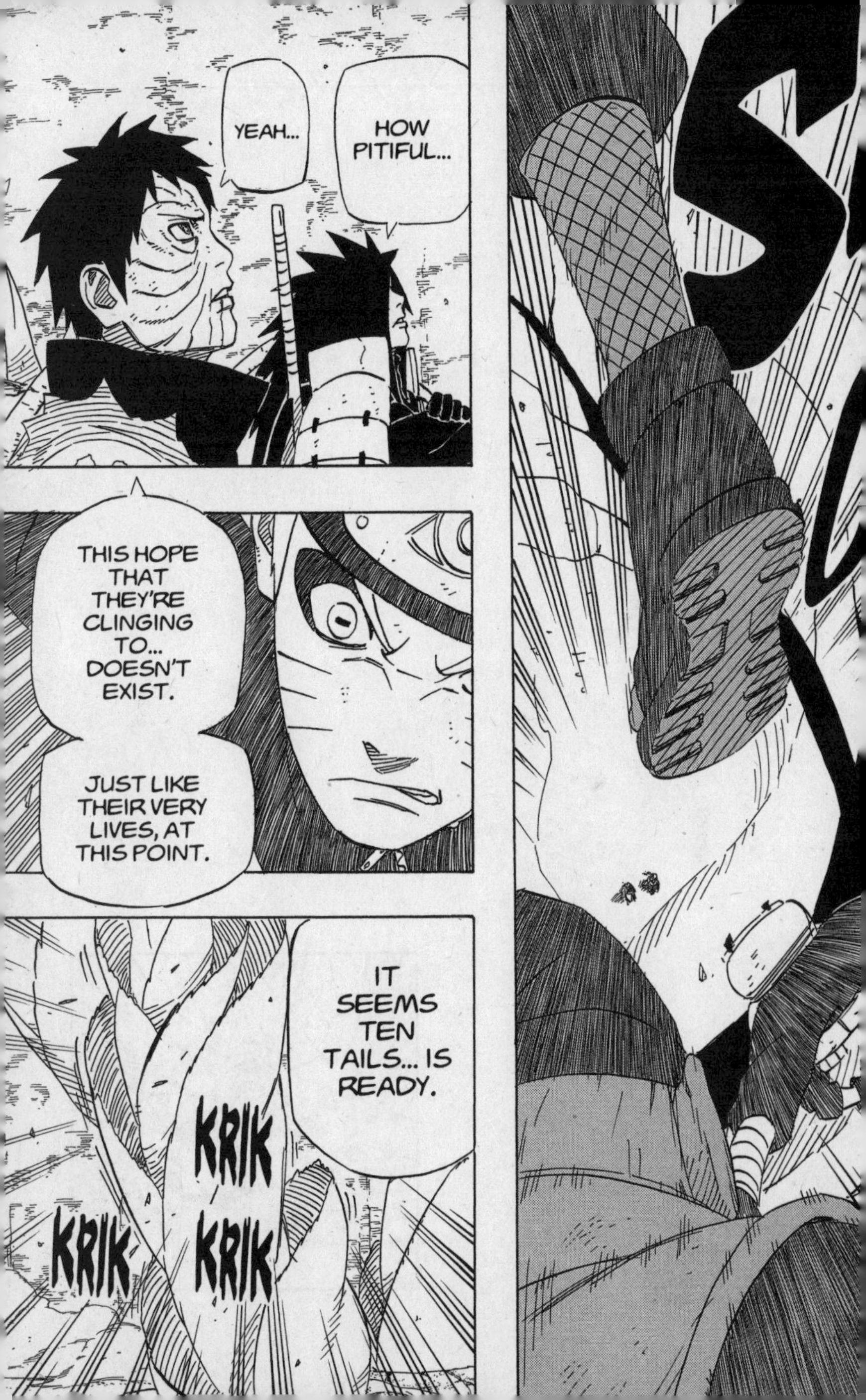
HOW PITIFUL...
YEAH...
THIS HOPE THAT THEY'RE CLINGING TO... DOESN'T EXIST.
JUST LIKE THEIR VERY LIVES, AT THIS POINT.
IT SEEMS TEN TAILS... IS READY.
KRIK
KRIK
KRIK

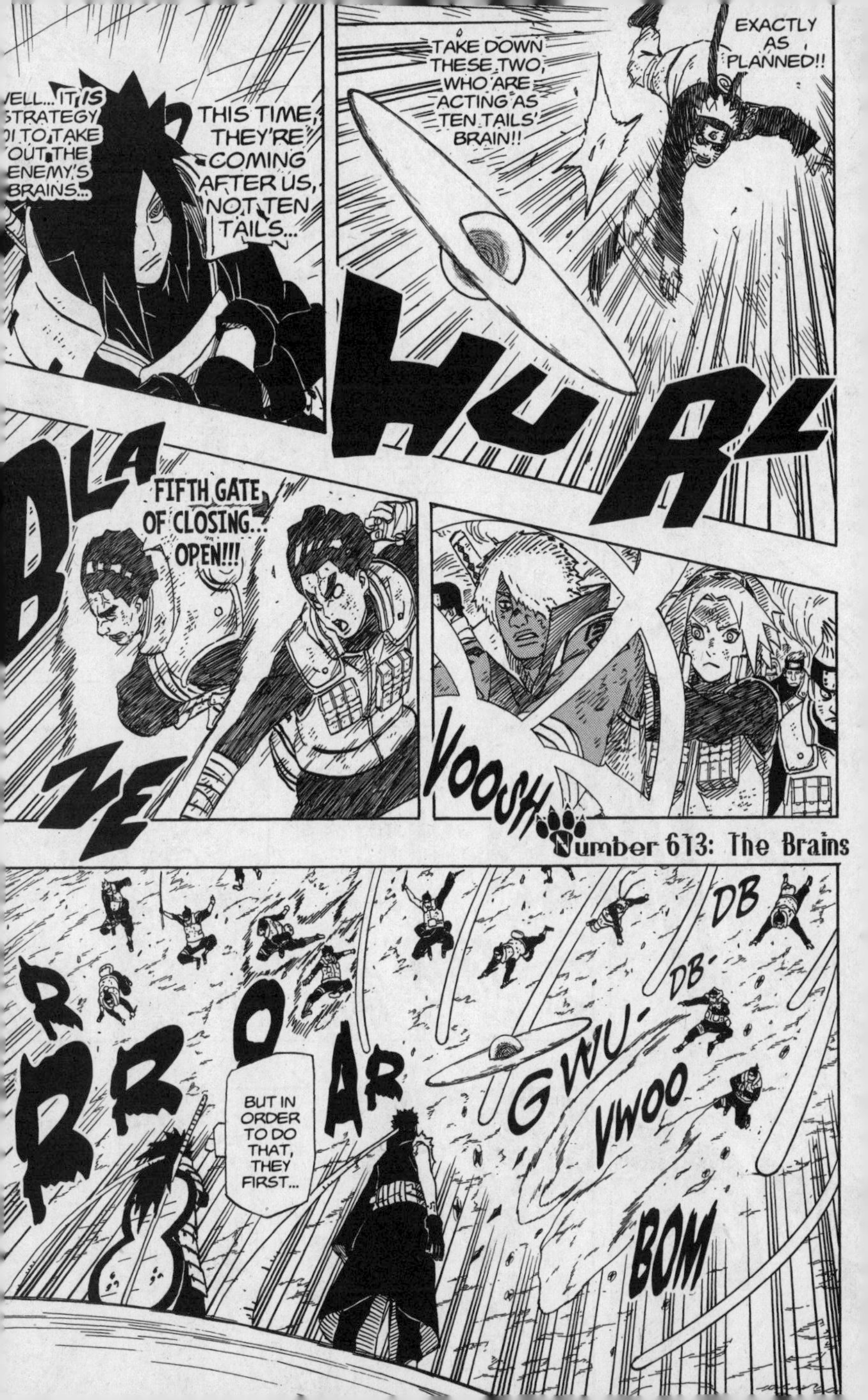
EXACTLY AS PLANNED!!
TAKE DOWN THESE TWO, WHO ARE ACTING AS TEN TAILS' BRAIN!!
WHURL
THIS TIME, THEY'RE COMING AFTER US, NOT TEN TAILS...
WELL... IT IS STRATEGY 101 TO TAKE OUT THE ENEMY'S BRAINS...
VOOSH
FIFTH GATE OF CLOSING... OPEN!!!
BLAZE
Number 613: The Brains
DB
DB
GWU-
VWOO
BOM
RRROAR
BUT IN ORDER TO DO THAT, THEY FIRST...

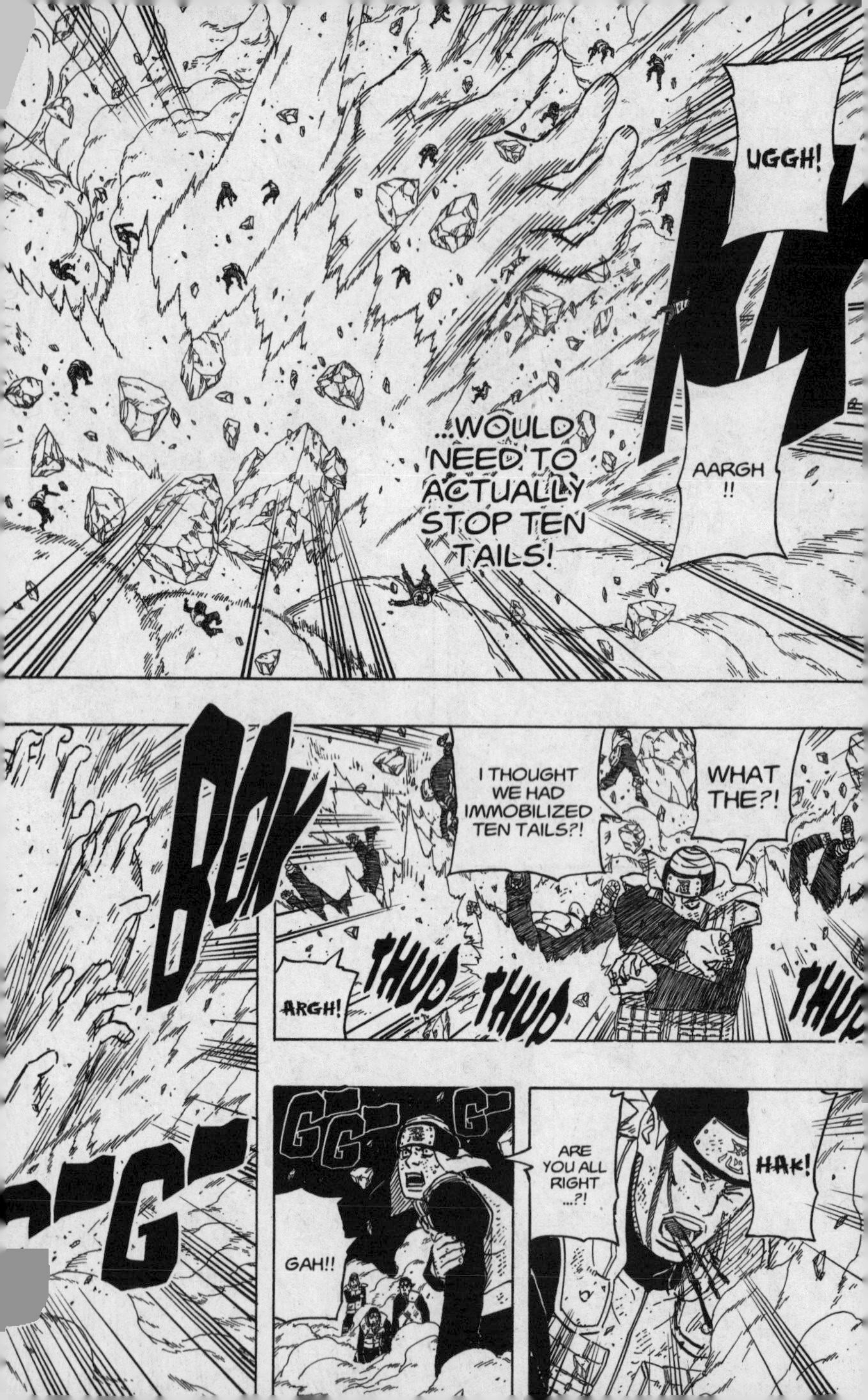

UGGH!
AARGH !!
...WOULD NEED TO ACTUALLY STOP TEN TAILS!
WHAT THE?!
I THOUGHT WE HAD IMMOBILIZED TEN TAILS?!
THUD
THUD
THUD
ARGH!
HAK!
ARE YOU ALL RIGHT ...?!
GG
G
GAH!!
BOK
G

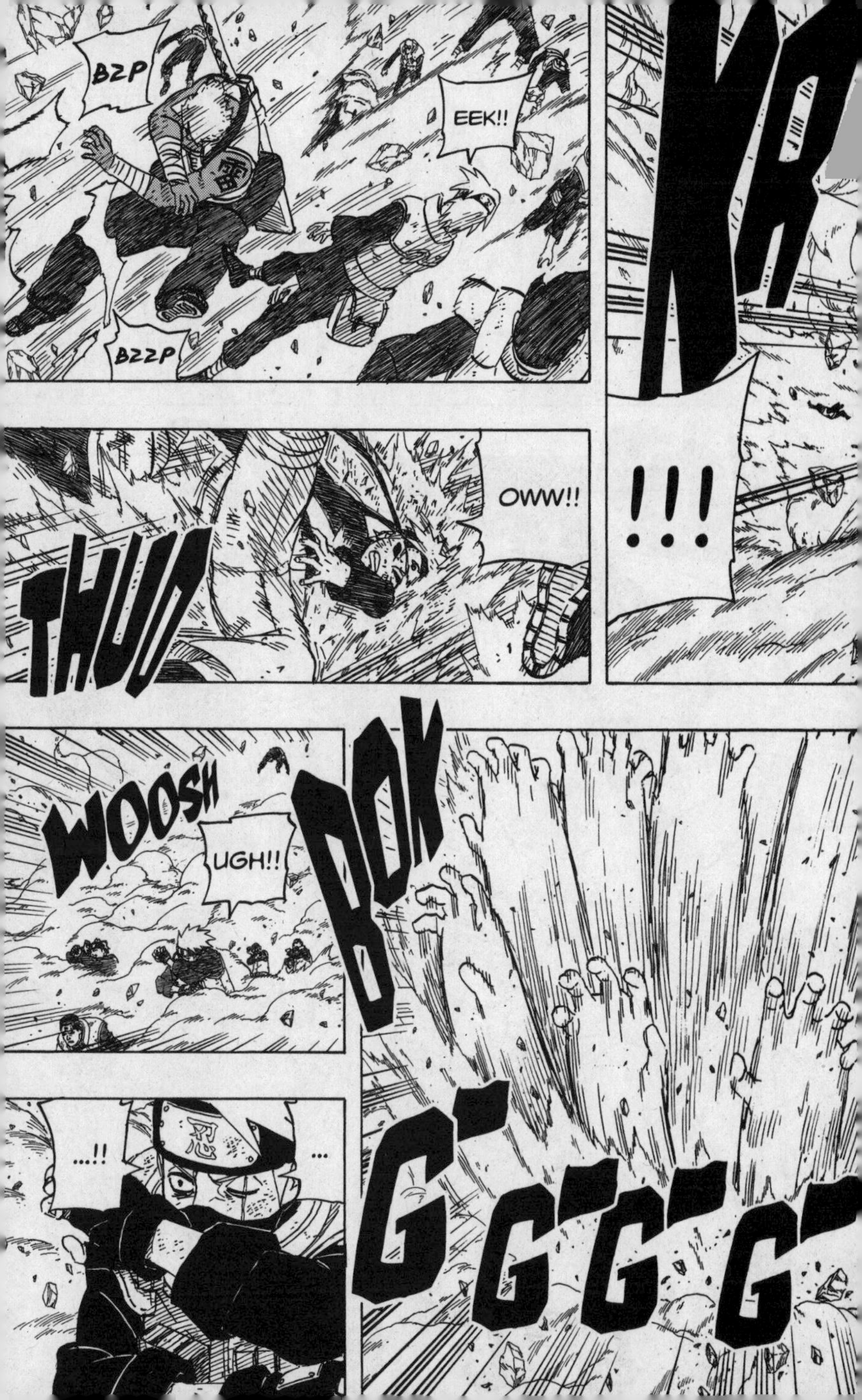
KR
!!!
EEK!!
BZP
BZZP
OWW!!
THUD
BOK
G'G'G'G
WOOSH
UGH!!
...
...!!

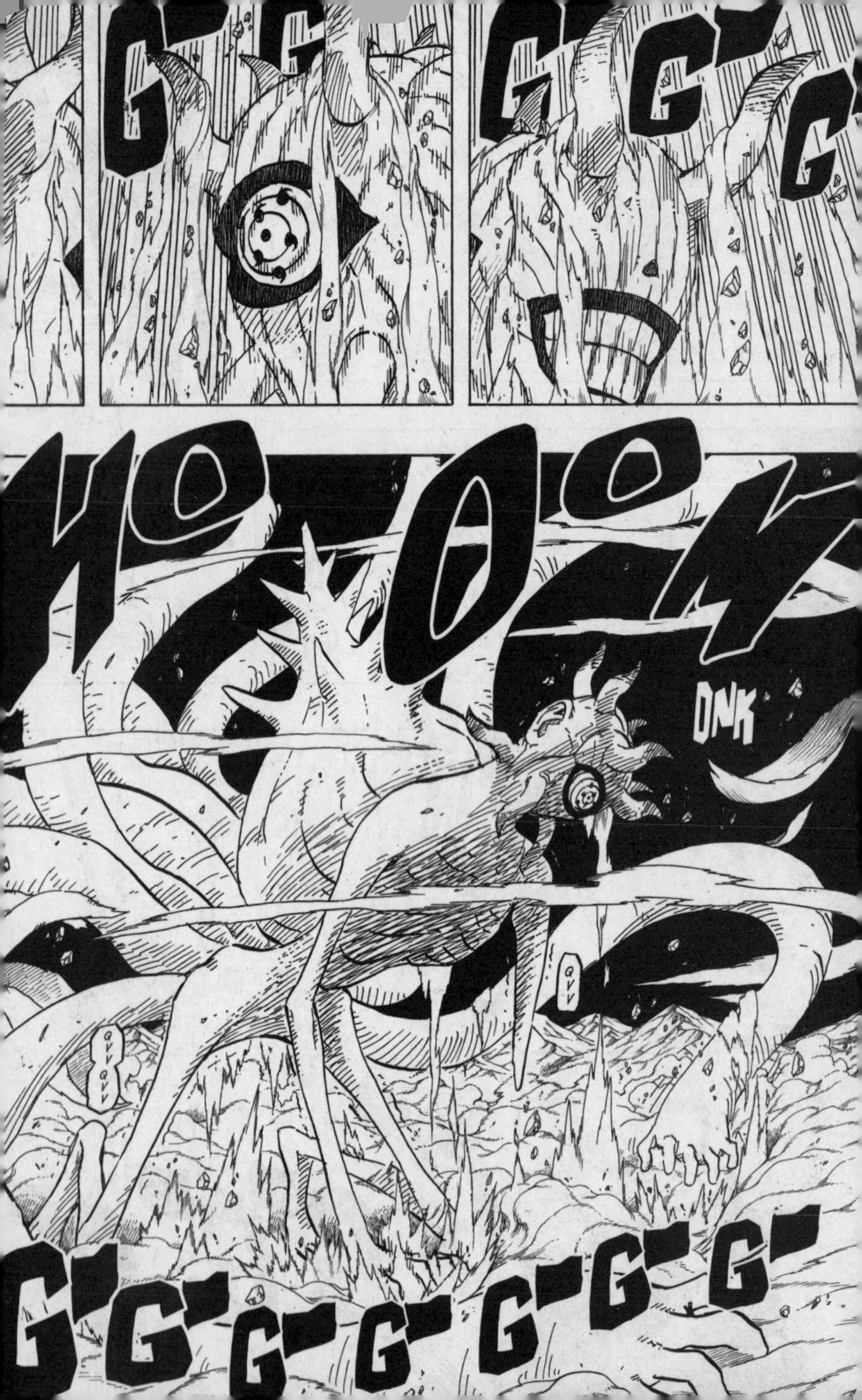
GGGG
GG
DNK
GGGGGGG

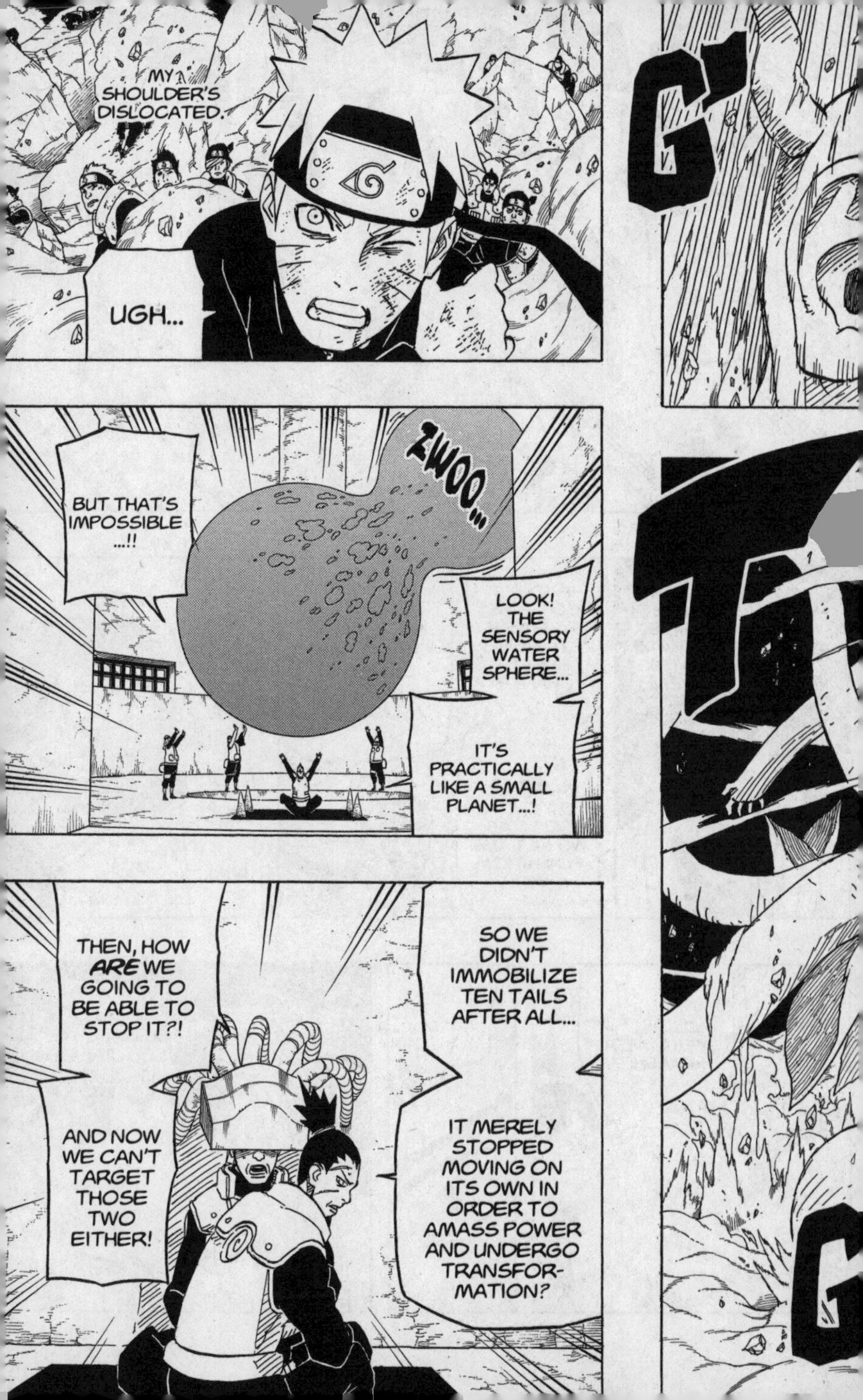
MY SHOULDER'S DISLOCATED.
UGH...
ZWOO...
LOOK! THE SENSORY WATER SPHERE...
IT'S PRACTICALLY LIKE A SMALL PLANET...!
BUT THAT'S IMPOSSIBLE ...!!
SO WE DIDN'T IMMOBILIZE TEN TAILS AFTER ALL...
IT MERELY STOPPED MOVING ON ITS OWN IN ORDER TO AMASS POWER AND UNDERGO TRANSFORMATION?
THEN, HOW *ARE* WE GOING TO BE ABLE TO STOP IT?!
AND NOW WE CAN'T TARGET THOSE TWO EITHER!

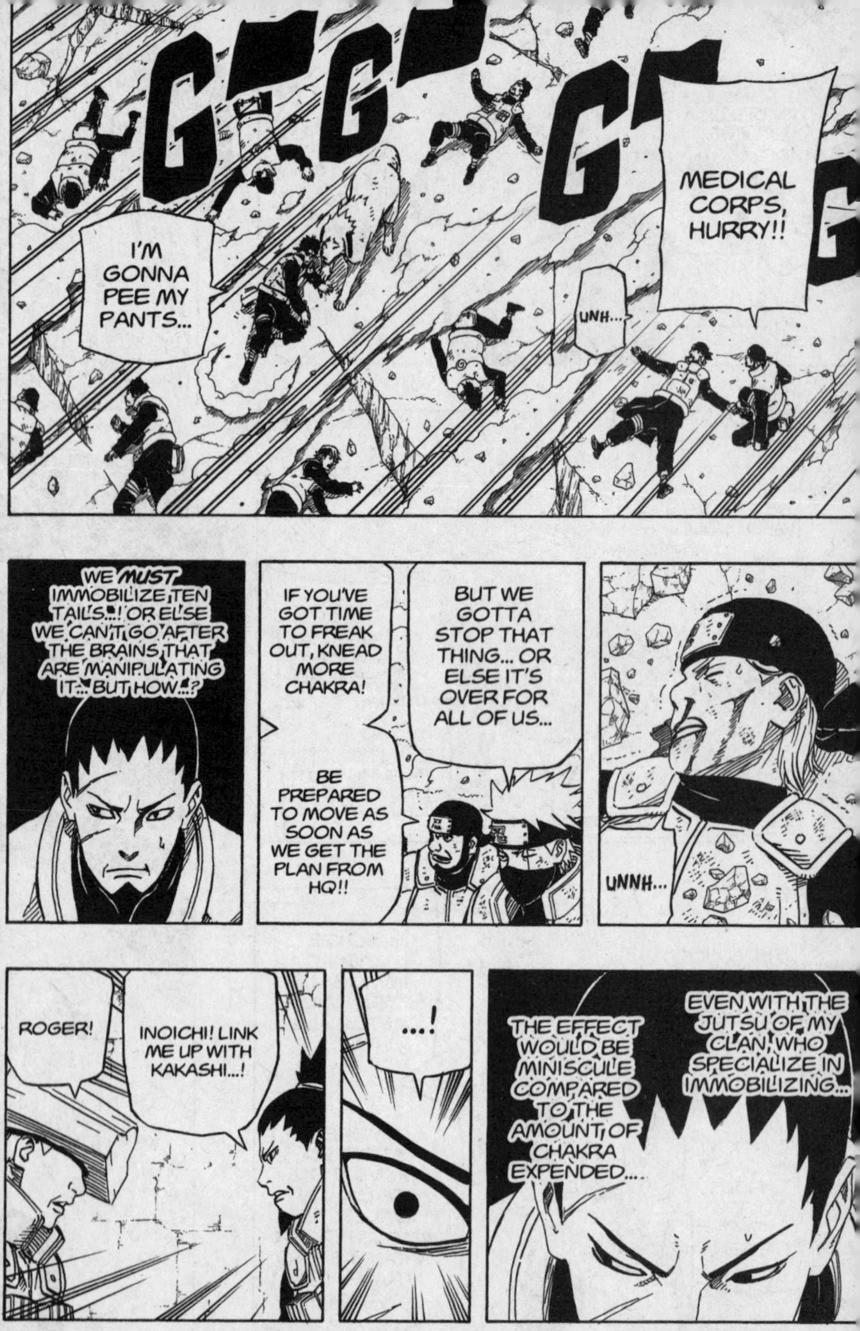

MEDICAL CORPS, HURRY!!
UNH...
I'M GONNA PEE MY PANTS...
UNNH...
BUT WE GOTTA STOP THAT THING... OR ELSE IT'S OVER FOR ALL OF US...
IF YOU'VE GOT TIME TO FREAK OUT, KNEAD MORE CHAKRA!
BE PREPARED TO MOVE AS SOON AS WE GET THE PLAN FROM HQ!!
WE MUST IMMOBILIZE TEN TAILS...! OR ELSE WE CAN'T GO AFTER THE BRAINS THAT ARE MANIPULATING IT... BUT HOW...?
EVEN WITH THE JUTSU OF MY CLAN, WHO SPECIALIZE IN IMMOBILIZING...
THE EFFECT WOULD BE MINISCULE COMPARED TO THE AMOUNT OF CHAKRA EXPENDED...
...!
INOICHI! LINK ME UP WITH KAKASHI...!
ROGER!

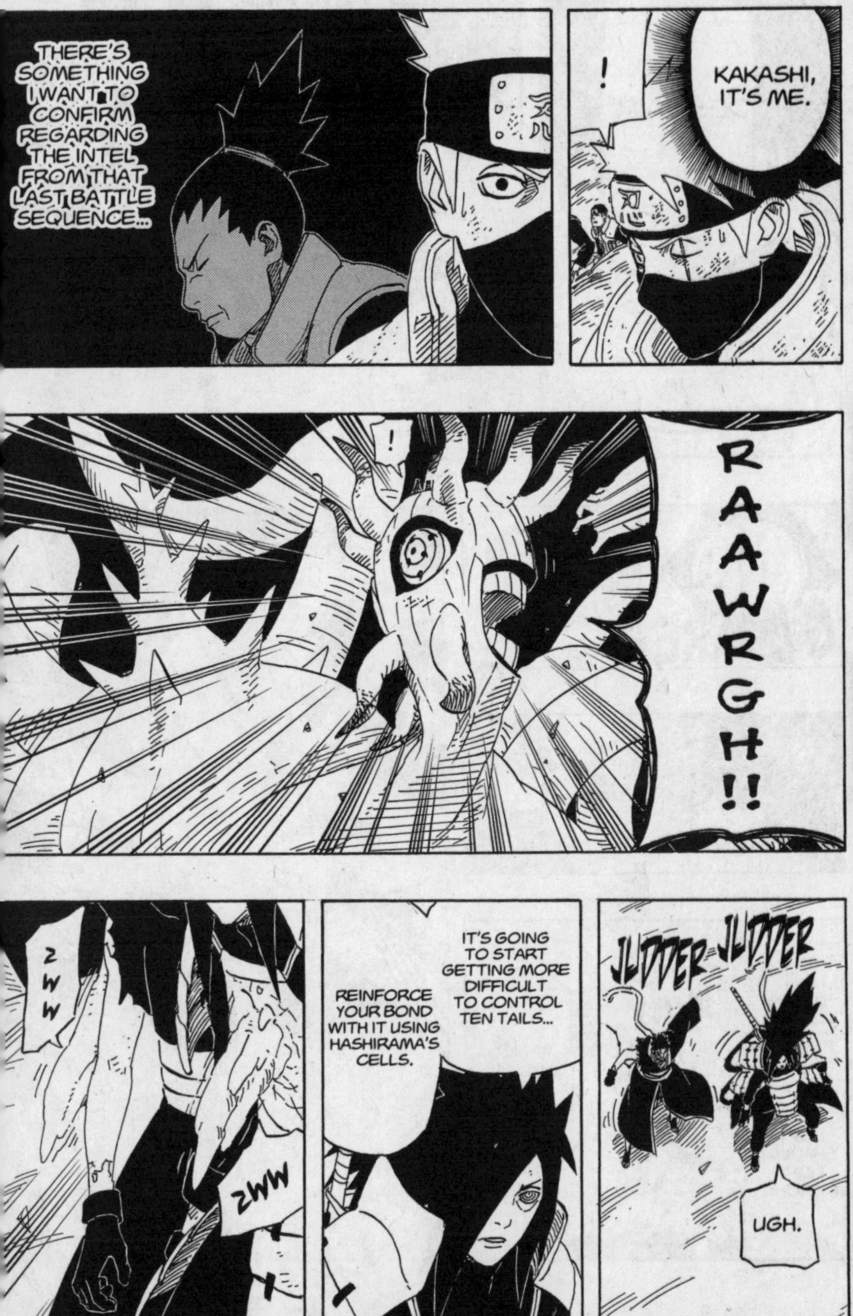
!
KAKASHI, IT'S ME.
THERE'S SOMETHING I WANT TO CONFIRM REGARDING THE INTEL FROM THAT LAST BATTLE SEQUENCE...
RAAWRGH!!
!
JUDDER JUDDER
UGH.
IT'S GOING TO START GETTING MORE DIFFICULT TO CONTROL TEN TAILS...
REINFORCE YOUR BOND WITH IT USING HASHIRAMA'S CELLS.
ZWW
ZWW

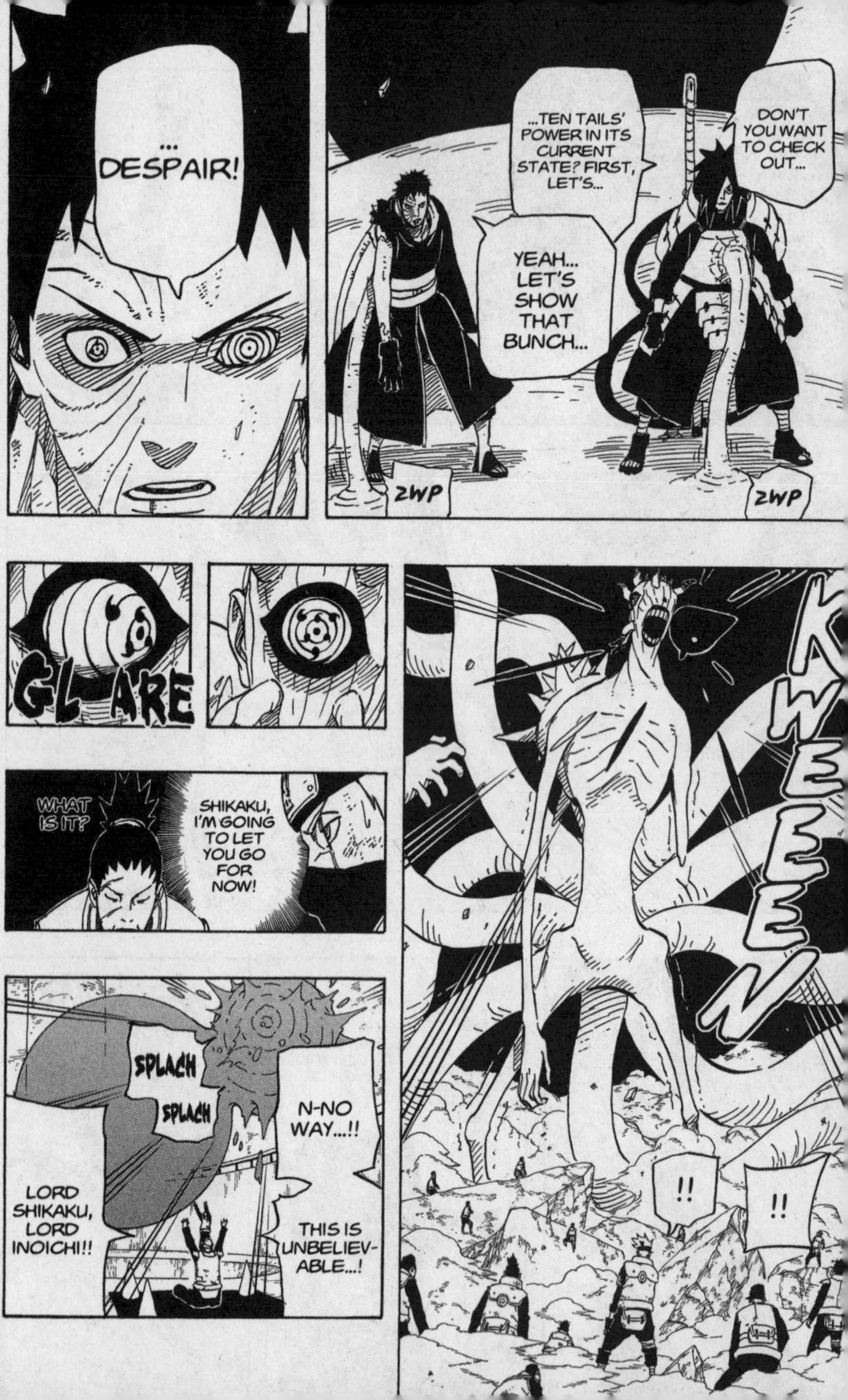
DON'T YOU WANT TO CHECK OUT...
...TEN TAILS' POWER IN ITS CURRENT STATE? FIRST, LET'S...
YEAH... LET'S SHOW THAT BUNCH...
ZWP
ZWP
... DESPAIR!
KWEEEEN
!!
!!
GLARE
SHIKAKU, I'M GOING TO LET YOU GO FOR NOW!
WHAT IS IT?
N-NO WAY...!!
SPLACH
SPLACH
THIS IS UNBELIEVABLE...!
LORD SHIKAKU, LORD INOICHI!!

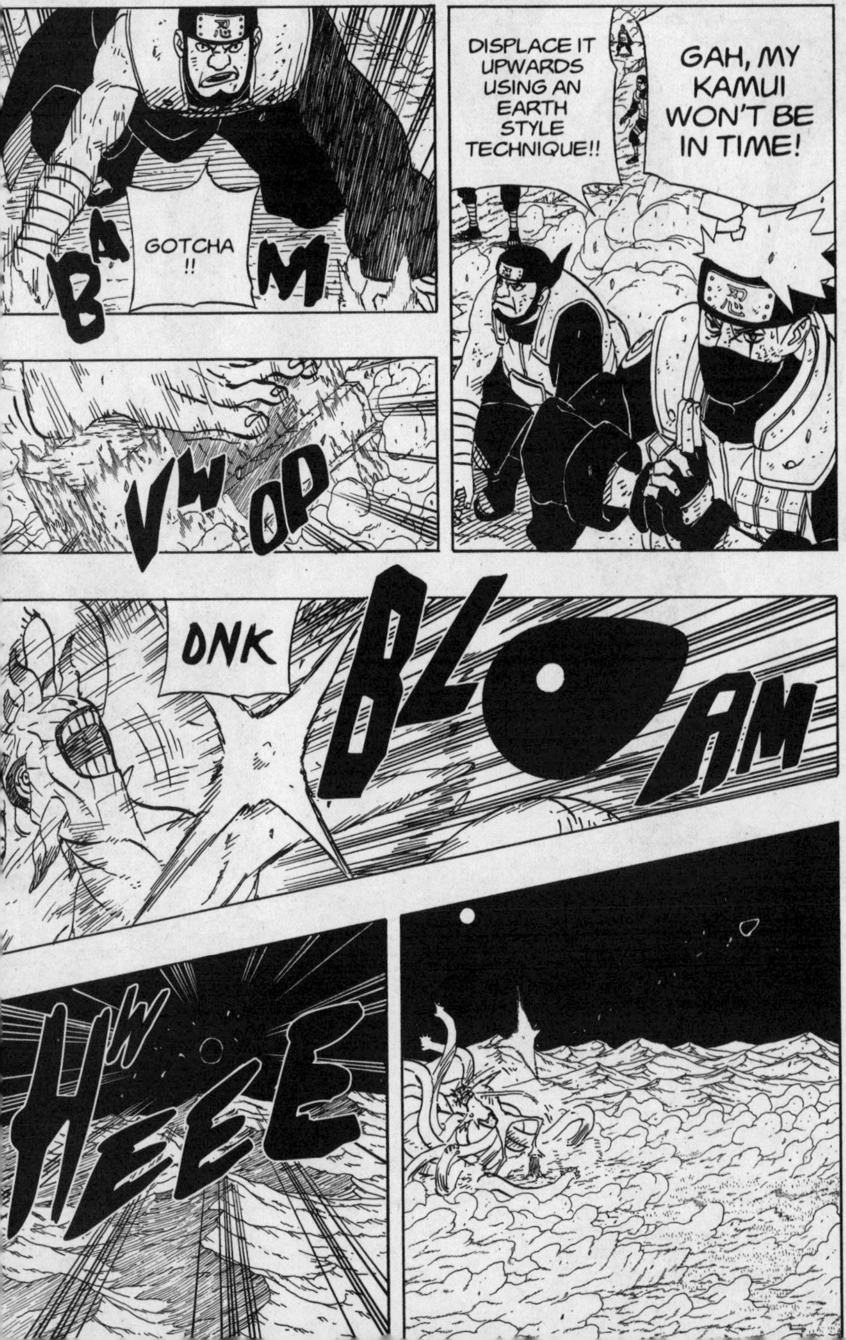
GAH, MY KAMUI WON'T BE IN TIME!
DISPLACE IT UPWARDS USING AN EARTH STYLE TECHNIQUE!!
BAM
GOTCHA!!
VWOOP
BLOAM
ONK
HWEEE

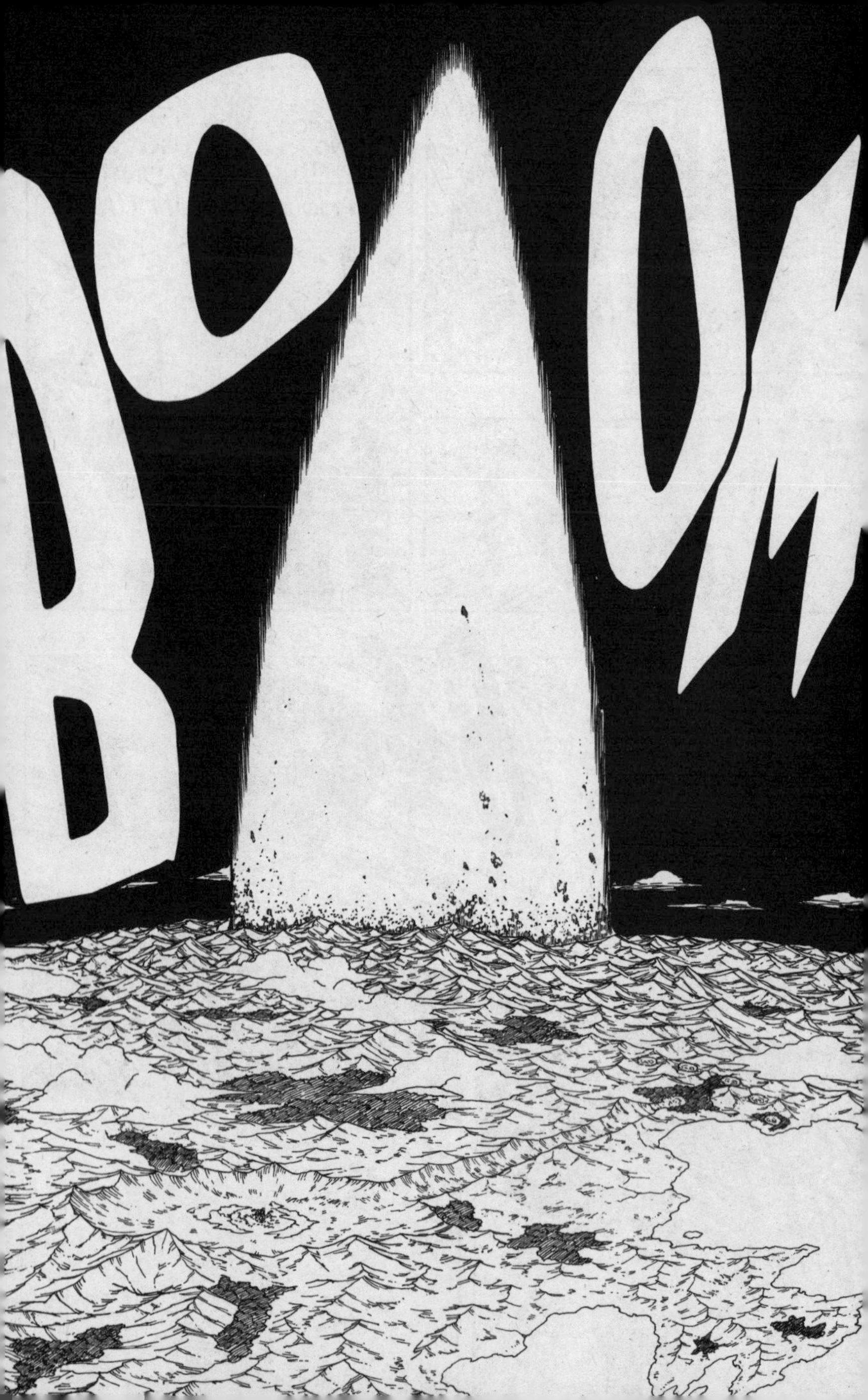
BOOM

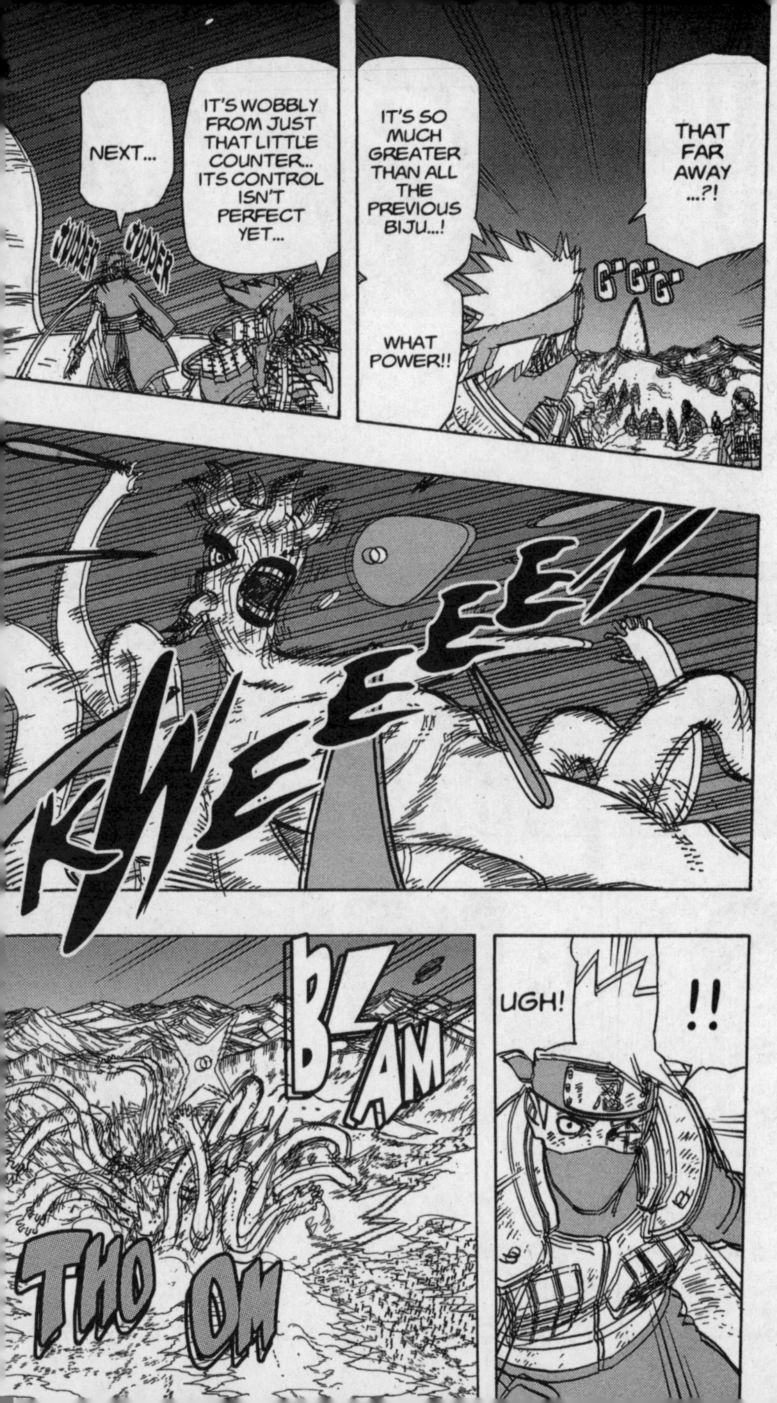
THAT FAR AWAY ...?!
G'G'G'
IT'S SO MUCH GREATER THAN ALL THE PREVIOUS BIJU...!
WHAT POWER!!
IT'S WOBBLY FROM JUST THAT LITTLE COUNTER.. ITS CONTROL ISN'T PERFECT YET...
NEXT...
SHUDDER SHUDDER
KWEEEEN
!!
UGH!
BLAM
THOOM

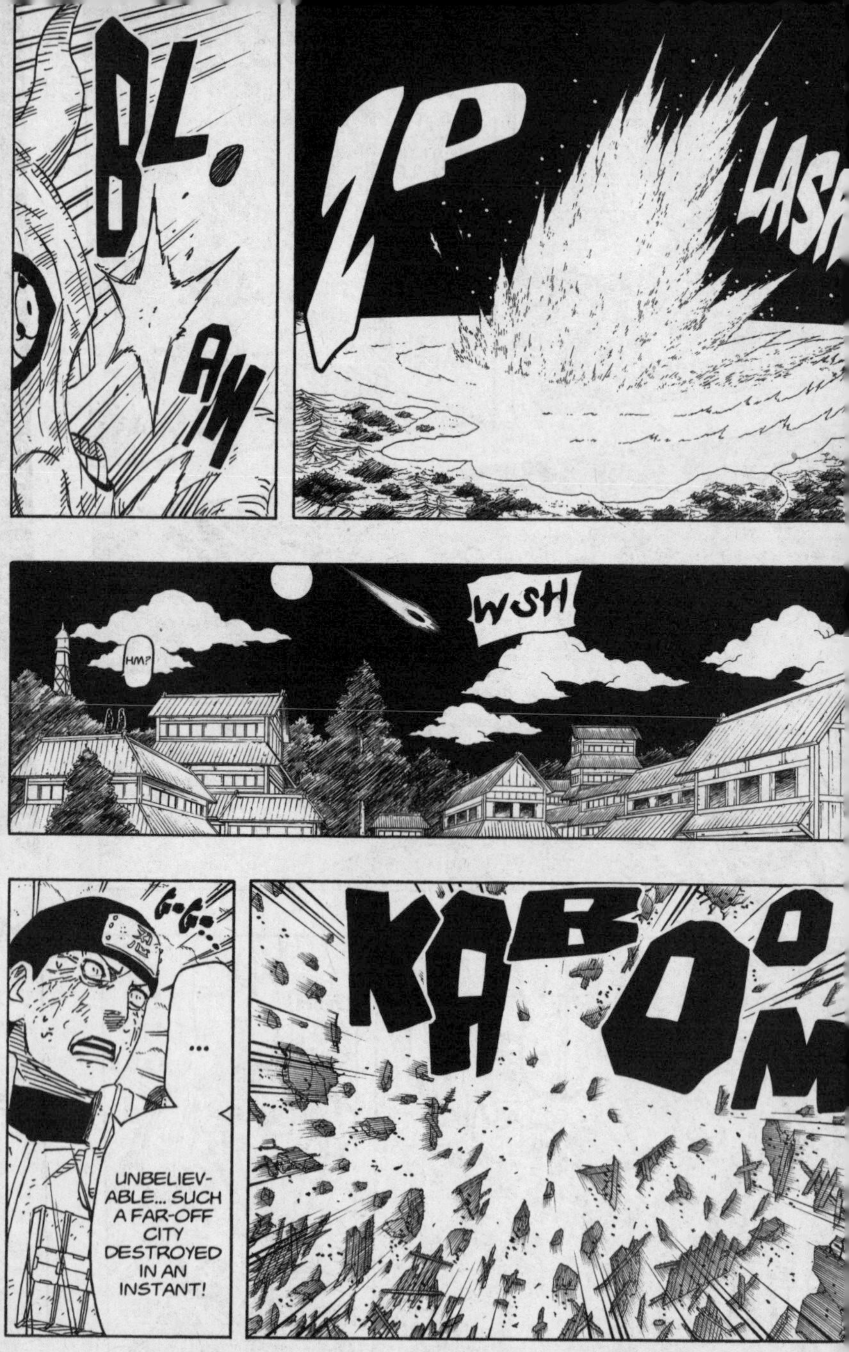
ZIP
LASH
BLAM
WSH
HM?
KABOOM
G-G-...
...
UNBELIEV-ABLE... SUCH A FAR-OFF CITY DESTROYED IN AN INSTANT!

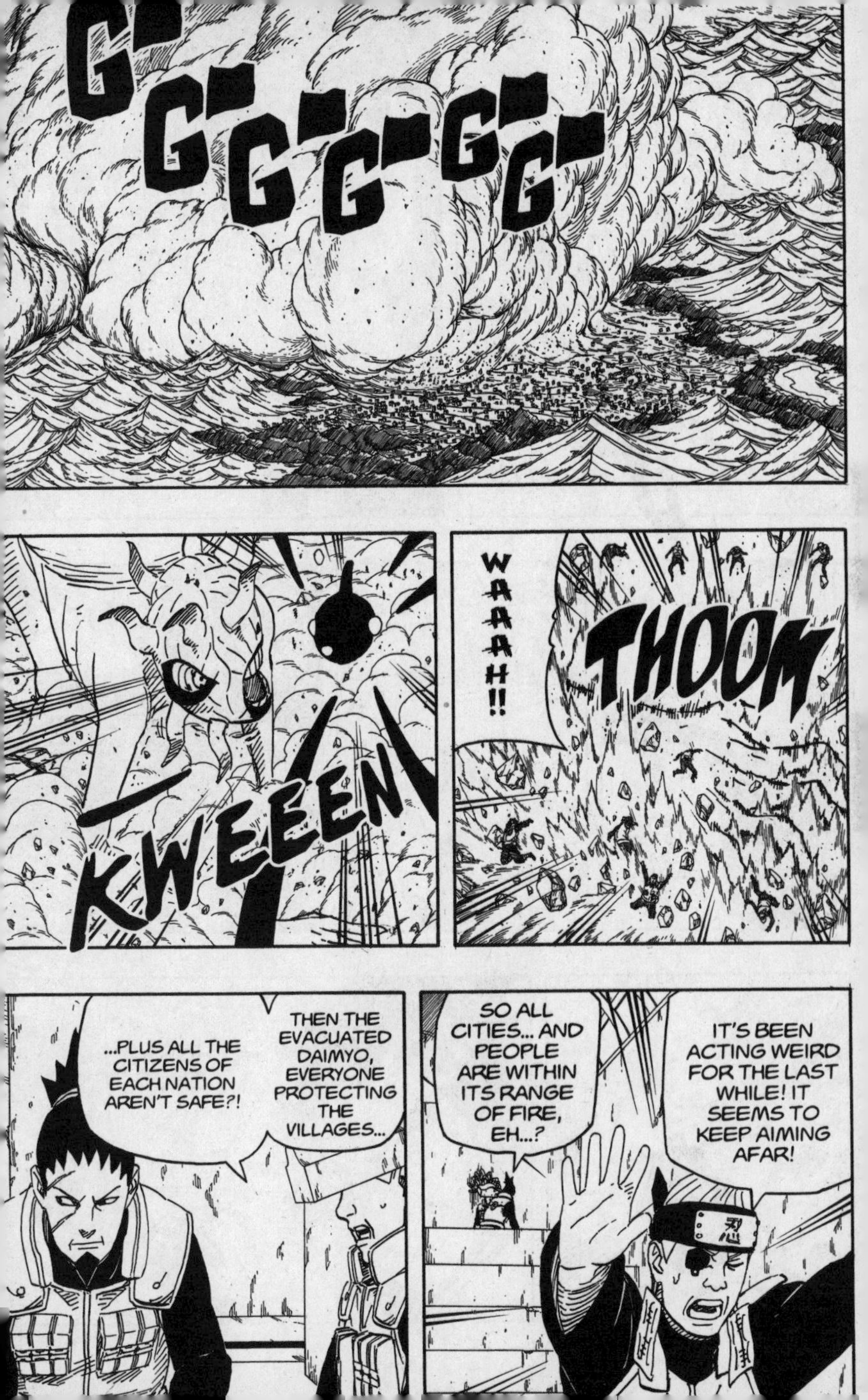
G-G-G-G-G-G-G-
WAAAAH!!
THOOM
KWEEEN
IT'S BEEN ACTING WEIRD FOR THE LAST WHILE! IT SEEMS TO KEEP AIMING AFAR!
SO ALL CITIES... AND PEOPLE ARE WITHIN ITS RANGE OF FIRE, EH...?
THEN THE EVACUATED DAIMYO, EVERYONE PROTECTING THE VILLAGES...
...PLUS ALL THE CITIZENS OF EACH NATION AREN'T SAFE?!

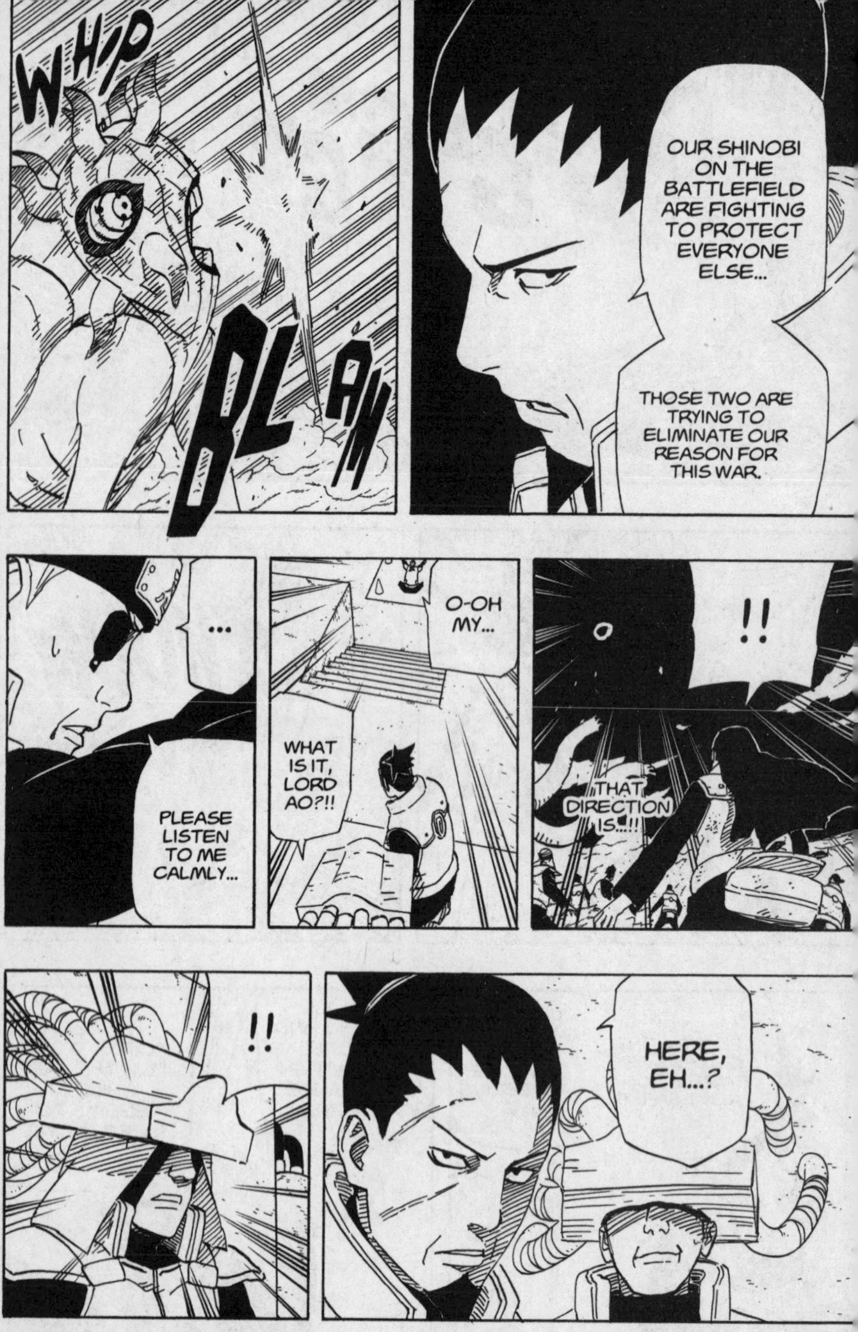
OUR SHINOBI ON THE BATTLEFIELD ARE FIGHTING TO PROTECT EVERYONE ELSE...
THOSE TWO ARE TRYING TO ELIMINATE OUR REASON FOR THIS WAR.
WHIP
BLAM
!!
THAT DIRECTION IS...!!
O-OH MY...
WHAT IS IT, LORD AO?!!
...
PLEASE LISTEN TO ME CALMLY...
HERE, EH...?
!!

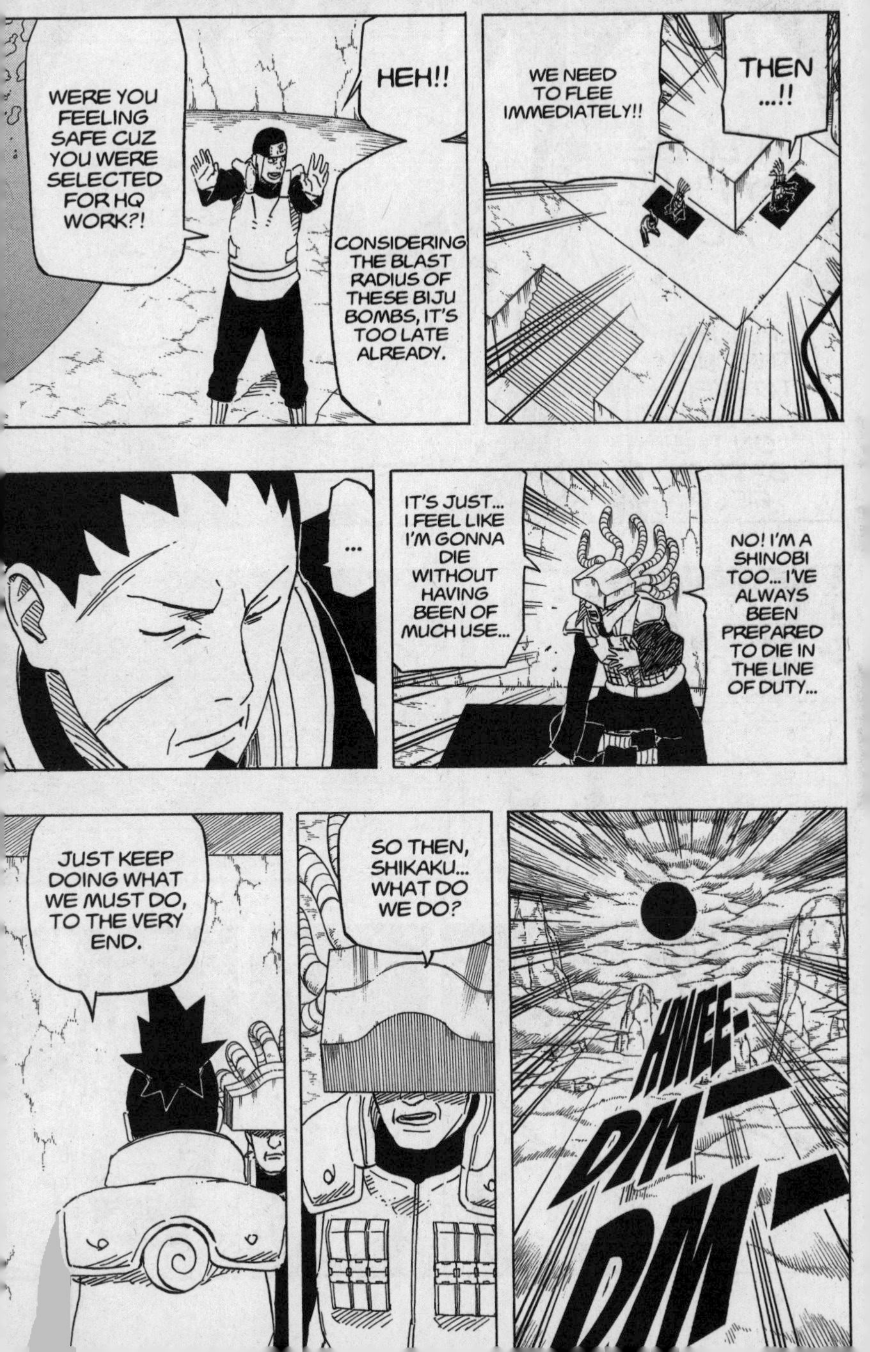
THEN ...!!
WE NEED TO FLEE IMMEDIATELY!!
HEH!!
WERE YOU FEELING SAFE CUZ YOU WERE SELECTED FOR HQ WORK?!
CONSIDERING THE BLAST RADIUS OF THESE BIJU BOMBS, IT'S TOO LATE ALREADY.
NO! I'M A SHINOBI TOO... I'VE ALWAYS BEEN PREPARED TO DIE IN THE LINE OF DUTY...
IT'S JUST... I FEEL LIKE I'M GONNA DIE WITHOUT HAVING BEEN OF MUCH USE...
...
HWEE-
DM-
DM-
SO THEN, SHIKAKU... WHAT DO WE DO?
JUST KEEP DOING WHAT WE MUST DO, TO THE VERY END.

IT'LL BE MY FINAL ACT.

PUT ME THROUGH TO EVERYONE ON THE BATTLEFIELD.

I HAVE A PLAN TO STOP TEN TAILS...

LISTEN UP, EVERYONE...

!!

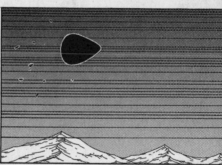

...

112

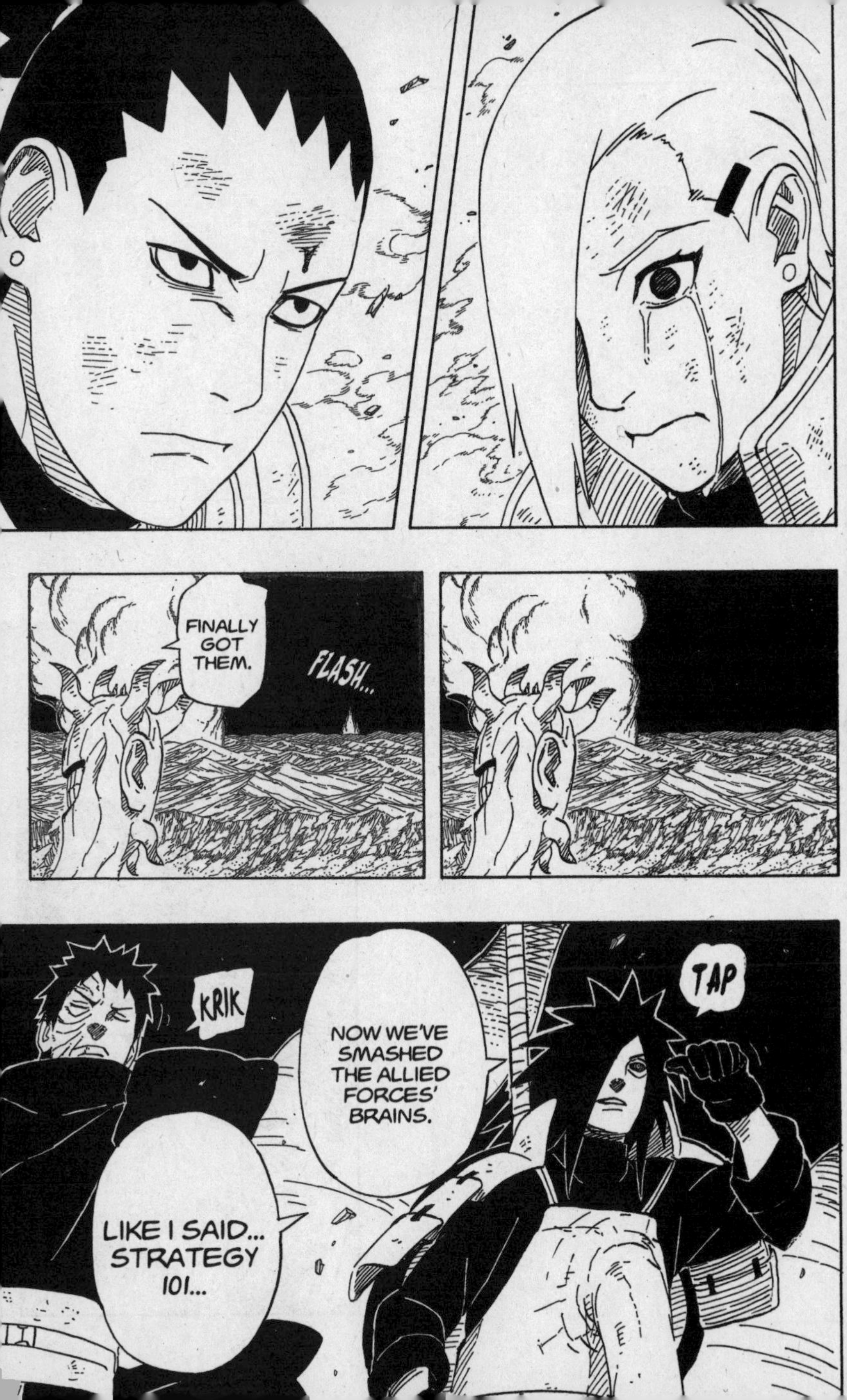
FINALLY GOT THEM.
FLASH...
TAP
NOW WE'VE SMASHED THE ALLIED FORCES' BRAINS.
KRIK
LIKE I SAID... STRATEGY 101...

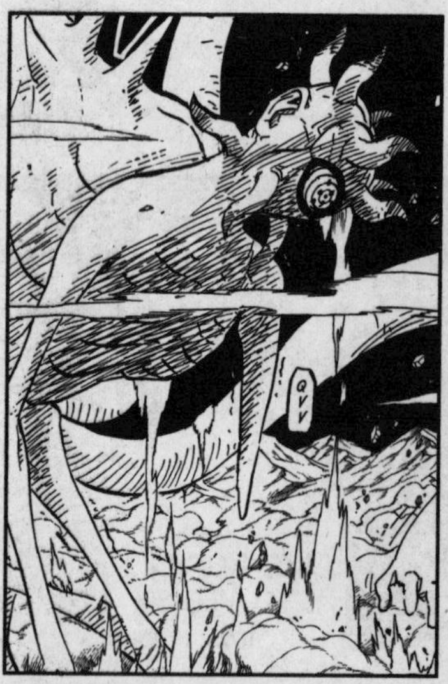
QVV

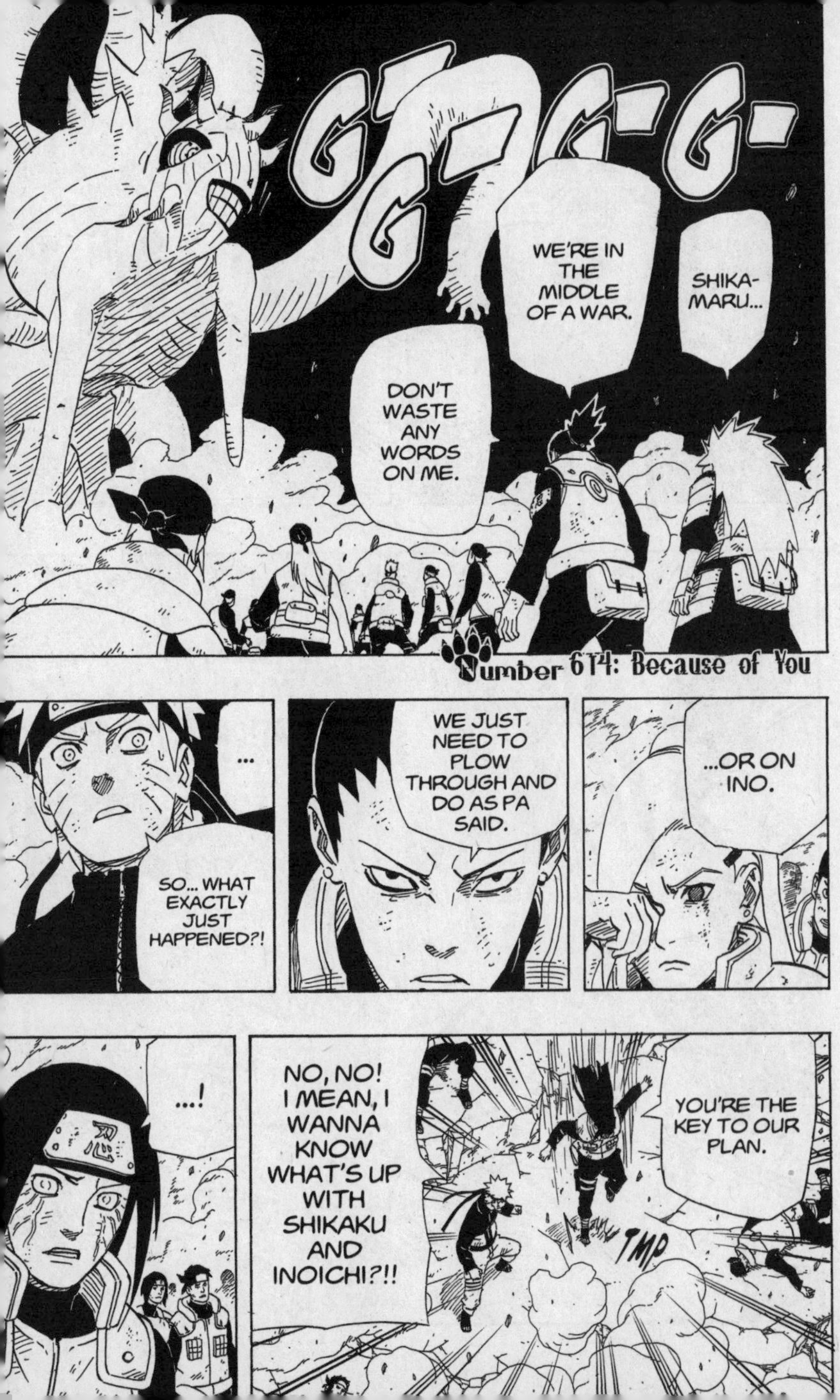
G-G-G-G-G-
SHIKA-MARU...
WE'RE IN THE MIDDLE OF A WAR.
DON'T WASTE ANY WORDS ON ME.
Number 614: Because of You
...OR ON INO.
WE JUST NEED TO PLOW THROUGH AND DO AS PA SAID.
...
SO... WHAT EXACTLY JUST HAPPENED?!
YOU'RE THE KEY TO OUR PLAN.
NO, NO! I MEAN, I WANNA KNOW WHAT'S UP WITH SHIKAKU AND INOICHI?!!
TMP
...!

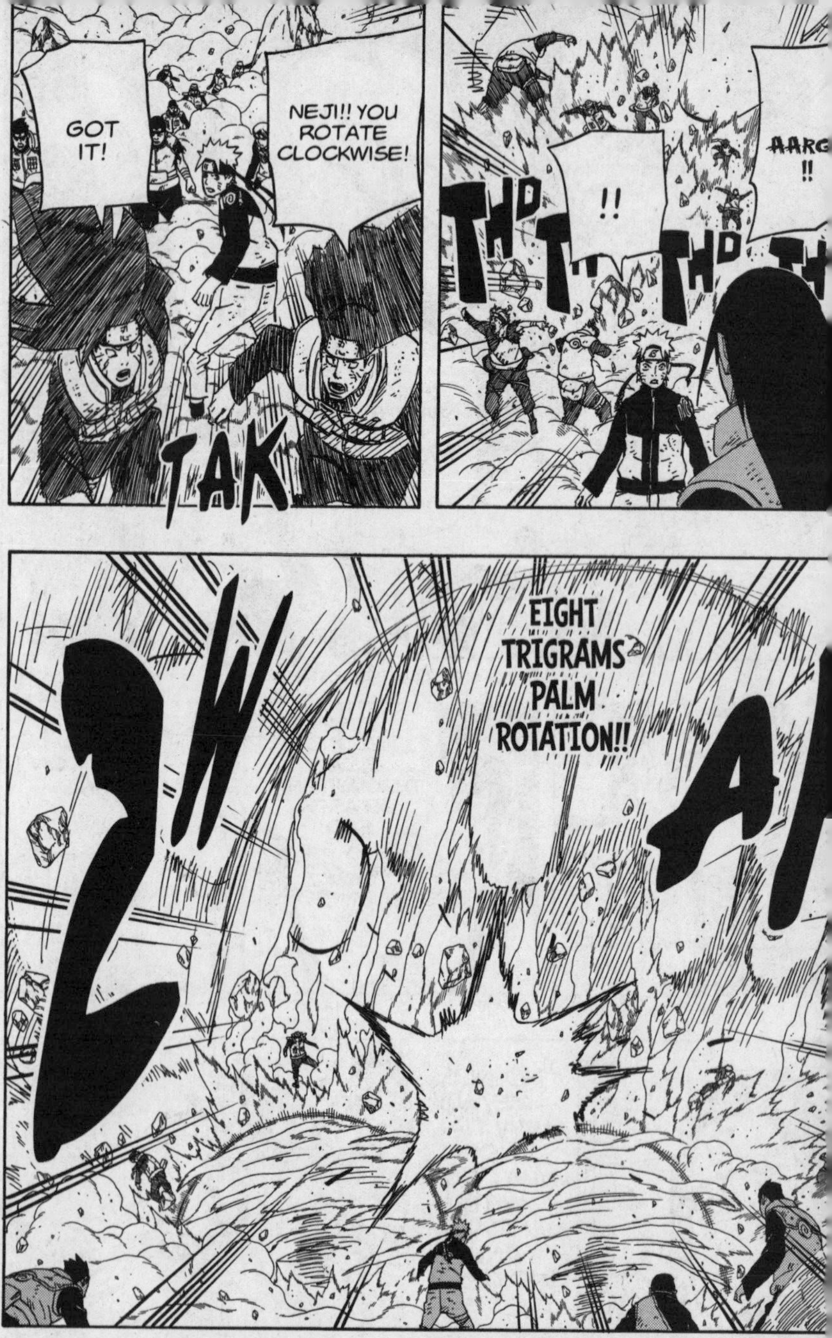
AARG !!
!!
THD
THD
NEJI!! YOU ROTATE CLOCKWISE!
GOT IT!
TAK
EIGHT TRIGRAMS PALM ROTATION!!

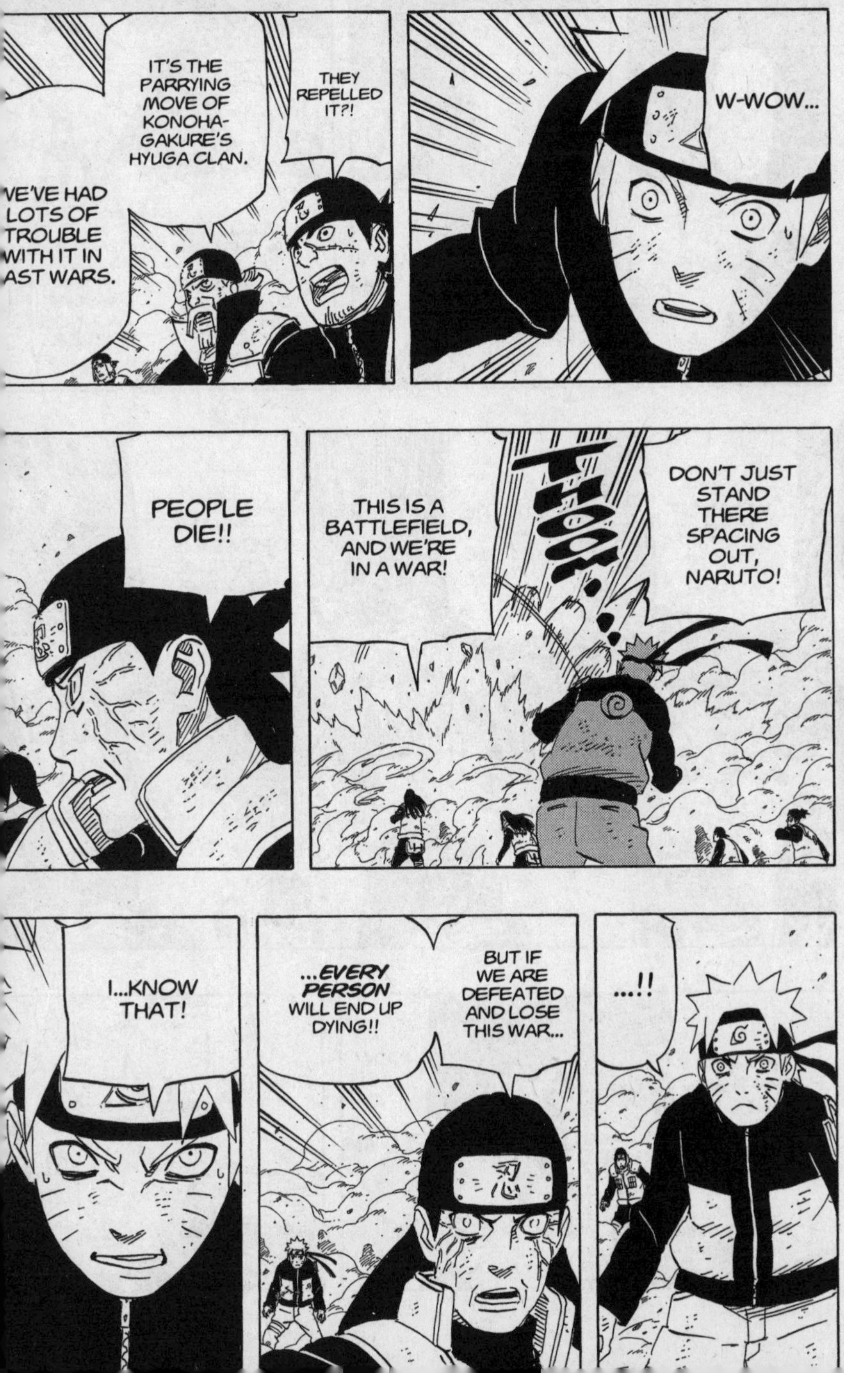
W-WOW...
THEY REPELLED IT?!
IT'S THE PARRYING MOVE OF KONOHA-GAKURE'S HYUGA CLAN.
VE'VE HAD LOTS OF TROUBLE WITH IT IN AST WARS.
DON'T JUST STAND THERE SPACING OUT, NARUTO!
THOOM...
THIS IS A BATTLEFIELD, AND WE'RE IN A WAR!
PEOPLE DIE!!
...!!
BUT IF WE ARE DEFEATED AND LOSE THIS WAR...
...*EVERY PERSON* WILL END UP DYING!!
I...KNOW THAT!

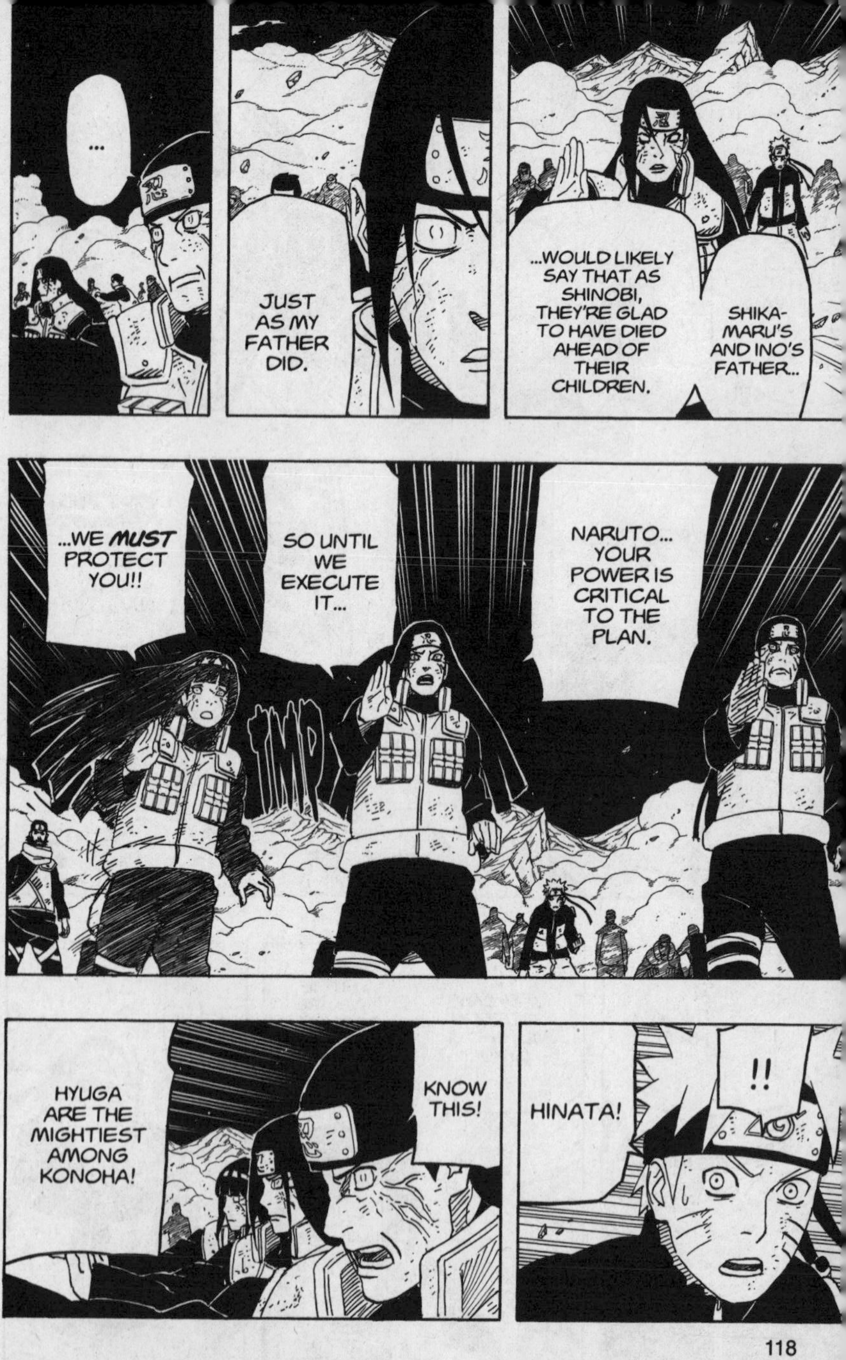
SHIKA-MARU'S AND INO'S FATHER...
...WOULD LIKELY SAY THAT AS SHINOBI, THEY'RE GLAD TO HAVE DIED AHEAD OF THEIR CHILDREN.
JUST AS MY FATHER DID.
...
NARUTO... YOUR POWER IS CRITICAL TO THE PLAN.
SO UNTIL WE EXECUTE IT...
TMP
...WE *MUST* PROTECT YOU!!
!!
HINATA!
KNOW THIS!
HYUGA ARE THE MIGHTIEST AMONG KONOHA!

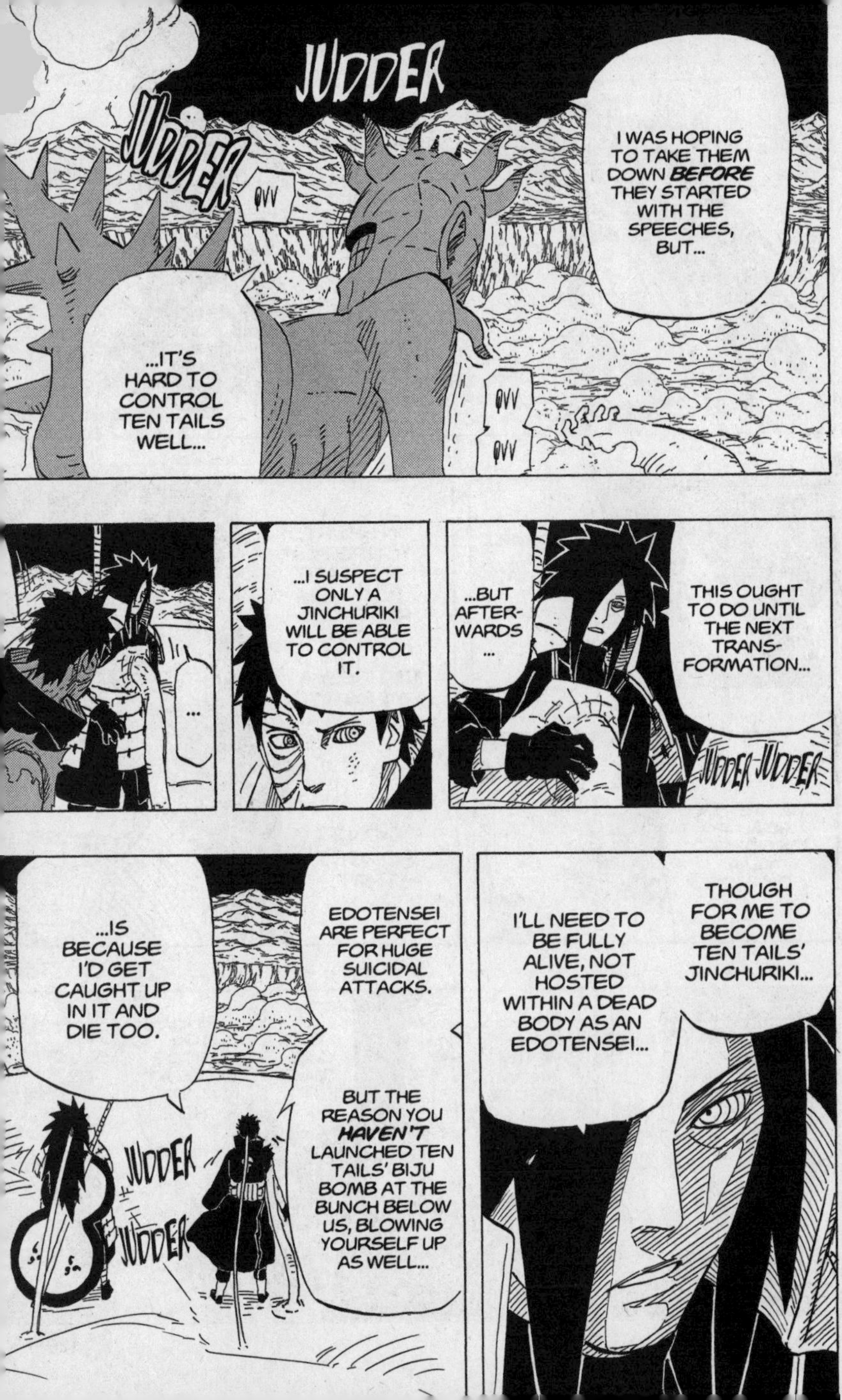
JUDDER
JUDDER
I WAS HOPING TO TAKE THEM DOWN **BEFORE** THEY STARTED WITH THE SPEECHES, BUT...
QVV
...IT'S HARD TO CONTROL TEN TAILS WELL...
QVV
QVV
THIS OUGHT TO DO UNTIL THE NEXT TRANS-FORMATION...
...BUT AFTER-WARDS...
JUDDER-JUDDER
...I SUSPECT ONLY A JINCHURIKI WILL BE ABLE TO CONTROL IT.
...
THOUGH FOR ME TO BECOME TEN TAILS' JINCHURIKI...
I'LL NEED TO BE FULLY ALIVE, NOT HOSTED WITHIN A DEAD BODY AS AN EDOTENSEI...
EDOTENSEI ARE PERFECT FOR HUGE SUICIDAL ATTACKS.
BUT THE REASON YOU ***HAVEN'T*** LAUNCHED TEN TAILS' BIJU BOMB AT THE BUNCH BELOW US, BLOWING YOURSELF UP AS WELL...
...IS BECAUSE I'D GET CAUGHT UP IN IT AND DIE TOO.
JUDDER
JUDDER

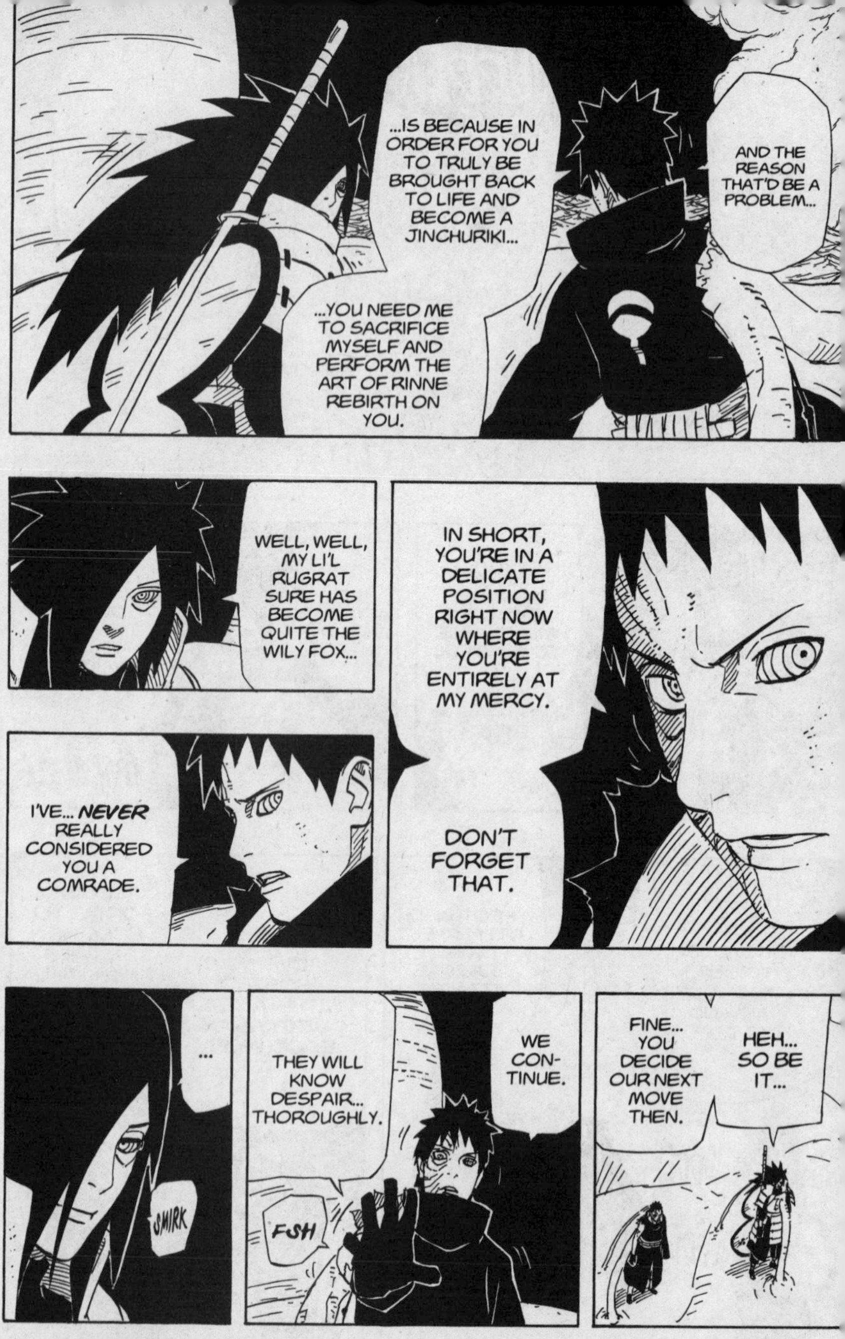
AND THE REASON THAT'D BE A PROBLEM...
...IS BECAUSE IN ORDER FOR YOU TO TRULY BE BROUGHT BACK TO LIFE AND BECOME A JINCHURIKI...
...YOU NEED ME TO SACRIFICE MYSELF AND PERFORM THE ART OF RINNE REBIRTH ON YOU.
IN SHORT, YOU'RE IN A DELICATE POSITION RIGHT NOW WHERE YOU'RE ENTIRELY AT MY MERCY.
DON'T FORGET THAT.
WELL, WELL, MY LI'L RUGRAT SURE HAS BECOME QUITE THE WILY FOX...
I'VE... ***NEVER*** REALLY CONSIDERED YOU A COMRADE.
HEH... SO BE IT...
FINE... YOU DECIDE OUR NEXT MOVE THEN.
WE CON-TINUE.
THEY WILL KNOW DESPAIR... THOROUGHLY.
FSH
...
SMIRK

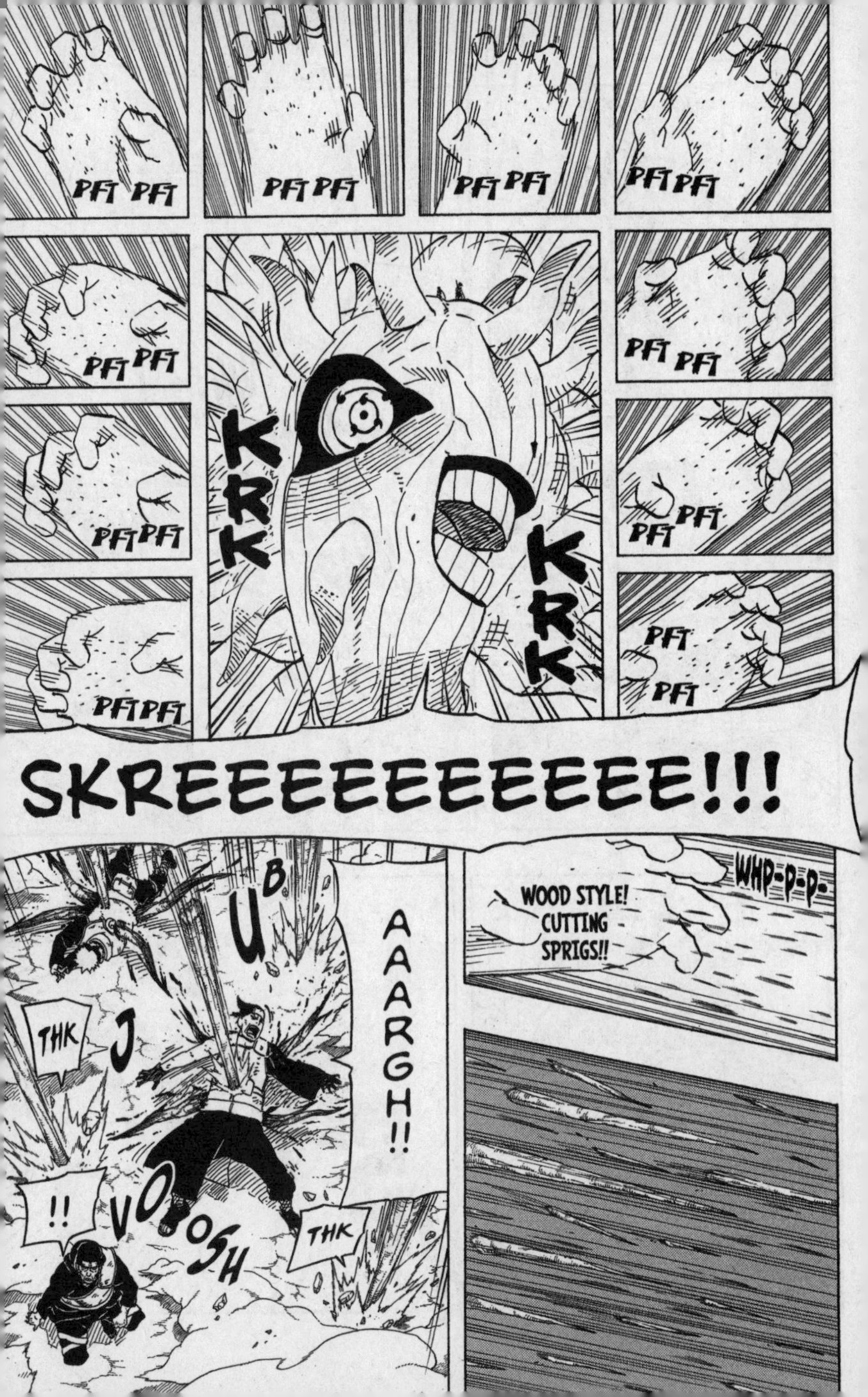
PFT PFT
PFT PFT
PFT PFT
PFT PFT
PFT PFT
PFT PFT
PFT PFT
KRK
KRK
PFT PFT
PFT PFT
PFT PFT
SKREEEEEEEEEEEE!!!
WHP-P-P-
WOOD STYLE! CUTTING SPRIGS!!
AAAARGH!!
B
U
J
THK
!!
VOOOSH
THK

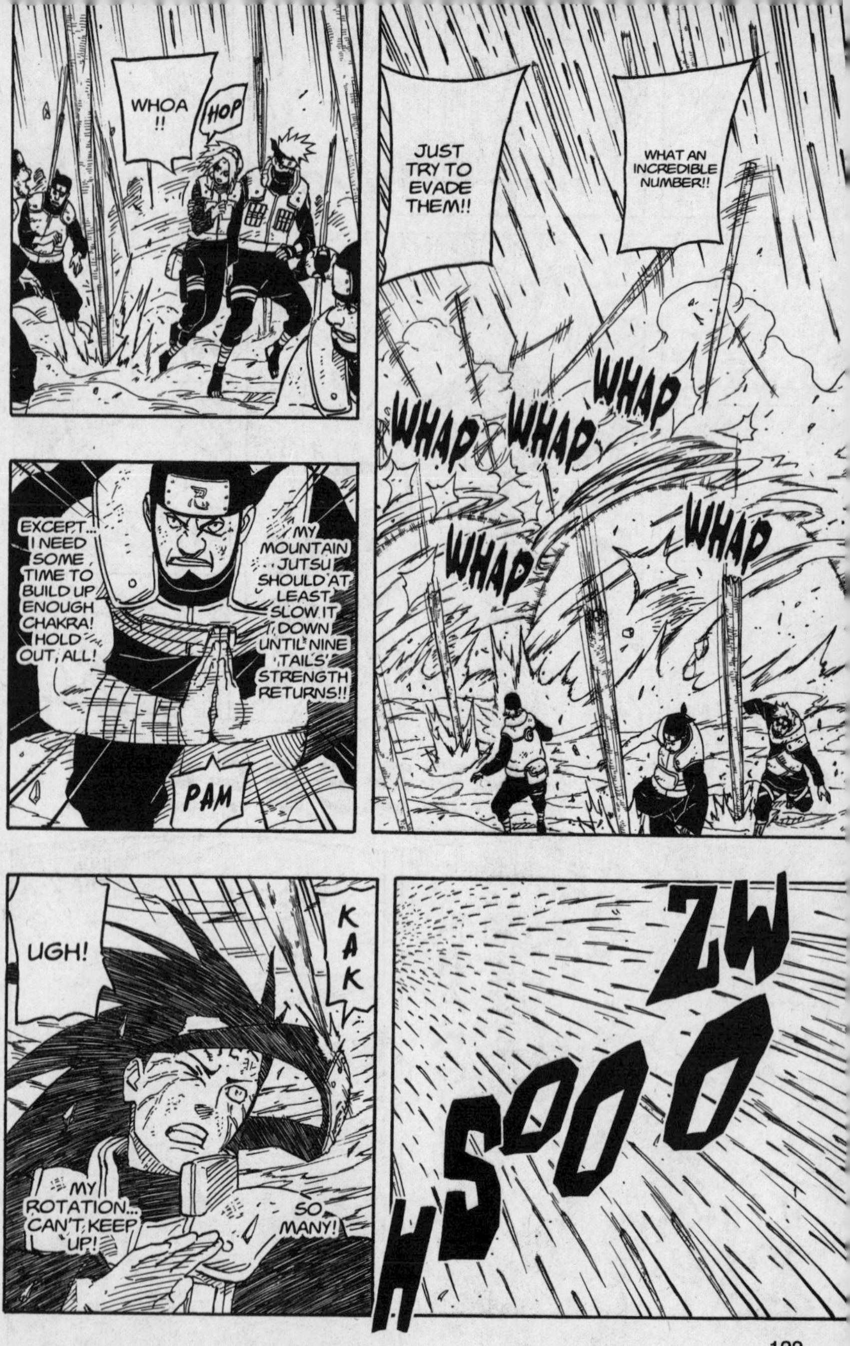
WHAT AN INCREDIBLE NUMBER!!
JUST TRY TO EVADE THEM!!
WHAP
WHAP
WHAP
WHAP
WHAP
WHOA !!
HOP
MY MOUNTAIN JUTSU SHOULD AT LEAST SLOW IT DOWN UNTIL NINE TAILS' STRENGTH RETURNS!!
EXCEPT... I NEED SOME TIME TO BUILD UP ENOUGH CHAKRA! HOLD OUT, ALL!
PAM
ZWOOOSH
KAK
UGH!
SO MANY!
MY ROTATION... CAN'T KEEP UP!

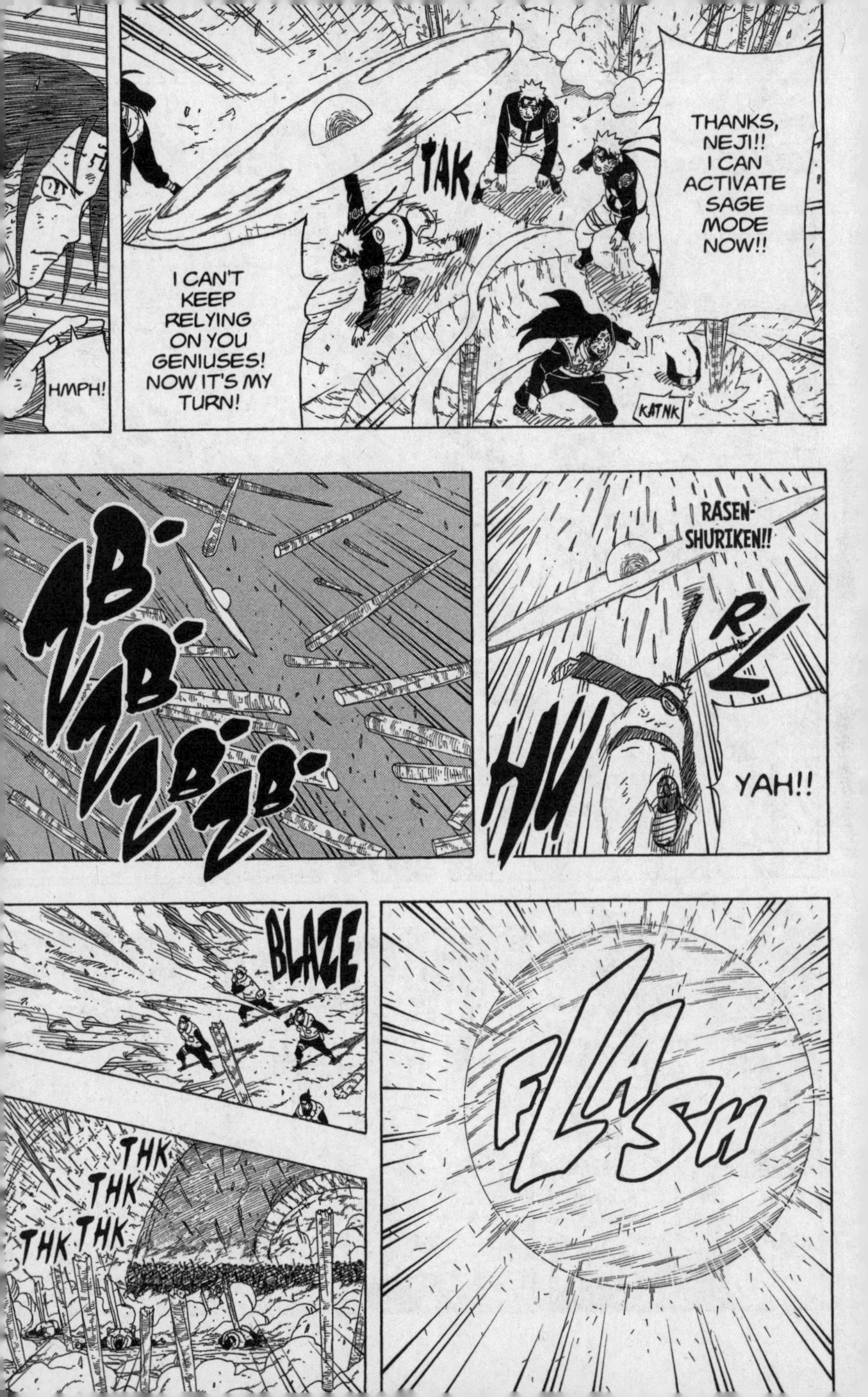
THANKS, NEJI!! I CAN ACTIVATE SAGE MODE NOW!!
TAK
I CAN'T KEEP RELYING ON YOU GENIUSES! NOW IT'S MY TURN!
KATNK
HMPH!
RASEN-SHURIKEN!!
YAH!!
FLASH
BLAZE
THK THK THK THK

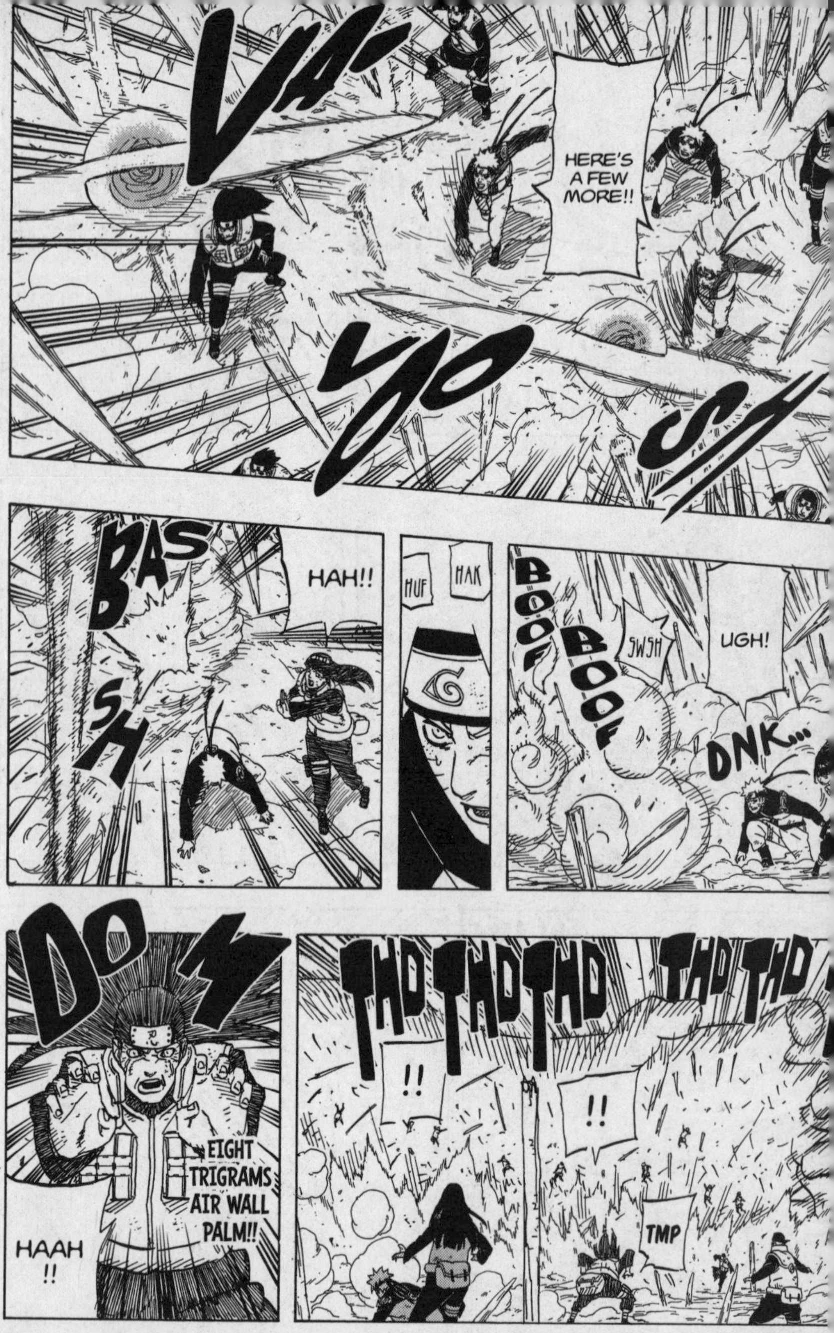
HERE'S A FEW MORE!!
VA
YO
SH
UGH!
SWSH
BOOF BOOF BOOF
DNK...
HAK
HUF
HAH!!
BAS
SH
THD THD
THD THD THD
!!
!!
TMP
DON
EIGHT TRIGRAMS AIR WALL PALM!!
HAAH!!

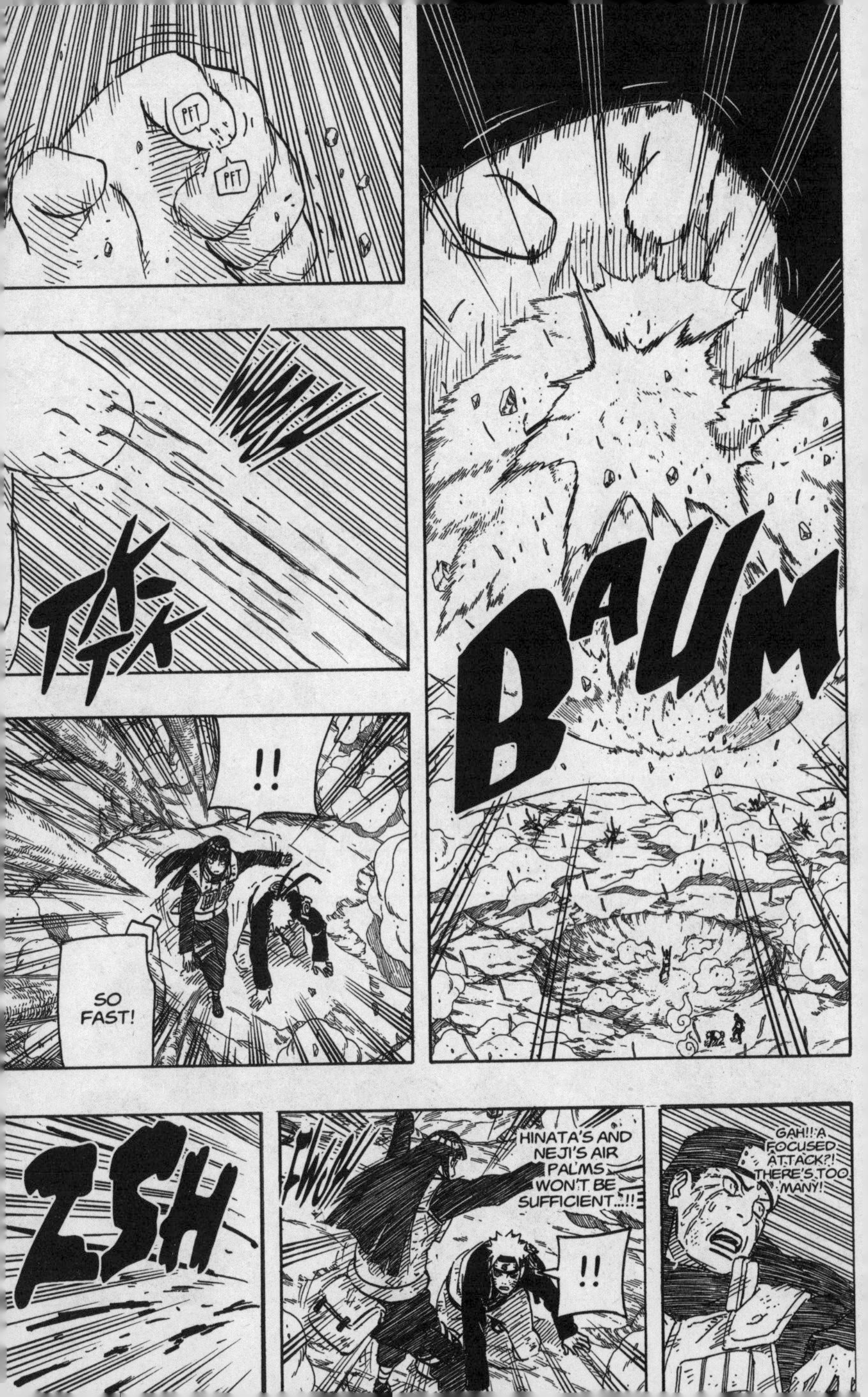
BAUM
PFT
PFT
WHAM
TAK
!!
SO FAST!
GAH!! A FOCUSED ATTACK?! THERE'S TOO MANY!
HINATA'S AND NEJI'S AIR PALMS WON'T BE SUFFICIENT...!!
FWSH
!!
ZSH

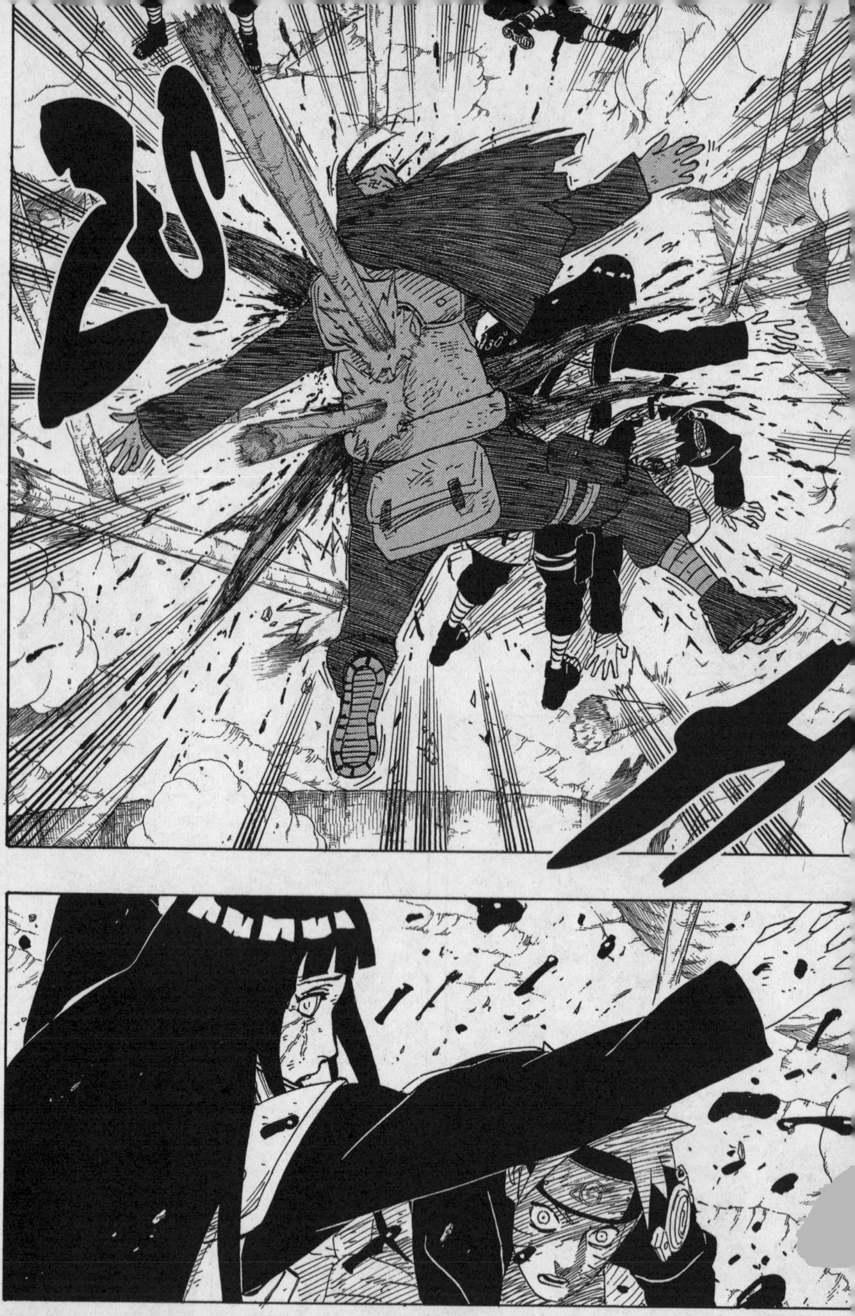

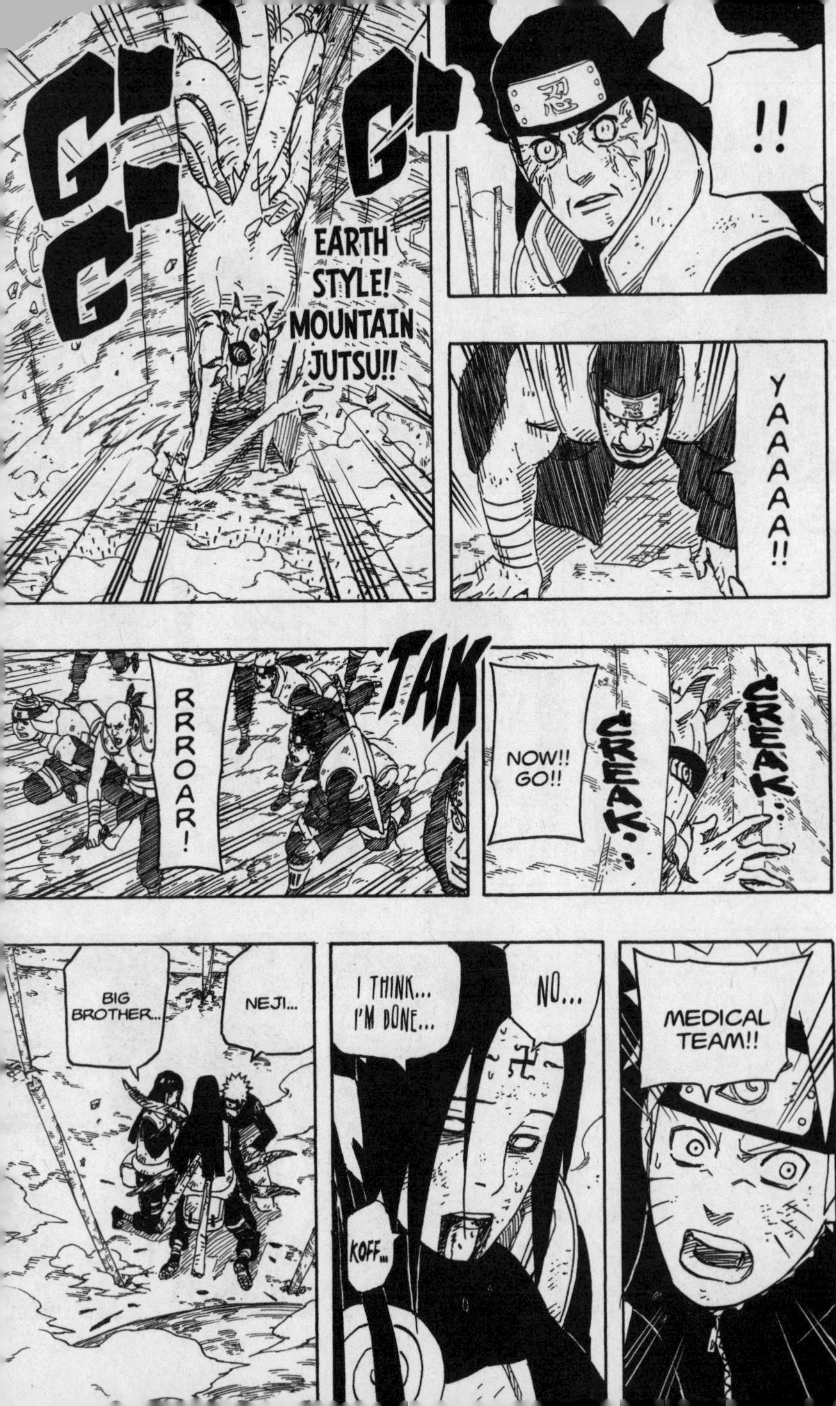
!!
YAAAAAA!!
G G G
EARTH STYLE! MOUNTAIN JUTSU!!
CREAK...
NOW!! GO!!
CREAK...
TAK
RRROAR!
MEDICAL TEAM!!
NO...
I THINK... I'M DONE...
KOFF...
NEJI...
BIG BROTHER...

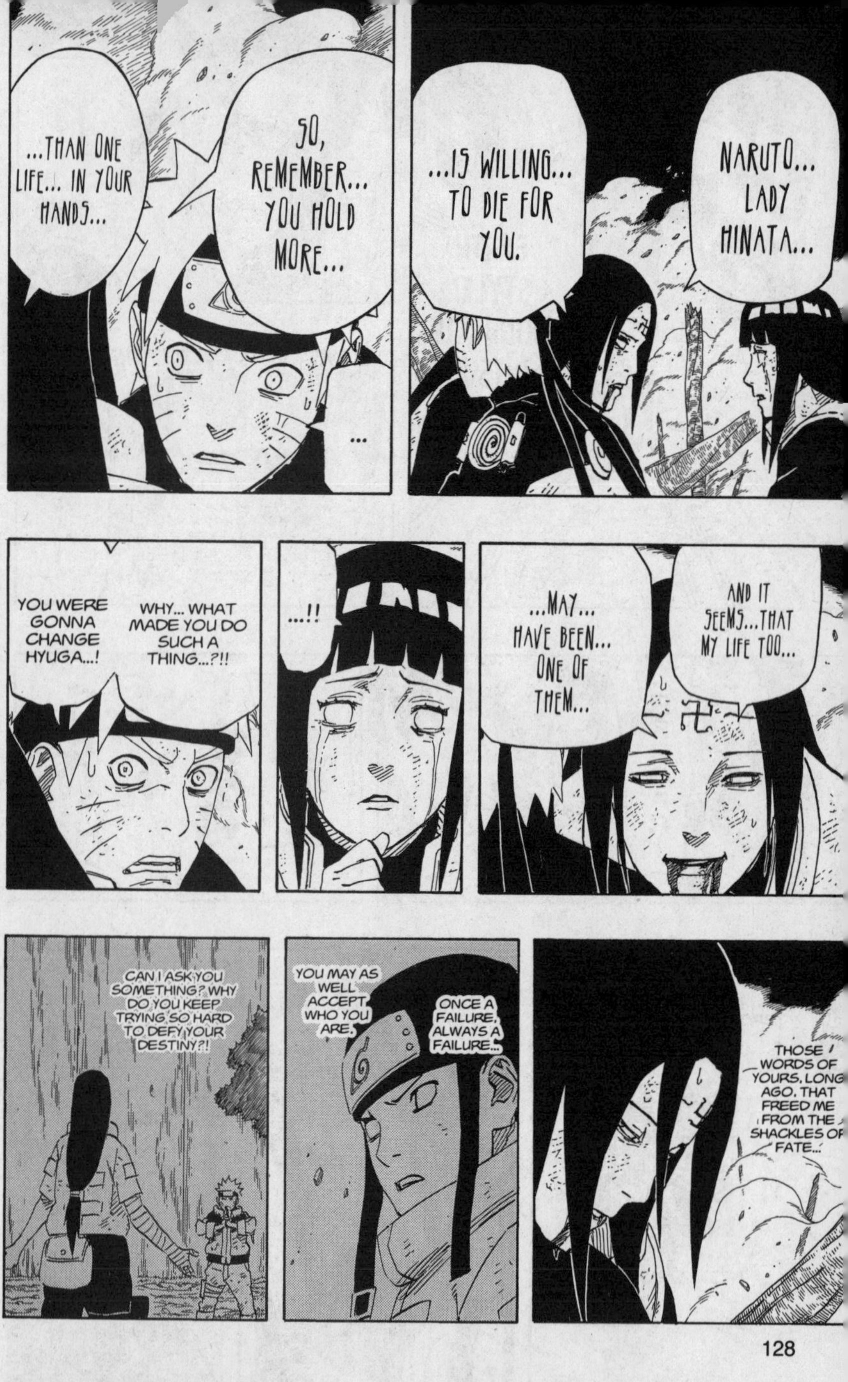
NARUTO... LADY HINATA...
...IS WILLING... TO DIE FOR YOU.
SO, REMEMBER... YOU HOLD MORE...
...THAN ONE LIFE... IN YOUR HANDS...
...
AND IT SEEMS...THAT MY LIFE TOO...
...MAY... HAVE BEEN... ONE OF THEM...
...!!
WHY... WHAT MADE YOU DO SUCH A THING...?!!
YOU WERE GONNA CHANGE HYUGA...!
THOSE WORDS OF YOURS, LONG AGO, THAT FREED ME FROM THE SHACKLES OF FATE...
ONCE A FAILURE, ALWAYS A FAILURE...
YOU MAY AS WELL ACCEPT WHO YOU ARE.
CAN I ASK YOU SOMETHING? WHY DO YOU KEEP TRYING SO HARD TO DEFY YOUR DESTINY?!

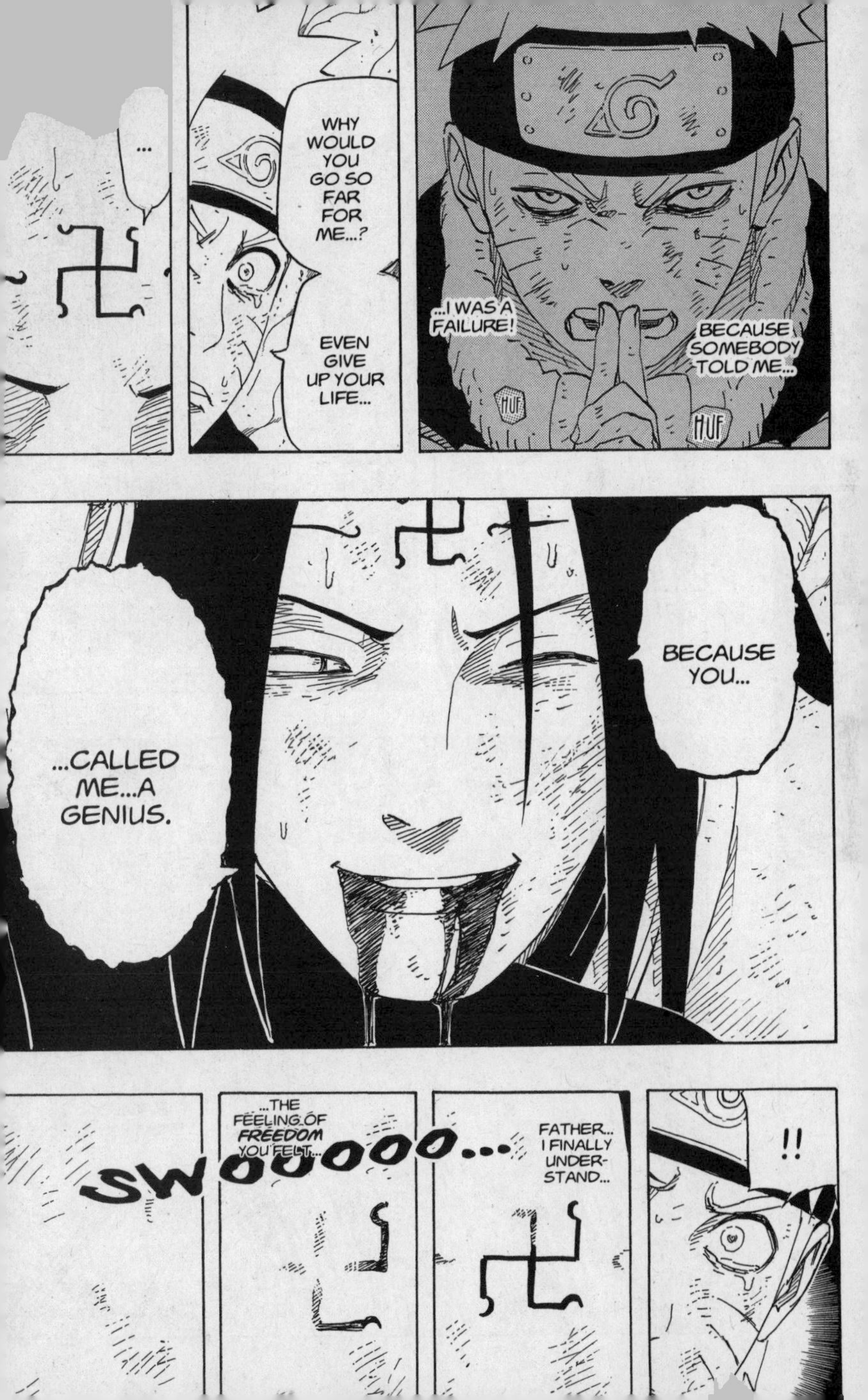
BECAUSE SOMEBODY TOLD ME...
...I WAS A FAILURE!
HUF
HUF
WHY WOULD YOU GO SO FAR FOR ME...?
EVEN GIVE UP YOUR LIFE...
...
BECAUSE YOU...
...CALLED ME...A GENIUS.
!!
FATHER... I FINALLY UNDERSTAND...
...THE FEELING OF *FREEDOM* YOU FELT...
SWOOOOO...

...CHOOSING TO DIE IN ORDER TO PROTECT YOUR COMRADES...

I THOUGHT YOU WEREN'T GOING TO LET ANY OF YOUR COMRADES DIE?

130

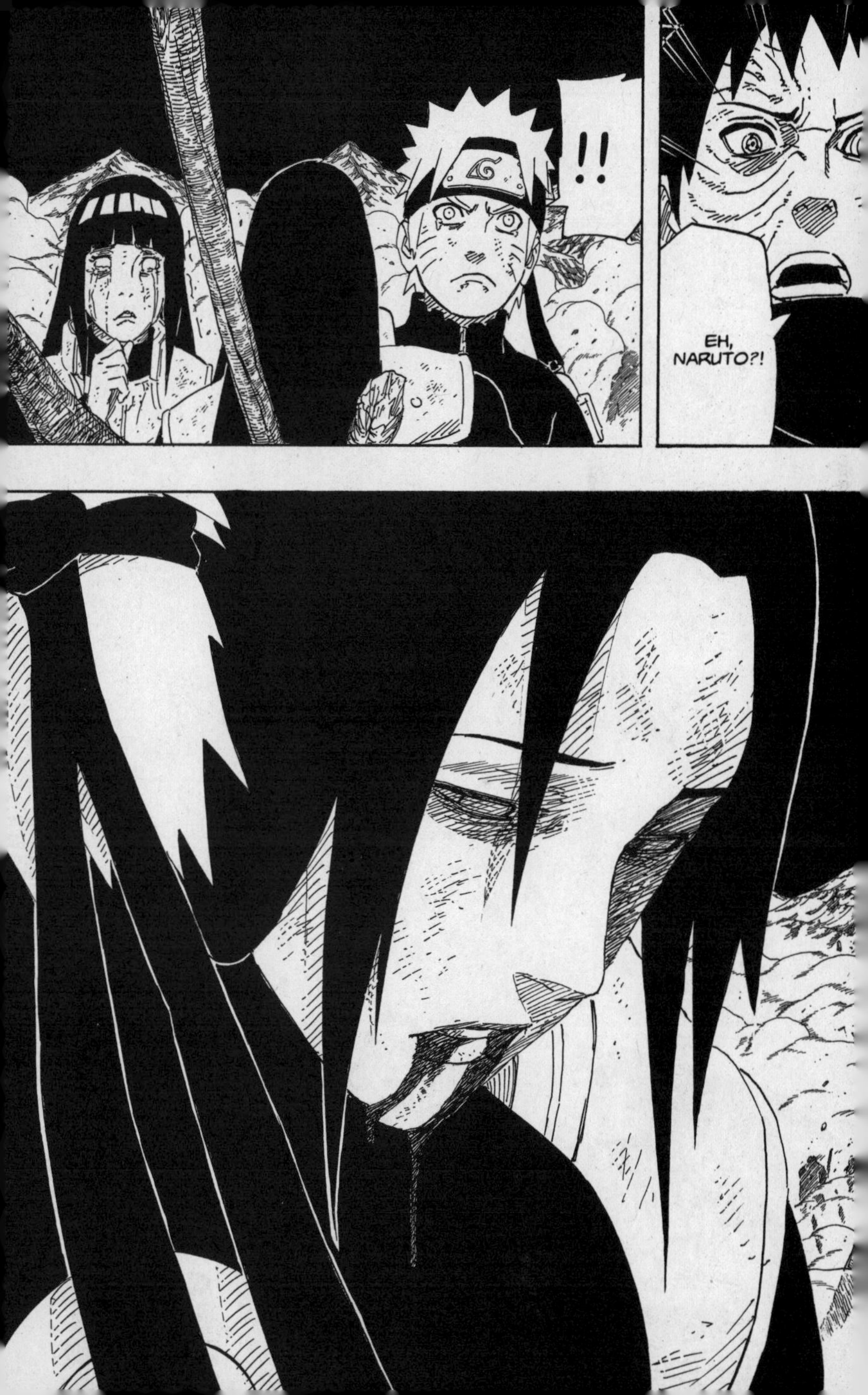
EH, NARUTO?!
!!

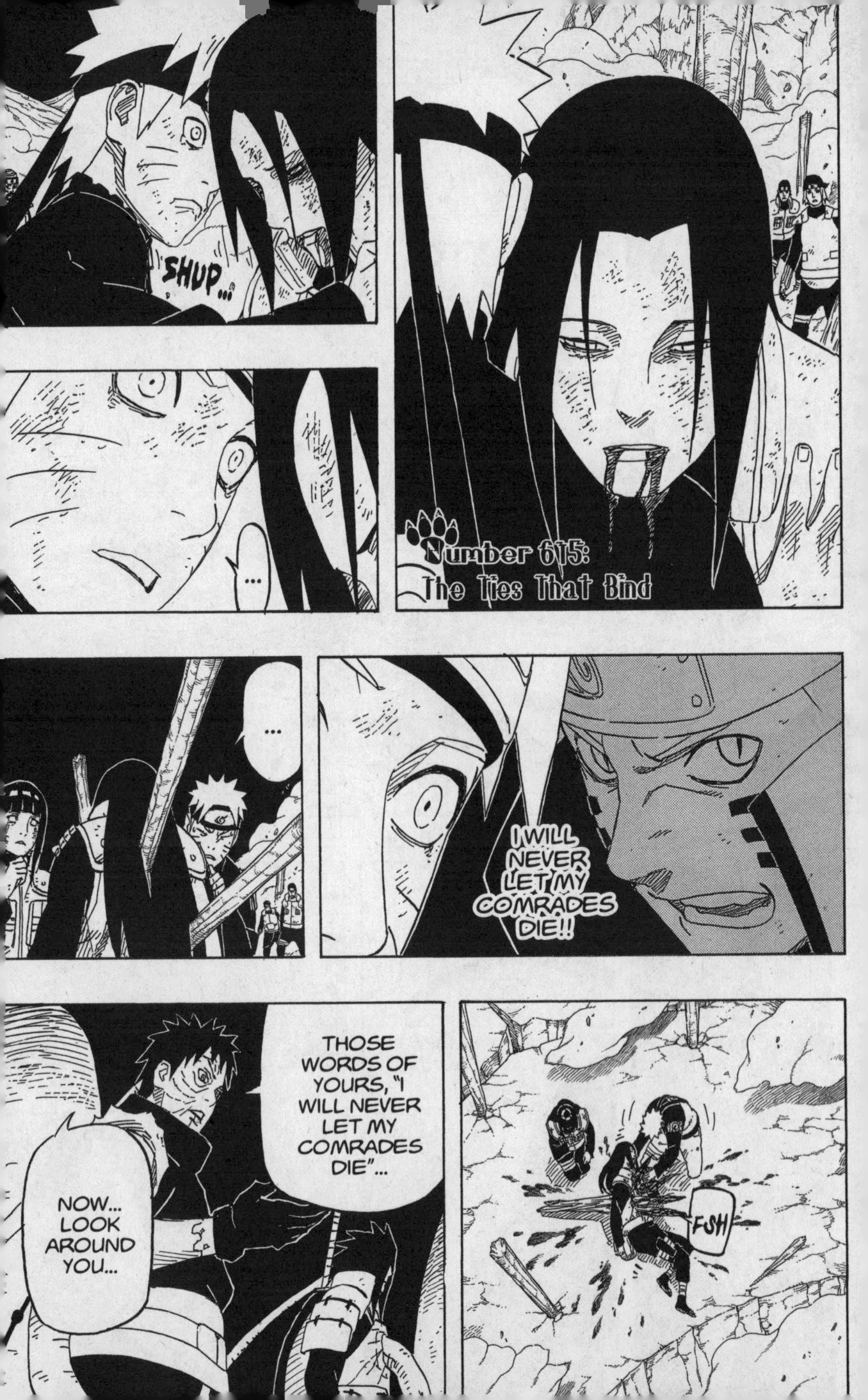
Number 615:
The Ties That Bind
SHUP...
...
I WILL NEVER LET MY COMRADES DIE!!
...
FSH
THOSE WORDS OF YOURS, "I WILL NEVER LET MY COMRADES DIE"...
NOW... LOOK AROUND YOU...

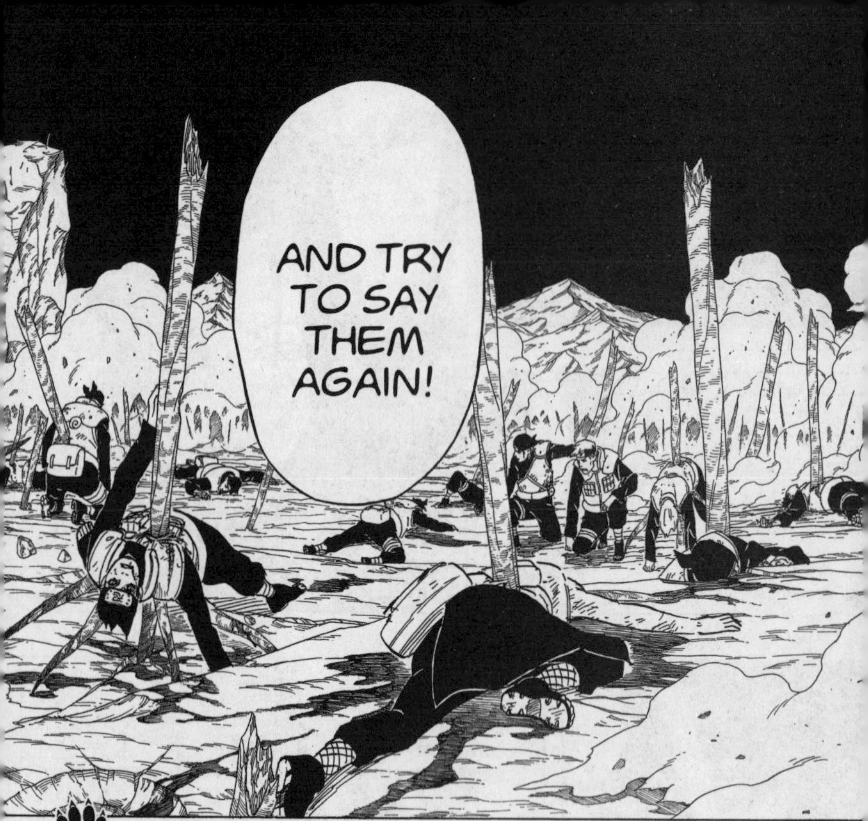
AND TRY TO SAY THEM AGAIN!

Number 615: The Ties That Bind

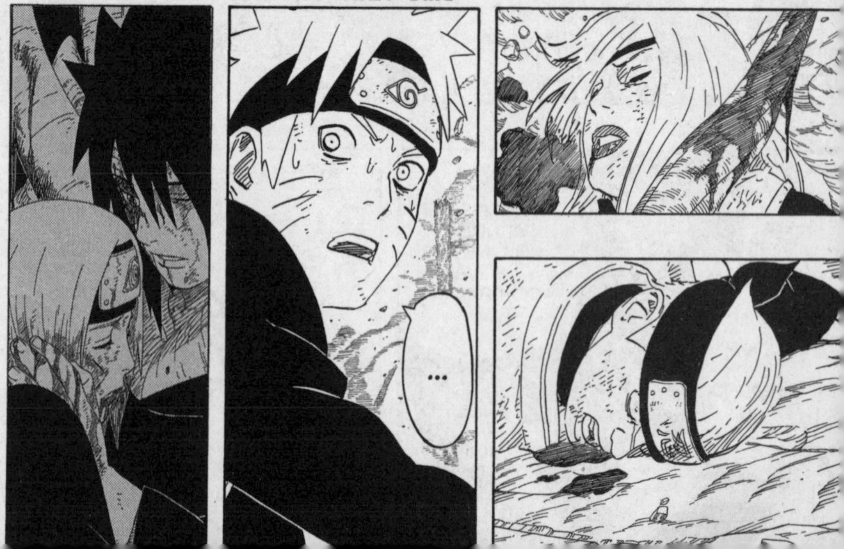
...

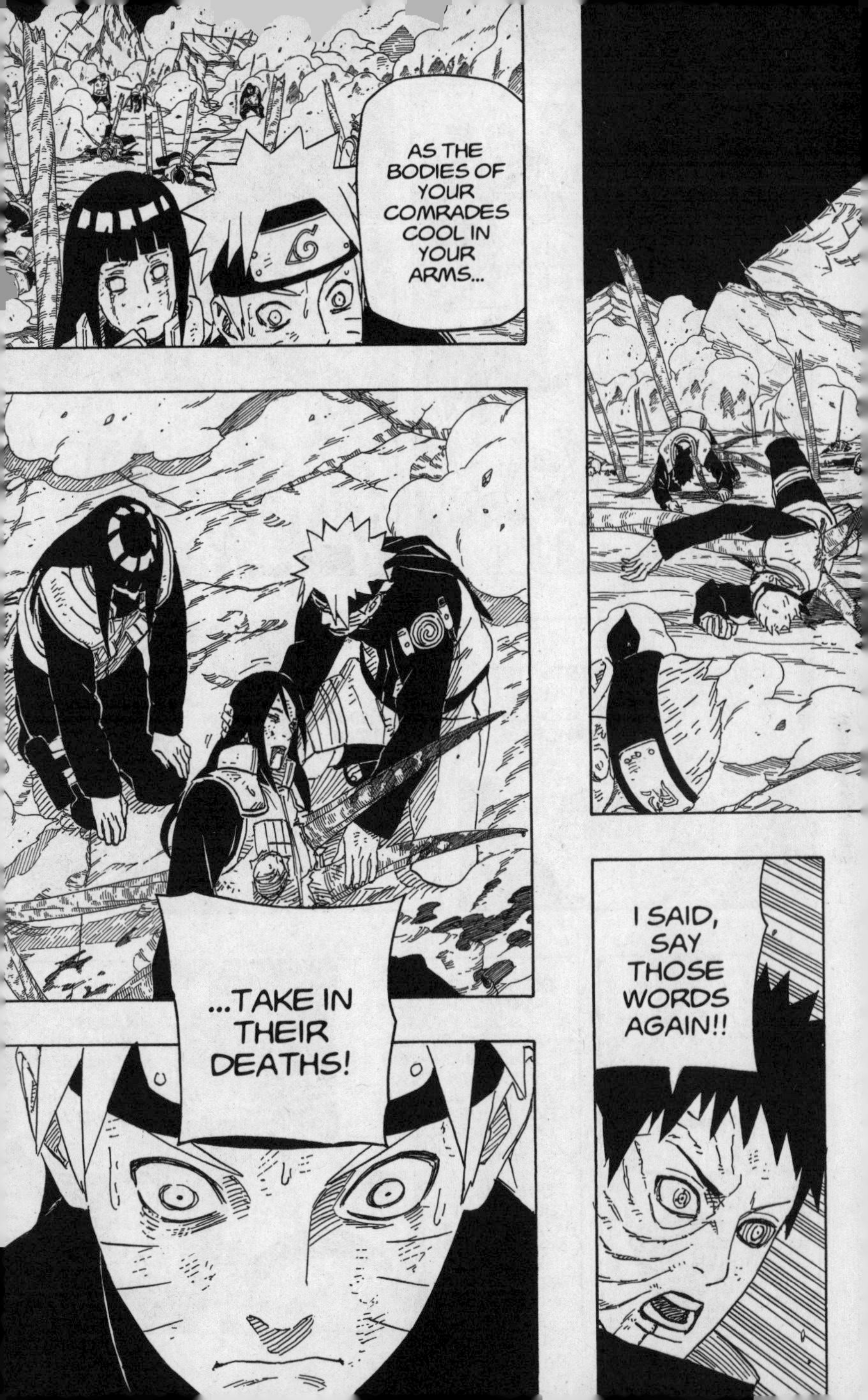
I SAID, SAY THOSE WORDS AGAIN!!
AS THE BODIES OF YOUR COMRADES COOL IN YOUR ARMS...
...TAKE IN THEIR DEATHS!

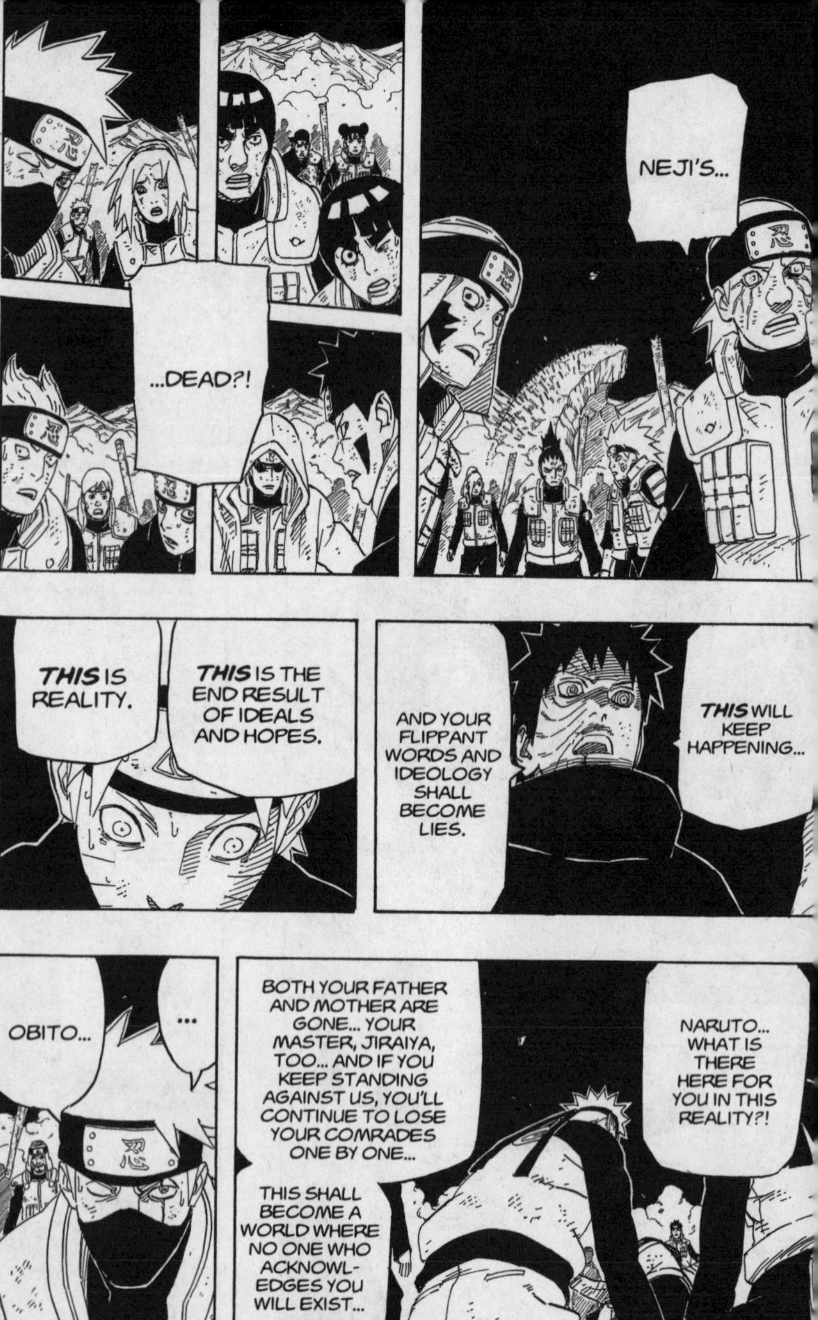
NEJI'S...
...DEAD?!
THIS WILL KEEP HAPPENING...
AND YOUR FLIPPANT WORDS AND IDEOLOGY SHALL BECOME LIES.
THIS IS THE END RESULT OF IDEALS AND HOPES.
THIS IS REALITY.
NARUTO... WHAT IS THERE HERE FOR YOU IN THIS REALITY?!
BOTH YOUR FATHER AND MOTHER ARE GONE... YOUR MASTER, JIRAIYA, TOO... AND IF YOU KEEP STANDING AGAINST US, YOU'LL CONTINUE TO LOSE YOUR COMRADES ONE BY ONE...
THIS SHALL BECOME A WORLD WHERE NO ONE WHO ACKNOWL-EDGES YOU WILL EXIST...
...
OBITO...

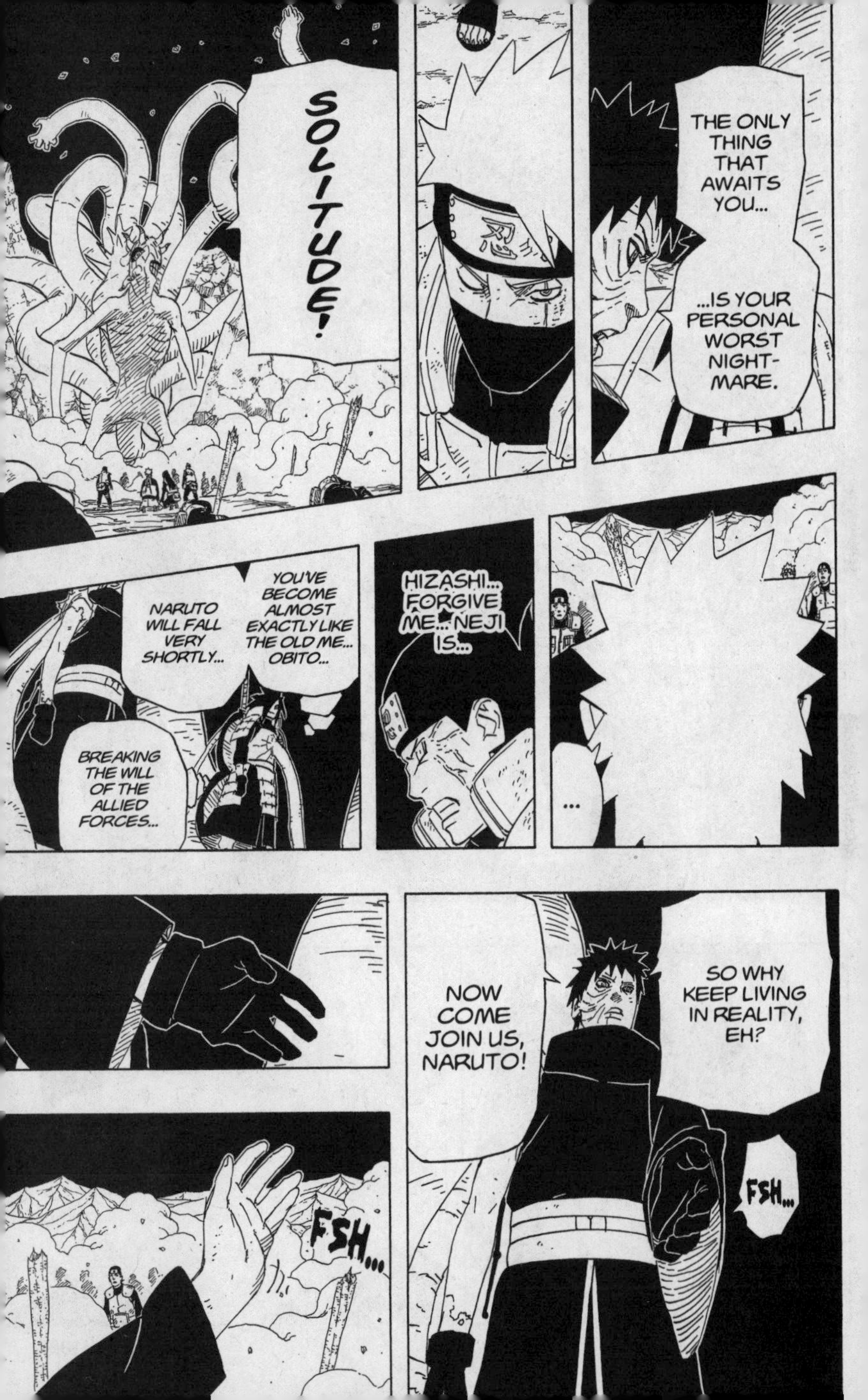

THE ONLY THING THAT AWAITS YOU...
...IS YOUR PERSONAL WORST NIGHT-MARE.
SOLITUDE!
...
HIZASHI... FORGIVE ME... NEJI IS...
YOU'VE BECOME ALMOST EXACTLY LIKE THE OLD ME... OBITO...
NARUTO WILL FALL VERY SHORTLY...
BREAKING THE WILL OF THE ALLIED FORCES...
SO WHY KEEP LIVING IN REALITY, EH?
NOW COME JOIN US, NARUTO!
FSH...
FSH...

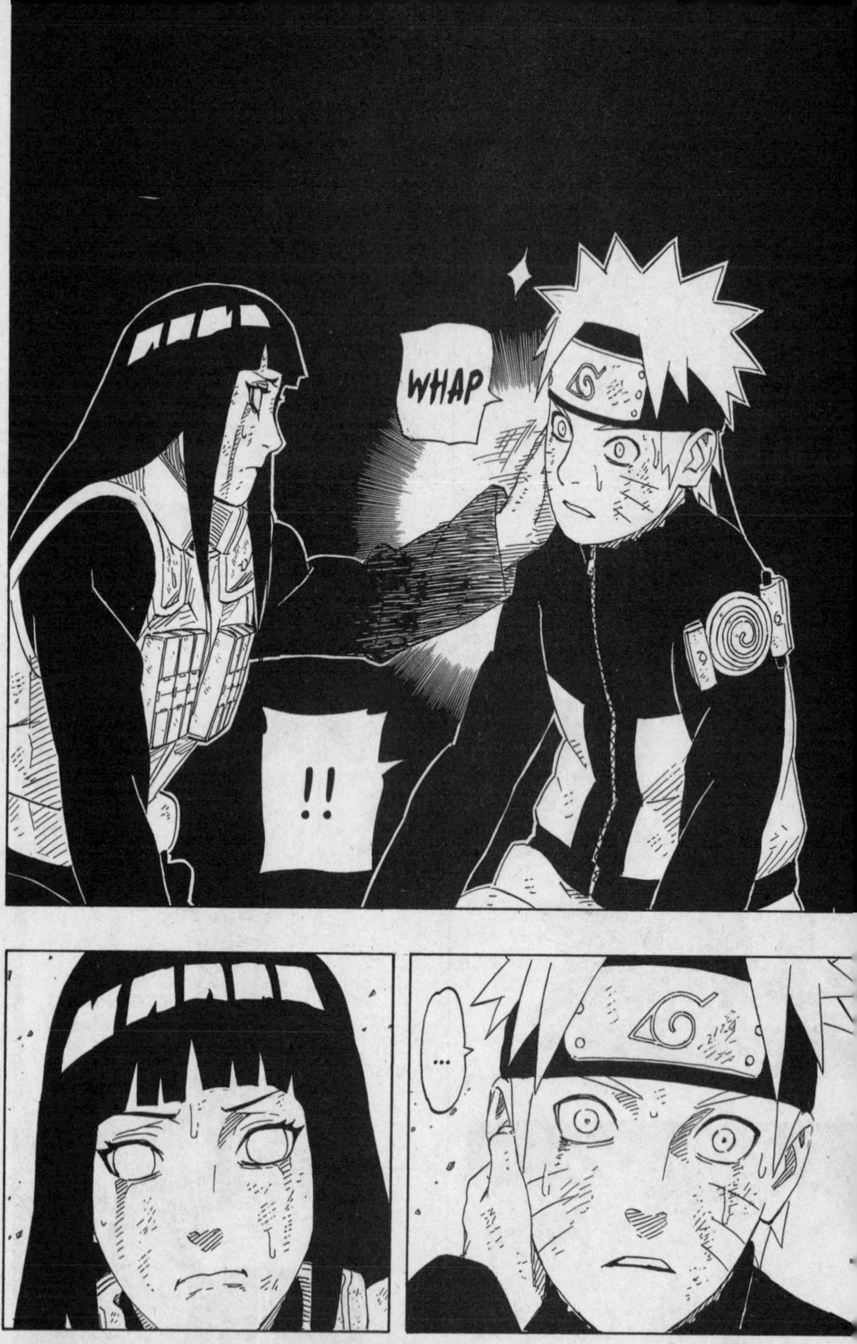
WHAP
!!
...

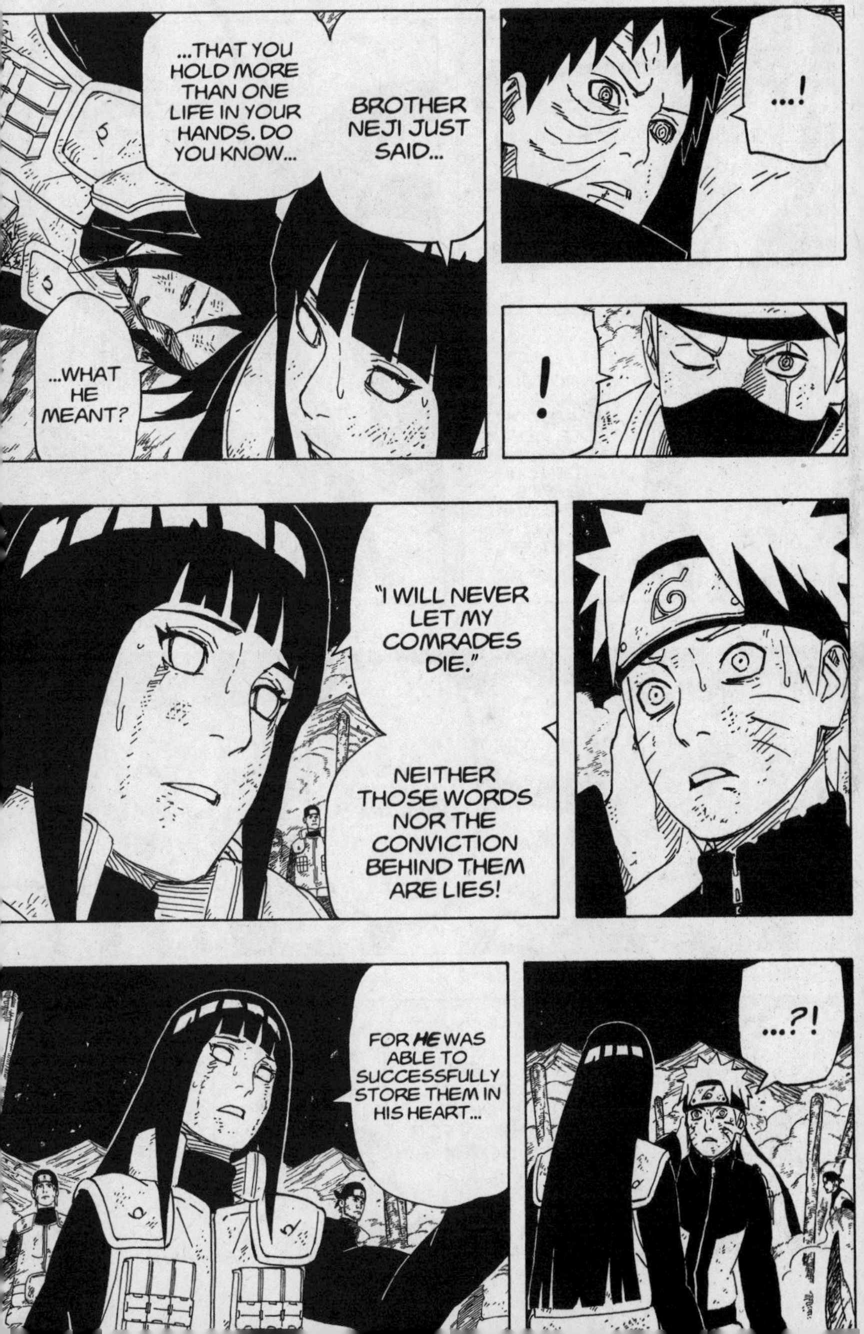
...!
!
BROTHER NEJI JUST SAID...
...THAT YOU HOLD MORE THAN ONE LIFE IN YOUR HANDS. DO YOU KNOW...
...WHAT HE MEANT?
"I WILL NEVER LET MY COMRADES DIE."
NEITHER THOSE WORDS NOR THE CONVICTION BEHIND THEM ARE LIES!
...?!
FOR ***HE*** WAS ABLE TO SUCCESSFULLY STORE THEM IN HIS HEART...

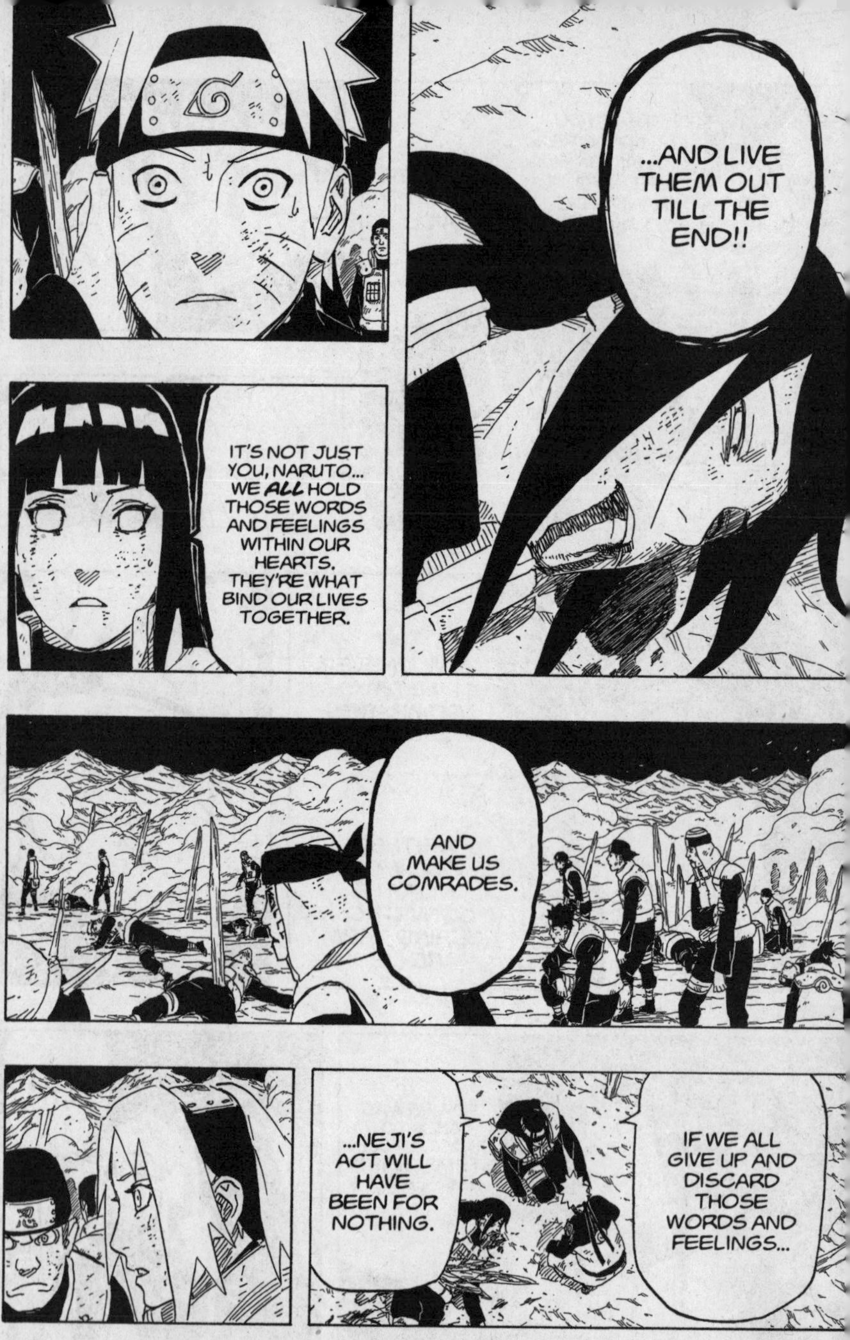
...AND LIVE THEM OUT TILL THE END!!
IT'S NOT JUST YOU, NARUTO... WE **ALL** HOLD THOSE WORDS AND FEELINGS WITHIN OUR HEARTS. THEY'RE WHAT BIND OUR LIVES TOGETHER.
AND MAKE US COMRADES.
IF WE ALL GIVE UP AND DISCARD THOSE WORDS AND FEELINGS...
...NEJI'S ACT WILL HAVE BEEN FOR NOTHING.

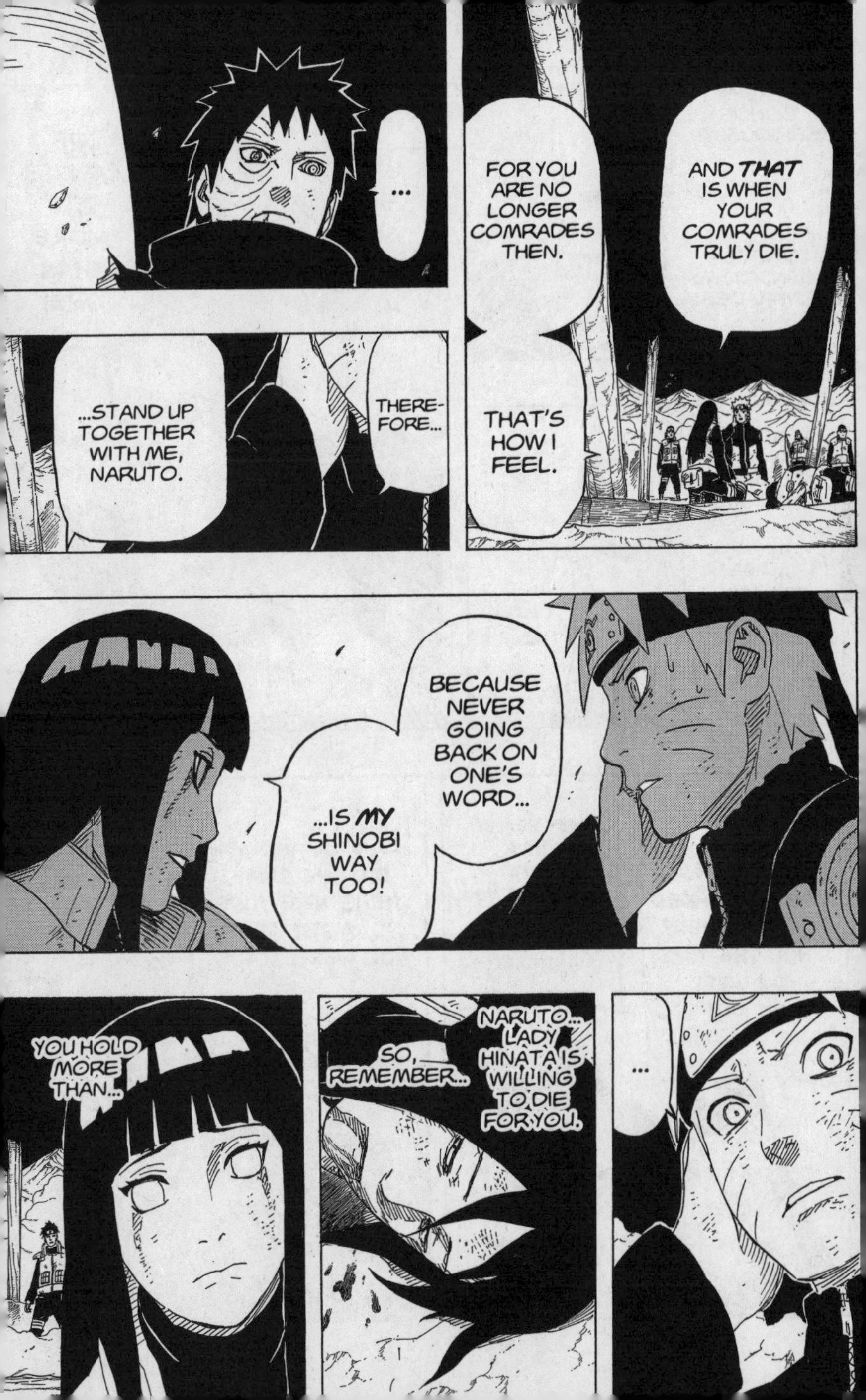
AND **THAT** IS WHEN YOUR COMRADES TRULY DIE.
FOR YOU ARE NO LONGER COMRADES THEN.
THAT'S HOW I FEEL.
...
THERE-FORE...
...STAND UP TOGETHER WITH ME, NARUTO.
BECAUSE NEVER GOING BACK ON ONE'S WORD...
...IS **MY** SHINOBI WAY TOO!
...
NARUTO... LADY HINATA IS WILLING TO DIE FOR YOU.
SO, REMEMBER...
YOU HOLD MORE THAN...

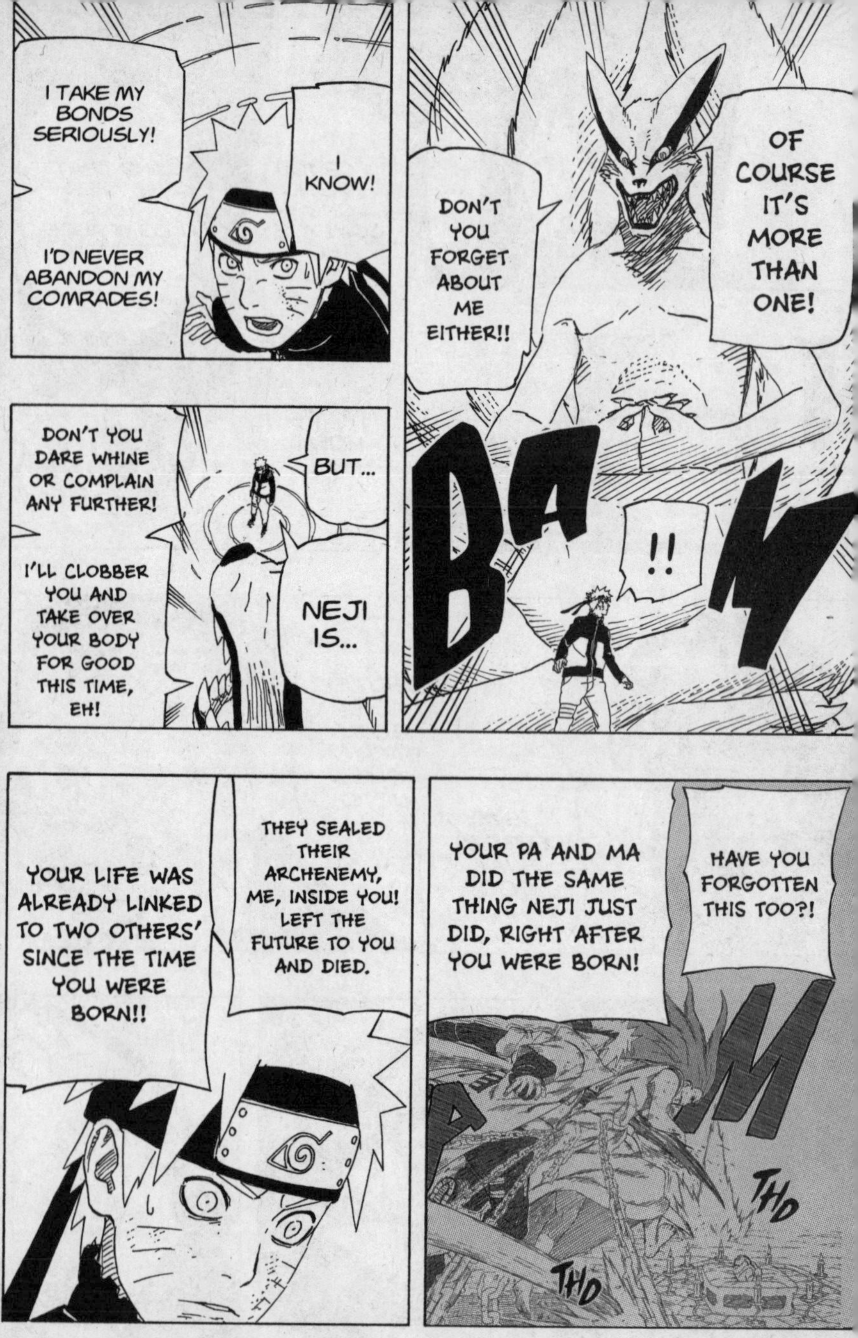
I TAKE MY BONDS SERIOUSLY!
I KNOW!
I'D NEVER ABANDON MY COMRADES!
DON'T YOU DARE WHINE OR COMPLAIN ANY FURTHER!
BUT...
I'LL CLOBBER YOU AND TAKE OVER YOUR BODY FOR GOOD THIS TIME, EH!
NEJI IS...
DON'T YOU FORGET ABOUT ME EITHER!!
OF COURSE IT'S MORE THAN ONE!
BAM
!!
YOUR LIFE WAS ALREADY LINKED TO TWO OTHERS' SINCE THE TIME YOU WERE BORN!!
THEY SEALED THEIR ARCHENEMY, ME, INSIDE YOU! LEFT THE FUTURE TO YOU AND DIED.
YOUR PA AND MA DID THE SAME THING NEJI JUST DID, RIGHT AFTER YOU WERE BORN!
HAVE YOU FORGOTTEN THIS TOO?!
THD
THD

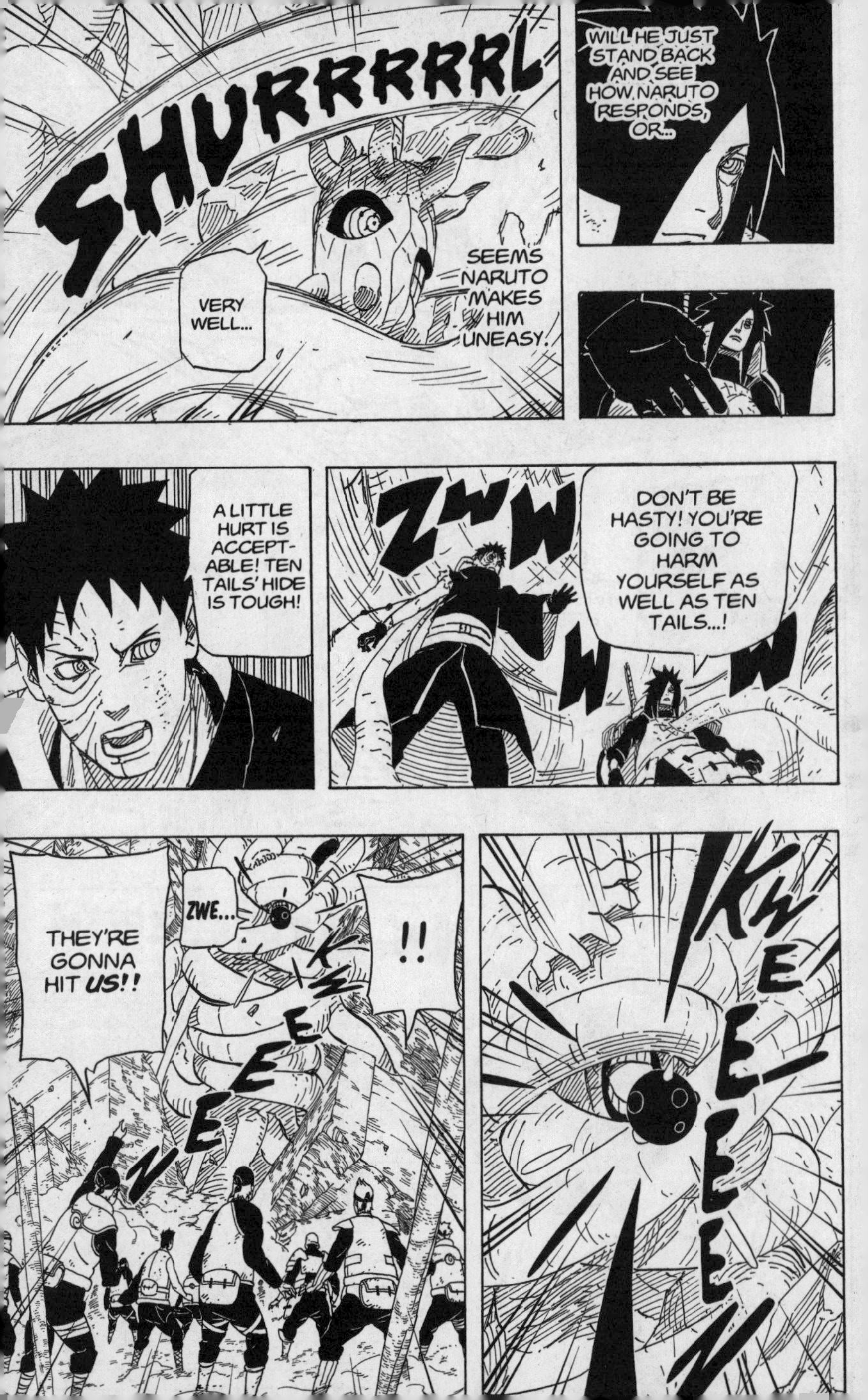
WILL HE JUST STAND BACK AND SEE HOW NARUTO RESPONDS, OR...
SEEMS NARUTO MAKES HIM UNEASY.
SHURRRRRL
VERY WELL...
DON'T BE HASTY! YOU'RE GOING TO HARM YOURSELF AS WELL AS TEN TAILS...!
ZWWWWW
A LITTLE HURT IS ACCEPTABLE! TEN TAILS' HIDE IS TOUGH!
KWEEEEEN
!!
ZWE...
KWEEEEEN
THEY'RE GONNA HIT *US*!!

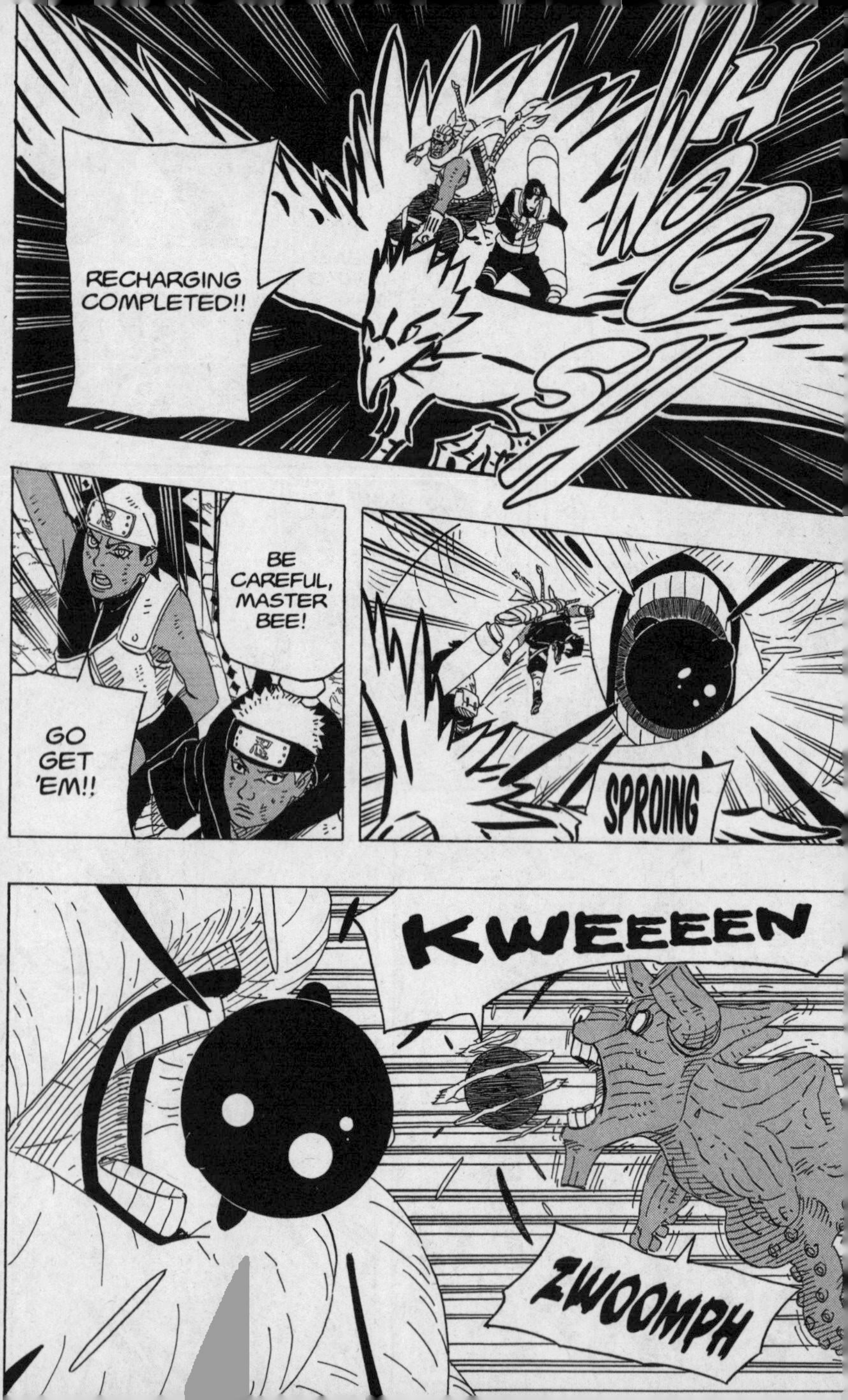
WHOOSH
RECHARGING COMPLETED!!
SPROING
BE CAREFUL, MASTER BEE!
GO GET 'EM!!
KWEEEEN
ZWOOMPH

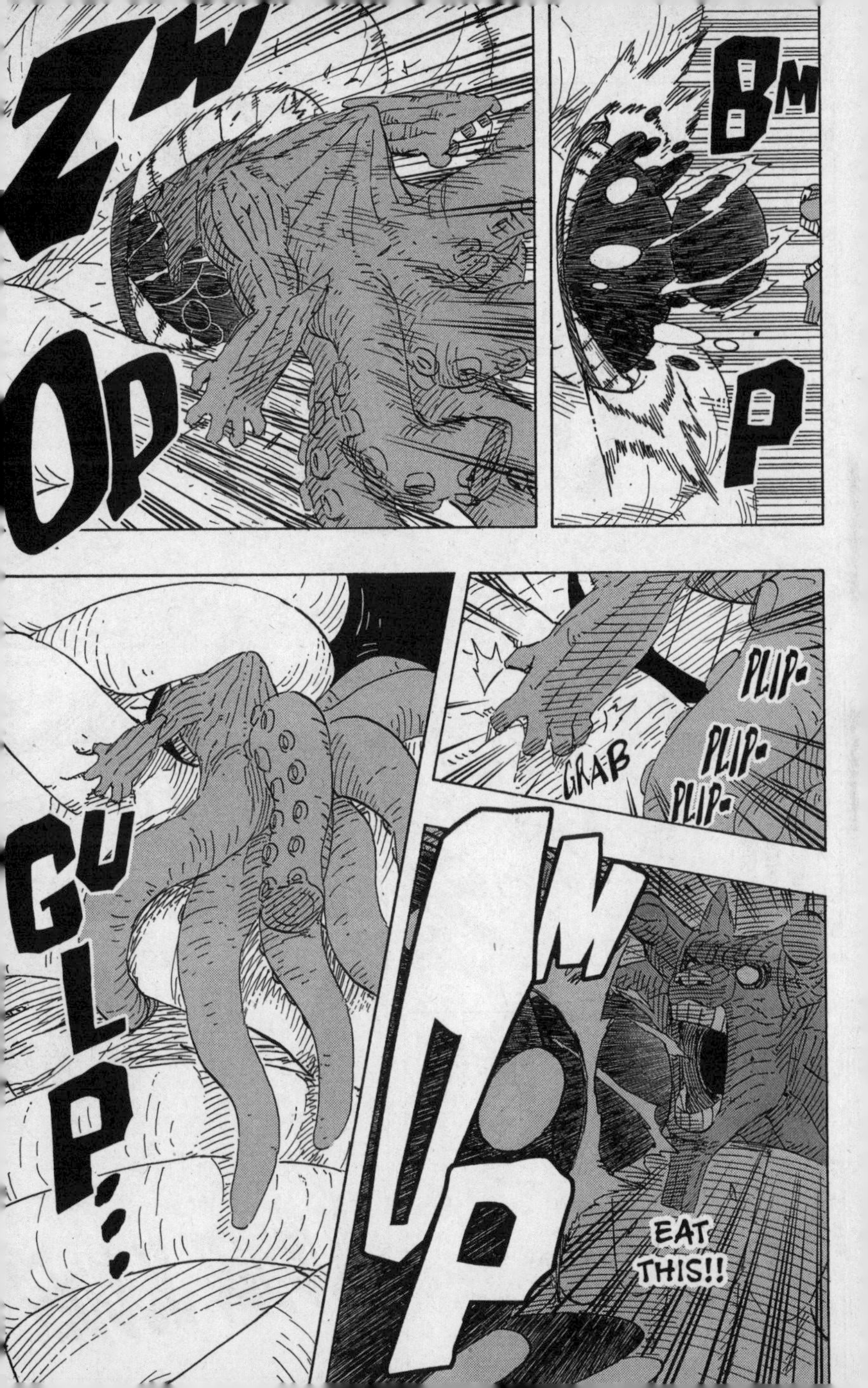
BMP
ZWOOP
GRAB
PLIP
PLIP
PLIP
EAT THIS!!
GULP...

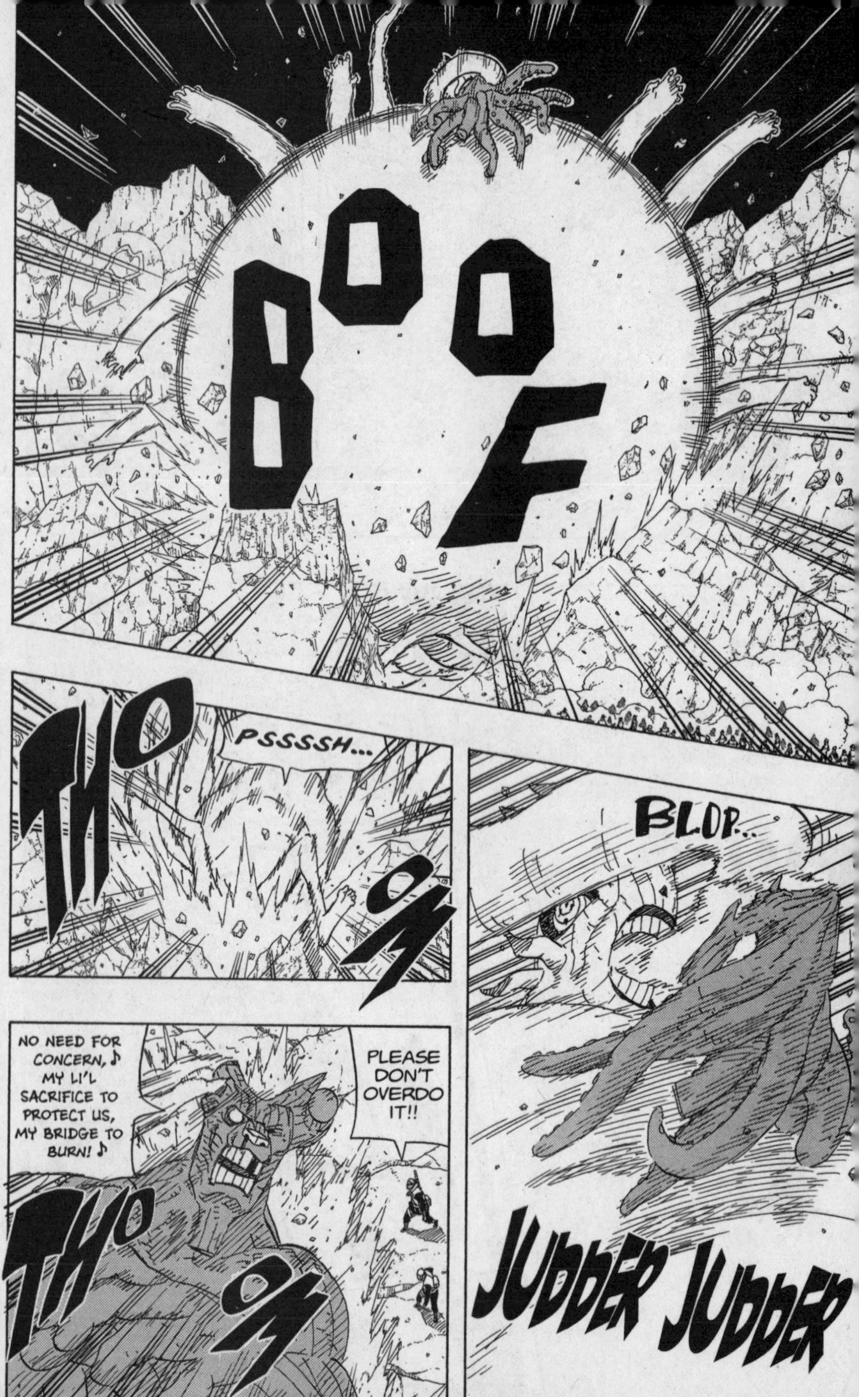
BOOOF
BLOP...
JUDDER JUDDER
PSSSSH...
THOOM
PLEASE DON'T OVERDO IT!!
NO NEED FOR CONCERN, ♪ MY LI'L SACRIFICE TO PROTECT US, MY BRIDGE TO BURN! ♪
THOOM

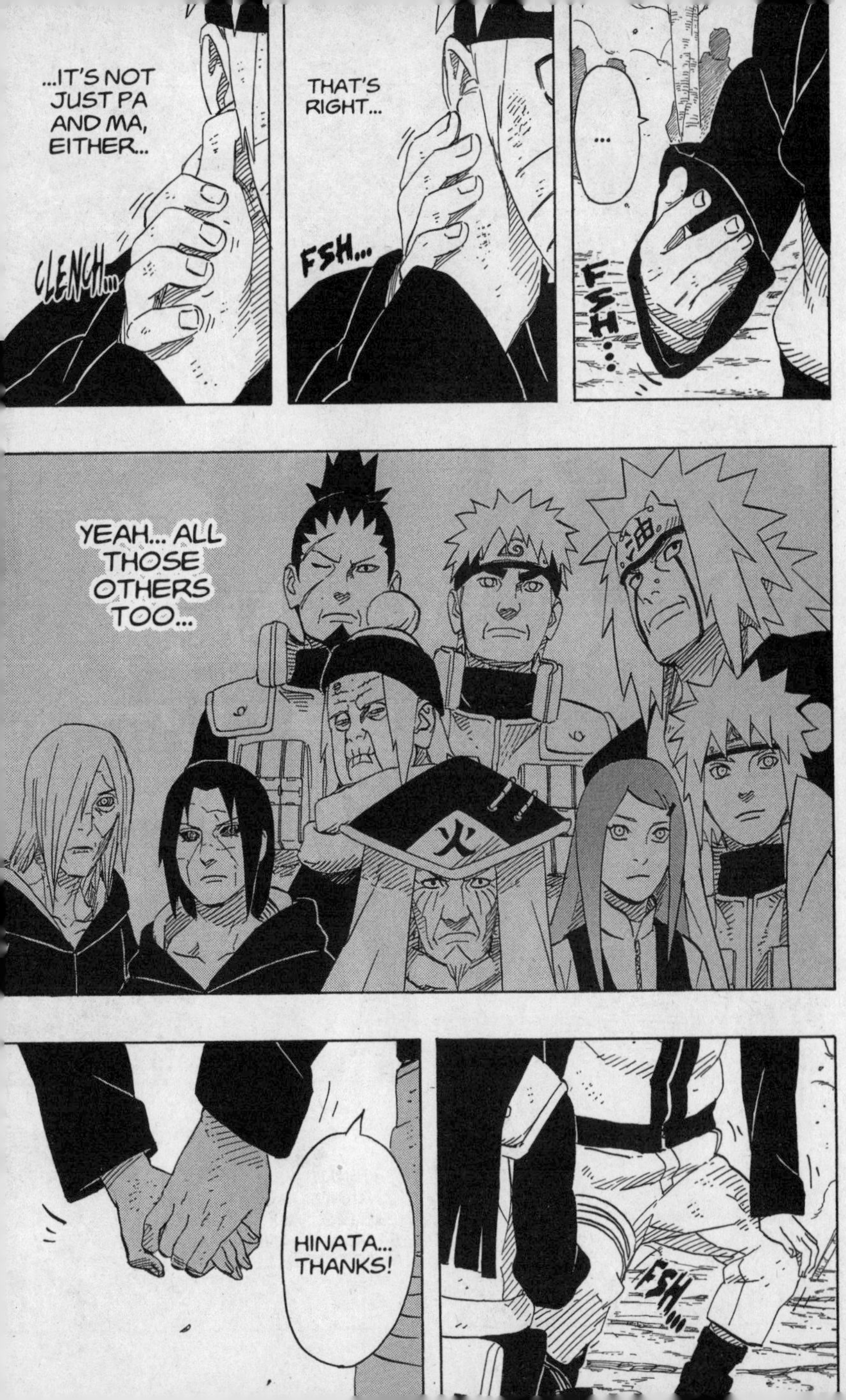
...
FSH...
THAT'S RIGHT...
FSH...
...IT'S NOT JUST PA AND MA, EITHER...
CLENCH...
YEAH... ALL THOSE OTHERS TOO...
FSH...
HINATA... THANKS!

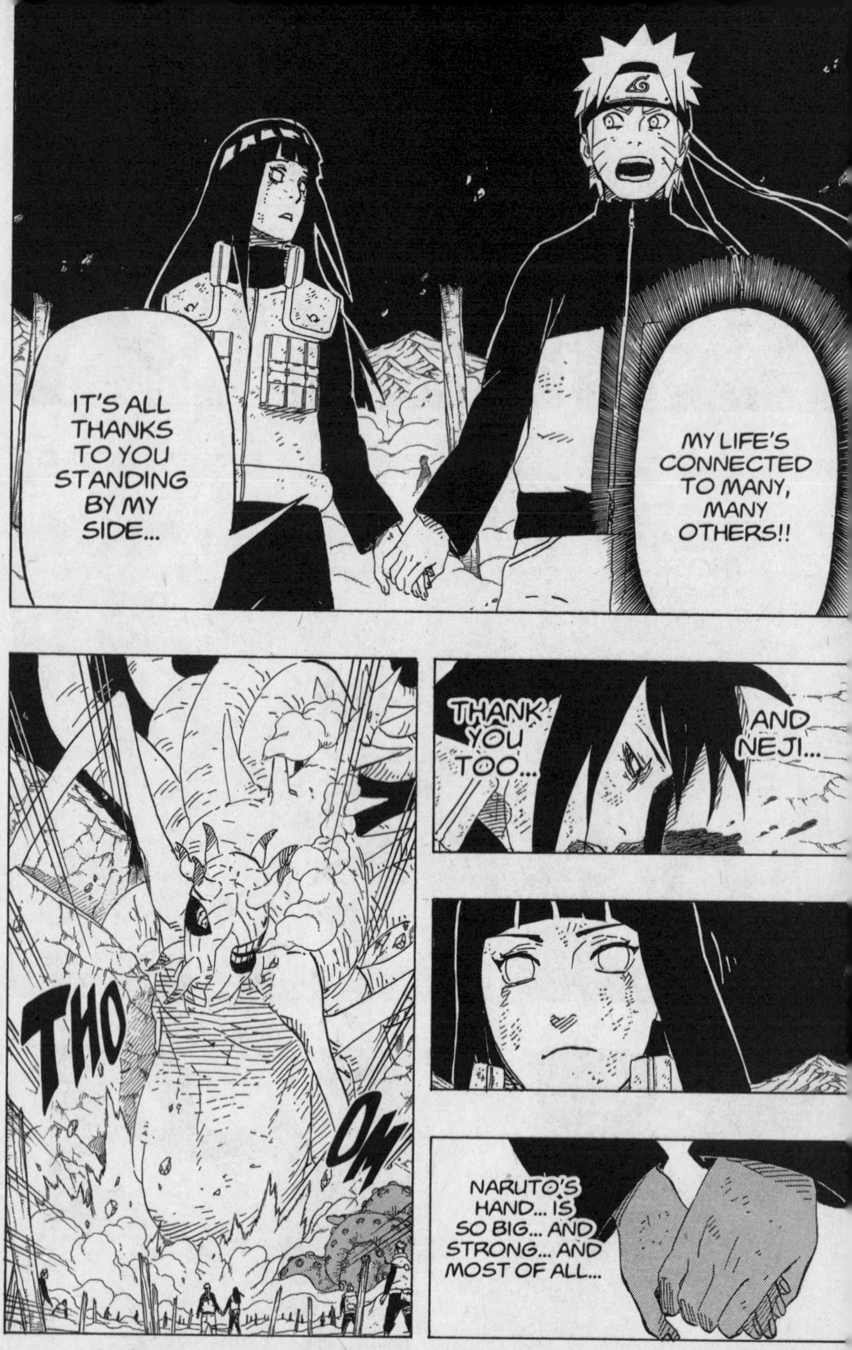
MY LIFE'S CONNECTED TO MANY, MANY OTHERS!!
IT'S ALL THANKS TO YOU STANDING BY MY SIDE...
AND NEJI...
THANK YOU TOO...
NARUTO'S HAND... IS SO BIG... AND STRONG... AND MOST OF ALL...
THOOM

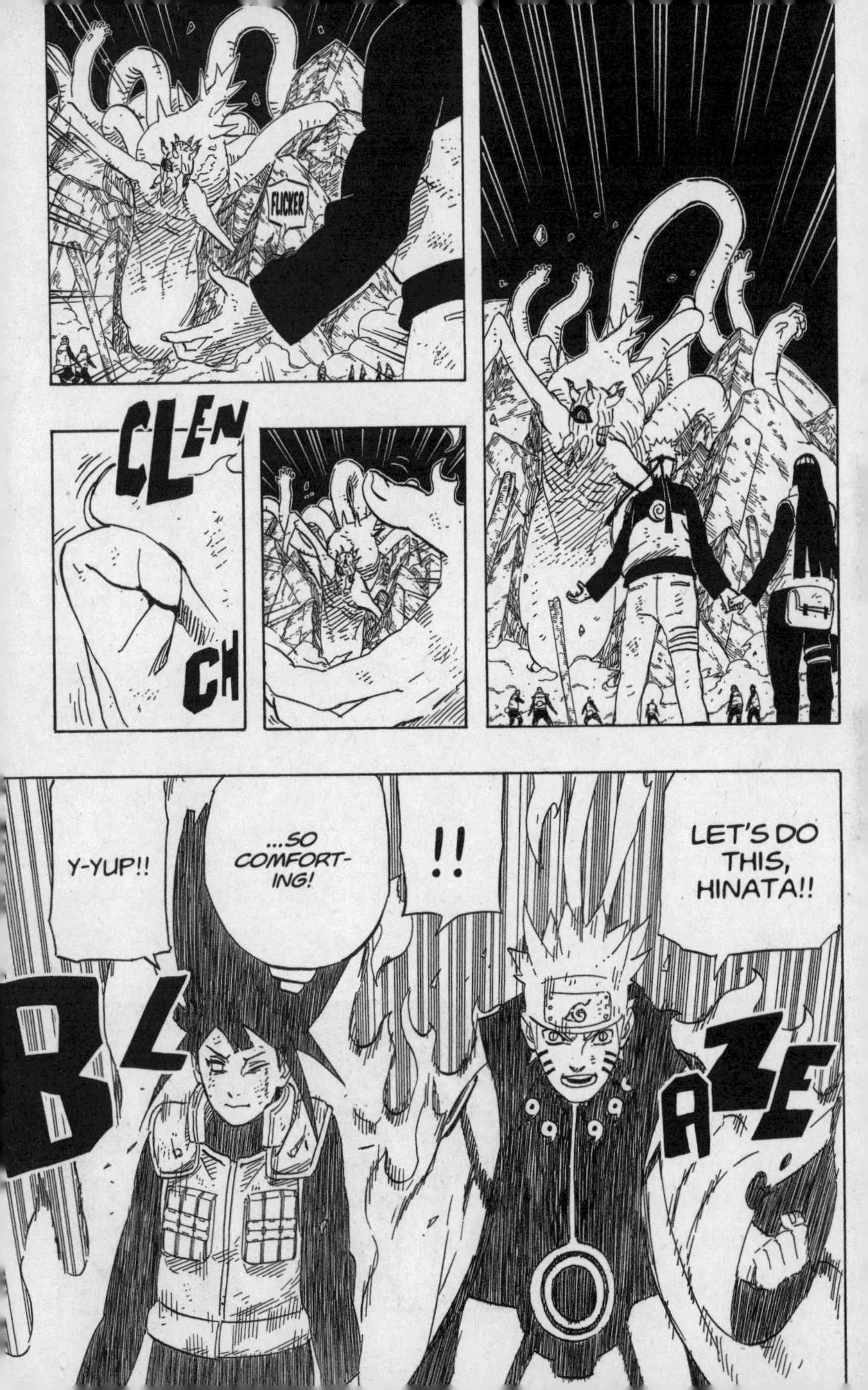
FLICKER
CLENCH
LET'S DO THIS, HINATA!!
!!
...SO COMFORT-ING!
Y-YUP!!
BLAZE

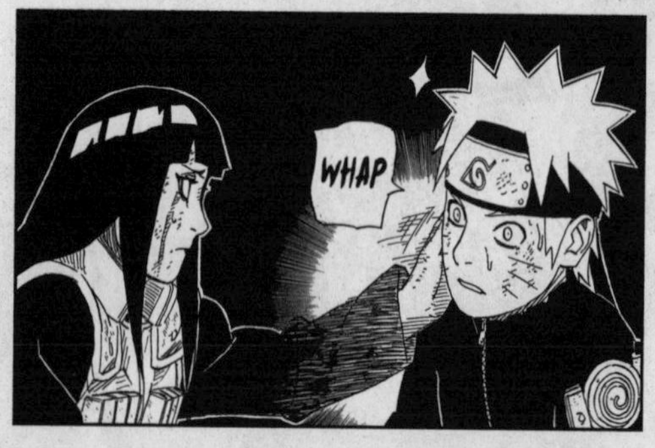
WHAP

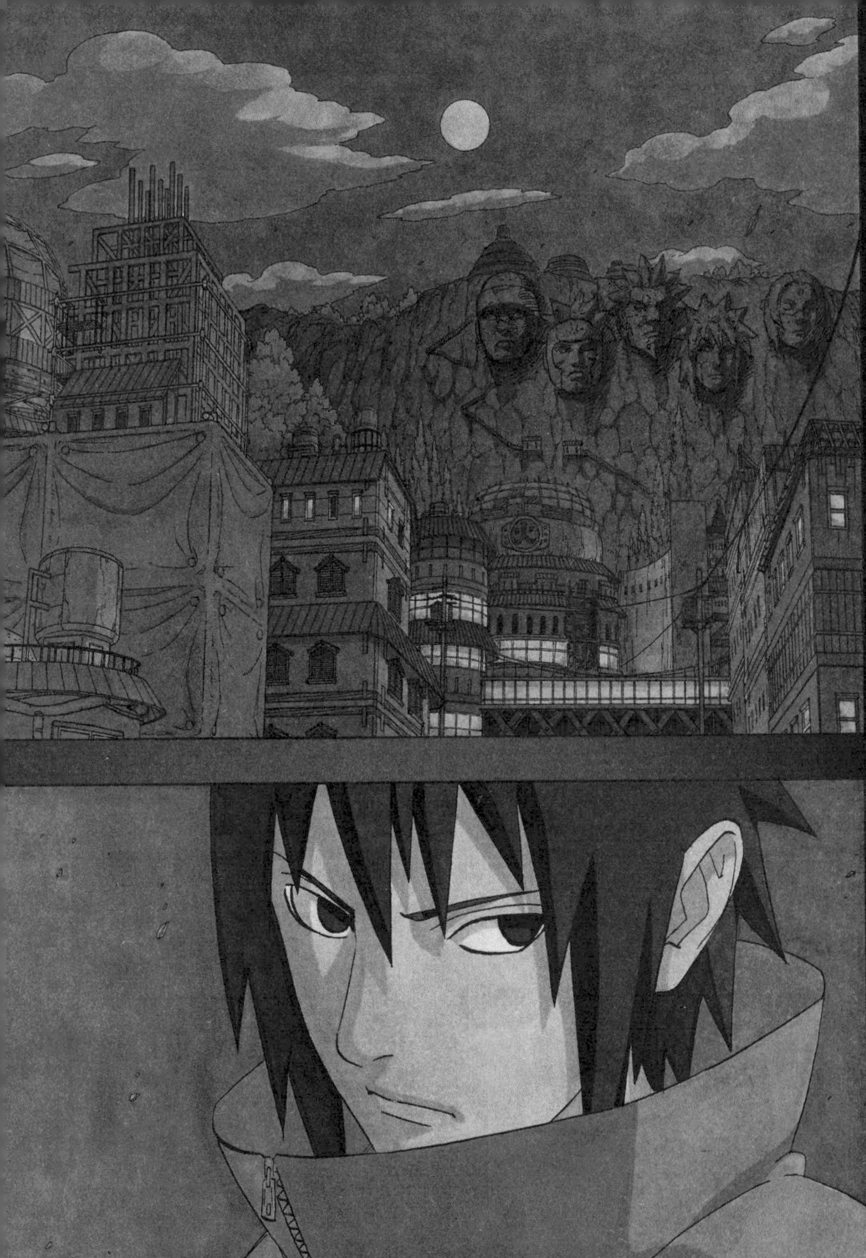

Number 616: Those Who Dance in the Shadows

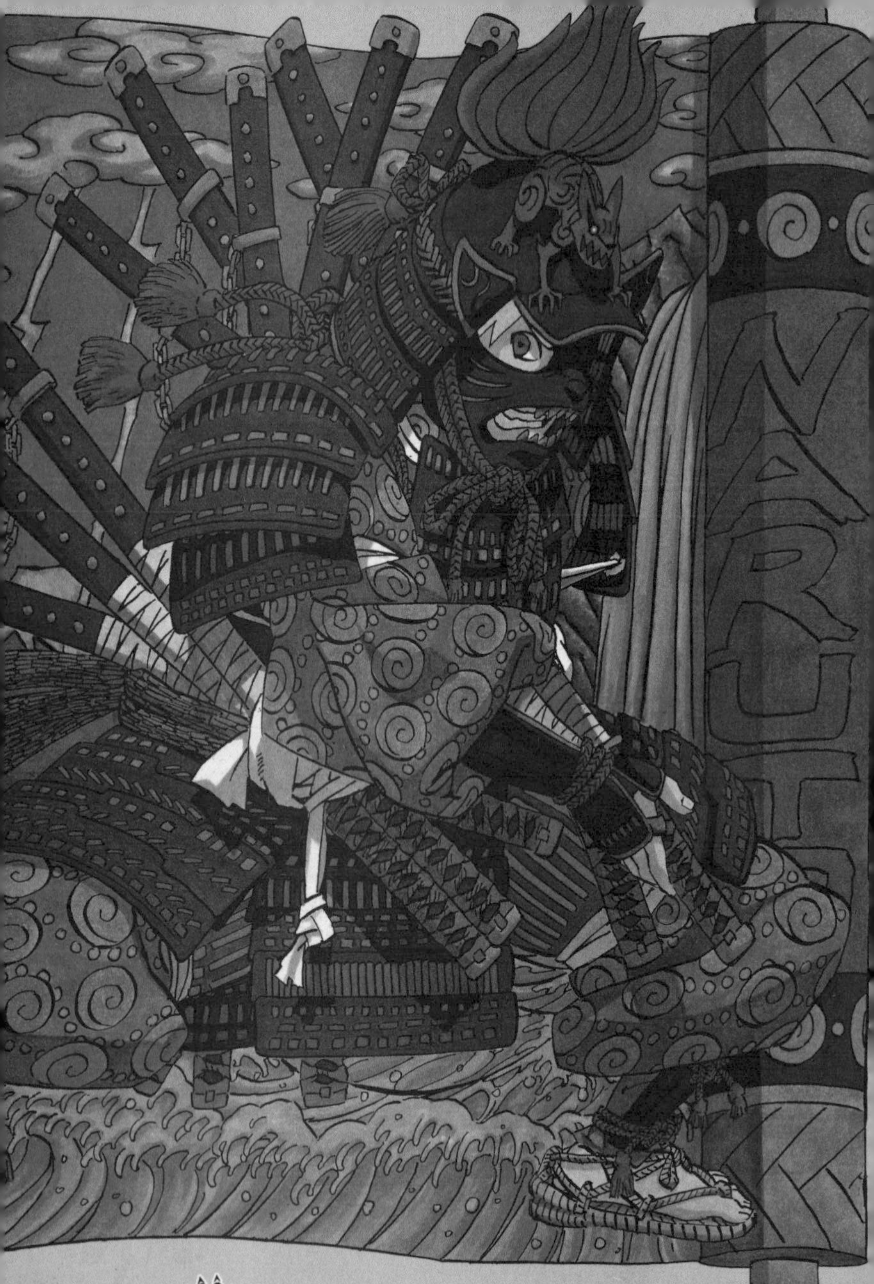

Number 616: Those Who Dance in the Shadows

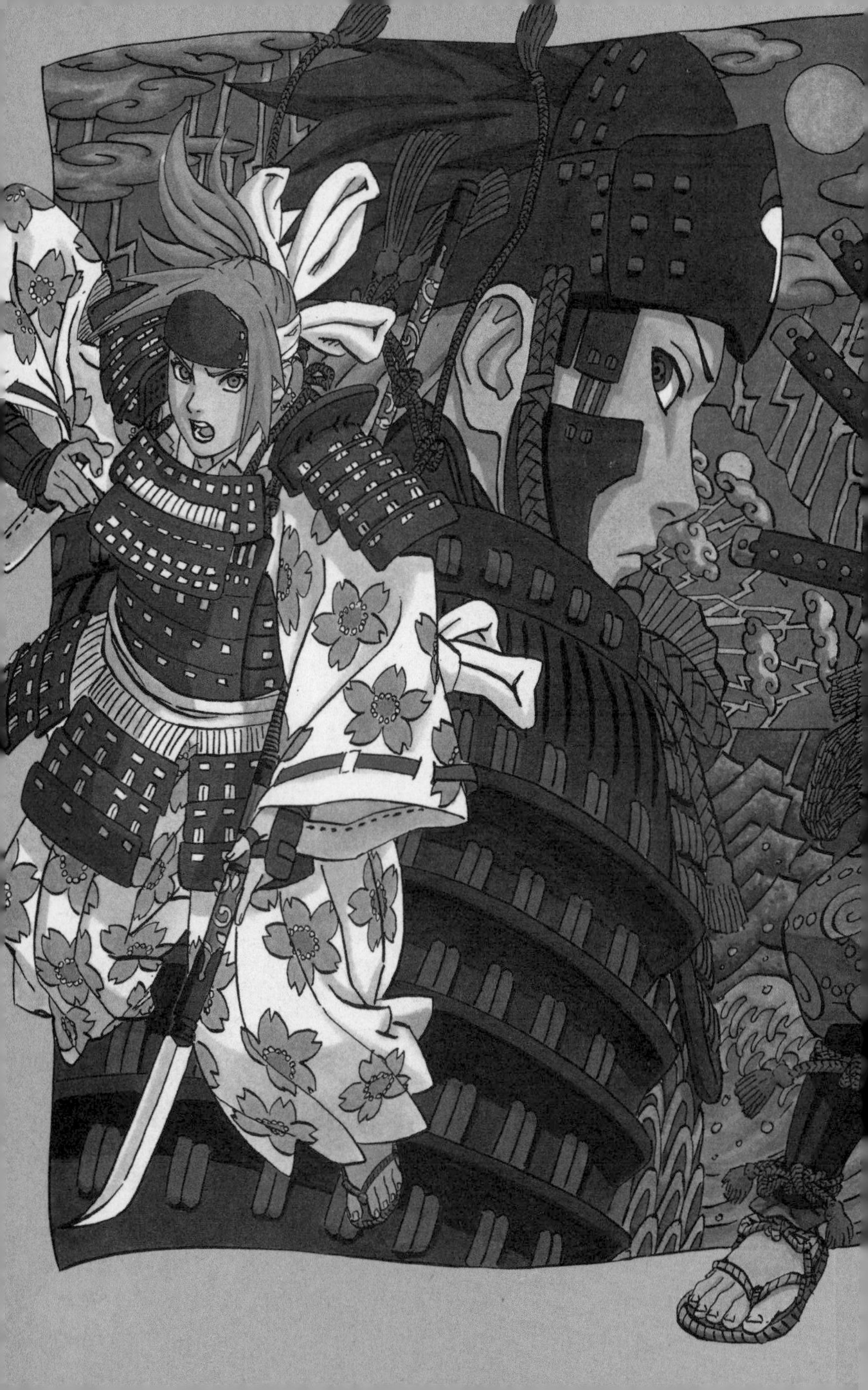

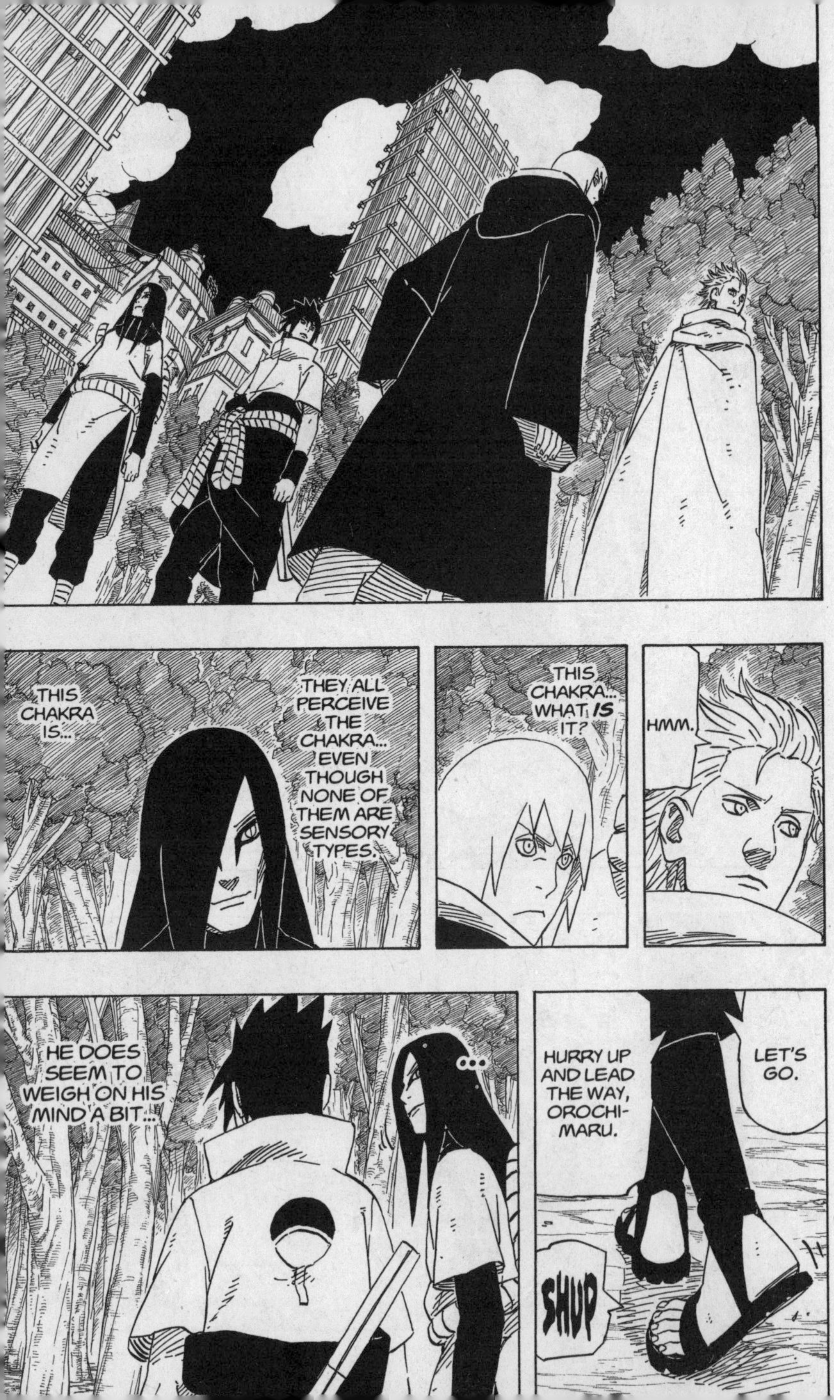
HMM.
THIS CHAKRA... WHAT IS IT?
THEY ALL PERCEIVE THE CHAKRA... EVEN THOUGH NONE OF THEM ARE SENSORY TYPES.
THIS CHAKRA IS...
LET'S GO.
HURRY UP AND LEAD THE WAY, OROCHIMARU.
SHUP
...
HE DOES SEEM TO WEIGH ON HIS MIND A BIT...

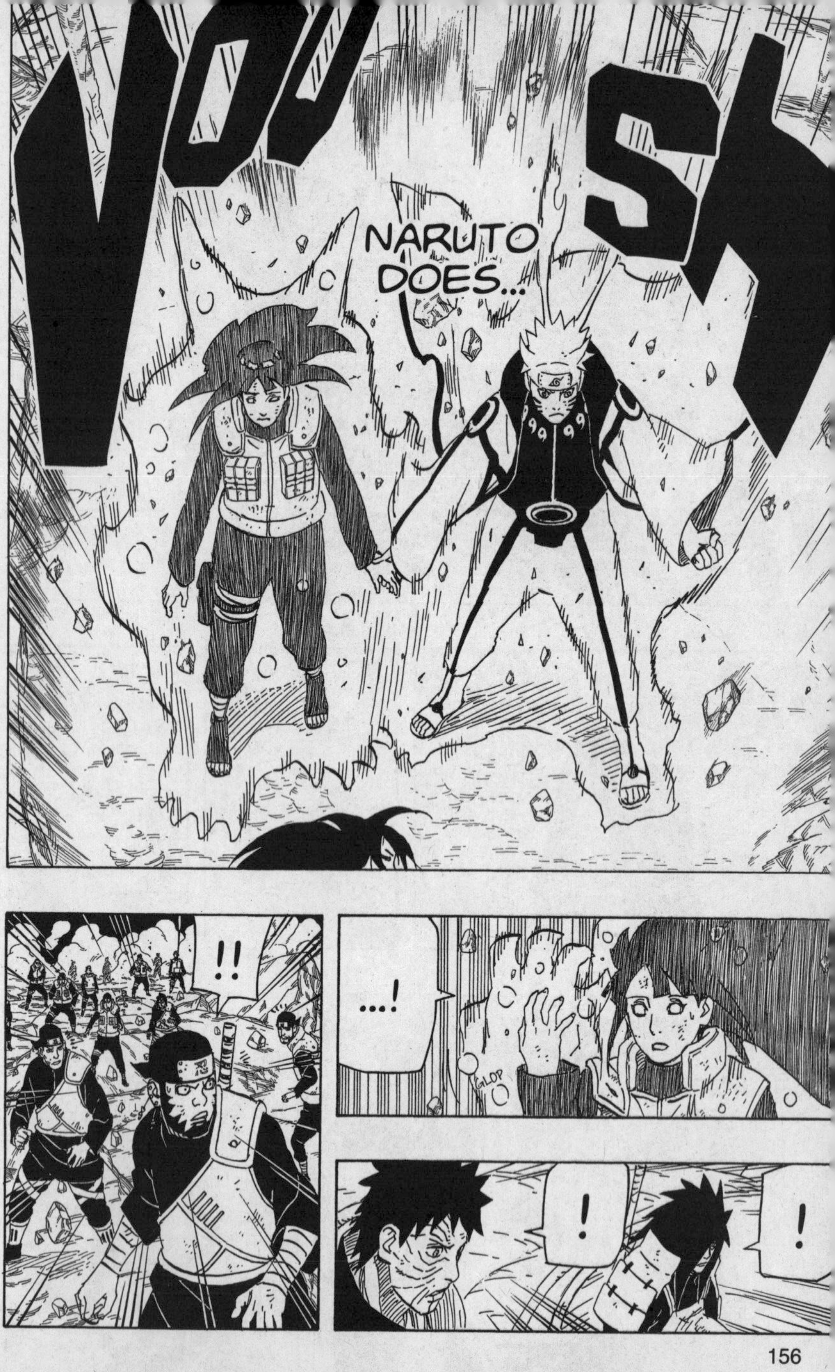
VOOSH
NARUTO DOES...
...!
GLOP
!
!
!!

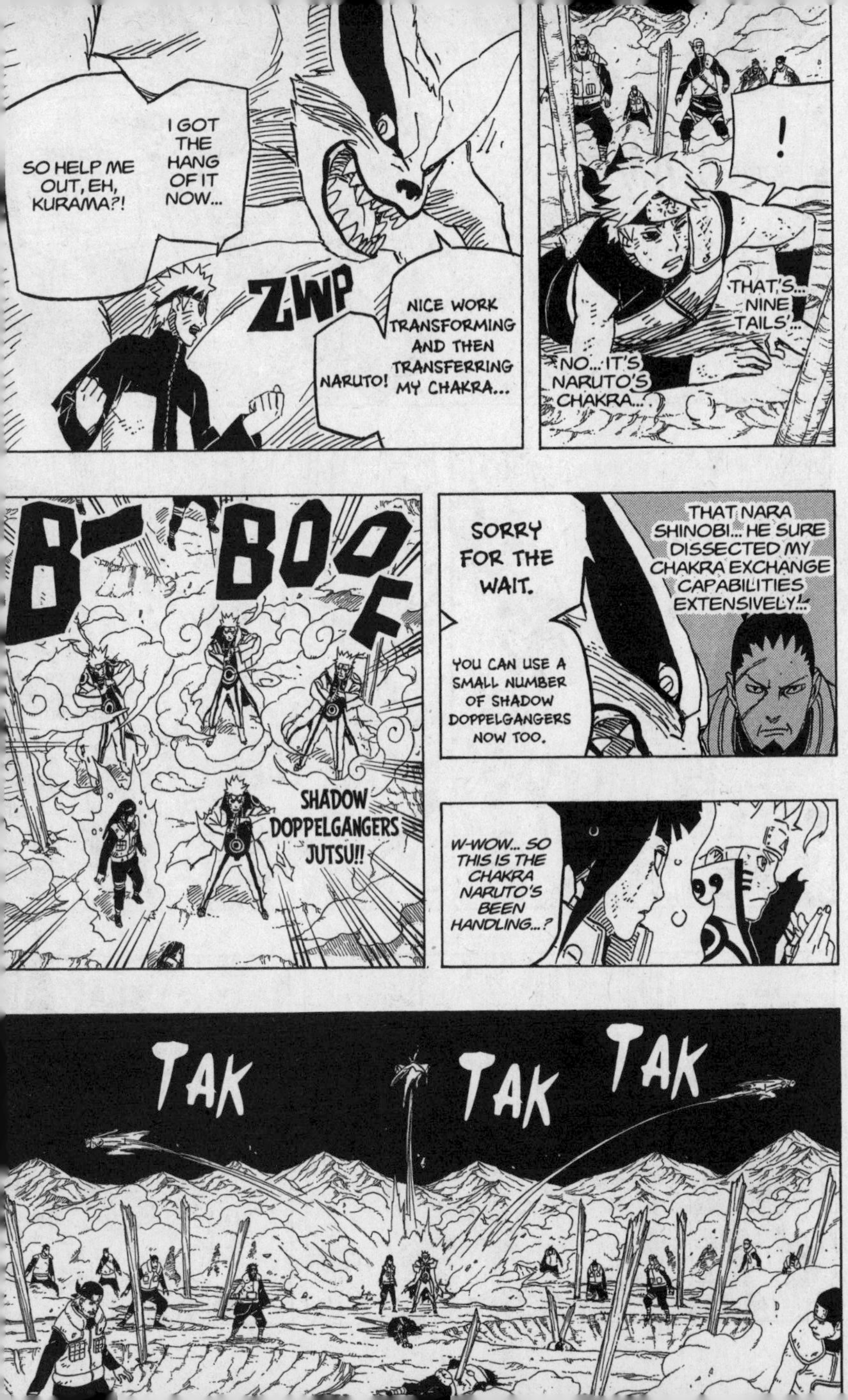
!
THAT'S... NINE TAILS'...
NO... IT'S NARUTO'S CHAKRA...
I GOT THE HANG OF IT NOW...
SO HELP ME OUT, EH, KURAMA?!
ZWP
NICE WORK TRANSFORMING AND THEN TRANSFERRING MY CHAKRA...
NARUTO!
THAT NARA SHINOBI... HE SURE DISSECTED MY CHAKRA EXCHANGE CAPABILITIES EXTENSIVELY...
SORRY FOR THE WAIT.
YOU CAN USE A SMALL NUMBER OF SHADOW DOPPELGANGERS NOW TOO.
W-WOW... SO THIS IS THE CHAKRA NARUTO'S BEEN HANDLING...?
B-BOOF
SHADOW DOPPELGANGERS JUTSU!!
TAK
TAK
TAK

SORRY!

FSH

OMP

YOU'RE LATE, NARUTO!

CHOJI!! INO!!

SHUP

Y-YUP!

SHOOM

GSH

HEY, CHOJI!! YOU'RE FILLING OUT AGAIN!!

TAK

PLUMP

PLUMP

W-WHAT THE... MY CALORIE COUNT'S...

SLAP

SLAP

158

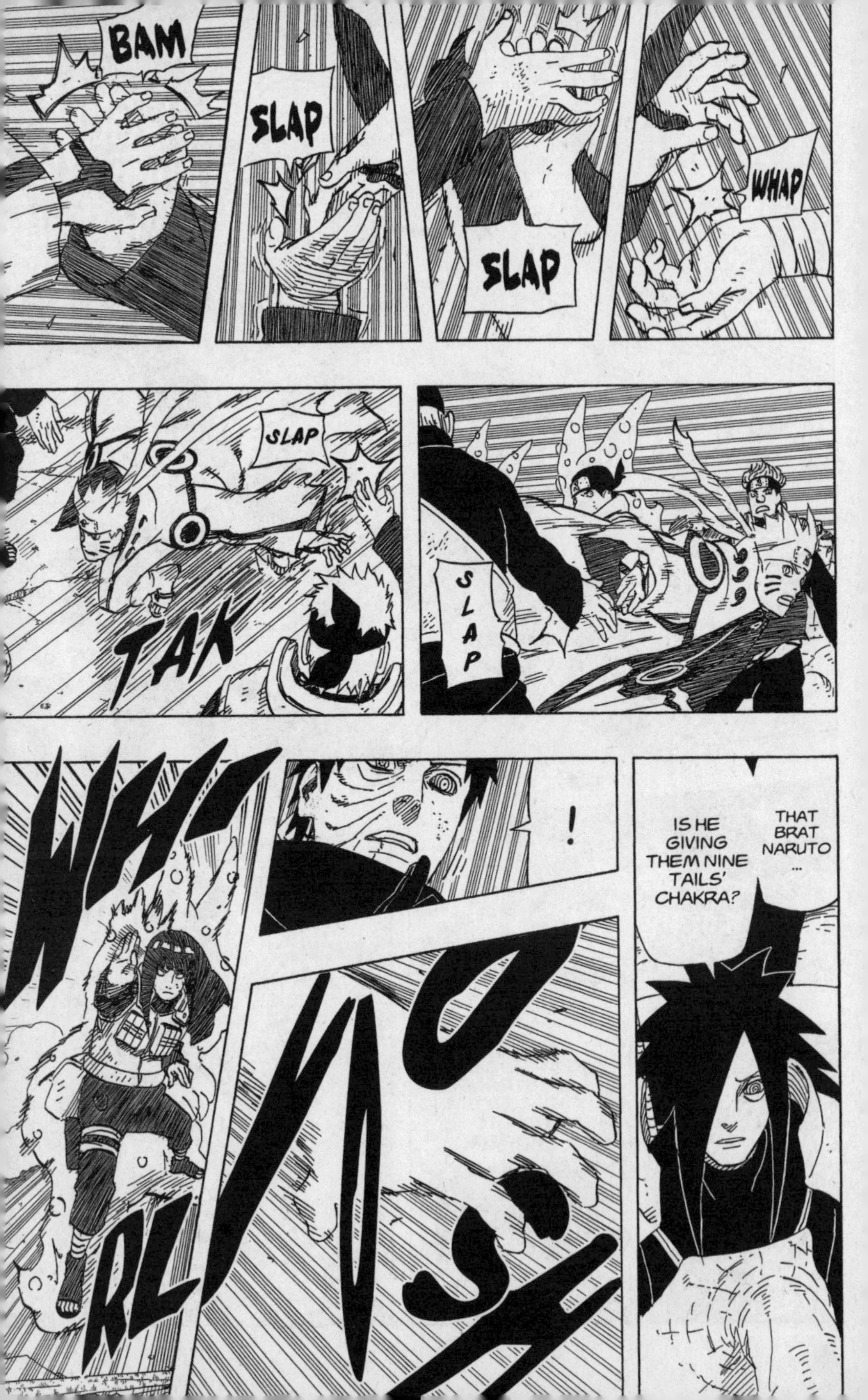
WHAP
SLAP
SLAP
BAM
SLAP
SLAP
TAK
THAT BRAT NARUTO ...
IS HE GIVING THEM NINE TAILS' CHAKRA?
!
WHOOSH

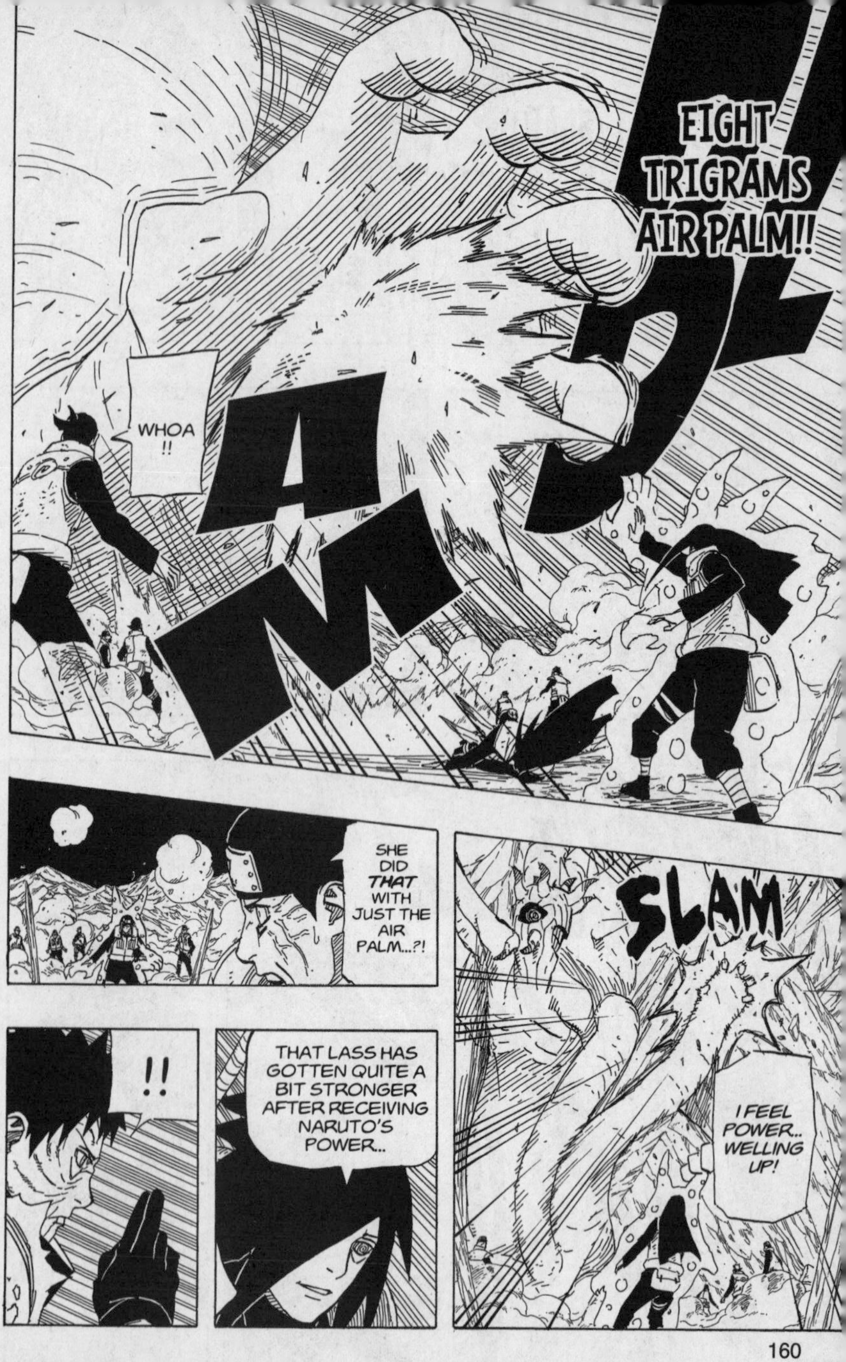
EIGHT TRIGRAMS AIR PALM!!
WHOA !!
SLAM
I FEEL POWER... WELLING UP!
SHE DID *THAT* WITH JUST THE AIR PALM...?!
THAT LASS HAS GOTTEN QUITE A BIT STRONGER AFTER RECEIVING NARUTO'S POWER...
!!

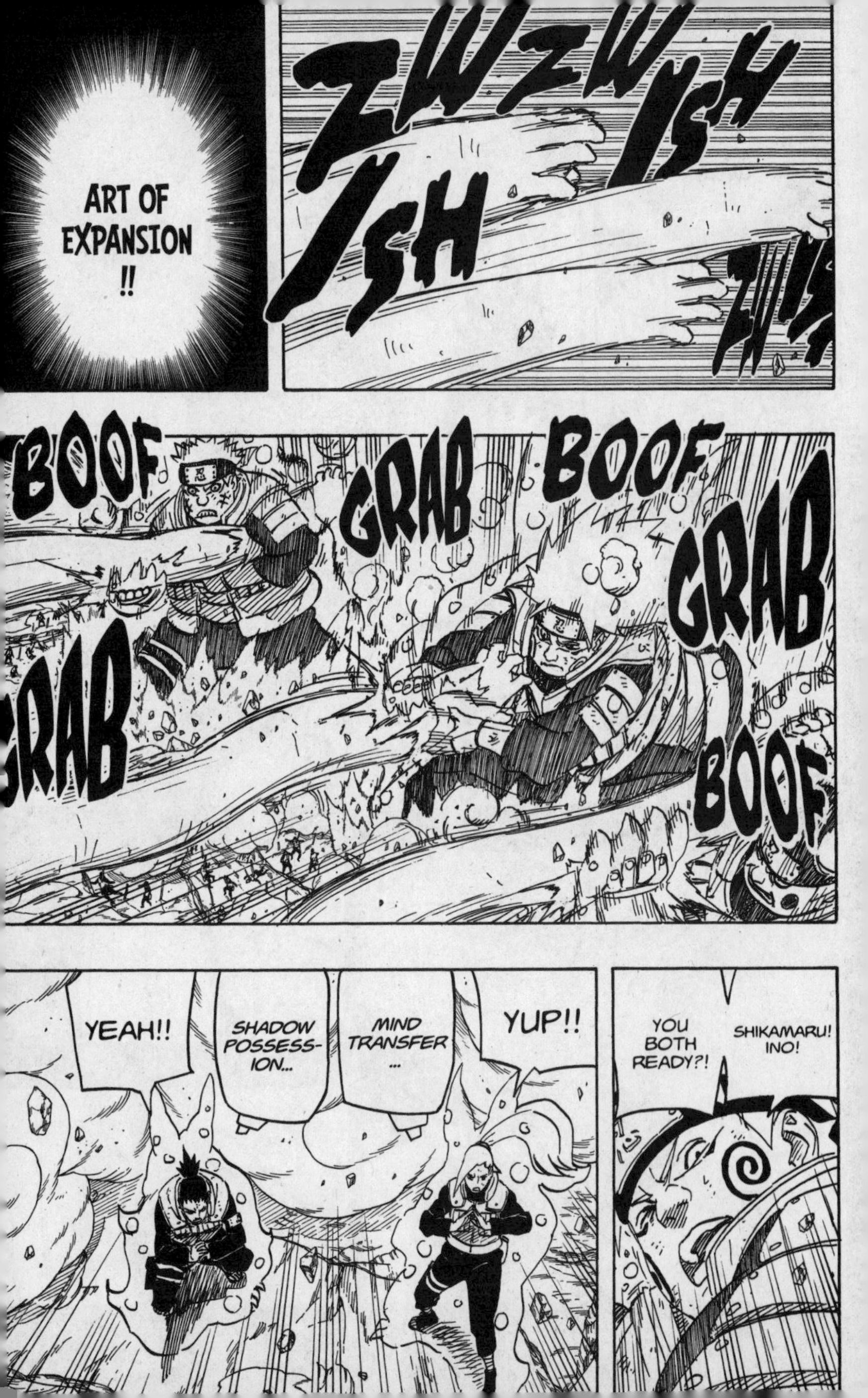
ZWISH
ZWISH
ART OF EXPANSION !!
GRAB
BOOF
BOOF
GRAB
GRAB
BOOF
GRAB
BOOF
SHIKAMARU! INO!
YOU BOTH READY?!
YUP!!
MIND TRANSFER ...
SHADOW POSSESS-ION...
YEAH!!

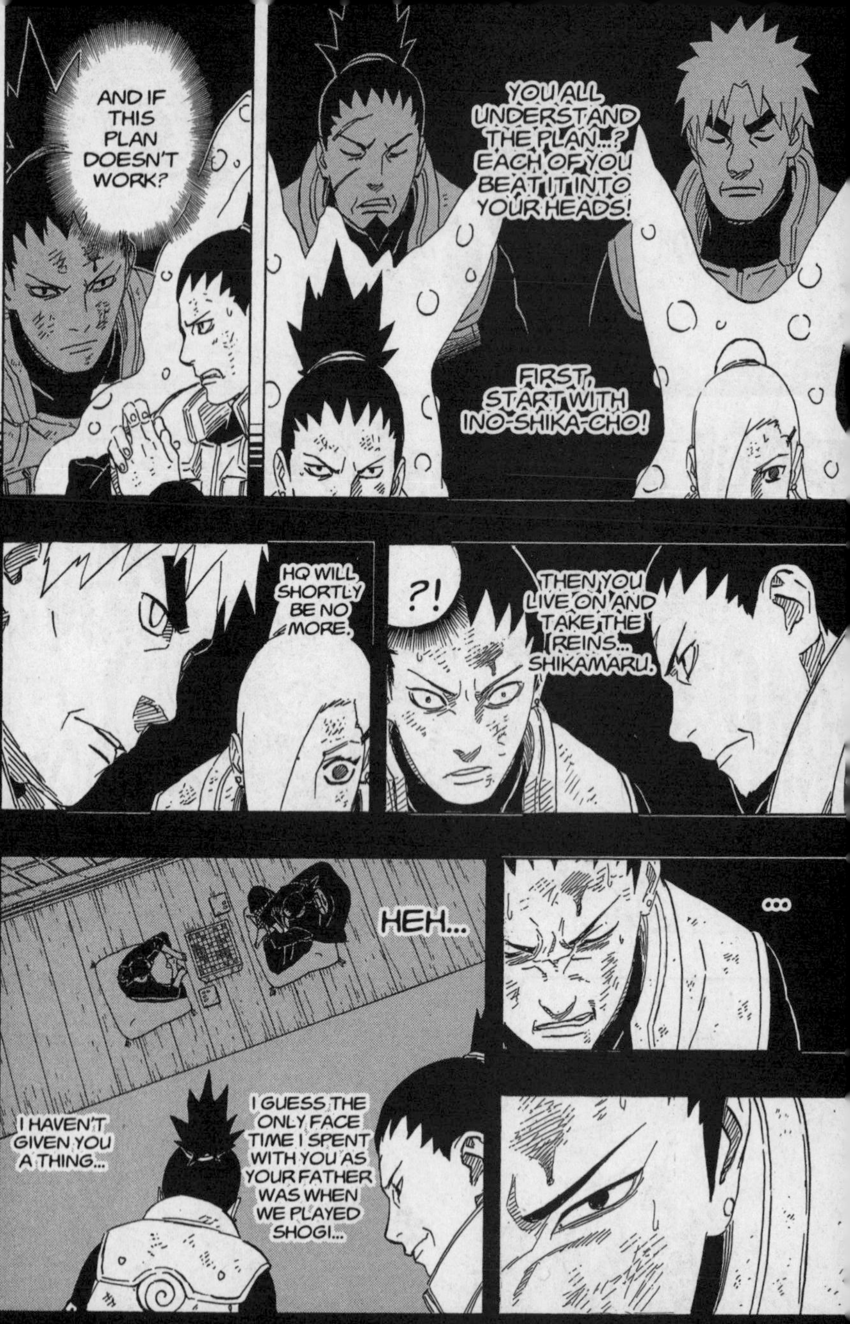
YOU ALL UNDERSTAND THE PLAN...? EACH OF YOU BEAT IT INTO YOUR HEADS!
FIRST, START WITH INO-SHIKA-CHO!
AND IF THIS PLAN DOESN'T WORK?
THEN YOU LIVE ON AND TAKE THE REINS... SHIKAMARU.
?!
HQ WILL SHORTLY BE NO MORE.
...
HEH...
I GUESS THE ONLY FACE TIME I SPENT WITH YOU AS YOUR FATHER WAS WHEN WE PLAYED SHOGI...
I HAVEN'T GIVEN YOU A THING...

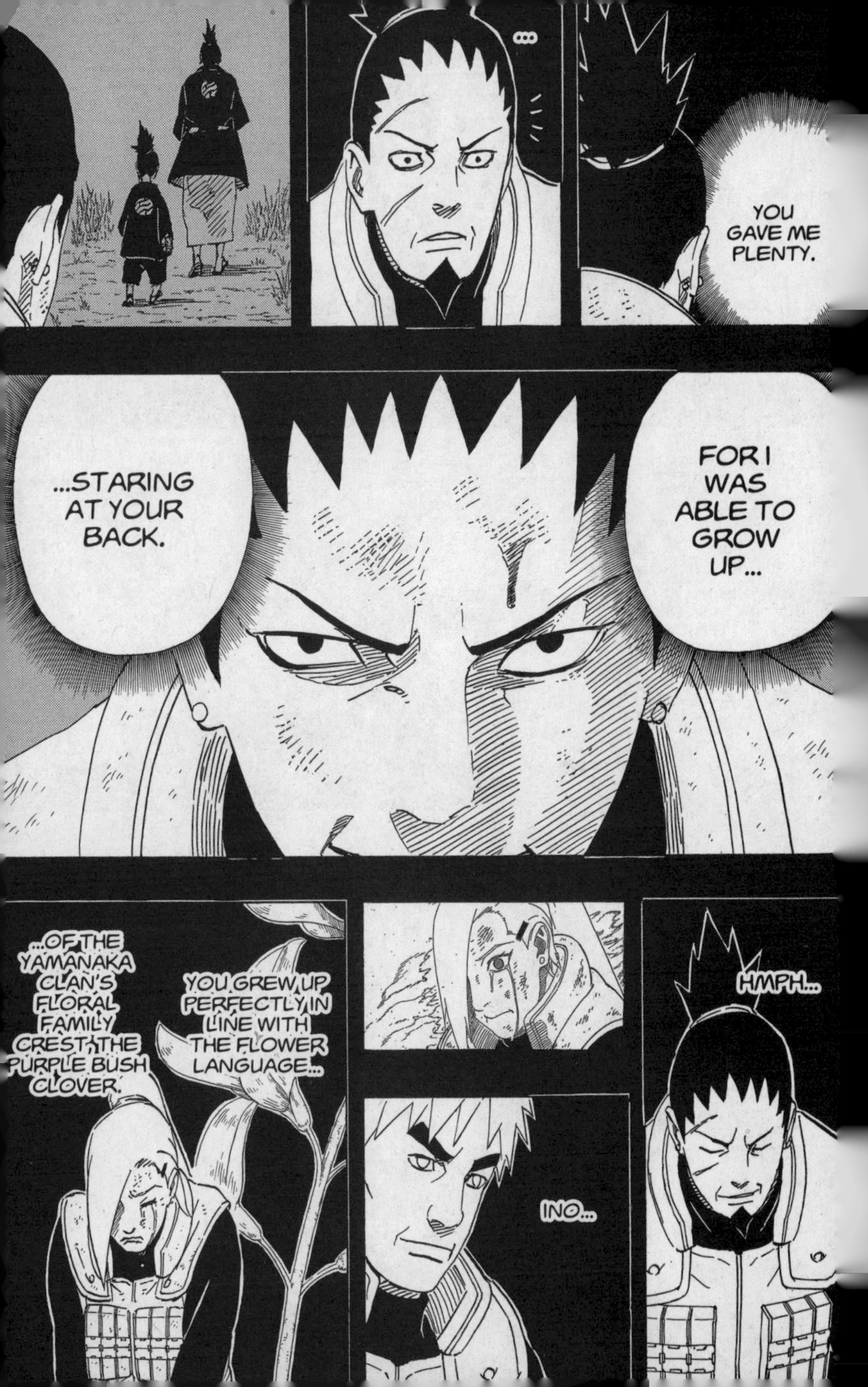
YOU GAVE ME PLENTY.
...
FOR I WAS ABLE TO GROW UP...
...STARING AT YOUR BACK.
HMPH...
INO...
YOU GREW UP PERFECTLY IN LINE WITH THE FLOWER LANGUAGE...
...OF THE YAMANAKA CLAN'S FLORAL FAMILY CREST, THE PURPLE BUSH CLOVER.

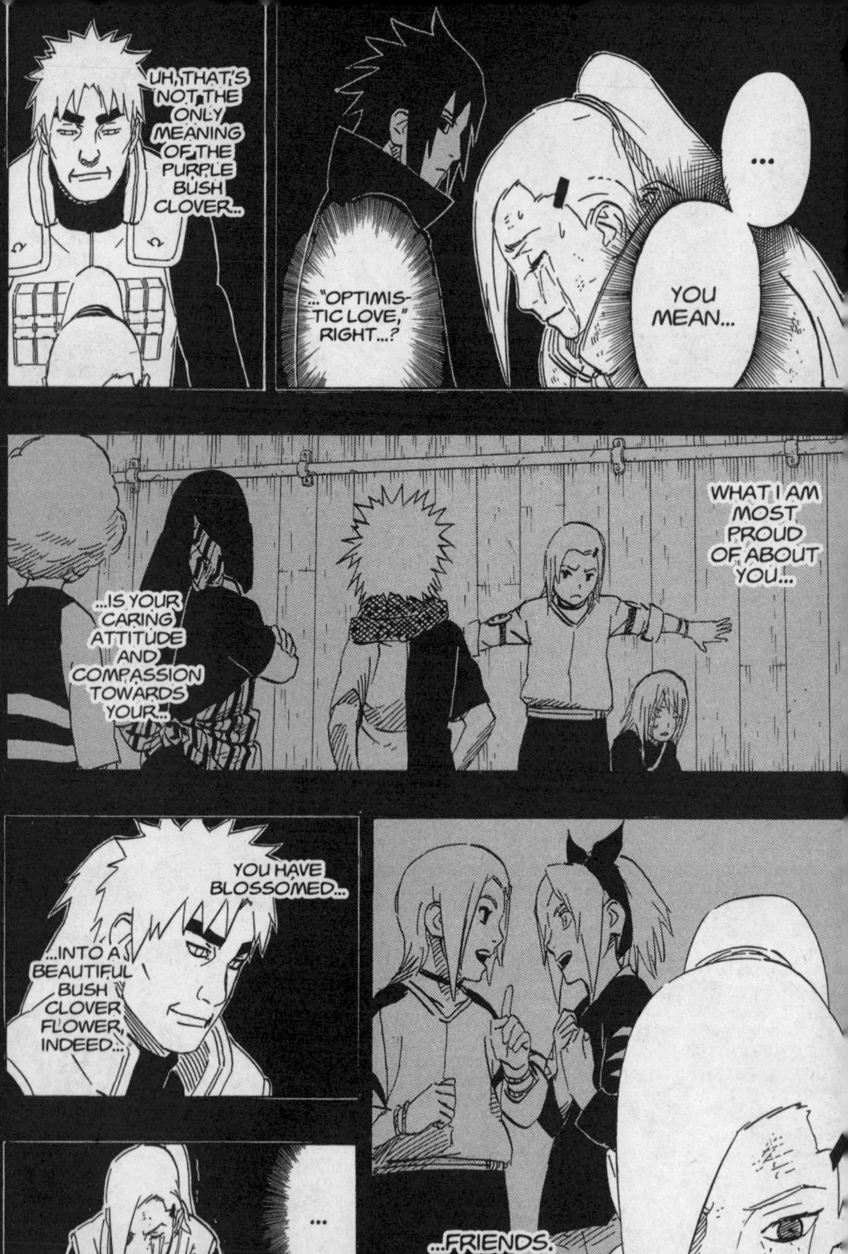
...
YOU MEAN...
..."OPTIMISTIC LOVE," RIGHT...?
UH, THAT'S NOT THE ONLY MEANING OF THE PURPLE BUSH CLOVER...
WHAT I AM MOST PROUD OF ABOUT YOU...
...IS YOUR CARING ATTITUDE AND COMPASSION TOWARDS YOUR...
...FRIENDS.
YOU HAVE BLOSSOMED...
...INTO A BEAUTIFUL BUSH CLOVER FLOWER, INDEED...
...

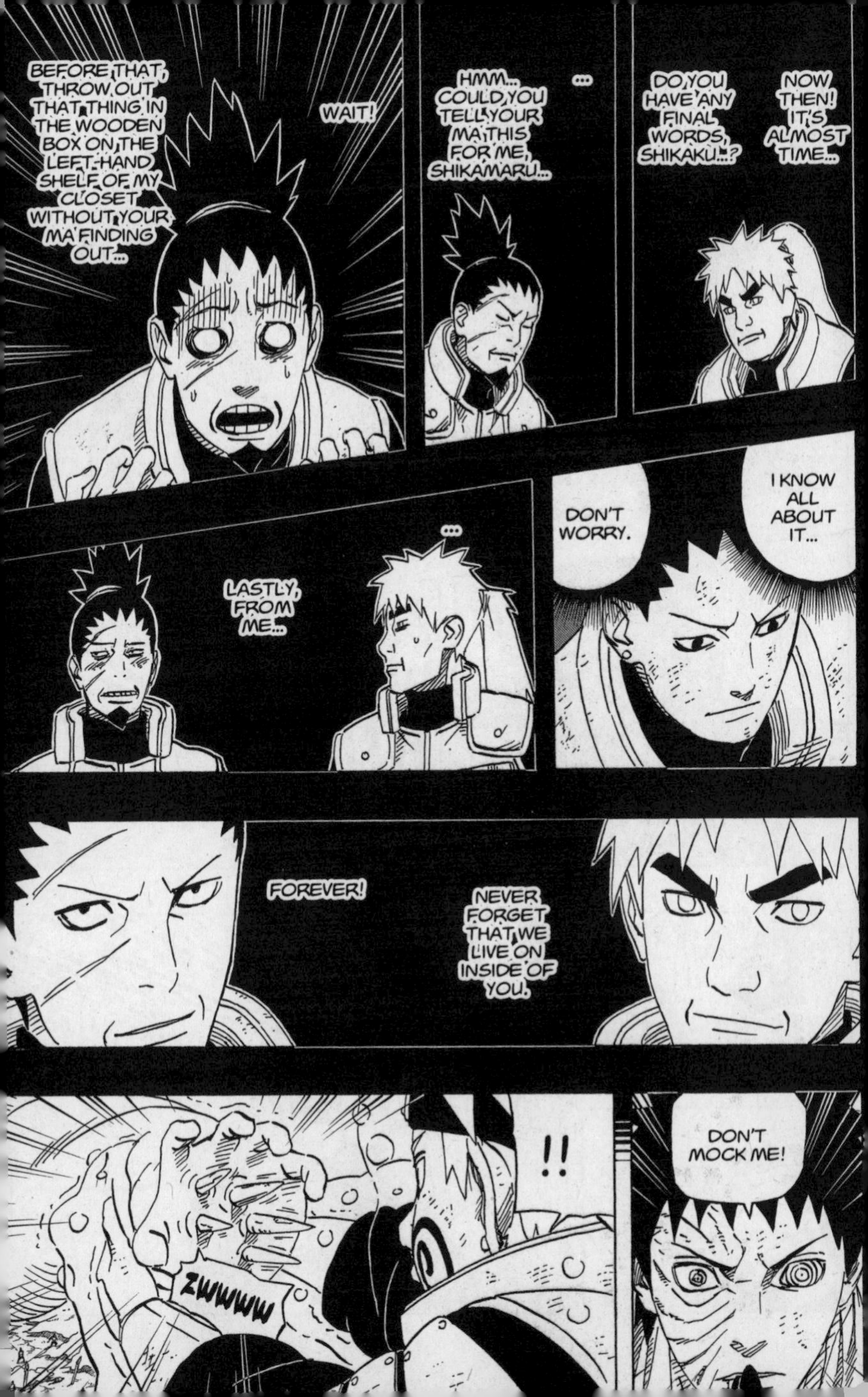
NOW THEN! IT'S ALMOST TIME...
DO YOU HAVE ANY FINAL WORDS, SHIKAKU...?
...
HMM... COULD YOU TELL YOUR MA THIS FOR ME, SHIKAMARU...
WAIT!
BEFORE THAT, THROW OUT THAT THING IN THE WOODEN BOX ON THE LEFT-HAND SHELF OF MY CLOSET WITHOUT YOUR MA FINDING OUT...
I KNOW ALL ABOUT IT...
DON'T WORRY.
...
LASTLY, FROM ME...
NEVER FORGET THAT WE LIVE ON INSIDE OF YOU.
FOREVER!
DON'T MOCK ME!
!!
ZWWWW

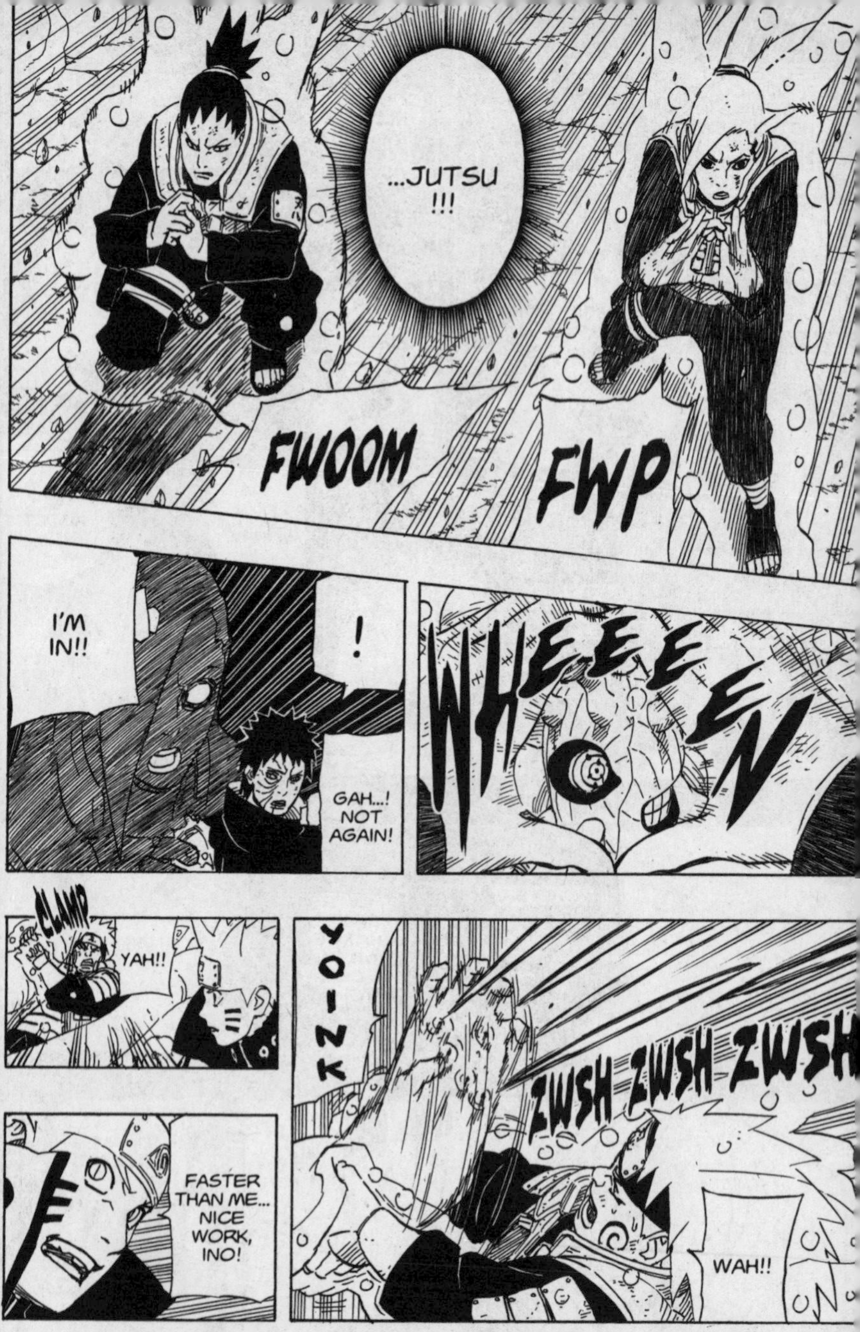
...JUTSU !!!
FWP
FWOOM
WHEEEEN
!
I'M IN!!
GAH...! NOT AGAIN!
YOINK
ZWSH ZWSH ZWSH
WAH!!
CLAMP
YAH!!
FASTER THAN ME... NICE WORK, INO!

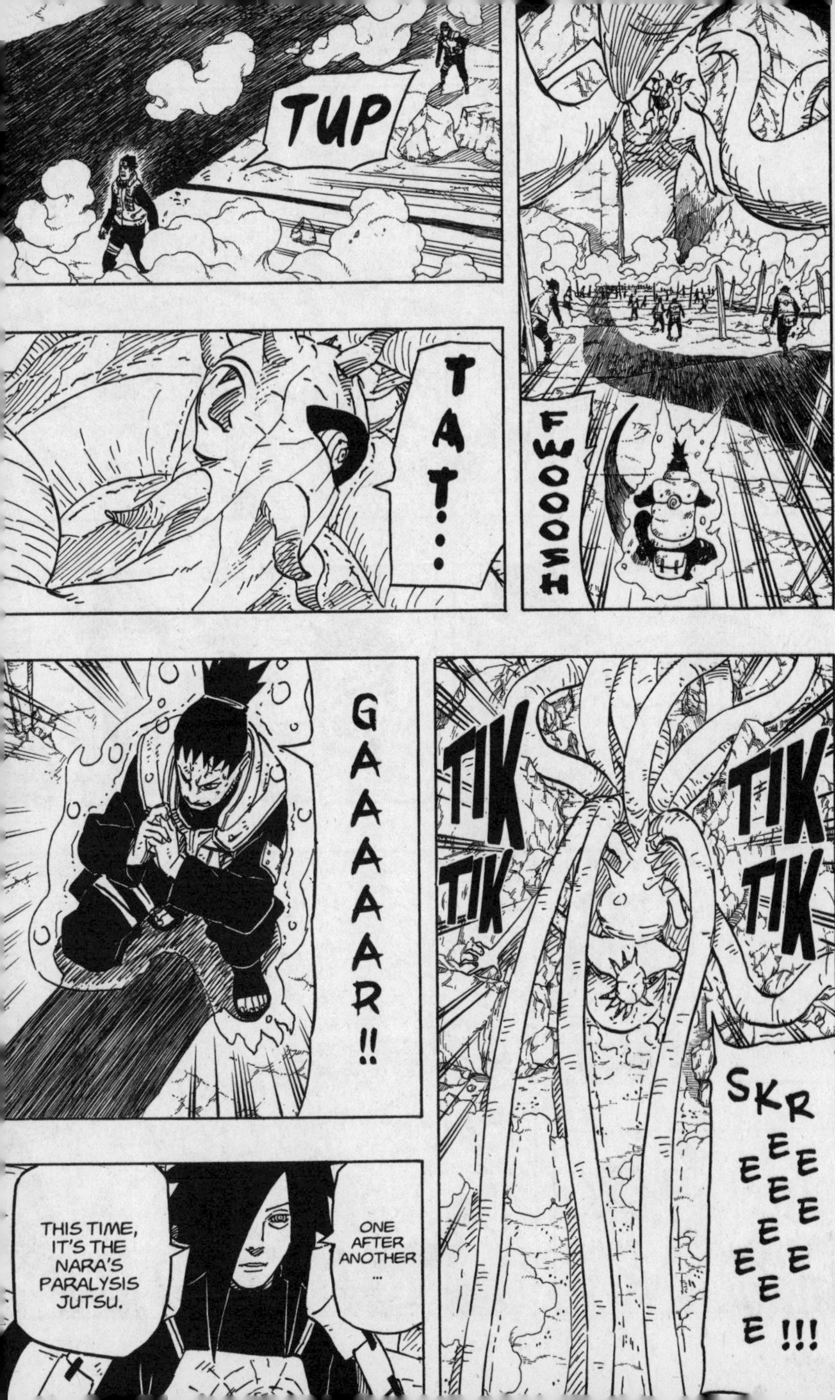
FWOOOSH
TUP
TAT...
TIK TIK
TIK TIK
SKREEEEEEEEEEE!!!
GAAAAAR!!
ONE AFTER ANOTHER...
THIS TIME, IT'S THE NARA'S PARALYSIS JUTSU.

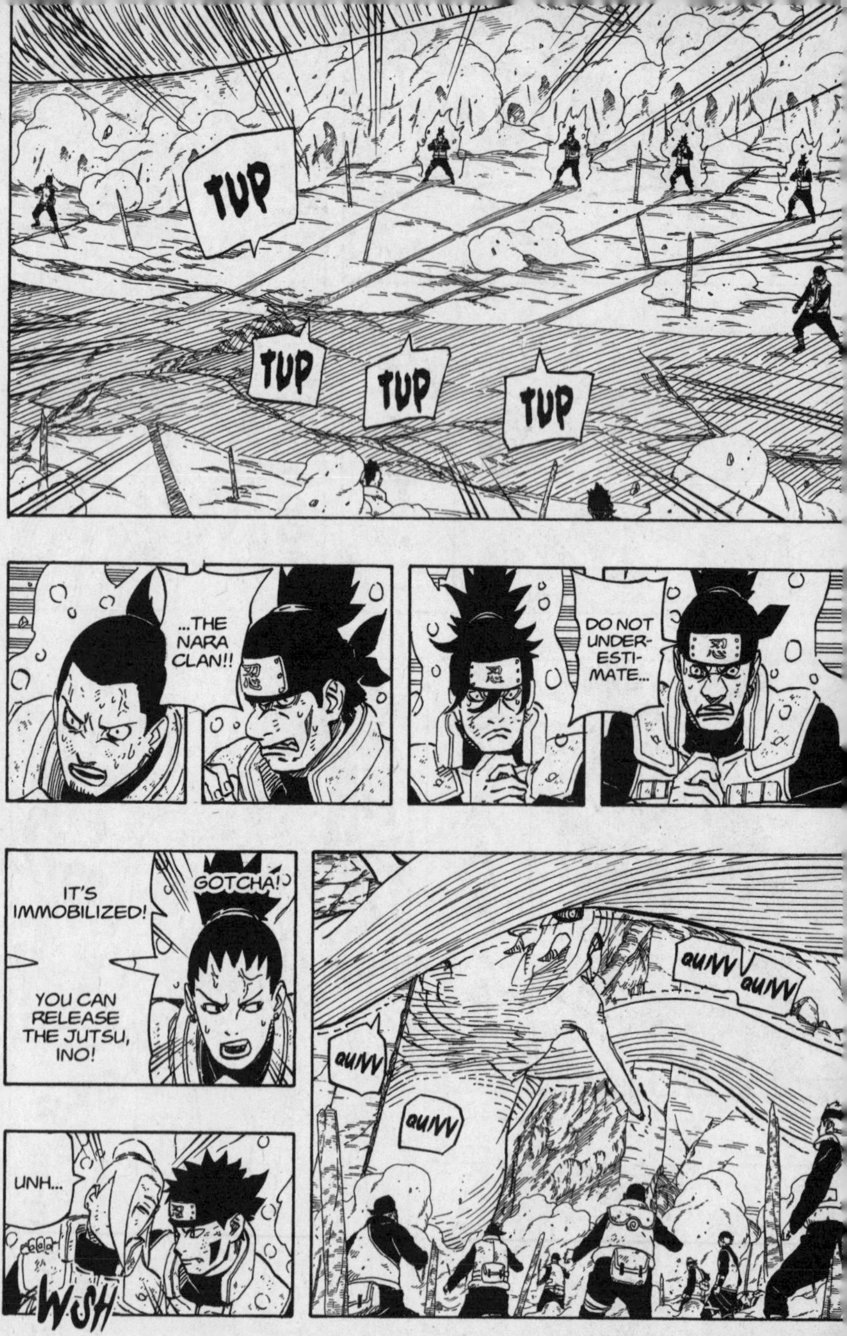
TUP
TUP
TUP
TUP
DO NOT UNDER-ESTIMATE...
...THE NARA CLAN!!
QUIVV
QUIVV
QUIVV
QUIVV
GOTCHA!
IT'S IMMOBILIZED!
YOU CAN RELEASE THE JUTSU, INO!
UNH...
WSH

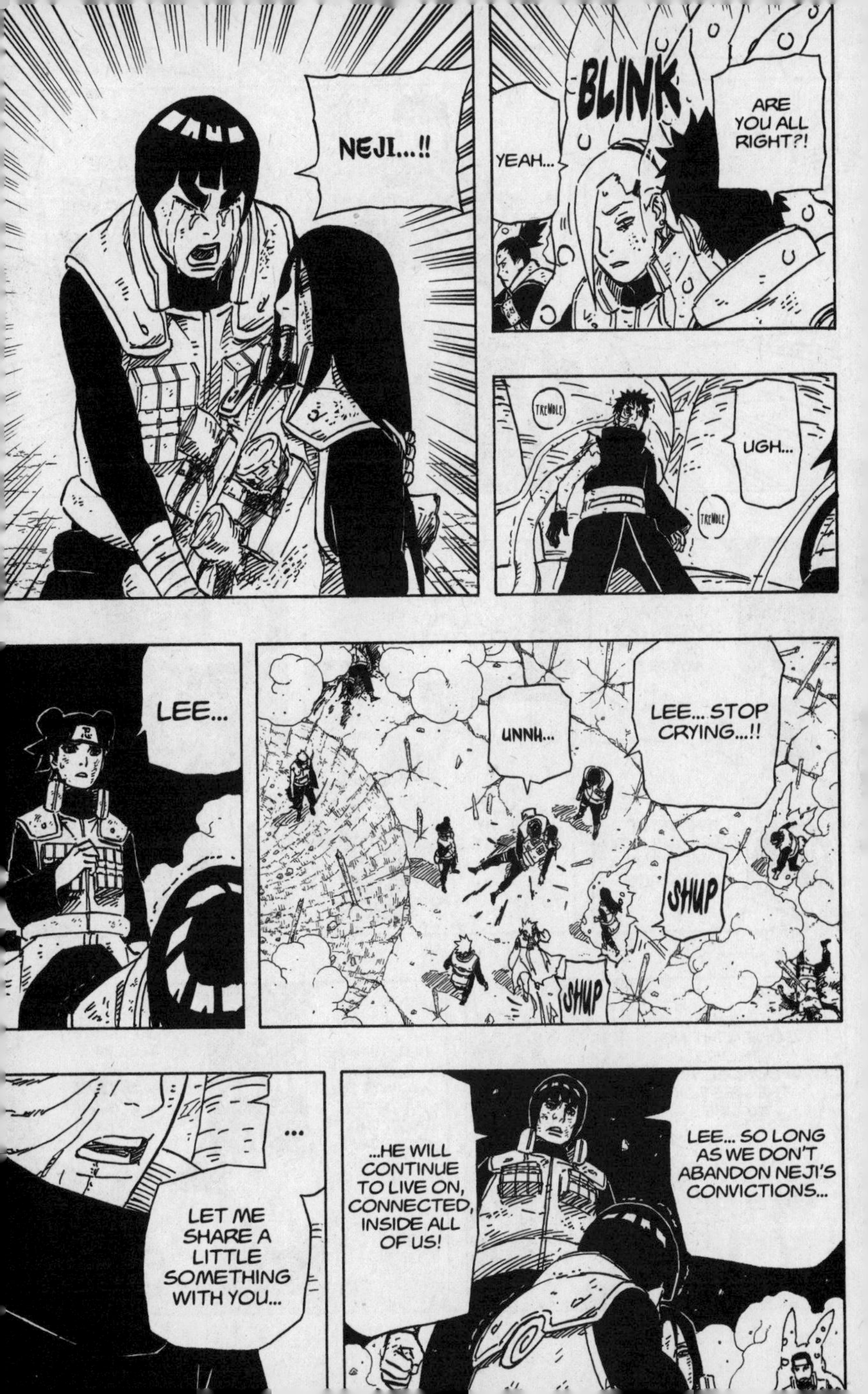
ARE YOU ALL RIGHT?!
BLINK
YEAH...
TREMBLE
UGH...
TREMBLE
NEJI...!!
LEE... STOP CRYING...!!
UNNH...
SHUP
SHUP
LEE...
LEE... SO LONG AS WE DON'T ABANDON NEJI'S CONVICTIONS...
...HE WILL CONTINUE TO LIVE ON, CONNECTED, INSIDE ALL OF US!
...
LET ME SHARE A LITTLE SOMETHING WITH YOU...

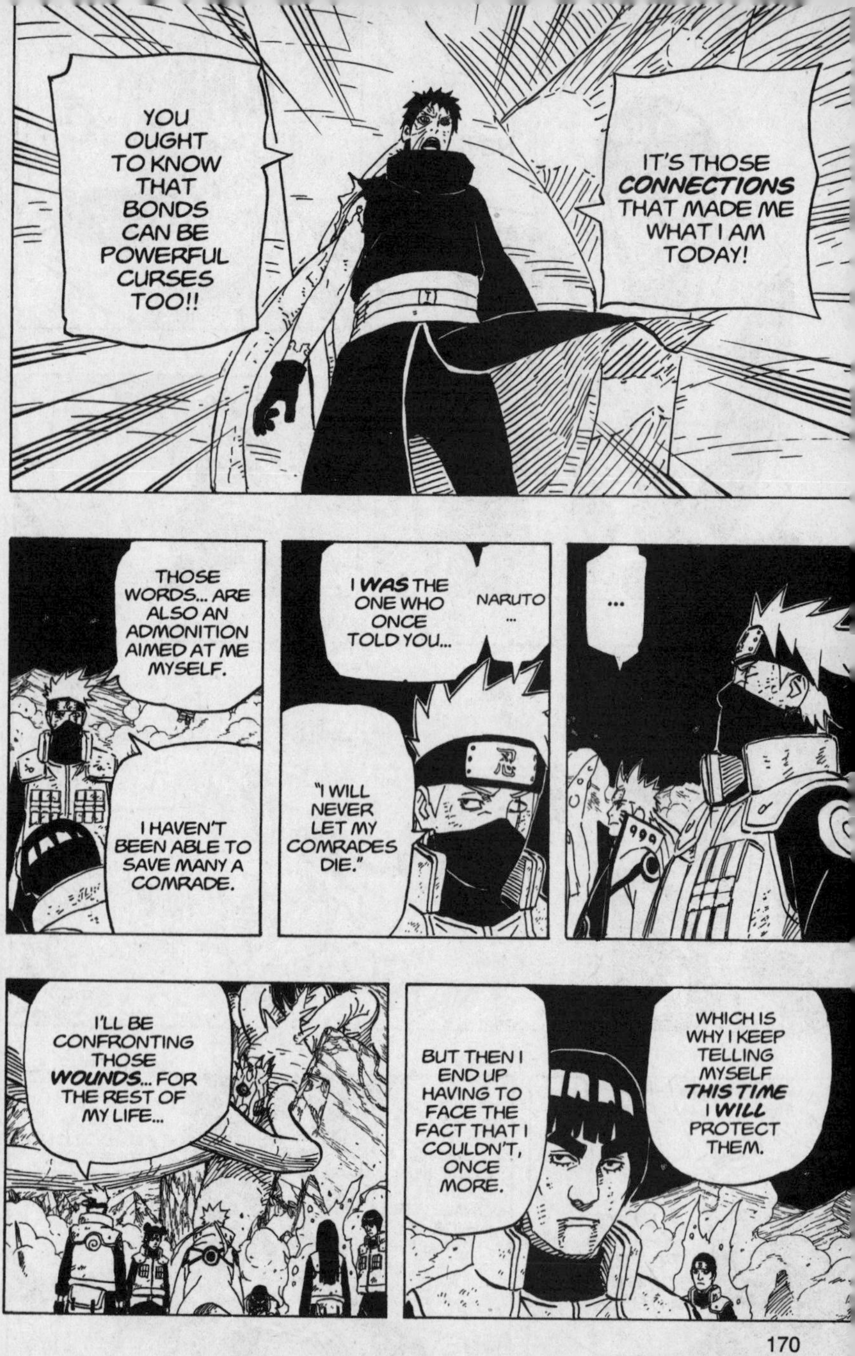
IT'S THOSE CONNECTIONS THAT MADE ME WHAT I AM TODAY!
YOU OUGHT TO KNOW THAT BONDS CAN BE POWERFUL CURSES TOO!!
...
NARUTO ...
I WAS THE ONE WHO ONCE TOLD YOU...
"I WILL NEVER LET MY COMRADES DIE."
THOSE WORDS... ARE ALSO AN ADMONITION AIMED AT ME MYSELF.
I HAVEN'T BEEN ABLE TO SAVE MANY A COMRADE.
WHICH IS WHY I KEEP TELLING MYSELF THIS TIME I WILL PROTECT THEM.
BUT THEN I END UP HAVING TO FACE THE FACT THAT I COULDN'T, ONCE MORE.
I'LL BE CONFRONTING THOSE WOUNDS... FOR THE REST OF MY LIFE...

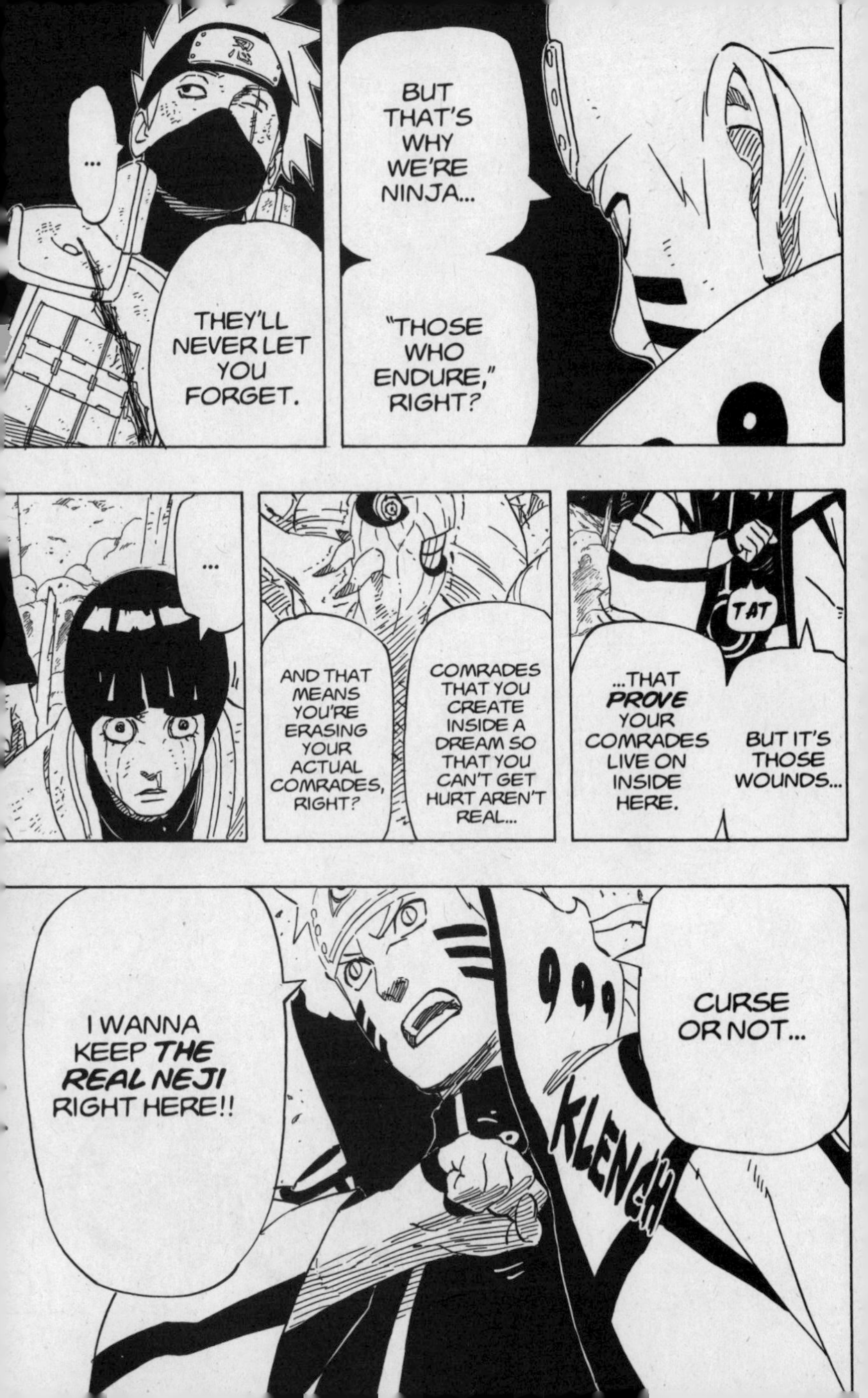
BUT THAT'S WHY WE'RE NINJA...
"THOSE WHO ENDURE," RIGHT?
...
THEY'LL NEVER LET YOU FORGET.
TAT
BUT IT'S THOSE WOUNDS...
...THAT **PROVE** YOUR COMRADES LIVE ON INSIDE HERE.
COMRADES THAT YOU CREATE INSIDE A DREAM SO THAT YOU CAN'T GET HURT AREN'T REAL...
AND THAT MEANS YOU'RE ERASING YOUR ACTUAL COMRADES, RIGHT?
...
CURSE OR NOT...
KLENCH
I WANNA KEEP **THE REAL NEJI** RIGHT HERE!!

NARUTO

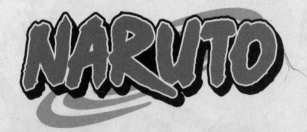

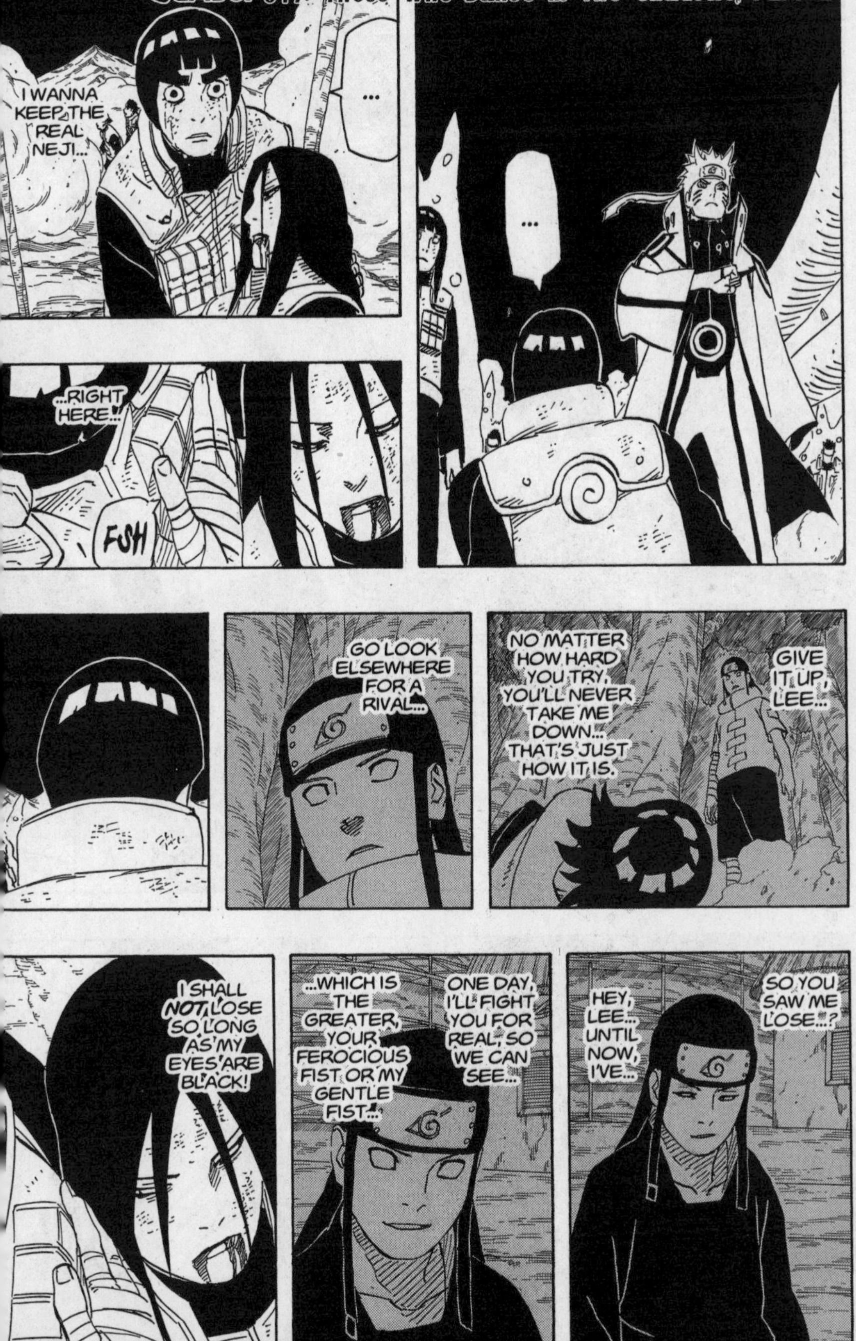
...
...
I WANNA KEEP THE REAL NEJI...
...RIGHT HERE...
FSH
GIVE IT UP, LEE...
NO MATTER HOW HARD YOU TRY, YOU'LL NEVER TAKE ME DOWN... THAT'S JUST HOW IT IS.
GO LOOK ELSEWHERE FOR A RIVAL...
SO YOU SAW ME LOSE...?
HEY, LEE... UNTIL NOW, I'VE...
ONE DAY, I'LL FIGHT YOU FOR REAL, SO WE CAN SEE...
...WHICH IS THE GREATER, YOUR FEROCIOUS FIST OR MY GENTLE FIST...
I SHALL *NOT* LOSE SO LONG AS MY EYES ARE BLACK!

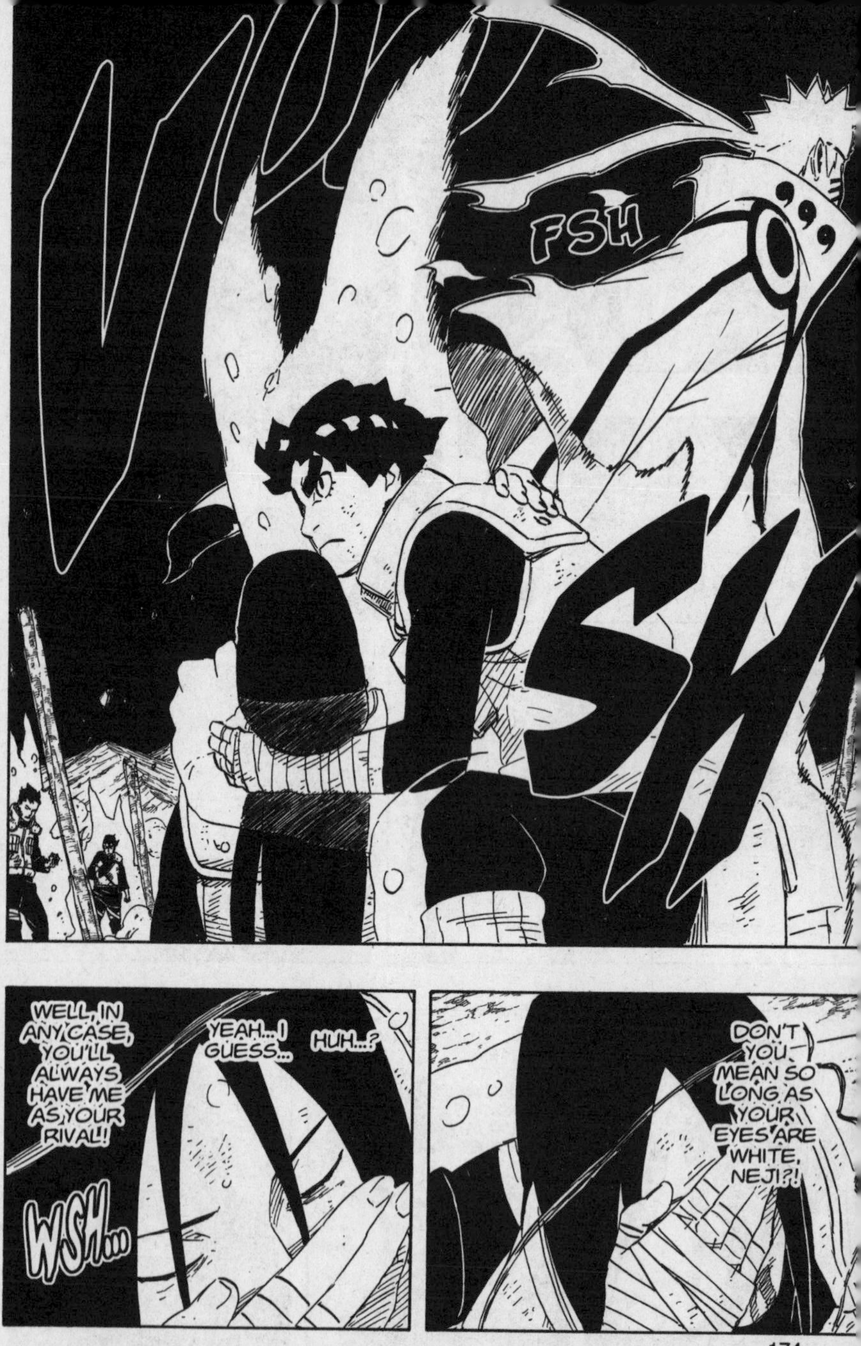
FSH
DON'T YOU MEAN SO LONG AS YOUR EYES ARE WHITE, NEJI?!
HUH...?
YEAH... I GUESS...
WELL, IN ANY CASE, YOU'LL ALWAYS HAVE ME AS YOUR RIVAL!
WSH...

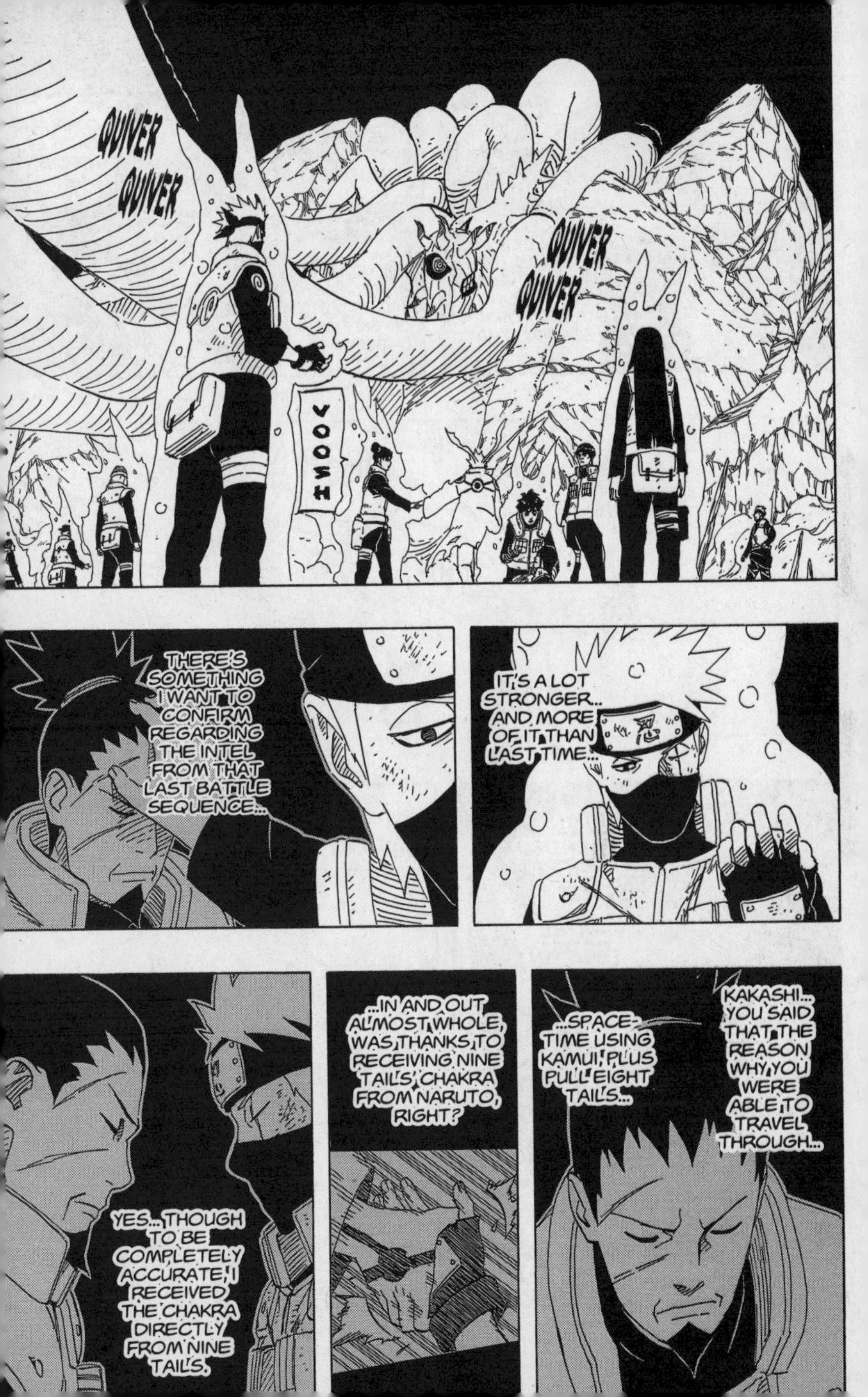
QUIVER QUIVER
QUIVER QUIVER
VOOSH
IT'S A LOT STRONGER... AND MORE OF IT THAN LAST TIME...
THERE'S SOMETHING I WANT TO CONFIRM REGARDING THE INTEL FROM THAT LAST BATTLE SEQUENCE...
KAKASHI... YOU SAID THAT THE REASON WHY YOU WERE ABLE TO TRAVEL THROUGH...
...SPACE-TIME USING KAMUI, PLUS PULL EIGHT TAILS...
...IN AND OUT ALMOST WHOLE, WAS THANKS TO RECEIVING NINE TAILS' CHAKRA FROM NARUTO, RIGHT?
YES... THOUGH TO BE COMPLETELY ACCURATE, I RECEIVED THE CHAKRA DIRECTLY FROM NINE TAILS.

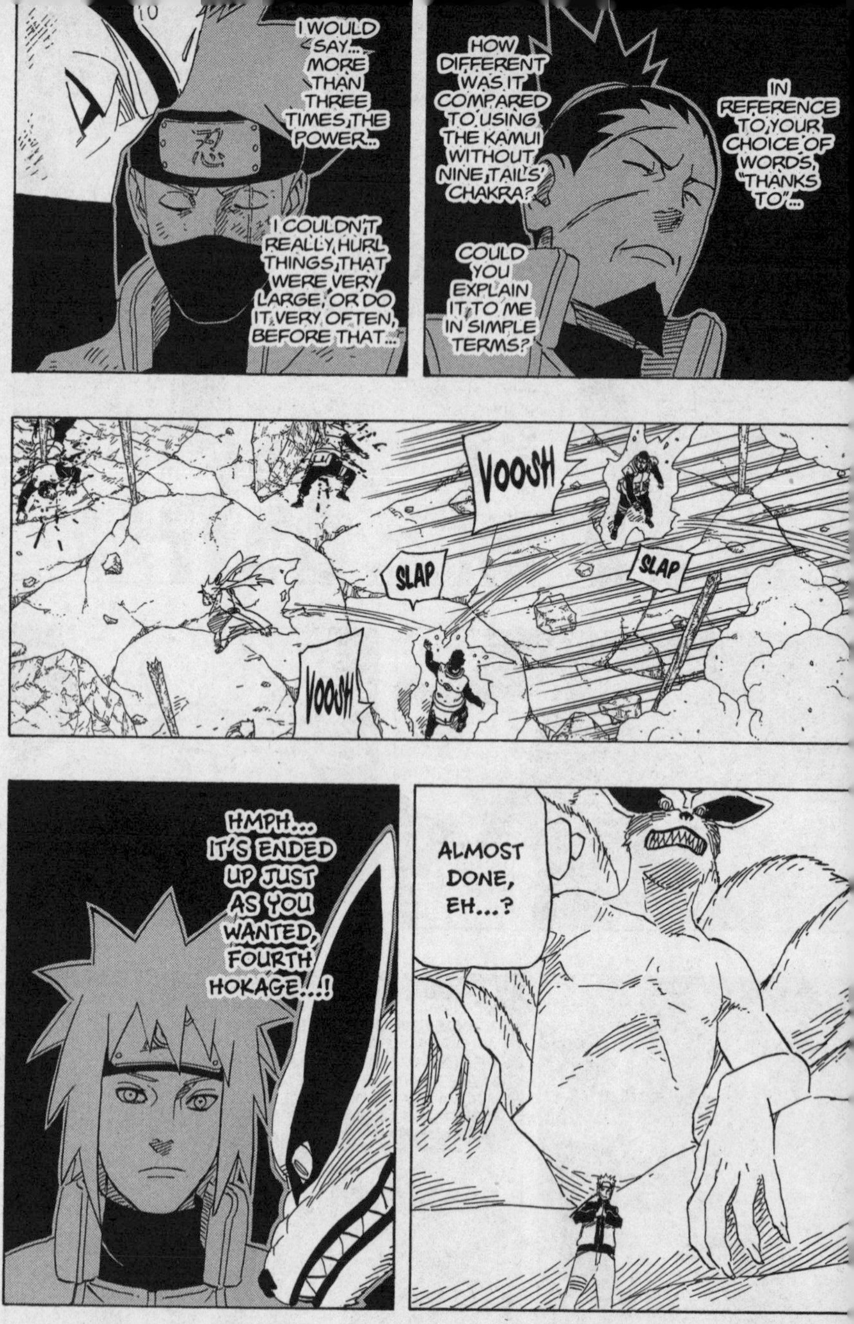
IN REFERENCE TO YOUR CHOICE OF WORDS, "THANKS TO"...
HOW DIFFERENT WAS IT COMPARED TO USING THE KAMUI WITHOUT NINE TAILS' CHAKRA?
COULD YOU EXPLAIN IT TO ME IN SIMPLE TERMS?
I WOULD SAY... MORE THAN THREE TIMES THE POWER...
I COULDN'T REALLY HURL THINGS THAT WERE VERY LARGE, OR DO IT VERY OFTEN, BEFORE THAT...
VOOSH
SLAP
SLAP
VOOSH
ALMOST DONE, EH...?
HMPH... IT'S ENDED UP JUST AS YOU WANTED, FOURTH HOKAGE...!

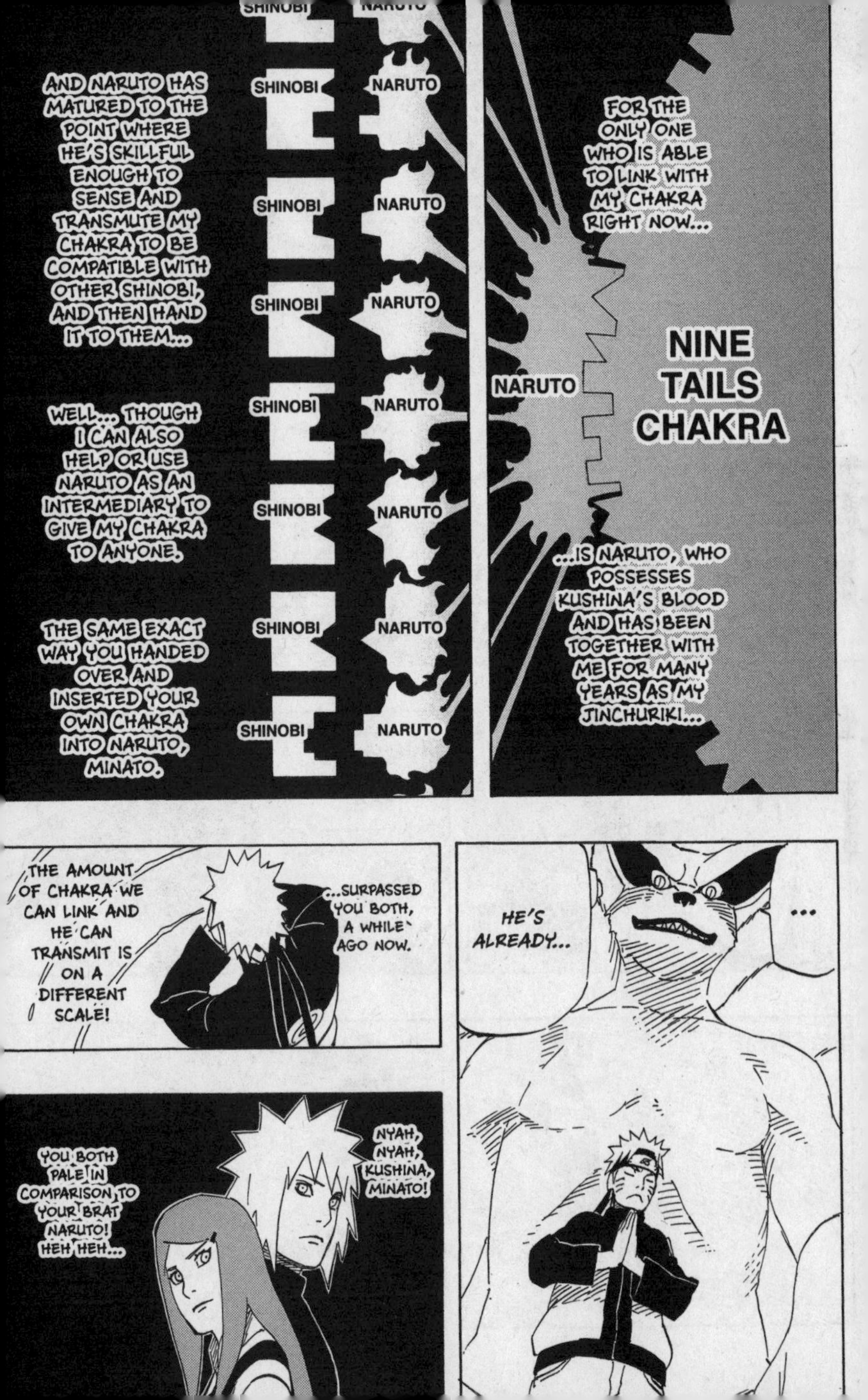
FOR THE ONLY ONE WHO IS ABLE TO LINK WITH MY CHAKRA RIGHT NOW...
NINE TAILS CHAKRA
NARUTO
...IS NARUTO, WHO POSSESSES KUSHINA'S BLOOD AND HAS BEEN TOGETHER WITH ME FOR MANY YEARS AS MY JINCHURIKI...
NARUTO
SHINOBI
NARUTO
SHINOBI
NARUTO
SHINOBI
NARUTO
SHINOBI
AND NARUTO HAS MATURED TO THE POINT WHERE HE'S SKILLFUL ENOUGH TO SENSE AND TRANSMUTE MY CHAKRA TO BE COMPATIBLE WITH OTHER SHINOBI, AND THEN HAND IT TO THEM...
NARUTO
SHINOBI
NARUTO
SHINOBI
WELL... THOUGH I CAN ALSO HELP OR USE NARUTO AS AN INTERMEDIARY TO GIVE MY CHAKRA TO ANYONE.
NARUTO
SHINOBI
NARUTO
SHINOBI
THE SAME EXACT WAY YOU HANDED OVER AND INSERTED YOUR OWN CHAKRA INTO NARUTO, MINATO.
...
HE'S ALREADY...
...SURPASSED YOU BOTH, A WHILE AGO NOW.
THE AMOUNT OF CHAKRA WE CAN LINK AND HE CAN TRANSMIT IS ON A DIFFERENT SCALE!
NYAH, NYAH, KUSHINA, MINATO!
YOU BOTH PALE IN COMPARISON TO YOUR BRAT NARUTO! HEH HEH...

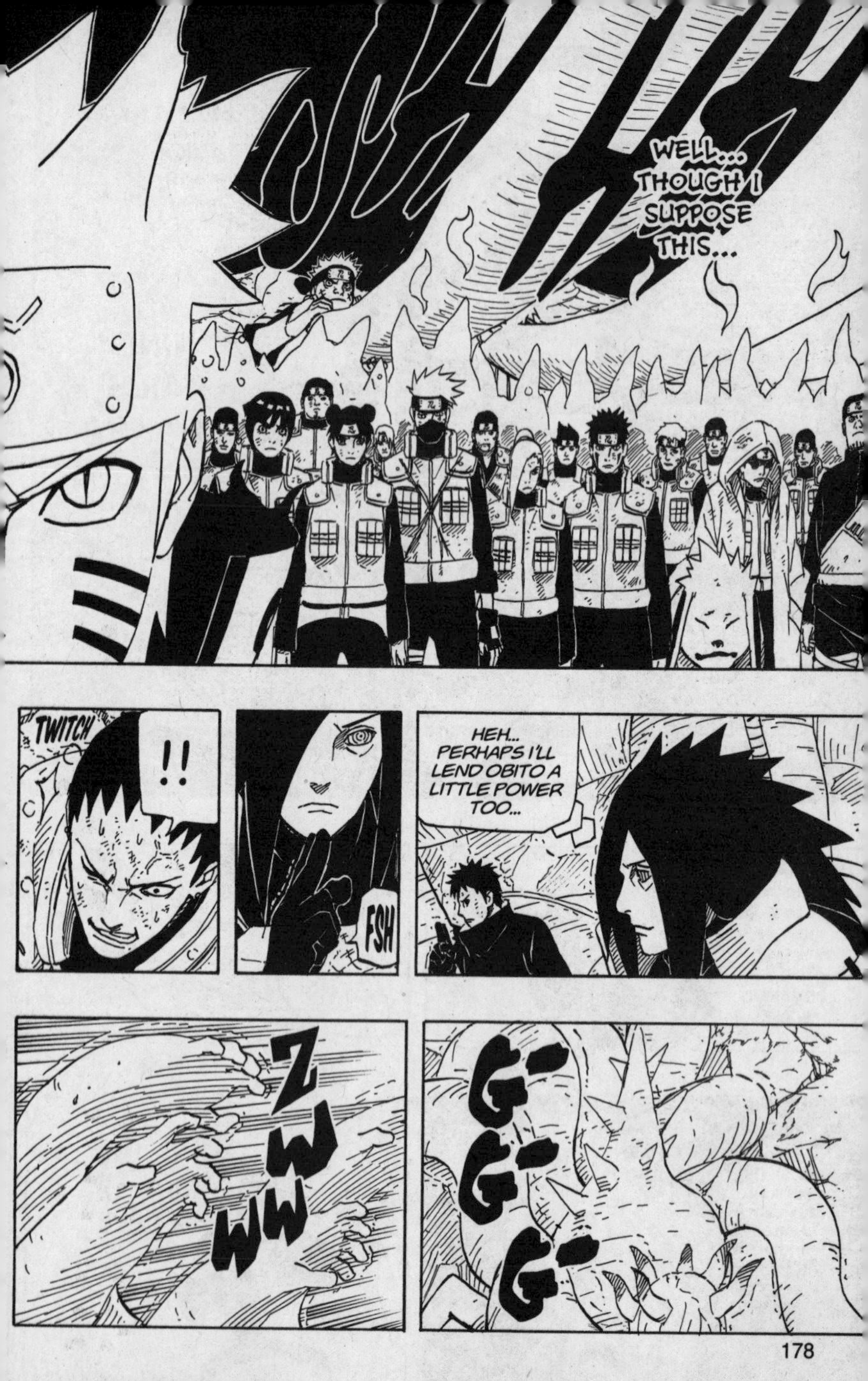
WELL... THOUGH I SUPPOSE THIS...
HEH... PERHAPS I'LL LEND OBITO A LITTLE POWER TOO...
FSH
!!
TWITCH
G-G-G-
ZWWW

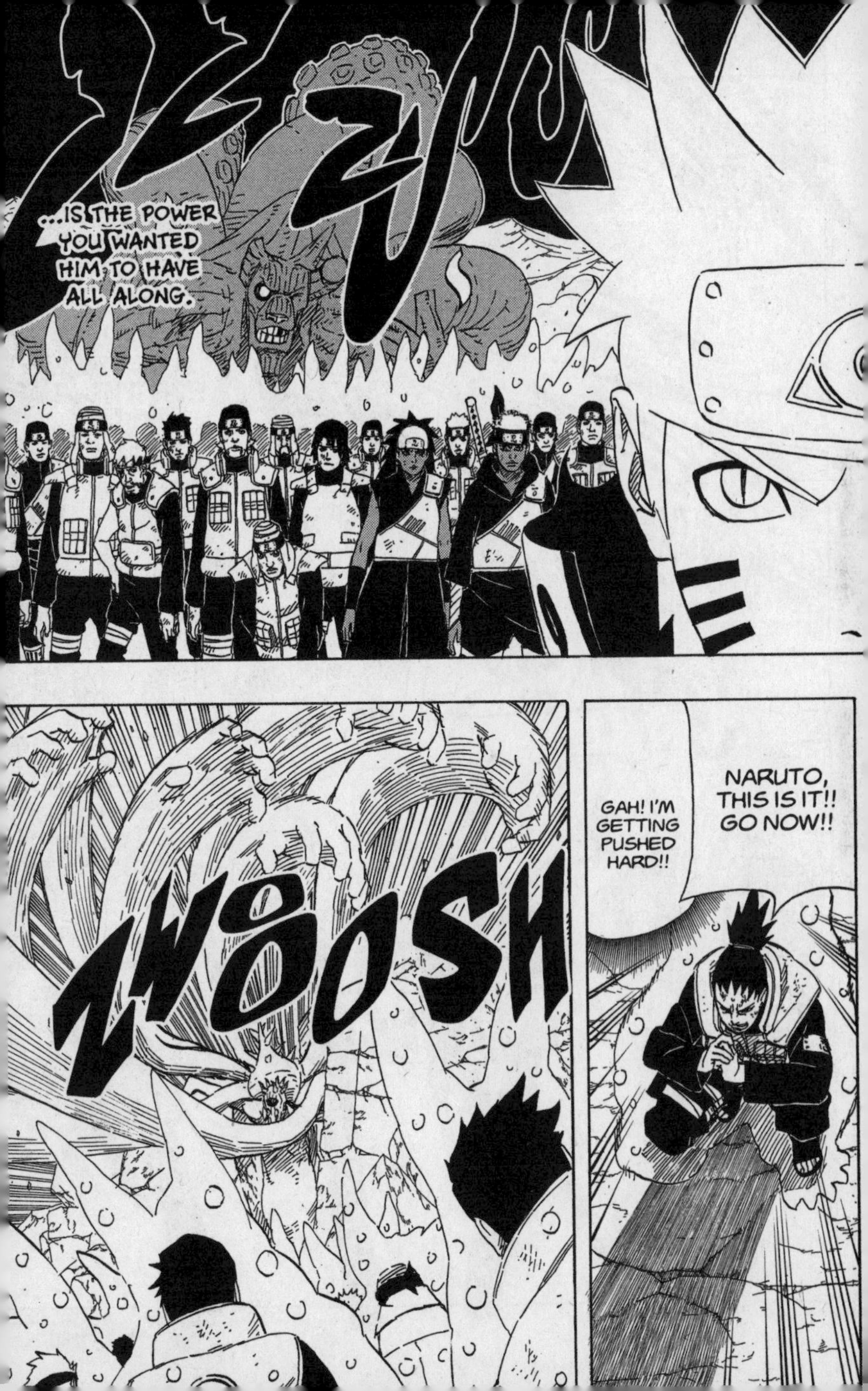
...IS THE POWER YOU WANTED HIM TO HAVE ALL ALONG.
NARUTO, THIS IS IT!! GO NOW!!
GAH! I'M GETTING PUSHED HARD!!
WHOOSH

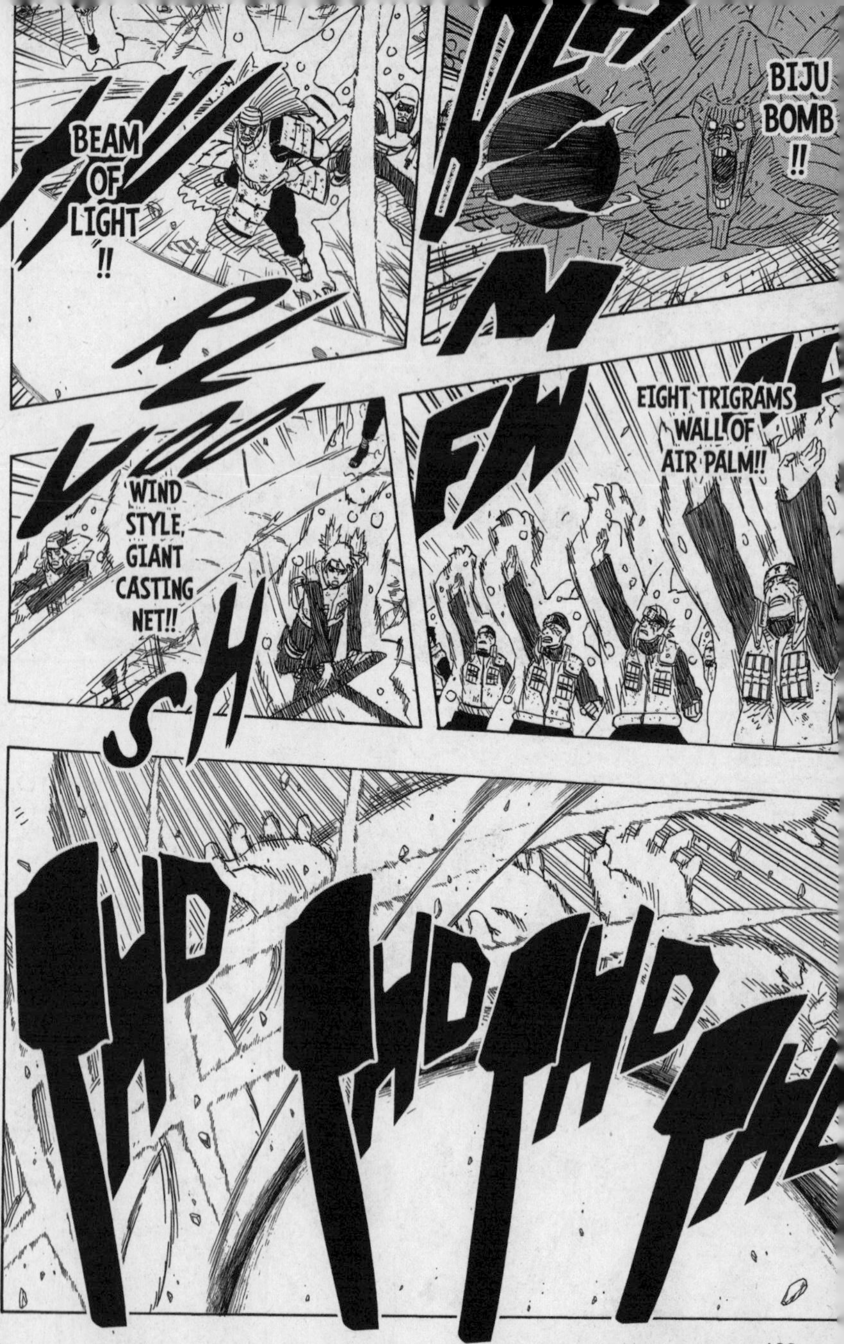
BIJU BOMB !!
BEAM OF LIGHT !!
EIGHT TRIGRAMS WALL OF AIR PALM!!
WIND STYLE, GIANT CASTING NET!!
THD
THD
THD
THD
TH

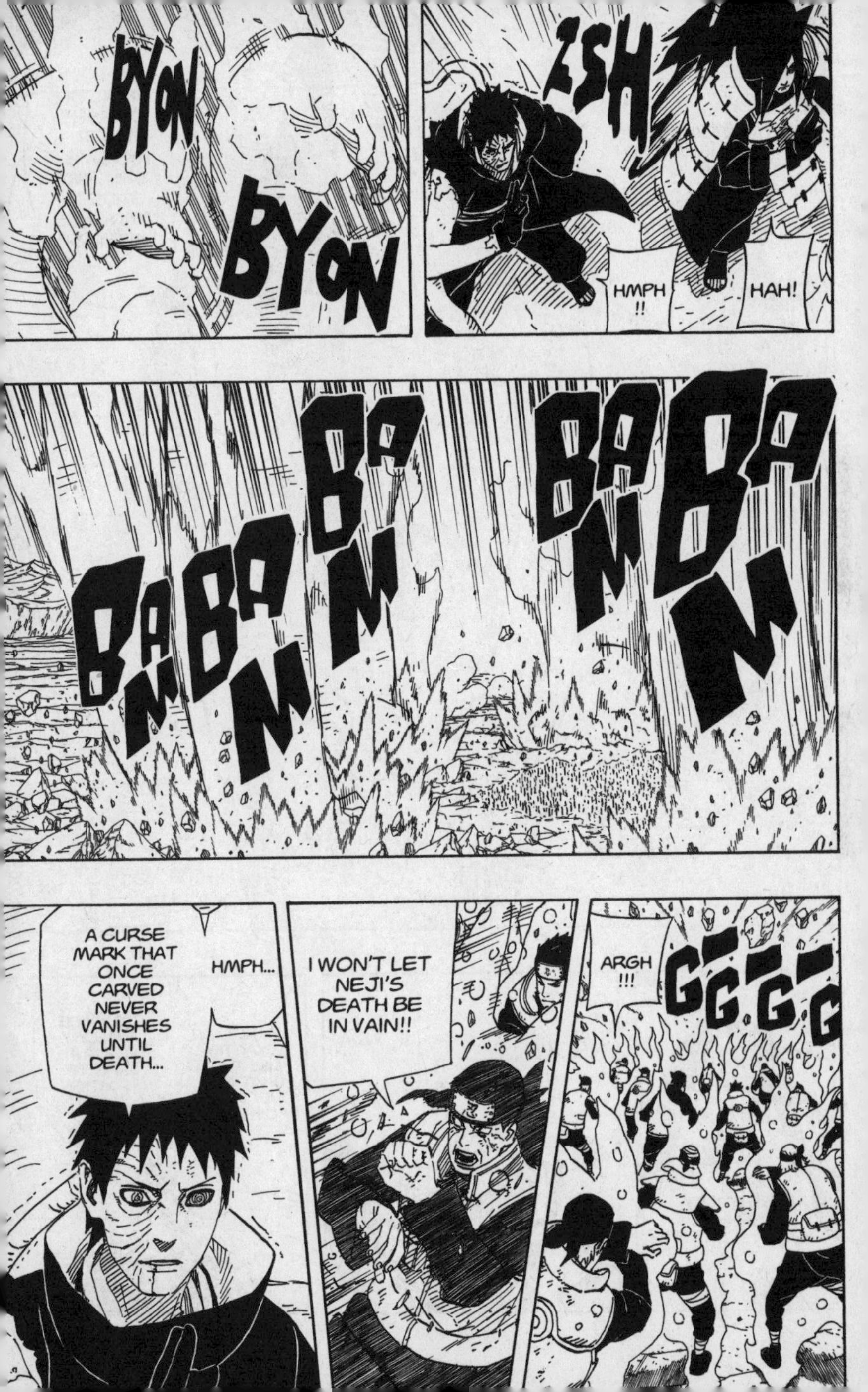
ISH
HAH!
HMPH !!
BYON
BYON
BABAM
BABAM
BABAM
BABAM
ARGH !!!
G-G-G-G
I WON'T LET NEJI'S DEATH BE IN VAIN!!
HMPH...
A CURSE MARK THAT ONCE CARVED NEVER VANISHES UNTIL DEATH...

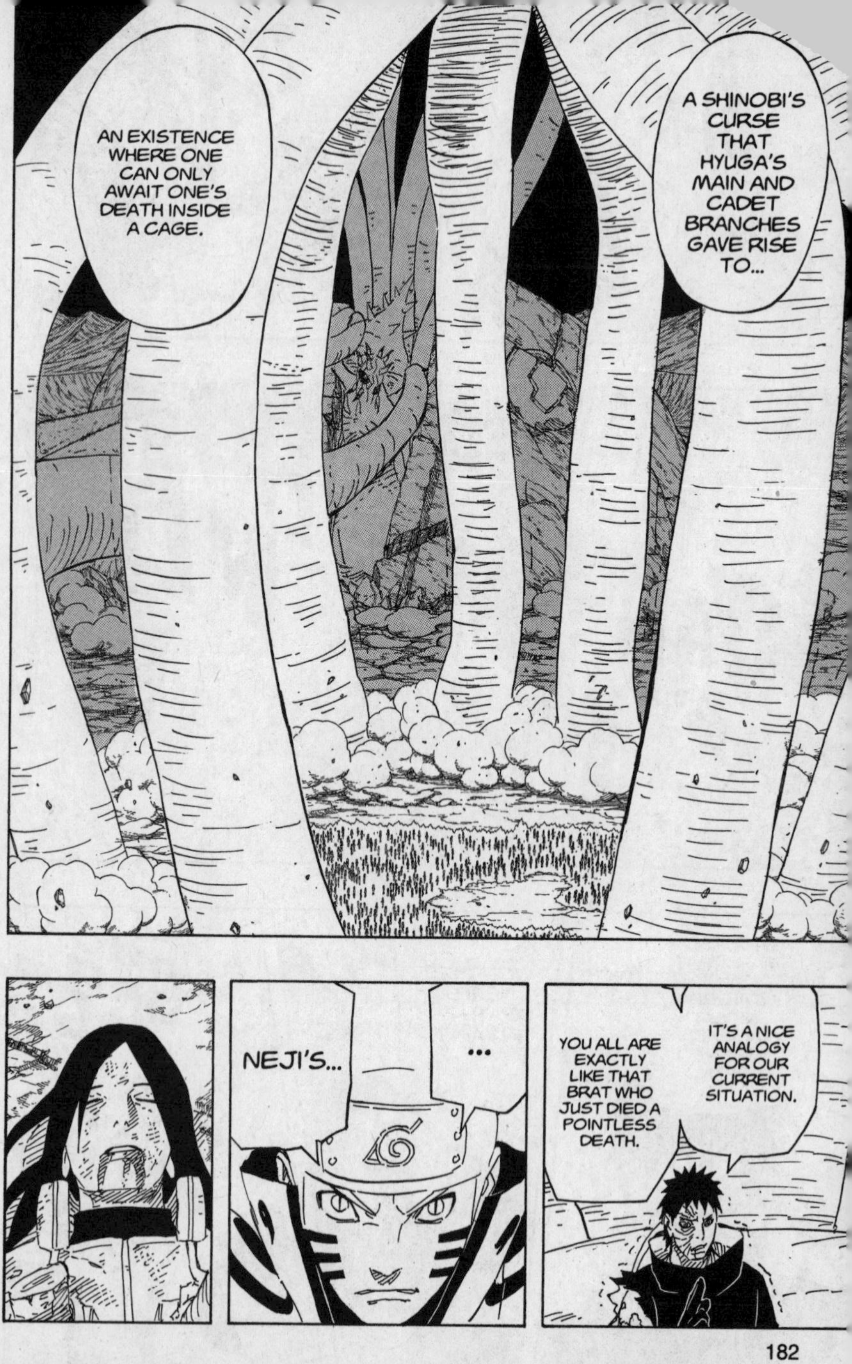
A SHINOBI'S CURSE THAT HYUGA'S MAIN AND CADET BRANCHES GAVE RISE TO...
AN EXISTENCE WHERE ONE CAN ONLY AWAIT ONE'S DEATH INSIDE A CAGE.
IT'S A NICE ANALOGY FOR OUR CURRENT SITUATION.
YOU ALL ARE EXACTLY LIKE THAT BRAT WHO JUST DIED A POINTLESS DEATH.
...
NEJI'S...

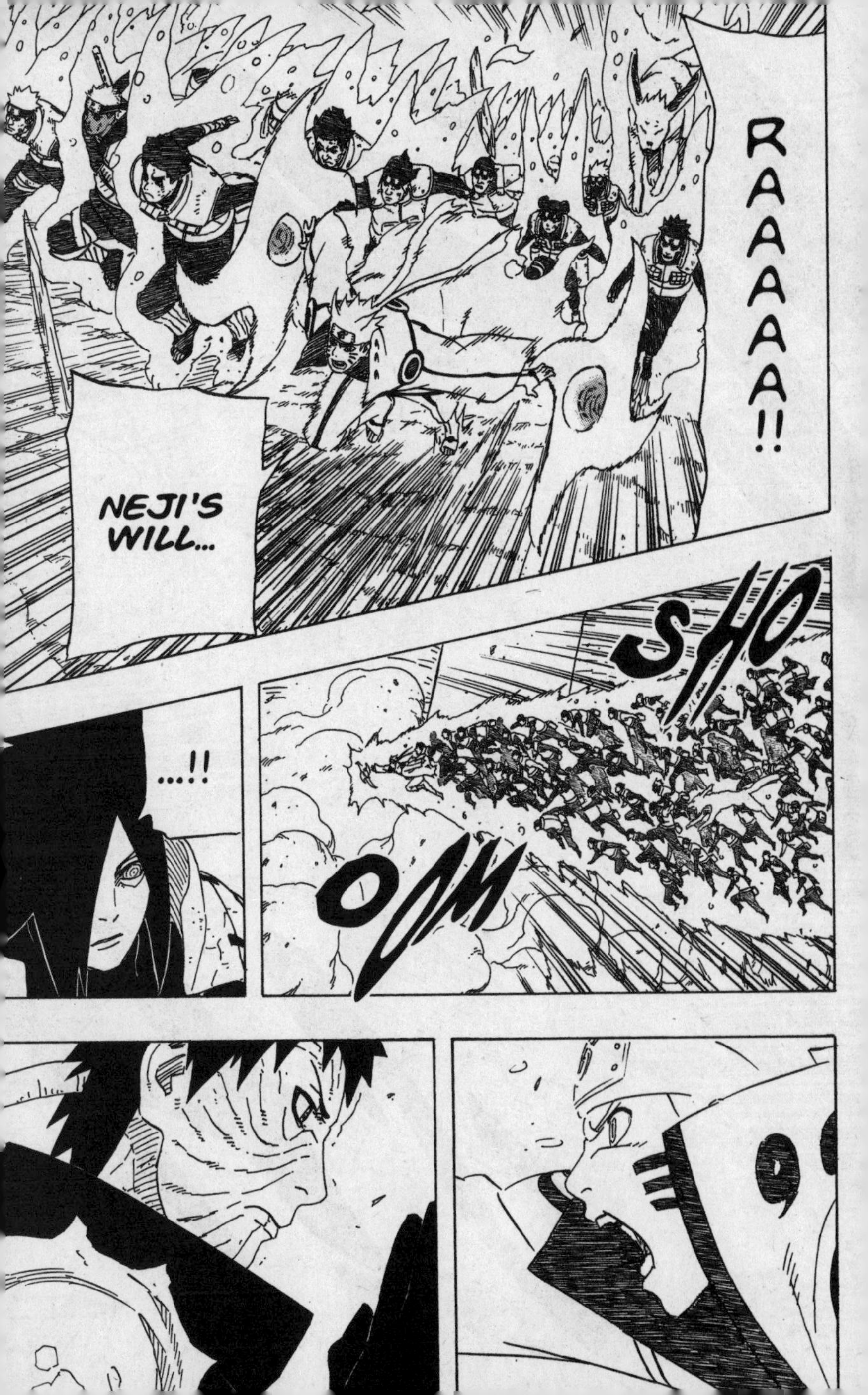
RAAAAA!!
NEJI'S WILL...
SHOOM
...!!

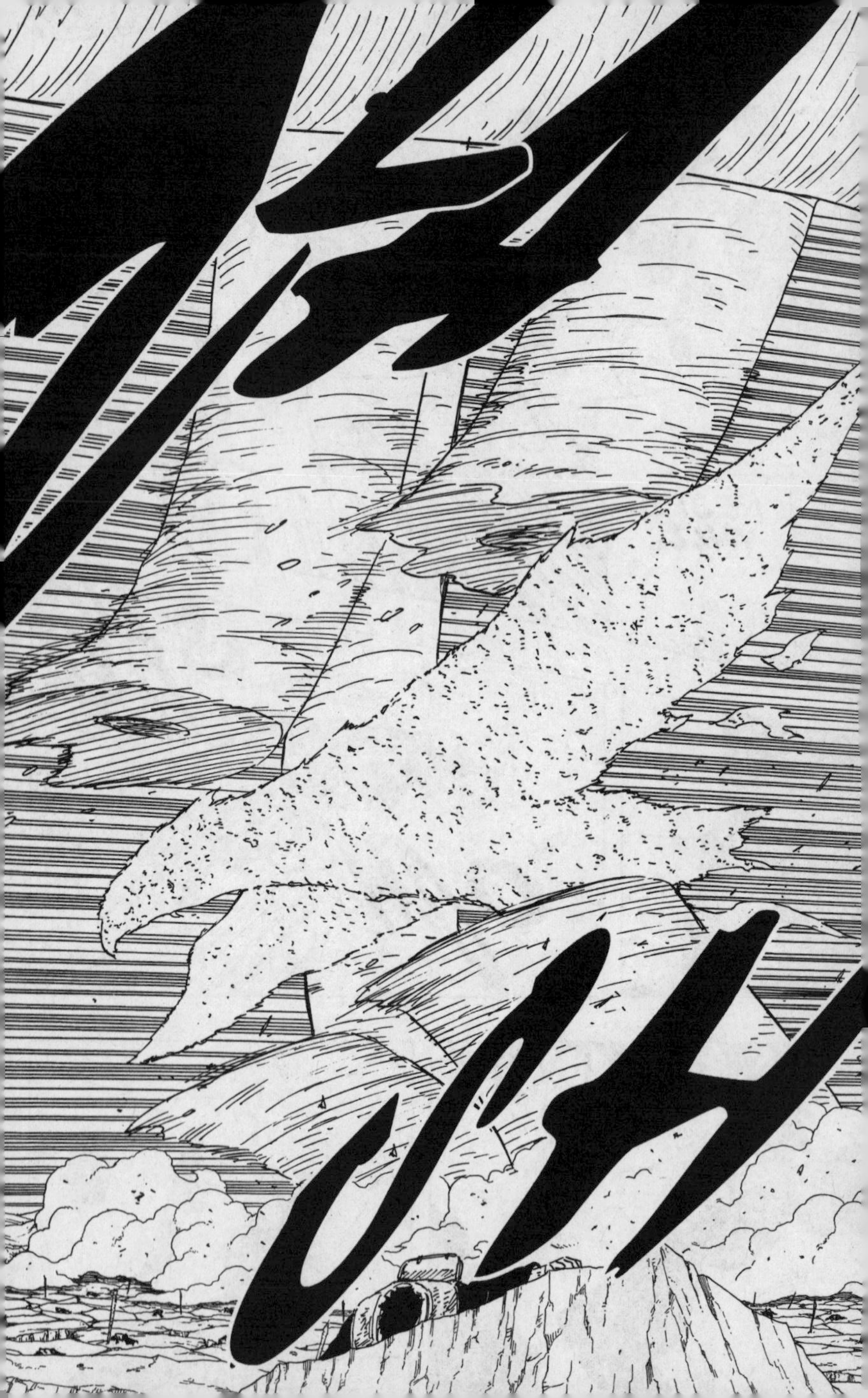

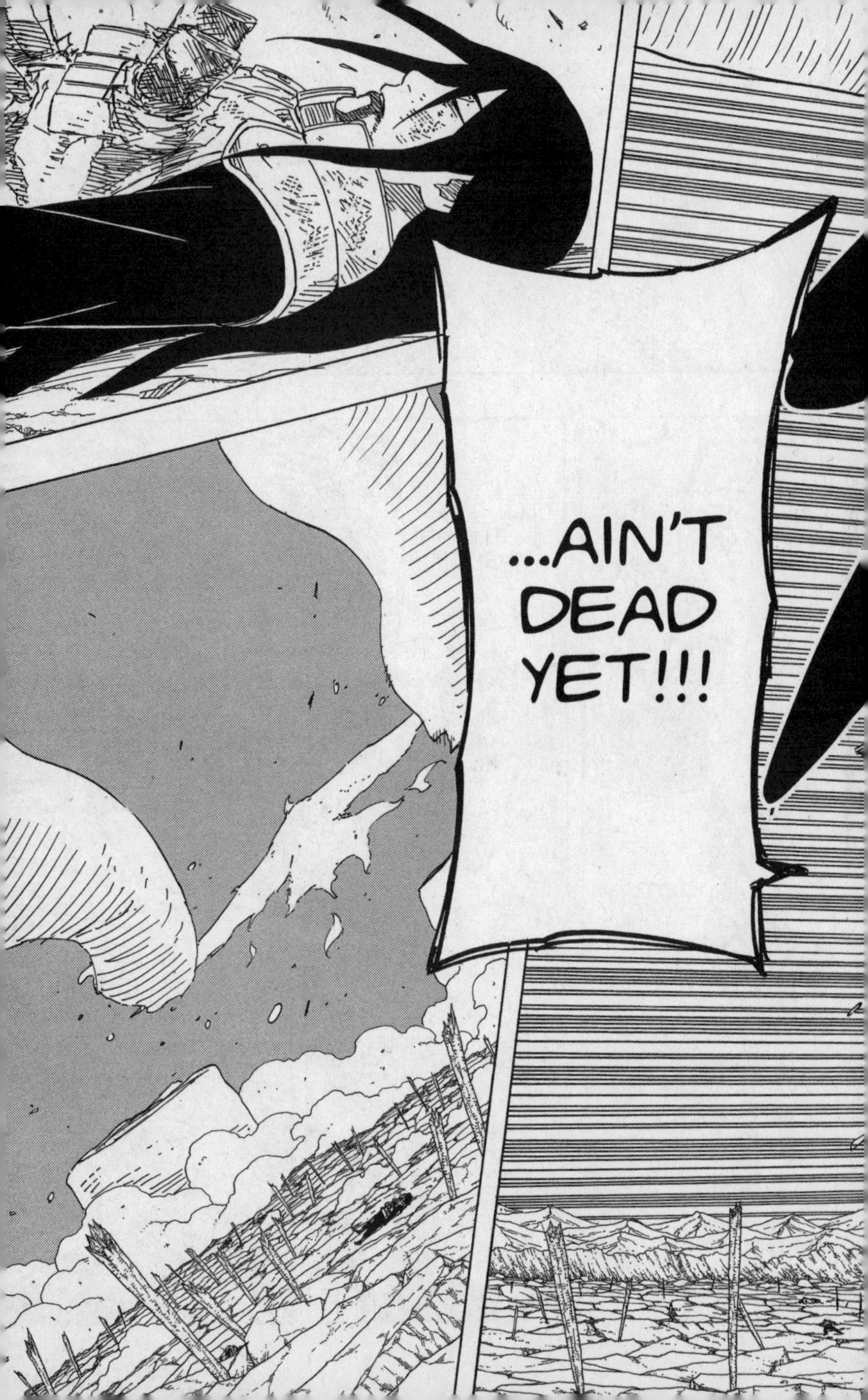
...AIN'T DEAD YET!!!

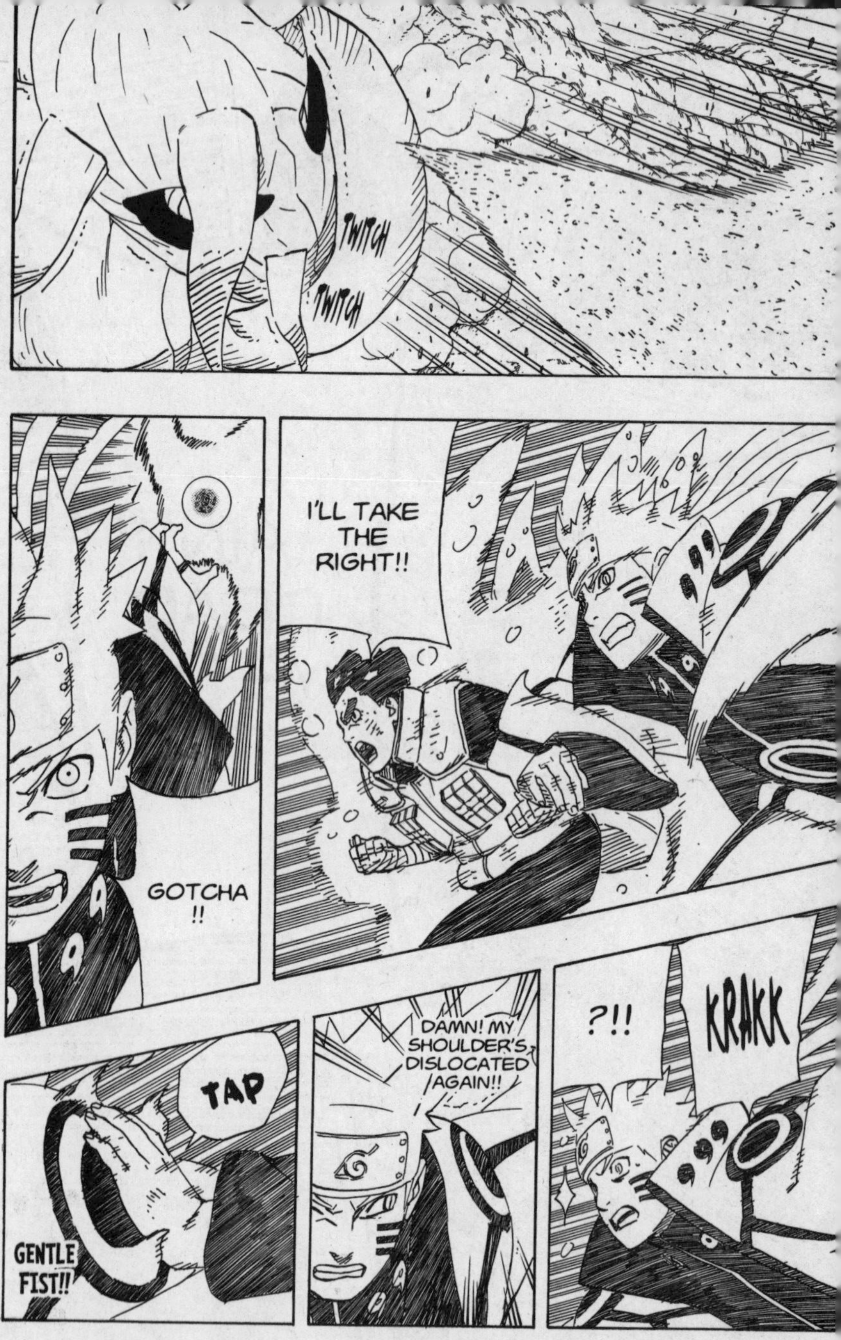
TWITCH
TWITCH
I'LL TAKE THE RIGHT!!
GOTCHA!!
KRAKK
?!!
DAMN! MY SHOULDER'S DISLOCATED AGAIN!!
TAP
GENTLE FIST!!

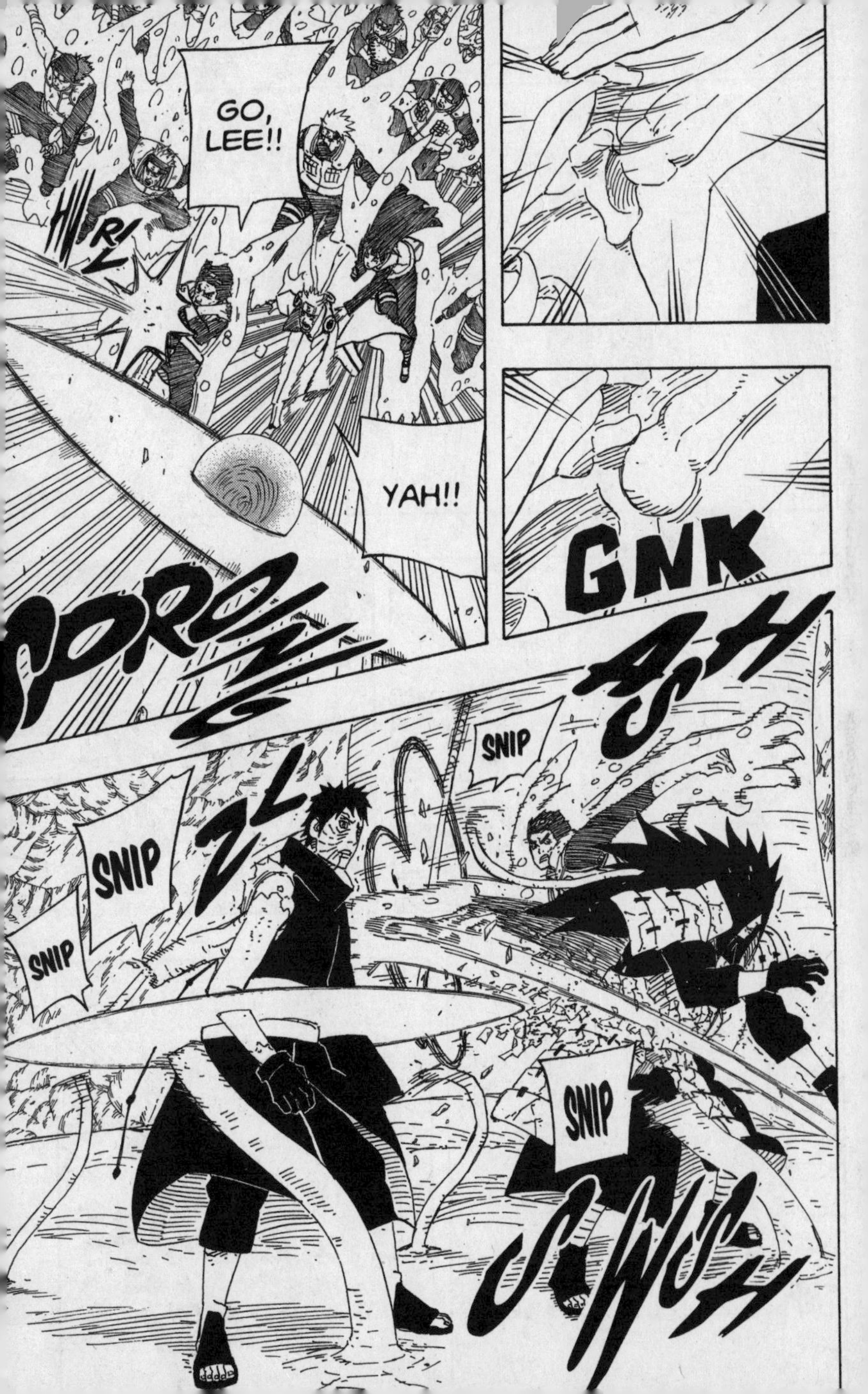
GNK
GO, LEE!!
YAH!!
SNIP
SNIP
SNIP
SNIP

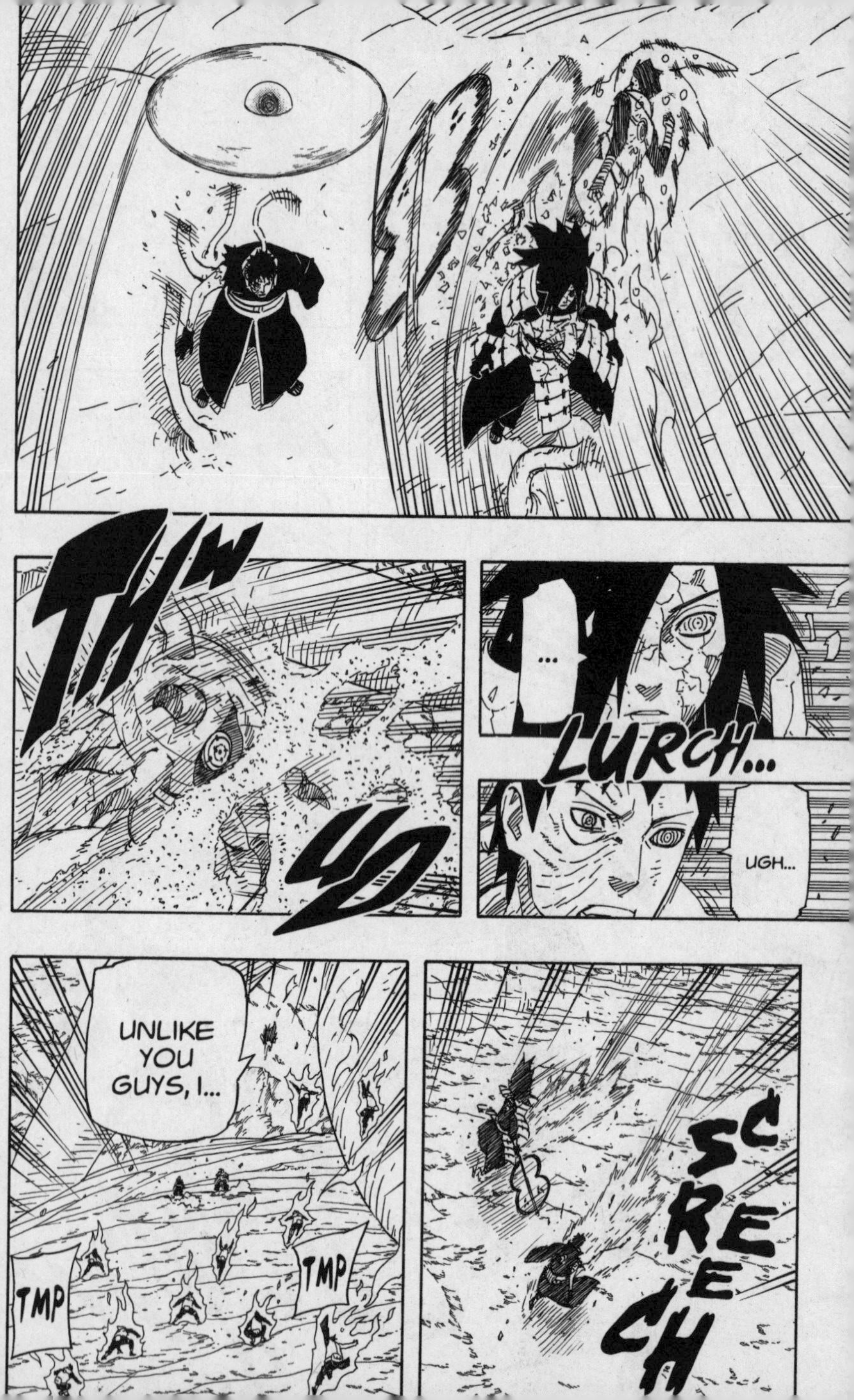
...
LURCH...
UGH...
THWUD
SCREECH
UNLIKE YOU GUYS, I...
TMP
TMP

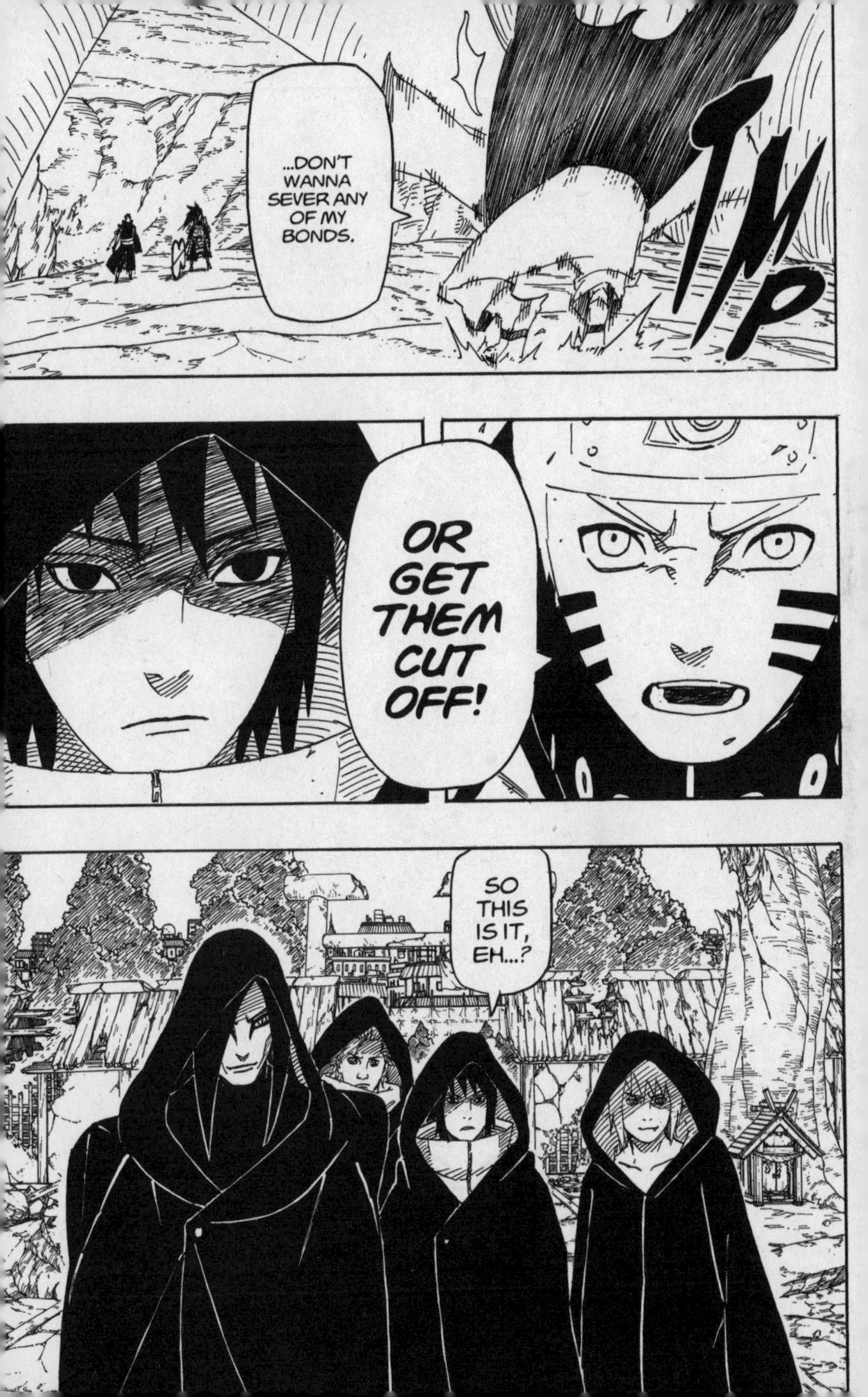
TMP
...DON'T WANNA SEVER ANY OF MY BONDS.
OR GET THEM CUT OFF!
SO THIS IS IT, EH...?

NARUTO

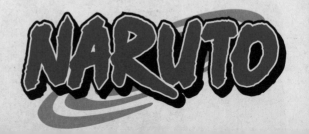

岸本斉史

I've recently starting going out to eat with my assistants after work. Once we get our drinks I always end up leading the toast... but my assistants' eyes seem to be stating that simply saying "thanks for your hard work today" is somewhat insufficient... Ah, but there ain't much variation that can be had there!!!

—Masashi Kishimoto, 2013

NARUTO

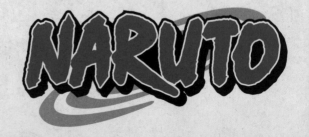

SHON[redacted]DITION

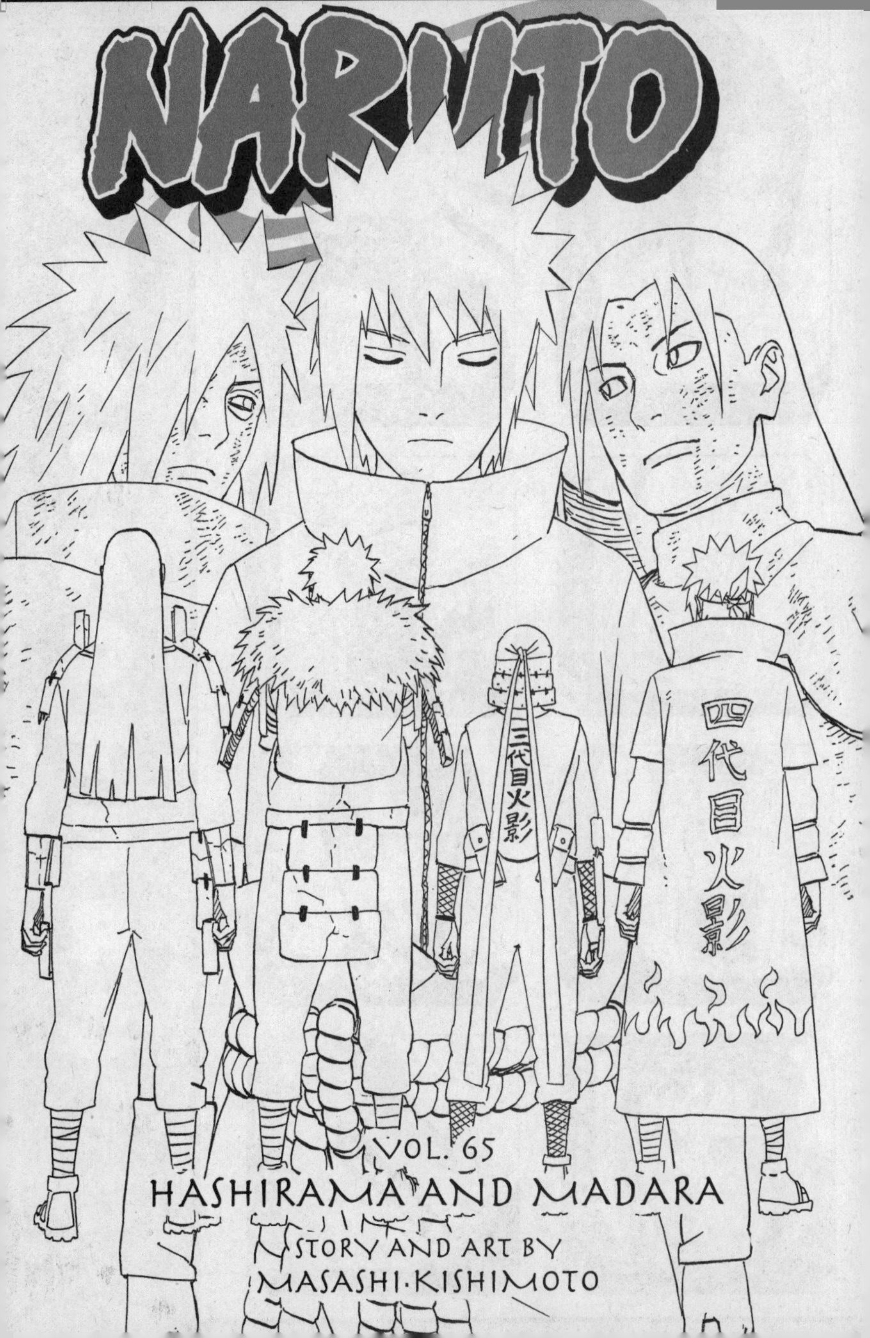
NARUTO
VOL. 65
HASHIRAMA AND MADARA
STORY AND ART BY
MASASHI·KISHIMOTO

Naruto うずまきナルト

Sasuke うちはサスケ

Sakura 春野サクラ

Kakashi はたけカカシ

Yamato ヤマト

Sai サイ

Obito うちはオビト

Kurama 九喇嘛

CHARACTERS

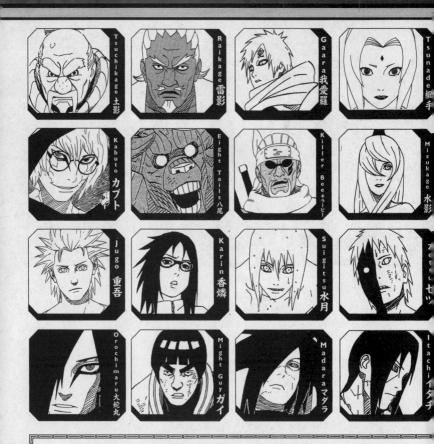

Tsunade 綱手
Gaara 我愛羅
Raikage 雷影
Tsuchikage 土影
Mizukage 水影
Killer Bee キラービー
Eight Tails 八尾
Kabuto カブト
Zetsu ゼツ
Suigitsu 水月
Karin 香燐
Jugo 重吾
Itachi イタチ
Madara マダラ
Might Guy ガイ
Orochimaru 大蛇丸

THE STORY SO FAR...

Naruto, the biggest troublemaker at the Ninja Academy in the Village of Konohagakure, finally becomes a ninja along with his classmates Sasuke and Sakura. They grow and mature through countless trials and battles. However, Sasuke, unable to give up his quest for vengeance, leaves Konohagakure to seek Orochimaru and his power…

Two years pass. Naruto grows up and engages in fierce battles against the Tailed Beast-targeting Akatsuki. Elsewhere, after winning the heroic battle against Itachi and learning his older brother's true intentions, Sasuke allies with the Akatsuki and sets out to destroy Konoha.

The Fourth Great Ninja War against the Akatsuki begins. Having stopped the Edotensei jutsu with the help of his brother, Sasuke now heads off with Orochimaru to fullfil a new objective. Meanwhile, Naruto and his allies try to stop Obito and Madara from reviving Ten Tails. And what will Sasuke's next move be?!

NARUTO

VOL. 65
HASHIRAMA AND MADARA

CONTENTS

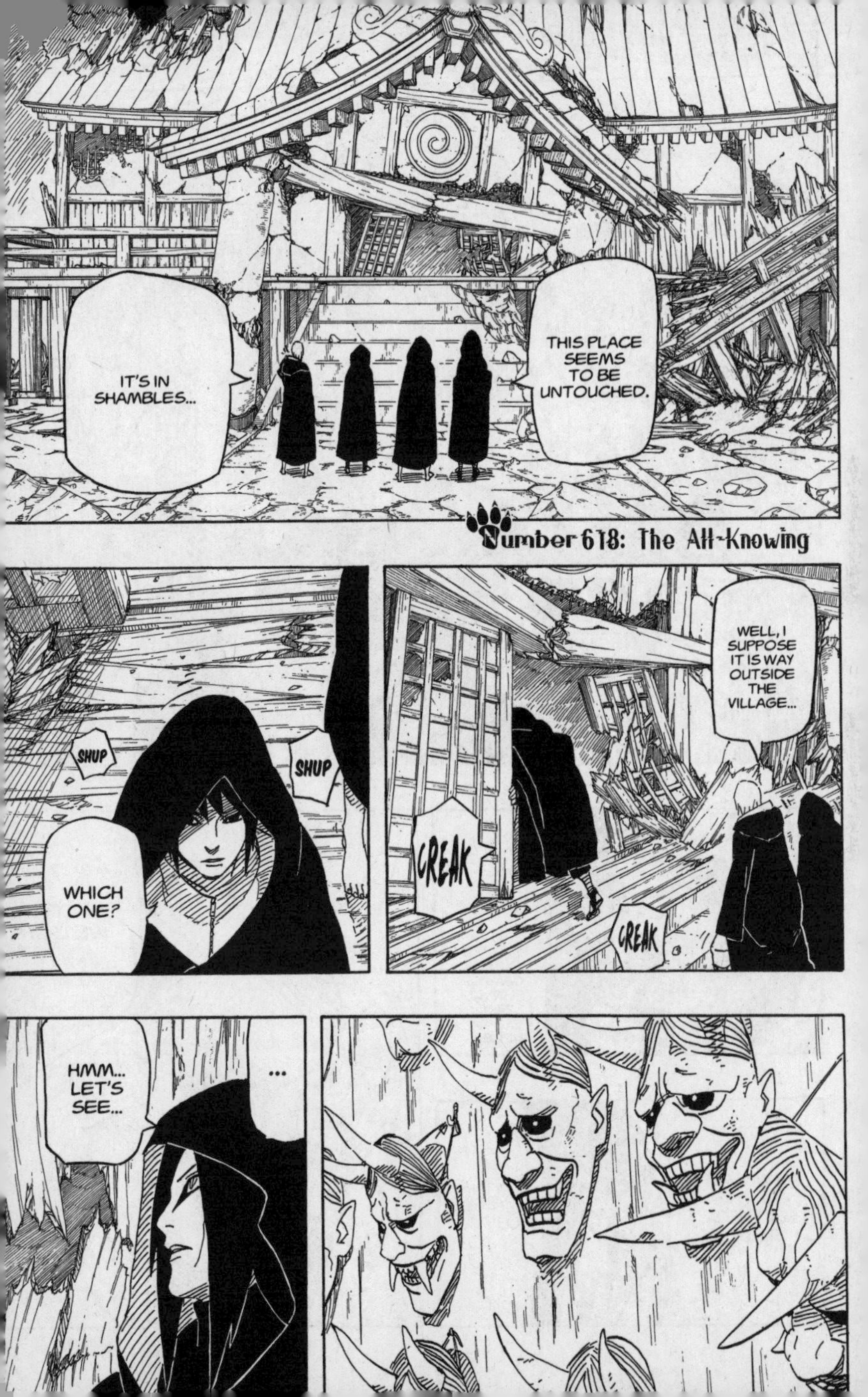
THIS PLACE SEEMS TO BE UNTOUCHED.
IT'S IN SHAMBLES...
Number 618: The All-Knowing
WELL, I SUPPOSE IT IS WAY OUTSIDE THE VILLAGE...
CREAK
CREAK
SHUP
SHUP
WHICH ONE?
...
HMM... LET'S SEE...

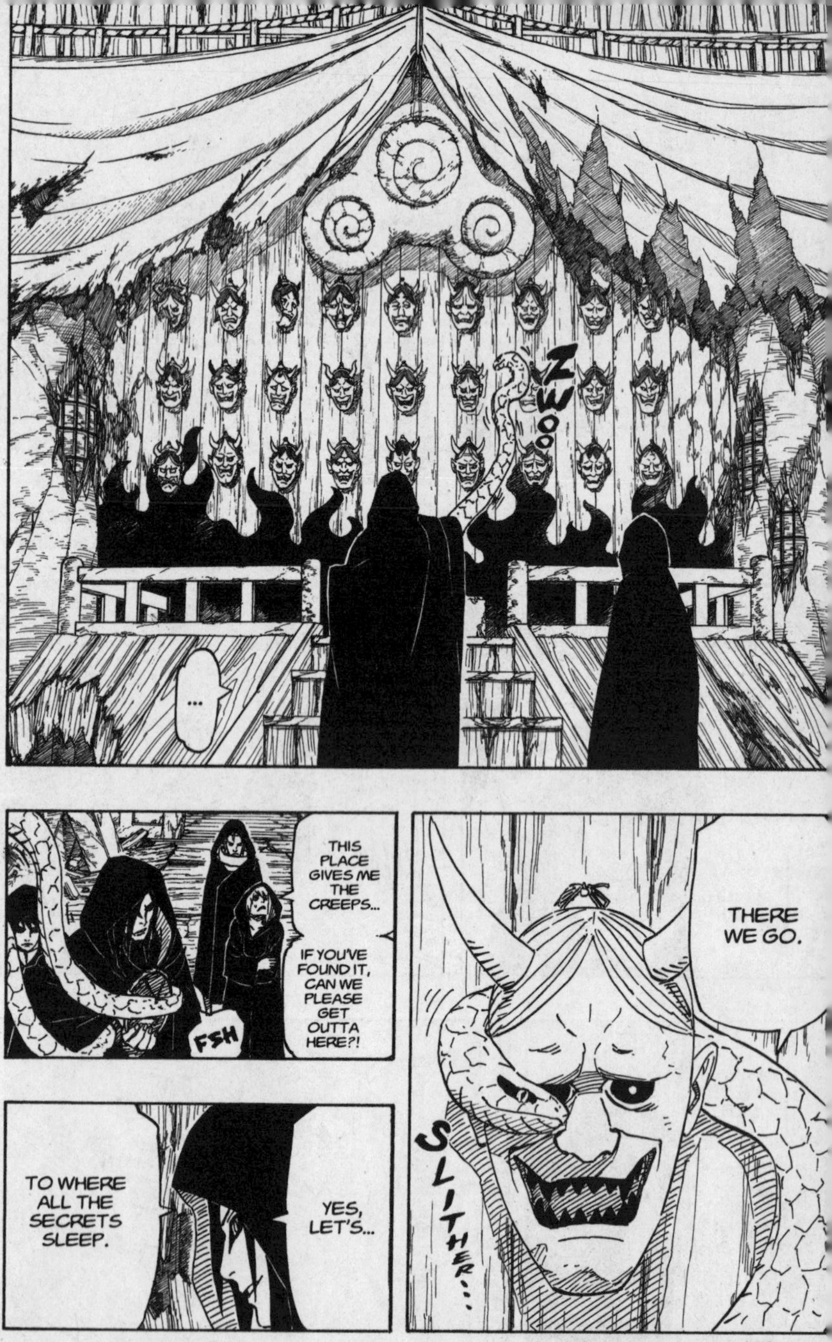
ZWOO
...
THERE WE GO.
SLITHER...
THIS PLACE GIVES ME THE CREEPS...
IF YOU'VE FOUND IT, CAN WE PLEASE GET OUTTA HERE?!
FSH
YES, LET'S...
TO WHERE ALL THE SECRETS SLEEP.

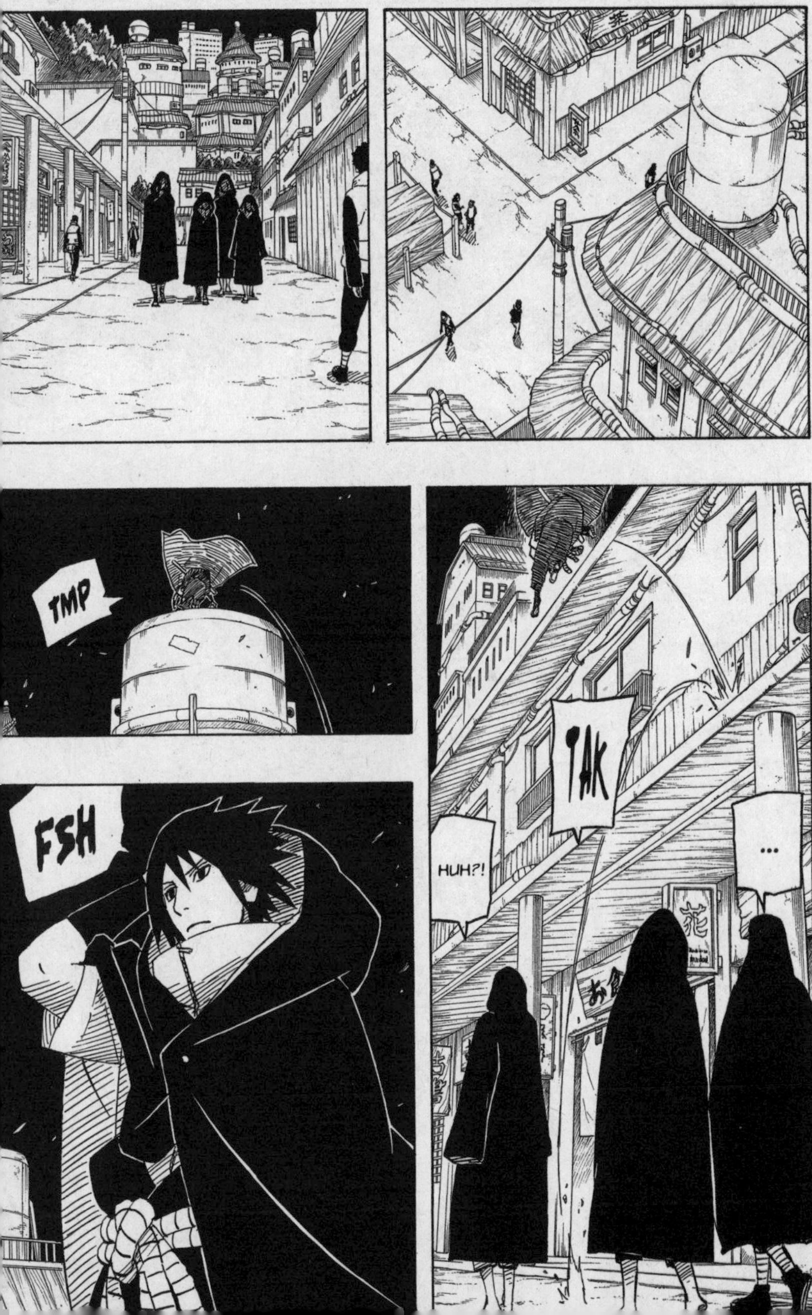
TAK
...
HUH?!
TMP
FSH

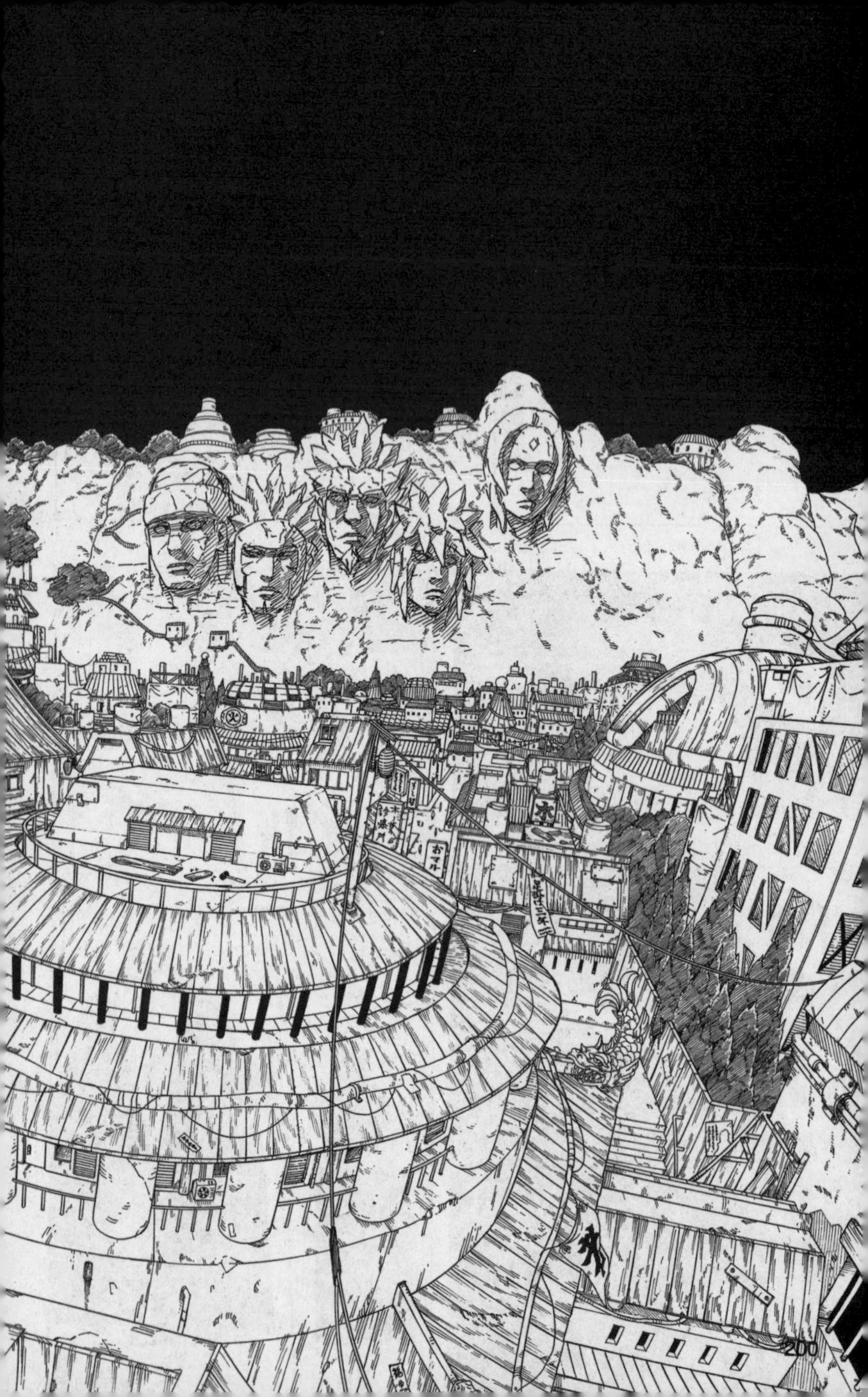

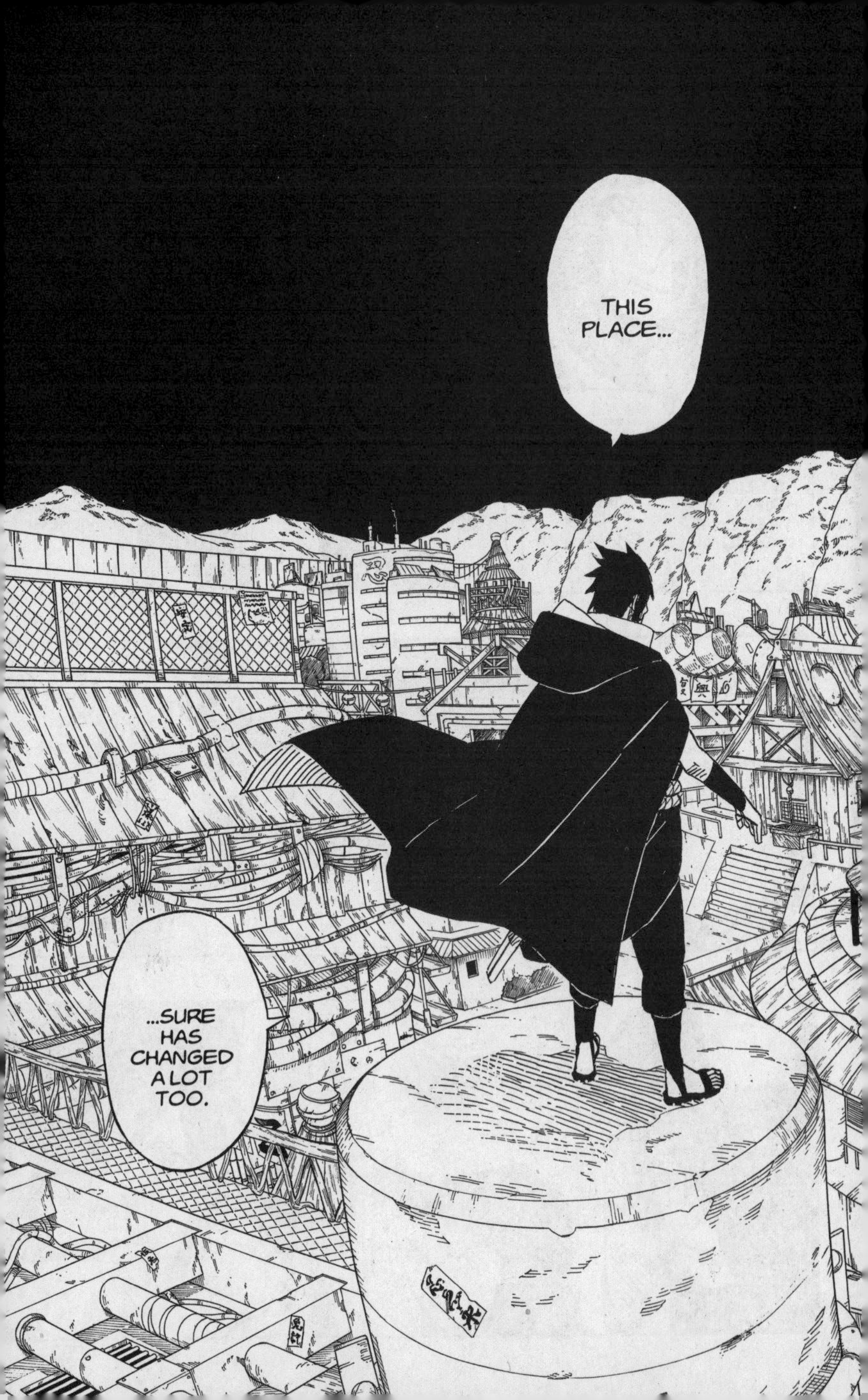
THIS PLACE...
...SURE HAS CHANGED A LOT TOO.

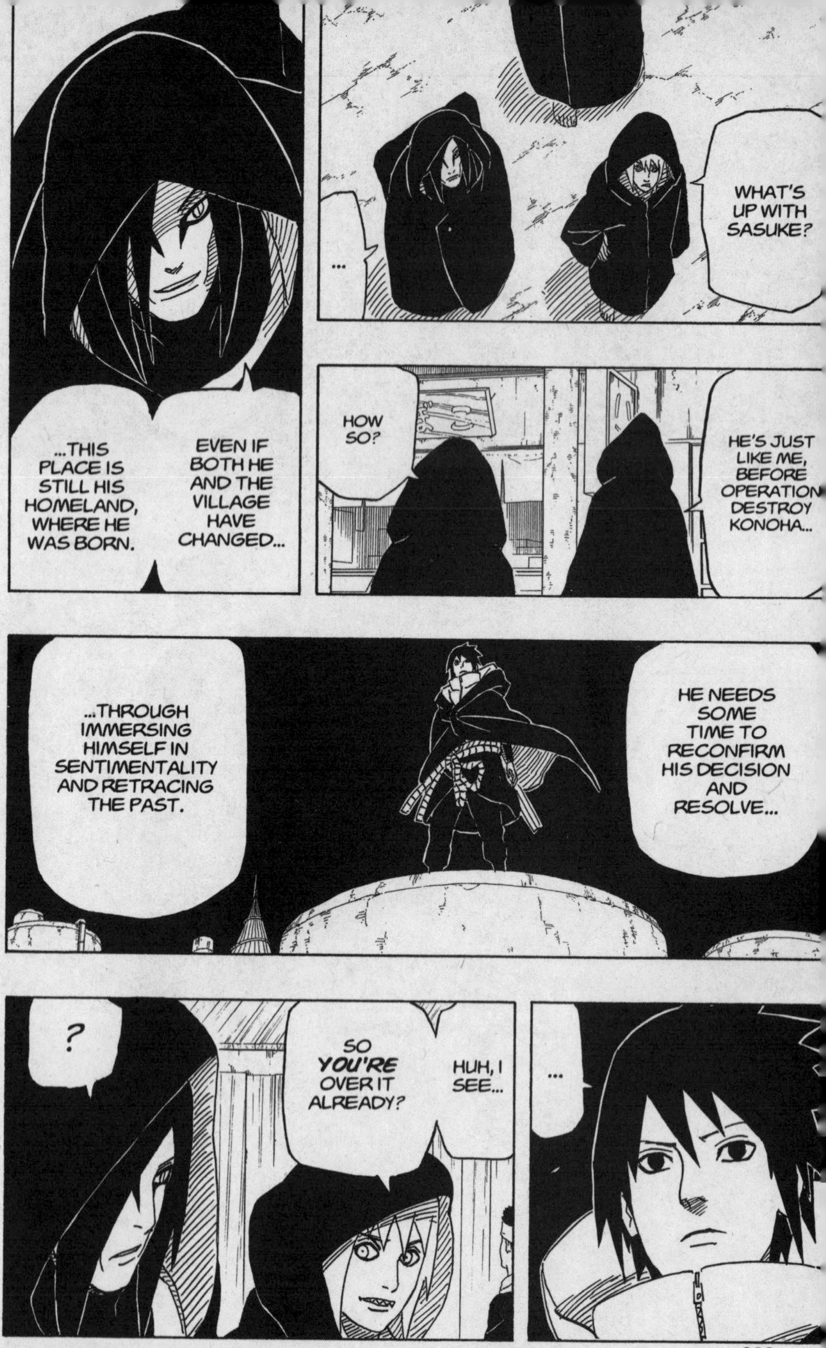
WHAT'S UP WITH SASUKE?
...
HE'S JUST LIKE ME, BEFORE OPERATION DESTROY KONOHA...
HOW SO?
EVEN IF BOTH HE AND THE VILLAGE HAVE CHANGED...
...THIS PLACE IS STILL HIS HOMELAND, WHERE HE WAS BORN.
HE NEEDS SOME TIME TO RECONFIRM HIS DECISION AND RESOLVE...
...THROUGH IMMERSING HIMSELF IN SENTIMENTALITY AND RETRACING THE PAST.
...
HUH, I SEE...
SO *YOU'RE* OVER IT ALREADY?
?

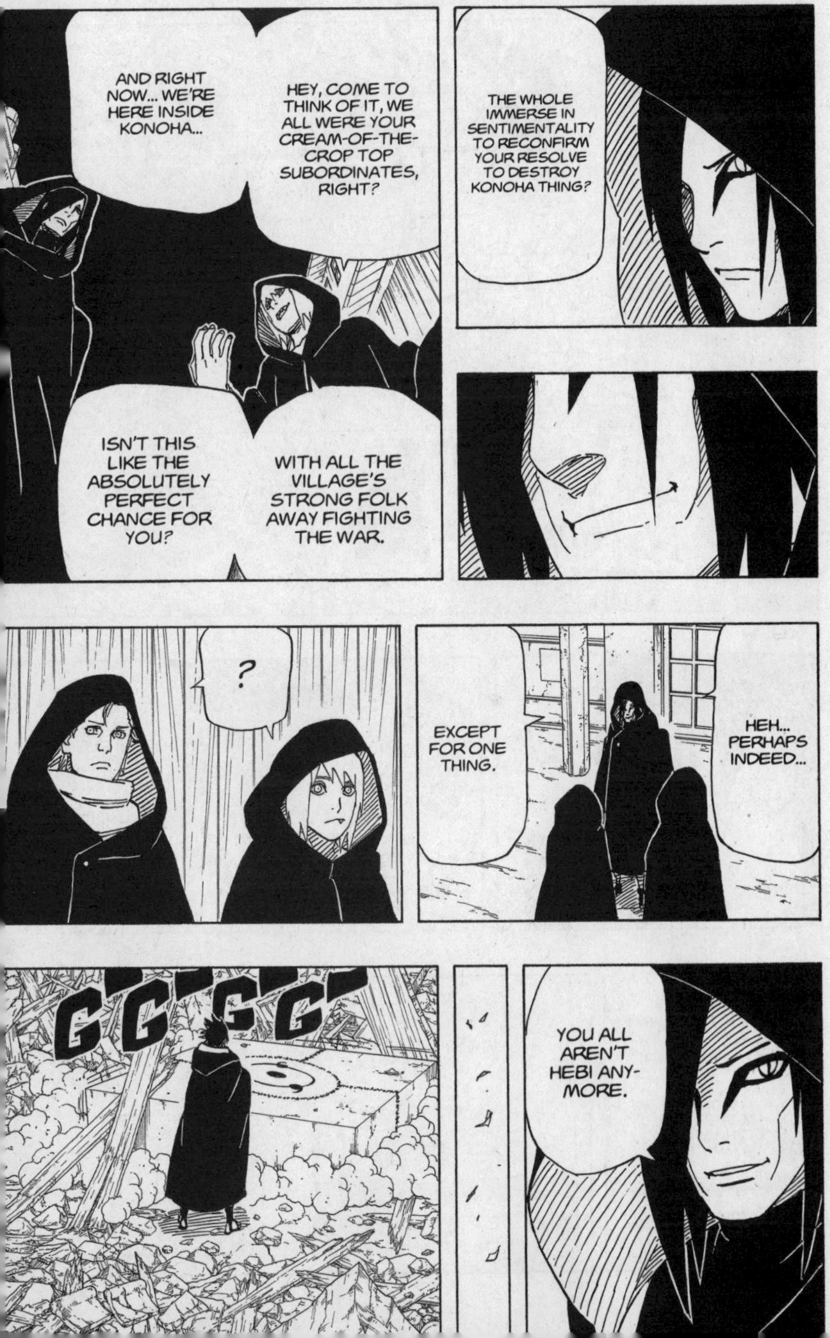
THE WHOLE IMMERSE IN SENTIMENTALITY TO RECONFIRM YOUR RESOLVE TO DESTROY KONOHA THING?
HEY, COME TO THINK OF IT, WE ALL WERE YOUR CREAM-OF-THE-CROP TOP SUBORDINATES, RIGHT?
AND RIGHT NOW... WE'RE HERE INSIDE KONOHA...
WITH ALL THE VILLAGE'S STRONG FOLK AWAY FIGHTING THE WAR.
ISN'T THIS LIKE THE ABSOLUTELY PERFECT CHANCE FOR YOU?
HEH... PERHAPS INDEED...
EXCEPT FOR ONE THING.
?
YOU ALL AREN'T HEBI ANY-MORE.
GGGG

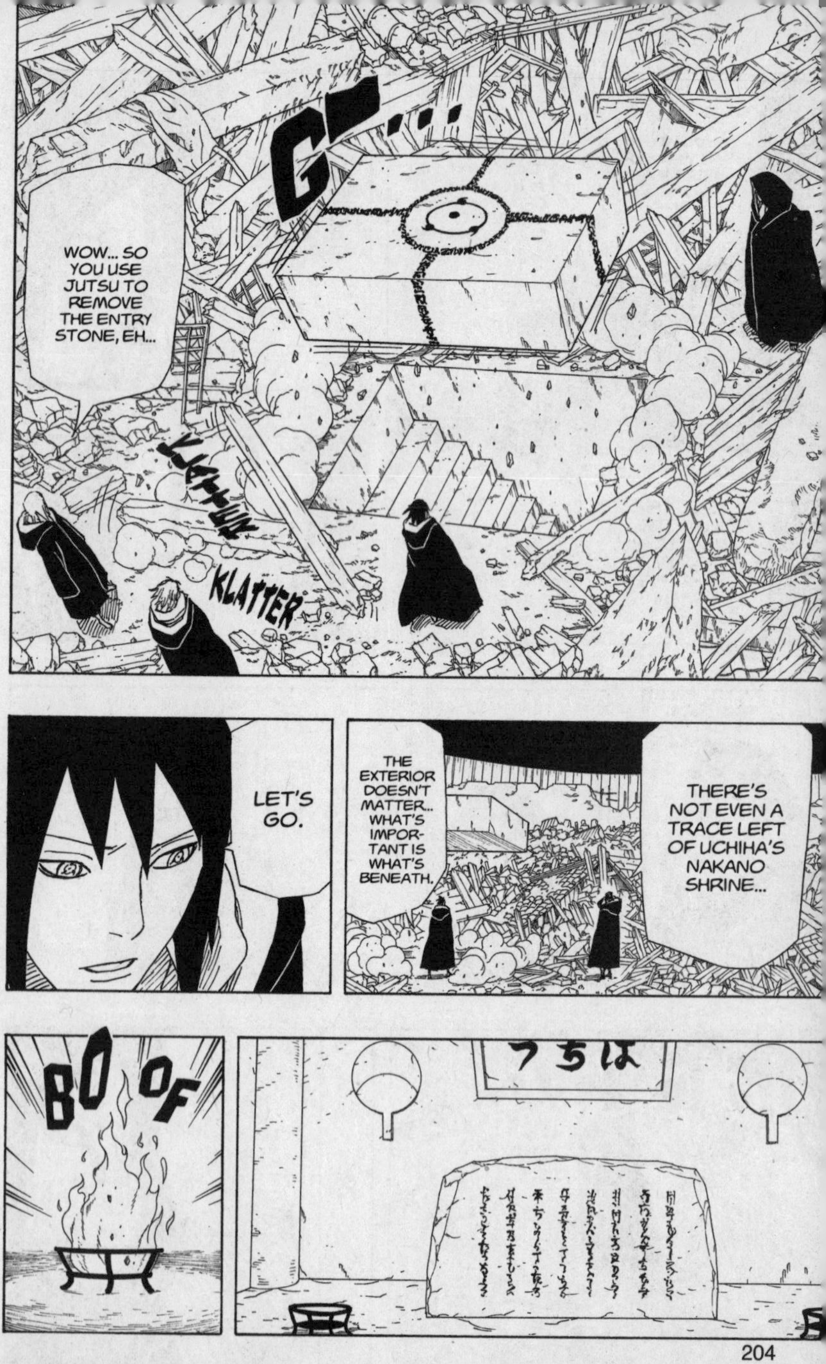
WOW... SO YOU USE JUTSU TO REMOVE THE ENTRY STONE, EH...
KLATTER
KLATTER
THERE'S NOT EVEN A TRACE LEFT OF UCHIHA'S NAKANO SHRINE...
THE EXTERIOR DOESN'T MATTER.. WHAT'S IMPORTANT IS WHAT'S BENEATH.
LET'S GO.
うちは
BOOF

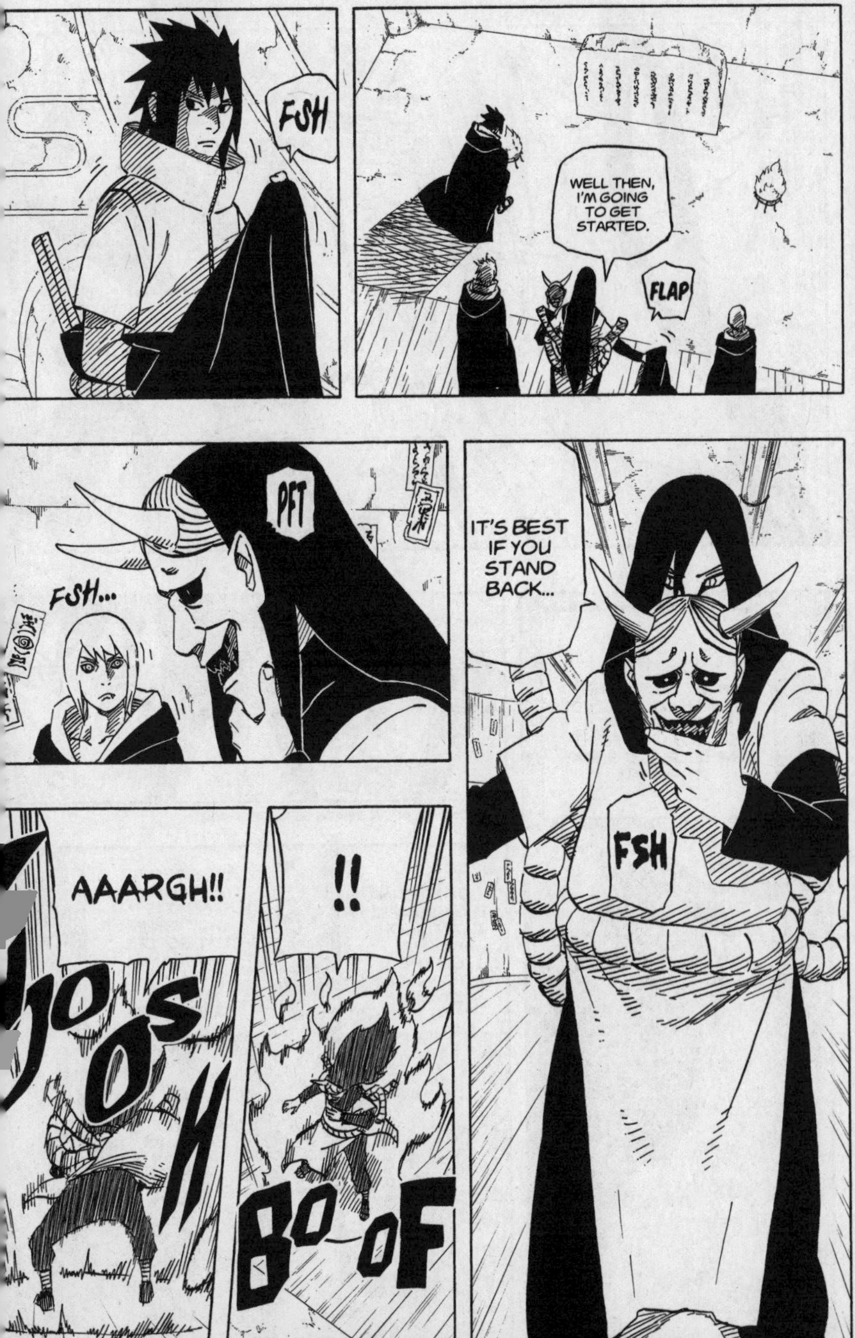
WELL THEN, I'M GOING TO GET STARTED.
FLAP
FSH
IT'S BEST IF YOU STAND BACK...
FSH
PFT
FSH...
!!
BO-OF
AAARGH!!

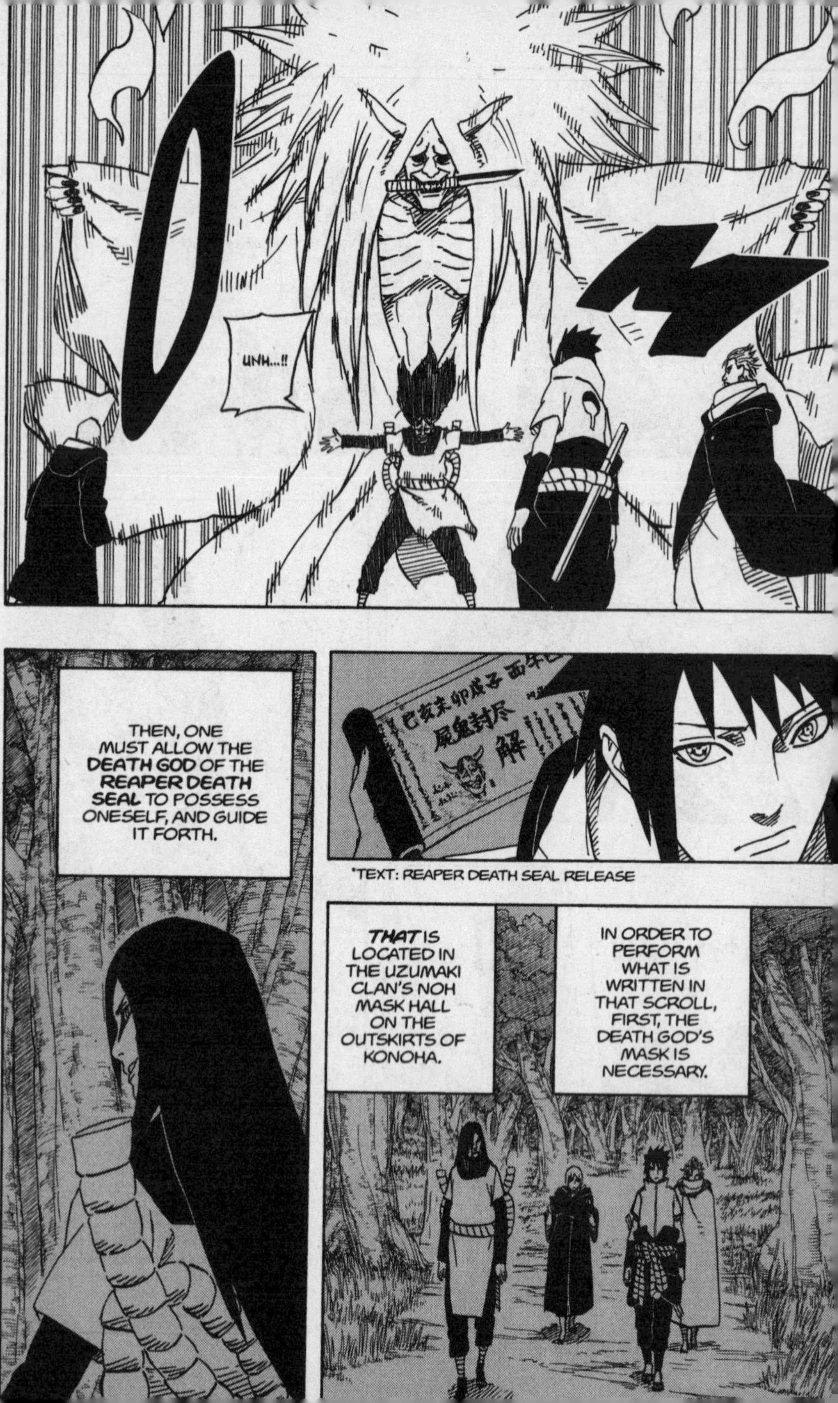
UNH...!!
*TEXT: REAPER DEATH SEAL RELEASE
IN ORDER TO PERFORM WHAT IS WRITTEN IN THAT SCROLL, FIRST, THE DEATH GOD'S MASK IS NECESSARY.
THAT IS LOCATED IN THE UZUMAKI CLAN'S NOH MASK HALL ON THE OUTSKIRTS OF KONOHA.
THEN, ONE MUST ALLOW THE DEATH GOD OF THE REAPER DEATH SEAL TO POSSESS ONESELF, AND GUIDE IT FORTH.

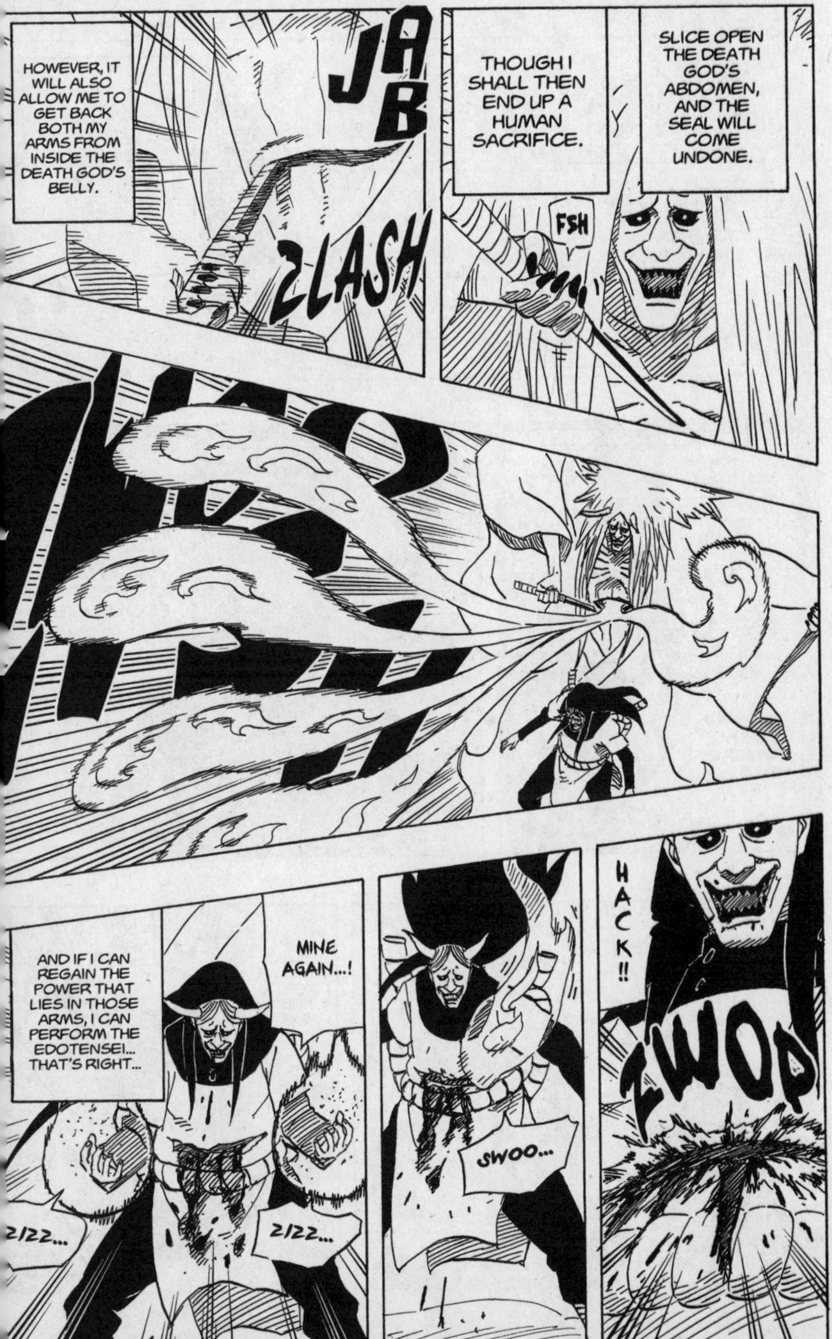
SLICE OPEN THE DEATH GOD'S ABDOMEN, AND THE SEAL WILL COME UNDONE.
THOUGH I SHALL THEN END UP A HUMAN SACRIFICE.
FSH
JAB
HOWEVER, IT WILL ALSO ALLOW ME TO GET BACK BOTH MY ARMS FROM INSIDE THE DEATH GOD'S BELLY.
ZLASH
HACK!!
ZWOP
SWOO...
MINE AGAIN...!
AND IF I CAN REGAIN THE POWER THAT LIES IN THOSE ARMS, I CAN PERFORM THE EDOTENSEI... THAT'S RIGHT...
ZIZZ...
ZIZZ...

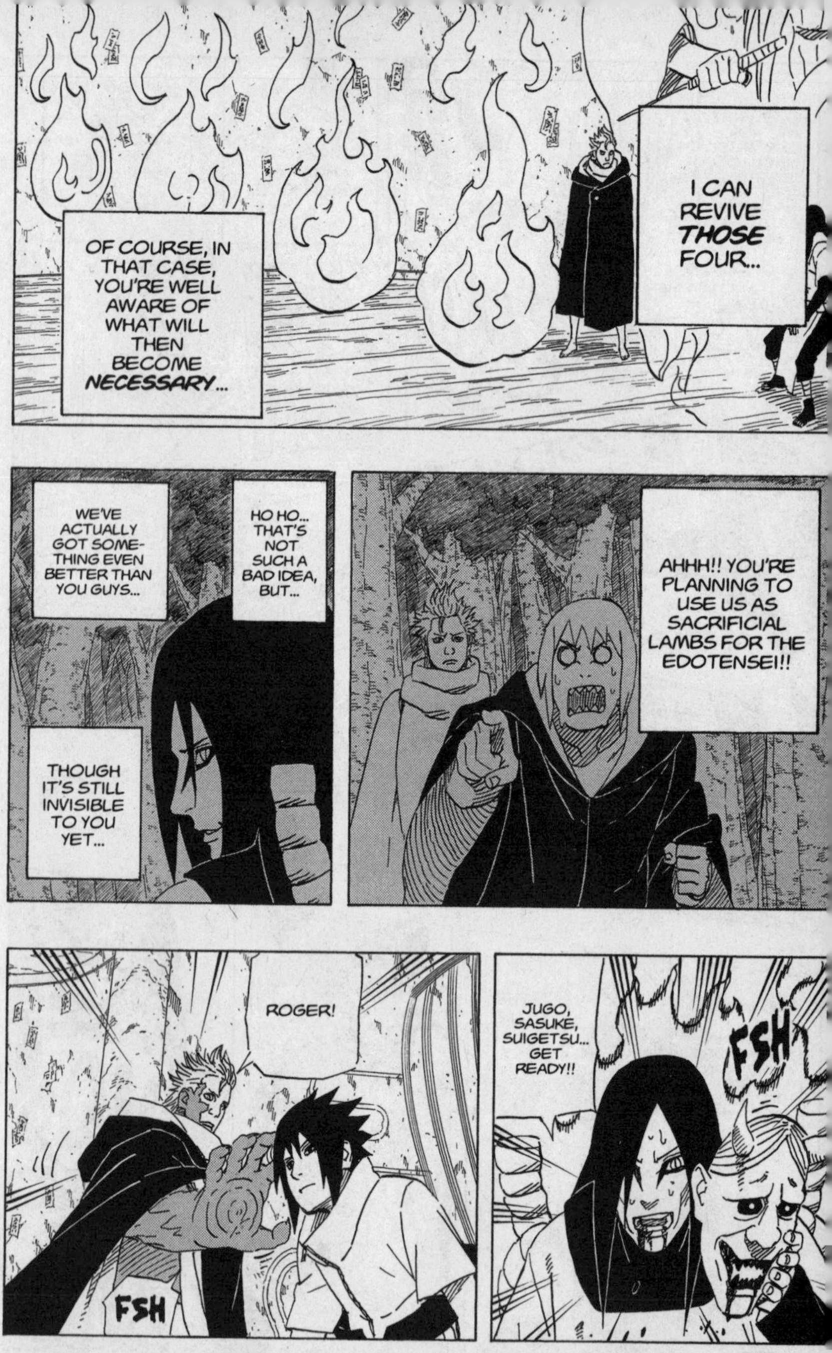
I CAN REVIVE *THOSE* FOUR...
OF COURSE, IN THAT CASE, YOU'RE WELL AWARE OF WHAT WILL THEN BECOME *NECESSARY*...
AHHH!! YOU'RE PLANNING TO USE US AS SACRIFICIAL LAMBS FOR THE EDOTENSEI!!
HO HO... THAT'S NOT SUCH A BAD IDEA, BUT...
WE'VE ACTUALLY GOT SOME-THING EVEN BETTER THAN YOU GUYS...
THOUGH IT'S STILL INVISIBLE TO YOU YET...
JUGO, SASUKE, SUIGETSU... GET READY!!
FSH
ROGER!
FSH

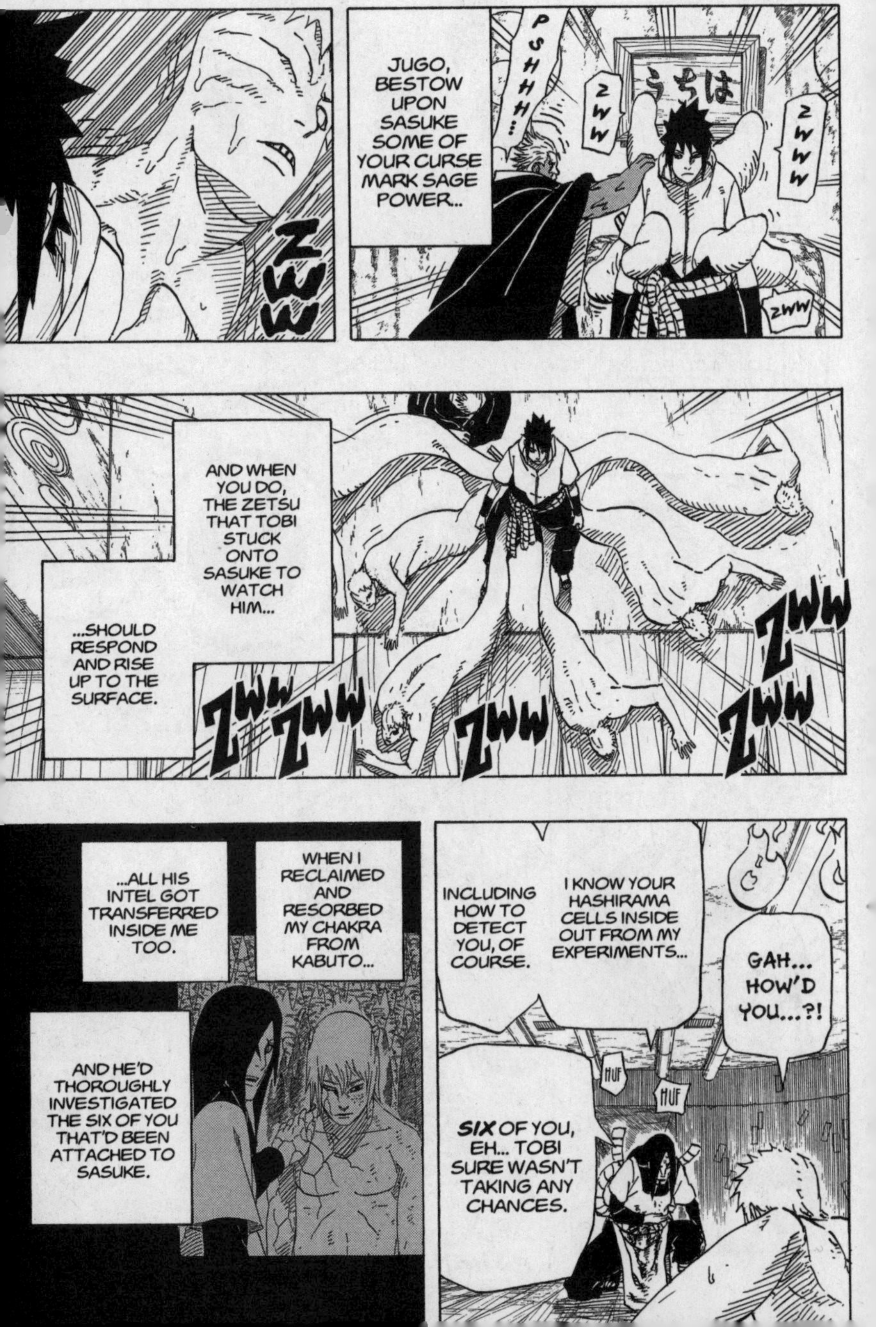
PSHHH...
JUGO, BESTOW UPON SASUKE SOME OF YOUR CURSE MARK SAGE POWER...
ZWW
うちは
ZWWW
ZWW
ZWW
AND WHEN YOU DO, THE ZETSU THAT TOBI STUCK ONTO SASUKE TO WATCH HIM...
...SHOULD RESPOND AND RISE UP TO THE SURFACE.
ZWW
ZWW
ZWW
ZWW
ZWW
ZWW
GAH... HOW'D YOU...?!
I KNOW YOUR HASHIRAMA CELLS INSIDE OUT FROM MY EXPERIMENTS...
INCLUDING HOW TO DETECT YOU, OF COURSE.
HUF
HUF
SIX OF YOU, EH... TOBI SURE WASN'T TAKING ANY CHANCES.
WHEN I RECLAIMED AND RESORBED MY CHAKRA FROM KABUTO...
...ALL HIS INTEL GOT TRANSFERRED INSIDE ME TOO.
AND HE'D THOROUGHLY INVESTIGATED THE SIX OF YOU THAT'D BEEN ATTACHED TO SASUKE.

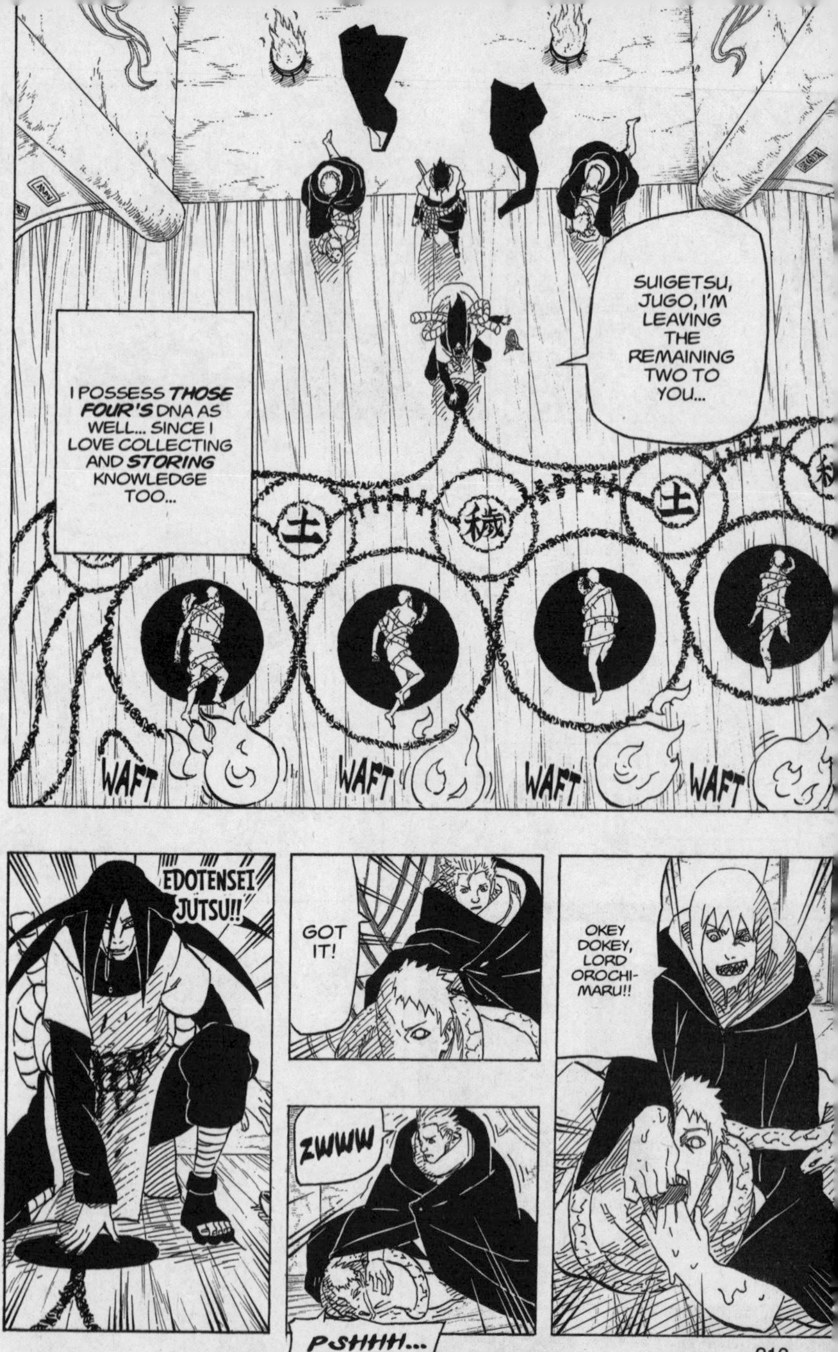
SUIGETSU, JUGO, I'M LEAVING THE REMAINING TWO TO YOU...
I POSSESS THOSE FOUR'S DNA AS WELL... SINCE I LOVE COLLECTING AND STORING KNOWLEDGE TOO...
土
穢
土
WAFT
WAFT
WAFT
WAFT
OKEY DOKEY, LORD OROCHI-MARU!!
GOT IT!
ZWWW
PSHHH...
EDOTENSEI JUTSU!!

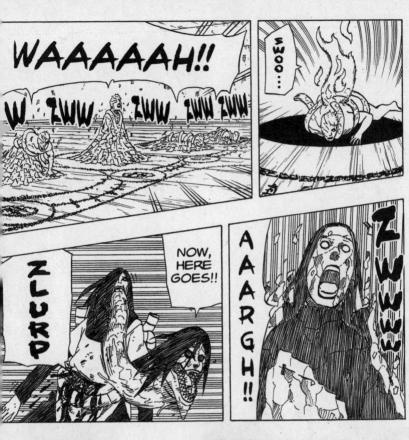

WAAAAAH!!

W ZWW ZWW ZWW ZWW

SWOO...

NOW, HERE GOES!!

ZLURP

AAARGH!!

ZWWWW

THEY WHO ARE ALL-KNOWING...

ZWW

ZWP

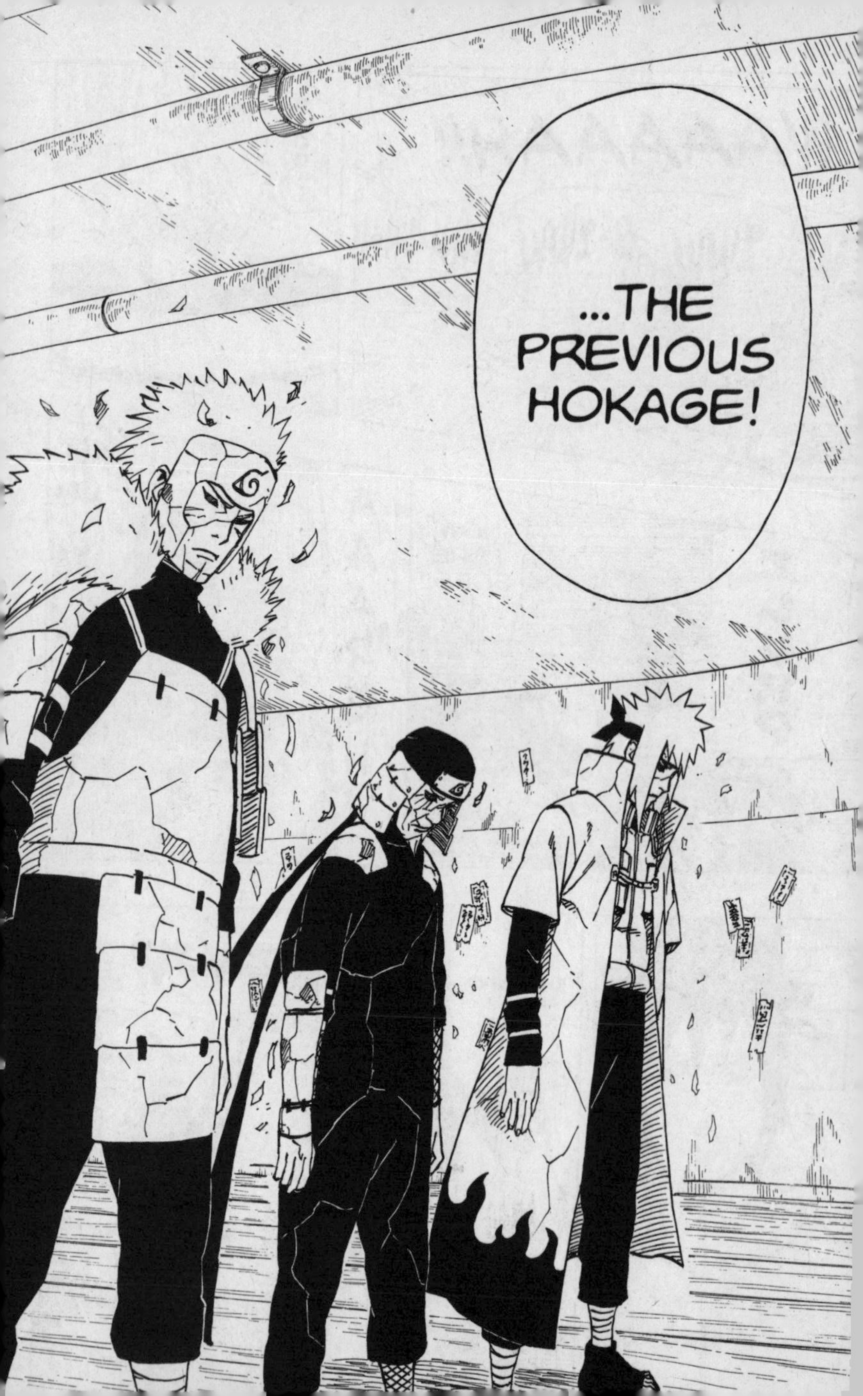
...THE PREVIOUS HOKAGE!

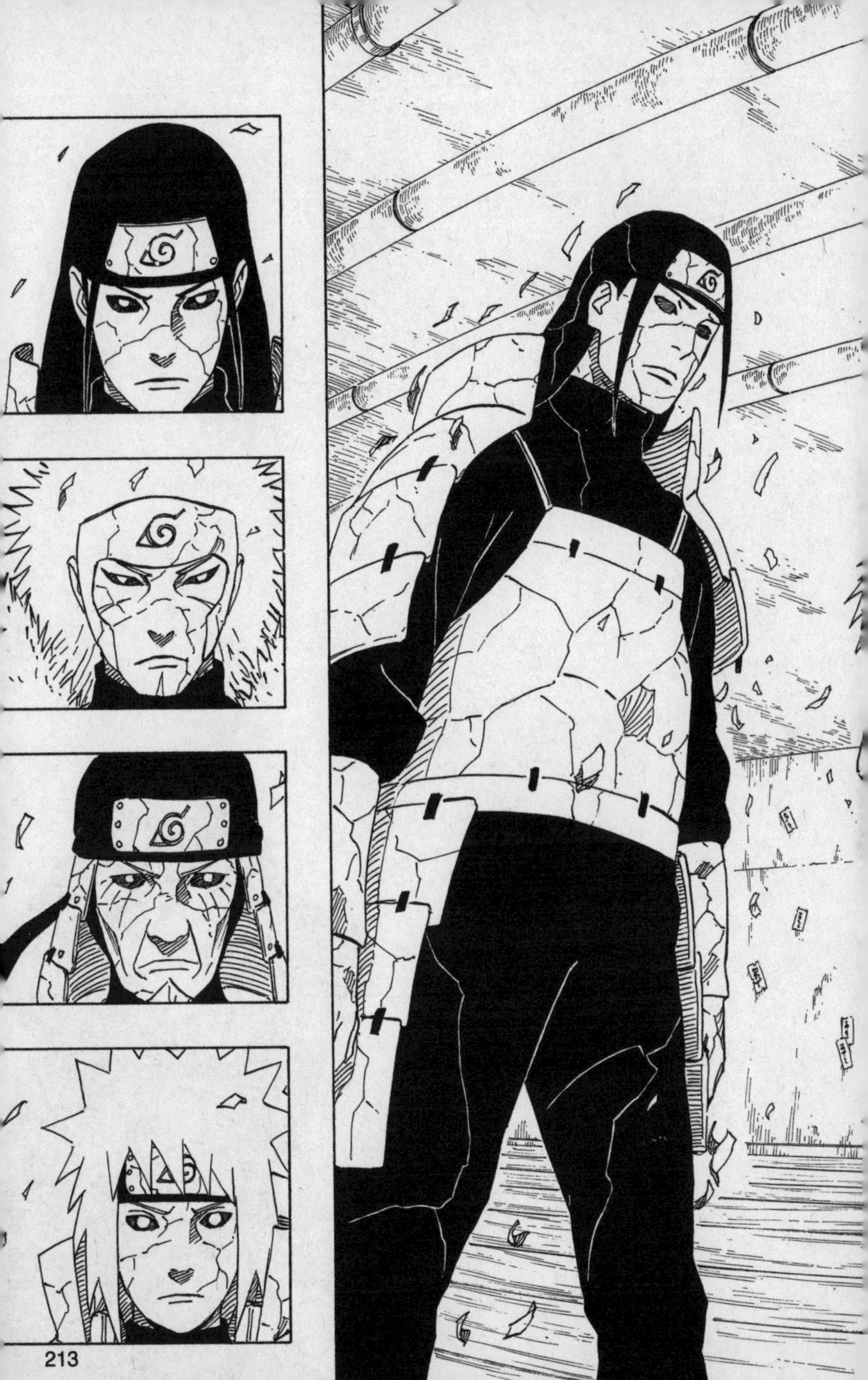

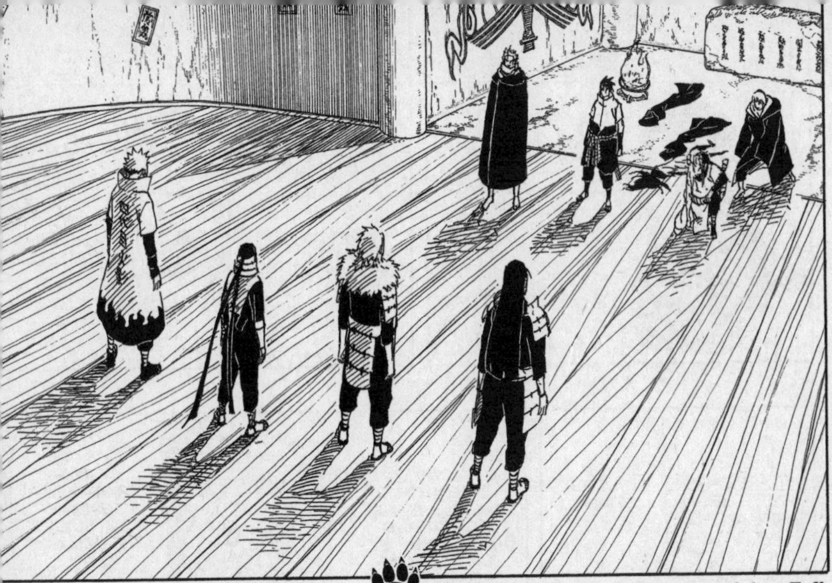

Number 619: A Clan Possessed by Evil

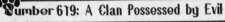

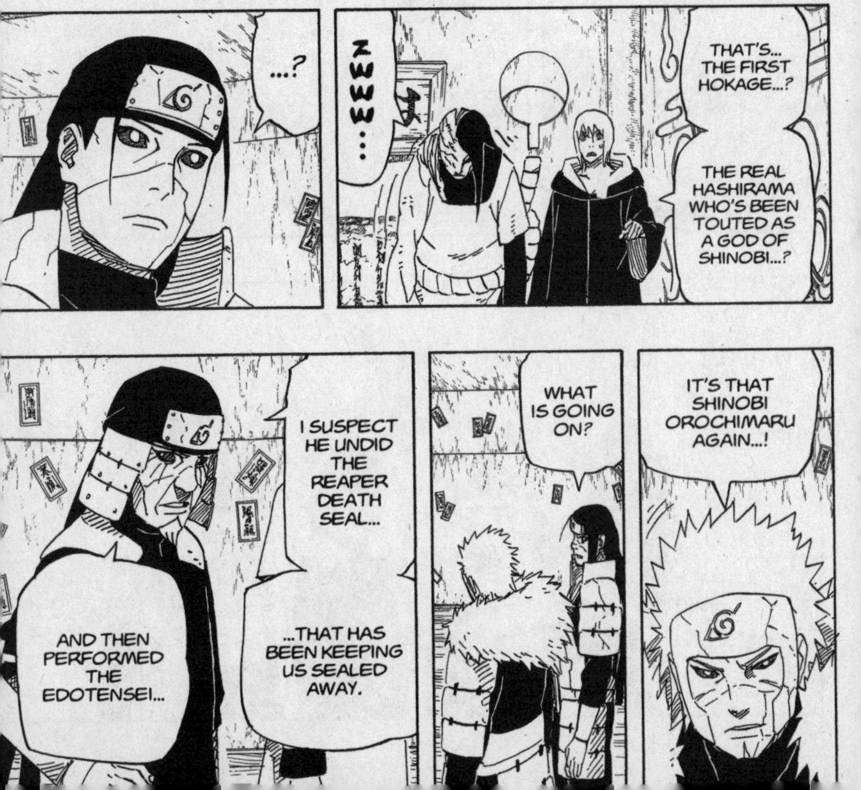
THAT'S... THE FIRST HOKAGE...?
THE REAL HASHIRAMA WHO'S BEEN TOUTED AS A GOD OF SHINOBI...?
ZWWW...
...?
IT'S THAT SHINOBI OROCHIMARU AGAIN...!
WHAT IS GOING ON?
I SUSPECT HE UNDID THE REAPER DEATH SEAL...
...THAT HAS BEEN KEEPING US SEALED AWAY.
AND THEN PERFORMED THE EDOTENSEI...

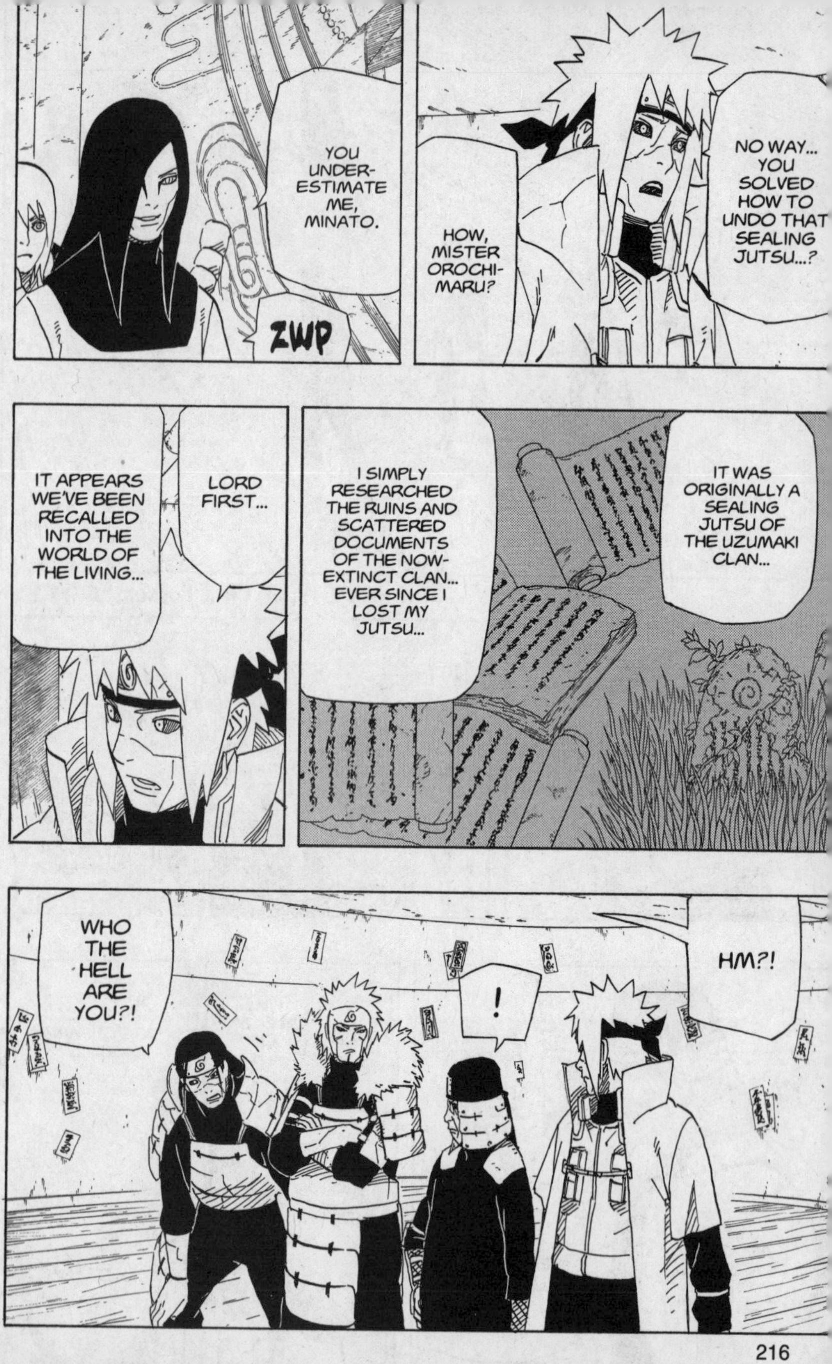
NO WAY... YOU SOLVED HOW TO UNDO THAT SEALING JUTSU...?
HOW, MISTER OROCHIMARU?
YOU UNDERESTIMATE ME, MINATO.
ZWP
IT WAS ORIGINALLY A SEALING JUTSU OF THE UZUMAKI CLAN...
I SIMPLY RESEARCHED THE RUINS AND SCATTERED DOCUMENTS OF THE NOW-EXTINCT CLAN... EVER SINCE I LOST MY JUTSU...
LORD FIRST...
IT APPEARS WE'VE BEEN RECALLED INTO THE WORLD OF THE LIVING...
HM?!
!
WHO THE HELL ARE YOU?!

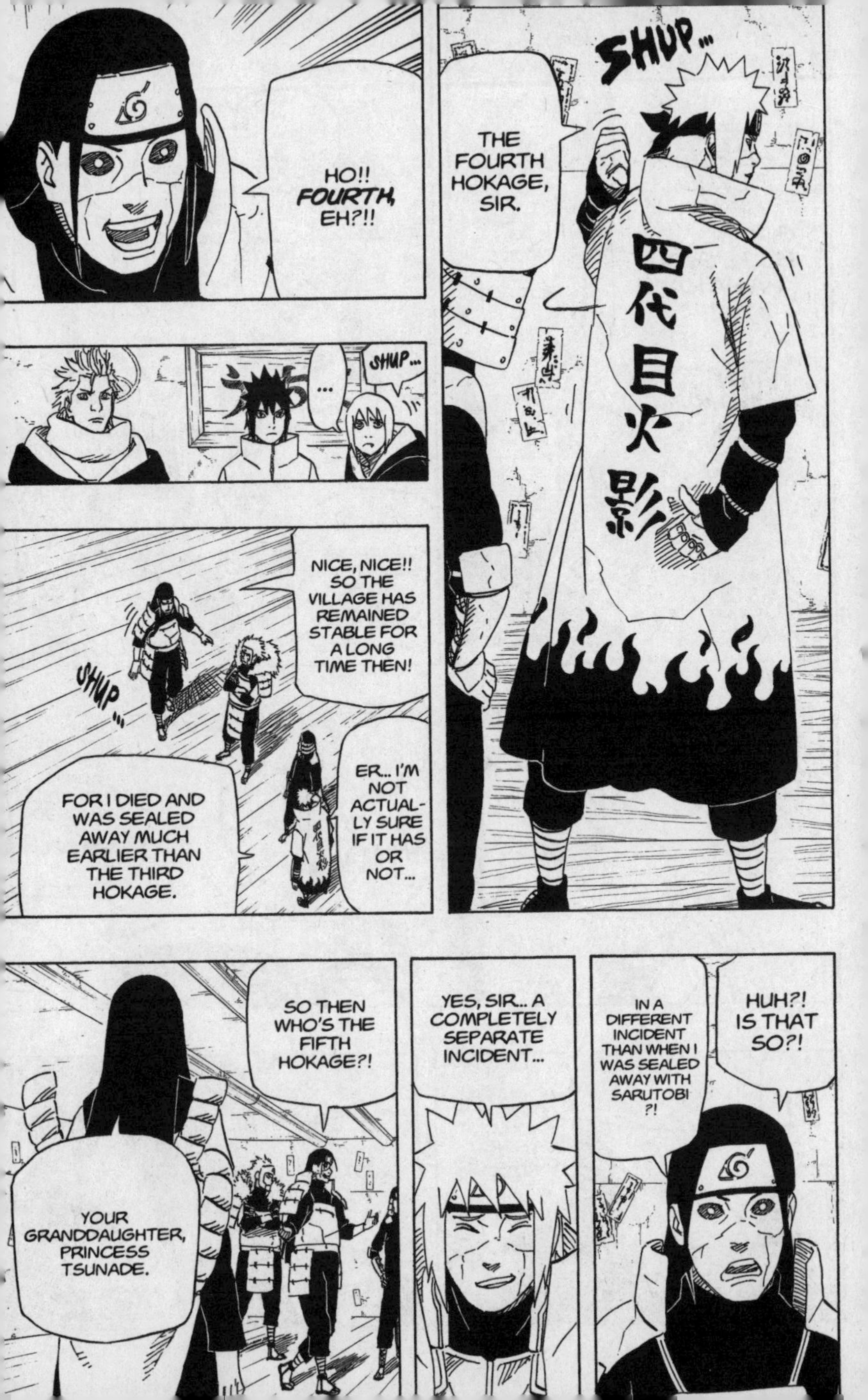
SHUP...
四代目火影
THE FOURTH HOKAGE, SIR.
HO!! FOURTH, EH?!!
SHUP...
...
NICE, NICE!! SO THE VILLAGE HAS REMAINED STABLE FOR A LONG TIME THEN!
SHUP...
ER... I'M NOT ACTUAL-LY SURE IF IT HAS OR NOT...
FOR I DIED AND WAS SEALED AWAY MUCH EARLIER THAN THE THIRD HOKAGE.
HUH?! IS THAT SO?!
IN A DIFFERENT INCIDENT THAN WHEN I WAS SEALED AWAY WITH SARUTOBI?!
YES, SIR... A COMPLETELY SEPARATE INCIDENT...
SO THEN WHO'S THE FIFTH HOKAGE?!
YOUR GRANDDAUGHTER, PRINCESS TSUNADE.

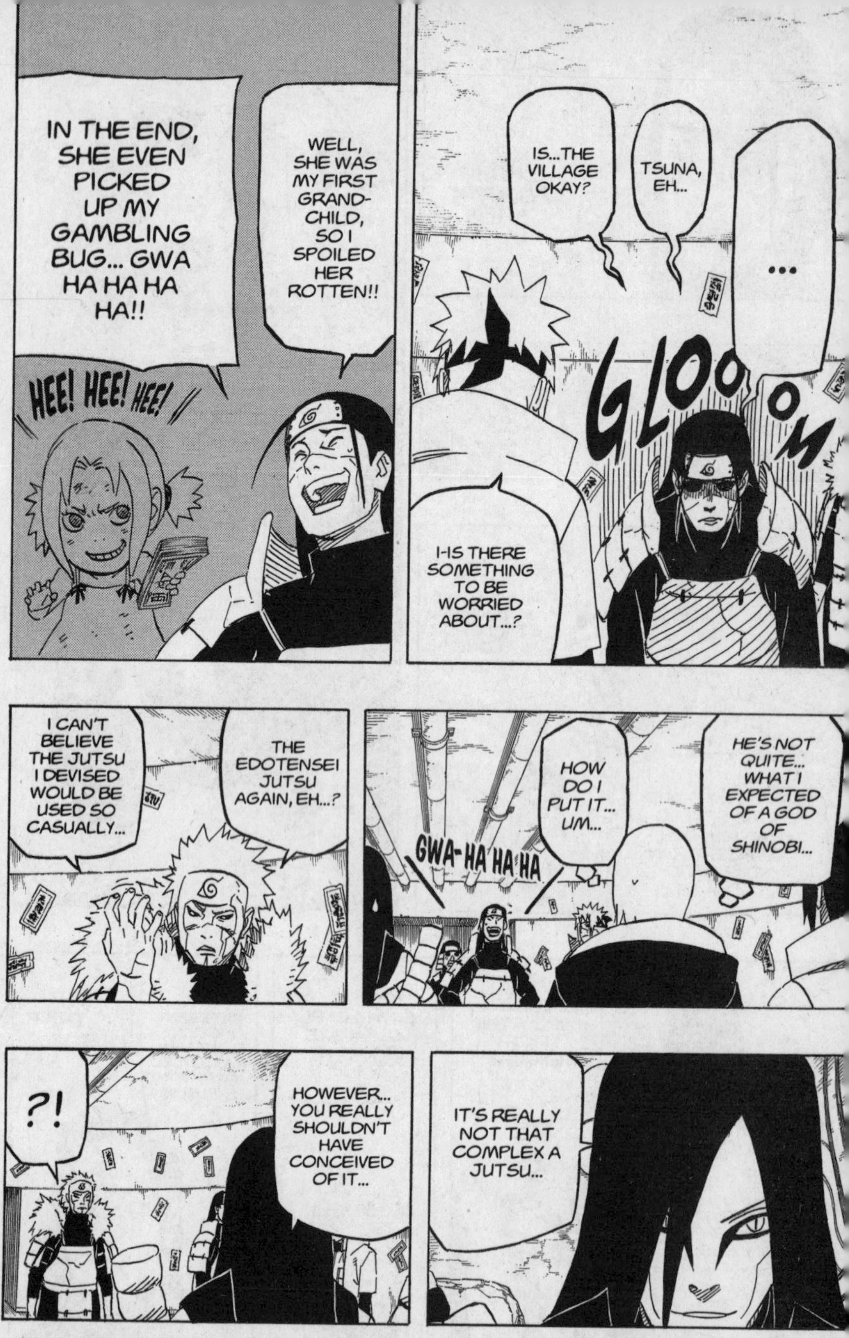
...
TSUNA, EH...
IS...THE VILLAGE OKAY?
GLOOOM
I-IS THERE SOMETHING TO BE WORRIED ABOUT...?
WELL, SHE WAS MY FIRST GRAND-CHILD, SO I SPOILED HER ROTTEN!!
IN THE END, SHE EVEN PICKED UP MY GAMBLING BUG... GWA HA HA HA HA!!
HEE! HEE! HEE!
HE'S NOT QUITE... WHAT I EXPECTED OF A GOD OF SHINOBI...
HOW DO I PUT IT... UM...
GWA-HA HA HA
THE EDOTENSEI JUTSU AGAIN, EH...?
I CAN'T BELIEVE THE JUTSU I DEVISED WOULD BE USED SO CASUALLY...
IT'S REALLY NOT THAT COMPLEX A JUTSU...
HOWEVER... YOU REALLY SHOULDN'T HAVE CONCEIVED OF IT...
?!

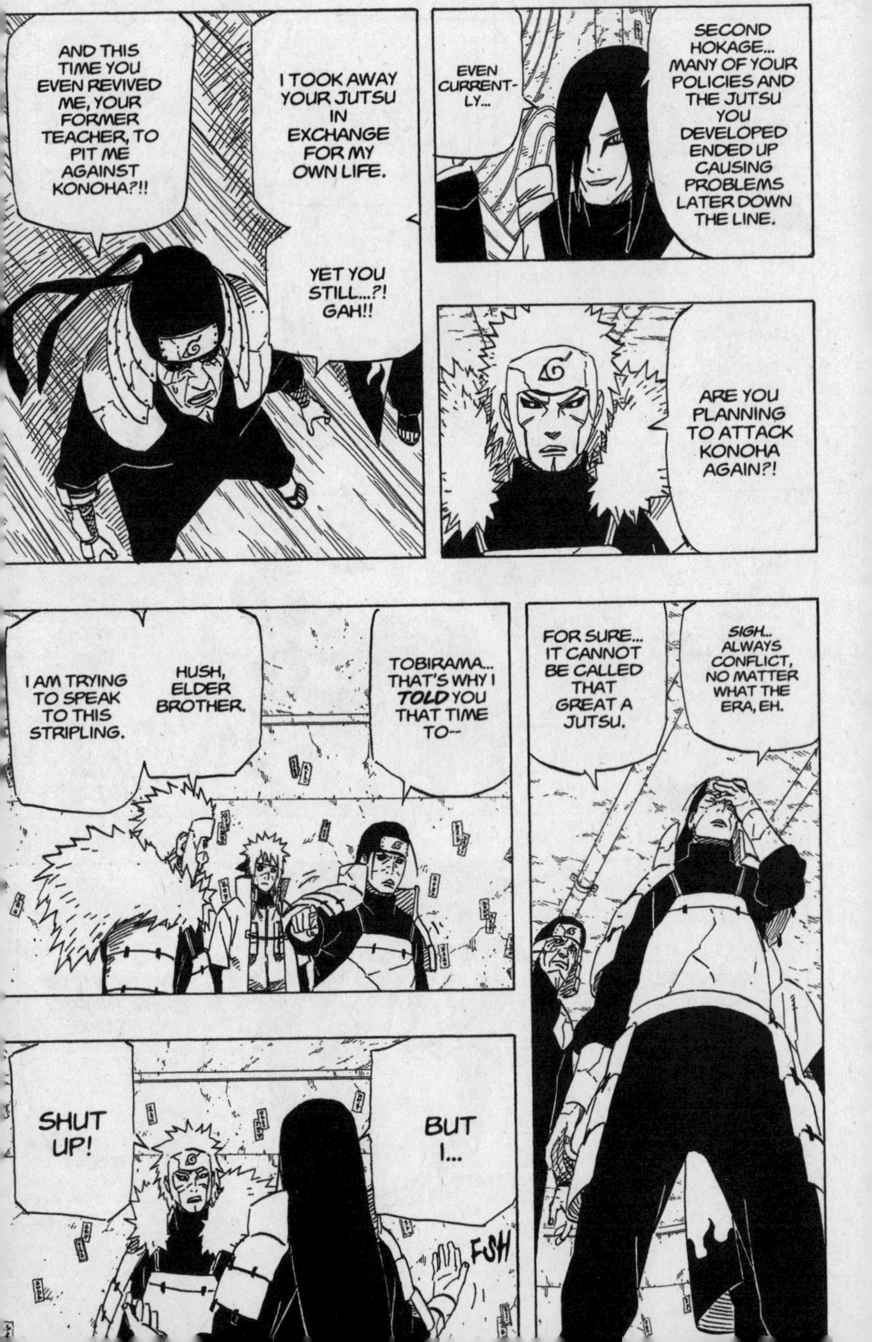
SECOND HOKAGE... MANY OF YOUR POLICIES AND THE JUTSU YOU DEVELOPED ENDED UP CAUSING PROBLEMS LATER DOWN THE LINE.
EVEN CURRENT-LY...
ARE YOU PLANNING TO ATTACK KONOHA AGAIN?!
I TOOK AWAY YOUR JUTSU IN EXCHANGE FOR MY OWN LIFE.
AND THIS TIME YOU EVEN REVIVED ME, YOUR FORMER TEACHER, TO PIT ME AGAINST KONOHA?!!
YET YOU STILL...?! GAH!!
SIGH.. ALWAYS CONFLICT, NO MATTER WHAT THE ERA, EH.
FOR SURE... IT CANNOT BE CALLED THAT GREAT A JUTSU.
TOBIRAMA... THAT'S WHY I **TOLD** YOU THAT TIME TO--
HUSH, ELDER BROTHER.
I AM TRYING TO SPEAK TO THIS STRIPLING.
BUT I...
SHUT UP!
FSH

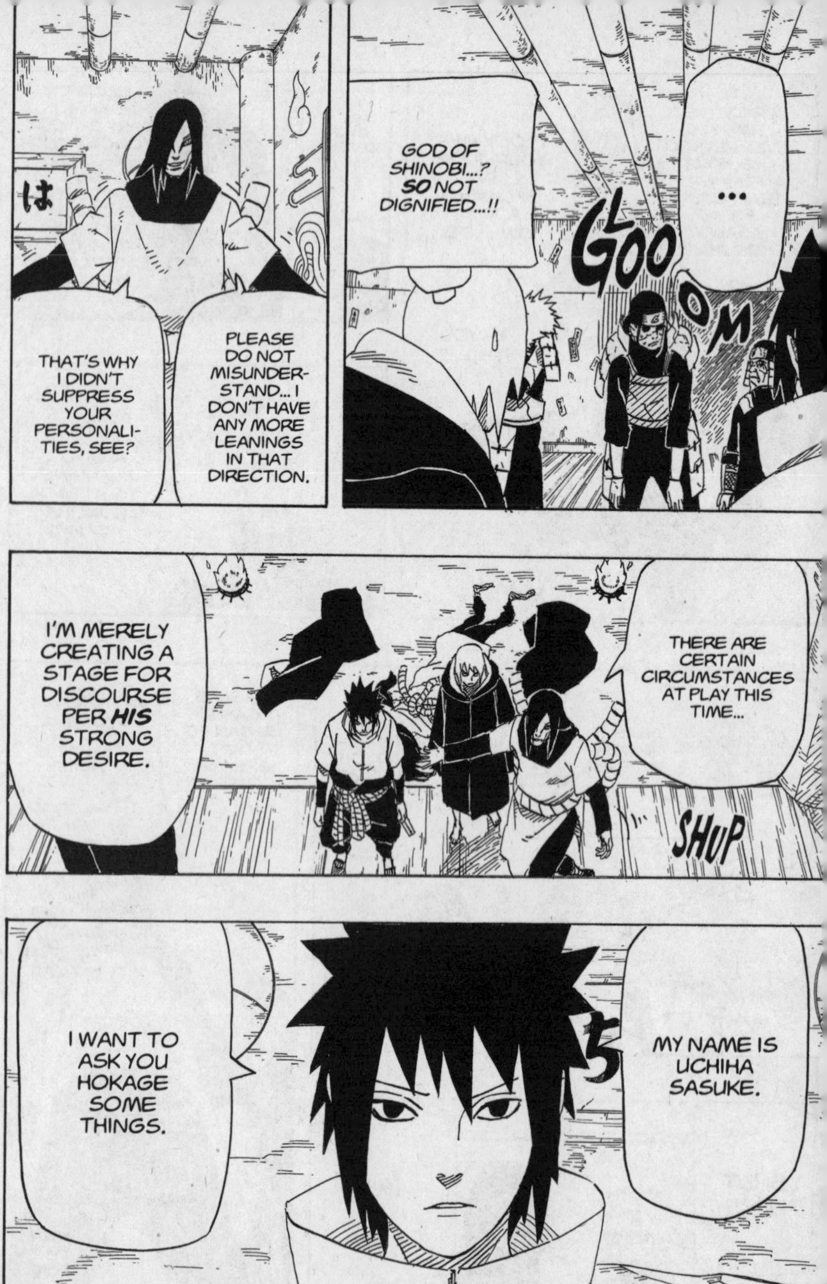
...
GOOOM
GOD OF SHINOBI...? SO NOT DIGNIFIED...!!
PLEASE DO NOT MISUNDERSTAND... I DON'T HAVE ANY MORE LEANINGS IN THAT DIRECTION.
THAT'S WHY I DIDN'T SUPPRESS YOUR PERSONALITIES, SEE?
THERE ARE CERTAIN CIRCUMSTANCES AT PLAY THIS TIME...
SHUP
I'M MERELY CREATING A STAGE FOR DISCOURSE PER HIS STRONG DESIRE.
MY NAME IS UCHIHA SASUKE.
I WANT TO ASK YOU HOKAGE SOME THINGS.

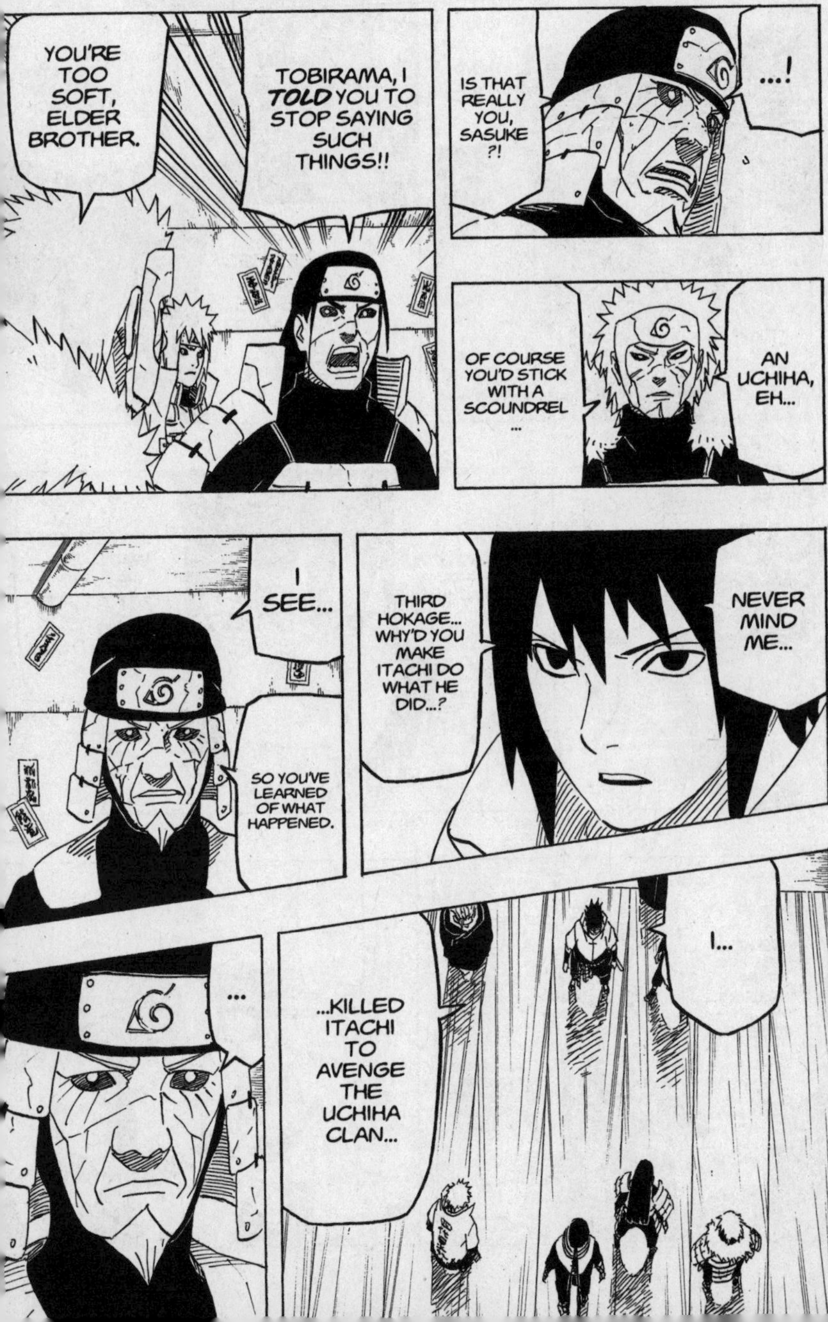
...!
IS THAT REALLY YOU, SASUKE ?!
AN UCHIHA, EH...
OF COURSE YOU'D STICK WITH A SCOUNDREL ...
TOBIRAMA, I TOLD YOU TO STOP SAYING SUCH THINGS!!
YOU'RE TOO SOFT, ELDER BROTHER.
NEVER MIND ME...
THIRD HOKAGE... WHY'D YOU MAKE ITACHI DO WHAT HE DID...?
I SEE...
SO YOU'VE LEARNED OF WHAT HAPPENED.
I...
...KILLED ITACHI TO AVENGE THE UCHIHA CLAN...
...

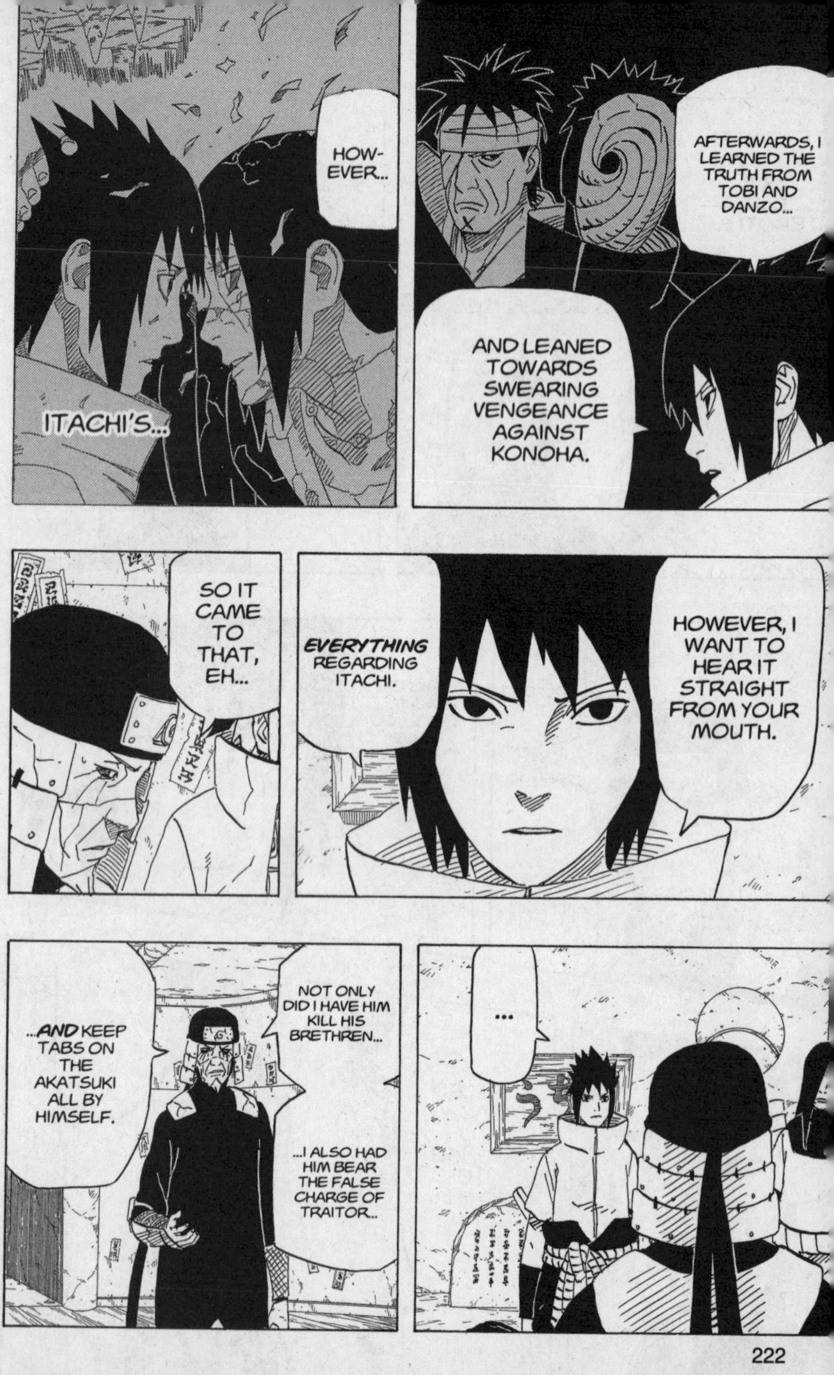
AFTERWARDS, I LEARNED THE TRUTH FROM TOBI AND DANZO...
AND LEANED TOWARDS SWEARING VENGEANCE AGAINST KONOHA.
HOW-EVER...
ITACHI'S...
HOWEVER, I WANT TO HEAR IT STRAIGHT FROM YOUR MOUTH.
EVERYTHING REGARDING ITACHI.
SO IT CAME TO THAT, EH...
...
NOT ONLY DID I HAVE HIM KILL HIS BRETHREN...
...I ALSO HAD HIM BEAR THE FALSE CHARGE OF TRAITOR...
...*AND* KEEP TABS ON THE AKATSUKI ALL BY HIMSELF.

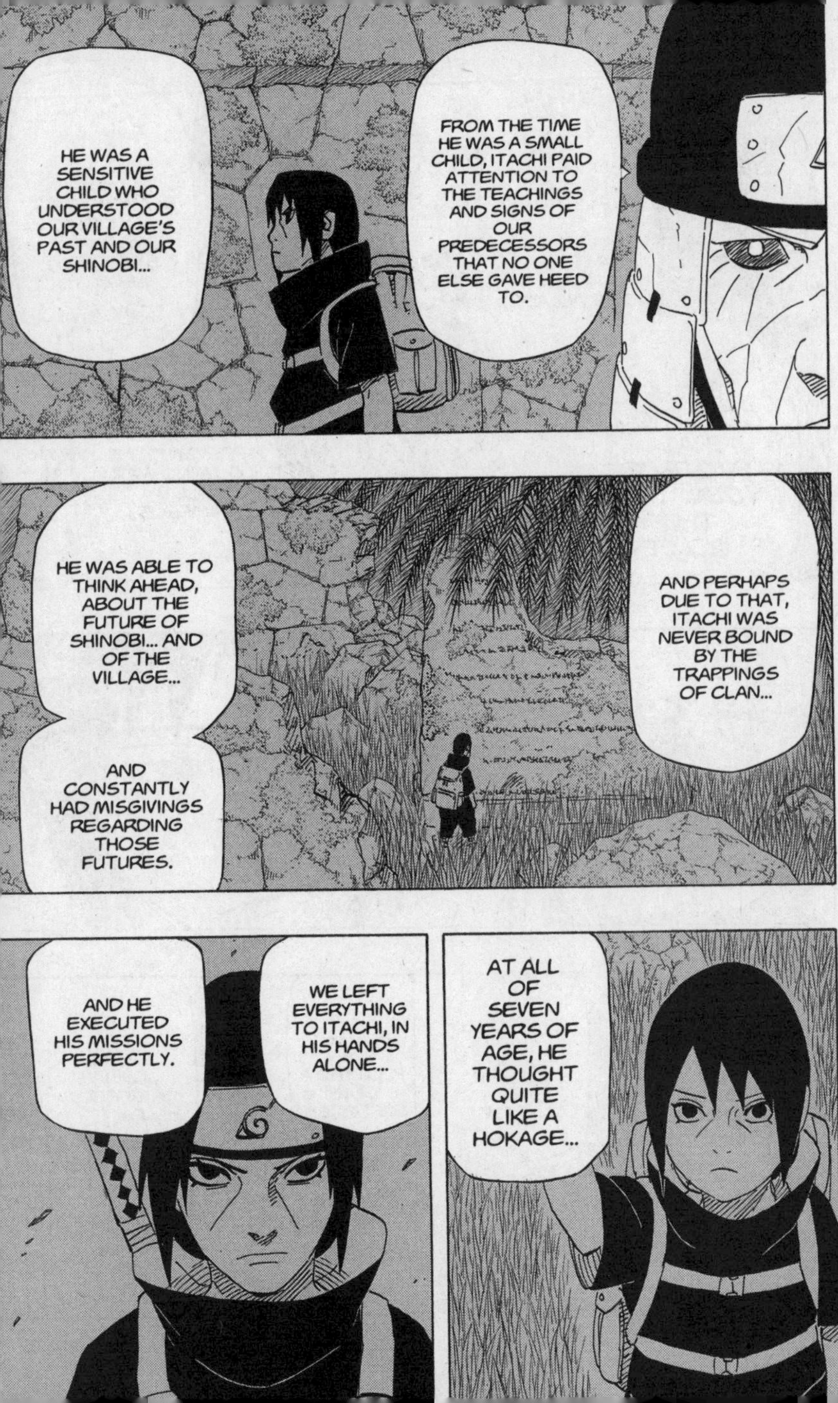
FROM THE TIME HE WAS A SMALL CHILD, ITACHI PAID ATTENTION TO THE TEACHINGS AND SIGNS OF OUR PREDECESSORS THAT NO ONE ELSE GAVE HEED TO.
HE WAS A SENSITIVE CHILD WHO UNDERSTOOD OUR VILLAGE'S PAST AND OUR SHINOBI...
AND PERHAPS DUE TO THAT, ITACHI WAS NEVER BOUND BY THE TRAPPINGS OF CLAN...
HE WAS ABLE TO THINK AHEAD, ABOUT THE FUTURE OF SHINOBI... AND OF THE VILLAGE...
AND CONSTANTLY HAD MISGIVINGS REGARDING THOSE FUTURES.
AT ALL OF SEVEN YEARS OF AGE, HE THOUGHT QUITE LIKE A HOKAGE...
WE LEFT EVERYTHING TO ITACHI, IN HIS HANDS ALONE...
AND HE EXECUTED HIS MISSIONS PERFECTLY.

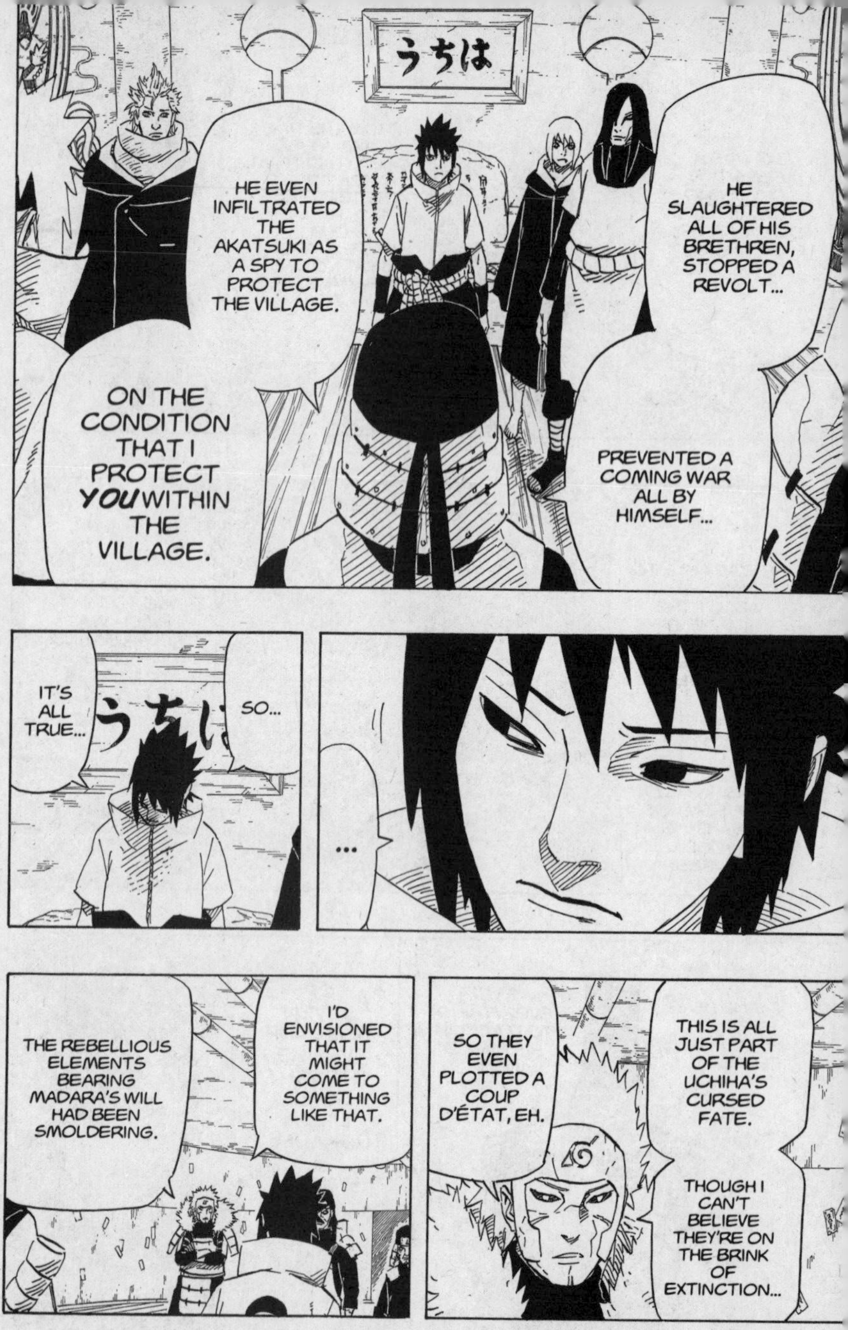
うちは
HE SLAUGHTERED ALL OF HIS BRETHREN, STOPPED A REVOLT...
PREVENTED A COMING WAR ALL BY HIMSELF...
HE EVEN INFILTRATED THE AKATSUKI AS A SPY TO PROTECT THE VILLAGE.
ON THE CONDITION THAT I PROTECT ***YOU*** WITHIN THE VILLAGE.
...
SO...
IT'S ALL TRUE...
うちは
THIS IS ALL JUST PART OF THE UCHIHA'S CURSED FATE.
THOUGH I CAN'T BELIEVE THEY'RE ON THE BRINK OF EXTINCTION...
SO THEY EVEN PLOTTED A COUP D'ÉTAT, EH.
I'D ENVISIONED THAT IT MIGHT COME TO SOMETHING LIKE THAT.
THE REBELLIOUS ELEMENTS BEARING MADARA'S WILL HAD BEEN SMOLDERING.

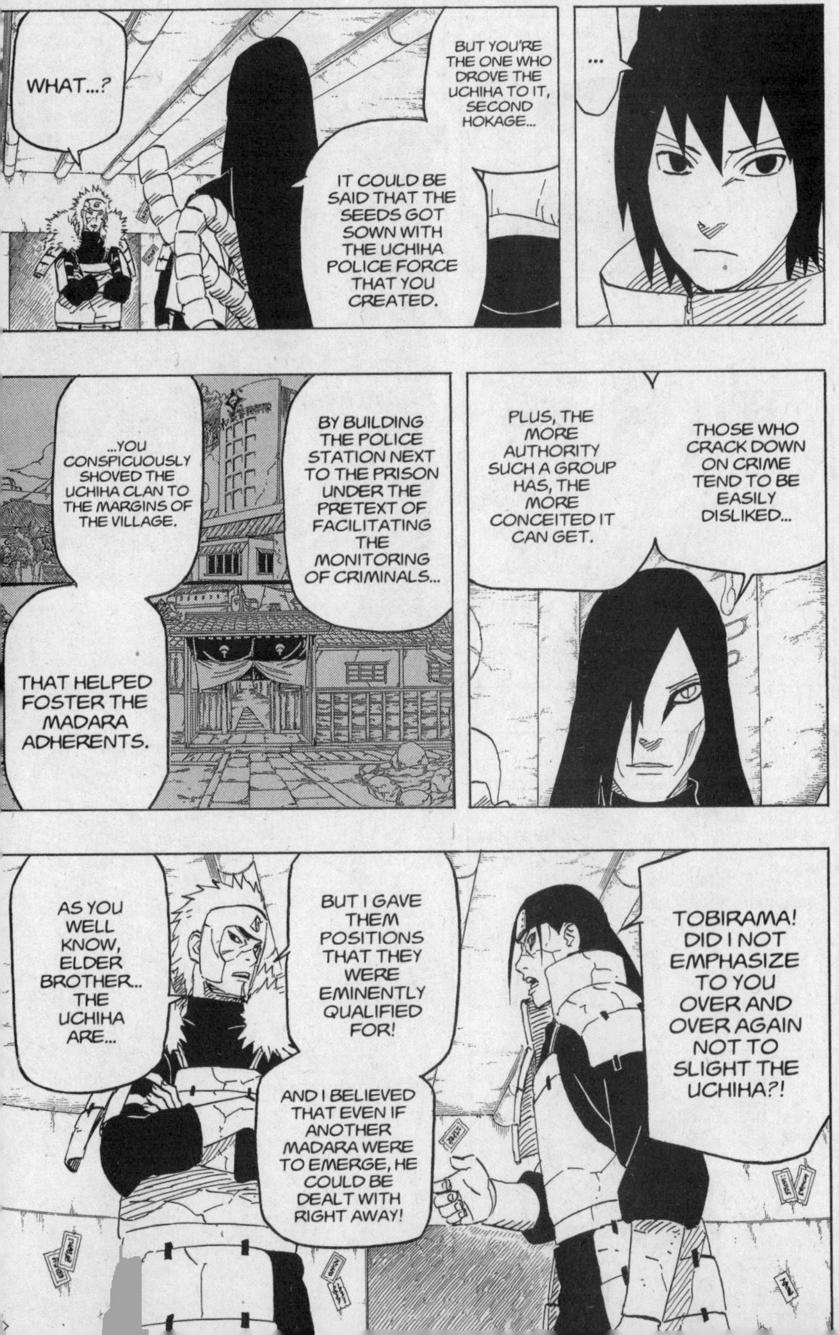
...
BUT YOU'RE THE ONE WHO DROVE THE UCHIHA TO IT, SECOND HOKAGE...
IT COULD BE SAID THAT THE SEEDS GOT SOWN WITH THE UCHIHA POLICE FORCE THAT YOU CREATED.
WHAT...?
THOSE WHO CRACK DOWN ON CRIME TEND TO BE EASILY DISLIKED...
PLUS, THE MORE AUTHORITY SUCH A GROUP HAS, THE MORE CONCEITED IT CAN GET.
BY BUILDING THE POLICE STATION NEXT TO THE PRISON UNDER THE PRETEXT OF FACILITATING THE MONITORING OF CRIMINALS...
...YOU CONSPICUOUSLY SHOVED THE UCHIHA CLAN TO THE MARGINS OF THE VILLAGE.
THAT HELPED FOSTER THE MADARA ADHERENTS.
TOBIRAMA! DID I NOT EMPHASIZE TO YOU OVER AND OVER AGAIN NOT TO SLIGHT THE UCHIHA?!
AS YOU WELL KNOW, ELDER BROTHER... THE UCHIHA ARE...
BUT I GAVE THEM POSITIONS THAT THEY WERE EMINENTLY QUALIFIED FOR!
AND I BELIEVED THAT EVEN IF ANOTHER MADARA WERE TO EMERGE, HE COULD BE DEALT WITH RIGHT AWAY!

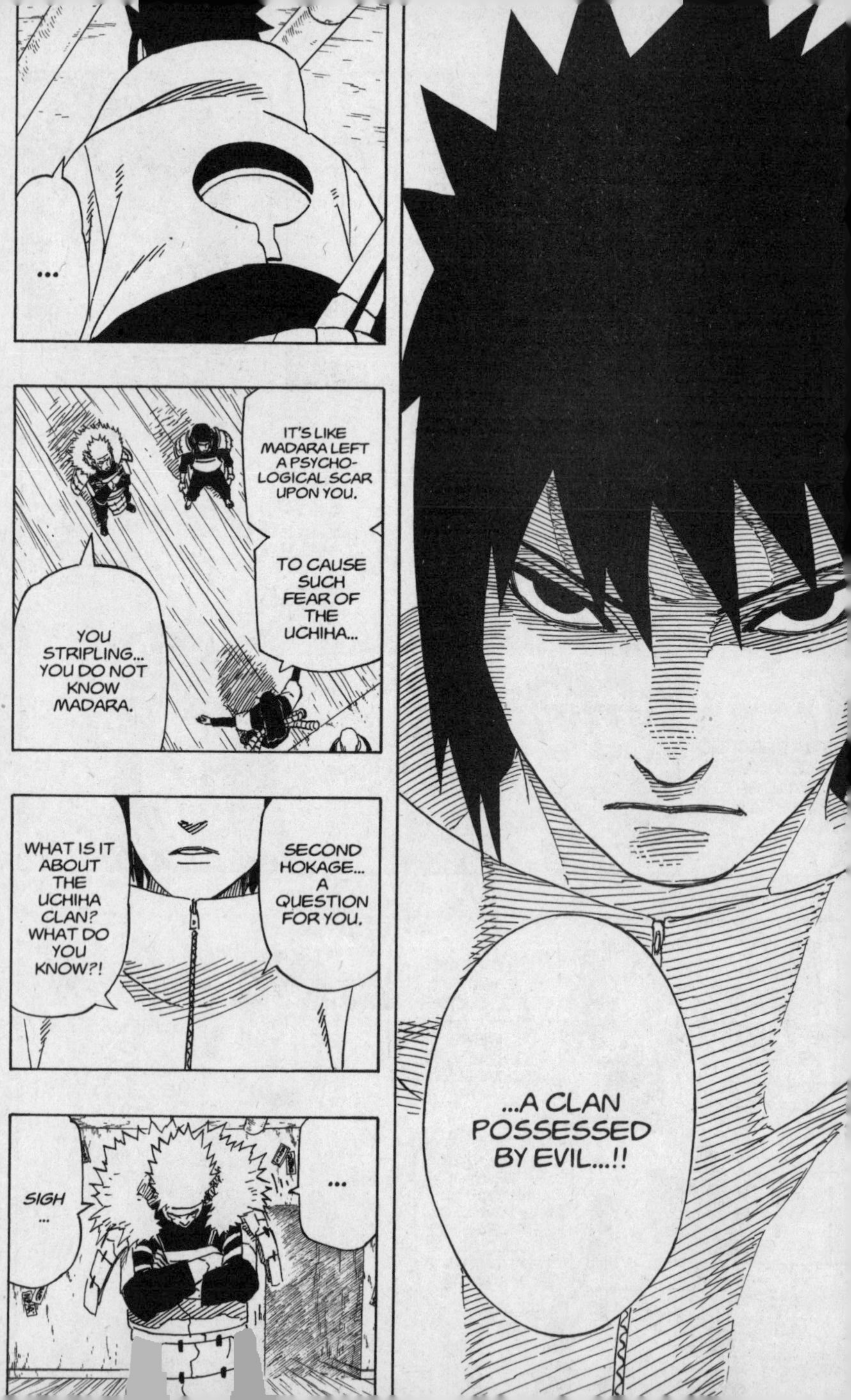
...A CLAN POSSESSED BY EVIL...!!
...
IT'S LIKE MADARA LEFT A PSYCHO-LOGICAL SCAR UPON YOU.
TO CAUSE SUCH FEAR OF THE UCHIHA...
YOU STRIPLING... YOU DO NOT KNOW MADARA.
SECOND HOKAGE... A QUESTION FOR YOU.
WHAT IS IT ABOUT THE UCHIHA CLAN? WHAT DO YOU KNOW?!
...
SIGH ...

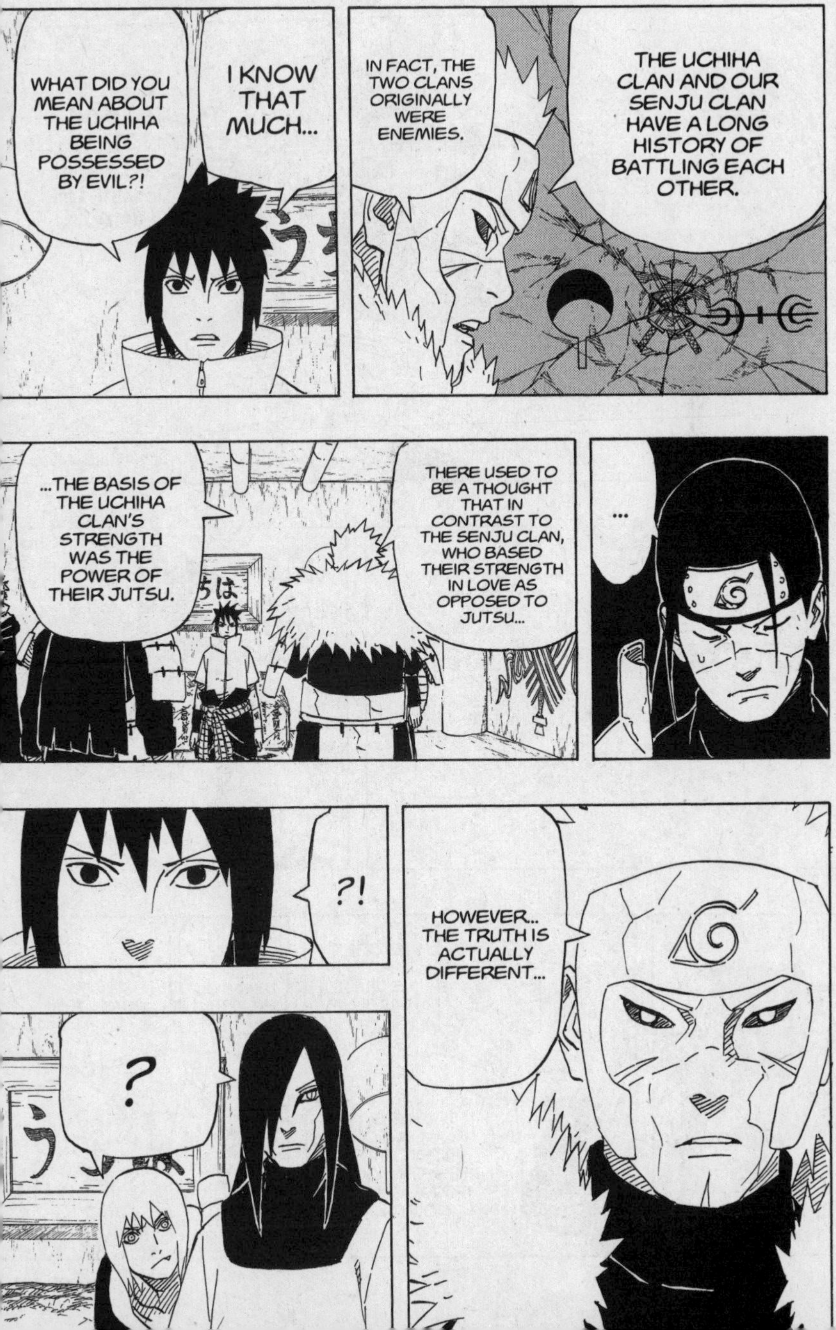
THE UCHIHA CLAN AND OUR SENJU CLAN HAVE A LONG HISTORY OF BATTLING EACH OTHER.
IN FACT, THE TWO CLANS ORIGINALLY WERE ENEMIES.
I KNOW THAT MUCH...
WHAT DID YOU MEAN ABOUT THE UCHIHA BEING POSSESSED BY EVIL?!
...
THERE USED TO BE A THOUGHT THAT IN CONTRAST TO THE SENJU CLAN, WHO BASED THEIR STRENGTH IN LOVE AS OPPOSED TO JUTSU...
...THE BASIS OF THE UCHIHA CLAN'S STRENGTH WAS THE POWER OF THEIR JUTSU.
HOWEVER... THE TRUTH IS ACTUALLY DIFFERENT...
?!
?

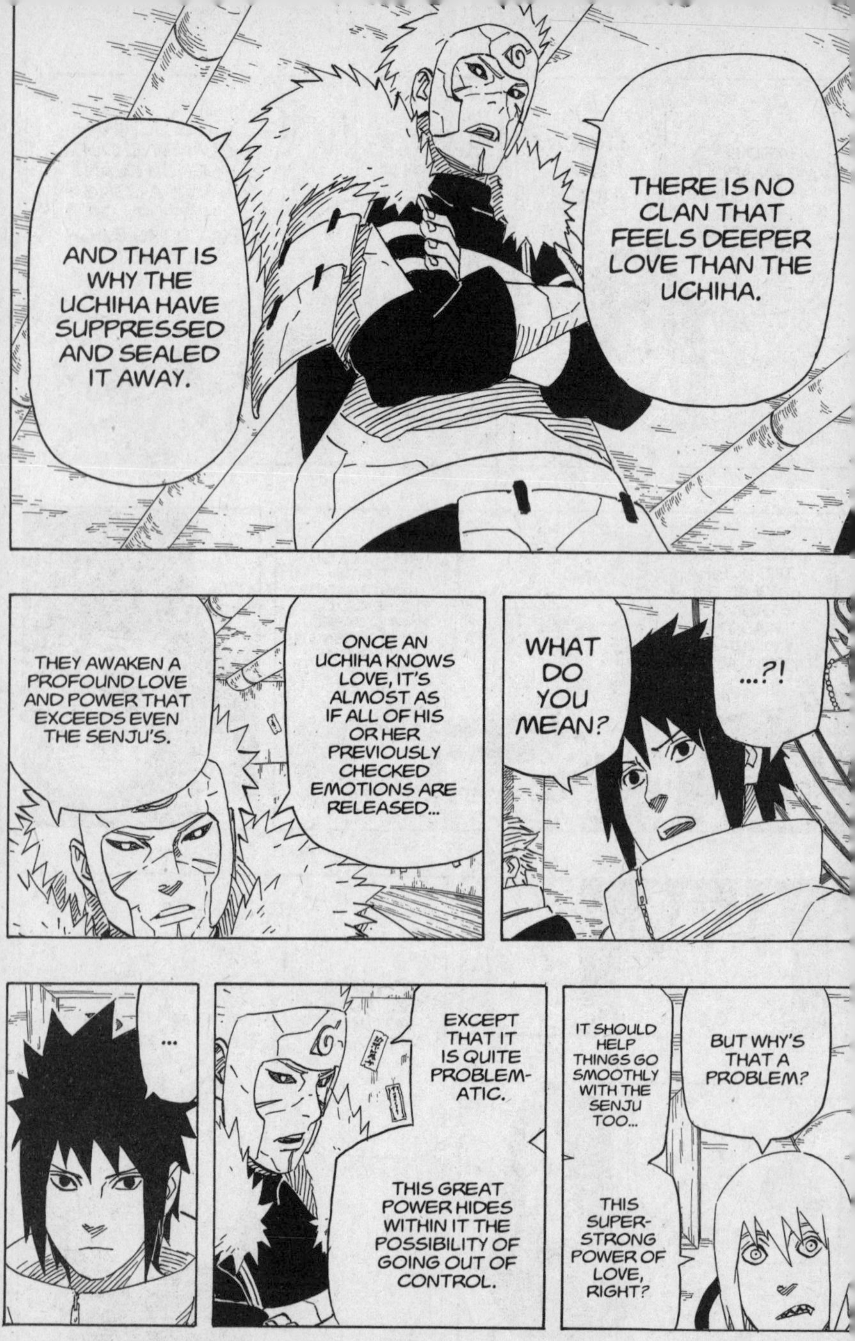
THERE IS NO CLAN THAT FEELS DEEPER LOVE THAN THE UCHIHA.
AND THAT IS WHY THE UCHIHA HAVE SUPPRESSED AND SEALED IT AWAY.
...?!
WHAT DO YOU MEAN?
ONCE AN UCHIHA KNOWS LOVE, IT'S ALMOST AS IF ALL OF HIS OR HER PREVIOUSLY CHECKED EMOTIONS ARE RELEASED...
THEY AWAKEN A PROFOUND LOVE AND POWER THAT EXCEEDS EVEN THE SENJU'S.
BUT WHY'S THAT A PROBLEM?
IT SHOULD HELP THINGS GO SMOOTHLY WITH THE SENJU TOO...
THIS SUPER-STRONG POWER OF LOVE, RIGHT?
EXCEPT THAT IT IS QUITE PROBLEM-ATIC.
THIS GREAT POWER HIDES WITHIN IT THE POSSIBILITY OF GOING OUT OF CONTROL.
...

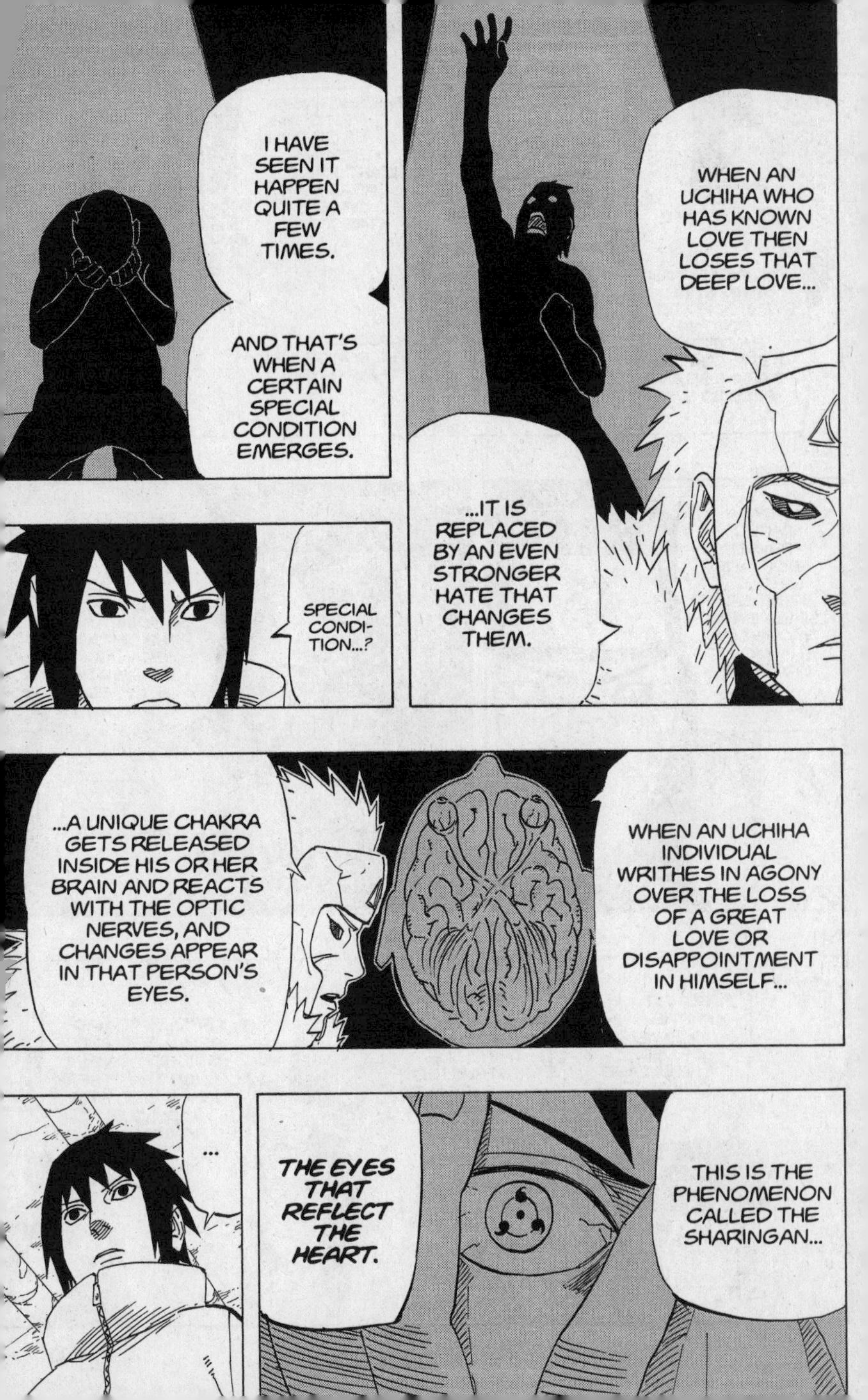
WHEN AN UCHIHA WHO HAS KNOWN LOVE THEN LOSES THAT DEEP LOVE...
...IT IS REPLACED BY AN EVEN STRONGER HATE THAT CHANGES THEM.
I HAVE SEEN IT HAPPEN QUITE A FEW TIMES.
AND THAT'S WHEN A CERTAIN SPECIAL CONDITION EMERGES.
SPECIAL CONDITION...?
WHEN AN UCHIHA INDIVIDUAL WRITHES IN AGONY OVER THE LOSS OF A GREAT LOVE OR DISAPPOINTMENT IN HIMSELF...
...A UNIQUE CHAKRA GETS RELEASED INSIDE HIS OR HER BRAIN AND REACTS WITH THE OPTIC NERVES, AND CHANGES APPEAR IN THAT PERSON'S EYES.
THIS IS THE PHENOMENON CALLED THE SHARINGAN...
THE EYES THAT REFLECT THE HEART.
...

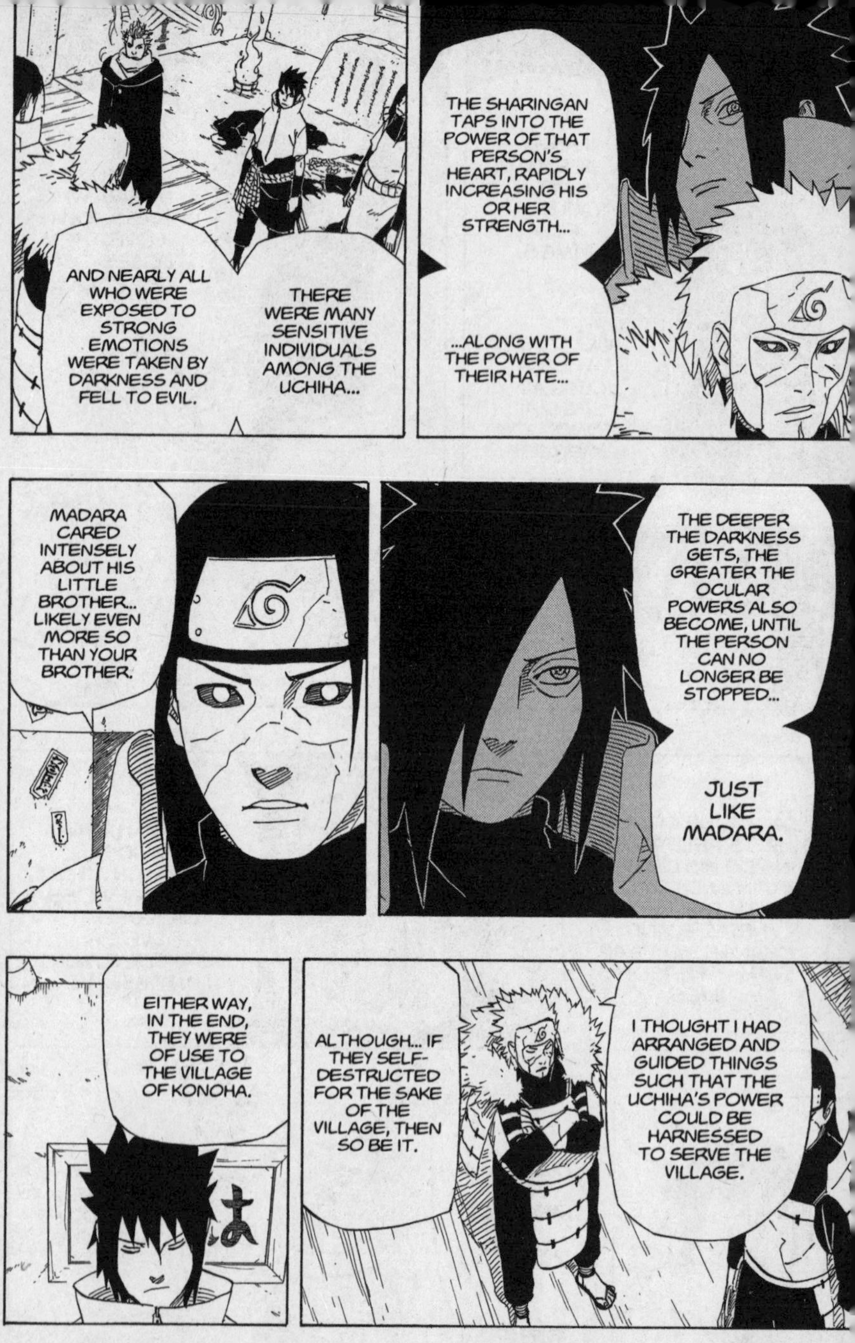
THE SHARINGAN TAPS INTO THE POWER OF THAT PERSON'S HEART, RAPIDLY INCREASING HIS OR HER STRENGTH...
...ALONG WITH THE POWER OF THEIR HATE...
THERE WERE MANY SENSITIVE INDIVIDUALS AMONG THE UCHIHA...
AND NEARLY ALL WHO WERE EXPOSED TO STRONG EMOTIONS WERE TAKEN BY DARKNESS AND FELL TO EVIL.
THE DEEPER THE DARKNESS GETS, THE GREATER THE OCULAR POWERS ALSO BECOME, UNTIL THE PERSON CAN NO LONGER BE STOPPED...
JUST LIKE MADARA.
MADARA CARED INTENSELY ABOUT HIS LITTLE BROTHER... LIKELY EVEN MORE SO THAN YOUR BROTHER.
I THOUGHT I HAD ARRANGED AND GUIDED THINGS SUCH THAT THE UCHIHA'S POWER COULD BE HARNESSED TO SERVE THE VILLAGE.
ALTHOUGH... IF THEY SELF-DESTRUCTED FOR THE SAKE OF THE VILLAGE, THEN SO BE IT.
EITHER WAY, IN THE END, THEY WERE OF USE TO THE VILLAGE OF KONOHA.

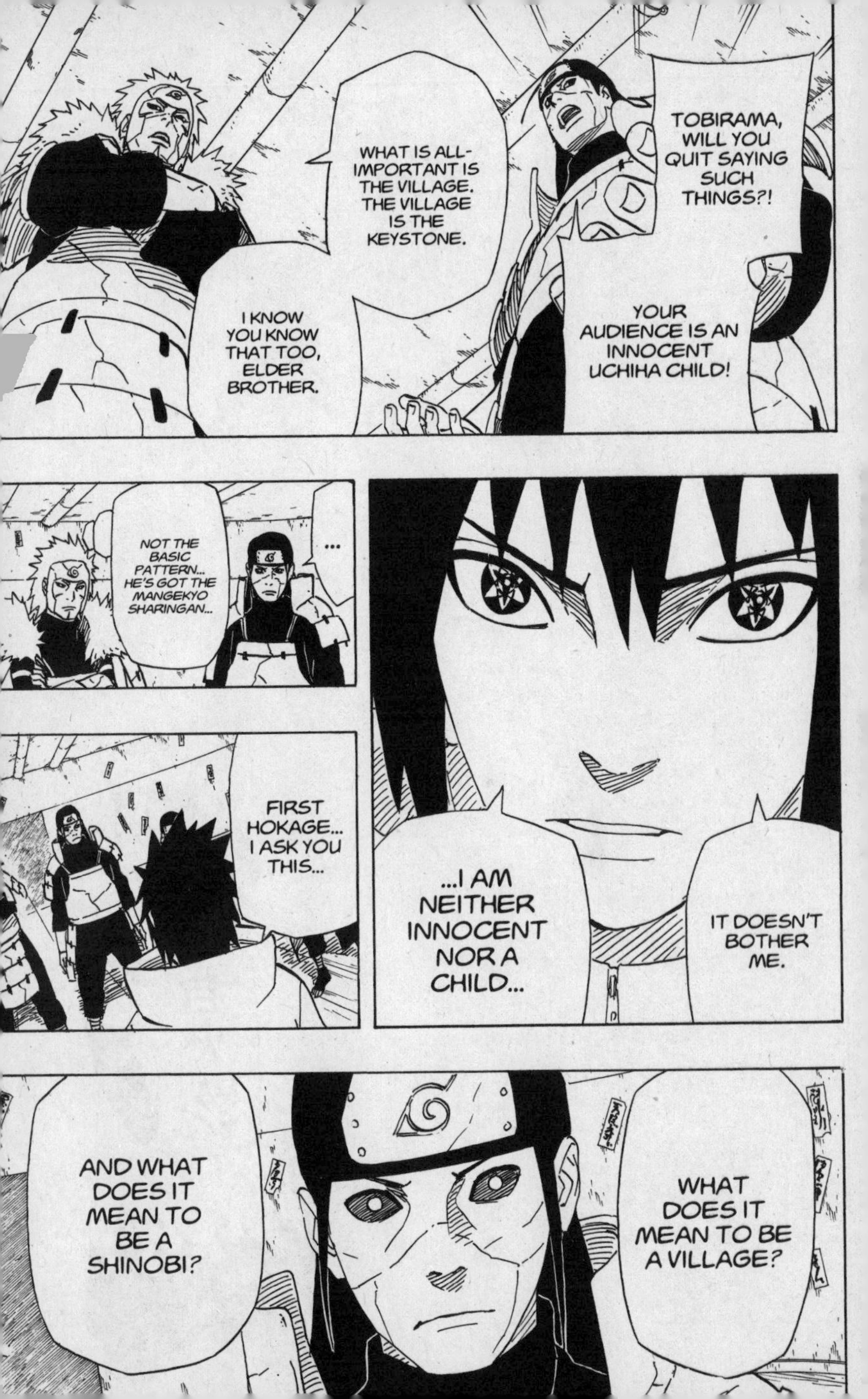
TOBIRAMA, WILL YOU QUIT SAYING SUCH THINGS?!
YOUR AUDIENCE IS AN INNOCENT UCHIHA CHILD!
WHAT IS ALL-IMPORTANT IS THE VILLAGE. THE VILLAGE IS THE KEYSTONE.
I KNOW YOU KNOW THAT TOO, ELDER BROTHER.
IT DOESN'T BOTHER ME.
...I AM NEITHER INNOCENT NOR A CHILD...
...
NOT THE BASIC PATTERN... HE'S GOT THE MANGEKYO SHARINGAN...
FIRST HOKAGE... I ASK YOU THIS...
WHAT DOES IT MEAN TO BE A VILLAGE?
AND WHAT DOES IT MEAN TO BE A SHINOBI?

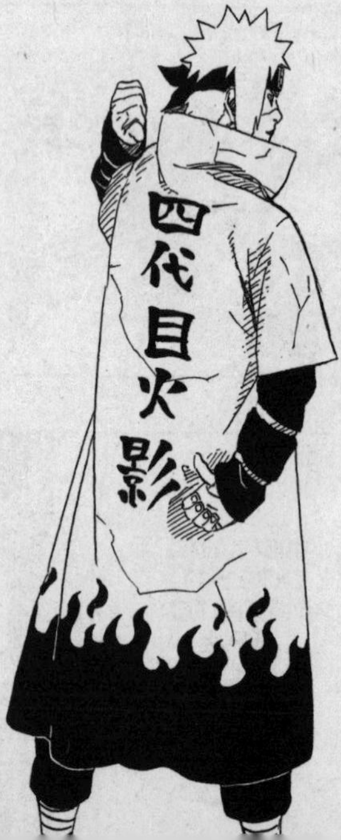
四代目火影

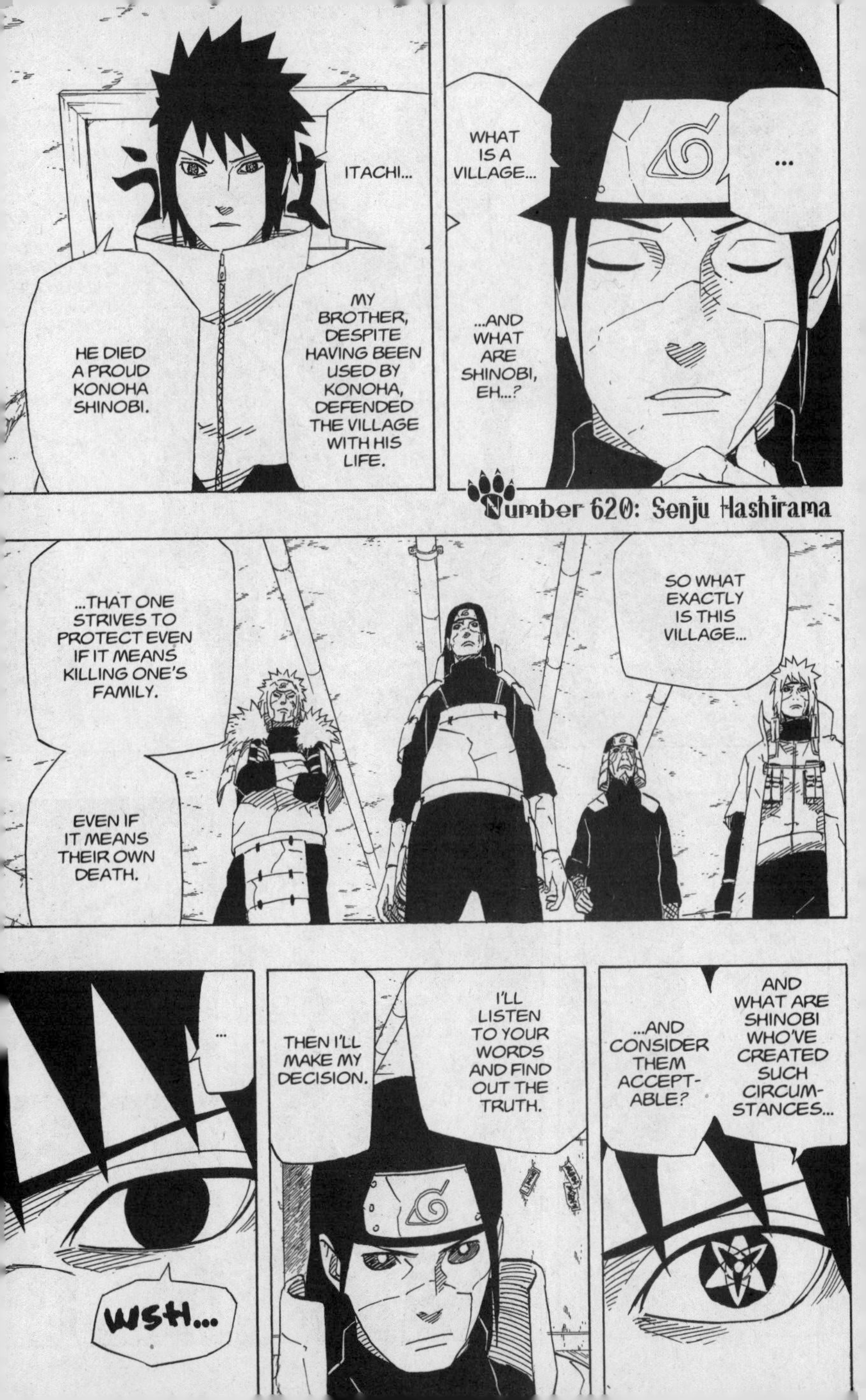
...
WHAT IS A VILLAGE...
...AND WHAT ARE SHINOBI, EH...?
ITACHI...
MY BROTHER, DESPITE HAVING BEEN USED BY KONOHA, DEFENDED THE VILLAGE WITH HIS LIFE.
HE DIED A PROUD KONOHA SHINOBI.
Number 620: Senju Hashirama
SO WHAT EXACTLY IS THIS VILLAGE...
...THAT ONE STRIVES TO PROTECT EVEN IF IT MEANS KILLING ONE'S FAMILY.
EVEN IF IT MEANS THEIR OWN DEATH.
AND WHAT ARE SHINOBI WHO'VE CREATED SUCH CIRCUMSTANCES...
...AND CONSIDER THEM ACCEPTABLE?
I'LL LISTEN TO YOUR WORDS AND FIND OUT THE TRUTH.
THEN I'LL MAKE MY DECISION.
...
WSH...

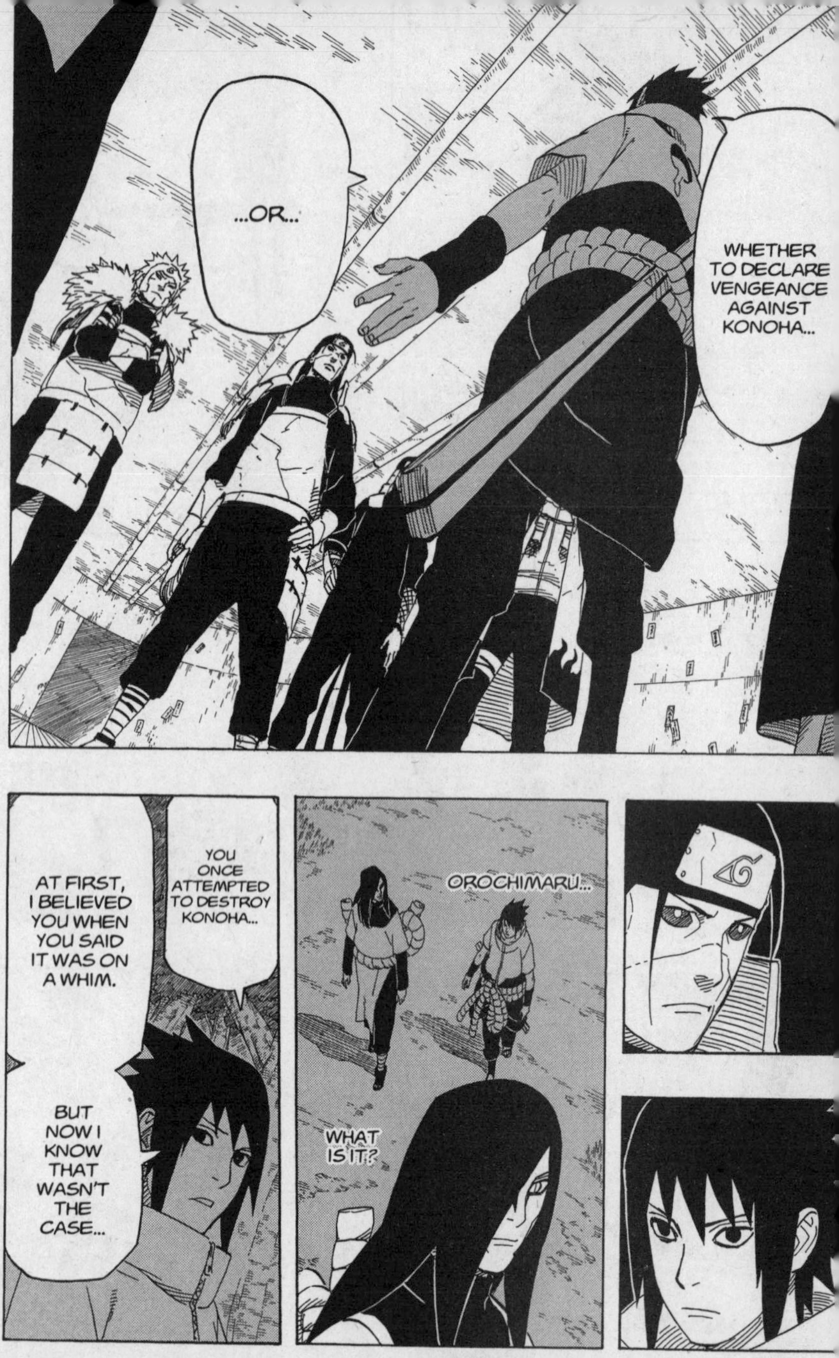
WHETHER TO DECLARE VENGEANCE AGAINST KONOHA...
...OR...
OROCHIMARU...
WHAT IS IT?
YOU ONCE ATTEMPTED TO DESTROY KONOHA...
AT FIRST, I BELIEVED YOU WHEN YOU SAID IT WAS ON A WHIM.
BUT NOW I KNOW THAT WASN'T THE CASE...

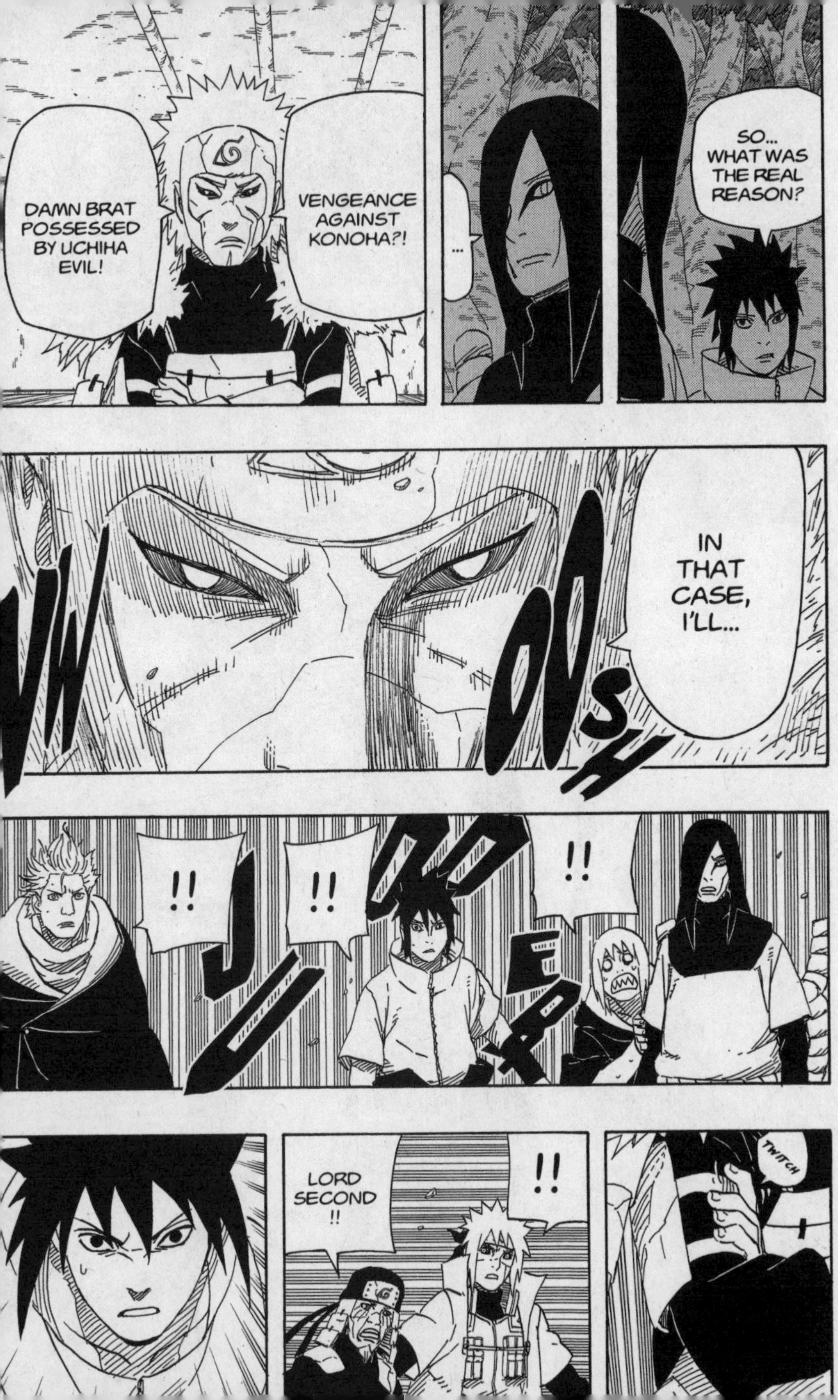

SO... WHAT WAS THE REAL REASON?
...
VENGEANCE AGAINST KONOHA?!
DAMN BRAT POSSESSED BY UCHIHA EVIL!
IN THAT CASE, I'LL...
!!
!!
!!
TWITCH
!!
LORD SECOND !!

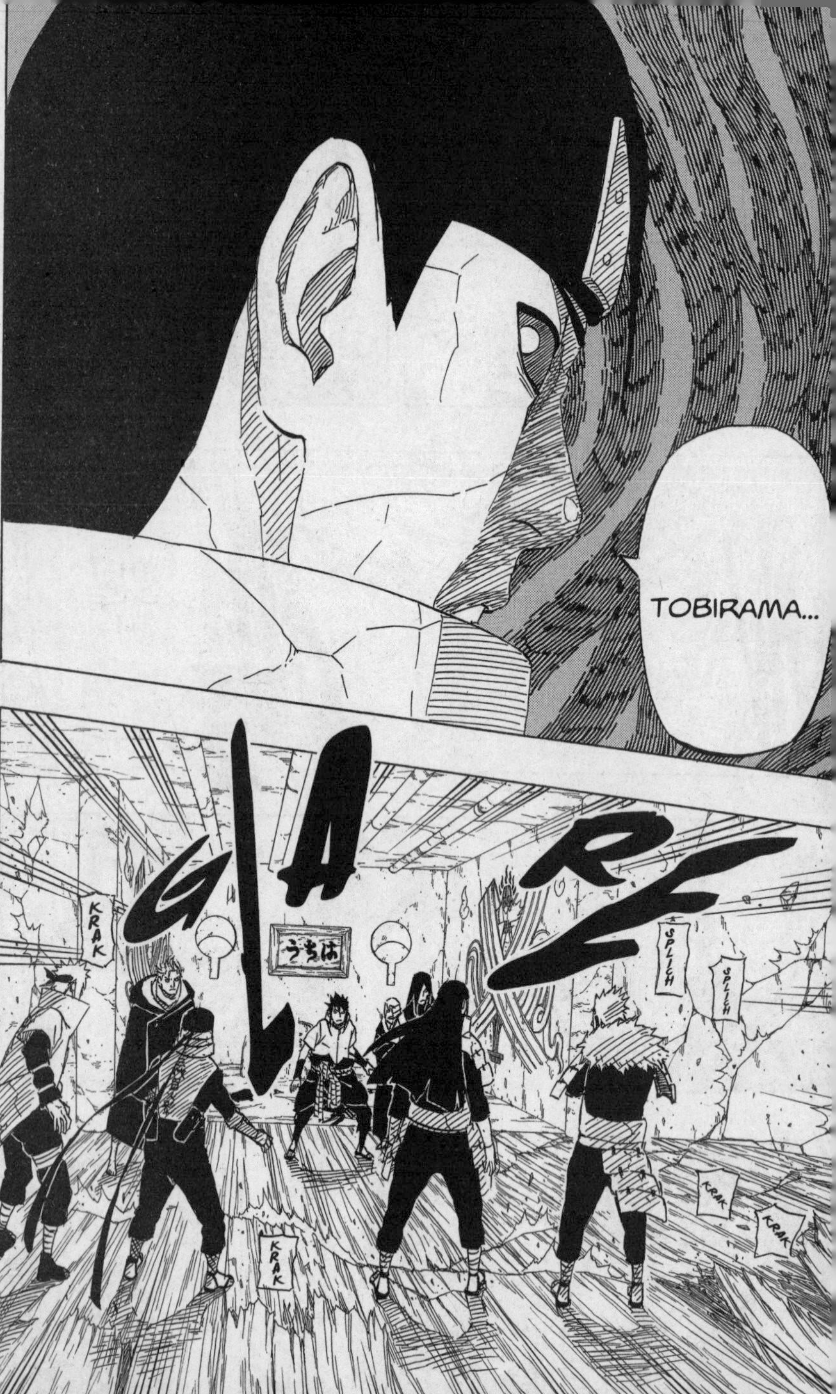
TOBIRAMA...
SPLICH
SPLICH
KRAK
KRAK
KRAK
うちは
KRAK

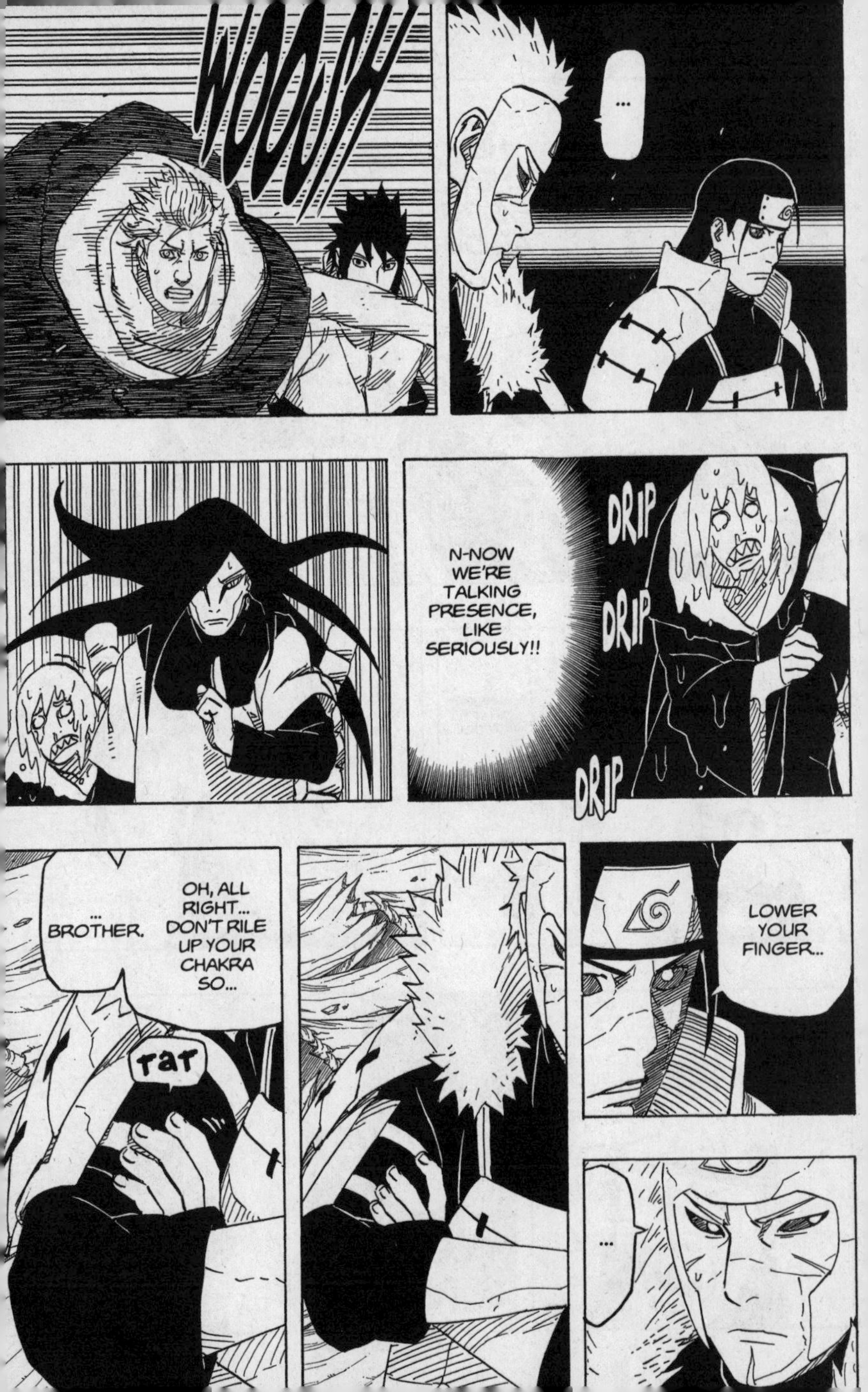
...
WOOSH
DRIP
DRIP
DRIP
N-NOW WE'RE TALKING PRESENCE, LIKE SERIOUSLY!!
LOWER YOUR FINGER...
OH, ALL RIGHT... DON'T RILE UP YOUR CHAKRA SO...
... BROTHER.
tat
...

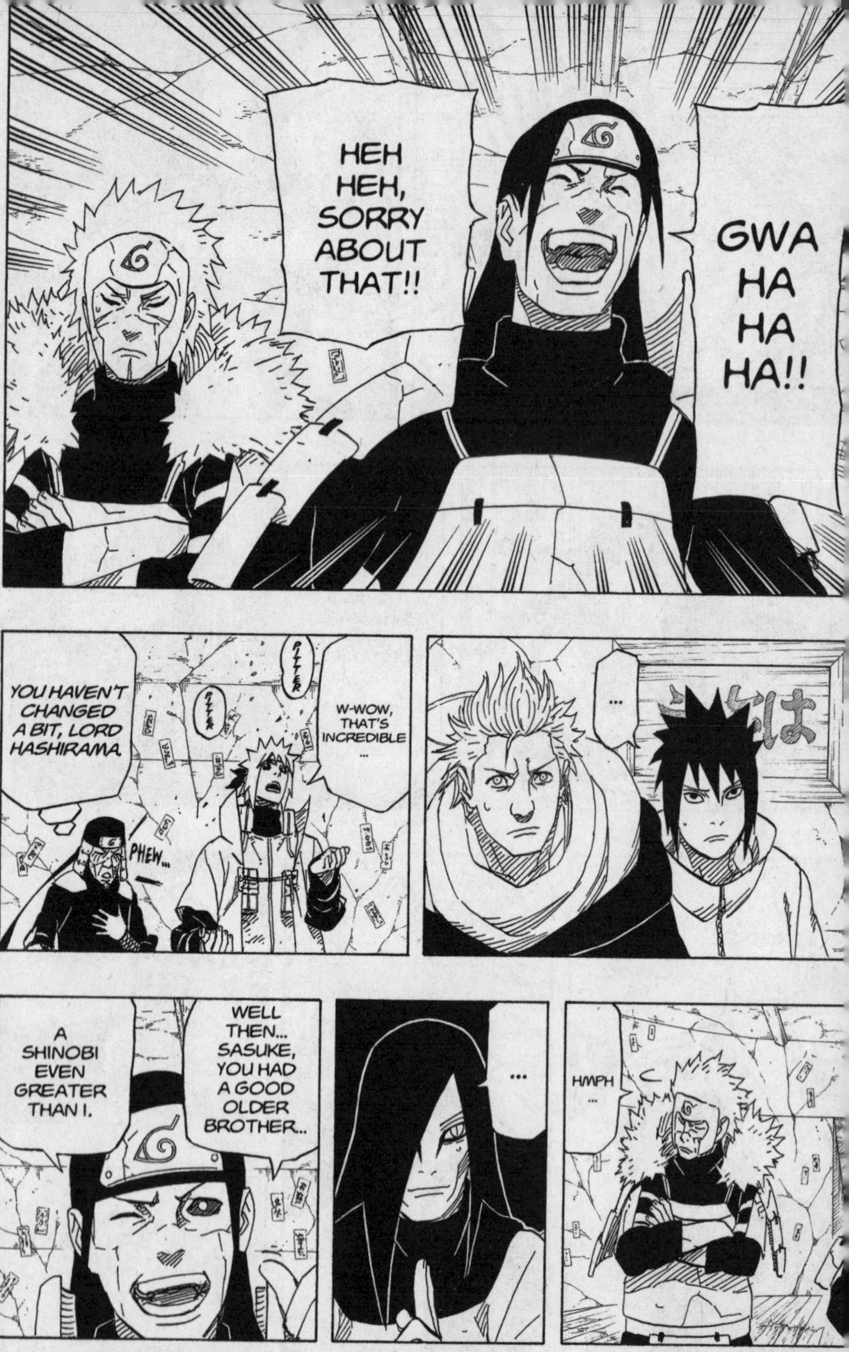
GWA HA HA HA!!
HEH HEH, SORRY ABOUT THAT!!
...
W-WOW, THAT'S INCREDIBLE ...
PITTER
PITTER
YOU HAVEN'T CHANGED A BIT, LORD HASHIRAMA.
PHEW...
HMPH ...
...
WELL THEN... SASUKE, YOU HAD A GOOD OLDER BROTHER...
A SHINOBI EVEN GREATER THAN I.

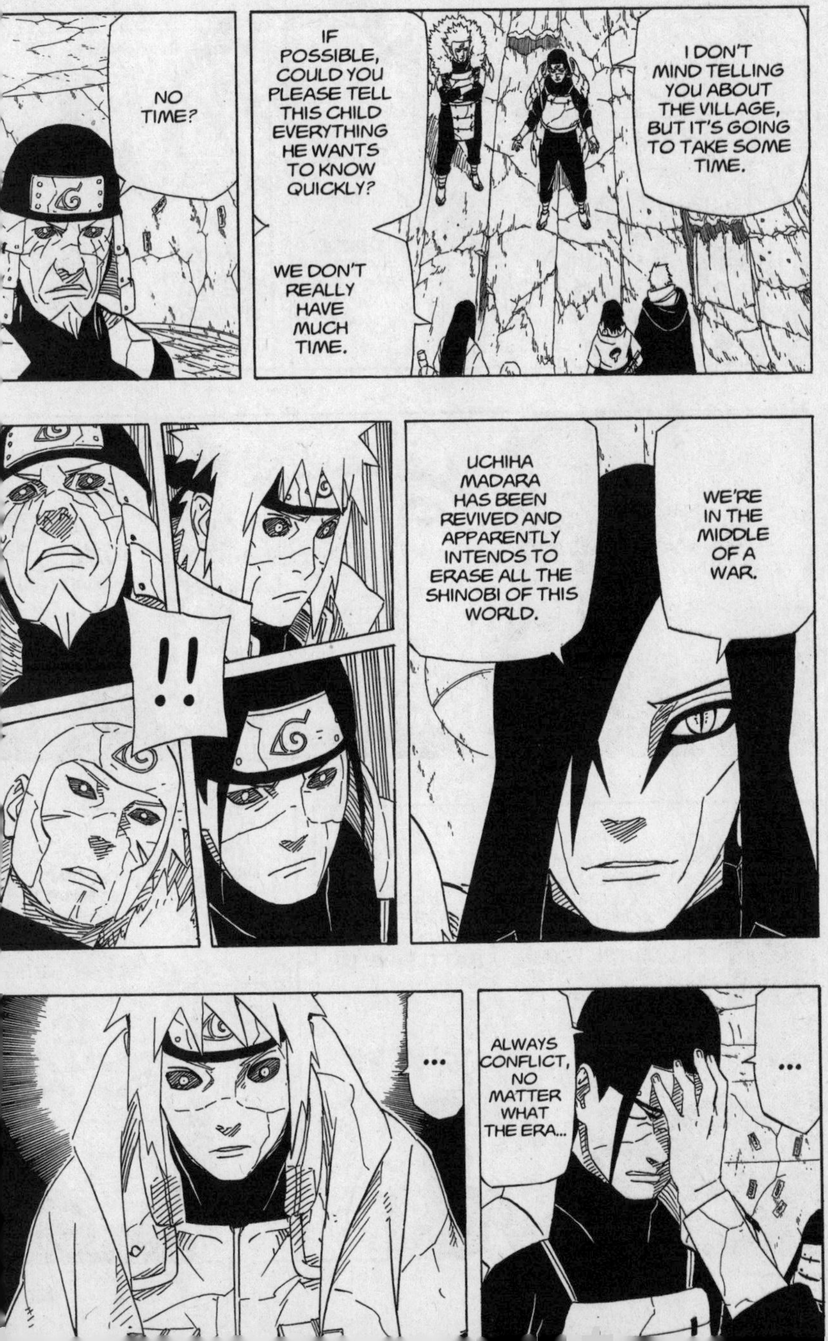
I DON'T MIND TELLING YOU ABOUT THE VILLAGE, BUT IT'S GOING TO TAKE SOME TIME.
IF POSSIBLE, COULD YOU PLEASE TELL THIS CHILD EVERYTHING HE WANTS TO KNOW QUICKLY?
WE DON'T REALLY HAVE MUCH TIME.
NO TIME?
WE'RE IN THE MIDDLE OF A WAR.
UCHIHA MADARA HAS BEEN REVIVED AND APPARENTLY INTENDS TO ERASE ALL THE SHINOBI OF THIS WORLD.
!!
...
ALWAYS CONFLICT, NO MATTER WHAT THE ERA...
...

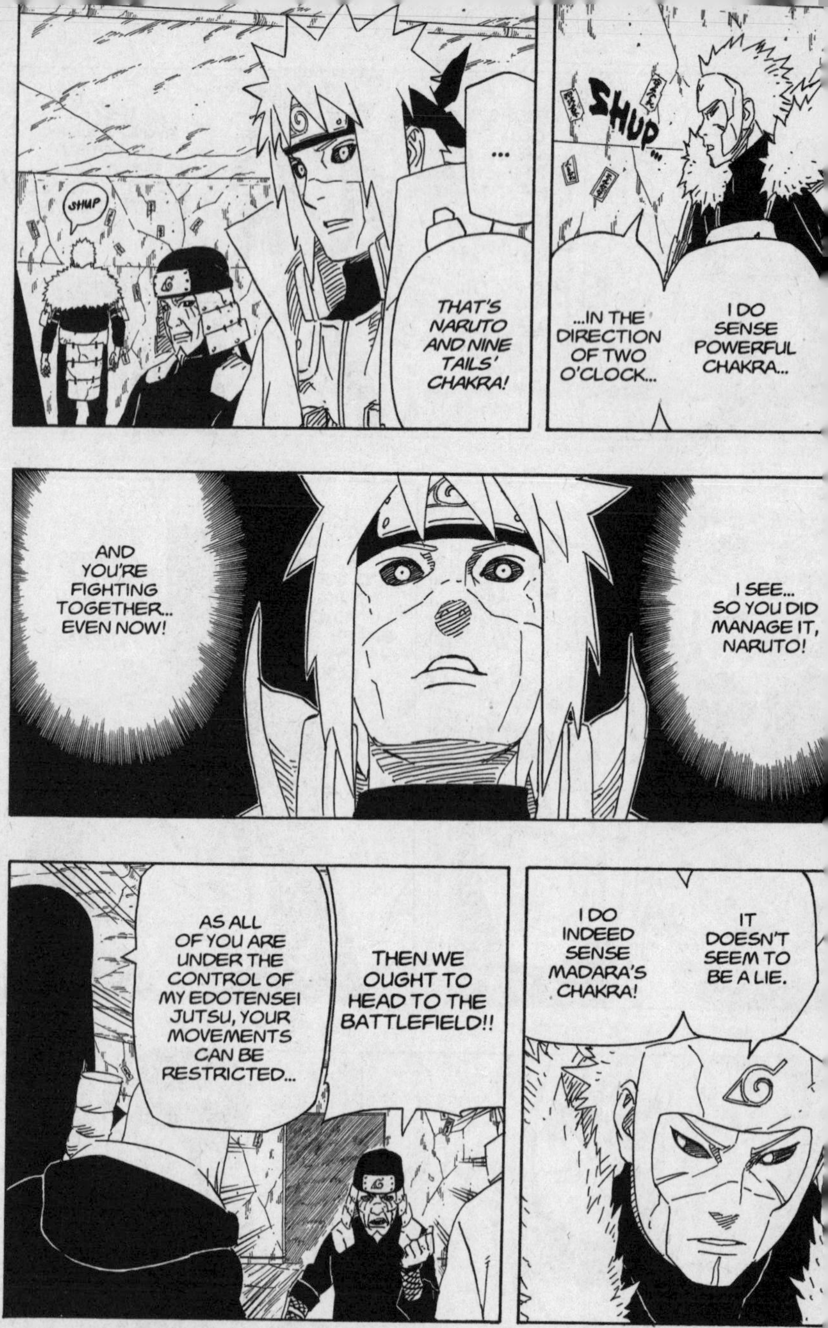
SHUP...
I DO SENSE POWERFUL CHAKRA...
...IN THE DIRECTION OF TWO O'CLOCK...
...
SHUP
THAT'S NARUTO AND NINE TAILS' CHAKRA!
I SEE... SO YOU DID MANAGE IT, NARUTO!
AND YOU'RE FIGHTING TOGETHER... EVEN NOW!
IT DOESN'T SEEM TO BE A LIE.
I DO INDEED SENSE MADARA'S CHAKRA!
THEN WE OUGHT TO HEAD TO THE BATTLEFIELD!!
AS ALL OF YOU ARE UNDER THE CONTROL OF MY EDOTENSEI JUTSU, YOUR MOVEMENTS CAN BE RESTRICTED...

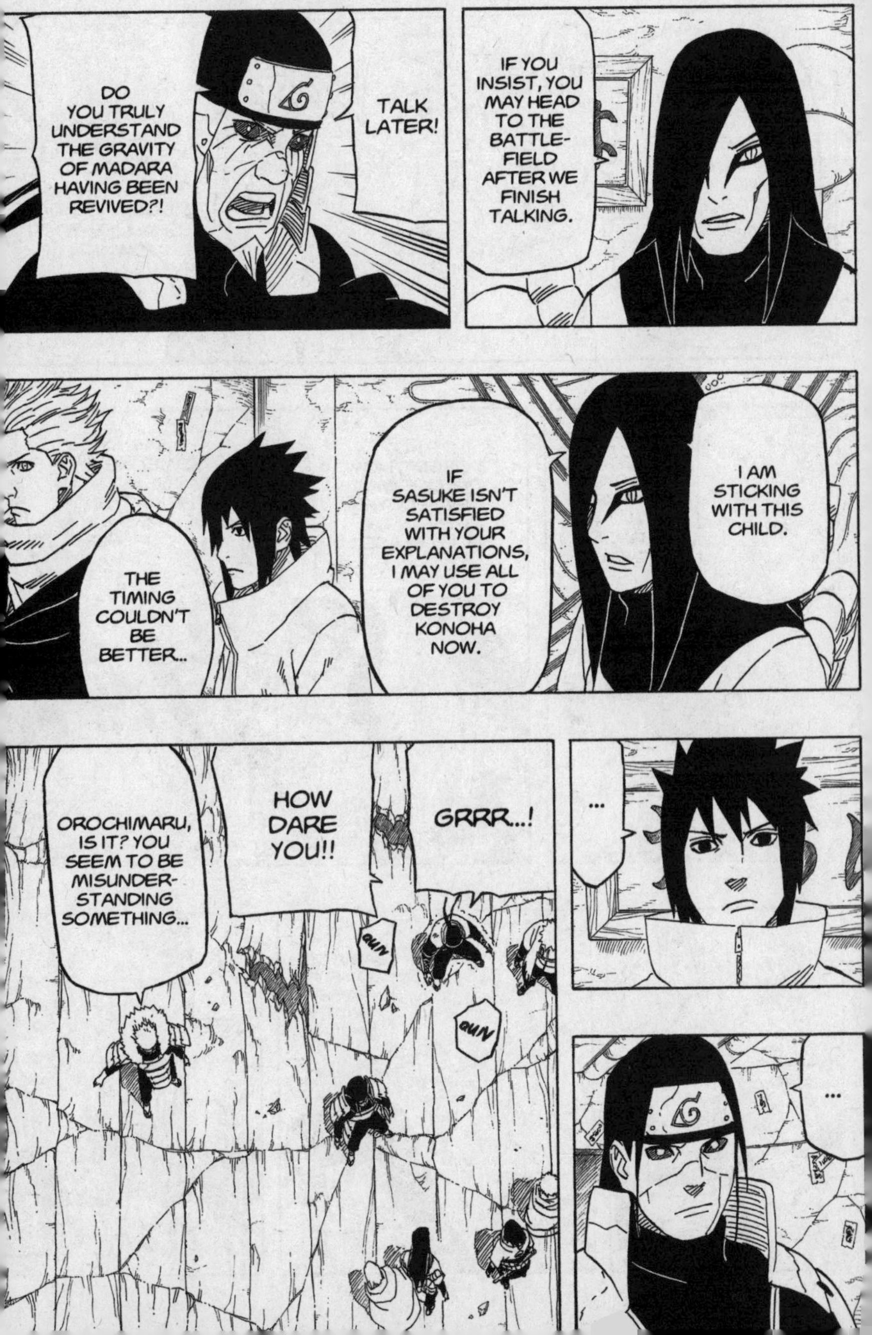
IF YOU INSIST, YOU MAY HEAD TO THE BATTLE-FIELD AFTER WE FINISH TALKING.
TALK LATER!
DO YOU TRULY UNDERSTAND THE GRAVITY OF MADARA HAVING BEEN REVIVED?!
I AM STICKING WITH THIS CHILD.
IF SASUKE ISN'T SATISFIED WITH YOUR EXPLANATIONS, I MAY USE ALL OF YOU TO DESTROY KONOHA NOW.
THE TIMING COULDN'T BE BETTER...
...
...
GRRR...!
HOW DARE YOU!!
OROCHIMARU, IS IT? YOU SEEM TO BE MISUNDER-STANDING SOMETHING...
QUN
QUN

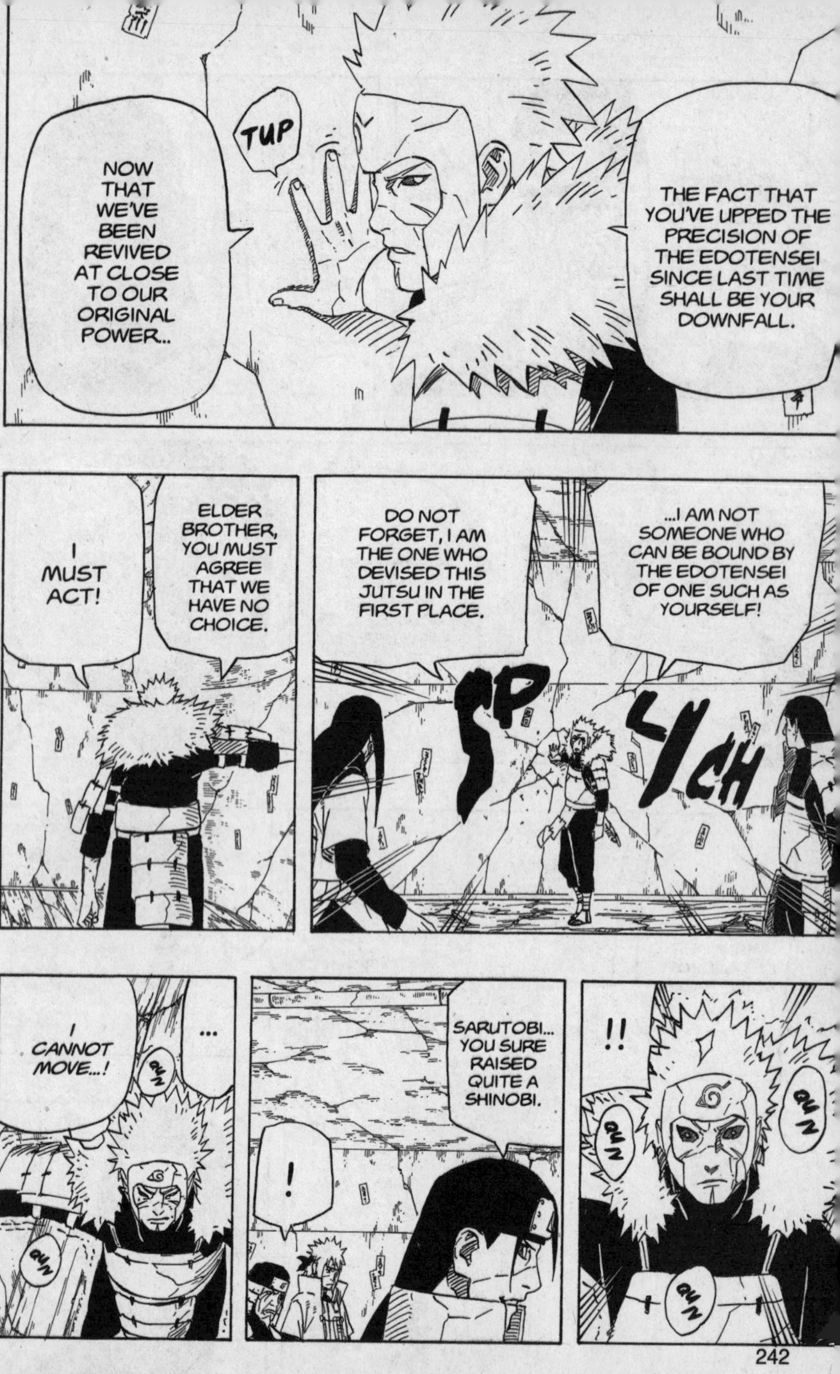
THE FACT THAT YOU'VE UPPED THE PRECISION OF THE EDOTENSEI SINCE LAST TIME SHALL BE YOUR DOWNFALL.
TUP
NOW THAT WE'VE BEEN REVIVED AT CLOSE TO OUR ORIGINAL POWER...
...I AM NOT SOMEONE WHO CAN BE BOUND BY THE EDOTENSEI OF ONE SUCH AS YOURSELF!
DO NOT FORGET, I AM THE ONE WHO DEVISED THIS JUTSU IN THE FIRST PLACE.
SPLCH
ELDER BROTHER, YOU MUST AGREE THAT WE HAVE NO CHOICE.
I MUST ACT!
!!
QUN
QUN
QUN
SARUTOBI... YOU SURE RAISED QUITE A SHINOBI.
!
...
I CANNOT MOVE...!
QUN
QUN

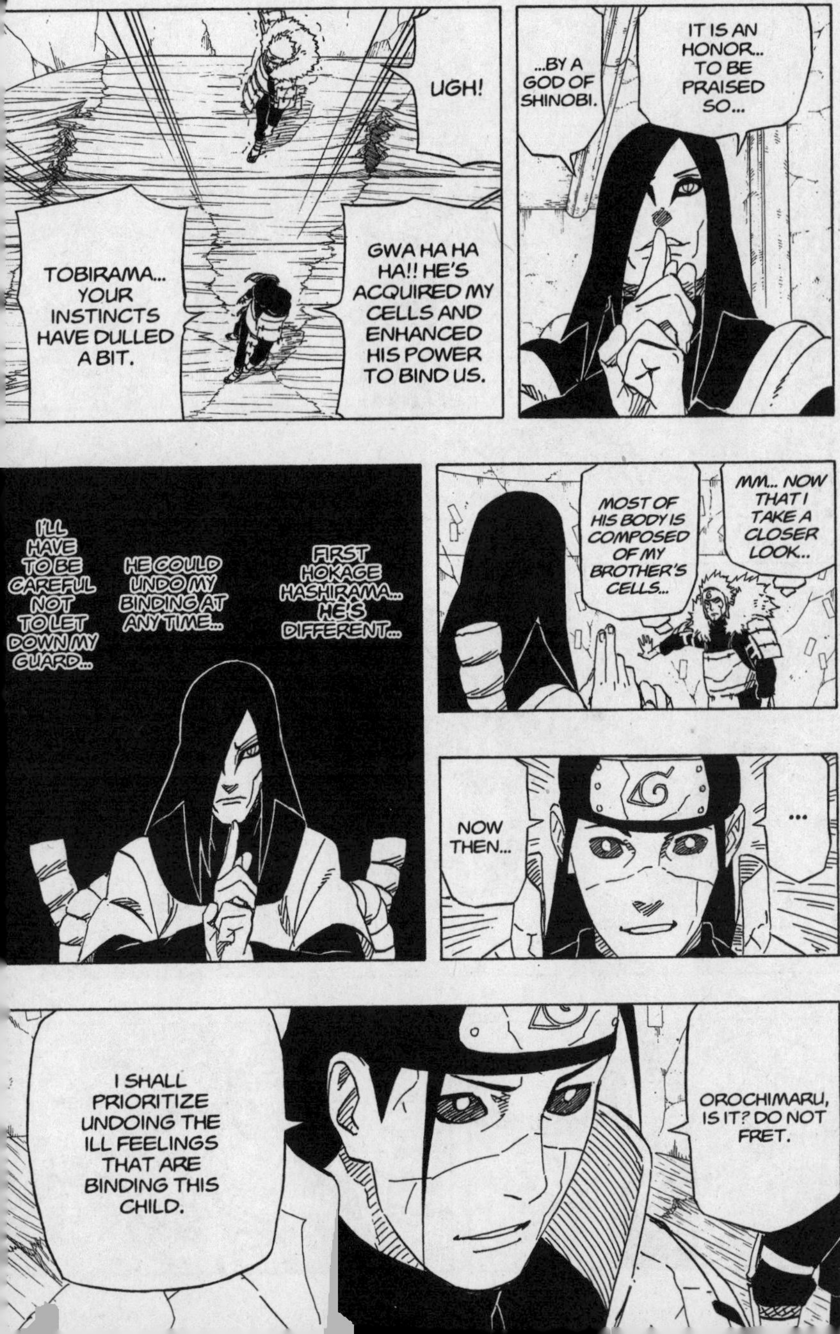
IT IS AN HONOR.. TO BE PRAISED SO...
...BY A GOD OF SHINOBI.
UGH!
GWA HA HA HA!! HE'S ACQUIRED MY CELLS AND ENHANCED HIS POWER TO BIND US.
TOBIRAMA... YOUR INSTINCTS HAVE DULLED A BIT.
MM... NOW THAT I TAKE A CLOSER LOOK...
MOST OF HIS BODY IS COMPOSED OF MY BROTHER'S CELLS...
...
NOW THEN...
FIRST HOKAGE HASHIRAMA... HE'S DIFFERENT...
HE COULD UNDO MY BINDING AT ANY TIME...
I'LL HAVE TO BE CAREFUL NOT TO LET DOWN MY GUARD...
OROCHIMARU, IS IT? DO NOT FRET.
I SHALL PRIORITIZE UNDOING THE ILL FEELINGS THAT ARE BINDING THIS CHILD.

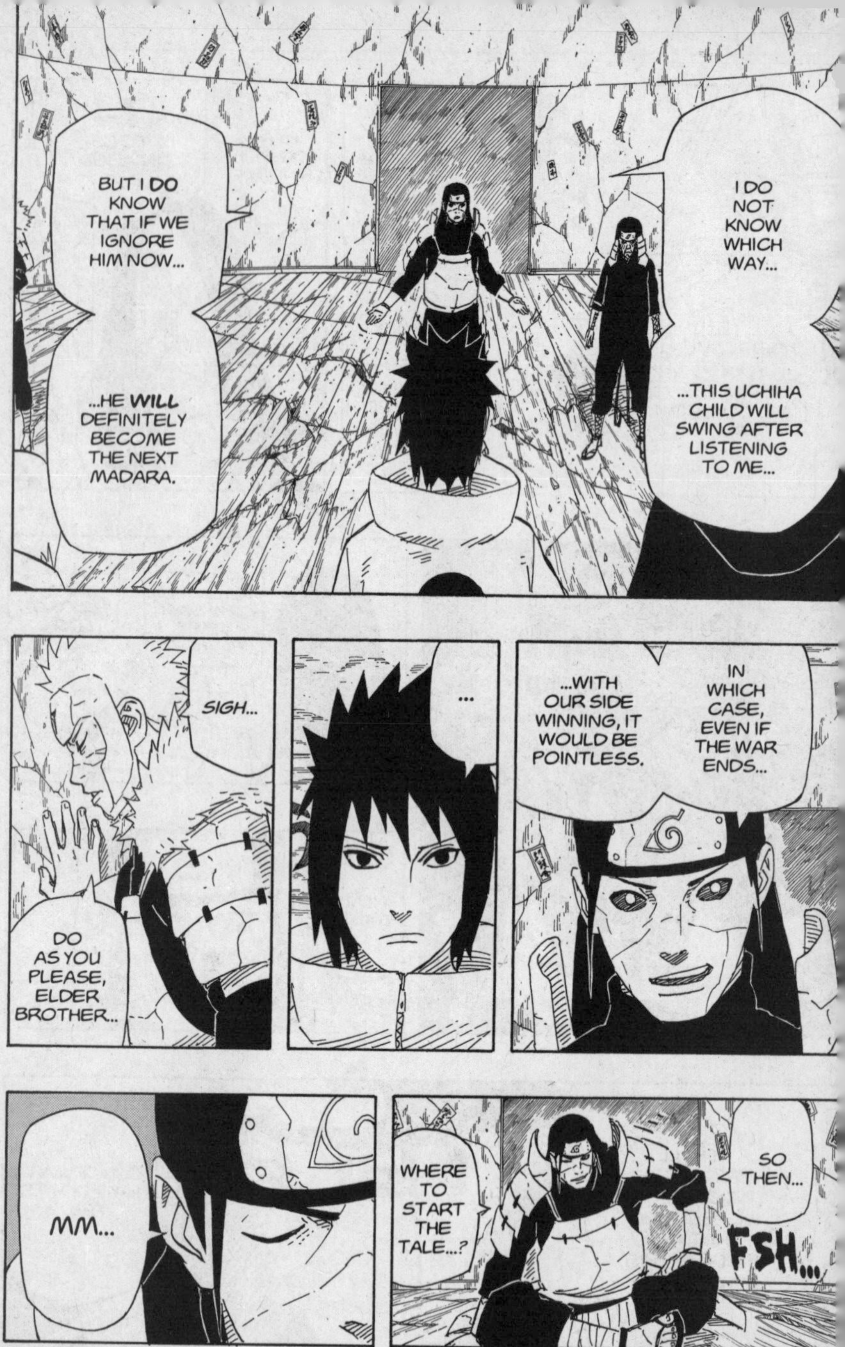
I DO NOT KNOW WHICH WAY...
...THIS UCHIHA CHILD WILL SWING AFTER LISTENING TO ME...
BUT I DO KNOW THAT IF WE IGNORE HIM NOW...
...HE WILL DEFINITELY BECOME THE NEXT MADARA.
IN WHICH CASE, EVEN IF THE WAR ENDS...
...WITH OUR SIDE WINNING, IT WOULD BE POINTLESS.
...
SIGH...
DO AS YOU PLEASE, ELDER BROTHER...
SO THEN...
FSH...
WHERE TO START THE TALE...?
MM...

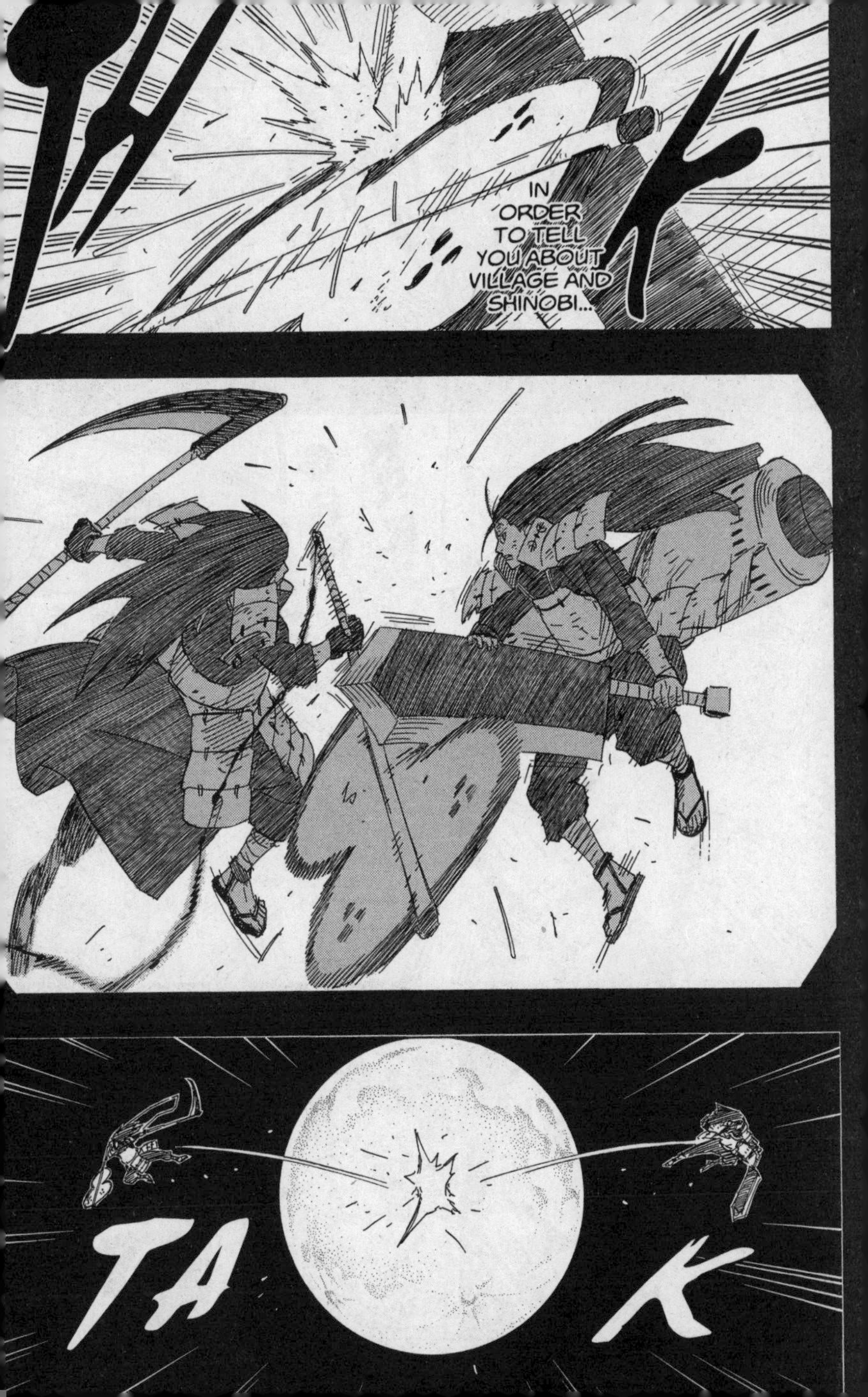
SHK
IN ORDER TO TELL YOU ABOUT VILLAGE AND SHINOBI...
TAK

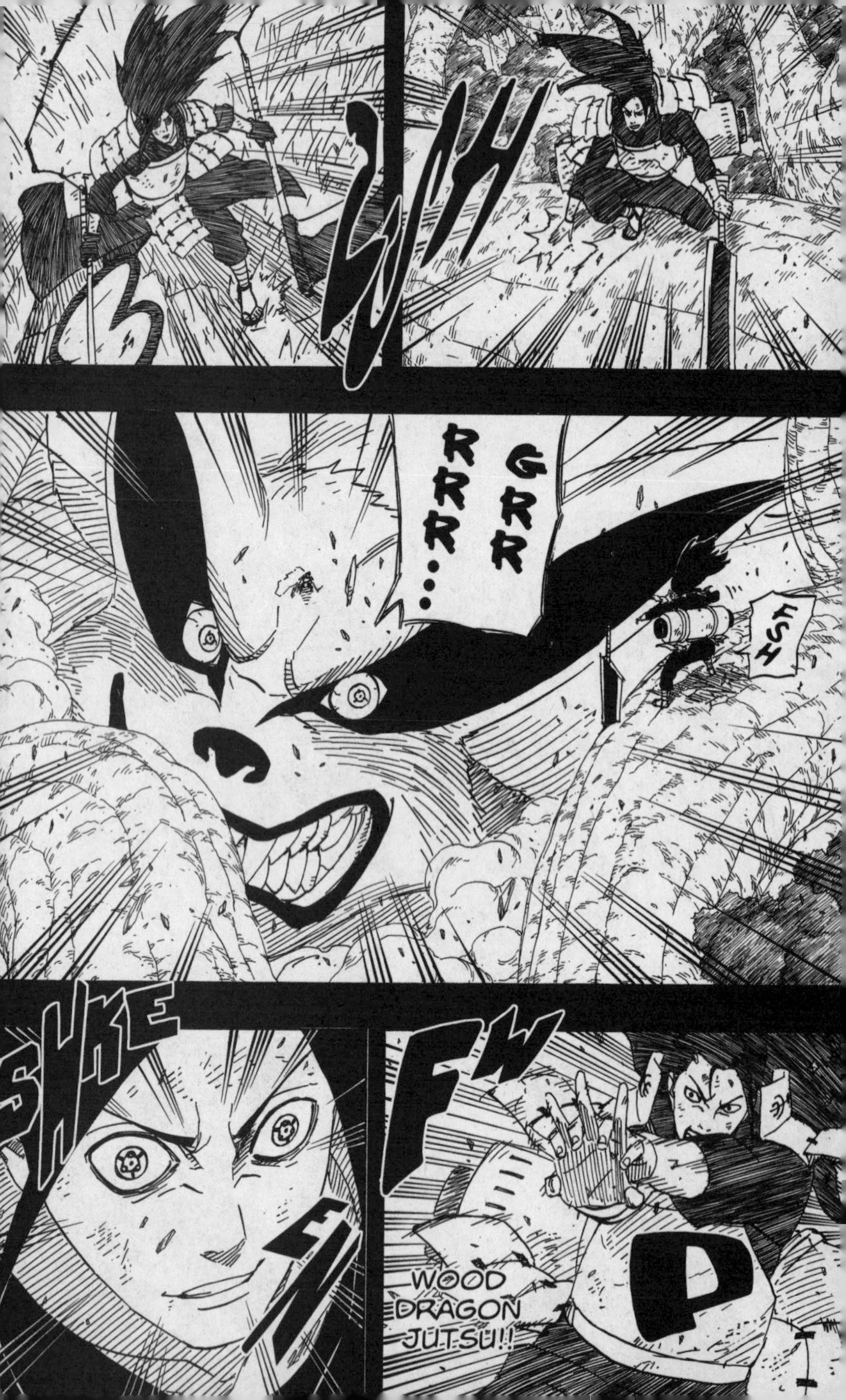
GRRR
RRRR...
FSH
FW
WOOD DRAGON JUTSU!!

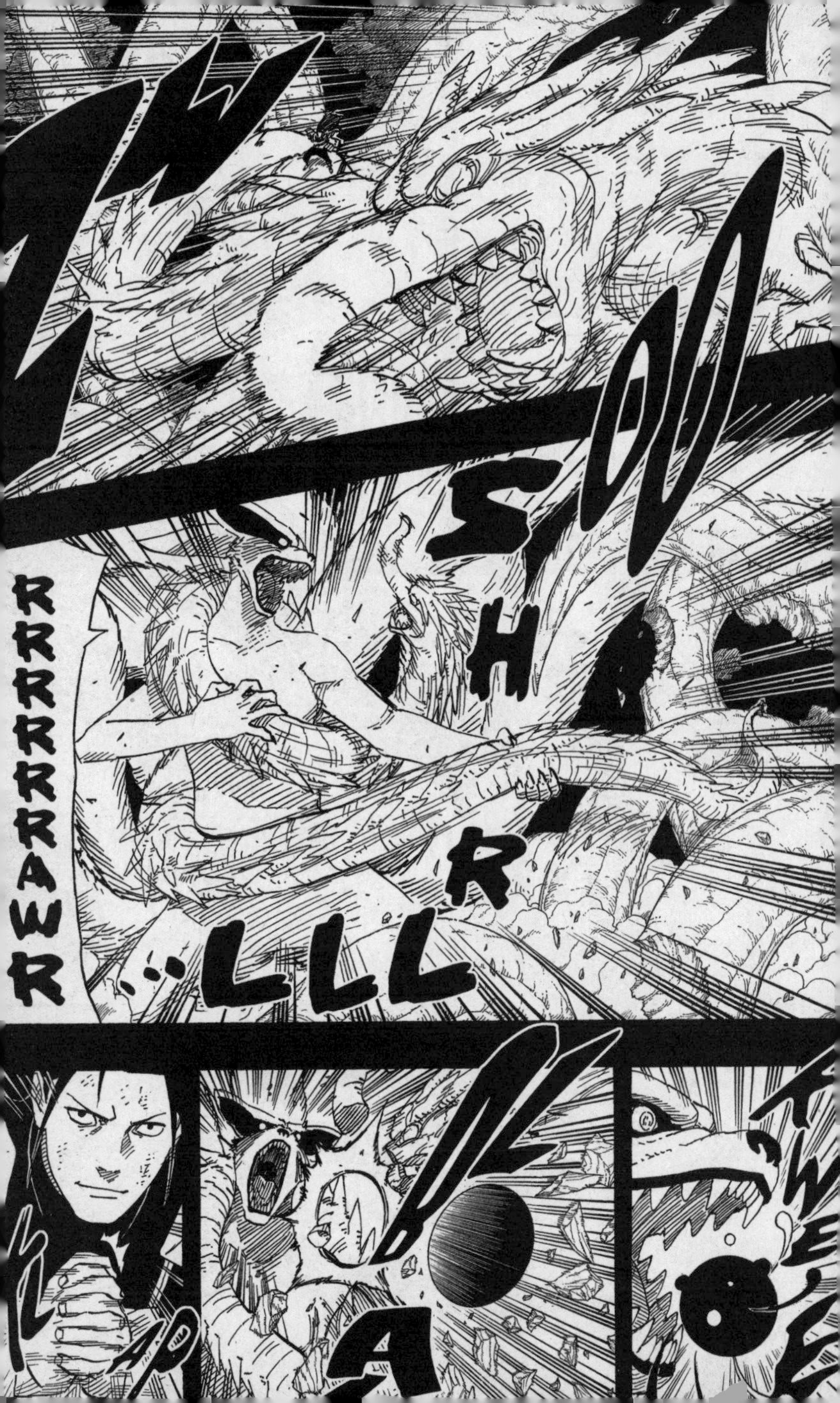
RRRRRRRAWR

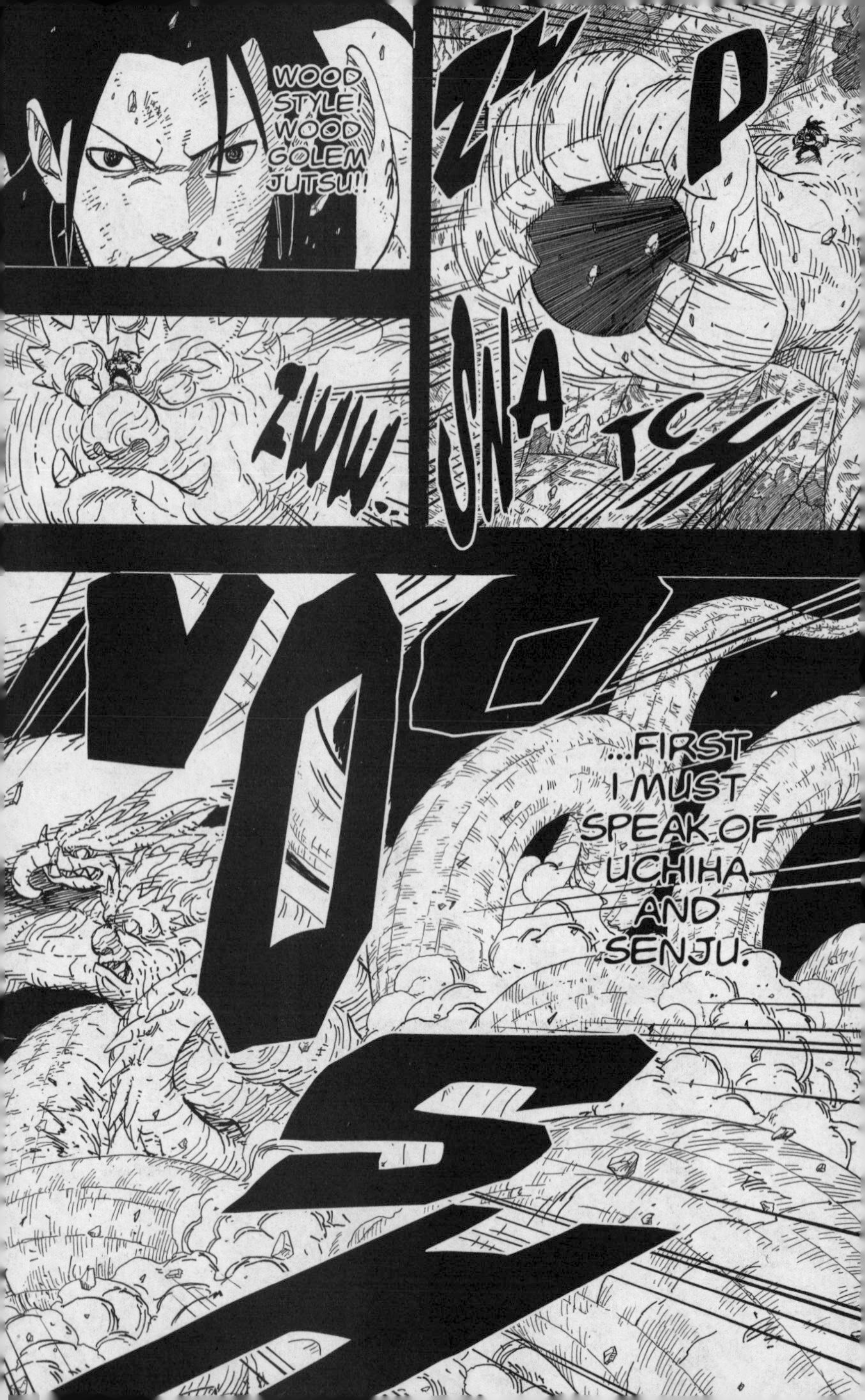
SNATCH
WOOD STYLE! WOOD GOLEM JUTSU!!
ZWWW
...FIRST I MUST SPEAK OF UCHIHA AND SENJU.

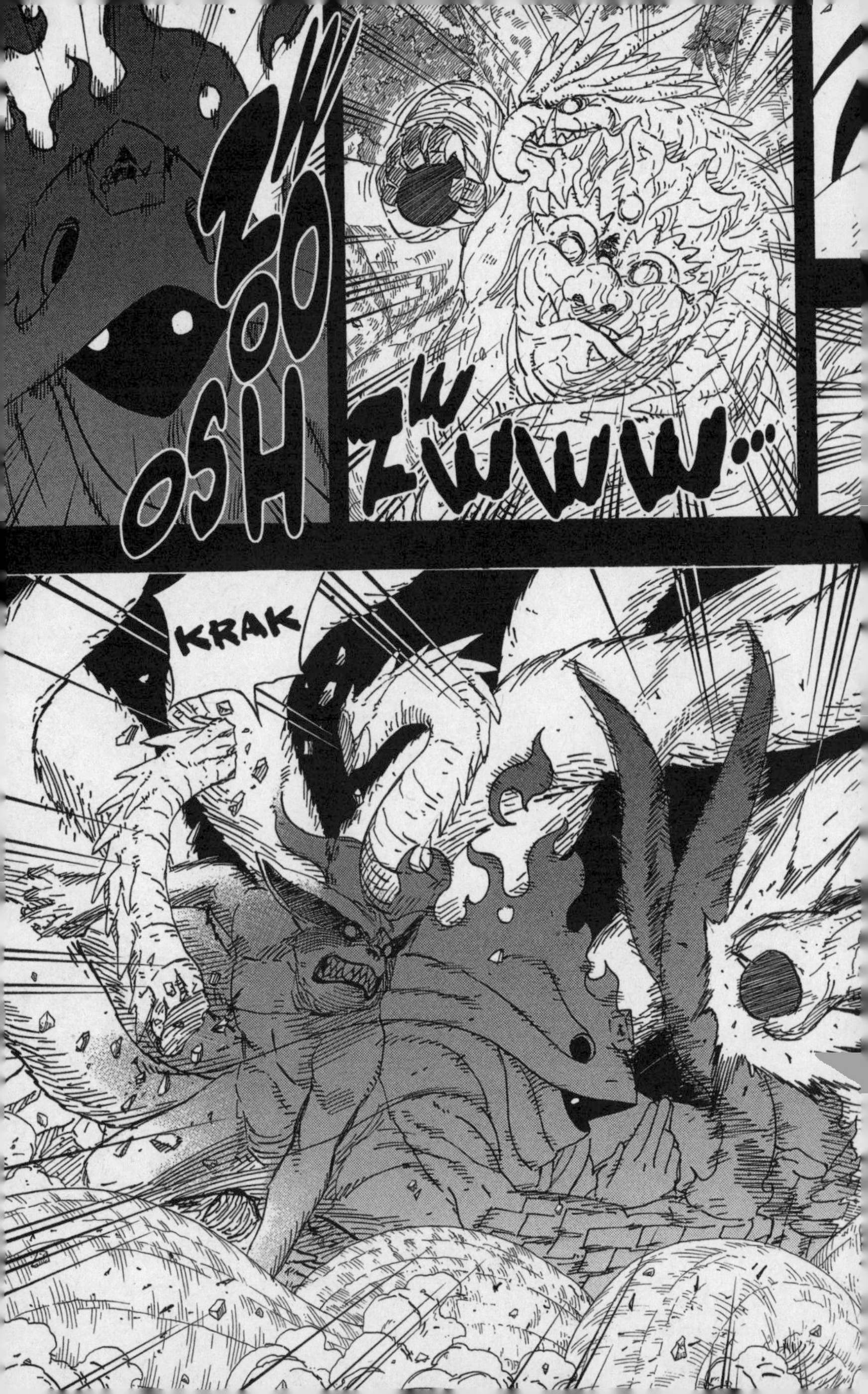

ZW
ZWWWW...
ZWOOOSH
KRAK

Number 621: Hashirama and Madara

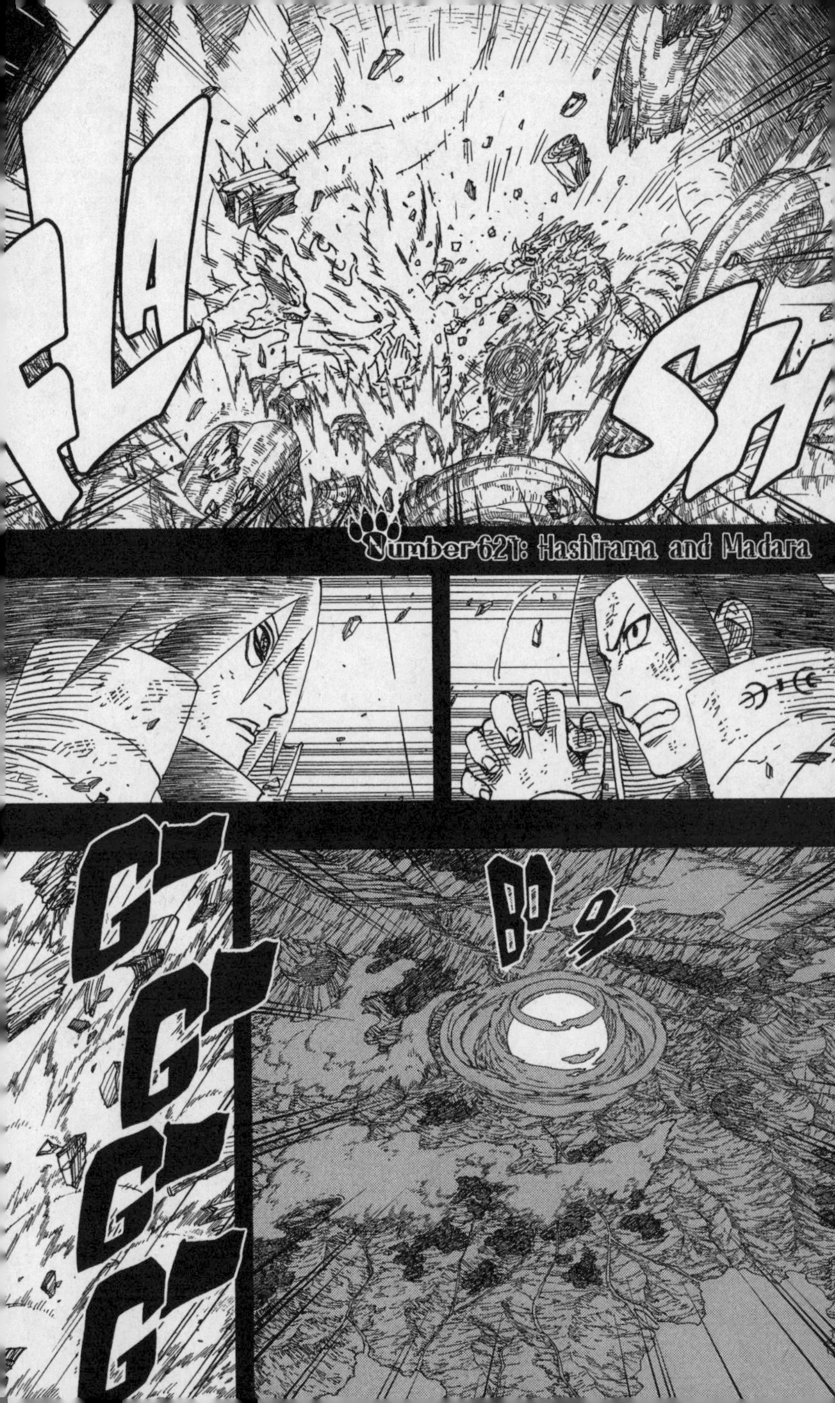
FLA
SH
BOOM
G
G
G
G

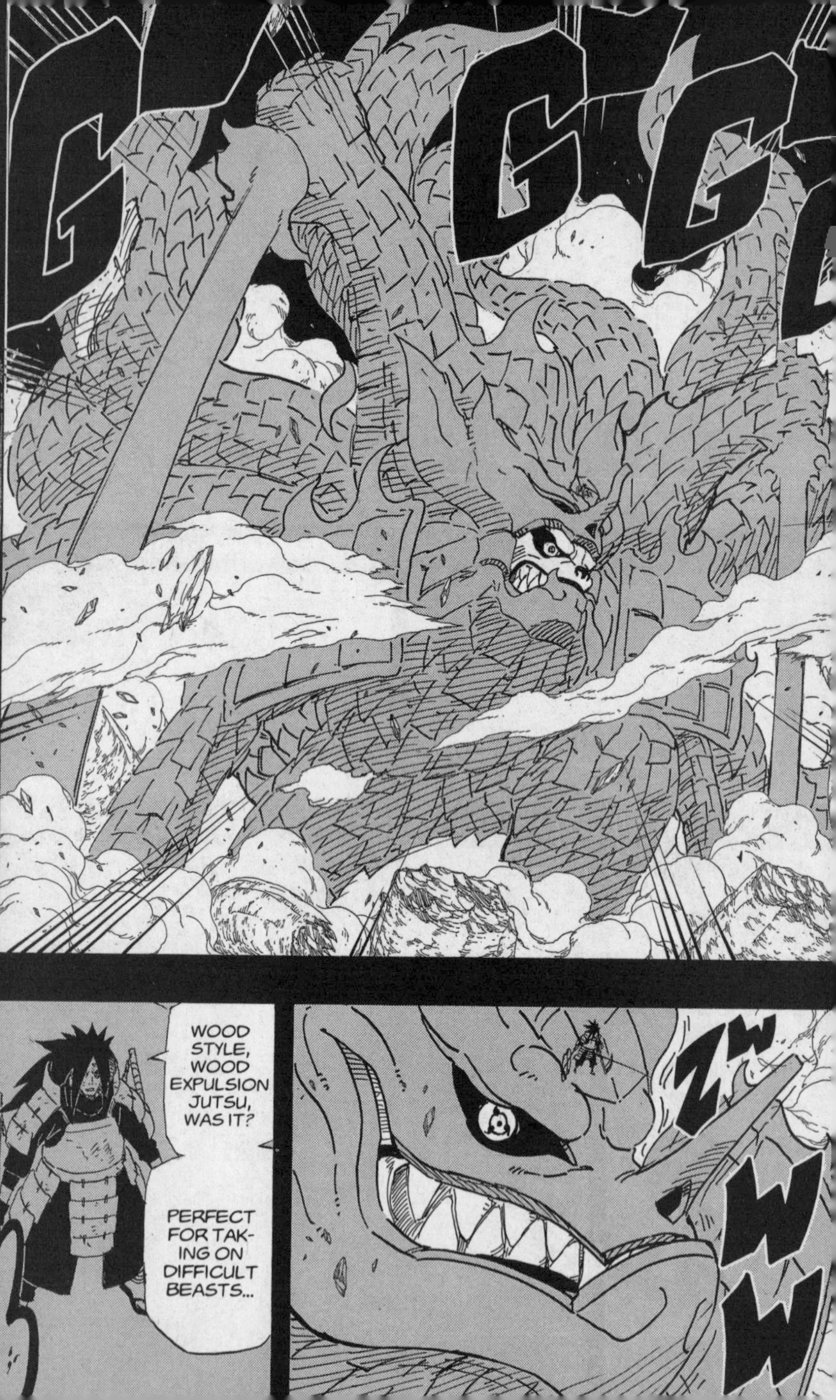
GGGG
ZWWW
WOOD STYLE, WOOD EXPULSION JUTSU, WAS IT?
PERFECT FOR TAKING ON DIFFICULT BEASTS...

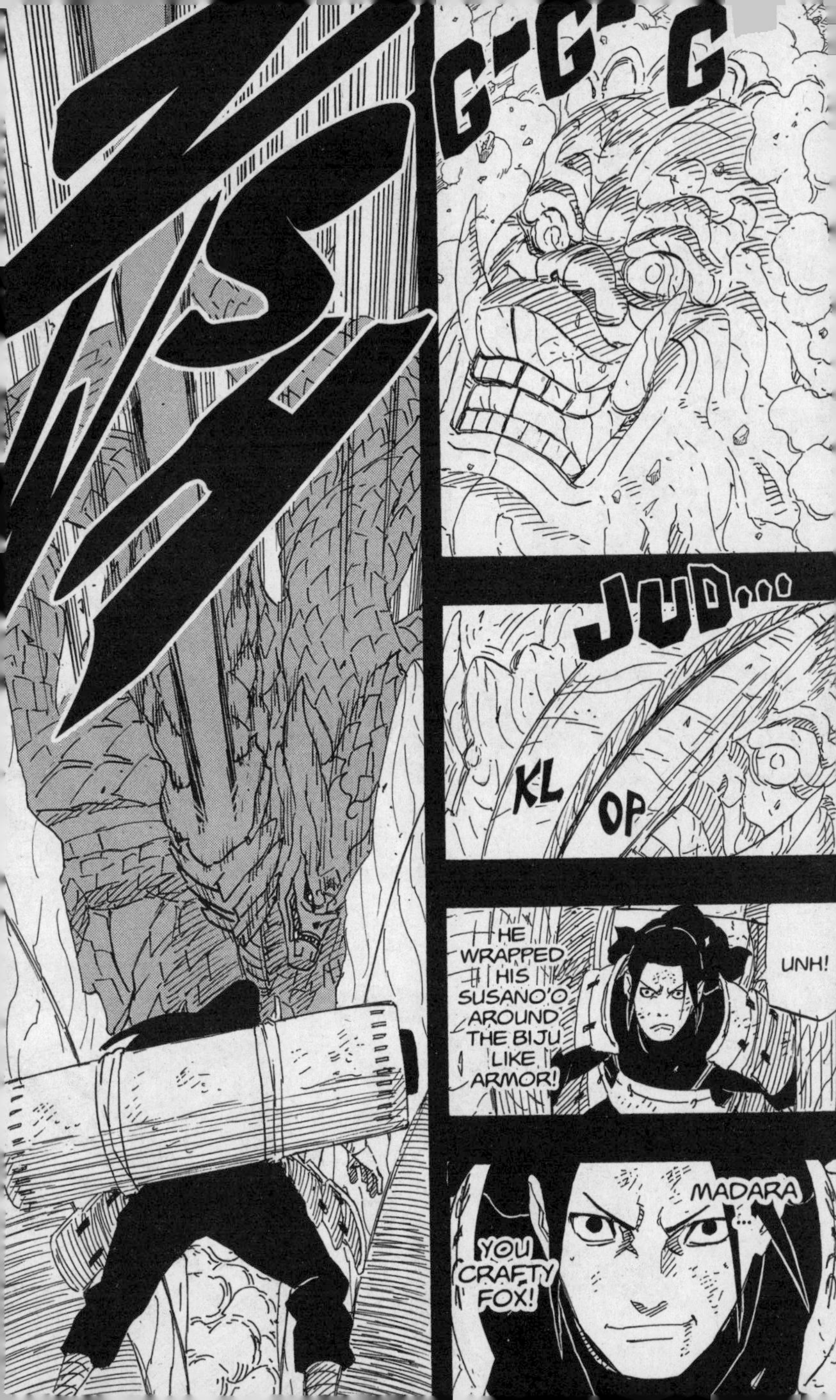
G-G-G
JUD...
KL OP
UNH!
HE WRAPPED HIS SUSANO'O AROUND THE BIJU LIKE ARMOR!
MADARA...
YOU CRAFTY FOX!

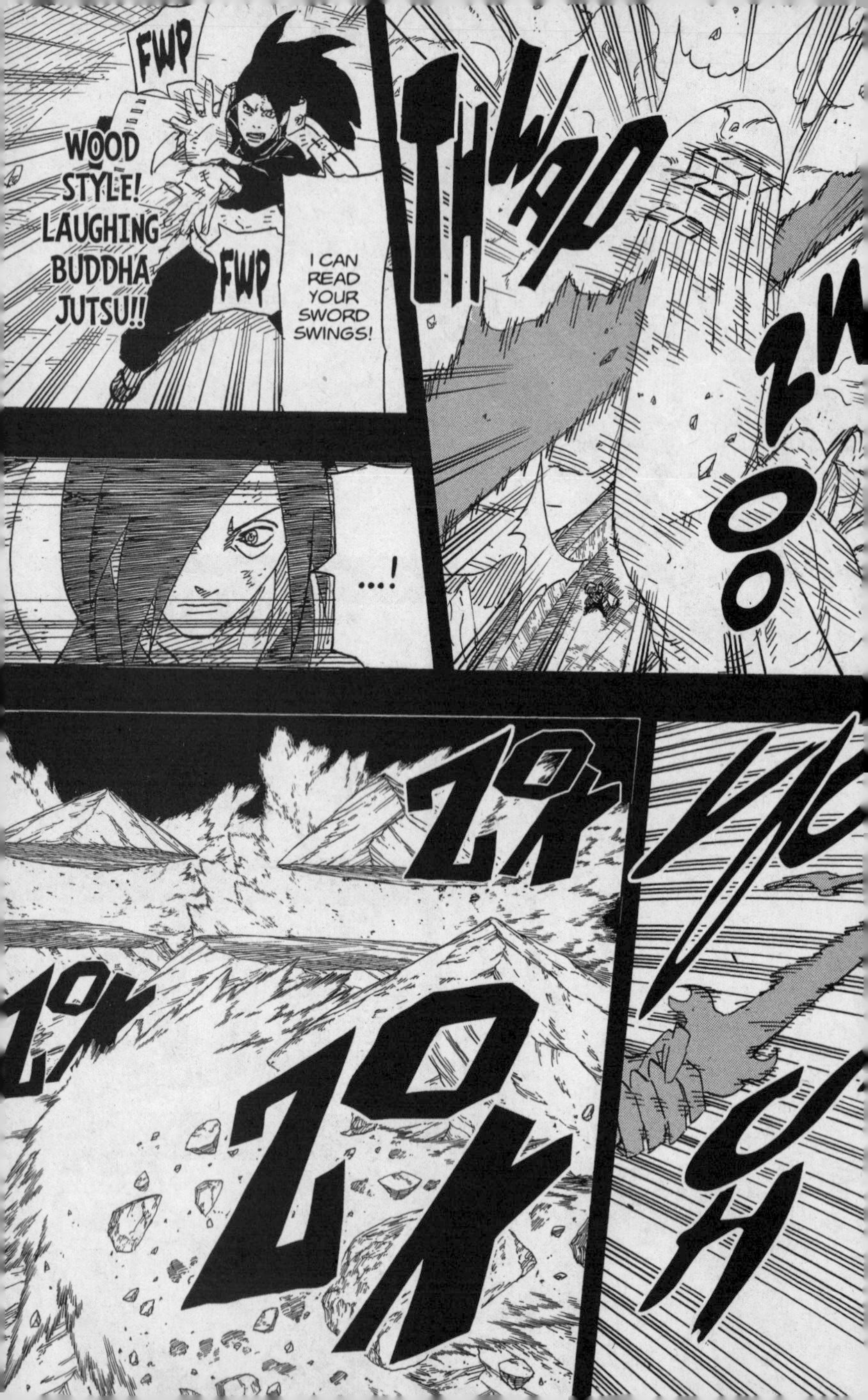
THWAP
FWP
WOOD STYLE! LAUGHING BUDDHA JUTSU!!
FWP
I CAN READ YOUR SWORD SWINGS!
...!

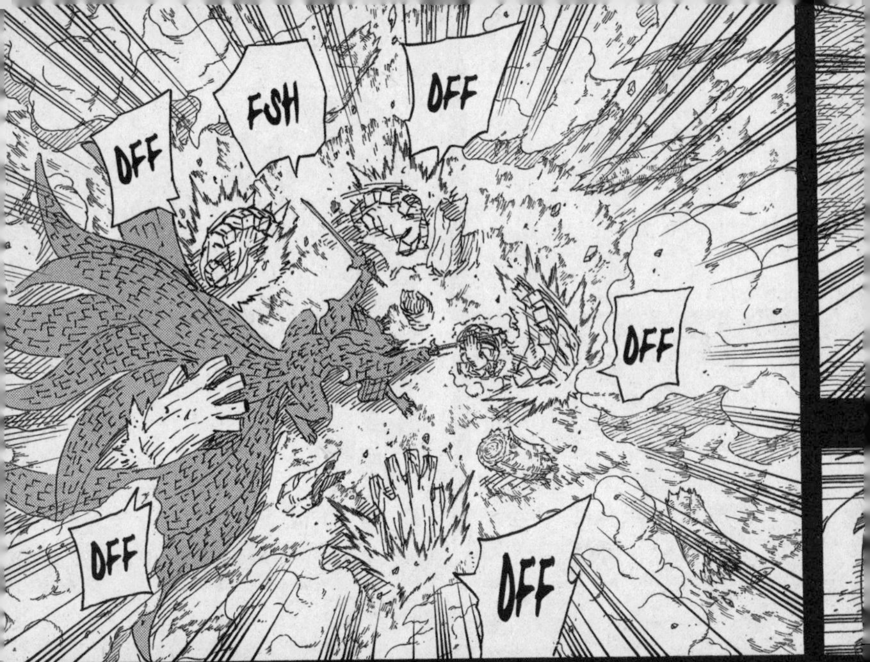
OFF
OFF
FSH
OFF
OFF
OFF
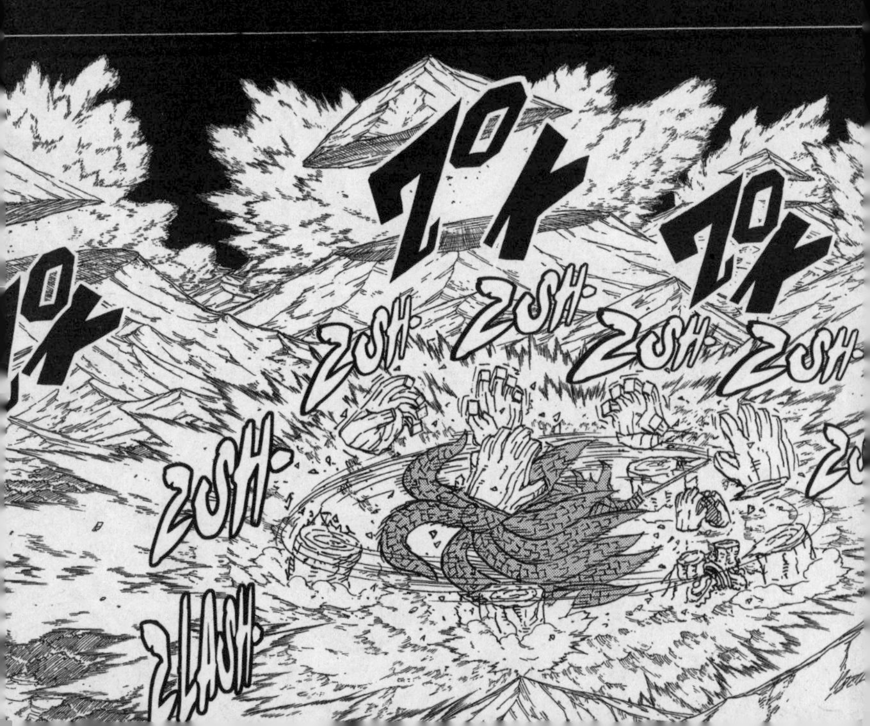
ZSH
ZSH
ZSH
ZSH
ZSH
SLASH

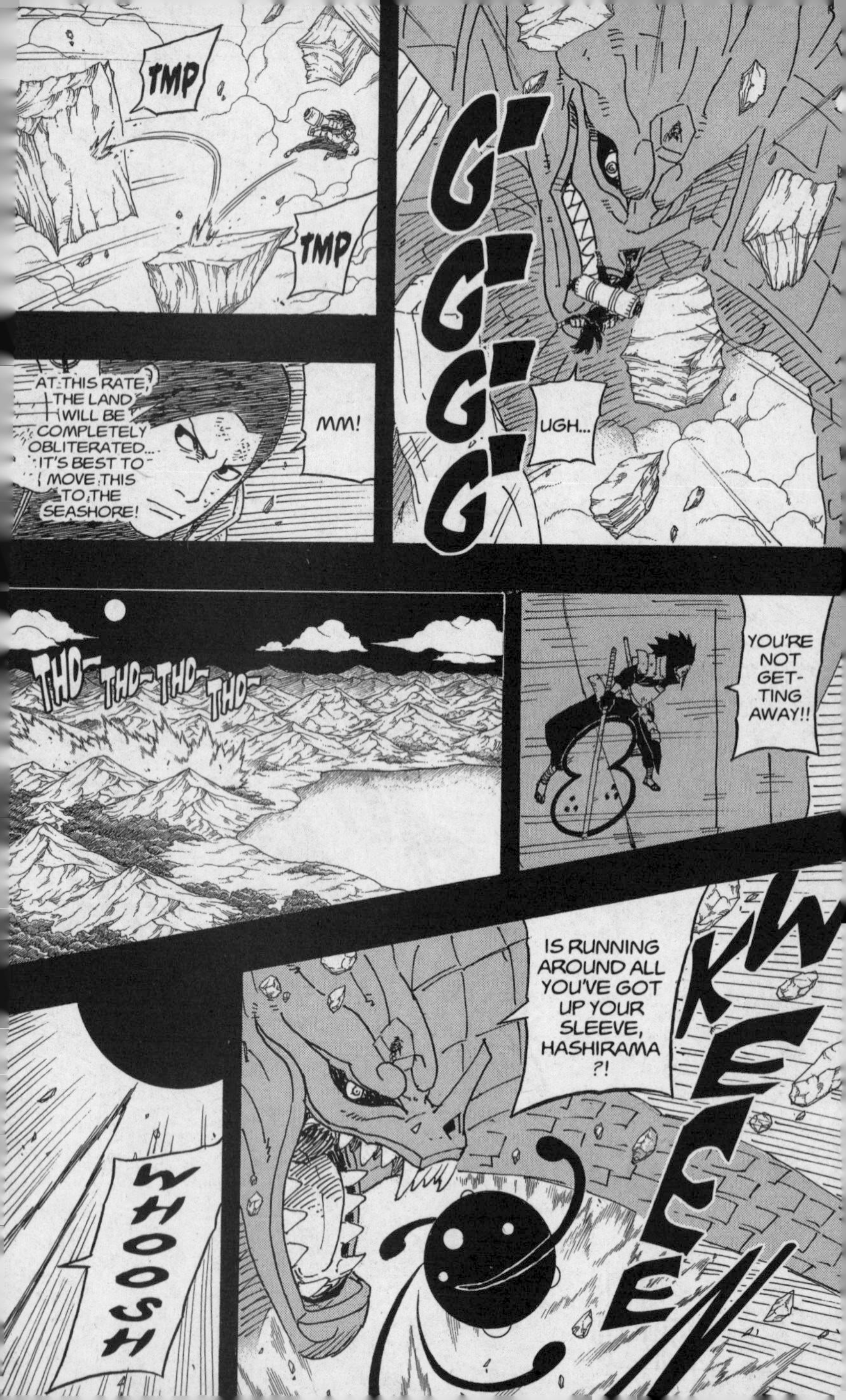

G-G-G-G-G
UGH...
TMP
TMP
MM!
AT THIS RATE, THE LAND WILL BE COMPLETELY OBLITERATED... IT'S BEST TO MOVE THIS TO THE SEASHORE!
YOU'RE NOT GET-TING AWAY!!
THD-THD-THD-THD-
KWEEEEN
IS RUNNING AROUND ALL YOU'VE GOT UP YOUR SLEEVE, HASHIRAMA?!
WHOOSH

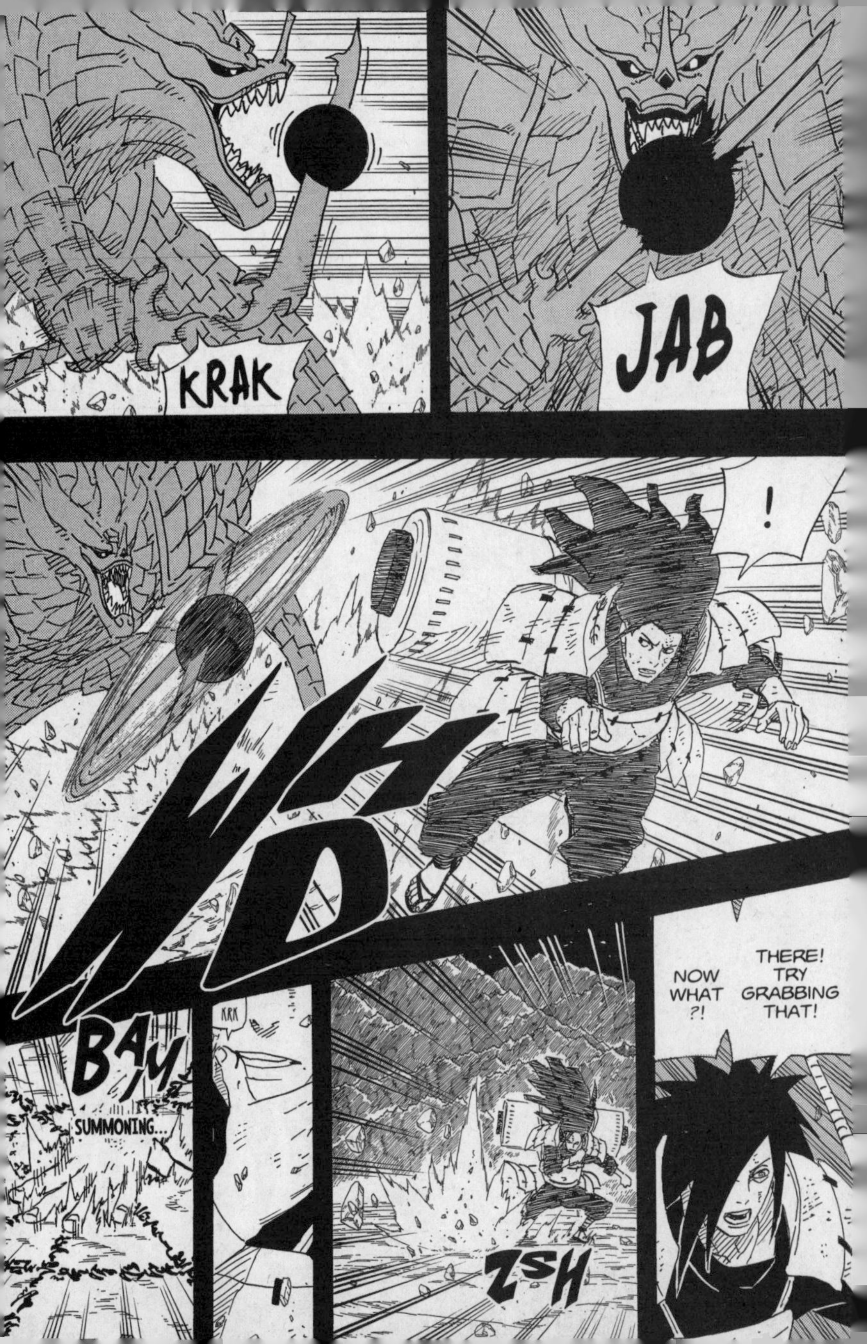
JAB
KRAK
!
WHD
THERE! TRY GRABBING THAT!
NOW WHAT ?!
ZSH
KRK
BAM
SUMMONING...

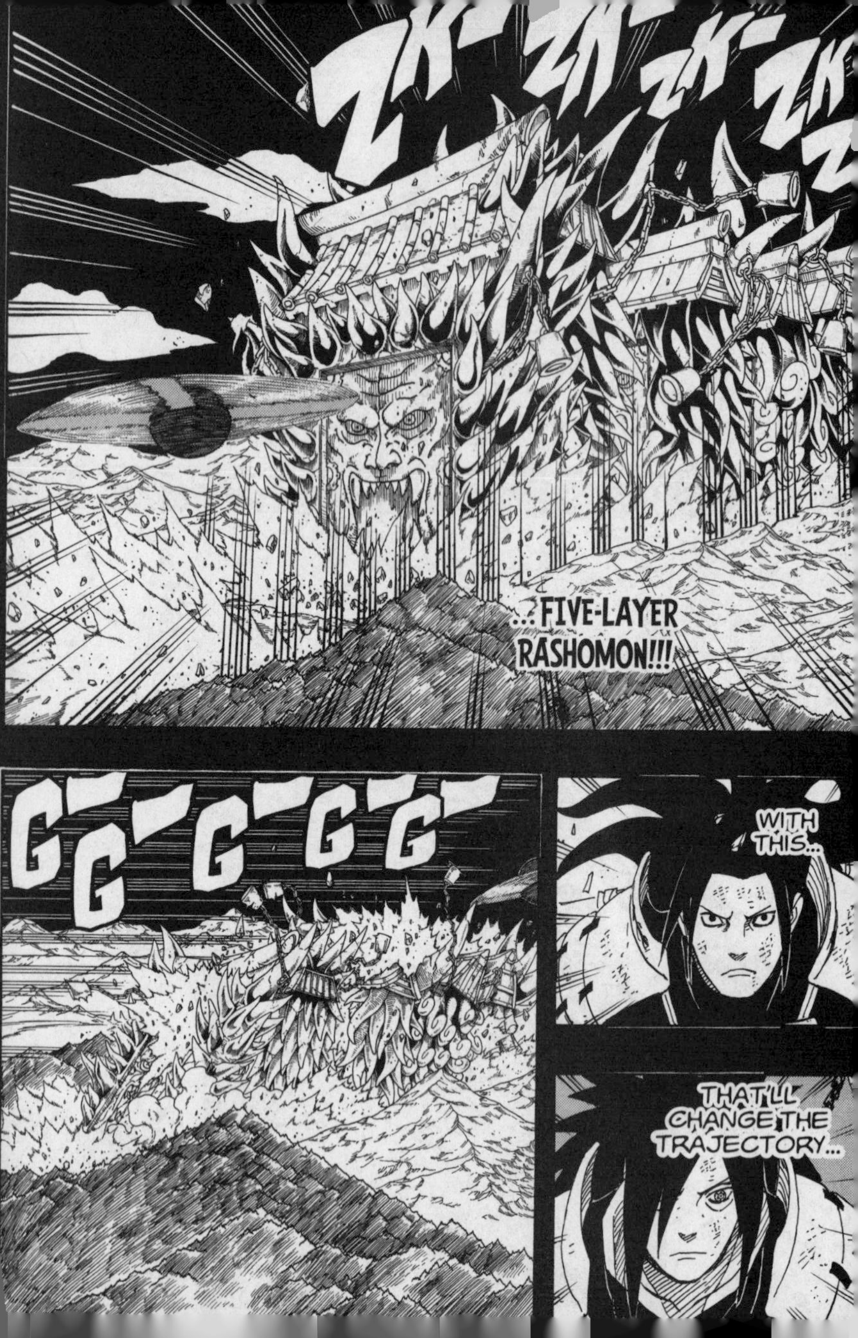
ZK-ZK-ZK-ZK
...FIVE-LAYER RASHOMON!!!
WITH THIS...
THAT'LL CHANGE THE TRAJECTORY...
G-G-G-G-G

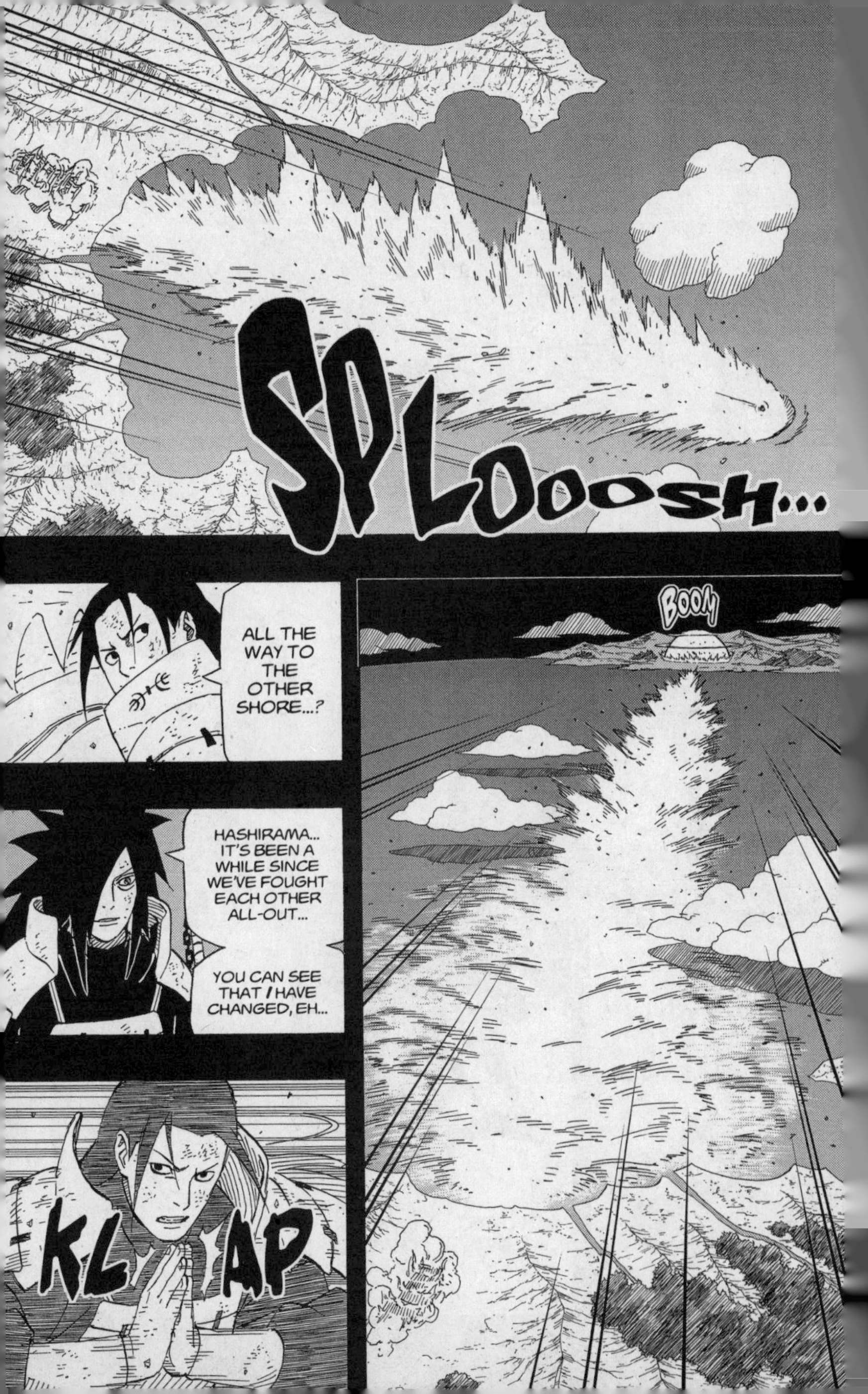
SPLOOOSH...
BOOM
ALL THE WAY TO THE OTHER SHORE...?
HASHIRAMA... IT'S BEEN A WHILE SINCE WE'VE FOUGHT EACH OTHER ALL-OUT...
YOU CAN SEE THAT I HAVE CHANGED, EH...
KLAP

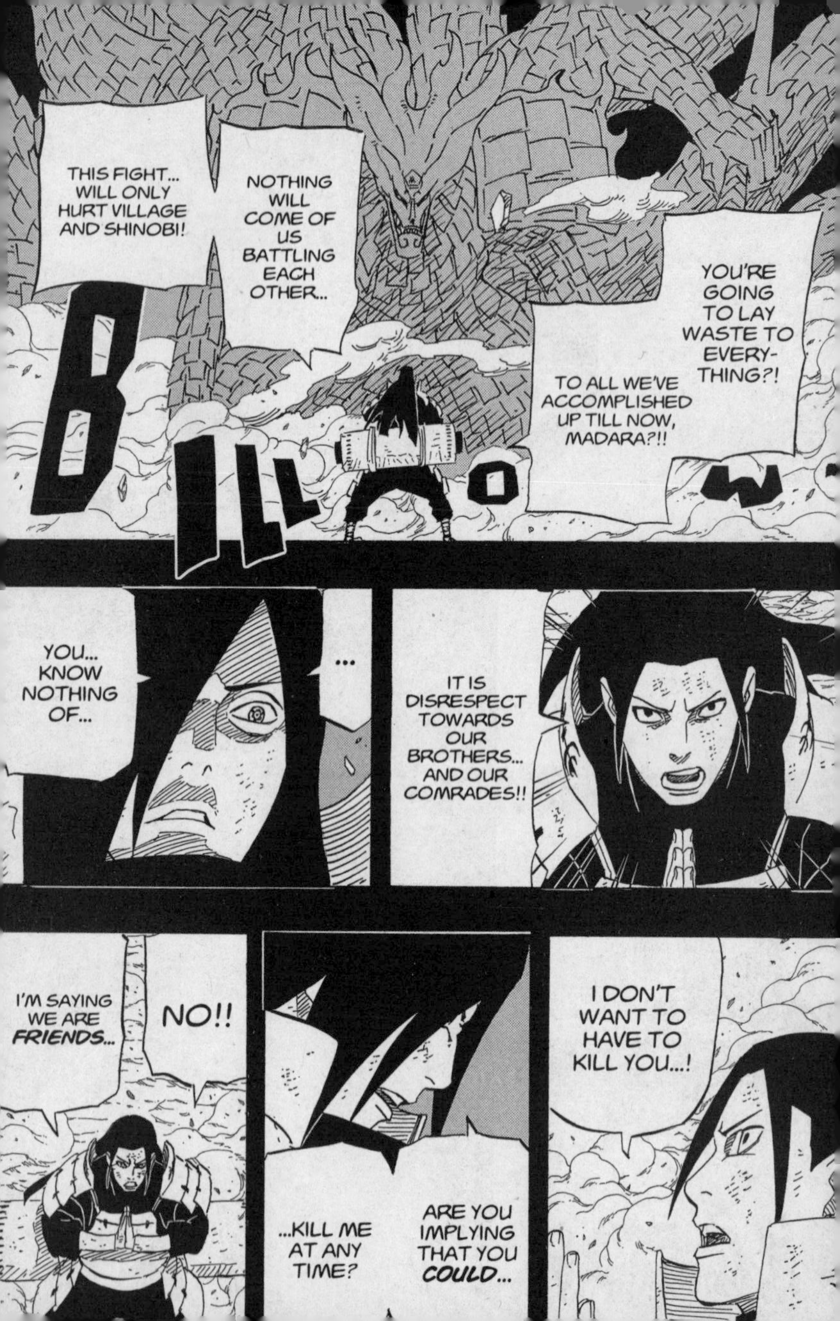
YOU'RE GOING TO LAY WASTE TO EVERYTHING?!
TO ALL WE'VE ACCOMPLISHED UP TILL NOW, MADARA?!!
NOTHING WILL COME OF US BATTLING EACH OTHER...
THIS FIGHT... WILL ONLY HURT VILLAGE AND SHINOBI!
BILLOW
IT IS DISRESPECT TOWARDS OUR BROTHERS... AND OUR COMRADES!!
...
YOU... KNOW NOTHING OF...
I DON'T WANT TO HAVE TO KILL YOU...!
ARE YOU IMPLYING THAT YOU **COULD**...
...KILL ME AT ANY TIME?
NO!!
I'M SAYING WE ARE **FRIENDS**...

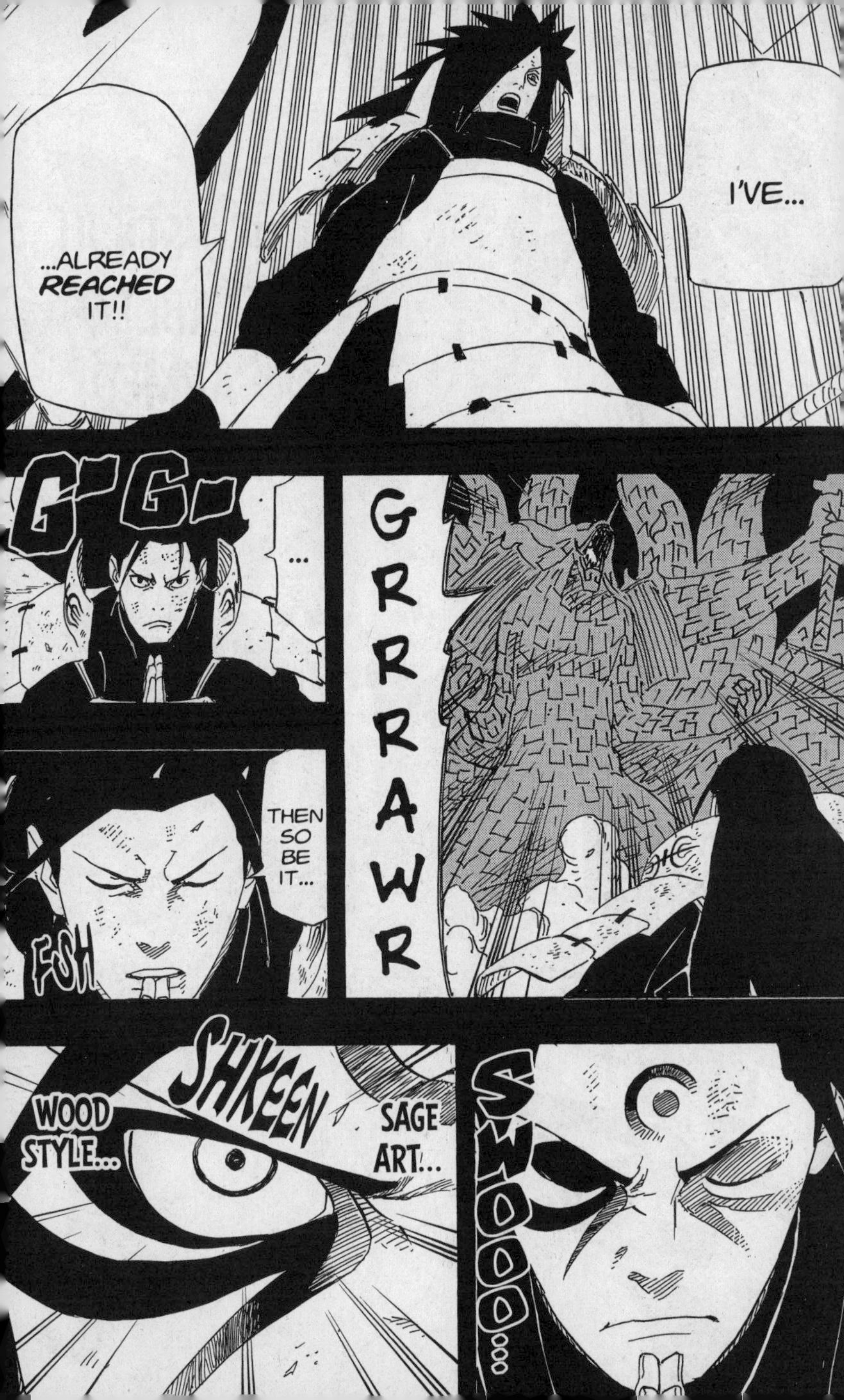
I'VE...
...ALREADY REACHED IT!!
GRRRAWR
G'G-
...
THEN SO BE IT...
FSH
SWOOOO...
SAGE ART...
SHKEEN
WOOD STYLE...

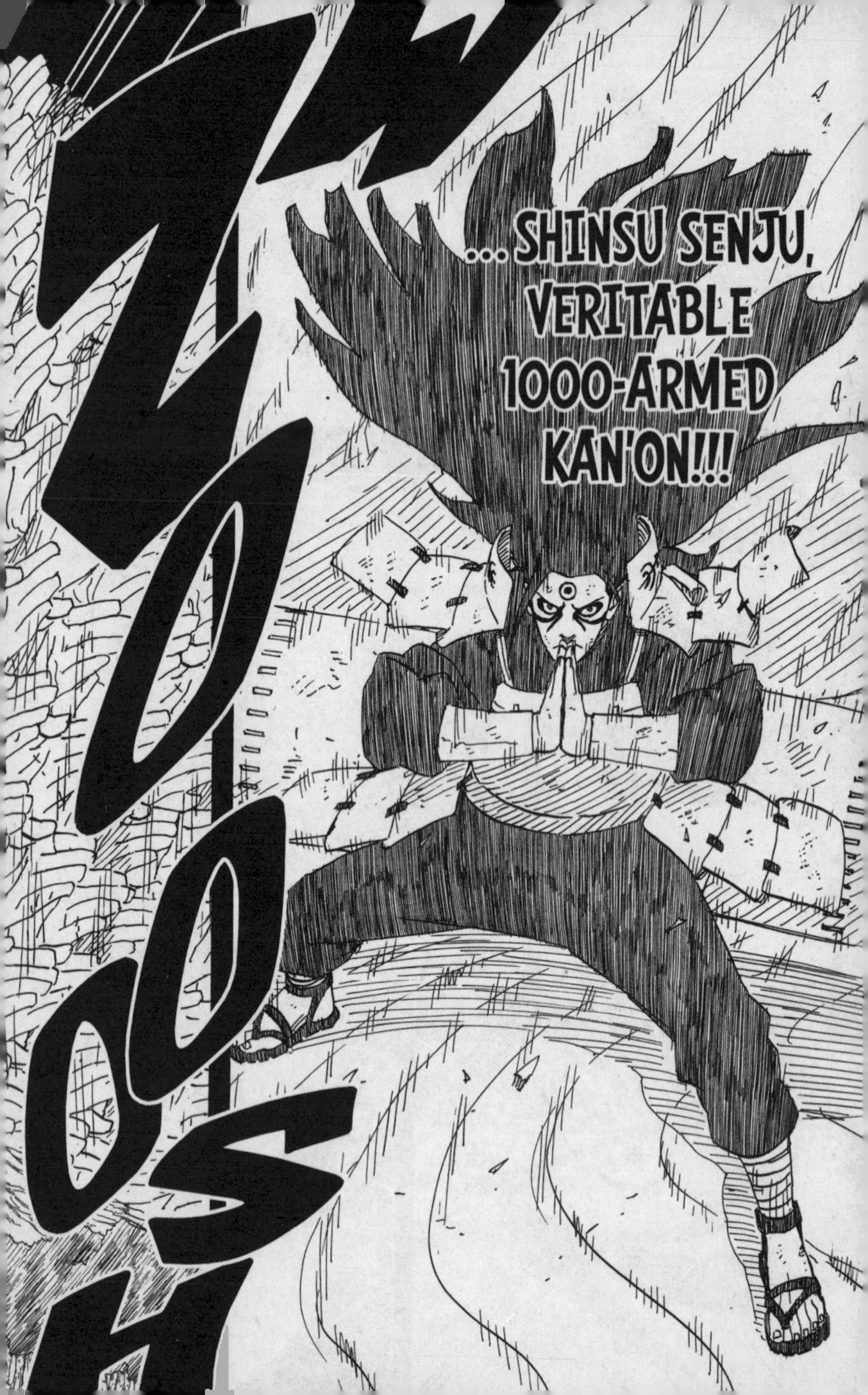
...SHINSU SENJU, VERITABLE 1000-ARMED KAN'ON!!!

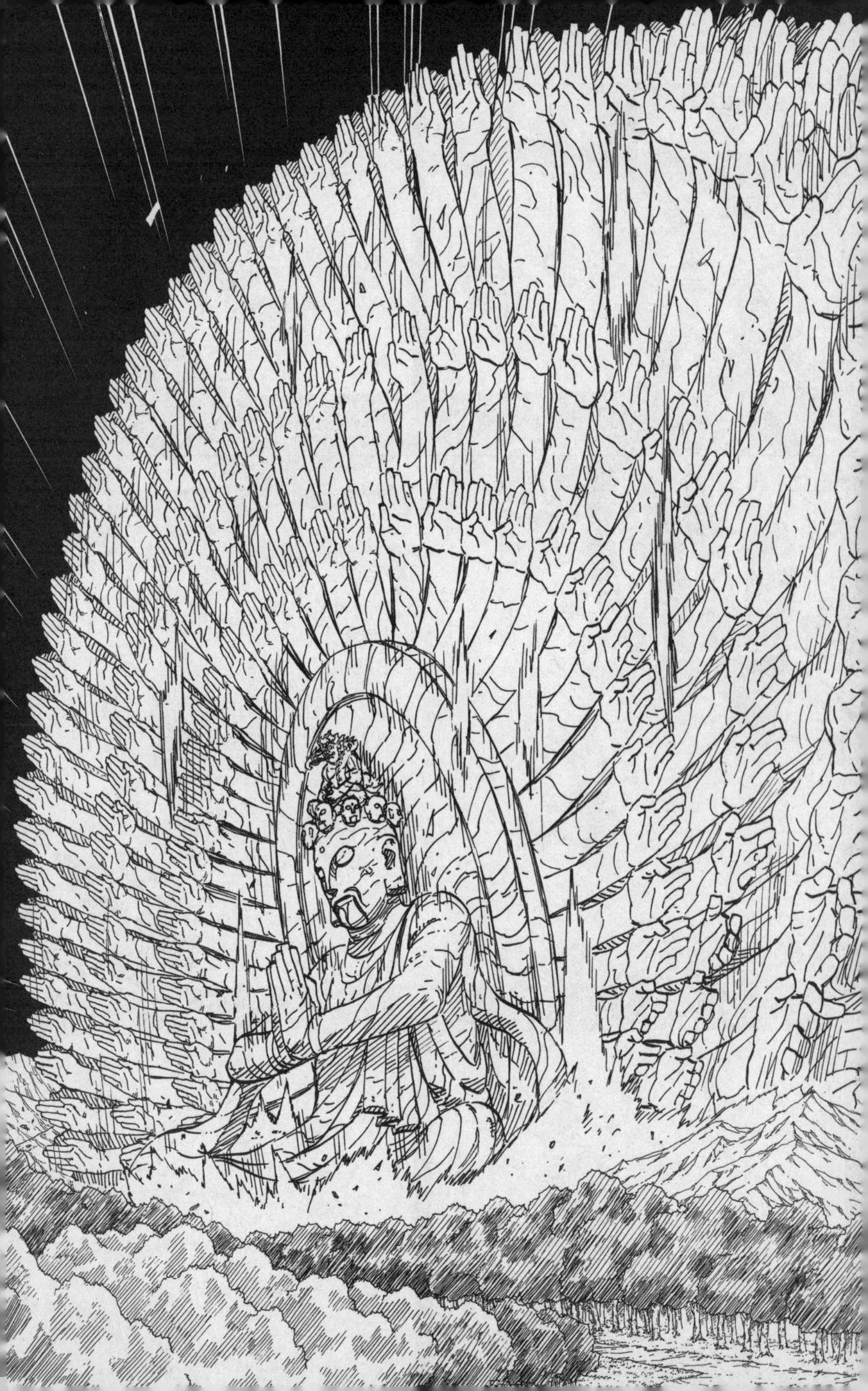

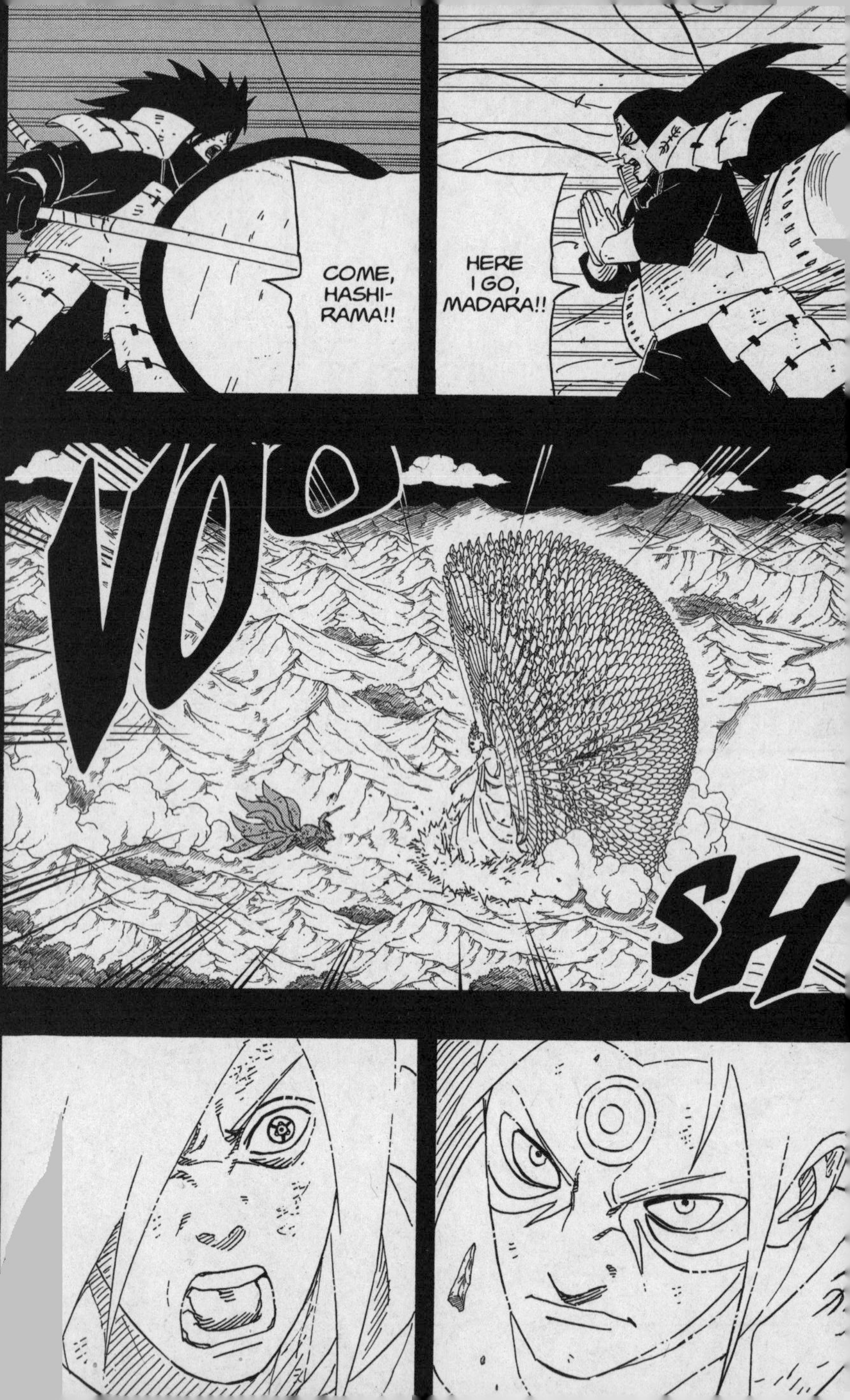
HERE I GO, MADARA!!
COME, HASHI-RAMA!!
VOO
SH

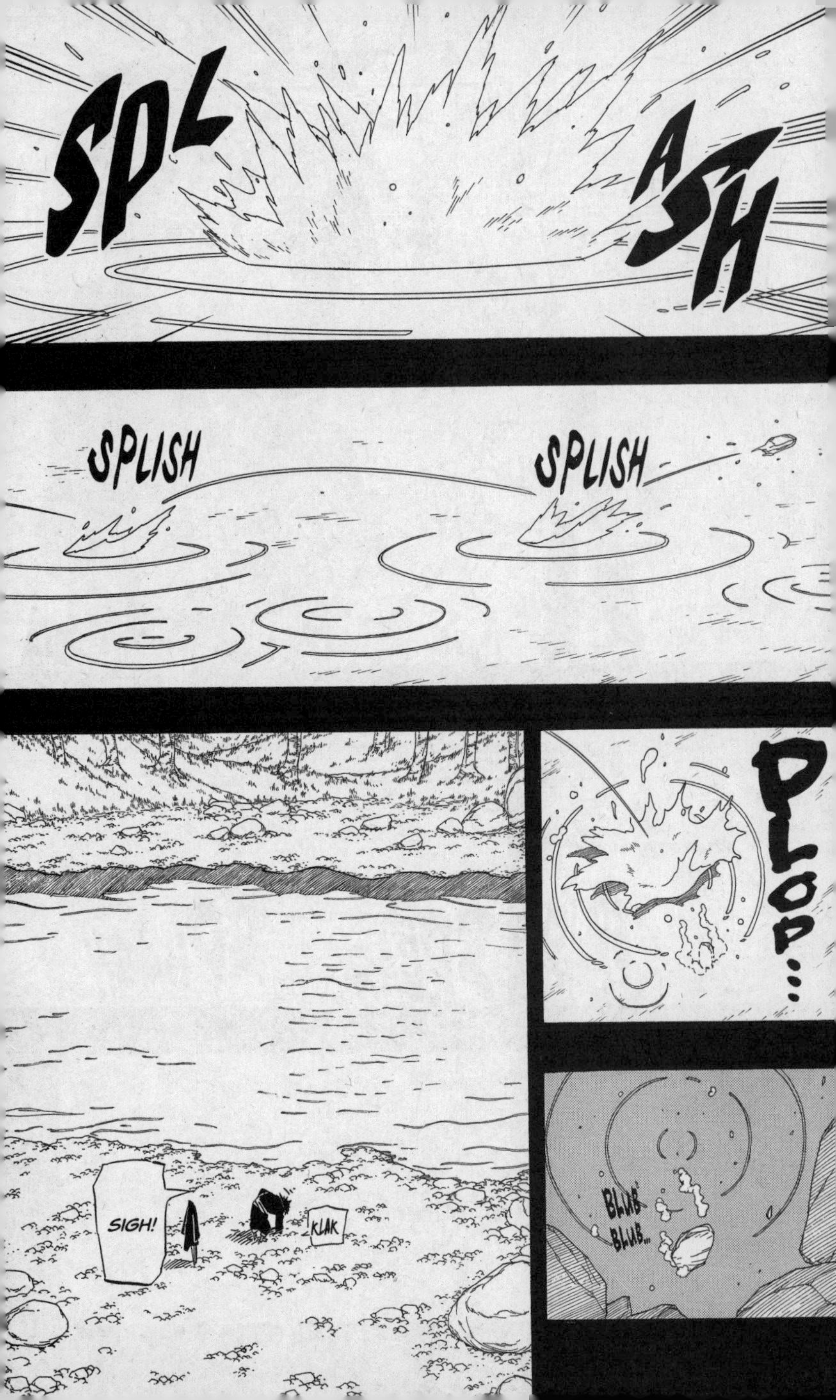
SPLASH
SPLISH
SPLISH
PLOP...
BLUB
BLUB...
KLAK
SIGH!

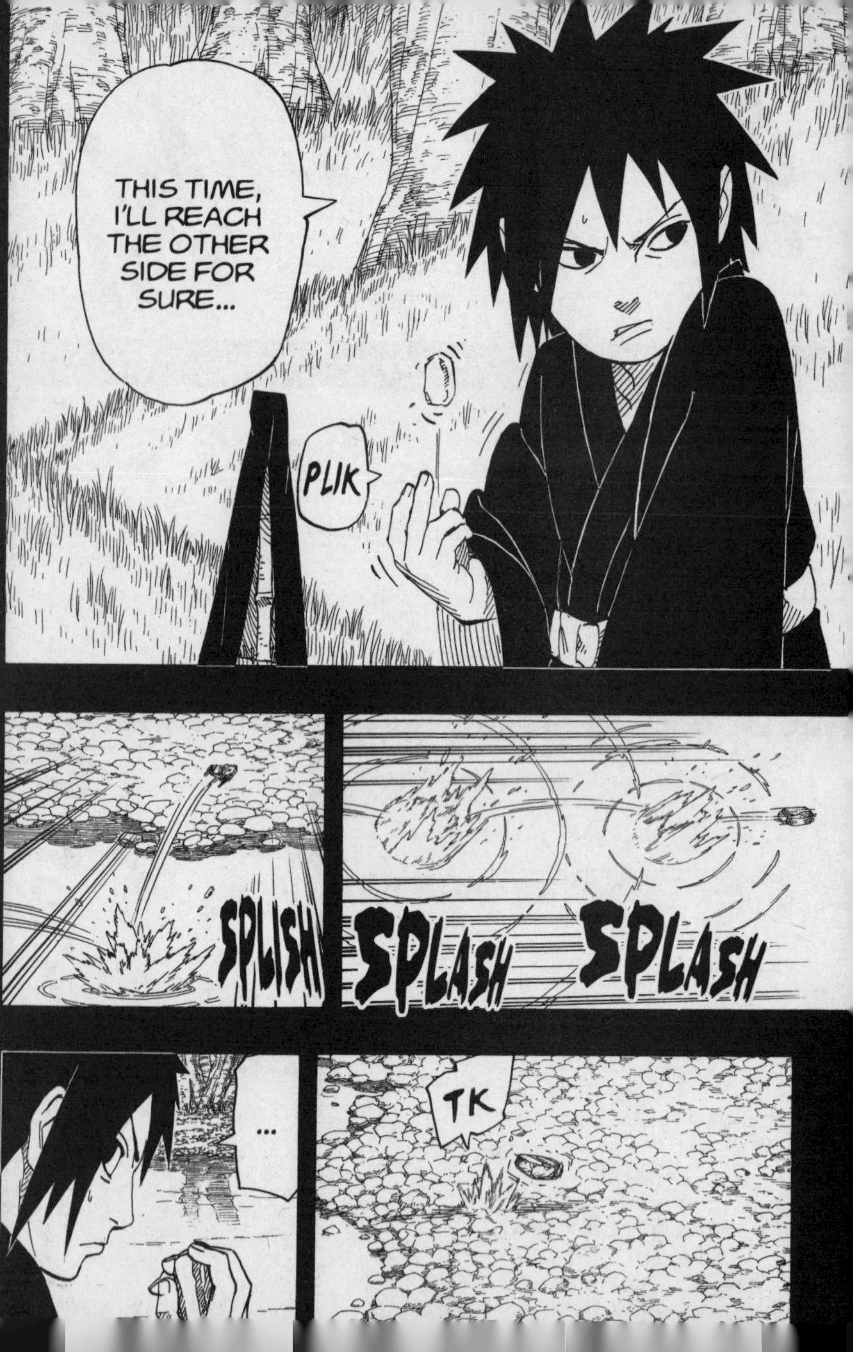
THIS TIME, I'LL REACH THE OTHER SIDE FOR SURE...
PLIK
SPLASH
SPLASH
SPLISH
TK
...

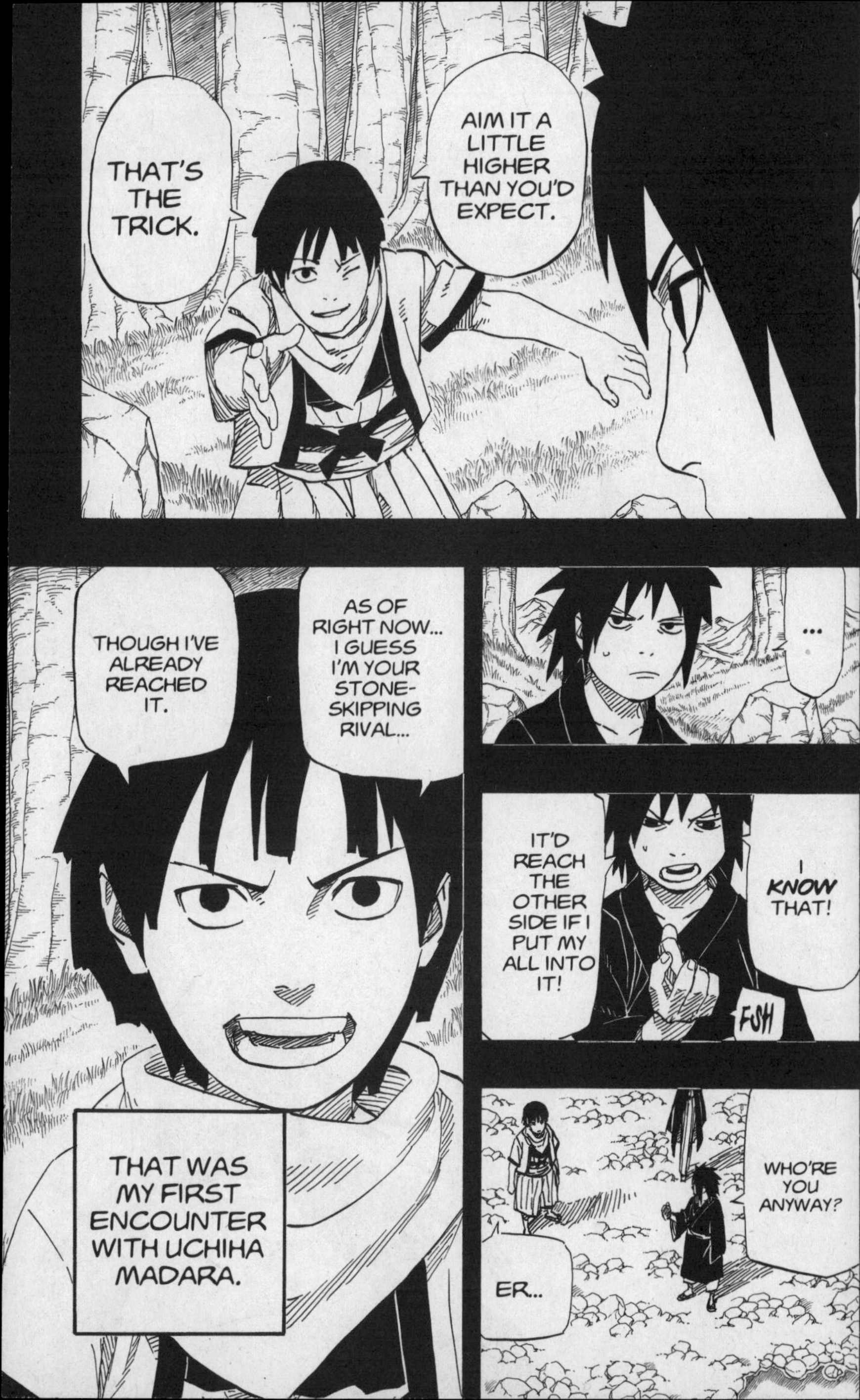
AIM IT A LITTLE HIGHER THAN YOU'D EXPECT.
THAT'S THE TRICK.
...
I KNOW THAT!
IT'D REACH THE OTHER SIDE IF I PUT MY ALL INTO IT!
FSH
WHO'RE YOU ANYWAY?
ER...
AS OF RIGHT NOW... I GUESS I'M YOUR STONE-SKIPPING RIVAL...
THOUGH I'VE ALREADY REACHED IT.
THAT WAS MY FIRST ENCOUNTER WITH UCHIHA MADARA.

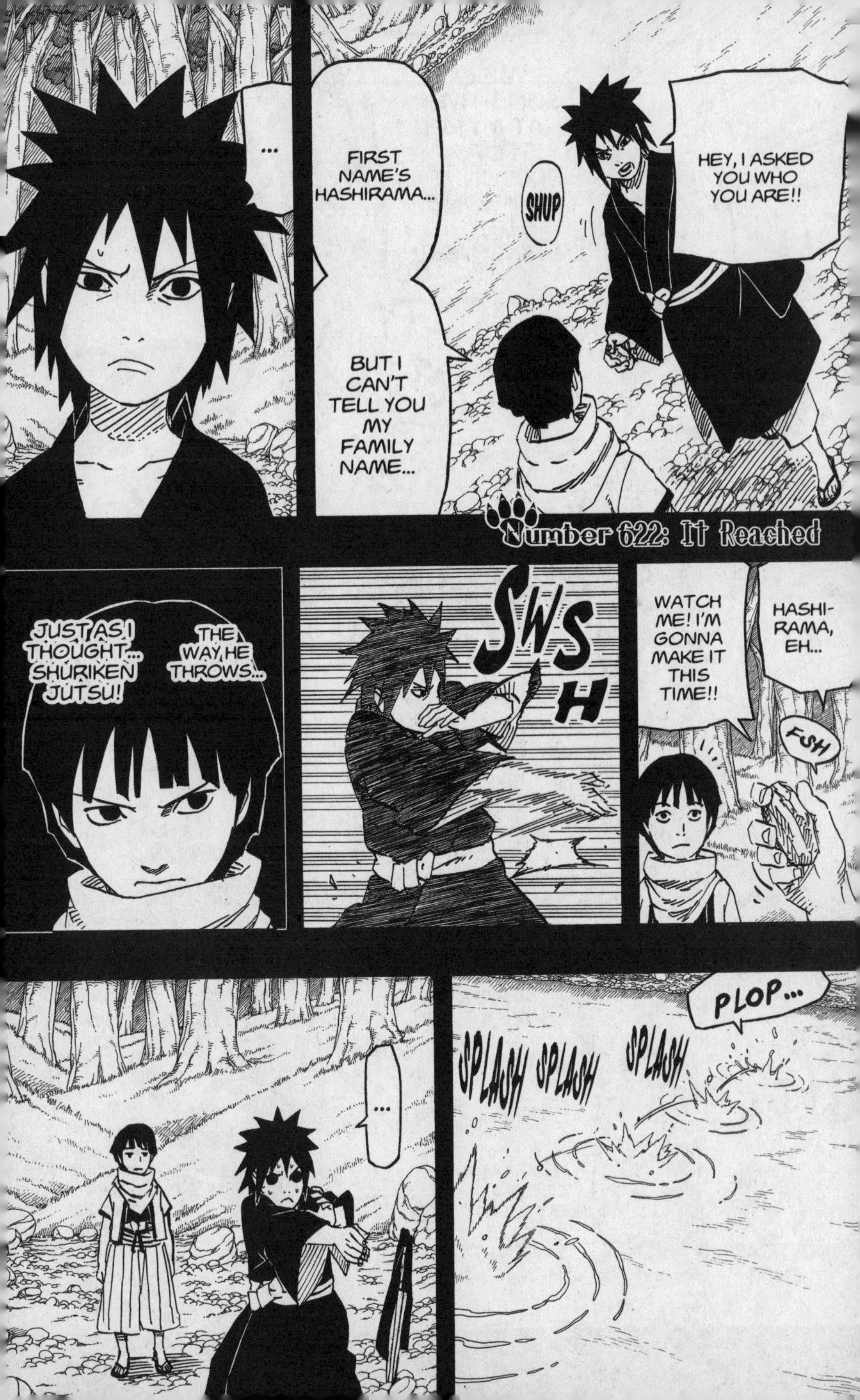
HEY, I ASKED YOU WHO YOU ARE!!
SHUP
FIRST NAME'S HASHIRAMA...
BUT I CAN'T TELL YOU MY FAMILY NAME...
...
Number 622: It Reached
HASHI-RAMA, EH...
WATCH ME! I'M GONNA MAKE IT THIS TIME!!
FSH
SWSH
THE WAY HE THROWS...
JUST AS I THOUGHT... SHURIKEN JUTSU!
PLOP...
SPLASH
SPLASH
SPLASH
...

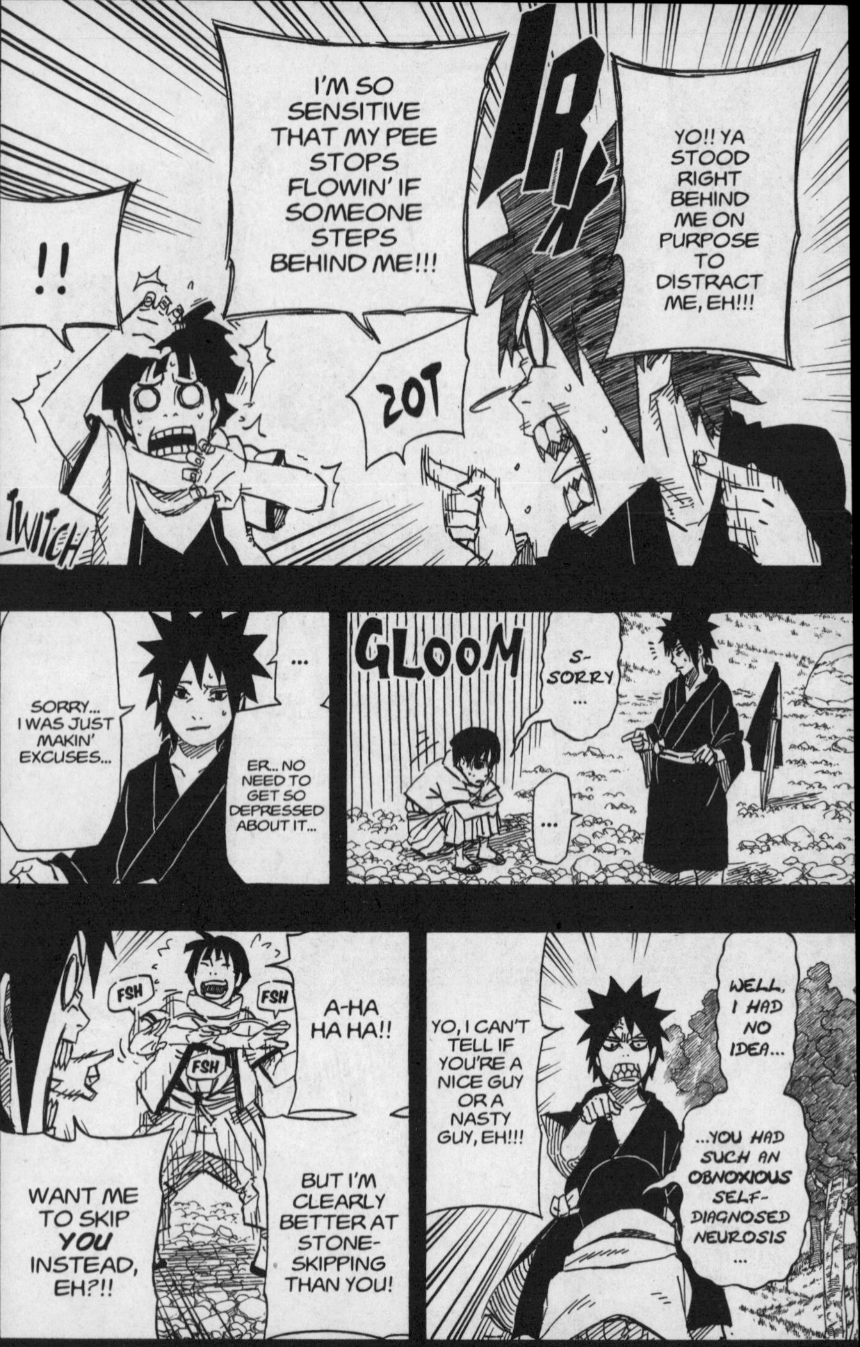
YO!! YA STOOD RIGHT BEHIND ME ON PURPOSE TO DISTRACT ME, EH!!!
ZOT
I'M SO SENSITIVE THAT MY PEE STOPS FLOWIN' IF SOMEONE STEPS BEHIND ME!!!
!!
TWITCH
S-SORRY...
...
GLOOM
...
ER... NO NEED TO GET SO DEPRESSED ABOUT IT...
SORRY... I WAS JUST MAKIN' EXCUSES...
WELL, I HAD NO IDEA...
...YOU HAD SUCH AN OBNOXIOUS SELF-DIAGNOSED NEUROSIS...
YO, I CAN'T TELL IF YOU'RE A NICE GUY OR A NASTY GUY, EH!!!
A-HA HA HA!!
BUT I'M CLEARLY BETTER AT STONE-SKIPPING THAN YOU!
FSH
FSH
FSH
WANT ME TO SKIP YOU INSTEAD, EH?!!

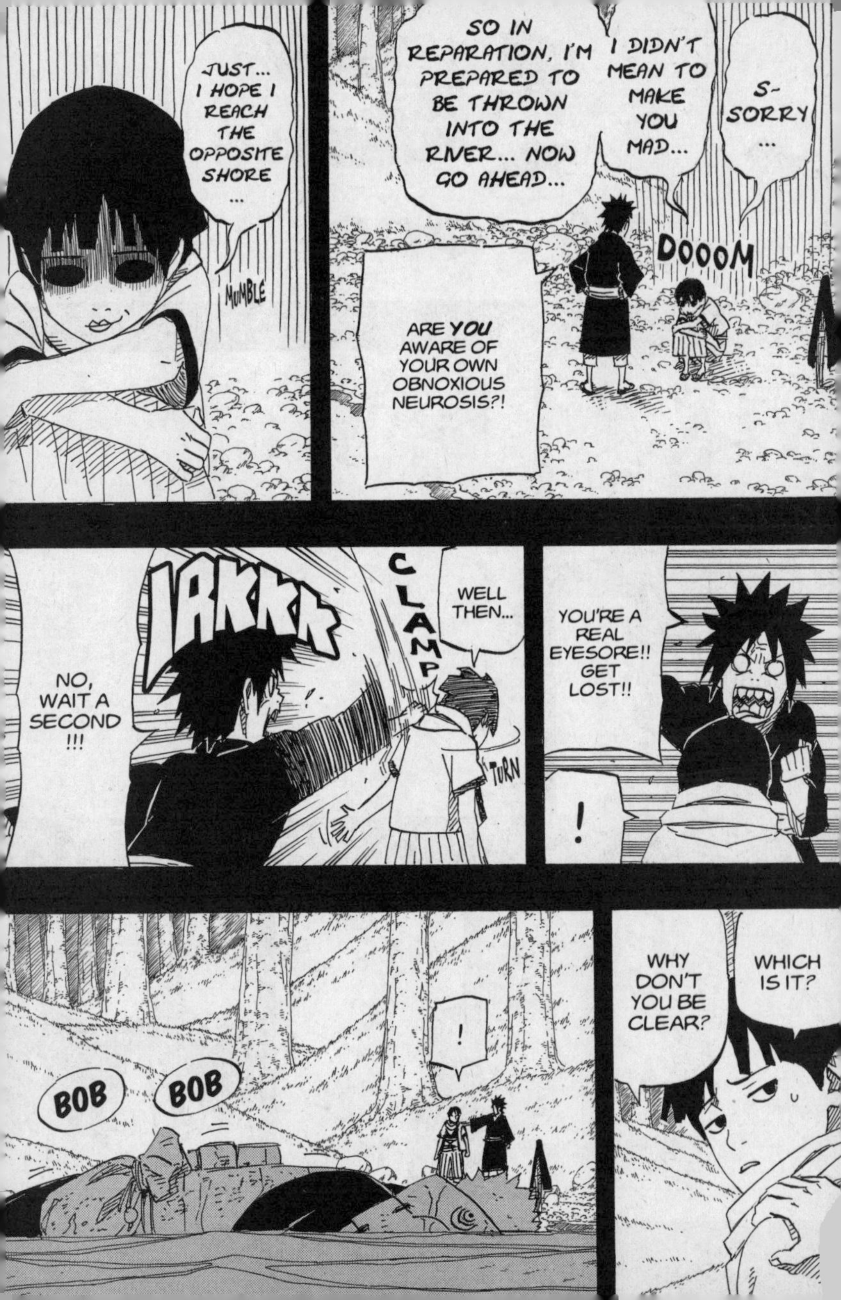
S-SORRY...
I DIDN'T MEAN TO MAKE YOU MAD...
SO IN REPARATION, I'M PREPARED TO BE THROWN INTO THE RIVER... NOW GO AHEAD...
DOOOM
ARE YOU AWARE OF YOUR OWN OBNOXIOUS NEUROSIS?!
JUST... I HOPE I REACH THE OPPOSITE SHORE ...
MUMBLE
YOU'RE A REAL EYESORE!! GET LOST!!
!
WELL THEN...
CLAMP
TURN
NO, WAIT A SECOND !!!
WHICH IS IT?
WHY DON'T YOU BE CLEAR?
!
BOB
BOB

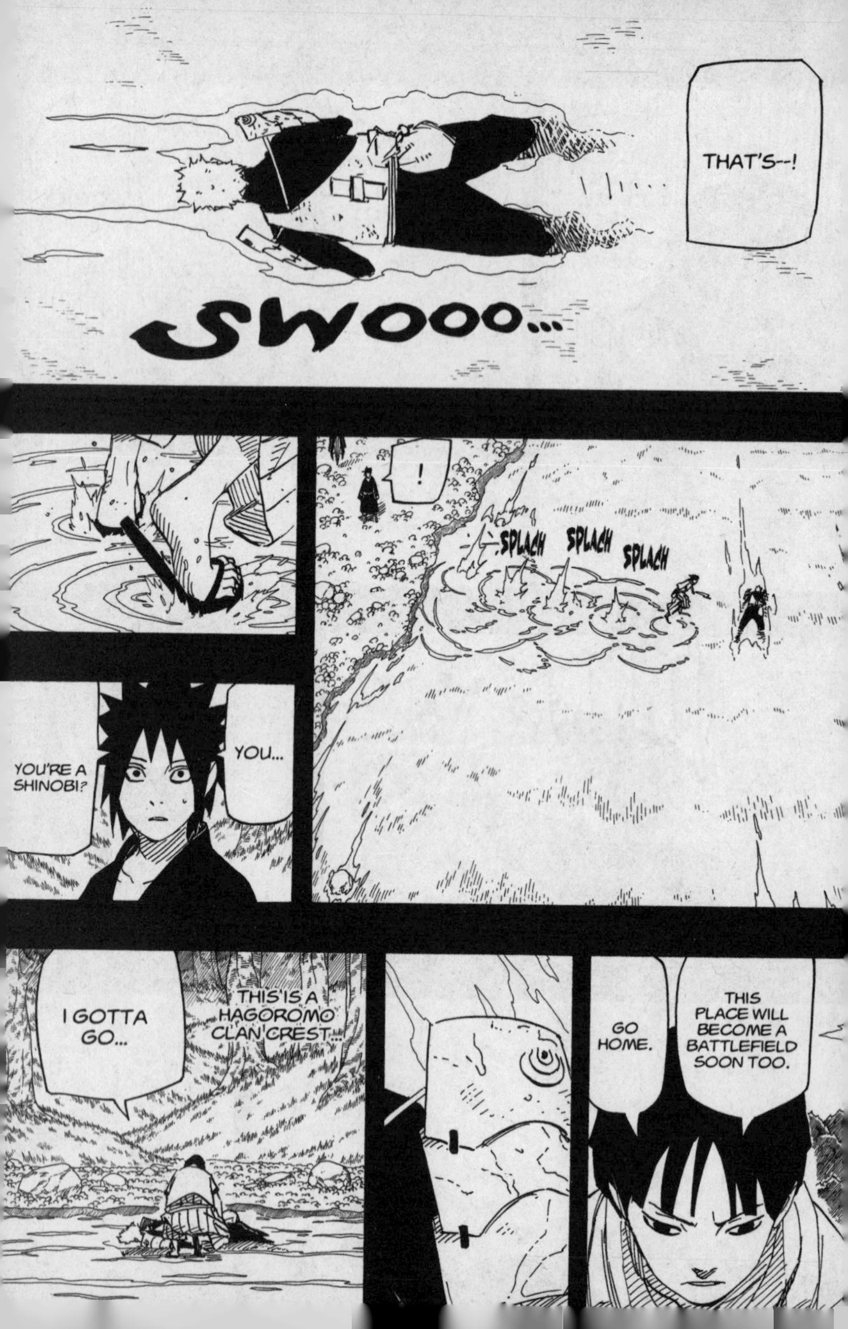
THAT'S--!
SWOOO...
!
SPLACH
SPLACH
SPLACH
THAT'S--!
YOU...
YOU'RE A SHINOBI?
THIS PLACE WILL BECOME A BATTLEFIELD SOON TOO.
GO HOME.
THIS IS A HAGOROMO CLAN CREST...
I GOTTA GO...

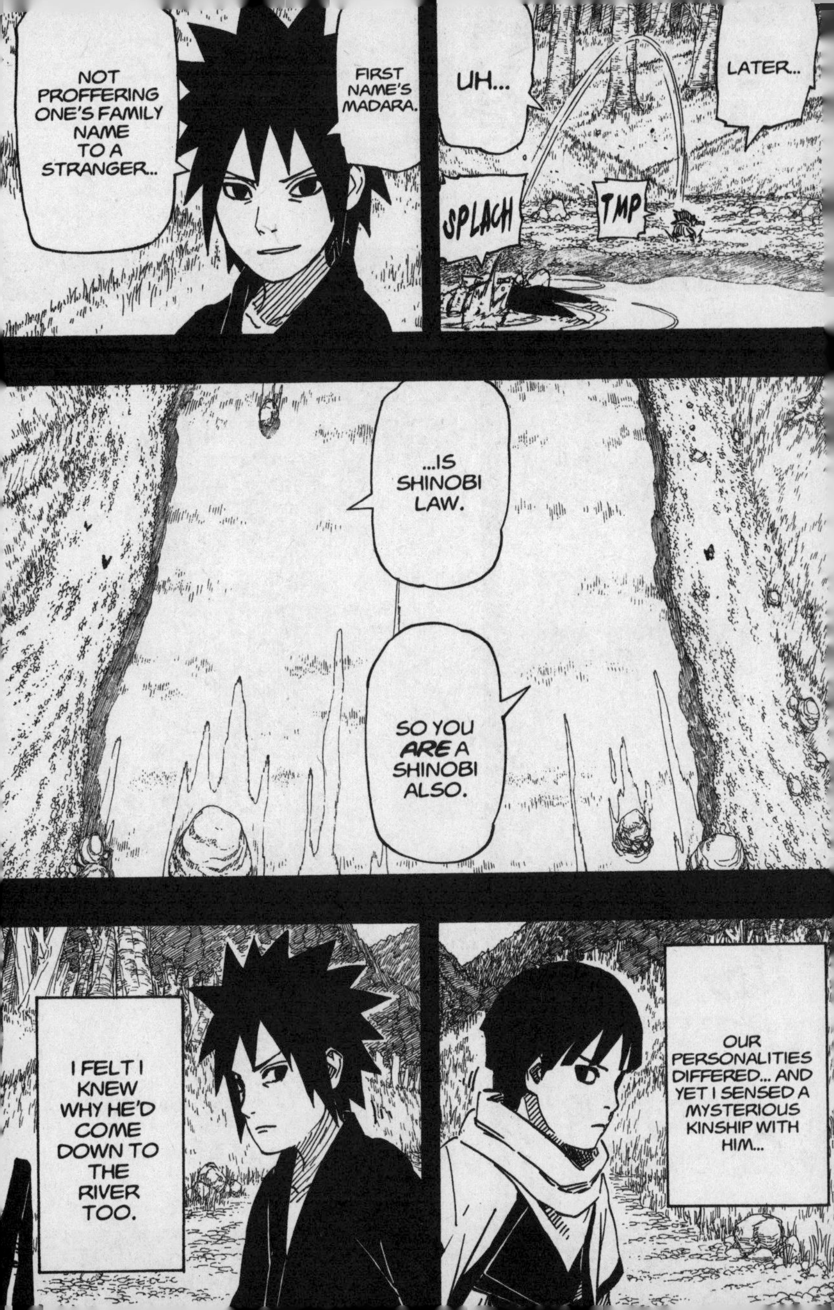
LATER..
UH...
TMP
SPLACH
FIRST NAME'S MADARA.
NOT PROFFERING ONE'S FAMILY NAME TO A STRANGER..
...IS SHINOBI LAW.
SO YOU ARE A SHINOBI ALSO.
OUR PERSONALITIES DIFFERED... AND YET I SENSED A MYSTERIOUS KINSHIP WITH HIM...
I FELT I KNEW WHY HE'D COME DOWN TO THE RIVER TOO.

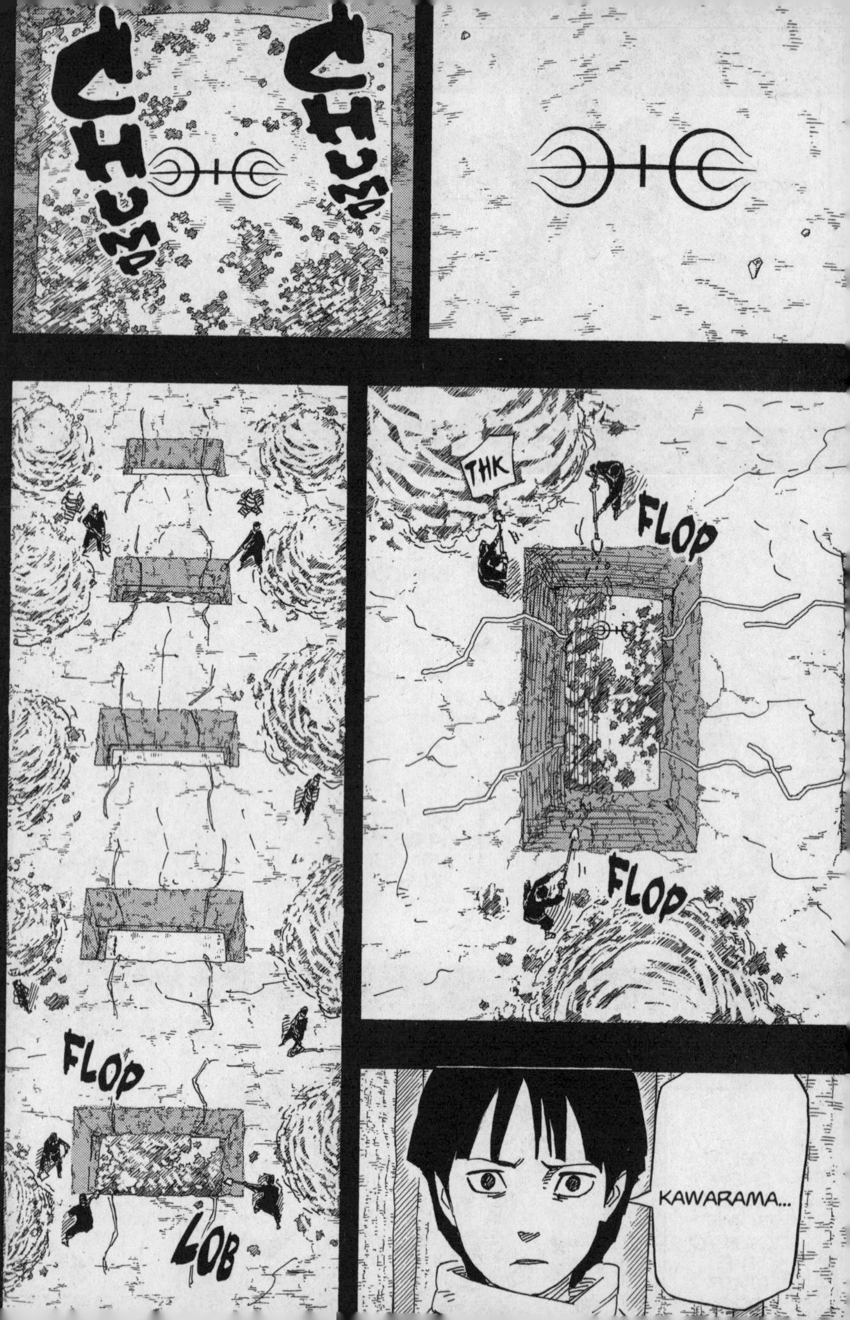
CHUMP
CHUMP
THK
FLOP
FLOP
KAWARAMA...
FLOP
LOB

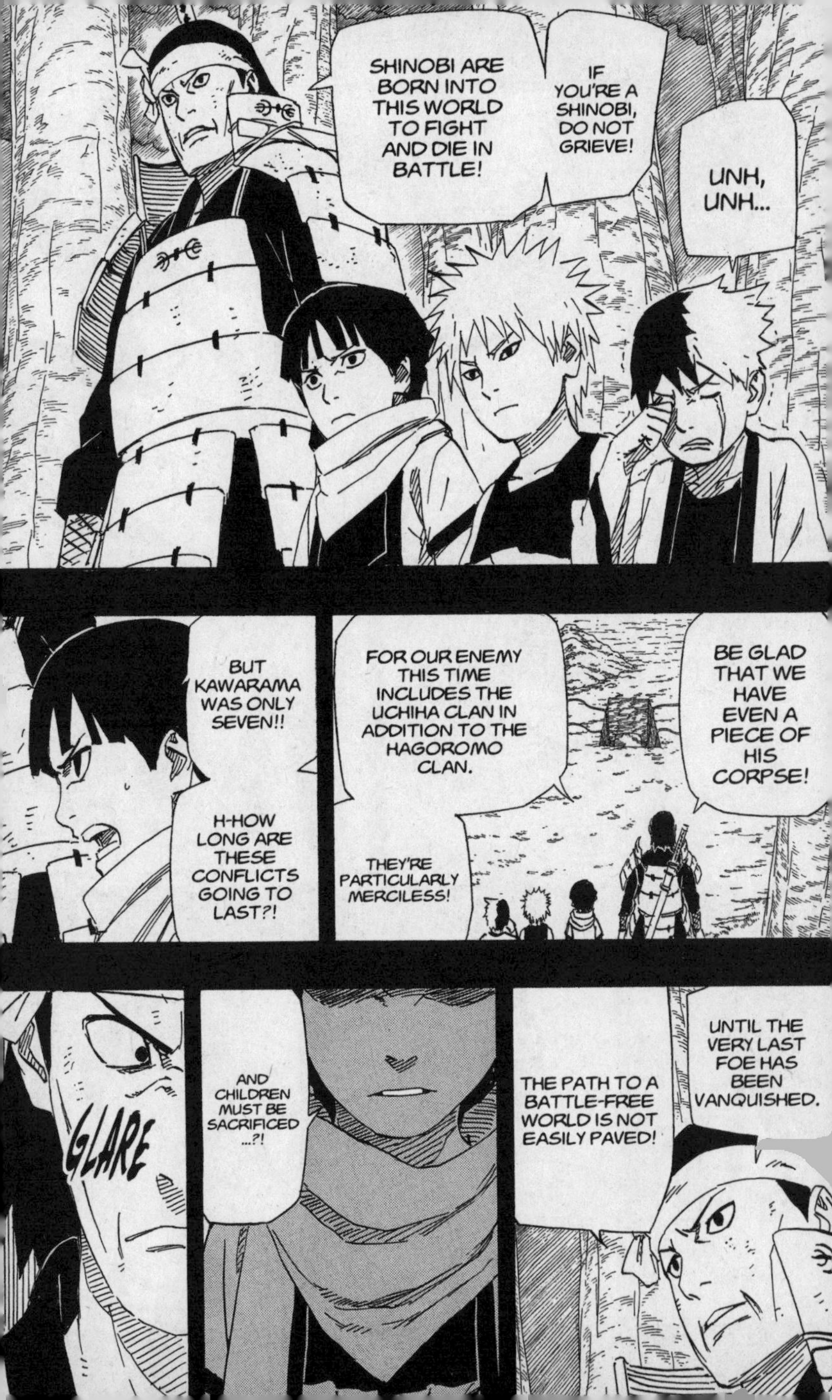
UNH, UNH...
IF YOU'RE A SHINOBI, DO NOT GRIEVE!
SHINOBI ARE BORN INTO THIS WORLD TO FIGHT AND DIE IN BATTLE!
BE GLAD THAT WE HAVE EVEN A PIECE OF HIS CORPSE!
FOR OUR ENEMY THIS TIME INCLUDES THE UCHIHA CLAN IN ADDITION TO THE HAGOROMO CLAN.
THEY'RE PARTICULARLY MERCILESS!
BUT KAWARAMA WAS ONLY SEVEN!!
H-HOW LONG ARE THESE CONFLICTS GOING TO LAST?!
UNTIL THE VERY LAST FOE HAS BEEN VANQUISHED.
THE PATH TO A BATTLE-FREE WORLD IS NOT EASILY PAVED!
AND CHILDREN MUST BE SACRIFICED ...?!
GLARE

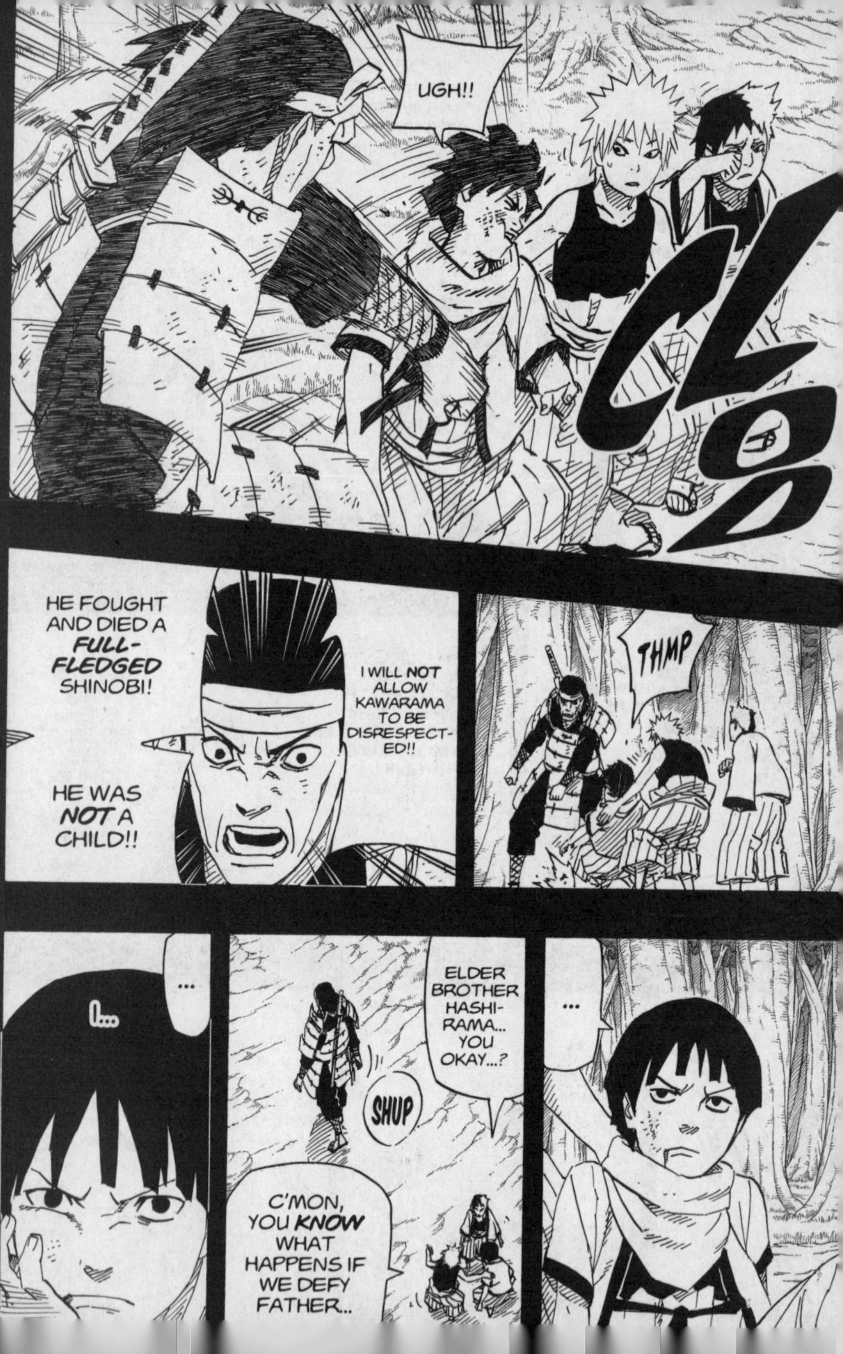
UGH!!
CLOD
THMP
I WILL **NOT** ALLOW KAWARAMA TO BE DISRESPECTED!!
HE FOUGHT AND DIED A ***FULL-FLEDGED*** SHINOBI!
HE WAS ***NOT*** A CHILD!!
...
ELDER BROTHER HASHIRAMA... YOU OKAY...?
SHUP
C'MON, YOU ***KNOW*** WHAT HAPPENS IF WE DEFY FATHER...
...
I...

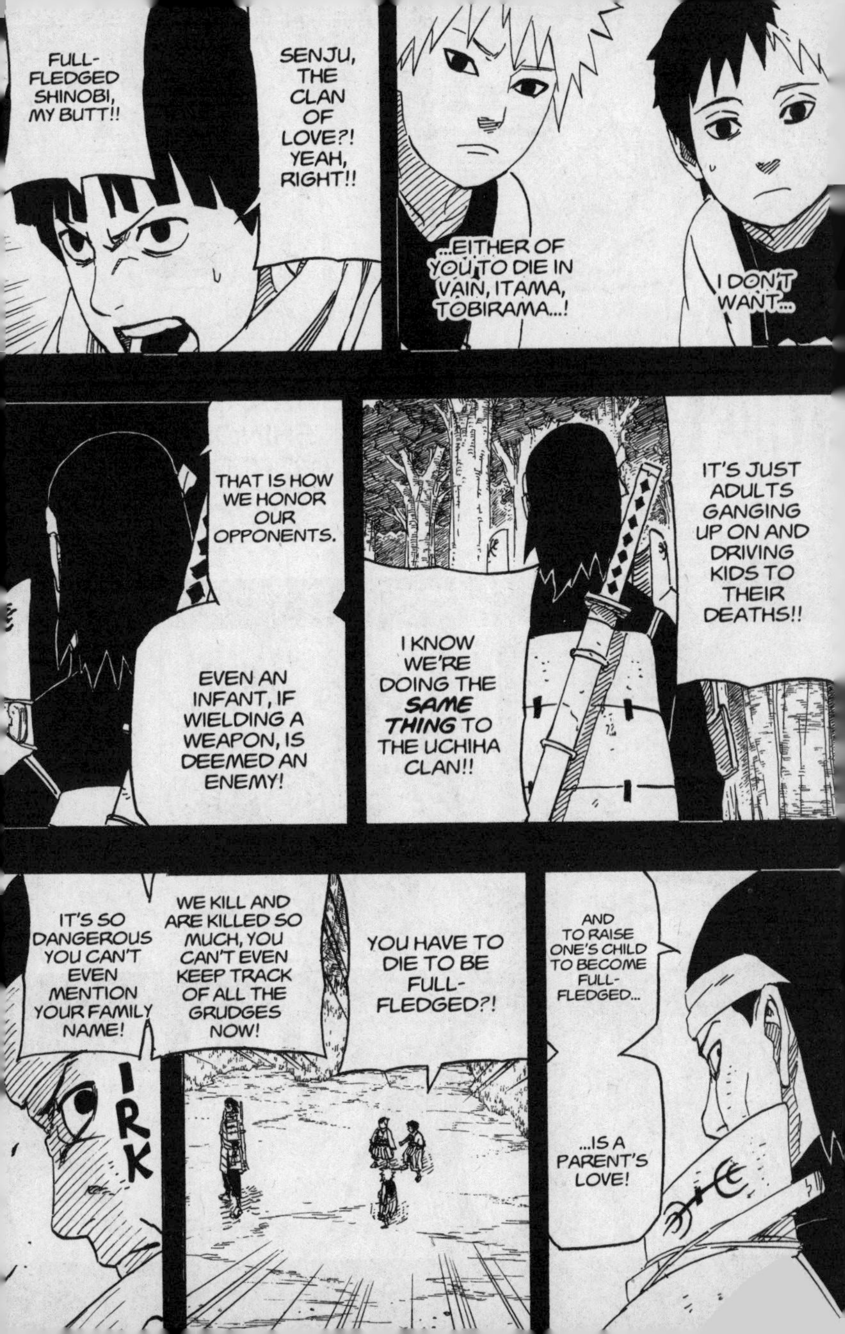
I DON'T WANT...
...EITHER OF YOU TO DIE IN VAIN, ITAMA, TOBIRAMA...!
SENJU, THE CLAN OF LOVE?! YEAH, RIGHT!!
FULL-FLEDGED SHINOBI, MY BUTT!!
IT'S JUST ADULTS GANGING UP ON AND DRIVING KIDS TO THEIR DEATHS!!
I KNOW WE'RE DOING THE SAME THING TO THE UCHIHA CLAN!!
THAT IS HOW WE HONOR OUR OPPONENTS.
EVEN AN INFANT, IF WIELDING A WEAPON, IS DEEMED AN ENEMY!
AND TO RAISE ONE'S CHILD TO BECOME FULL-FLEDGED...
...IS A PARENT'S LOVE!
YOU HAVE TO DIE TO BE FULL-FLEDGED?!
WE KILL AND ARE KILLED SO MUCH, YOU CAN'T EVEN KEEP TRACK OF ALL THE GRUDGES NOW!
IT'S SO DANGEROUS YOU CAN'T EVEN MENTION YOUR FAMILY NAME!
IRK

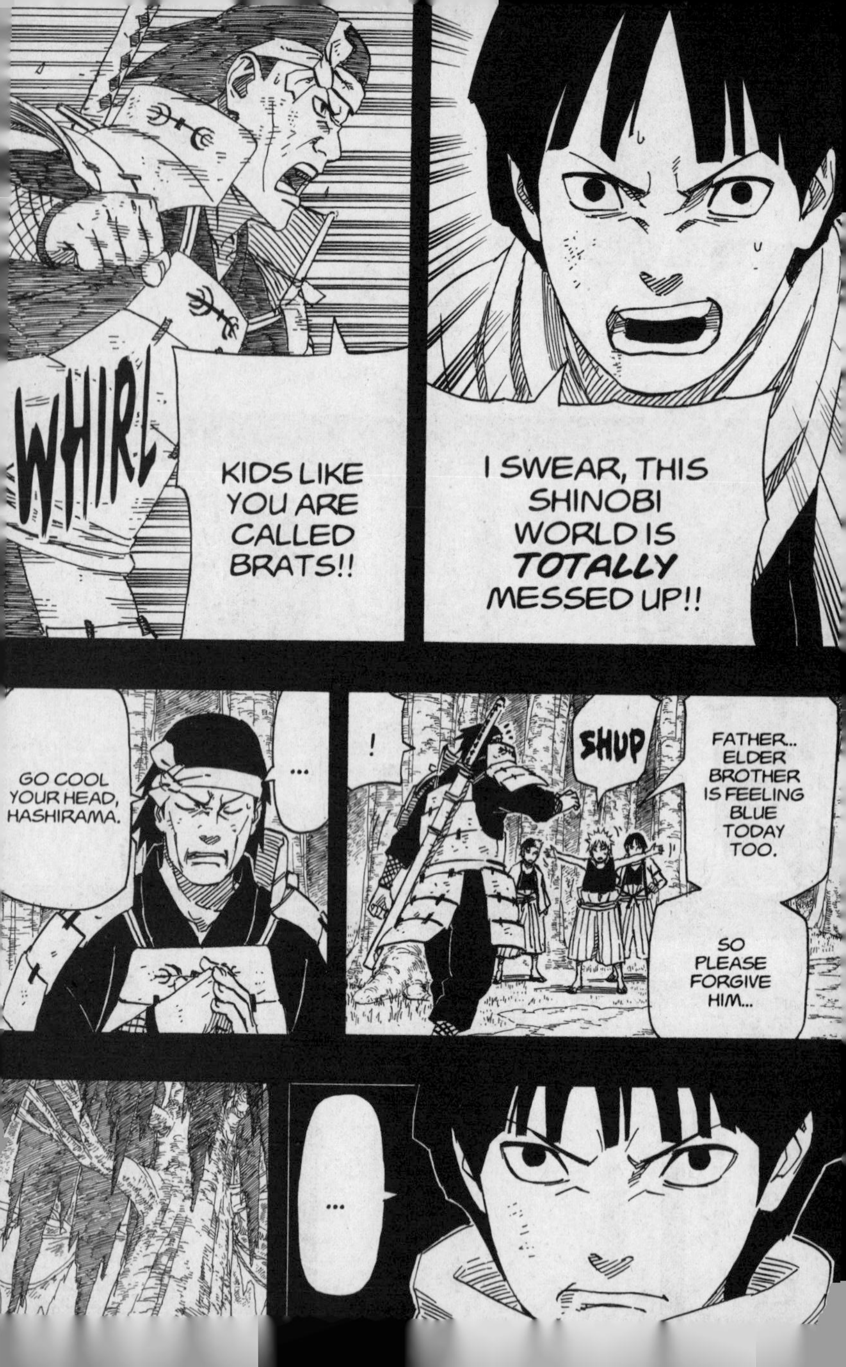
I SWEAR, THIS SHINOBI WORLD IS ***TOTALLY*** MESSED UP!!
WHIRL
KIDS LIKE YOU ARE CALLED BRATS!!
FATHER... ELDER BROTHER IS FEELING BLUE TODAY TOO.
SO PLEASE FORGIVE HIM...
SHUP
!
...
GO COOL YOUR HEAD, HASHIRAMA.
...

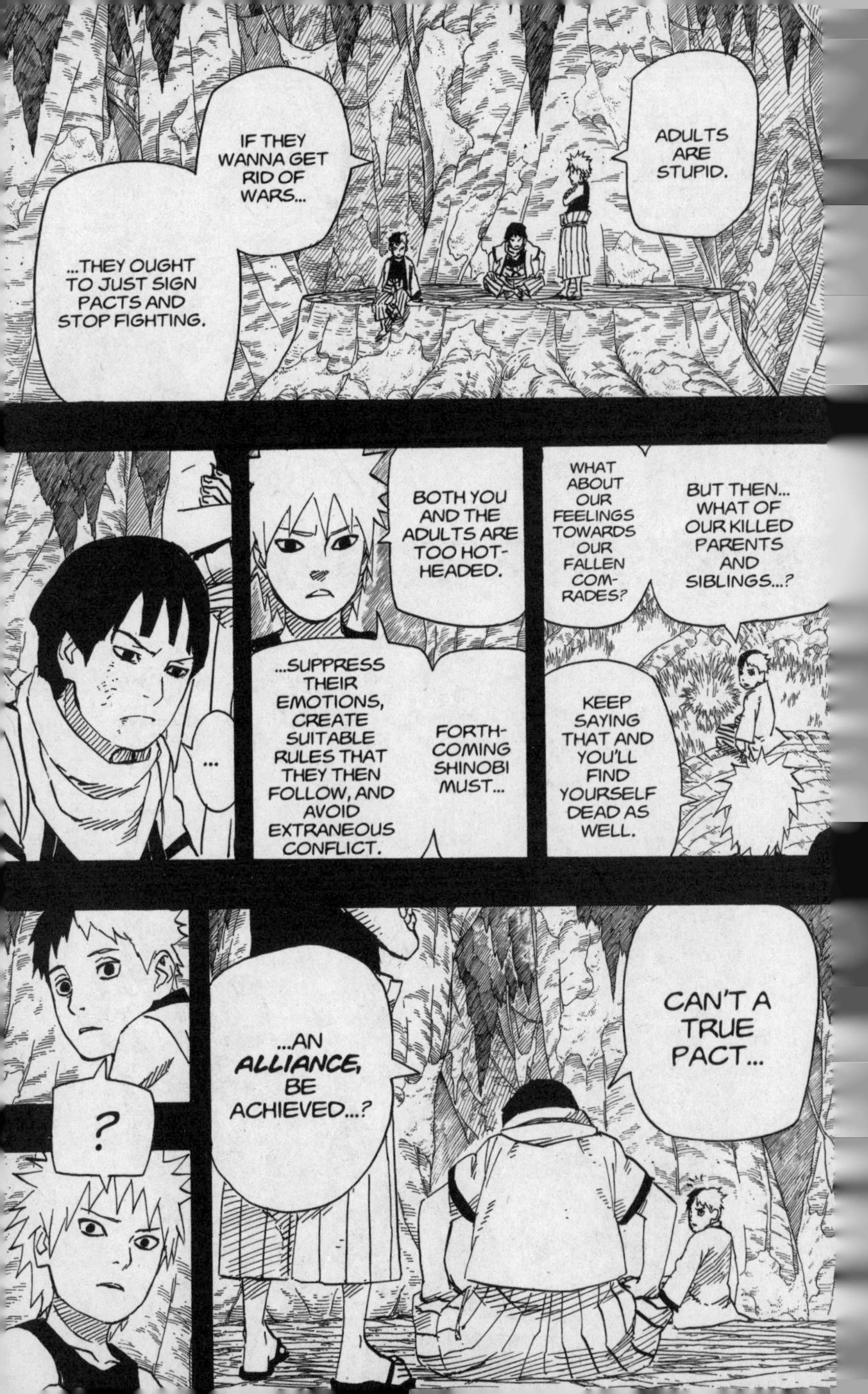
ADULTS ARE STUPID.
IF THEY WANNA GET RID OF WARS...
...THEY OUGHT TO JUST SIGN PACTS AND STOP FIGHTING.
BUT THEN... WHAT OF OUR KILLED PARENTS AND SIBLINGS...?
WHAT ABOUT OUR FEELINGS TOWARDS OUR FALLEN COM-RADES?
KEEP SAYING THAT AND YOU'LL FIND YOURSELF DEAD AS WELL.
BOTH YOU AND THE ADULTS ARE TOO HOT-HEADED.
FORTH-COMING SHINOBI MUST...
...SUPPRESS THEIR EMOTIONS, CREATE SUITABLE RULES THAT THEY THEN FOLLOW, AND AVOID EXTRANEOUS CONFLICT.
...
CAN'T A TRUE PACT...
...AN ***ALLIANCE,*** BE ACHIEVED...?
?

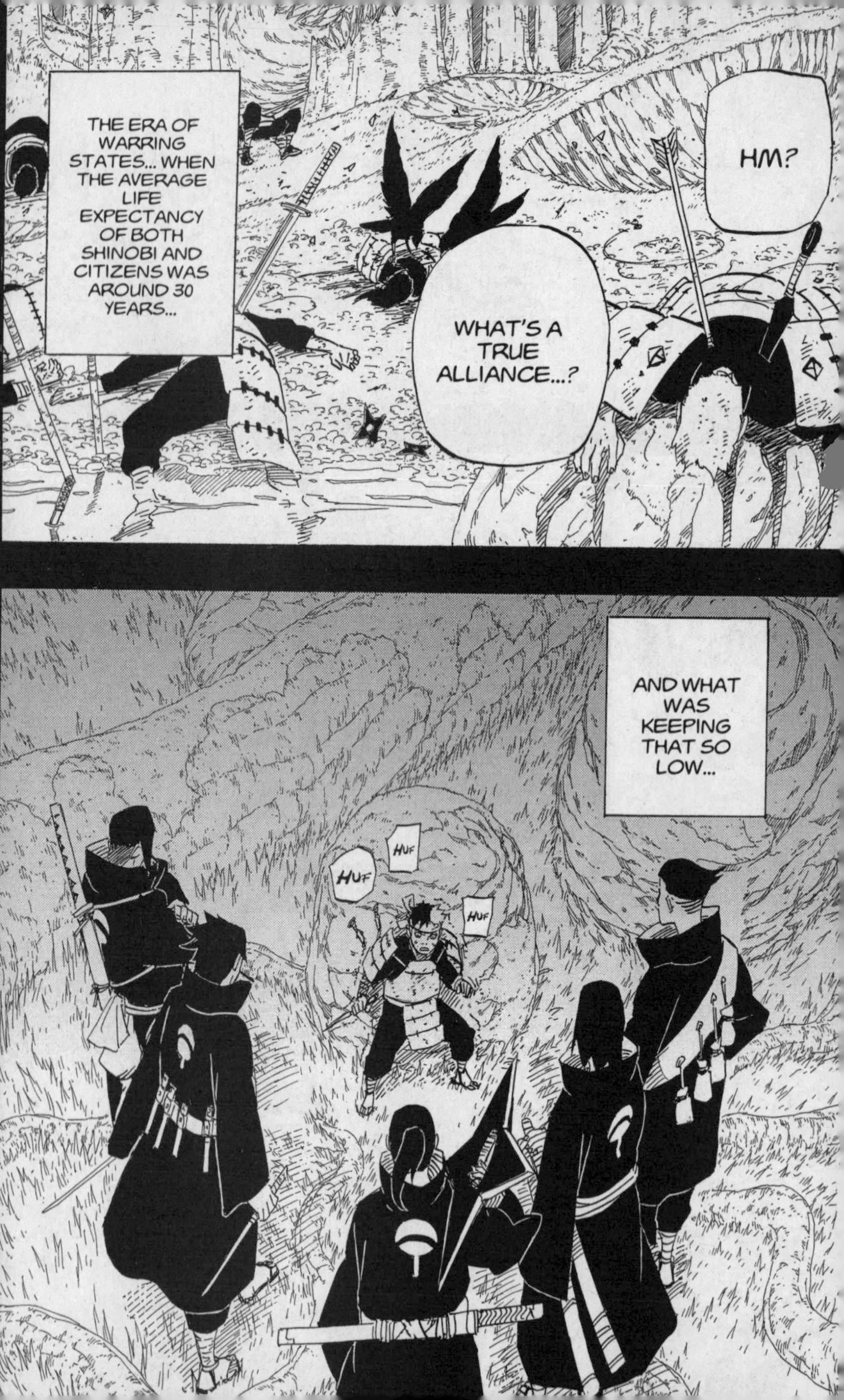
HM?
WHAT'S A TRUE ALLIANCE...?
THE ERA OF WARRING STATES... WHEN THE AVERAGE LIFE EXPECTANCY OF BOTH SHINOBI AND CITIZENS WAS AROUND 30 YEARS...
AND WHAT WAS KEEPING THAT SO LOW...
HUF
HUF
HUF

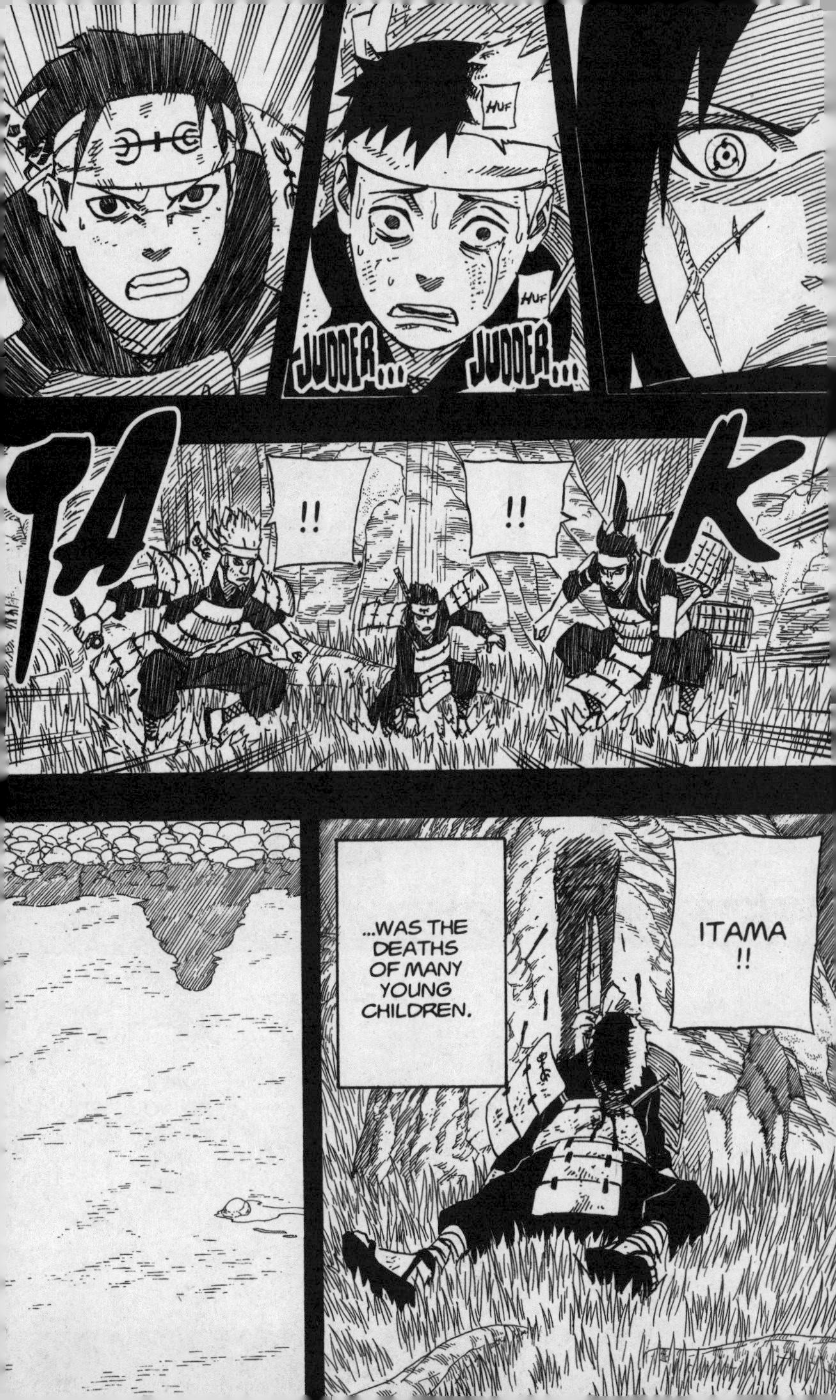
HUF
HUF
JUDDER...
JUDDER...
K
!!
!!
TA
ITAMA !!
...WAS THE DEATHS OF MANY YOUNG CHILDREN.

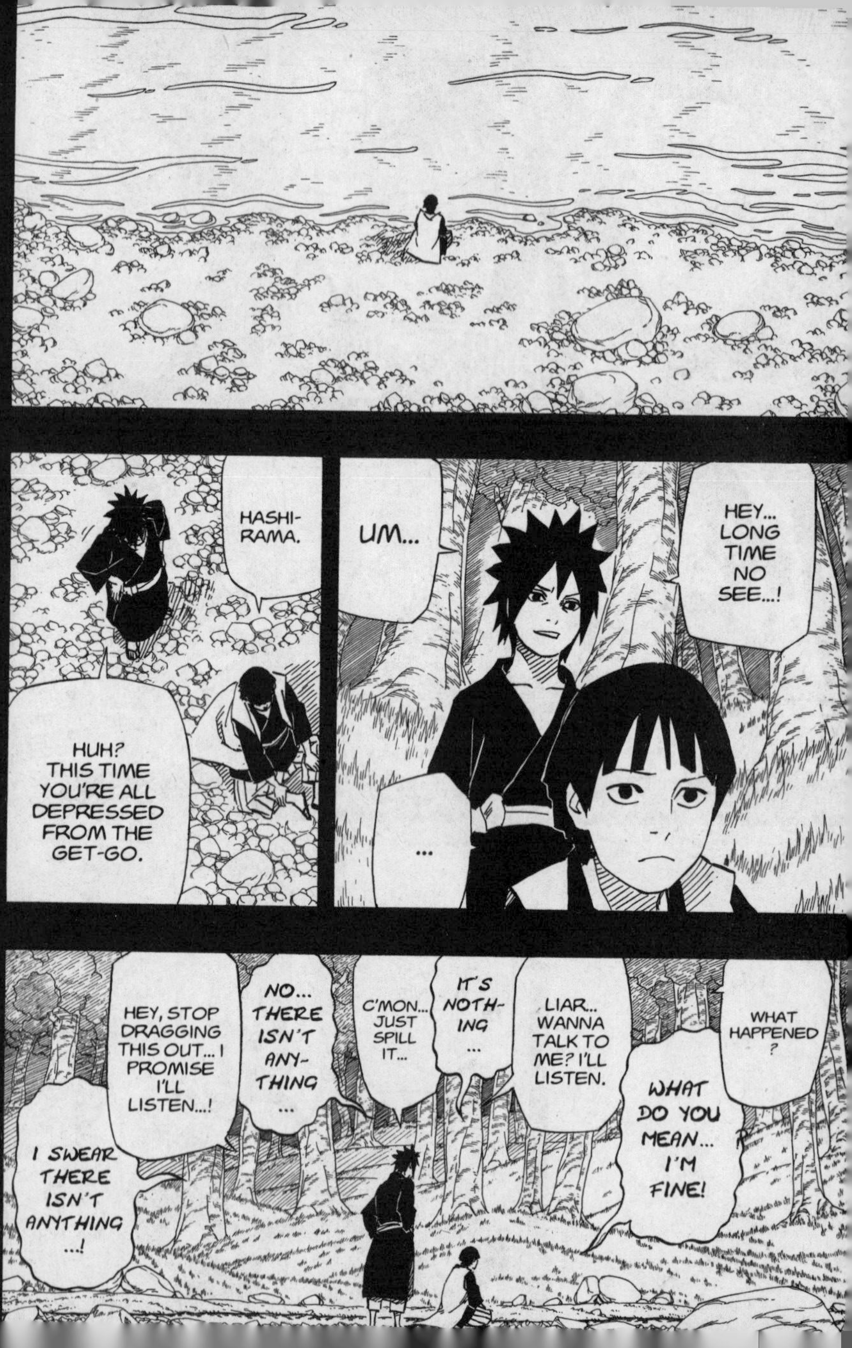
HEY... LONG TIME NO SEE...!
UM...
...
HASHI-RAMA.
HUH? THIS TIME YOU'RE ALL DEPRESSED FROM THE GET-GO.
WHAT HAPPENED?
WHAT DO YOU MEAN... I'M FINE!
LIAR... WANNA TALK TO ME? I'LL LISTEN.
IT'S NOTH-ING...
C'MON... JUST SPILL IT...
NO... THERE ISN'T ANY-THING...
HEY, STOP DRAGGING THIS OUT... I PROMISE I'LL LISTEN...!
I SWEAR THERE ISN'T ANYTHING...!

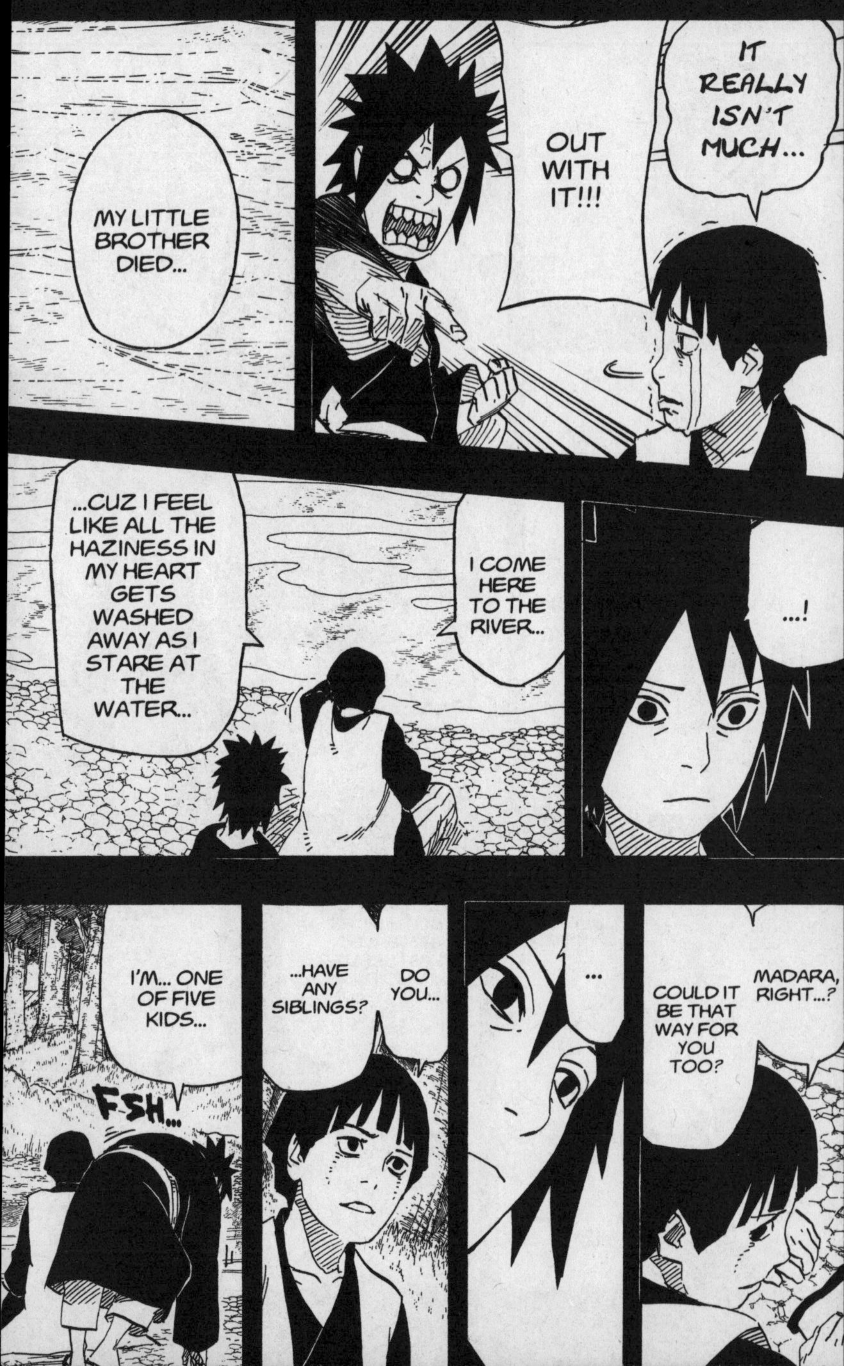
IT REALLY ISN'T MUCH...
OUT WITH IT!!!
MY LITTLE BROTHER DIED...
...!
I COME HERE TO THE RIVER...
...CUZ I FEEL LIKE ALL THE HAZINESS IN MY HEART GETS WASHED AWAY AS I STARE AT THE WATER...
MADARA, RIGHT...?
COULD IT BE THAT WAY FOR YOU TOO?
...
DO YOU...
...HAVE ANY SIBLINGS?
I'M... ONE OF FIVE KIDS...
FSH...

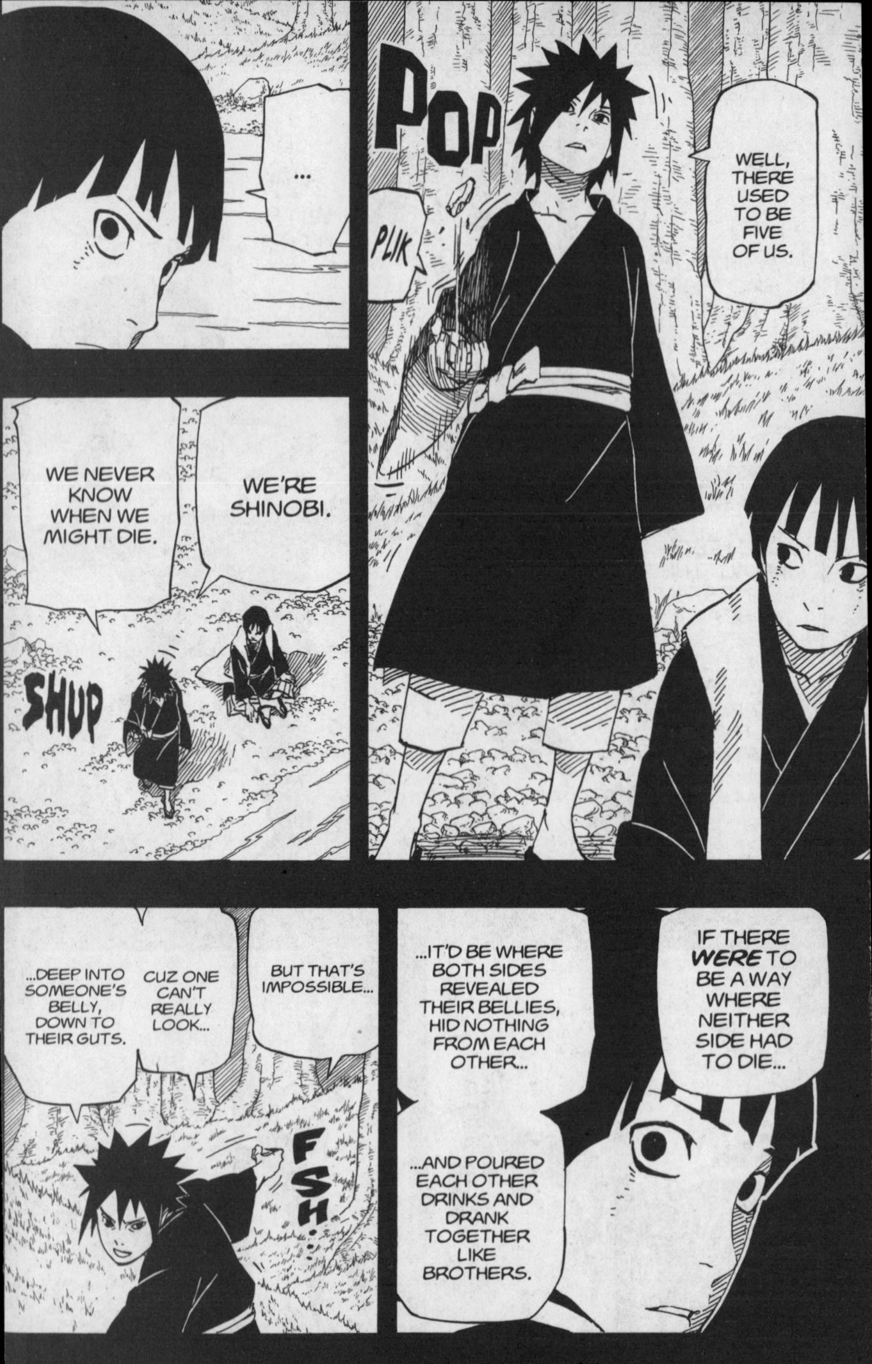
WELL, THERE USED TO BE FIVE OF US.
POP
PLIK
...
WE'RE SHINOBI.
WE NEVER KNOW WHEN WE MIGHT DIE.
SHUP
IF THERE *WERE* TO BE A WAY WHERE NEITHER SIDE HAD TO DIE...
...IT'D BE WHERE BOTH SIDES REVEALED THEIR BELLIES, HID NOTHING FROM EACH OTHER...
...AND POURED EACH OTHER DRINKS AND DRANK TOGETHER LIKE BROTHERS.
BUT THAT'S IMPOSSIBLE...
CUZ ONE CAN'T REALLY LOOK...
...DEEP INTO SOMEONE'S BELLY, DOWN TO THEIR GUTS.
FSH

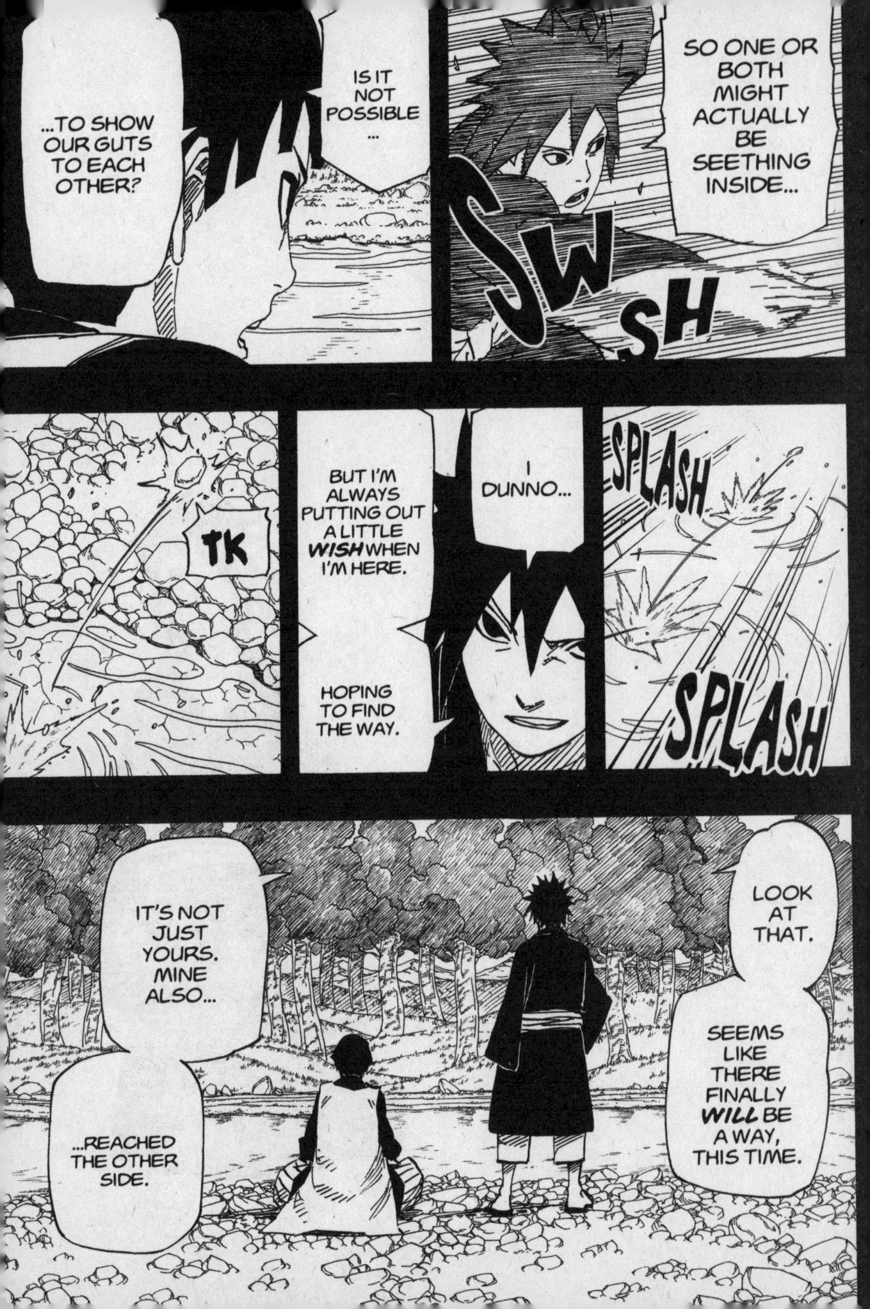
SO ONE OR BOTH MIGHT ACTUALLY BE SEETHING INSIDE...
SWSH
IS IT NOT POSSIBLE...
...TO SHOW OUR GUTS TO EACH OTHER?
SPLASH
SPLASH
I DUNNO...
BUT I'M ALWAYS PUTTING OUT A LITTLE WISH WHEN I'M HERE.
HOPING TO FIND THE WAY.
TK
LOOK AT THAT.
SEEMS LIKE THERE FINALLY WILL BE A WAY, THIS TIME.
IT'S NOT JUST YOURS. MINE ALSO...
...REACHED THE OTHER SIDE.

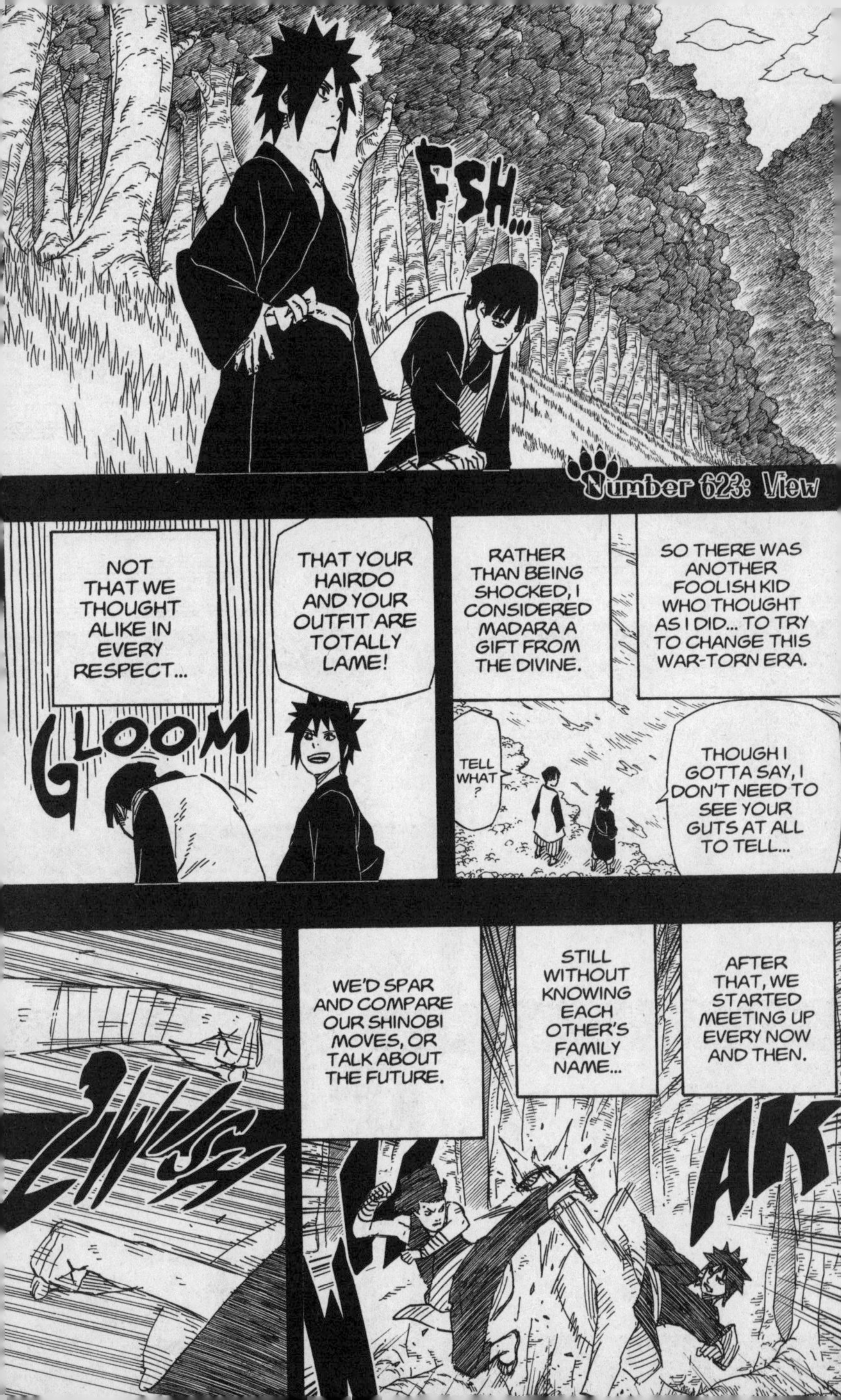
FSH...
Number 623: View
SO THERE WAS ANOTHER FOOLISH KID WHO THOUGHT AS I DID... TO TRY TO CHANGE THIS WAR-TORN ERA.
RATHER THAN BEING SHOCKED, I CONSIDERED MADARA A GIFT FROM THE DIVINE.
THOUGH I GOTTA SAY, I DON'T NEED TO SEE YOUR GUTS AT ALL TO TELL...
TELL WHAT?
THAT YOUR HAIRDO AND YOUR OUTFIT ARE TOTALLY LAME!
NOT THAT WE THOUGHT ALIKE IN EVERY RESPECT...
GLOOM
AFTER THAT, WE STARTED MEETING UP EVERY NOW AND THEN.
STILL WITHOUT KNOWING EACH OTHER'S FAMILY NAME...
WE'D SPAR AND COMPARE OUR SHINOBI MOVES, OR TALK ABOUT THE FUTURE.
AK
ZWISH

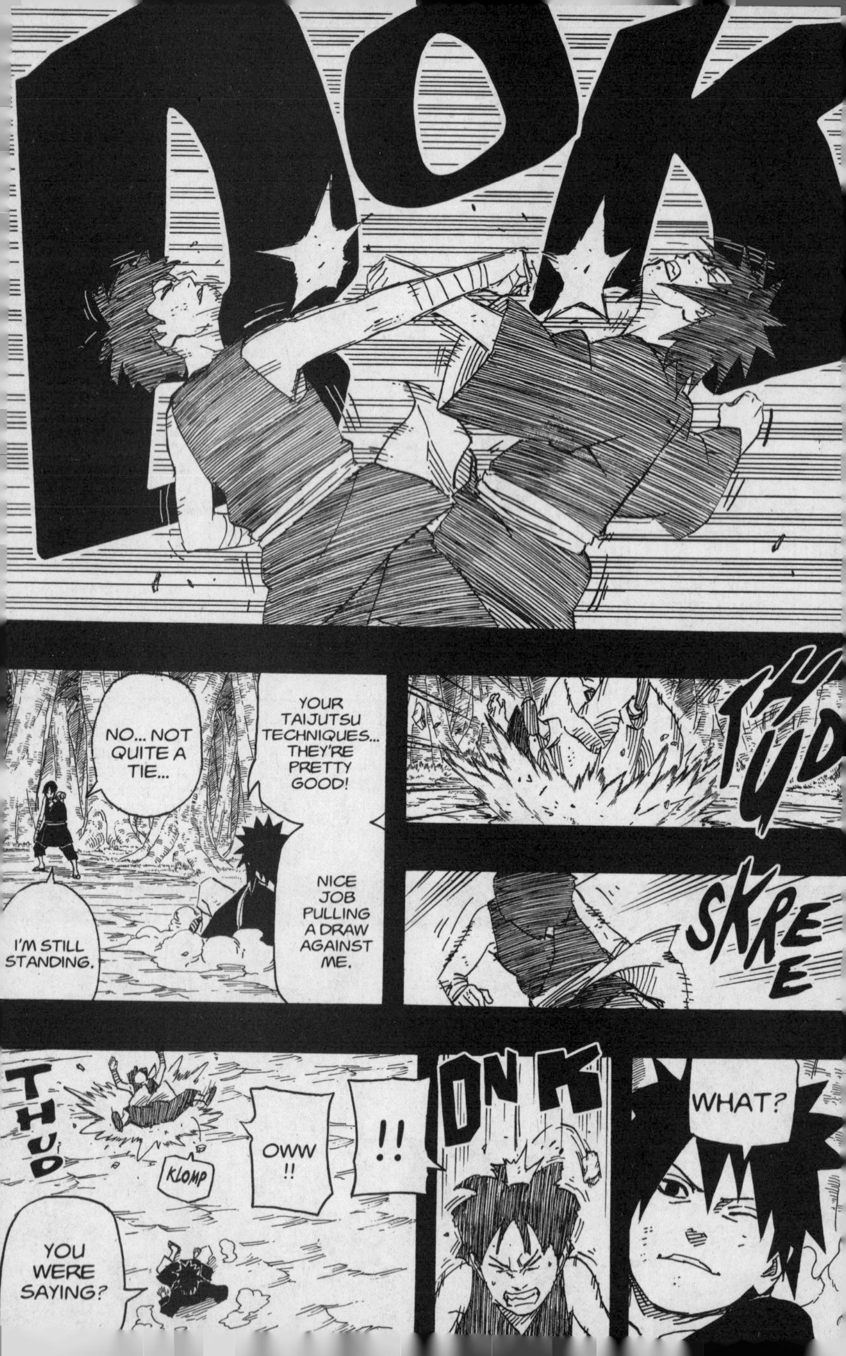
DOK
THUD
SKREE
YOUR TAIJUTSU TECHNIQUES... THEY'RE PRETTY GOOD!
NO... NOT QUITE A TIE...
NICE JOB PULLING A DRAW AGAINST ME.
I'M STILL STANDING.
WHAT?
DNK
!!
OWW !!
THUD
KLOMP
YOU WERE SAYING?

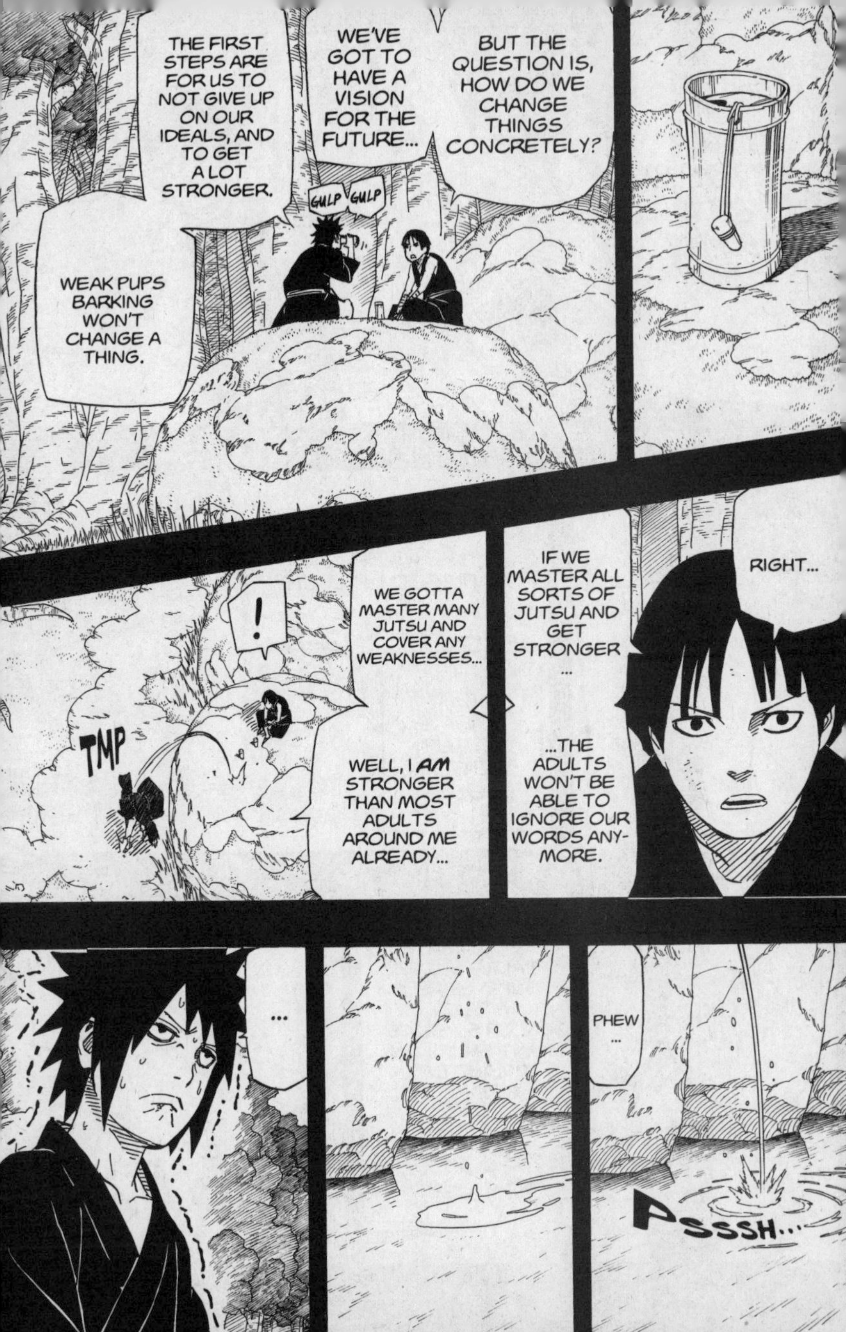
BUT THE QUESTION IS, HOW DO WE CHANGE THINGS CONCRETELY?
WE'VE GOT TO HAVE A VISION FOR THE FUTURE...
THE FIRST STEPS ARE FOR US TO NOT GIVE UP ON OUR IDEALS, AND TO GET A LOT STRONGER.
GULP GULP
WEAK PUPS BARKING WON'T CHANGE A THING.
RIGHT...
IF WE MASTER ALL SORTS OF JUTSU AND GET STRONGER ...
...THE ADULTS WON'T BE ABLE TO IGNORE OUR WORDS ANY-MORE.
WE GOTTA MASTER MANY JUTSU AND COVER ANY WEAKNESSES...
WELL, I *AM* STRONGER THAN MOST ADULTS AROUND ME ALREADY...
!
TMP
PHEW ...
PSSSH...
...

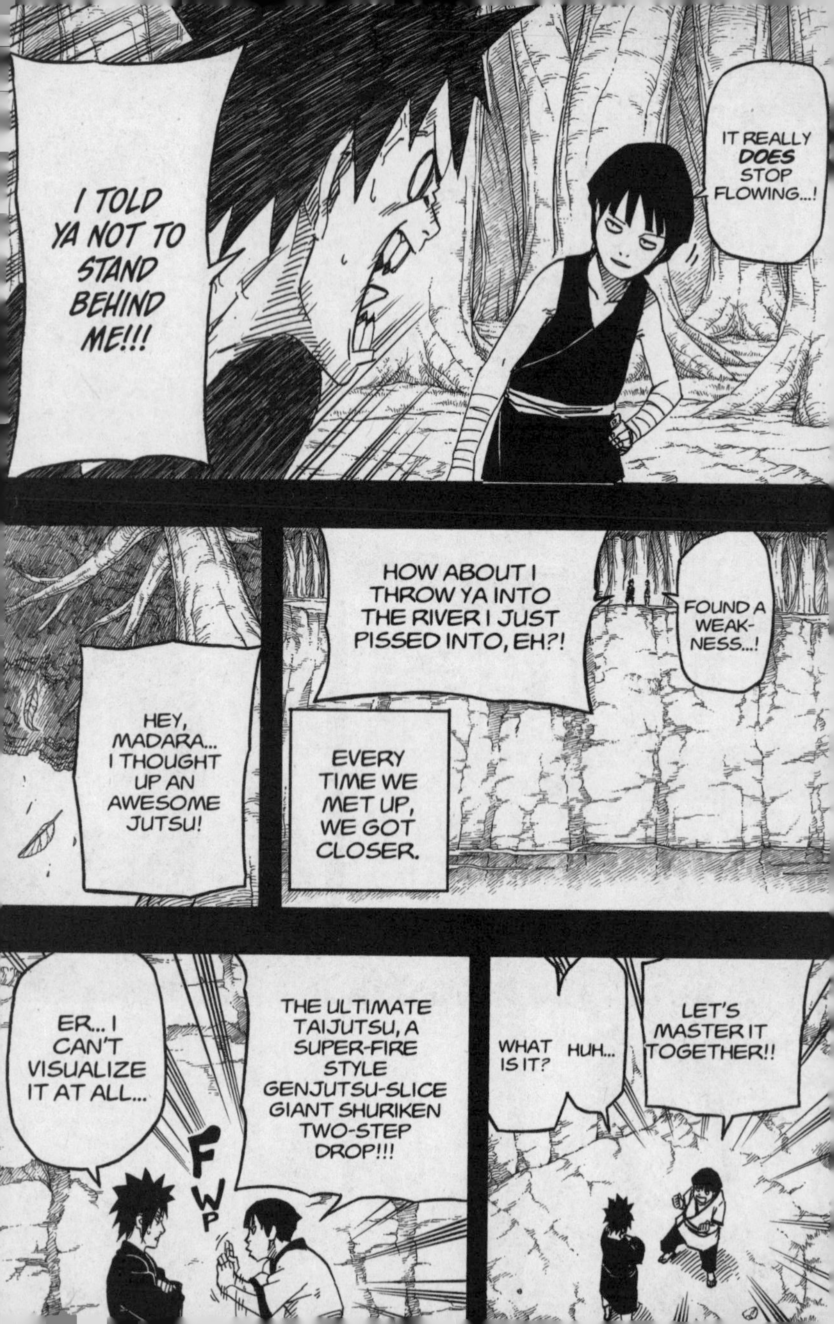
IT REALLY DOES STOP FLOWING...!
I TOLD YA NOT TO STAND BEHIND ME!!!
FOUND A WEAK-NESS...!
HOW ABOUT I THROW YA INTO THE RIVER I JUST PISSED INTO, EH?!
EVERY TIME WE MET UP, WE GOT CLOSER.
HEY, MADARA... I THOUGHT UP AN AWESOME JUTSU!
LET'S MASTER IT TOGETHER!!
HUH...
WHAT IS IT?
THE ULTIMATE TAIJUTSU, A SUPER-FIRE STYLE GENJUTSU-SLICE GIANT SHURIKEN TWO-STEP DROP!!!
FWP
ER... I CAN'T VISUALIZE IT AT ALL...

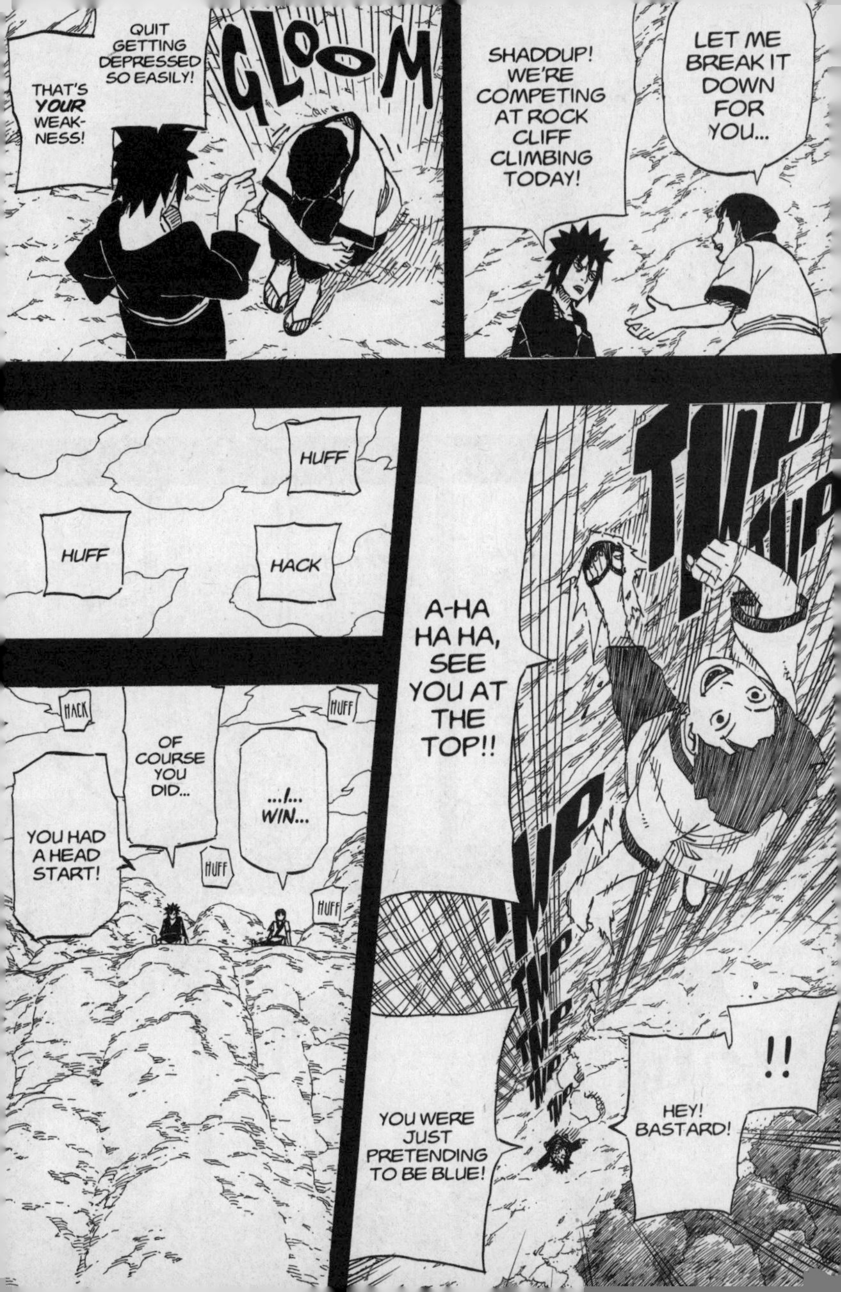
LET ME BREAK IT DOWN FOR YOU...
SHADDUP! WE'RE COMPETING AT ROCK CLIFF CLIMBING TODAY!
GLOOM
QUIT GETTING DEPRESSED SO EASILY!
THAT'S *YOUR* WEAK-NESS!
TMP
TMP
A-HA HA HA, SEE YOU AT THE TOP!!
TMP
TMP
TMP
TMP
!!
HEY! BASTARD!
YOU WERE JUST PRETENDING TO BE BLUE!
HUFF
HUFF
HACK
HUFF
HACK
...I... WIN...
OF COURSE YOU DID...
HUFF
HUFF
YOU HAD A HEAD START!

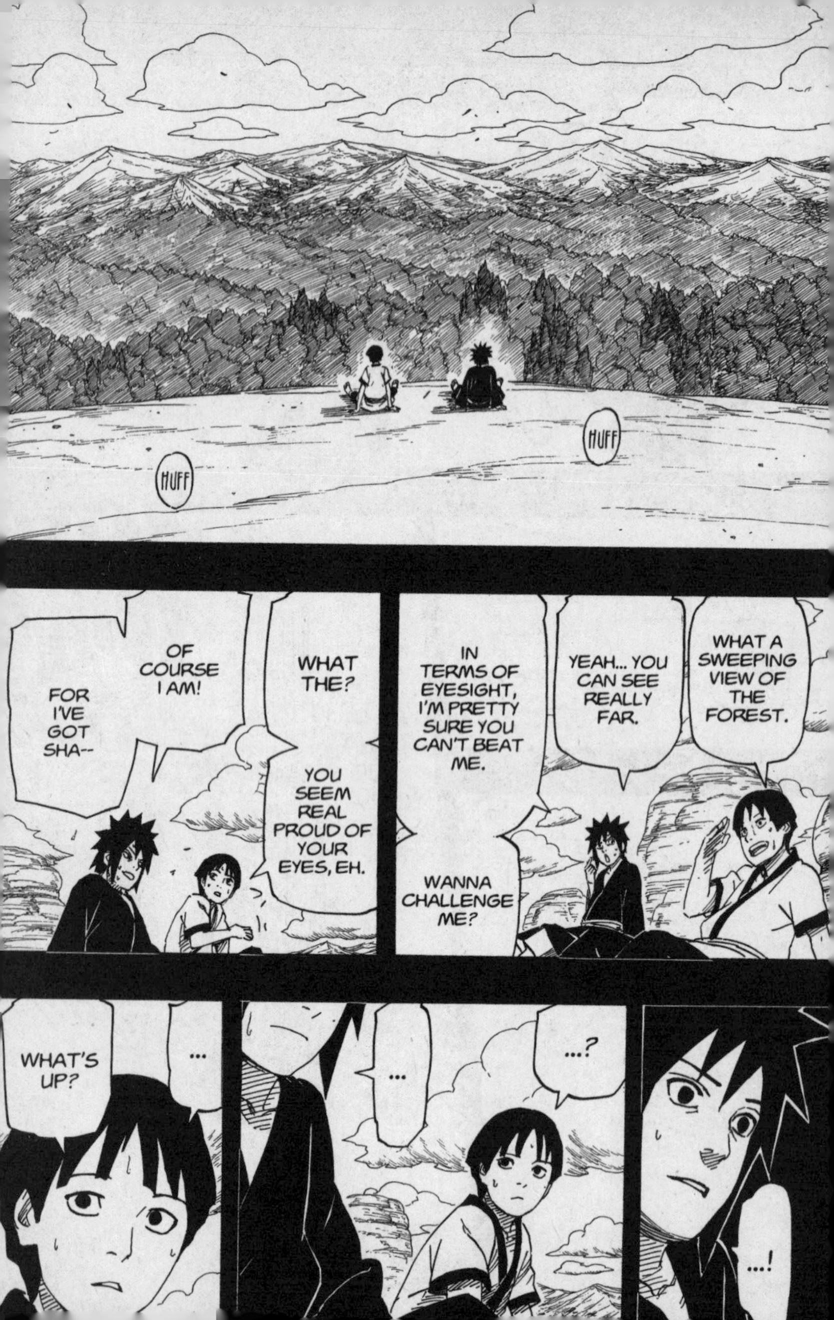
HUFF
HUFF
WHAT A SWEEPING VIEW OF THE FOREST.
YEAH... YOU CAN SEE REALLY FAR.
IN TERMS OF EYESIGHT, I'M PRETTY SURE YOU CAN'T BEAT ME.
WANNA CHALLENGE ME?
WHAT THE?
YOU SEEM REAL PROUD OF YOUR EYES, EH.
OF COURSE I AM!
FOR I'VE GOT SHA--
...!
...?
...
...
WHAT'S UP?

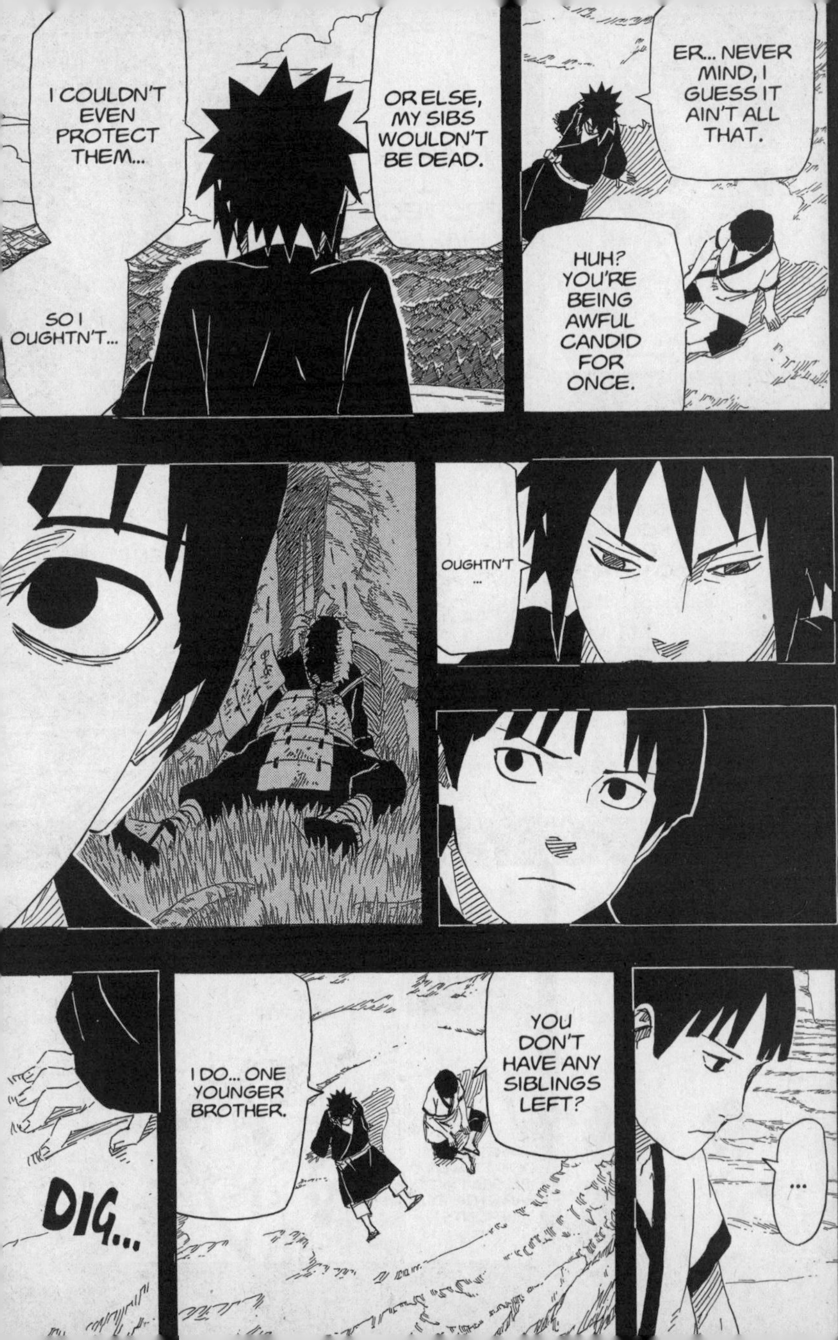
ER... NEVER MIND, I GUESS IT AIN'T ALL THAT.
HUH? YOU'RE BEING AWFUL CANDID FOR ONCE.
OR ELSE, MY SIBS WOULDN'T BE DEAD.
I COULDN'T EVEN PROTECT THEM...
SO I OUGHTN'T...
OUGHTN'T ...
...
YOU DON'T HAVE ANY SIBLINGS LEFT?
I DO... ONE YOUNGER BROTHER.
DIG...

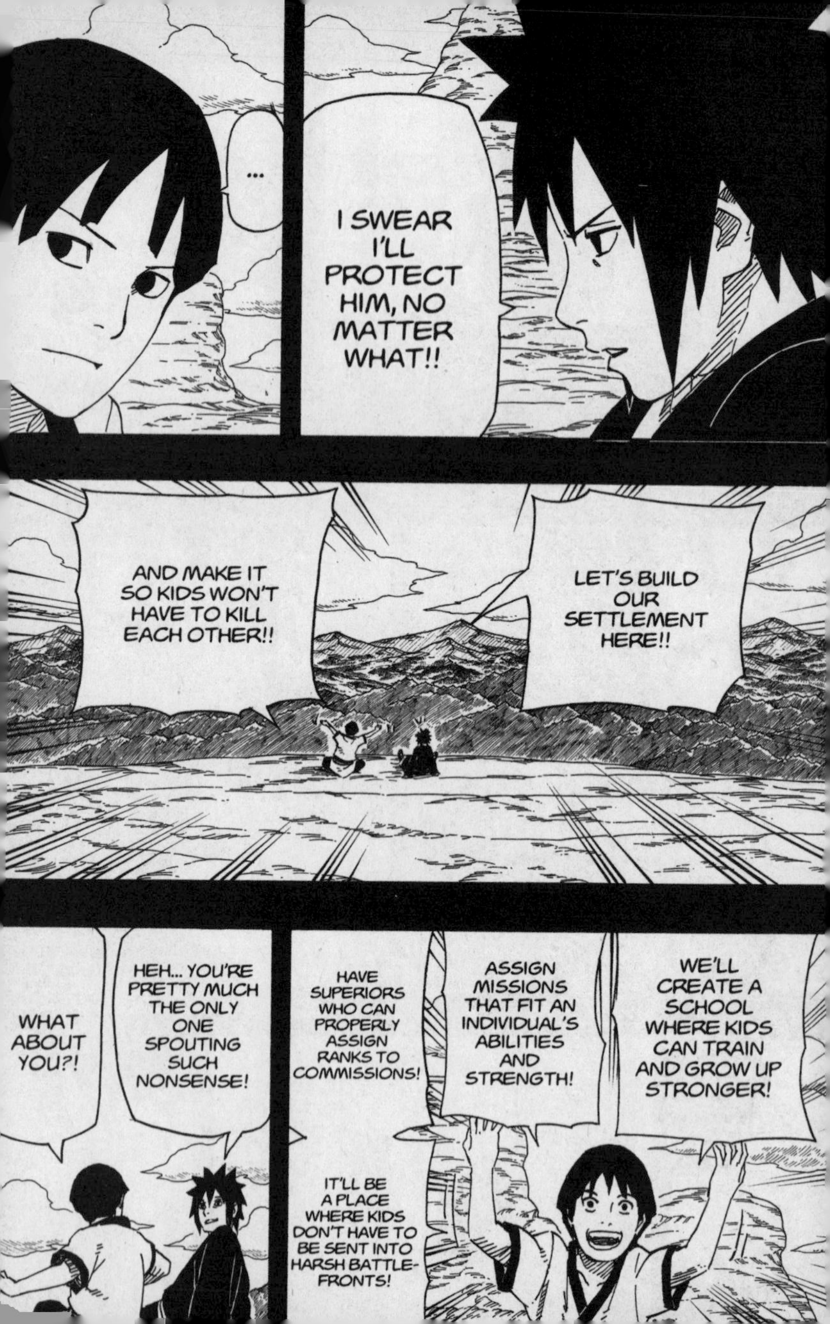
I SWEAR I'LL PROTECT HIM, NO MATTER WHAT!!
...
LET'S BUILD OUR SETTLEMENT HERE!!
AND MAKE IT SO KIDS WON'T HAVE TO KILL EACH OTHER!!
WE'LL CREATE A SCHOOL WHERE KIDS CAN TRAIN AND GROW UP STRONGER!
ASSIGN MISSIONS THAT FIT AN INDIVIDUAL'S ABILITIES AND STRENGTH!
HAVE SUPERIORS WHO CAN PROPERLY ASSIGN RANKS TO COMMISSIONS!
IT'LL BE A PLACE WHERE KIDS DON'T HAVE TO BE SENT INTO HARSH BATTLE-FRONTS!
HEH... YOU'RE PRETTY MUCH THE ONLY ONE SPOUTING SUCH NONSENSE!
WHAT ABOUT YOU?!

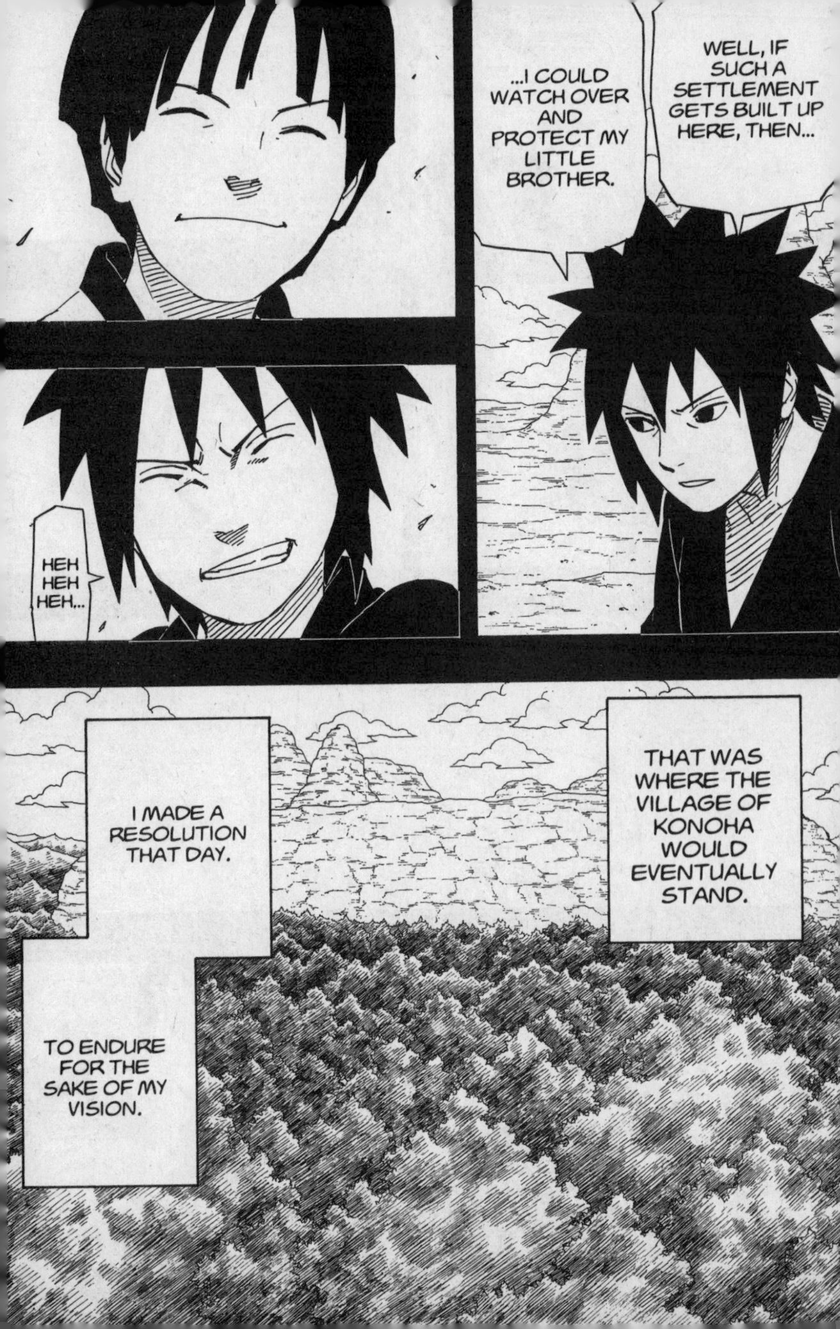
WELL, IF SUCH A SETTLEMENT GETS BUILT UP HERE, THEN...
...I COULD WATCH OVER AND PROTECT MY LITTLE BROTHER.
HEH HEH HEH...
THAT WAS WHERE THE VILLAGE OF KONOHA WOULD EVENTUALLY STAND.
I MADE A RESOLUTION THAT DAY.
TO ENDURE FOR THE SAKE OF MY VISION.

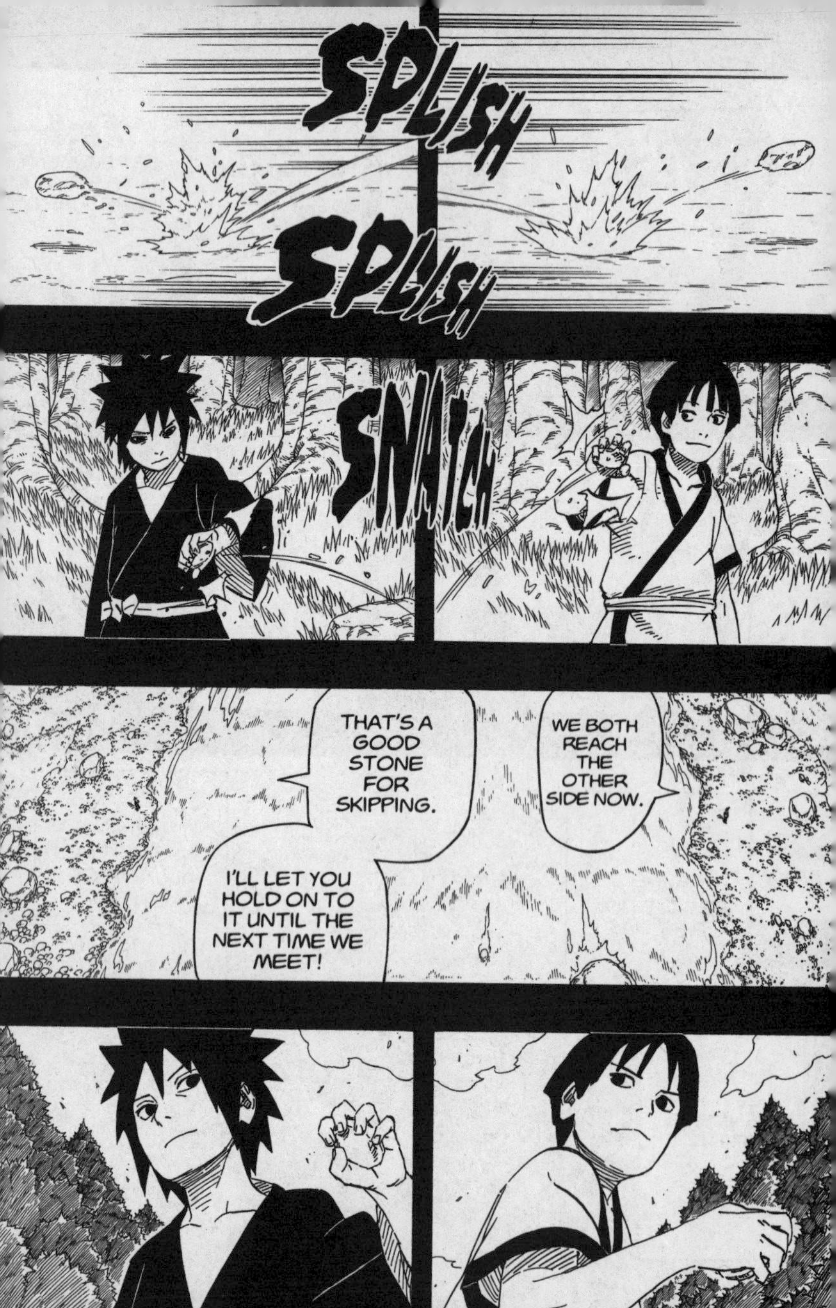
SPLISH
SPLISH
SNATCH
WE BOTH REACH THE OTHER SIDE NOW.
THAT'S A GOOD STONE FOR SKIPPING.
I'LL LET YOU HOLD ON TO IT UNTIL THE NEXT TIME WE MEET!

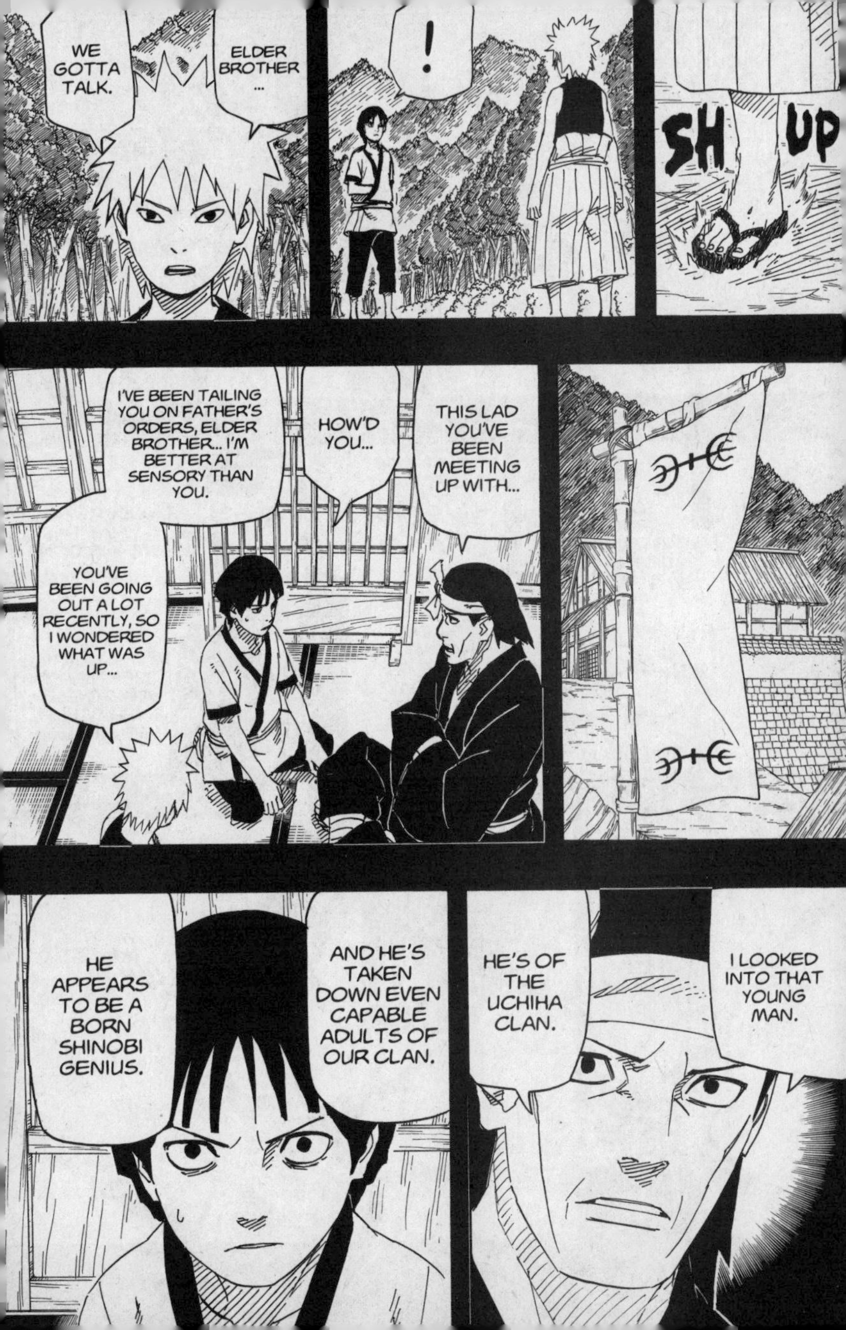
SH UP
!
ELDER BROTHER ...
WE GOTTA TALK.
THIS LAD YOU'VE BEEN MEETING UP WITH...
HOW'D YOU...
I'VE BEEN TAILING YOU ON FATHER'S ORDERS, ELDER BROTHER... I'M BETTER AT SENSORY THAN YOU.
YOU'VE BEEN GOING OUT A LOT RECENTLY, SO I WONDERED WHAT WAS UP...
I LOOKED INTO THAT YOUNG MAN.
HE'S OF THE UCHIHA CLAN.
AND HE'S TAKEN DOWN EVEN CAPABLE ADULTS OF OUR CLAN.
HE APPEARS TO BE A BORN SHINOBI GENIUS.

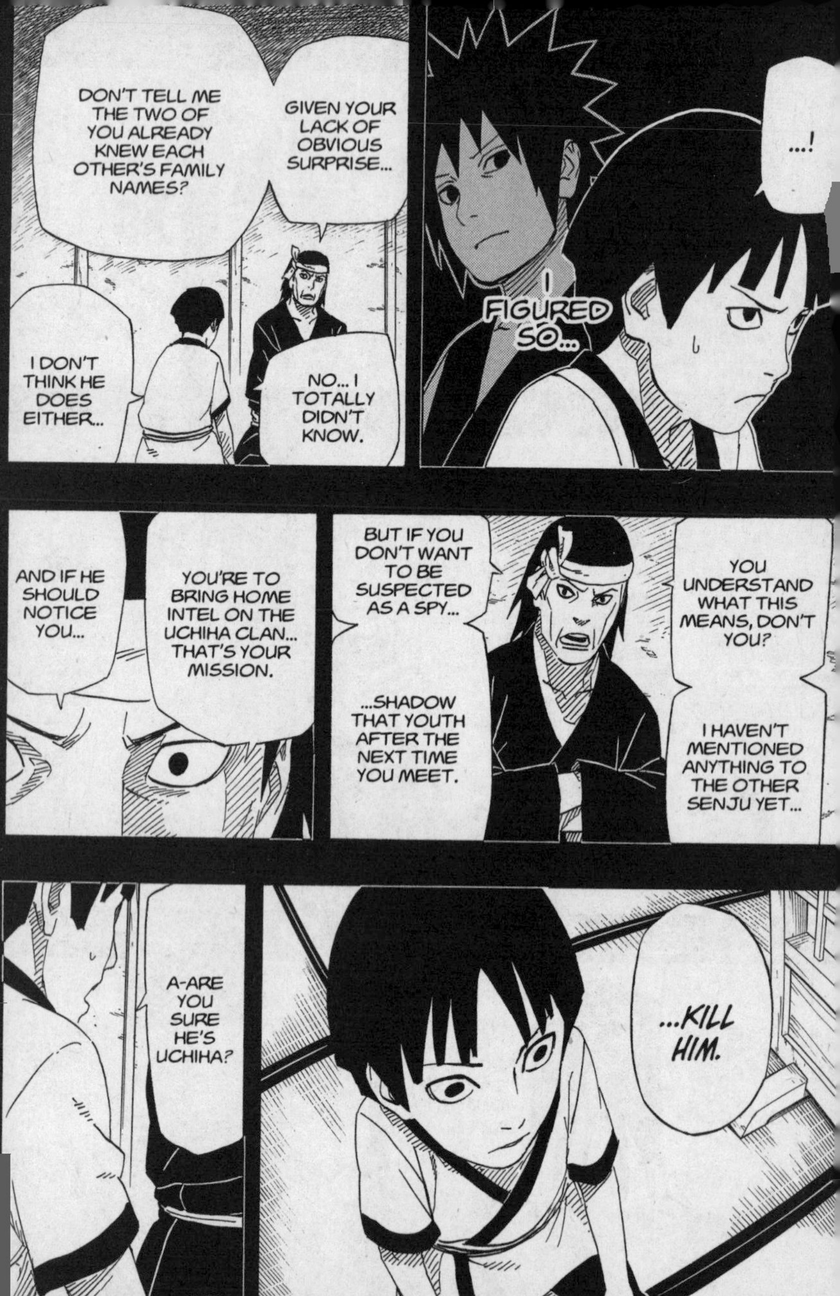
...!
I FIGURED SO...
GIVEN YOUR LACK OF OBVIOUS SURPRISE...
DON'T TELL ME THE TWO OF YOU ALREADY KNEW EACH OTHER'S FAMILY NAMES?
NO... I TOTALLY DIDN'T KNOW.
I DON'T THINK HE DOES EITHER...
YOU UNDERSTAND WHAT THIS MEANS, DON'T YOU?
I HAVEN'T MENTIONED ANYTHING TO THE OTHER SENJU YET...
BUT IF YOU DON'T WANT TO BE SUSPECTED AS A SPY...
...SHADOW THAT YOUTH AFTER THE NEXT TIME YOU MEET.
YOU'RE TO BRING HOME INTEL ON THE UCHIHA CLAN... THAT'S YOUR MISSION.
AND IF HE SHOULD NOTICE YOU...
...KILL HIM.
A-ARE YOU SURE HE'S UCHIHA?

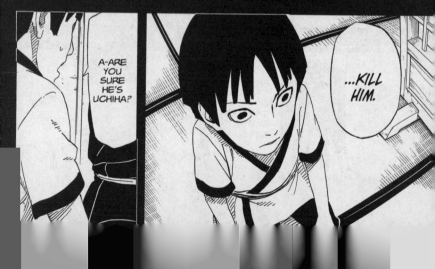

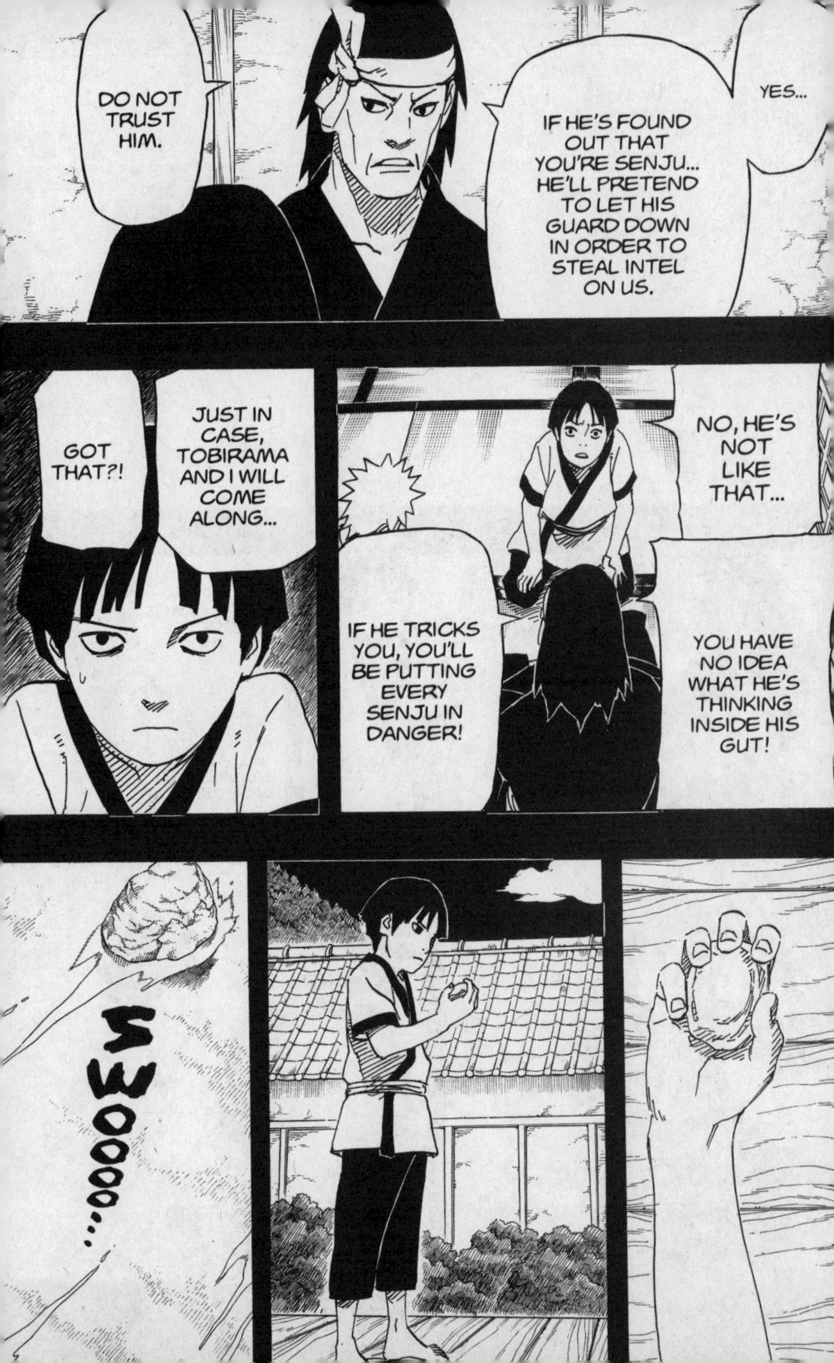
YES...
IF HE'S FOUND OUT THAT YOU'RE SENJU... HE'LL PRETEND TO LET HIS GUARD DOWN IN ORDER TO STEAL INTEL ON US.
DO NOT TRUST HIM.
NO, HE'S NOT LIKE THAT...
YOU HAVE NO IDEA WHAT HE'S THINKING INSIDE HIS GUT!
IF HE TRICKS YOU, YOU'LL BE PUTTING EVERY SENJU IN DANGER!
JUST IN CASE, TOBIRAMA AND I WILL COME ALONG...
GOT THAT?!
SWOOOOO...

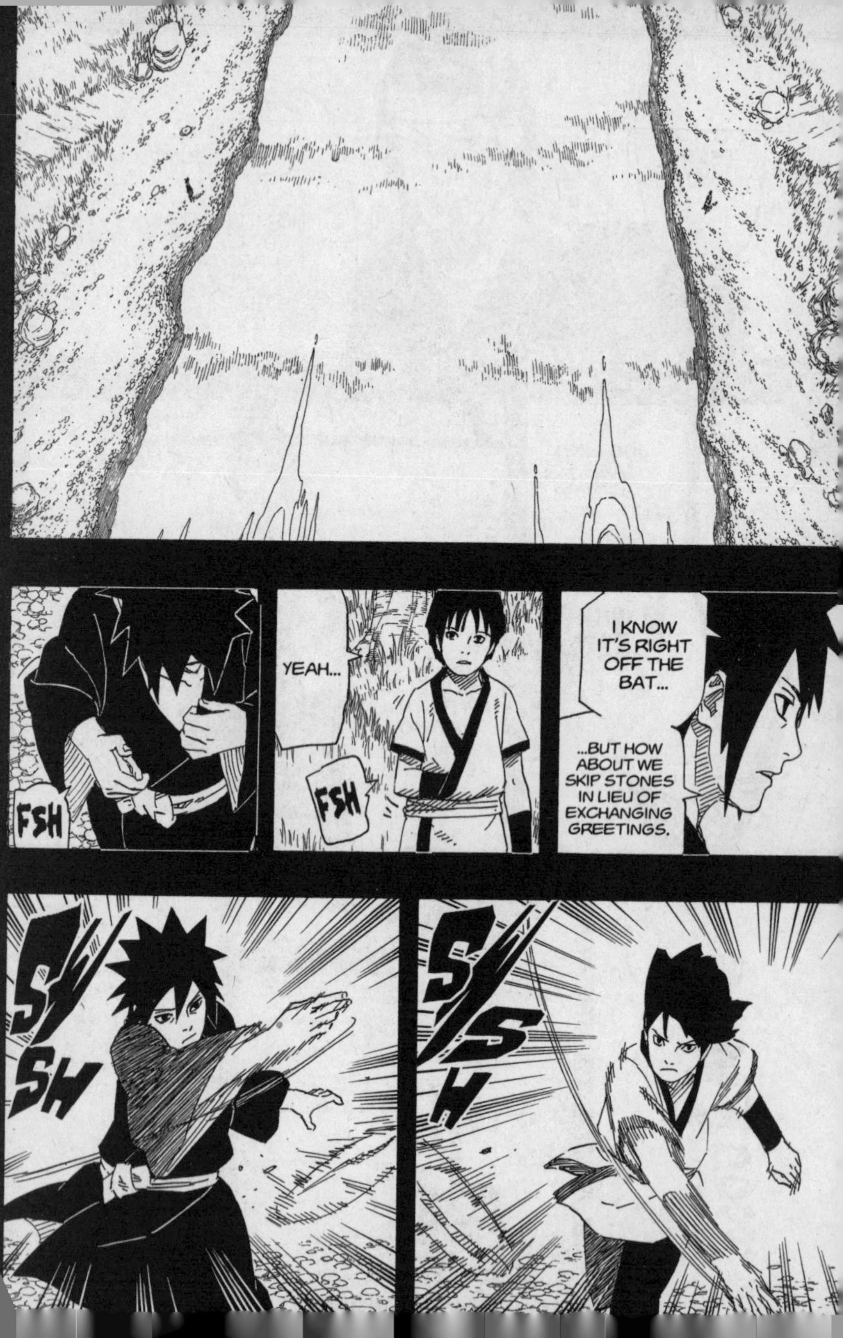
I KNOW IT'S RIGHT OFF THE BAT...
...BUT HOW ABOUT WE SKIP STONES IN LIEU OF EXCHANGING GREETINGS.
YEAH...
FSH
FSH
SSH
SSH

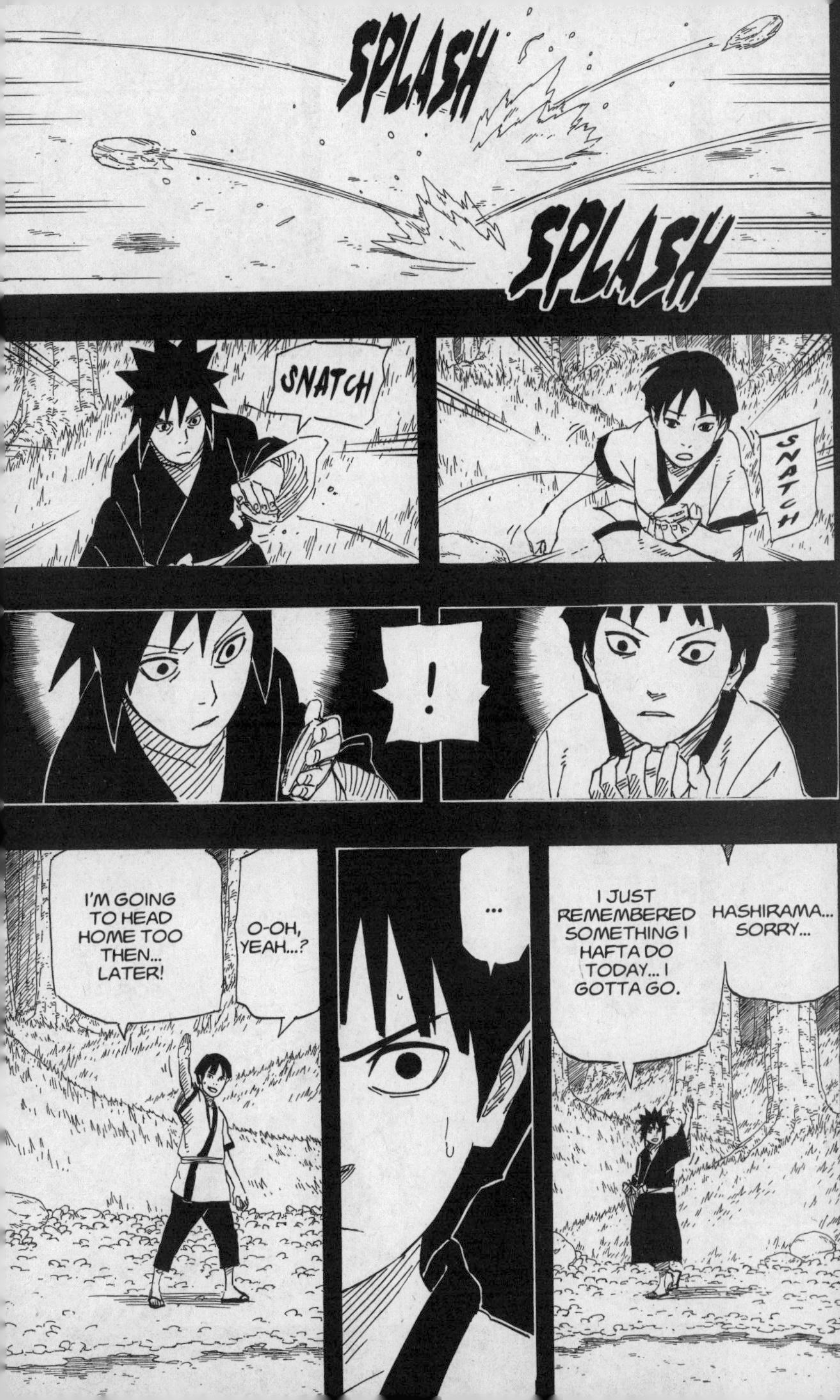
SPLASH
SPLASH
SNATCH
SNATCH
!
HASHIRAMA... SORRY...
I JUST REMEMBERED SOMETHING I HAFTA DO TODAY... I GOTTA GO.
...
O-OH, YEAH...?
I'M GOING TO HEAD HOME TOO THEN... LATER!

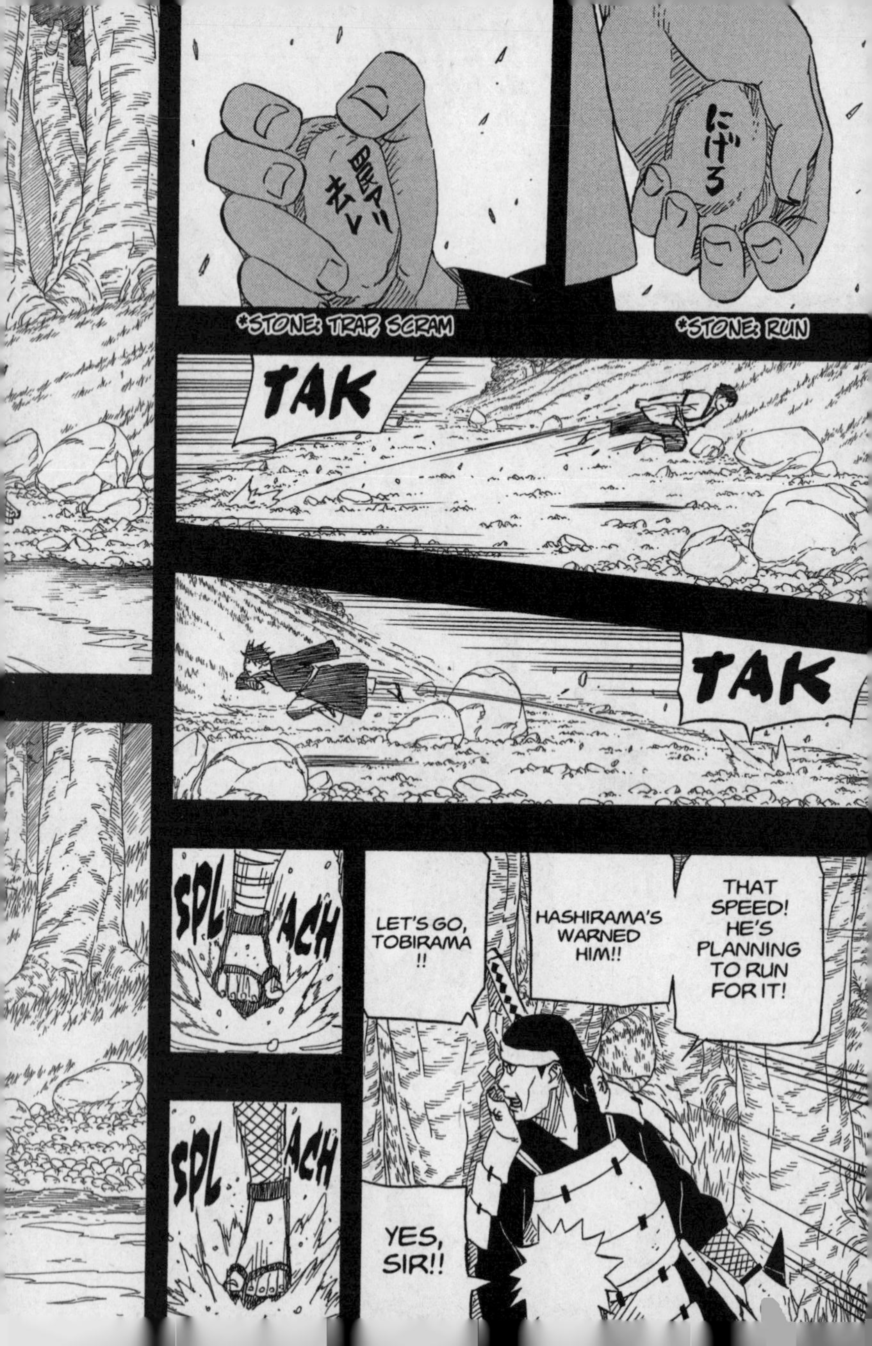
にげる
*STONE: RUN
罠アリ去レ
*STONE: TRAP, SCRAM
TAK
TAK
THAT SPEED! HE'S PLANNING TO RUN FOR IT!
HASHIRAMA'S WARNED HIM!!
LET'S GO, TOBIRAMA!!
YES, SIR!!
SPLACH
SPLACH

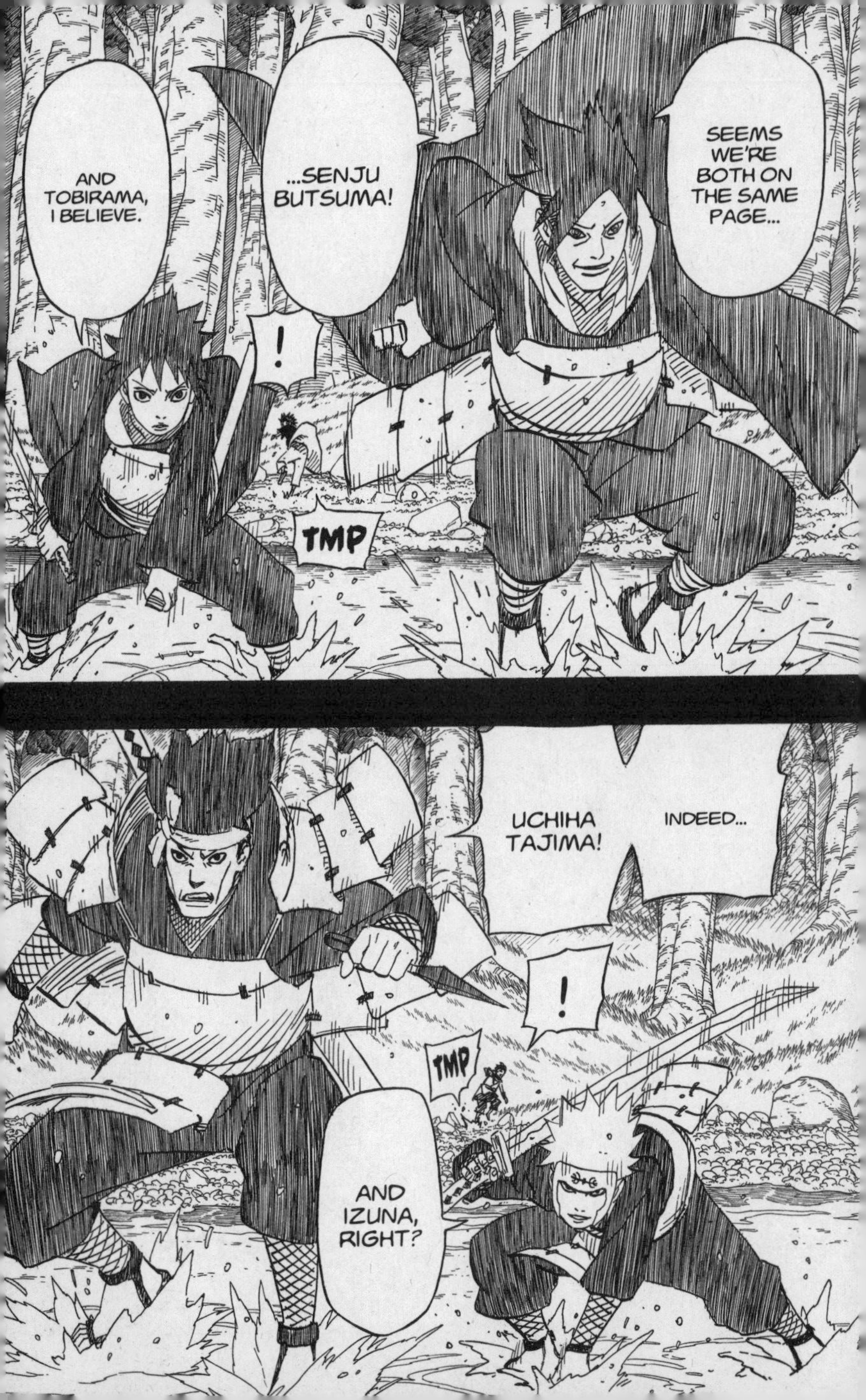
SEEMS WE'RE BOTH ON THE SAME PAGE...
...SENJU BUTSUMA!
AND TOBIRAMA, I BELIEVE.
!
TMP
INDEED...
UCHIHA TAJIMA!
!
TMP
AND IZUNA, RIGHT?

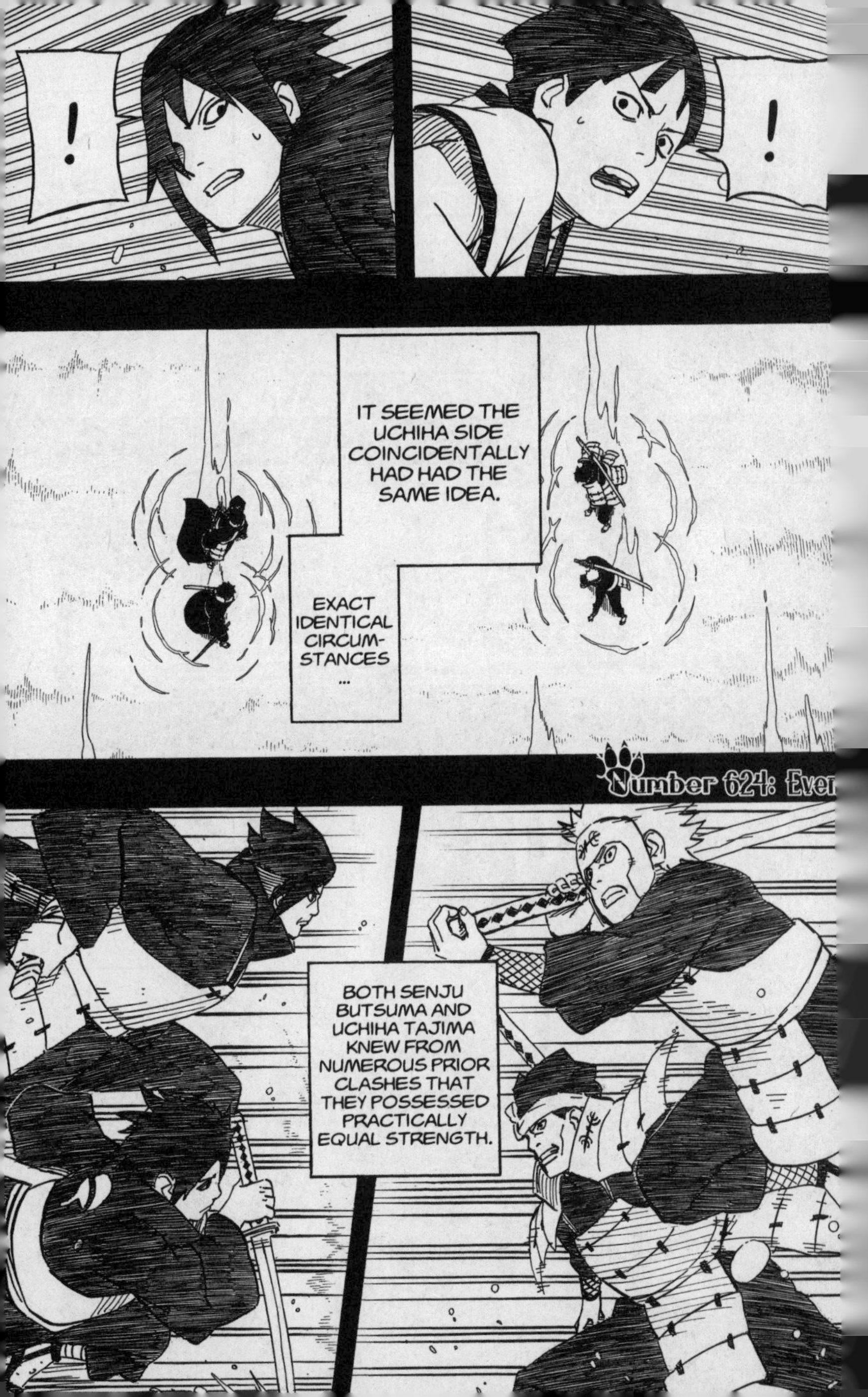
!
!
IT SEEMED THE UCHIHA SIDE COINCIDENTALLY HAD HAD THE SAME IDEA.
EXACT IDENTICAL CIRCUM-STANCES ...
Number 624: Even
BOTH SENJU BUTSUMA AND UCHIHA TAJIMA KNEW FROM NUMEROUS PRIOR CLASHES THAT THEY POSSESSED PRACTICALLY EQUAL STRENGTH.

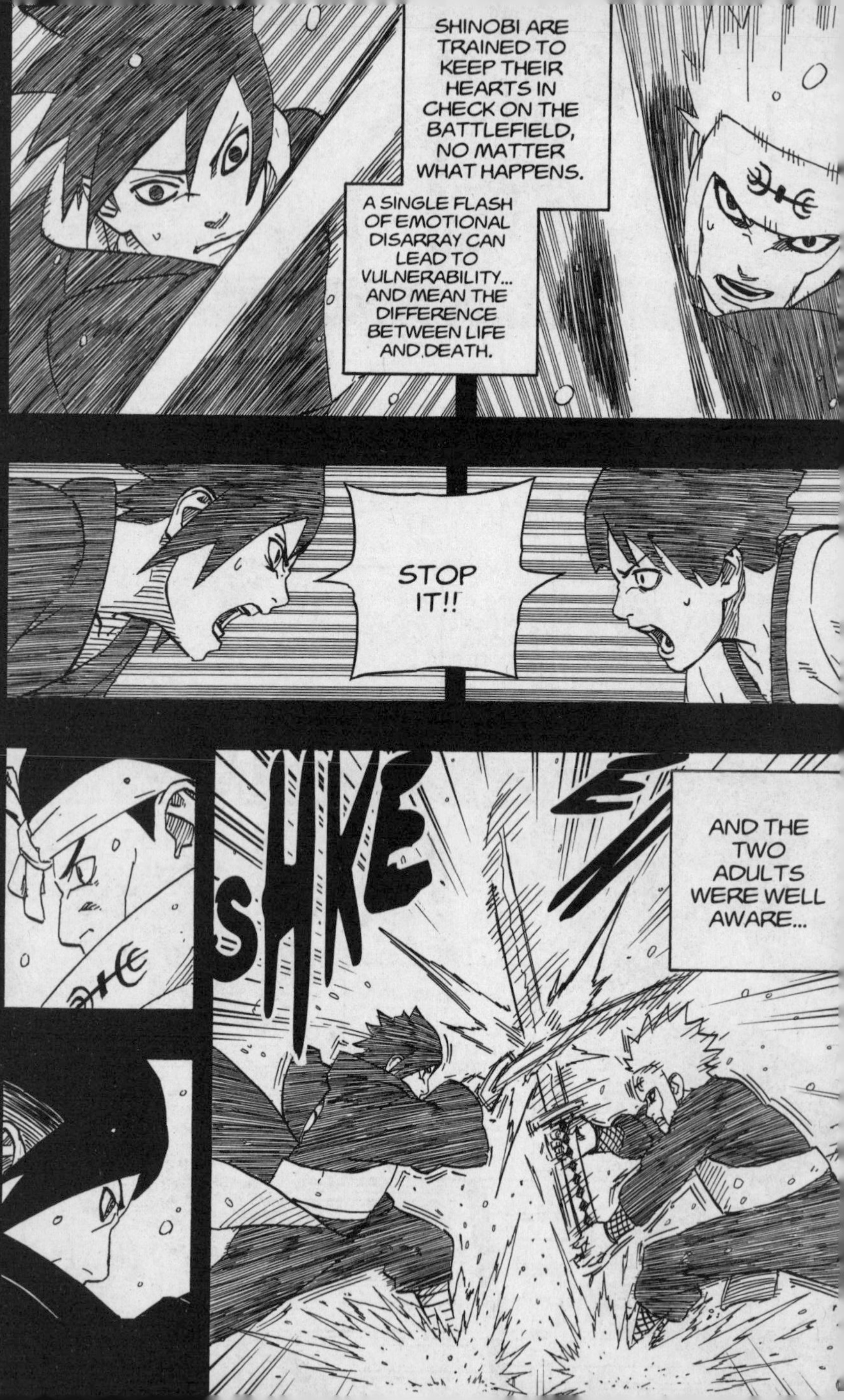

SHINOBI ARE TRAINED TO KEEP THEIR HEARTS IN CHECK ON THE BATTLEFIELD, NO MATTER WHAT HAPPENS.
A SINGLE FLASH OF EMOTIONAL DISARRAY CAN LEAD TO VULNERABILITY... AND MEAN THE DIFFERENCE BETWEEN LIFE AND DEATH.
STOP IT!!
AND THE TWO ADULTS WERE WELL AWARE...
SHKE

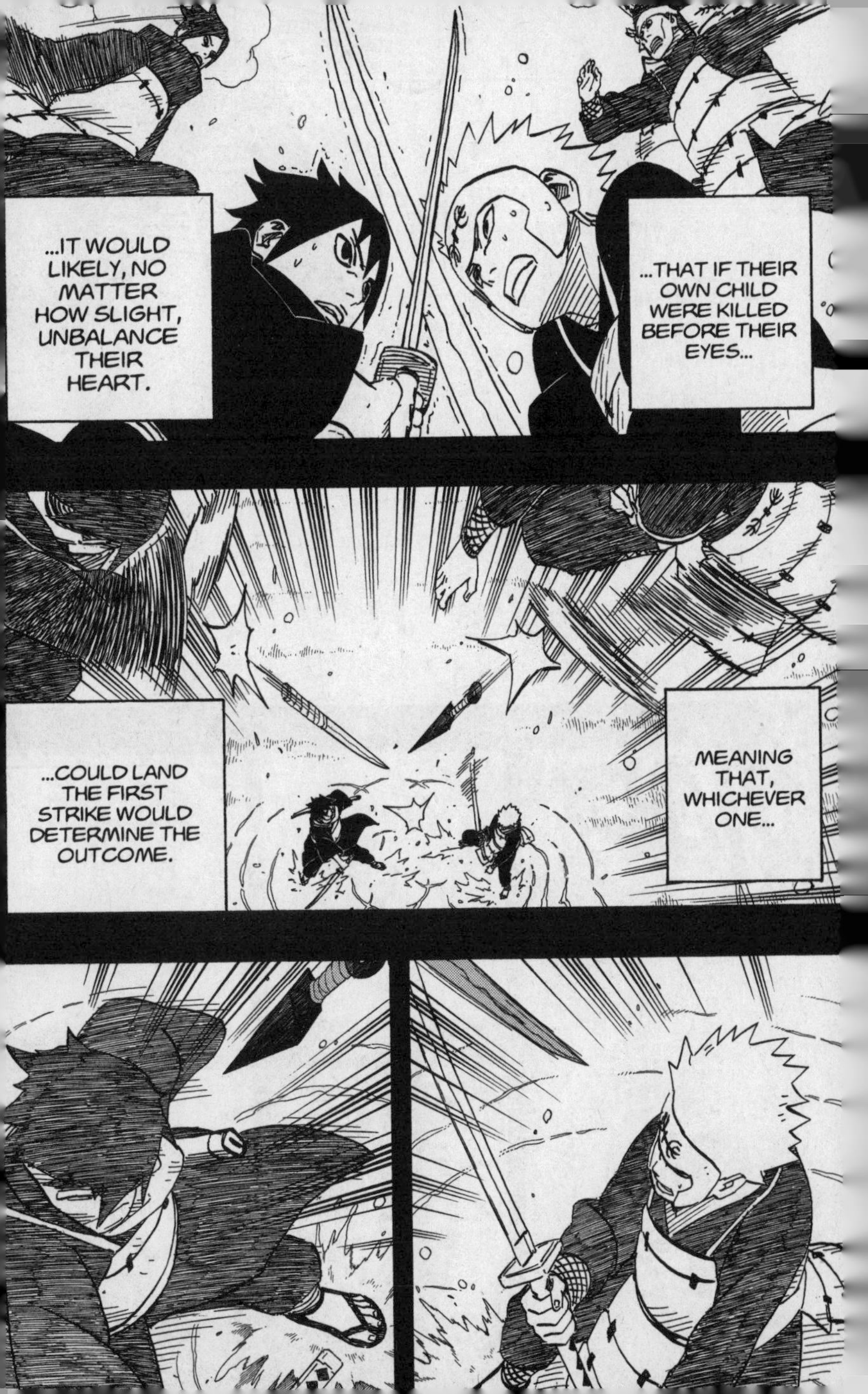
...THAT IF THEIR OWN CHILD WERE KILLED BEFORE THEIR EYES...
...IT WOULD LIKELY, NO MATTER HOW SLIGHT, UNBALANCE THEIR HEART.
MEANING THAT, WHICHEVER ONE...
...COULD LAND THE FIRST STRIKE WOULD DETERMINE THE OUTCOME.

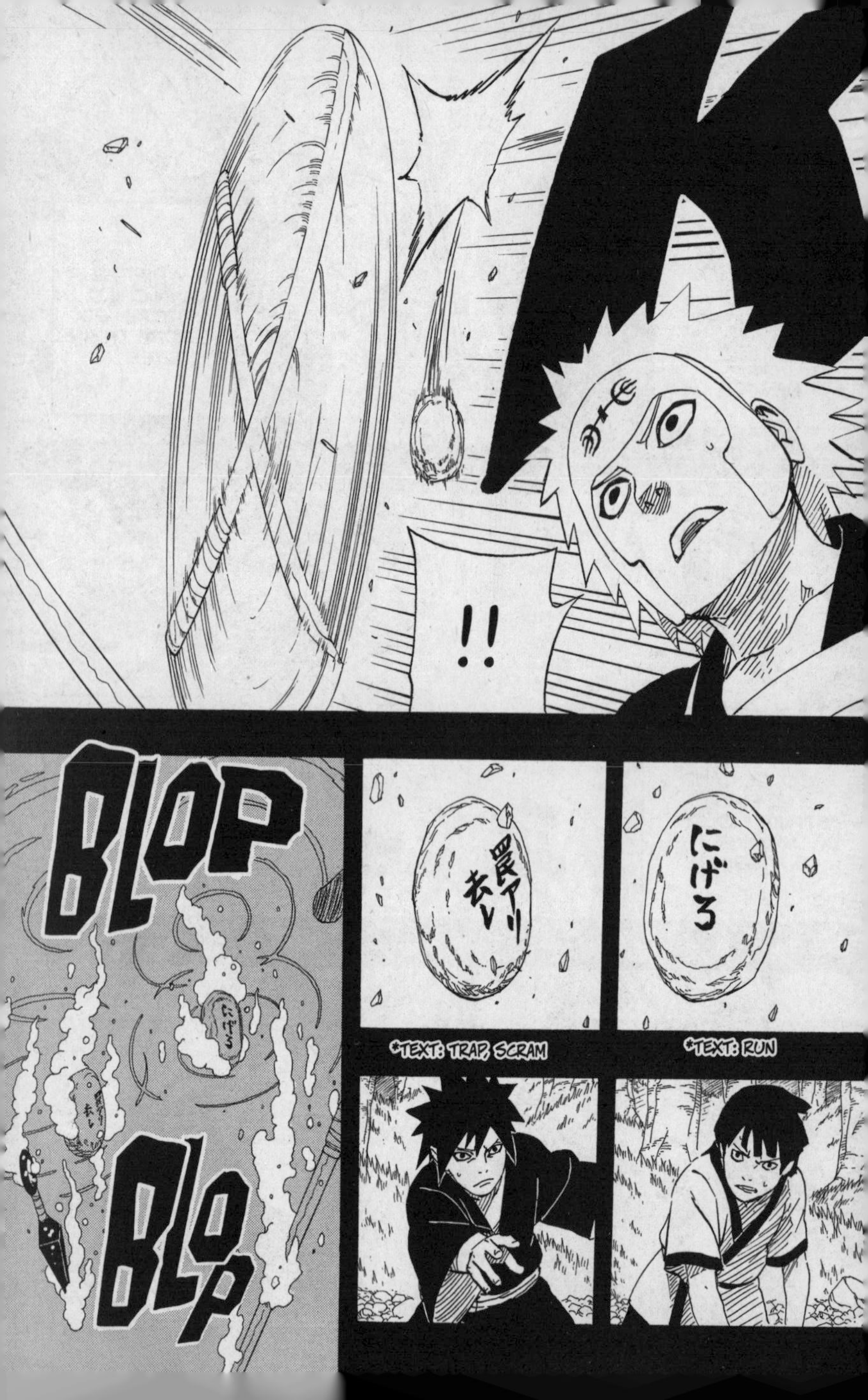
!!
にげろ
*TEXT: RUN
罠アリ去レ
*TEXT: TRAP, SCRAM
BLOP
にげろ
BLOP

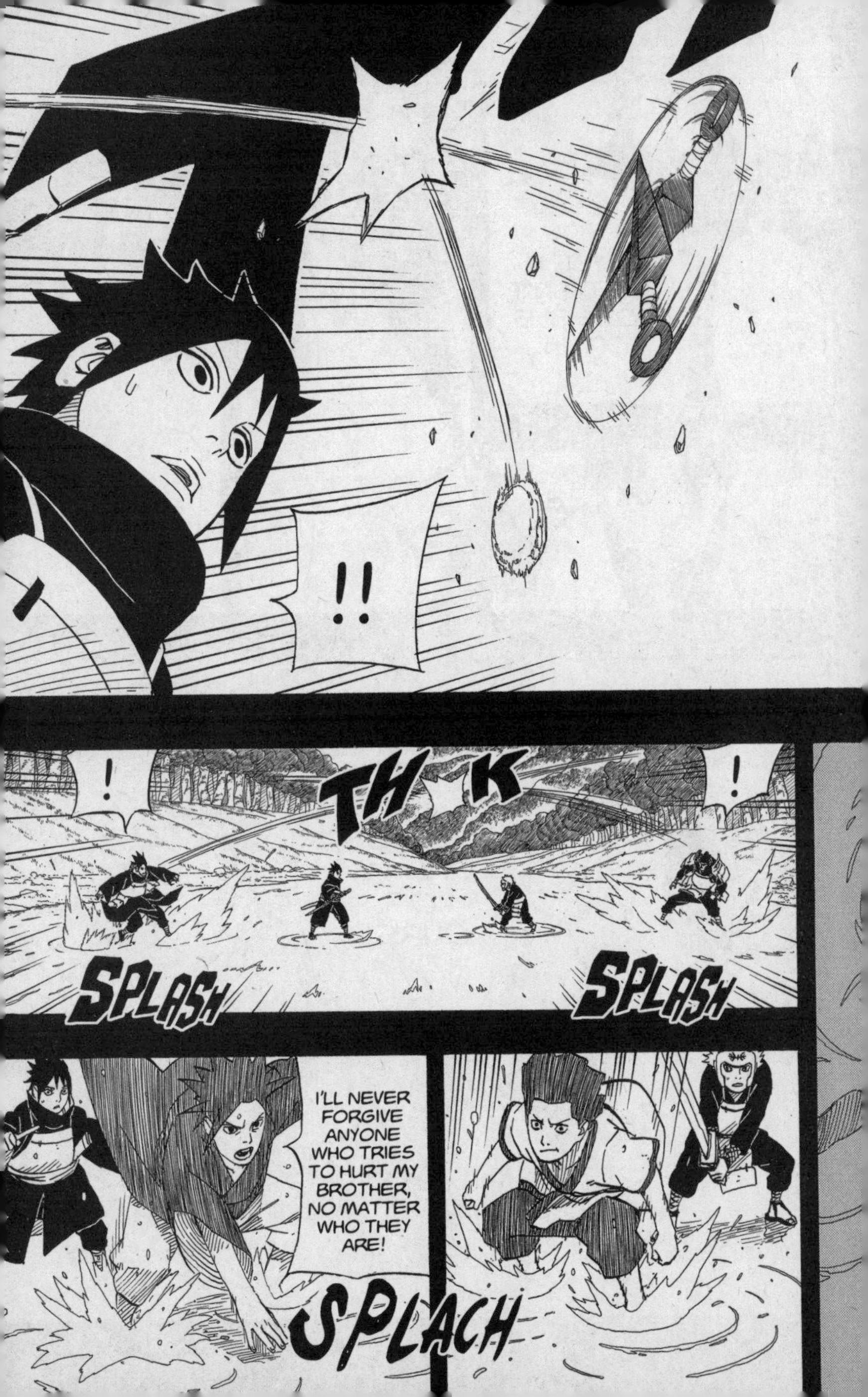
!!
!
TH K
!
SPLASH
SPLASH
I'LL NEVER FORGIVE ANYONE WHO TRIES TO HURT MY BROTHER, NO MATTER WHO THEY ARE!
SPLACH

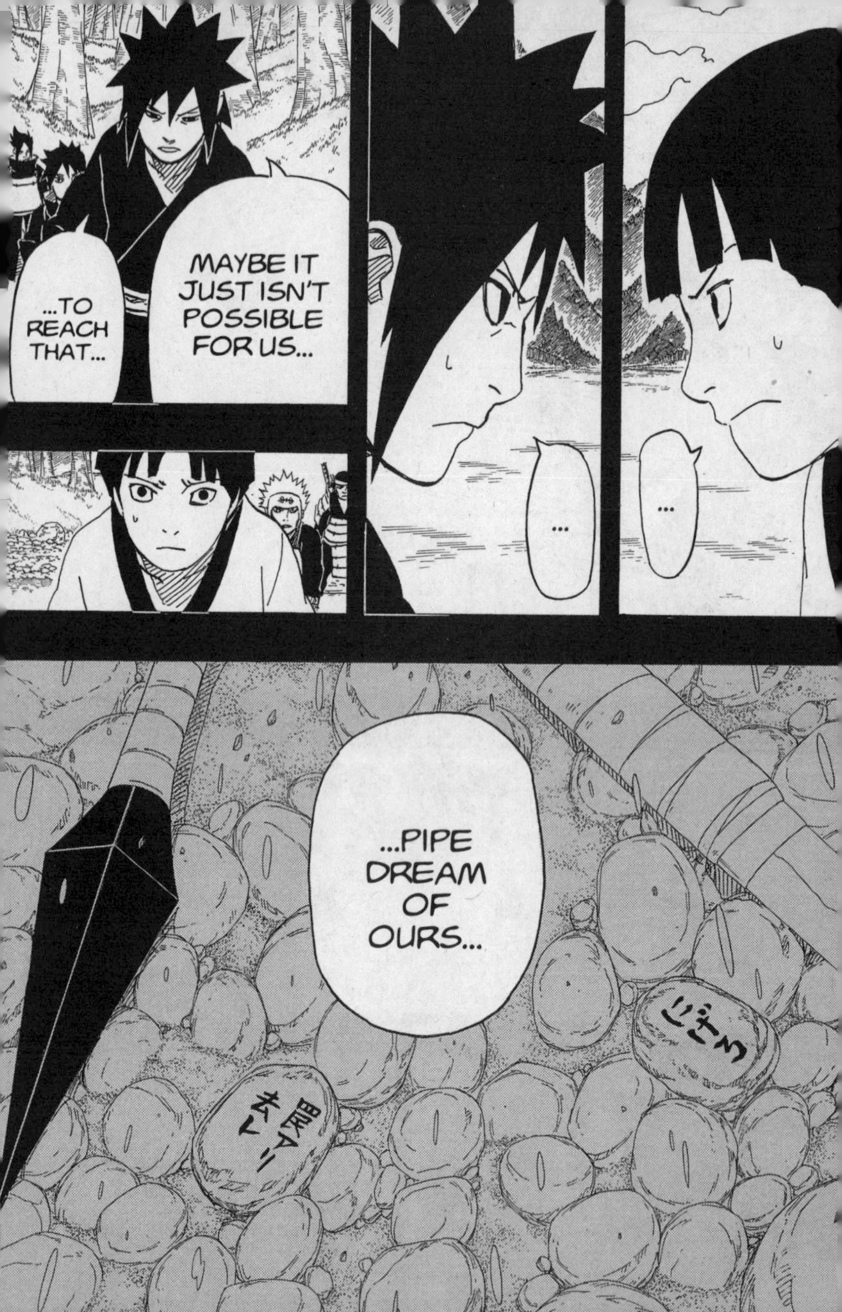
...
...
MAYBE IT JUST ISN'T POSSIBLE FOR US...
...TO REACH THAT...
...PIPE DREAM OF OURS...

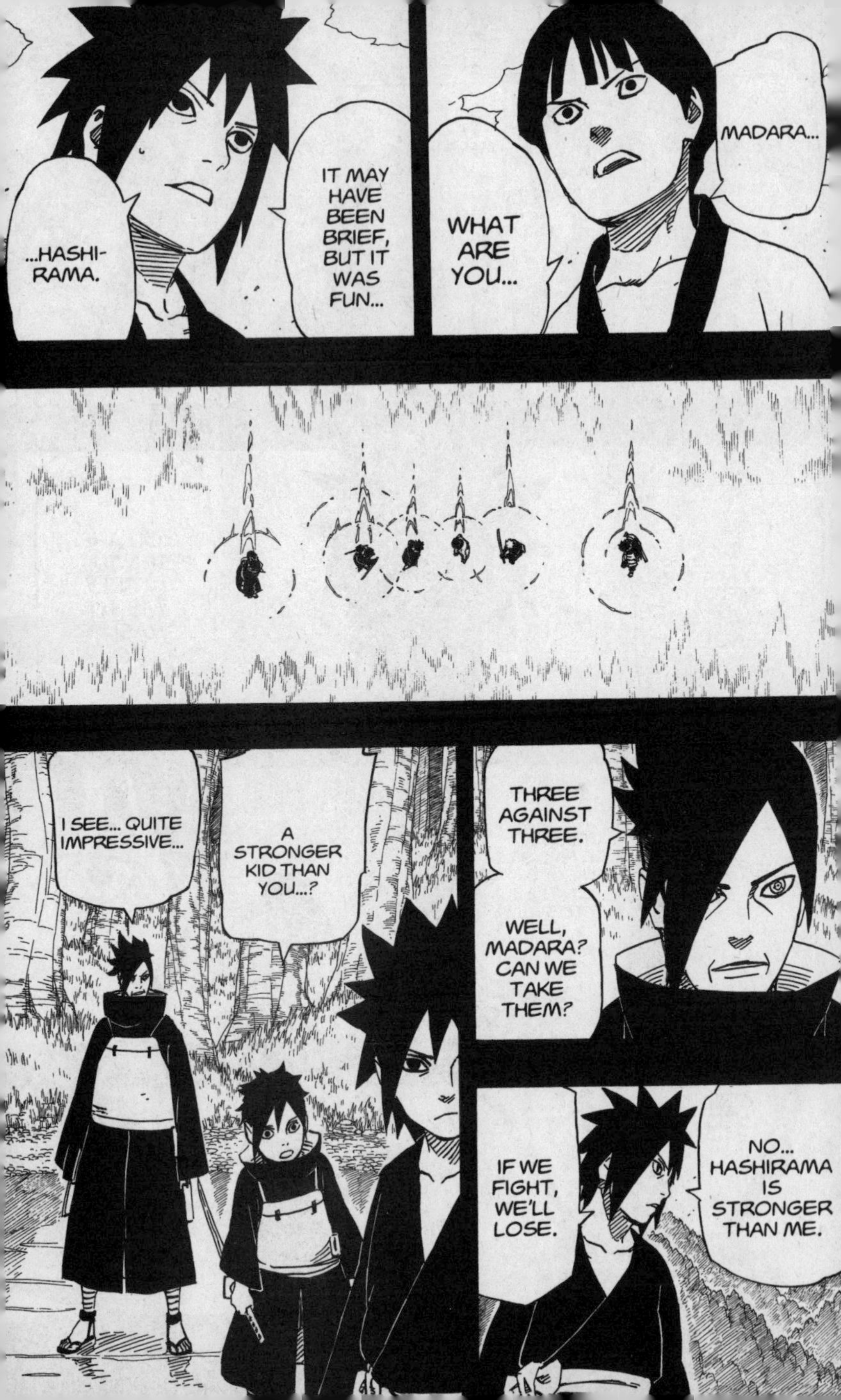
MADARA...
WHAT ARE YOU...
IT MAY HAVE BEEN BRIEF, BUT IT WAS FUN...
...HASHIRAMA.
THREE AGAINST THREE.
WELL, MADARA? CAN WE TAKE THEM?
NO... HASHIRAMA IS STRONGER THAN ME.
IF WE FIGHT, WE'LL LOSE.
A STRONGER KID THAN YOU...?
I SEE... QUITE IMPRESSIVE...

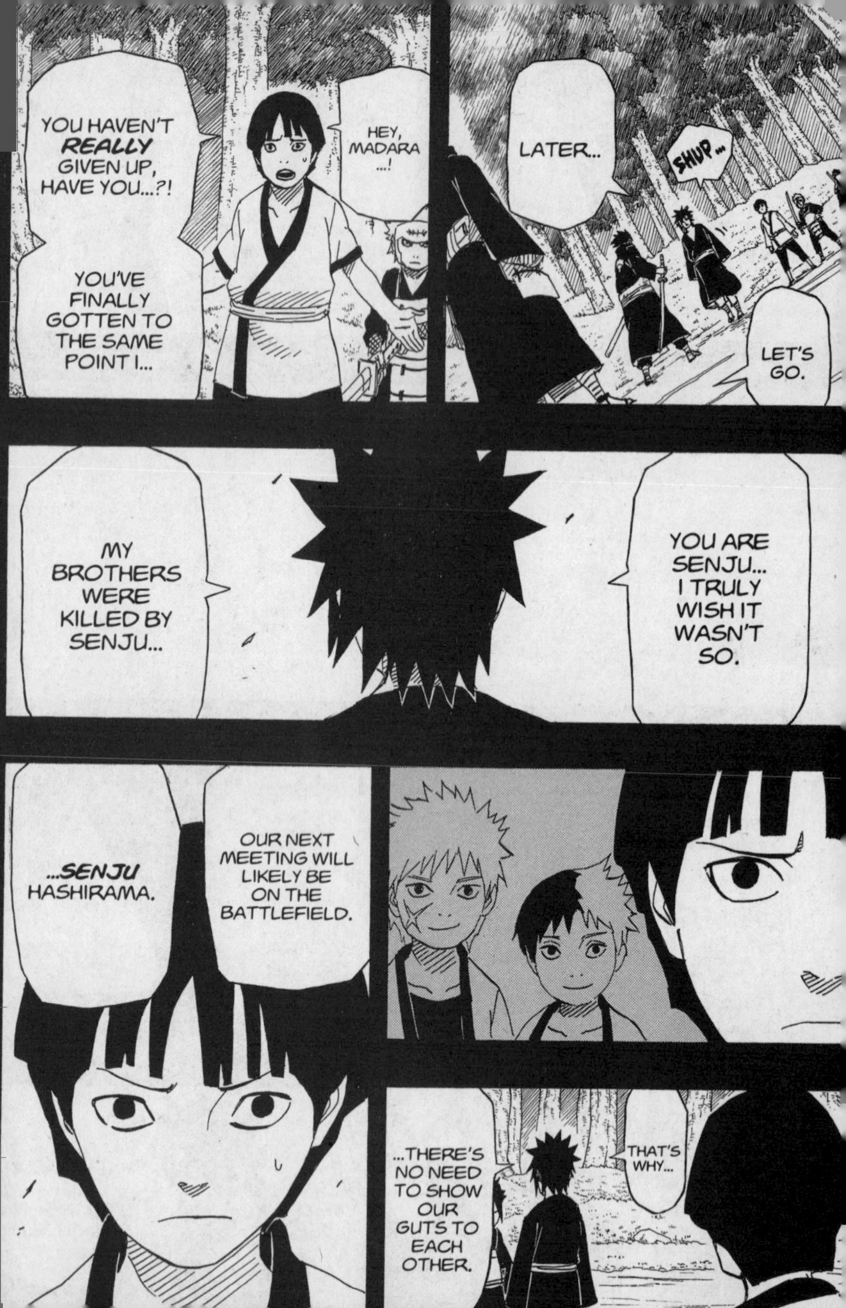
LATER...
SHUP...
LET'S GO.
HEY, MADARA ...!
YOU HAVEN'T *REALLY* GIVEN UP, HAVE YOU...?!
YOU'VE FINALLY GOTTEN TO THE SAME POINT I...
YOU ARE SENJU... I TRULY WISH IT WASN'T SO.
MY BROTHERS WERE KILLED BY SENJU...
THAT'S WHY...
...THERE'S NO NEED TO SHOW OUR GUTS TO EACH OTHER.
OUR NEXT MEETING WILL LIKELY BE ON THE BATTLEFIELD.
...*SENJU* HASHIRAMA.

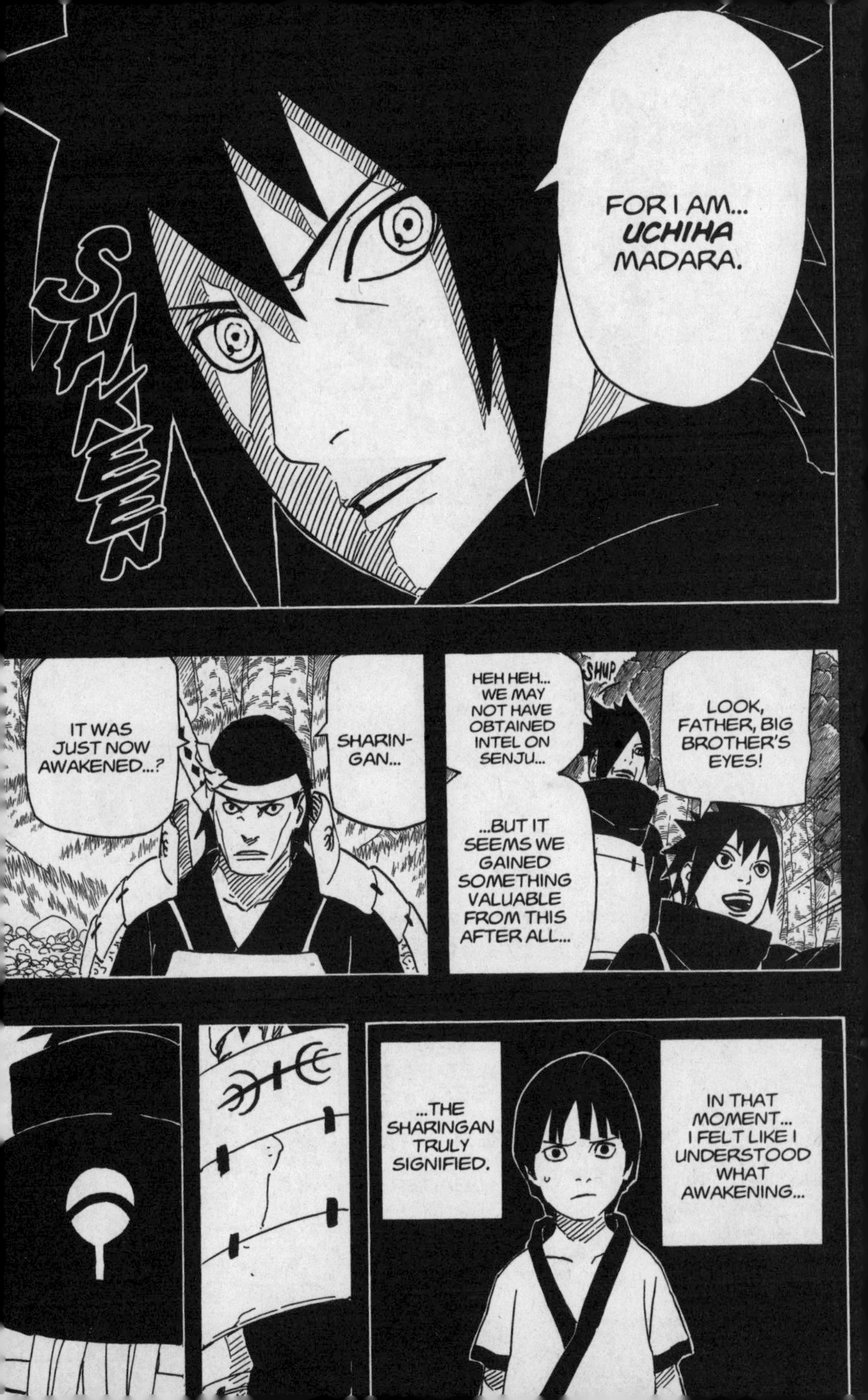
FOR I AM... UCHIHA MADARA.
SHAKEER
LOOK, FATHER, BIG BROTHER'S EYES!
SHUP
HEH HEH... WE MAY NOT HAVE OBTAINED INTEL ON SENJU...
...BUT IT SEEMS WE GAINED SOMETHING VALUABLE FROM THIS AFTER ALL...
SHARIN-GAN...
IT WAS JUST NOW AWAKENED...?
IN THAT MOMENT... I FELT LIKE I UNDERSTOOD WHAT AWAKENING...
...THE SHARINGAN TRULY SIGNIFIED.

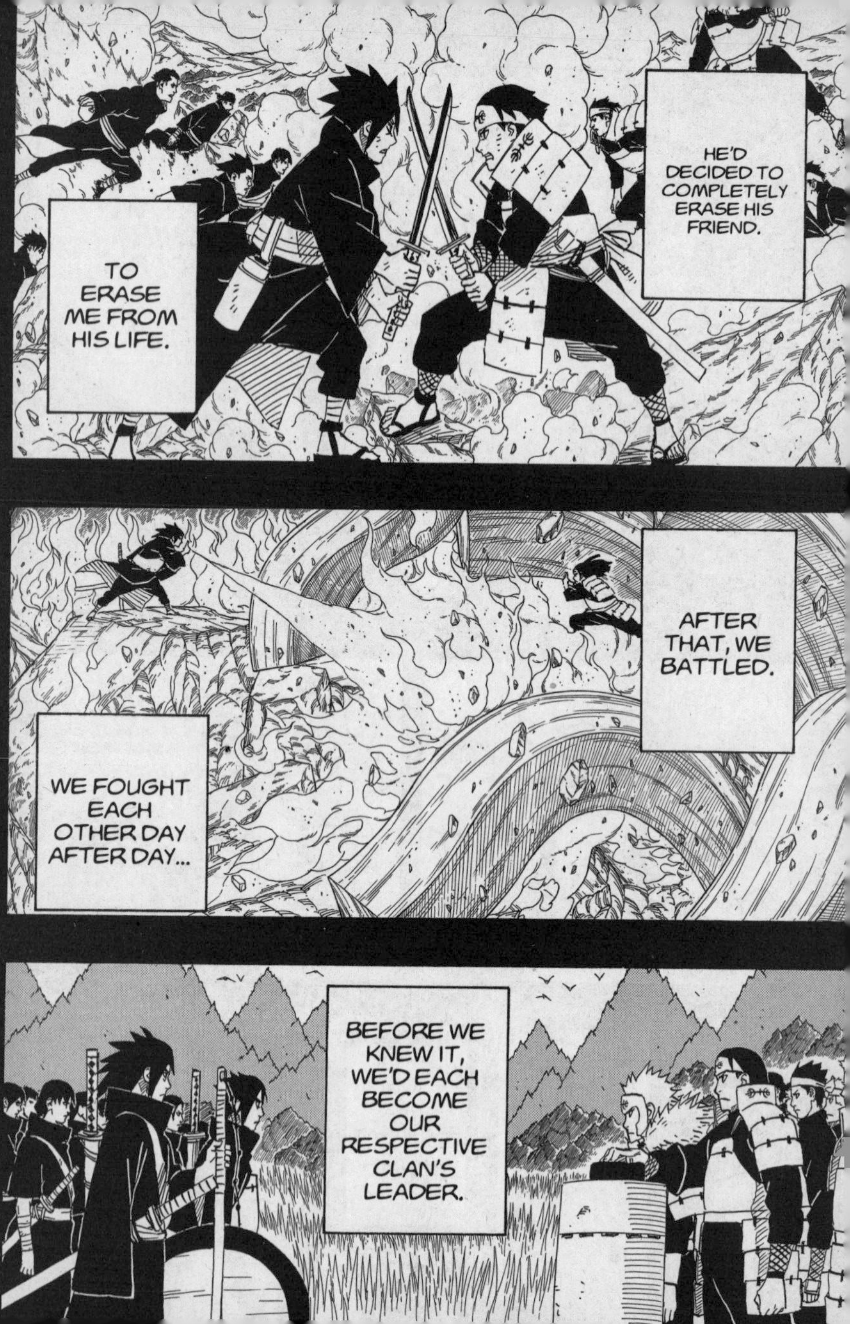
HE'D DECIDED TO COMPLETELY ERASE HIS FRIEND.
TO ERASE ME FROM HIS LIFE.
AFTER THAT, WE BATTLED.
WE FOUGHT EACH OTHER DAY AFTER DAY...
BEFORE WE KNEW IT, WE'D EACH BECOME OUR RESPECTIVE CLAN'S LEADER.

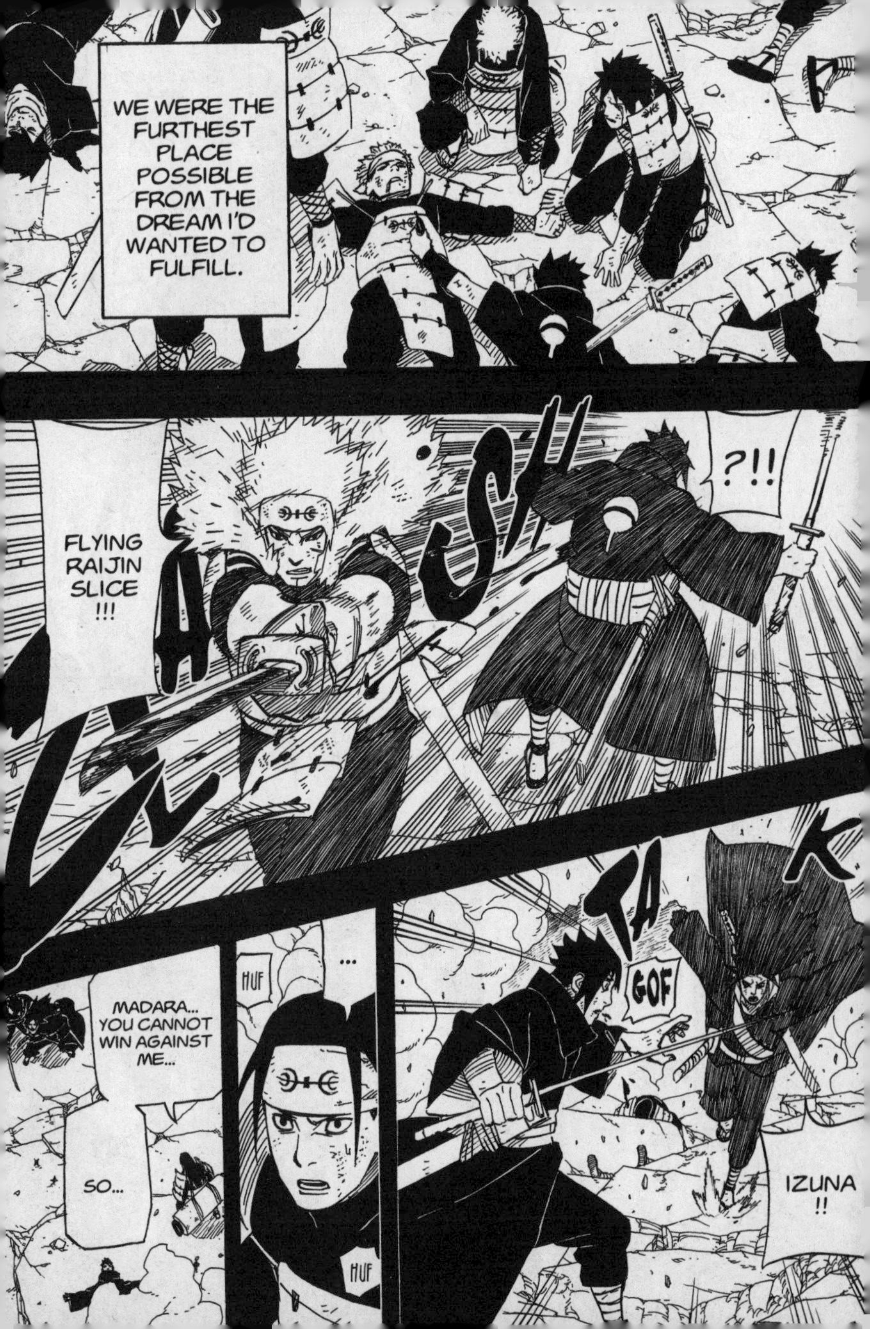
WE WERE THE FURTHEST PLACE POSSIBLE FROM THE DREAM I'D WANTED TO FULFILL.
?!!
FLYING RAIJIN SLICE !!!
TAK
IZUNA !!
GOF
...
HUF
HUF
MADARA... YOU CANNOT WIN AGAINST ME...
SO...

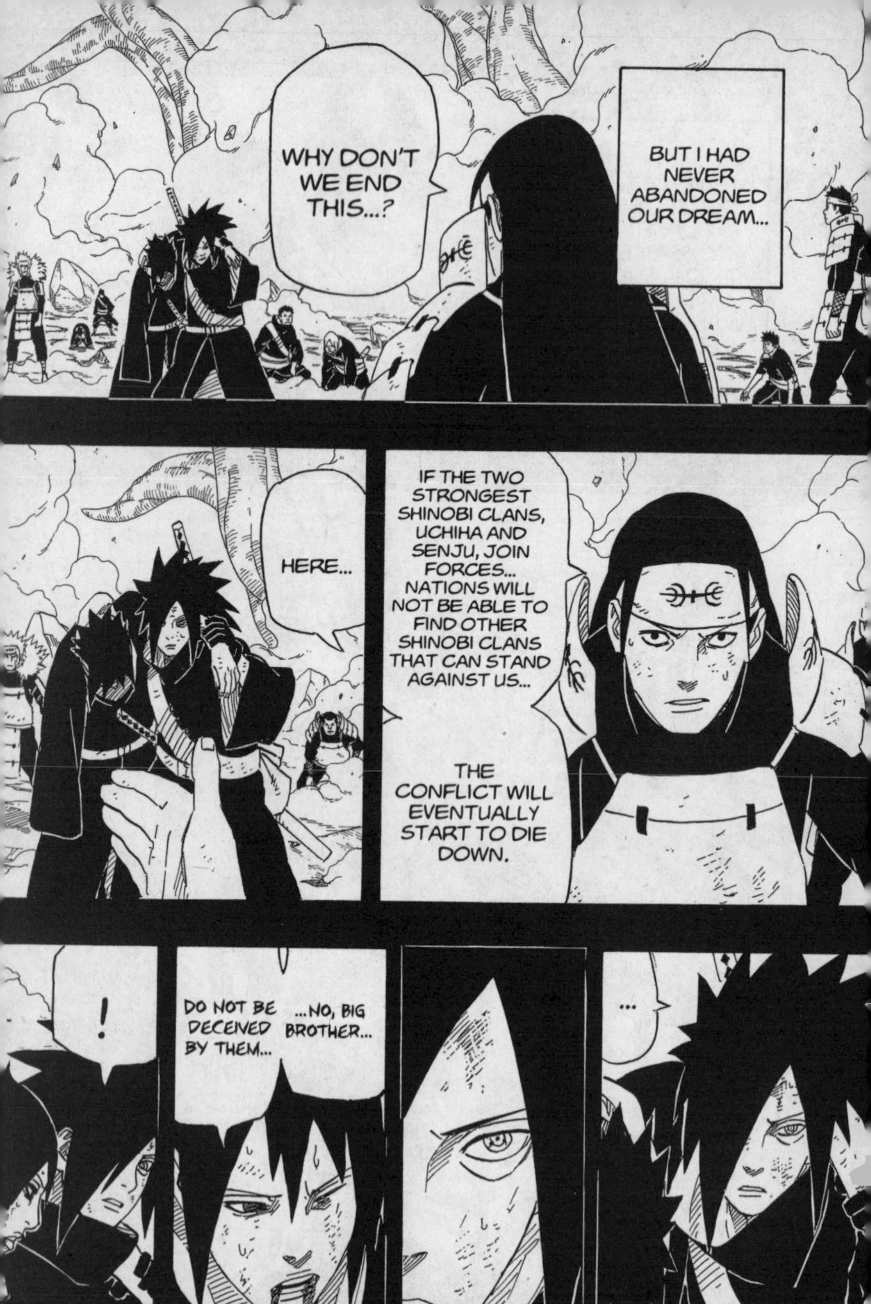
BUT I HAD NEVER ABANDONED OUR DREAM...
WHY DON'T WE END THIS...?
IF THE TWO STRONGEST SHINOBI CLANS, UCHIHA AND SENJU, JOIN FORCES... NATIONS WILL NOT BE ABLE TO FIND OTHER SHINOBI CLANS THAT CAN STAND AGAINST US...
THE CONFLICT WILL EVENTUALLY START TO DIE DOWN.
HERE...
...
...NO, BIG BROTHER...
DO NOT BE DECEIVED BY THEM...
!

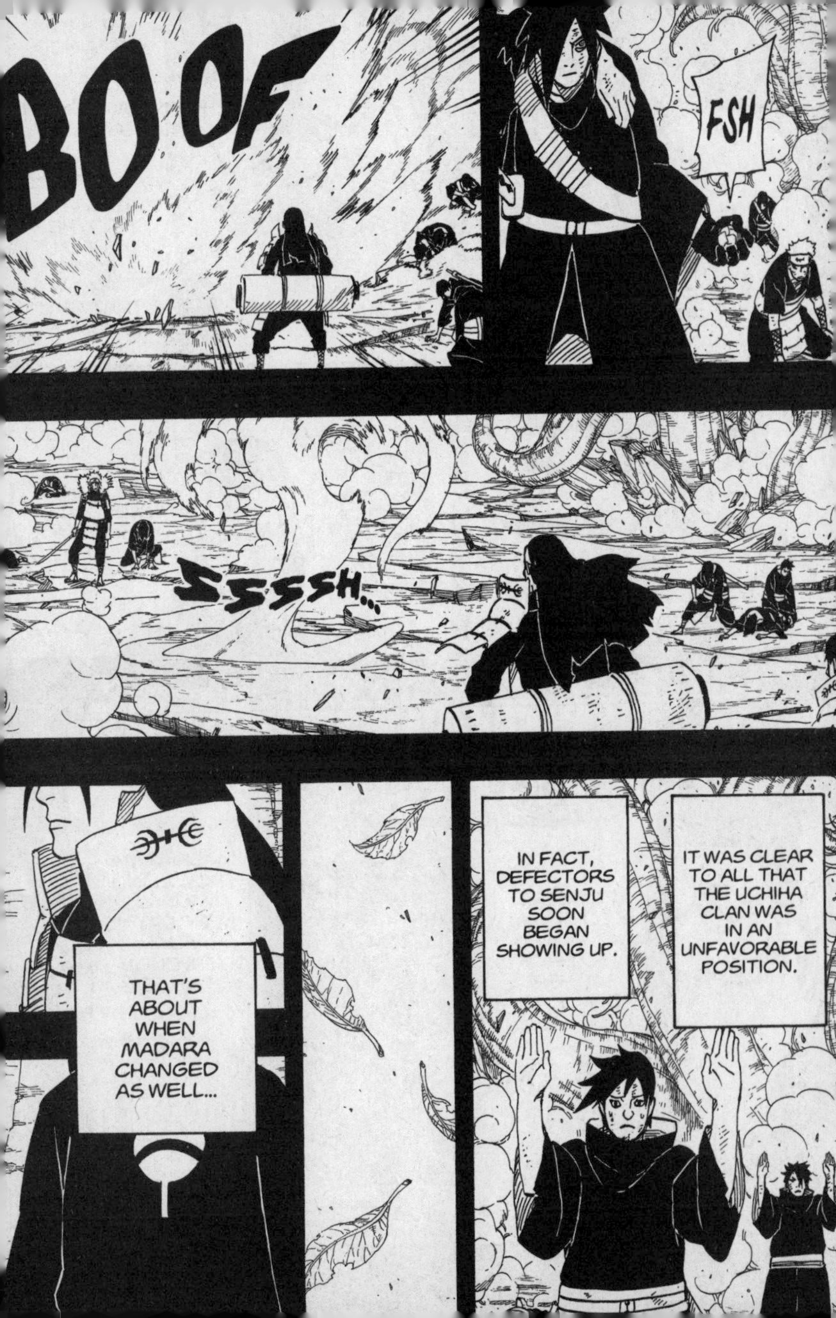
FSH
BOOF
SSSSH...
IT WAS CLEAR TO ALL THAT THE UCHIHA CLAN WAS IN AN UNFAVORABLE POSITION.
IN FACT, DEFECTORS TO SENJU SOON BEGAN SHOWING UP.
THAT'S ABOUT WHEN MADARA CHANGED AS WELL...

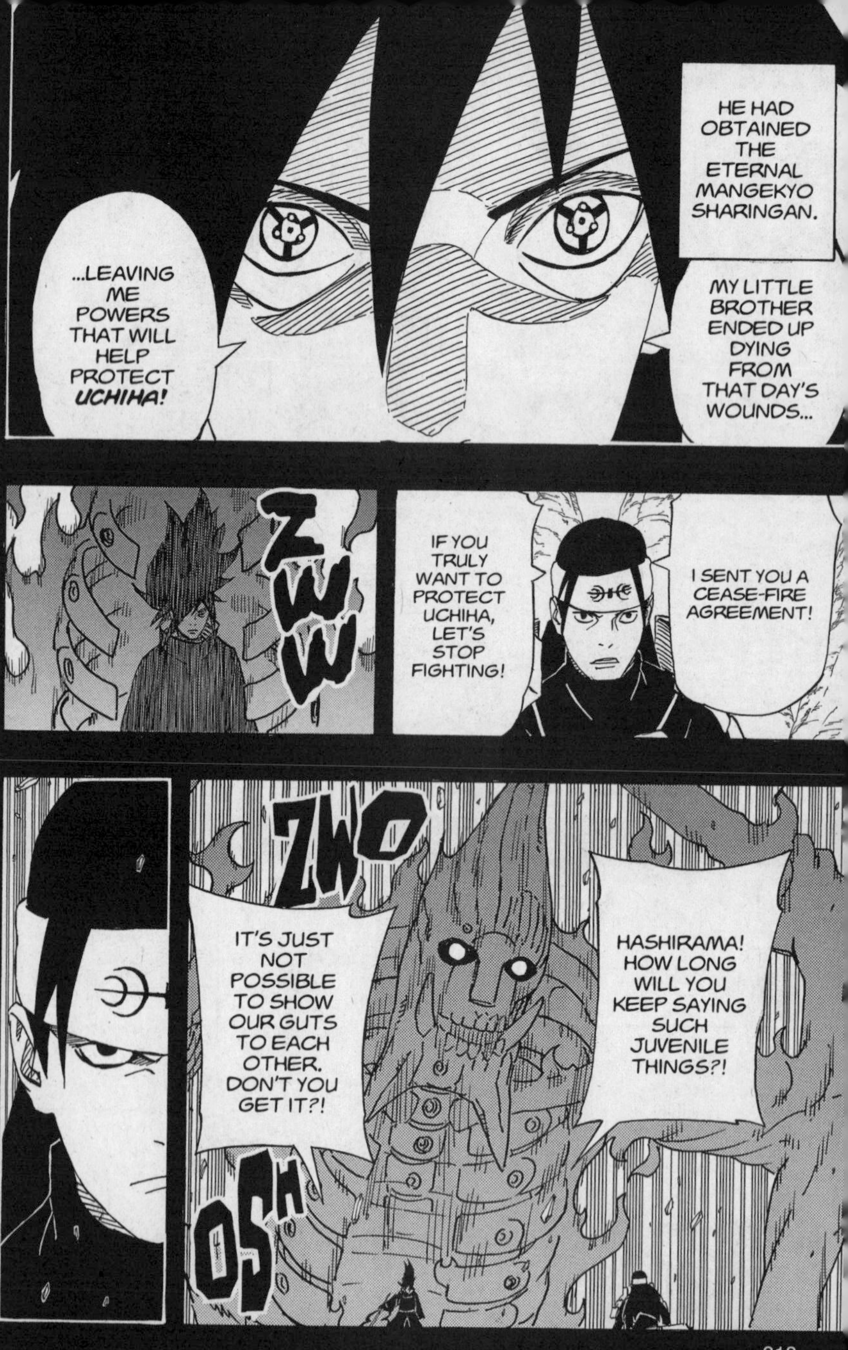
HE HAD OBTAINED THE ETERNAL MANGEKYO SHARINGAN.
MY LITTLE BROTHER ENDED UP DYING FROM THAT DAY'S WOUNDS...
...LEAVING ME POWERS THAT WILL HELP PROTECT *UCHIHA!*
I SENT YOU A CEASE-FIRE AGREEMENT!
IF YOU TRULY WANT TO PROTECT UCHIHA, LET'S STOP FIGHTING!
ZWW
HASHIRAMA! HOW LONG WILL YOU KEEP SAYING SUCH JUVENILE THINGS?!
IT'S JUST NOT POSSIBLE TO SHOW OUR GUTS TO EACH OTHER. DON'T YOU GET IT?!
ZWO
OSH

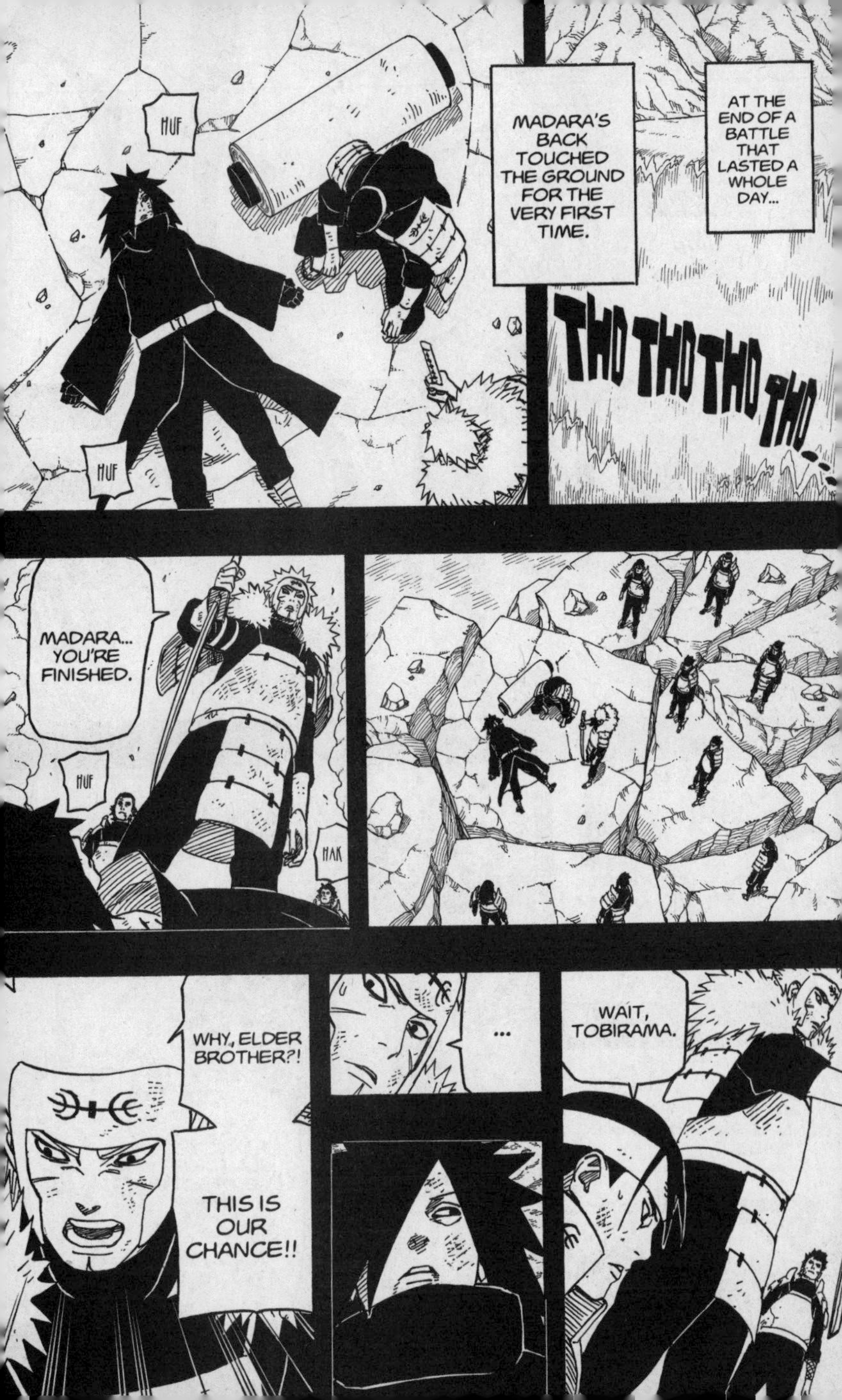
AT THE END OF A BATTLE THAT LASTED A WHOLE DAY...
MADARA'S BACK TOUCHED THE GROUND FOR THE VERY FIRST TIME.
THO THO THO THO THO...
HUF
HUF
MADARA... YOU'RE FINISHED.
HAK
HUF
WAIT, TOBIRAMA.
...
WHY, ELDER BROTHER?!
THIS IS OUR CHANCE!!

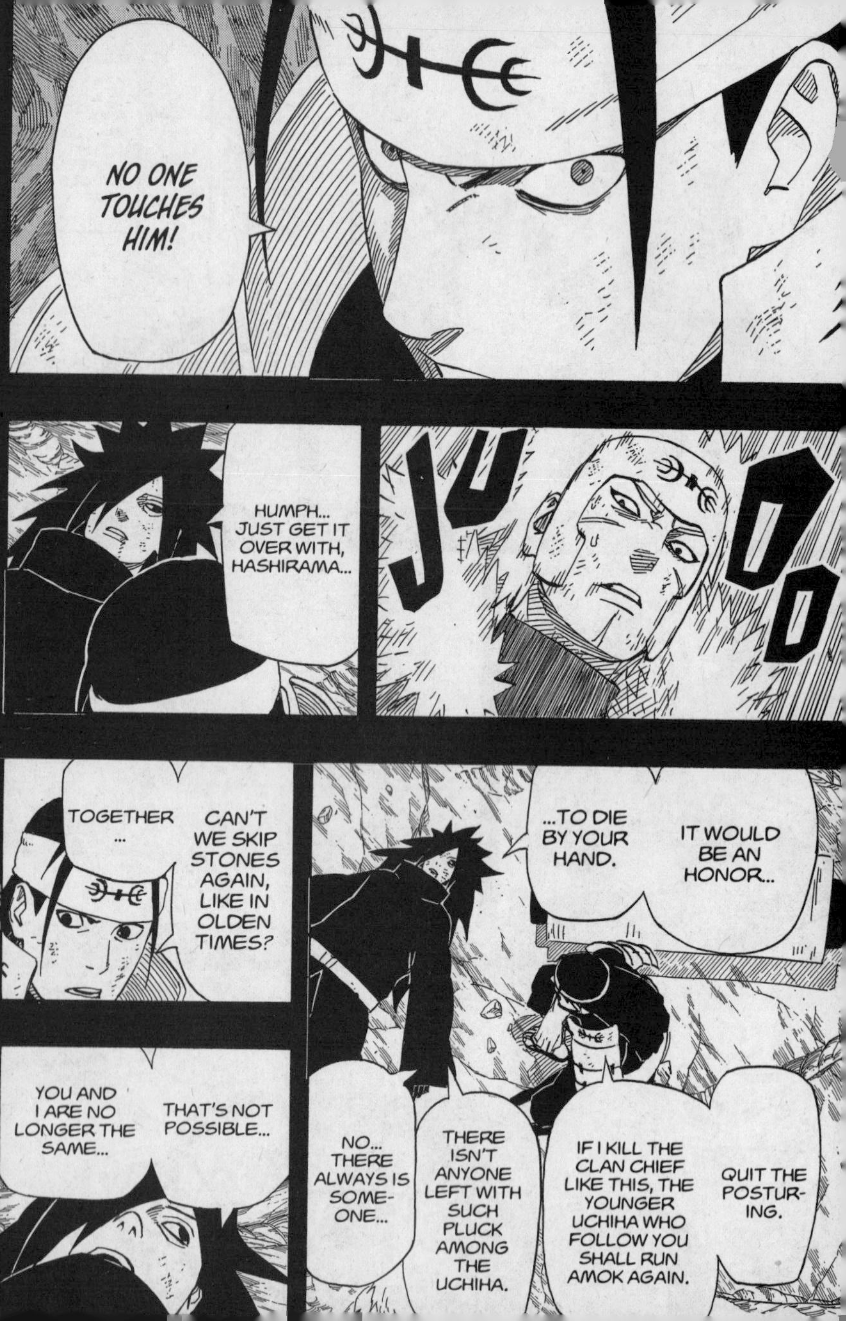
NO ONE TOUCHES HIM!
JUDO
HUMPH... JUST GET IT OVER WITH, HASHIRAMA...
IT WOULD BE AN HONOR...
...TO DIE BY YOUR HAND.
QUIT THE POSTUR-ING.
IF I KILL THE CLAN CHIEF LIKE THIS, THE YOUNGER UCHIHA WHO FOLLOW YOU SHALL RUN AMOK AGAIN.
THERE ISN'T ANYONE LEFT WITH SUCH PLUCK AMONG THE UCHIHA.
NO... THERE ALWAYS IS SOME-ONE...
CAN'T WE SKIP STONES AGAIN, LIKE IN OLDEN TIMES?
TOGETHER ...
THAT'S NOT POSSIBLE...
YOU AND I ARE NO LONGER THE SAME...

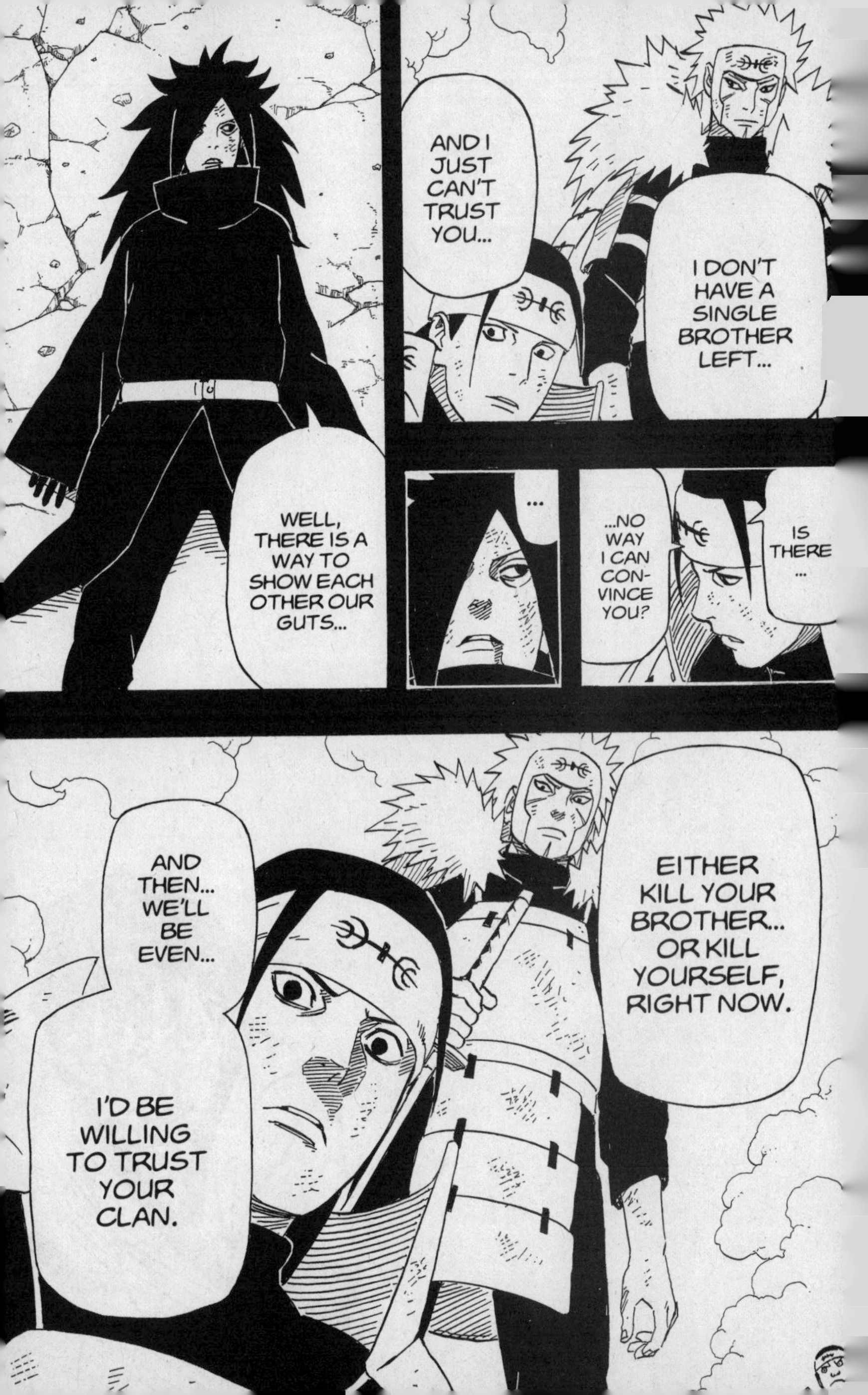
I DON'T HAVE A SINGLE BROTHER LEFT...
AND I JUST CAN'T TRUST YOU...
IS THERE...
...NO WAY I CAN CON-VINCE YOU?
...
WELL, THERE IS A WAY TO SHOW EACH OTHER OUR GUTS...
EITHER KILL YOUR BROTHER... OR KILL YOURSELF, RIGHT NOW.
AND THEN... WE'LL BE EVEN...
I'D BE WILLING TO TRUST YOUR CLAN.

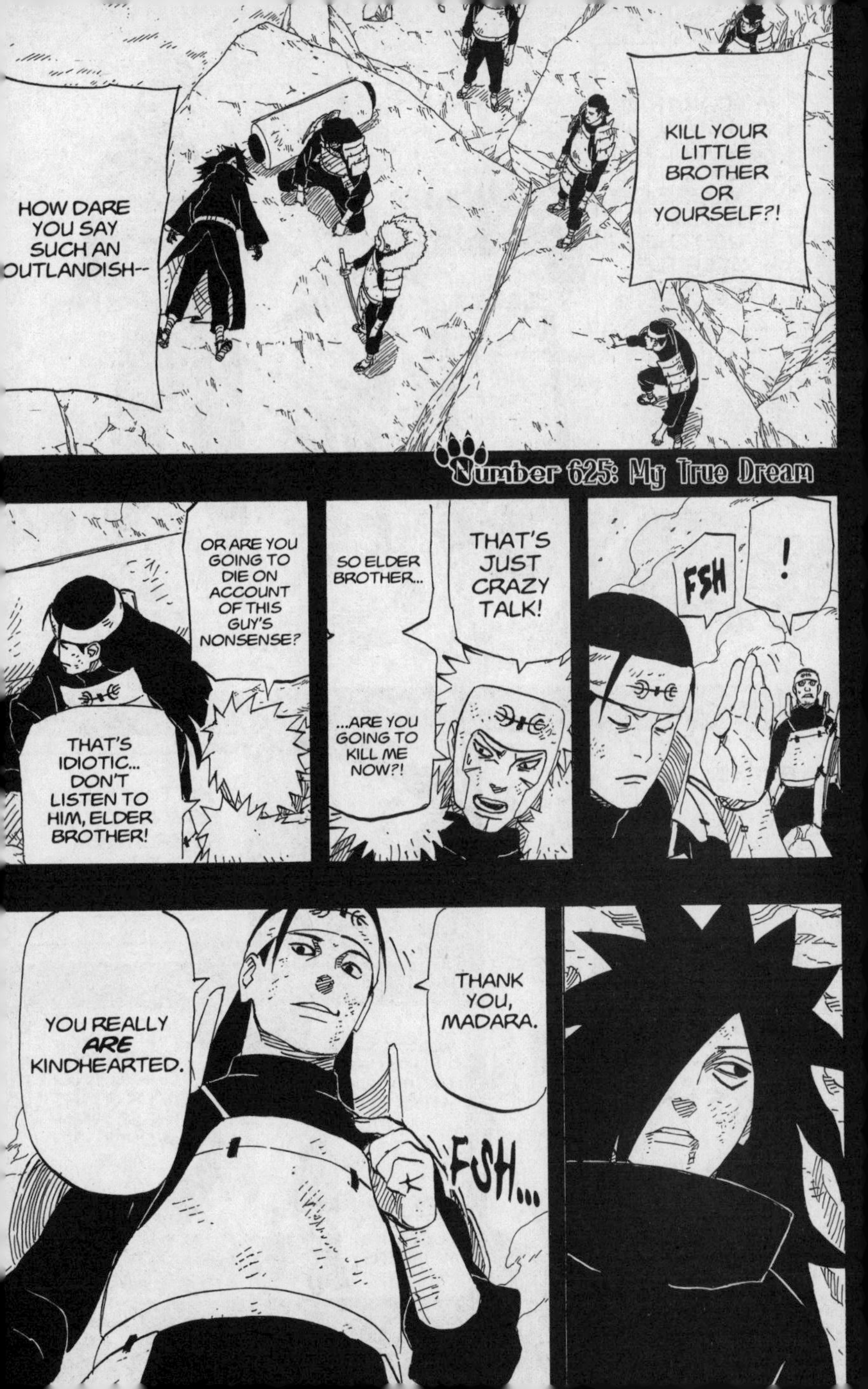

KILL YOUR LITTLE BROTHER OR YOURSELF?!
HOW DARE YOU SAY SUCH AN OUTLANDISH--
Number 625: My True Dream
!
FSH
THAT'S JUST CRAZY TALK!
SO ELDER BROTHER...
...ARE YOU GOING TO KILL ME NOW?!
OR ARE YOU GOING TO DIE ON ACCOUNT OF THIS GUY'S NONSENSE?
THAT'S IDIOTIC... DON'T LISTEN TO HIM, ELDER BROTHER!
FSH...
THANK YOU, MADARA.
YOU REALLY *ARE* KINDHEARTED.

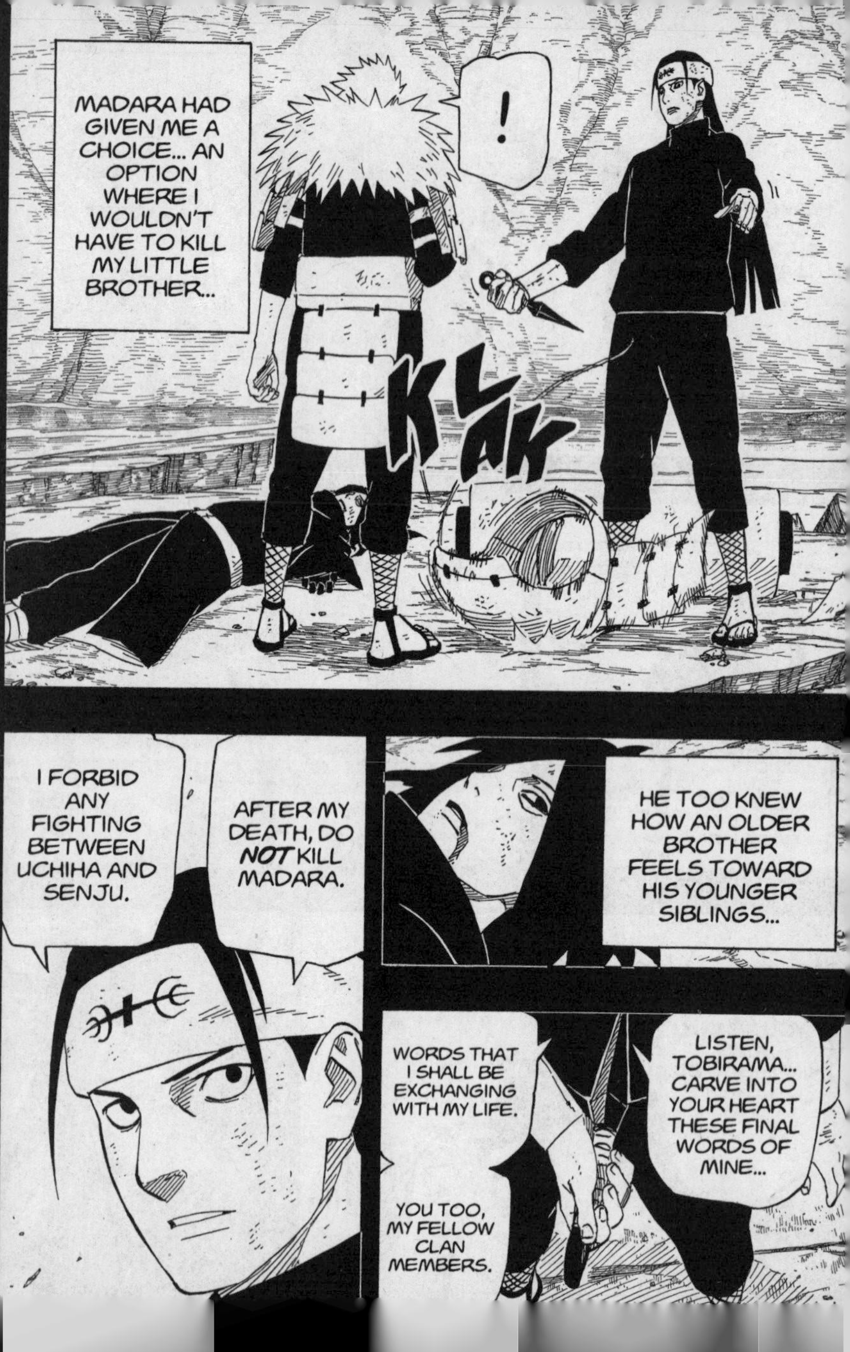
!
MADARA HAD GIVEN ME A CHOICE... AN OPTION WHERE I WOULDN'T HAVE TO KILL MY LITTLE BROTHER...
KLAK
HE TOO KNEW HOW AN OLDER BROTHER FEELS TOWARD HIS YOUNGER SIBLINGS...
LISTEN, TOBIRAMA... CARVE INTO YOUR HEART THESE FINAL WORDS OF MINE...
WORDS THAT I SHALL BE EXCHANGING WITH MY LIFE.
YOU TOO, MY FELLOW CLAN MEMBERS.
AFTER MY DEATH, DO *NOT* KILL MADARA.
I FORBID ANY FIGHTING BETWEEN UCHIHA AND SENJU.

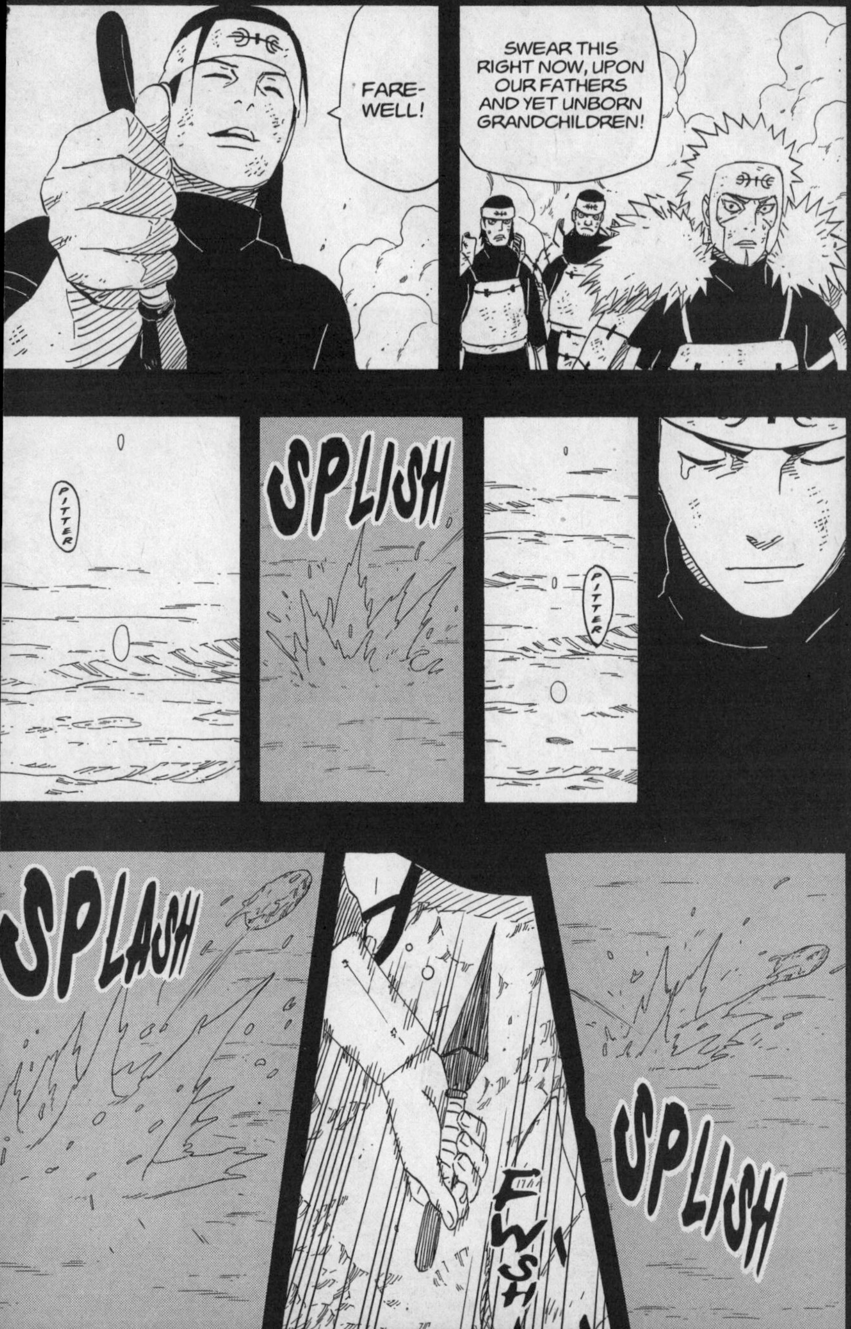
SWEAR THIS RIGHT NOW, UPON OUR FATHERS AND YET UNBORN GRANDCHILDREN!
FARE-WELL!
PITTER
SPLISH
PITTER
SPLISH
FWSH
SPLASH

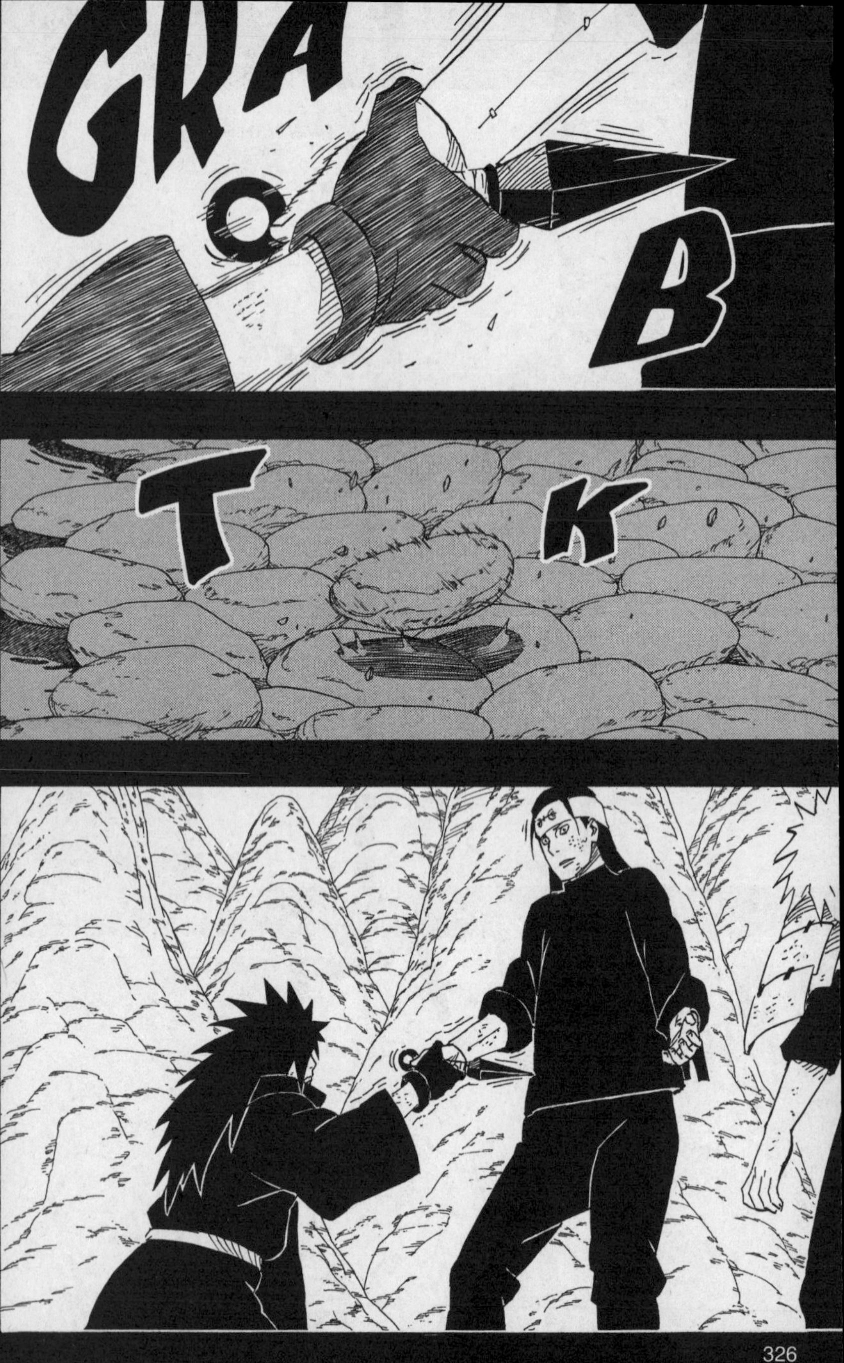
GRAB
TK

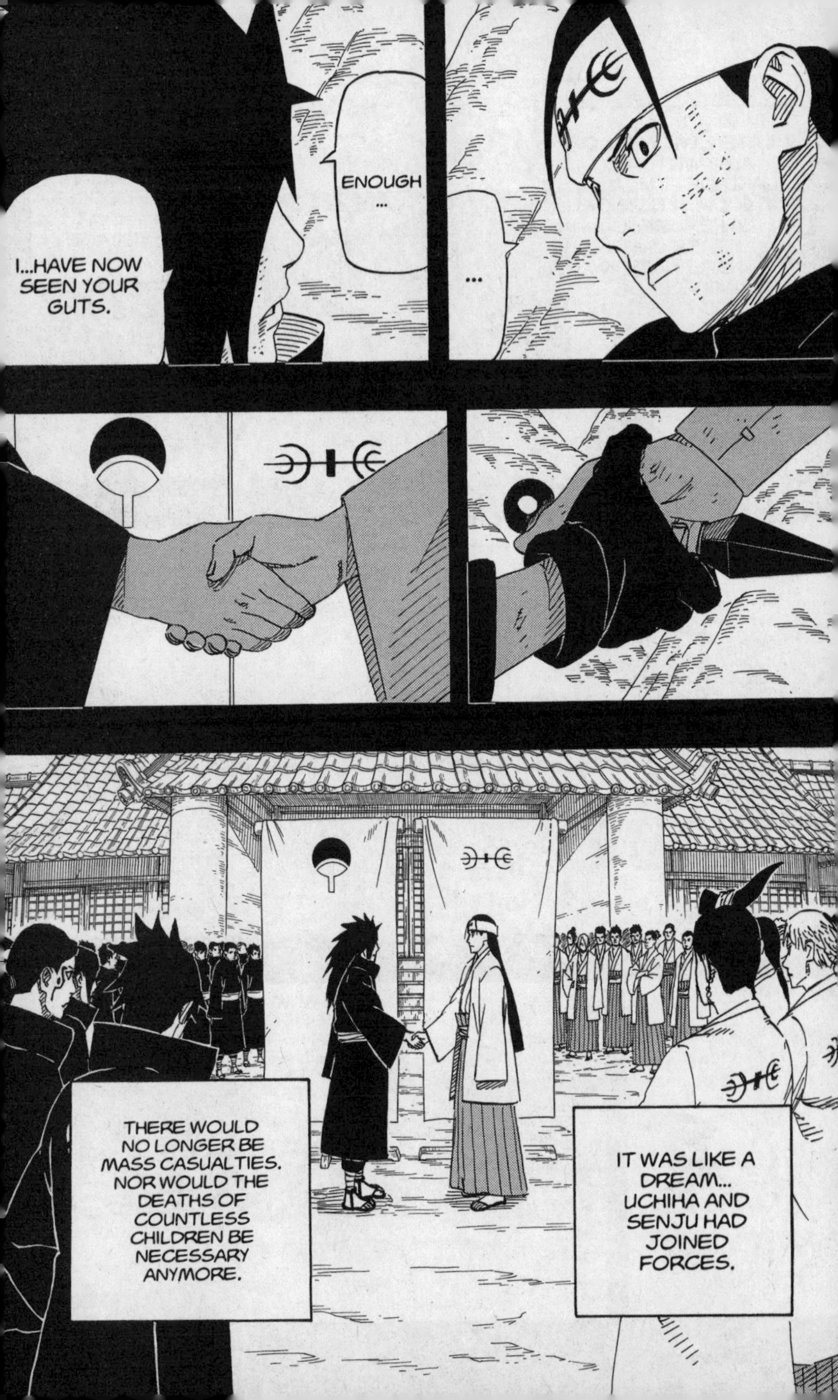
...
ENOUGH ...
I...HAVE NOW SEEN YOUR GUTS.
IT WAS LIKE A DREAM... UCHIHA AND SENJU HAD JOINED FORCES.
THERE WOULD NO LONGER BE MASS CASUALTIES. NOR WOULD THE DEATHS OF COUNTLESS CHILDREN BE NECESSARY ANYMORE.

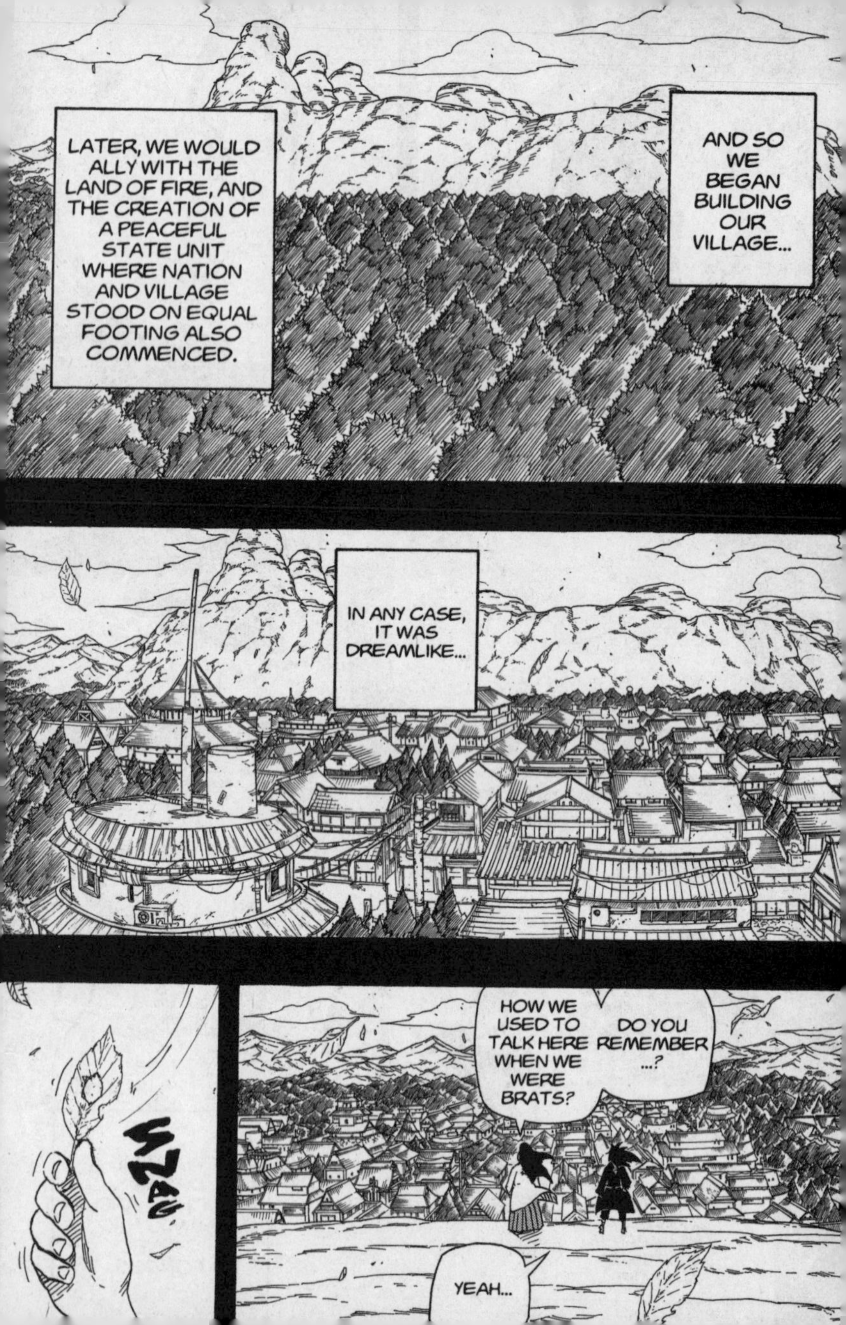
AND SO WE BEGAN BUILDING OUR VILLAGE...
LATER, WE WOULD ALLY WITH THE LAND OF FIRE, AND THE CREATION OF A PEACEFUL STATE UNIT WHERE NATION AND VILLAGE STOOD ON EQUAL FOOTING ALSO COMMENCED.
IN ANY CASE, IT WAS DREAMLIKE...
DO YOU REMEMBER ...?
HOW WE USED TO TALK HERE WHEN WE WERE BRATS?
YEAH...
SNAG

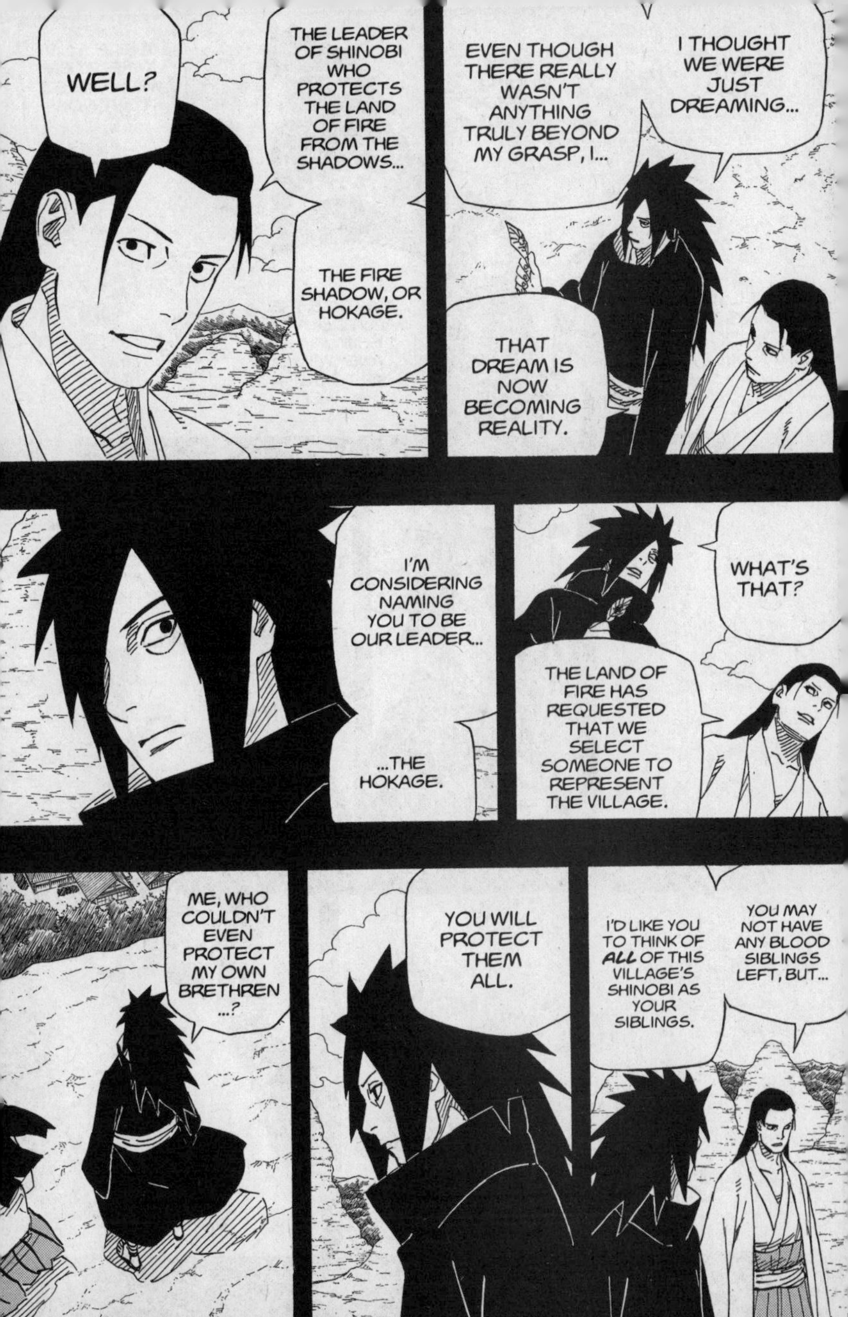
I THOUGHT WE WERE JUST DREAMING...
EVEN THOUGH THERE REALLY WASN'T ANYTHING TRULY BEYOND MY GRASP, I...
THAT DREAM IS NOW BECOMING REALITY.
THE LEADER OF SHINOBI WHO PROTECTS THE LAND OF FIRE FROM THE SHADOWS...
WELL?
THE FIRE SHADOW, OR HOKAGE.
WHAT'S THAT?
THE LAND OF FIRE HAS REQUESTED THAT WE SELECT SOMEONE TO REPRESENT THE VILLAGE.
I'M CONSIDERING NAMING YOU TO BE OUR LEADER...
...THE HOKAGE.
YOU MAY NOT HAVE ANY BLOOD SIBLINGS LEFT, BUT...
I'D LIKE YOU TO THINK OF ***ALL*** OF THIS VILLAGE'S SHINOBI AS YOUR SIBLINGS.
YOU WILL PROTECT THEM ALL.
ME, WHO COULDN'T EVEN PROTECT MY OWN BRETHREN...?

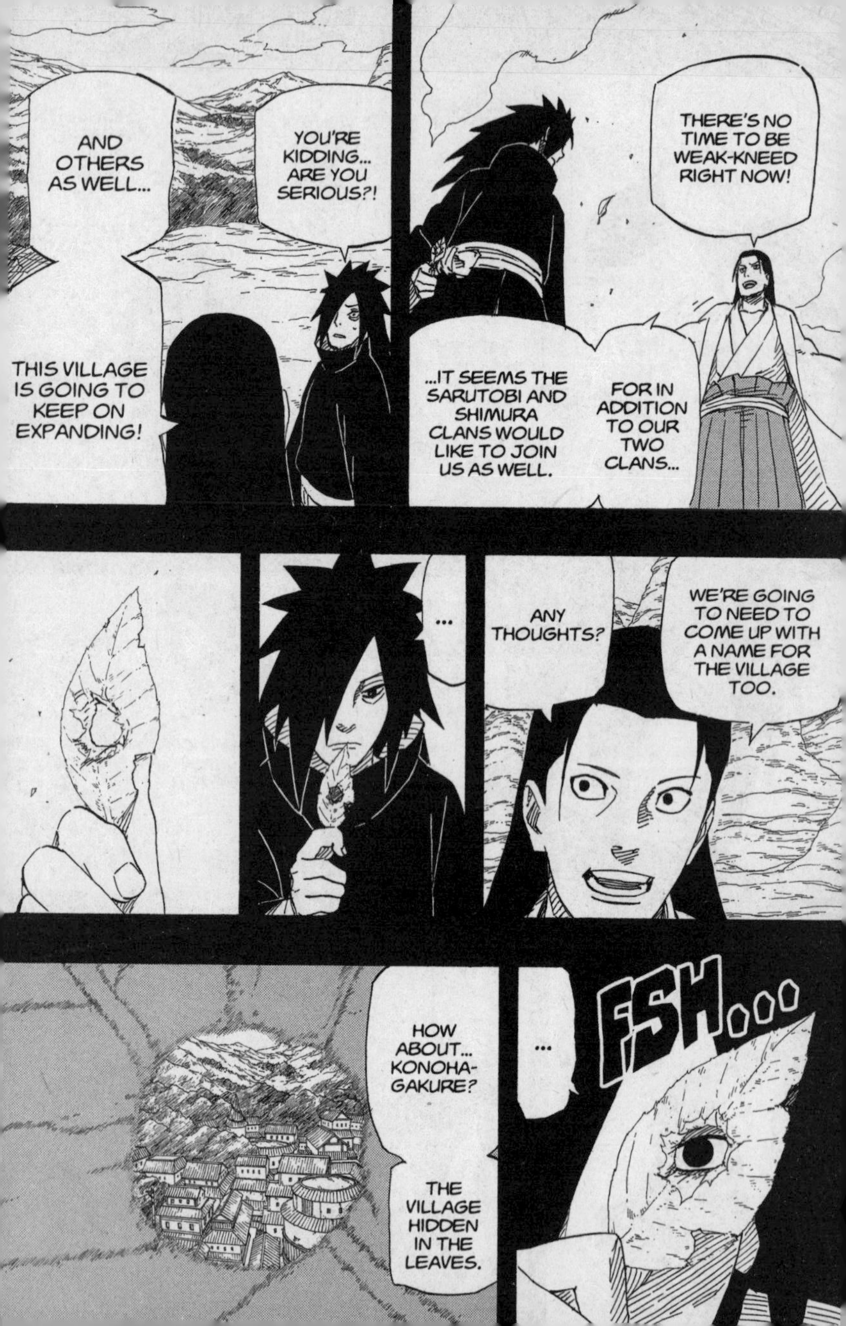
THERE'S NO TIME TO BE WEAK-KNEED RIGHT NOW!
FOR IN ADDITION TO OUR TWO CLANS...
...IT SEEMS THE SARUTOBI AND SHIMURA CLANS WOULD LIKE TO JOIN US AS WELL.
YOU'RE KIDDING... ARE YOU SERIOUS?!
AND OTHERS AS WELL...
THIS VILLAGE IS GOING TO KEEP ON EXPANDING!
WE'RE GOING TO NEED TO COME UP WITH A NAME FOR THE VILLAGE TOO.
ANY THOUGHTS?
...
FSH...
...
HOW ABOUT... KONOHA-GAKURE?
THE VILLAGE HIDDEN IN THE LEAVES.

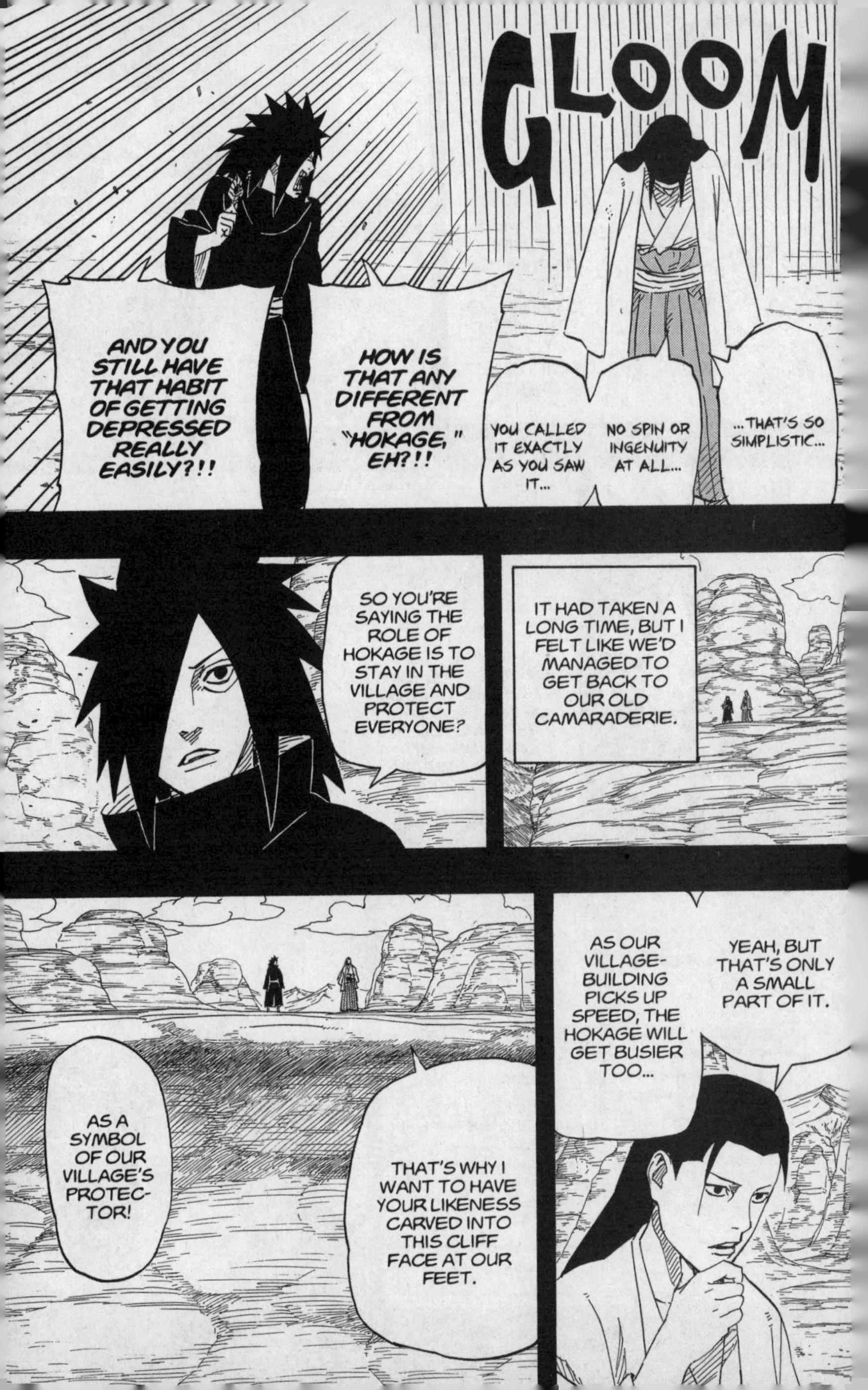
GLOOM
...THAT'S SO SIMPLISTIC...
NO SPIN OR INGENUITY AT ALL...
YOU CALLED IT EXACTLY AS YOU SAW IT...
HOW IS THAT ANY DIFFERENT FROM "HOKAGE," EH?!!
AND YOU STILL HAVE THAT HABIT OF GETTING DEPRESSED REALLY EASILY?!!
IT HAD TAKEN A LONG TIME, BUT I FELT LIKE WE'D MANAGED TO GET BACK TO OUR OLD CAMARADERIE.
SO YOU'RE SAYING THE ROLE OF HOKAGE IS TO STAY IN THE VILLAGE AND PROTECT EVERYONE?
YEAH, BUT THAT'S ONLY A SMALL PART OF IT.
AS OUR VILLAGE-BUILDING PICKS UP SPEED, THE HOKAGE WILL GET BUSIER TOO...
THAT'S WHY I WANT TO HAVE YOUR LIKENESS CARVED INTO THIS CLIFF FACE AT OUR FEET.
AS A SYMBOL OF OUR VILLAGE'S PROTECTOR!

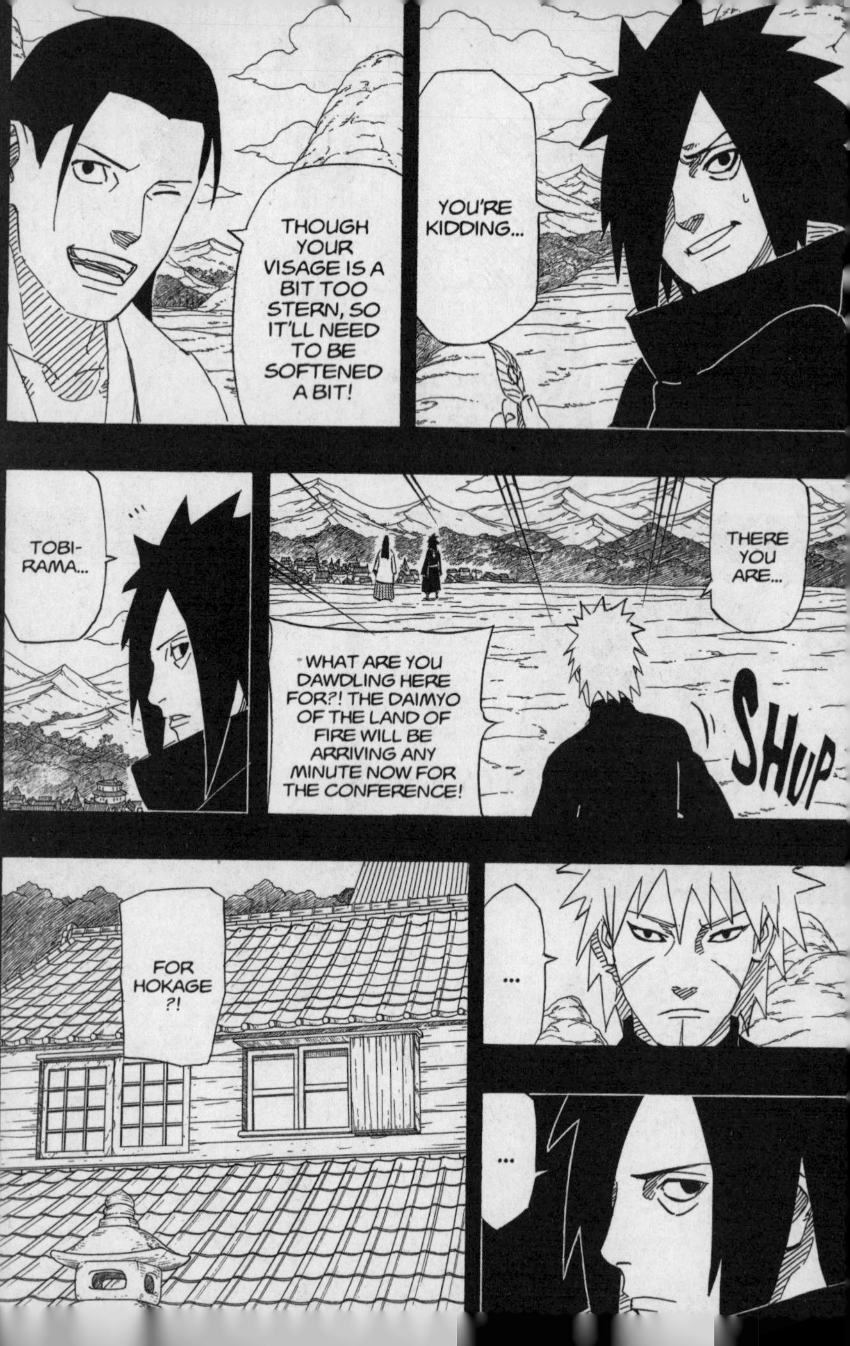
YOU'RE KIDDING...
THOUGH YOUR VISAGE IS A BIT TOO STERN, SO IT'LL NEED TO BE SOFTENED A BIT!
THERE YOU ARE...
SHUP
WHAT ARE YOU DAWDLING HERE FOR?! THE DAIMYO OF THE LAND OF FIRE WILL BE ARRIVING ANY MINUTE NOW FOR THE CONFERENCE!
TOBI-RAMA...
...
...
FOR HOKAGE ?!

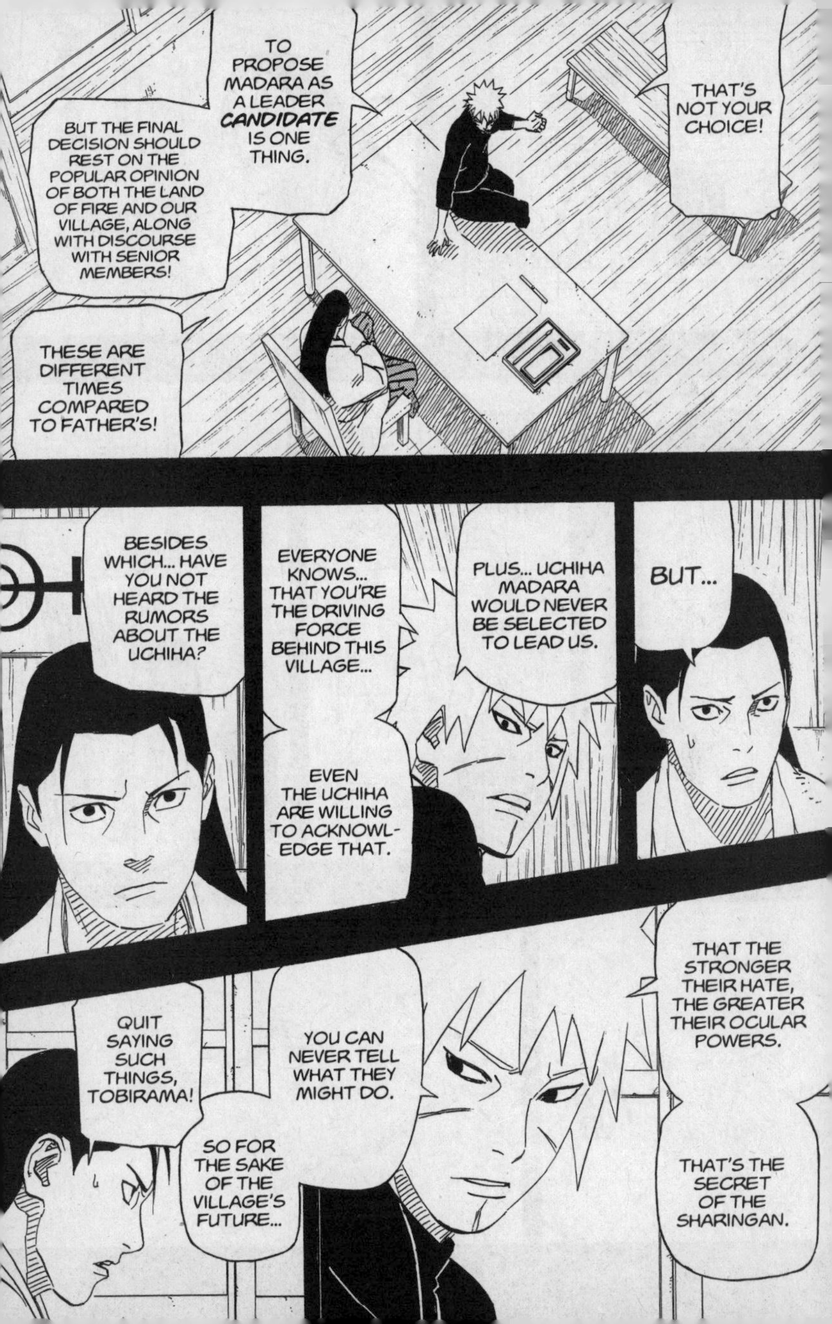
THAT'S NOT YOUR CHOICE!
TO PROPOSE MADARA AS A LEADER **CANDIDATE** IS ONE THING.
BUT THE FINAL DECISION SHOULD REST ON THE POPULAR OPINION OF BOTH THE LAND OF FIRE AND OUR VILLAGE, ALONG WITH DISCOURSE WITH SENIOR MEMBERS!
THESE ARE DIFFERENT TIMES COMPARED TO FATHER'S!
BUT...
PLUS... UCHIHA MADARA WOULD NEVER BE SELECTED TO LEAD US.
EVERYONE KNOWS... THAT YOU'RE THE DRIVING FORCE BEHIND THIS VILLAGE...
EVEN THE UCHIHA ARE WILLING TO ACKNOWL-EDGE THAT.
BESIDES WHICH... HAVE YOU NOT HEARD THE RUMORS ABOUT THE UCHIHA?
THAT THE STRONGER THEIR HATE, THE GREATER THEIR OCULAR POWERS.
THAT'S THE SECRET OF THE SHARINGAN.
YOU CAN NEVER TELL WHAT THEY MIGHT DO.
SO FOR THE SAKE OF THE VILLAGE'S FUTURE...
QUIT SAYING SUCH THINGS, TOBIRAMA!

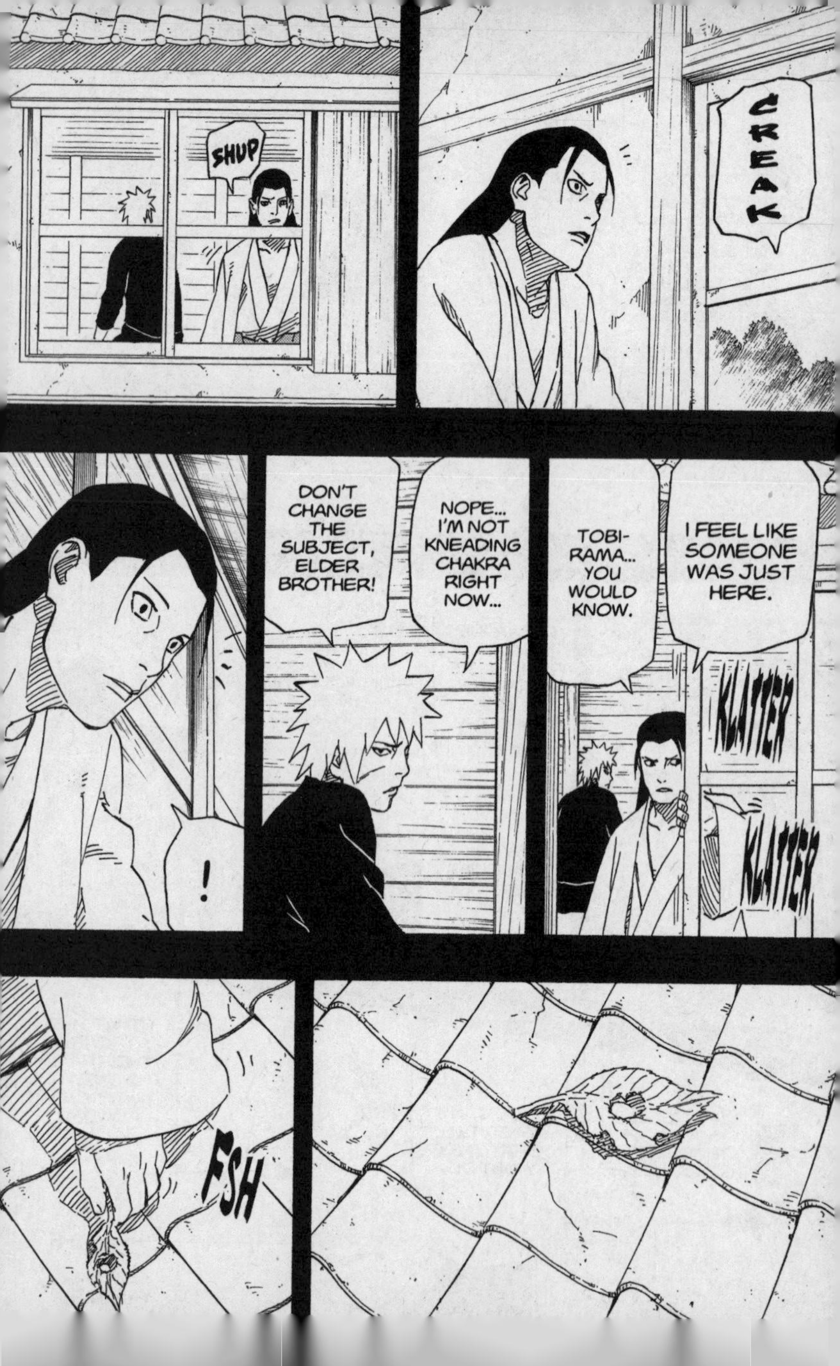
CREAK
SHUP
I FEEL LIKE SOMEONE WAS JUST HERE.
TOBI-RAMA... YOU WOULD KNOW.
KLATTER
KLATTER
NOPE... I'M NOT KNEADING CHAKRA RIGHT NOW...
DON'T CHANGE THE SUBJECT, ELDER BROTHER!
!
FSH

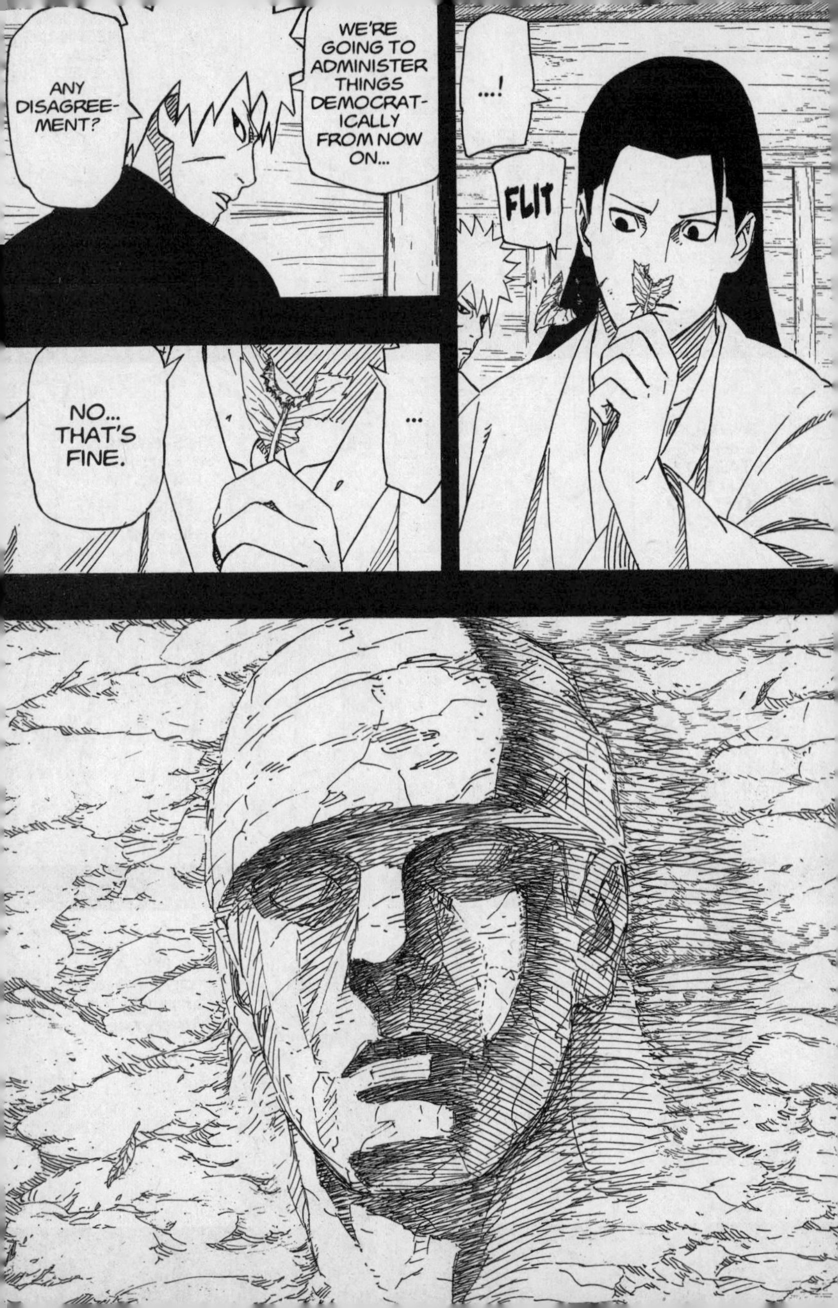
...!
FLIT
WE'RE GOING TO ADMINISTER THINGS DEMOCRATICALLY FROM NOW ON...
ANY DISAGREEMENT?
...
NO... THAT'S FINE.

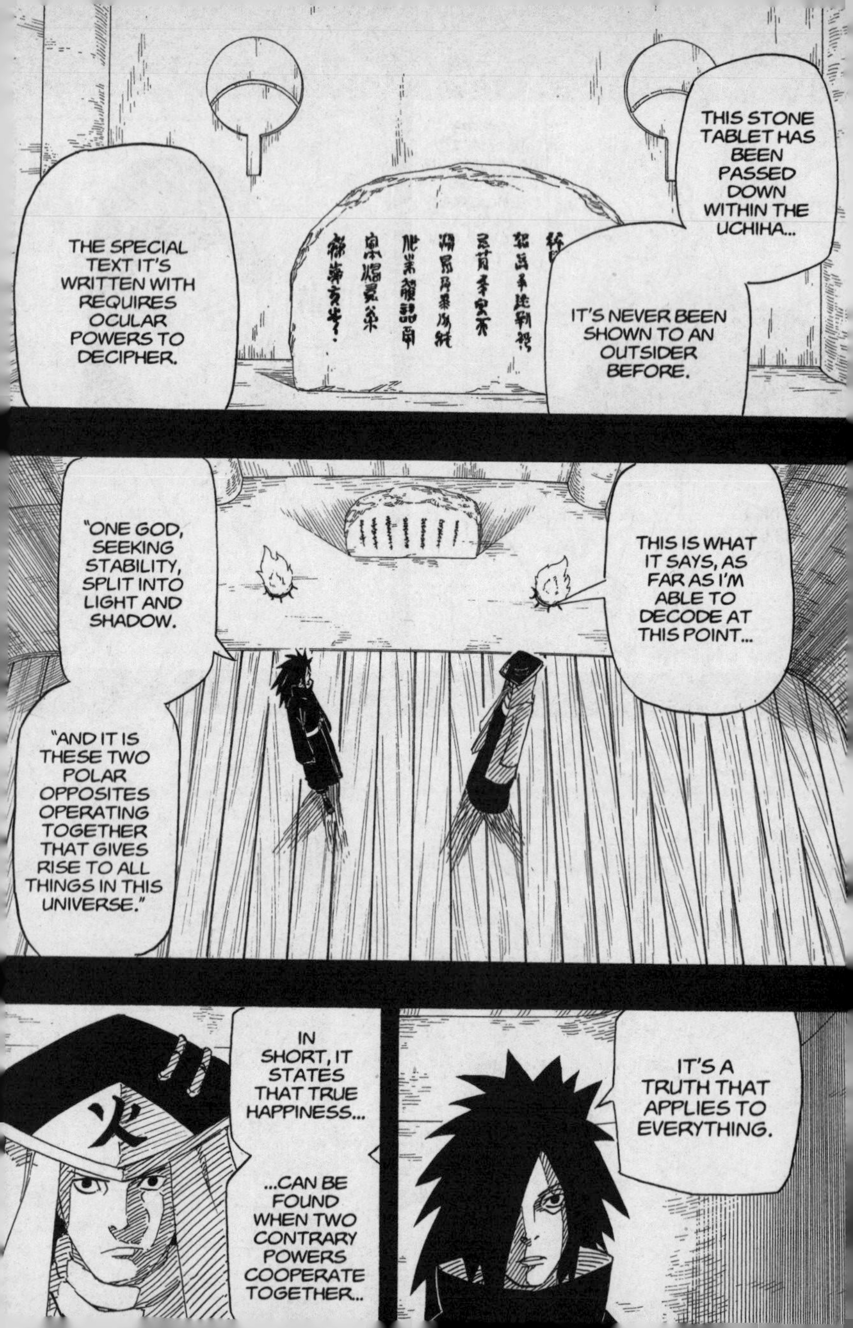
THIS STONE TABLET HAS BEEN PASSED DOWN WITHIN THE UCHIHA...
IT'S NEVER BEEN SHOWN TO AN OUTSIDER BEFORE.
THE SPECIAL TEXT IT'S WRITTEN WITH REQUIRES OCULAR POWERS TO DECIPHER.
THIS IS WHAT IT SAYS, AS FAR AS I'M ABLE TO DECODE AT THIS POINT...
"ONE GOD, SEEKING STABILITY, SPLIT INTO LIGHT AND SHADOW.
"AND IT IS THESE TWO POLAR OPPOSITES OPERATING TOGETHER THAT GIVES RISE TO ALL THINGS IN THIS UNIVERSE."
IT'S A TRUTH THAT APPLIES TO EVERYTHING.
IN SHORT, IT STATES THAT TRUE HAPPINESS...
...CAN BE FOUND WHEN TWO CONTRARY POWERS COOPERATE TOGETHER..

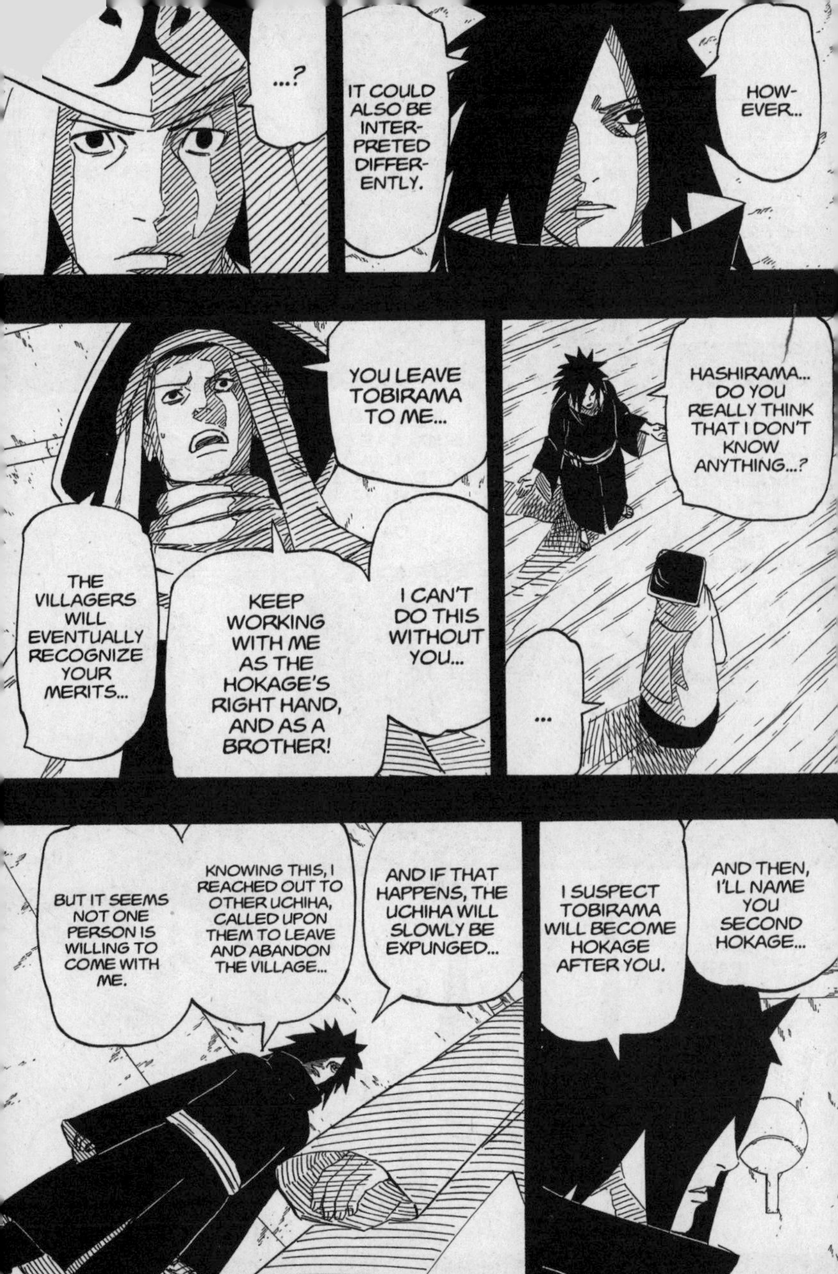
HOW-EVER...
IT COULD ALSO BE INTERPRETED DIFFERENTLY.
...?
HASHIRAMA... DO YOU REALLY THINK THAT I DON'T KNOW ANYTHING...?
...
YOU LEAVE TOBIRAMA TO ME...
I CAN'T DO THIS WITHOUT YOU...
KEEP WORKING WITH ME AS THE HOKAGE'S RIGHT HAND, AND AS A BROTHER!
THE VILLAGERS WILL EVENTUALLY RECOGNIZE YOUR MERITS...
AND THEN, I'LL NAME YOU SECOND HOKAGE...
I SUSPECT TOBIRAMA WILL BECOME HOKAGE AFTER YOU.
AND IF THAT HAPPENS, THE UCHIHA WILL SLOWLY BE EXPUNGED...
KNOWING THIS, I REACHED OUT TO OTHER UCHIHA, CALLED UPON THEM TO LEAVE AND ABANDON THE VILLAGE...
BUT IT SEEMS NOT ONE PERSON IS WILLING TO COME WITH ME.

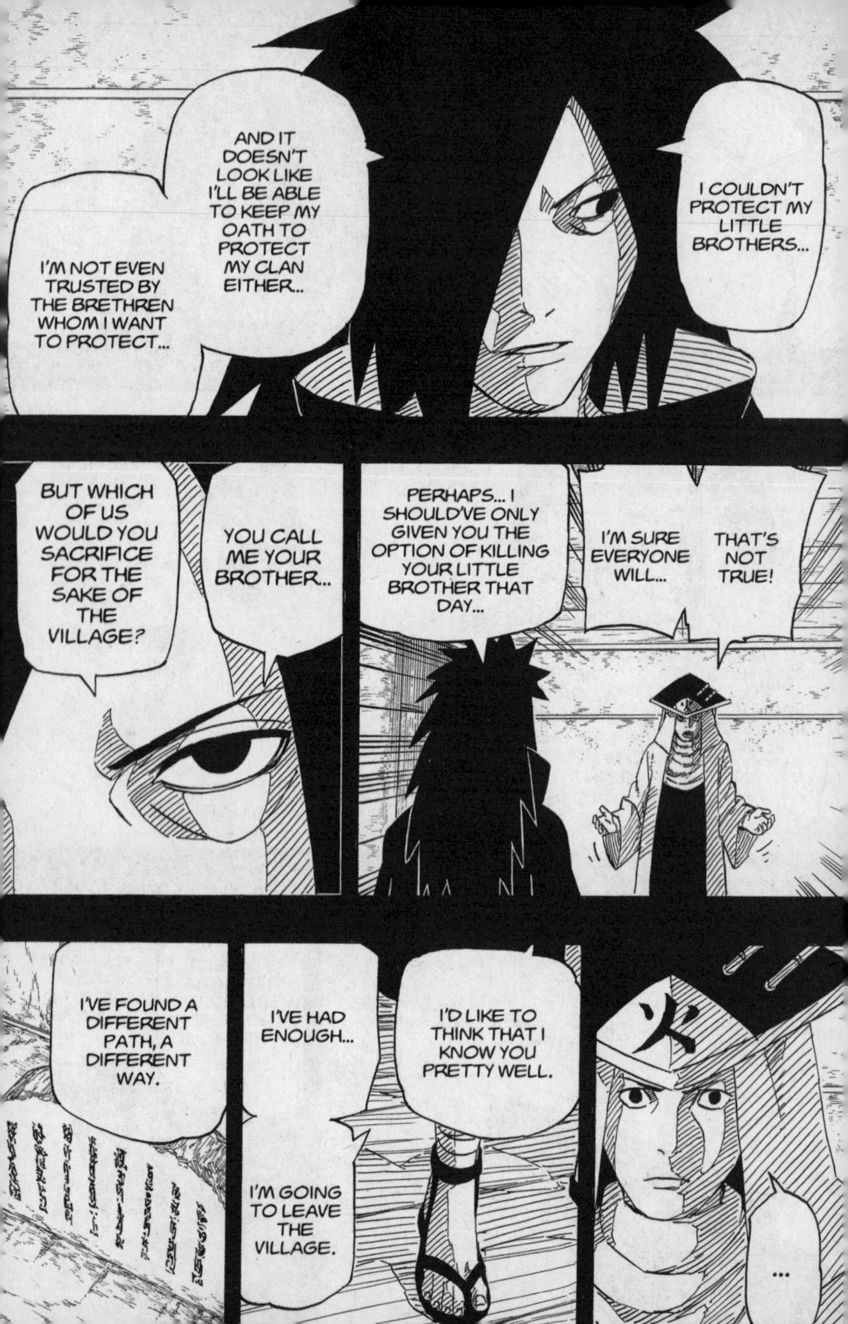
I COULDN'T PROTECT MY LITTLE BROTHERS...
AND IT DOESN'T LOOK LIKE I'LL BE ABLE TO KEEP MY OATH TO PROTECT MY CLAN EITHER...
I'M NOT EVEN TRUSTED BY THE BRETHREN WHOM I WANT TO PROTECT...
THAT'S NOT TRUE!
I'M SURE EVERYONE WILL...
PERHAPS... I SHOULD'VE ONLY GIVEN YOU THE OPTION OF KILLING YOUR LITTLE BROTHER THAT DAY...
YOU CALL ME YOUR BROTHER...
BUT WHICH OF US WOULD YOU SACRIFICE FOR THE SAKE OF THE VILLAGE?
...
I'D LIKE TO THINK THAT I KNOW YOU PRETTY WELL.
I'VE HAD ENOUGH...
I'M GOING TO LEAVE THE VILLAGE.
I'VE FOUND A DIFFERENT PATH, A DIFFERENT WAY.

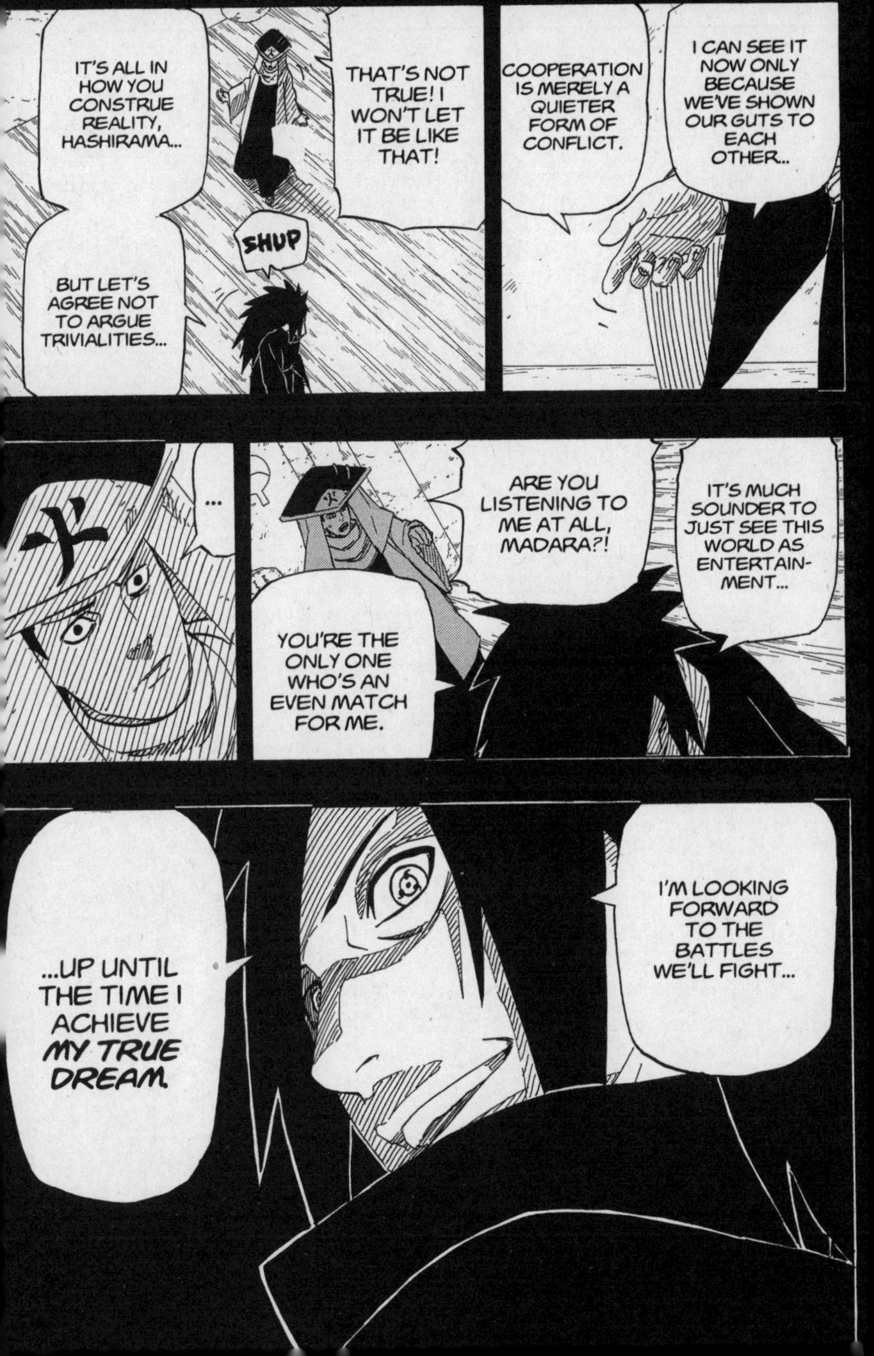
I CAN SEE IT NOW ONLY BECAUSE WE'VE SHOWN OUR GUTS TO EACH OTHER...
COOPERATION IS MERELY A QUIETER FORM OF CONFLICT.
THAT'S NOT TRUE! I WON'T LET IT BE LIKE THAT!
IT'S ALL IN HOW YOU CONSTRUE REALITY, HASHIRAMA...
SHUP
BUT LET'S AGREE NOT TO ARGUE TRIVIALITIES...
IT'S MUCH SOUNDER TO JUST SEE THIS WORLD AS ENTERTAIN-MENT...
ARE YOU LISTENING TO ME AT ALL, MADARA?!
YOU'RE THE ONLY ONE WHO'S AN EVEN MATCH FOR ME.
...
I'M LOOKING FORWARD TO THE BATTLES WE'LL FIGHT...
...UP UNTIL THE TIME I ACHIEVE ***MY TRUE DREAM.***

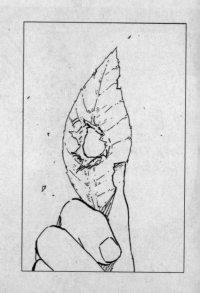

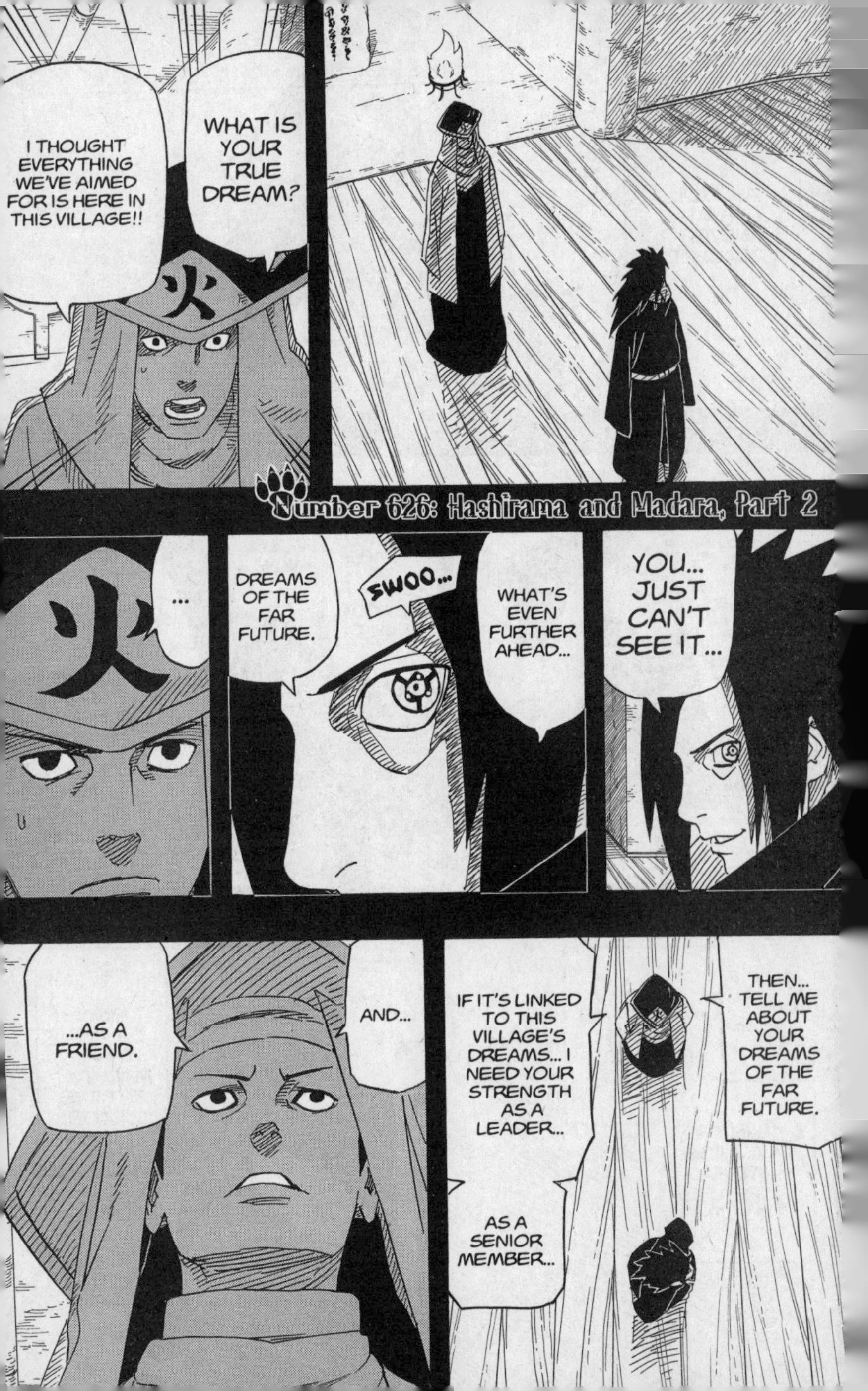
WHAT IS YOUR TRUE DREAM?
I THOUGHT EVERYTHING WE'VE AIMED FOR IS HERE IN THIS VILLAGE!!
Number 626: Hashirama and Madara, Part 2
YOU... JUST CAN'T SEE IT...
WHAT'S EVEN FURTHER AHEAD...
SWOO...
DREAMS OF THE FAR FUTURE.
...
THEN... TELL ME ABOUT YOUR DREAMS OF THE FAR FUTURE.
IF IT'S LINKED TO THIS VILLAGE'S DREAMS... I NEED YOUR STRENGTH AS A LEADER...
AS A SENIOR MEMBER...
AND...
...AS A FRIEND.

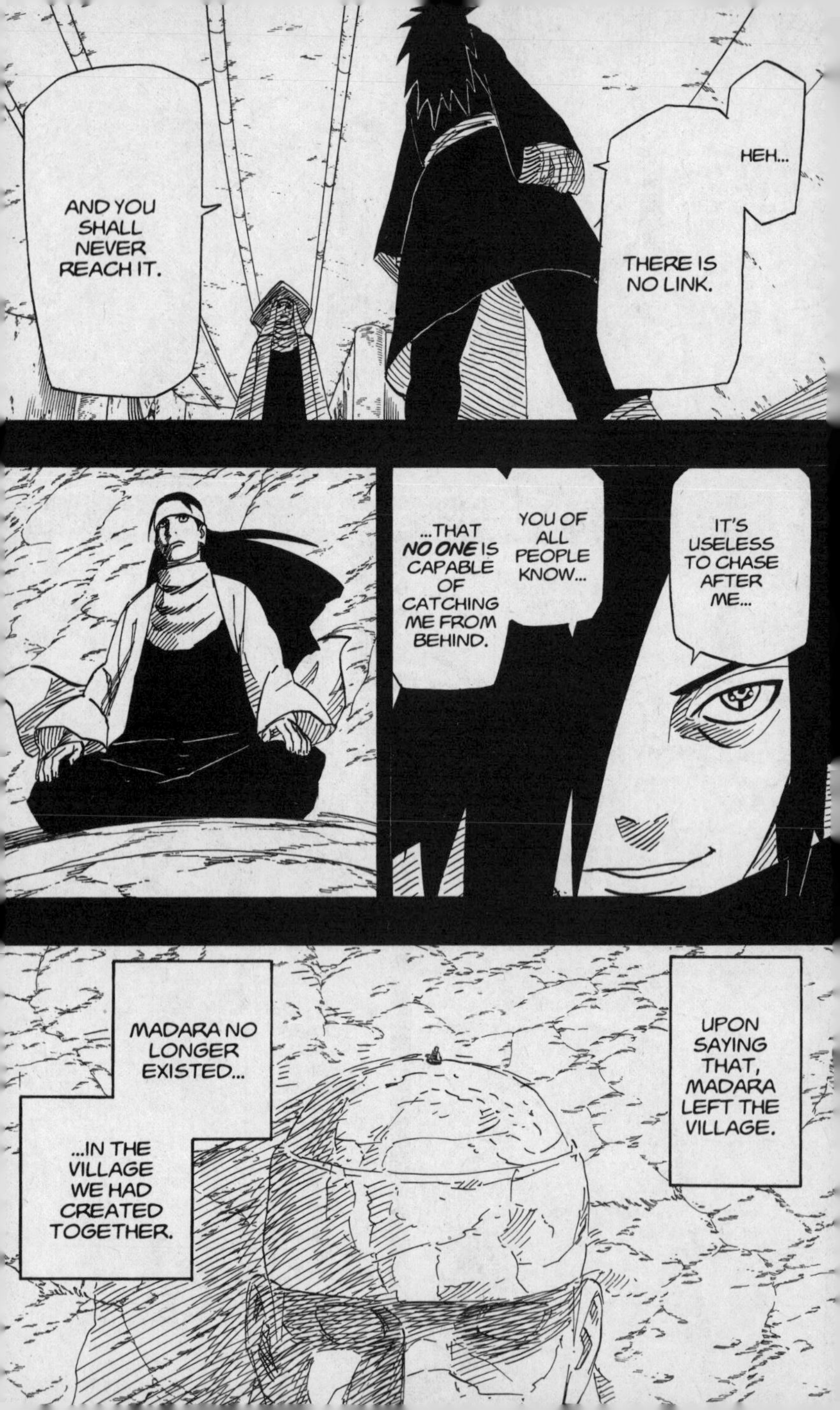
HEH...
THERE IS NO LINK.
AND YOU SHALL NEVER REACH IT.
IT'S USELESS TO CHASE AFTER ME...
YOU OF ALL PEOPLE KNOW...
...THAT *NO ONE* IS CAPABLE OF CATCHING ME FROM BEHIND.
UPON SAYING THAT, MADARA LEFT THE VILLAGE.
MADARA NO LONGER EXISTED...
...IN THE VILLAGE WE HAD CREATED TOGETHER.

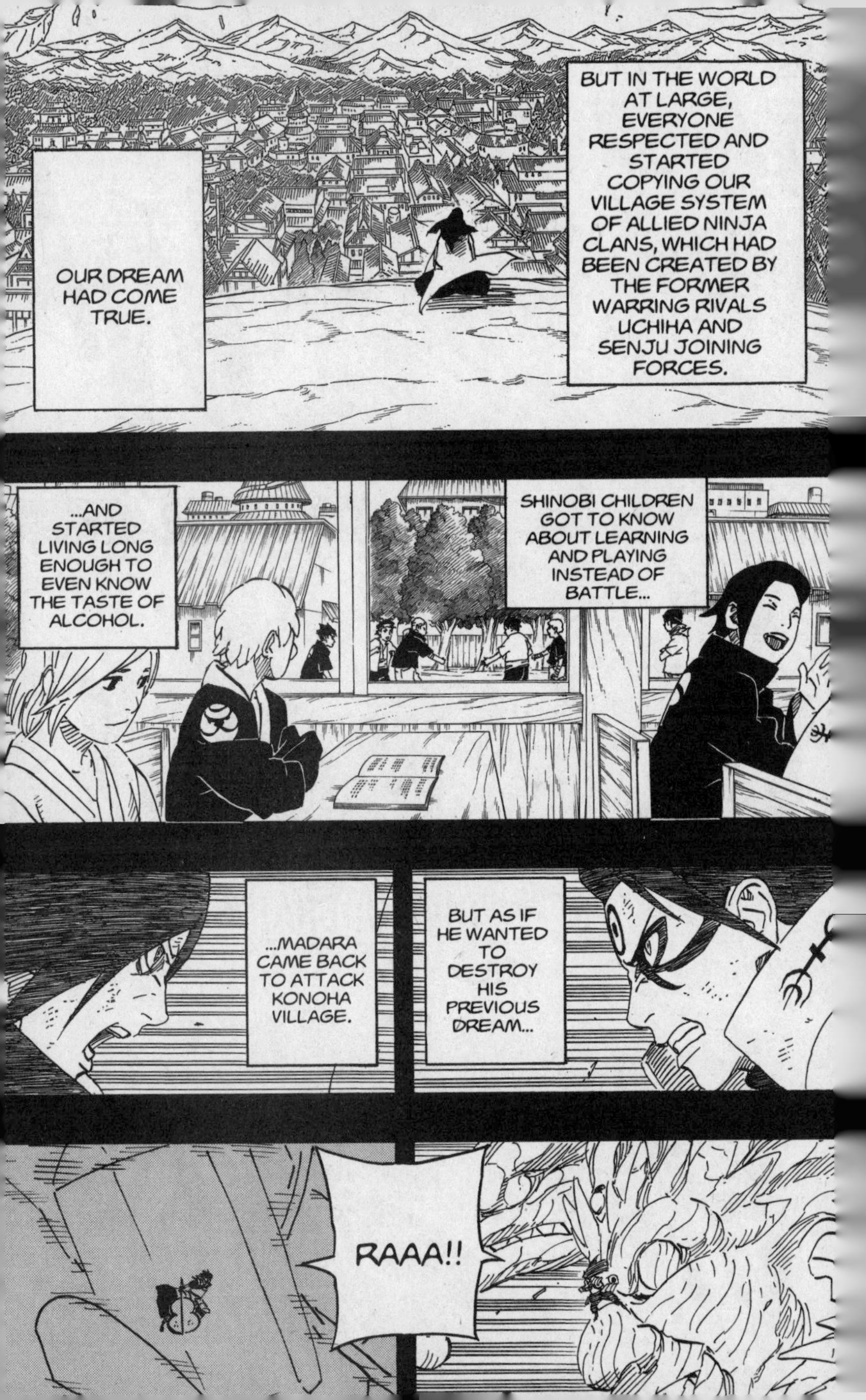
BUT IN THE WORLD AT LARGE, EVERYONE RESPECTED AND STARTED COPYING OUR VILLAGE SYSTEM OF ALLIED NINJA CLANS, WHICH HAD BEEN CREATED BY THE FORMER WARRING RIVALS UCHIHA AND SENJU JOINING FORCES.
OUR DREAM HAD COME TRUE.
SHINOBI CHILDREN GOT TO KNOW ABOUT LEARNING AND PLAYING INSTEAD OF BATTLE...
...AND STARTED LIVING LONG ENOUGH TO EVEN KNOW THE TASTE OF ALCOHOL.
BUT AS IF HE WANTED TO DESTROY HIS PREVIOUS DREAM...
...MADARA CAME BACK TO ATTACK KONOHA VILLAGE.
RAAA!!

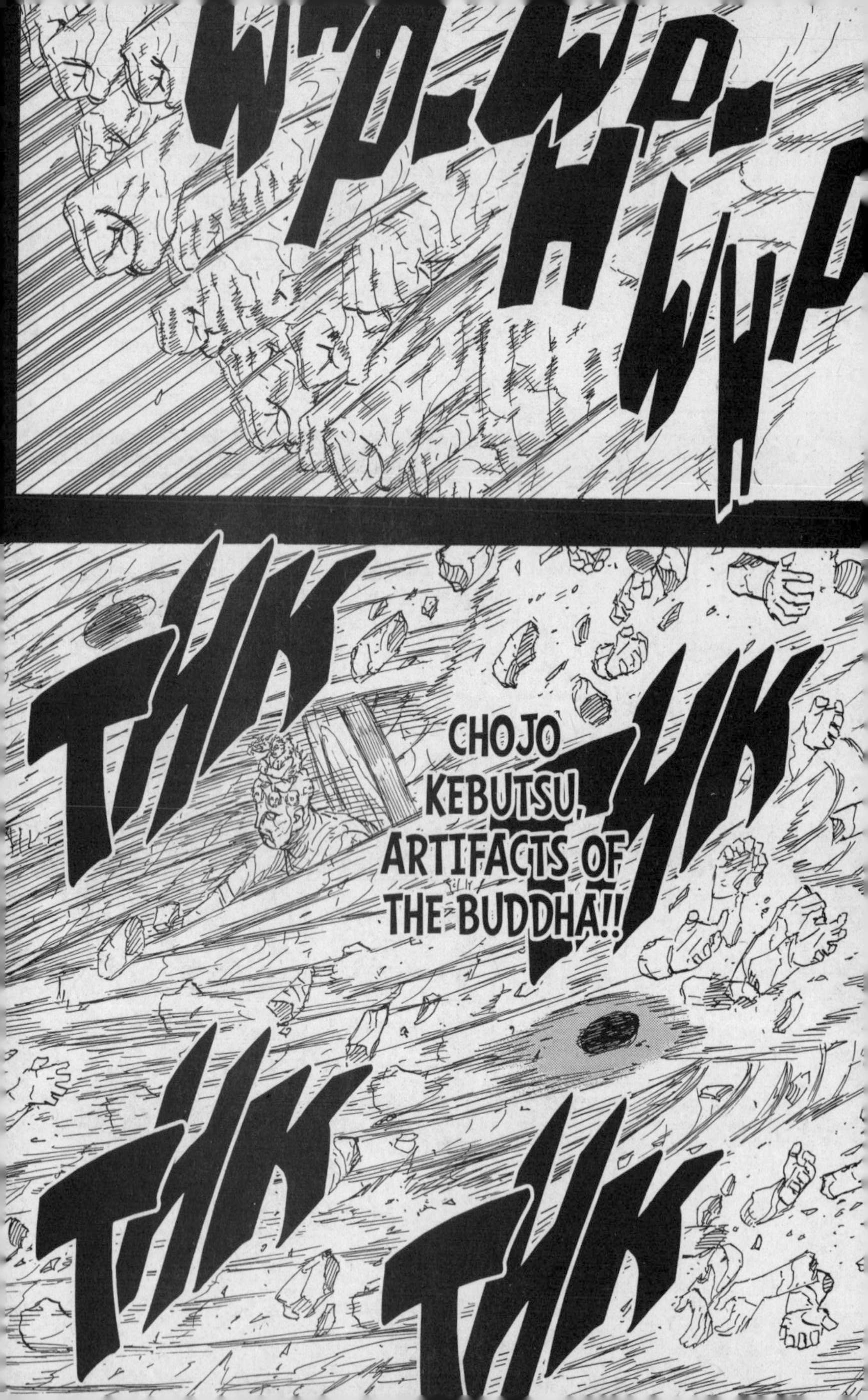
WHD-WHD-WHD-WHP
THK
THK
CHOJO KEBUTSU, ARTIFACTS OF THE BUDDHA!!
THK
THK
THK

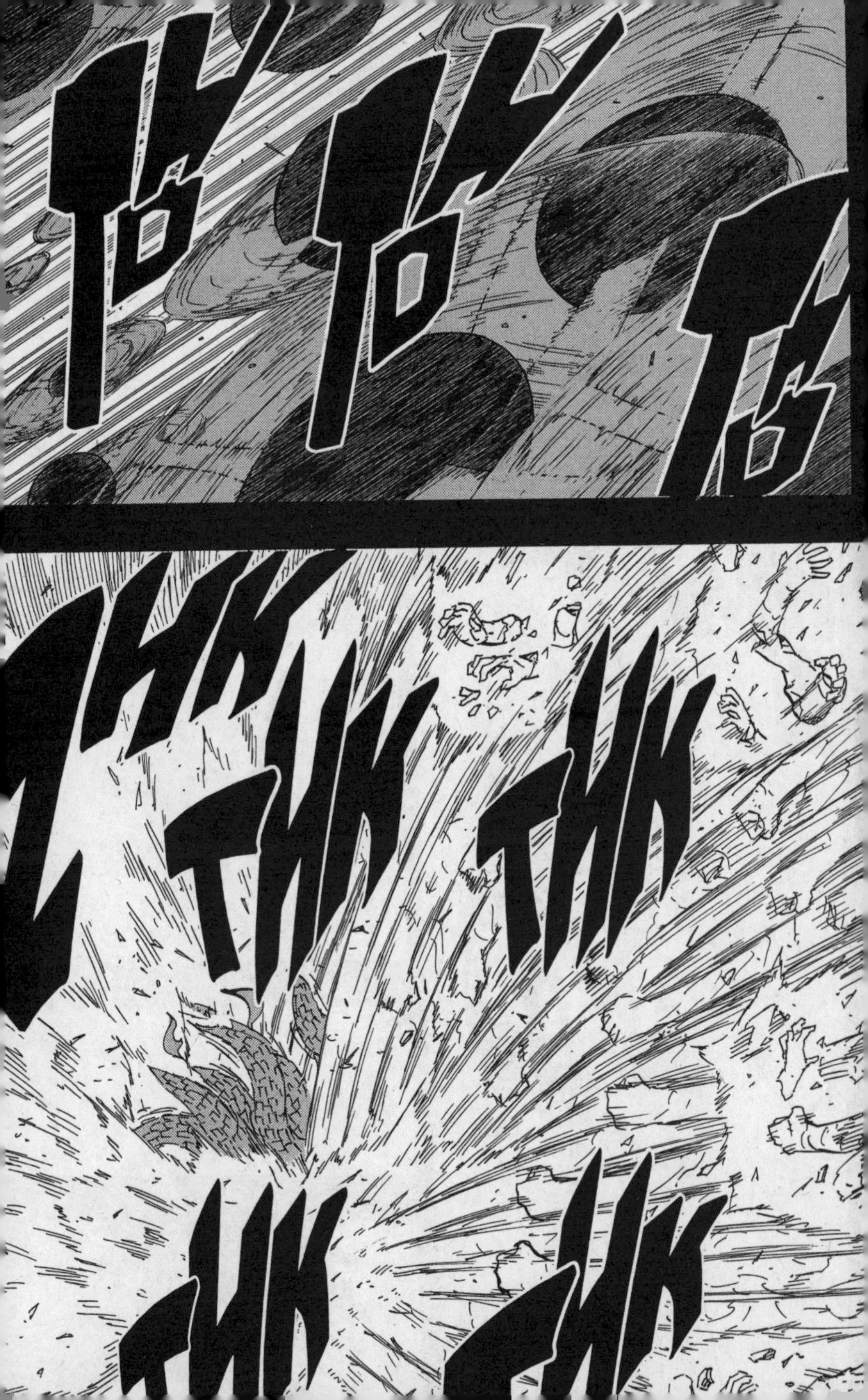
THK
THK
THK
THK
THK

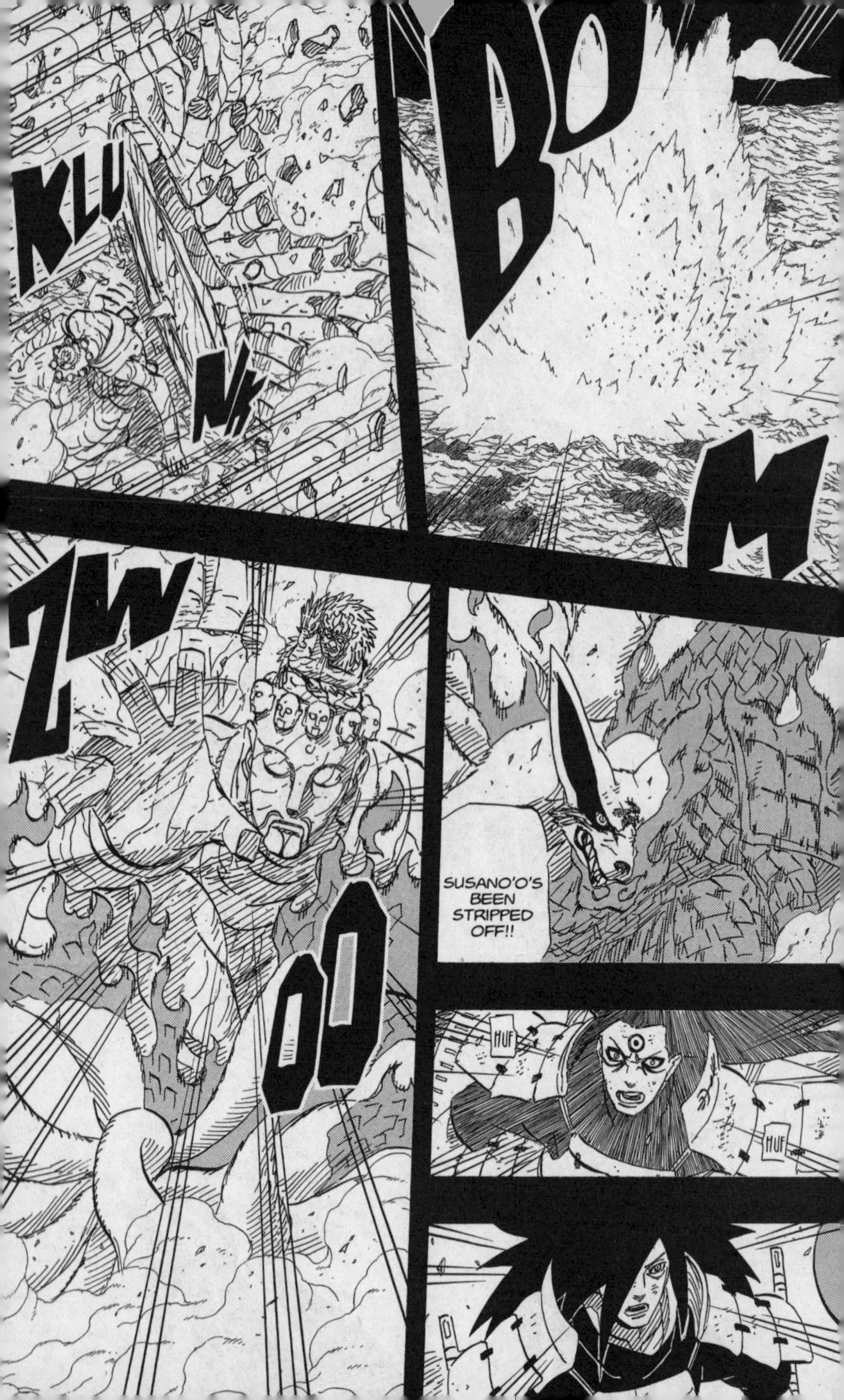
BOOM
KLUNK
SUSANO'O'S BEEN STRIPPED OFF!!
ZWOO
HUF
HUF

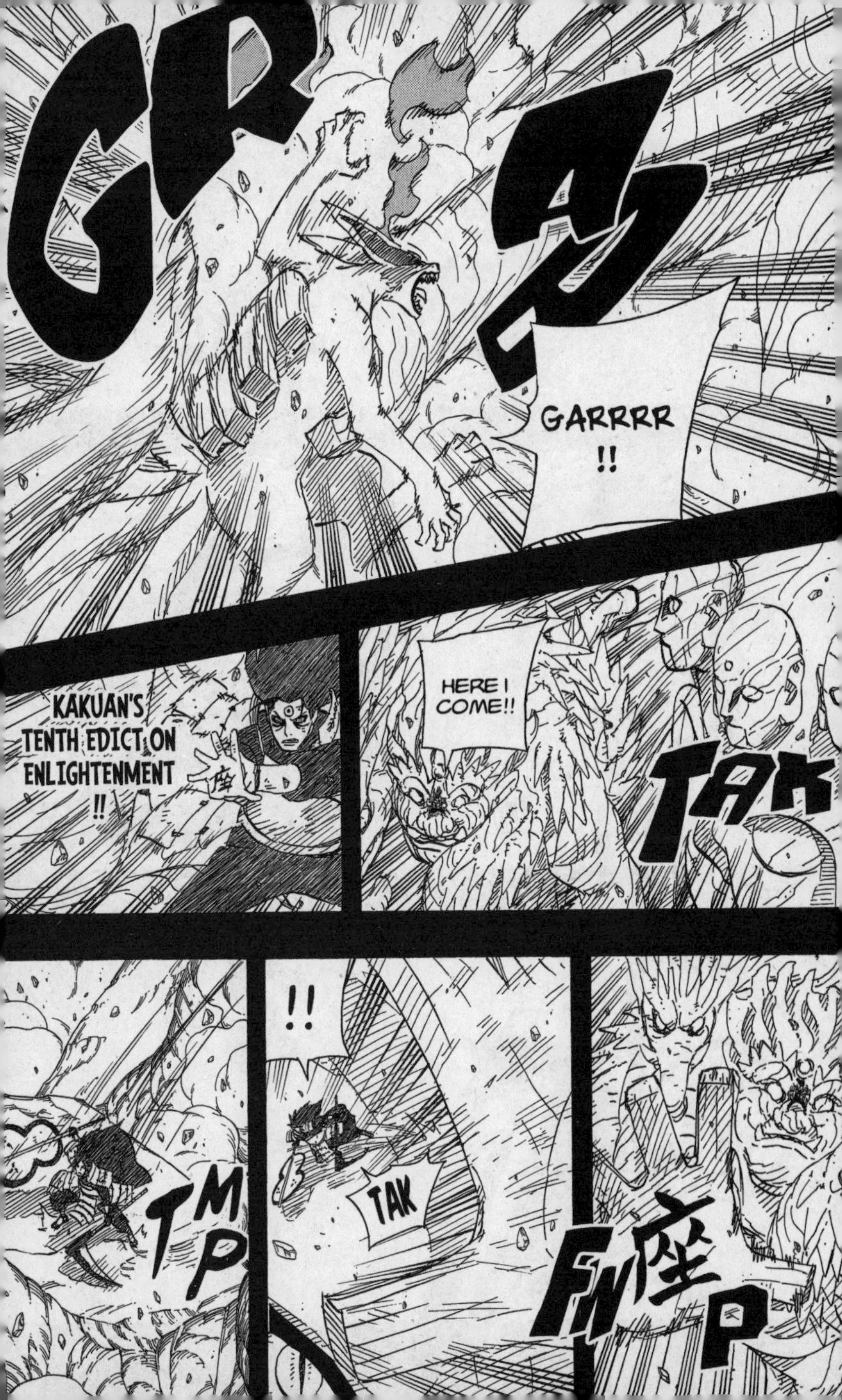
GRAA
GARRRR !!
HERE I COME!!
TAK
KAKUAN'S TENTH EDICT ON ENLIGHTENMENT !!
FWIP
!!
TAK
TMP

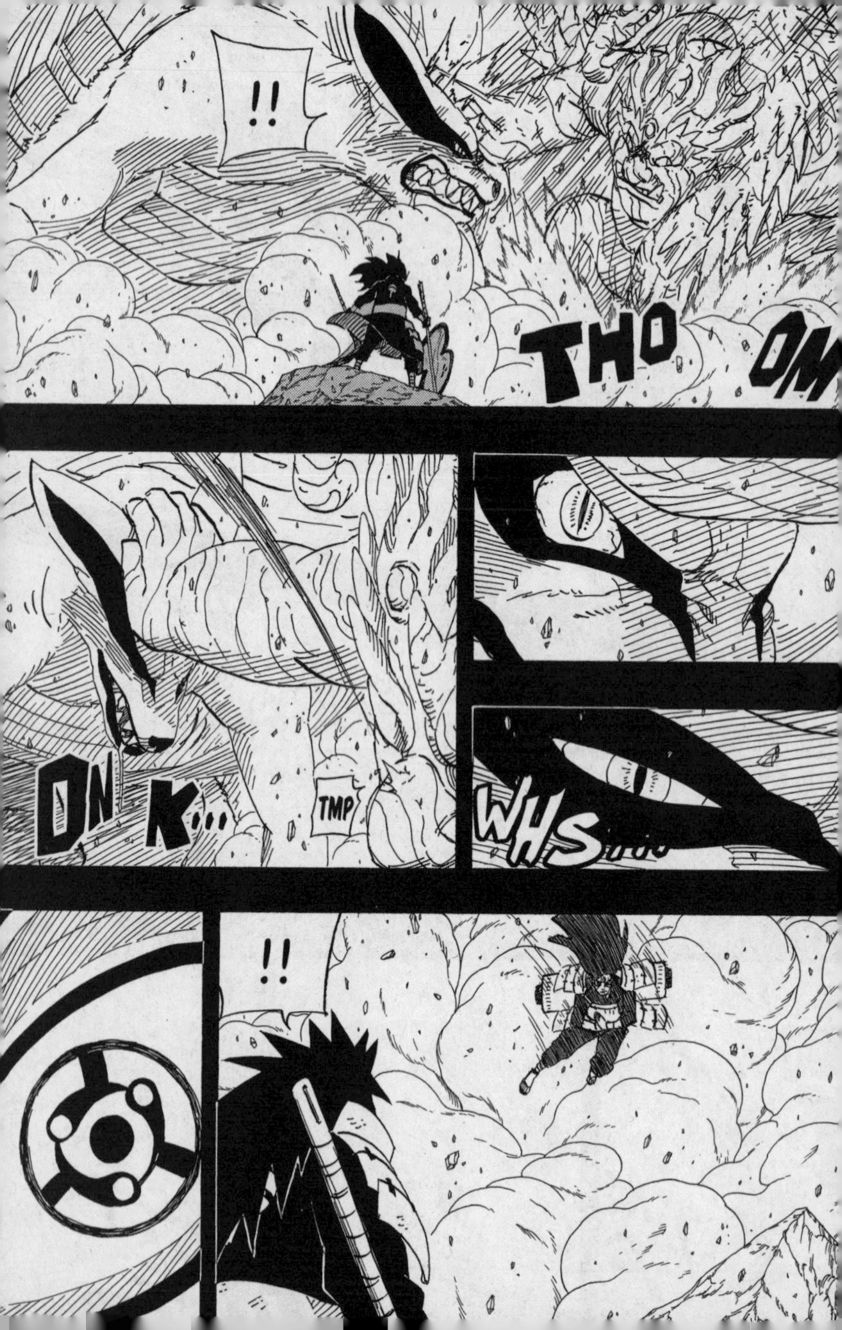

!!
THO OM
WHS
TMP
DN K...
!!

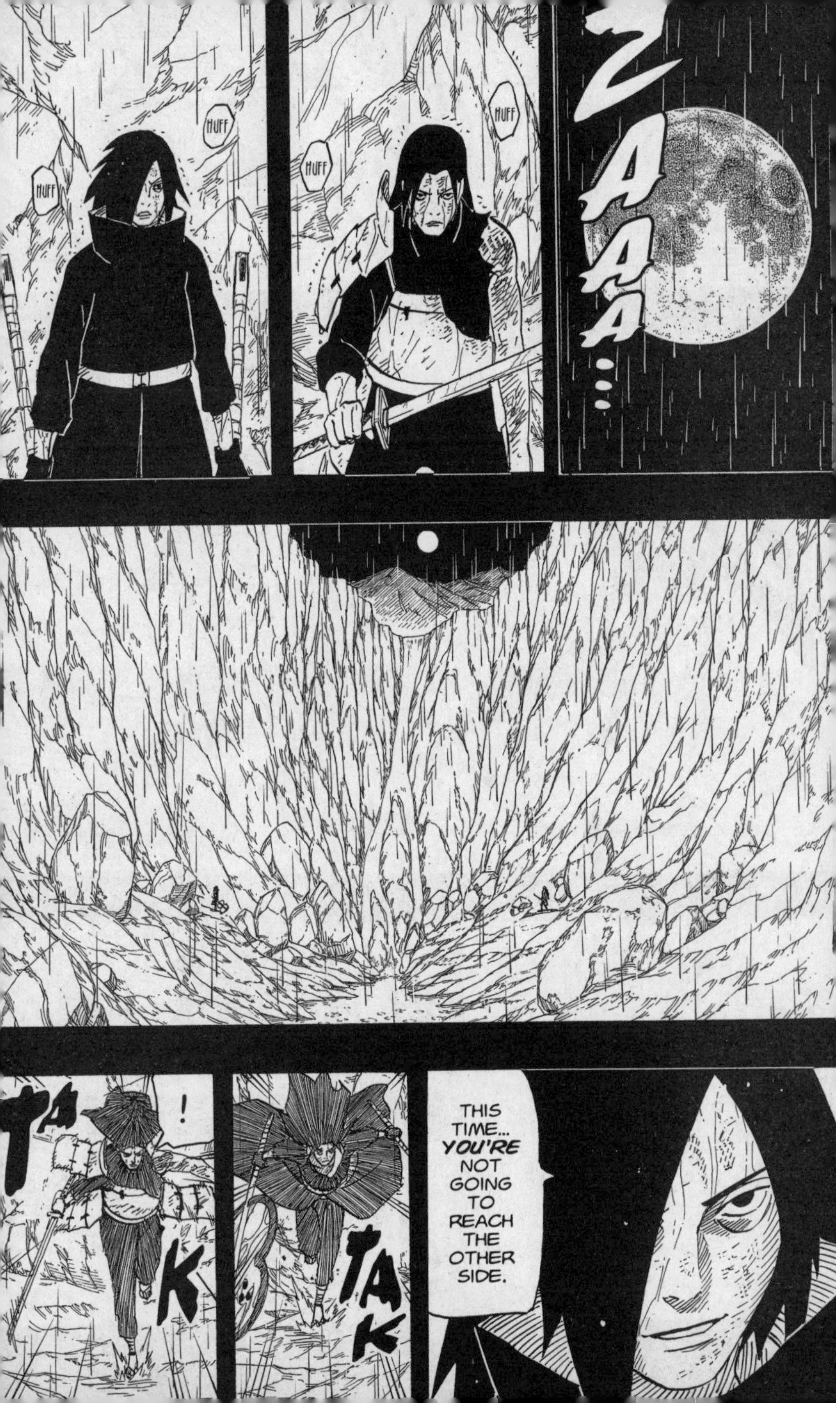
ZAAAA...
HUFF
HUFF
HUFF
HUFF
THIS TIME... *YOU'RE* NOT GOING TO REACH THE OTHER SIDE.
TAK
!
TAK

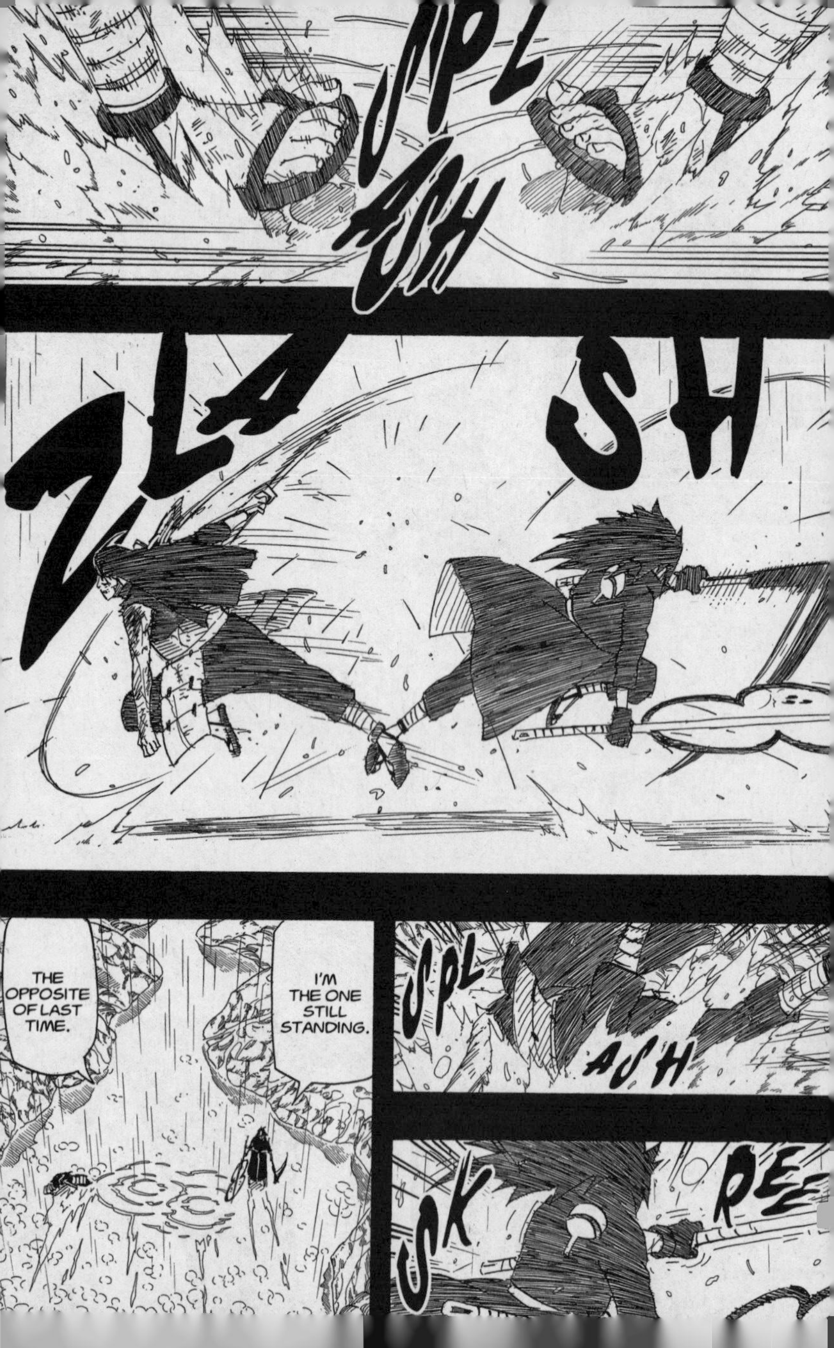
SPLASH
ZLASH
SPLASH
SKREE
I'M THE ONE STILL STANDING.
THE OPPOSITE OF LAST TIME.

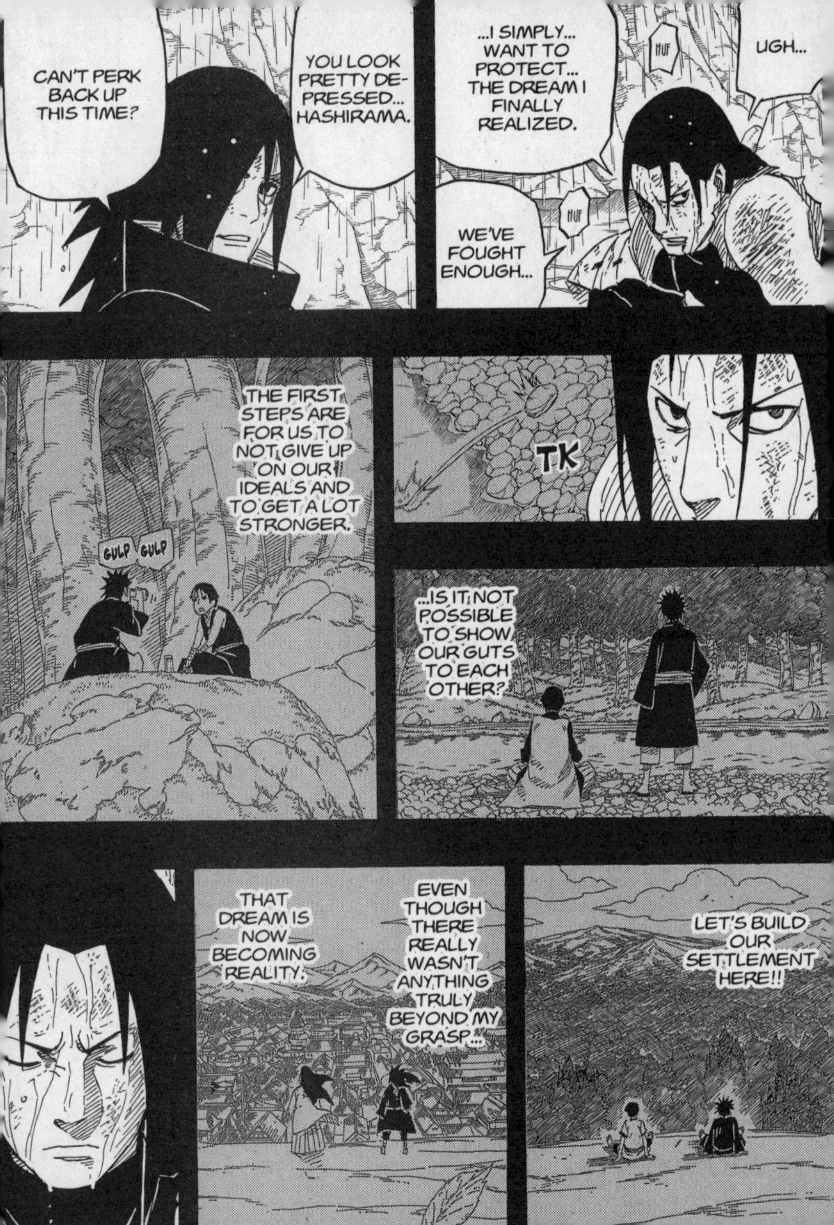
UGH...
HUF
...I SIMPLY... WANT TO PROTECT... THE DREAM I FINALLY REALIZED.
HUF
WE'VE FOUGHT ENOUGH...
YOU LOOK PRETTY DE-PRESSED... HASHIRAMA.
CAN'T PERK BACK UP THIS TIME?
TK
...IS IT NOT POSSIBLE TO SHOW OUR GUTS TO EACH OTHER?
THE FIRST STEPS ARE FOR US TO NOT GIVE UP ON OUR IDEALS AND TO GET A LOT STRONGER.
GULP GULP
LET'S BUILD OUR SETTLEMENT HERE!!
EVEN THOUGH THERE REALLY WASN'T ANYTHING TRULY BEYOND MY GRASP...
THAT DREAM IS NOW BECOMING REALITY.

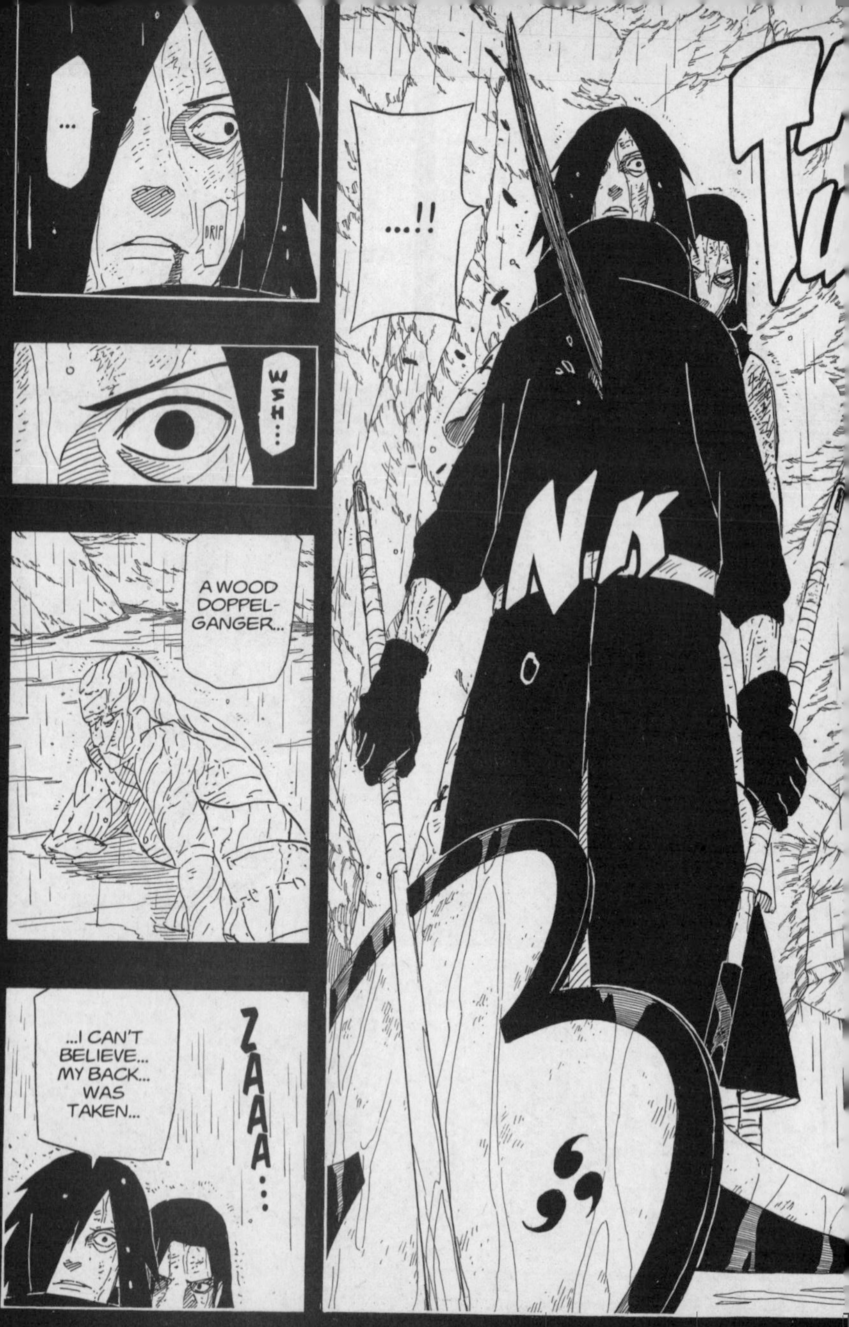

...!!
...
DRIP
WSH...
A WOOD DOPPEL-GANGER...
...I CAN'T BELIEVE... MY BACK... WAS TAKEN...
ZAAA...

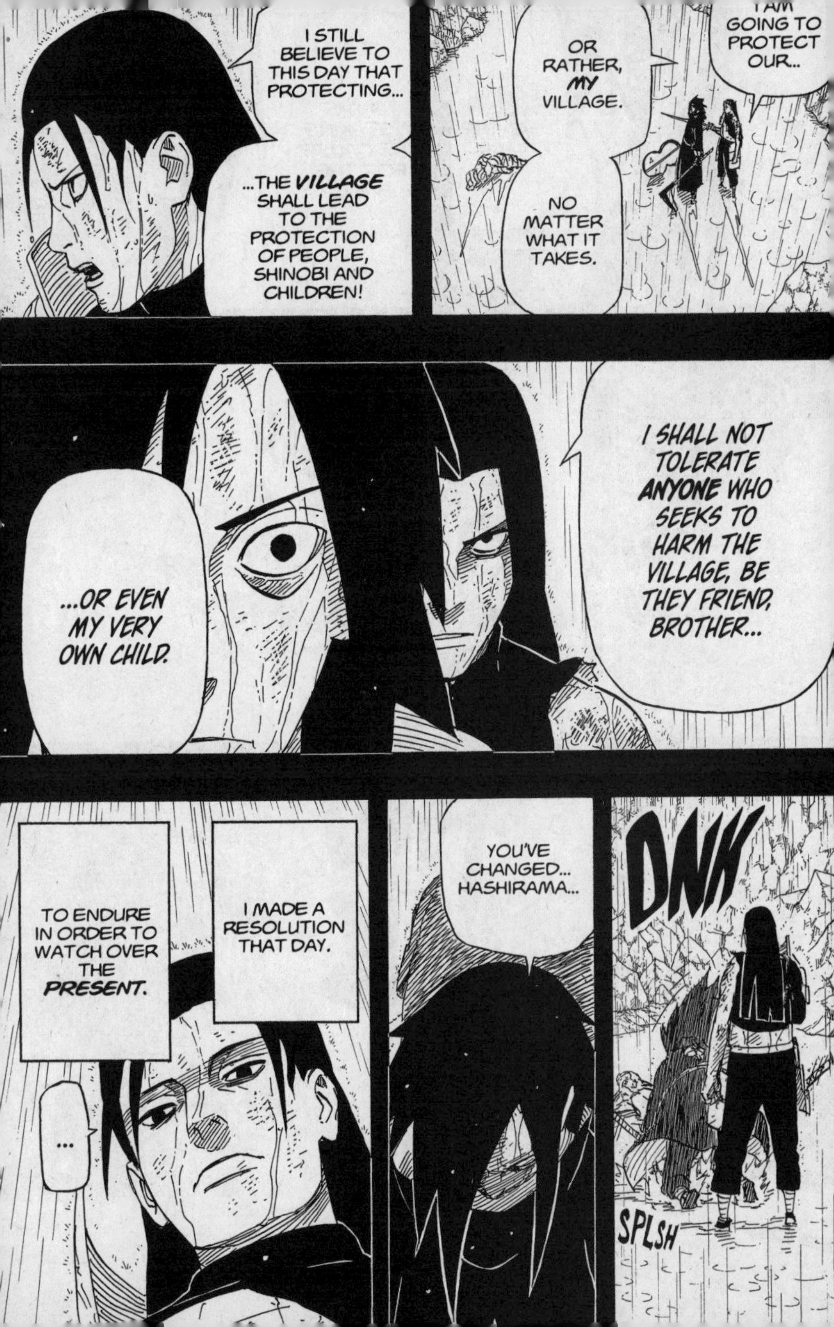
I AM GOING TO PROTECT OUR...
OR RATHER, MY VILLAGE.
NO MATTER WHAT IT TAKES.
I STILL BELIEVE TO THIS DAY THAT PROTECTING...
...THE VILLAGE SHALL LEAD TO THE PROTECTION OF PEOPLE, SHINOBI AND CHILDREN!
I SHALL NOT TOLERATE ANYONE WHO SEEKS TO HARM THE VILLAGE, BE THEY FRIEND, BROTHER...
...OR EVEN MY VERY OWN CHILD.
DNK
SPLSH
YOU'VE CHANGED... HASHIRAMA...
I MADE A RESOLUTION THAT DAY.
TO ENDURE IN ORDER TO WATCH OVER THE PRESENT.
...

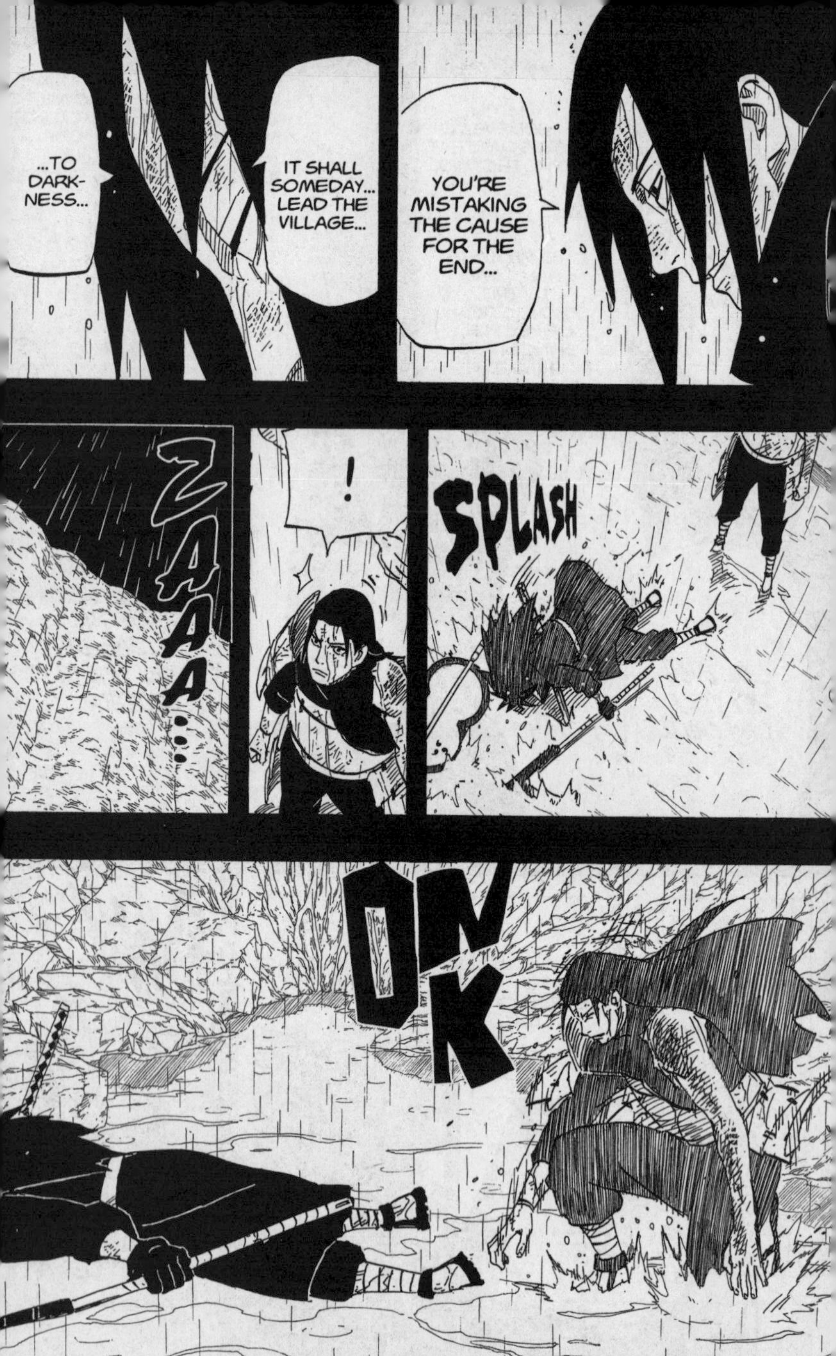
YOU'RE MISTAKING THE CAUSE FOR THE END...
IT SHALL SOMEDAY... LEAD THE VILLAGE...
...TO DARKNESS...
SPLASH
!
ZAAAA....
ONK

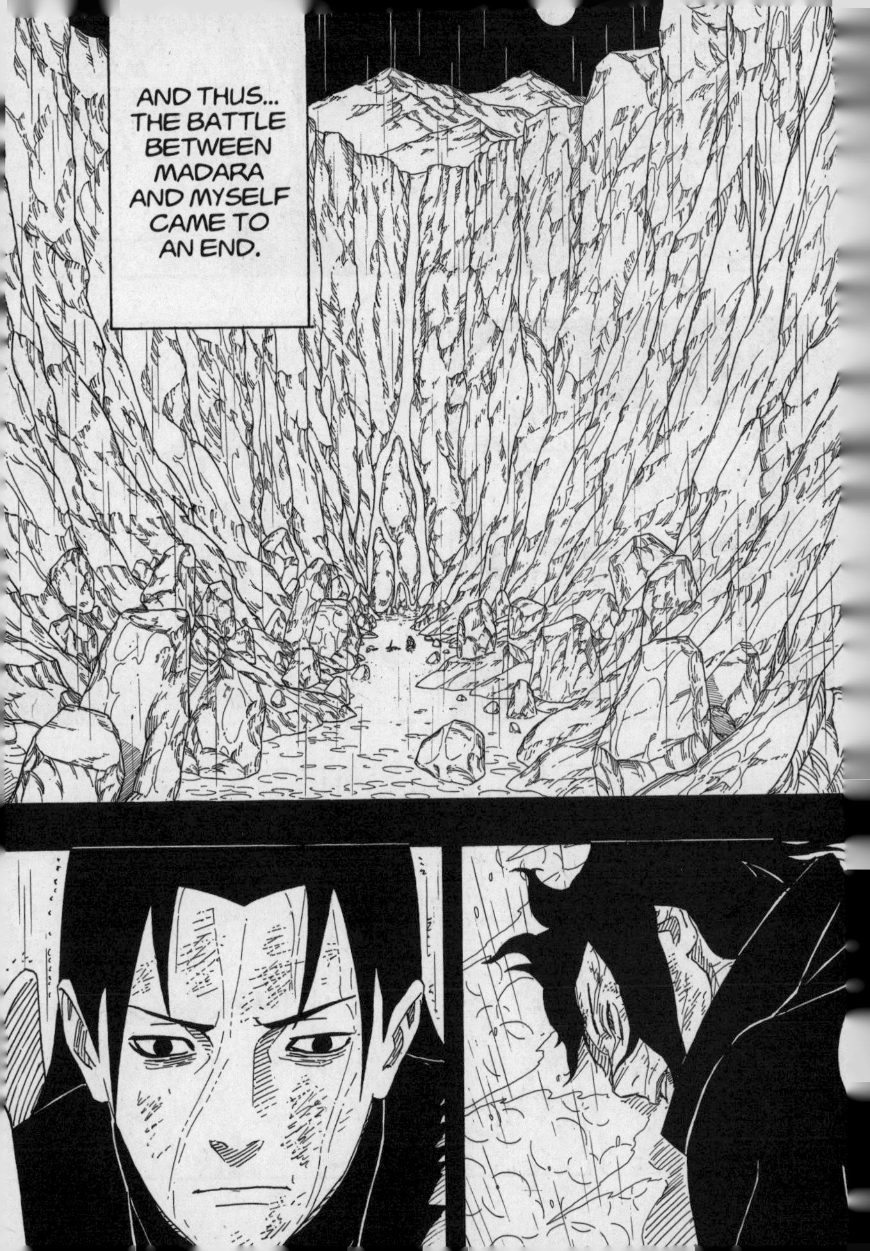
AND THUS... THE BATTLE BETWEEN MADARA AND MYSELF CAME TO AN END.

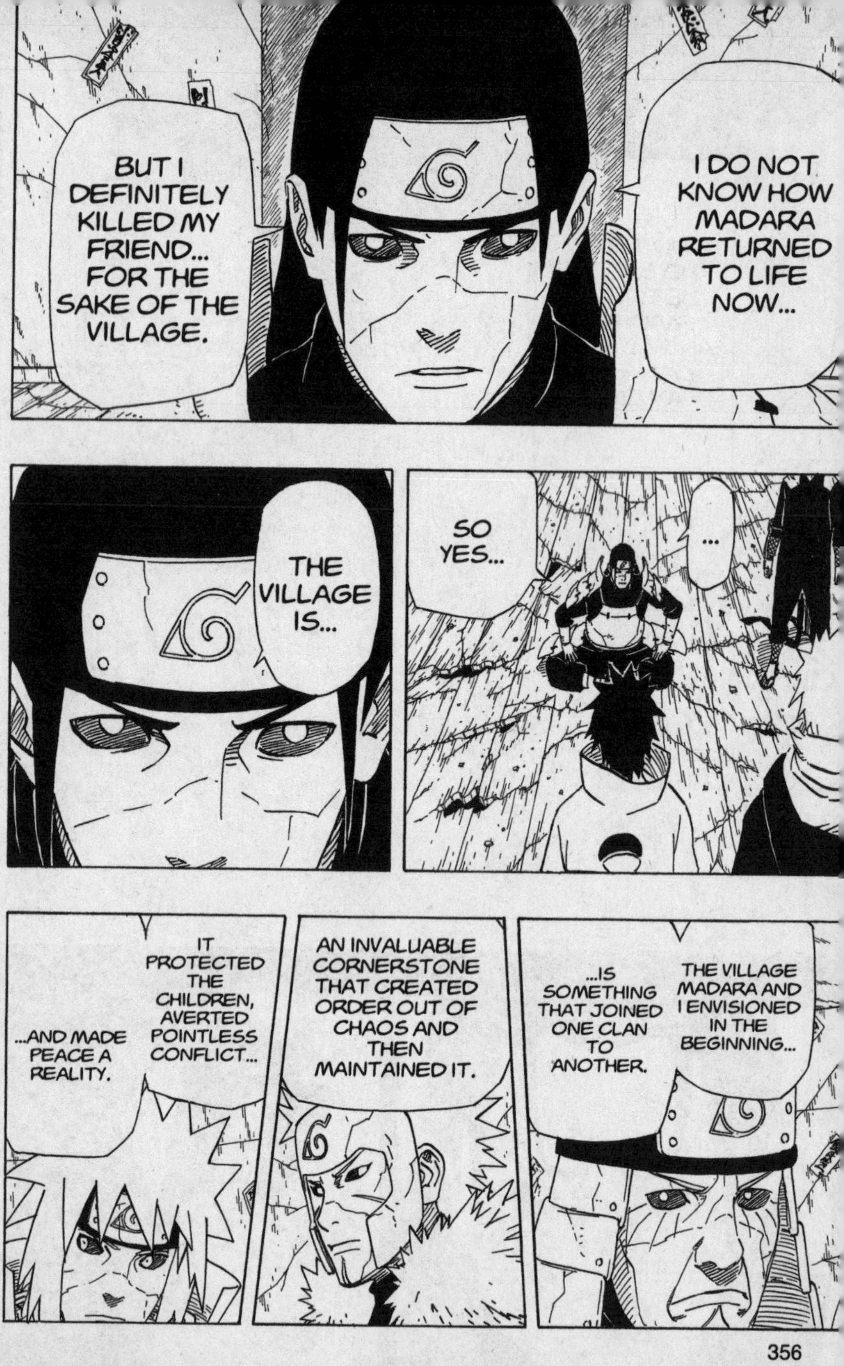
I DO NOT KNOW HOW MADARA RETURNED TO LIFE NOW...
BUT I DEFINITELY KILLED MY FRIEND... FOR THE SAKE OF THE VILLAGE.
...
SO YES...
THE VILLAGE IS...
THE VILLAGE MADARA AND I ENVISIONED IN THE BEGINNING...
...IS SOMETHING THAT JOINED ONE CLAN TO ANOTHER.
AN INVALUABLE CORNERSTONE THAT CREATED ORDER OUT OF CHAOS AND THEN MAINTAINED IT.
IT PROTECTED THE CHILDREN, AVERTED POINTLESS CONFLICT...
...AND MADE PEACE A REALITY.

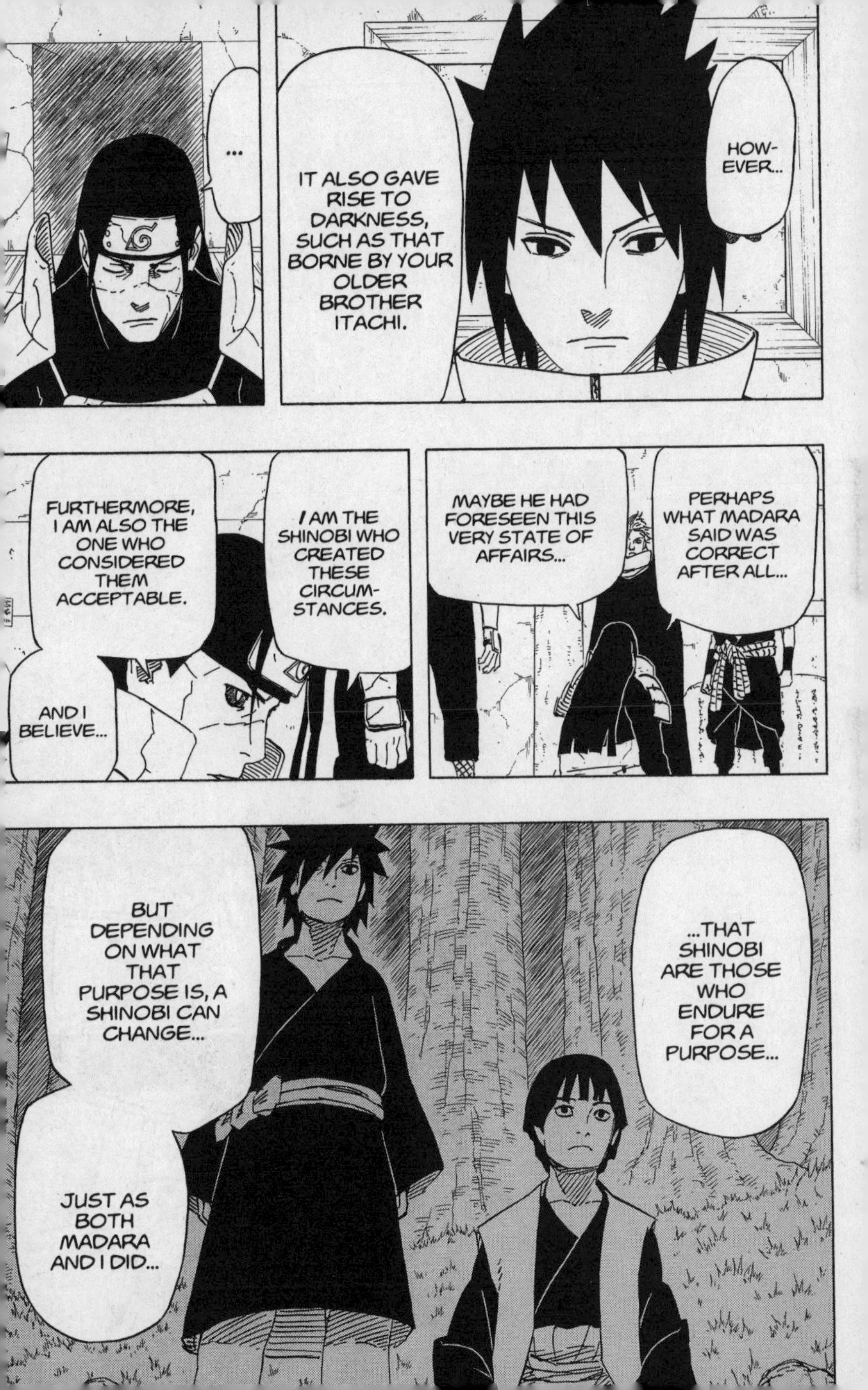
HOWEVER...
IT ALSO GAVE RISE TO DARKNESS, SUCH AS THAT BORNE BY YOUR OLDER BROTHER ITACHI.
...
PERHAPS WHAT MADARA SAID WAS CORRECT AFTER ALL...
MAYBE HE HAD FORESEEN THIS VERY STATE OF AFFAIRS...
I AM THE SHINOBI WHO CREATED THESE CIRCUMSTANCES.
FURTHERMORE, I AM ALSO THE ONE WHO CONSIDERED THEM ACCEPTABLE.
AND I BELIEVE...
...THAT SHINOBI ARE THOSE WHO ENDURE FOR A PURPOSE...
BUT DEPENDING ON WHAT THAT PURPOSE IS, A SHINOBI CAN CHANGE...
JUST AS BOTH MADARA AND I DID...

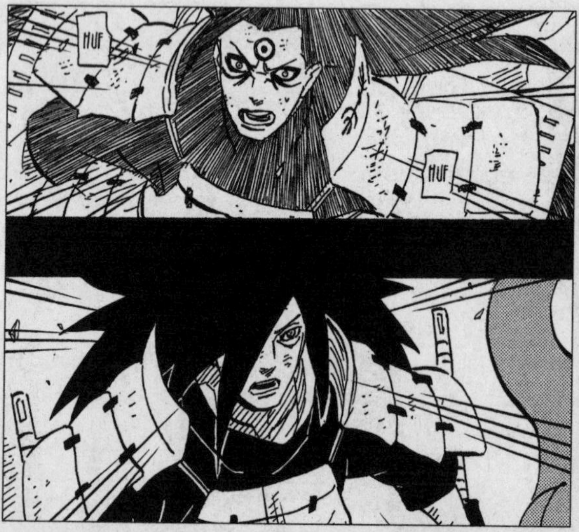
HUF
HUF

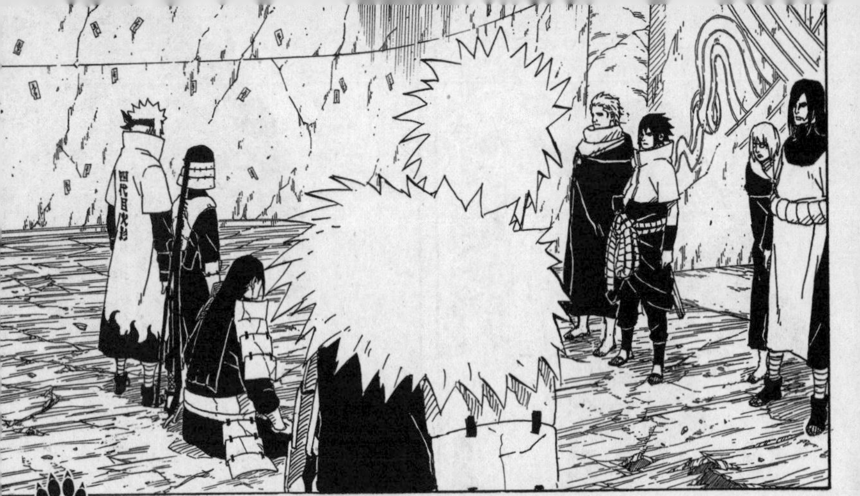

Number 627: Sasuke's Answer

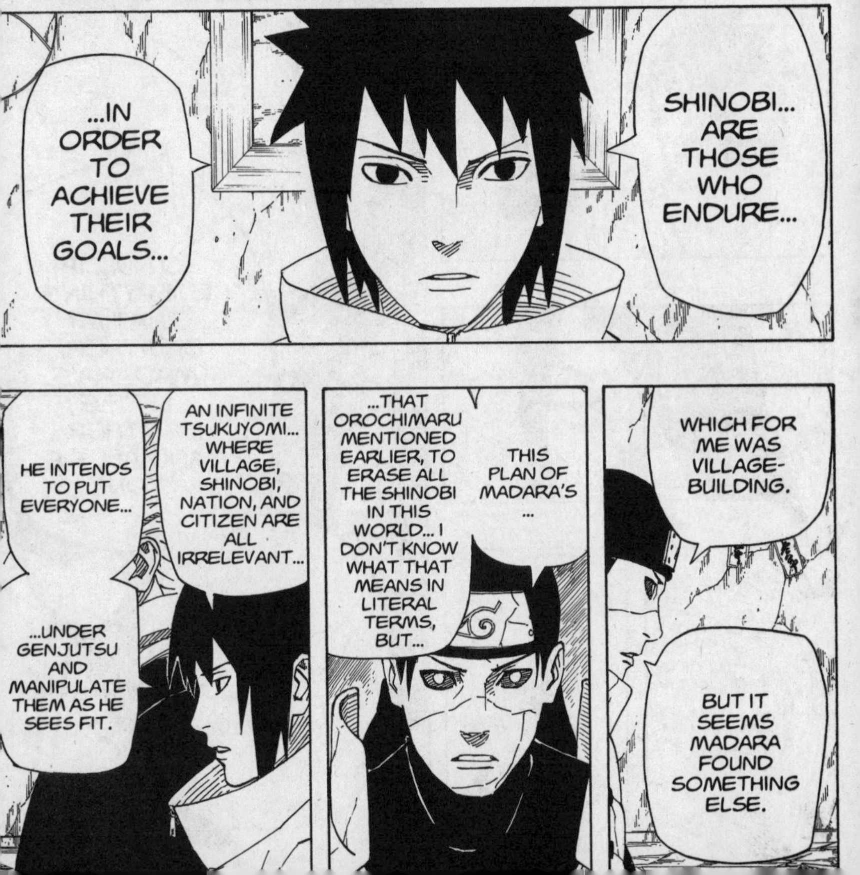

SHINOBI... ARE THOSE WHO ENDURE...
...IN ORDER TO ACHIEVE THEIR GOALS...
WHICH FOR ME WAS VILLAGE-BUILDING.
BUT IT SEEMS MADARA FOUND SOMETHING ELSE.
THIS PLAN OF MADARA'S...
...THAT OROCHIMARU MENTIONED EARLIER, TO ERASE ALL THE SHINOBI IN THIS WORLD... I DON'T KNOW WHAT THAT MEANS IN LITERAL TERMS, BUT...
AN INFINITE TSUKUYOMI... WHERE VILLAGE, SHINOBI, NATION, AND CITIZEN ARE ALL IRRELEVANT...
HE INTENDS TO PUT EVERYONE...
...UNDER GENJUTSU AND MANIPULATE THEM AS HE SEES FIT.

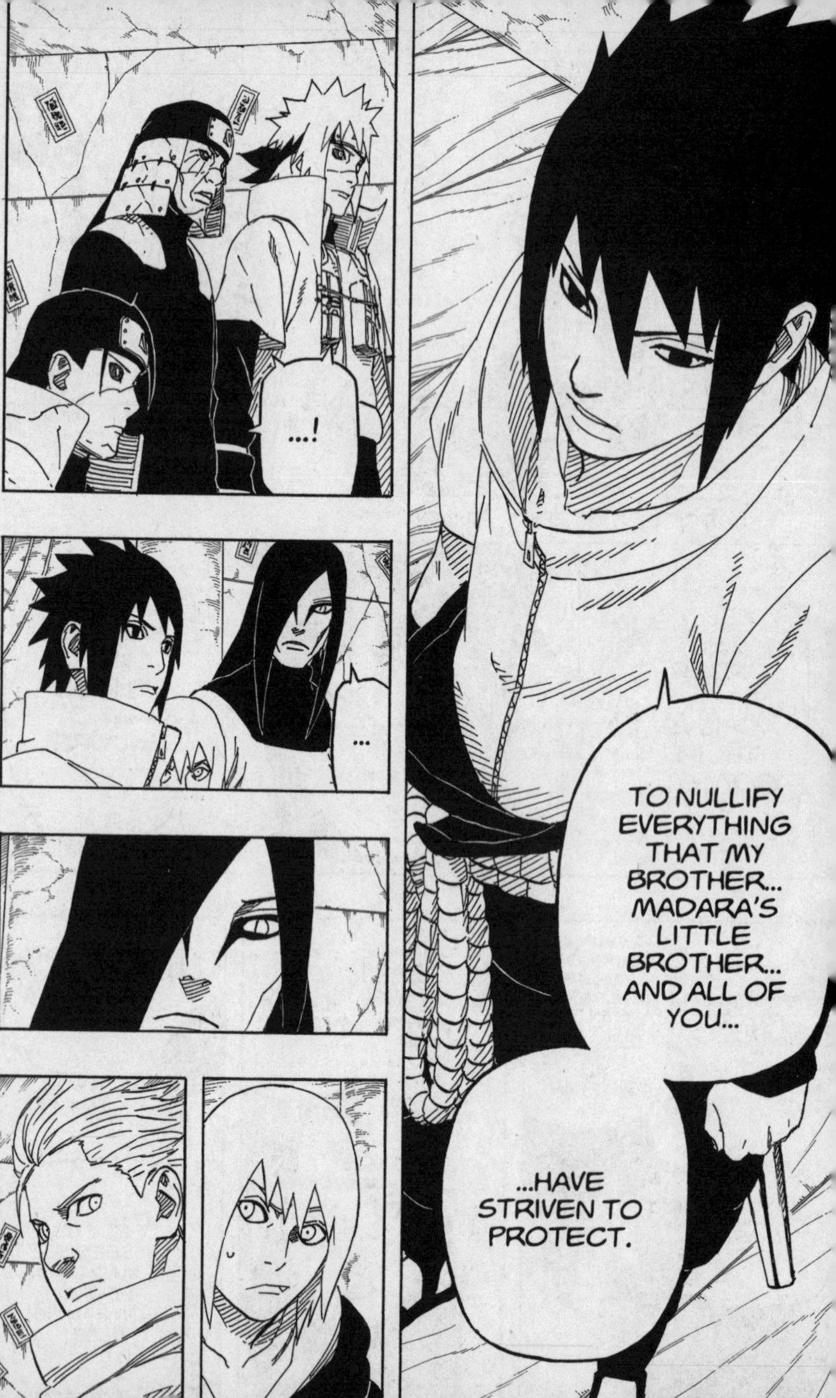
TO NULLIFY EVERYTHING THAT MY BROTHER... MADARA'S LITTLE BROTHER... AND ALL OF YOU...
...HAVE STRIVEN TO PROTECT.
...!
...

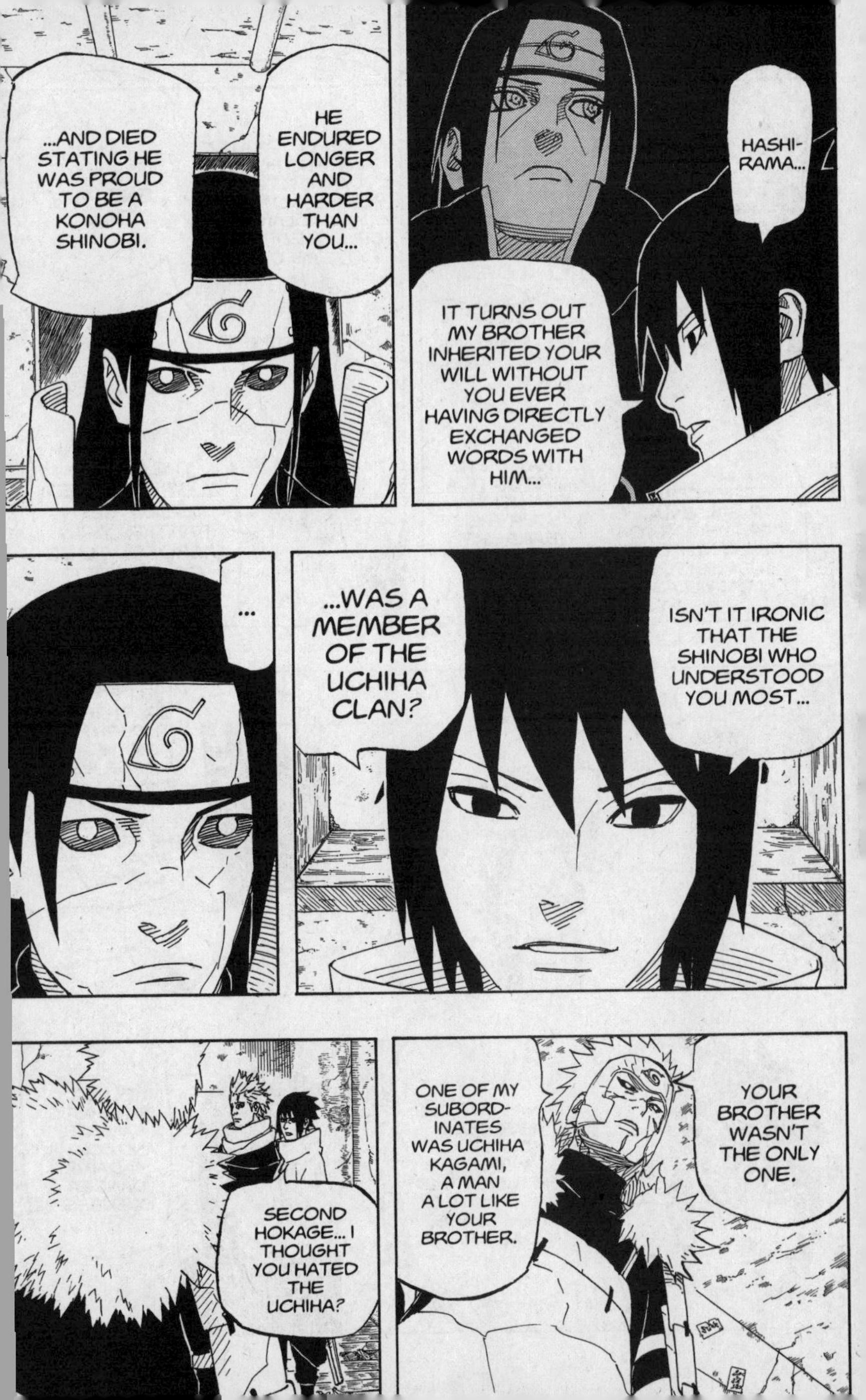
HASHI-RAMA...
IT TURNS OUT MY BROTHER INHERITED YOUR WILL WITHOUT YOU EVER HAVING DIRECTLY EXCHANGED WORDS WITH HIM...
HE ENDURED LONGER AND HARDER THAN YOU...
...AND DIED STATING HE WAS PROUD TO BE A KONOHA SHINOBI.
ISN'T IT IRONIC THAT THE SHINOBI WHO UNDERSTOOD YOU MOST...
...WAS A MEMBER OF THE UCHIHA CLAN?
...
YOUR BROTHER WASN'T THE ONLY ONE.
ONE OF MY SUBORD-INATES WAS UCHIHA KAGAMI, A MAN A LOT LIKE YOUR BROTHER.
SECOND HOKAGE... I THOUGHT YOU HATED THE UCHIHA?

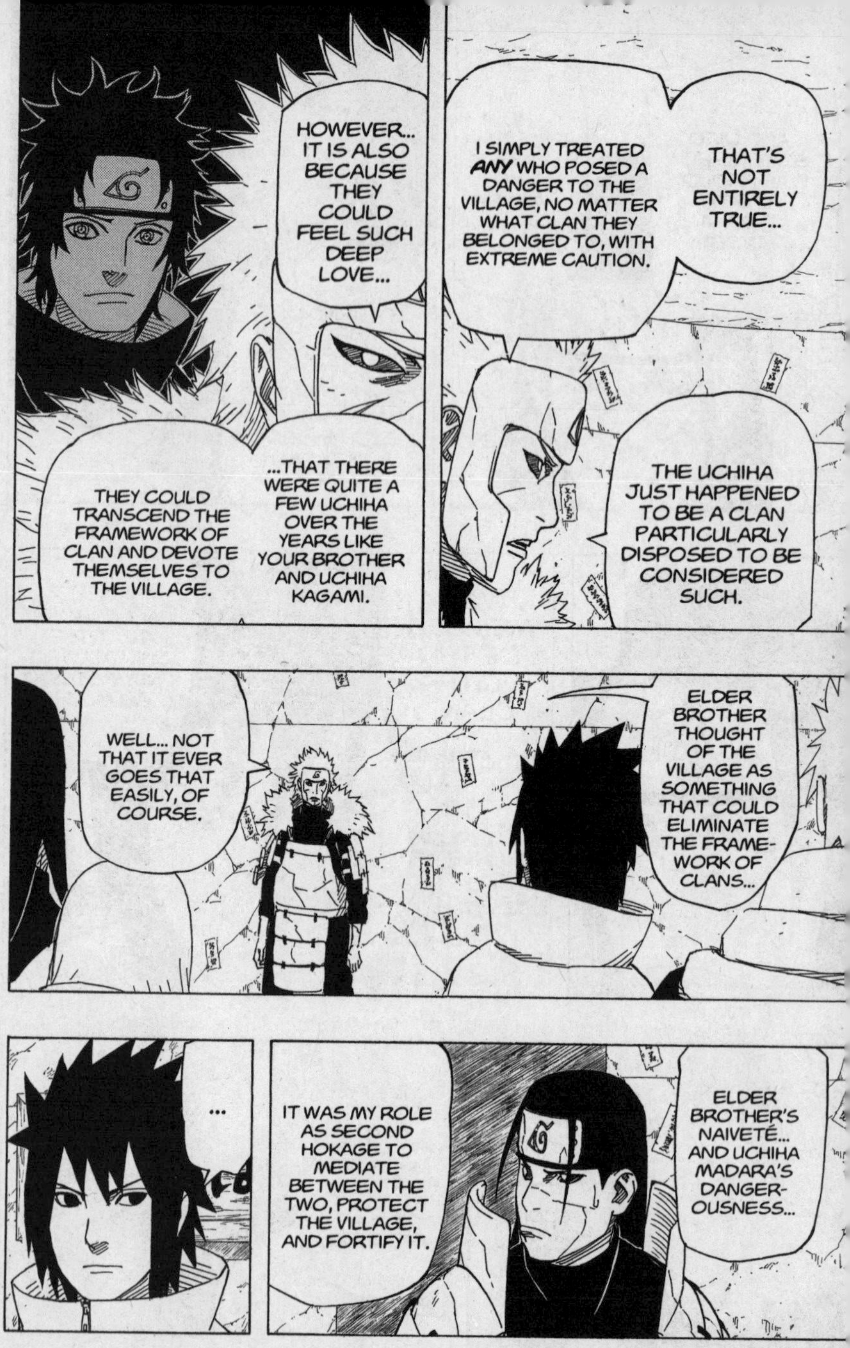
THAT'S NOT ENTIRELY TRUE...
I SIMPLY TREATED ANY WHO POSED A DANGER TO THE VILLAGE, NO MATTER WHAT CLAN THEY BELONGED TO, WITH EXTREME CAUTION.
THE UCHIHA JUST HAPPENED TO BE A CLAN PARTICULARLY DISPOSED TO BE CONSIDERED SUCH.
HOWEVER... IT IS ALSO BECAUSE THEY COULD FEEL SUCH DEEP LOVE...
...THAT THERE WERE QUITE A FEW UCHIHA OVER THE YEARS LIKE YOUR BROTHER AND UCHIHA KAGAMI.
THEY COULD TRANSCEND THE FRAMEWORK OF CLAN AND DEVOTE THEMSELVES TO THE VILLAGE.
ELDER BROTHER THOUGHT OF THE VILLAGE AS SOMETHING THAT COULD ELIMINATE THE FRAMEWORK OF CLANS...
WELL... NOT THAT IT EVER GOES THAT EASILY, OF COURSE.
ELDER BROTHER'S NAIVETÉ... AND UCHIHA MADARA'S DANGEROUSNESS...
IT WAS MY ROLE AS SECOND HOKAGE TO MEDIATE BETWEEN THE TWO, PROTECT THE VILLAGE, AND FORTIFY IT.
...

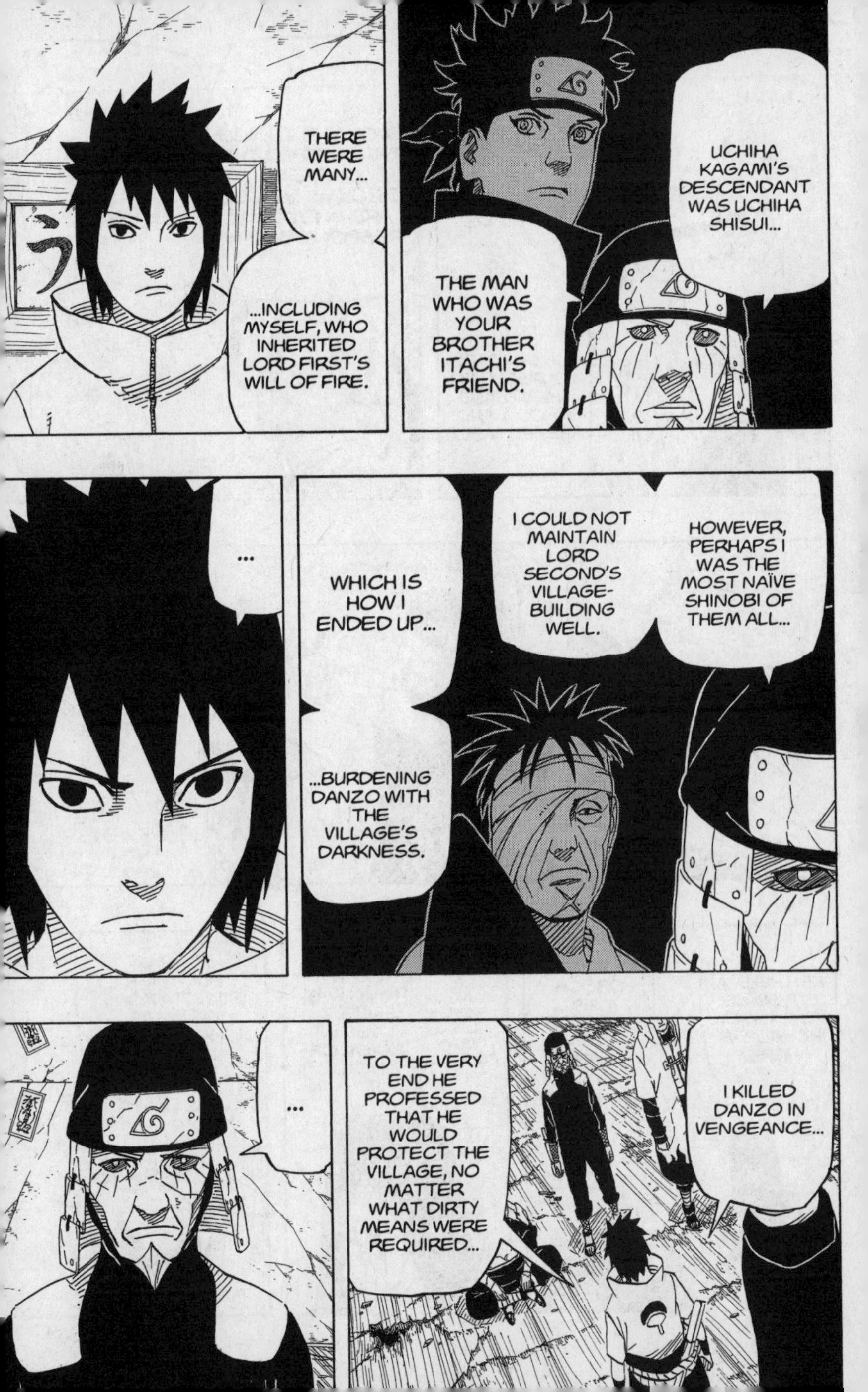
UCHIHA KAGAMI'S DESCENDANT WAS UCHIHA SHISUI...
THE MAN WHO WAS YOUR BROTHER ITACHI'S FRIEND.
THERE WERE MANY...
...INCLUDING MYSELF, WHO INHERITED LORD FIRST'S WILL OF FIRE.
HOWEVER, PERHAPS I WAS THE MOST NAÏVE SHINOBI OF THEM ALL...
I COULD NOT MAINTAIN LORD SECOND'S VILLAGE-BUILDING WELL.
WHICH IS HOW I ENDED UP...
...BURDENING DANZO WITH THE VILLAGE'S DARKNESS.
...
I KILLED DANZO IN VENGEANCE...
TO THE VERY END HE PROFESSED THAT HE WOULD PROTECT THE VILLAGE, NO MATTER WHAT DIRTY MEANS WERE REQUIRED...
...

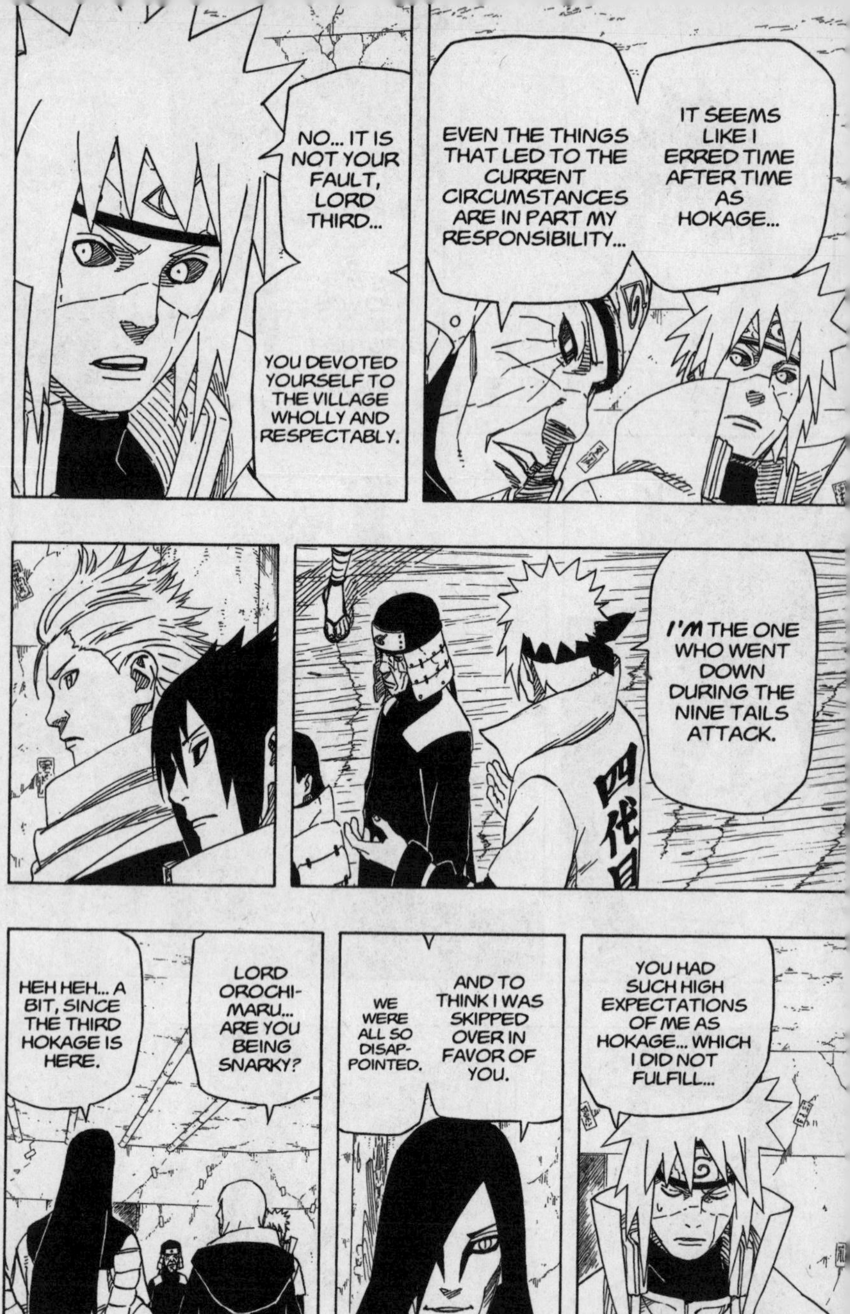
IT SEEMS LIKE I ERRED TIME AFTER TIME AS HOKAGE...
EVEN THE THINGS THAT LED TO THE CURRENT CIRCUMSTANCES ARE IN PART MY RESPONSIBILITY...
NO... IT IS NOT YOUR FAULT, LORD THIRD...
YOU DEVOTED YOURSELF TO THE VILLAGE WHOLLY AND RESPECTABLY.
I'M THE ONE WHO WENT DOWN DURING THE NINE TAILS ATTACK.
四代目
YOU HAD SUCH HIGH EXPECTATIONS OF ME AS HOKAGE... WHICH I DID NOT FULFILL...
AND TO THINK I WAS SKIPPED OVER IN FAVOR OF YOU.
WE WERE ALL SO DISAPPOINTED.
LORD OROCHIMARU... ARE YOU BEING SNARKY?
HEH HEH... A BIT, SINCE THE THIRD HOKAGE IS HERE.

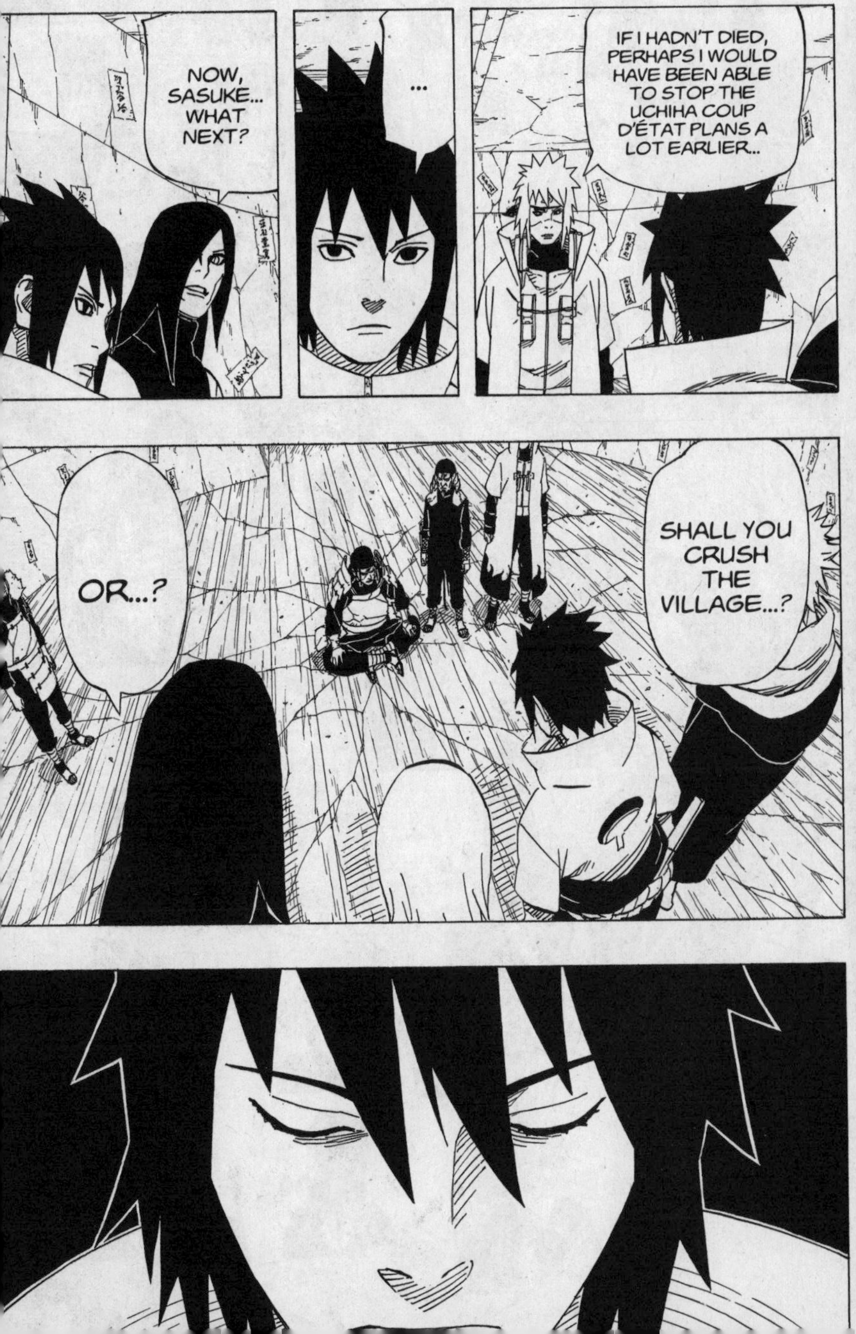
IF I HADN'T DIED, PERHAPS I WOULD HAVE BEEN ABLE TO STOP THE UCHIHA COUP D'ÉTAT PLANS A LOT EARLIER...
...
NOW, SASUKE... WHAT NEXT?
SHALL YOU CRUSH THE VILLAGE...?
OR...?

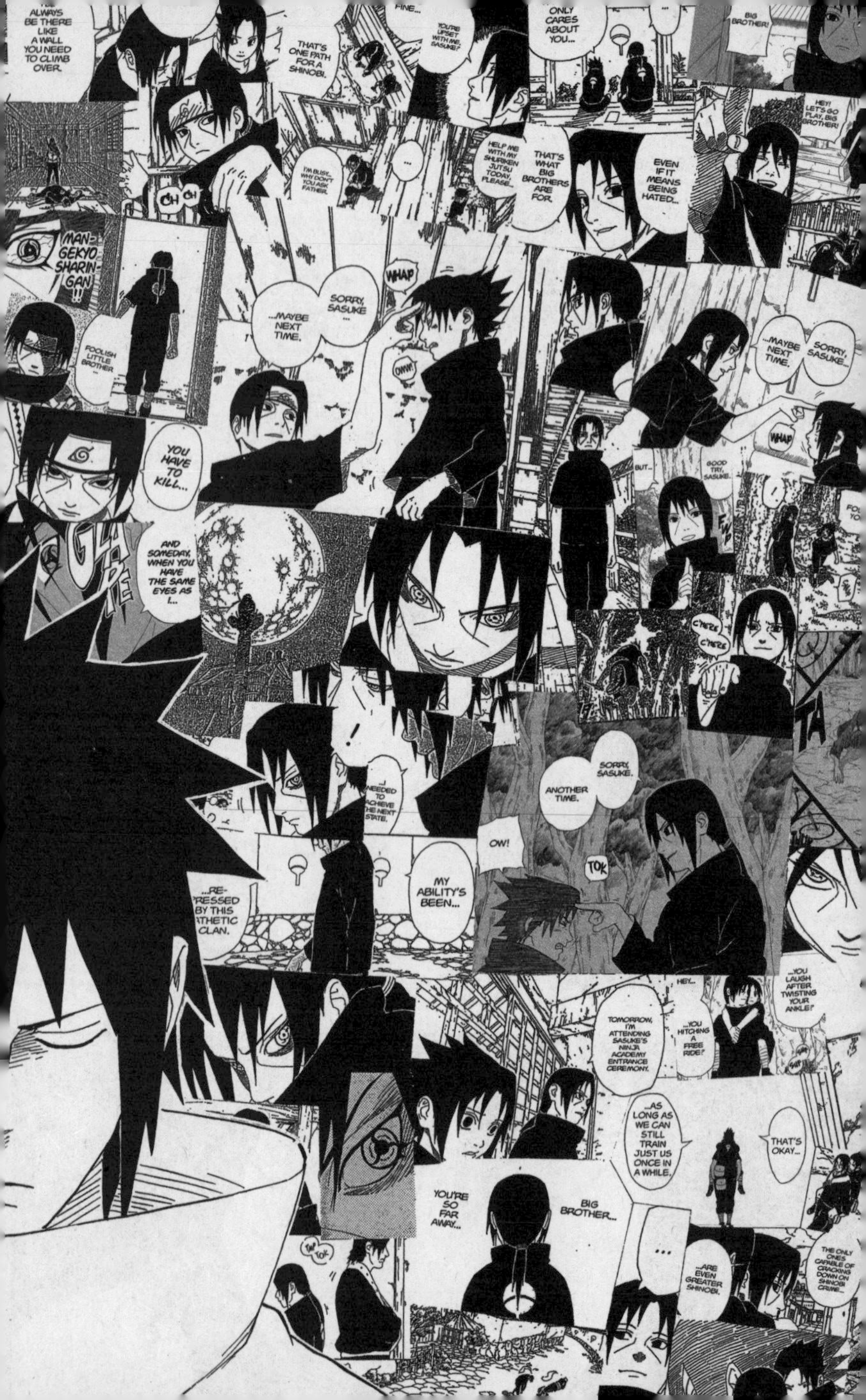
BIG BROTHER!
ONLY CARES ABOUT YOU...
FINE...
YOU'RE UPSET WITH ME, SASUKE?
THAT'S ONE PATH FOR A SHINOBI.
ALWAYS BE THERE LIKE A WALL YOU NEED TO CLIMB OVER.
HEY! LET'S GO PLAY, BIG BROTHER!
EVEN IF IT MEANS BEING HATED...
THAT'S WHAT BIG BROTHERS ARE FOR.
HELP ME WITH MY SHURIKEN JUTSU TODAY, PLEASE...
...
I'M BUSY... WHY DON'T YOU ASK FATHER.
CH CH
SORRY, SASUKE...
...MAYBE NEXT TIME.
WHAP
SORRY, SASUKE ...
...MAYBE NEXT TIME.
OWW!
MAN-GEKYO SHARIN-GAN!!
FOOLISH LITTLE BROTHER ...
WHAP
GOOD TRY, SASUKE.
BUT...
!
FWP
YOU HAVE TO KILL...
AND SOMEDAY, WHEN YOU HAVE THE SAME EYES AS I...
GLARE
C'MERE C'MERE
TA
!
...I NEEDED TO ACHIEVE HE NEXT STATE.
SORRY, SASUKE.
ANOTHER TIME.
OW!
TOK
MY ABILITY'S BEEN...
...RE-PRESSED BY THIS ATHETIC CLAN.
...YOU LAUGH AFTER TWISTING YOUR ANKLE?
HEY...
...YOU HITCHING A FREE RIDE?
TOMORROW, I'M ATTENDING SASUKE'S NINJA ACADEMY ENTRANCE CEREMONY.
THAT'S OKAY...
...AS LONG AS WE CAN STILL TRAIN JUST US ONCE IN A WHILE.
BIG BROTHER...
YOU'RE SO FAR AWAY...
THE ONLY ONES CAPABLE OF CRACKING DOWN ON SHINOBI CRIME...
...ARE EVEN GREATER SHINOBI.
...

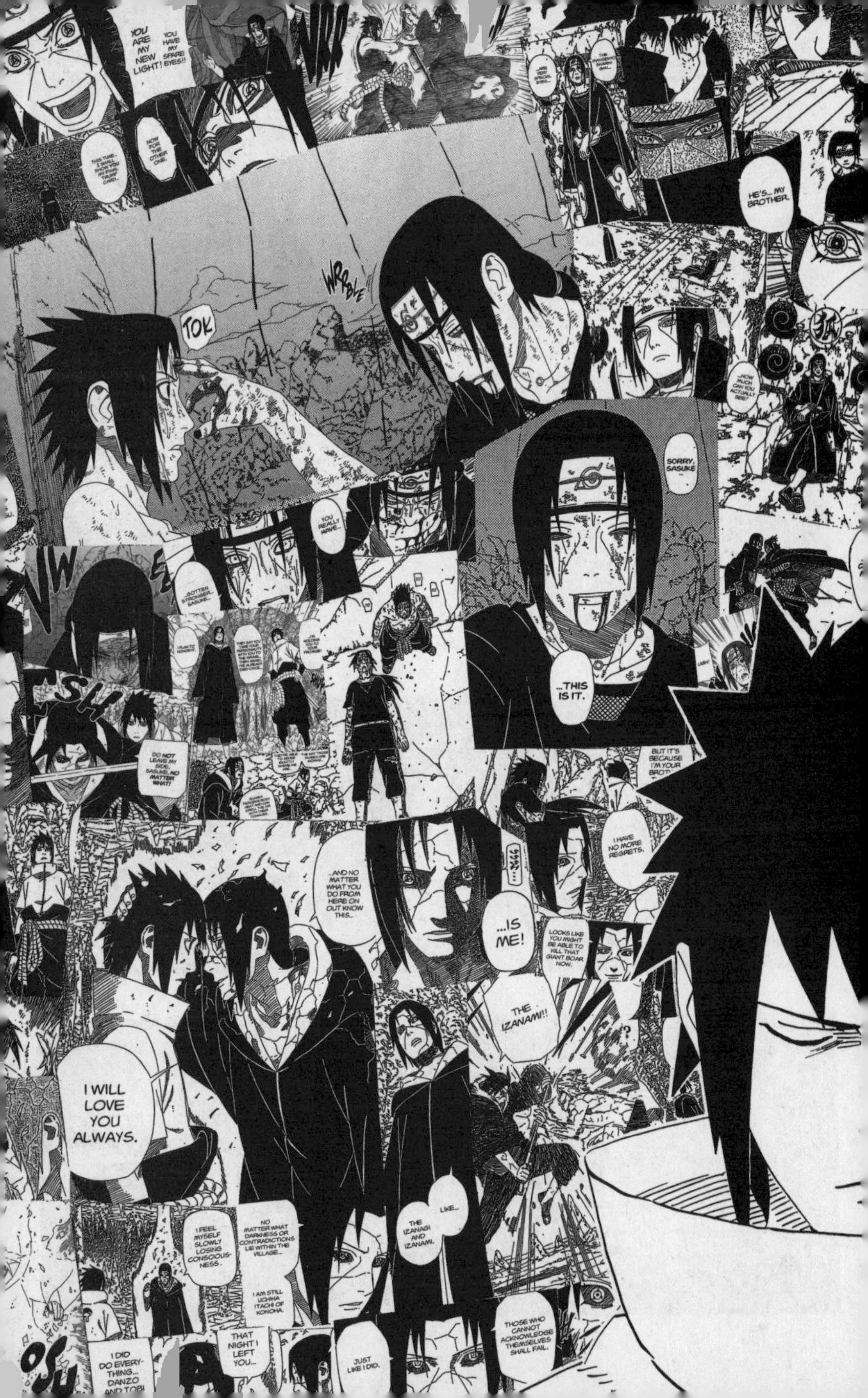

YOU HAVE MY SPARE EYES!!
YOU ARE MY NEW LIGHT!
NOW FOR THE OTHER ONE.
HE'S... MY BROTHER.
TOK
...HOW MUCH CAN YOU ACTUALLY SEE?
SORRY, SASUKE...
YOU REALLY HAVE...
...GOTTEN STRONGER, SASUKE...
...THIS IS IT.
DO NOT LEAVE MY SIDE, SASUKE, NO MATTER WHAT!
BUT IT'S BECAUSE I'M YOUR BROT-
I HAVE NO MORE REGRETS.
...AND NO MATTER WHAT YOU DO FROM HERE ON OUT KNOW THIS...
...IS ME!
LOOKS LIKE YOU MIGHT BE ABLE TO KILL THAT GIANT BOAR NOW.
THE IZANAMI!!
I WILL LOVE YOU ALWAYS.
LIKE...
THE IZANAGI AND IZANAMI.
NO MATTER WHAT DARKNESS OR CONTRADICTIONS LIE WITHIN THE VILLAGE...
I AM STILL UCHIHA ITACHI OF KONOHA.
I FEEL MYSELF SLOWLY LOSING CONSCIOUS-NESS.
THOSE WHO CANNOT ACKNOWLEDGE THEMSELVES SHALL FAIL.
JUST LIKE I DID.
THAT NIGHT I LEFT YOU...
I DID DO EVERY-THING... DANZO AND TOBI

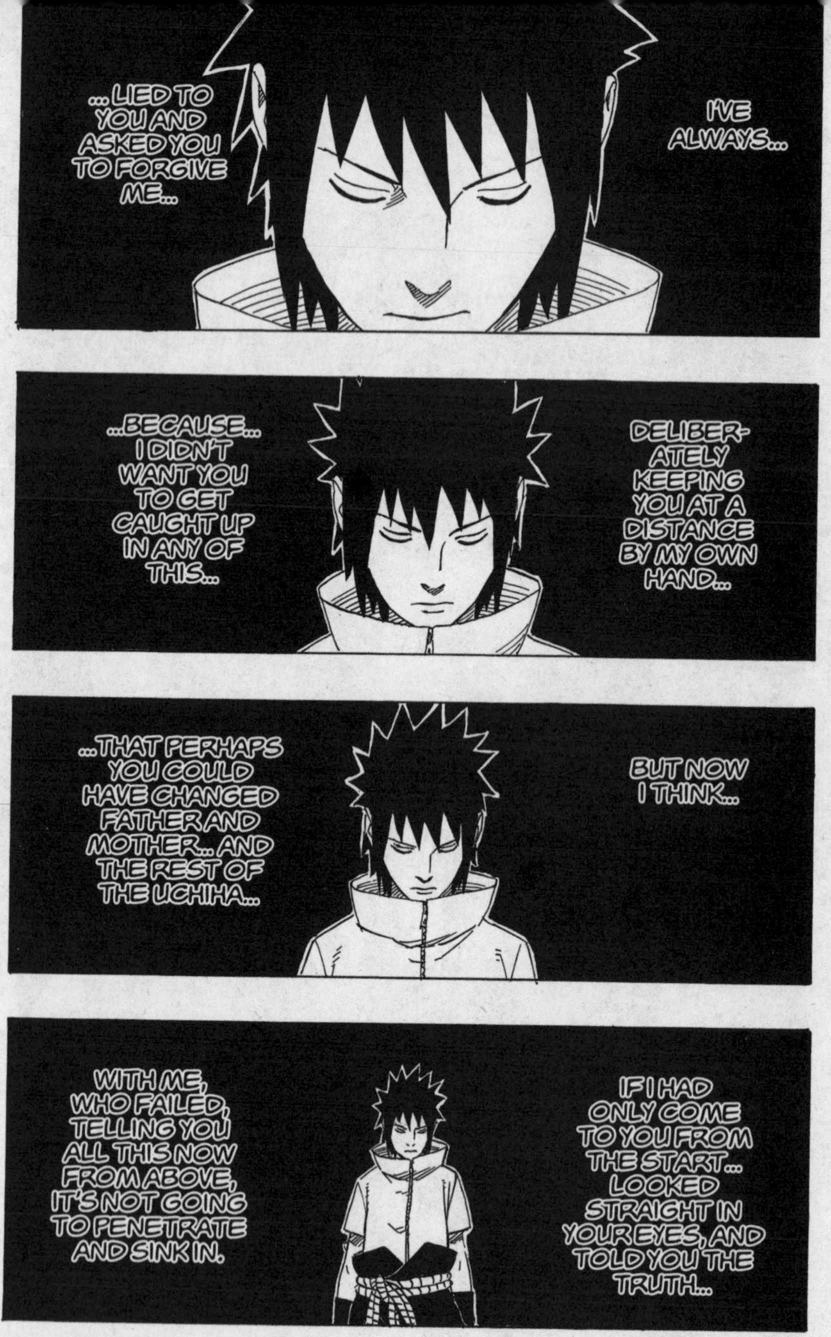
I'VE ALWAYS...
...LIED TO YOU AND ASKED YOU TO FORGIVE ME...
DELIBER-ATELY KEEPING YOU AT A DISTANCE BY MY OWN HAND...
...BECAUSE... I DIDN'T WANT YOU TO GET CAUGHT UP IN ANY OF THIS...
BUT NOW I THINK...
...THAT PERHAPS YOU COULD HAVE CHANGED FATHER AND MOTHER... AND THE REST OF THE UCHIHA...
IF I HAD ONLY COME TO YOU FROM THE START... LOOKED STRAIGHT IN YOUR EYES, AND TOLD YOU THE TRUTH...
WITH ME, WHO FAILED, TELLING YOU ALL THIS NOW FROM ABOVE, IT'S NOT GOING TO PENETRATE AND SINK IN.

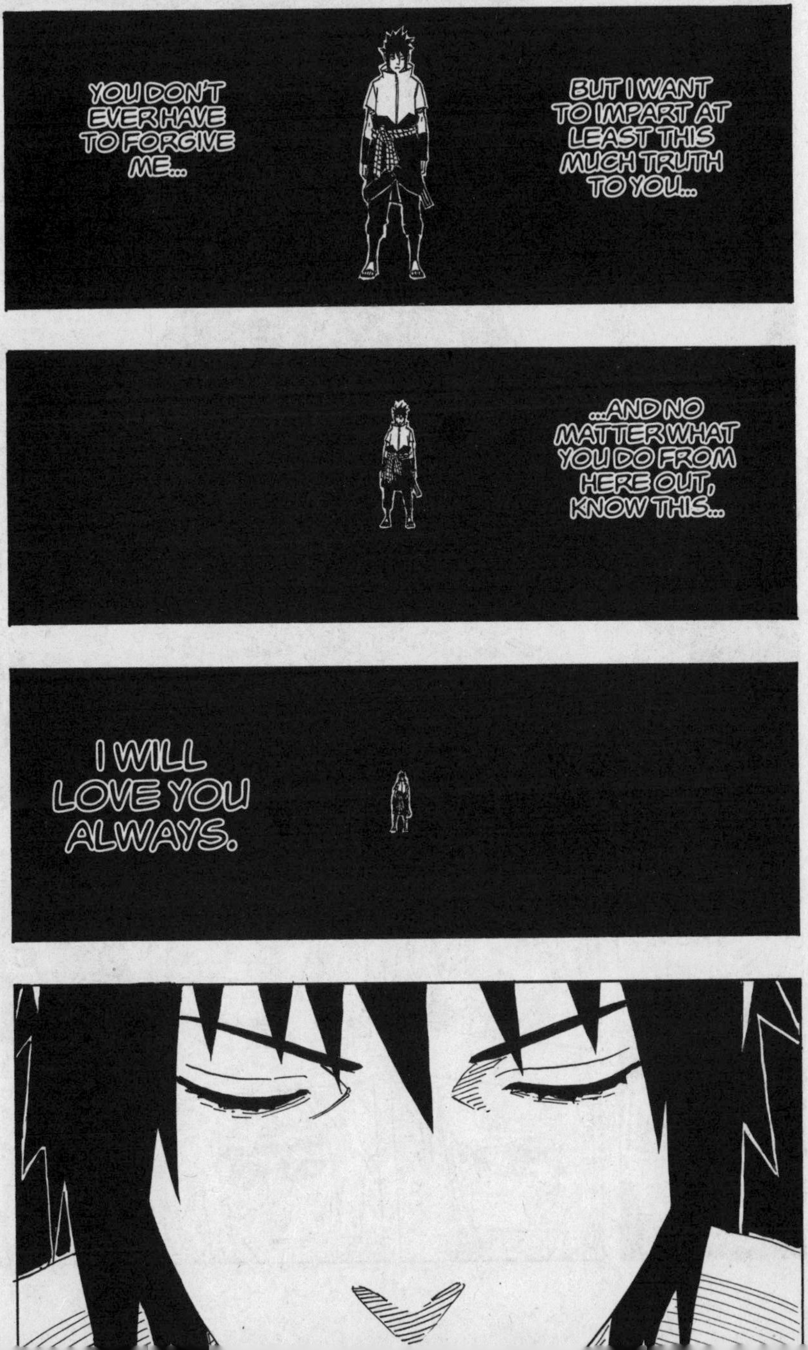
BUT I WANT TO IMPART AT LEAST THIS MUCH TRUTH TO YOU...
YOU DON'T EVER HAVE TO FORGIVE ME...
...AND NO MATTER WHAT YOU DO FROM HERE OUT, KNOW THIS...
I WILL LOVE YOU ALWAYS.

I WON'T LET THE VILLAGE AND ITACHI... BECOME NOTHING!

I'M GOING TO HEAD TO THE BATTLEFIELD.

IT'S DECIDED THEN!

370

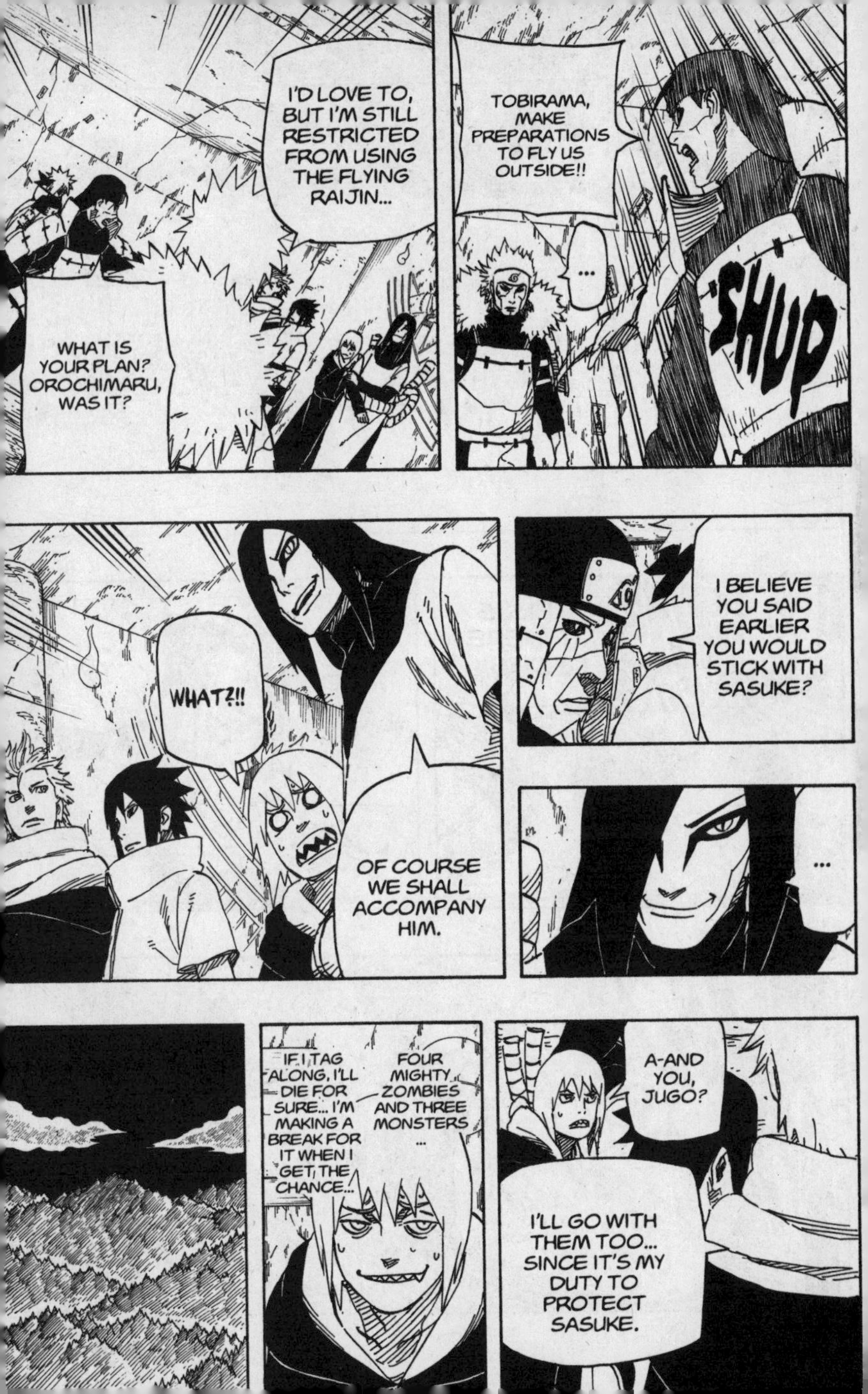
TOBIRAMA, MAKE PREPARATIONS TO FLY US OUTSIDE!!
...
SHUP
I'D LOVE TO, BUT I'M STILL RESTRICTED FROM USING THE FLYING RAIJIN...
WHAT IS YOUR PLAN? OROCHIMARU, WAS IT?
I BELIEVE YOU SAID EARLIER YOU WOULD STICK WITH SASUKE?
...
OF COURSE WE SHALL ACCOMPANY HIM.
WHAT?!!
A-AND YOU, JUGO?
I'LL GO WITH THEM TOO... SINCE IT'S MY DUTY TO PROTECT SASUKE.
FOUR MIGHTY ZOMBIES AND THREE MONSTERS...
IF I TAG ALONG, I'LL DIE FOR SURE... I'M MAKING A BREAK FOR IT WHEN I GET THE CHANCE...

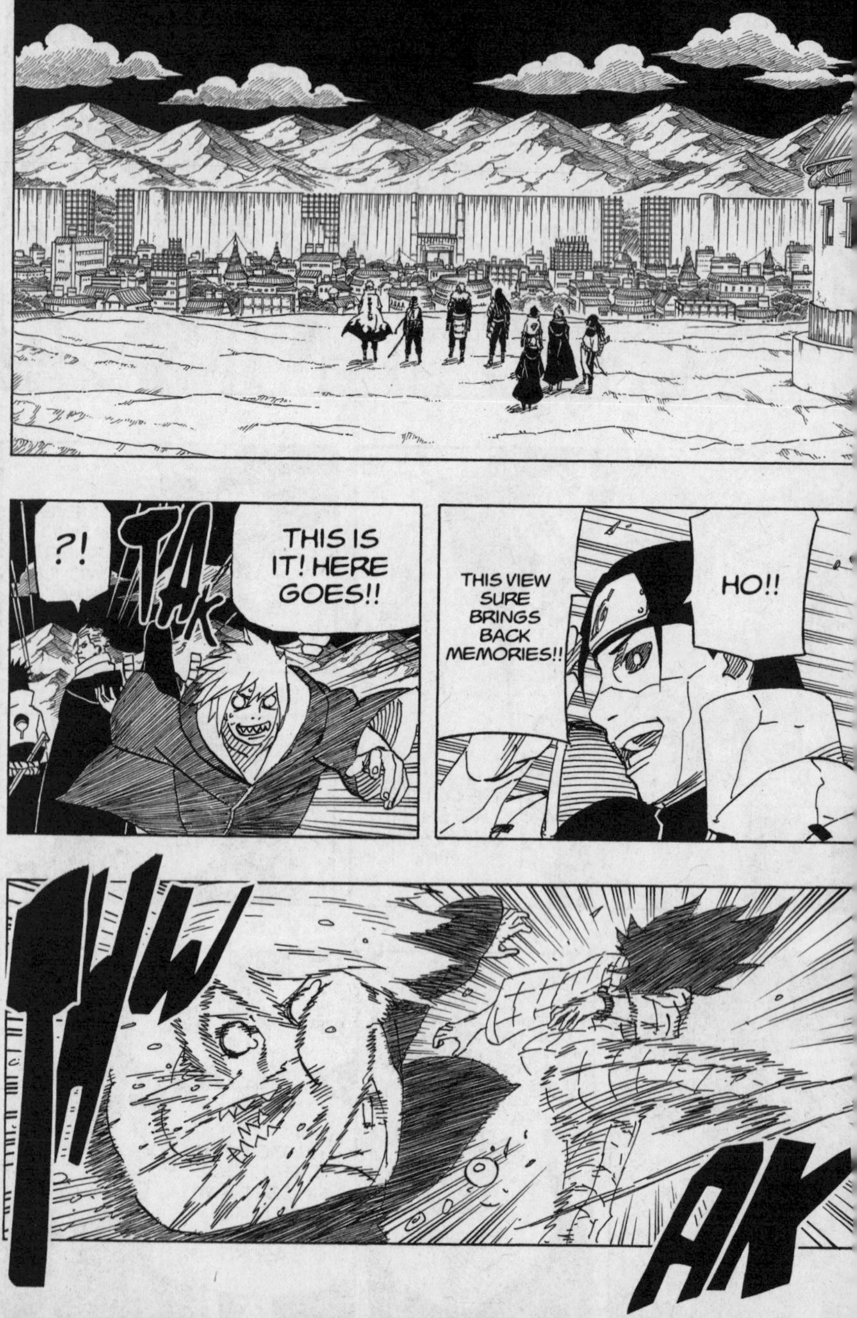
HO!!
THIS VIEW SURE BRINGS BACK MEMORIES!!
THIS IS IT! HERE GOES!!
TAK
?!
THWAK

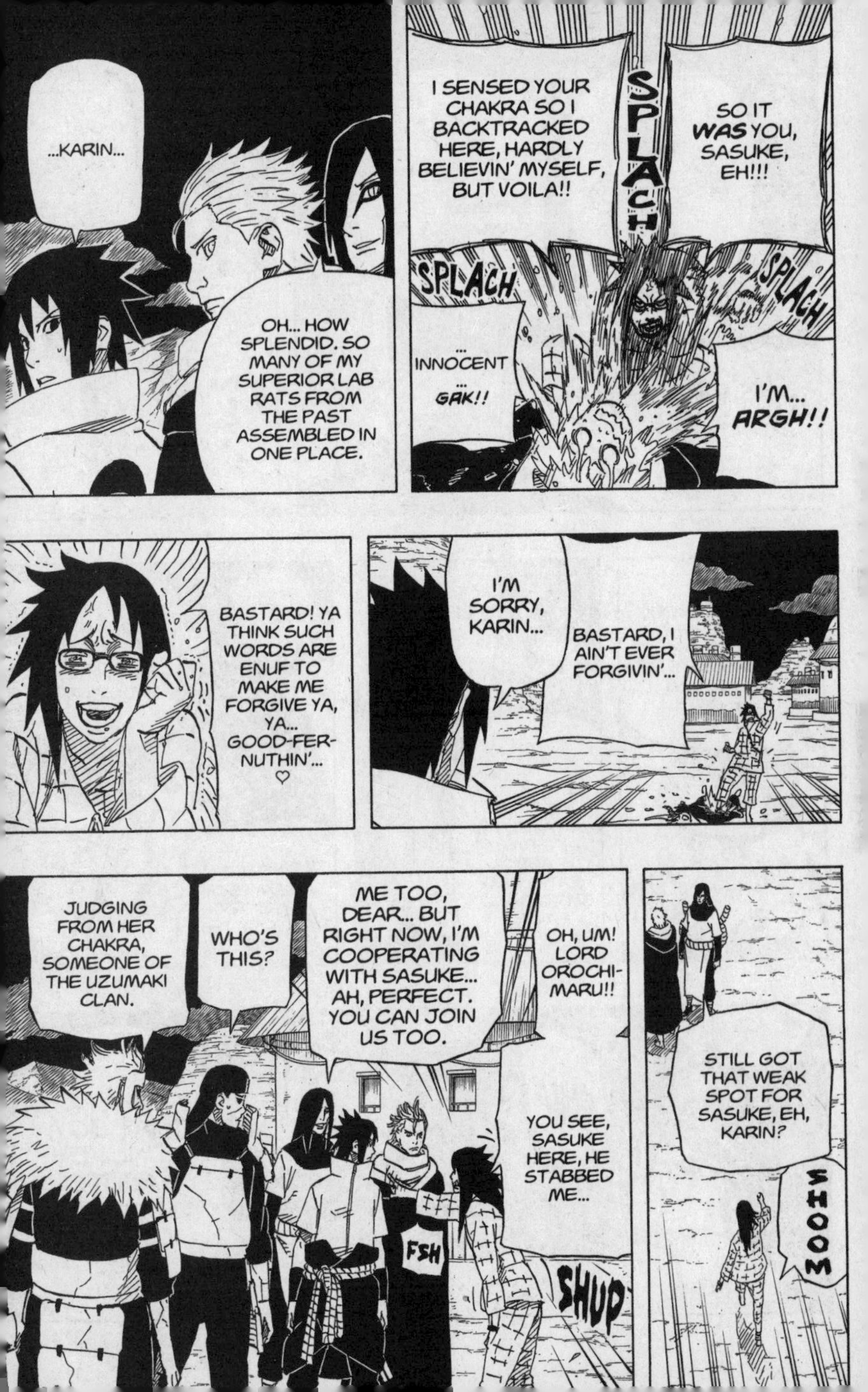
SO IT WAS YOU, SASUKE, EH!!!
I SENSED YOUR CHAKRA SO I BACKTRACKED HERE, HARDLY BELIEVIN' MYSELF, BUT VOILA!!
SPLACH
SPLACH
SPLACH
I'M... ARGH!!
... INNOCENT ... GAK!!
...KARIN...
OH... HOW SPLENDID. SO MANY OF MY SUPERIOR LAB RATS FROM THE PAST ASSEMBLED IN ONE PLACE.
I'M SORRY, KARIN...
BASTARD, I AIN'T EVER FORGIVIN'...
BASTARD! YA THINK SUCH WORDS ARE ENUF TO MAKE ME FORGIVE YA, YA... GOOD-FER-NUTHIN'... ♡
STILL GOT THAT WEAK SPOT FOR SASUKE, EH, KARIN?
SHOOM
OH, UM! LORD OROCHI-MARU!!
YOU SEE, SASUKE HERE, HE STABBED ME...
ME TOO, DEAR... BUT RIGHT NOW, I'M COOPERATING WITH SASUKE... AH, PERFECT. YOU CAN JOIN US TOO.
WHO'S THIS?
JUDGING FROM HER CHAKRA, SOMEONE OF THE UZUMAKI CLAN.
FSH
SHUP

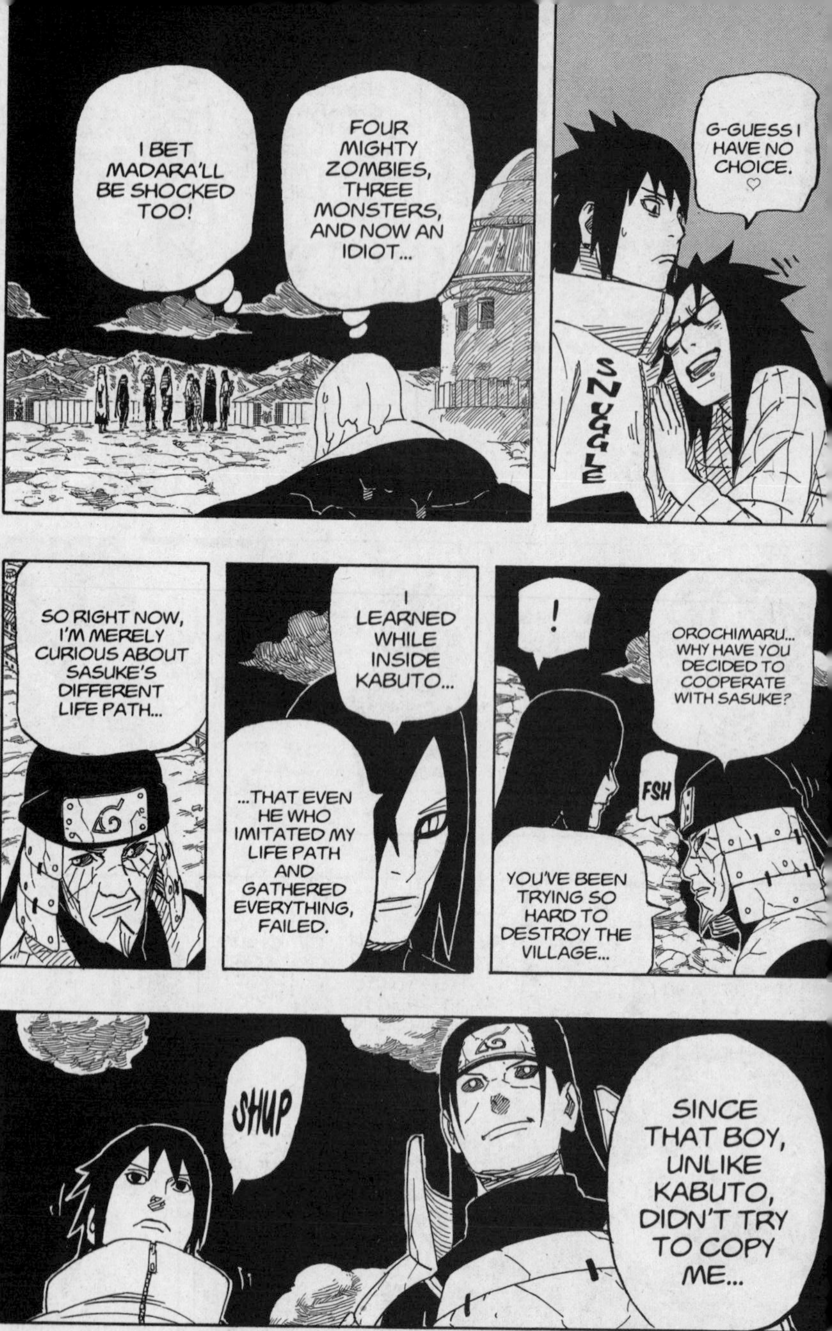
G-GUESS I HAVE NO CHOICE. ♡
SNUGGLE
FOUR MIGHTY ZOMBIES, THREE MONSTERS, AND NOW AN IDIOT...
I BET MADARA'LL BE SHOCKED TOO!
OROCHIMARU... WHY HAVE YOU DECIDED TO COOPERATE WITH SASUKE?
!
FSH
YOU'VE BEEN TRYING SO HARD TO DESTROY THE VILLAGE...
I LEARNED WHILE INSIDE KABUTO...
...THAT EVEN HE WHO IMITATED MY LIFE PATH AND GATHERED EVERYTHING, FAILED.
SO RIGHT NOW, I'M MERELY CURIOUS ABOUT SASUKE'S DIFFERENT LIFE PATH...
SINCE THAT BOY, UNLIKE KABUTO, DIDN'T TRY TO COPY ME...
SHUP

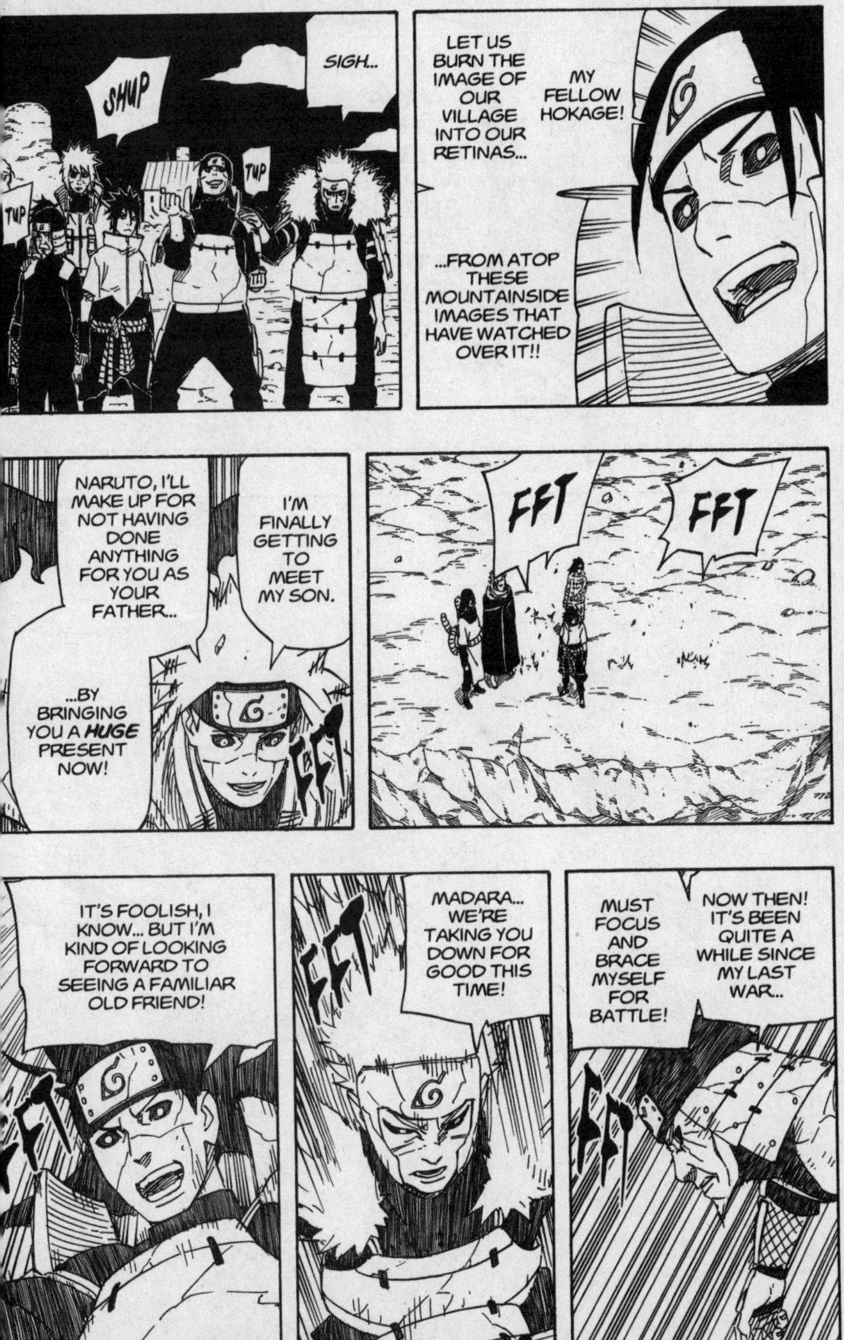
MY FELLOW HOKAGE!
LET US BURN THE IMAGE OF OUR VILLAGE INTO OUR RETINAS...
...FROM ATOP THESE MOUNTAINSIDE IMAGES THAT HAVE WATCHED OVER IT!!
SIGH...
SHUP
TUP
TUP
FFT
FFT
I'M FINALLY GETTING TO MEET MY SON.
NARUTO, I'LL MAKE UP FOR NOT HAVING DONE ANYTHING FOR YOU AS YOUR FATHER...
...BY BRINGING YOU A HUGE PRESENT NOW!
FFT
NOW THEN! IT'S BEEN QUITE A WHILE SINCE MY LAST WAR...
MUST FOCUS AND BRACE MYSELF FOR BATTLE!
FFT
MADARA... WE'RE TAKING YOU DOWN FOR GOOD THIS TIME!
FFT
IT'S FOOLISH, I KNOW... BUT I'M KIND OF LOOKING FORWARD TO SEEING A FAMILIAR OLD FRIEND!
FFT

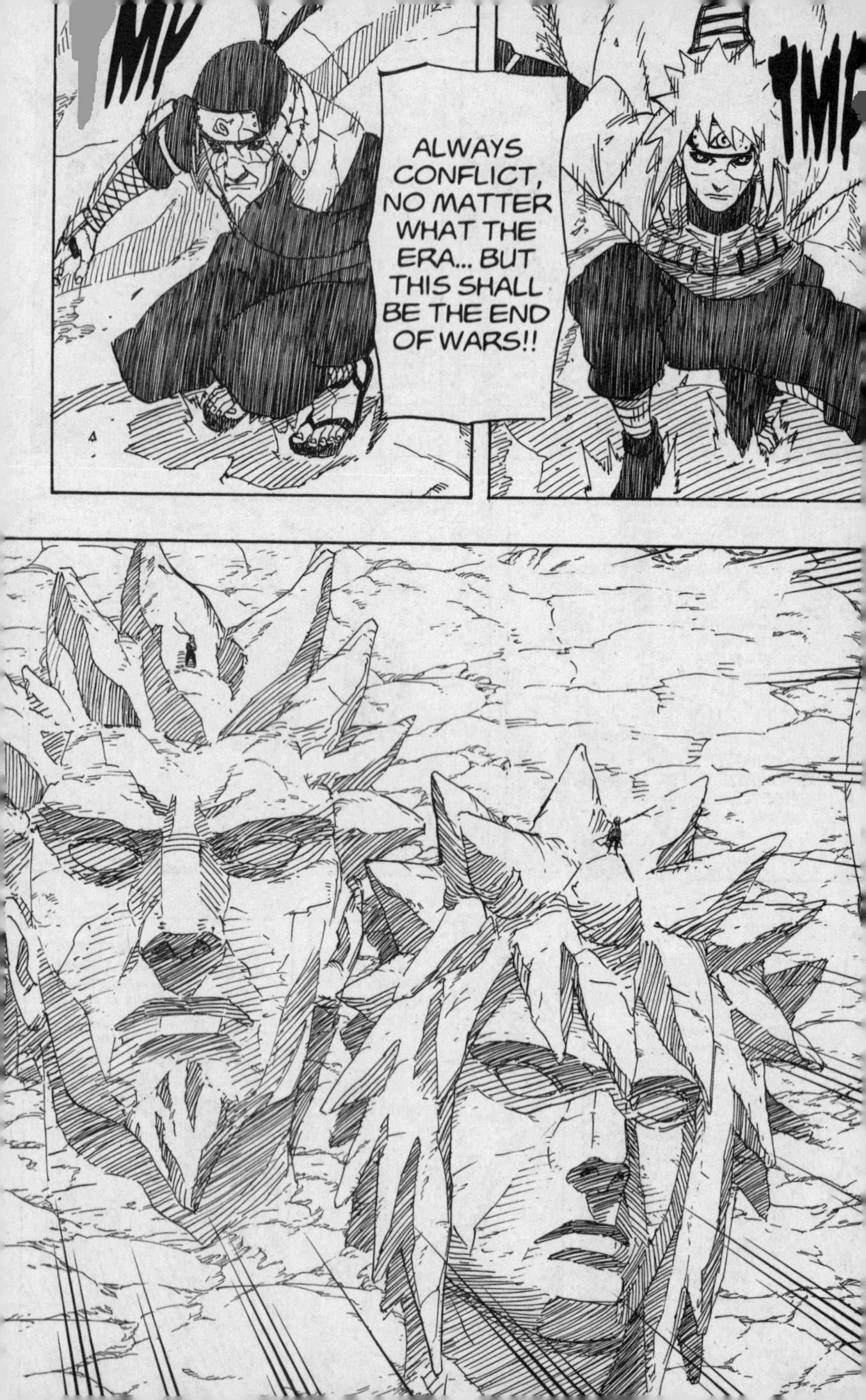
ALWAYS CONFLICT, NO MATTER WHAT THE ERA... BUT THIS SHALL BE THE END OF WARS!!

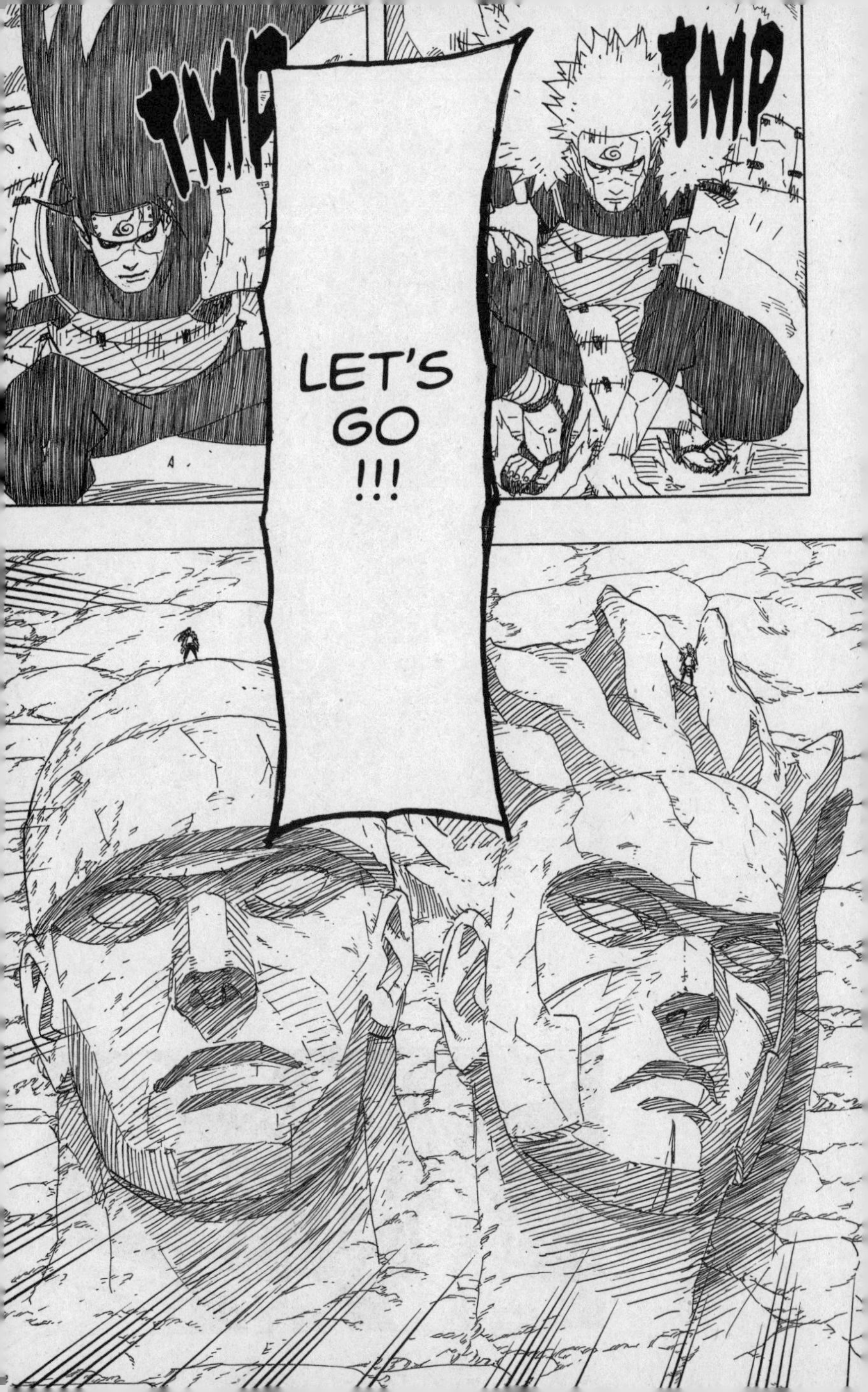
TMP
TMP
LET'S GO !!!

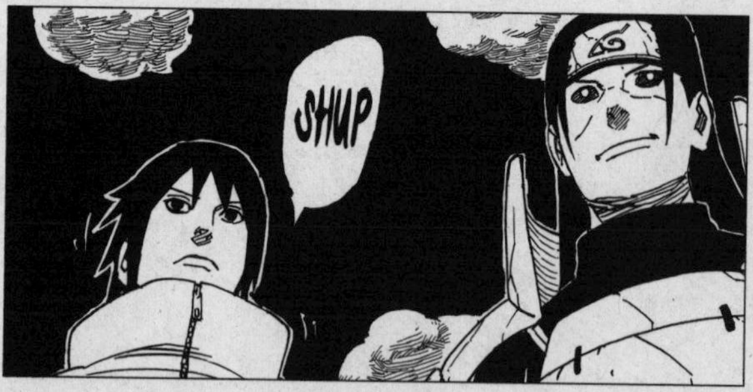
SHUP

V1~
~A LOT
HAPPENS~
~V66

岸本斉史

Naruto is really starting to enter its climax. It's gone on longer than I expected, but it's definitely inching closer to the finale. This volume's cover is an updated version of the chapter 4 title page illustration from volume 1. The image I thought up back then is finally coming true in this volume...

—Masashi Kishimoto, 2013

NARUTO

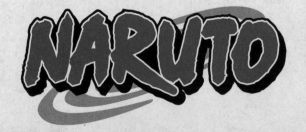

SHON[redacted]DITION

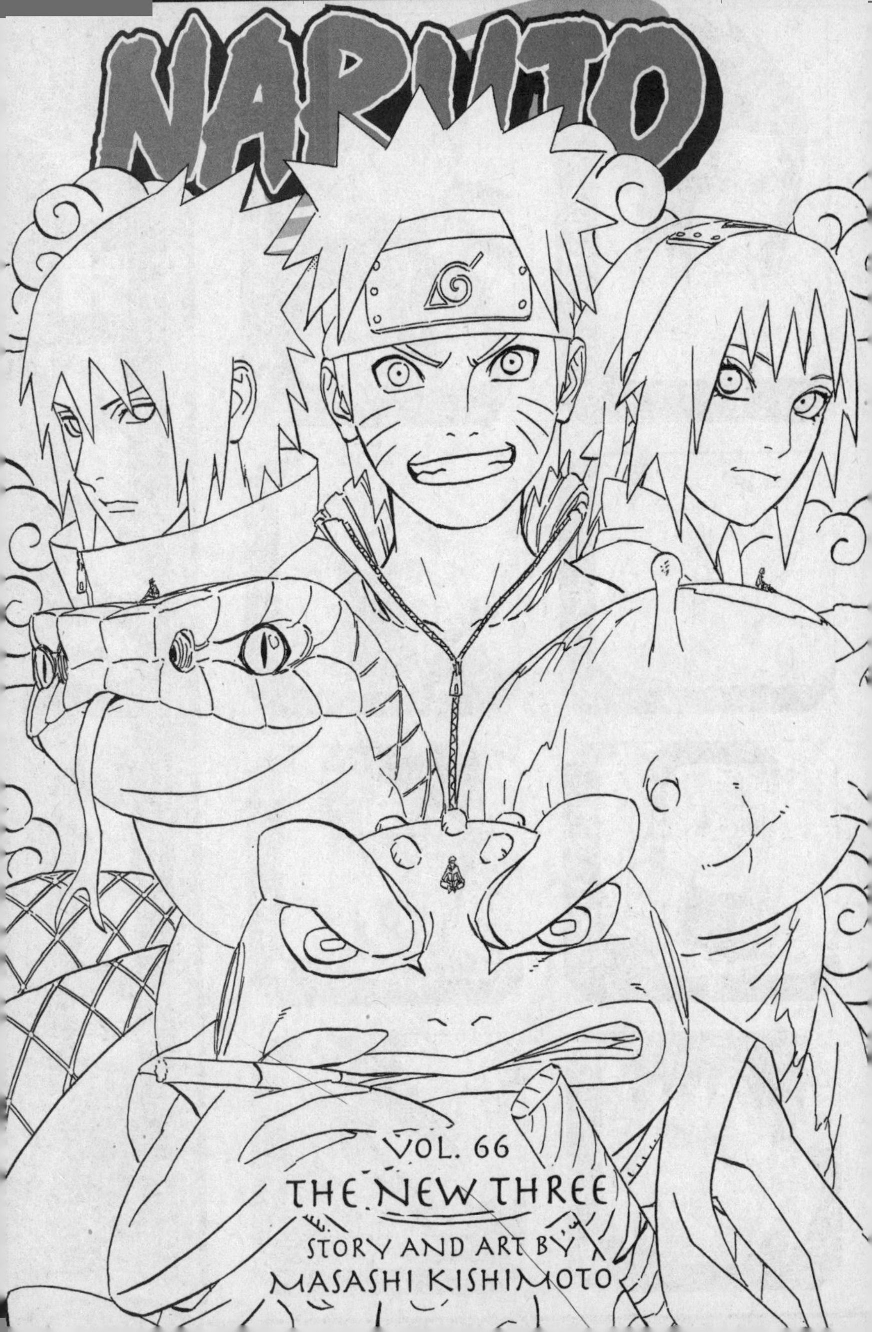
NARUTO
VOL. 66
THE NEW THREE
STORY AND ART BY
MASASHI KISHIMOTO

CHARACTERS

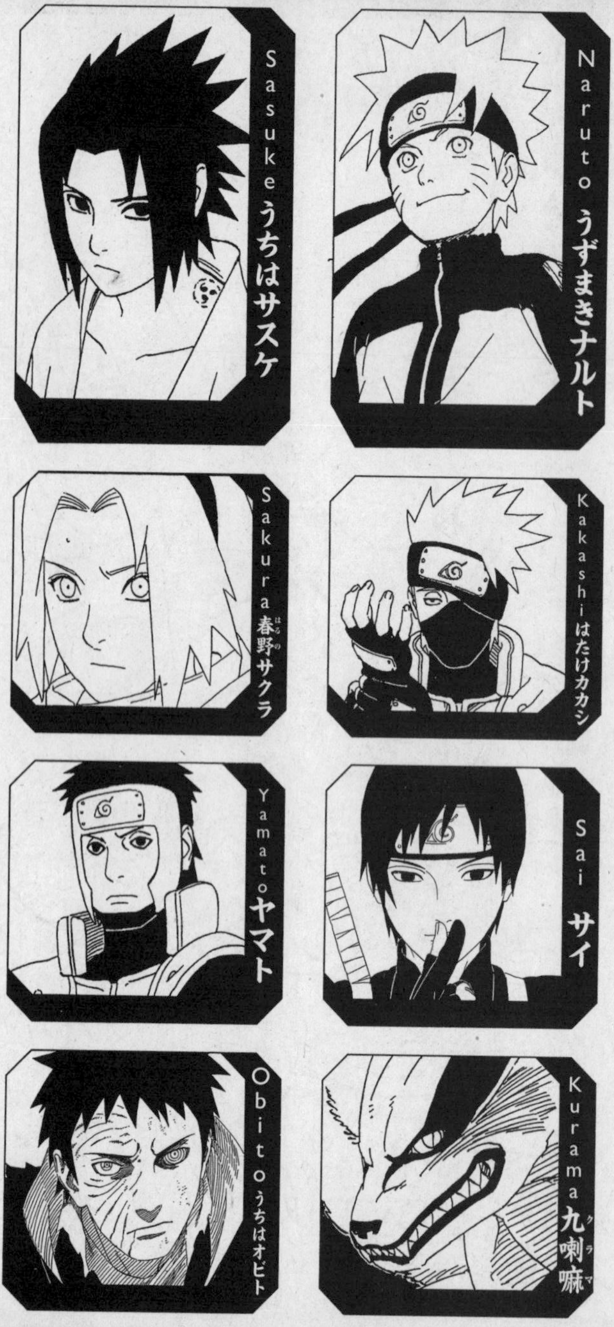
Naruto うずまきナルト
Sasuke うちはサスケ
Kakashi はたけカカシ
Sakura 春野サクラ
Sai サイ
Yamato ヤマト
Kurama 九喇嘛
Obito うちはオビト

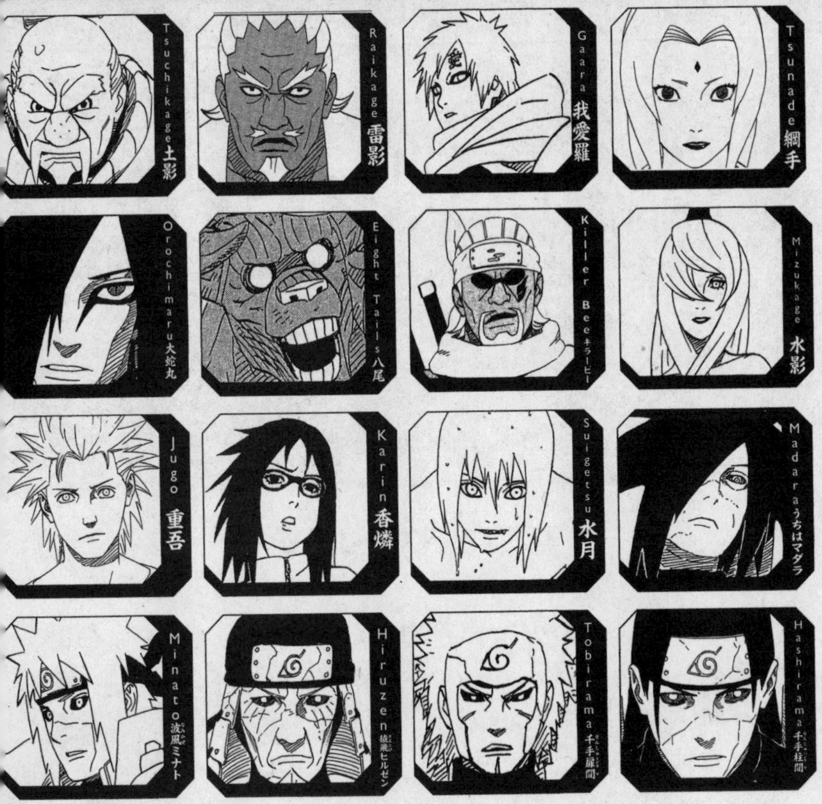

Tsunade 綱手
Gaara 我愛羅
Raikage 雷影
Tsuchikage 土影
Mizukage 水影
Killer Bee キラービー
Eight Tails 八尾
Orochimaru 大蛇丸
Madara うちはマダラ
Suigetsu 水月
Karin 香燐
Jugo 重吾
Hashirama 千手柱間
Tobirama 千手扉間
Hiruzen 猿飛ヒルゼン
Minato 波風ミナト

THE STORY SO FAR...

Naruto, the biggest troublemaker at the Ninja Academy in the Village of Konohagakure, finally becomes a ninja along with his classmates Sasuke and Sakura. They grow and mature through countless trials and battles. However, Sasuke, unable to give up his quest for vengeance, leaves Konohagakure to seek Orochimaru and his power…

Two years pass. Naruto grows up and engages in fierce battles against the Tailed Beast-targeting Akatsuki. And the Fourth Great Ninja War against the Akatsuki finally begins. Naruto and his companions face off against the reunited Obito and Madara in order to stop the resurrected Ten Tails! Meanwhile, Sasuke borrows the help of a revived Orochimaru to bring back the previous Hokage using Edotensei. After hearing the truth about the village and what shinobi are from Senju Hashirama, Sasuke adopts his brother's will and decides to head to the battlefield to protect his village!!

NARUTO

VOL. 66
THE NEW THREE

CONTENTS

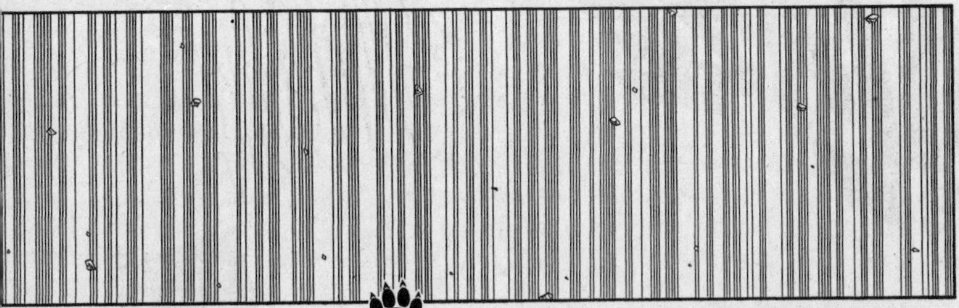

Number 628: Here and Now, and Hereafter

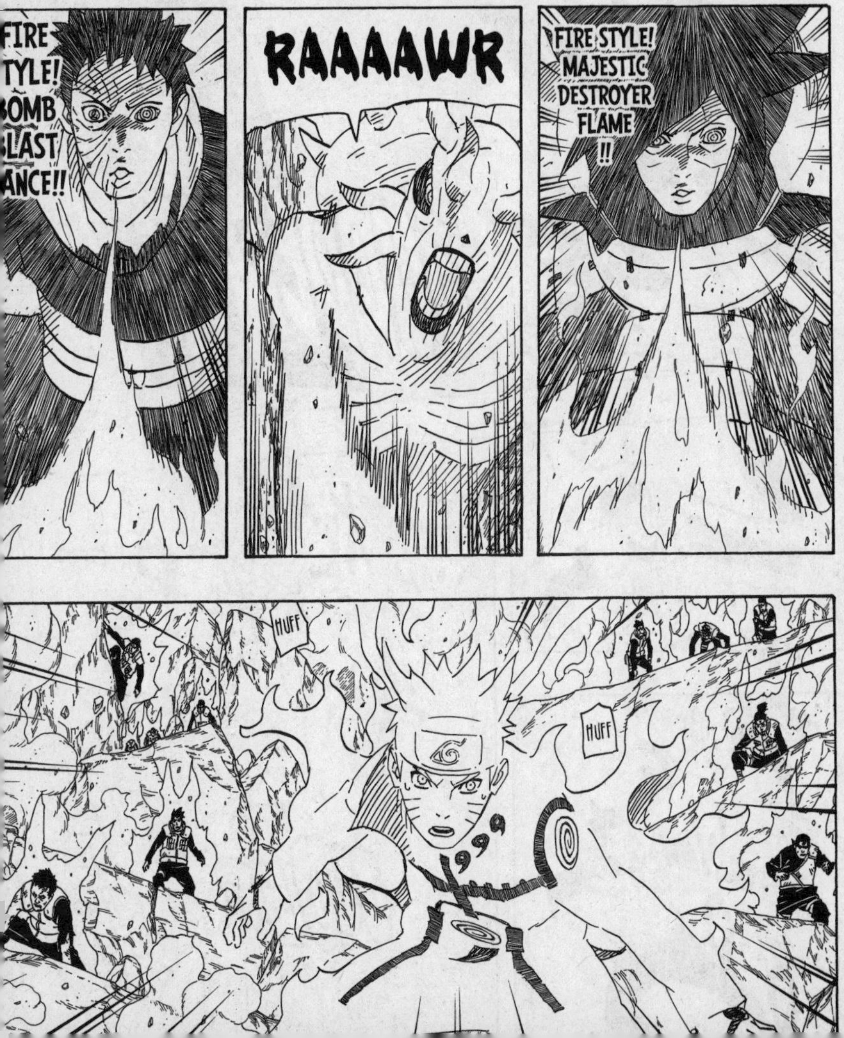
FIRE STYLE! MAJESTIC DESTROYER FLAME!!
RAAAAWR
FIRE TYLE! OMB LAST ANCE!!
HUFF
HUFF

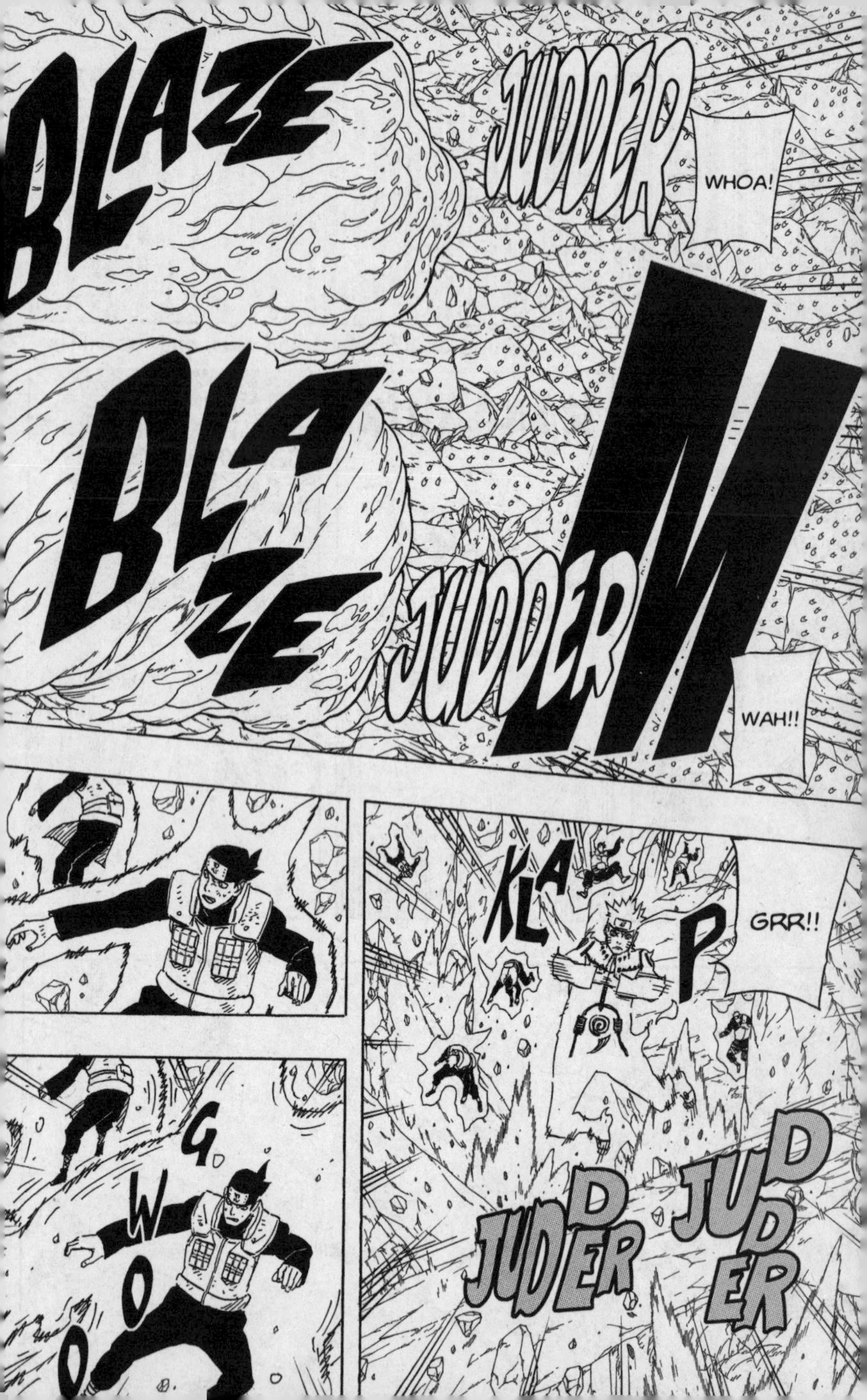
JUDDER
WHOA!
BLAZE
BLAZE
JUDDER
WAH!!
KLAP
GRR!!
JUDDER
JUDDER
GWOO

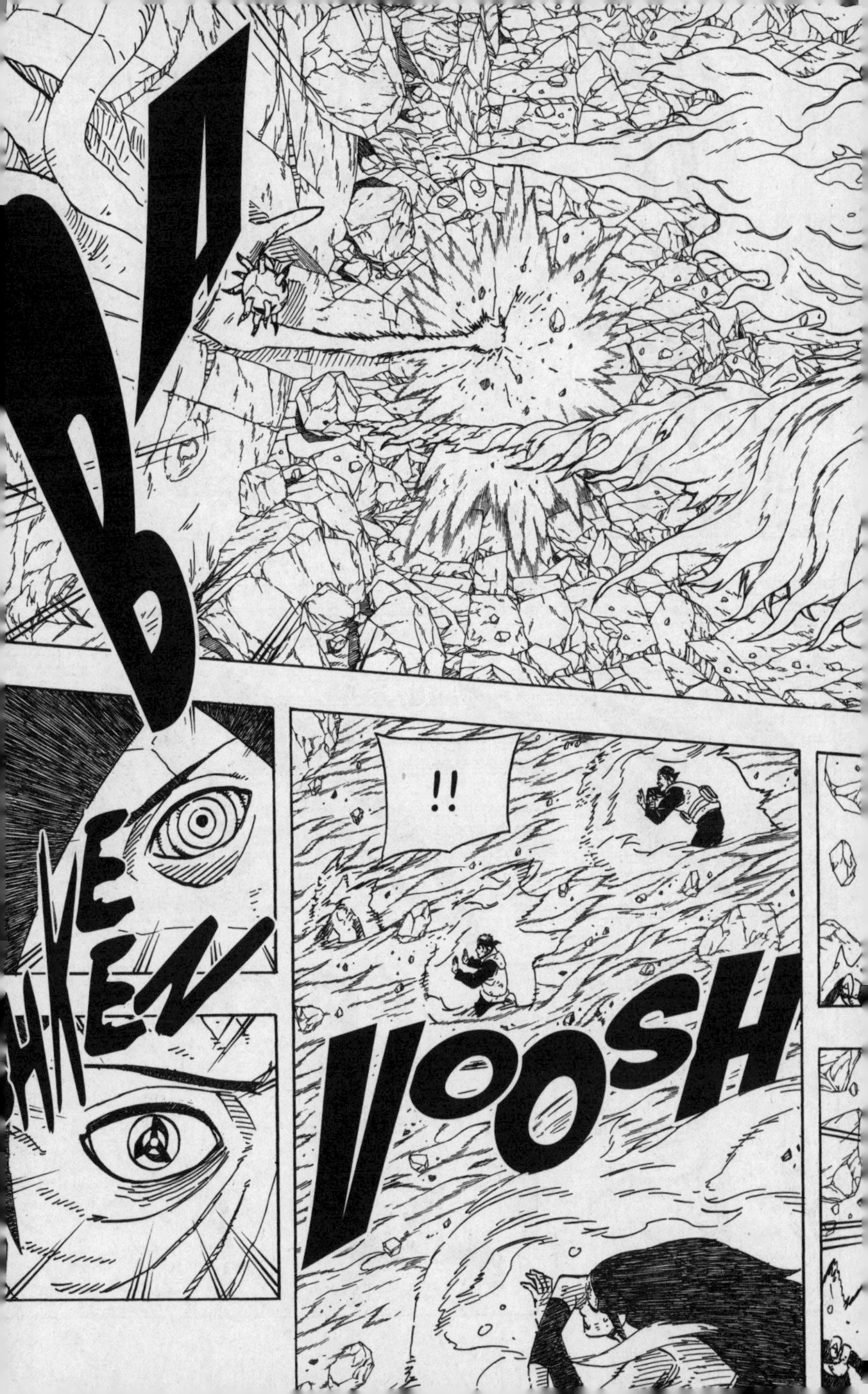
!!
WOOSH

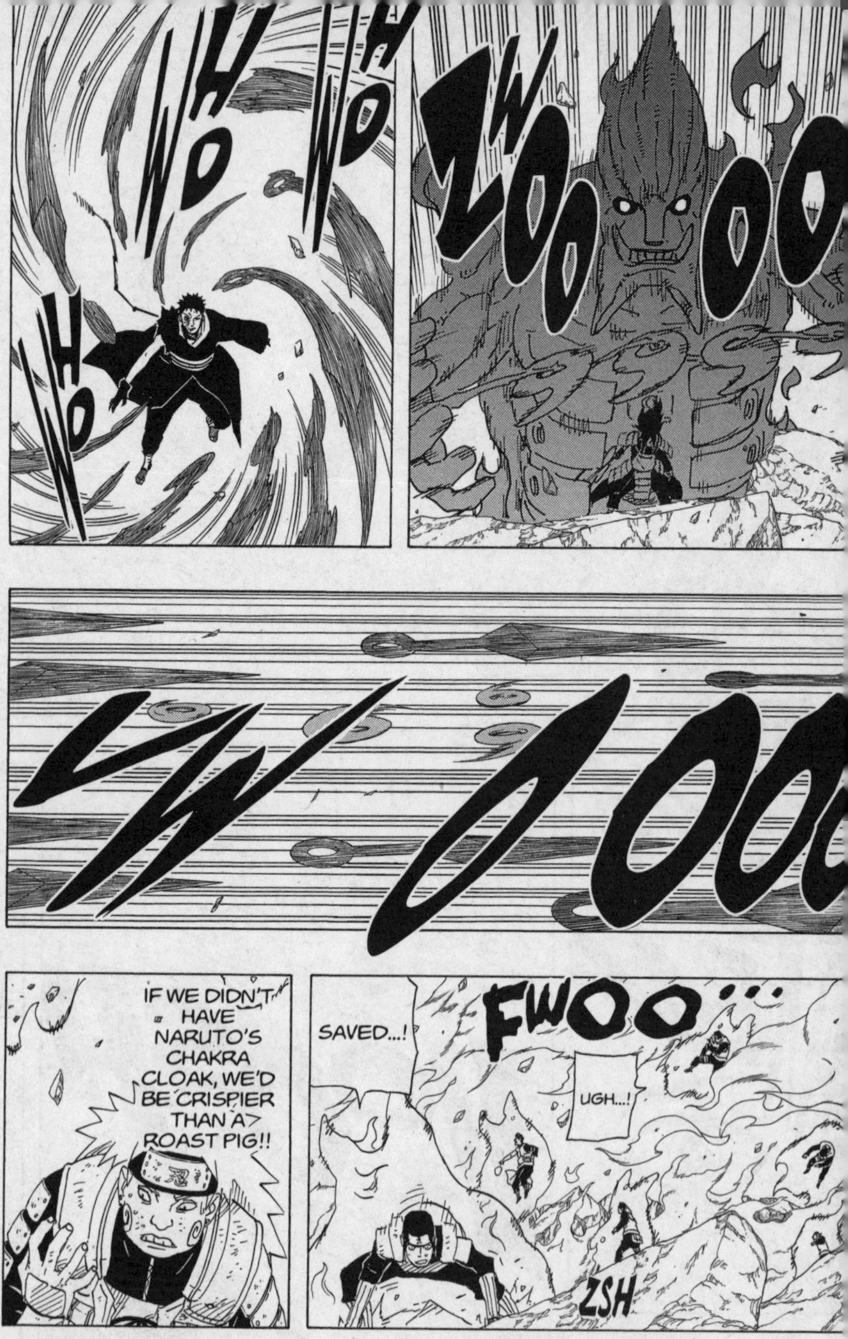
ZWOOOO
WHO
WHO
WHO
WHO
FWOO...
UGH...!
SAVED...!
ZSH
IF WE DIDN'T HAVE NARUTO'S CHAKRA CLOAK, WE'D BE CRISPIER THAN A ROAST PIG!!

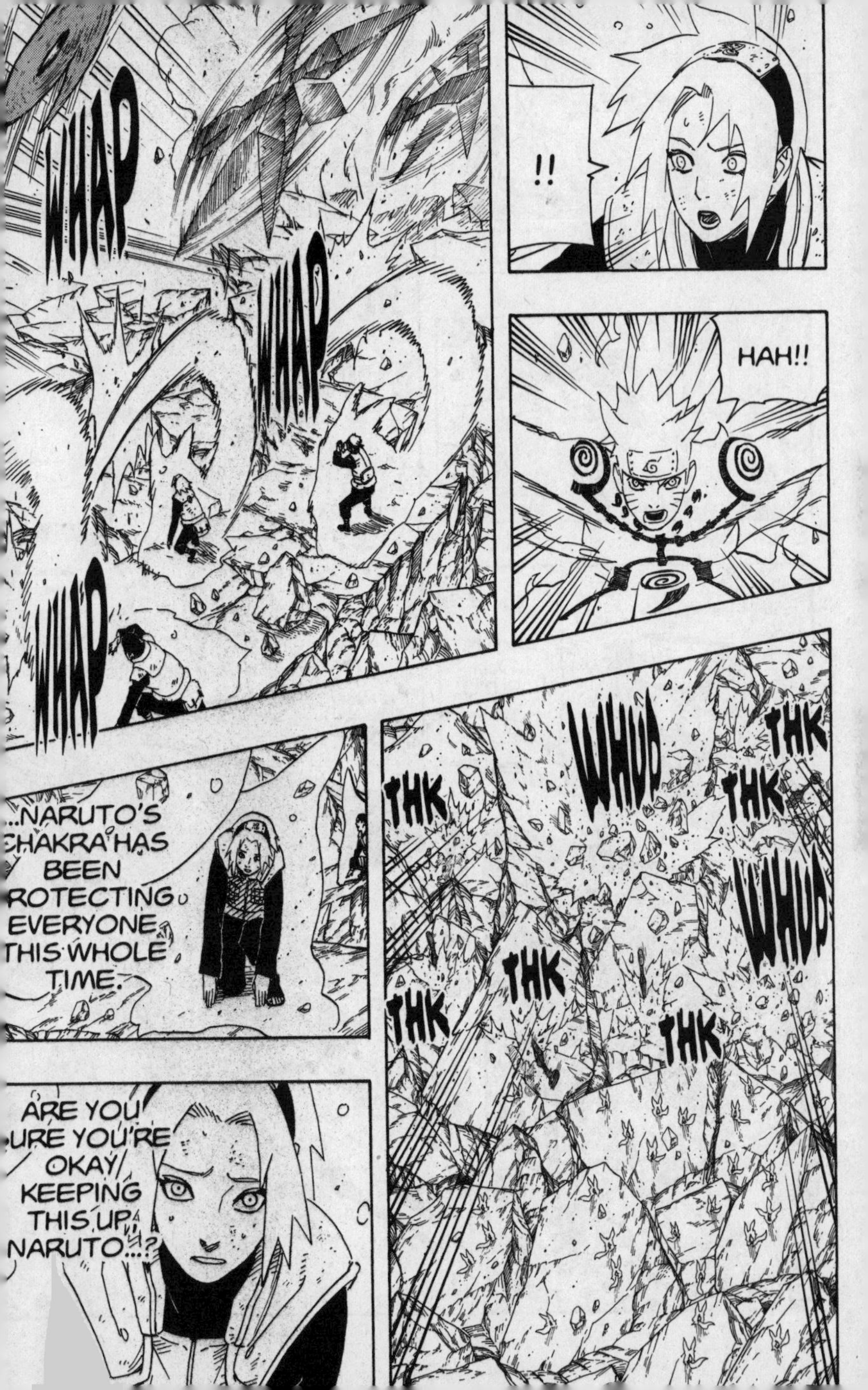

!!
HAH!!
WHAP
WHAP
WHAP
THK
THK
WHUD
WHUD
THK
THK
THK
THK
...NARUTO'S CHAKRA HAS BEEN ROTECTING EVERYONE THIS WHOLE TIME.
ARE YOU URE YOU'RE OKAY KEEPING THIS UP, NARUTO...?

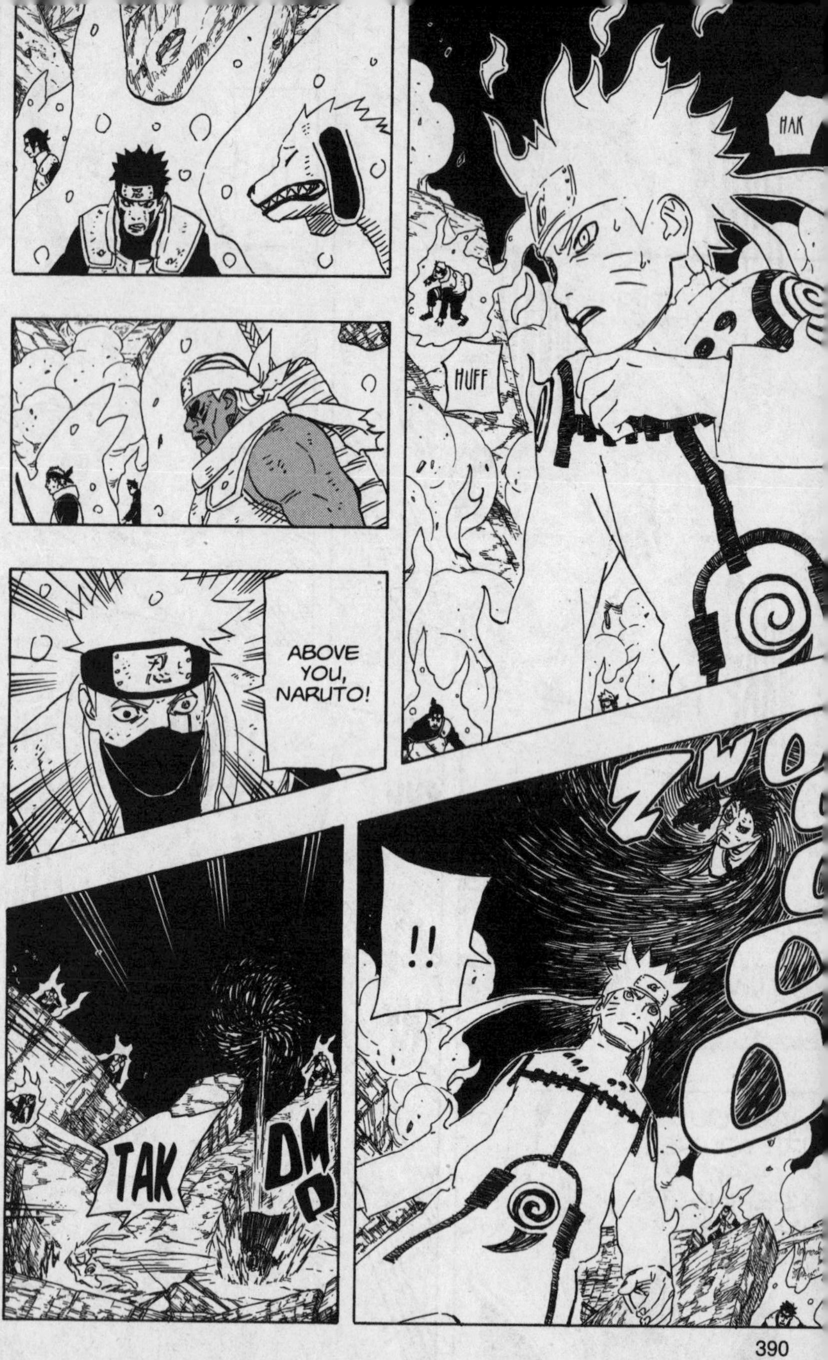
HAK
HUFF
ABOVE YOU, NARUTO!
ZWOOO
!!
DMP
TAK

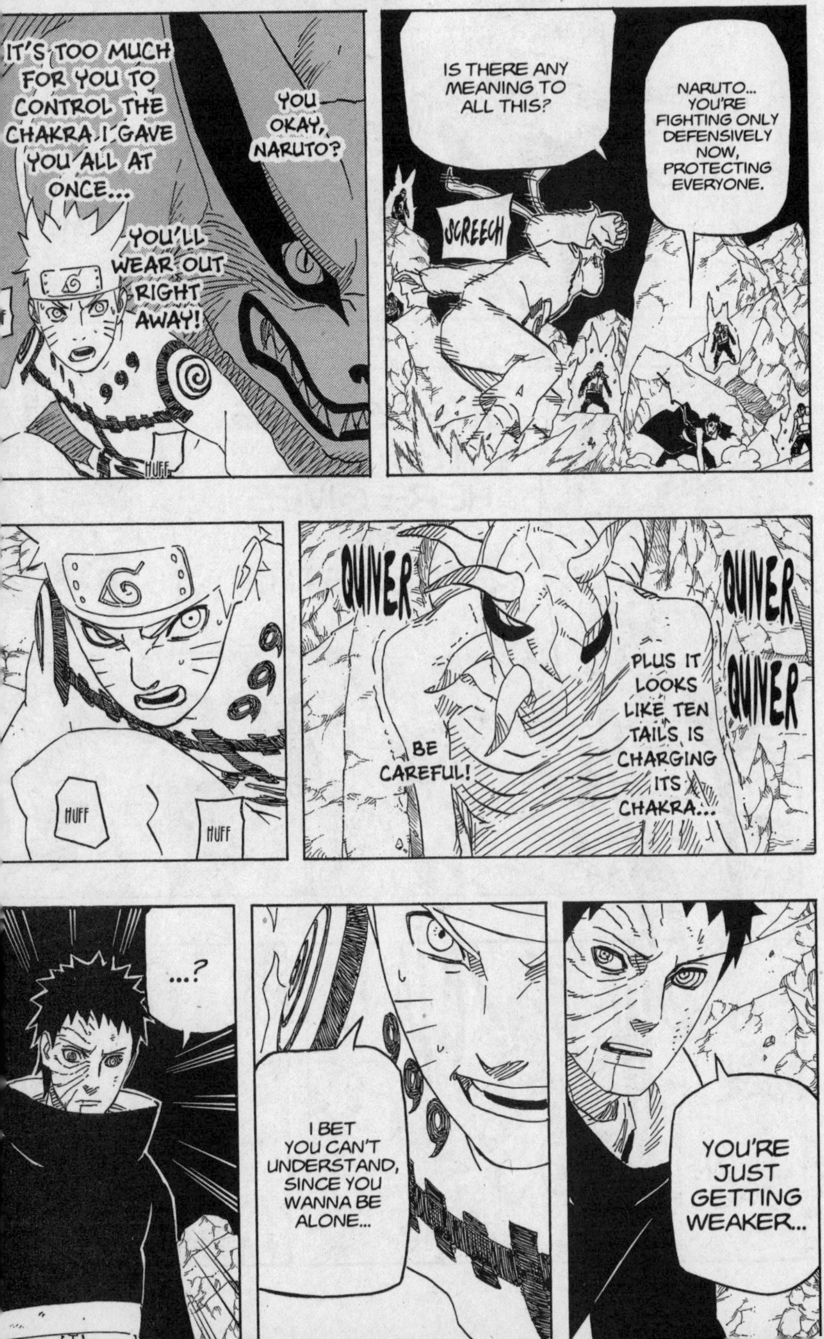
NARUTO... YOU'RE FIGHTING ONLY DEFENSIVELY NOW, PROTECTING EVERYONE.
IS THERE ANY MEANING TO ALL THIS?
SCREECH
YOU OKAY, NARUTO?
IT'S TOO MUCH FOR YOU TO CONTROL THE CHAKRA I GAVE YOU ALL AT ONCE...
YOU'LL WEAR OUT RIGHT AWAY!
HUFF
QUIVER
QUIVER
PLUS IT LOOKS LIKE TEN TAILS IS CHARGING ITS CHAKRA...
BE CAREFUL!
QUIVER
HUFF
HUFF
YOU'RE JUST GETTING WEAKER...
I BET YOU CAN'T UNDERSTAND, SINCE YOU WANNA BE ALONE...
...?

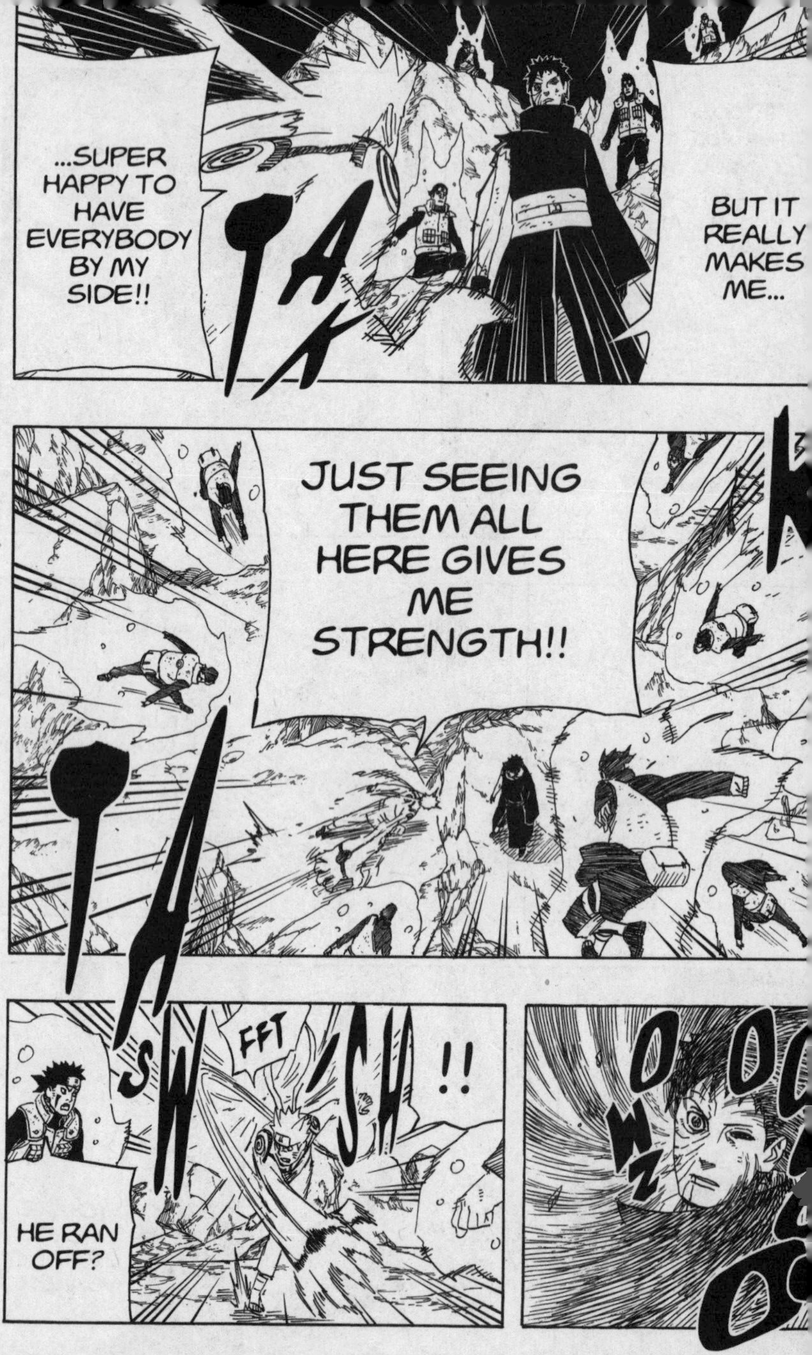
BUT IT REALLY MAKES ME...
...SUPER HAPPY TO HAVE EVERYBODY BY MY SIDE!!
TAK
JUST SEEING THEM ALL HERE GIVES ME STRENGTH!!
TAK
SWISH
FFT
!!
HE RAN OFF?

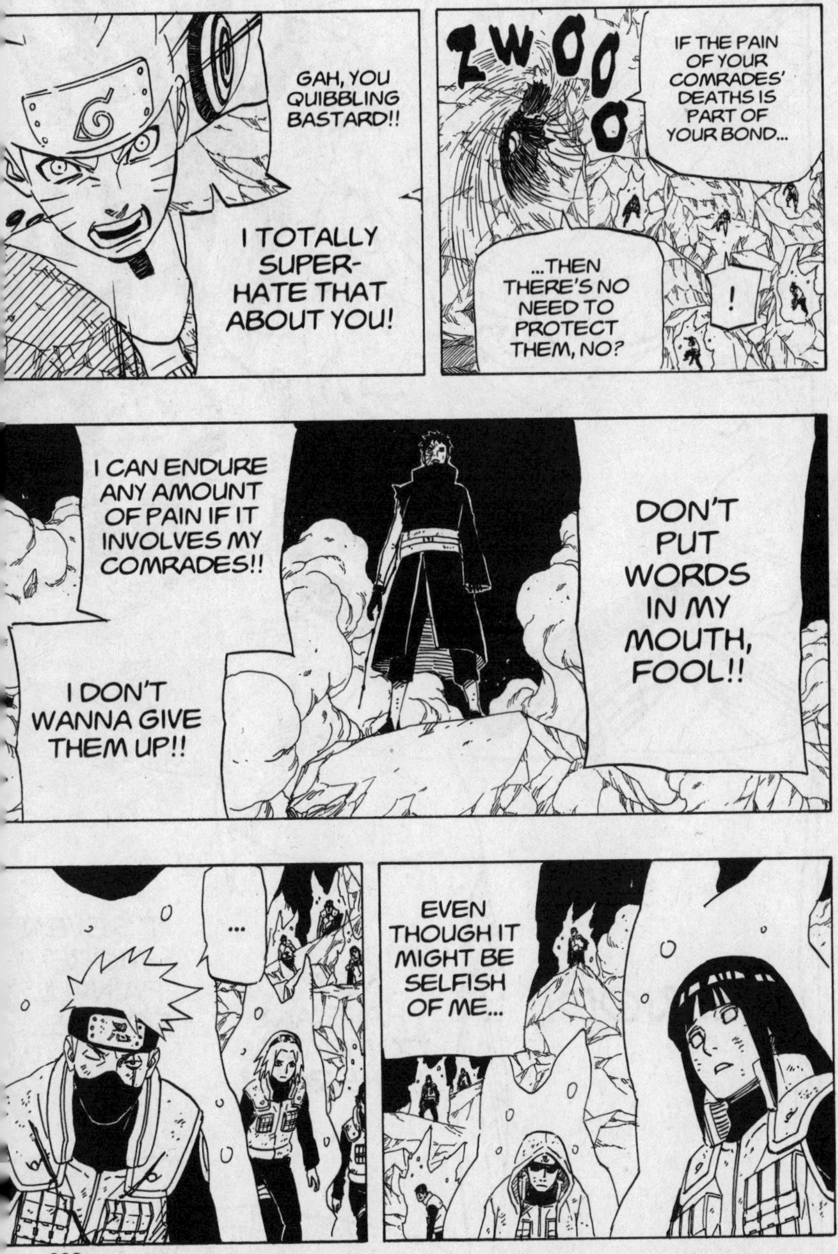
ZWOOO
IF THE PAIN OF YOUR COMRADES' DEATHS IS PART OF YOUR BOND...
...THEN THERE'S NO NEED TO PROTECT THEM, NO?
!
GAH, YOU QUIBBLING BASTARD!!
I TOTALLY SUPER-HATE THAT ABOUT YOU!
DON'T PUT WORDS IN MY MOUTH, FOOL!!
I CAN ENDURE ANY AMOUNT OF PAIN IF IT INVOLVES MY COMRADES!!
I DON'T WANNA GIVE THEM UP!!
EVEN THOUGH IT MIGHT BE SELFISH OF ME...
...

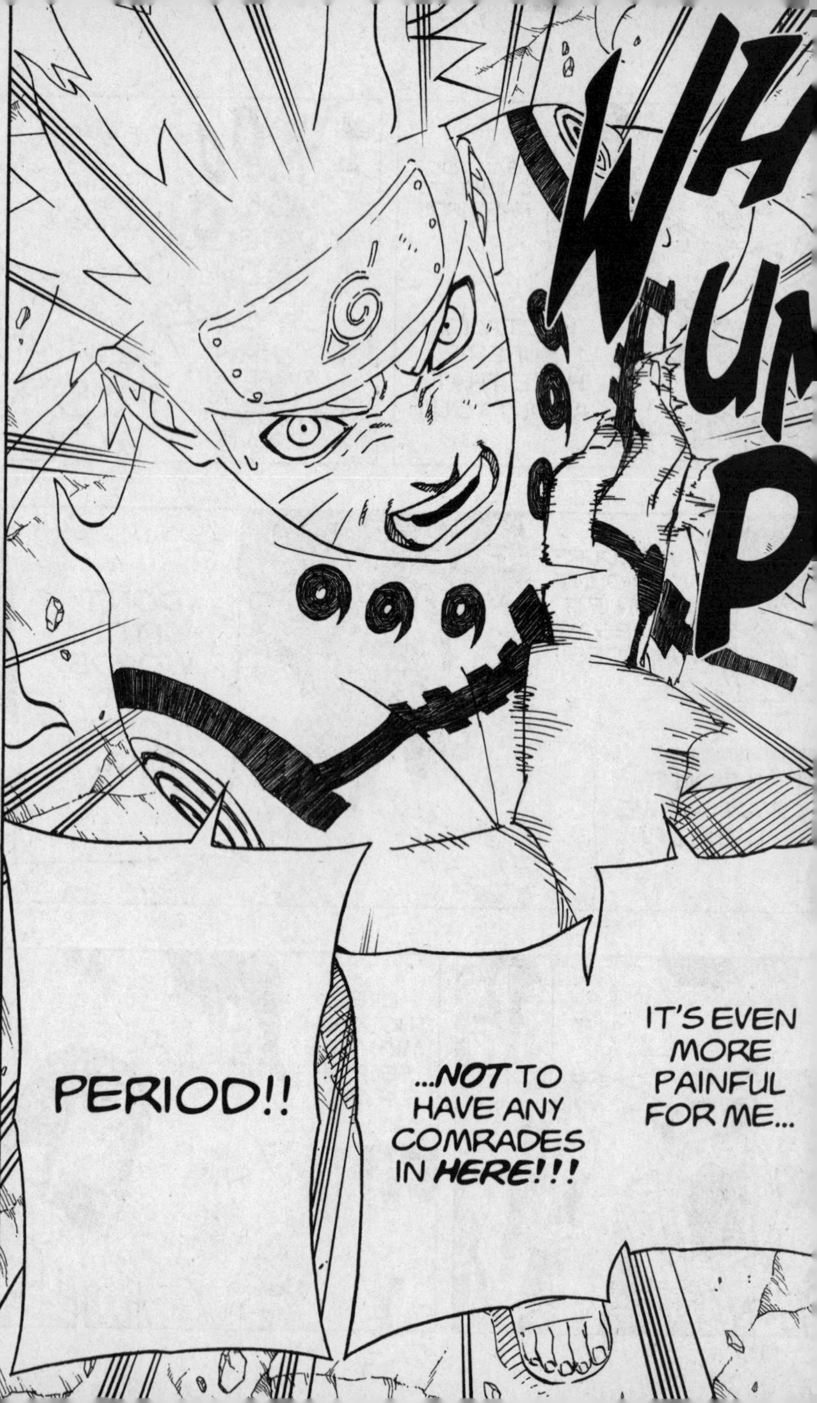
WHUMP
IT'S EVEN MORE PAINFUL FOR ME...
...*NOT* TO HAVE ANY COMRADES IN *HERE*!!!
PERIOD!!

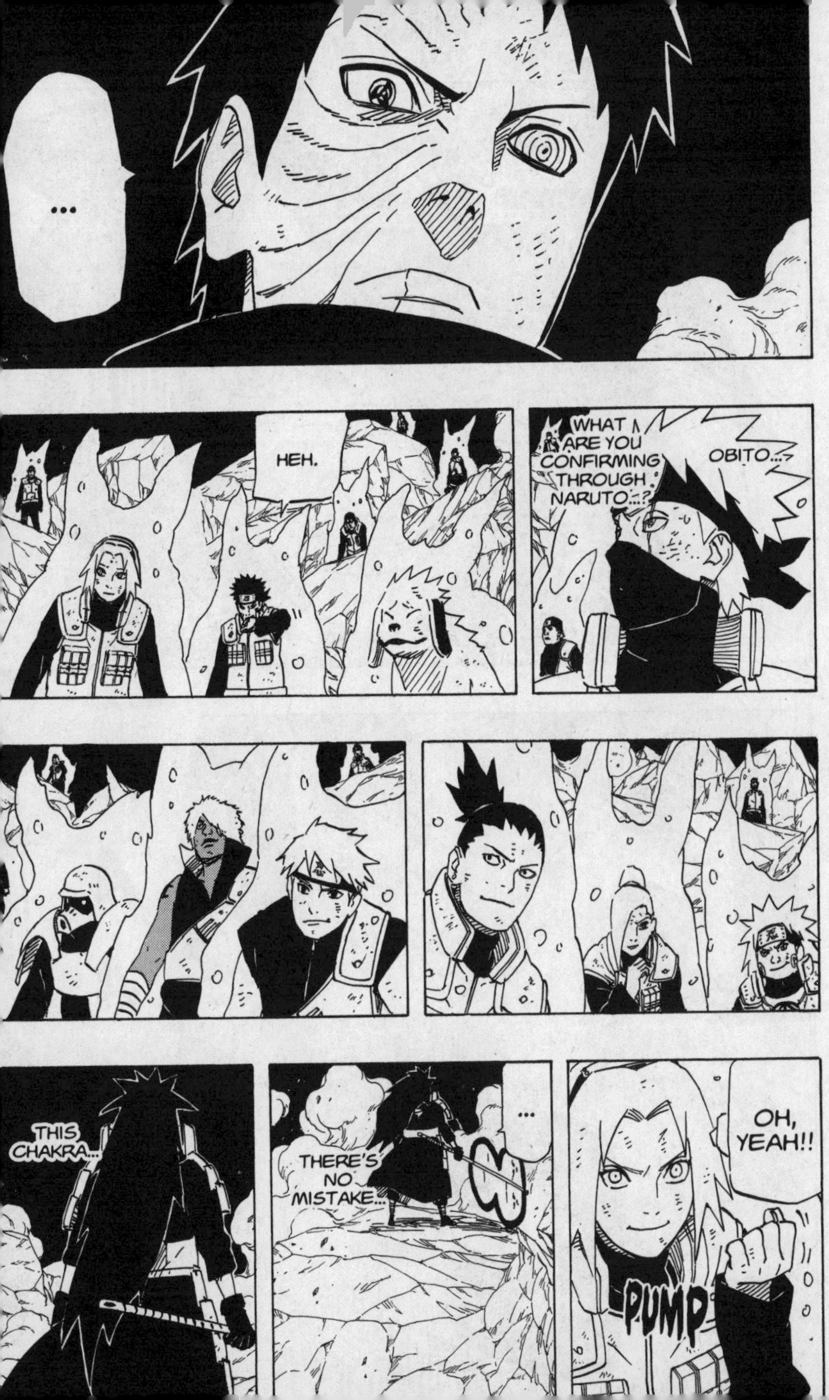
...
OBITO...?
WHAT ARE YOU CONFIRMING THROUGH NARUTO...?
HEH.
OH, YEAH!!
PUMP
...
THERE'S NO MISTAKE...
THIS CHAKRA...

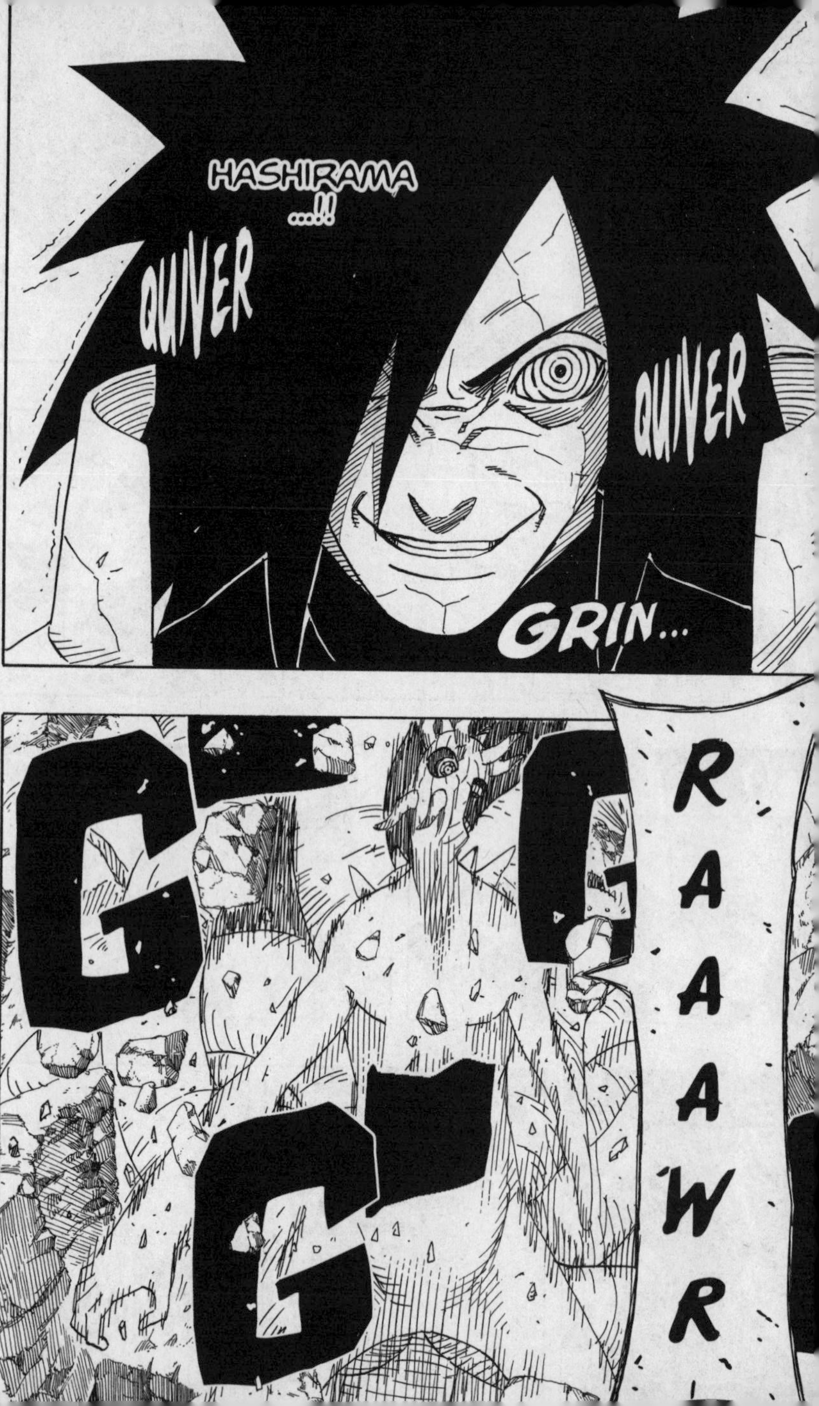
HASHIRAMA ...!!
QUIVER
QUIVER
GRIN...
GOGOGO
RAAAWR

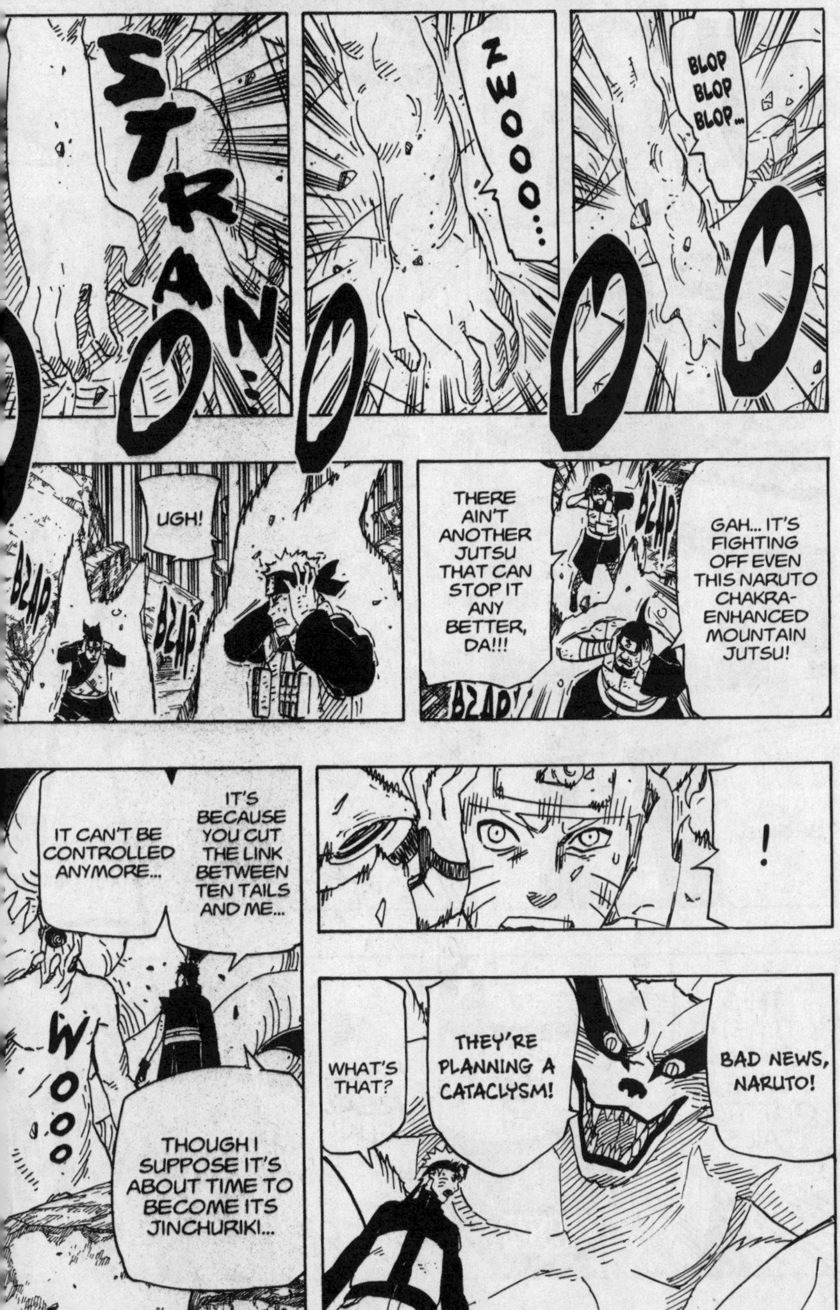

BLOP BLOP BLOP...
ZWOOO...
STRANOOOO
GAH... IT'S FIGHTING OFF EVEN THIS NARUTO CHAKRA-ENHANCED MOUNTAIN JUTSU!
BZAP
THERE AIN'T ANOTHER JUTSU THAT CAN STOP IT ANY BETTER, DA!!!
BZAP
UGH!
BZAP
BZAP
!
BAD NEWS, NARUTO!
THEY'RE PLANNING A CATACLYSM!
WHAT'S THAT?
IT'S BECAUSE YOU CUT THE LINK BETWEEN TEN TAILS AND ME...
IT CAN'T BE CONTROLLED ANYMORE...
THOUGH I SUPPOSE IT'S ABOUT TIME TO BECOME ITS JINCHURIKI...
WOOO

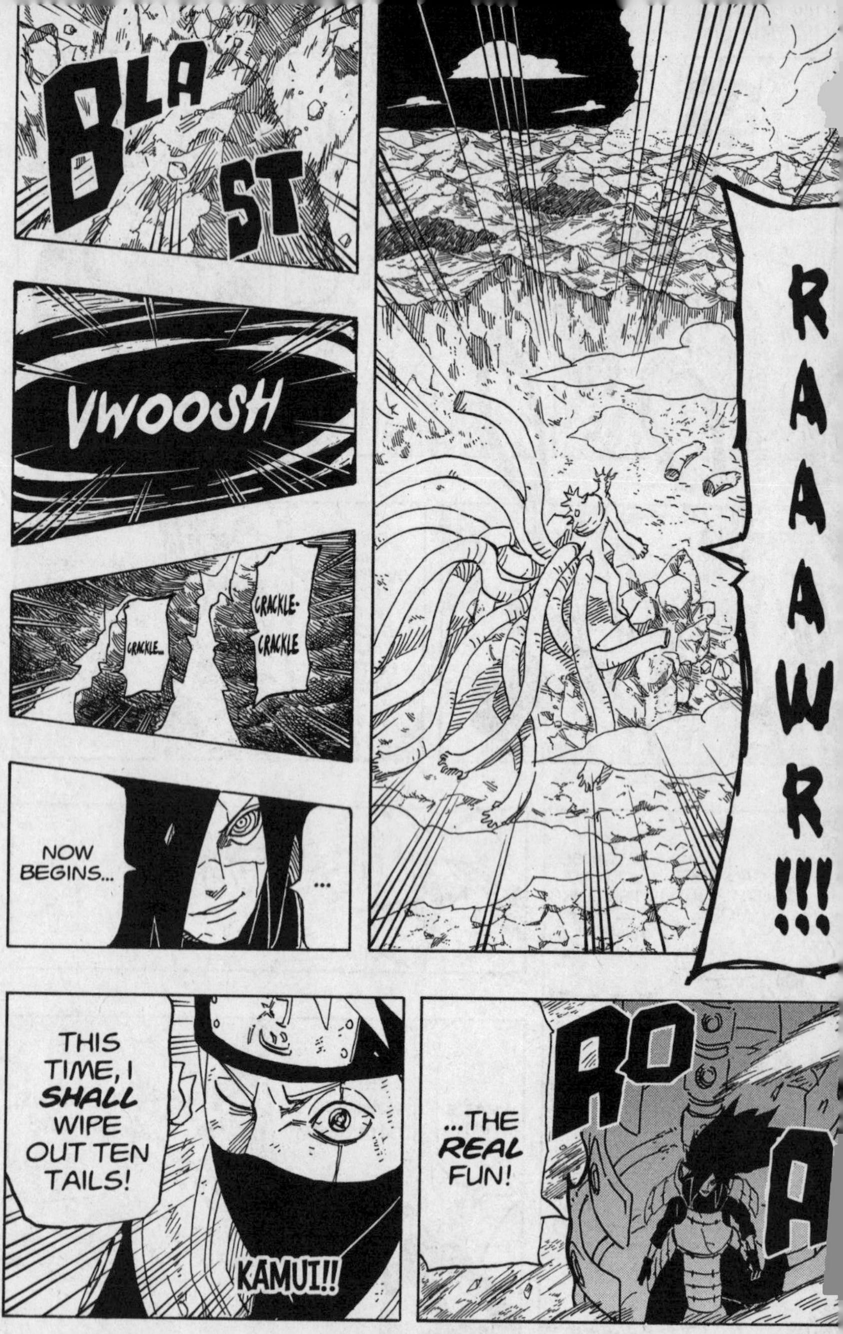
RAAAWR!!!
BLAST
VWOOSH
CRACKLE-CRACKLE
CRACKLE...
...
NOW BEGINS...
ROAA
...THE REAL FUN!
THIS TIME, I SHALL WIPE OUT TEN TAILS!
KAMUI!!

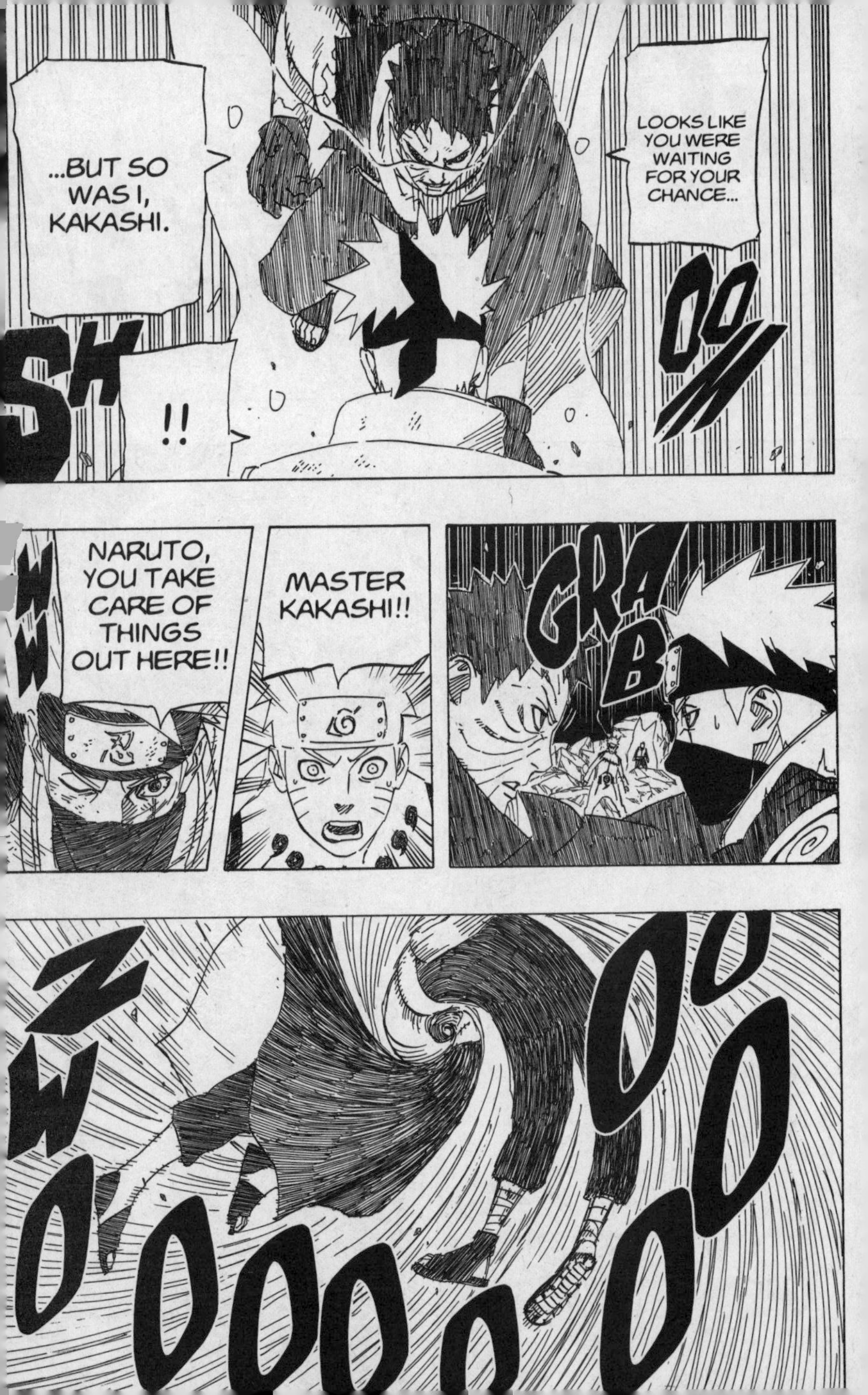
LOOKS LIKE YOU WERE WAITING FOR YOUR CHANCE...
...BUT SO WAS I, KAKASHI.
!!
SH
GRAB
MASTER KAKASHI!!
NARUTO, YOU TAKE CARE OF THINGS OUT HERE!!

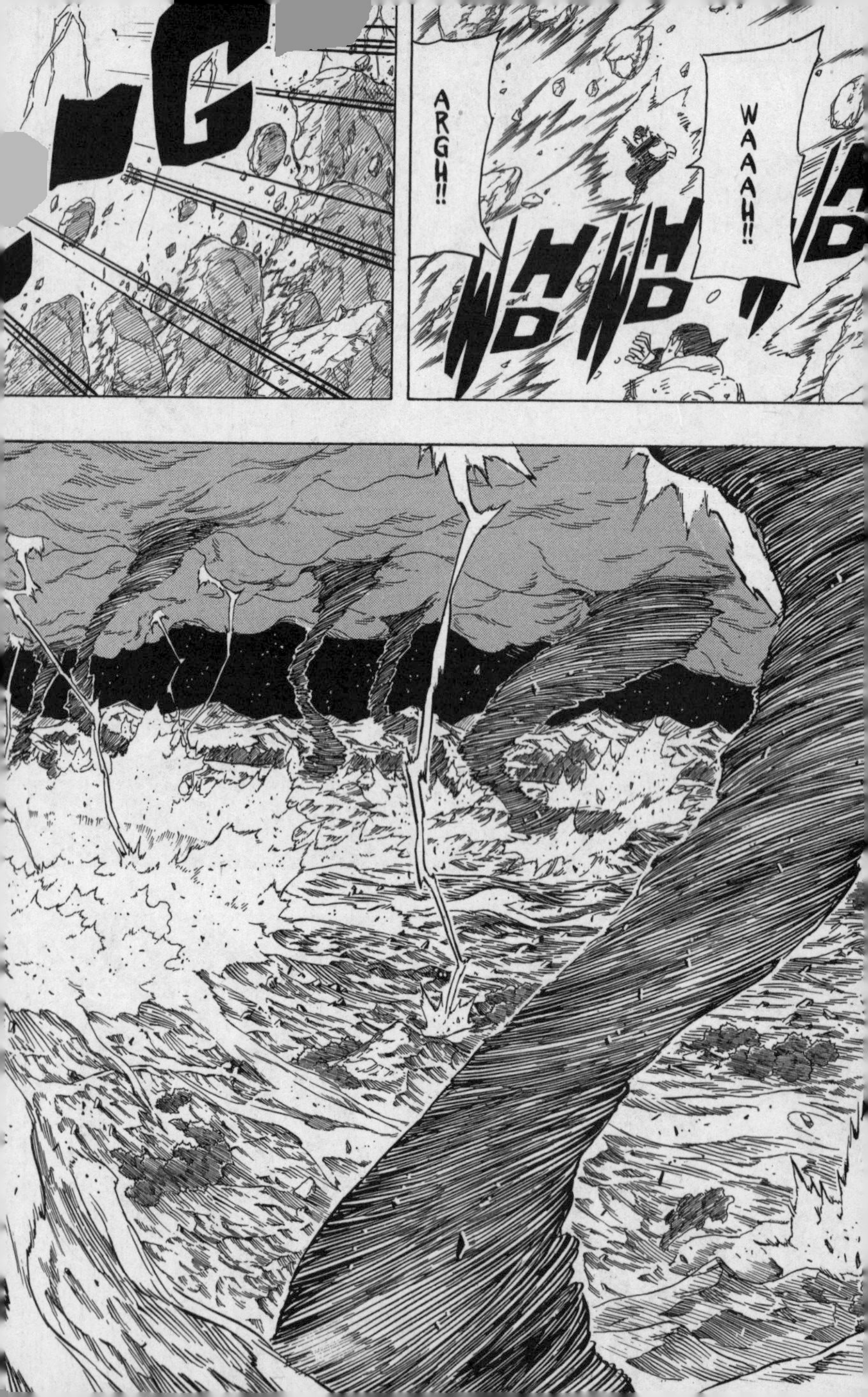
WAAAAH!!
ARGH!!

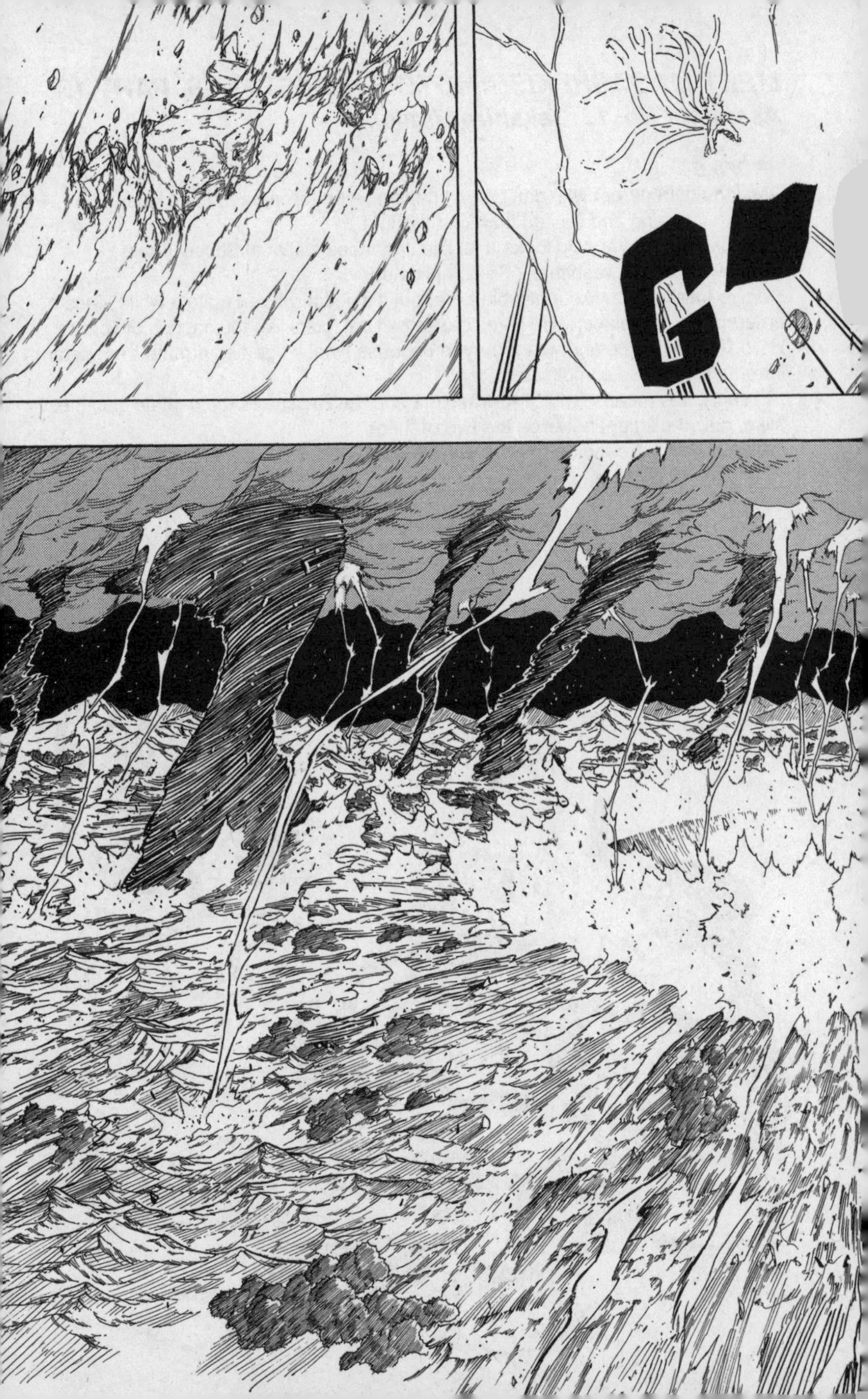
G

MEET MASASHI KISHIMOTO'S ASSISTANTS, PART 13
Assistant No. 13: Takahiro Hiraishi

PROFILE

- An indulgent parent who can't stop grinning when talking about his kids.
- More scheming and wicked than first thought.
- A basketball player who looks a lot like Japanese National Soccer Team goalkeeper Eiji Kawashima... So complicated.
- We're treating him like a newbie here, but it's actually been quite a while since he entered the workplace... He loves basketball but looks like the captain of Tomica Hero Rescue Force and was annoyed because I wasn't getting around to assistant introductions... So complicated.
- In short, this means GK Eiji Kawashima and the Rescue Force captain also look alike, but...he's right between the two of them.
- Always walks around on the tips of his toes.
- Fundamentally nice.

[Tasks] Coloring, screentone, backgrounds

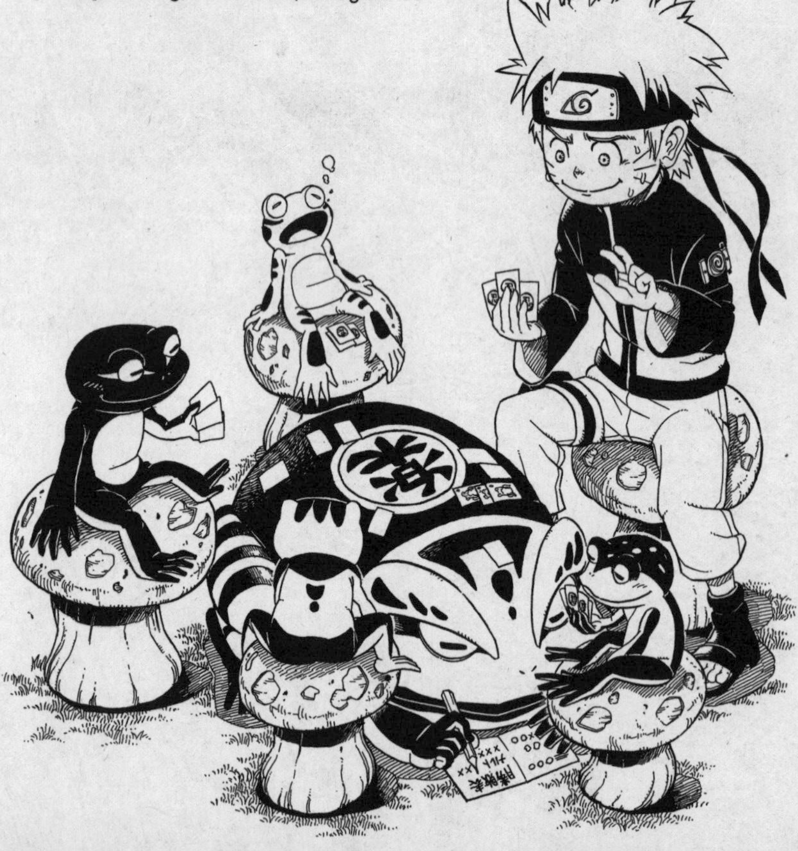

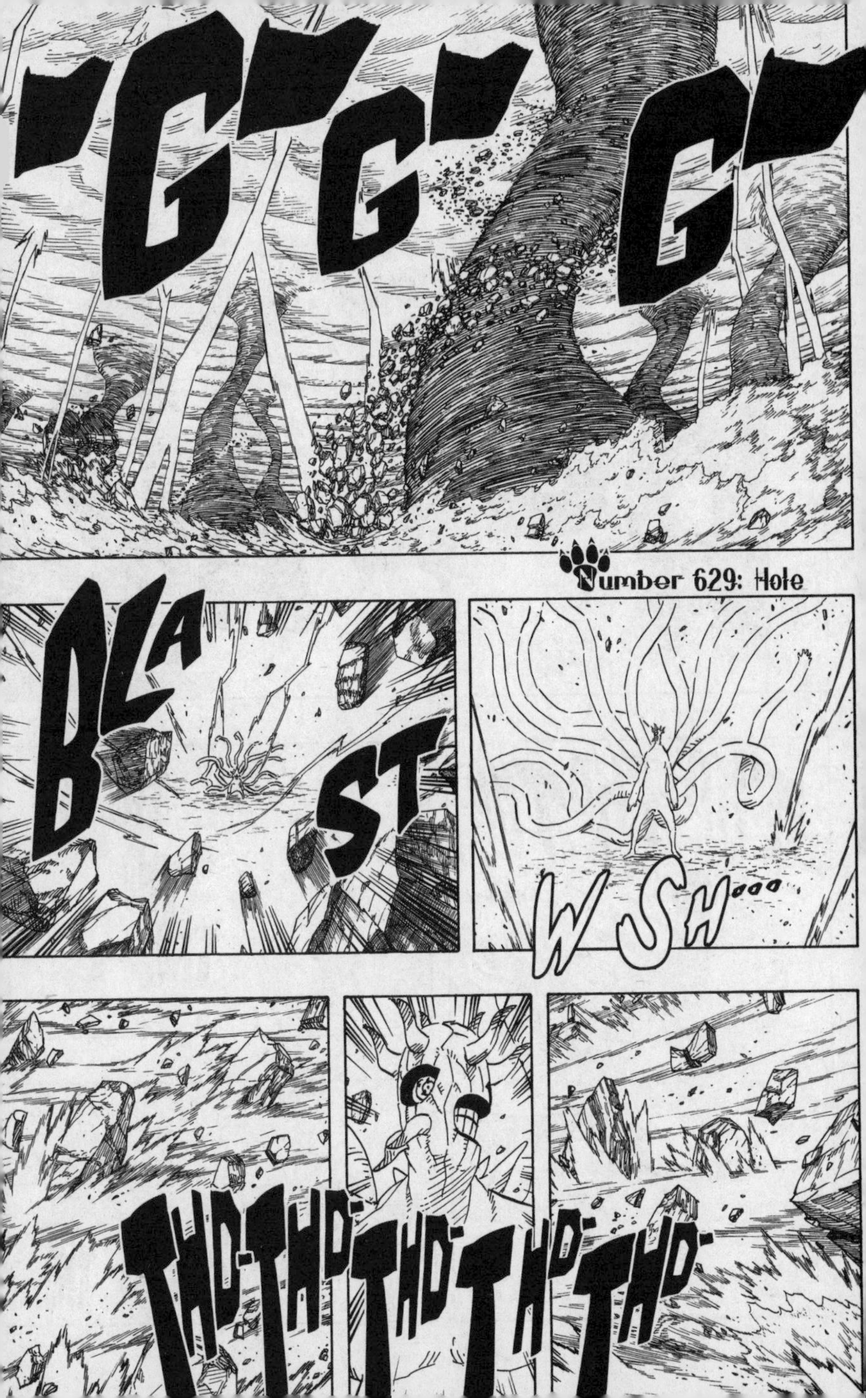
GGG
Number 629: Hole
WSH...
BLAST
THD-THD-THD-THD-THD-

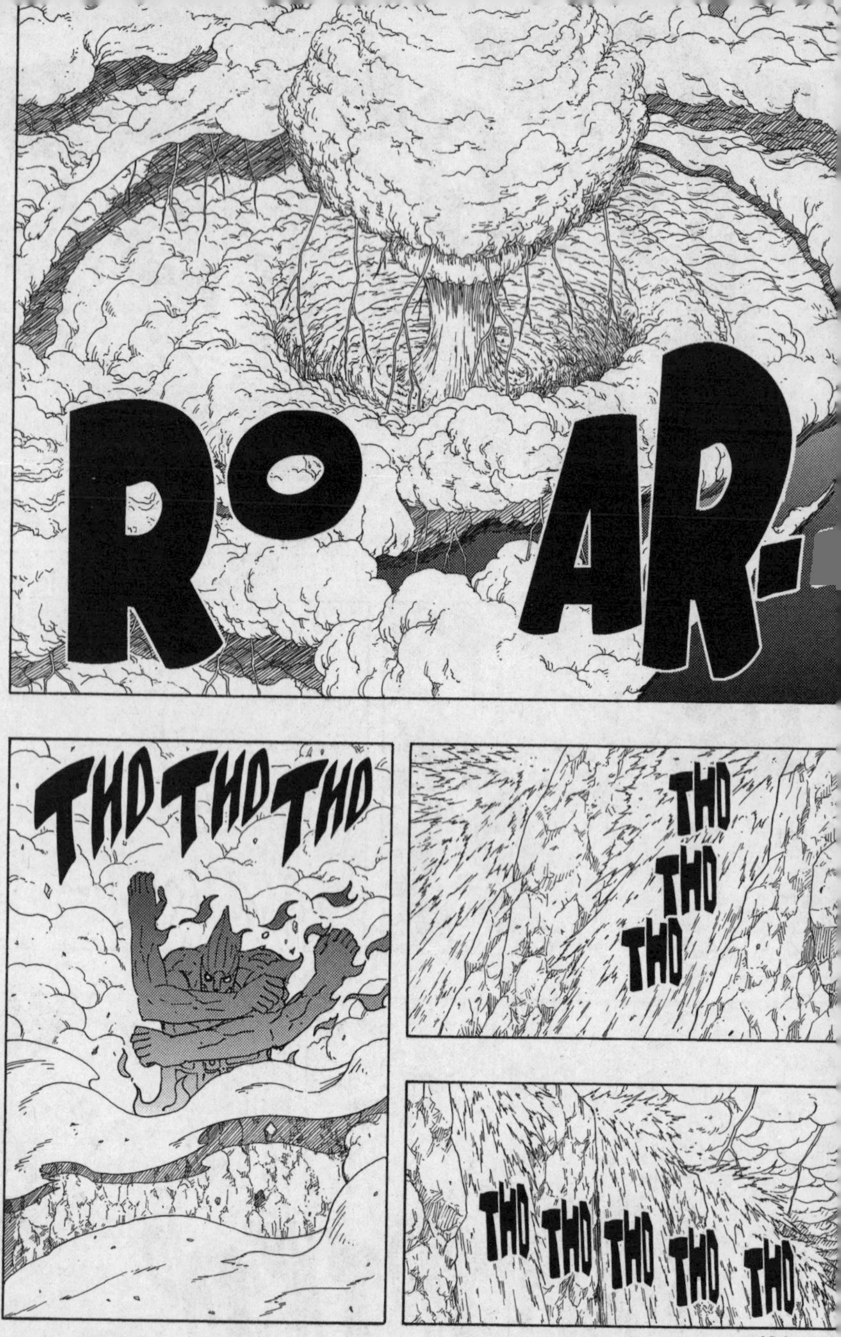
ROAR-
THD THD THD
THD THD THD THD THD
THD THD THD

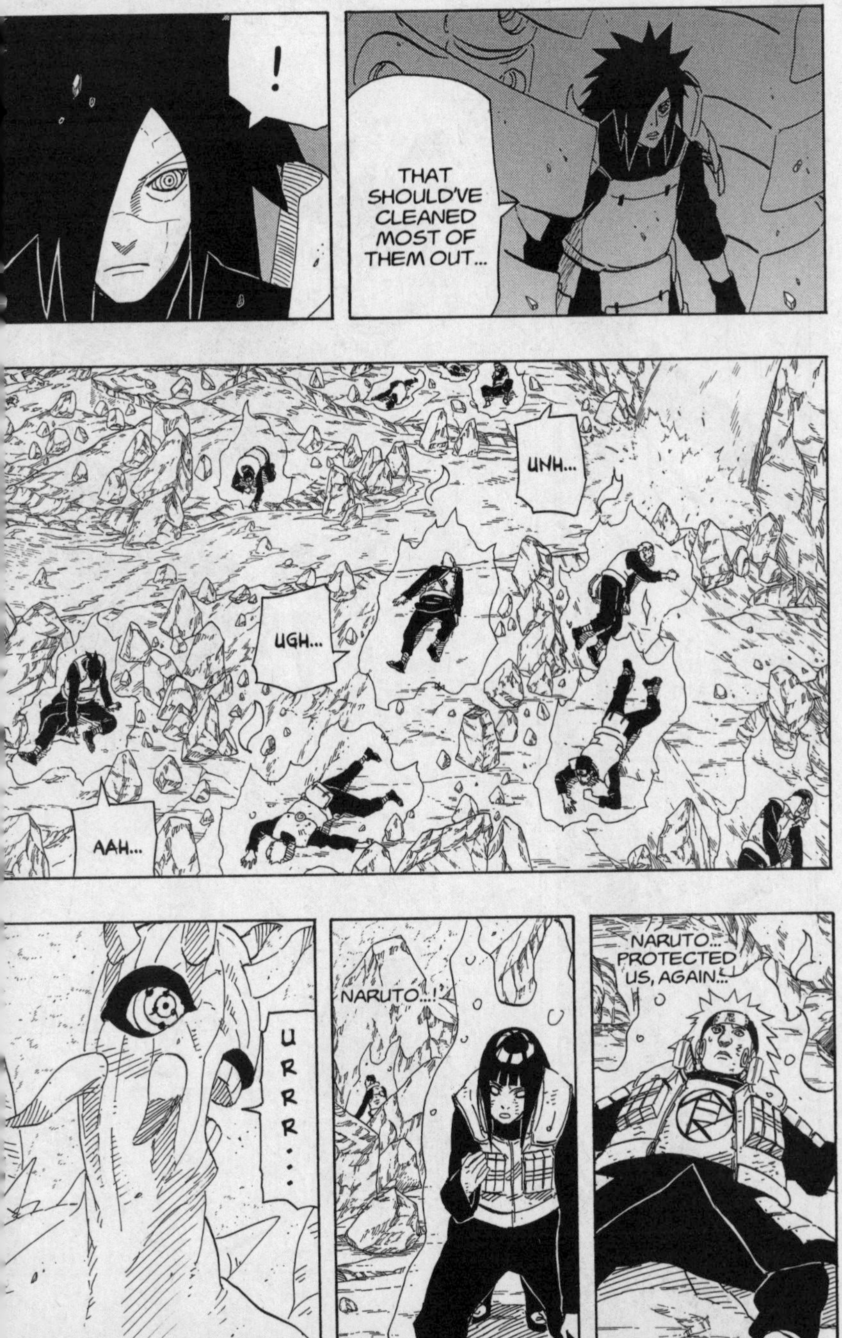
THAT SHOULD'VE CLEANED MOST OF THEM OUT...
!
UNH...
UGH...
AAH...
NARUTO... PROTECTED US, AGAIN...
NARUTO...!
URRR...

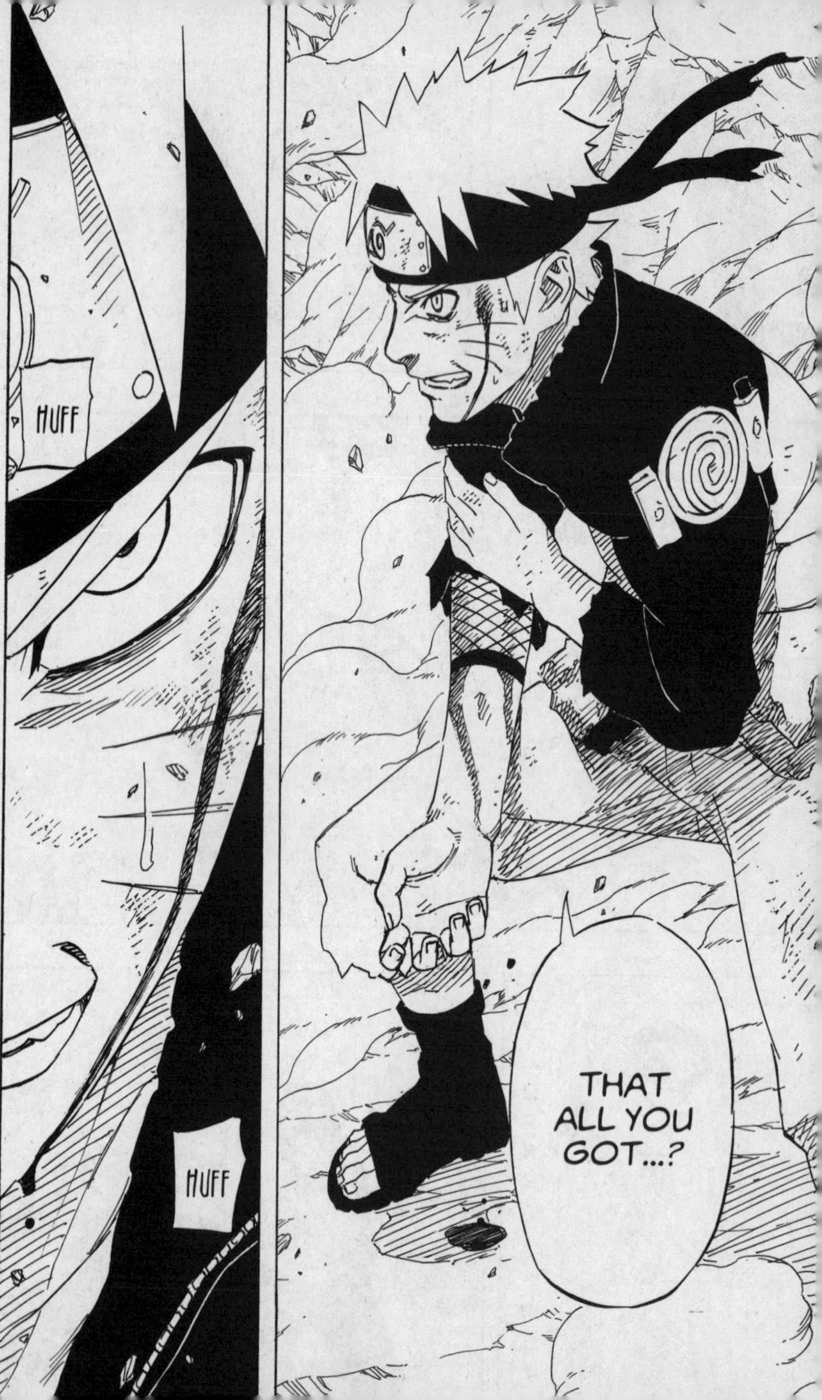
THAT ALL YOU GOT...?
HUFF
HUFF

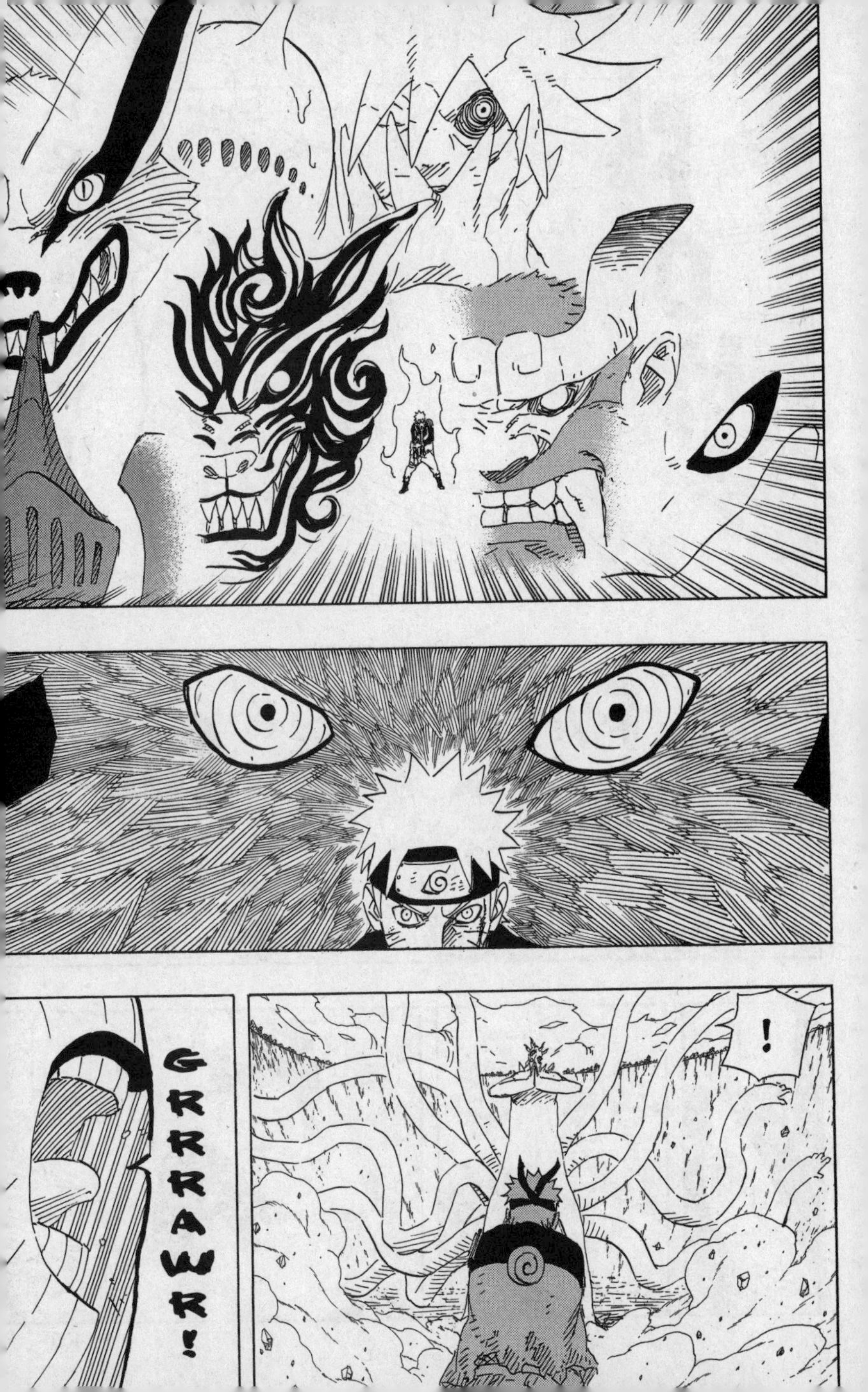
!
GRRRAWR!

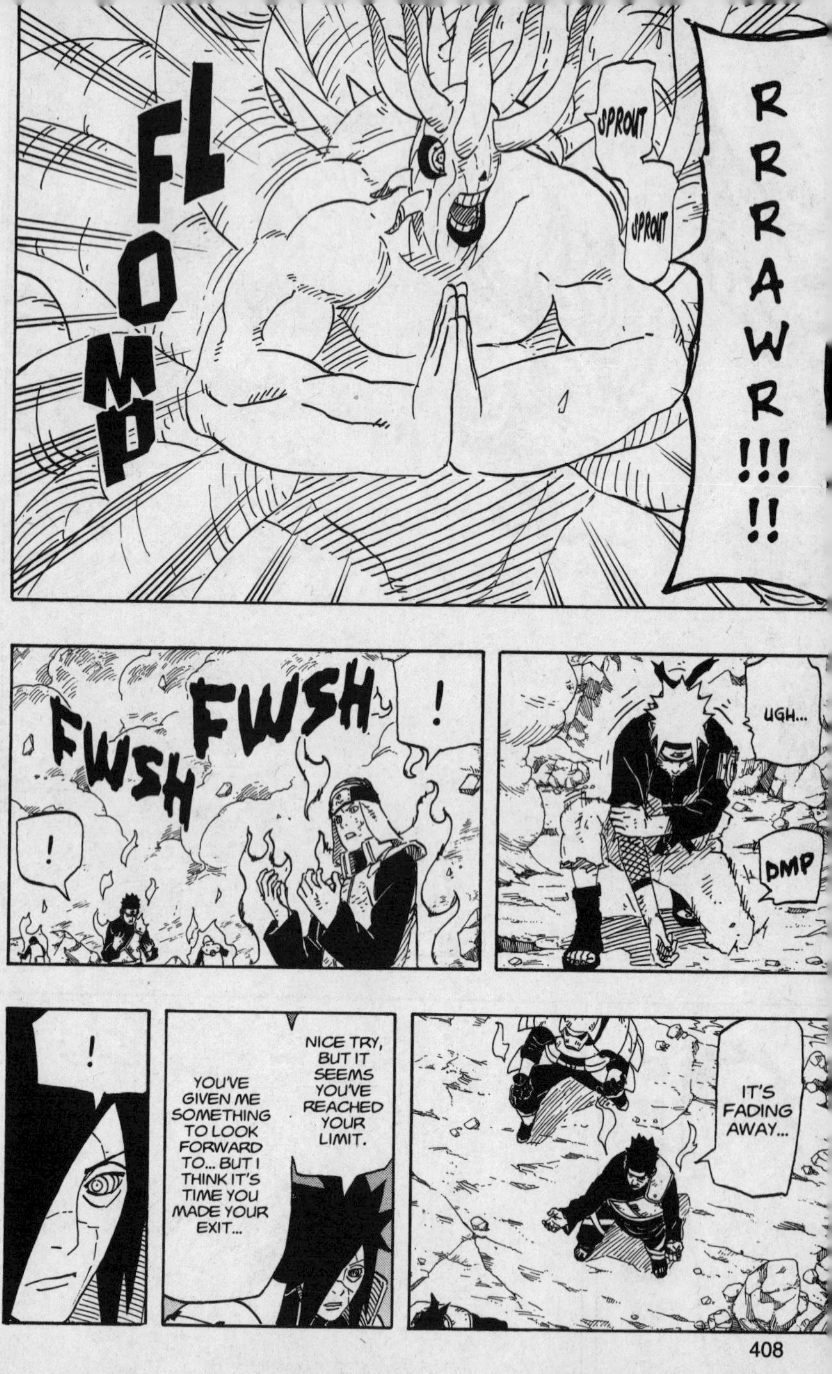
RRRAWR!!!!!
SPROUT
SPROUT
FLOMP
UGH...
DMP
!
FWSH
FWSH
!
IT'S FADING AWAY...
NICE TRY, BUT IT SEEMS YOU'VE REACHED YOUR LIMIT.
YOU'VE GIVEN ME SOMETHING TO LOOK FORWARD TO... BUT I THINK IT'S TIME YOU MADE YOUR EXIT...
!

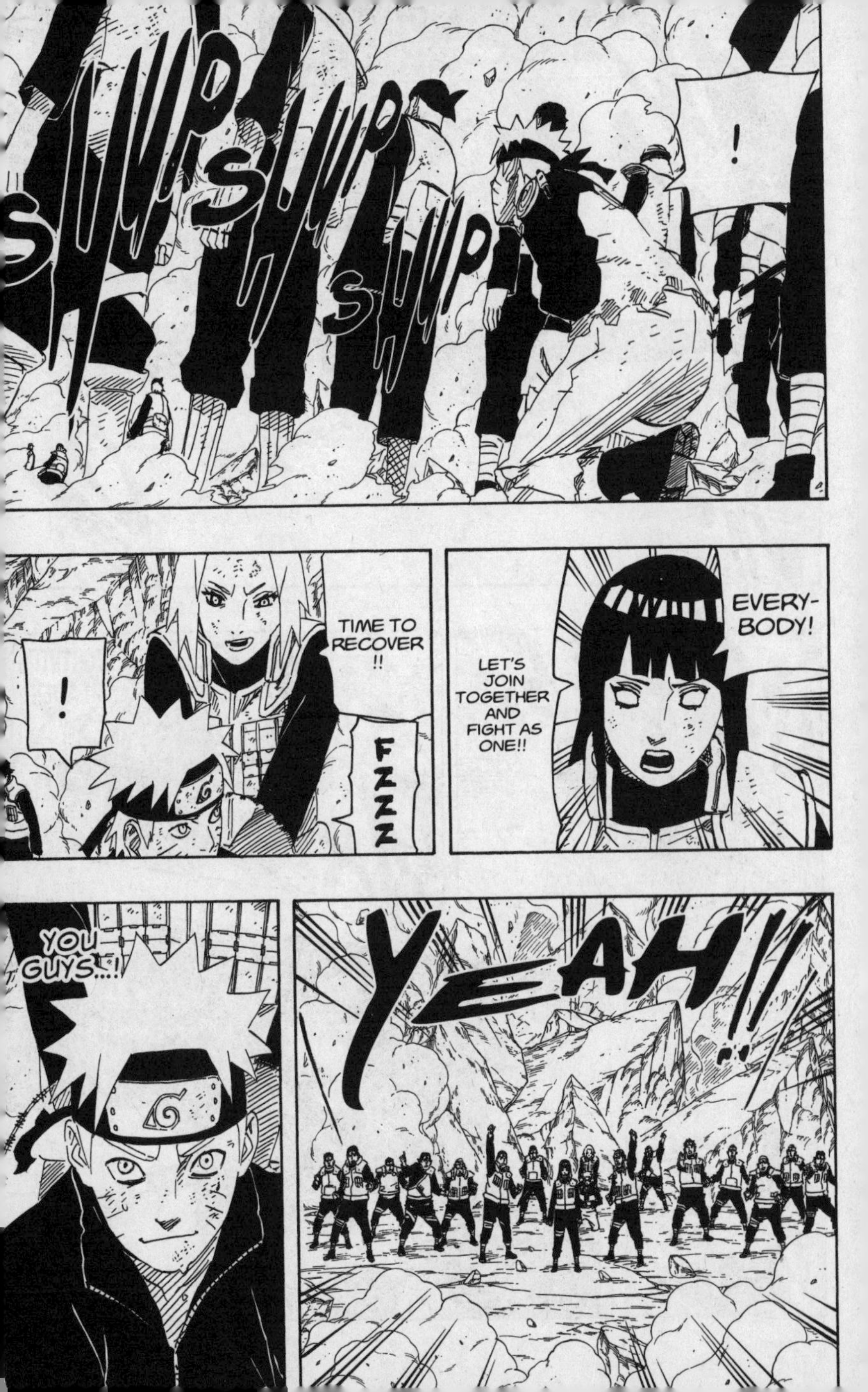
!
SHUP
SHUP
SHUP
SHUP
EVERY-BODY!
LET'S JOIN TOGETHER AND FIGHT AS ONE!!
TIME TO RECOVER!!
FZZZ
!
YEAH!!
YOU GUYS...!

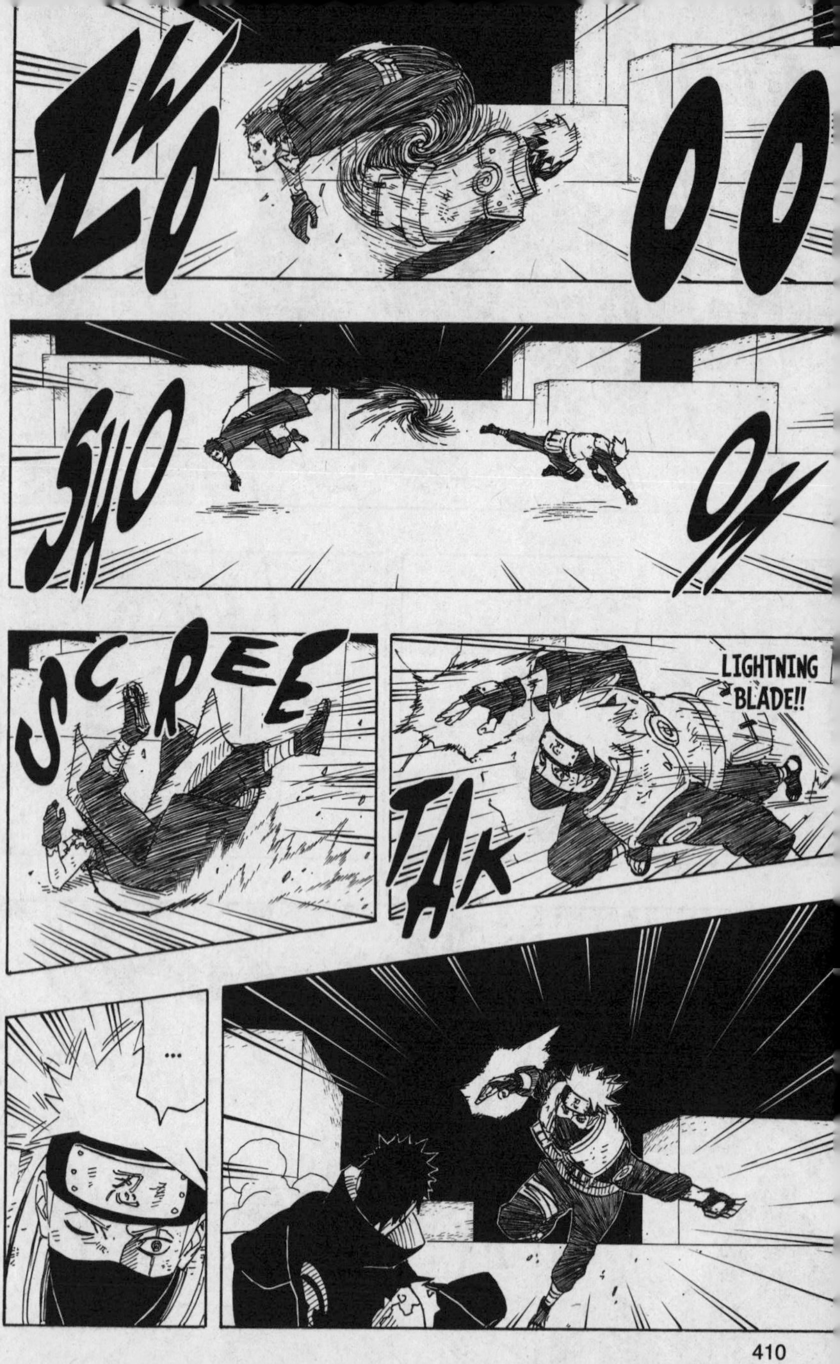

ZWOOOO
SHOOM
LIGHTNING BLADE!!
TAK
SCREE
...

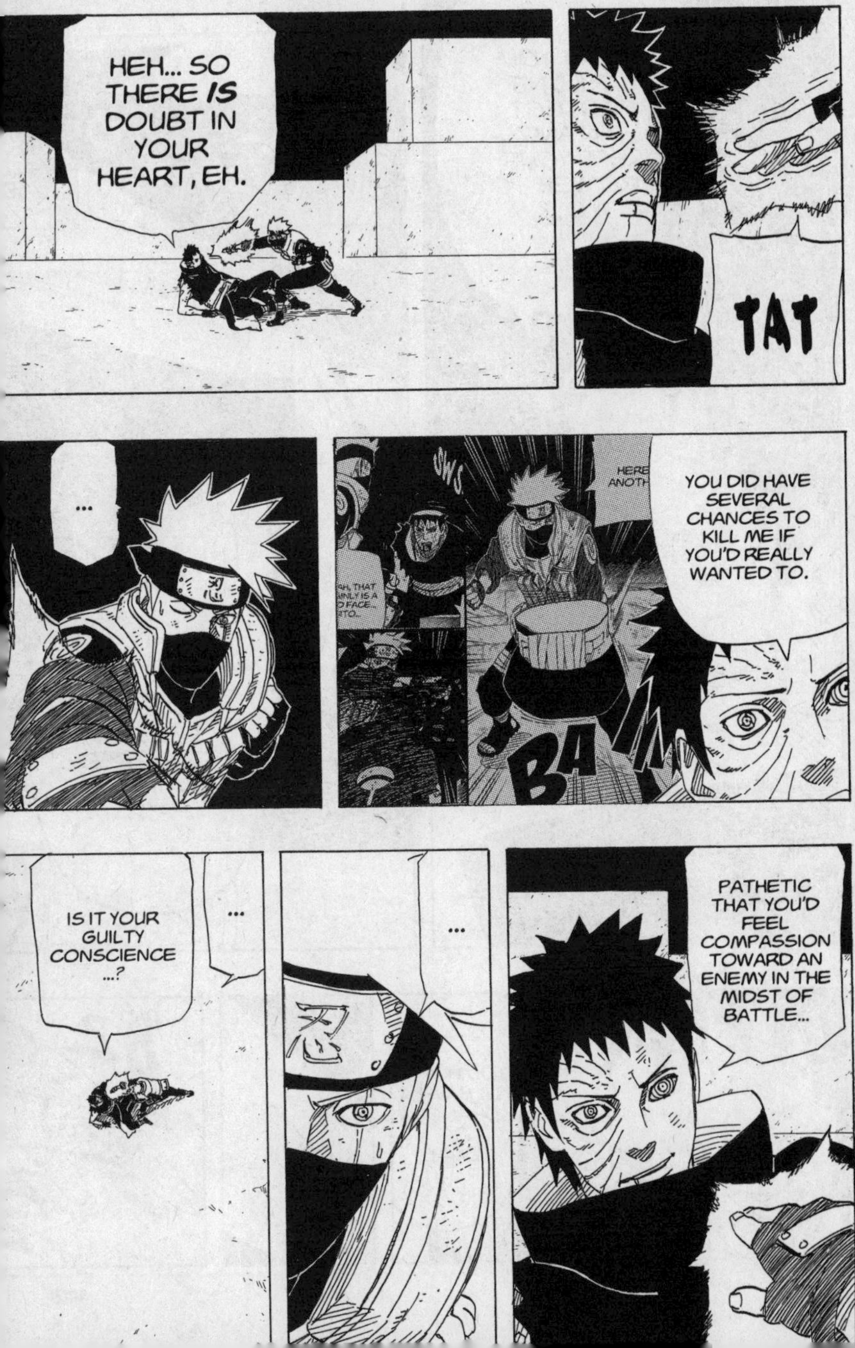
TAT
HEH... SO THERE *IS* DOUBT IN YOUR HEART, EH.
YOU DID HAVE SEVERAL CHANCES TO KILL ME IF YOU'D REALLY WANTED TO.
BA
...
PATHETIC THAT YOU'D FEEL COMPASSION TOWARD AN ENEMY IN THE MIDST OF BATTLE...
...
...
IS IT YOUR GUILTY CONSCIENCE ...?

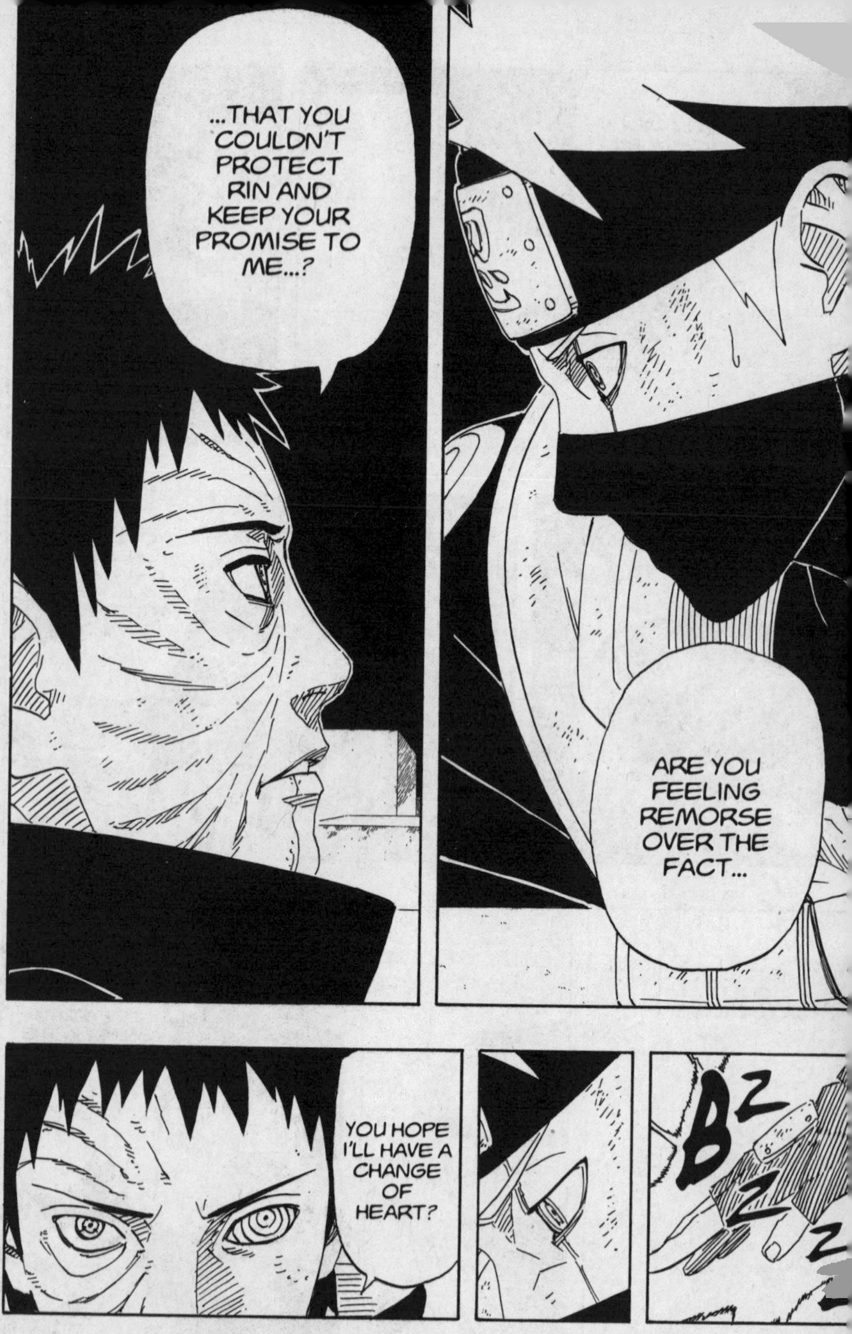
ARE YOU FEELING REMORSE OVER THE FACT...
...THAT YOU COULDN'T PROTECT RIN AND KEEP YOUR PROMISE TO ME...?
BZZZ
YOU HOPE I'LL HAVE A CHANGE OF HEART?

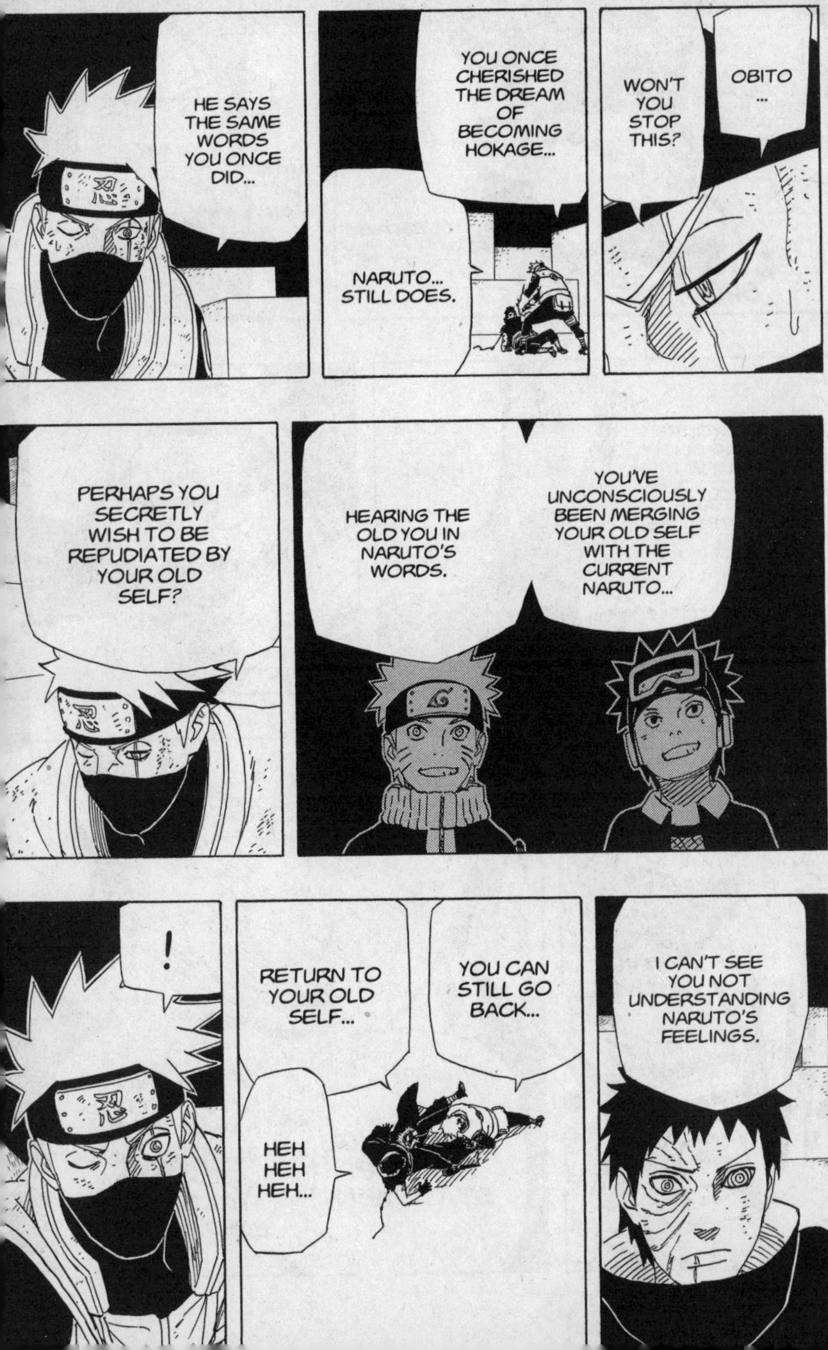
OBITO...
WON'T YOU STOP THIS?
YOU ONCE CHERISHED THE DREAM OF BECOMING HOKAGE...
NARUTO... STILL DOES.
HE SAYS THE SAME WORDS YOU ONCE DID...
YOU'VE UNCONSCIOUSLY BEEN MERGING YOUR OLD SELF WITH THE CURRENT NARUTO...
HEARING THE OLD YOU IN NARUTO'S WORDS.
PERHAPS YOU SECRETLY WISH TO BE REPUDIATED BY YOUR OLD SELF?
I CAN'T SEE YOU NOT UNDERSTANDING NARUTO'S FEELINGS.
YOU CAN STILL GO BACK...
RETURN TO YOUR OLD SELF...
HEH HEH HEH...
!

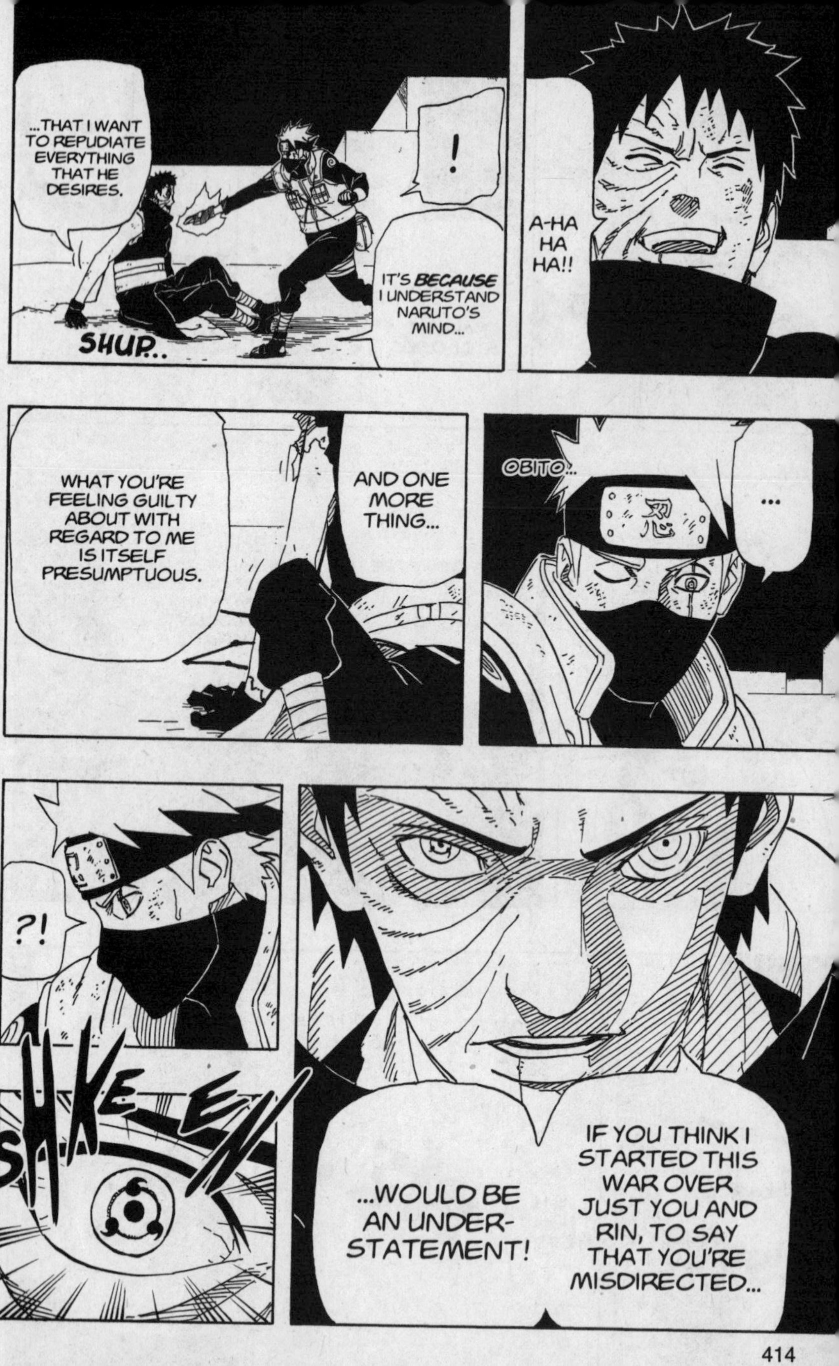
A-HA
HA
HA!!
!
IT'S *BECAUSE* I UNDERSTAND NARUTO'S MIND...
...THAT I WANT TO REPUDIATE EVERYTHING THAT HE DESIRES.
SHUP...
...
OBITO...
AND ONE MORE THING...
WHAT YOU'RE FEELING GUILTY ABOUT WITH REGARD TO ME IS ITSELF PRESUMPTUOUS.
IF YOU THINK I STARTED THIS WAR OVER JUST YOU AND RIN, TO SAY THAT YOU'RE MISDIRECTED...
...WOULD BE AN UNDER-STATEMENT!
?!
SHKEEN

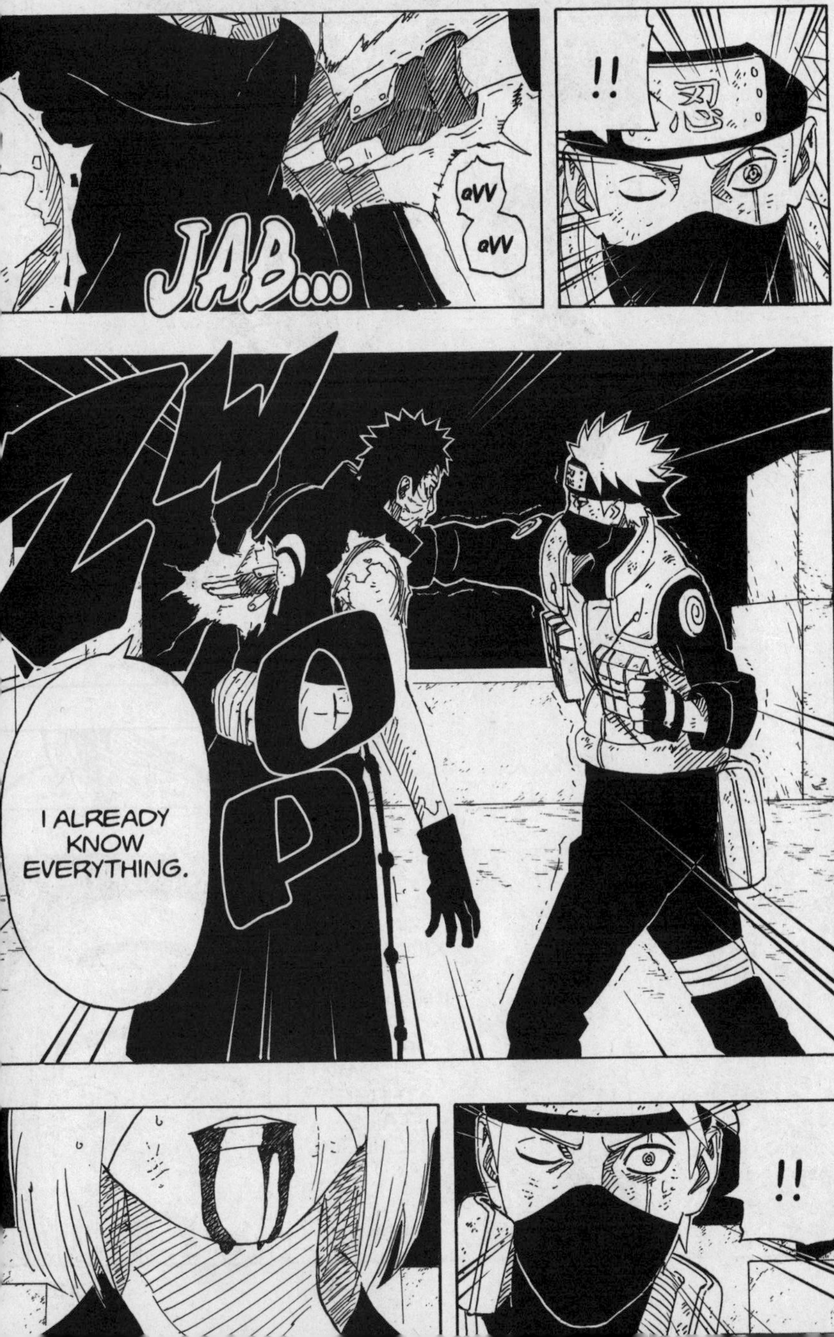
!!
JAB...
GAV
GAV
ZWOP
I ALREADY KNOW EVERYTHING.
!!

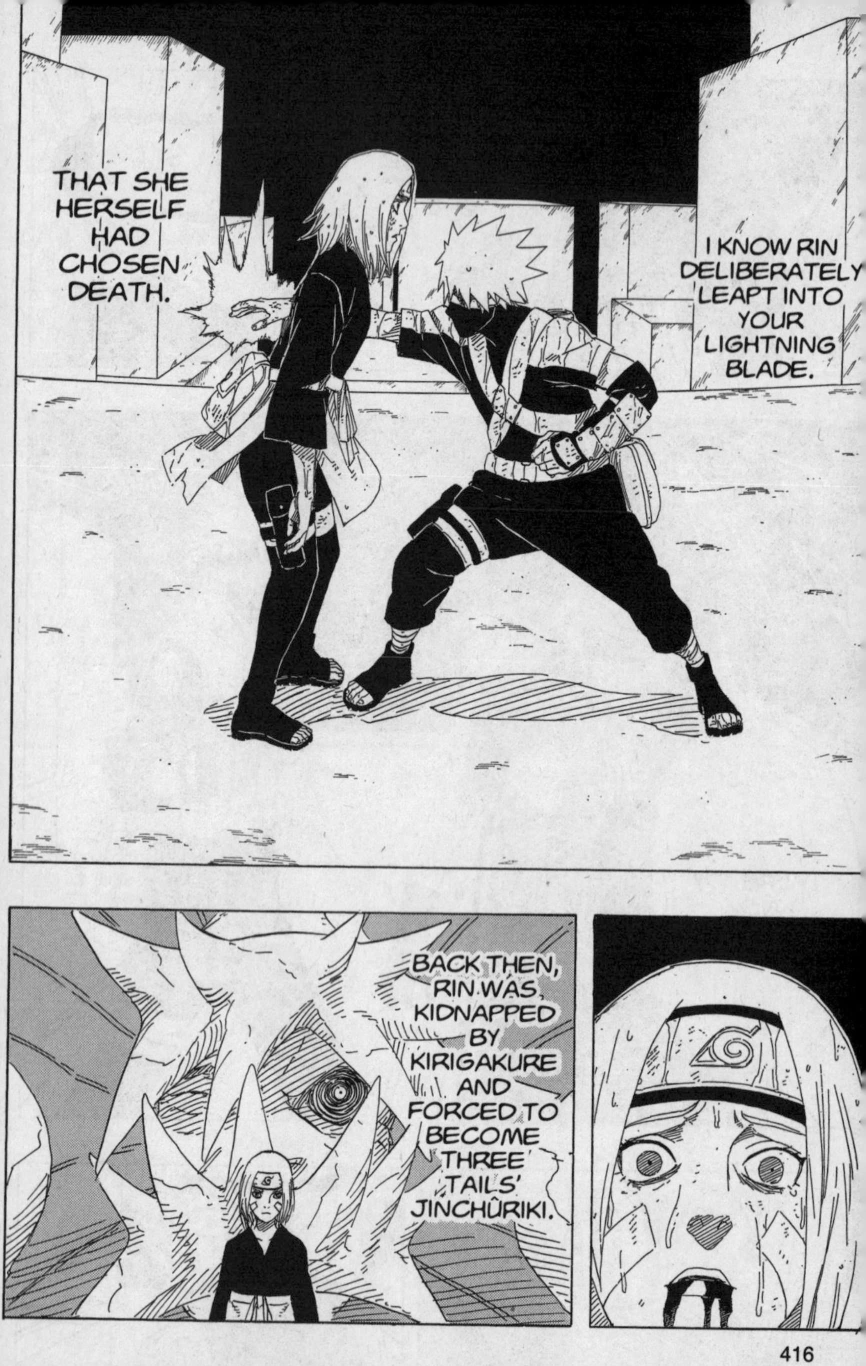
I KNOW RIN DELIBERATELY LEAPT INTO YOUR LIGHTNING BLADE.
THAT SHE HERSELF HAD CHOSEN DEATH.
BACK THEN, RIN WAS KIDNAPPED BY KIRIGAKURE AND FORCED TO BECOME THREE TAILS' JINCHÛRIKI.

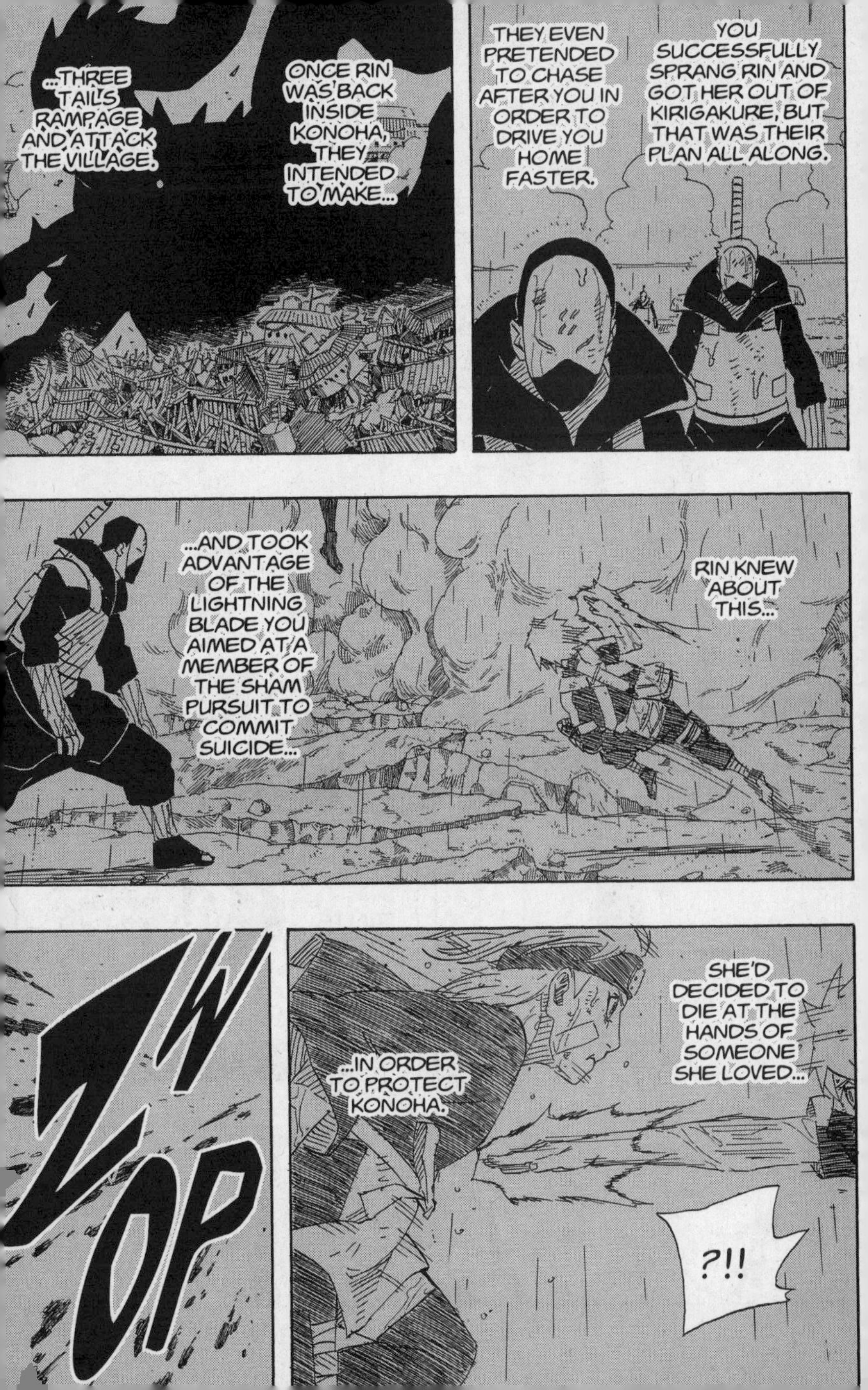
YOU SUCCESSFULLY SPRANG RIN AND GOT HER OUT OF KIRIGAKURE, BUT THAT WAS THEIR PLAN ALL ALONG.
THEY EVEN PRETENDED TO CHASE AFTER YOU IN ORDER TO DRIVE YOU HOME FASTER.
ONCE RIN WAS BACK INSIDE KONOHA, THEY INTENDED TO MAKE...
...THREE TAILS RAMPAGE AND ATTACK THE VILLAGE.
RIN KNEW ABOUT THIS...
...AND TOOK ADVANTAGE OF THE LIGHTNING BLADE YOU AIMED AT A MEMBER OF THE SHAM PURSUIT TO COMMIT SUICIDE...
SHE'D DECIDED TO DIE AT THE HANDS OF SOMEONE SHE LOVED...
...IN ORDER TO PROTECT KONOHA.
?!!
ZWOP

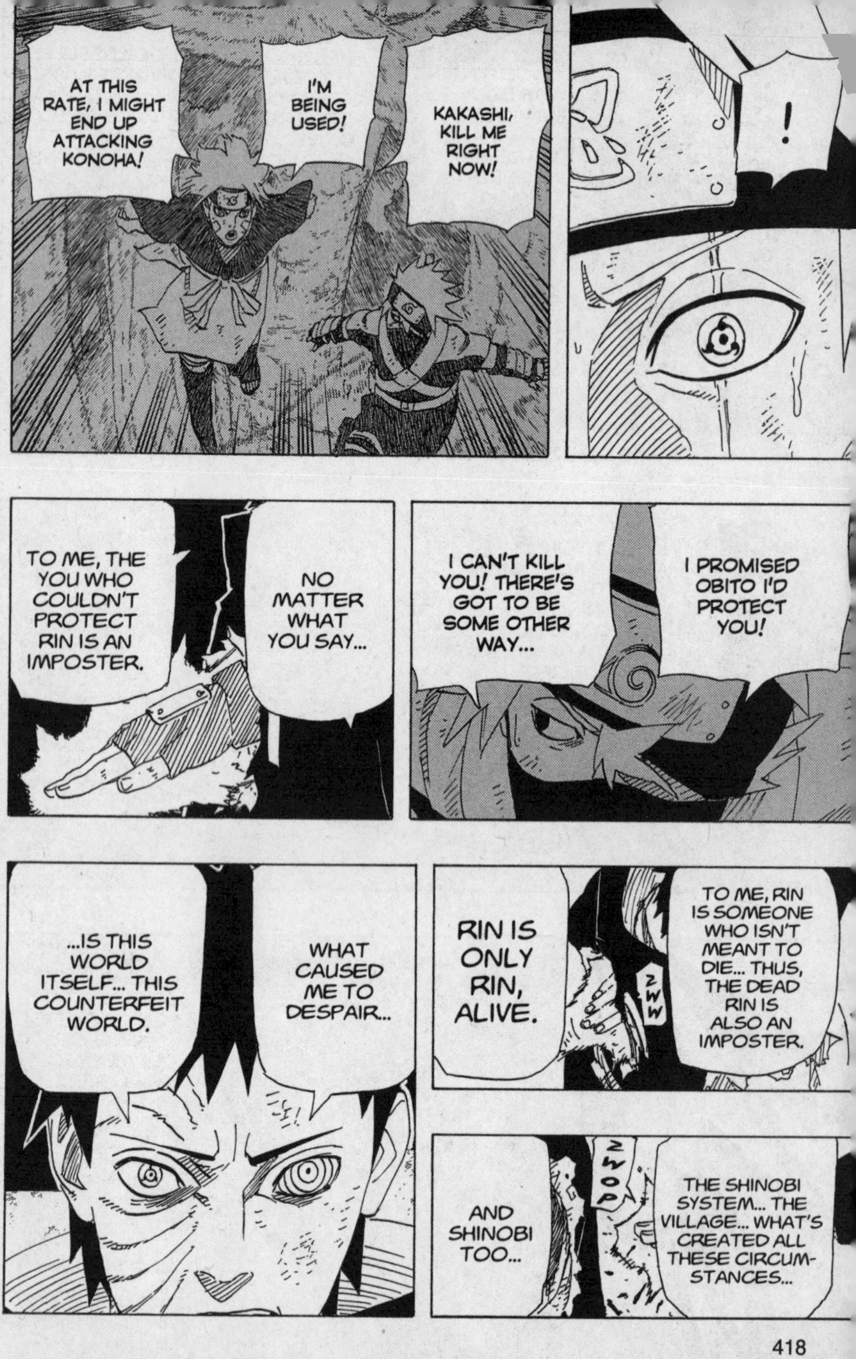
!
KAKASHI, KILL ME RIGHT NOW!
I'M BEING USED!
AT THIS RATE, I MIGHT END UP ATTACKING KONOHA!
I PROMISED OBITO I'D PROTECT YOU!
I CAN'T KILL YOU! THERE'S GOT TO BE SOME OTHER WAY...
NO MATTER WHAT YOU SAY...
TO ME, THE YOU WHO COULDN'T PROTECT RIN IS AN IMPOSTER.
TO ME, RIN IS SOMEONE WHO ISN'T MEANT TO DIE... THUS, THE DEAD RIN IS ALSO AN IMPOSTER.
ZWW
RIN IS ONLY RIN, ALIVE.
ZWOP
THE SHINOBI SYSTEM... THE VILLAGE... WHAT'S CREATED ALL THESE CIRCUMSTANCES...
AND SHINOBI TOO...
WHAT CAUSED ME TO DESPAIR...
...IS THIS WORLD ITSELF... THIS COUNTERFEIT WORLD.

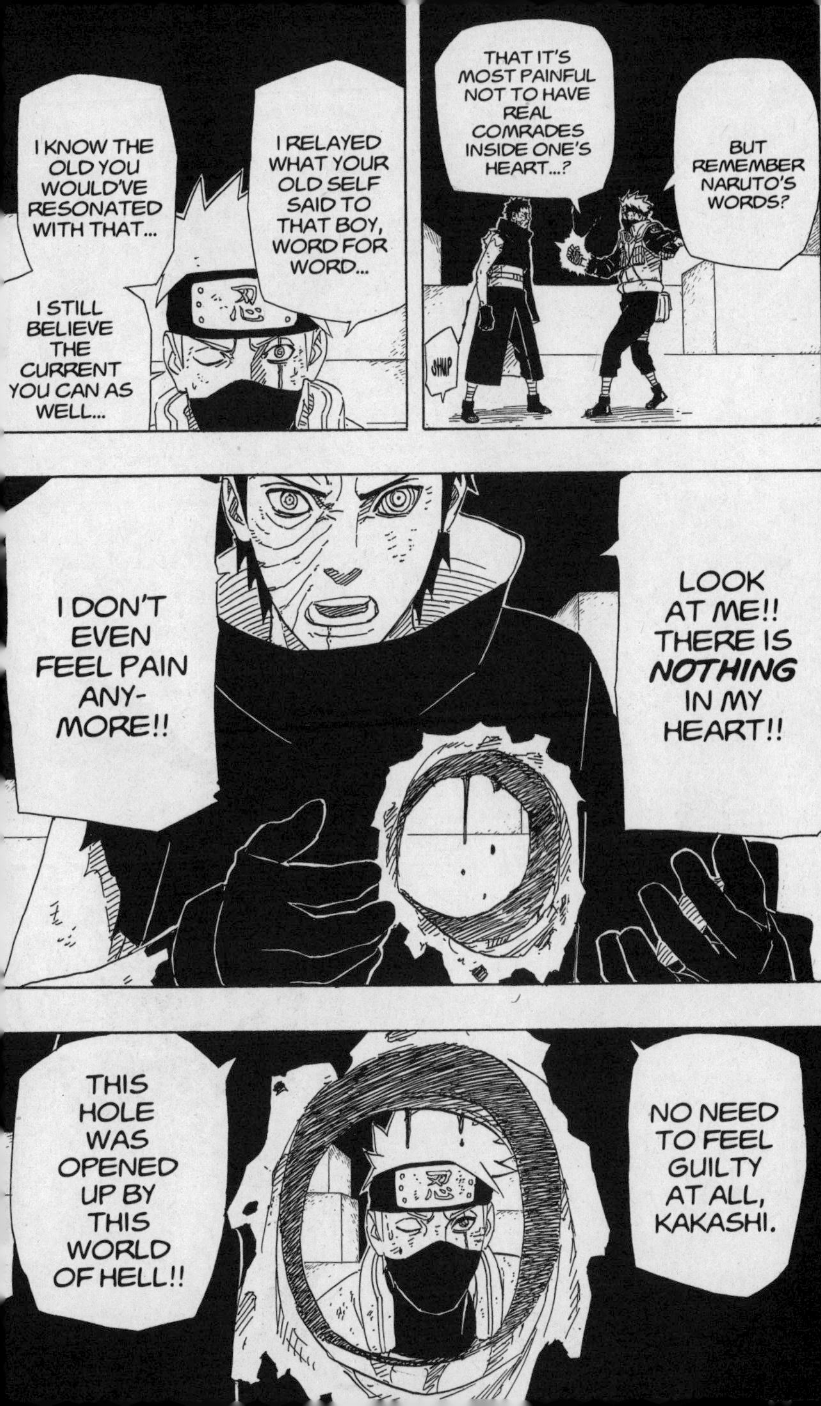
BUT REMEMBER NARUTO'S WORDS?
THAT IT'S MOST PAINFUL NOT TO HAVE REAL COMRADES INSIDE ONE'S HEART...?
I RELAYED WHAT YOUR OLD SELF SAID TO THAT BOY, WORD FOR WORD...
I KNOW THE OLD YOU WOULD'VE RESONATED WITH THAT...
I STILL BELIEVE THE CURRENT YOU CAN AS WELL...
LOOK AT ME!! THERE IS NOTHING IN MY HEART!!
I DON'T EVEN FEEL PAIN ANY-MORE!!
NO NEED TO FEEL GUILTY AT ALL, KAKASHI.
THIS HOLE WAS OPENED UP BY THIS WORLD OF HELL!!

Number 630: Something to Fill the Hole

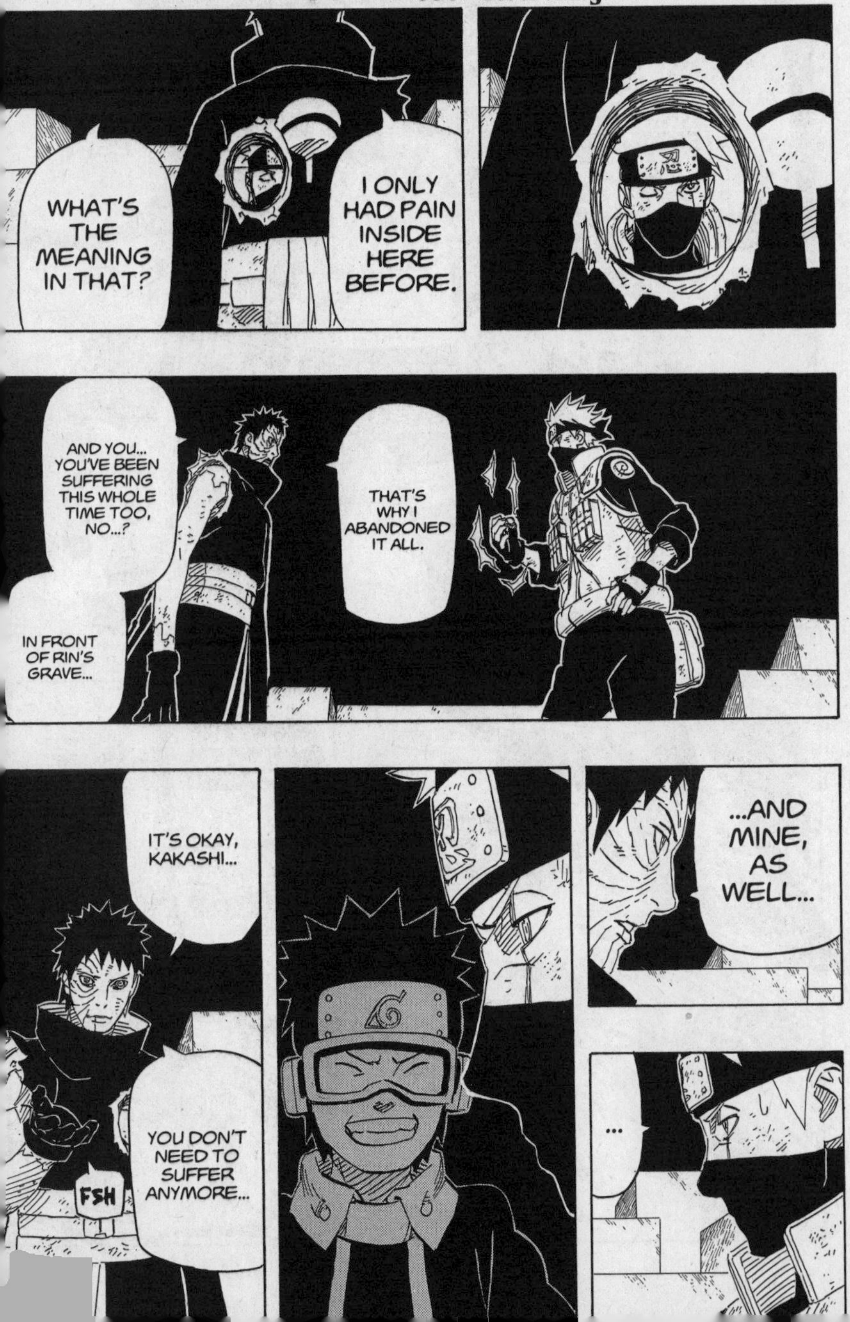
I ONLY HAD PAIN INSIDE HERE BEFORE.
WHAT'S THE MEANING IN THAT?
THAT'S WHY I ABANDONED IT ALL.
AND YOU... YOU'VE BEEN SUFFERING THIS WHOLE TIME TOO, NO...?
IN FRONT OF RIN'S GRAVE...
...AND MINE, AS WELL...
...
IT'S OKAY, KAKASHI...
YOU DON'T NEED TO SUFFER ANYMORE...
FSH

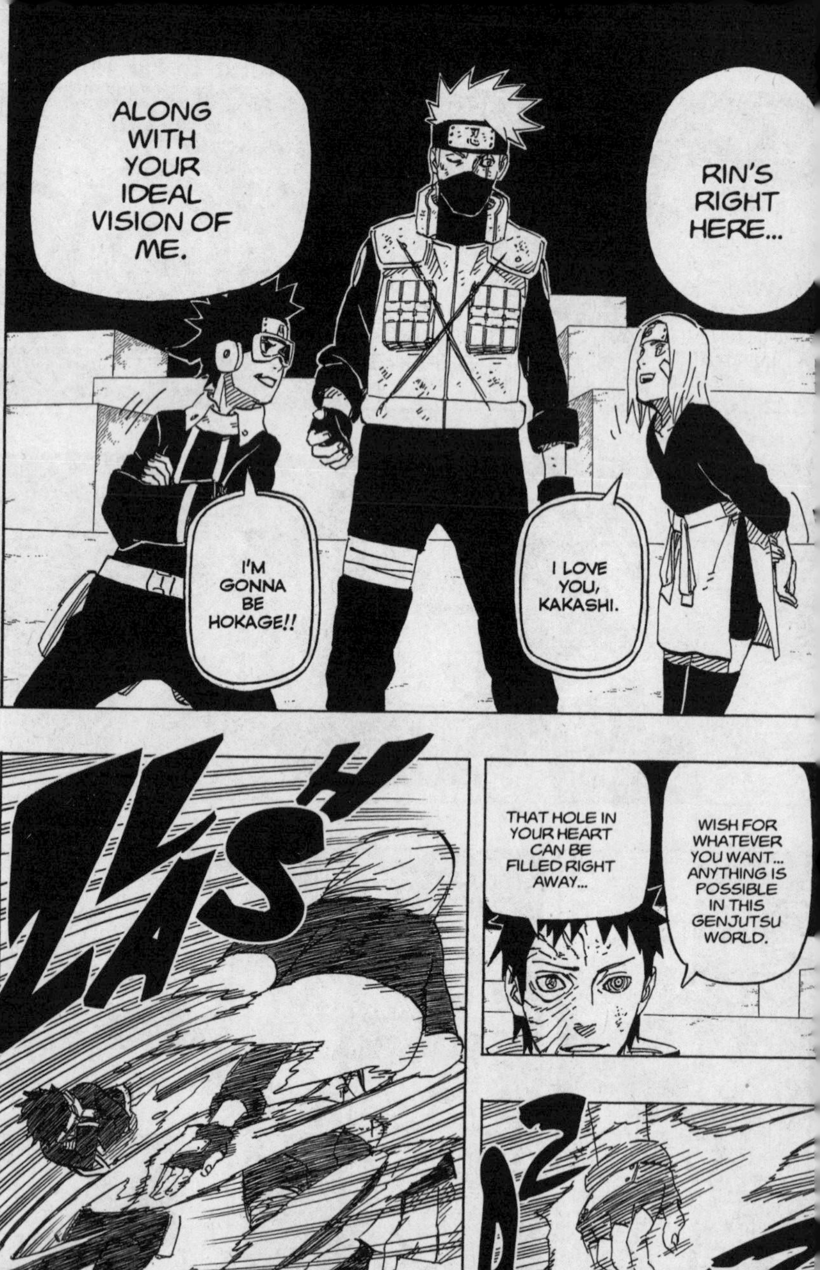
RIN'S RIGHT HERE...
ALONG WITH YOUR IDEAL VISION OF ME.
I LOVE YOU, KAKASHI.
I'M GONNA BE HOKAGE!!
WISH FOR WHATEVER YOU WANT... ANYTHING IS POSSIBLE IN THIS GENJUTSU WORLD.
THAT HOLE IN YOUR HEART CAN BE FILLED RIGHT AWAY...
BZZ
ZWASH

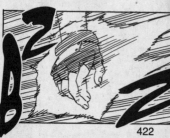

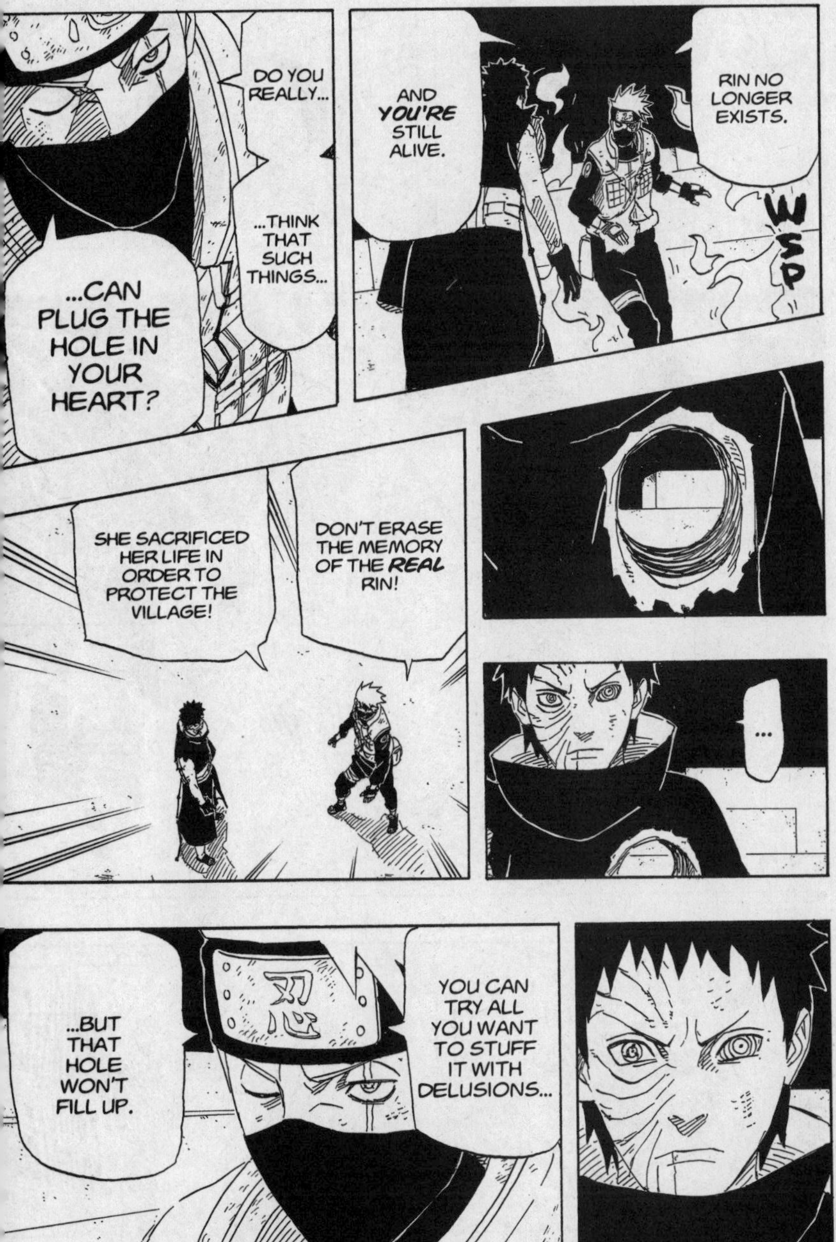
RIN NO LONGER EXISTS.
WSP
AND YOU'RE STILL ALIVE.
DO YOU REALLY...
...THINK THAT SUCH THINGS...
...CAN PLUG THE HOLE IN YOUR HEART?
...
DON'T ERASE THE MEMORY OF THE REAL RIN!
SHE SACRIFICED HER LIFE IN ORDER TO PROTECT THE VILLAGE!
YOU CAN TRY ALL YOU WANT TO STUFF IT WITH DELUSIONS...
...BUT THAT HOLE WON'T FILL UP.

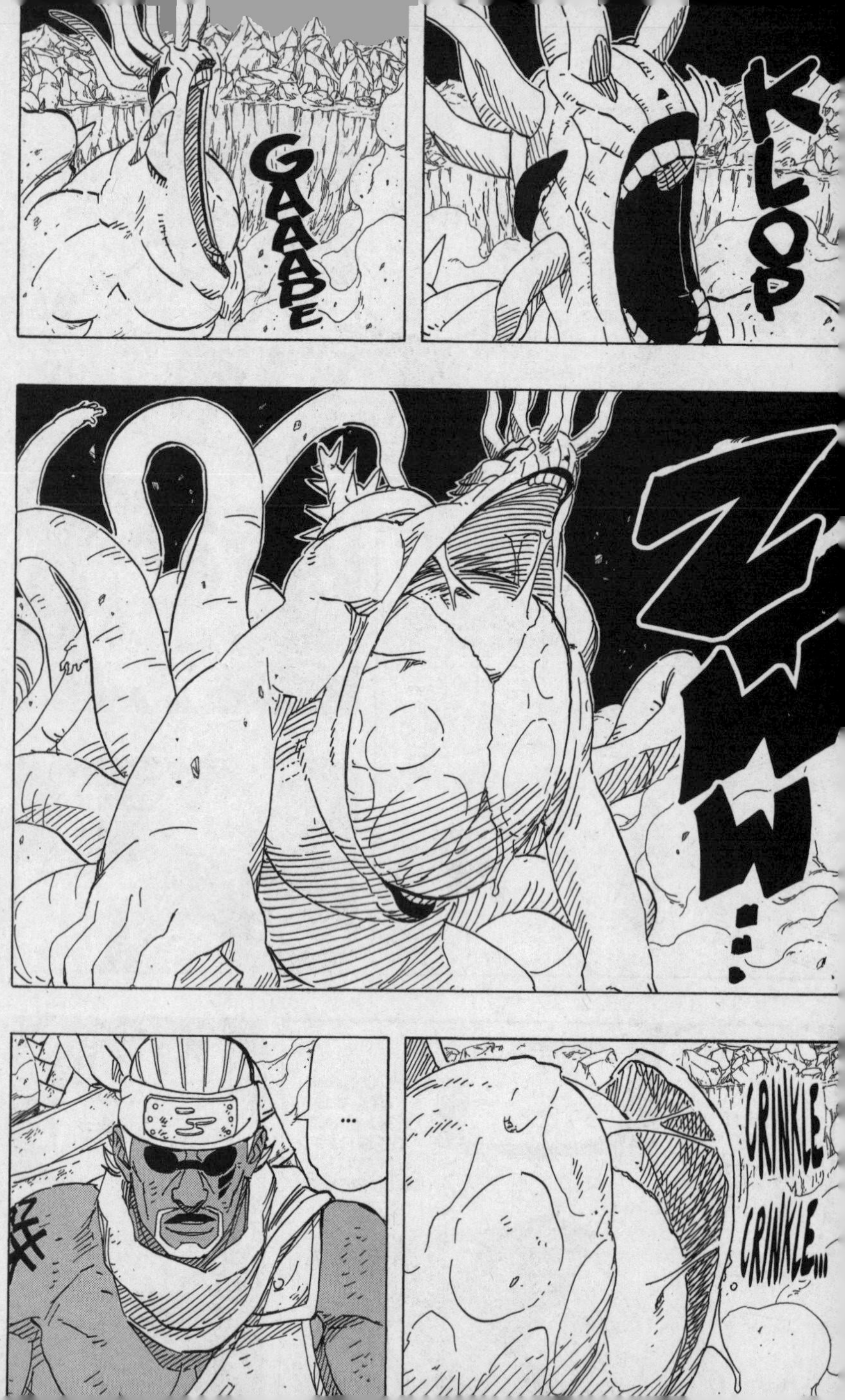
KLOP
GAAADE
ZWW...
CRINKLE
CRINKLE...
...

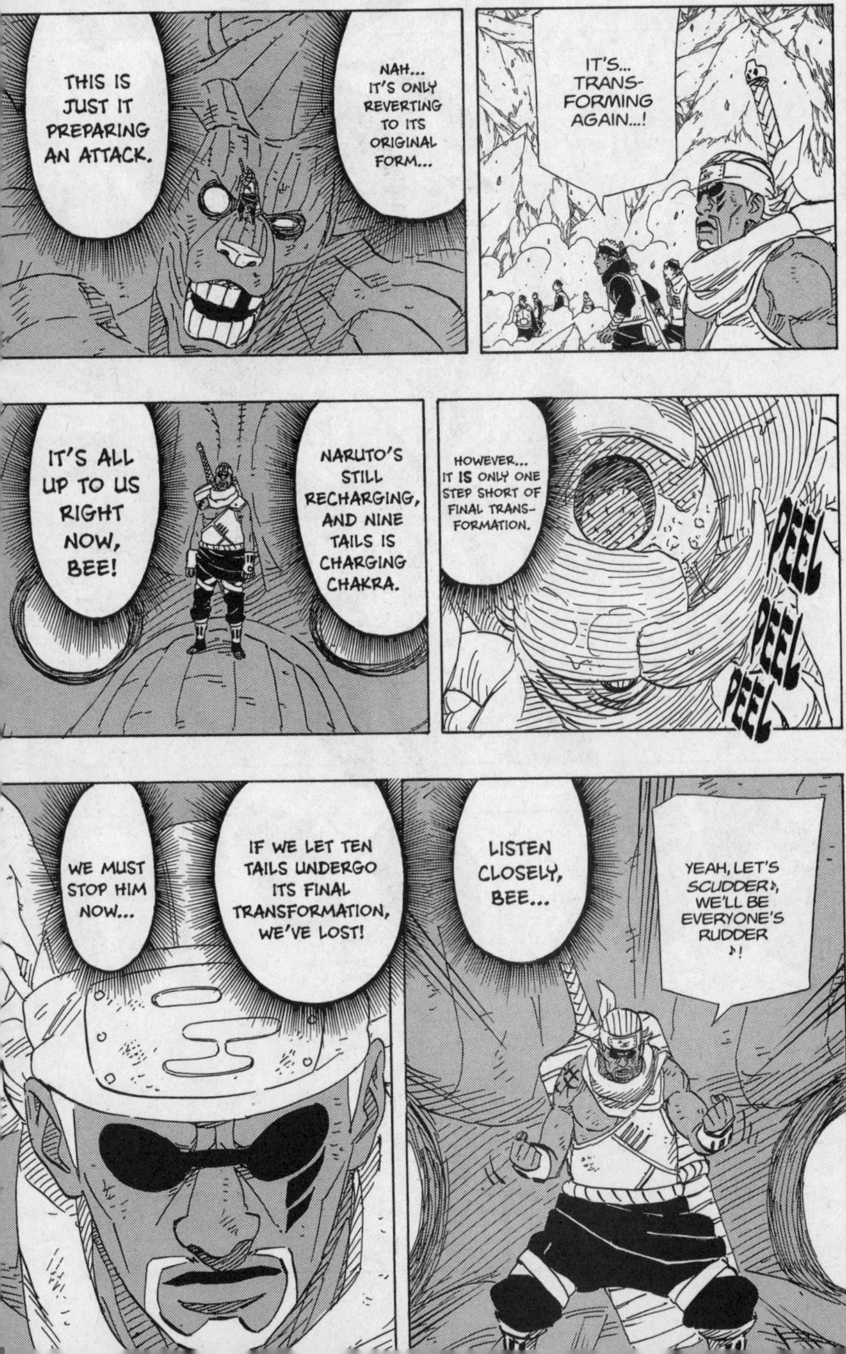
IT'S... TRANS-FORMING AGAIN...!
NAH... IT'S ONLY REVERTING TO ITS ORIGINAL FORM...
THIS IS JUST IT PREPARING AN ATTACK.
HOWEVER... IT IS ONLY ONE STEP SHORT OF FINAL TRANS-FORMATION.
PEEL PEEL PEEL
NARUTO'S STILL RECHARGING, AND NINE TAILS IS CHARGING CHAKRA.
IT'S ALL UP TO US RIGHT NOW, BEE!
YEAH, LET'S SCUDDER♪, WE'LL BE EVERYONE'S RUDDER ♪!
LISTEN CLOSELY, BEE...
IF WE LET TEN TAILS UNDERGO ITS FINAL TRANSFORMATION, WE'VE LOST!
WE MUST STOP HIM NOW...

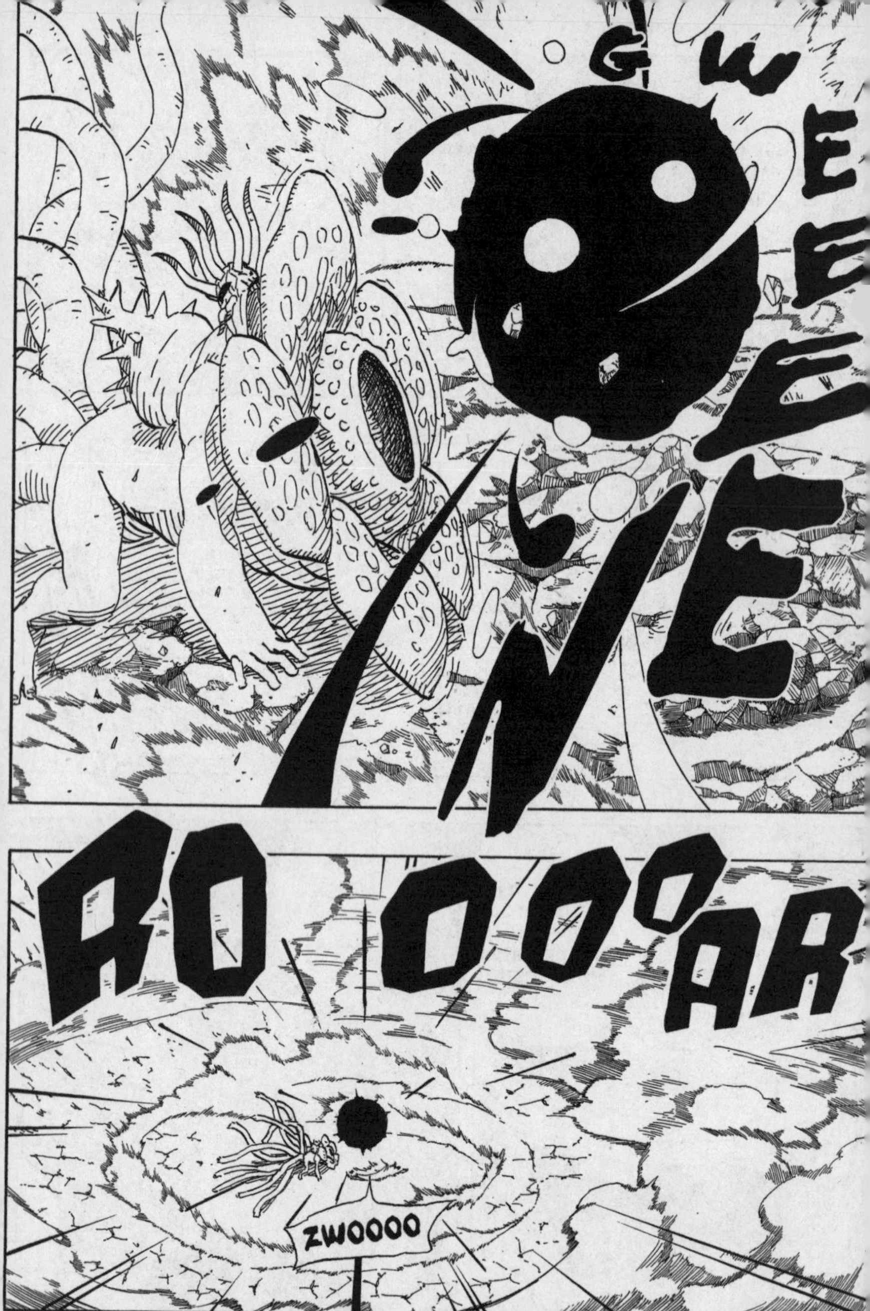
ROOOOAR
ZWOOOO

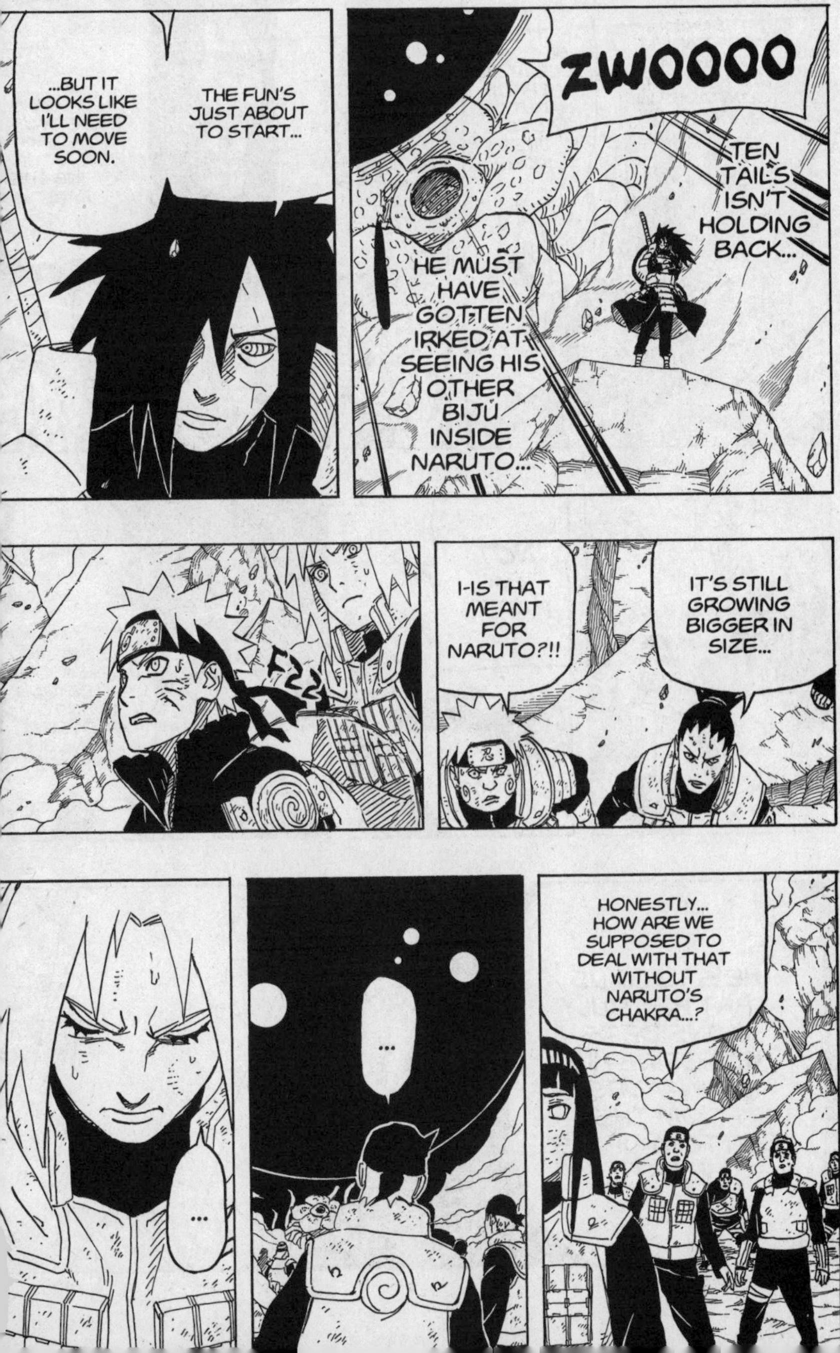
ZWOOOO
TEN TAILS ISN'T HOLDING BACK...
HE MUST HAVE GOTTEN IRKED AT SEEING HIS OTHER BIJU INSIDE NARUTO...
THE FUN'S JUST ABOUT TO START...
...BUT IT LOOKS LIKE I'LL NEED TO MOVE SOON.
IT'S STILL GROWING BIGGER IN SIZE...
I-IS THAT MEANT FOR NARUTO?!!
FZZ
HONESTLY... HOW ARE WE SUPPOSED TO DEAL WITH THAT WITHOUT NARUTO'S CHAKRA...?
...
...

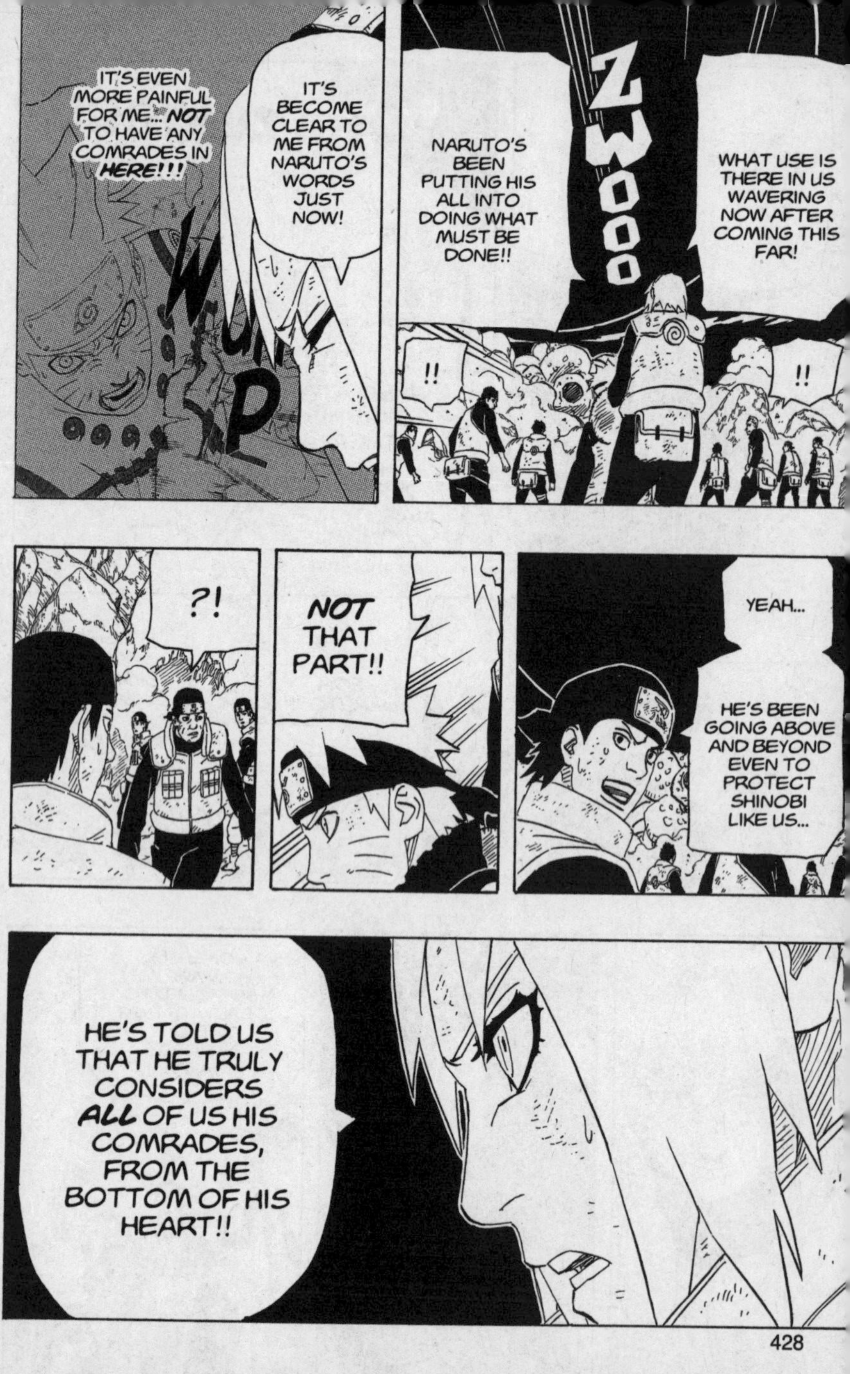
WHAT USE IS THERE IN US WAVERING NOW AFTER COMING THIS FAR!
NARUTO'S BEEN PUTTING HIS ALL INTO DOING WHAT MUST BE DONE!!
ZWOOO
!!
!!
IT'S BECOME CLEAR TO ME FROM NARUTO'S WORDS JUST NOW!
IT'S EVEN MORE PAINFUL FOR ME... **NOT** TO HAVE ANY COMRADES IN **HERE!!!**
WUMP
YEAH...
HE'S BEEN GOING ABOVE AND BEYOND EVEN TO PROTECT SHINOBI LIKE US...
NOT THAT PART!!
?!
HE'S TOLD US THAT HE TRULY CONSIDERS **ALL** OF US HIS COMRADES, FROM THE BOTTOM OF HIS HEART!!

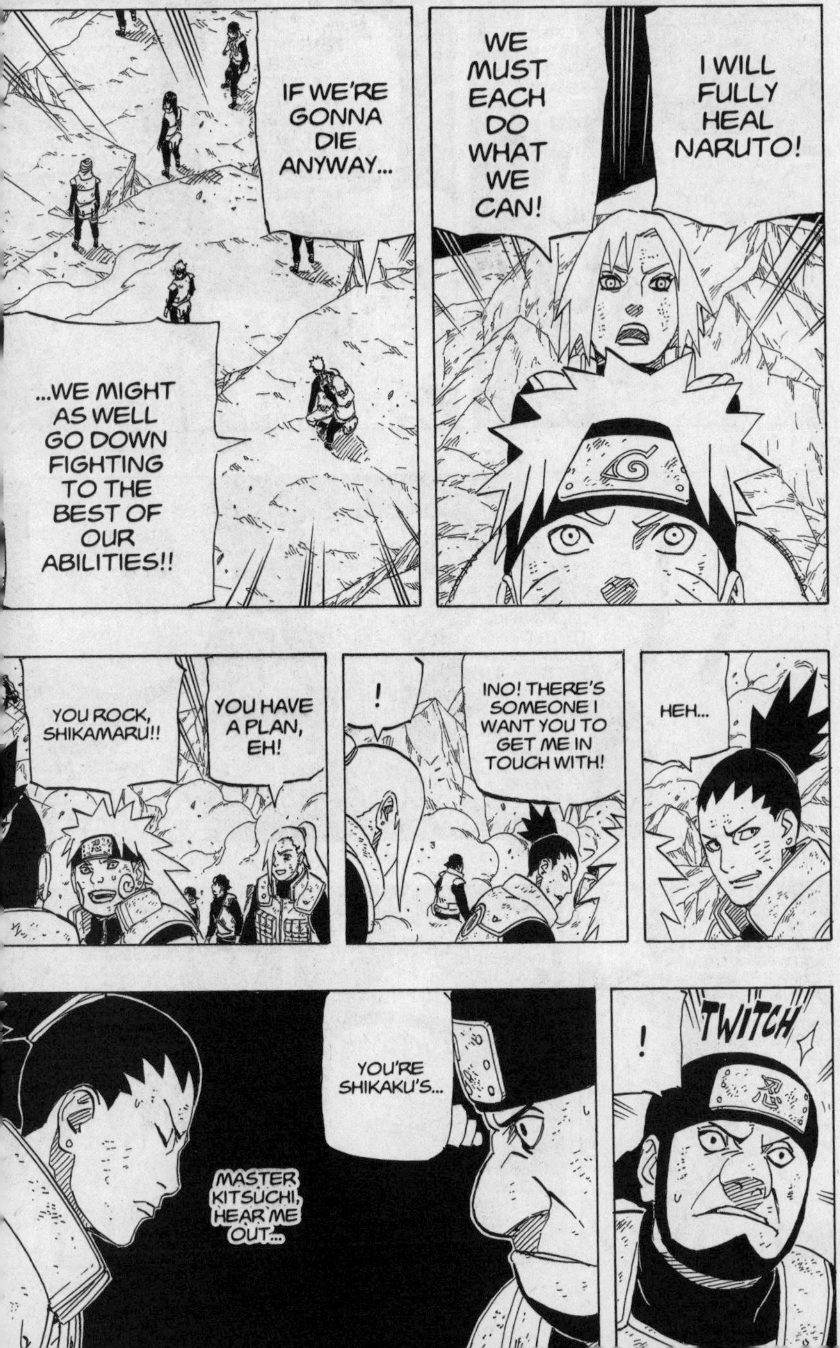
I WILL FULLY HEAL NARUTO!
WE MUST EACH DO WHAT WE CAN!
IF WE'RE GONNA DIE ANYWAY...
...WE MIGHT AS WELL GO DOWN FIGHTING TO THE BEST OF OUR ABILITIES!!
HEH...
INO! THERE'S SOMEONE I WANT YOU TO GET ME IN TOUCH WITH!
!
YOU HAVE A PLAN, EH!
YOU ROCK, SHIKAMARU!!
TWITCH
!
YOU'RE SHIKAKU'S...
MASTER KITSUCHI, HEAR ME OUT...

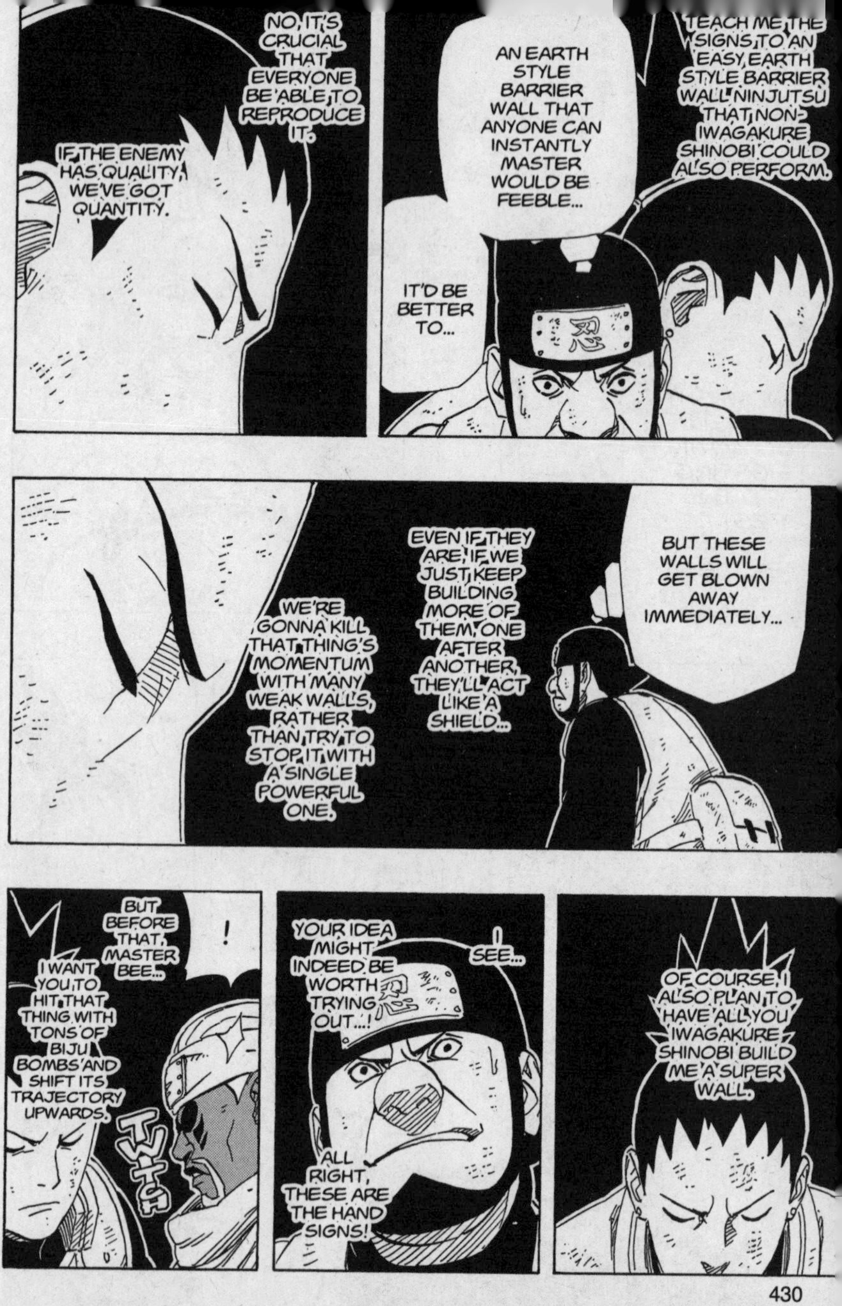
TEACH ME THE SIGNS TO AN EASY EARTH STYLE BARRIER WALL NINJUTSU THAT NON-IWAGAKURE SHINOBI COULD ALSO PERFORM.
AN EARTH STYLE BARRIER WALL THAT ANYONE CAN INSTANTLY MASTER WOULD BE FEEBLE...
IT'D BE BETTER TO...
NO, IT'S CRUCIAL THAT EVERYONE BE ABLE TO REPRODUCE IT.
IF THE ENEMY HAS QUALITY, WE'VE GOT QUANTITY.
BUT THESE WALLS WILL GET BLOWN AWAY IMMEDIATELY...
EVEN IF THEY ARE, IF WE JUST KEEP BUILDING MORE OF THEM, ONE AFTER ANOTHER, THEY'LL ACT LIKE A SHIELD...
WE'RE GONNA KILL THAT THING'S MOMENTUM WITH MANY WEAK WALLS, RATHER THAN TRY TO STOP IT WITH A SINGLE POWERFUL ONE.
OF COURSE, I ALSO PLAN TO HAVE ALL YOU IWAGAKURE SHINOBI BUILD ME A SUPER WALL.
I SEE...
YOUR IDEA MIGHT INDEED BE WORTH TRYING OUT...!
ALL RIGHT, THESE ARE THE HAND SIGNS!
!
BUT BEFORE THAT, MASTER BEE...
I WANT YOU TO HIT THAT THING WITH TONS OF BIJU BOMBS AND SHIFT ITS TRAJECTORY UPWARDS.
TWITCH

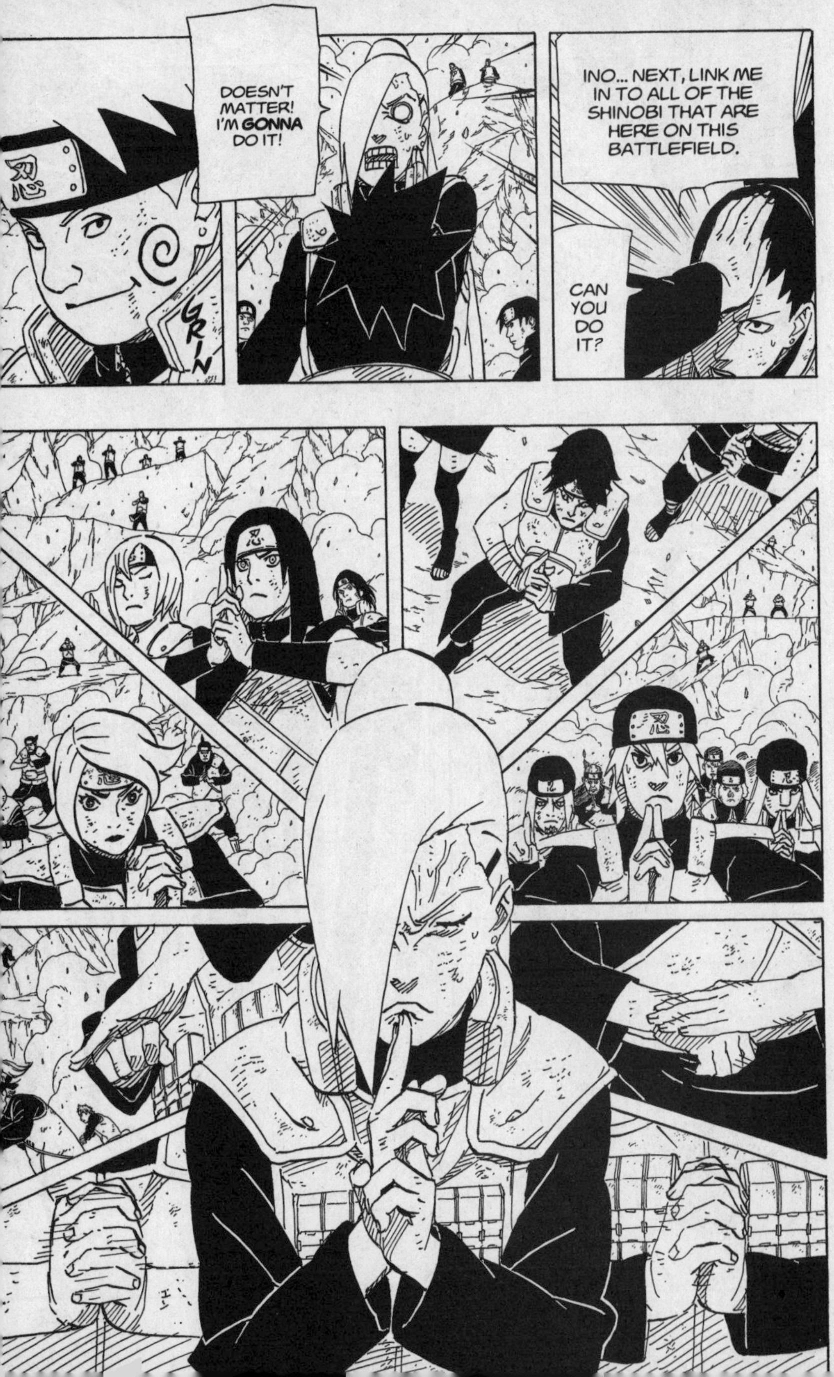

INO... NEXT, LINK ME IN TO ALL OF THE SHINOBI THAT ARE HERE ON THIS BATTLEFIELD.
CAN YOU DO IT?
DOESN'T MATTER! I'M **GONNA** DO IT!
GRIN

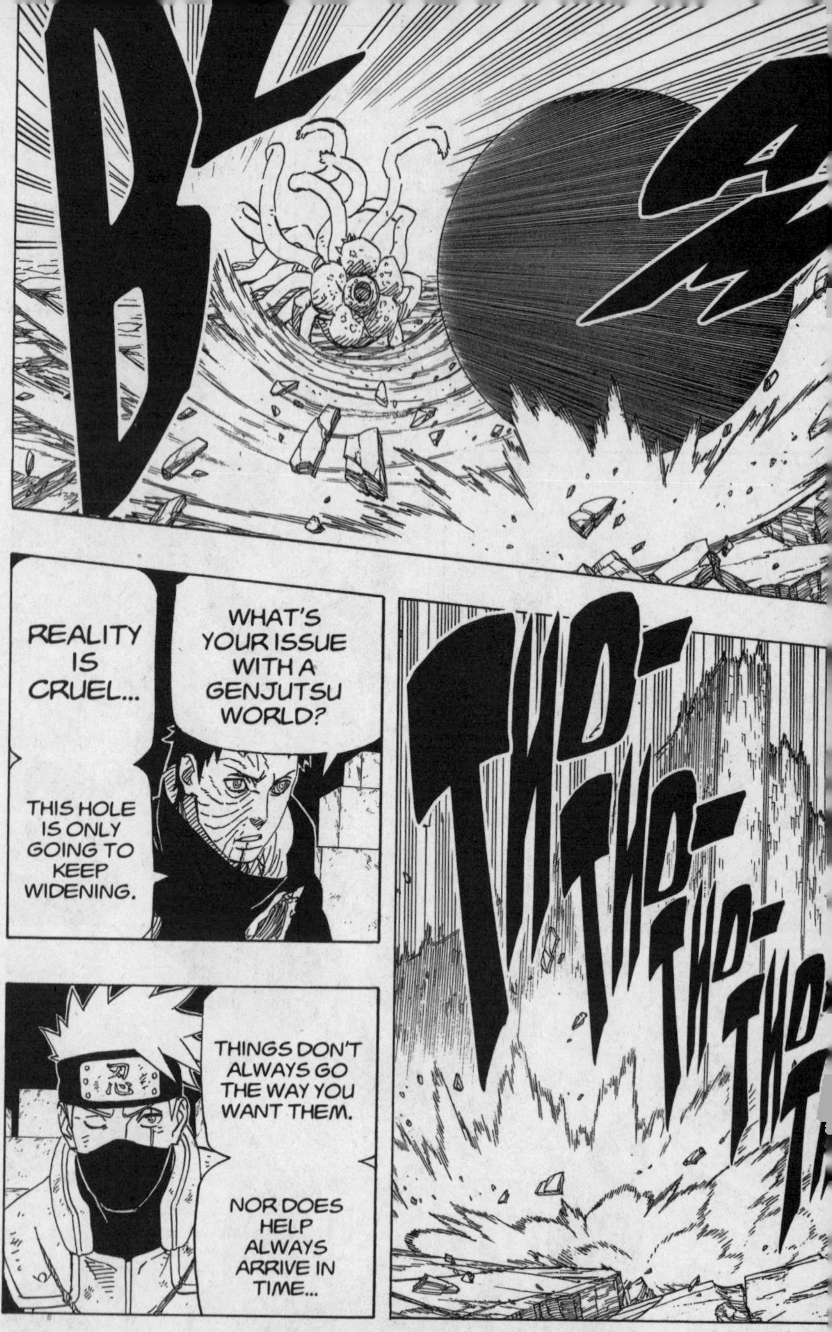
THO-THO-THO-THO-TH...
WHAT'S YOUR ISSUE WITH A GENJUTSU WORLD?
REALITY IS CRUEL...
THIS HOLE IS ONLY GOING TO KEEP WIDENING.
THINGS DON'T ALWAYS GO THE WAY YOU WANT THEM.
NOR DOES HELP ALWAYS ARRIVE IN TIME...

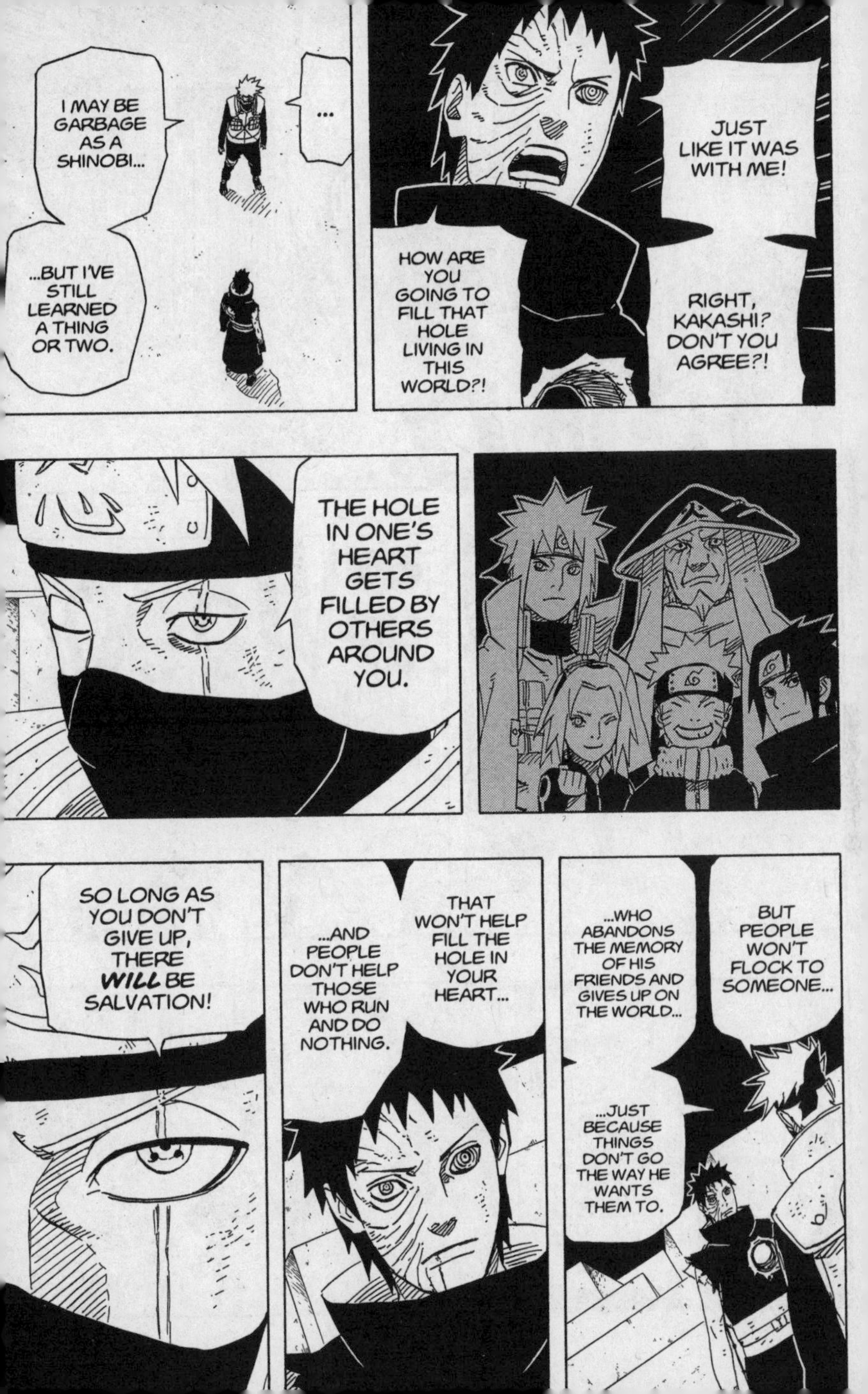
JUST LIKE IT WAS WITH ME!
HOW ARE YOU GOING TO FILL THAT HOLE LIVING IN THIS WORLD?!
RIGHT, KAKASHI? DON'T YOU AGREE?!
...
I MAY BE GARBAGE AS A SHINOBI...
...BUT I'VE STILL LEARNED A THING OR TWO.
THE HOLE IN ONE'S HEART GETS FILLED BY OTHERS AROUND YOU.
BUT PEOPLE WON'T FLOCK TO SOMEONE...
...WHO ABANDONS THE MEMORY OF HIS FRIENDS AND GIVES UP ON THE WORLD...
...JUST BECAUSE THINGS DON'T GO THE WAY HE WANTS THEM TO.
THAT WON'T HELP FILL THE HOLE IN YOUR HEART...
...AND PEOPLE DON'T HELP THOSE WHO RUN AND DO NOTHING.
SO LONG AS YOU DON'T GIVE UP, THERE **WILL** BE SALVATION!

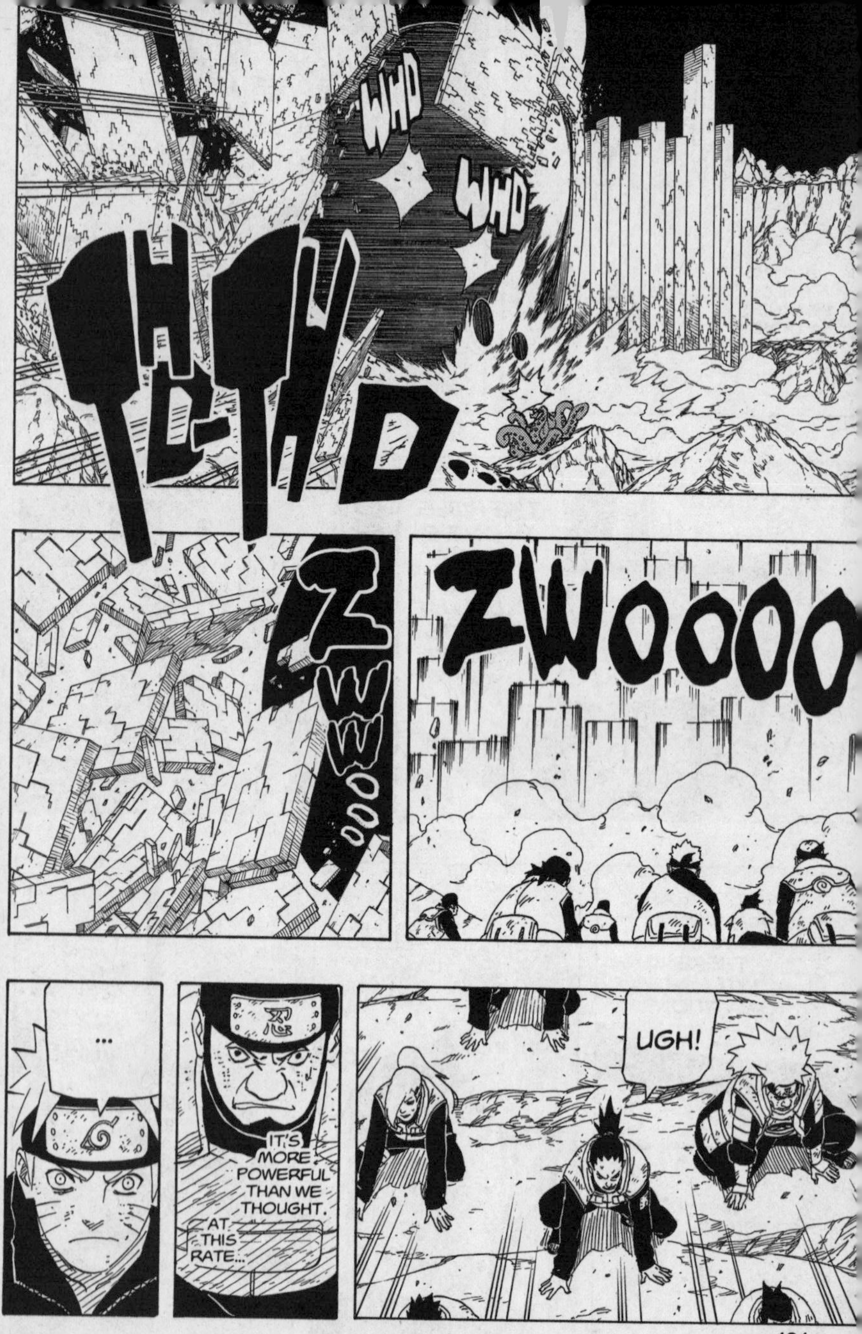
WHD
WHD
THD-THD...
ZWOOOO
ZWWOOOO
UGH!
IT'S MORE POWERFUL THAN WE THOUGHT.
AT THIS RATE...
...

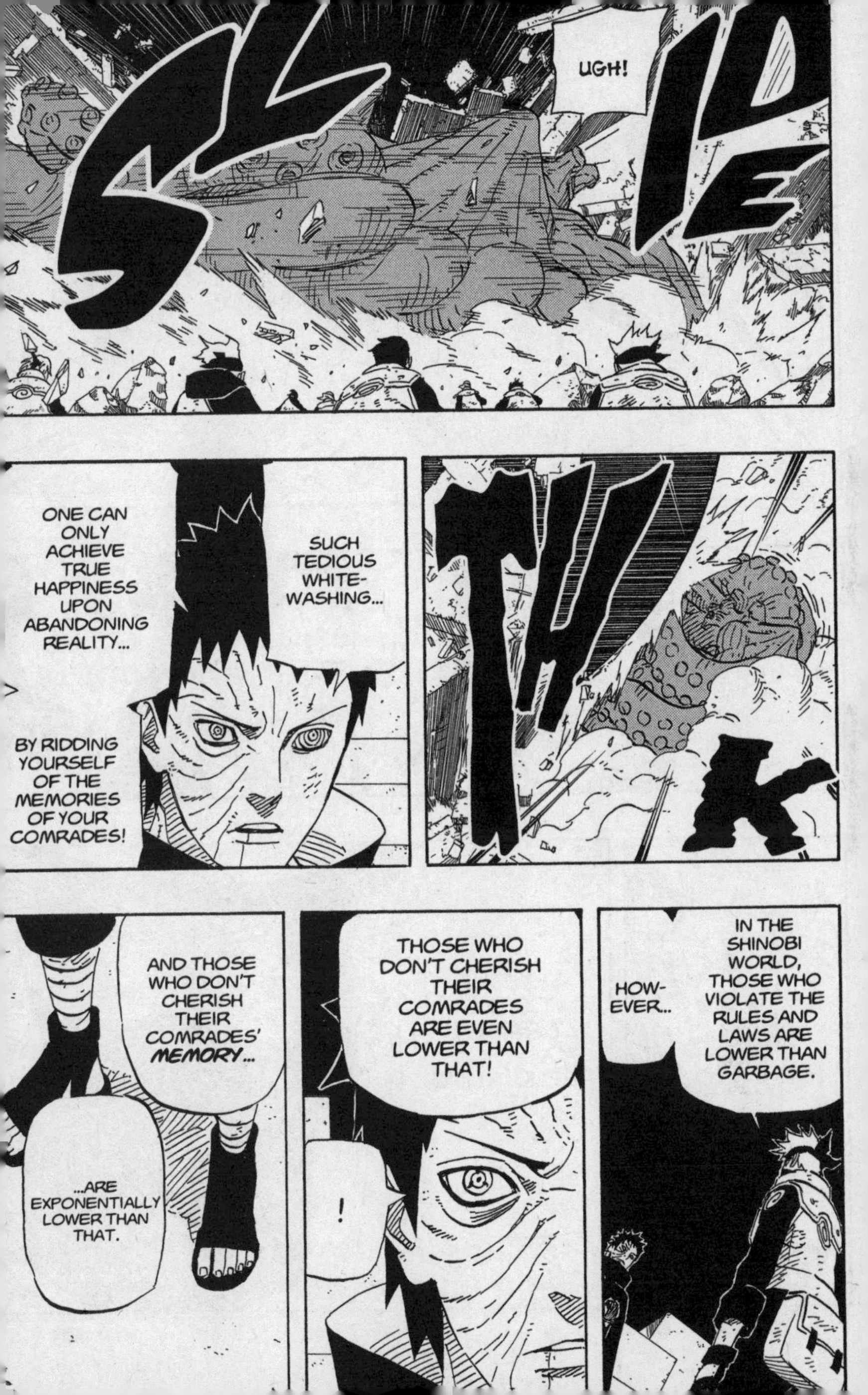
SLIDE
UGH!
SUCH TEDIOUS WHITE-WASHING...
ONE CAN ONLY ACHIEVE TRUE HAPPINESS UPON ABANDONING REALITY...
BY RIDDING YOURSELF OF THE MEMORIES OF YOUR COMRADES!
IN THE SHINOBI WORLD, THOSE WHO VIOLATE THE RULES AND LAWS ARE LOWER THAN GARBAGE.
HOW-EVER...
THOSE WHO DON'T CHERISH THEIR COMRADES ARE EVEN LOWER THAN THAT!
!
AND THOSE WHO DON'T CHERISH THEIR COMRADES' ***MEMORY***...
...ARE EXPONENTIALLY LOWER THAN THAT.

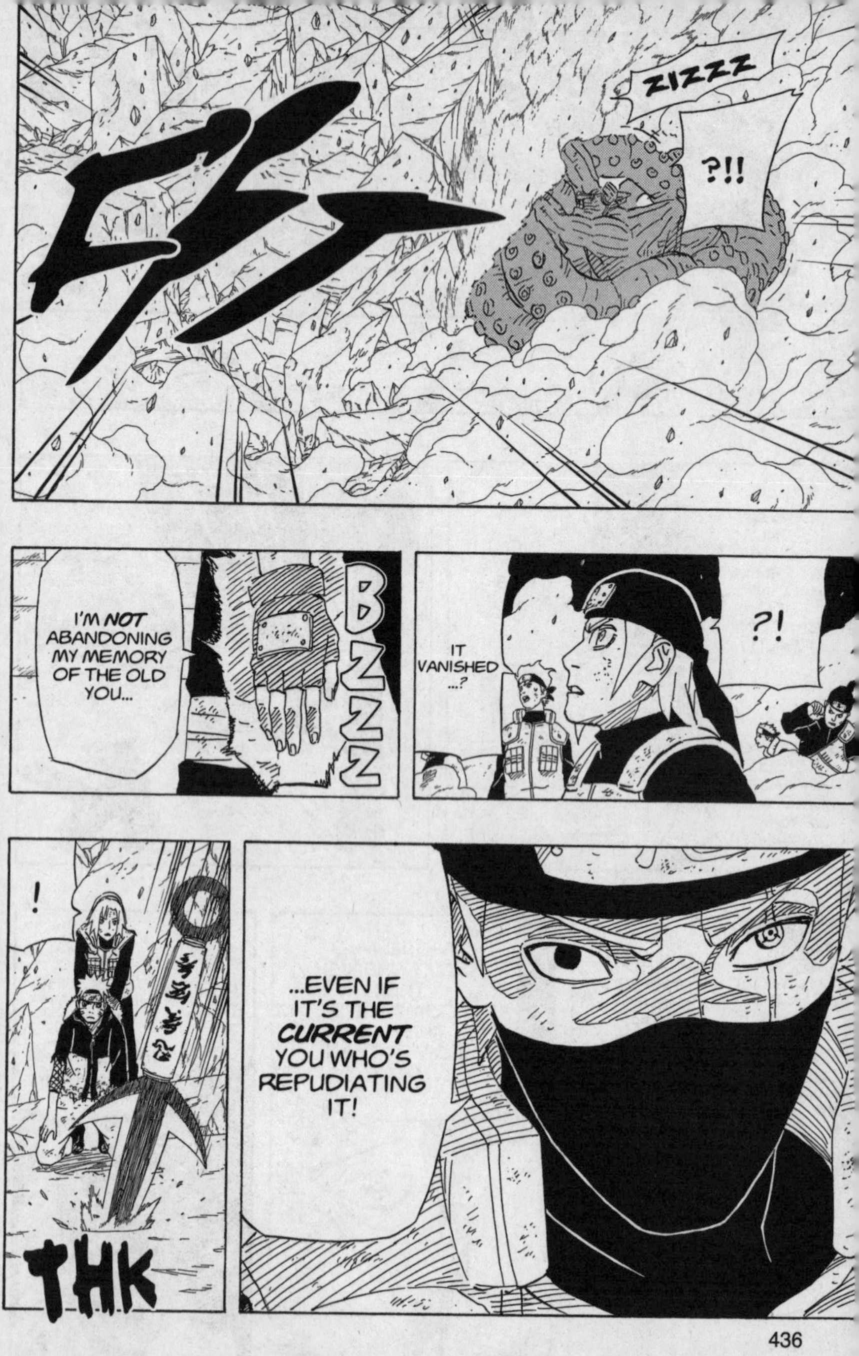
ZIZZZ
?!!
?!
IT VANISHED ...?
I'M NOT ABANDONING MY MEMORY OF THE OLD YOU...
BZZZ
...EVEN IF IT'S THE CURRENT YOU WHO'S REPUDIATING IT!
!
THK

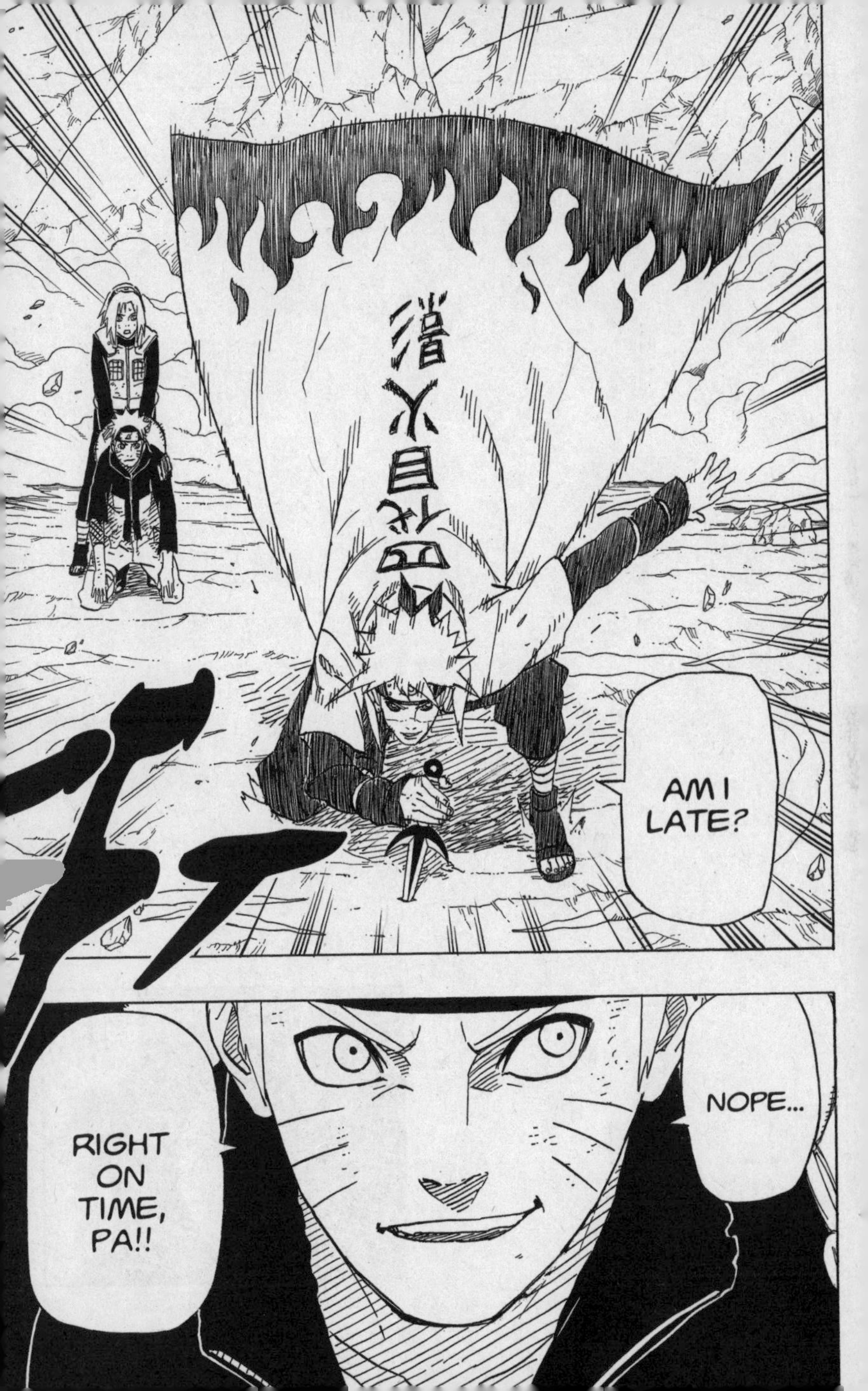
AM I LATE?
NOPE...
RIGHT ON TIME, PA!!

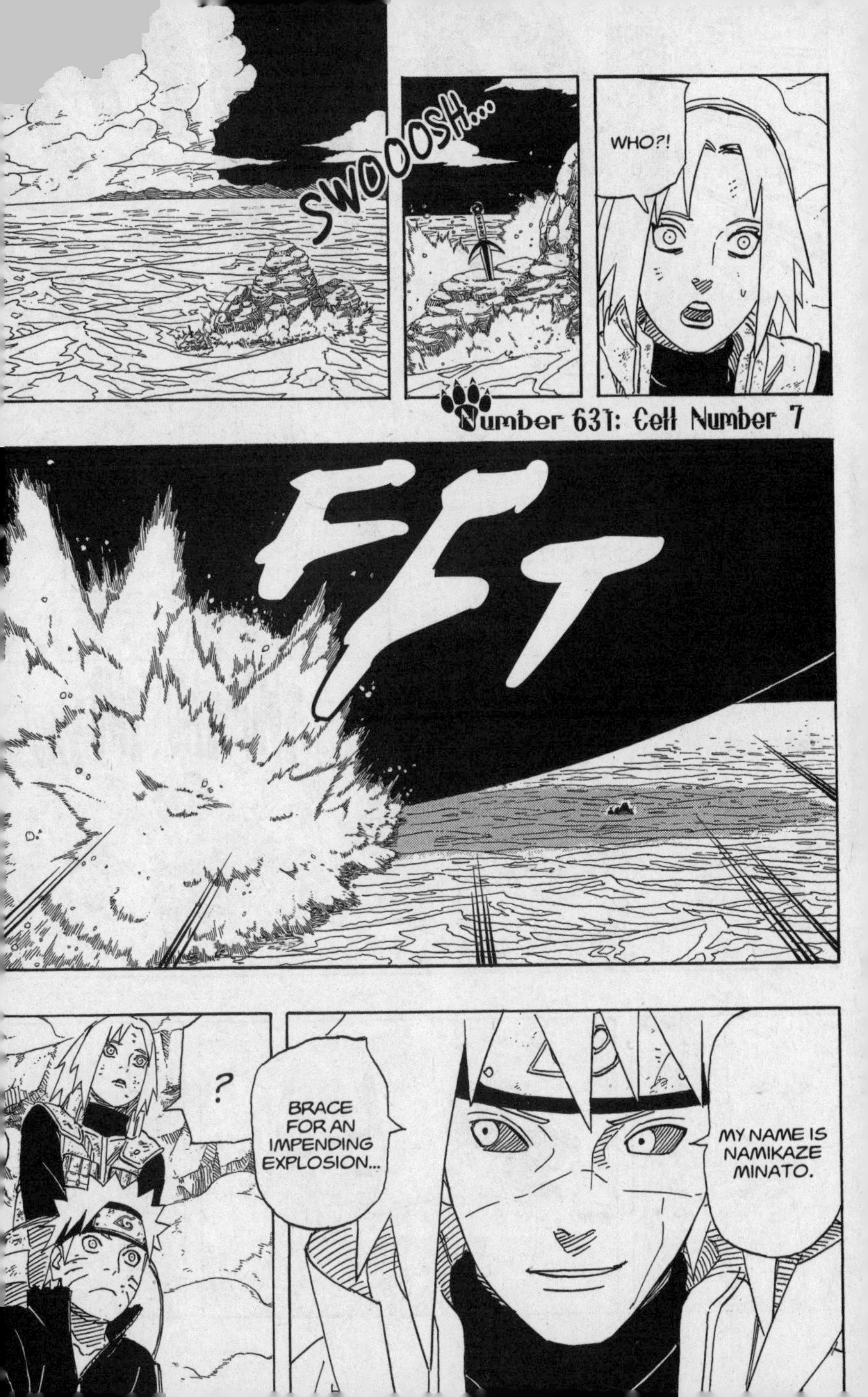
WHO?!
SWOOOSH...
Number 631: Cell Number 7
FFT
MY NAME IS NAMIKAZE MINATO.
BRACE FOR AN IMPENDING EXPLOSION...
?

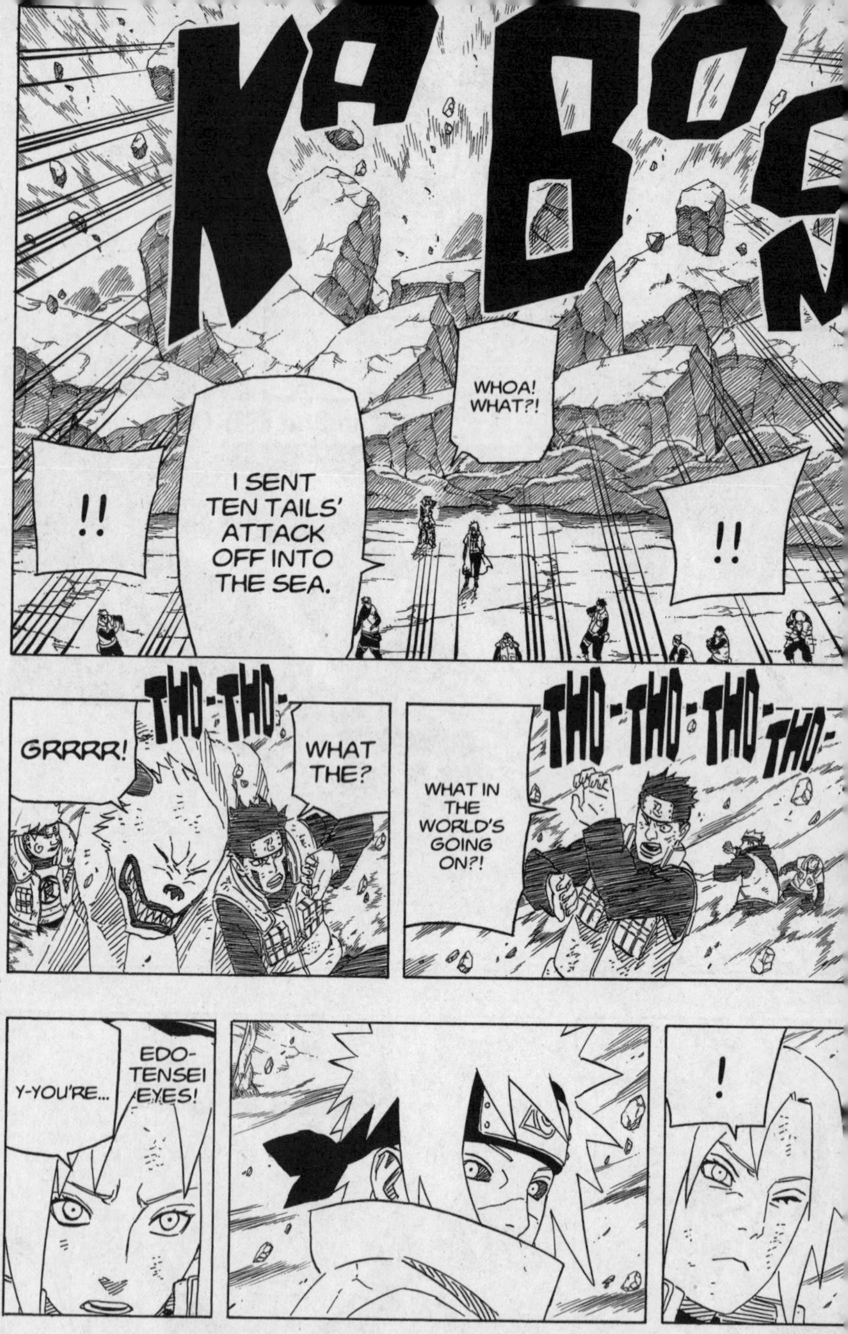
KA-BOOM
!!
WHOA! WHAT?!
I SENT TEN TAILS' ATTACK OFF INTO THE SEA.
!!
THO-THO-THO-THO-
WHAT IN THE WORLD'S GOING ON?!
THO-THO-
WHAT THE?
GRRRR!
!
EDO-TENSEI EYES!
Y-YOU'RE...

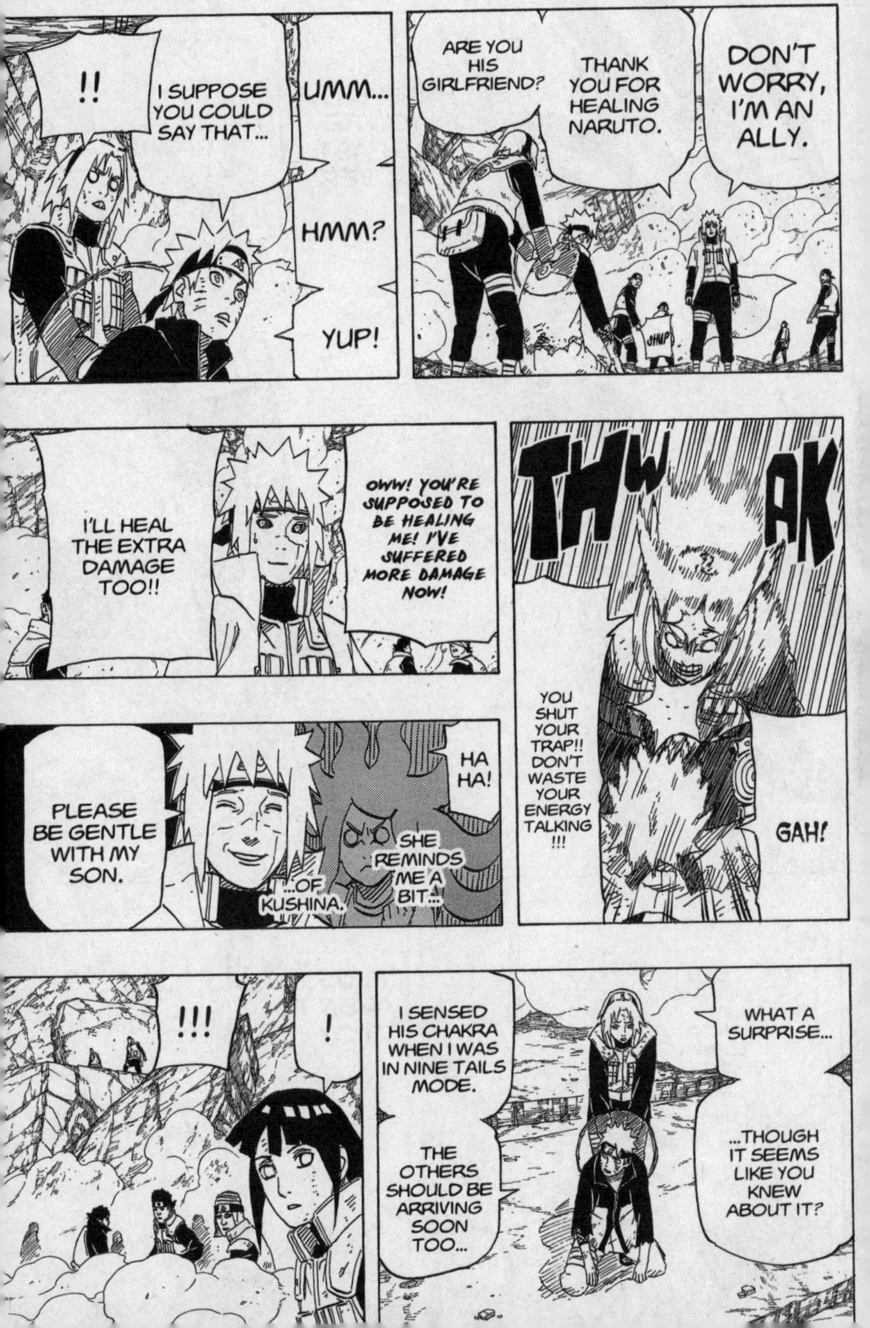
DON'T WORRY, I'M AN ALLY.
THANK YOU FOR HEALING NARUTO.
ARE YOU HIS GIRLFRIEND?
SHUP
UMM...
HMM?
YUP!
I SUPPOSE YOU COULD SAY THAT...
!!
THWAK
GAH!
YOU SHUT YOUR TRAP!! DON'T WASTE YOUR ENERGY TALKING!!!
OWW! YOU'RE SUPPOSED TO BE HEALING ME! I'VE SUFFERED MORE DAMAGE NOW!
I'LL HEAL THE EXTRA DAMAGE TOO!!
HA HA!
SHE REMINDS ME A BIT...
...OF KUSHINA.
PLEASE BE GENTLE WITH MY SON.
WHAT A SURPRISE...
...THOUGH IT SEEMS LIKE YOU KNEW ABOUT IT?
I SENSED HIS CHAKRA WHEN I WAS IN NINE TAILS MODE.
THE OTHERS SHOULD BE ARRIVING SOON TOO...
!
!!!

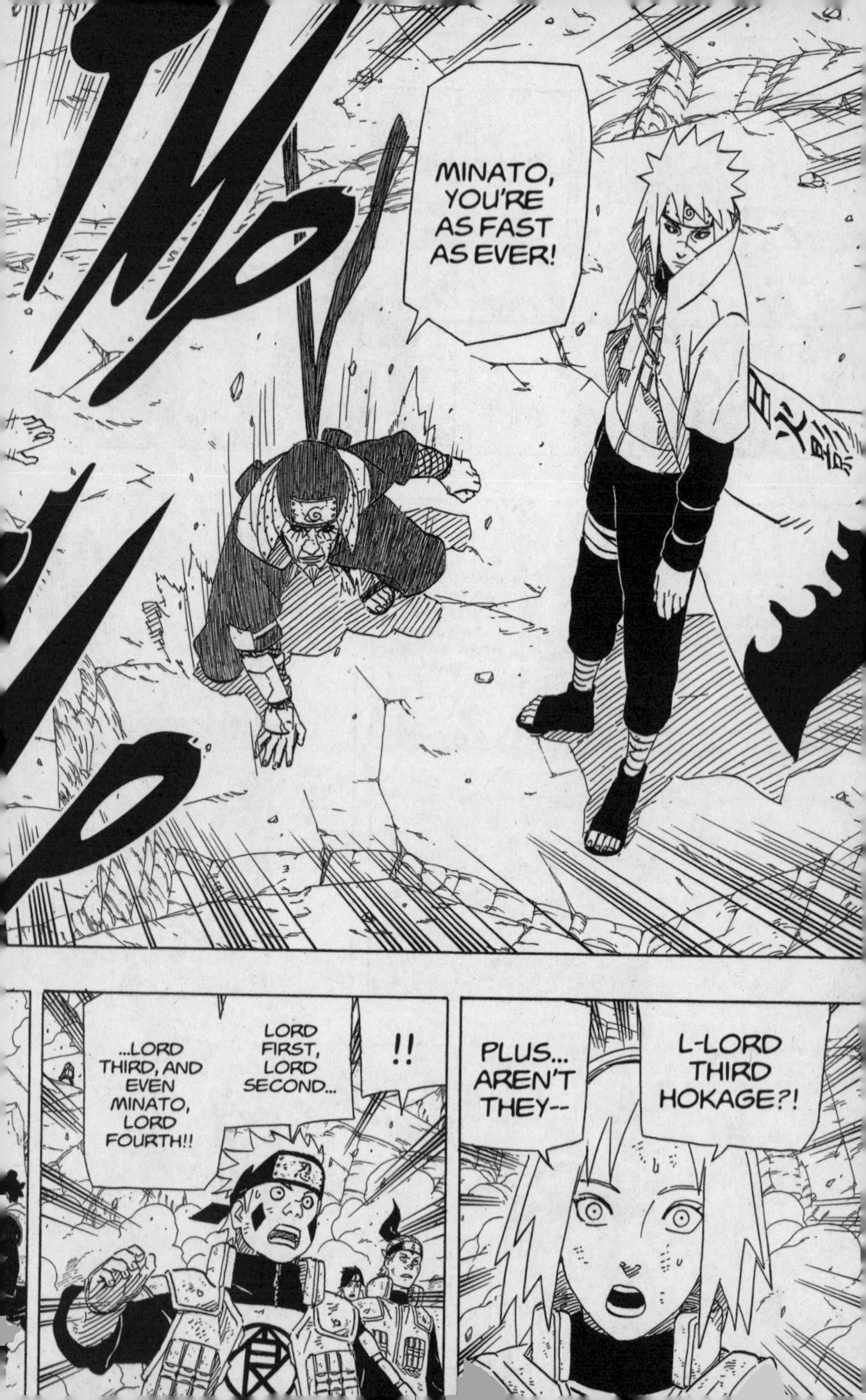
MINATO, YOU'RE AS FAST AS EVER!
L-LORD THIRD HOKAGE?!
PLUS... AREN'T THEY--
!!
LORD FIRST, LORD SECOND...
...LORD THIRD, AND EVEN MINATO, LORD FOURTH!!

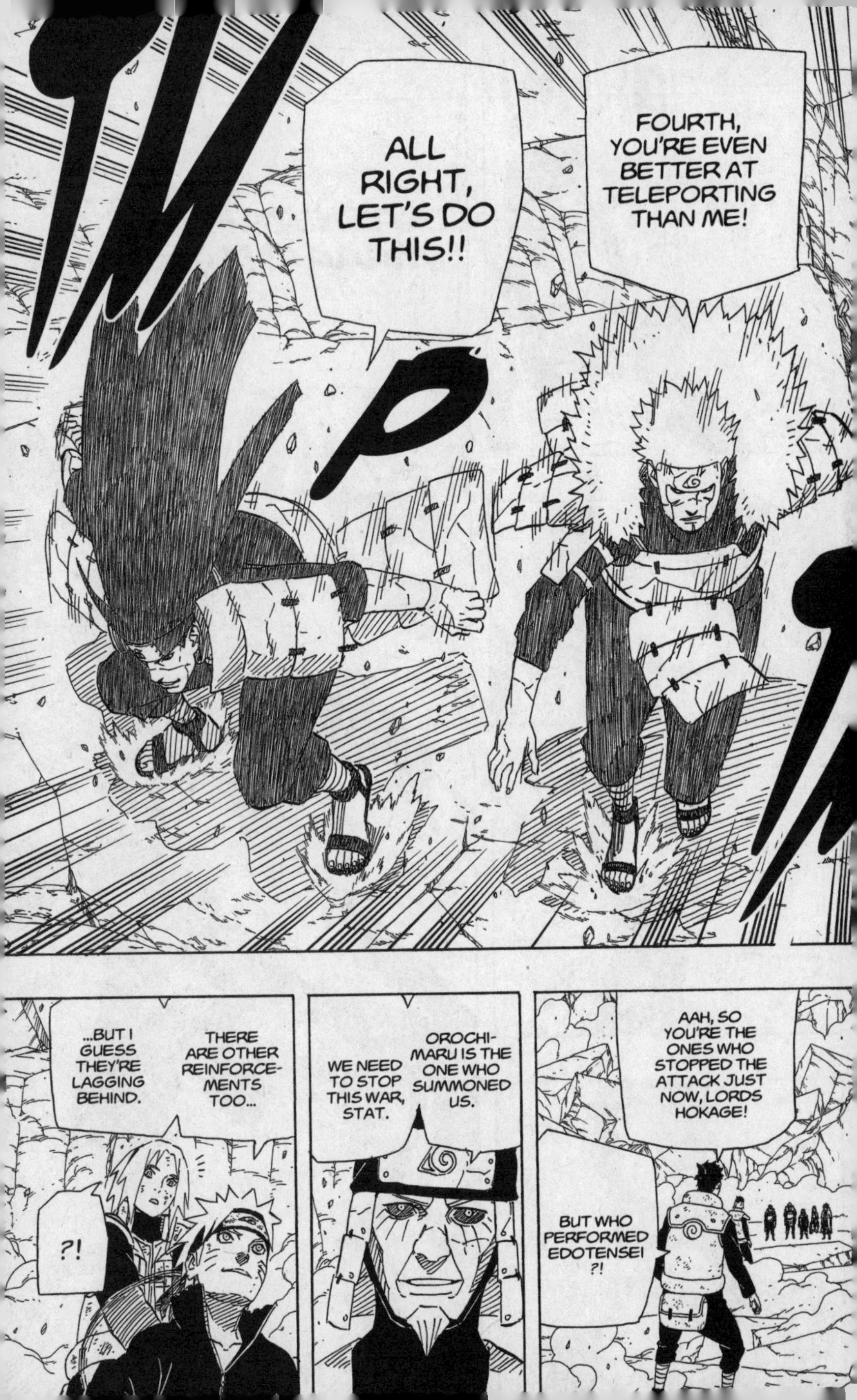
FOURTH, YOU'RE EVEN BETTER AT TELEPORTING THAN ME!
ALL RIGHT, LET'S DO THIS!!
AAH, SO YOU'RE THE ONES WHO STOPPED THE ATTACK JUST NOW, LORDS HOKAGE!
BUT WHO PERFORMED EDOTENSEI ?!
OROCHIMARU IS THE ONE WHO SUMMONED US.
WE NEED TO STOP THIS WAR, STAT.
THERE ARE OTHER REINFORCEMENTS TOO...
...BUT I GUESS THEY'RE LAGGING BEHIND.
?!

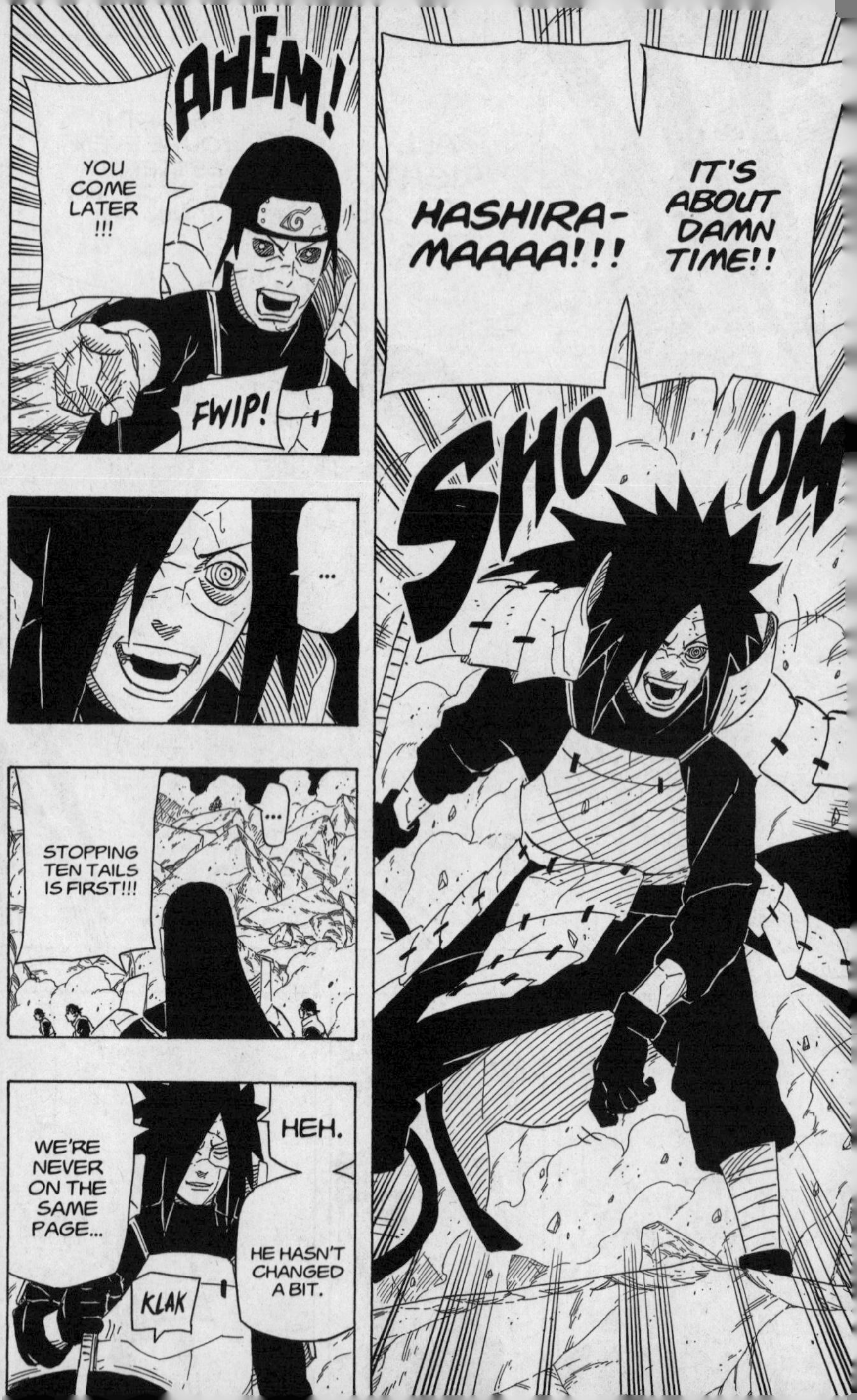

IT'S ABOUT DAMN TIME!!
HASHIRA-MAAAAA!!!
SHO
OM
AHEM!
YOU COME LATER!!!
FWIP!
...
...
STOPPING TEN TAILS IS FIRST!!!
HEH.
WE'RE NEVER ON THE SAME PAGE...
HE HASN'T CHANGED A BIT.
KLAK

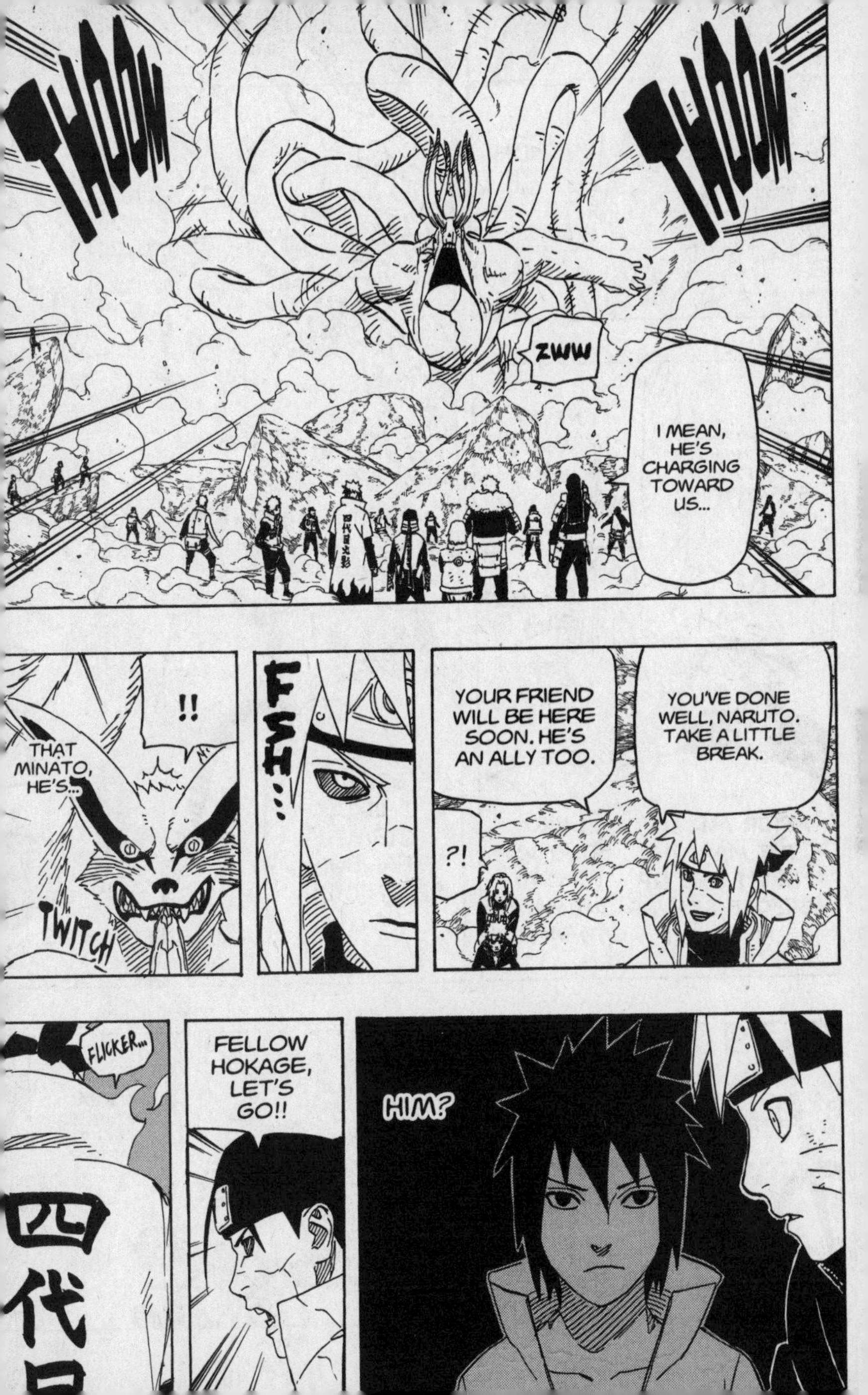
THOOM
THOOM
ZWW
I MEAN, HE'S CHARGING TOWARD US...
YOU'VE DONE WELL, NARUTO. TAKE A LITTLE BREAK.
YOUR FRIEND WILL BE HERE SOON. HE'S AN ALLY TOO.
?!
FSH...
!!
THAT MINATO, HE'S...
TWITCH
HIM?
FELLOW HOKAGE, LET'S GO!!
FLICKER...
四代

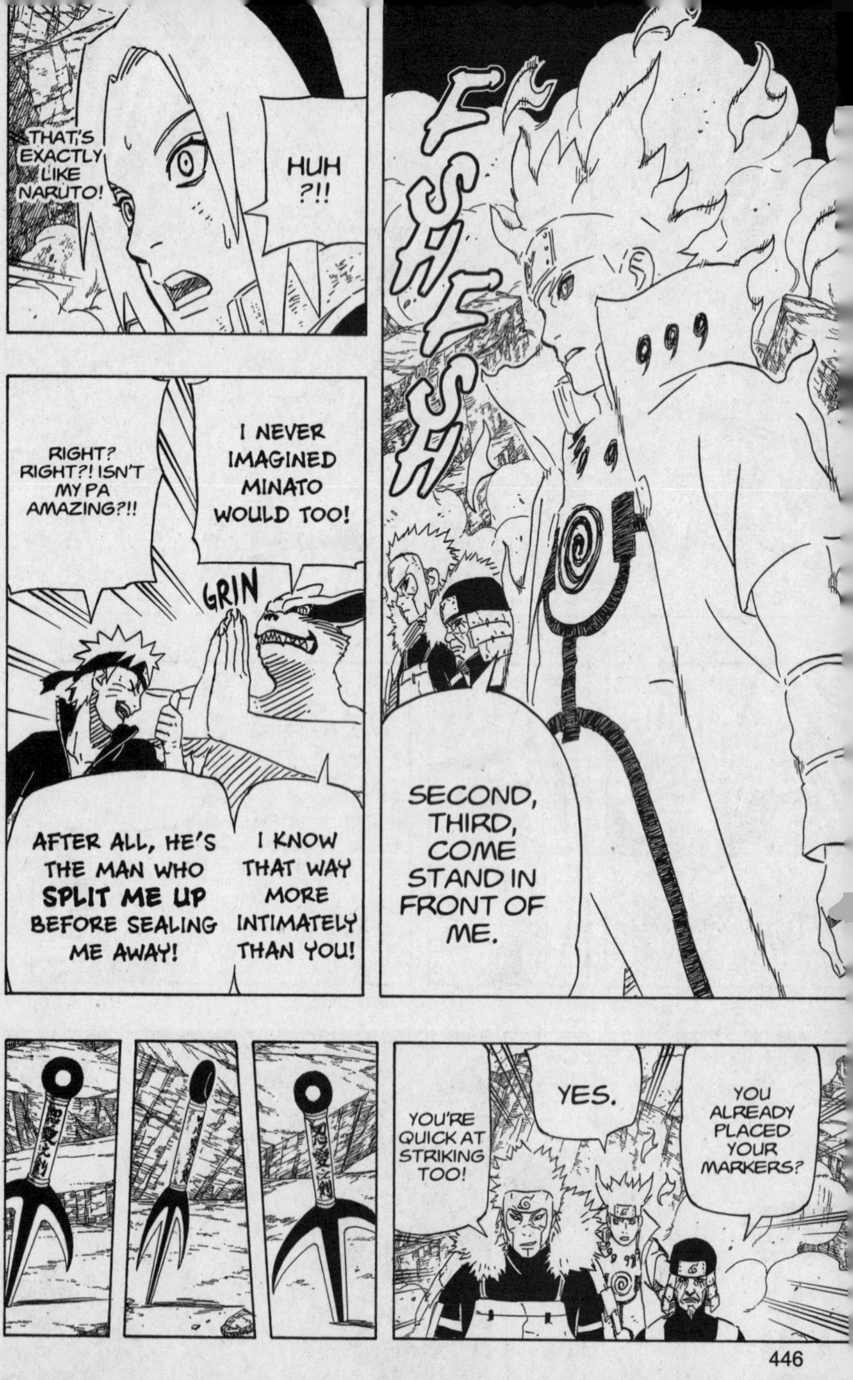
FSHSH
SECOND, THIRD, COME STAND IN FRONT OF ME.
HUH?!!
THAT'S EXACTLY LIKE NARUTO!
I NEVER IMAGINED MINATO WOULD TOO!
RIGHT? RIGHT?! ISN'T MY PA AMAZING?!!
GRIN
I KNOW THAT WAY MORE INTIMATELY THAN YOU!
AFTER ALL, HE'S THE MAN WHO **SPLIT ME UP** BEFORE SEALING ME AWAY!
YOU ALREADY PLACED YOUR MARKERS?
YES.
YOU'RE QUICK AT STRIKING TOO!

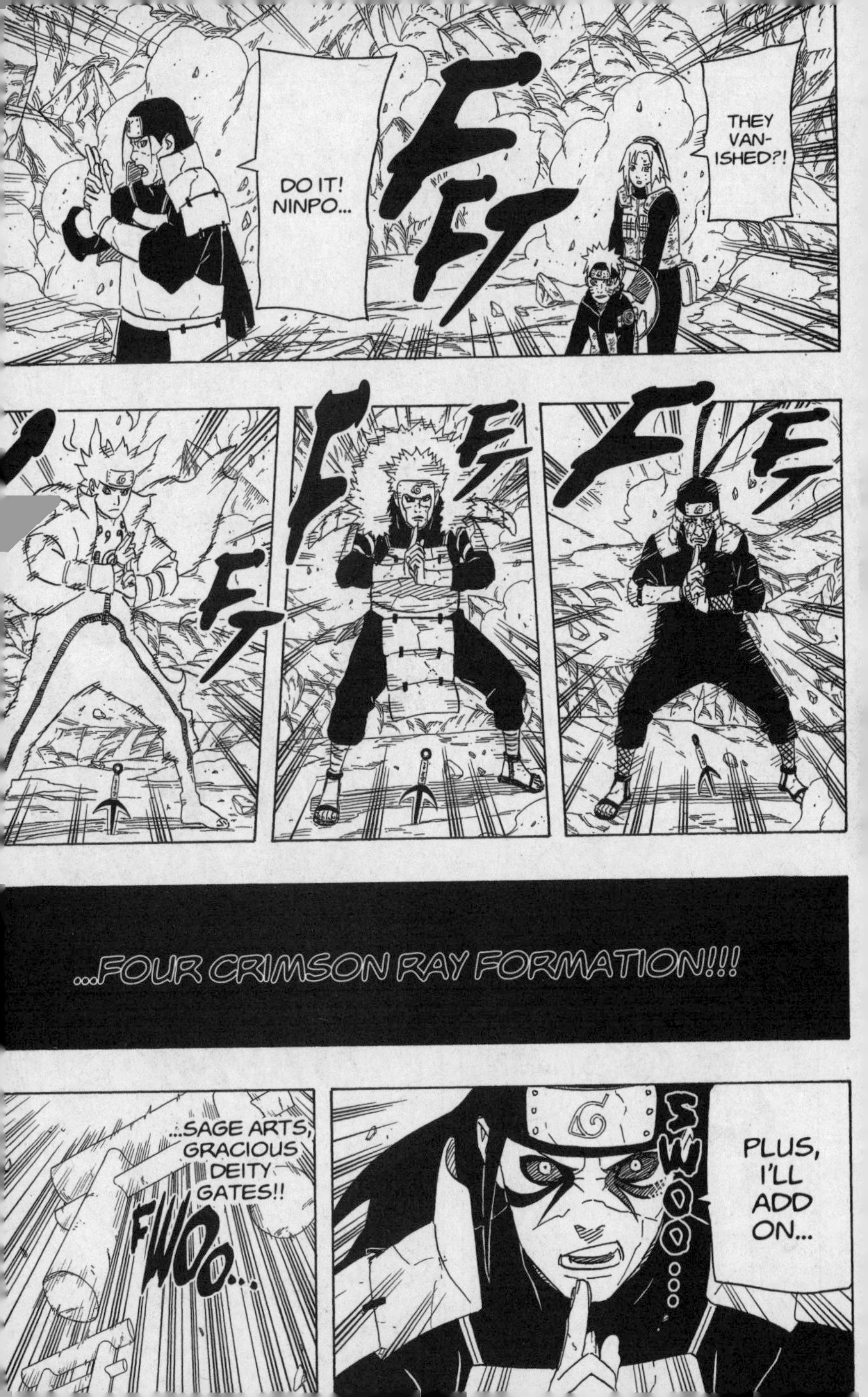
THEY VAN-ISHED?!
DO IT! NINPO...
...FOUR CRIMSON RAY FORMATION!!!
PLUS, I'LL ADD ON...
SWOOO...
...SAGE ARTS, GRACIOUS DEITY GATES!!
FWOO...

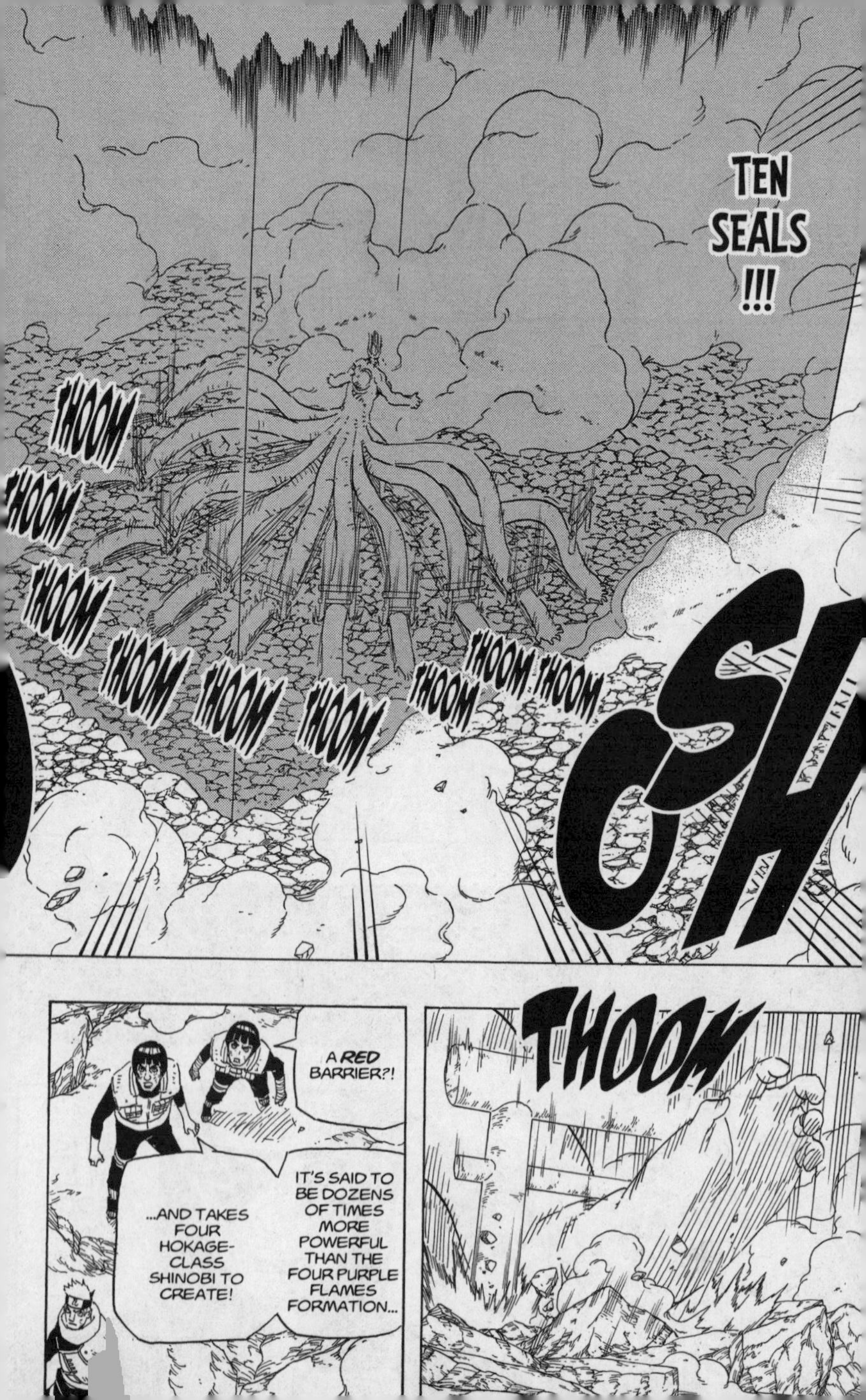
TEN SEALS !!!
THOOM THOOM
THOOM
THOOM
THOOM
THOOM
THOOM
THOOM
THOOM
THOOM
THOOM
A RED BARRIER?!
IT'S SAID TO BE DOZENS OF TIMES MORE POWERFUL THAN THE FOUR PURPLE FLAMES FORMATION...
...AND TAKES FOUR HOKAGE-CLASS SHINOBI TO CREATE!

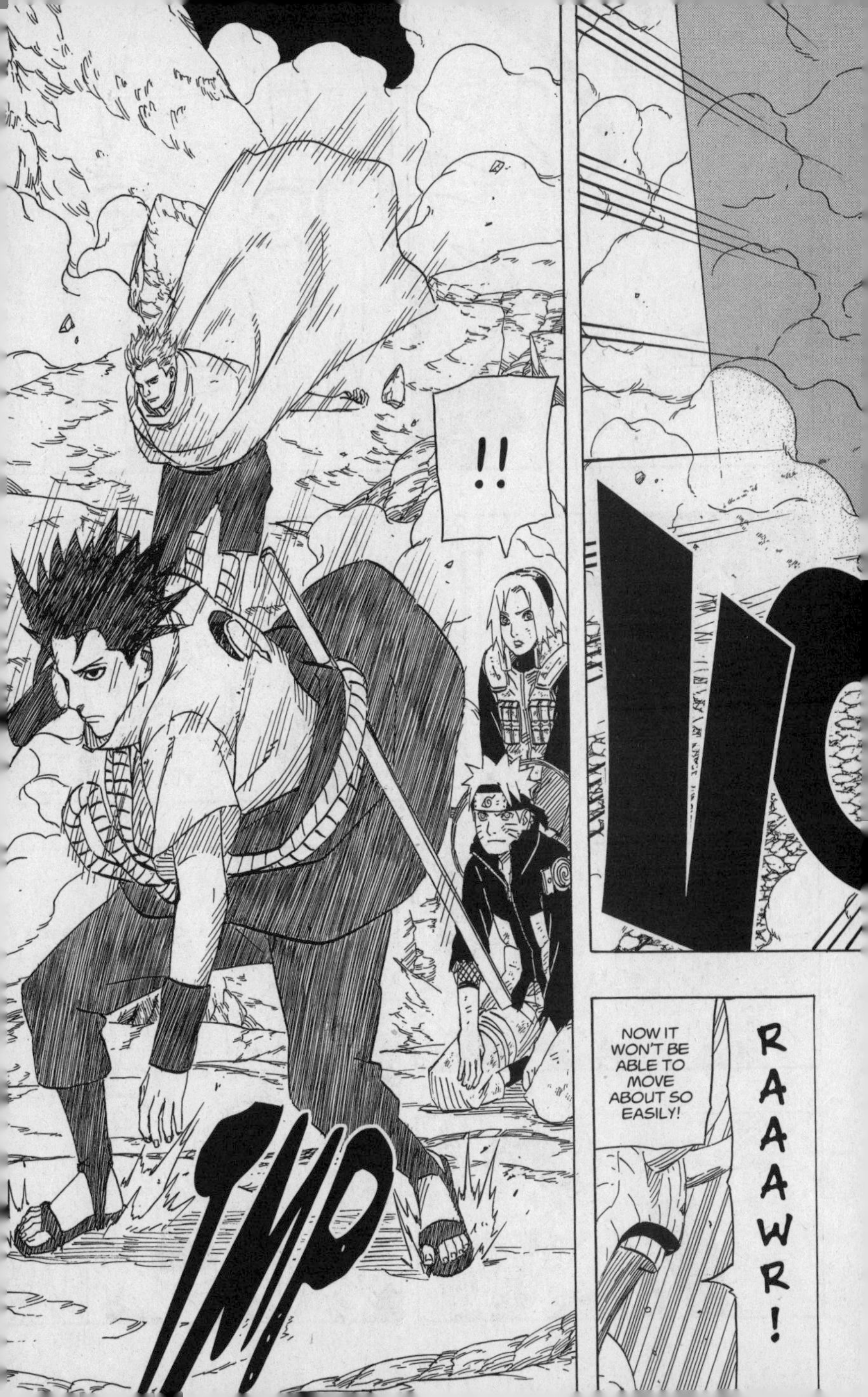
RAAAWR!
NOW IT WON'T BE ABLE TO MOVE ABOUT SO EASILY!
!!

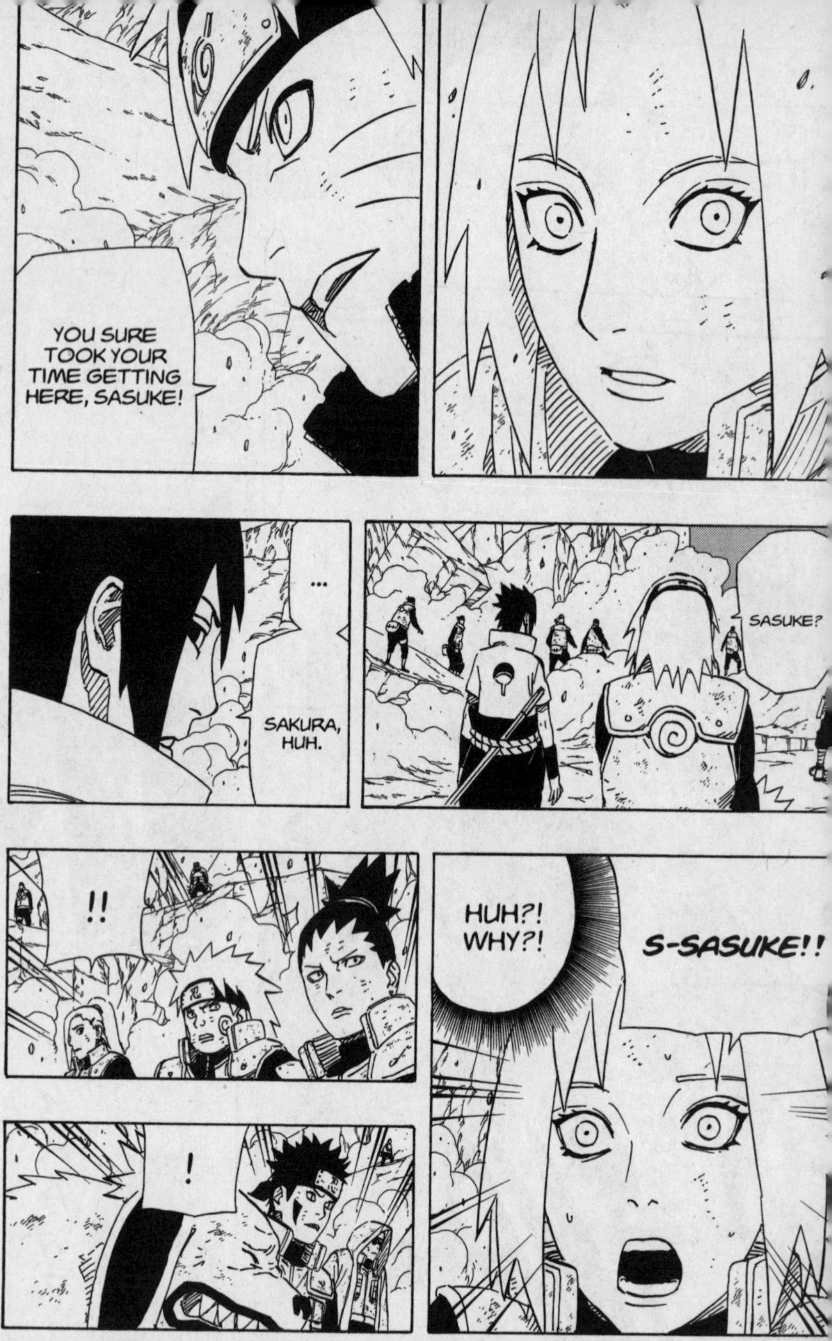
YOU SURE TOOK YOUR TIME GETTING HERE, SASUKE!
SASUKE?
...
SAKURA, HUH.
S-SASUKE!!
HUH?! WHY?!
!!
!

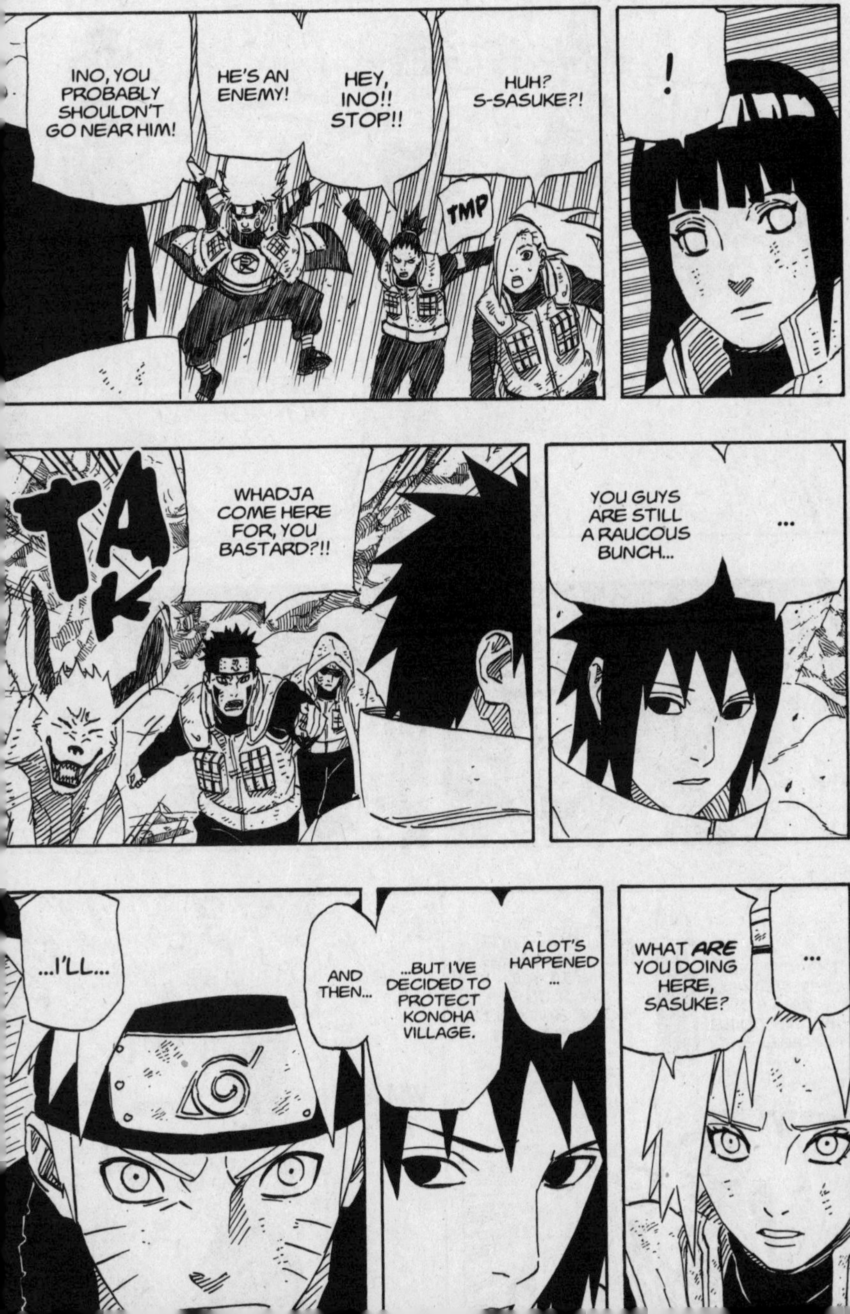
!
HUH? S-SASUKE?!
TMP
HEY, INO!! STOP!!
HE'S AN ENEMY!
INO, YOU PROBABLY SHOULDN'T GO NEAR HIM!
...
YOU GUYS ARE STILL A RAUCOUS BUNCH...
WHADJA COME HERE FOR, YOU BASTARD?!!
TAK
...
WHAT *ARE* YOU DOING HERE, SASUKE?
A LOT'S HAPPENED ...
...BUT I'VE DECIDED TO PROTECT KONOHA VILLAGE.
AND THEN...
...I'LL...

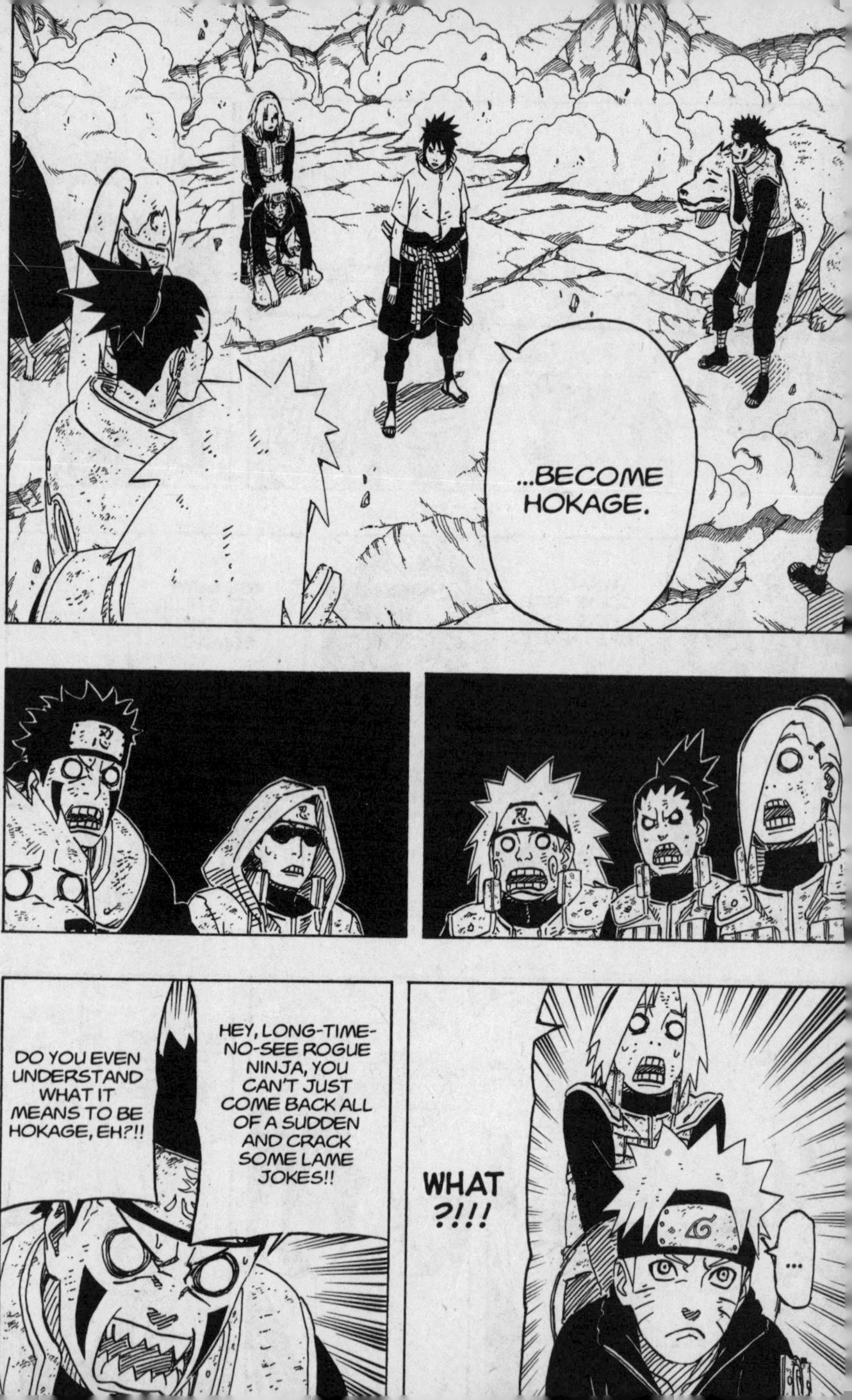
...BECOME HOKAGE.
WHAT ?!!!
...
HEY, LONG-TIME-NO-SEE ROGUE NINJA, YOU CAN'T JUST COME BACK ALL OF A SUDDEN AND CRACK SOME LAME JOKES!!
DO YOU EVEN UNDERSTAND WHAT IT MEANS TO BE HOKAGE, EH?!!

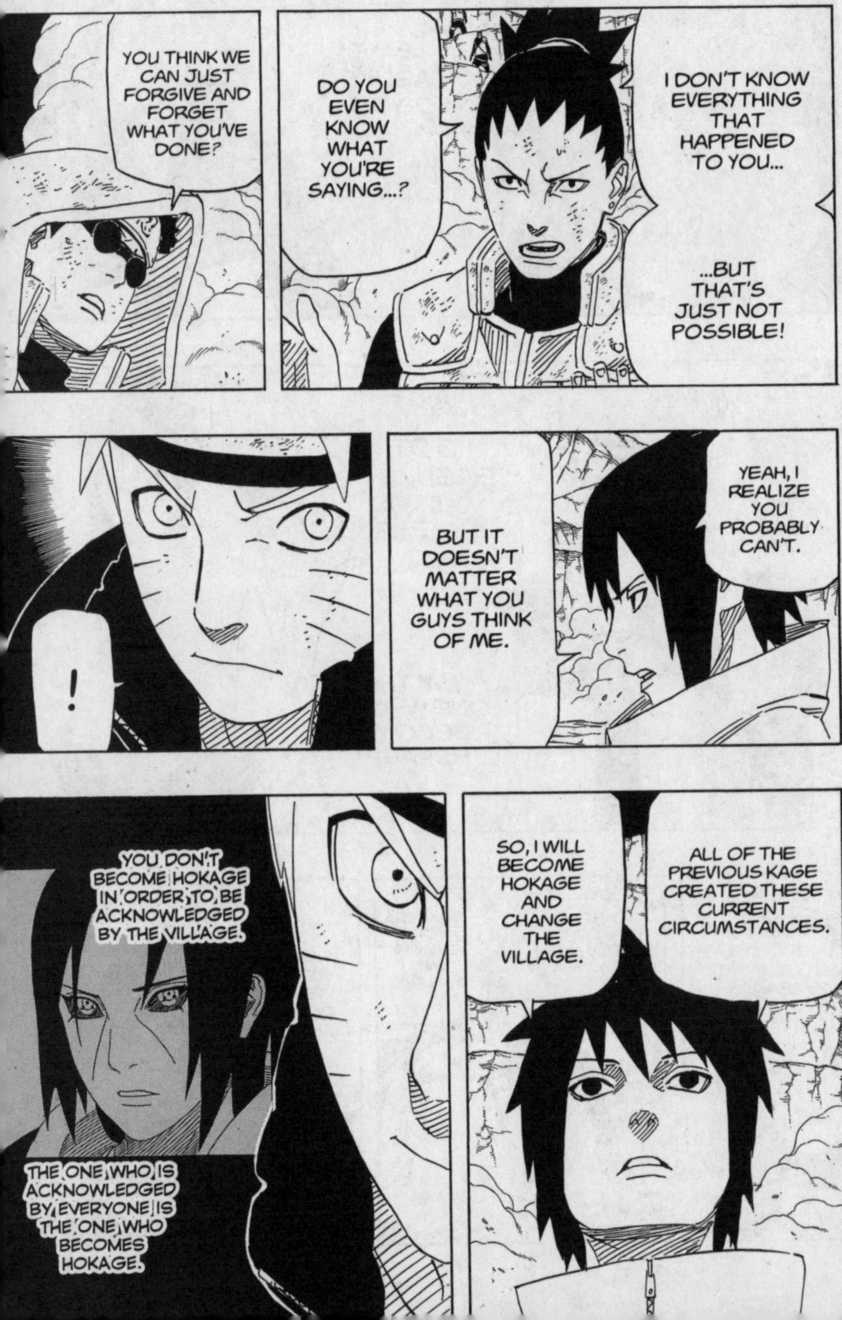
I DON'T KNOW EVERYTHING THAT HAPPENED TO YOU...
...BUT THAT'S JUST NOT POSSIBLE!
DO YOU EVEN KNOW WHAT YOU'RE SAYING...?
YOU THINK WE CAN JUST FORGIVE AND FORGET WHAT YOU'VE DONE?
YEAH, I REALIZE YOU PROBABLY CAN'T.
BUT IT DOESN'T MATTER WHAT YOU GUYS THINK OF ME.
!
ALL OF THE PREVIOUS KAGE CREATED THESE CURRENT CIRCUMSTANCES.
SO, I WILL BECOME HOKAGE AND CHANGE THE VILLAGE.
YOU DON'T BECOME HOKAGE IN ORDER TO BE ACKNOWLEDGED BY THE VILLAGE.
THE ONE WHO IS ACKNOWLEDGED BY EVERYONE IS THE ONE WHO BECOMES HOKAGE.

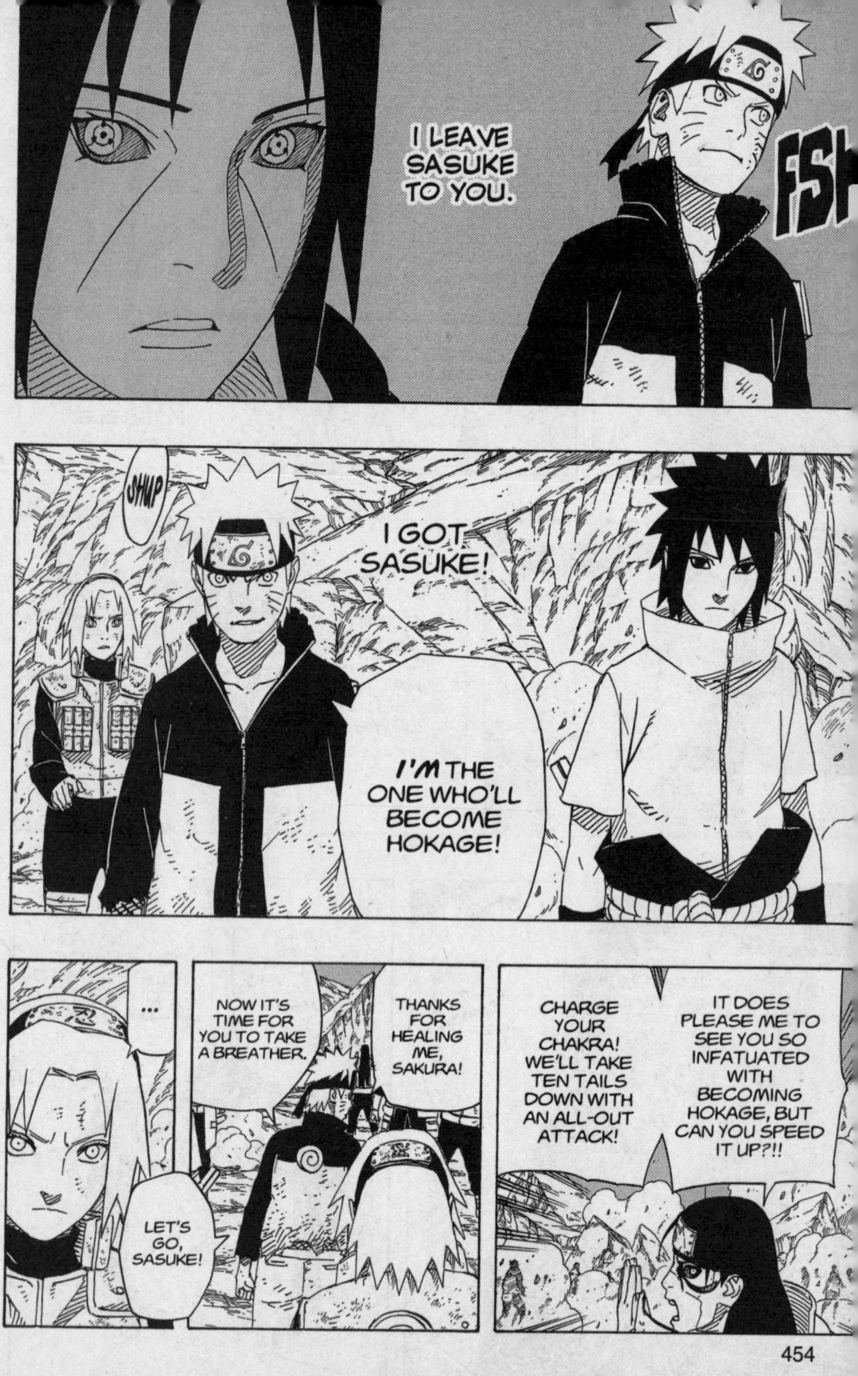
FSH
I LEAVE SASUKE TO YOU.
SHUP
I GOT SASUKE!
I'M THE ONE WHO'LL BECOME HOKAGE!
IT DOES PLEASE ME TO SEE YOU SO INFATUATED WITH BECOMING HOKAGE, BUT CAN YOU SPEED IT UP?!!
CHARGE YOUR CHAKRA! WE'LL TAKE TEN TAILS DOWN WITH AN ALL-OUT ATTACK!
THANKS FOR HEALING ME, SAKURA!
NOW IT'S TIME FOR YOU TO TAKE A BREATHER.
...
LET'S GO, SASUKE!

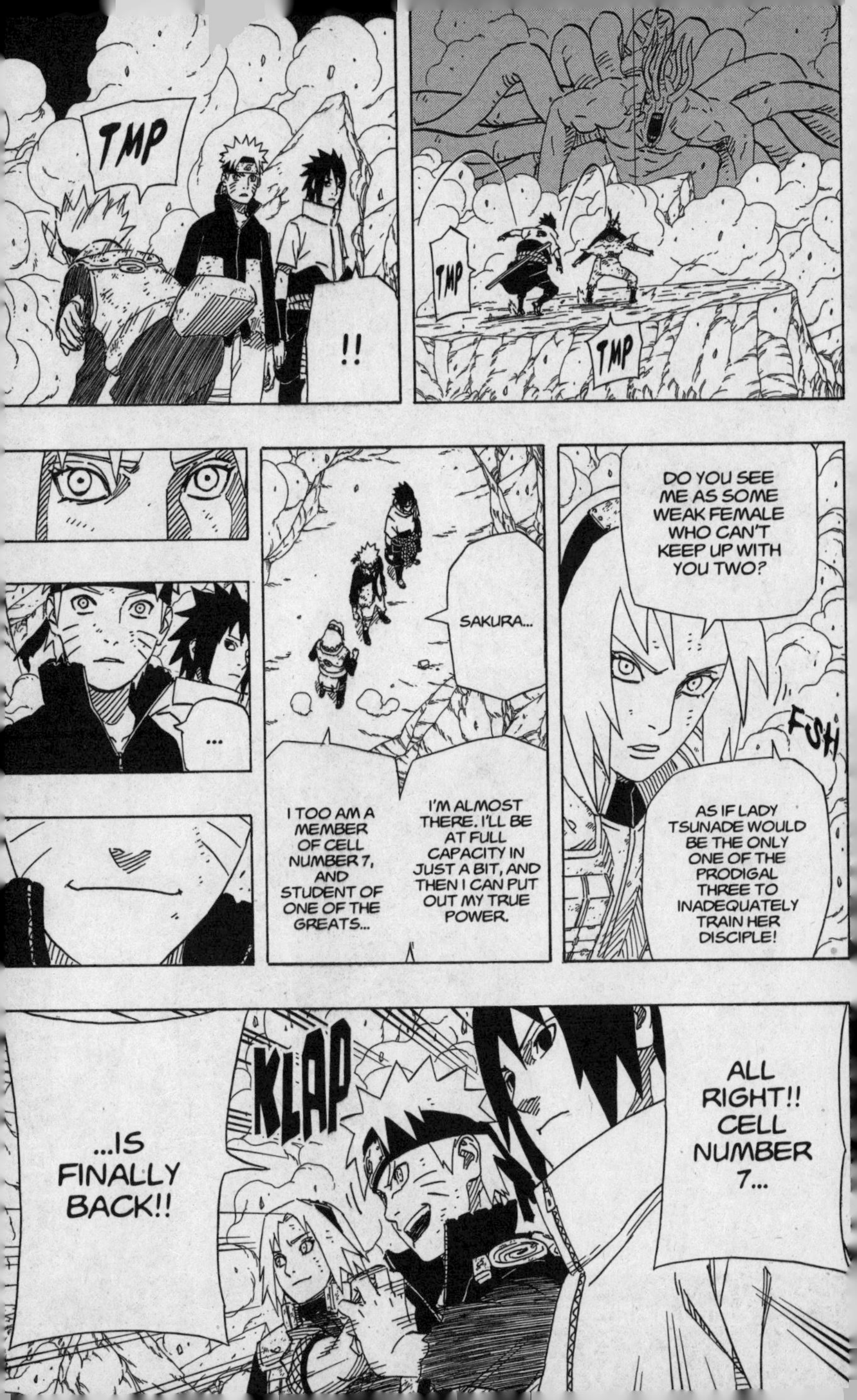
TMP
TMP
TMP
!!
DO YOU SEE ME AS SOME WEAK FEMALE WHO CAN'T KEEP UP WITH YOU TWO?
FSH
AS IF LADY TSUNADE WOULD BE THE ONLY ONE OF THE PRODIGAL THREE TO INADEQUATELY TRAIN HER DISCIPLE!
SAKURA...
I'M ALMOST THERE. I'LL BE AT FULL CAPACITY IN JUST A BIT, AND THEN I CAN PUT OUT MY TRUE POWER.
I TOO AM A MEMBER OF CELL NUMBER 7, AND STUDENT OF ONE OF THE GREATS...
...
ALL RIGHT!! CELL NUMBER 7...
KLAP
...IS FINALLY BACK!!

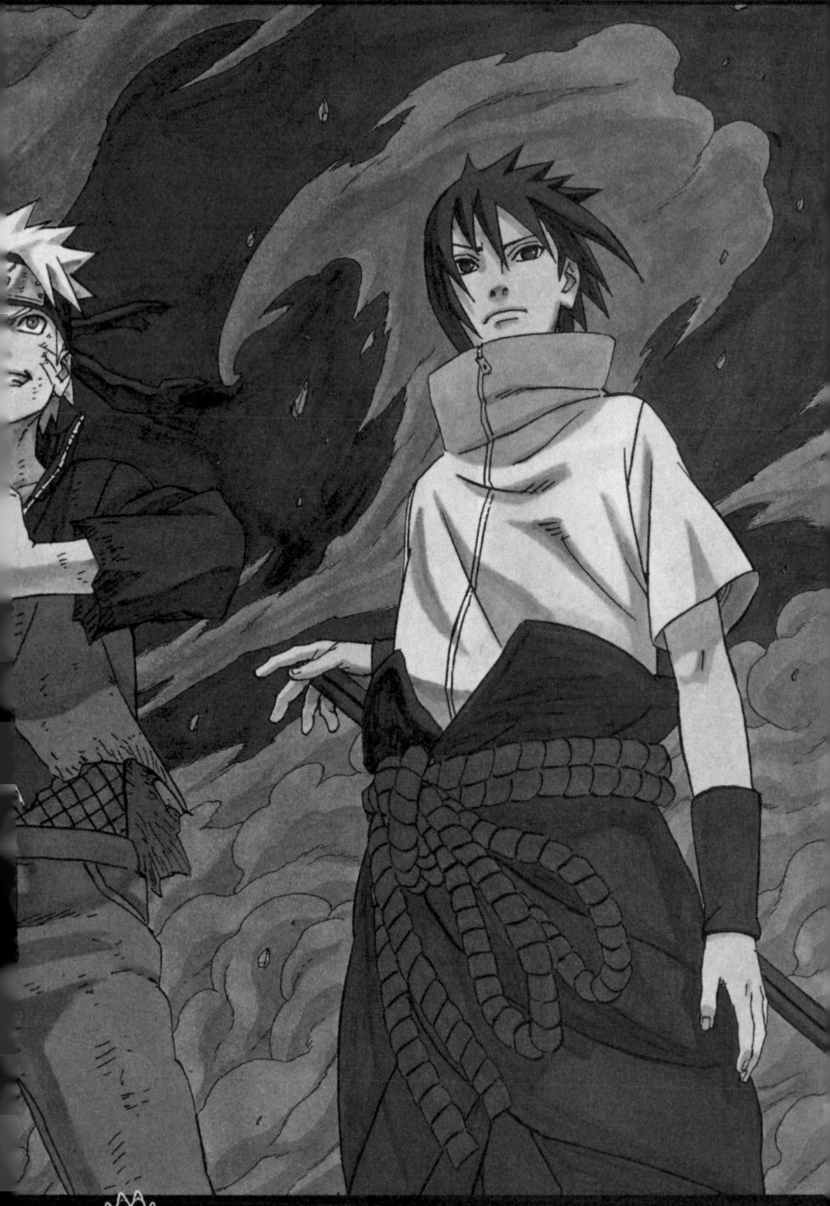

Number 632: A United Front

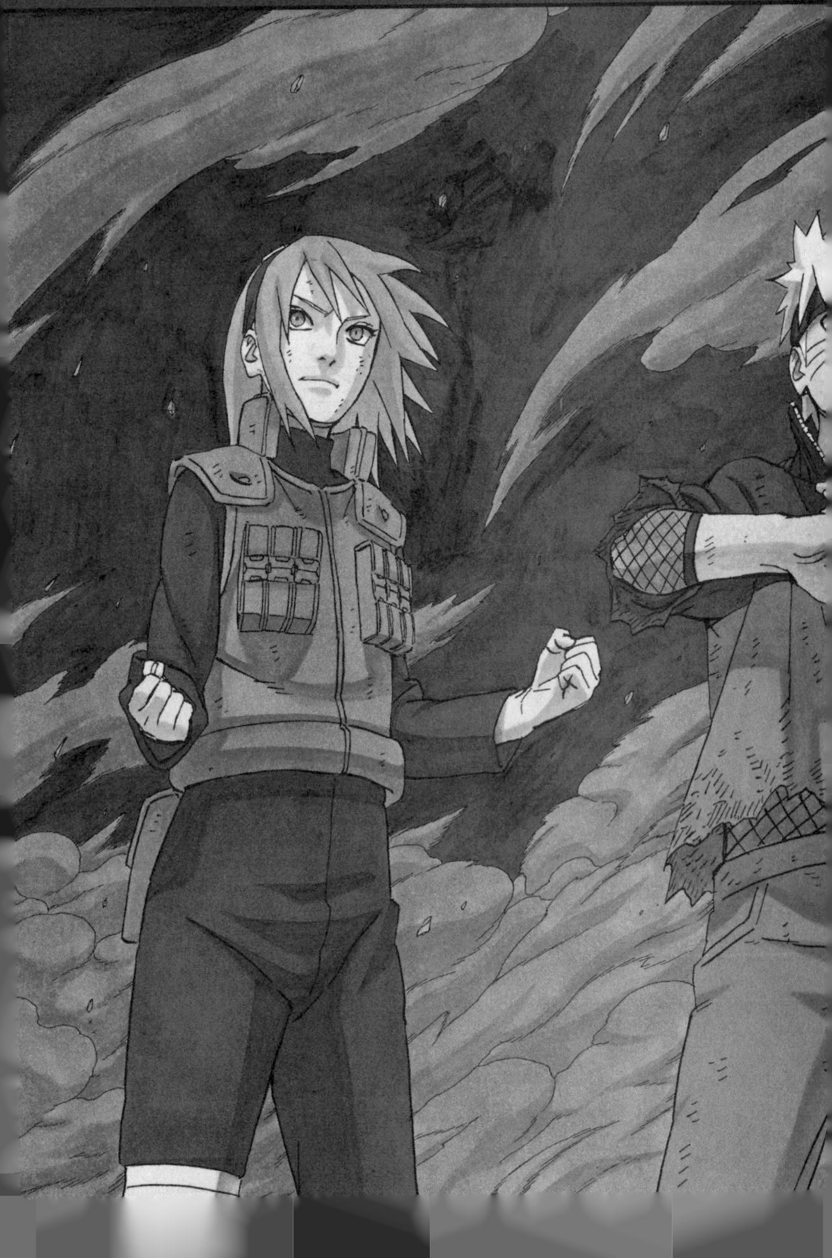

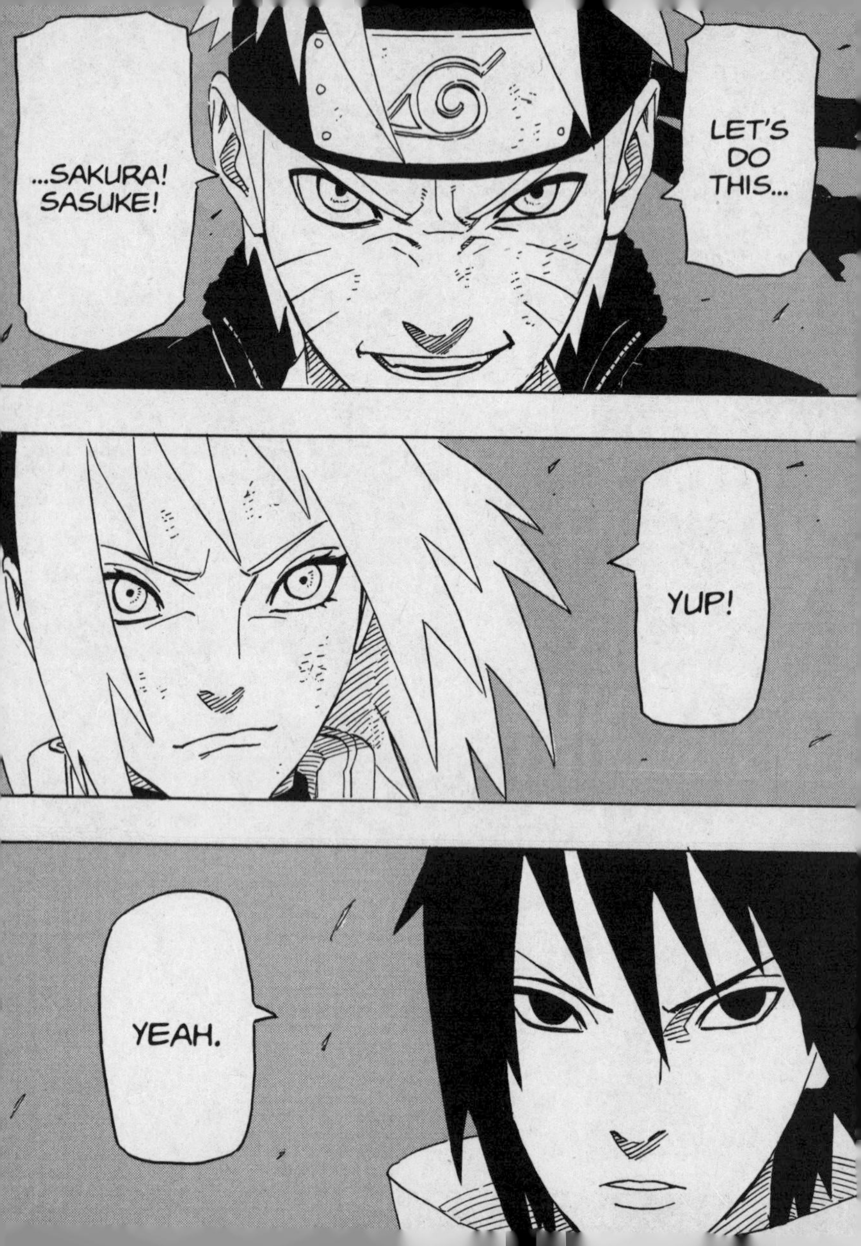
LET'S DO THIS...
...SAKURA! SASUKE!
YUP!
YEAH.

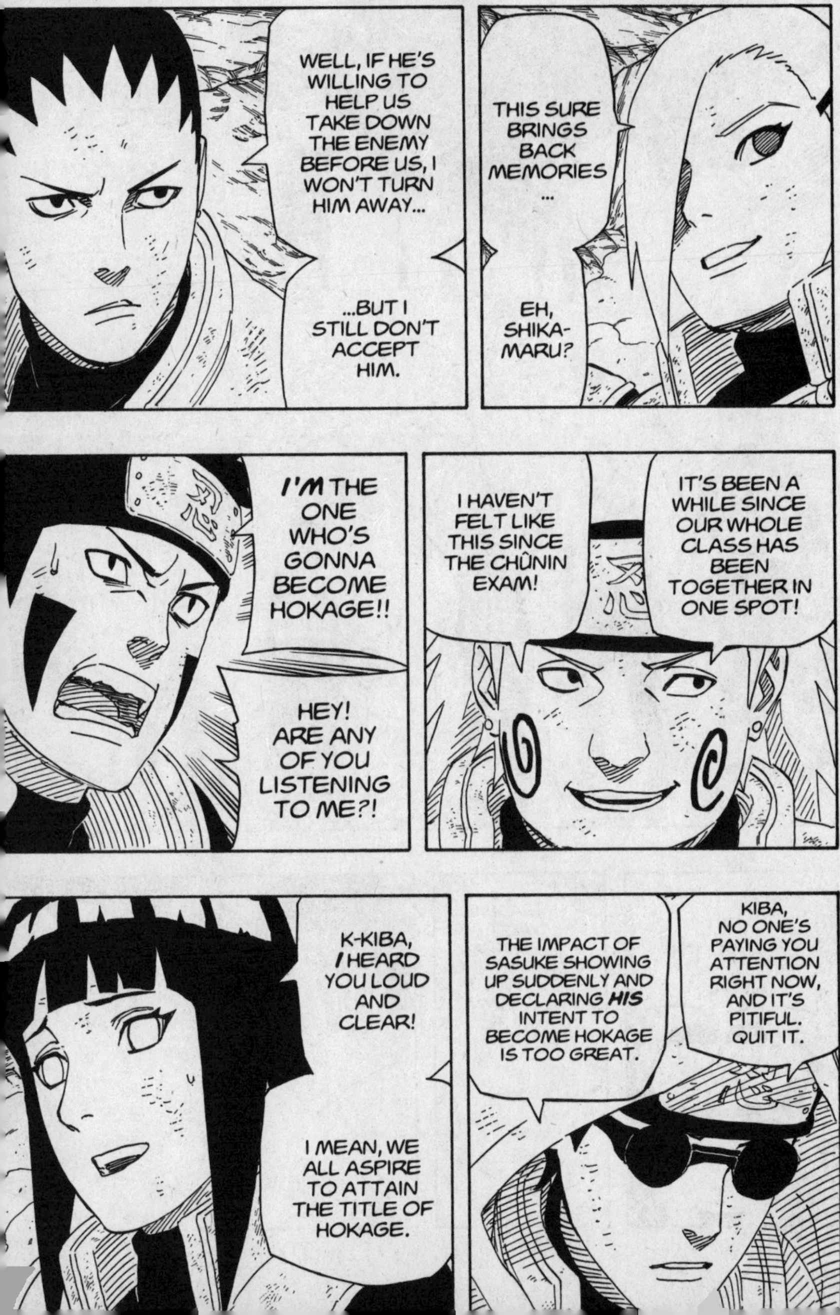
THIS SURE BRINGS BACK MEMORIES...
EH, SHIKA-MARU?
WELL, IF HE'S WILLING TO HELP US TAKE DOWN THE ENEMY BEFORE US, I WON'T TURN HIM AWAY...
...BUT I STILL DON'T ACCEPT HIM.
IT'S BEEN A WHILE SINCE OUR WHOLE CLASS HAS BEEN TOGETHER IN ONE SPOT!
I HAVEN'T FELT LIKE THIS SINCE THE CHÛNIN EXAM!
I'M THE ONE WHO'S GONNA BECOME HOKAGE!!
HEY! ARE ANY OF YOU LISTENING TO ME?!
KIBA, NO ONE'S PAYING YOU ATTENTION RIGHT NOW, AND IT'S PITIFUL. QUIT IT.
THE IMPACT OF SASUKE SHOWING UP SUDDENLY AND DECLARING *HIS* INTENT TO BECOME HOKAGE IS TOO GREAT.
K-KIBA, *I* HEARD YOU LOUD AND CLEAR!
I MEAN, WE ALL ASPIRE TO ATTAIN THE TITLE OF HOKAGE.

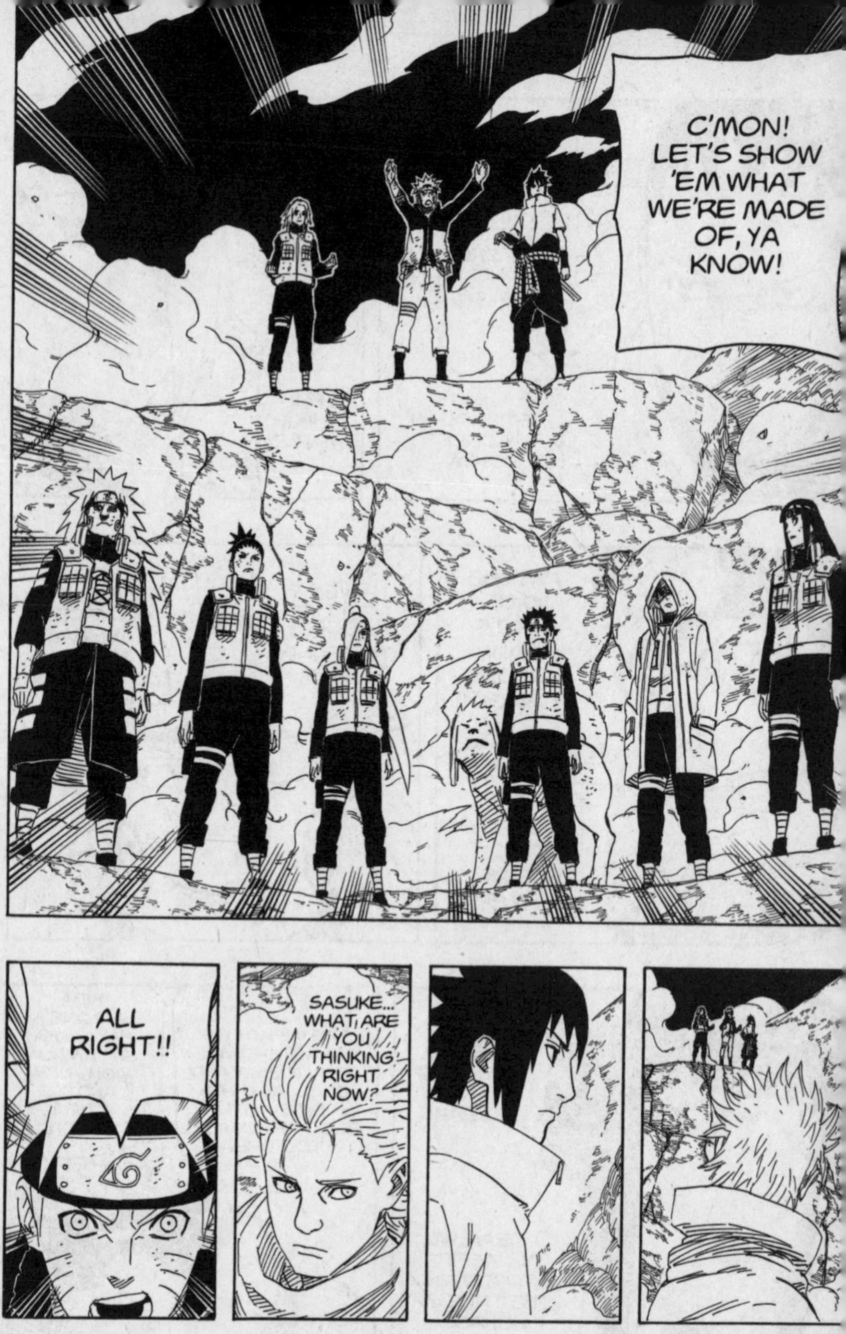
C'MON! LET'S SHOW 'EM WHAT WE'RE MADE OF, YA KNOW!
SASUKE... WHAT ARE YOU THINKING RIGHT NOW?
ALL RIGHT!!

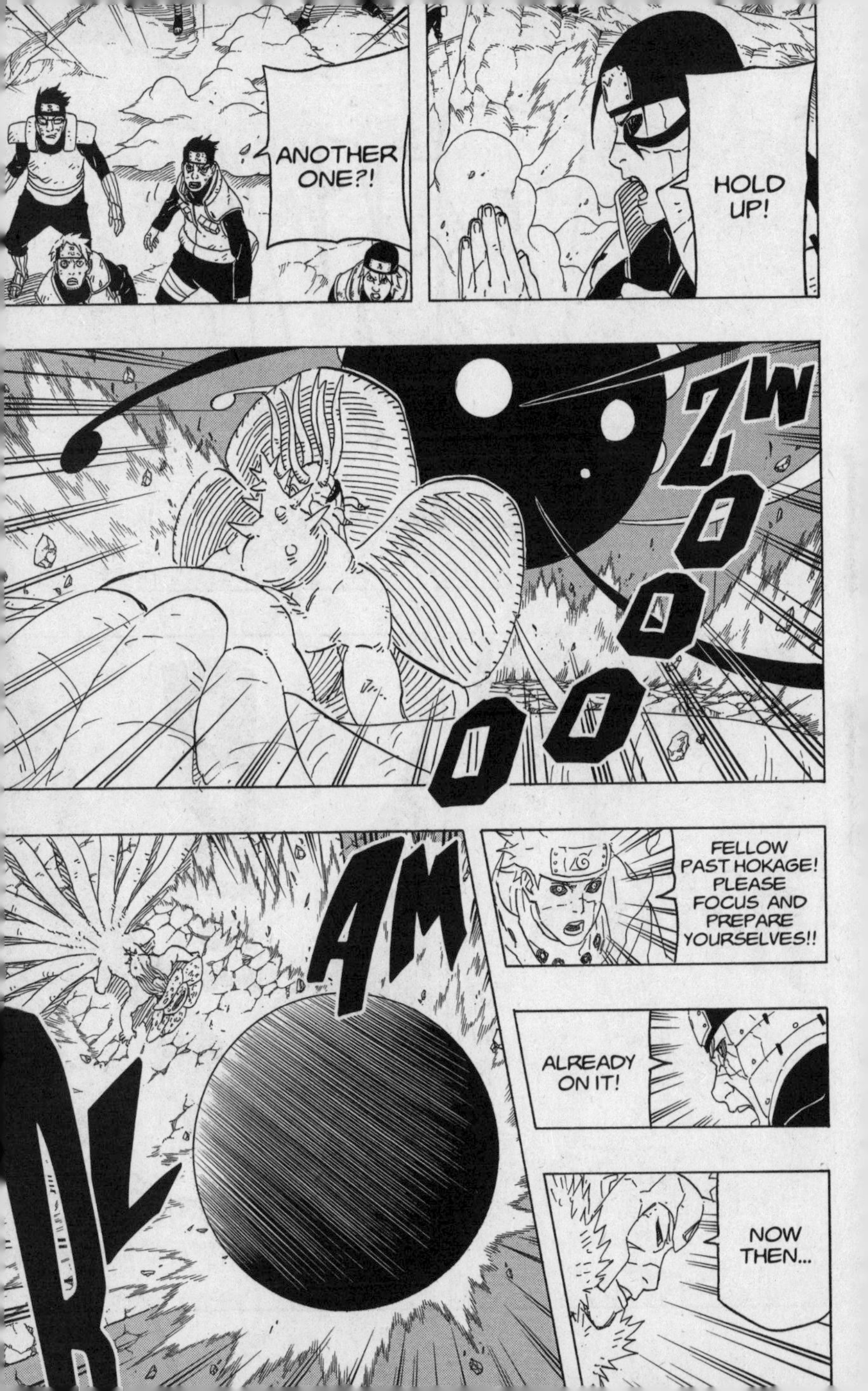
HOLD UP!
ANOTHER ONE?!
ZWOOOOO
FELLOW PAST HOKAGE! PLEASE FOCUS AND PREPARE YOURSELVES!!
ALREADY ON IT!
NOW THEN...
AM

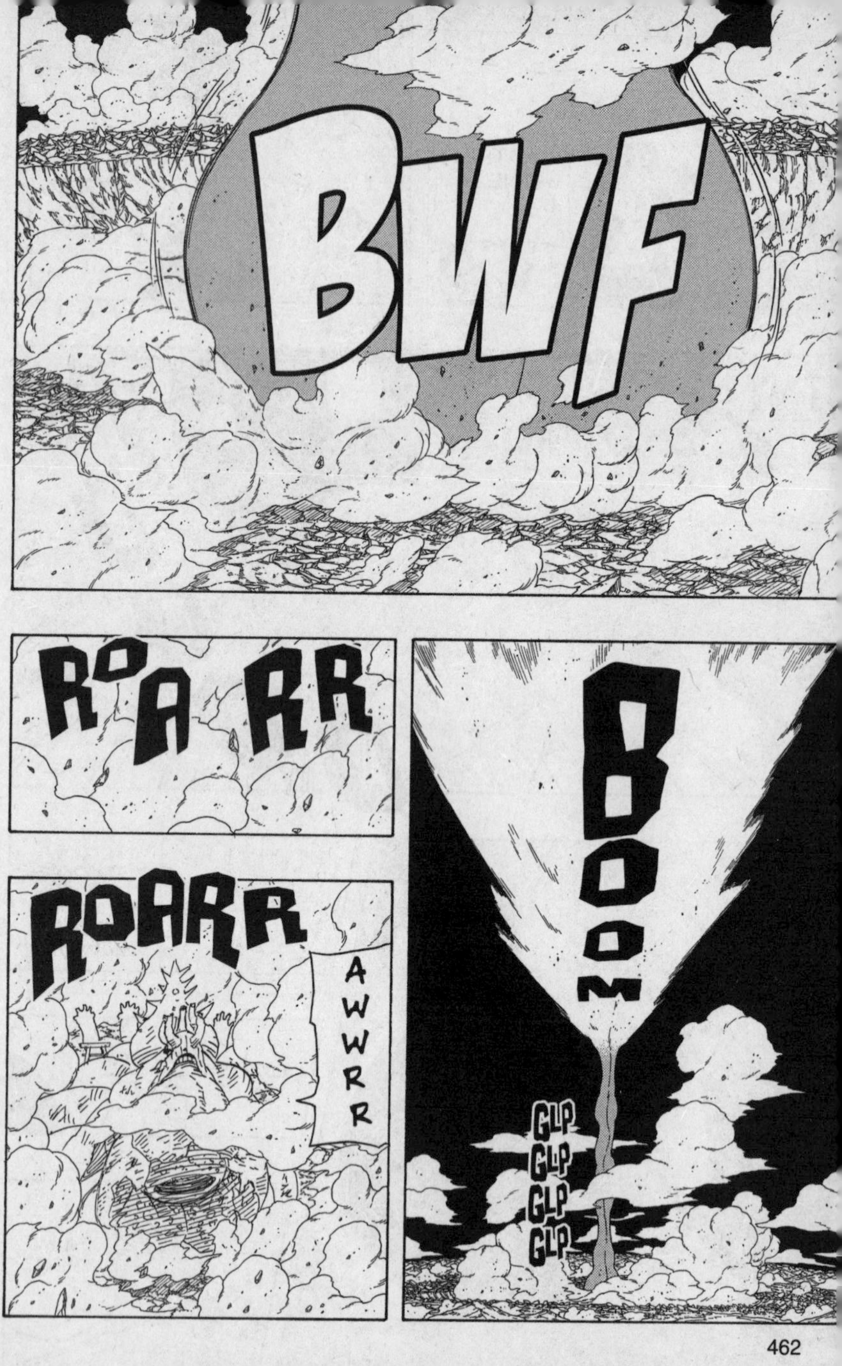
BWF
BOOM
GLP
GLP
GLP
GLP
ROARR
ROARR
AWWRR

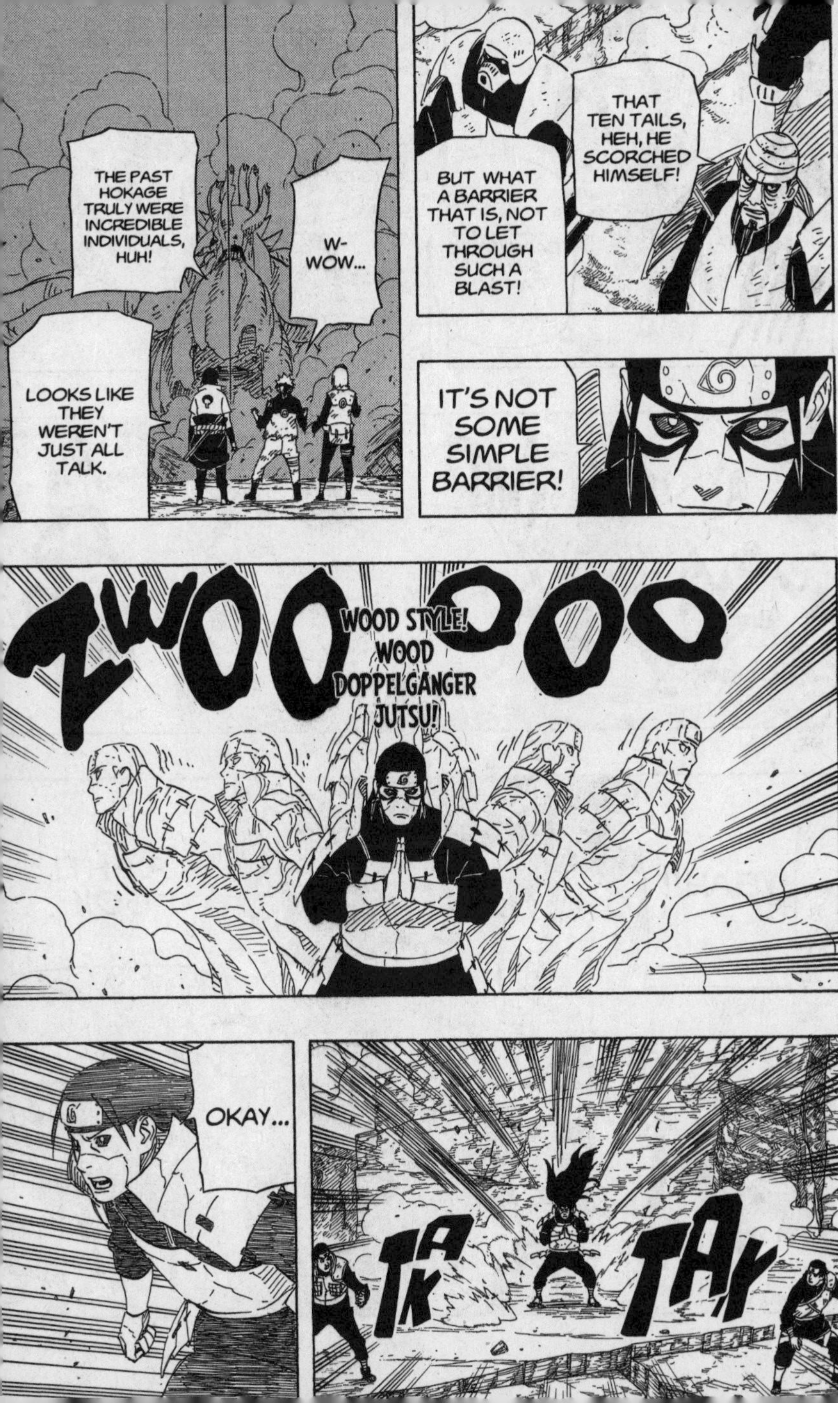
THAT TEN TAILS, HEH, HE SCORCHED HIMSELF!
BUT WHAT A BARRIER THAT IS, NOT TO LET THROUGH SUCH A BLAST!
IT'S NOT SOME SIMPLE BARRIER!
W-WOW...
THE PAST HOKAGE TRULY WERE INCREDIBLE INDIVIDUALS, HUH!
LOOKS LIKE THEY WEREN'T JUST ALL TALK.
ZWOOOOOO
WOOD STYLE! WOOD DOPPELGANGER JUTSU!
TAK
TAK
OKAY...

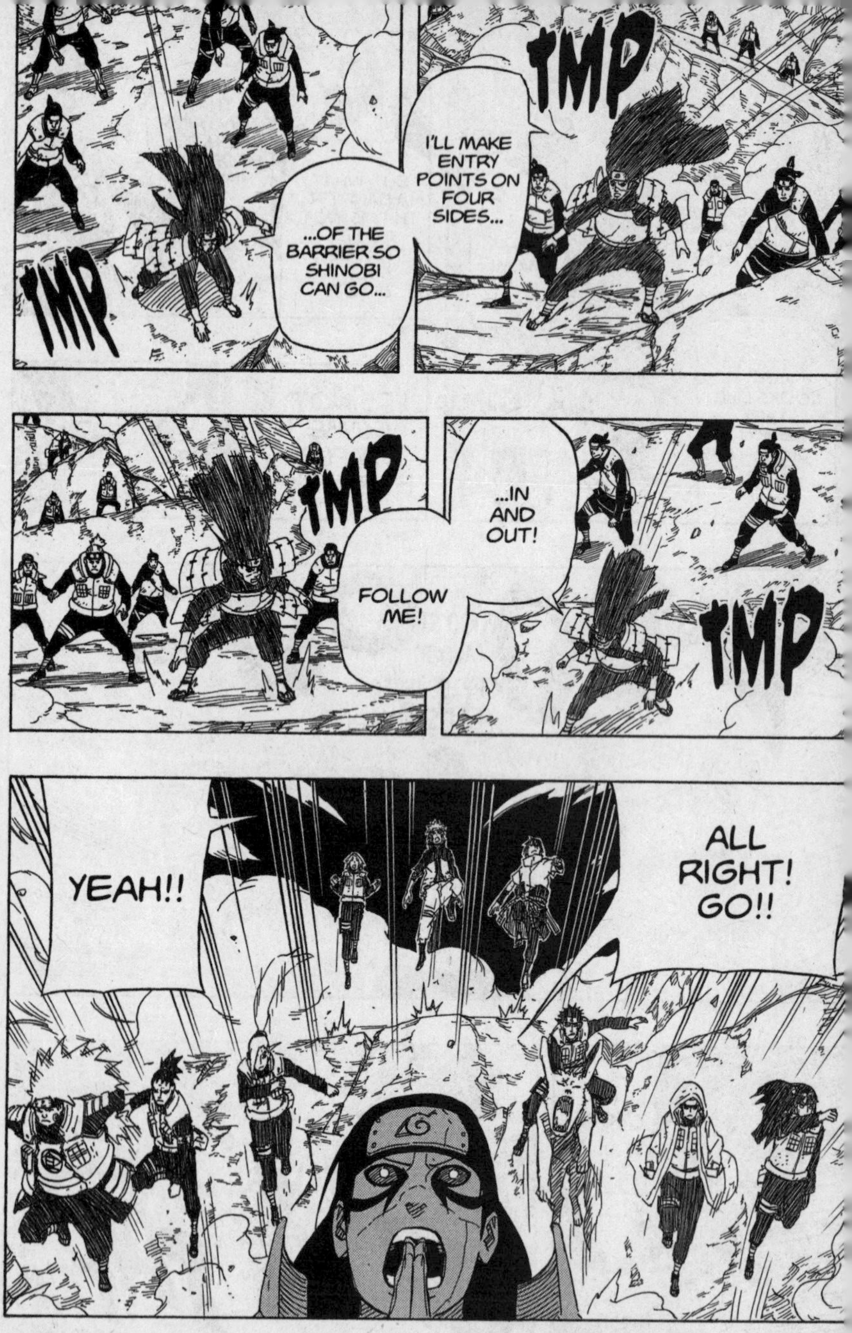
TMP
I'LL MAKE ENTRY POINTS ON FOUR SIDES...
...OF THE BARRIER SO SHINOBI CAN GO...
TMP
TMP
...IN AND OUT!
TMP
FOLLOW ME!
ALL RIGHT! GO!!
YEAH!!

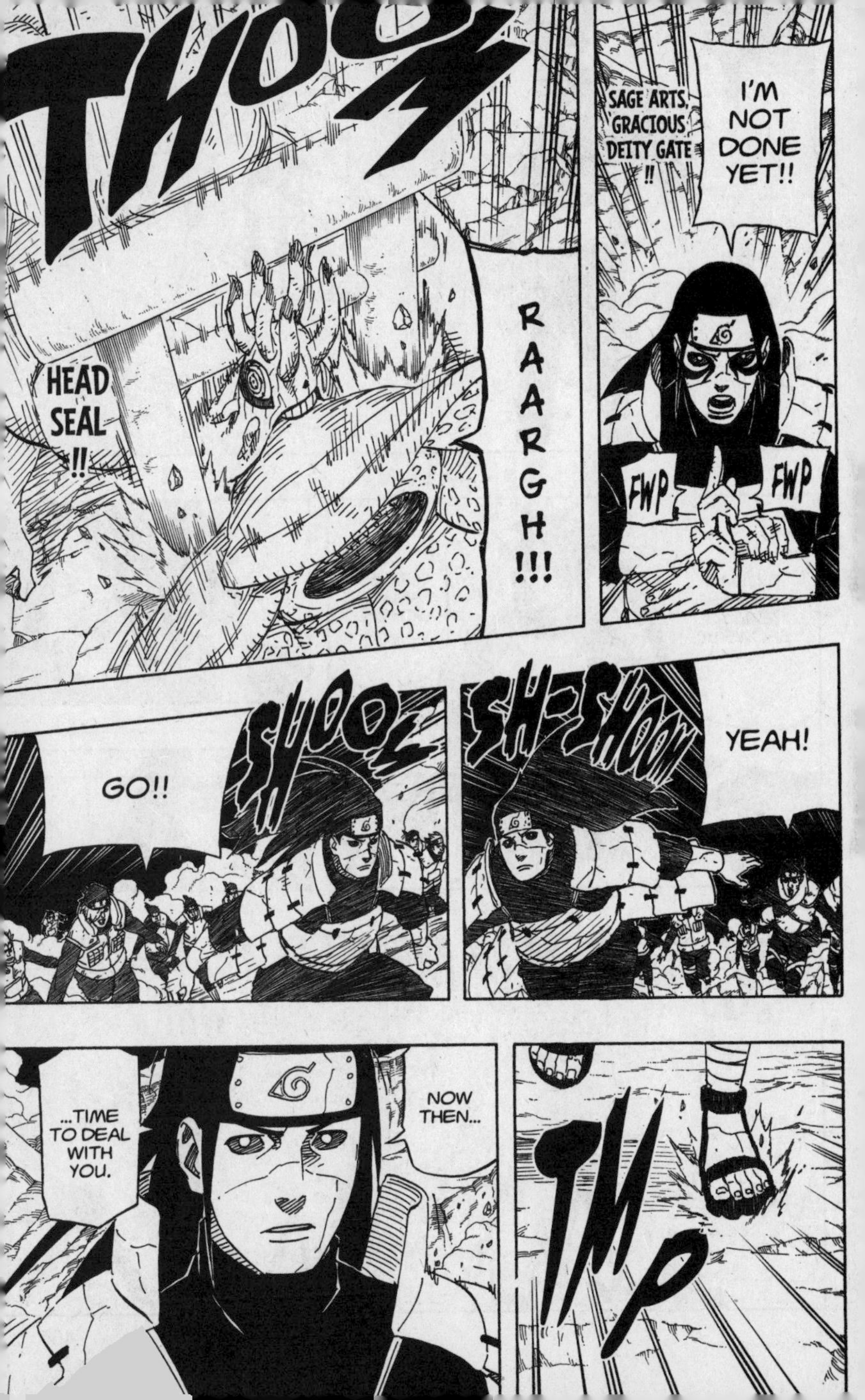
I'M NOT DONE YET!!
SAGE ARTS, GRACIOUS DEITY GATE!!
FWP
FWP
THOOM
RAARGH!!!
HEAD SEAL!!
YEAH!
SH-SHOOM
SHOOM
GO!!
THMP
NOW THEN...
...TIME TO DEAL WITH YOU.

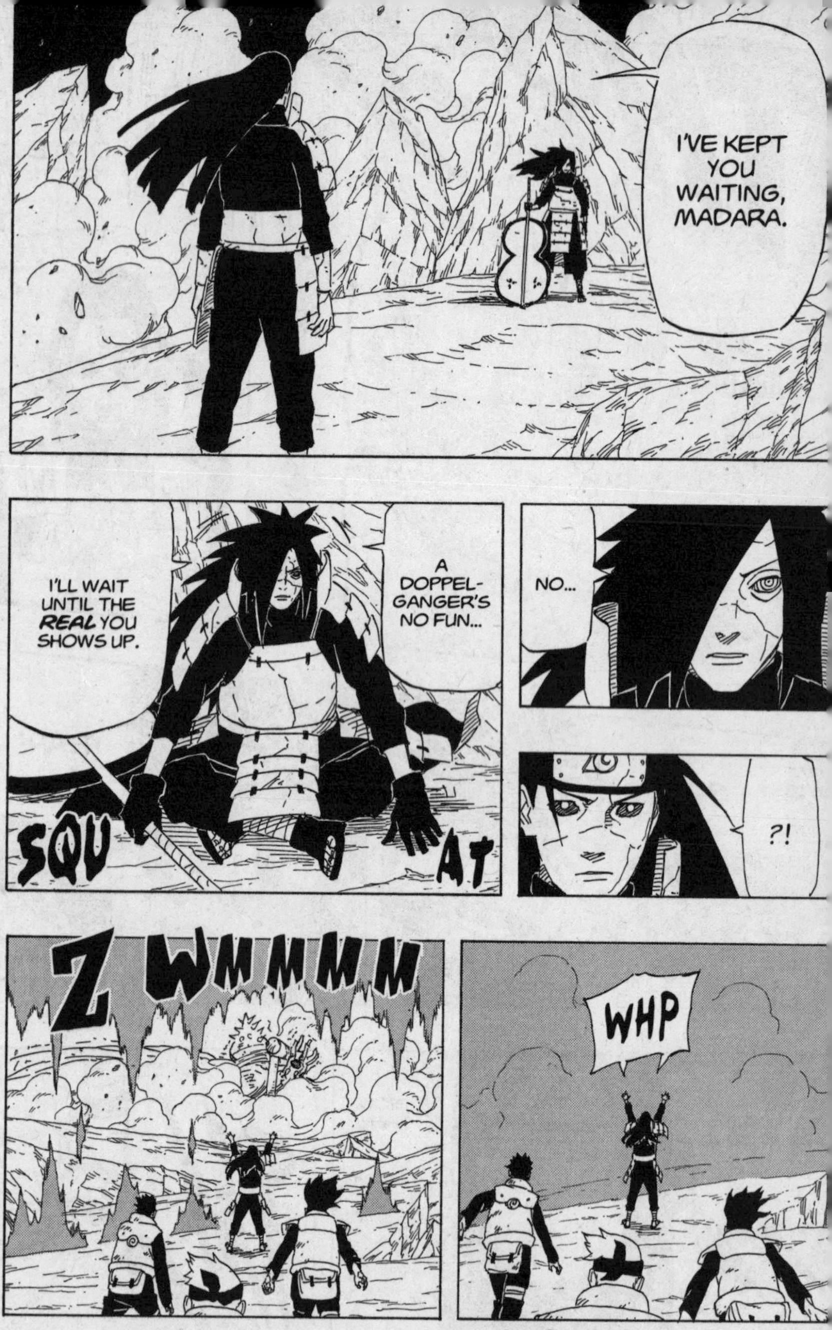
I'VE KEPT YOU WAITING, MADARA.
NO...
?!
A DOPPEL-GANGER'S NO FUN...
I'LL WAIT UNTIL THE **REAL** YOU SHOWS UP.
SQUAT
WHP
ZWMMMM

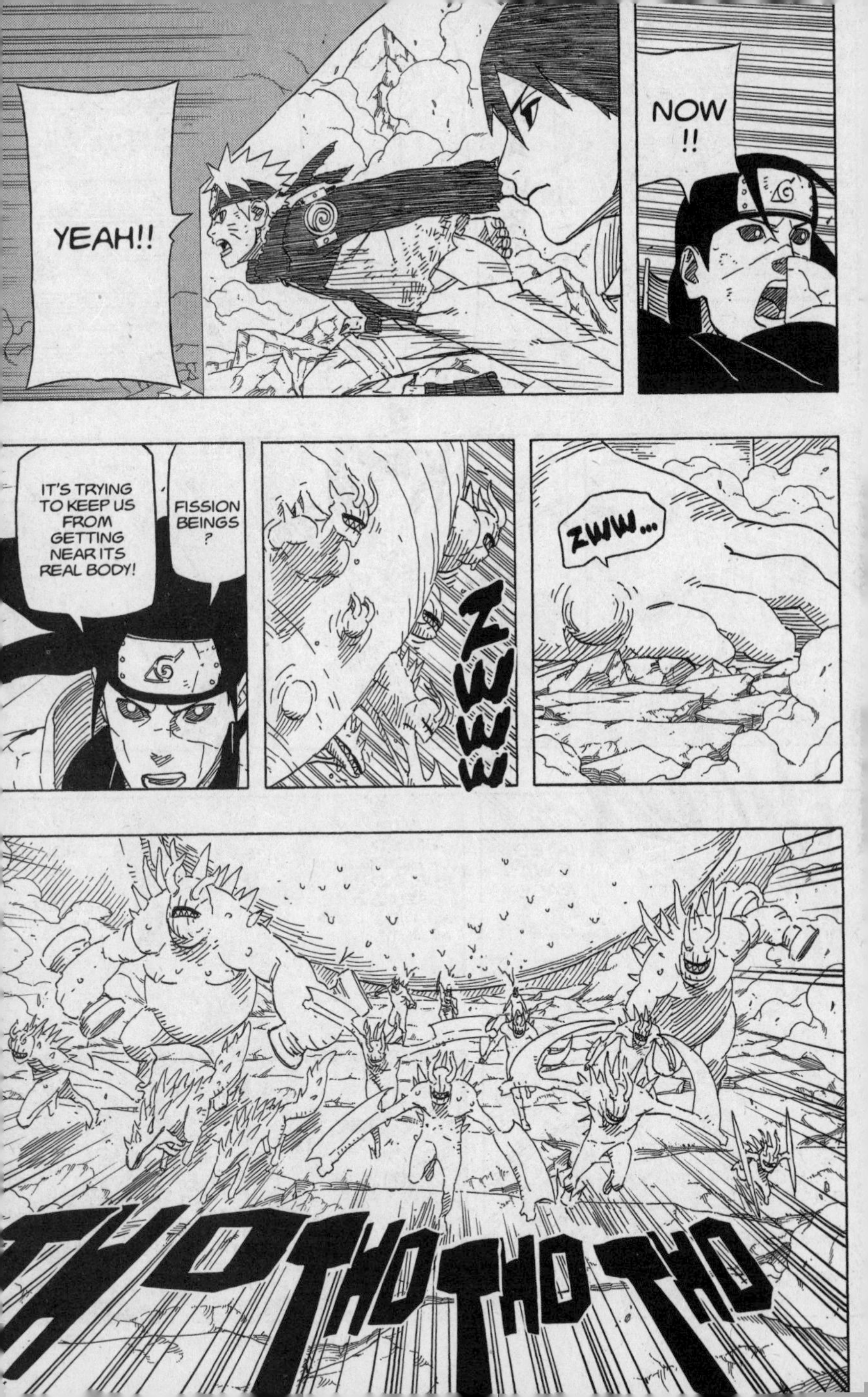
NOW !!
YEAH!!
ZWW...
ZWWW
FISSION BEINGS ?
IT'S TRYING TO KEEP US FROM GETTING NEAR ITS REAL BODY!
THD THD THD THD

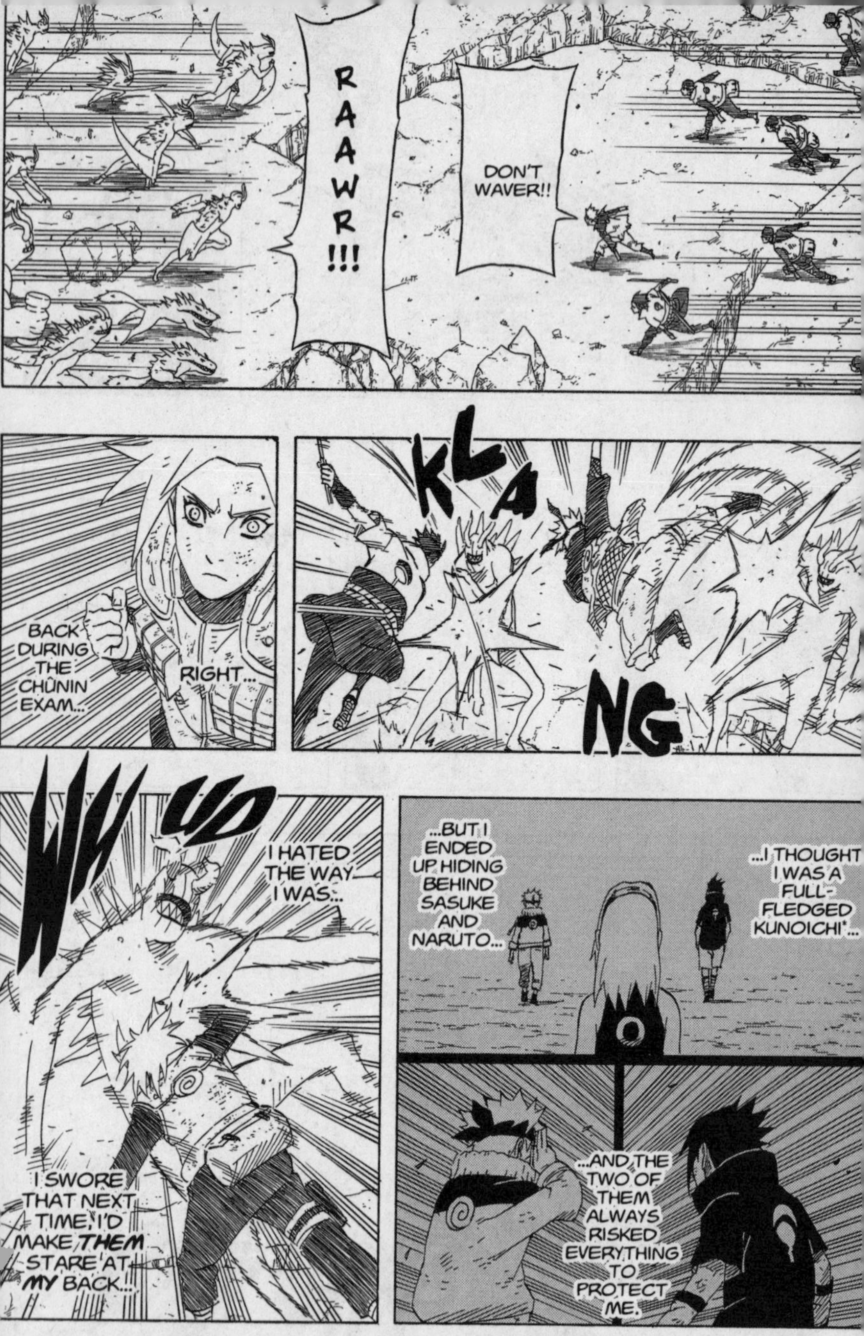
DON'T WAVER!!
RAAAWR!!!
KLANG
RIGHT...
BACK DURING THE CHŪNIN EXAM...
...I THOUGHT I WAS A FULL-FLEDGED KUNOICHI*...
...BUT I ENDED UP HIDING BEHIND SASUKE AND NARUTO...
...AND THE TWO OF THEM ALWAYS RISKED EVERYTHING TO PROTECT ME.
WHUD
I HATED THE WAY I WAS...
I SWORE THAT NEXT TIME, I'D MAKE *THEM* STARE AT *MY* BACK...

*KUNOICHI = FEMALE NINJA

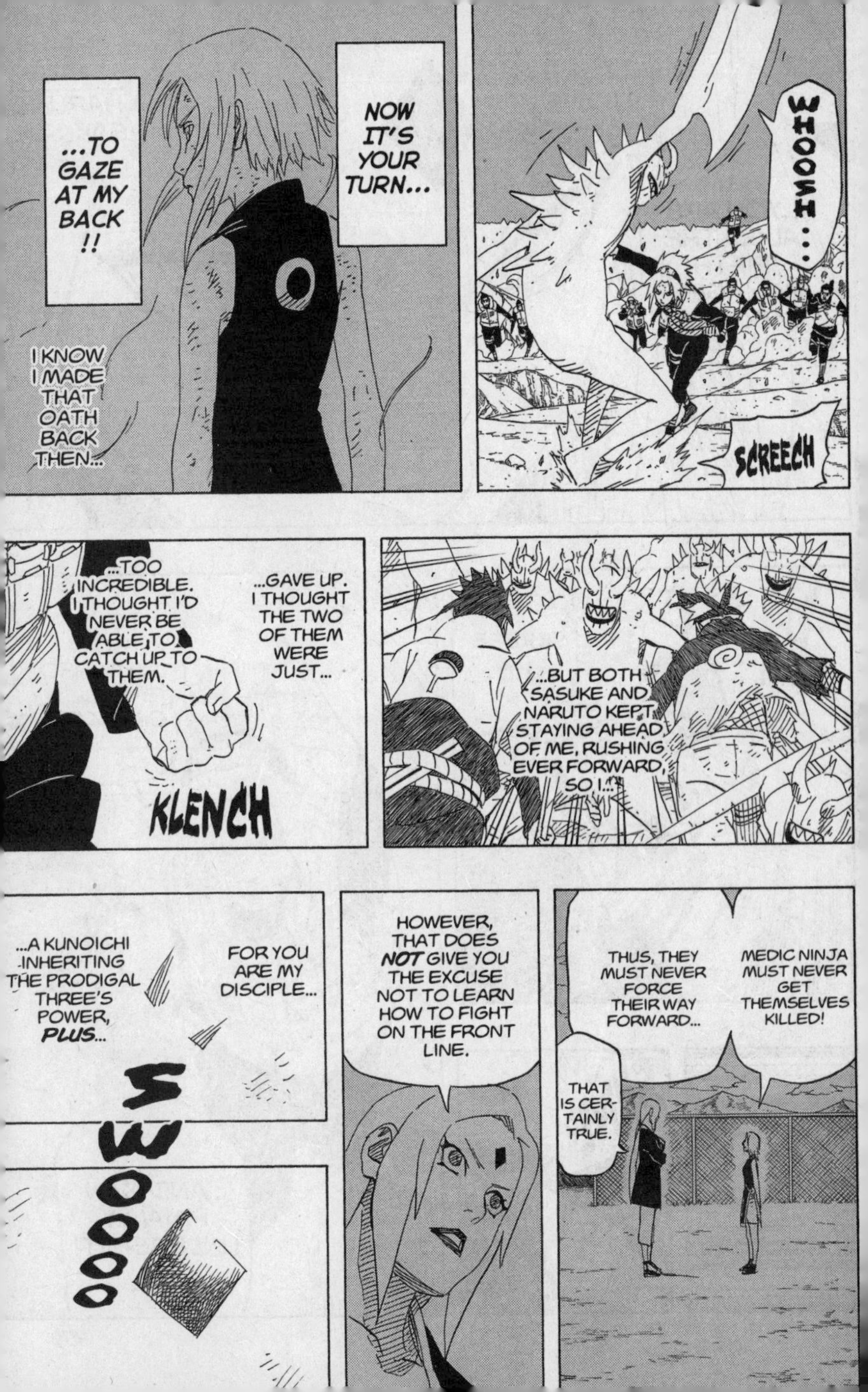
WHOOSH...
SCREECH
NOW IT'S YOUR TURN...
...TO GAZE AT MY BACK!!
I KNOW I MADE THAT OATH BACK THEN...
...BUT BOTH SASUKE AND NARUTO KEPT STAYING AHEAD OF ME, RUSHING EVER FORWARD, SO I...!
...GAVE UP. I THOUGHT THE TWO OF THEM WERE JUST...
...TOO INCREDIBLE. I THOUGHT I'D NEVER BE ABLE TO CATCH UP TO THEM.
KLENCH
MEDIC NINJA MUST NEVER GET THEMSELVES KILLED!
THUS, THEY MUST NEVER FORCE THEIR WAY FORWARD...
THAT IS CERTAINLY TRUE.
HOWEVER, THAT DOES **NOT** GIVE YOU THE EXCUSE NOT TO LEARN HOW TO FIGHT ON THE FRONT LINE.
FOR YOU ARE MY DISCIPLE...
...A KUNOICHI INHERITING THE PRODIGAL THREE'S POWER, **PLUS**...
SWOOOOO

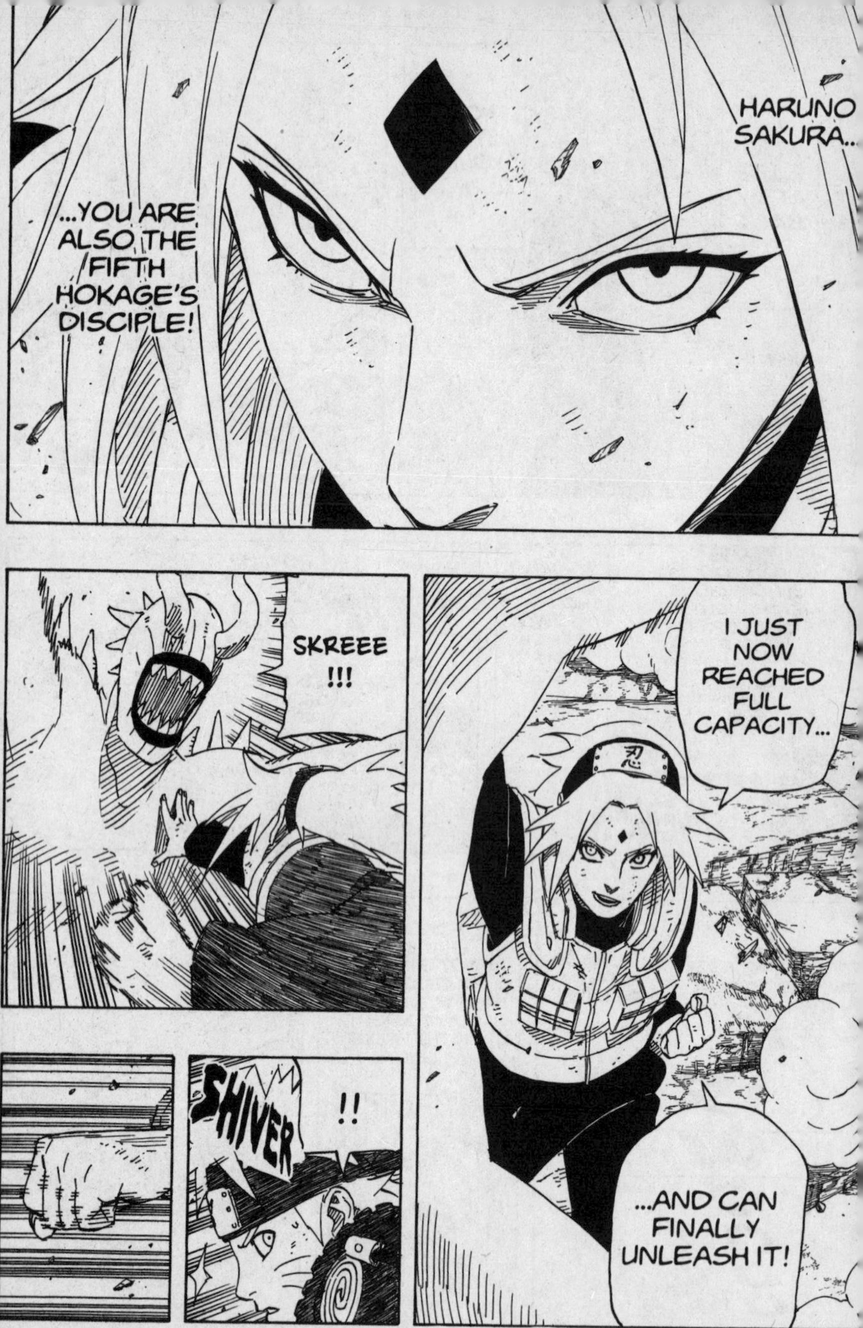
HARUNO SAKURA...
...YOU ARE ALSO THE FIFTH HOKAGE'S DISCIPLE!
I JUST NOW REACHED FULL CAPACITY...
...AND CAN FINALLY UNLEASH IT!
SKREEE !!!
!!
SHIVER

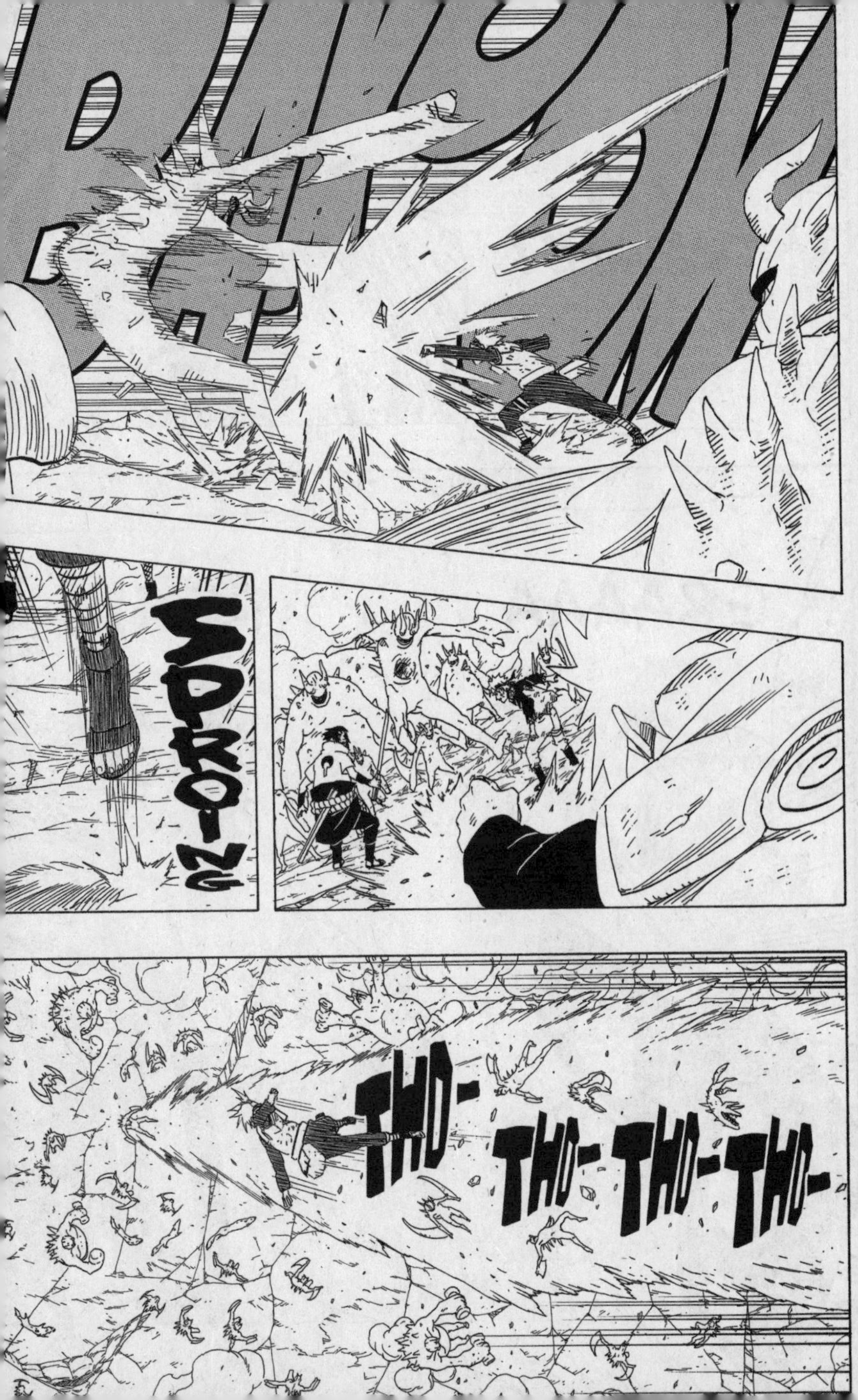
SPROING
THD- THD- THD- THD-

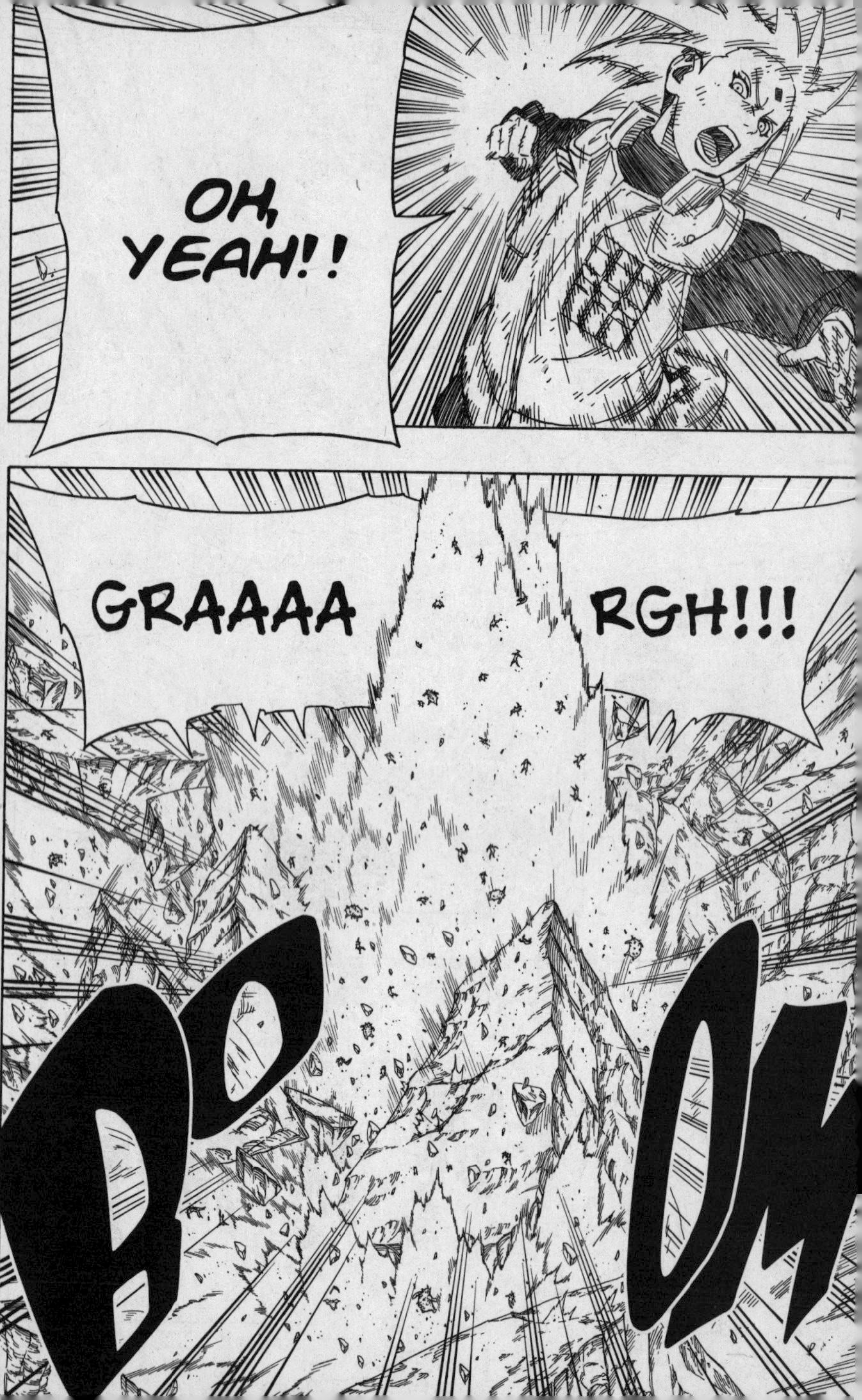
OH, YEAH!!
GRAAAA RGH!!!
BOOM

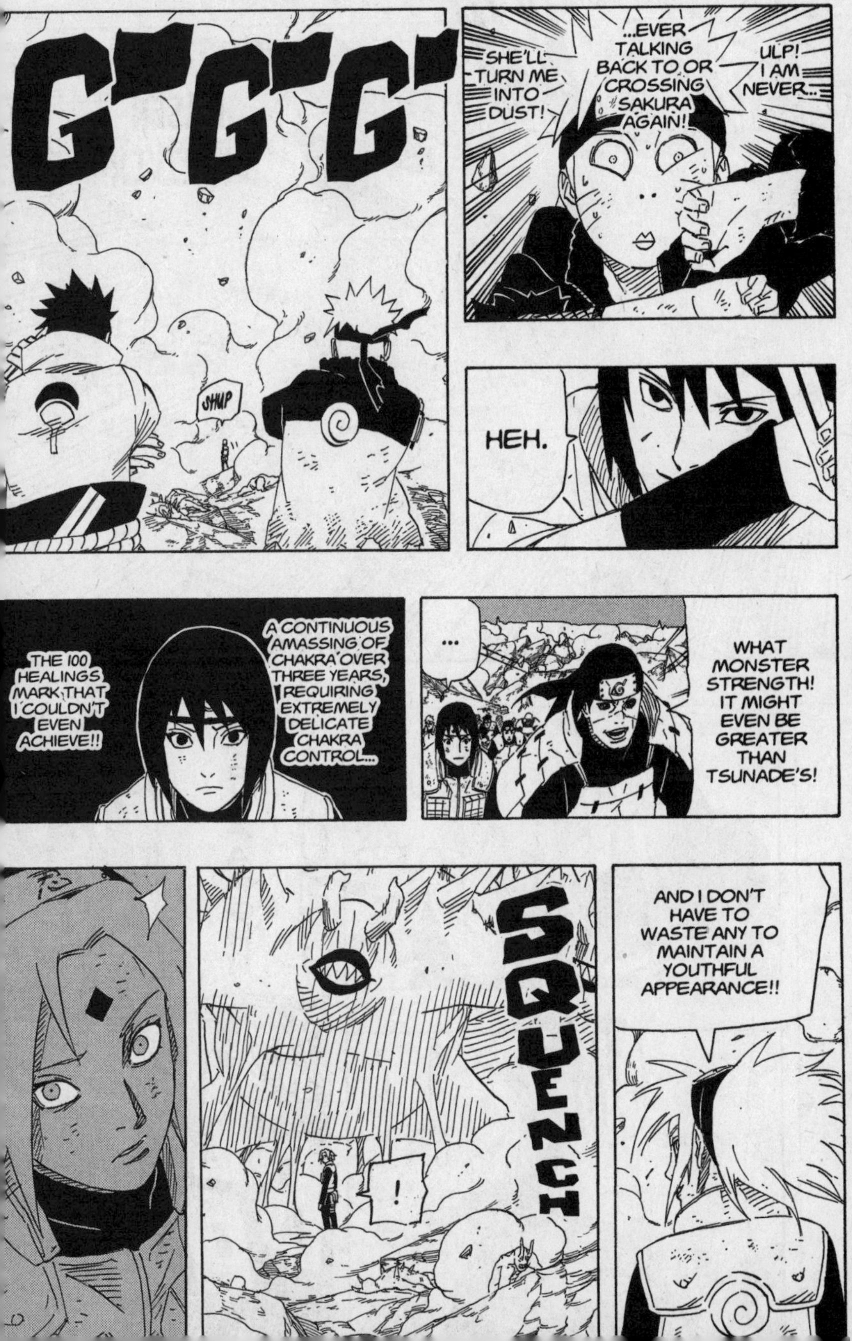
ULP! I AM NEVER...
...EVER TALKING BACK TO OR CROSSING SAKURA AGAIN!
SHE'LL TURN ME INTO DUST!
HEH.
G'G'G'
SHUP
WHAT MONSTER STRENGTH! IT MIGHT EVEN BE GREATER THAN TSUNADE'S!
...
A CONTINUOUS AMASSING OF CHAKRA OVER THREE YEARS, REQUIRING EXTREMELY DELICATE CHAKRA CONTROL...
THE 100 HEALINGS MARK THAT I COULDN'T EVEN ACHIEVE!!
AND I DON'T HAVE TO WASTE ANY TO MAINTAIN A YOUTHFUL APPEARANCE!!
SQUENCH
!

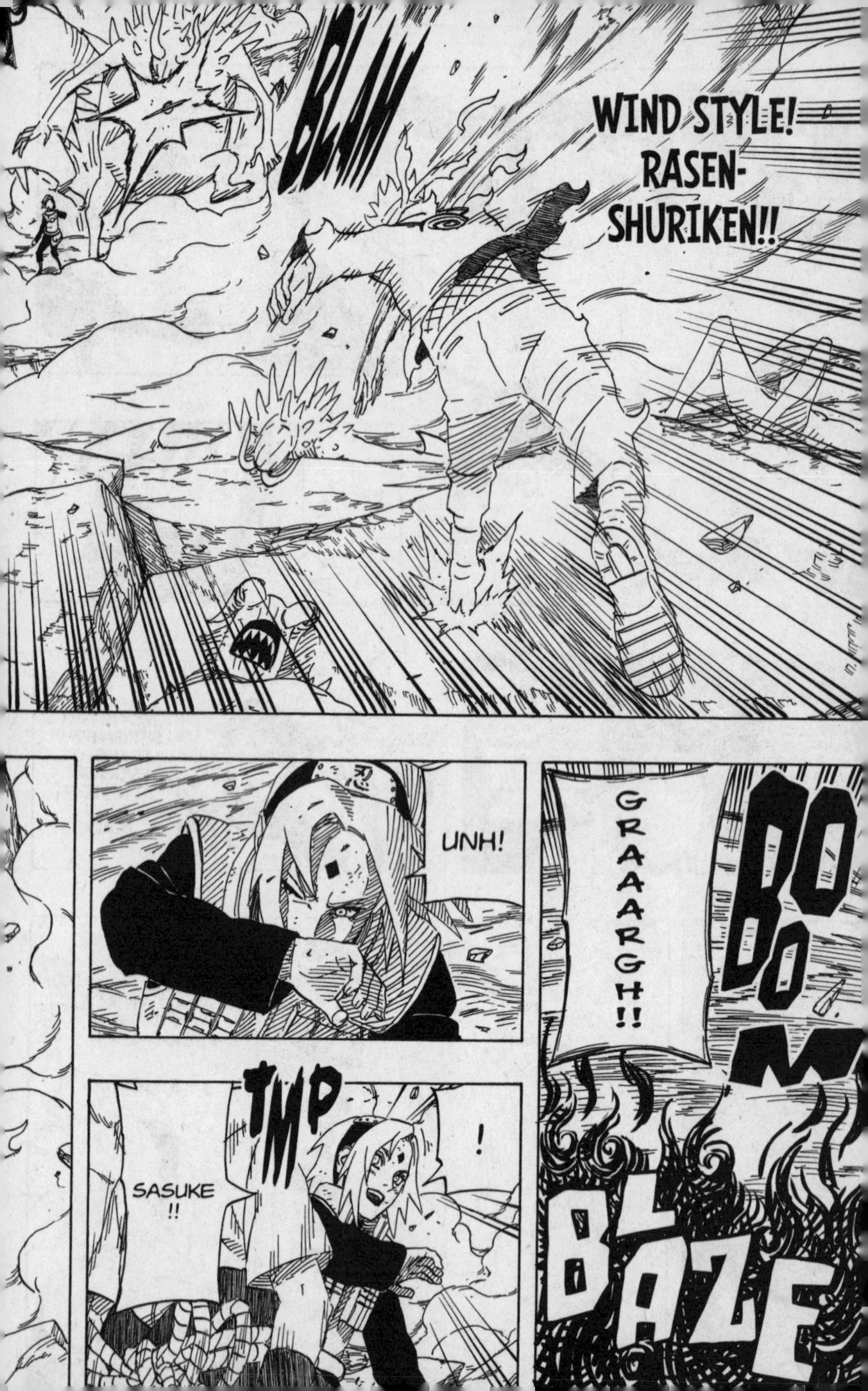

WIND STYLE! RASEN-SHURIKEN!!
BLAM
BOOM
GRAAARGH!!
BLAZE
UNH!
!
TMP
SASUKE!!

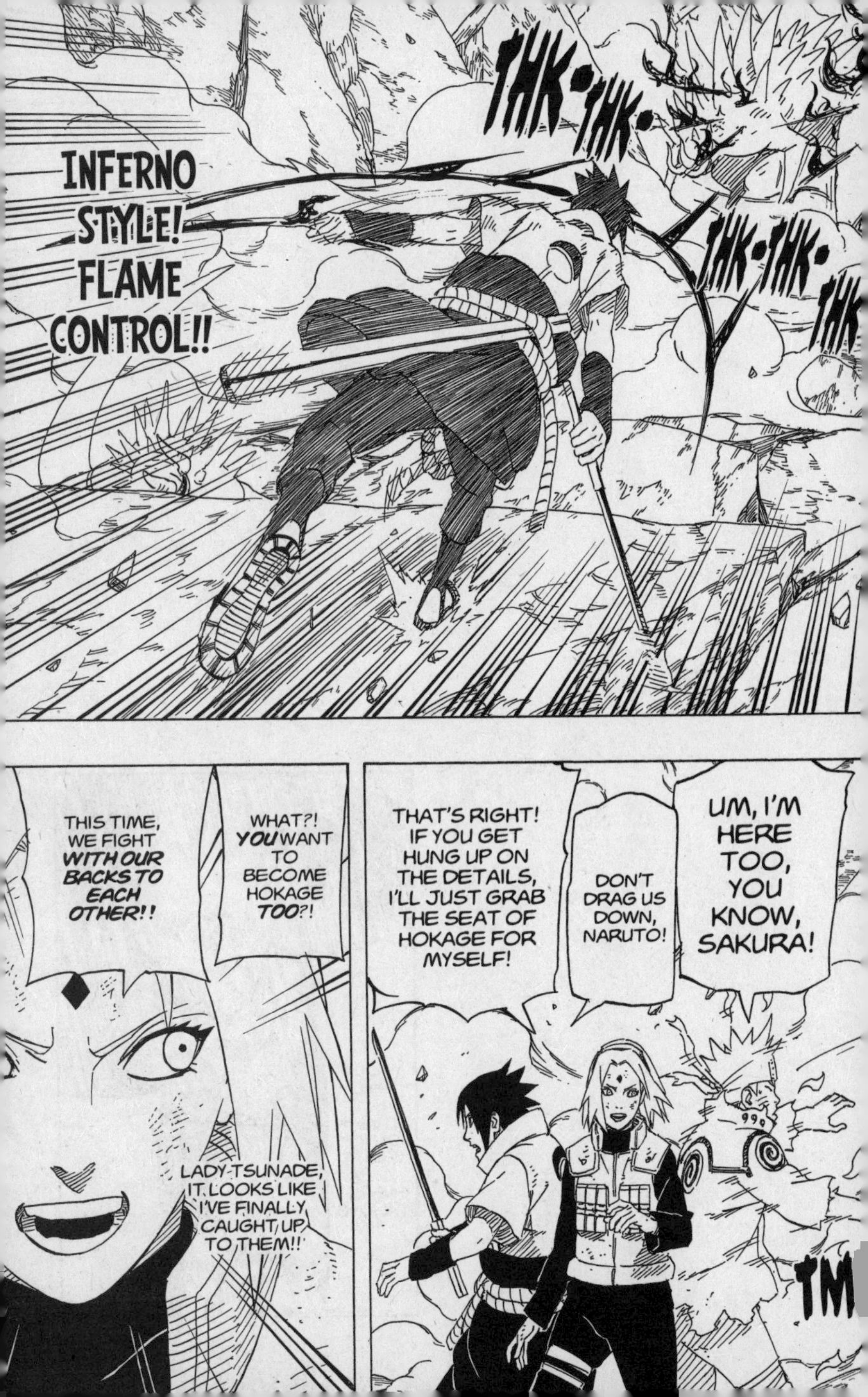
THK·THK·
THK·THK·THK
INFERNO STYLE! FLAME CONTROL!!
UM, I'M HERE TOO, YOU KNOW, SAKURA!
DON'T DRAG US DOWN, NARUTO!
THAT'S RIGHT! IF YOU GET HUNG UP ON THE DETAILS, I'LL JUST GRAB THE SEAT OF HOKAGE FOR MYSELF!
TM
WHAT?! ***YOU*** WANT TO BECOME HOKAGE ***TOO***?!
THIS TIME, WE FIGHT ***WITH OUR BACKS TO EACH OTHER!!***
LADY TSUNADE, IT LOOKS LIKE I'VE FINALLY CAUGHT UP TO THEM!!

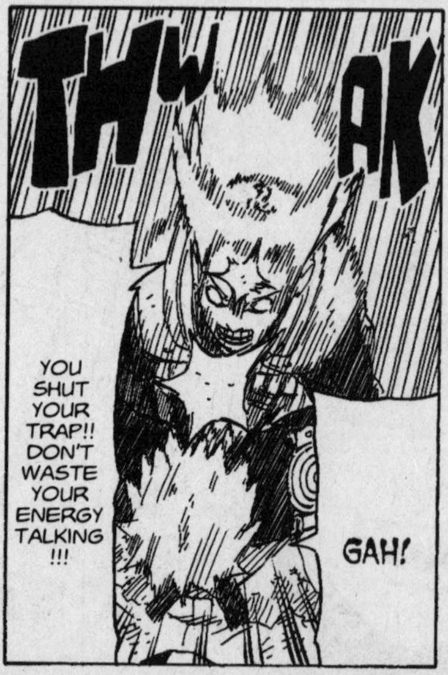
THWAK
YOU SHUT YOUR TRAP!! DON'T WASTE YOUR ENERGY TALKING!!!
GAH!

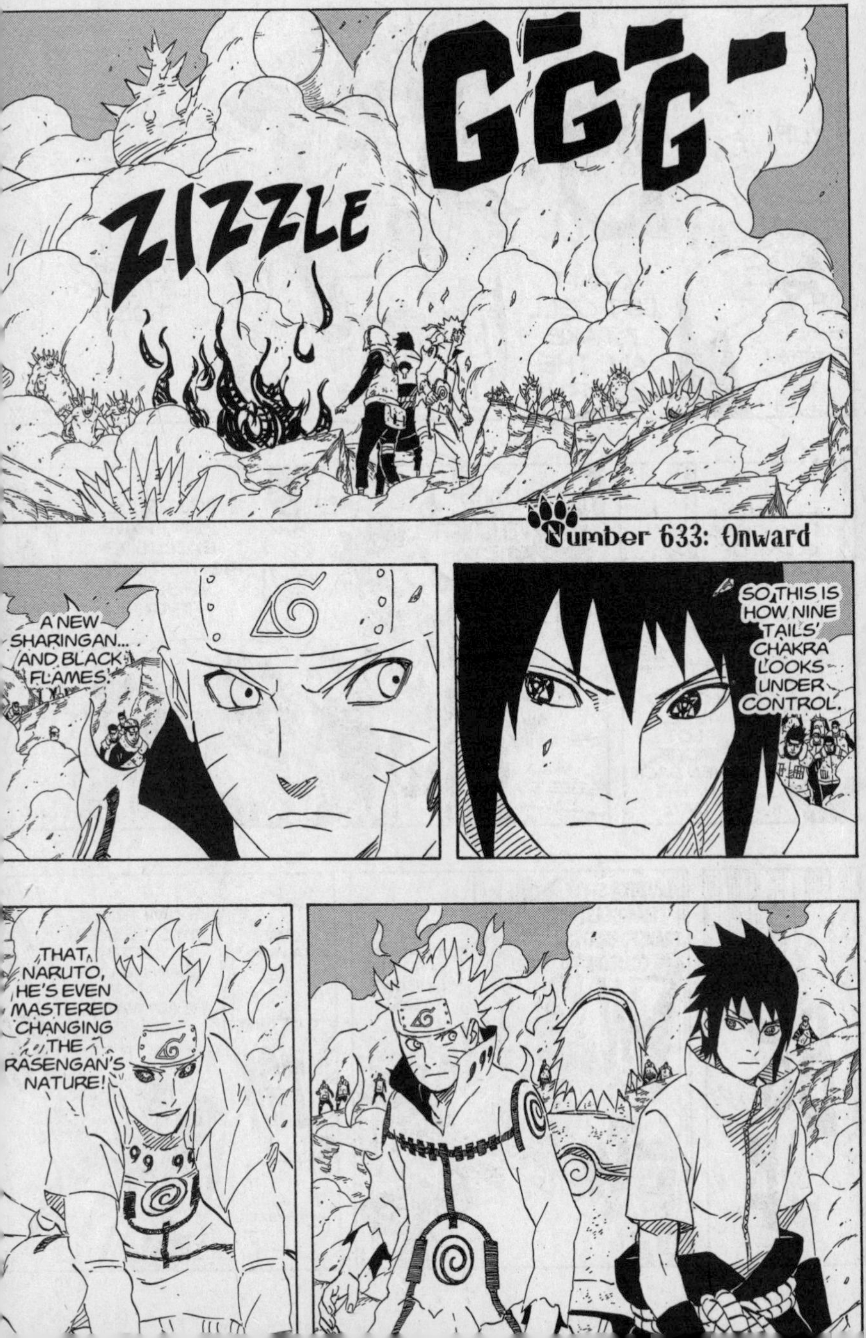
G-G-G-
ZIZZLE
Number 633: Onward
SO THIS IS HOW NINE TAILS' CHAKRA LOOKS UNDER CONTROL.
A NEW SHARINGAN... AND BLACK FLAMES.
THAT NARUTO, HE'S EVEN MASTERED CHANGING THE RASENGAN'S NATURE!

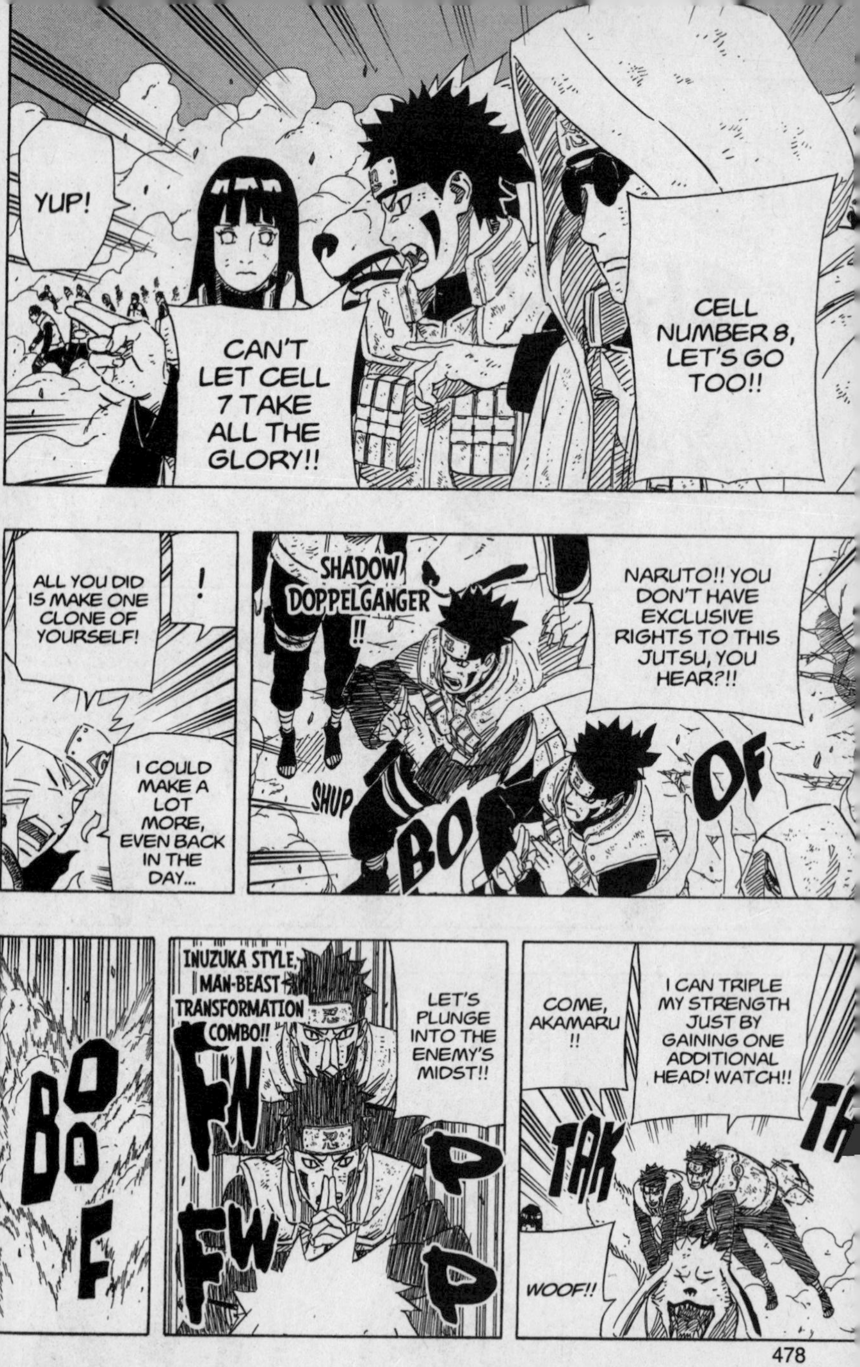
CELL NUMBER 8, LET'S GO TOO!!
CAN'T LET CELL 7 TAKE ALL THE GLORY!!
YUP!
NARUTO!! YOU DON'T HAVE EXCLUSIVE RIGHTS TO THIS JUTSU, YOU HEAR?!!
SHADOW DOPPELGANGER!!
SHUP
BOOF
!
ALL YOU DID IS MAKE ONE CLONE OF YOURSELF!
I COULD MAKE A LOT MORE, EVEN BACK IN THE DAY...
I CAN TRIPLE MY STRENGTH JUST BY GAINING ONE ADDITIONAL HEAD! WATCH!!
COME, AKAMARU!!
TAK
WOOF!!
LET'S PLUNGE INTO THE ENEMY'S MIDST!!
INUZUKA STYLE, MAN-BEAST TRANSFORMATION COMBO!!
FWP
FWP
BOOOF

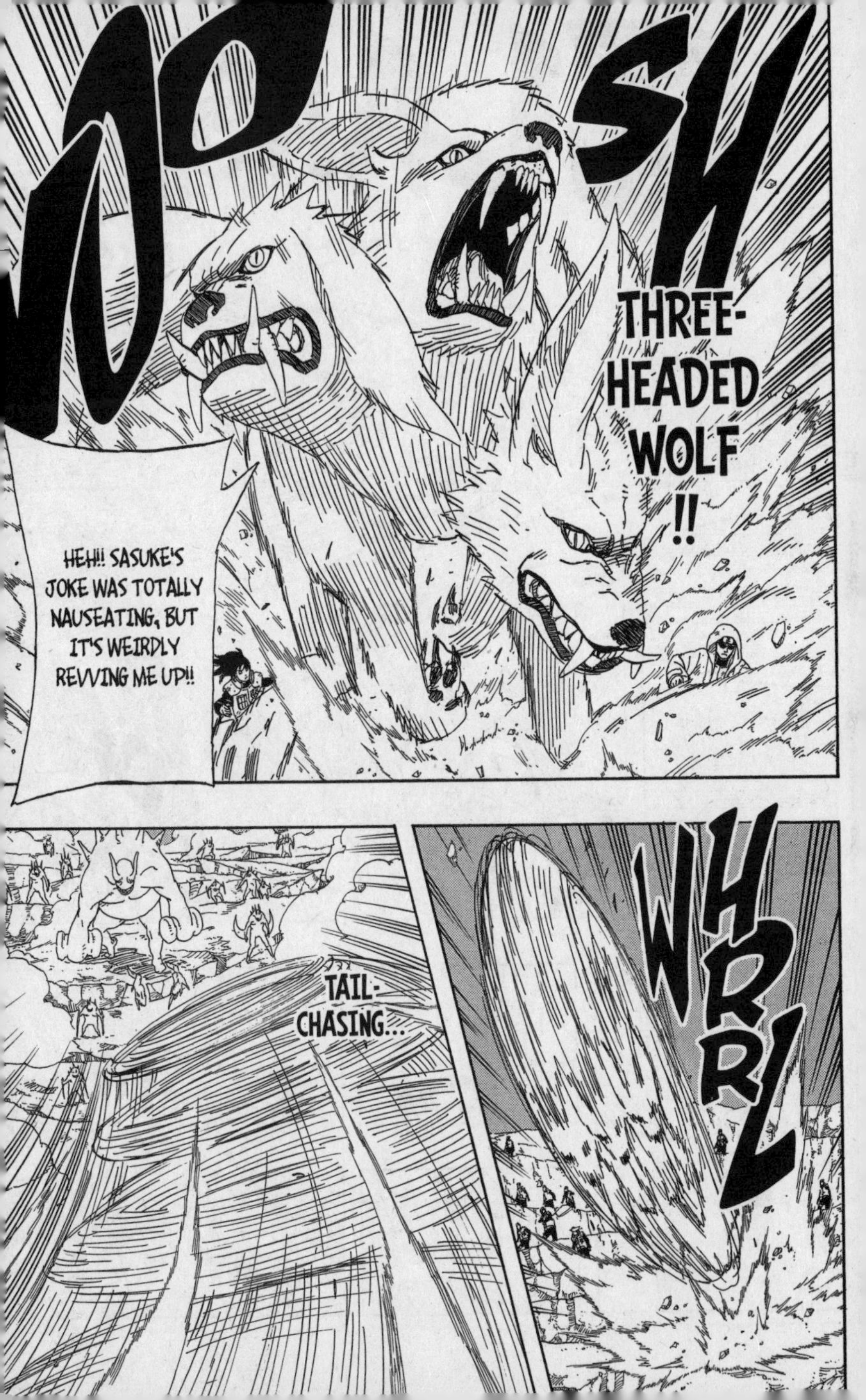
WOOSH
THREE-HEADED WOLF!!
HEH!! SASUKE'S JOKE WAS TOTALLY NAUSEATING, BUT IT'S WEIRDLY REVVING ME UP!!
WHRRL
TAIL-CHASING...

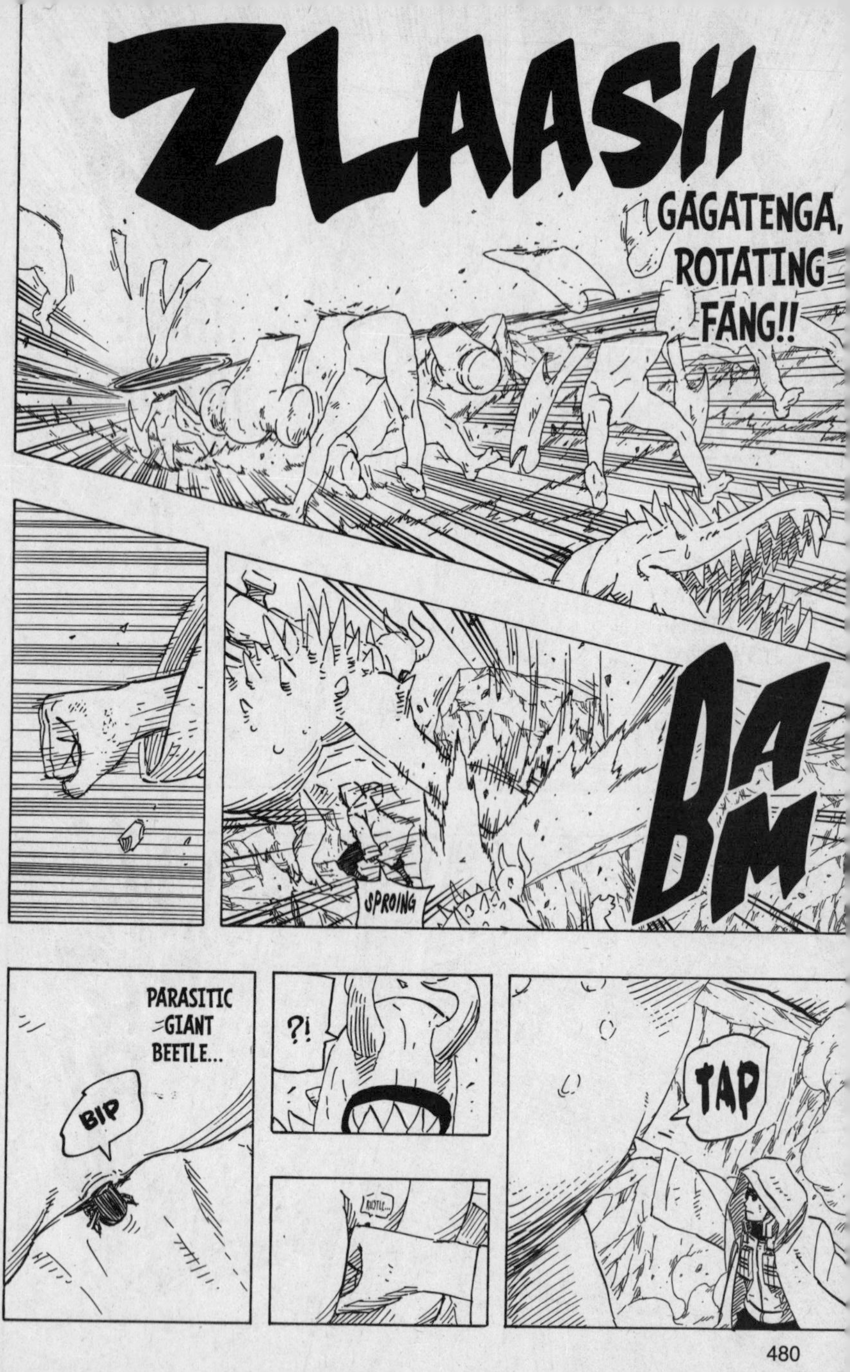
ZLAASH
GAGATENGA, ROTATING FANG!!
DABAM
SPROING
TAP
?!
RUSTLE...
PARASITIC GIANT BEETLE...
BIP

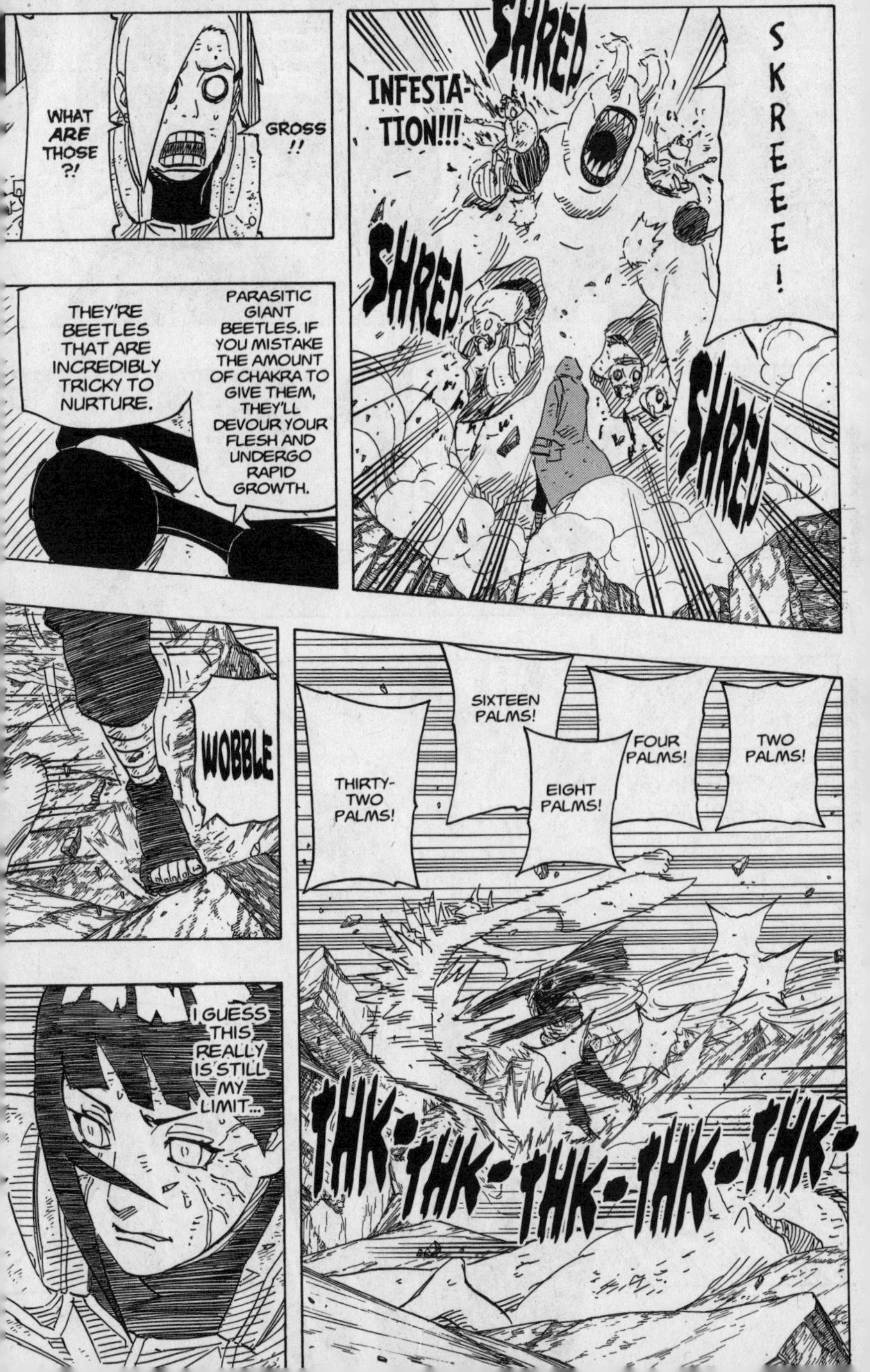
SKREEE!
SHRED
INFESTATION!!!
SHRED
SHRED
GROSS!!
WHAT ARE THOSE?!
PARASITIC GIANT BEETLES. IF YOU MISTAKE THE AMOUNT OF CHAKRA TO GIVE THEM, THEY'LL DEVOUR YOUR FLESH AND UNDERGO RAPID GROWTH.
THEY'RE BEETLES THAT ARE INCREDIBLY TRICKY TO NURTURE.
TWO PALMS!
FOUR PALMS!
EIGHT PALMS!
SIXTEEN PALMS!
THIRTY-TWO PALMS!
THK-THK-THK-THK-THK-
WOBBLE
I GUESS THIS REALLY IS STILL MY LIMIT...

YOU MUST FEARLESSLY TAKE A GIANT LEAP FORWARD.

THAT'S THE...

...TRICK TO ACHIEVING 64 PALMS.

SIXTY-FOUR PALMS!!

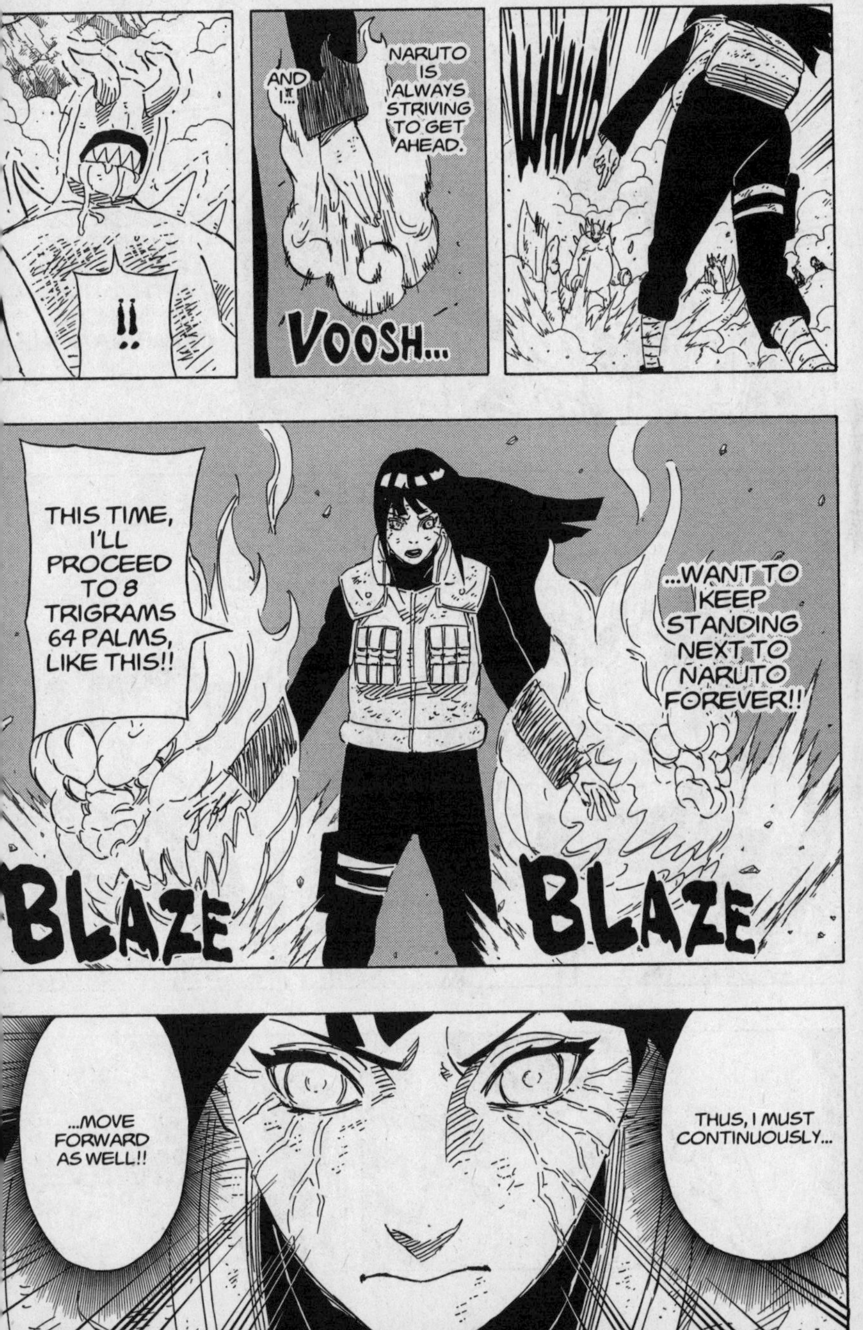
WHUD
NARUTO IS ALWAYS STRIVING TO GET AHEAD.
AND I...
VOOSH...
!!
...WANT TO KEEP STANDING NEXT TO NARUTO FOREVER!!
THIS TIME, I'LL PROCEED TO 8 TRIGRAMS 64 PALMS, LIKE THIS!!
BLAZE
BLAZE
THUS, I MUST CONTINUOUSLY...
...MOVE FORWARD AS WELL!!

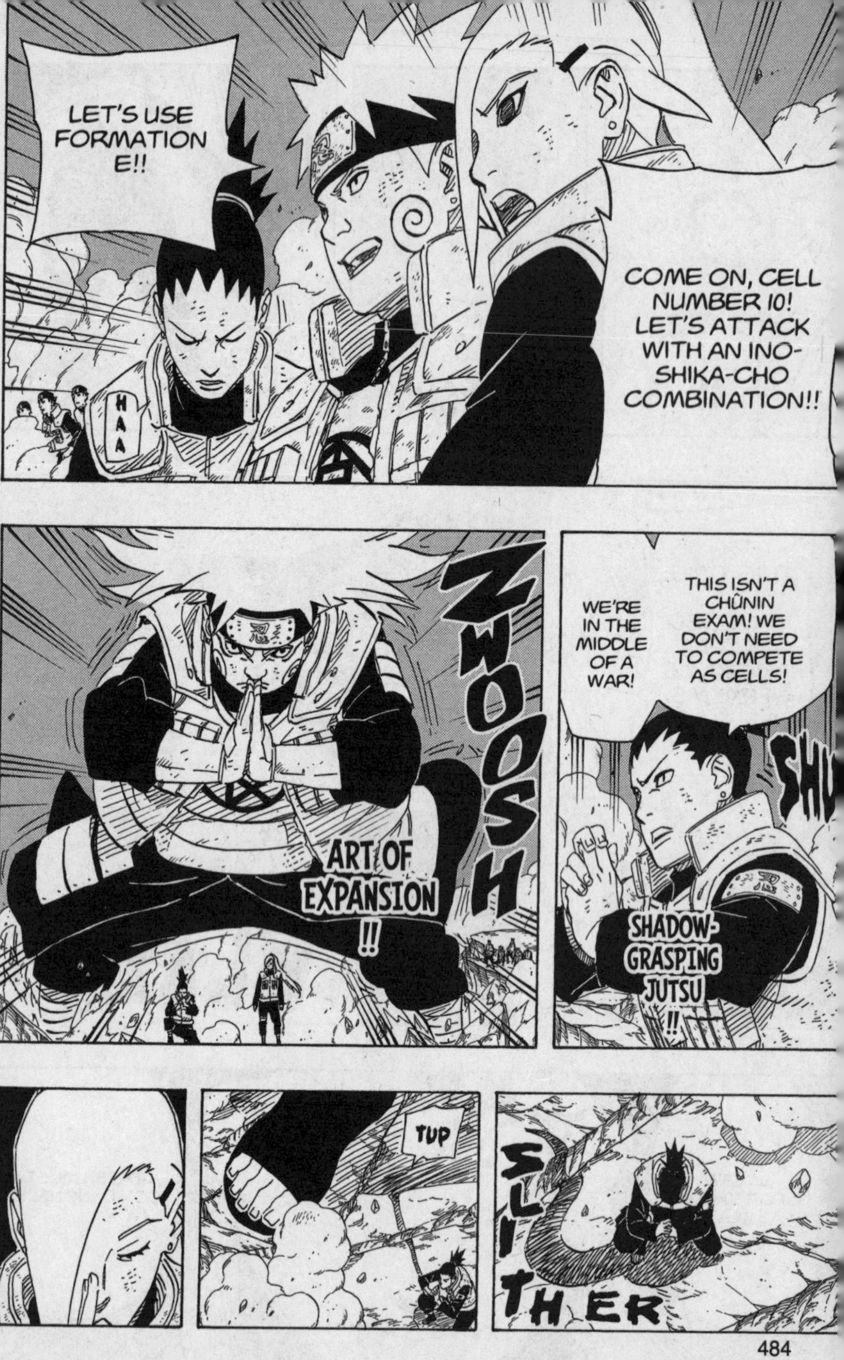
COME ON, CELL NUMBER 10! LET'S ATTACK WITH AN INO-SHIKA-CHO COMBINATION!!
LET'S USE FORMATION E!!
HAA
THIS ISN'T A CHŪNIN EXAM! WE DON'T NEED TO COMPETE AS CELLS!
WE'RE IN THE MIDDLE OF A WAR!
SHU
SHADOW-GRASPING JUTSU!!
WHOOSH
ART OF EXPANSION!!
SLITHER
TUP

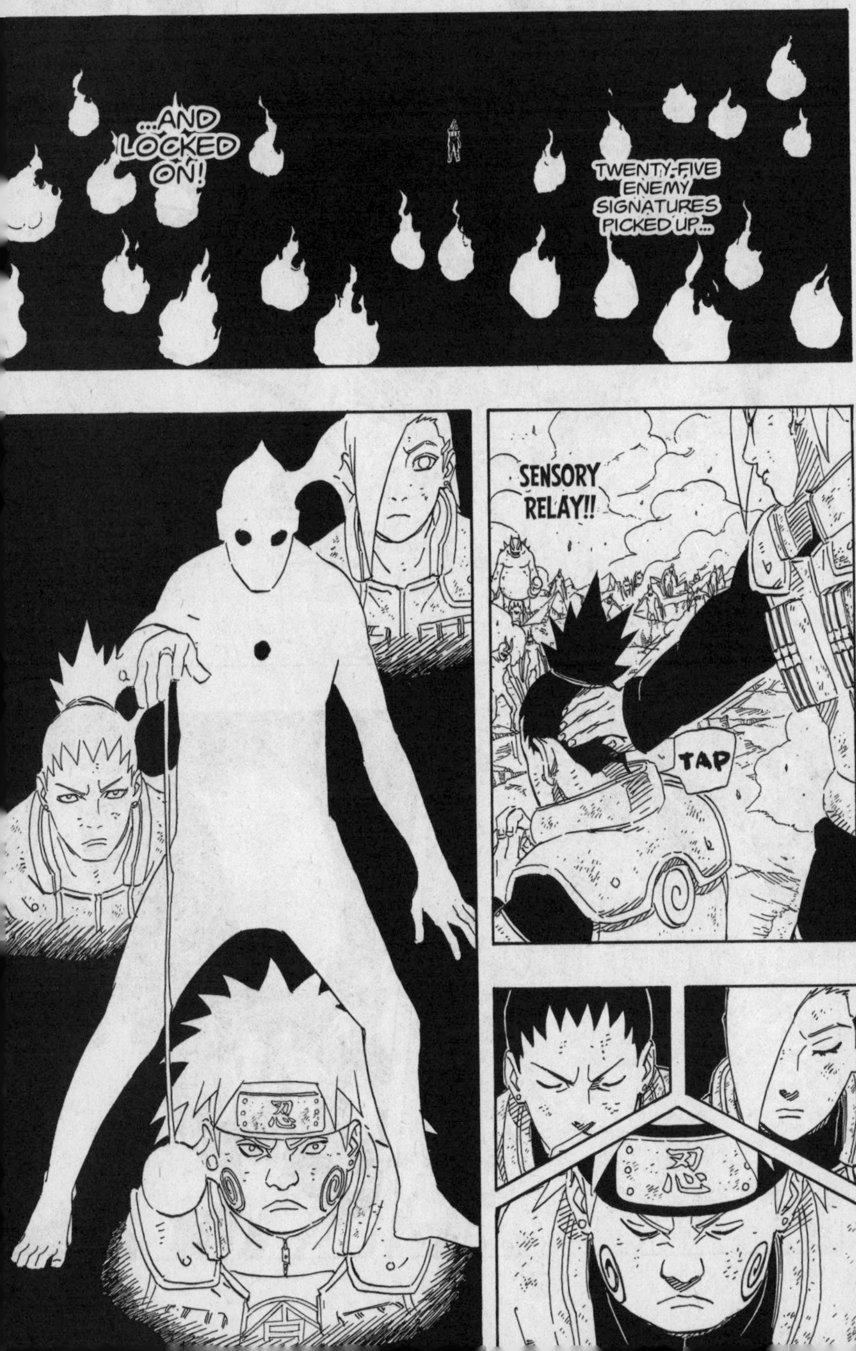
TWENTY-FIVE ENEMY SIGNATURES PICKED UP...
...AND LOCKED ON!
SENSORY RELAY!!
TAP

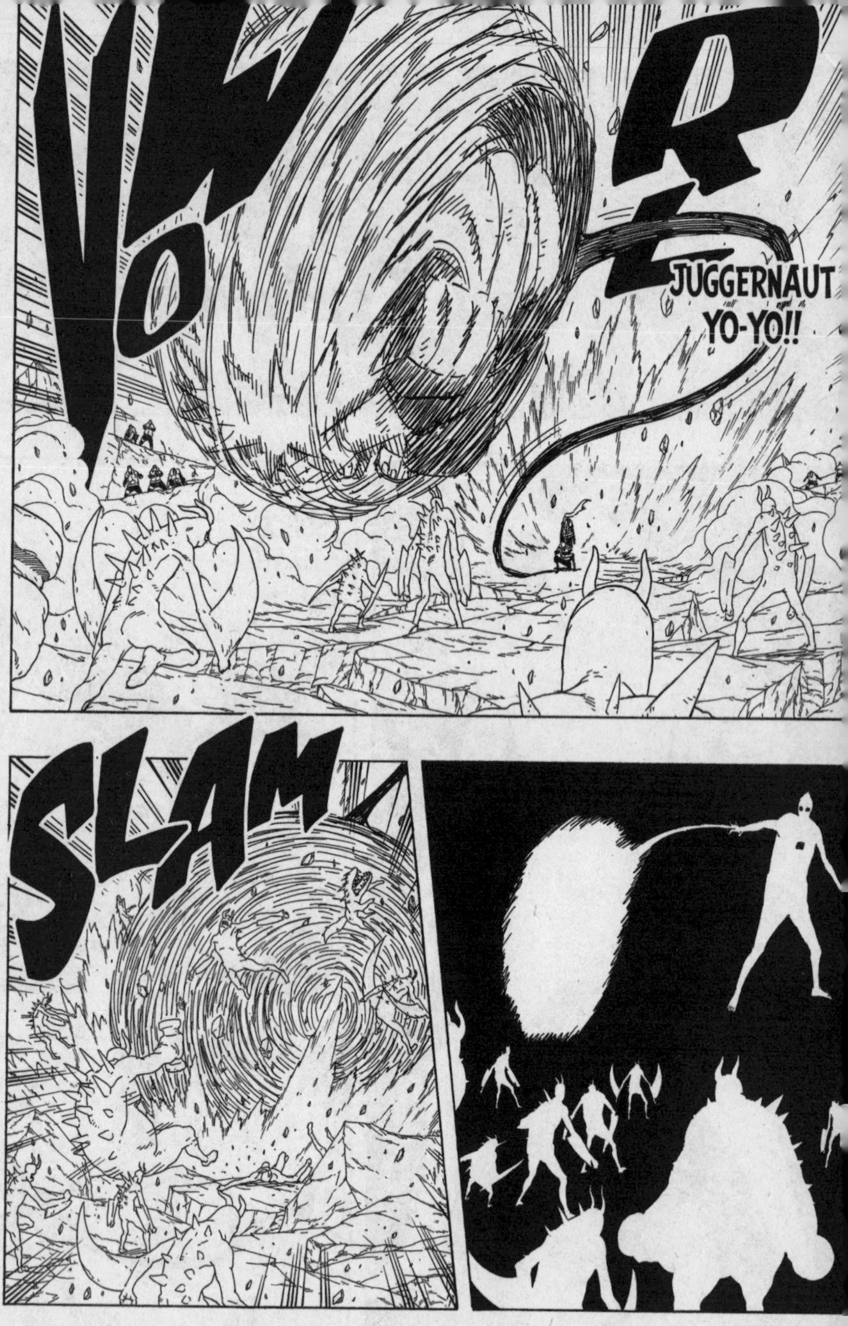
JUGGERNAUT YO-YO!!
SLAM

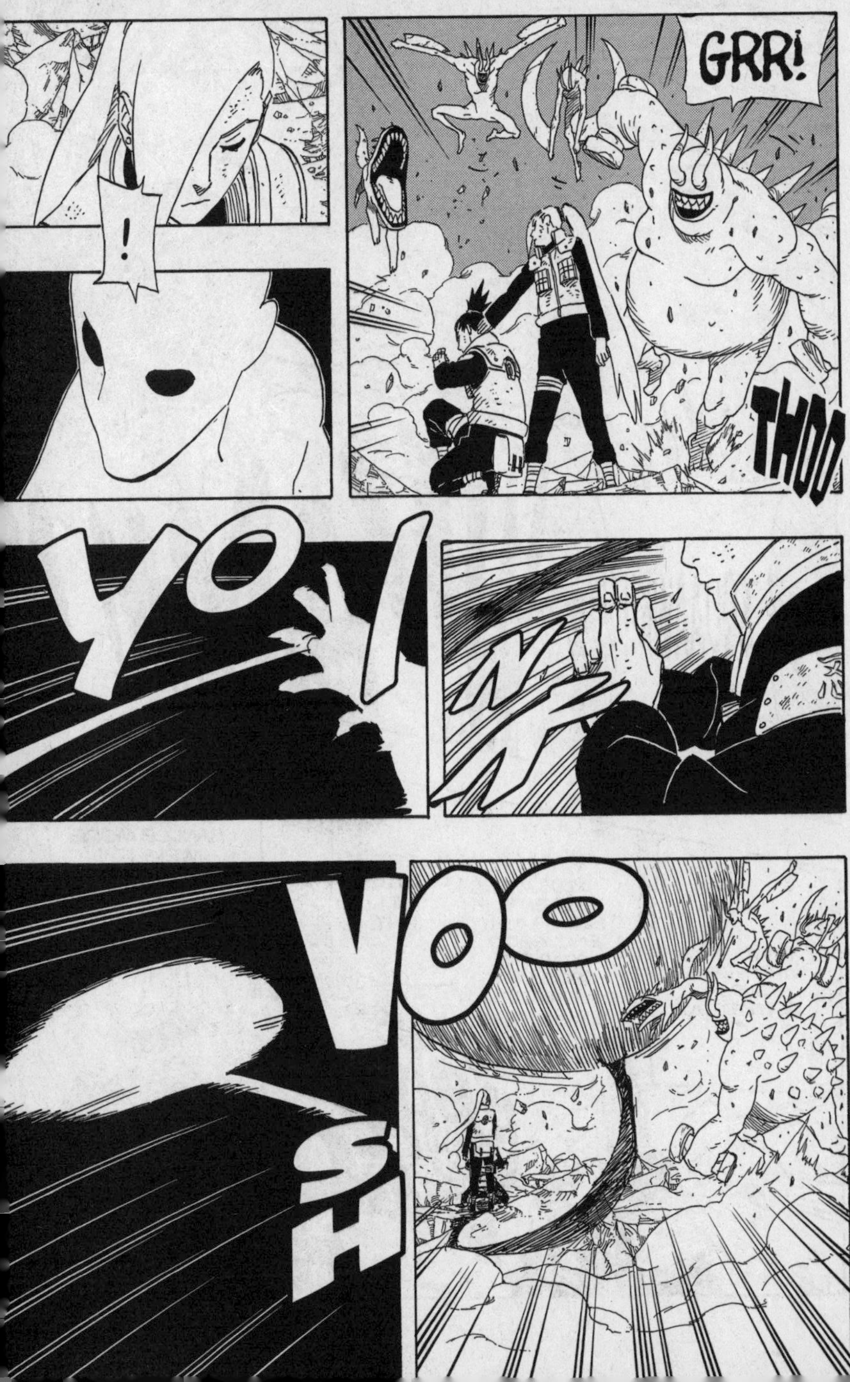
GRR!
THOO
!
N
YOI
VOOSH

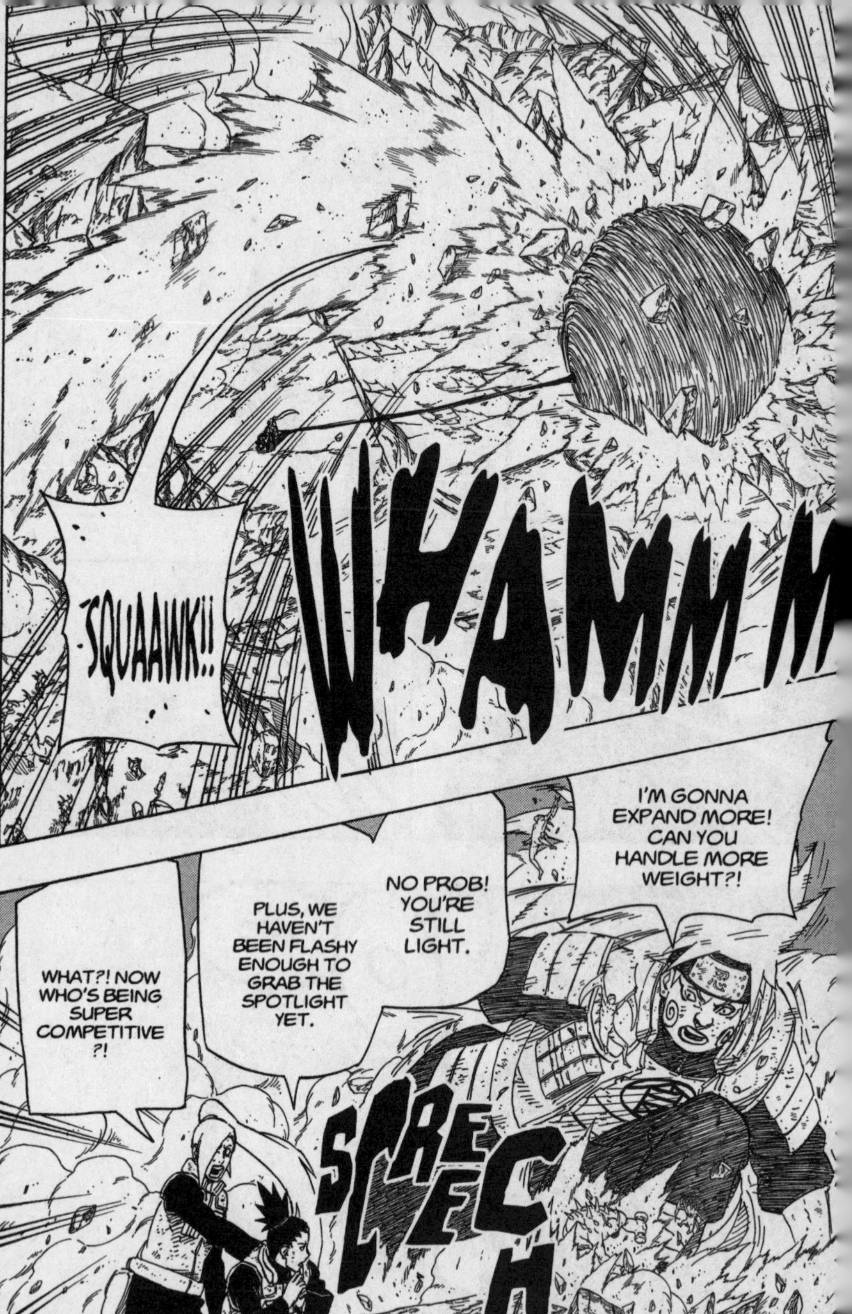
WHAMMM
SQUAAWK!!
I'M GONNA EXPAND MORE! CAN YOU HANDLE MORE WEIGHT?!
NO PROB! YOU'RE STILL LIGHT.
PLUS, WE HAVEN'T BEEN FLASHY ENOUGH TO GRAB THE SPOTLIGHT YET.
WHAT?! NOW WHO'S BEING SUPER COMPETITIVE ?!
SCREECH

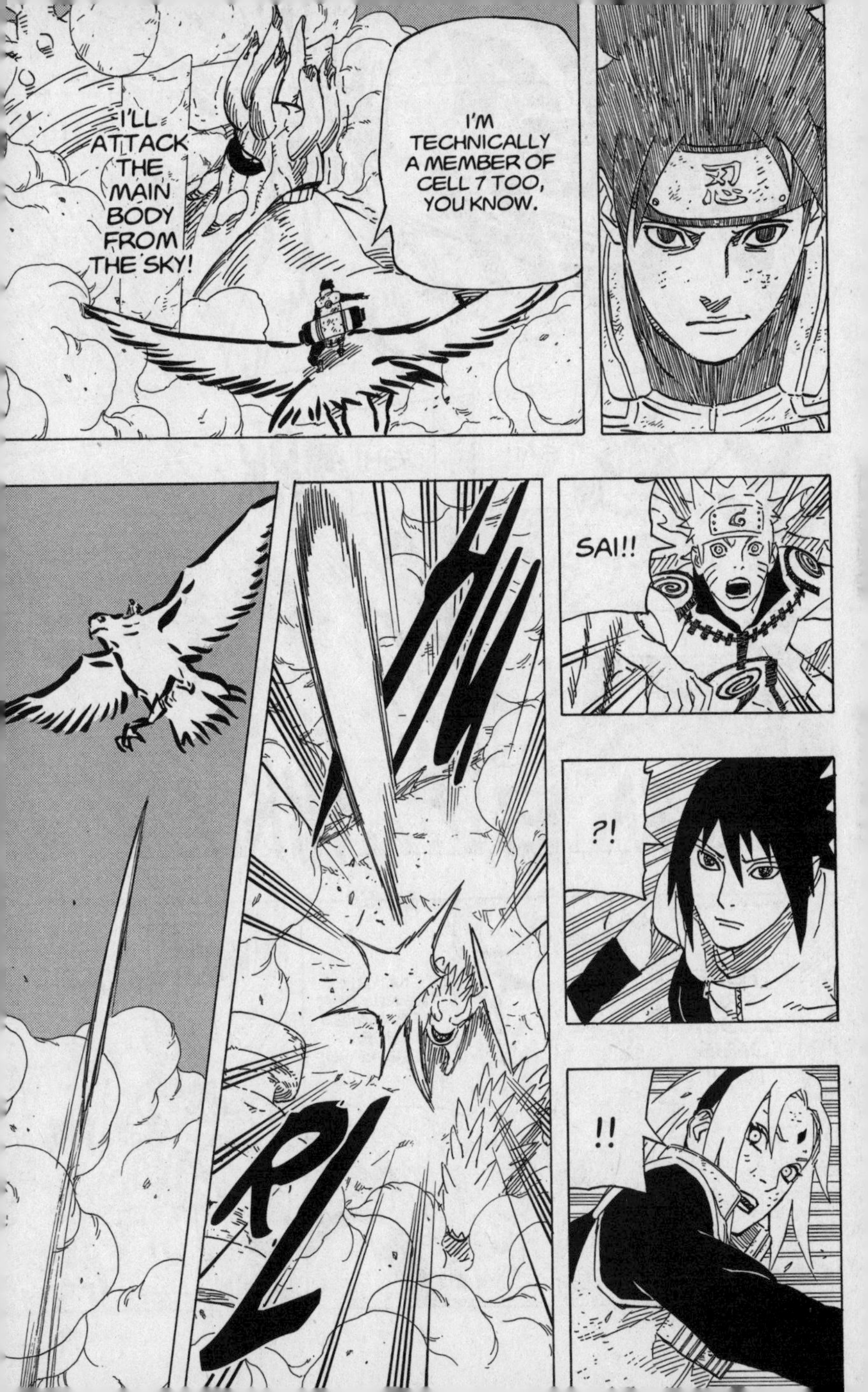
I'M TECHNICALLY A MEMBER OF CELL 7 TOO, YOU KNOW.
I'LL ATTACK THE MAIN BODY FROM THE SKY!
SAI!!
?!
!!

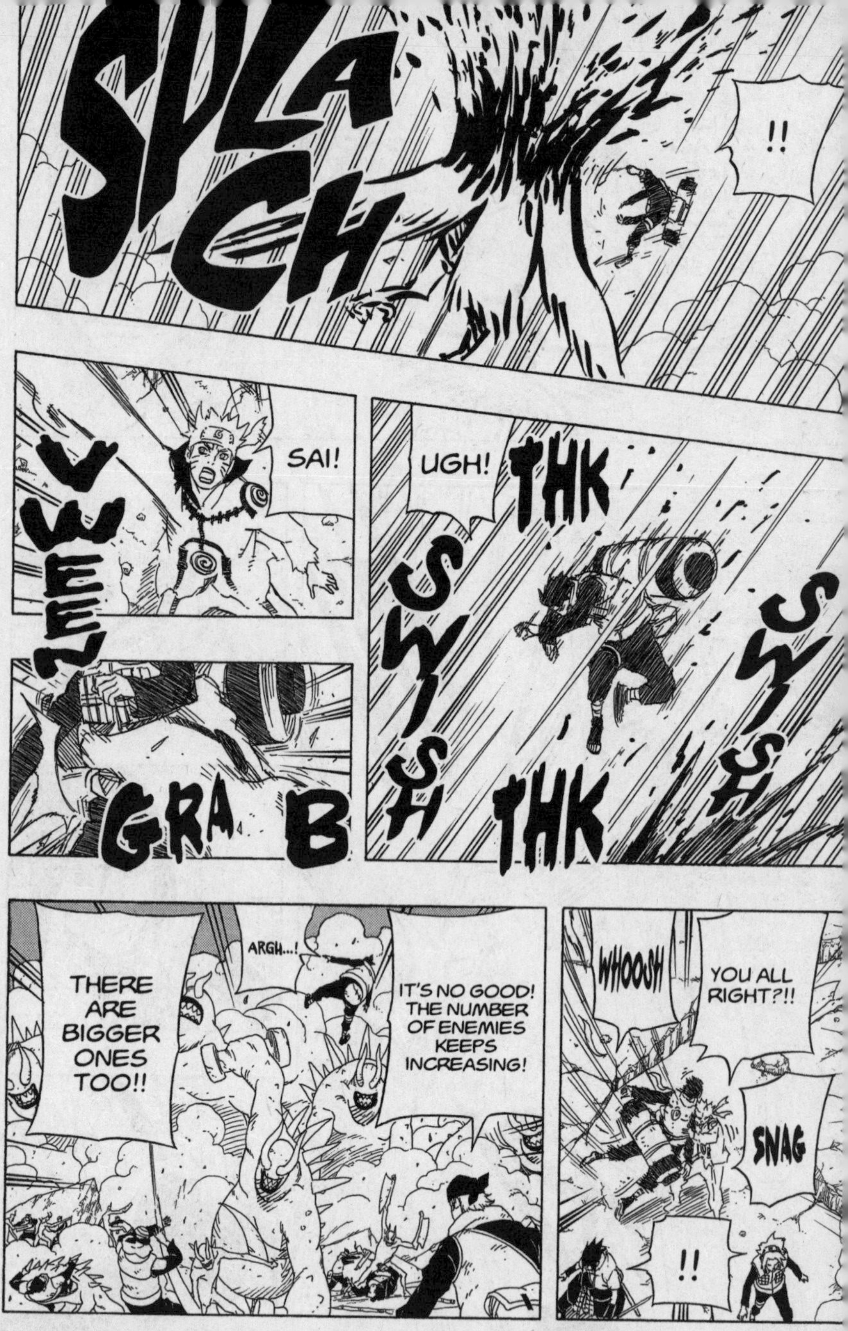
!!
SPLACH
UGH!
THK
SWISH
THK
SWISH
SAI!
GRAB
YOU ALL RIGHT?!!
WHOOSH
SNAG
!!
IT'S NO GOOD! THE NUMBER OF ENEMIES KEEPS INCREASING!
ARGH...!
THERE ARE BIGGER ONES TOO!!

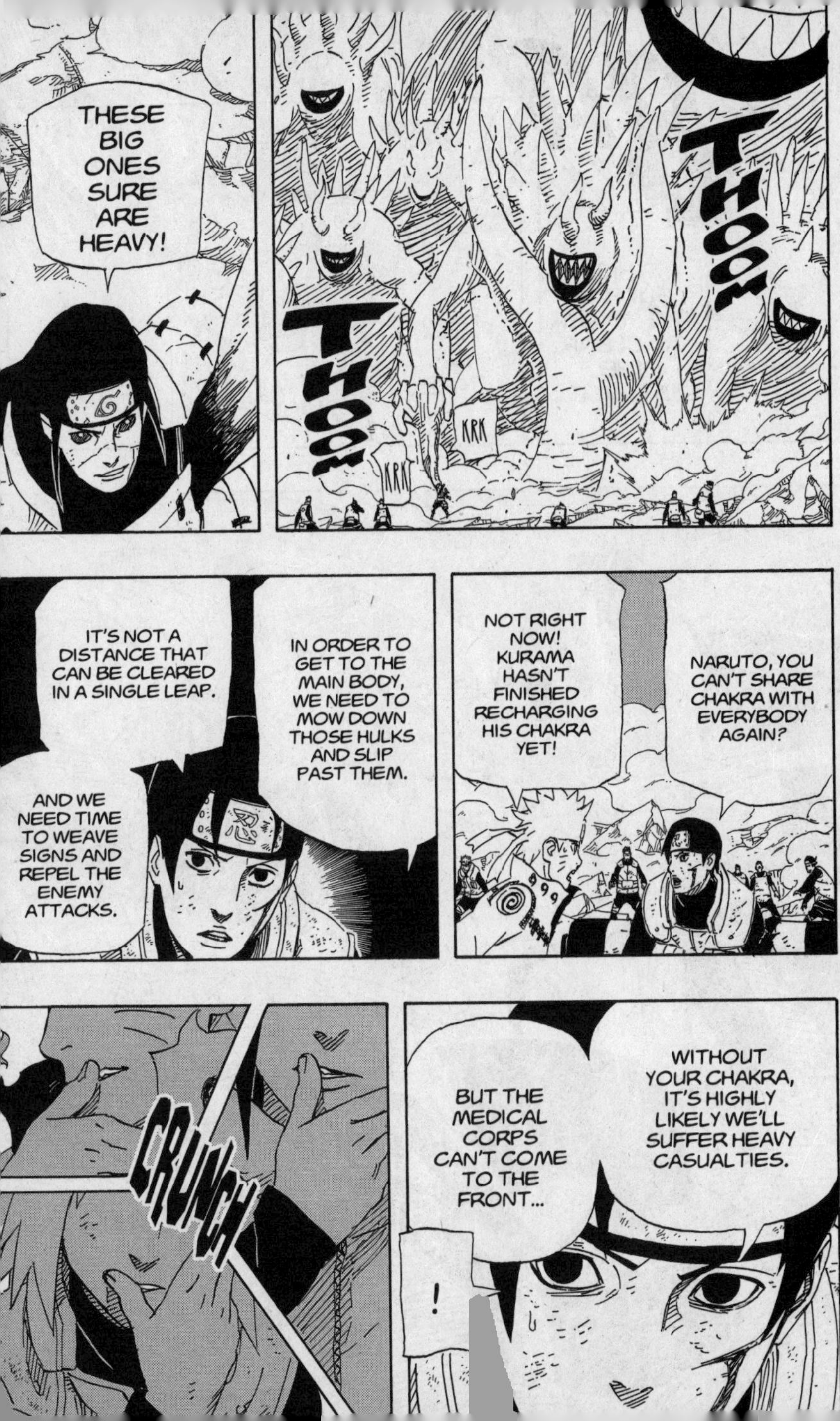
THOOM
THOOM
KRK
KRK
THESE BIG ONES SURE ARE HEAVY!
NARUTO, YOU CAN'T SHARE CHAKRA WITH EVERYBODY AGAIN?
NOT RIGHT NOW! KURAMA HASN'T FINISHED RECHARGING HIS CHAKRA YET!
IN ORDER TO GET TO THE MAIN BODY, WE NEED TO MOW DOWN THOSE HULKS AND SLIP PAST THEM.
IT'S NOT A DISTANCE THAT CAN BE CLEARED IN A SINGLE LEAP.
AND WE NEED TIME TO WEAVE SIGNS AND REPEL THE ENEMY ATTACKS.
WITHOUT YOUR CHAKRA, IT'S HIGHLY LIKELY WE'LL SUFFER HEAVY CASUALTIES.
BUT THE MEDICAL CORPS CAN'T COME TO THE FRONT...
!
CRUNCH

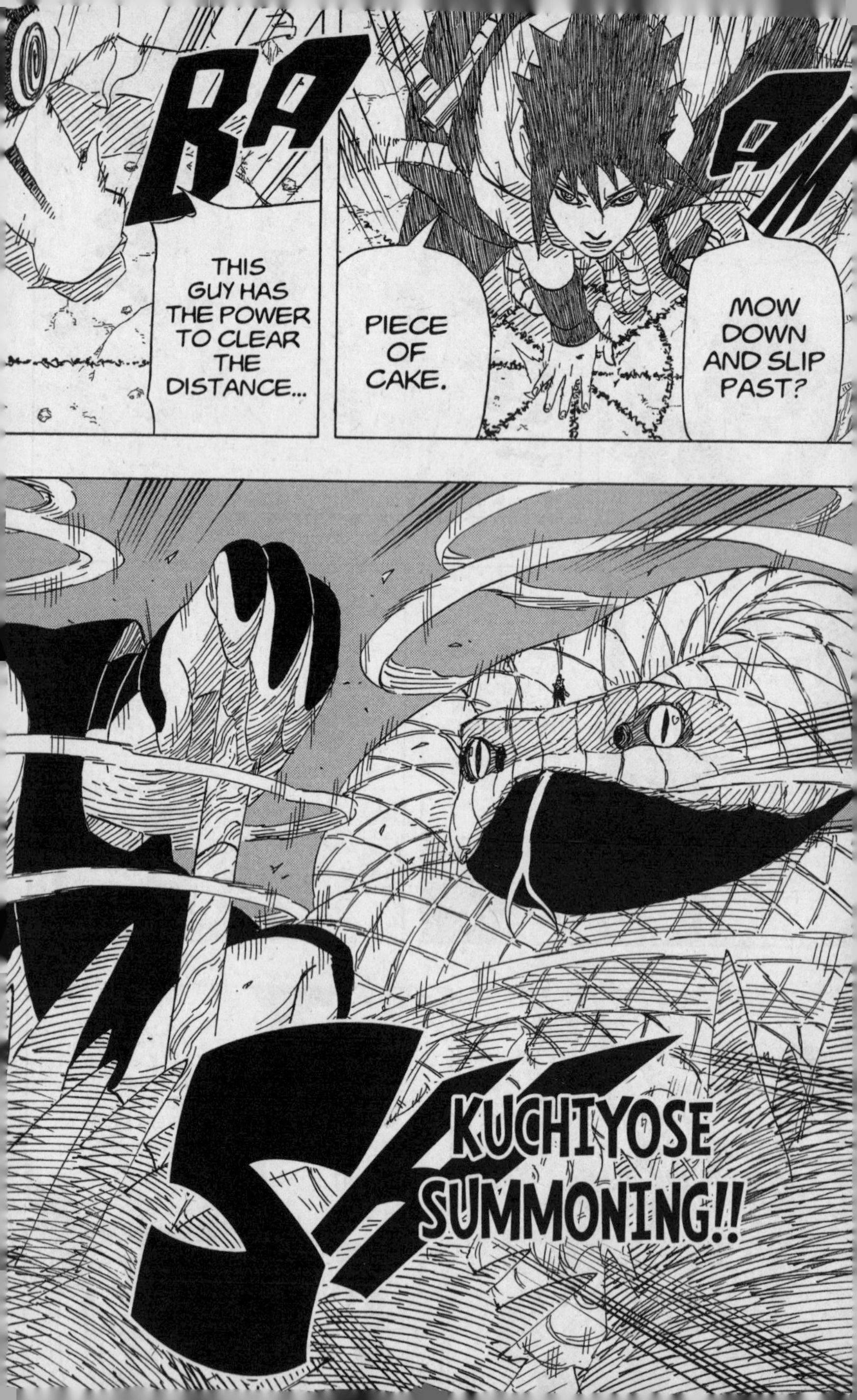
MOW DOWN AND SLIP PAST?
PIECE OF CAKE.
THIS GUY HAS THE POWER TO CLEAR THE DISTANCE...
KUCHIYOSE SUMMONING!!

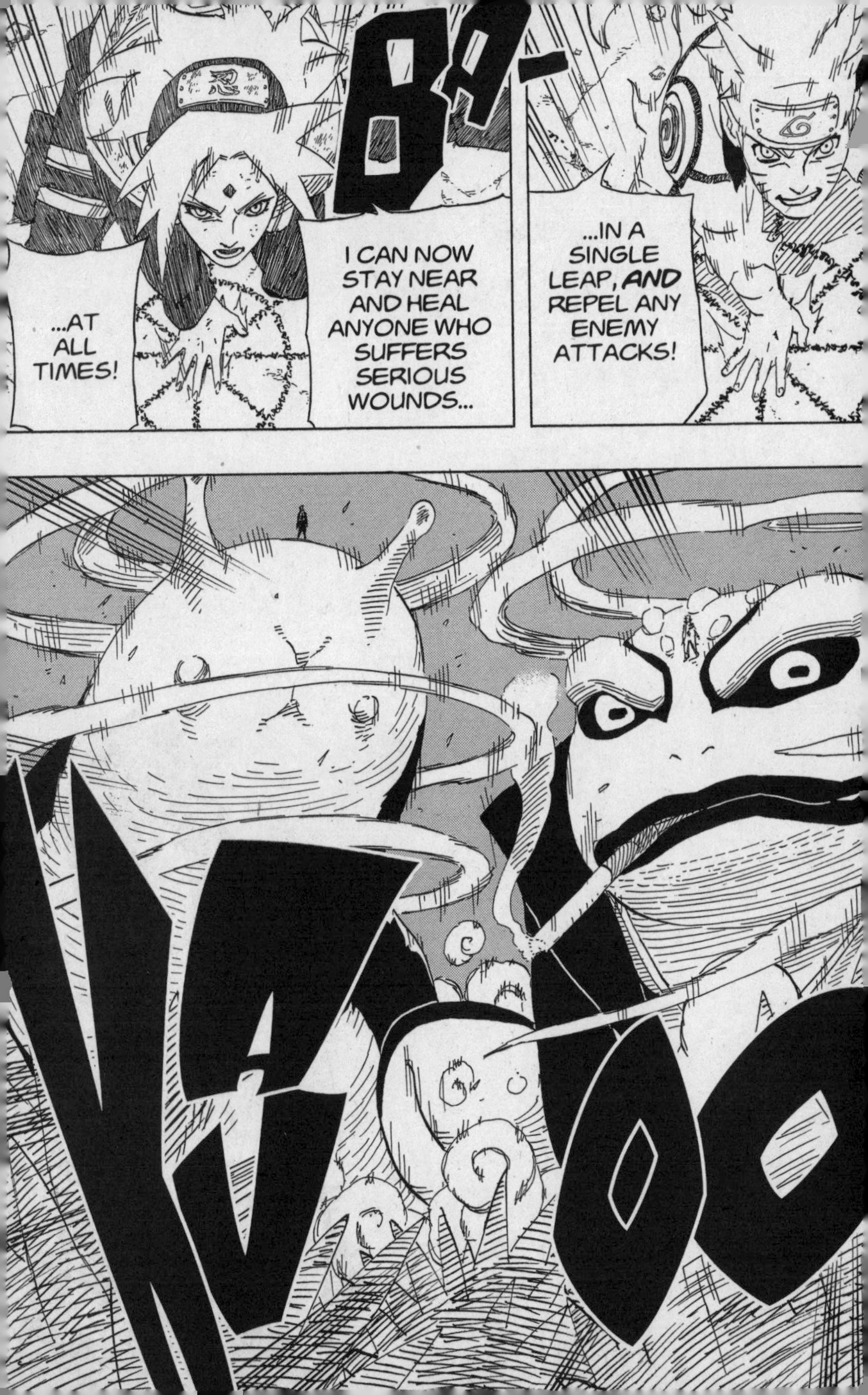
...IN A SINGLE LEAP, AND REPEL ANY ENEMY ATTACKS!
I CAN NOW STAY NEAR AND HEAL ANYONE WHO SUFFERS SERIOUS WOUNDS...
...AT ALL TIMES!

Number 634: The New Three

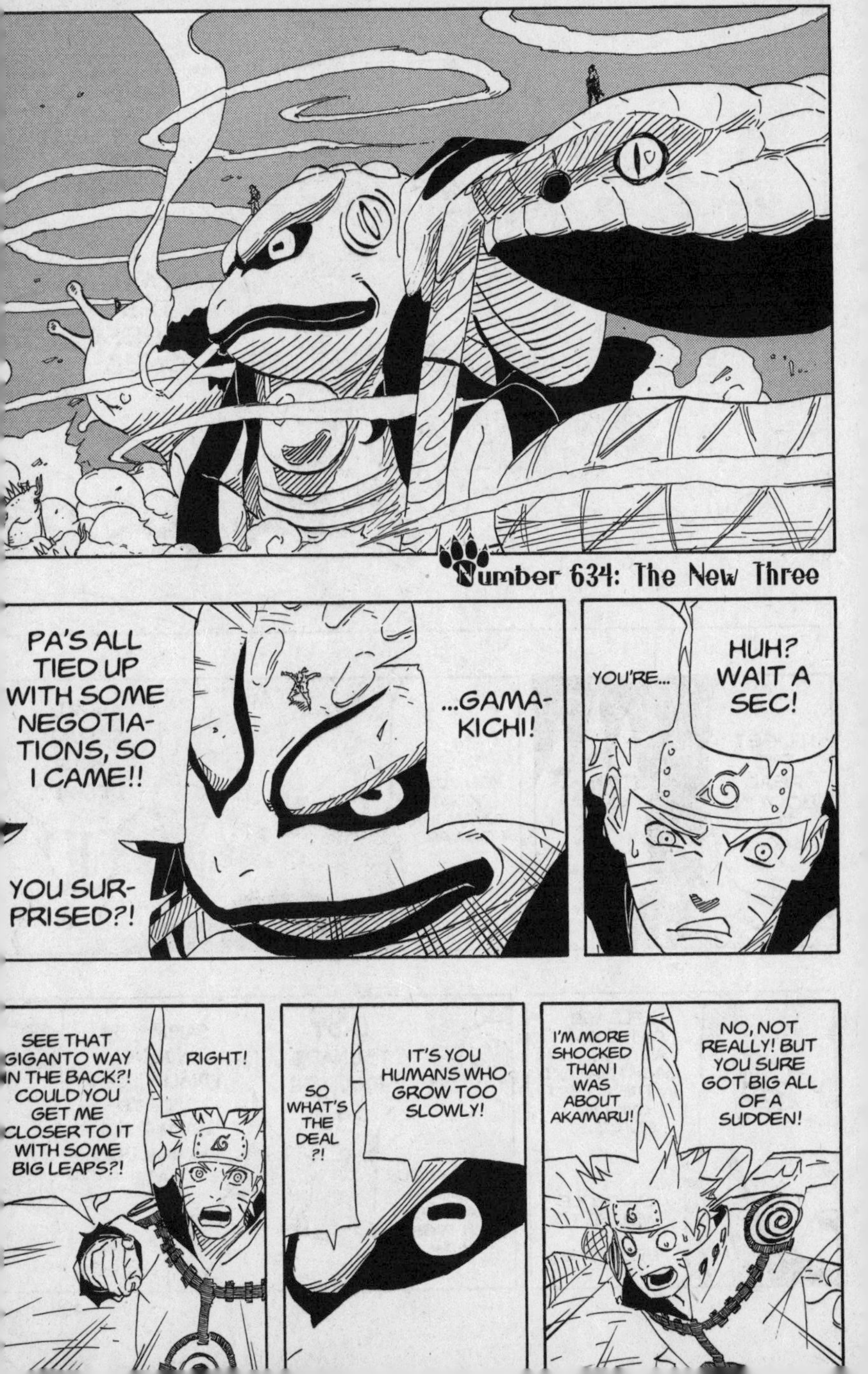
HUH? WAIT A SEC!
YOU'RE...
...GAMA-KICHI!
PA'S ALL TIED UP WITH SOME NEGOTIA-TIONS, SO I CAME!!
YOU SUR-PRISED?!
NO, NOT REALLY! BUT YOU SURE GOT BIG ALL OF A SUDDEN!
I'M MORE SHOCKED THAN I WAS ABOUT AKAMARU!
IT'S YOU HUMANS WHO GROW TOO SLOWLY!
SO WHAT'S THE DEAL ?!
SEE THAT GIGANTO WAY IN THE BACK?! COULD YOU GET ME CLOSER TO IT WITH SOME BIG LEAPS?!
RIGHT!

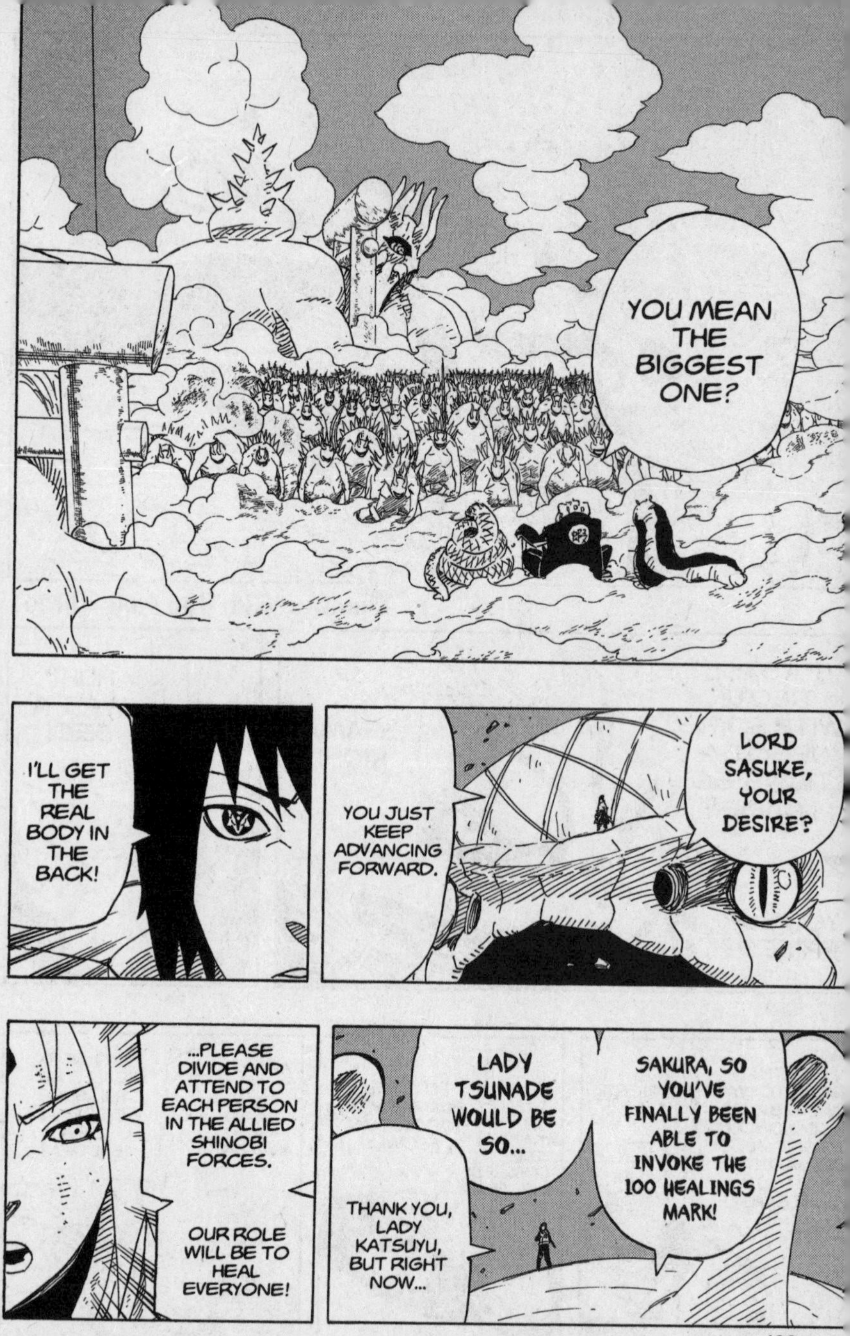
YOU MEAN THE BIGGEST ONE?
LORD SASUKE, YOUR DESIRE?
YOU JUST KEEP ADVANCING FORWARD.
I'LL GET THE REAL BODY IN THE BACK!
SAKURA, SO YOU'VE FINALLY BEEN ABLE TO INVOKE THE 100 HEALINGS MARK!
LADY TSUNADE WOULD BE SO...
THANK YOU, LADY KATSUYU, BUT RIGHT NOW...
...PLEASE DIVIDE AND ATTEND TO EACH PERSON IN THE ALLIED SHINOBI FORCES.
OUR ROLE WILL BE TO HEAL EVERYONE!

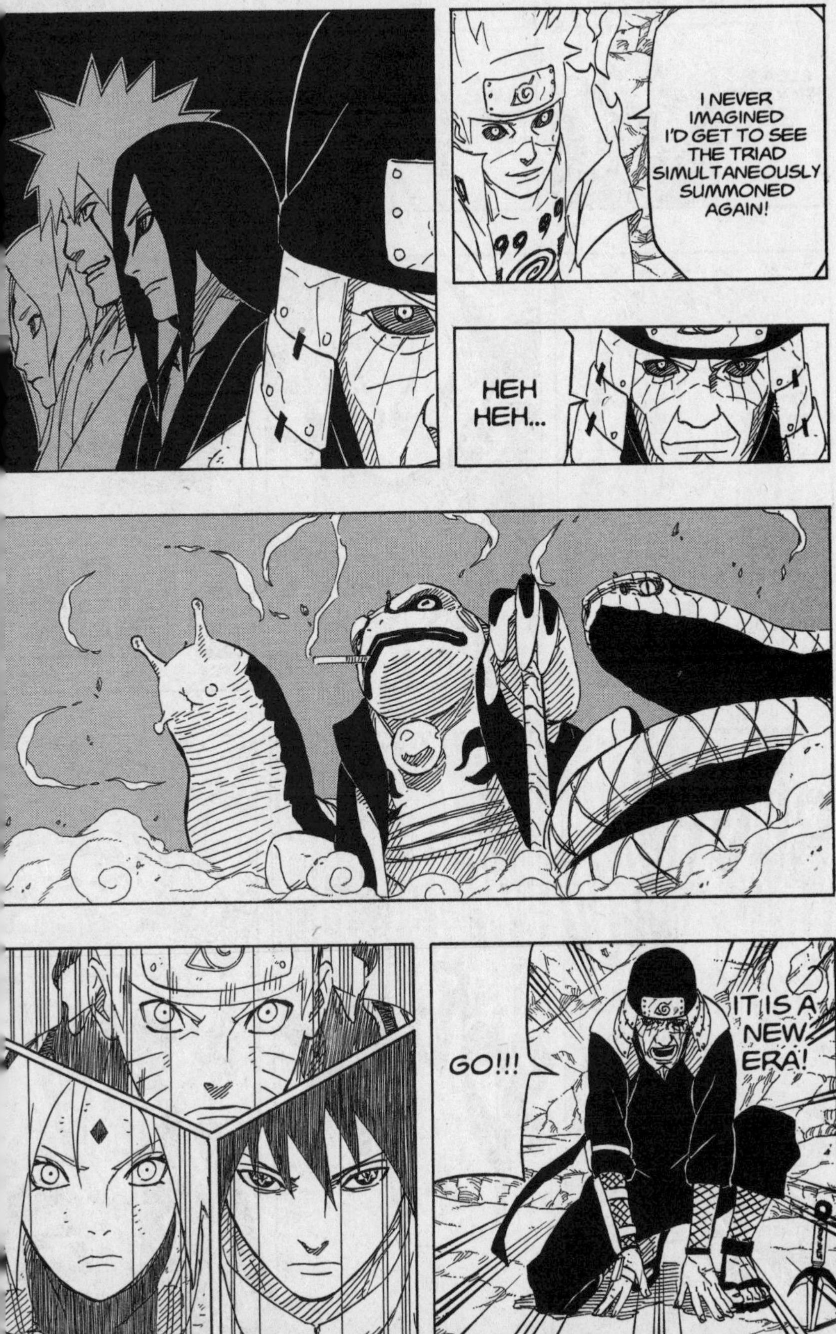
I NEVER IMAGINED I'D GET TO SEE THE TRIAD SIMULTANEOUSLY SUMMONED AGAIN!
HEH HEH...
IT IS A NEW ERA!
GO!!!

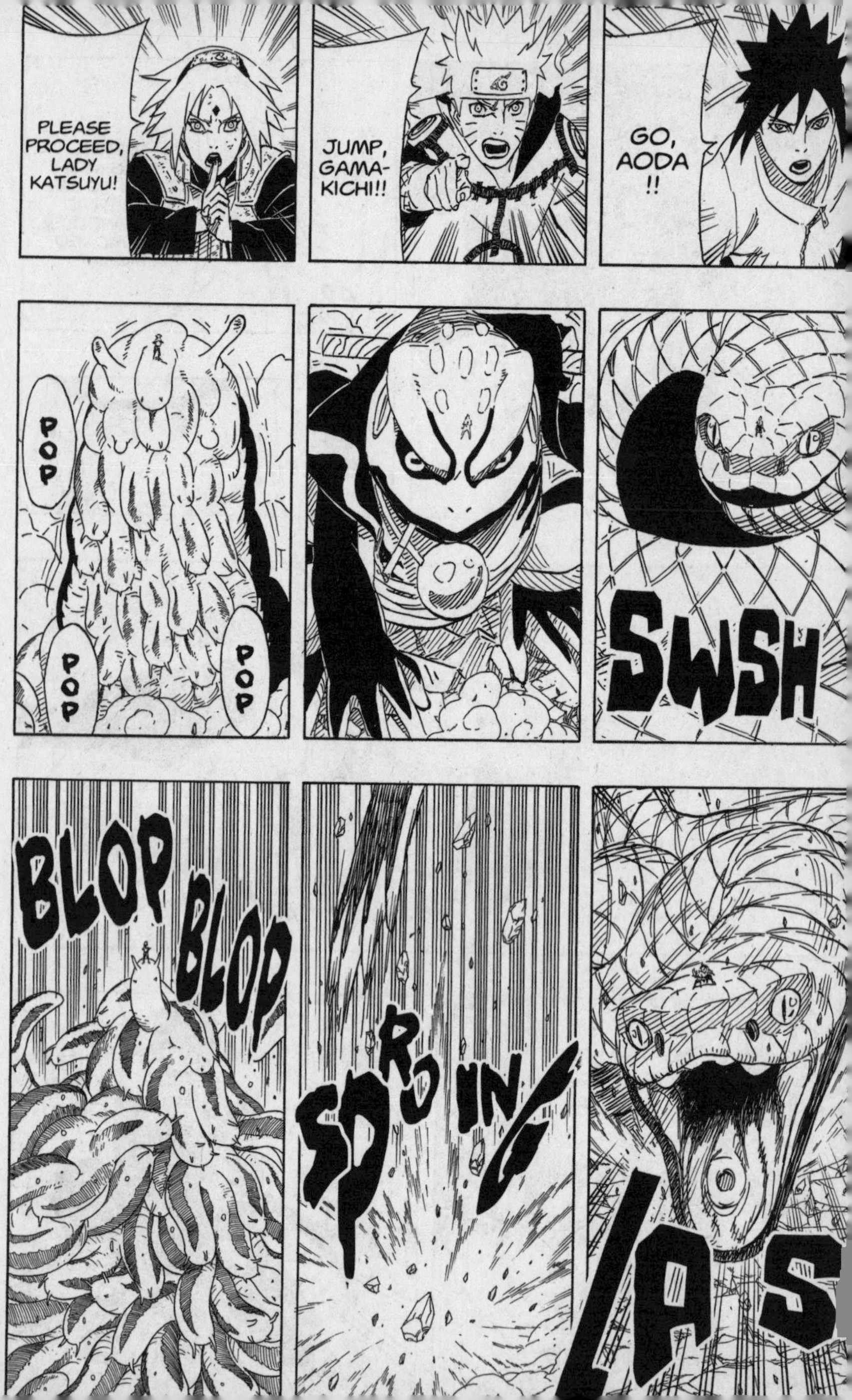
GO, AODA!!
JUMP, GAMAKICHI!!
PLEASE PROCEED, LADY KATSUYU!
SWSH
POP
POP
POP
SPROING
BLOP
BLOP

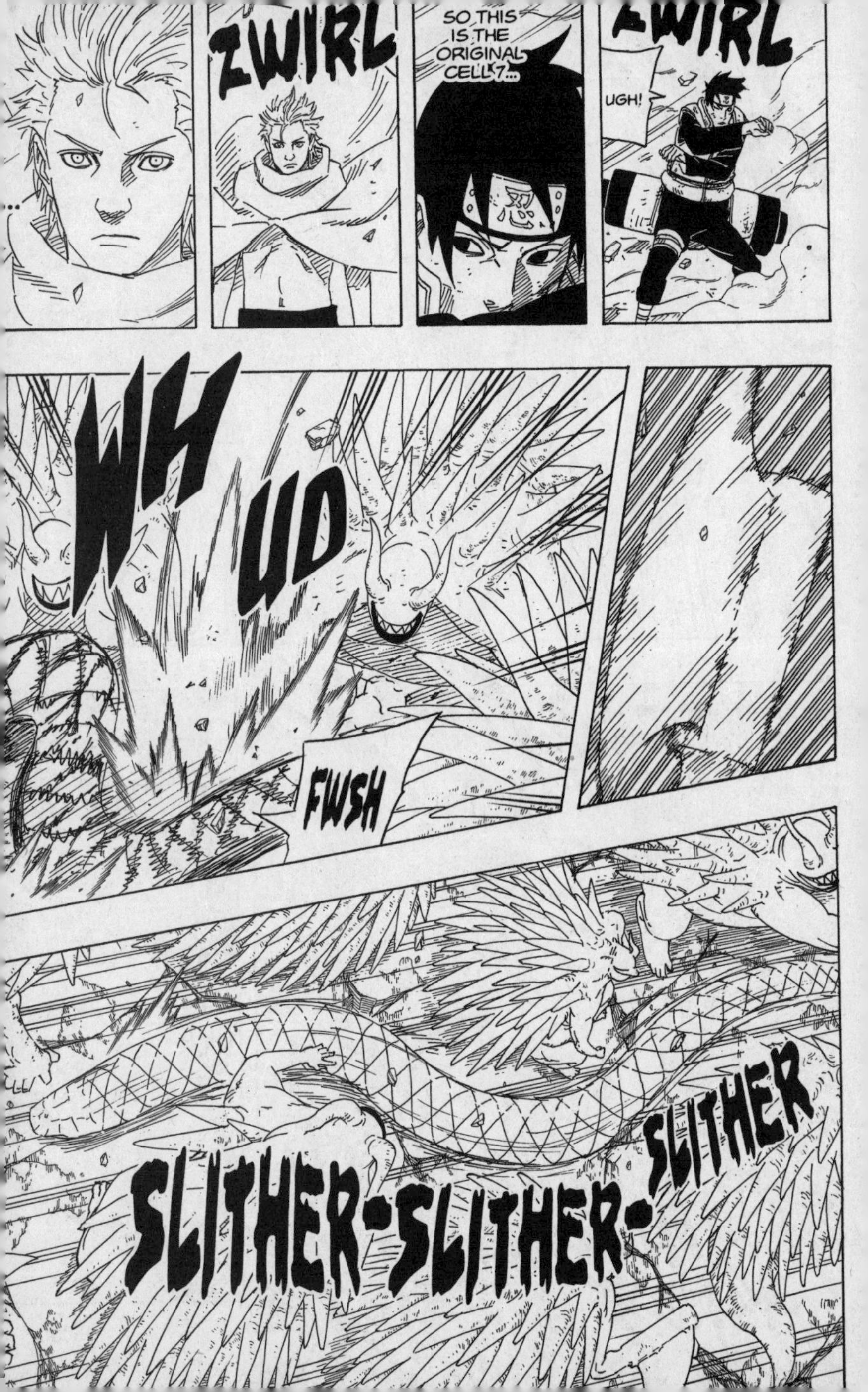

ZWIRL
UGH!
SO THIS IS THE ORIGINAL CELL 7...
ZWIRL
...
WHUD
FWSH
SLITHER-SLITHER-SLITHER

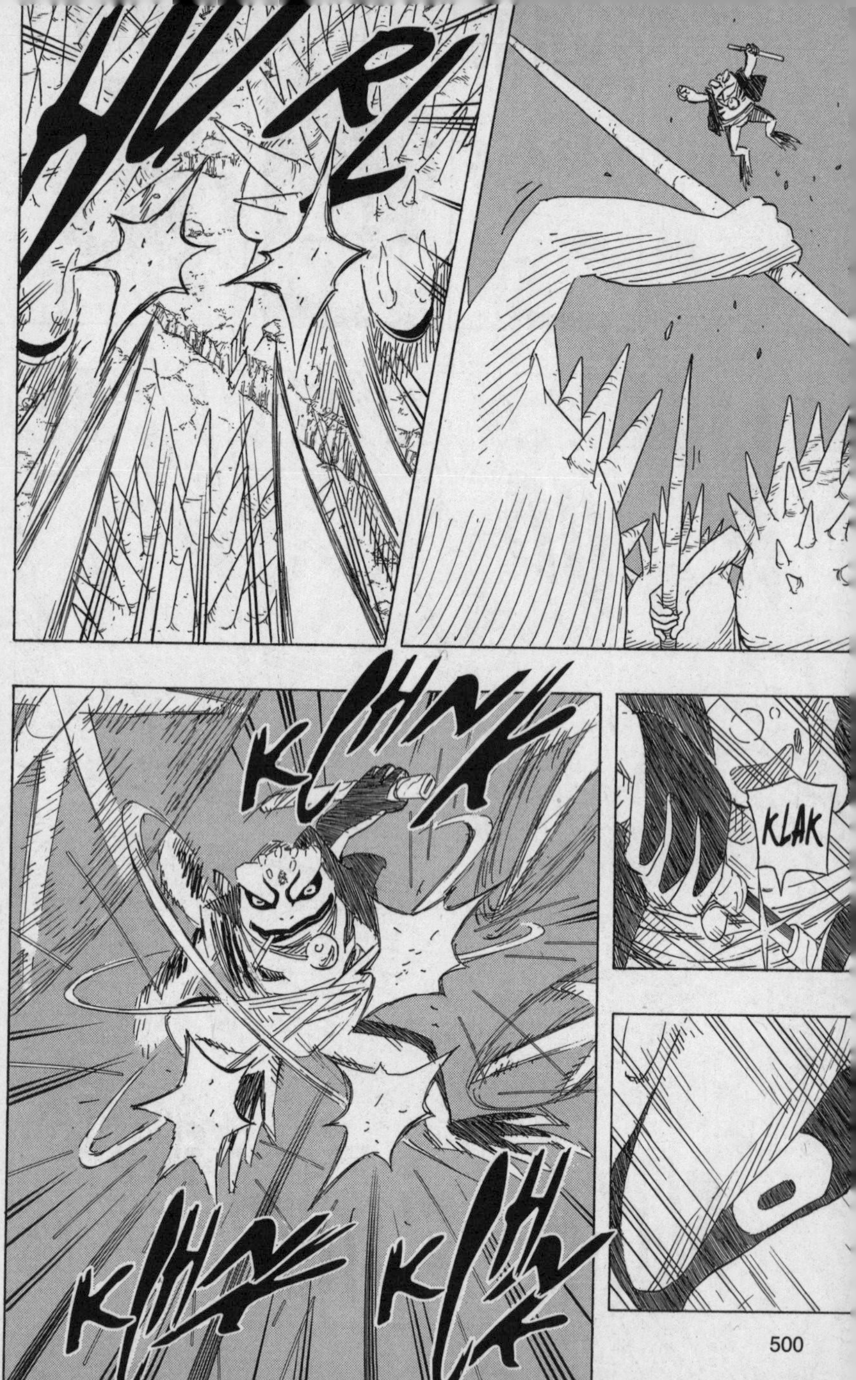
KLAK

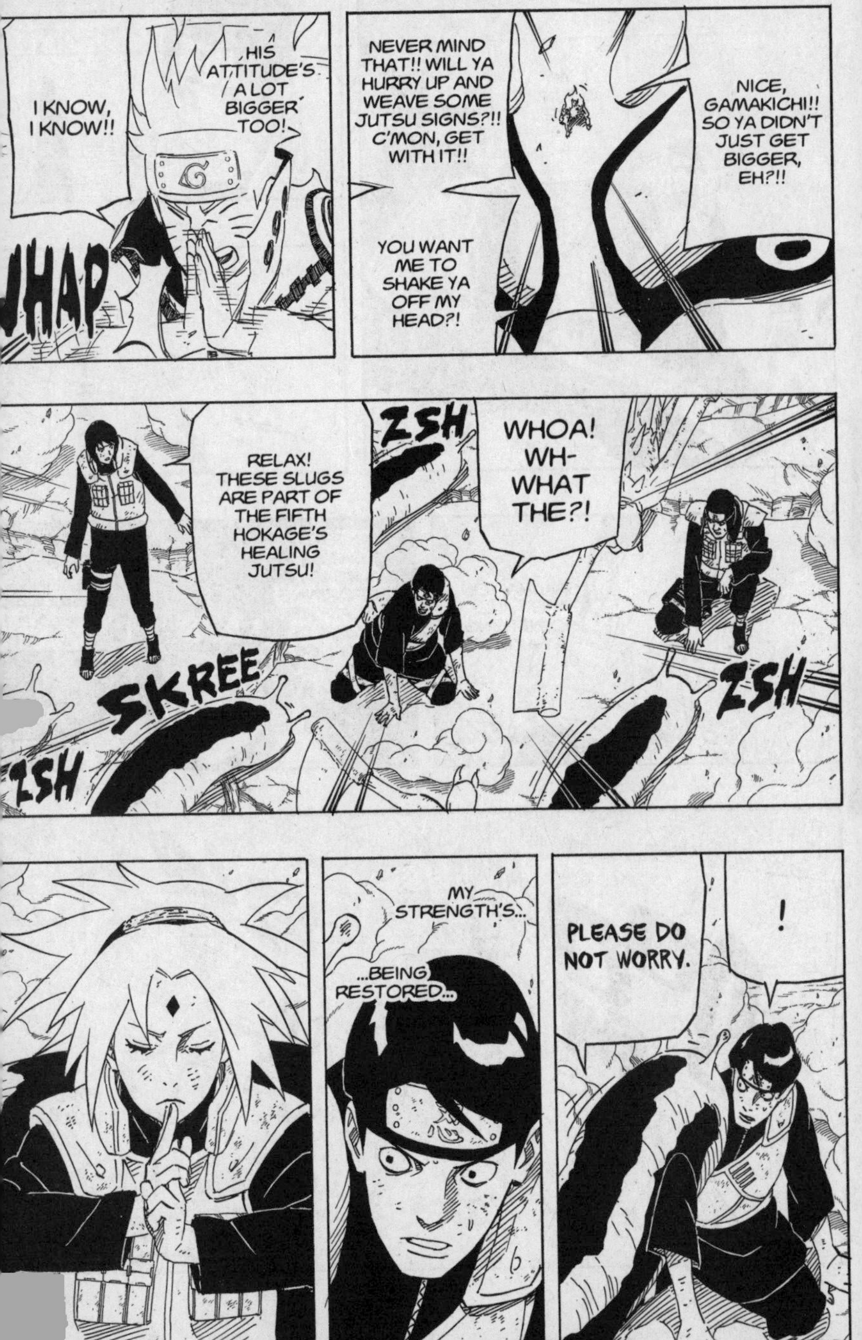
NICE, GAMAKICHI!! SO YA DIDN'T JUST GET BIGGER, EH?!!
NEVER MIND THAT!! WILL YA HURRY UP AND WEAVE SOME JUTSU SIGNS?!! C'MON, GET WITH IT!!
YOU WANT ME TO SHAKE YA OFF MY HEAD?!
HIS ATTITUDE'S A LOT BIGGER TOO!
I KNOW, I KNOW!!
WHOA! WH- WHAT THE?!
ZSH
RELAX! THESE SLUGS ARE PART OF THE FIFTH HOKAGE'S HEALING JUTSU!
ZSH
SKREE
ZSH
!
PLEASE DO NOT WORRY.
MY STRENGTH'S...
...BEING RESTORED...

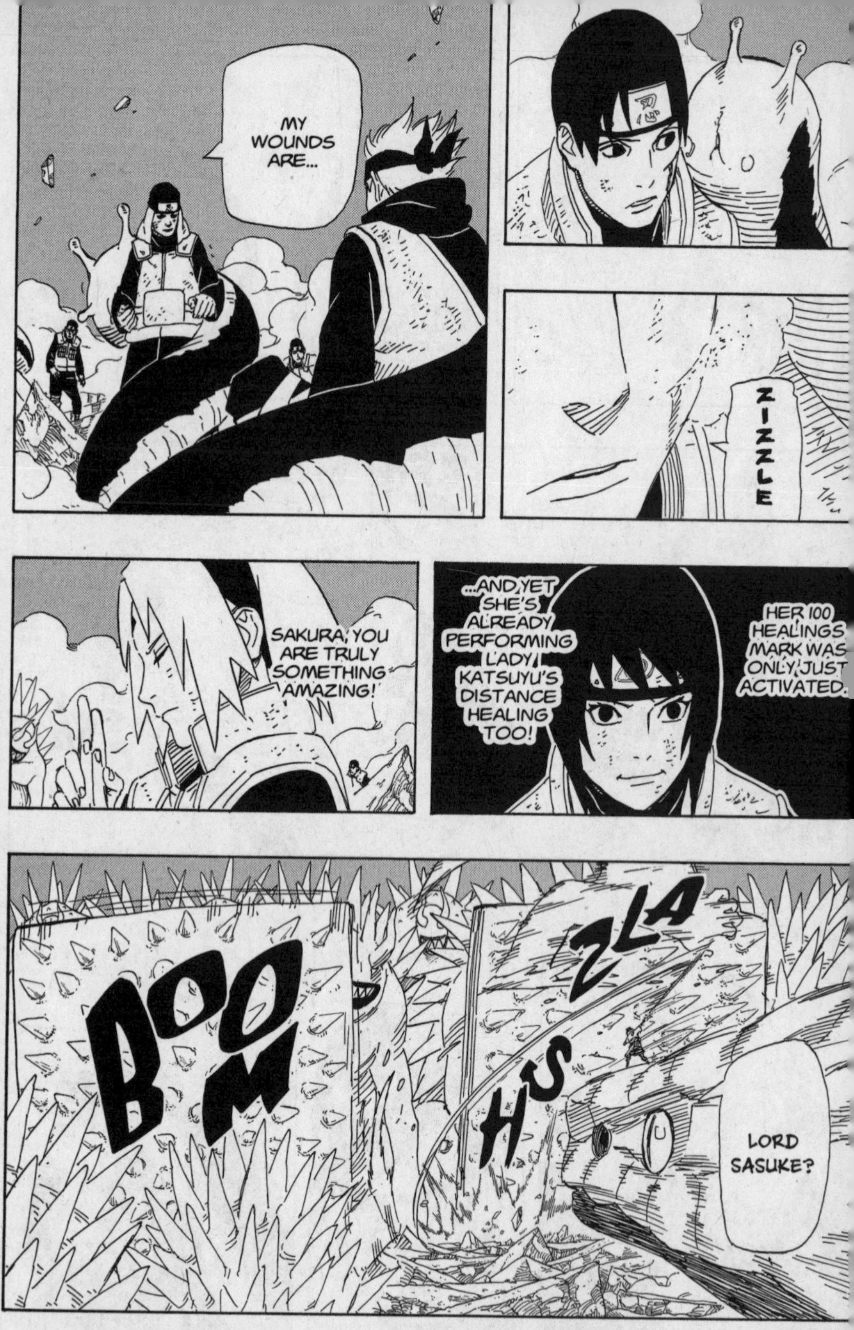
ZIZZLE
MY WOUNDS ARE...
HER 100 HEALINGS MARK WAS ONLY JUST ACTIVATED.
...AND YET SHE'S ALREADY PERFORMING LADY KATSUYU'S DISTANCE HEALING TOO!
SAKURA, YOU ARE TRULY SOMETHING AMAZING!
HSZLA
LORD SASUKE?
BOOM

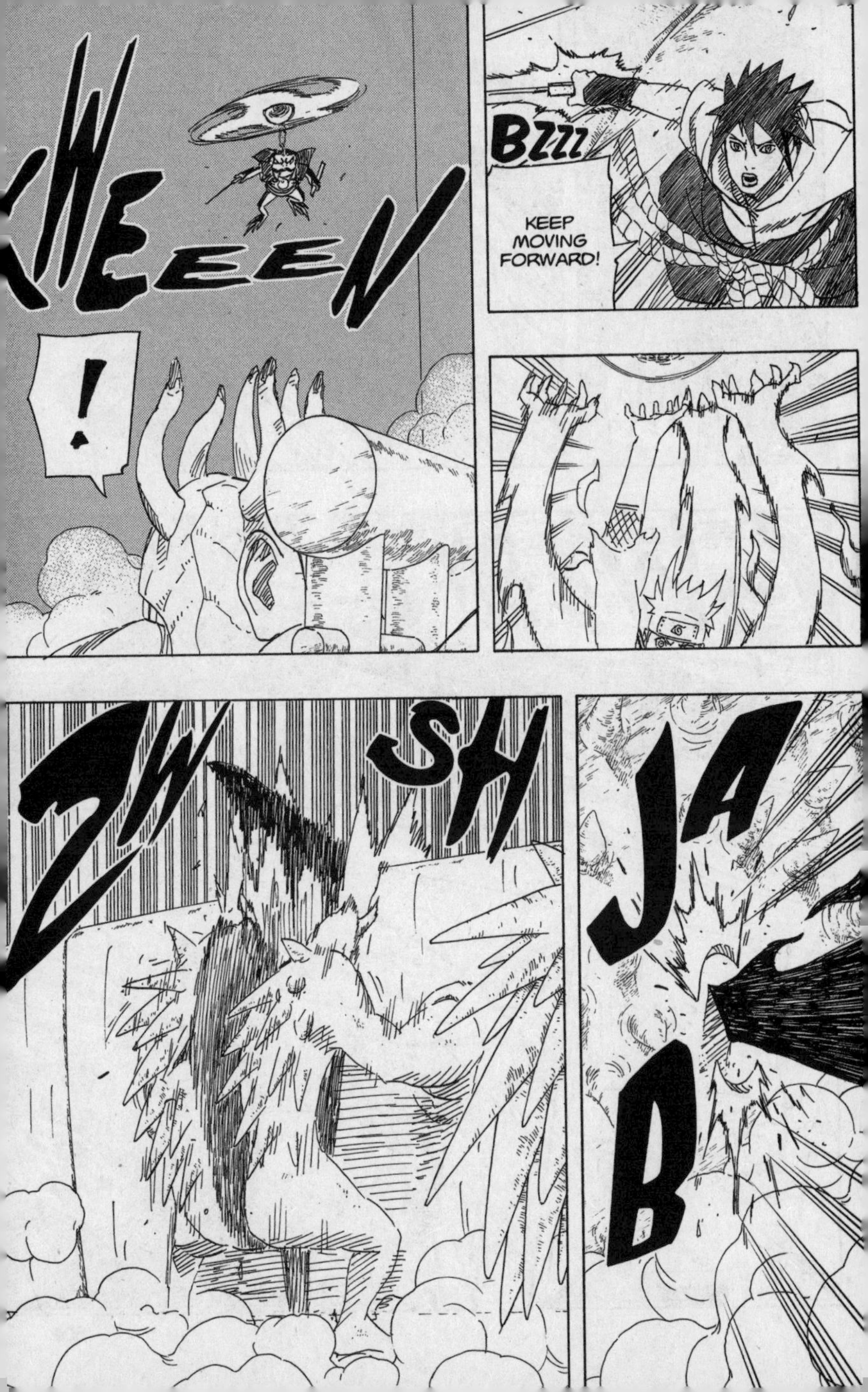
BZZZZ
KEEP MOVING FORWARD!
CHEEEN
!
JABB
ZWSH

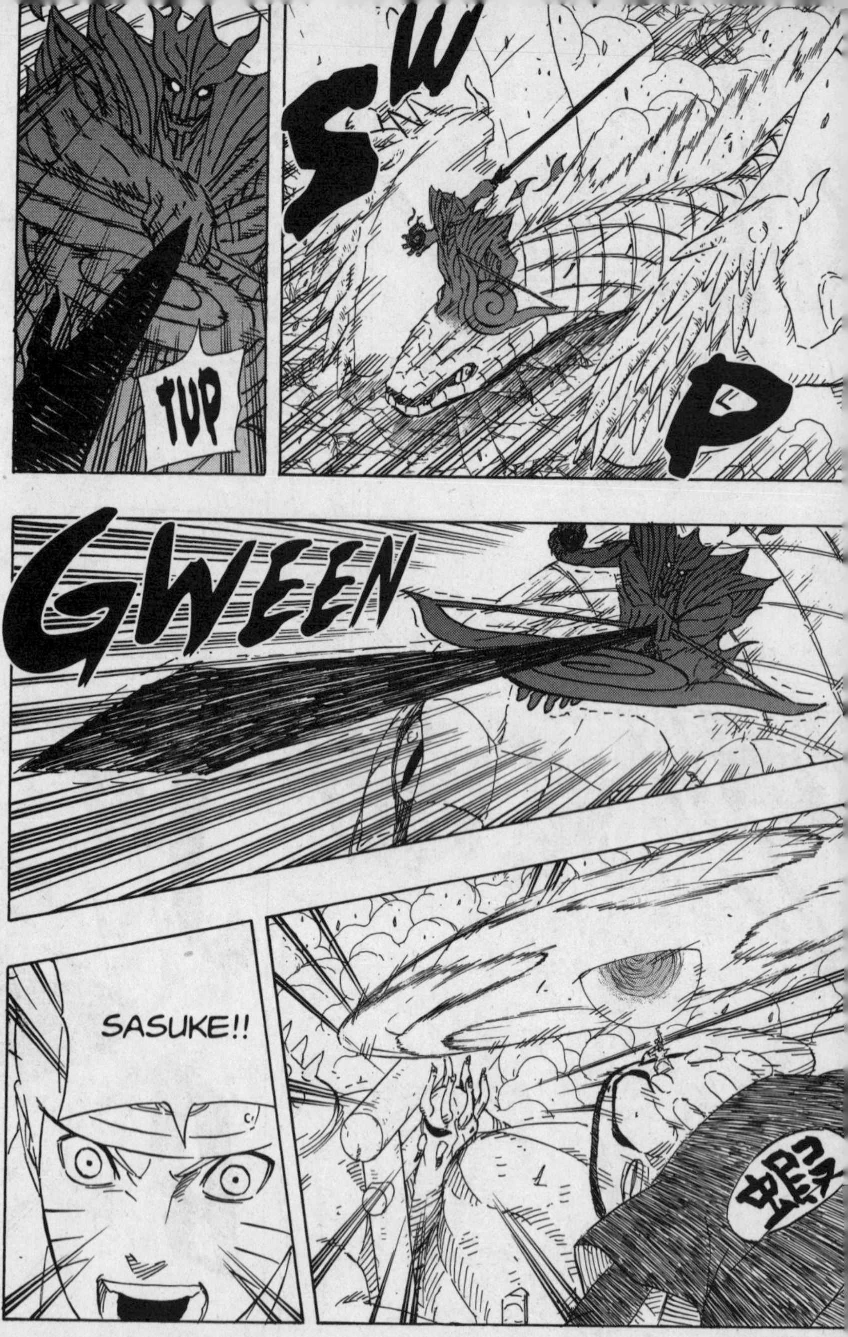
SWP
TUP
GWEEN
SASUKE!!

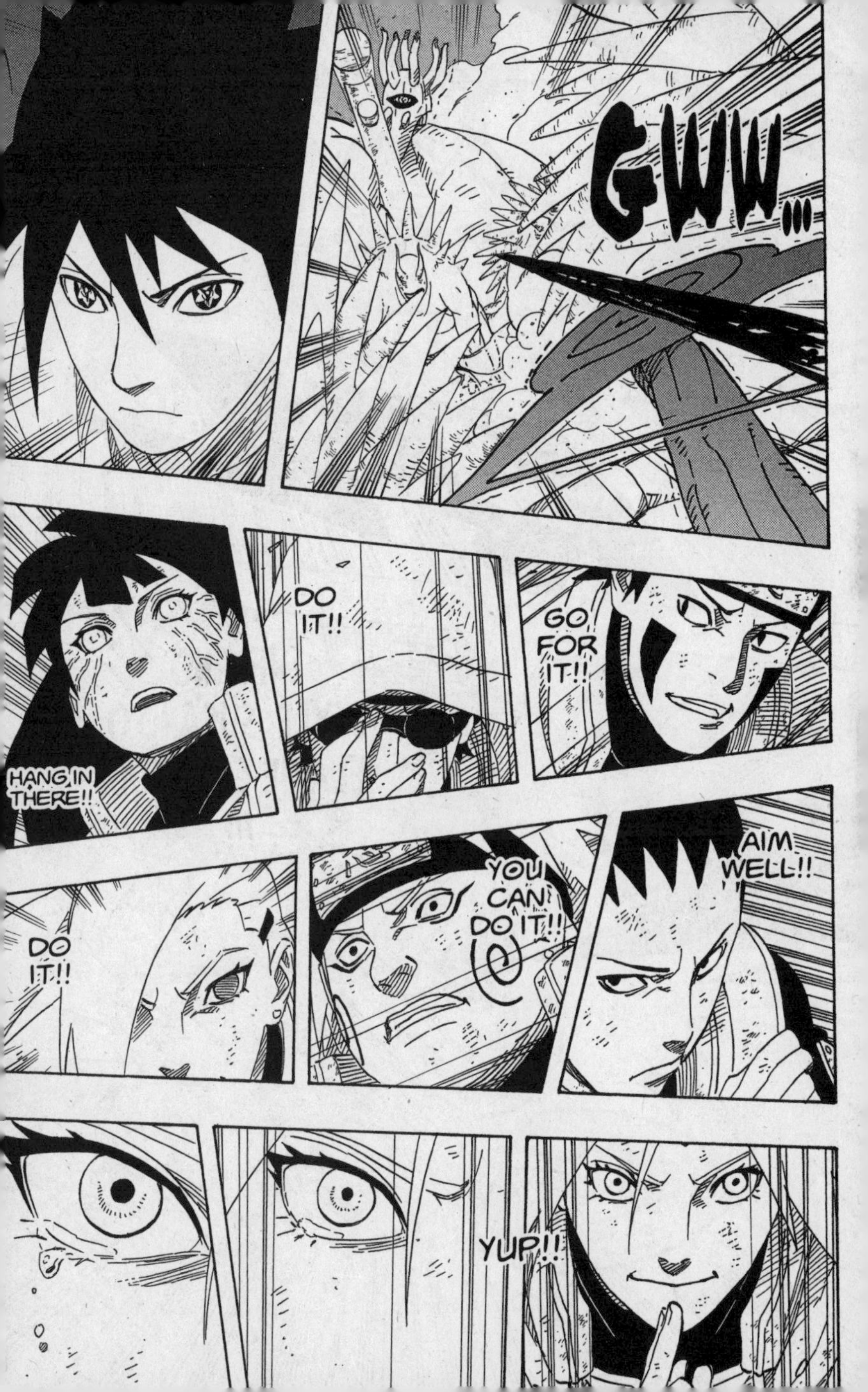
GWW!!!
GO FOR IT!!
DO IT!!
HANG IN THERE!!
AIM WELL!!
YOU CAN DO IT!!
DO IT!!
YUP!!

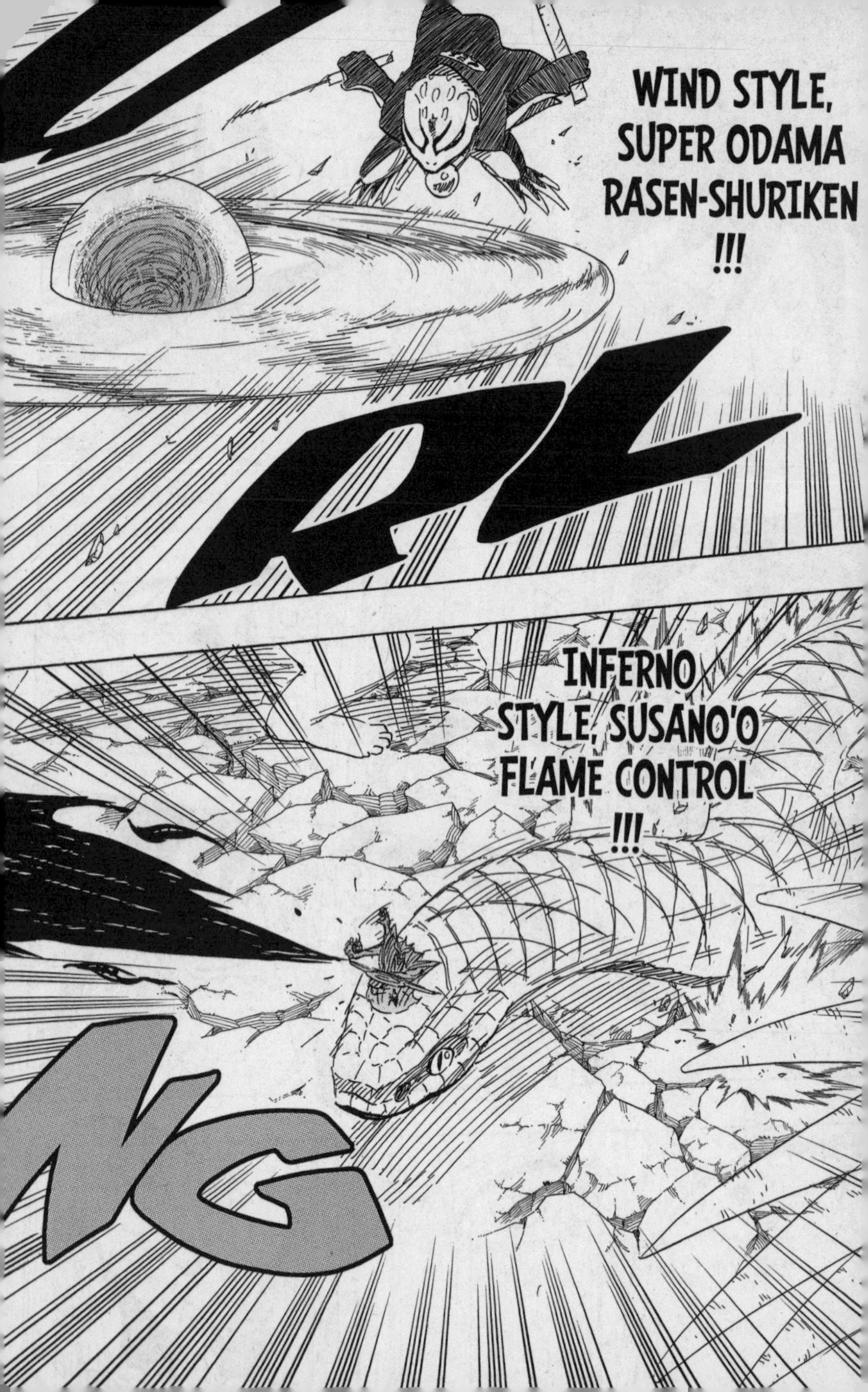
WIND STYLE, SUPER ODAMA RASEN-SHURIKEN !!!
INFERNO STYLE, SUSANO'O FLAME CONTROL !!!

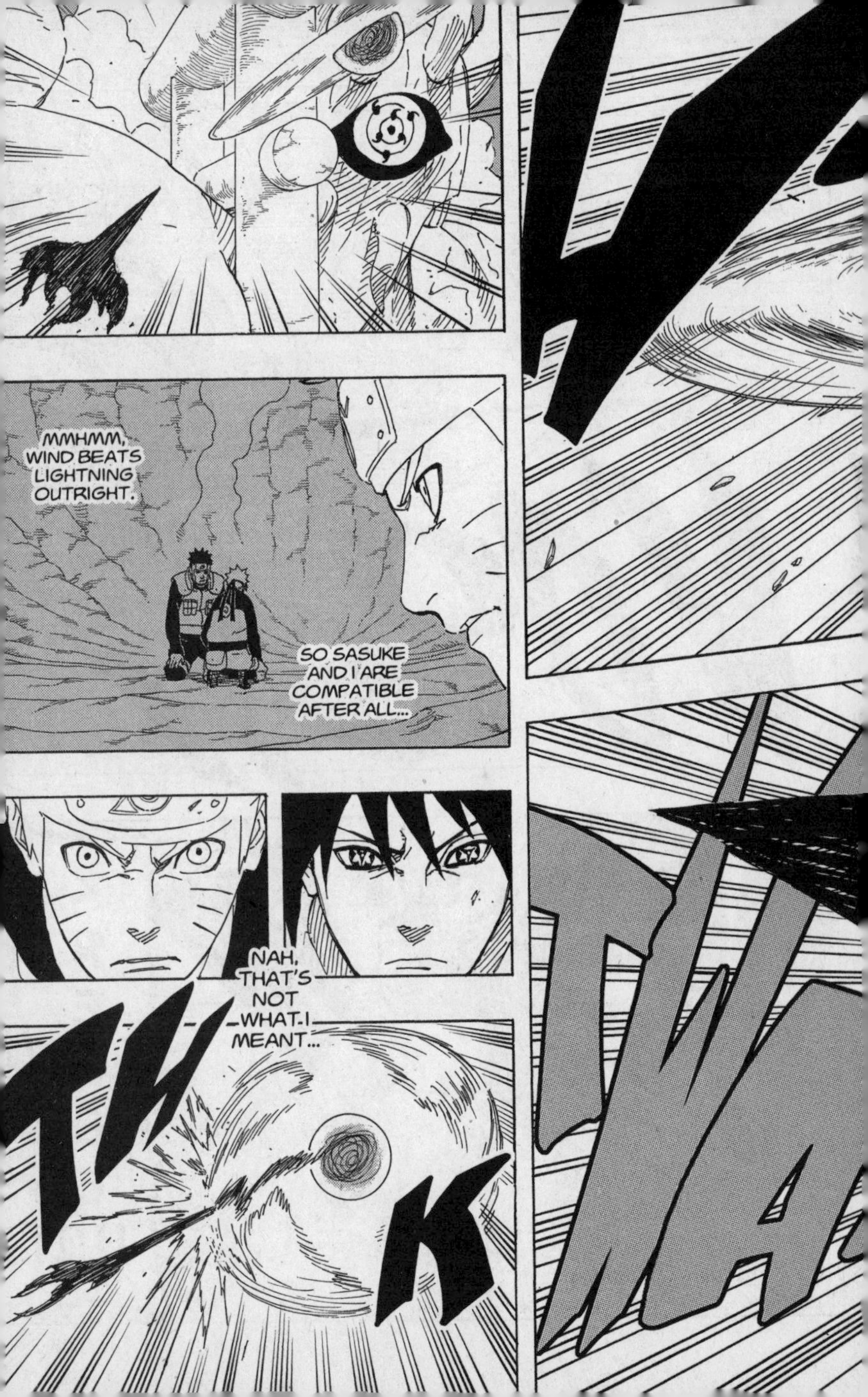

MMHMM, WIND BEATS LIGHTNING OUTRIGHT.
SO SASUKE AND I ARE COMPATIBLE AFTER ALL...
NAH, THAT'S NOT WHAT I MEANT...

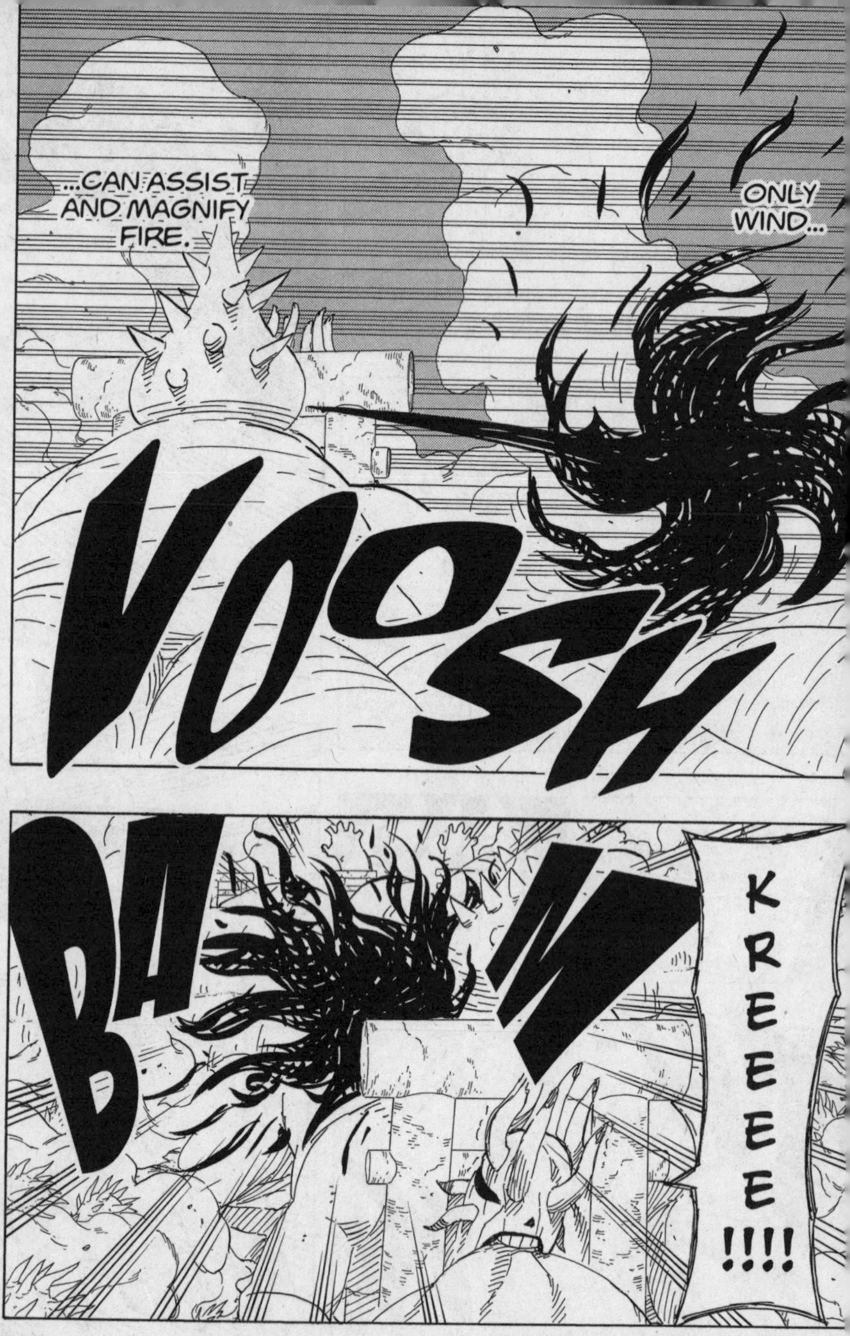
ONLY WIND...
...CAN ASSIST AND MAGNIFY FIRE.
VOOSH
KREEEE!!!!
BAN

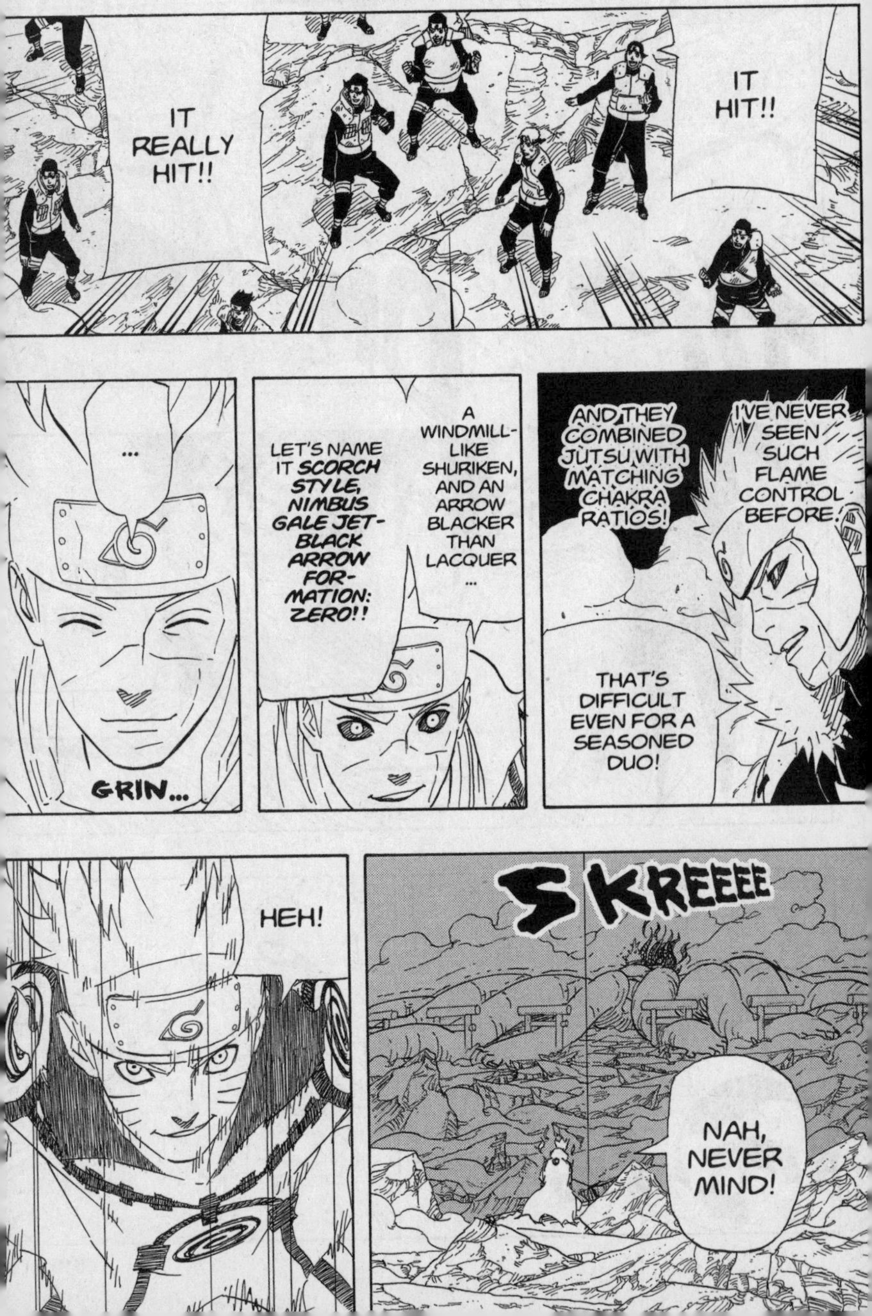
IT HIT!!
IT REALLY HIT!!
I'VE NEVER SEEN SUCH FLAME CONTROL BEFORE.
AND THEY COMBINED JUTSU WITH MATCHING CHAKRA RATIOS!
THAT'S DIFFICULT EVEN FOR A SEASONED DUO!
A WINDMILL-LIKE SHURIKEN, AND AN ARROW BLACKER THAN LACQUER ...
LET'S NAME IT SCORCH STYLE, NIMBUS GALE JET-BLACK ARROW FORMATION: ZERO!!
...
GRIN...
SKREEEE
NAH, NEVER MIND!
HEH!

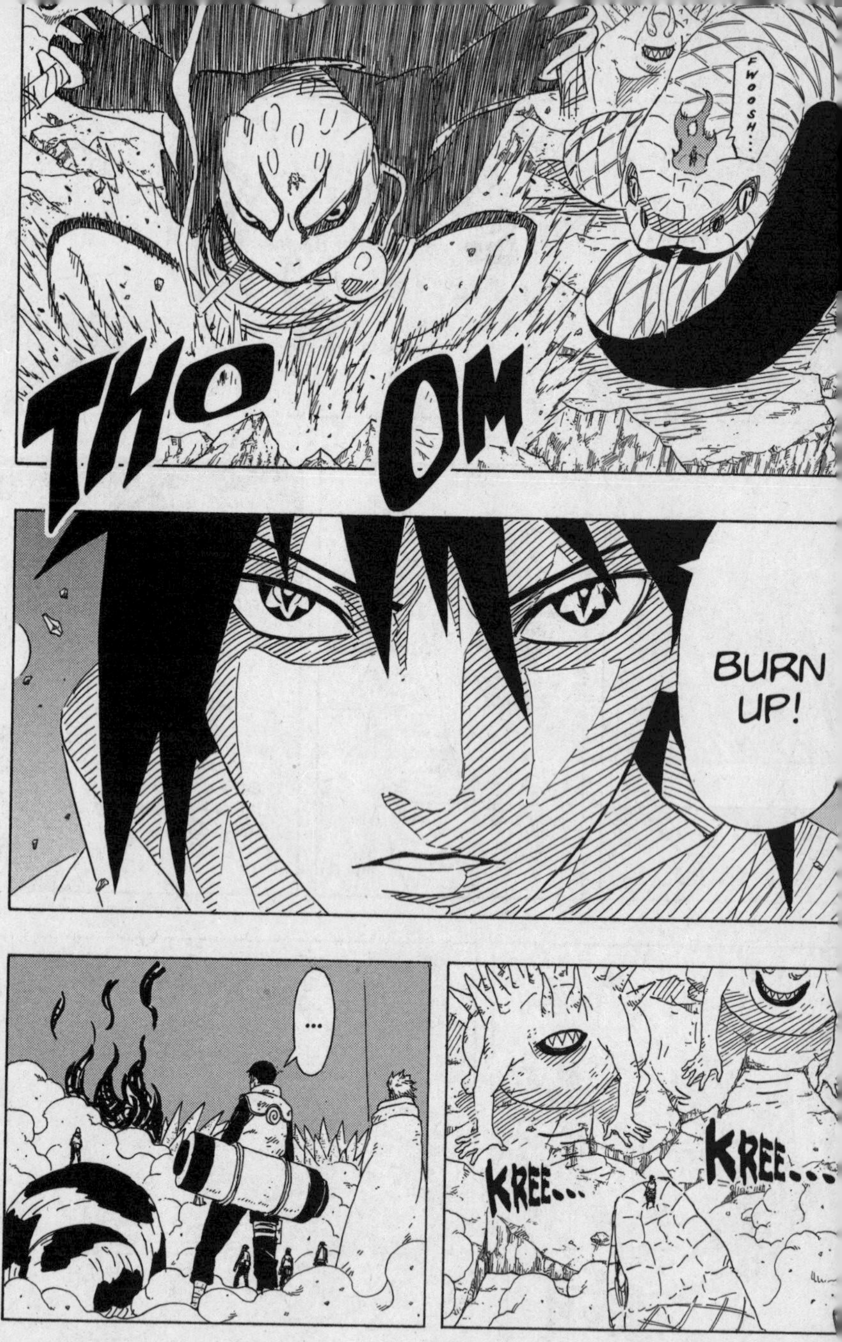
FWOOSH...
THOOM
BURN UP!
KREE...
KREE...
...

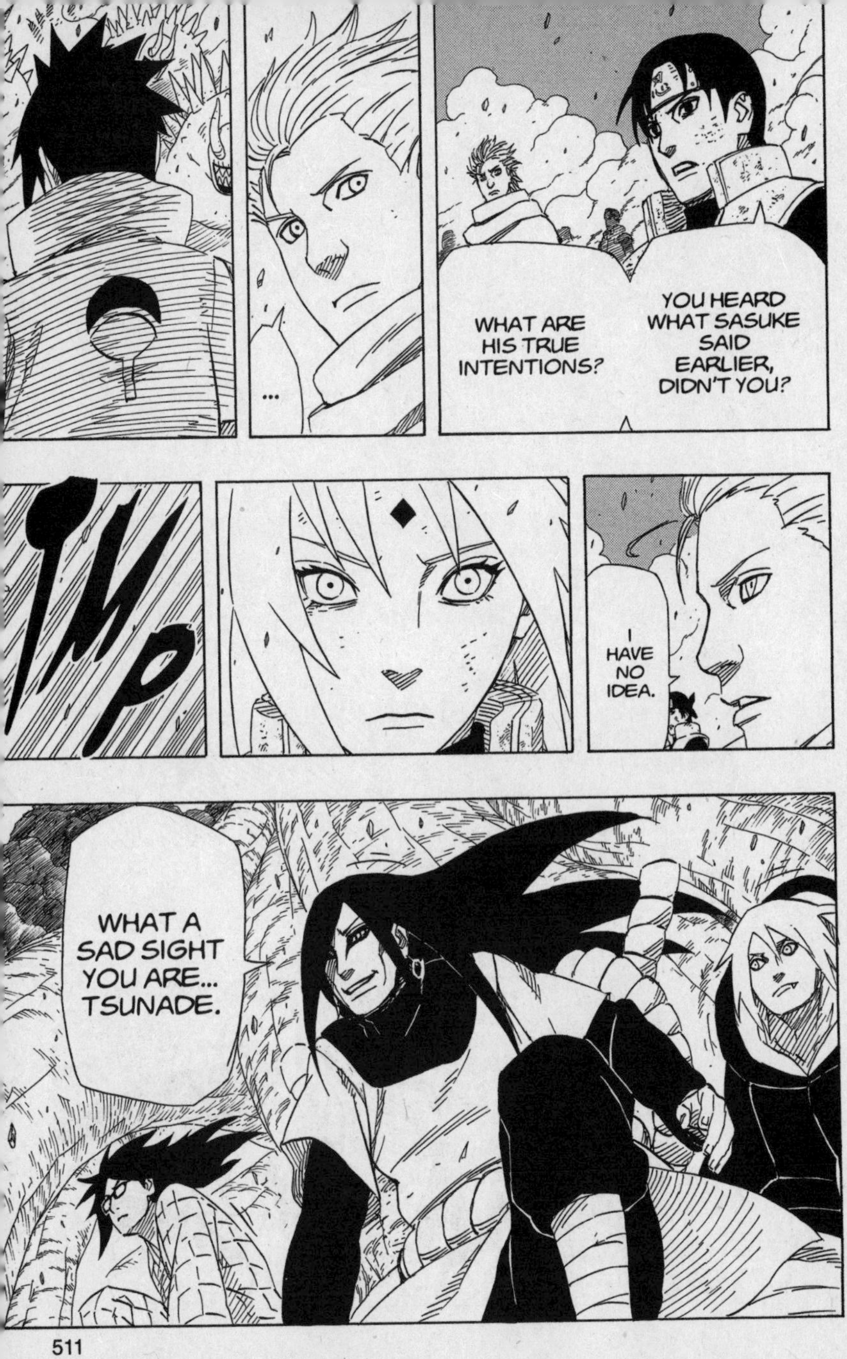
YOU HEARD WHAT SASUKE SAID EARLIER, DIDN'T YOU?
WHAT ARE HIS TRUE INTENTIONS?
...
I HAVE NO IDEA.
TMP
WHAT A SAD SIGHT YOU ARE... TSUNADE.

Number 635: A New Wind

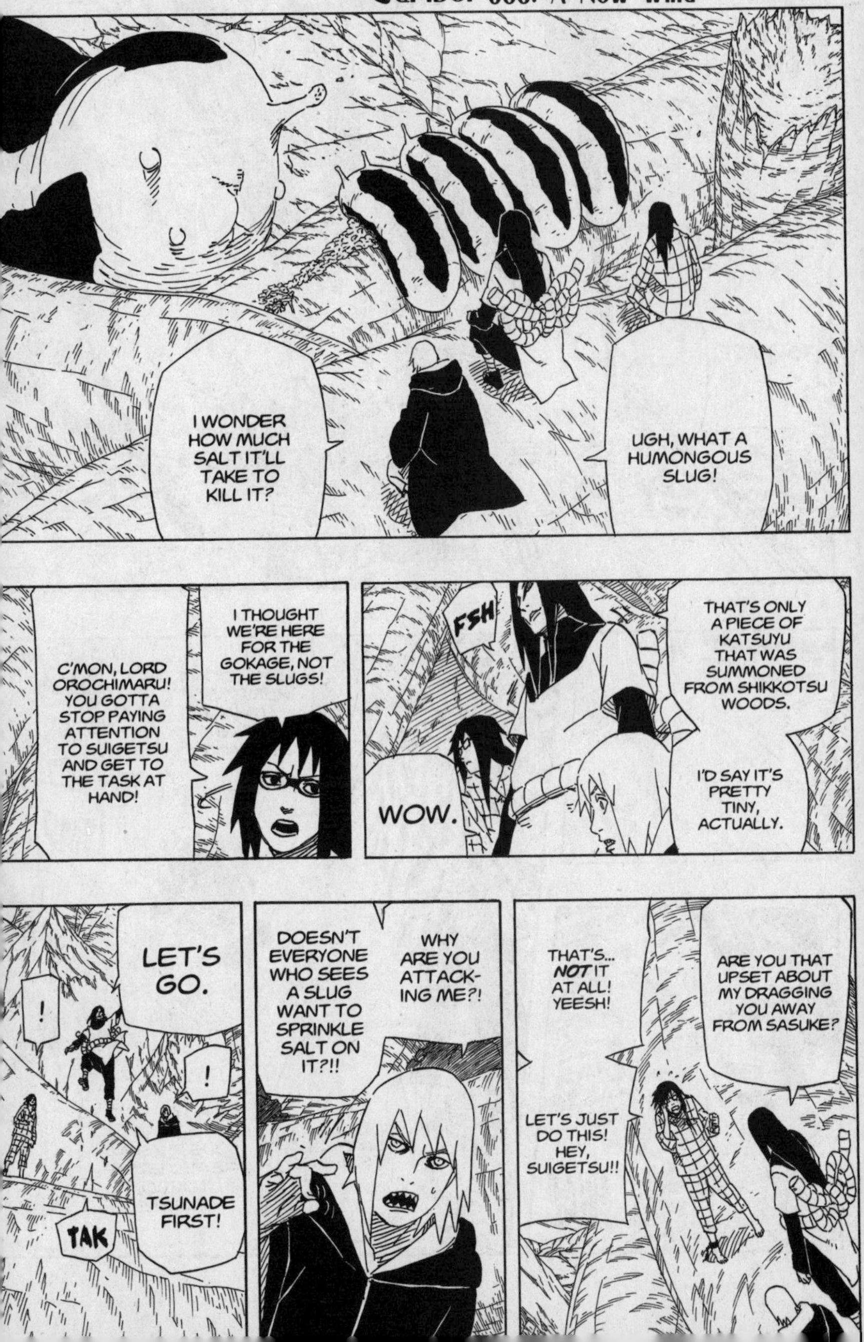
UGH, WHAT A HUMONGOUS SLUG!
I WONDER HOW MUCH SALT IT'LL TAKE TO KILL IT?
THAT'S ONLY A PIECE OF KATSUYU THAT WAS SUMMONED FROM SHIKKOTSU WOODS.
I'D SAY IT'S PRETTY TINY, ACTUALLY.
FSH
WOW.
I THOUGHT WE'RE HERE FOR THE GOKAGE, NOT THE SLUGS!
C'MON, LORD OROCHIMARU! YOU GOTTA STOP PAYING ATTENTION TO SUIGETSU AND GET TO THE TASK AT HAND!
ARE YOU THAT UPSET ABOUT MY DRAGGING YOU AWAY FROM SASUKE?
THAT'S... *NOT* IT AT ALL! YEESH!
LET'S JUST DO THIS! HEY, SUIGETSU!!
WHY ARE YOU ATTACKING ME?!
DOESN'T EVERYONE WHO SEES A SLUG WANT TO SPRINKLE SALT ON IT?!!
LET'S GO.
!
!
TSUNADE FIRST!
TAK

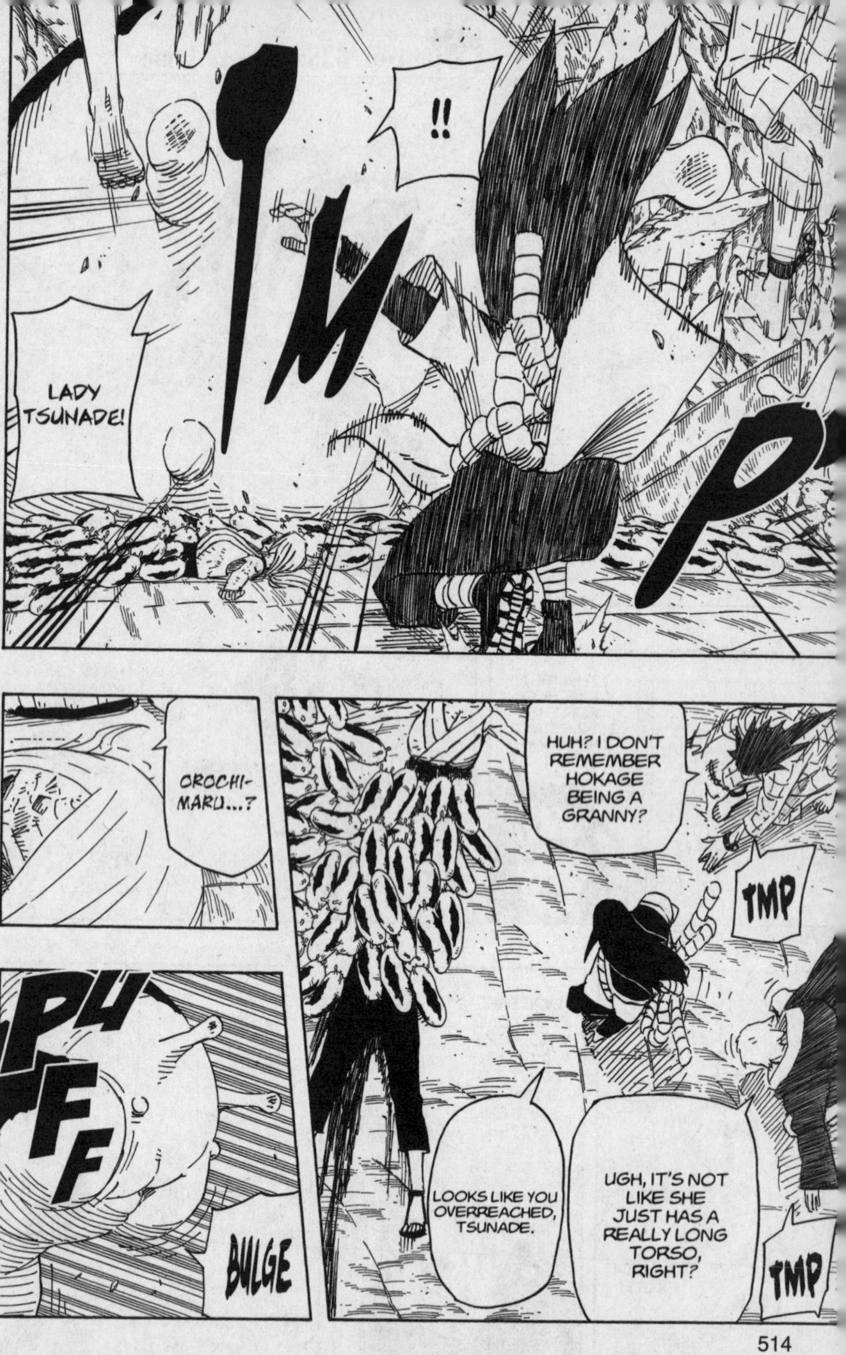
!!
LADY TSUNADE!
HUH? I DON'T REMEMBER HOKAGE BEING A GRANNY?
TMP
UGH, IT'S NOT LIKE SHE JUST HAS A REALLY LONG TORSO, RIGHT?
TMP
LOOKS LIKE YOU OVERREACHED, TSUNADE.
OROCHI-MARU...?
PUFF
BULGE

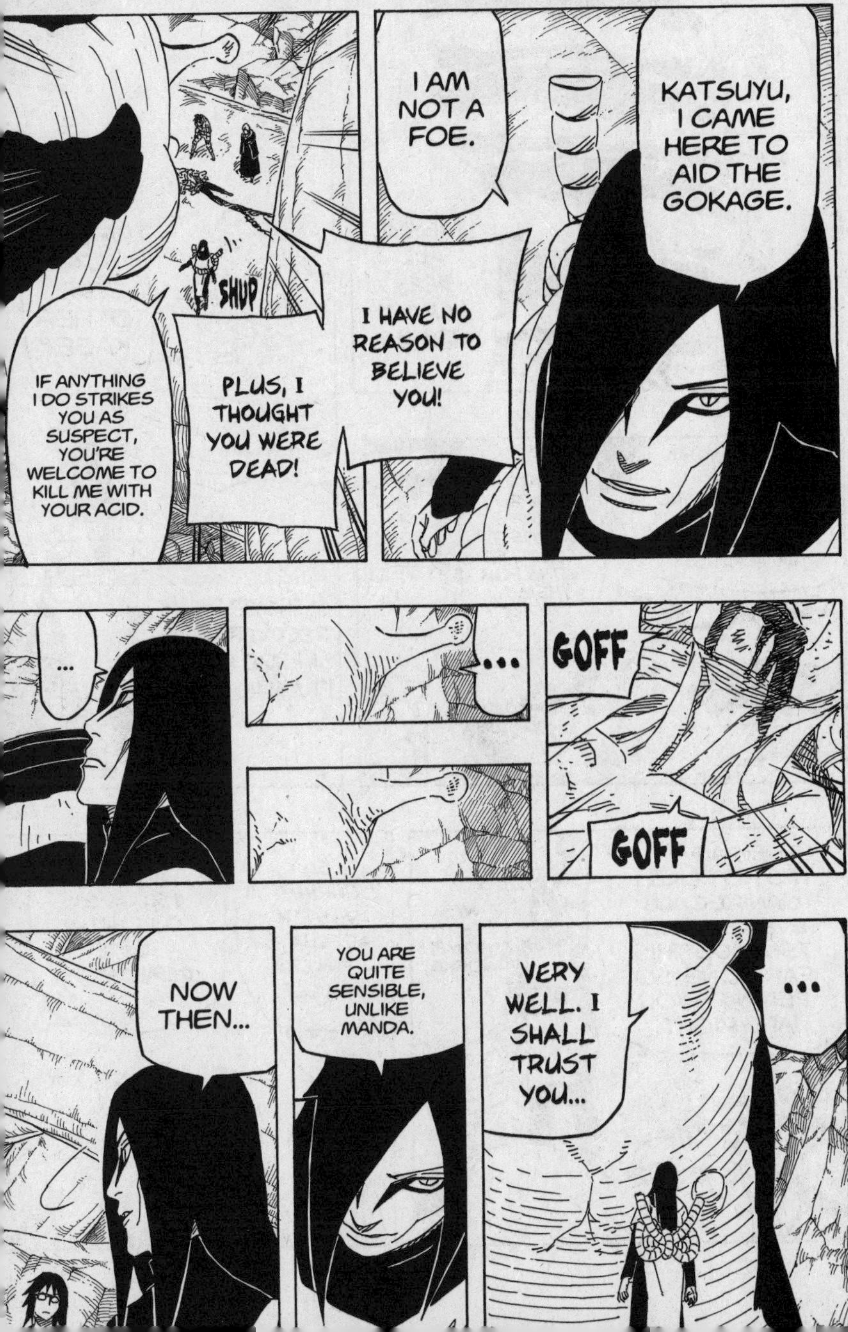
KATSUYU, I CAME HERE TO AID THE GOKAGE.
I AM NOT A FOE.
I HAVE NO REASON TO BELIEVE YOU!
PLUS, I THOUGHT YOU WERE DEAD!
SHUP
IF ANYTHING I DO STRIKES YOU AS SUSPECT, YOU'RE WELCOME TO KILL ME WITH YOUR ACID.
GOFF
GOFF
...
...
...
VERY WELL. I SHALL TRUST YOU...
YOU ARE QUITE SENSIBLE, UNLIKE MANDA.
NOW THEN...

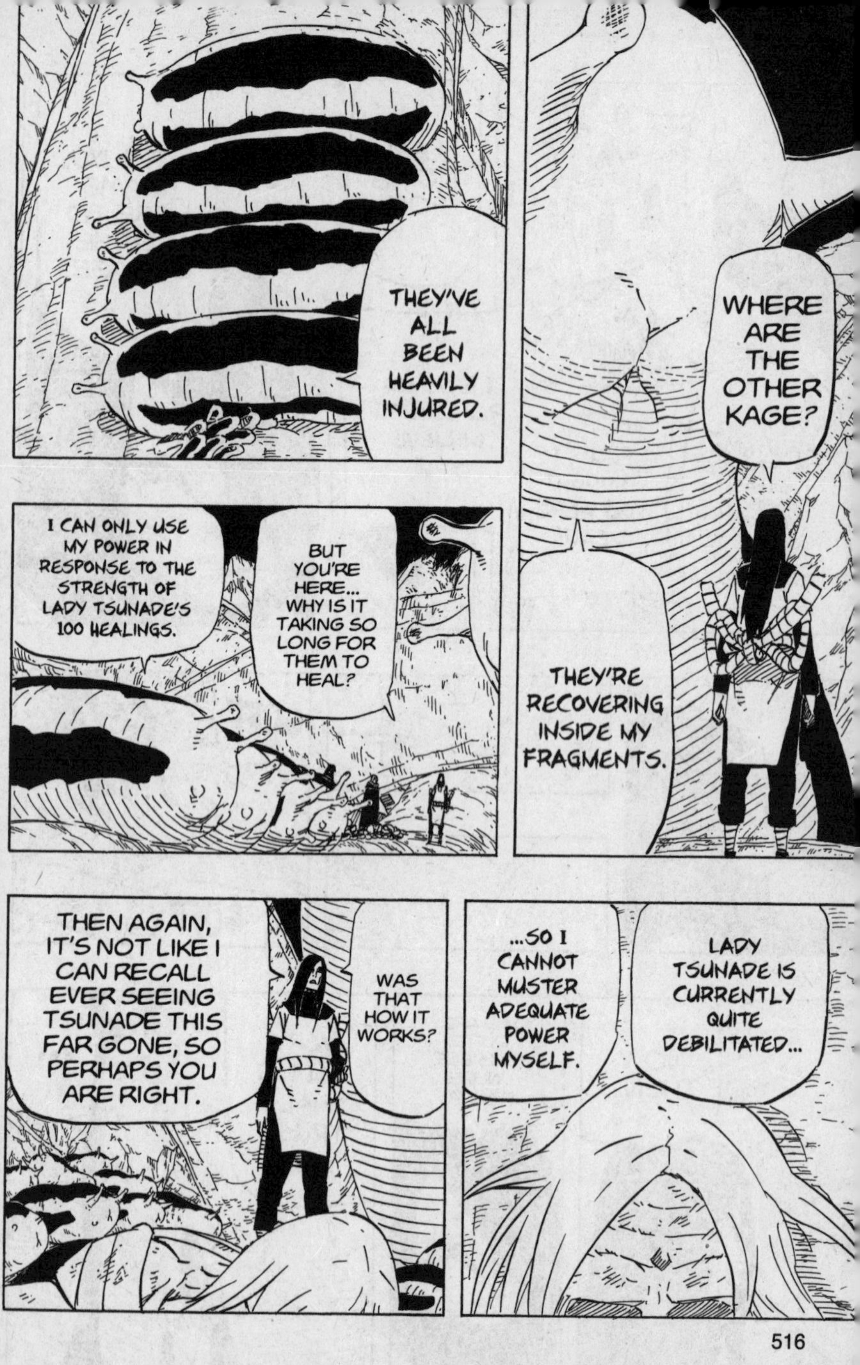
WHERE ARE THE OTHER KAGE?
THEY'RE RECOVERING INSIDE MY FRAGMENTS.
THEY'VE ALL BEEN HEAVILY INJURED.
BUT YOU'RE HERE... WHY IS IT TAKING SO LONG FOR THEM TO HEAL?
I CAN ONLY USE MY POWER IN RESPONSE TO THE STRENGTH OF LADY TSUNADE'S 100 HEALINGS.
LADY TSUNADE IS CURRENTLY QUITE DEBILITATED...
...SO I CANNOT MUSTER ADEQUATE POWER MYSELF.
WAS THAT HOW IT WORKS?
THEN AGAIN, IT'S NOT LIKE I CAN RECALL EVER SEEING TSUNADE THIS FAR GONE, SO PERHAPS YOU ARE RIGHT.

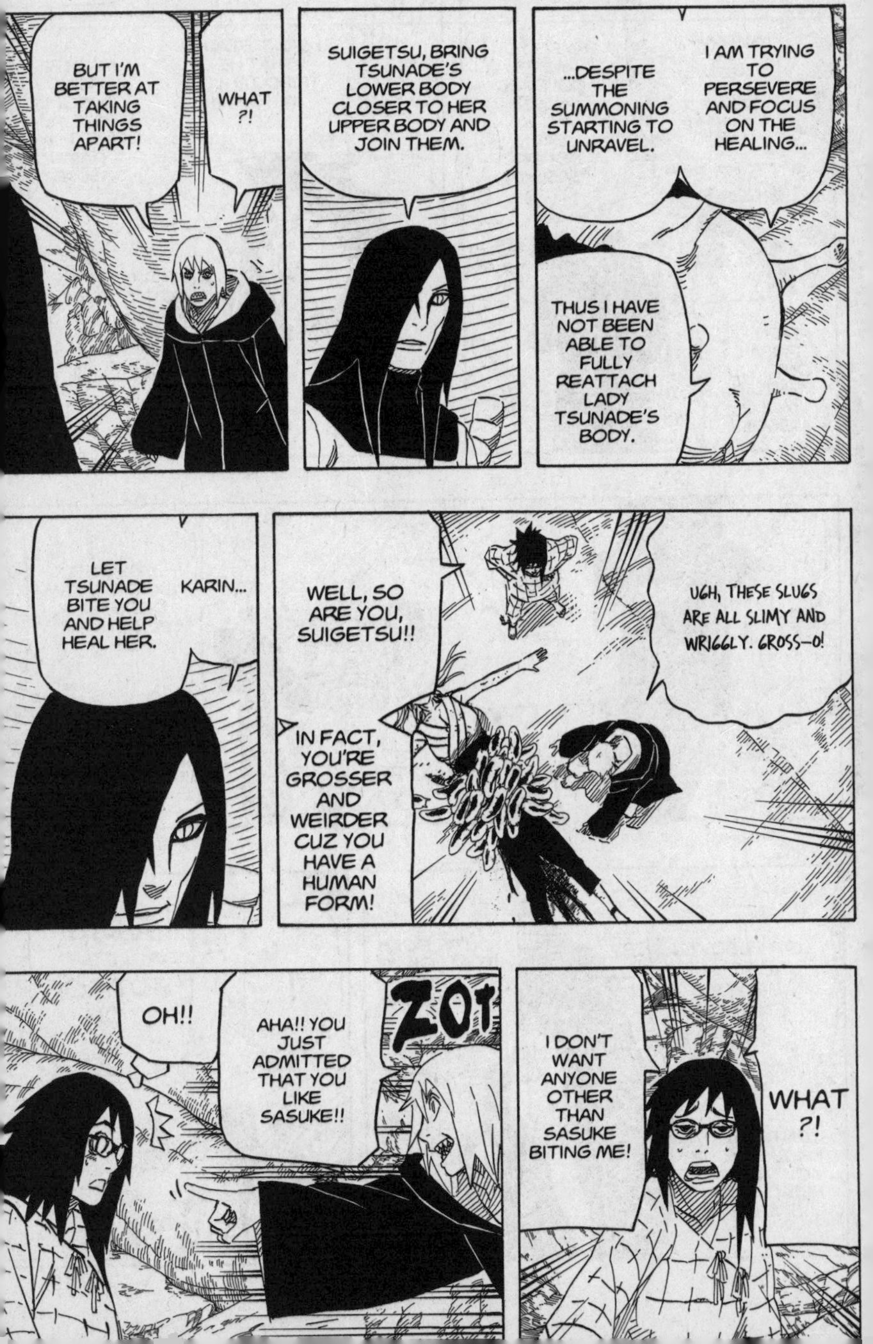
I AM TRYING TO PERSEVERE AND FOCUS ON THE HEALING...
...DESPITE THE SUMMONING STARTING TO UNRAVEL.
THUS I HAVE NOT BEEN ABLE TO FULLY REATTACH LADY TSUNADE'S BODY.
SUIGETSU, BRING TSUNADE'S LOWER BODY CLOSER TO HER UPPER BODY AND JOIN THEM.
WHAT?!
BUT I'M BETTER AT TAKING THINGS APART!
UGH, THESE SLUGS ARE ALL SLIMY AND WRIGGLY. GROSS-O!
WELL, SO ARE YOU, SUIGETSU!!
IN FACT, YOU'RE GROSSER AND WEIRDER CUZ YOU HAVE A HUMAN FORM!
KARIN...
LET TSUNADE BITE YOU AND HELP HEAL HER.
WHAT?!
I DON'T WANT ANYONE OTHER THAN SASUKE BITING ME!
ZOT
AHA!! YOU JUST ADMITTED THAT YOU LIKE SASUKE!!
OH!!

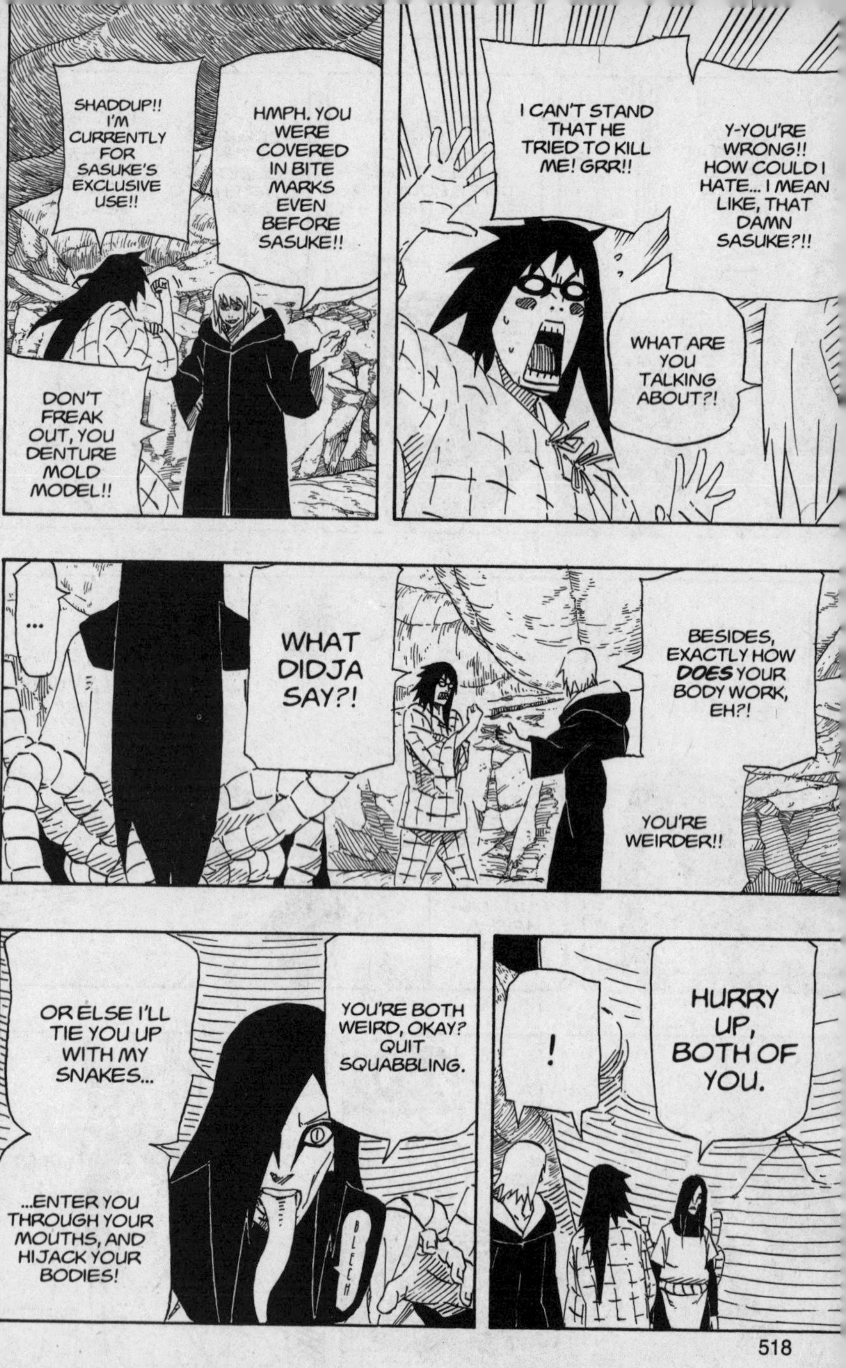
Y-YOU'RE WRONG!! HOW COULD I HATE... I MEAN LIKE, THAT DAMN SASUKE?!!
I CAN'T STAND THAT HE TRIED TO KILL ME! GRR!!
WHAT ARE YOU TALKING ABOUT?!
HMPH. YOU WERE COVERED IN BITE MARKS EVEN BEFORE SASUKE!!
SHADDUP!! I'M CURRENTLY FOR SASUKE'S EXCLUSIVE USE!!
DON'T FREAK OUT, YOU DENTURE MOLD MODEL!!
BESIDES, EXACTLY HOW **DOES** YOUR BODY WORK, EH?!
YOU'RE WEIRDER!!
WHAT DIDJA SAY?!
...
HURRY UP, BOTH OF YOU.
!
YOU'RE BOTH WEIRD, OKAY? QUIT SQUABBLING.
OR ELSE I'LL TIE YOU UP WITH MY SNAKES...
...ENTER YOU THROUGH YOUR MOUTHS, AND HIJACK YOUR BODIES!
BLECH

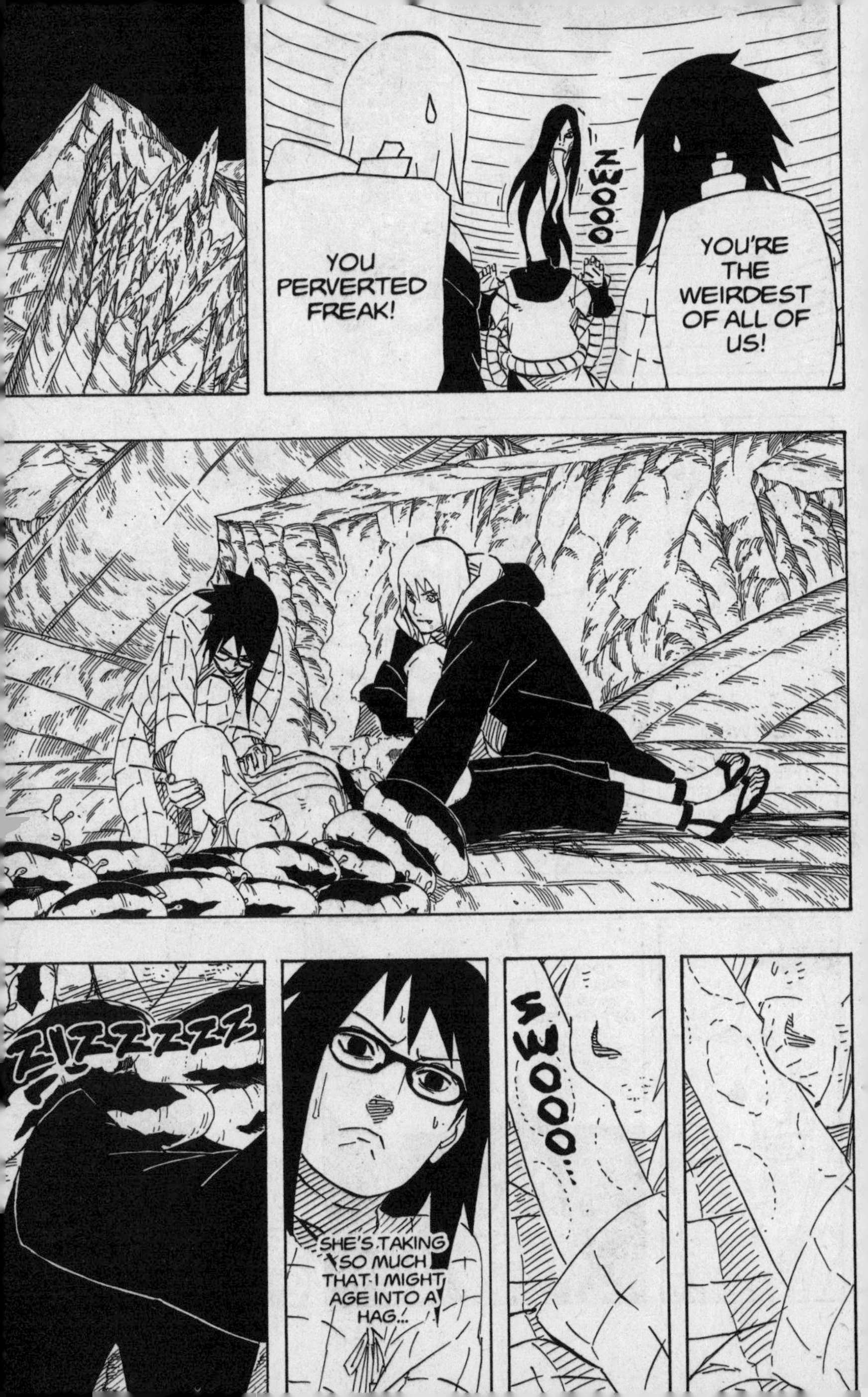
YOU'RE THE WEIRDEST OF ALL OF US!
ZWOOO
YOU PERVERTED FREAK!
SWOOO...
SHE'S TAKING SO MUCH THAT I MIGHT AGE INTO A HAG...
ZIZZZZZZ

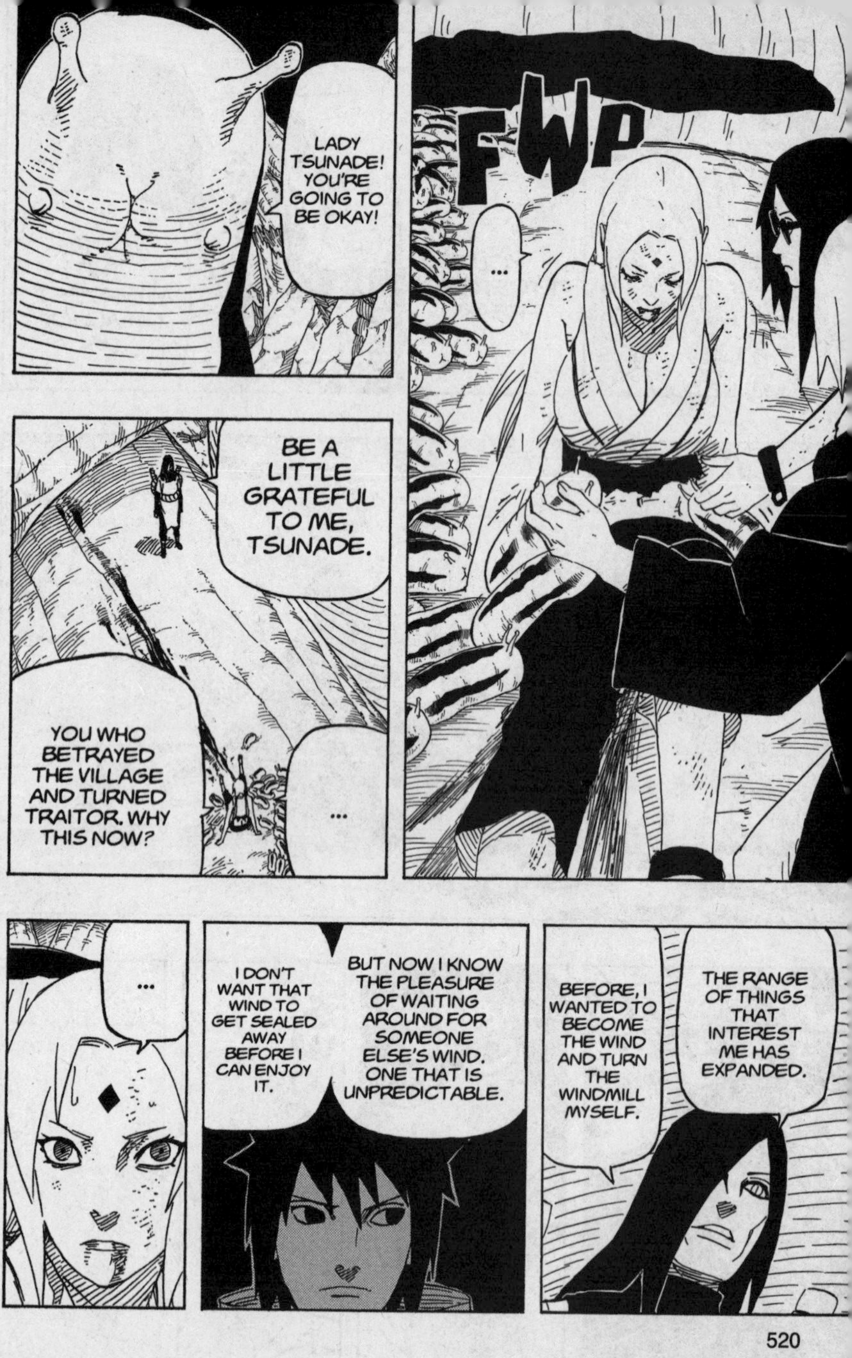
FWP
...
LADY TSUNADE! YOU'RE GOING TO BE OKAY!
BE A LITTLE GRATEFUL TO ME, TSUNADE.
...
YOU WHO BETRAYED THE VILLAGE AND TURNED TRAITOR. WHY THIS NOW?
THE RANGE OF THINGS THAT INTEREST ME HAS EXPANDED.
BEFORE, I WANTED TO BECOME THE WIND AND TURN THE WINDMILL MYSELF.
BUT NOW I KNOW THE PLEASURE OF WAITING AROUND FOR SOMEONE ELSE'S WIND. ONE THAT IS UNPREDICTABLE.
I DON'T WANT THAT WIND TO GET SEALED AWAY BEFORE I CAN ENJOY IT.
...

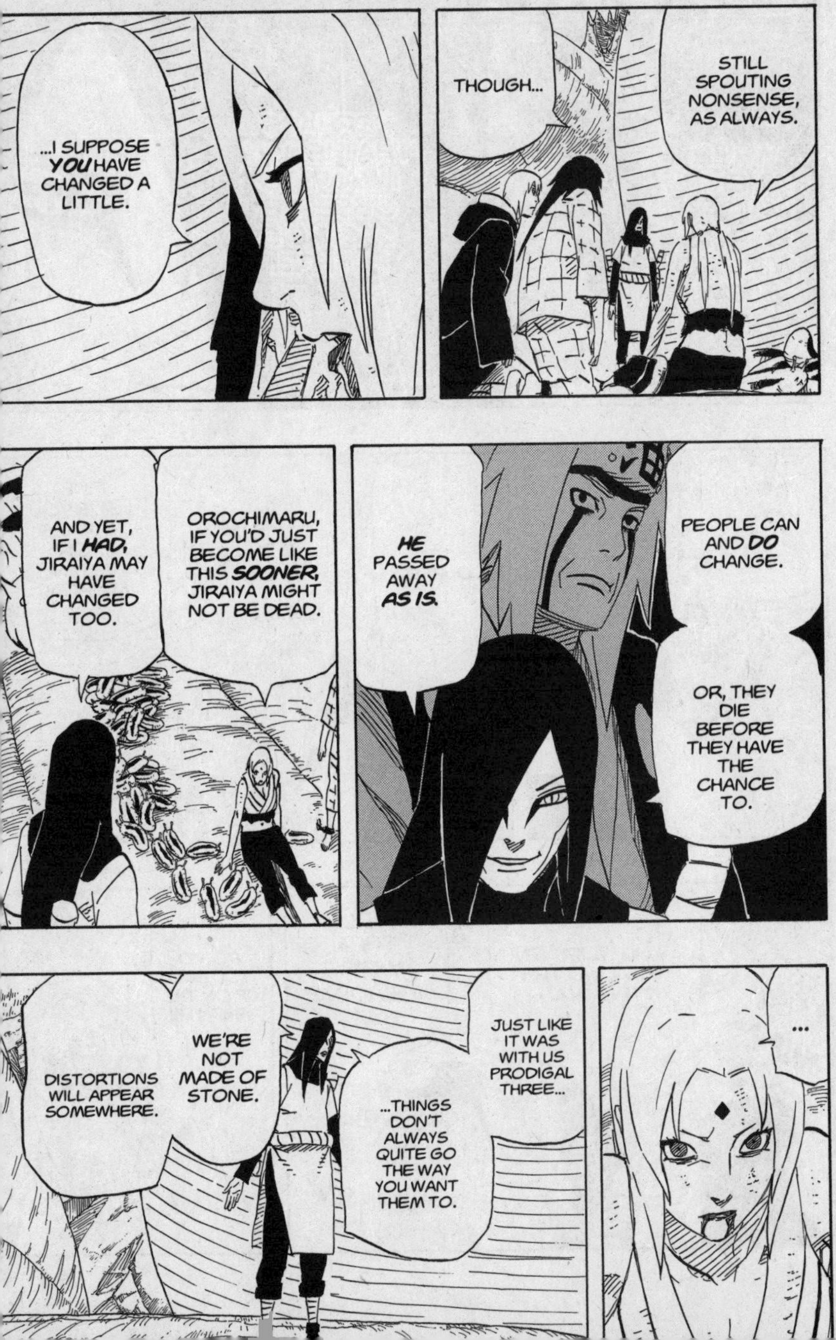
STILL SPOUTING NONSENSE, AS ALWAYS.
THOUGH...
...I SUPPOSE **YOU** HAVE CHANGED A LITTLE.
PEOPLE CAN AND **DO** CHANGE.
OR, THEY DIE BEFORE THEY HAVE THE CHANCE TO.
HE PASSED AWAY **AS IS.**
OROCHIMARU, IF YOU'D JUST BECOME LIKE THIS **SOONER,** JIRAIYA MIGHT NOT BE DEAD.
AND YET, IF I **HAD,** JIRAIYA MAY HAVE CHANGED TOO.
...
JUST LIKE IT WAS WITH US PRODIGAL THREE...
...THINGS DON'T ALWAYS QUITE GO THE WAY YOU WANT THEM TO.
WE'RE NOT MADE OF STONE.
DISTORTIONS WILL APPEAR SOMEWHERE.

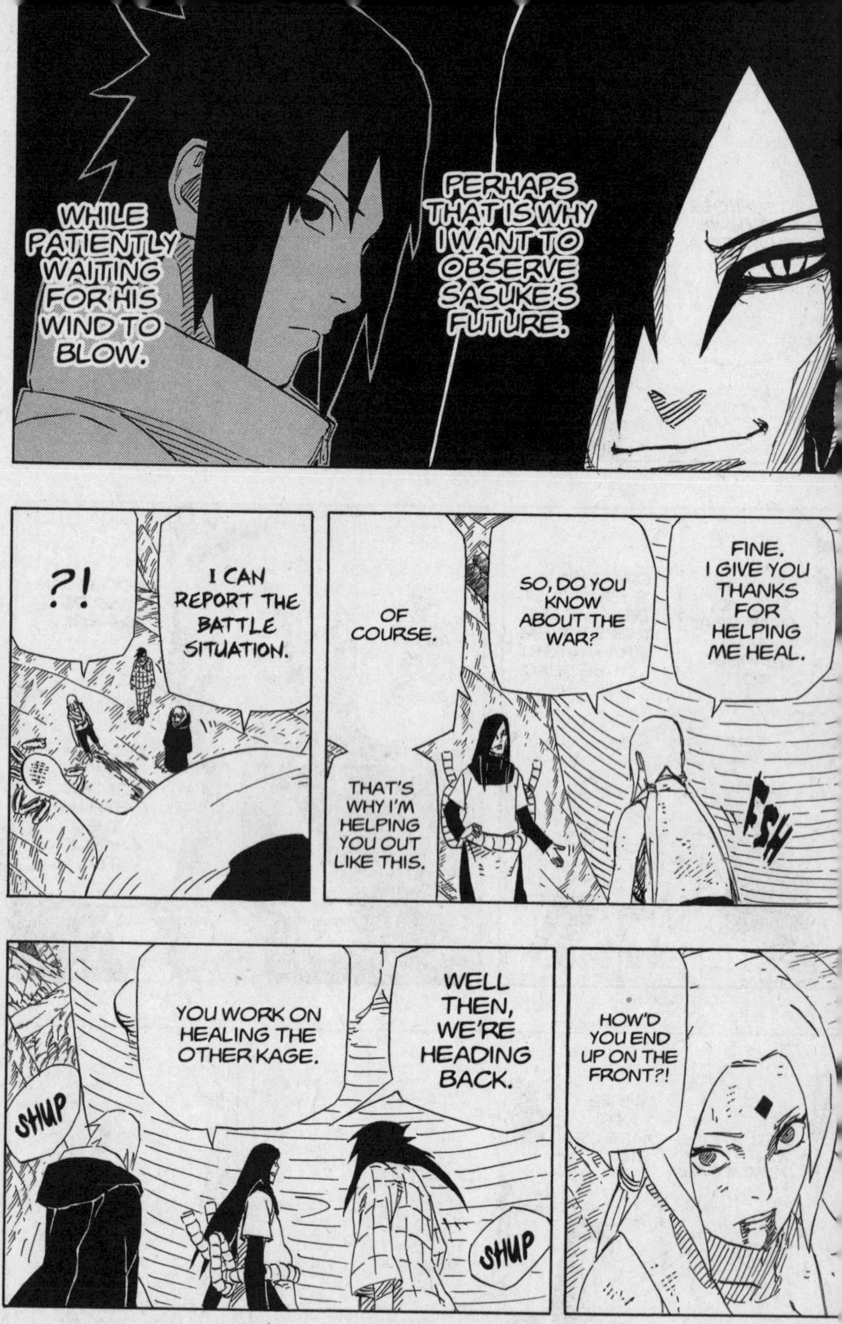
PERHAPS THAT IS WHY I WANT TO OBSERVE SASUKE'S FUTURE.
WHILE PATIENTLY WAITING FOR HIS WIND TO BLOW.
FINE. I GIVE YOU THANKS FOR HELPING ME HEAL.
FSH
SO, DO YOU KNOW ABOUT THE WAR?
OF COURSE.
THAT'S WHY I'M HELPING YOU OUT LIKE THIS.
I CAN REPORT THE BATTLE SITUATION.
?!
HOW'D YOU END UP ON THE FRONT?!
WELL THEN, WE'RE HEADING BACK.
SHUP
YOU WORK ON HEALING THE OTHER KAGE.
SHUP

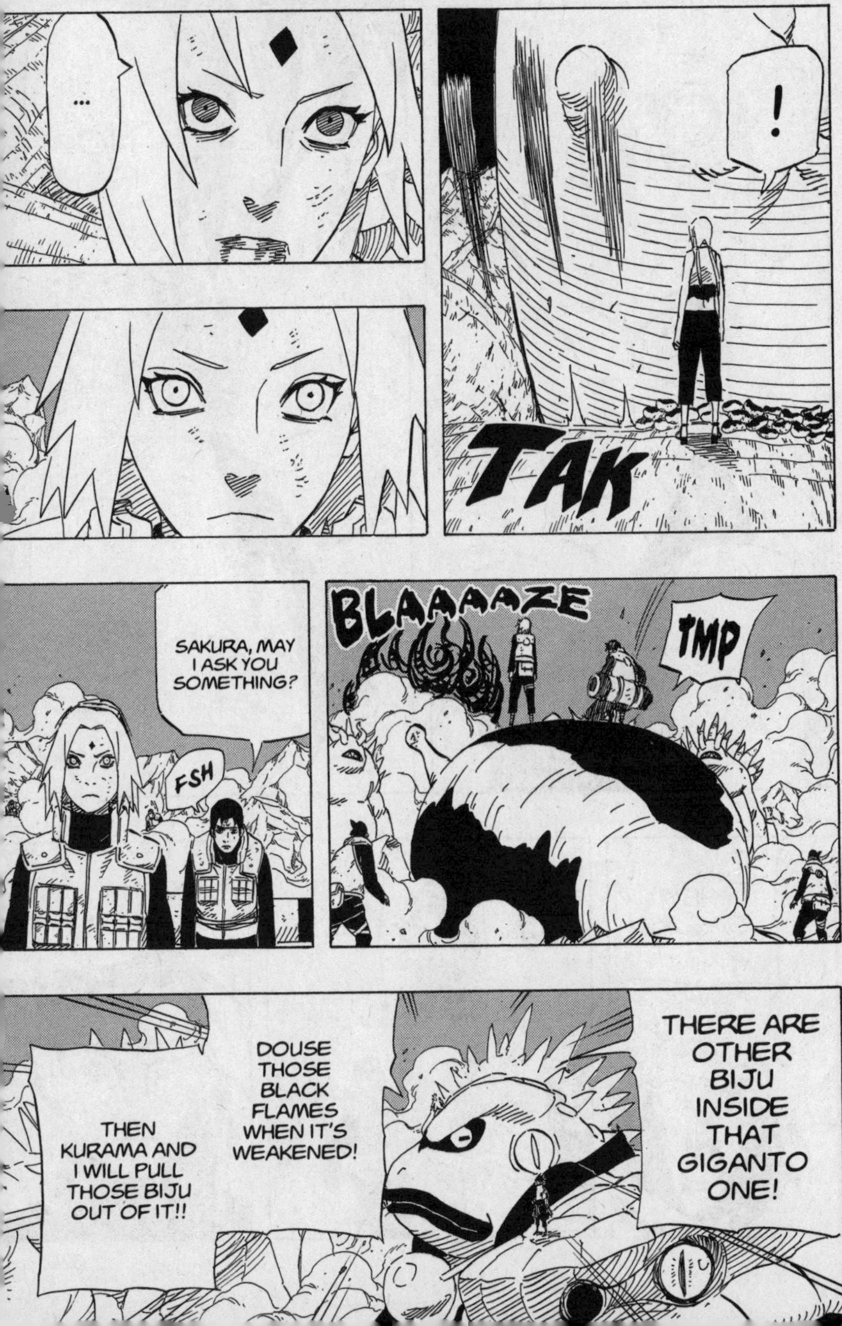
!
TAK
...
BLAAAAZE
TMP
SAKURA, MAY I ASK YOU SOMETHING?
FSH
THERE ARE OTHER BIJU INSIDE THAT GIGANTO ONE!
DOUSE THOSE BLACK FLAMES WHEN IT'S WEAKENED!
THEN KURAMA AND I WILL PULL THOSE BIJU OUT OF IT!!

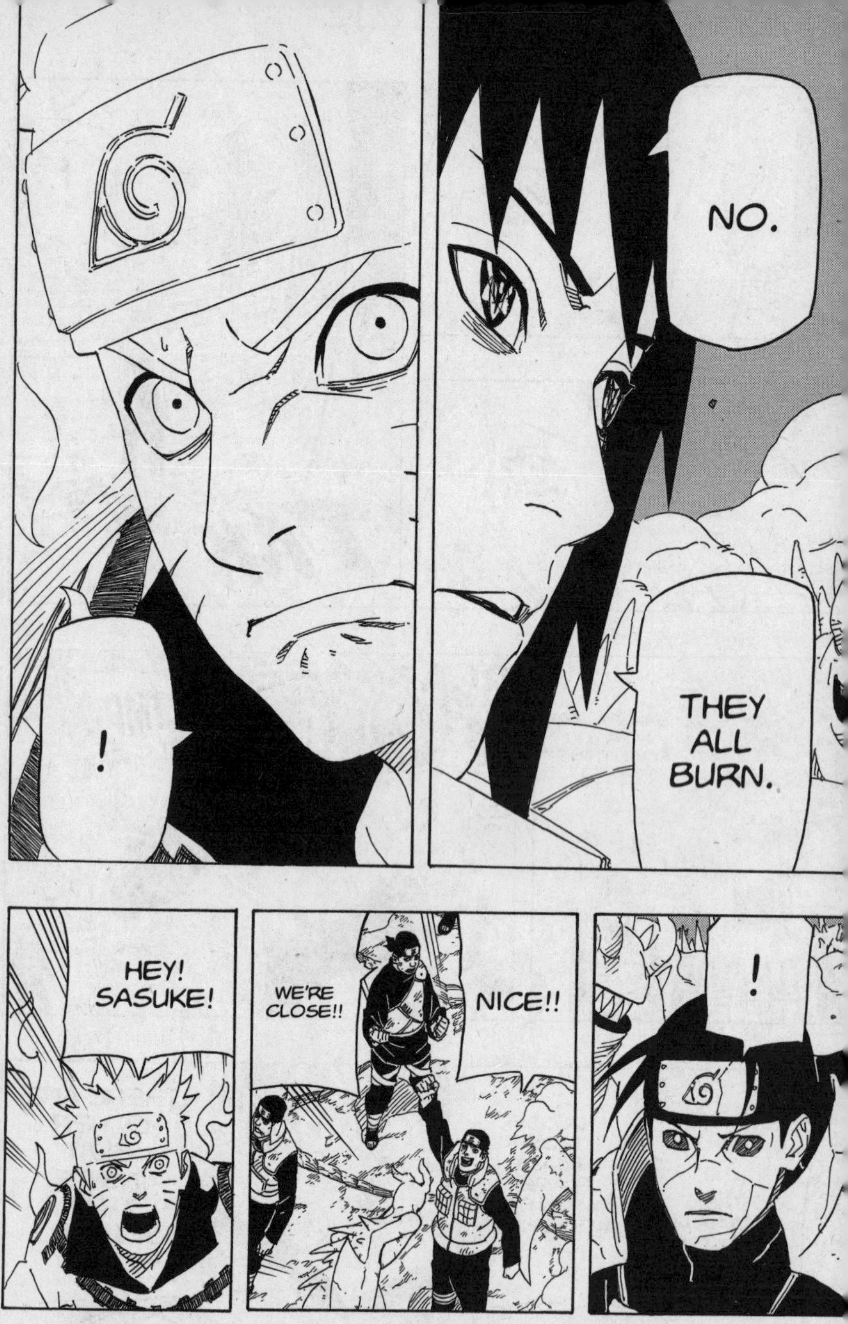
NO.
THEY ALL BURN.
!
!
NICE!!
WE'RE CLOSE!!
HEY! SASUKE!

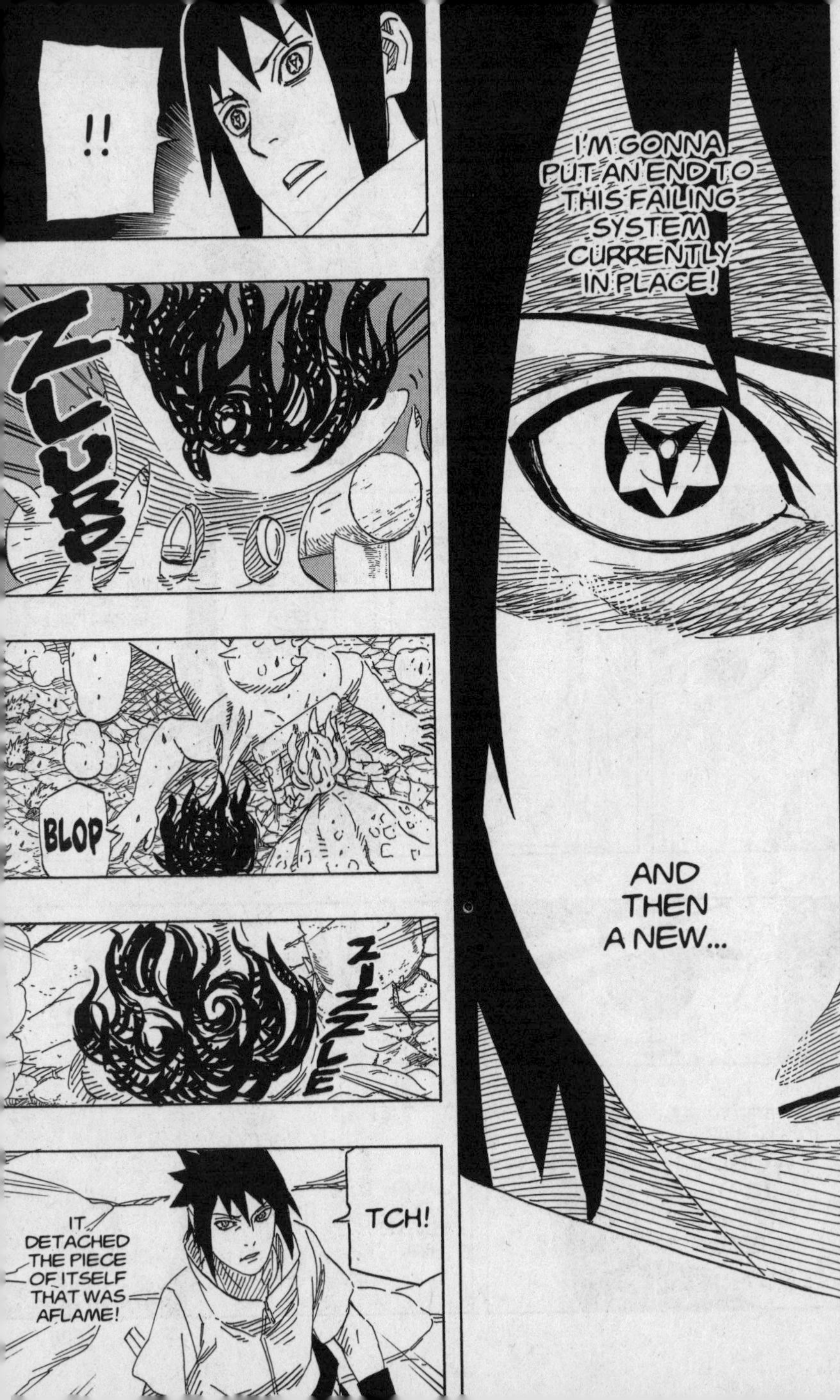
I'M GONNA PUT AN END TO THIS FAILING SYSTEM CURRENTLY IN PLACE!
AND THEN A NEW...
!!
BLOP
ZIZZLE
TCH!
IT DETACHED THE PIECE OF ITSELF THAT WAS AFLAME!

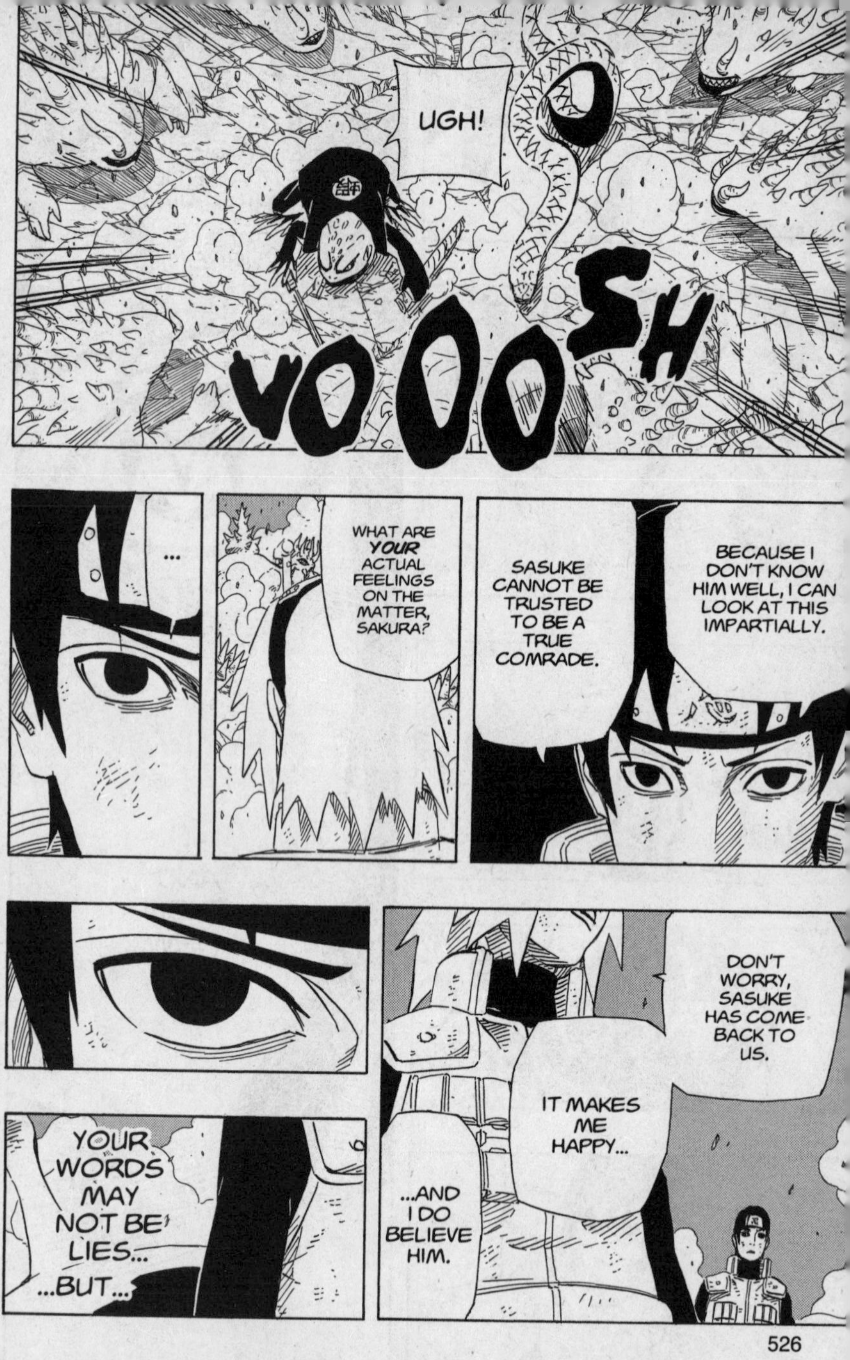
UGH!
VOOOSH
BECAUSE I DON'T KNOW HIM WELL, I CAN LOOK AT THIS IMPARTIALLY.
SASUKE CANNOT BE TRUSTED TO BE A TRUE COMRADE.
WHAT ARE **YOUR** ACTUAL FEELINGS ON THE MATTER, SAKURA?
...
DON'T WORRY, SASUKE HAS COME BACK TO US.
IT MAKES ME HAPPY...
...AND I DO BELIEVE HIM.
YOUR WORDS MAY NOT BE LIES...
...BUT...

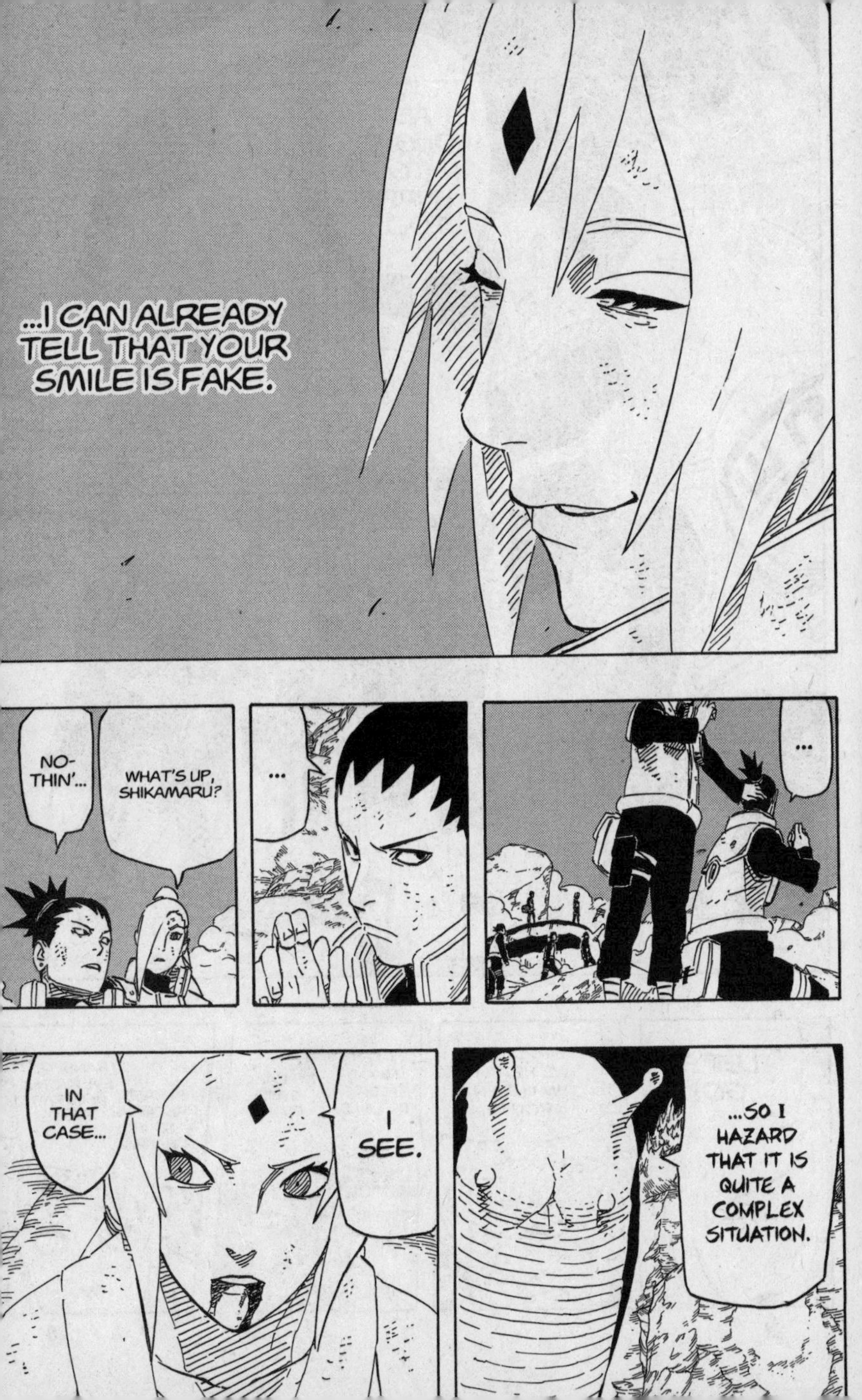
...I CAN ALREADY TELL THAT YOUR SMILE IS FAKE.
...
...
WHAT'S UP, SHIKAMARU?
NO-THIN'...
...SO I HAZARD THAT IT IS QUITE A COMPLEX SITUATION.
I SEE.
IN THAT CASE...

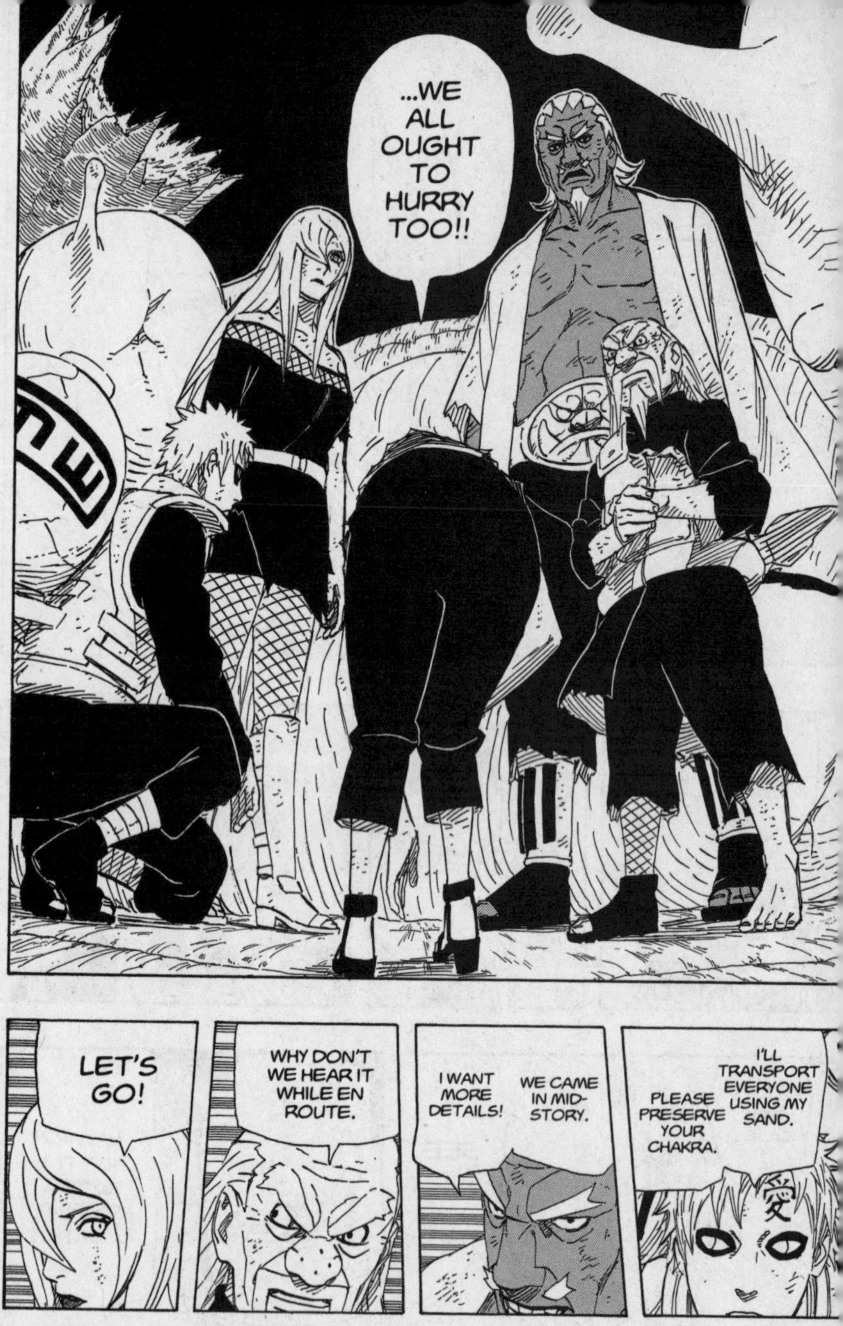
...WE ALL OUGHT TO HURRY TOO!!
I'LL TRANSPORT EVERYONE USING MY SAND.
PLEASE PRESERVE YOUR CHAKRA.
WE CAME IN MID-STORY.
I WANT MORE DETAILS!
WHY DON'T WE HEAR IT WHILE EN ROUTE.
LET'S GO!

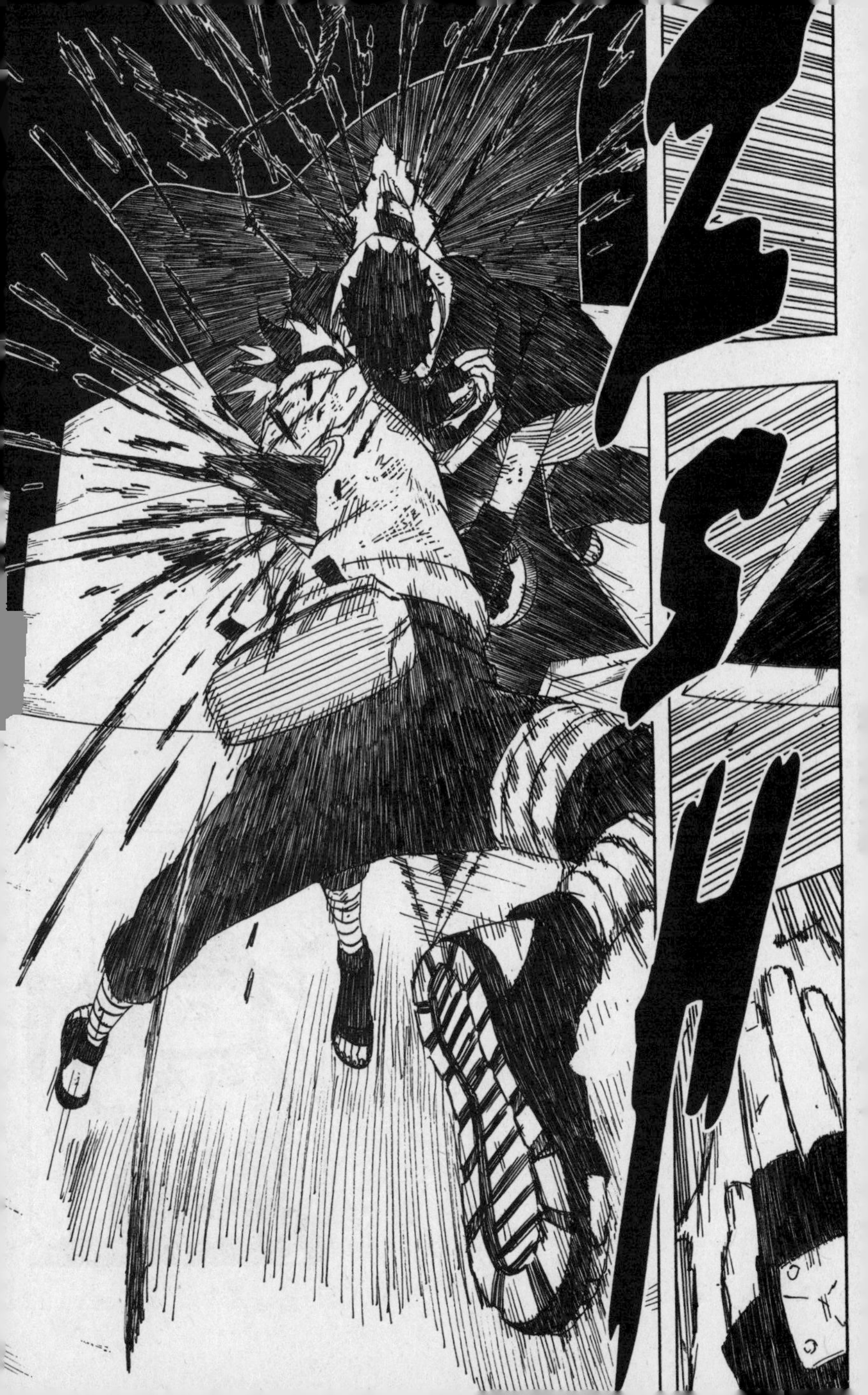

Number 636: The Current Obito

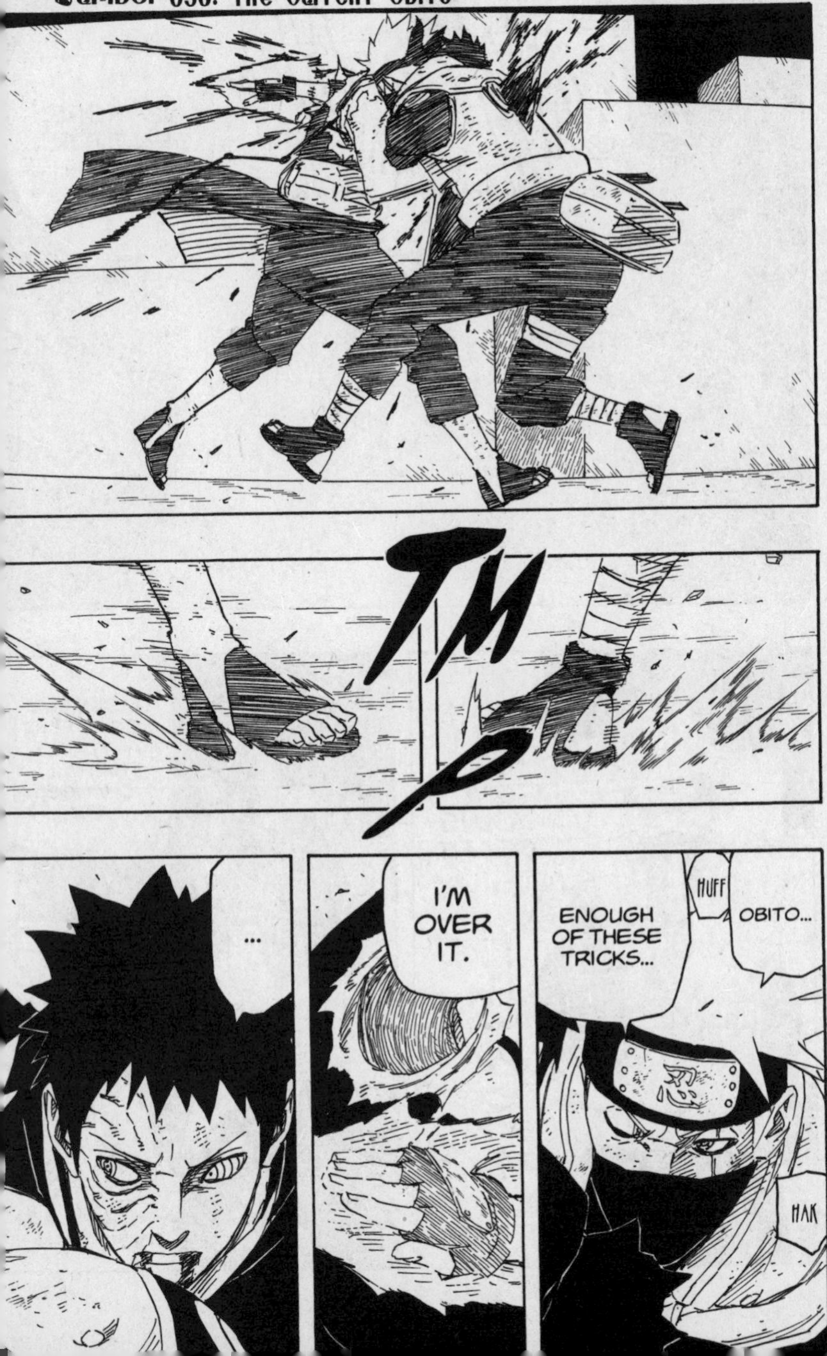
TMP
OBITO...
HUFF
ENOUGH OF THESE TRICKS...
HAK
I'M OVER IT.
...

NO MORE GENJUTSU.

ALL I CAN GIVE YOU IS DEATH.

SWOO...

LOOKS LIKE I CAN'T FIND ANYTHING THAT WILL CHANGE YOU.

WISP

RIGHT NOW...

FSH

LET'S END THIS!

SWOO

FSH

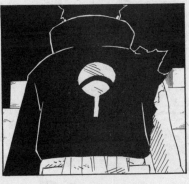

THEN I SHALL DO THE SAME...

...

...BEGIN SHINOBI HAND-TO-HAND COMBAT!

WELL THEN...

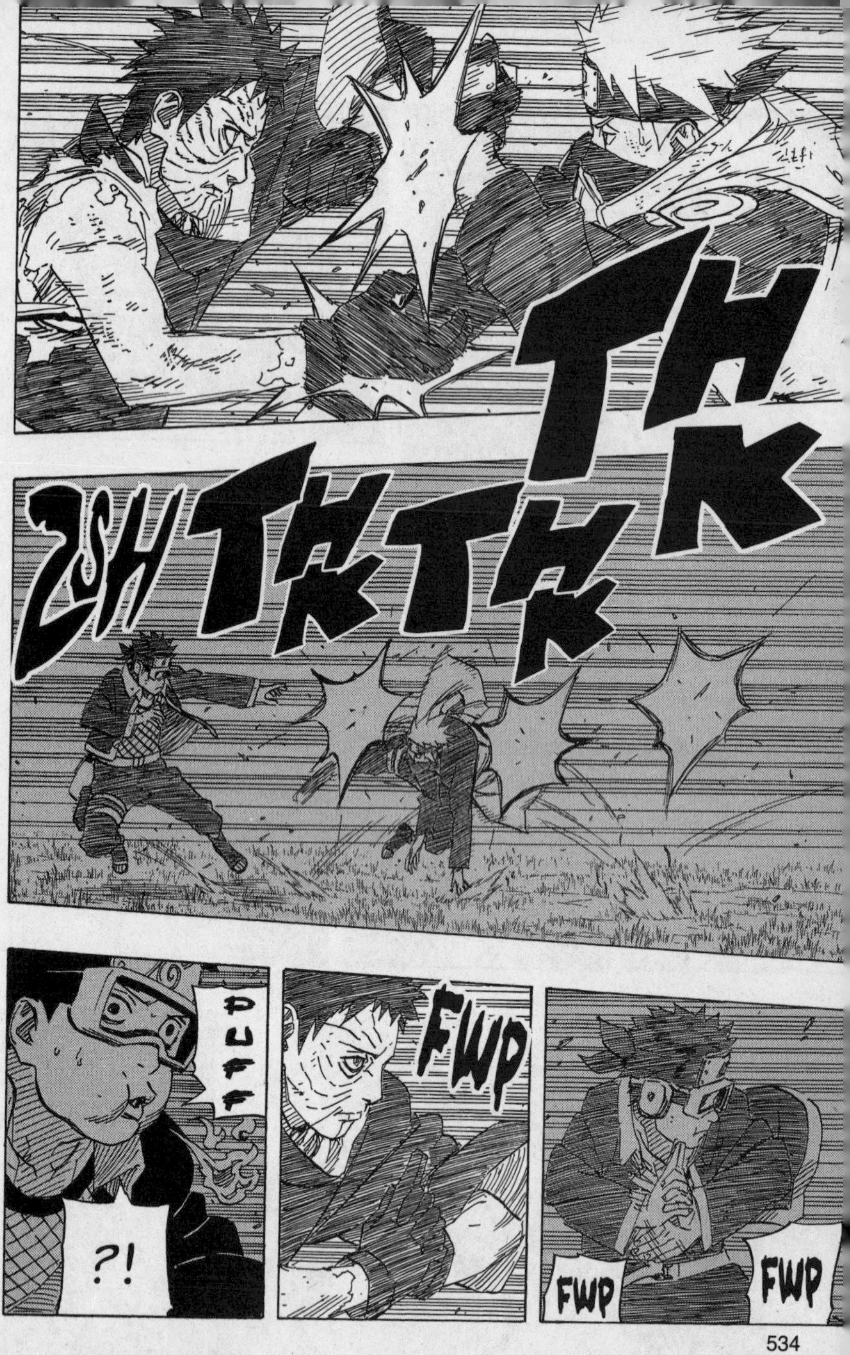
ZSH
THK THK THK
FWP
FWP
FWP
PUFF
?!

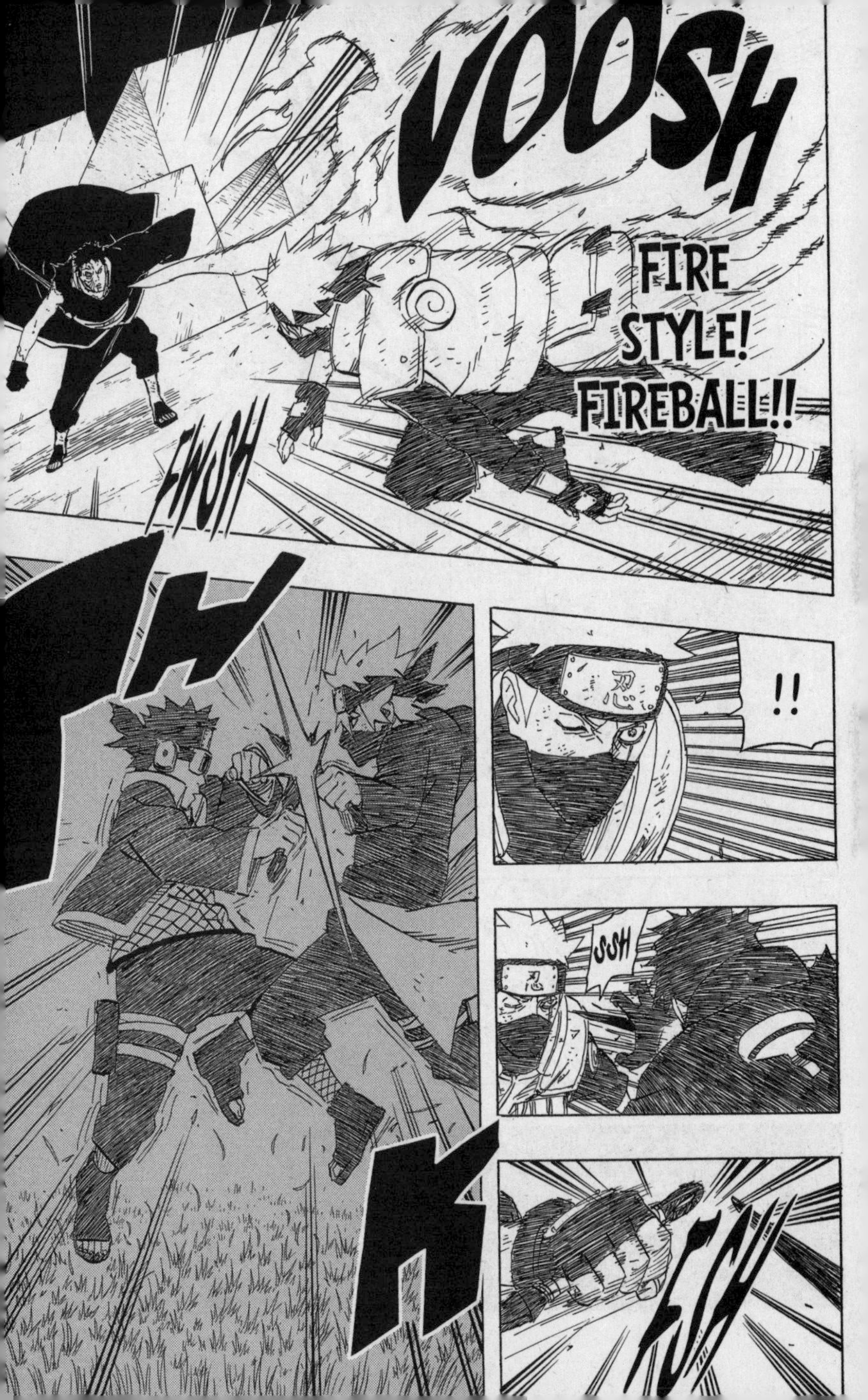
VOOSH
FIRE STYLE! FIREBALL!!
FWOSH
!!
SSH
FSH

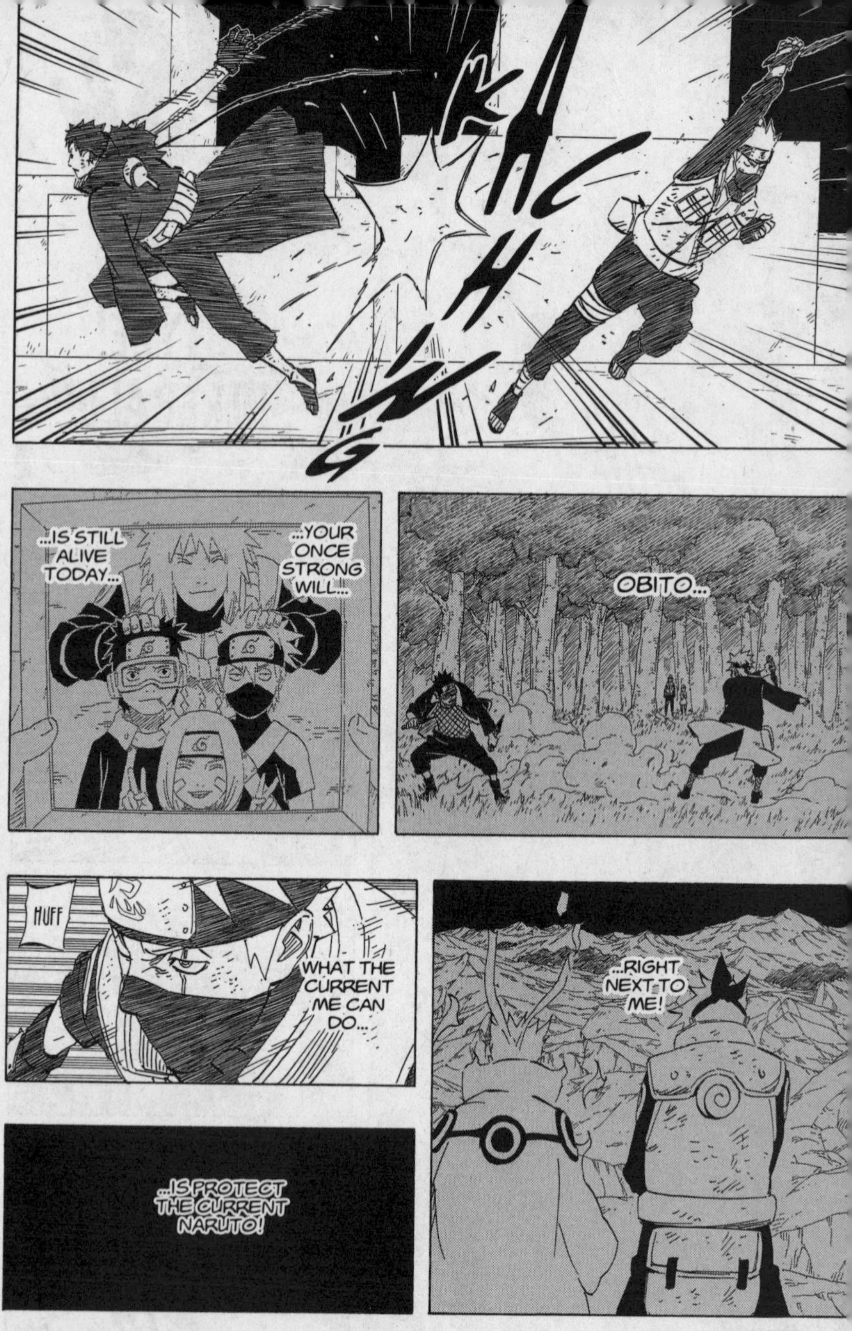
KACHING
OBITO...
...YOUR ONCE STRONG WILL...
...IS STILL ALIVE TODAY...
...RIGHT NEXT TO ME!
HUFF
WHAT THE CURRENT ME CAN DO...
...IS PROTECT THE CURRENT NARUTO!

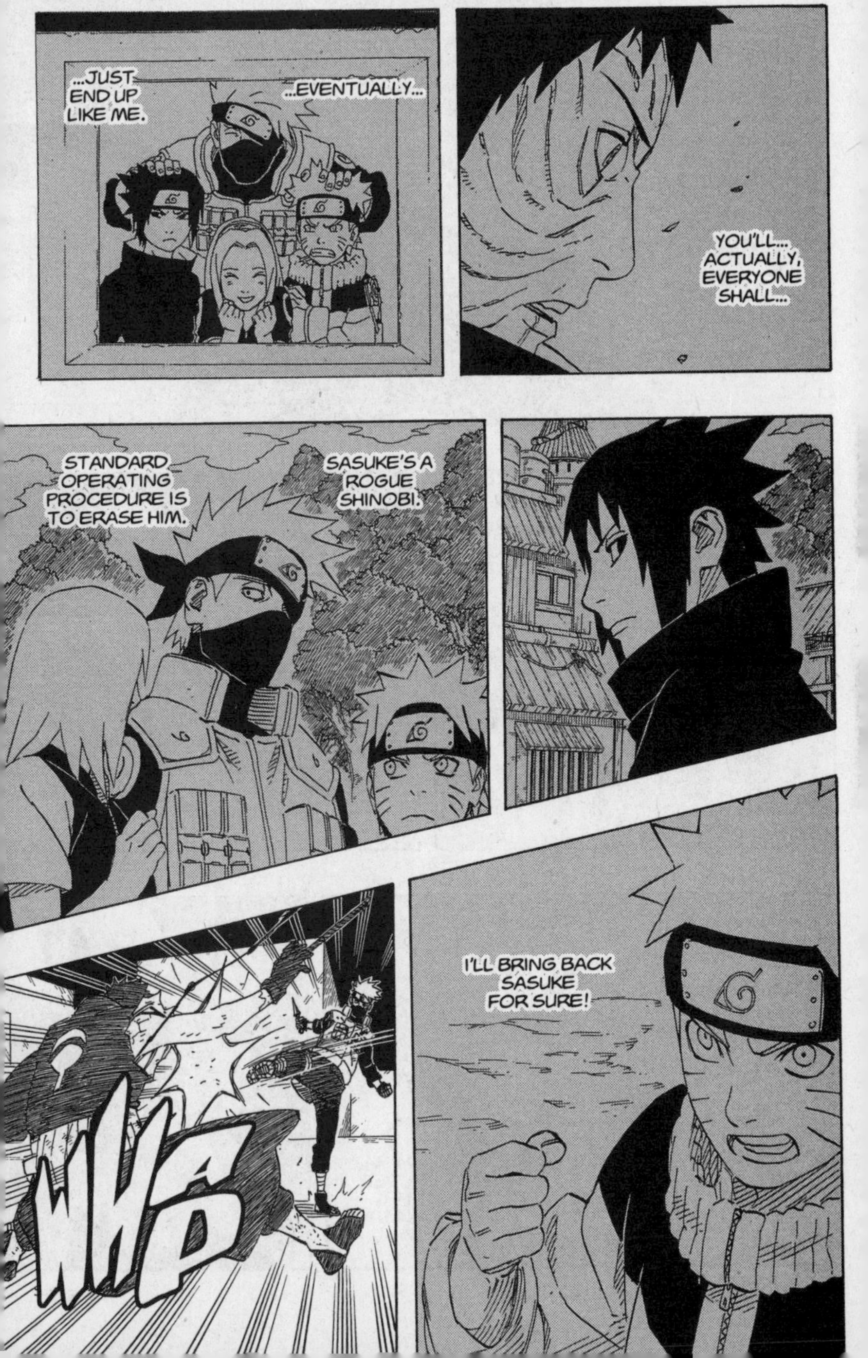
YOU'LL... ACTUALLY, EVERYONE SHALL...
...EVENTUALLY...
...JUST END UP LIKE ME.
SASUKE'S A ROGUE SHINOBI.
STANDARD OPERATING PROCEDURE IS TO ERASE HIM.
I'LL BRING BACK SASUKE FOR SURE!
WHAP

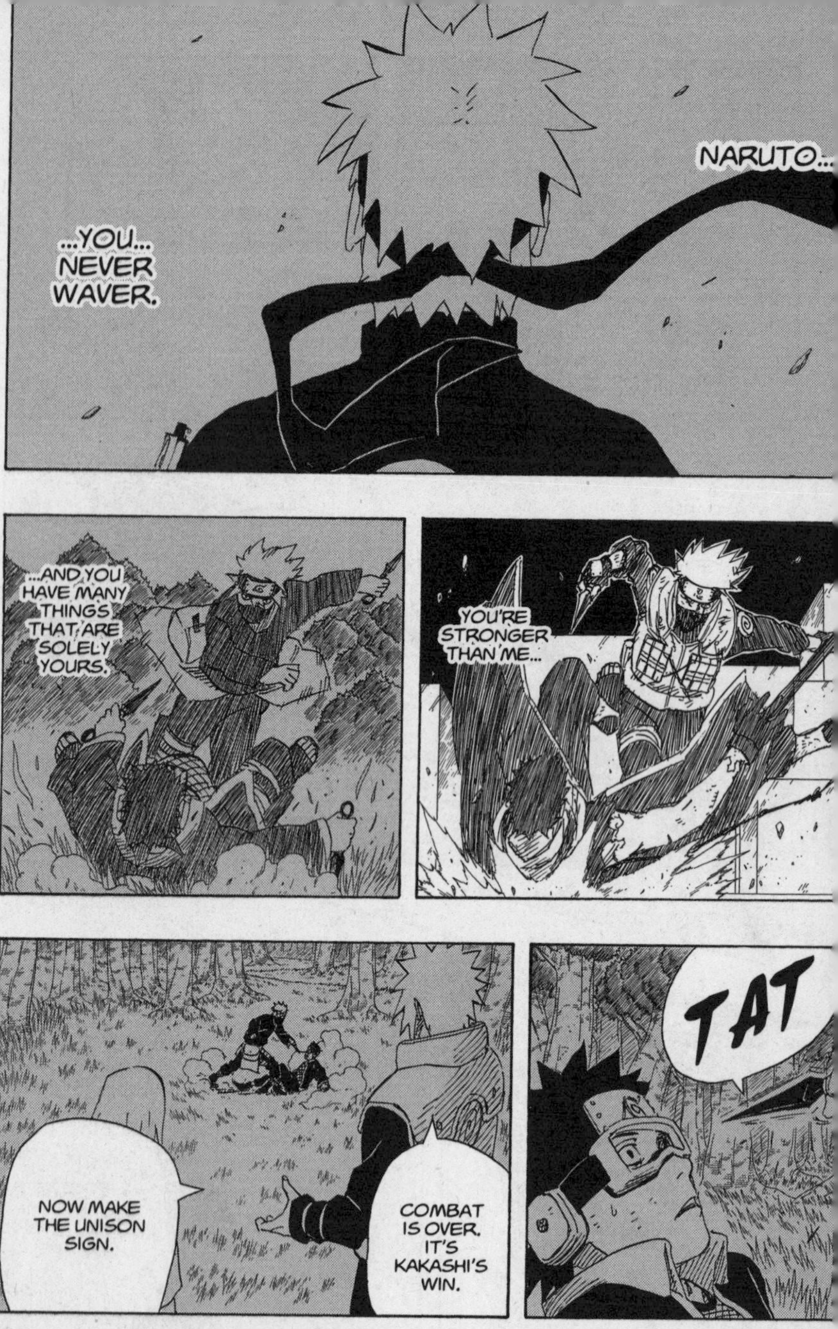
NARUTO...
...YOU... NEVER WAVER.
YOU'RE STRONGER THAN ME...
...AND YOU HAVE MANY THINGS THAT ARE SOLELY YOURS.
TAT
COMBAT IS OVER. IT'S KAKASHI'S WIN.
NOW MAKE THE UNISON SIGN.

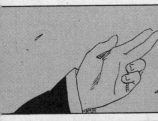

THIS IS ALL THAT THE CURRENT ME CAN DO.

AND THAT IS...

FSh

BZZZ

...TO PROTECT THIS WORLD, MY COMRADES AND THE OBITO OF THE PAST...

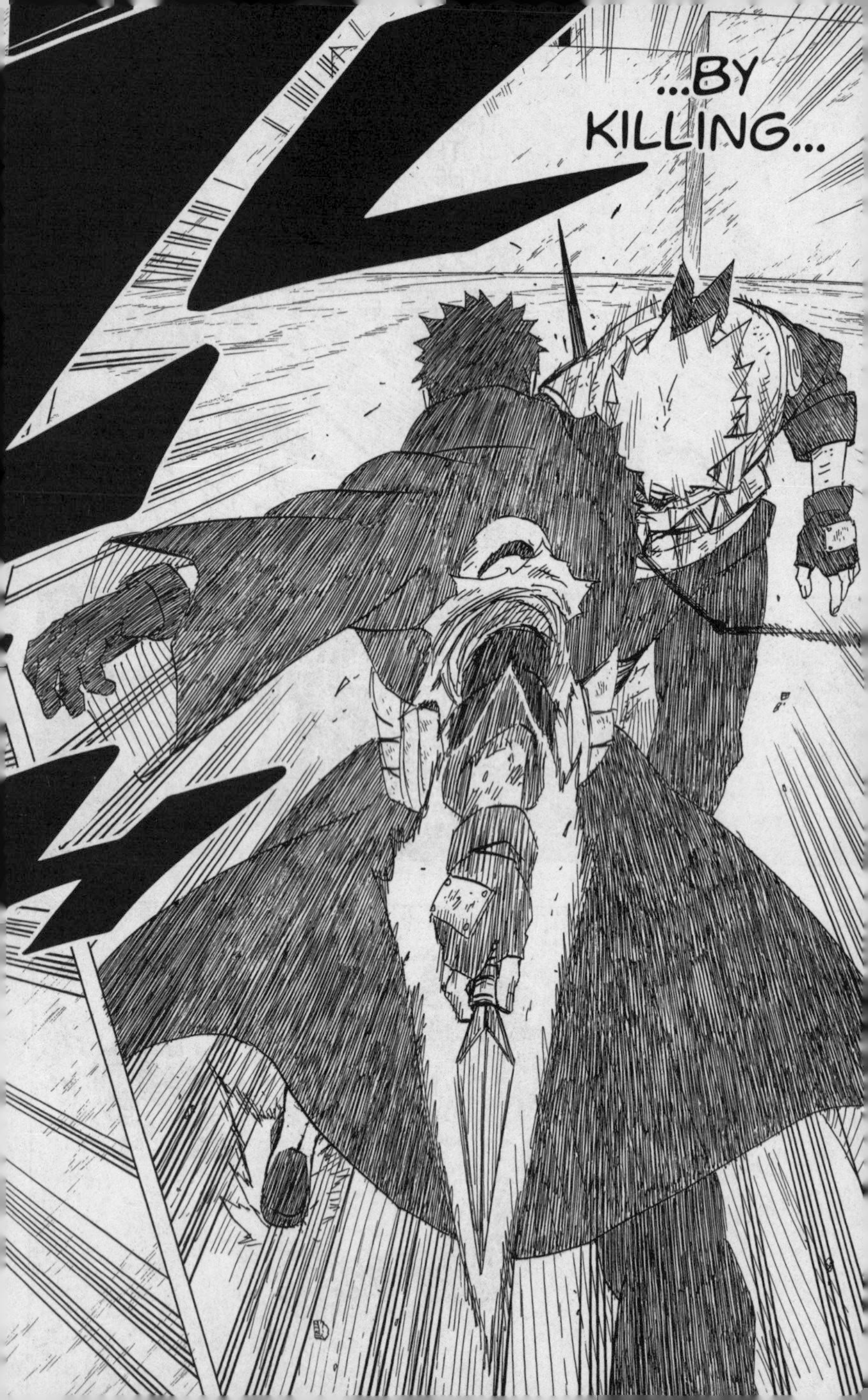
...BY
KILLING...

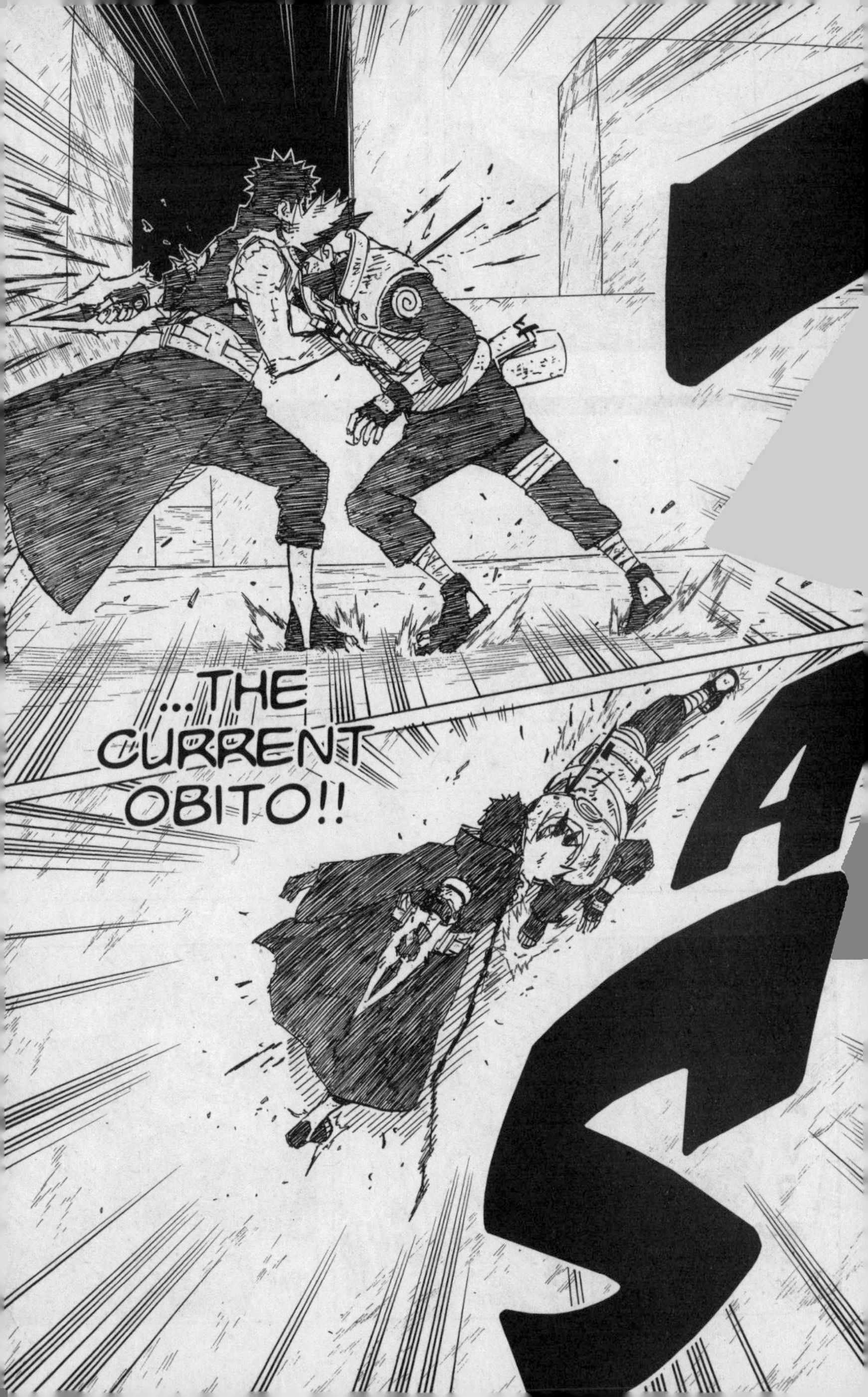
...THE CURRENT OBITO!!

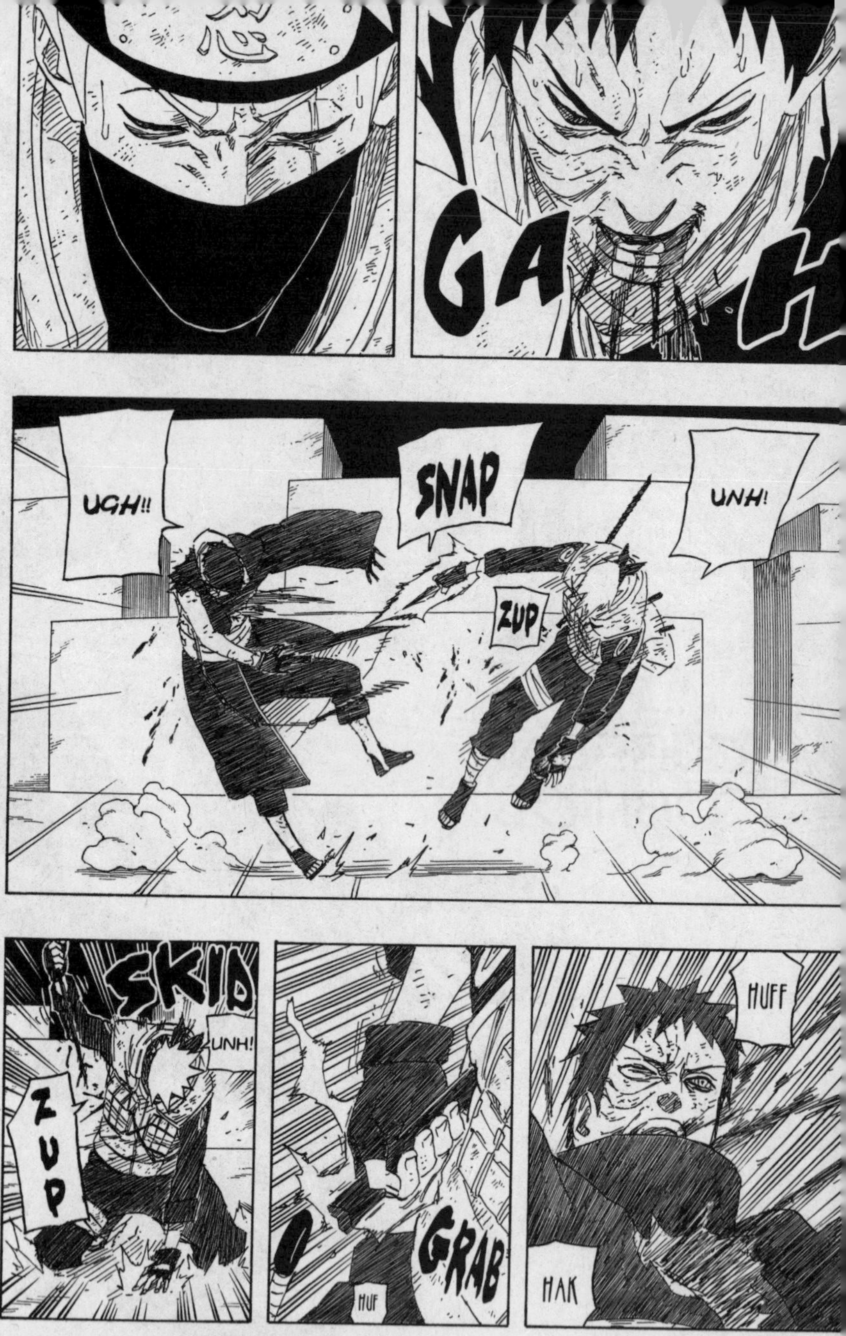
GAH
UNH!
SNAP
ZUP
UGH!!
HUFF
HAK
GRAB
HUF
SKID
UNH!
ZUP

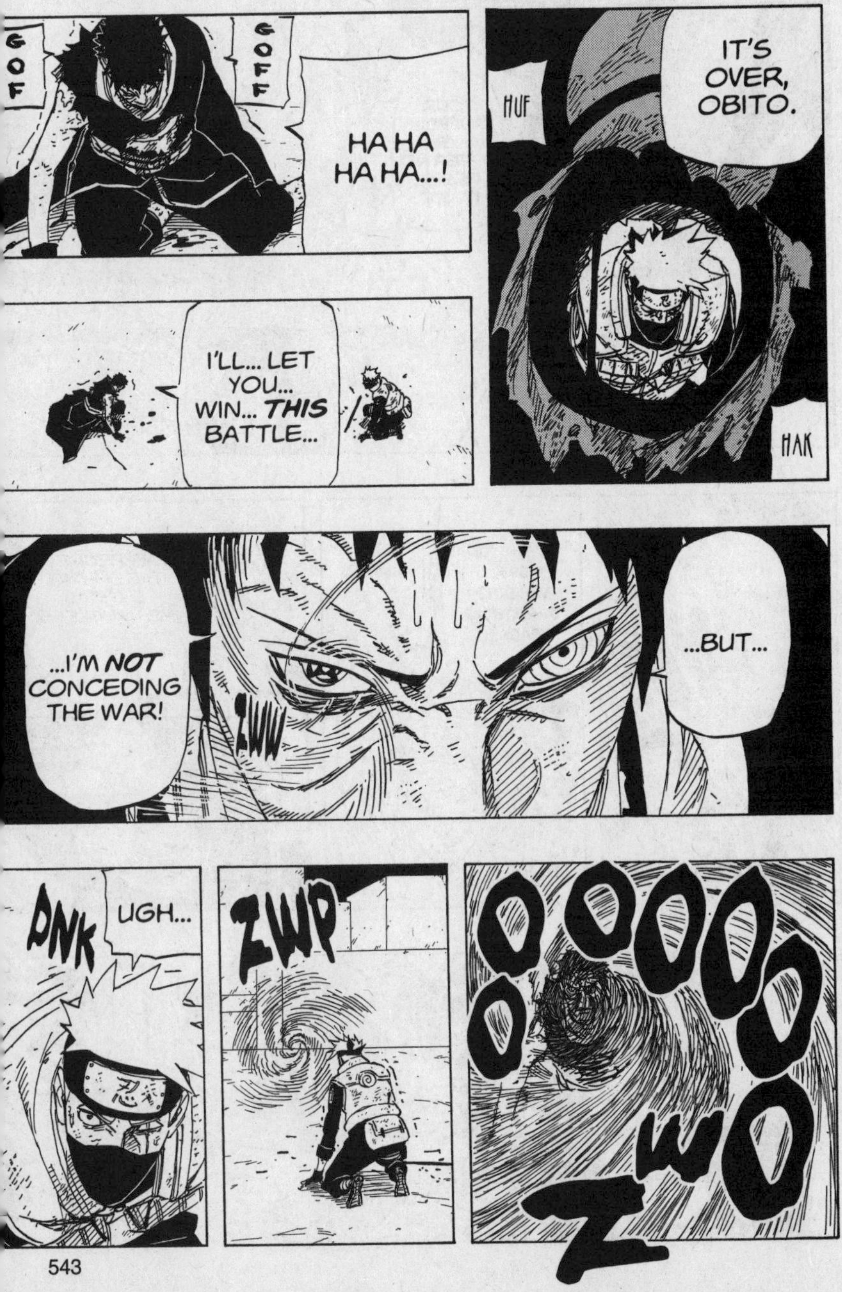
HUF
IT'S OVER, OBITO.
HAK
GOFF
GOF
HA HA HA HA...!
I'LL... LET YOU... WIN... *THIS* BATTLE...
...BUT...
...I'M *NOT* CONCEDING THE WAR!
ZWW
ZWOOOOOOOOO
ZWP
UGH...
DNK

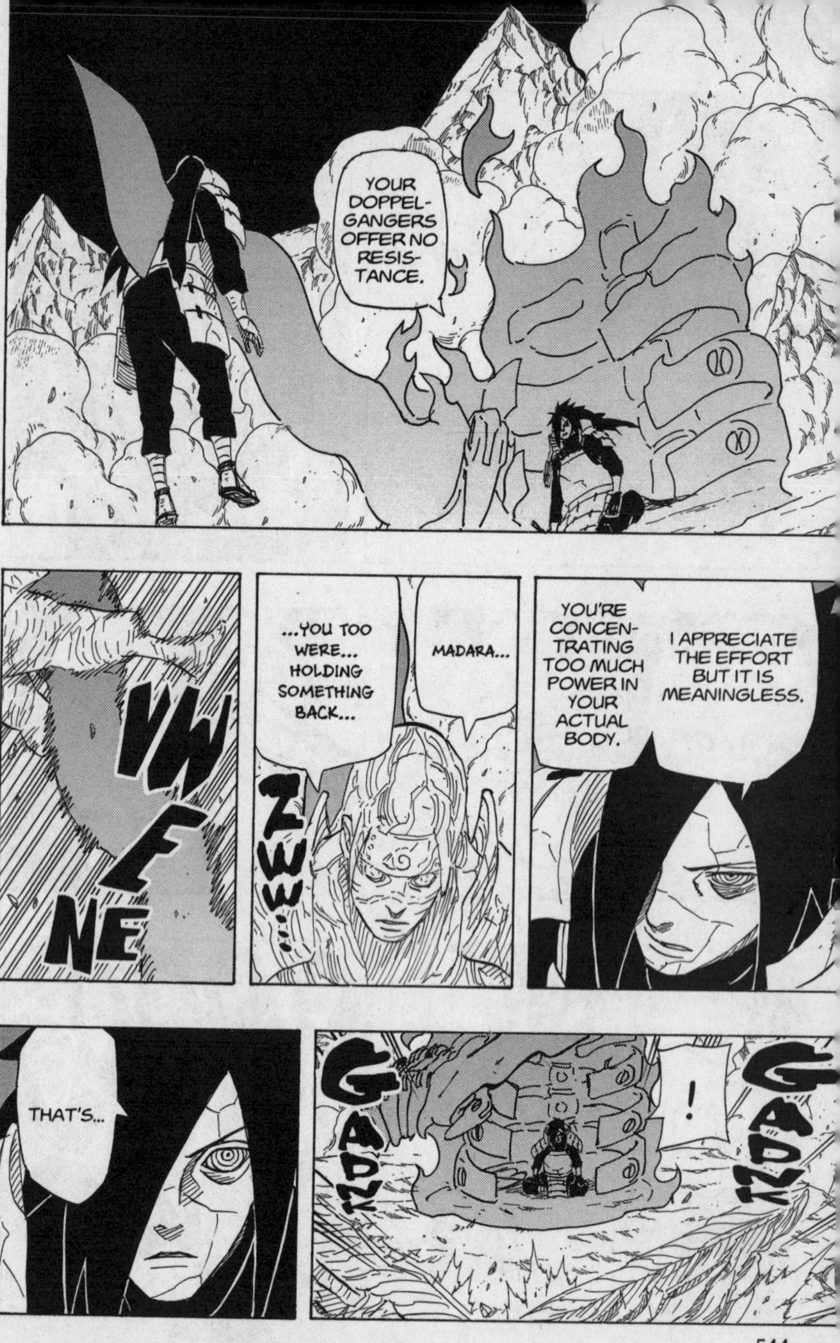
YOUR DOPPEL-GANGERS OFFER NO RESIS-TANCE.
I APPRECIATE THE EFFORT BUT IT IS MEANINGLESS.
YOU'RE CONCEN-TRATING TOO MUCH POWER IN YOUR ACTUAL BODY.
MADARA...
...YOU TOO WERE... HOLDING SOMETHING BACK...
ZWWW...
!
THAT'S...

HAK

HUFF

AHHH!

ZWOOOOOO

UNH!

WHUD

IT CANNOT BE HELPED...

FSH

I WANTED TO FIGHT HASHIRAMA BEFORE I BECAME A JINCHURIKI, BUT, OH WELL!

LOOKS LIKE THAT IS OF NO USE TO ME ANYMORE...

M-MY BODY'S...!

Z WWW OOO

SPURT SPURT

SPURT

AARGH!!

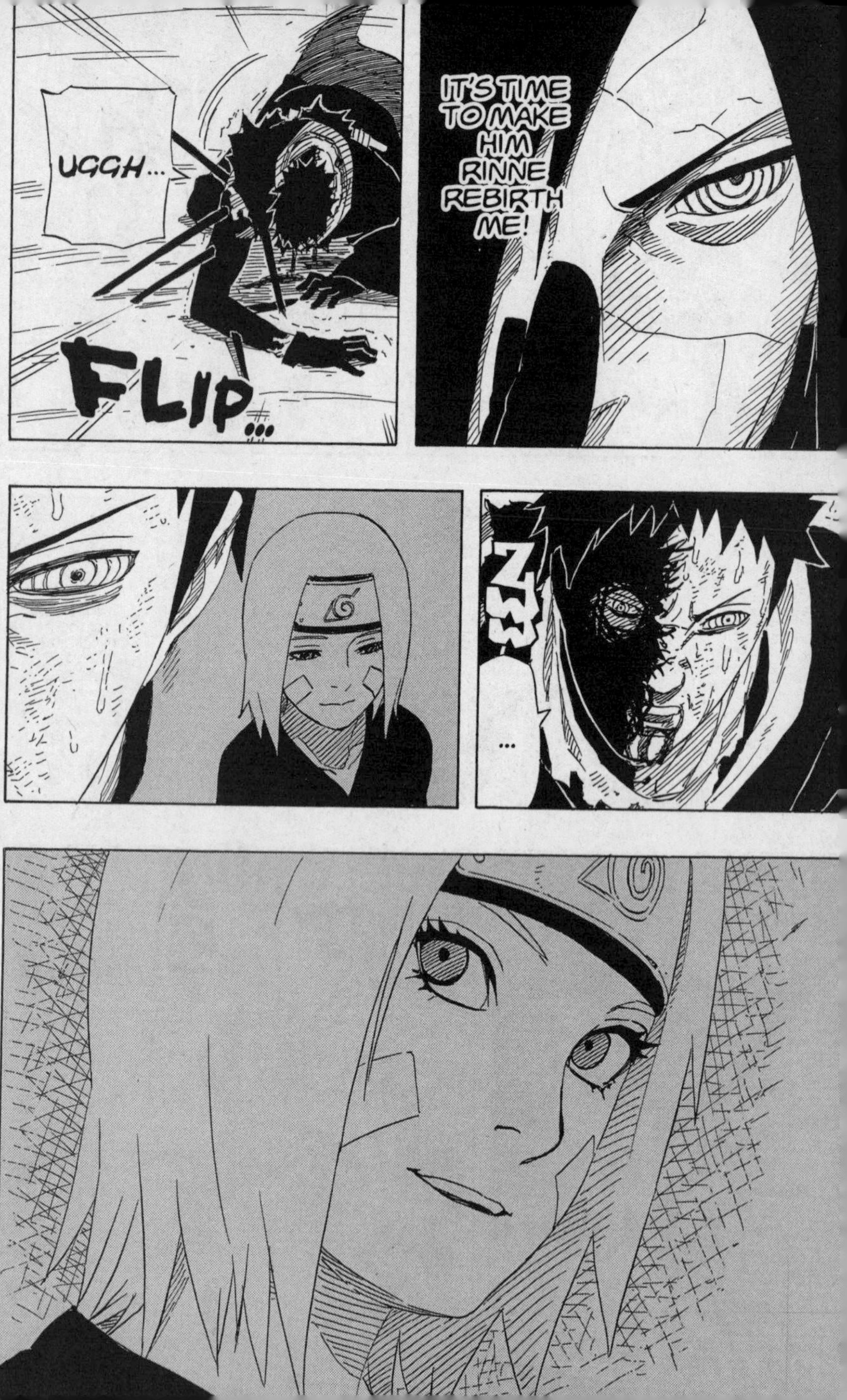
IT'S TIME TO MAKE HIM RINNE REBIRTH ME!
UGGH...
FLIP...
ZWW
...

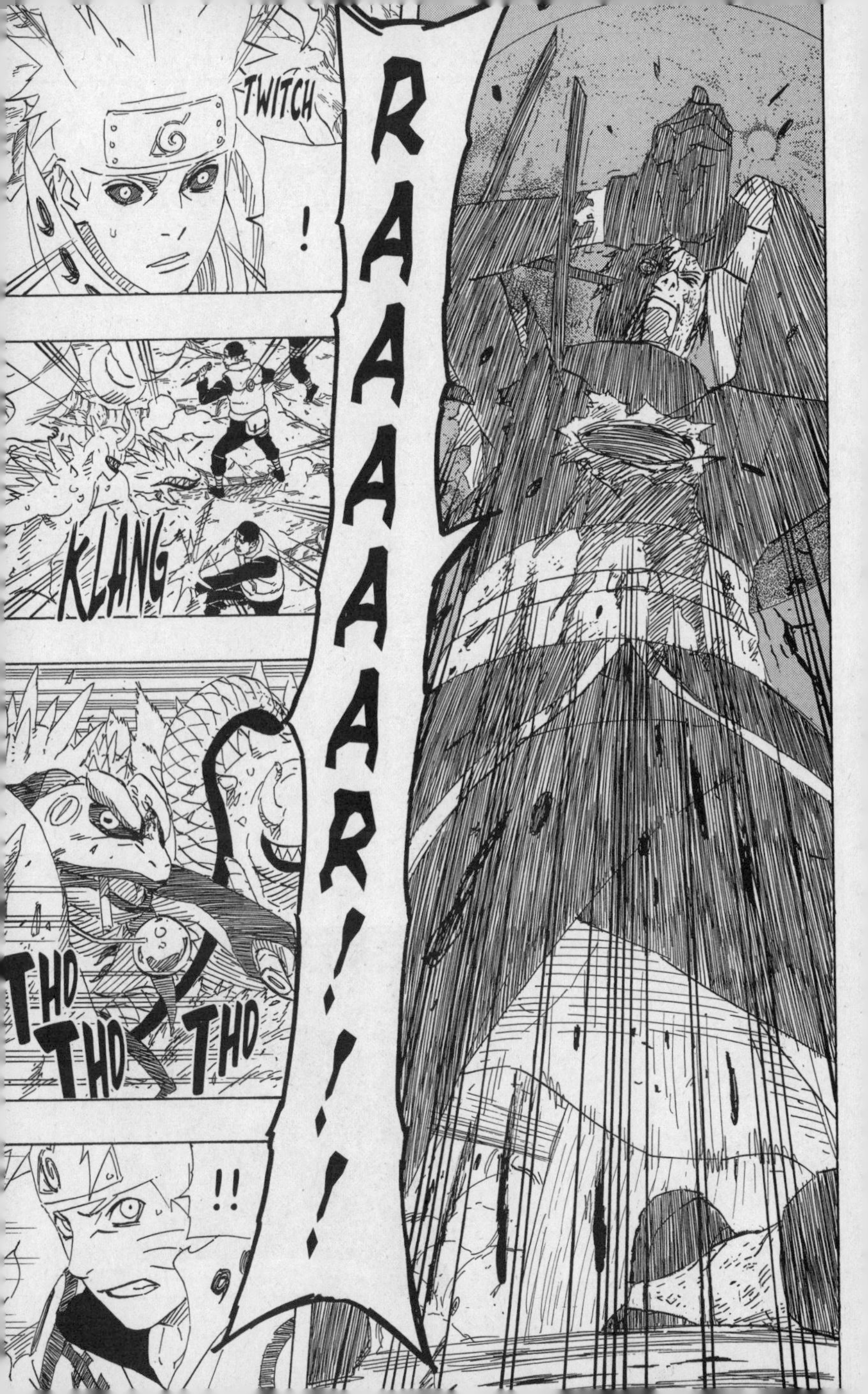
RAAAAAR!!!!
TWITCH
!
KLANG
THO THO THO
!!

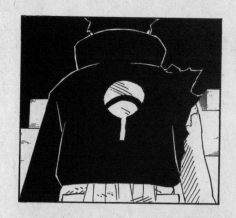

Number 637: The Ten Tails Jinchuriki

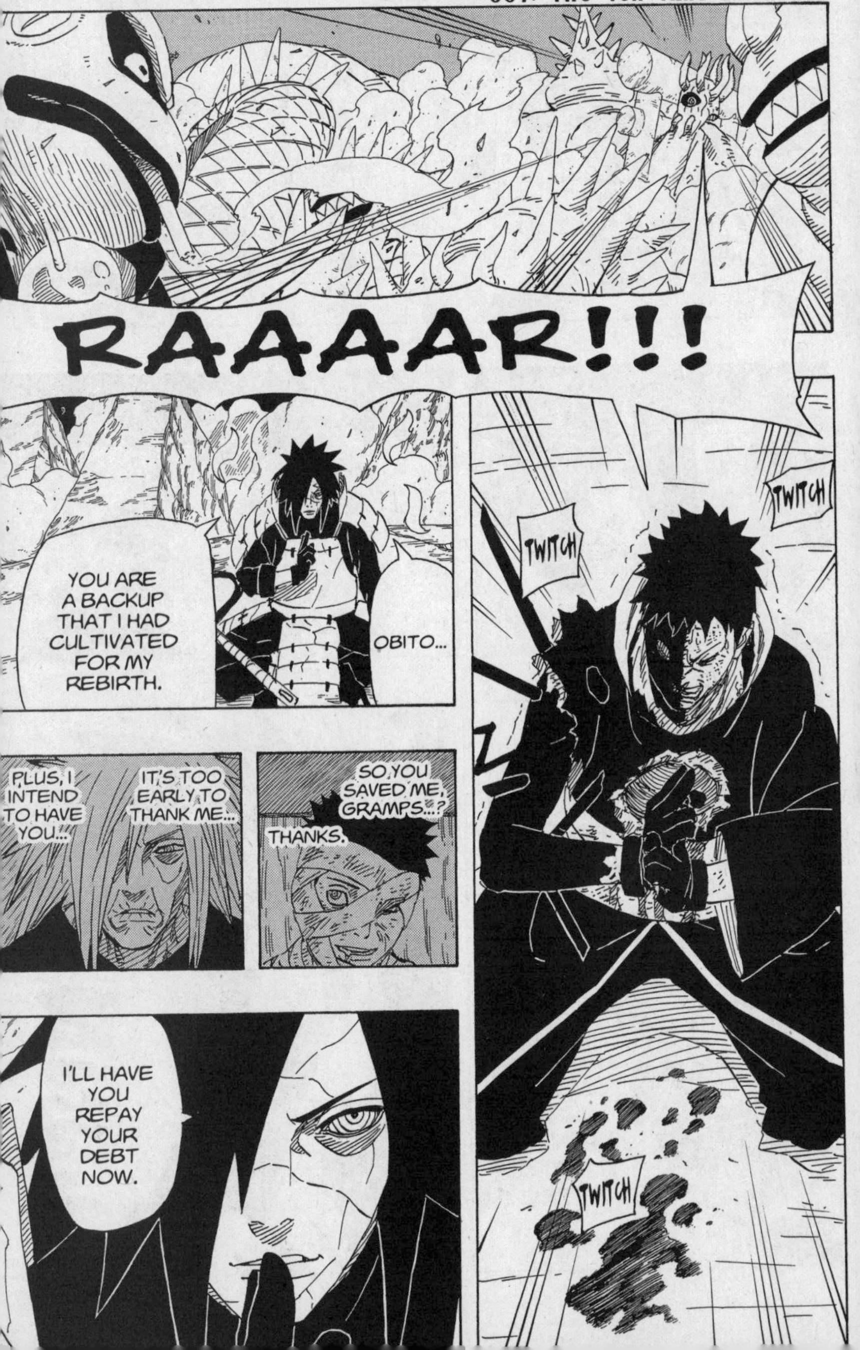
RAAAAR!!!
TWITCH
TWITCH
TWITCH
OBITO...
YOU ARE A BACKUP THAT I HAD CULTIVATED FOR MY REBIRTH.
SO YOU SAVED ME, GRAMPS...?
THANKS.
IT'S TOO EARLY TO THANK ME...
PLUS, I INTEND TO HAVE YOU...
I'LL HAVE YOU REPAY YOUR DEBT NOW.

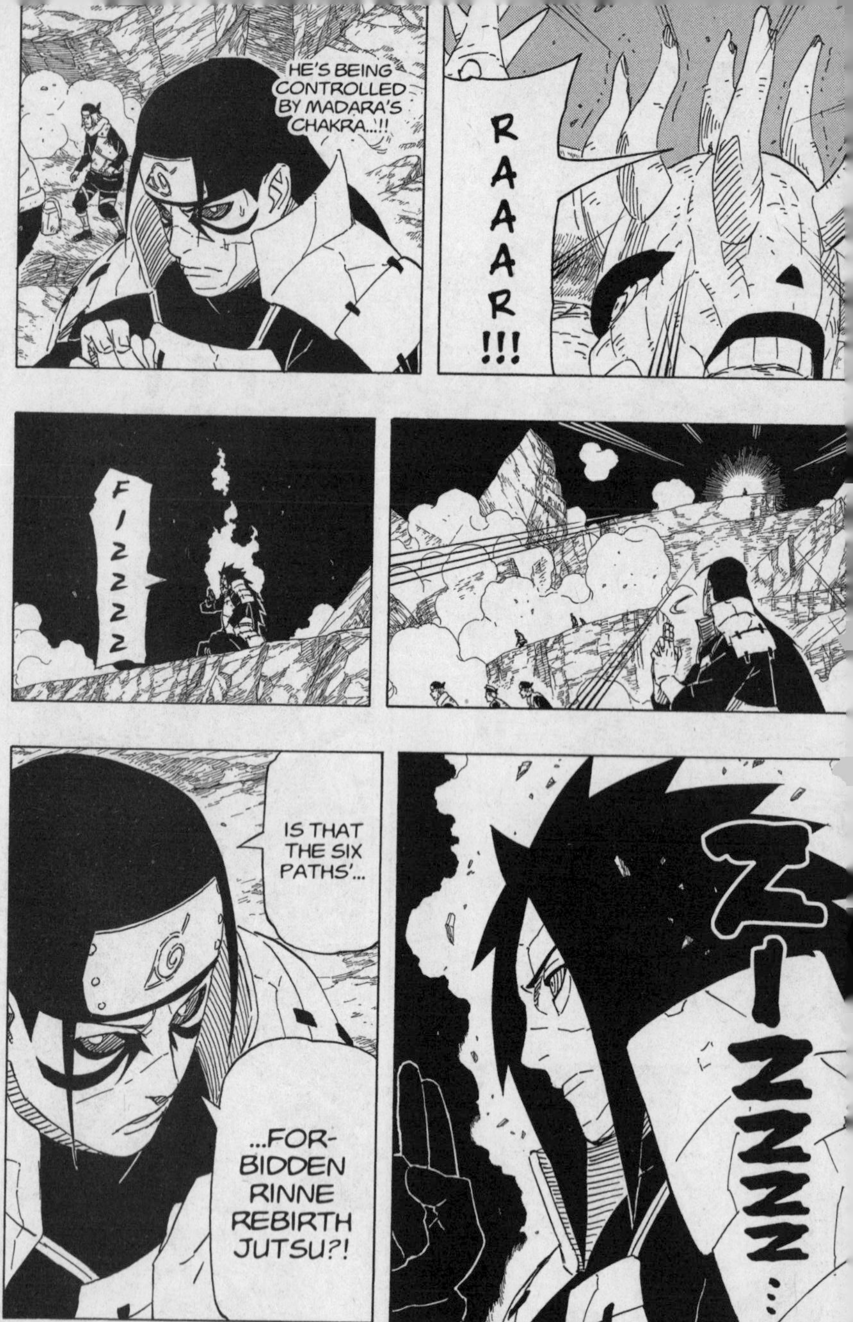
RAAAR!!!
HE'S BEING CONTROLLED BY MADARA'S CHAKRA...!!
FIZZZZ
ZZZZZZ...
IS THAT THE SIX PATHS'...
...FORBIDDEN RINNE REBIRTH JUTSU?!

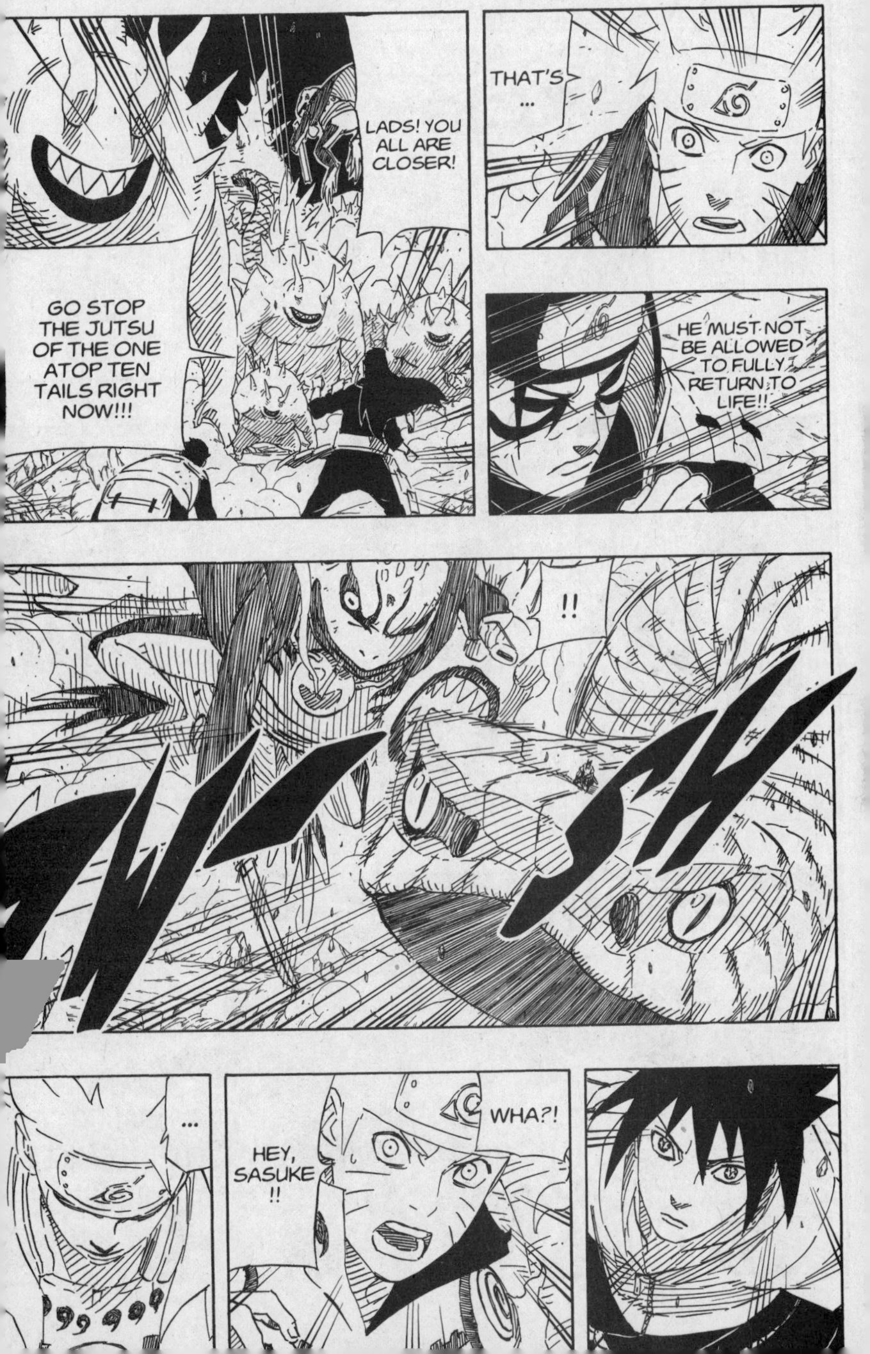
THAT'S ...
HE MUST NOT BE ALLOWED TO FULLY RETURN TO LIFE!!
LADS! YOU ALL ARE CLOSER!
GO STOP THE JUTSU OF THE ONE ATOP TEN TAILS RIGHT NOW!!!
!!
WHA?!
HEY, SASUKE !!
...

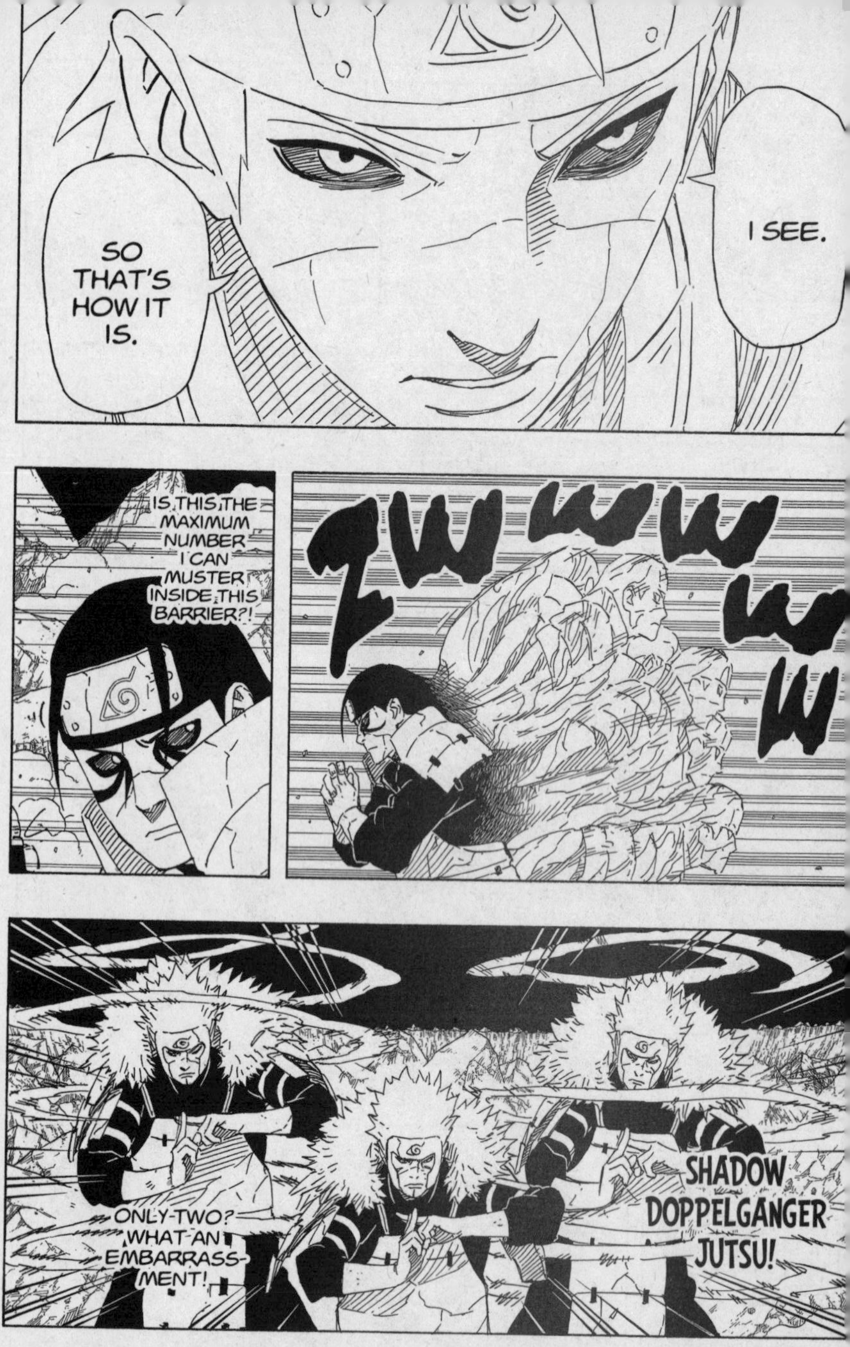

I SEE.
SO THAT'S HOW IT IS.
ZWWWWWW
IS THIS THE MAXIMUM NUMBER I CAN MUSTER INSIDE THIS BARRIER?!
SHADOW DOPPELGANGER JUTSU!
ONLY TWO? WHAT AN EMBARRASS-MENT!

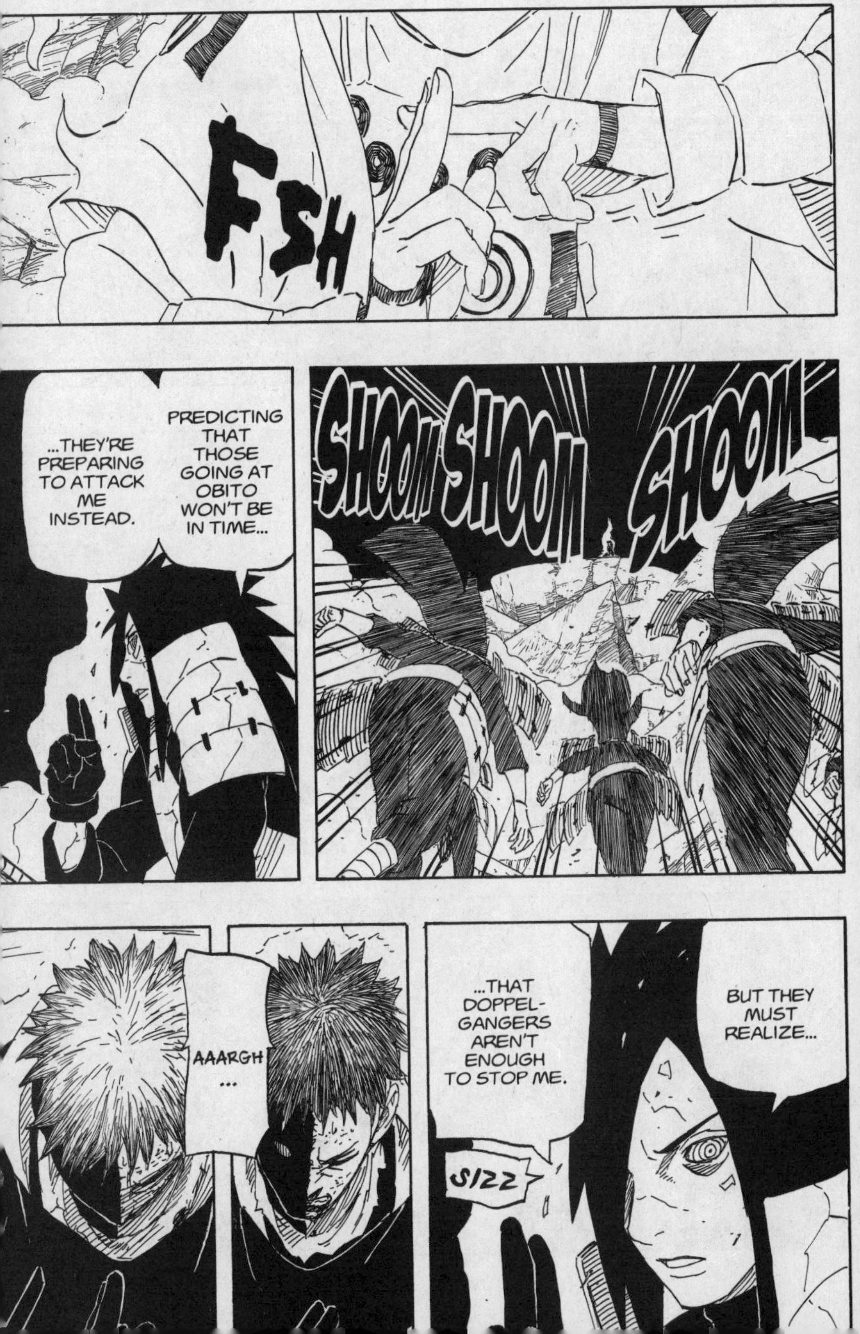
FSH
SHOOM SHOOM
SHOOM
PREDICTING THAT THOSE GOING AT OBITO WON'T BE IN TIME...
...THEY'RE PREPARING TO ATTACK ME INSTEAD.
BUT THEY MUST REALIZE...
...THAT DOPPEL-GANGERS AREN'T ENOUGH TO STOP ME.
SIZZ
AAARGH...

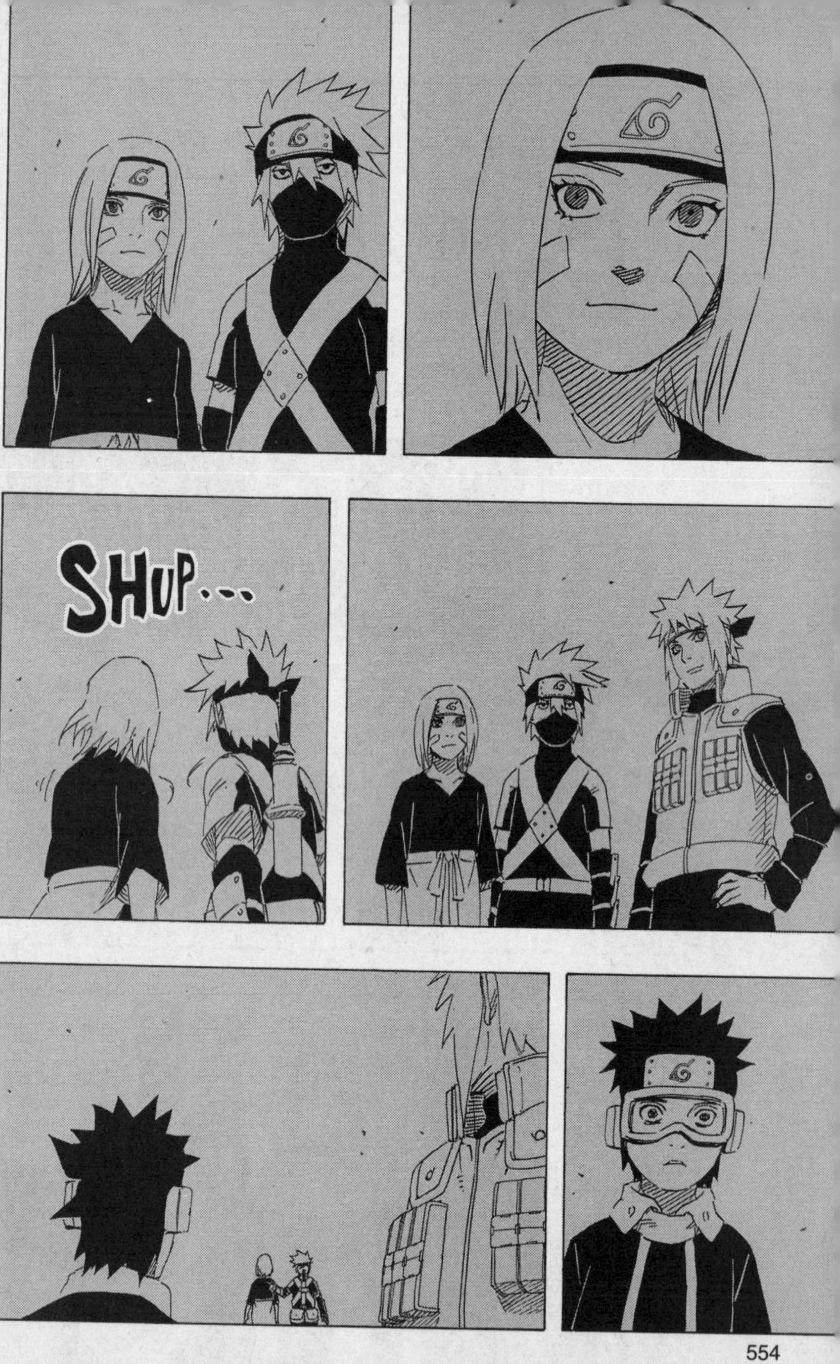
SHUP...

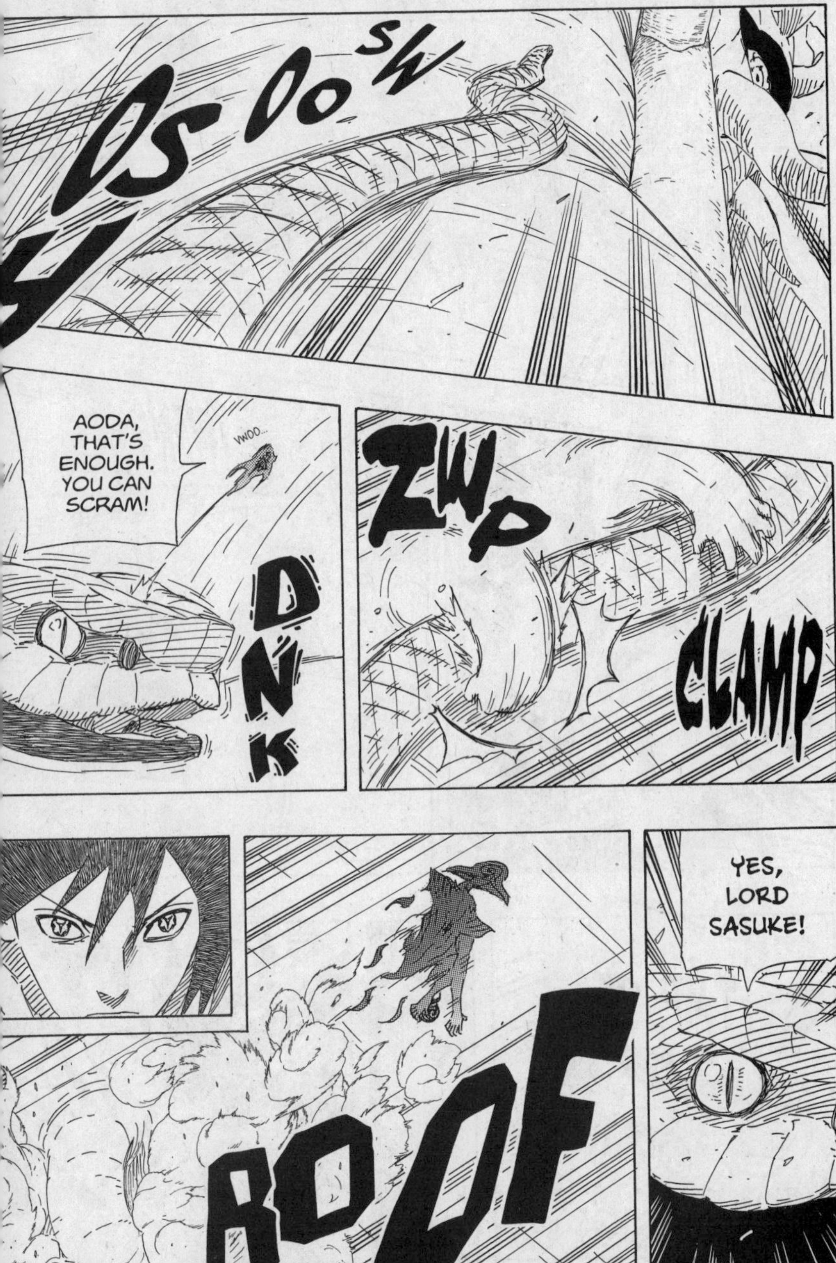
SWOOSH
ZWP
CLAMP
AODA, THAT'S ENOUGH. YOU CAN SCRAM!
VWOO...
DNK
YES, LORD SASUKE!
BOOF

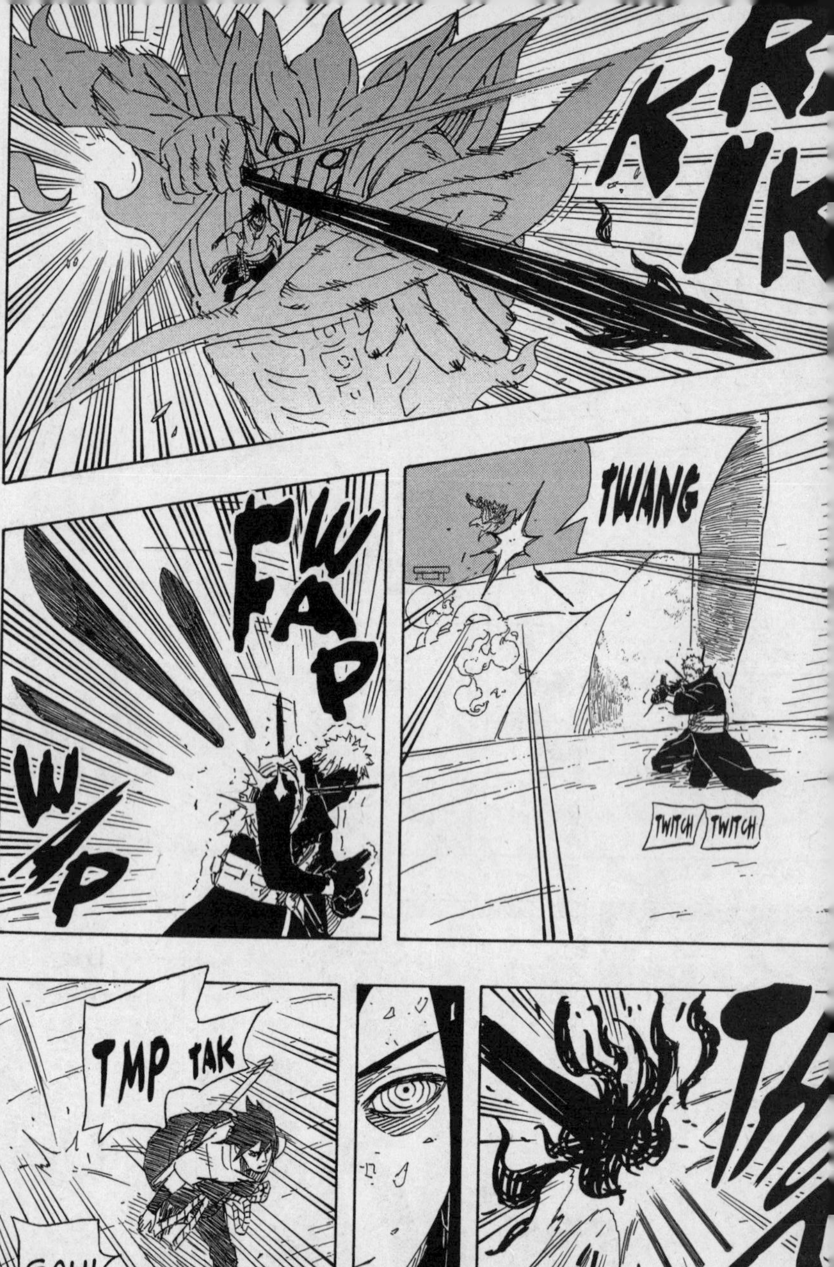
TWANG
TWITCH TWITCH
FWAP
WAP
TMP TAK
GAH!

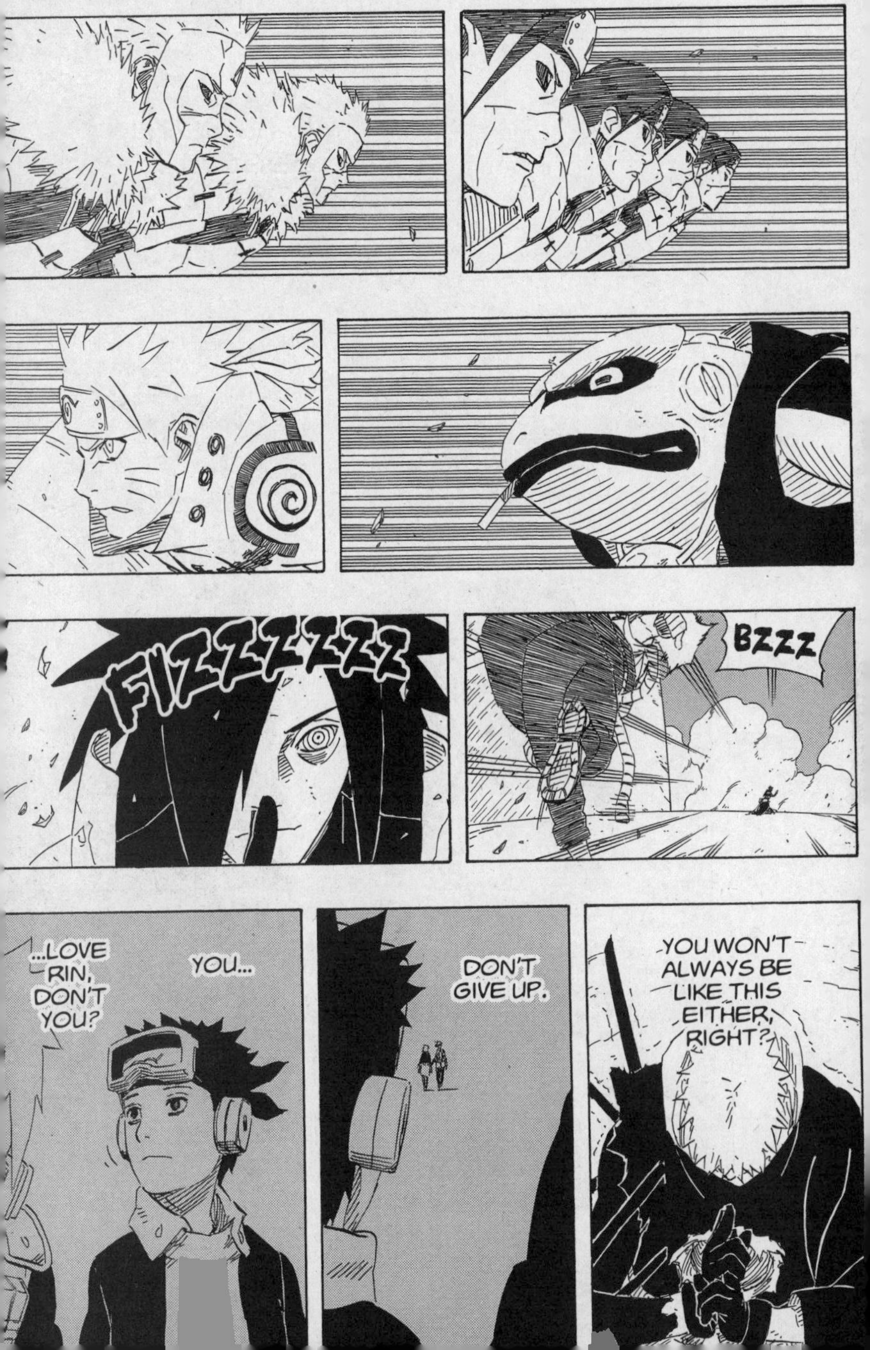
BZZZ
FIZZZZZZ
YOU WON'T ALWAYS BE LIKE THIS EITHER, RIGHT?
DON'T GIVE UP.
YOU...
...LOVE RIN, DON'T YOU?

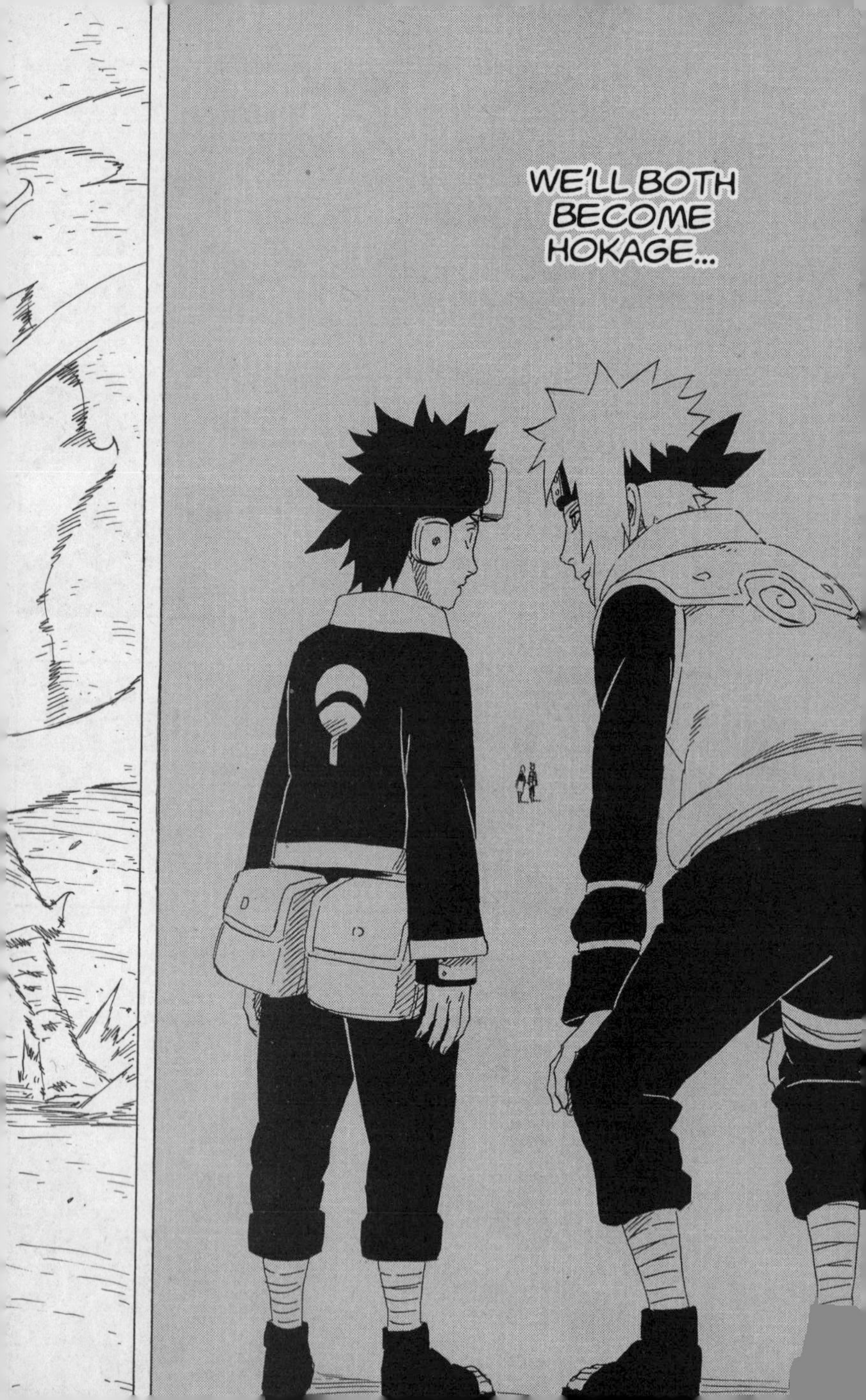
WE'LL BOTH BECOME HOKAGE...

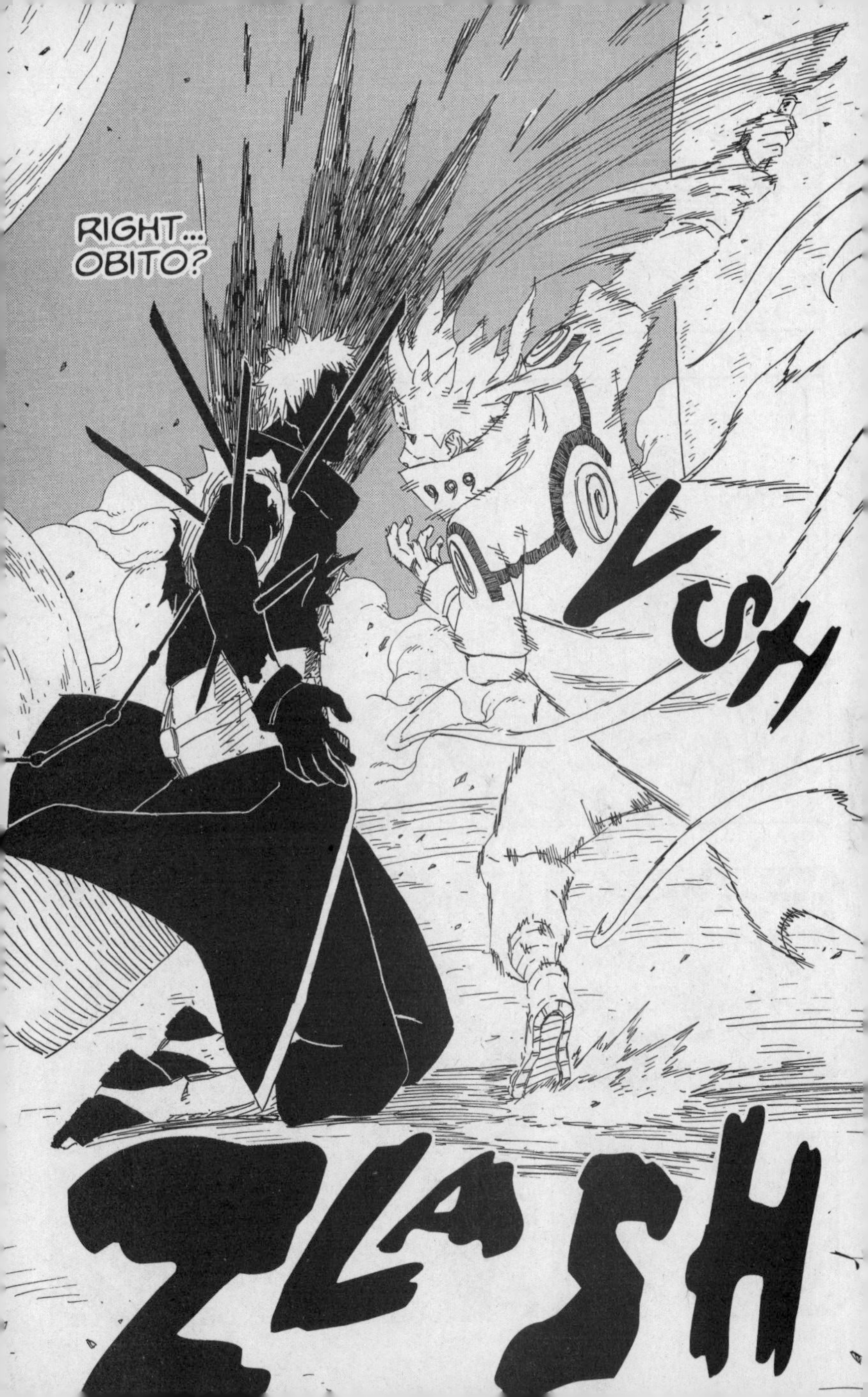
RIGHT... OBITO?
VSH
ZLASH

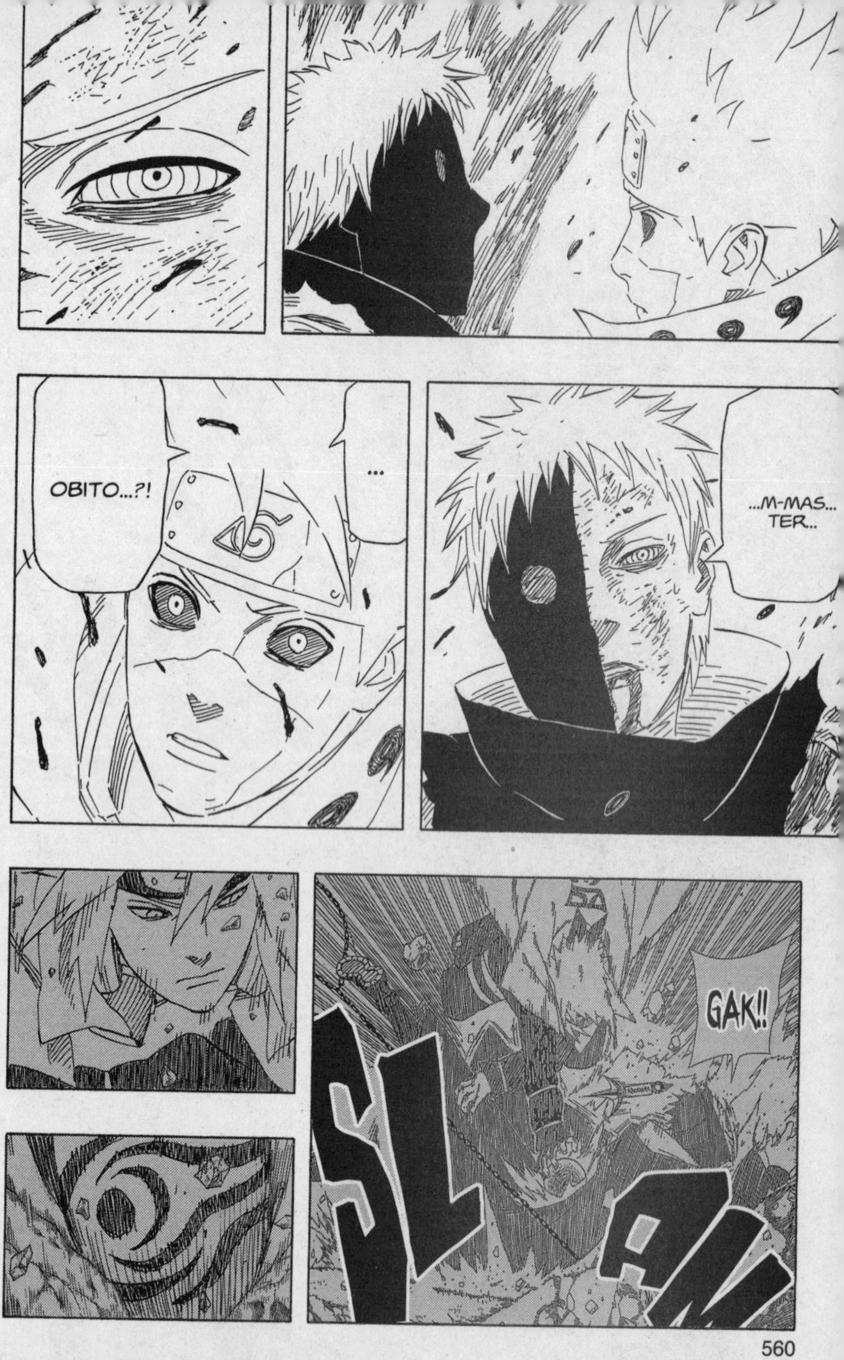
...M-MAS...
TER...
...
OBITO...?!
GAK!!
SLAM!!

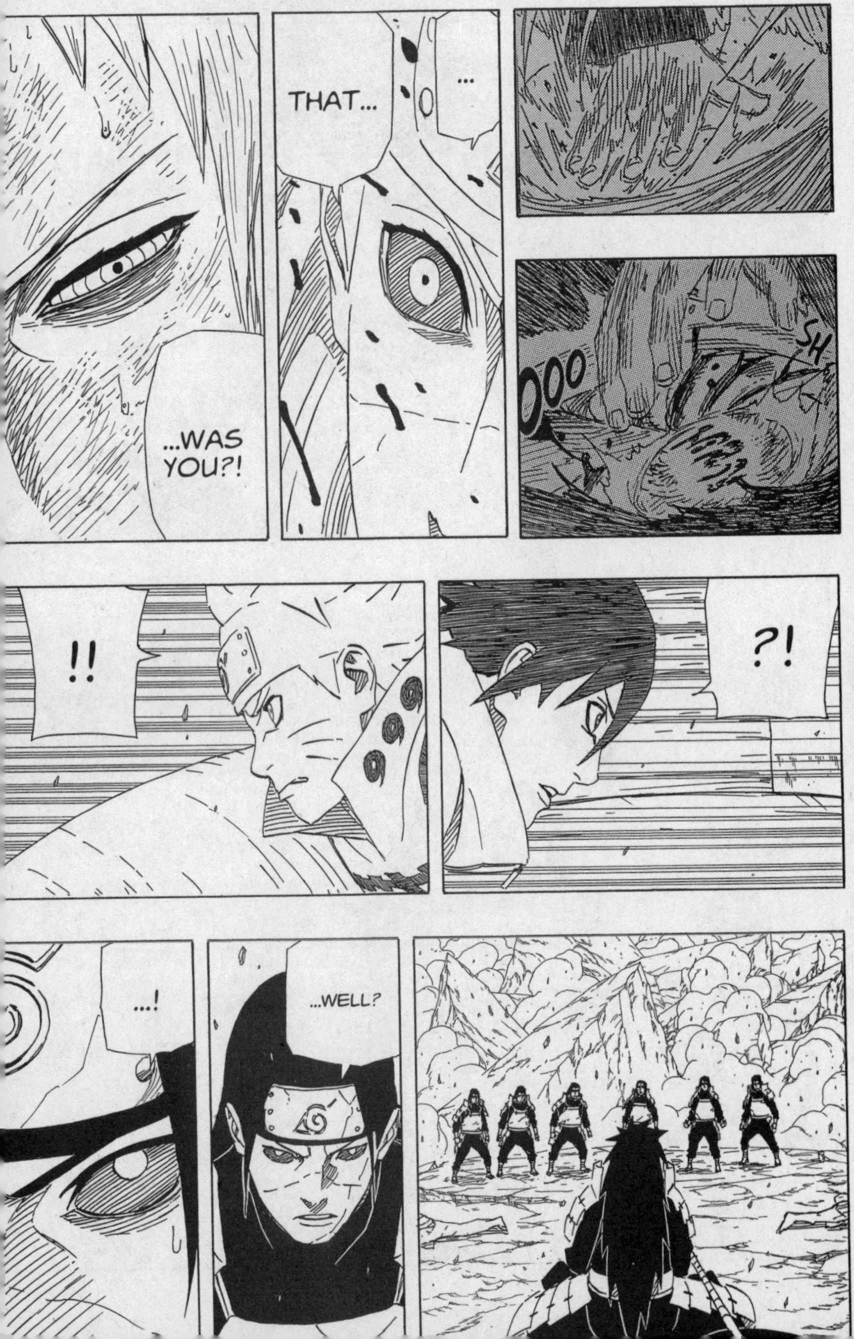
SH
OOO
...
THAT...
...WAS YOU?!
?!
!!
...WELL?
...!

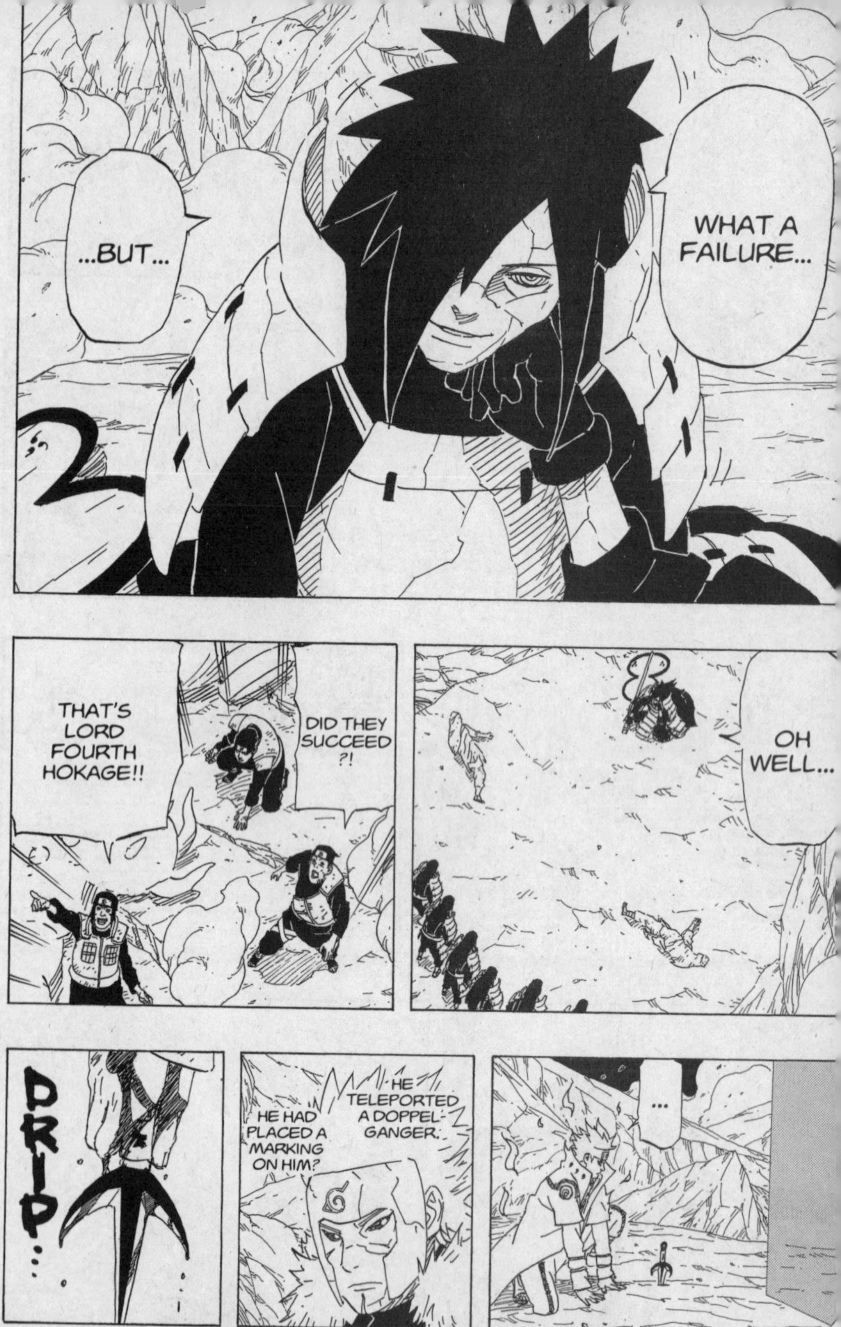
WHAT A FAILURE...
...BUT...
OH WELL...
DID THEY SUCCEED?!
THAT'S LORD FOURTH HOKAGE!!
...
HE TELEPORTED A DOPPEL-GANGER.
HE HAD PLACED A MARKING ON HIM?
DRIP...

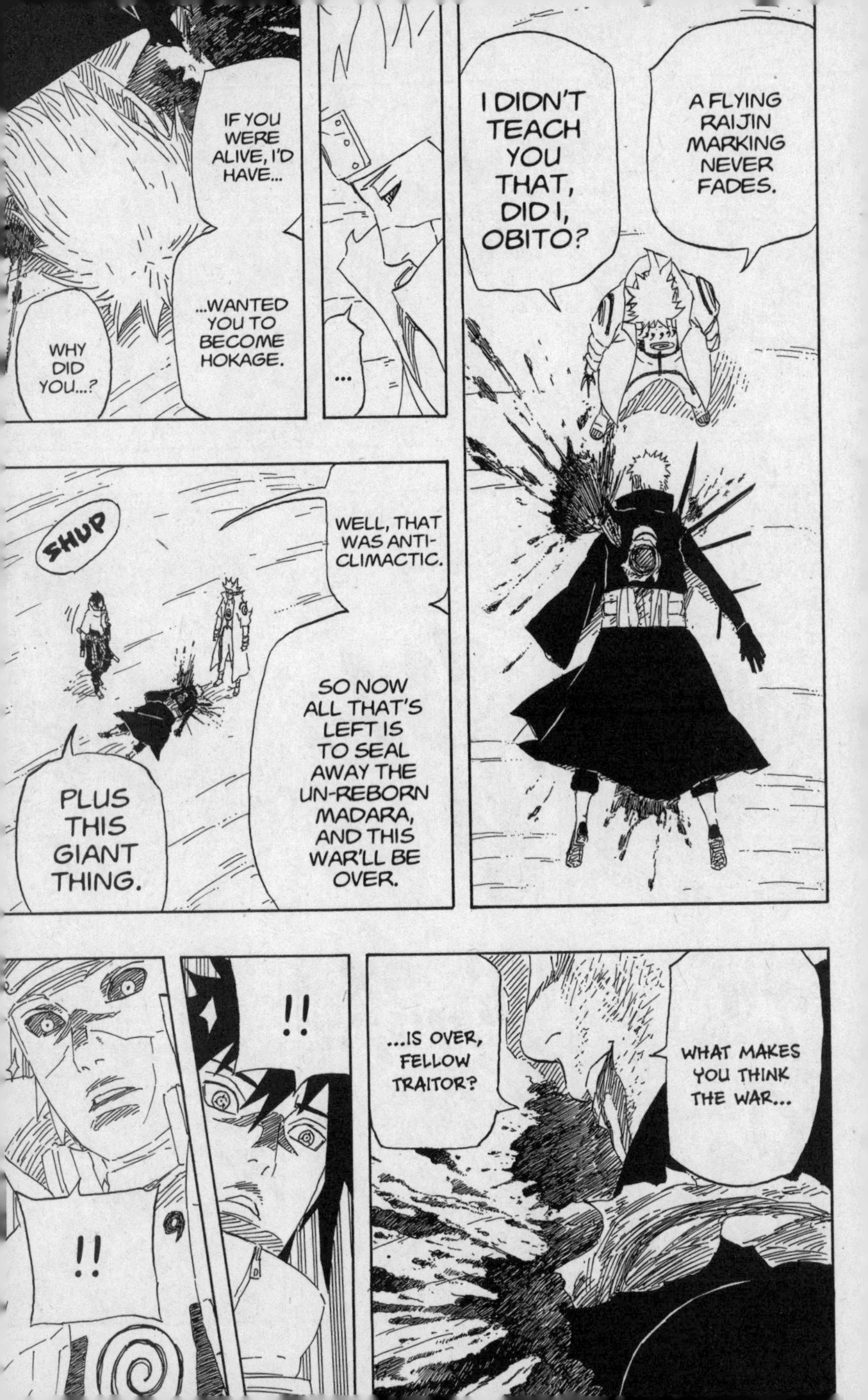
A FLYING RAIJIN MARKING NEVER FADES.
I DIDN'T TEACH YOU THAT, DID I, OBITO?
...
IF YOU WERE ALIVE, I'D HAVE...
...WANTED YOU TO BECOME HOKAGE.
WHY DID YOU...?
WELL, THAT WAS ANTI-CLIMACTIC.
SO NOW ALL THAT'S LEFT IS TO SEAL AWAY THE UN-REBORN MADARA, AND THIS WAR'LL BE OVER.
SHUP
PLUS THIS GIANT THING.
WHAT MAKES YOU THINK THE WAR...
...IS OVER, FELLOW TRAITOR?
!!
!!

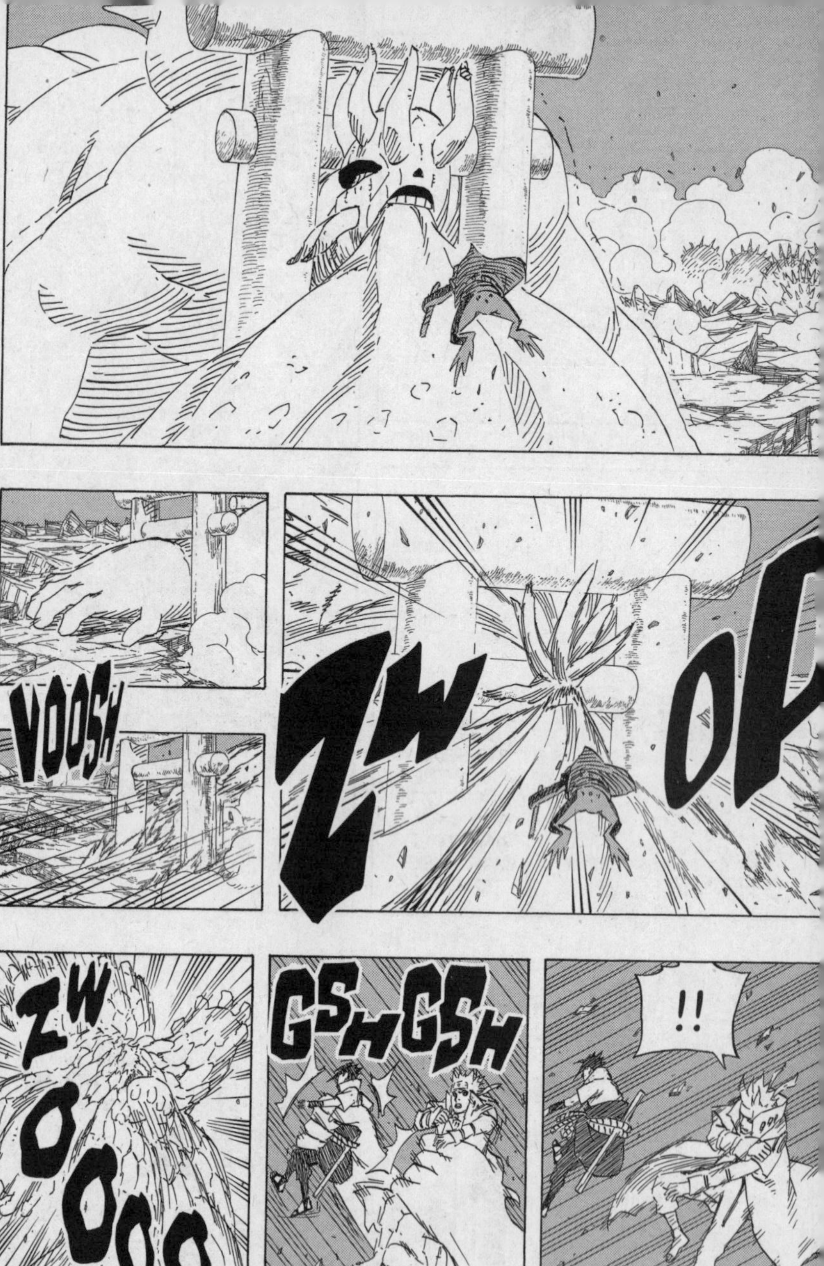
ZW
O
VOOSH
!!
GSH GSH
ZWOOOO

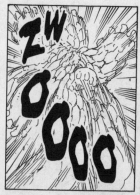

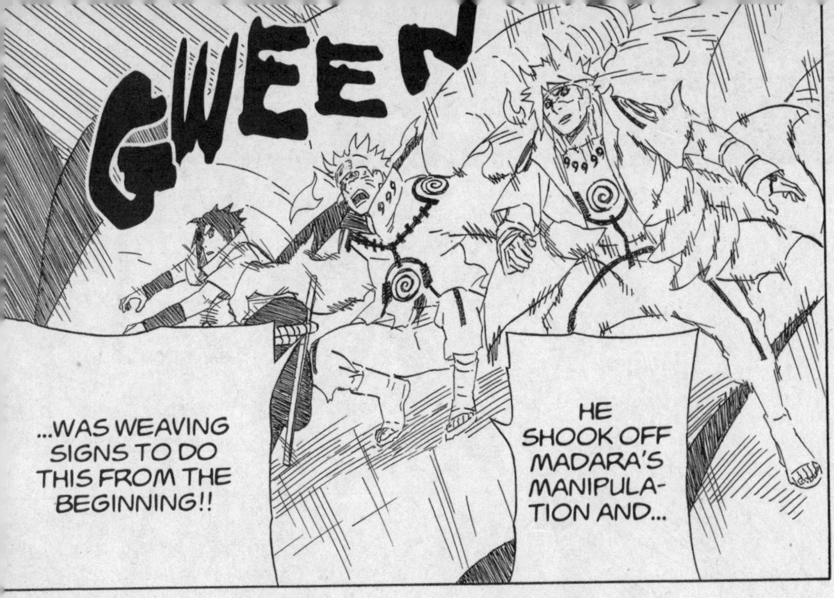
GWEEN
HE SHOOK OFF MADARA'S MANIPULATION AND...
...WAS WEAVING SIGNS TO DO THIS FROM THE BEGINNING!!

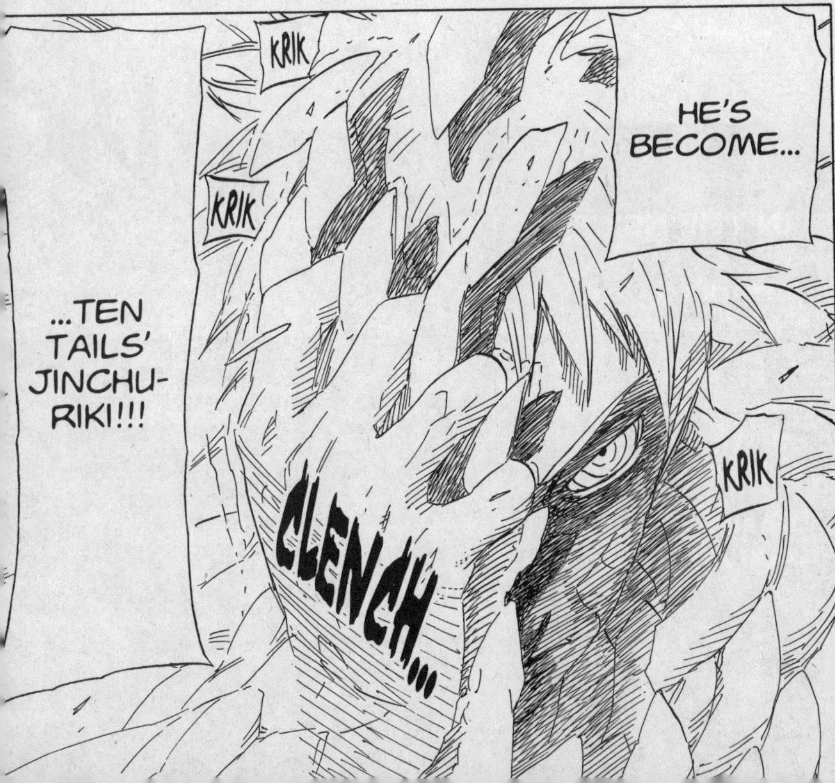
HE'S BECOME...
...TEN TAILS' JINCHURIKI!!!
KRIK
KRIK
KRIK
CLENCH...

IN THE NEXT VOLUME...

ASSAULT

Obito has shocked the ninja world by absorbing Ten Tails into himself and transforming into the ultimate Jinchuriki. Even as the Shinobi Alliance's resolve begins to falter in the face of Obito's overwhelming power, Naruto refuses to give in. But how can he turn the tables with the odds so stacked against him? Can Naruto and Sasuke work together long enough to lead the ninja world to victory?!

NARUTO 3-IN-1 EDITION VOLUME 23 AVAILABLE AUGUST 2018!

MY HERO ACADEMIA

IZUKU MIDORIYA WANTS TO BE A HERO MORE THAN ANYTHING, BUT HE HASN'T GOT AN OUNCE OF POWER IN HIM. WITH NO CHANCE OF GETTING INTO THE U.A. HIGH SCHOOL FOR HEROES, HIS LIFE IS LOOKING LIKE A DEAD END. THEN AN ENCOUNTER WITH ALL MIGHT, THE GREATEST HERO OF ALL, GIVES HIM A CHANCE TO CHANGE HIS DESTINY...

www.viz.com

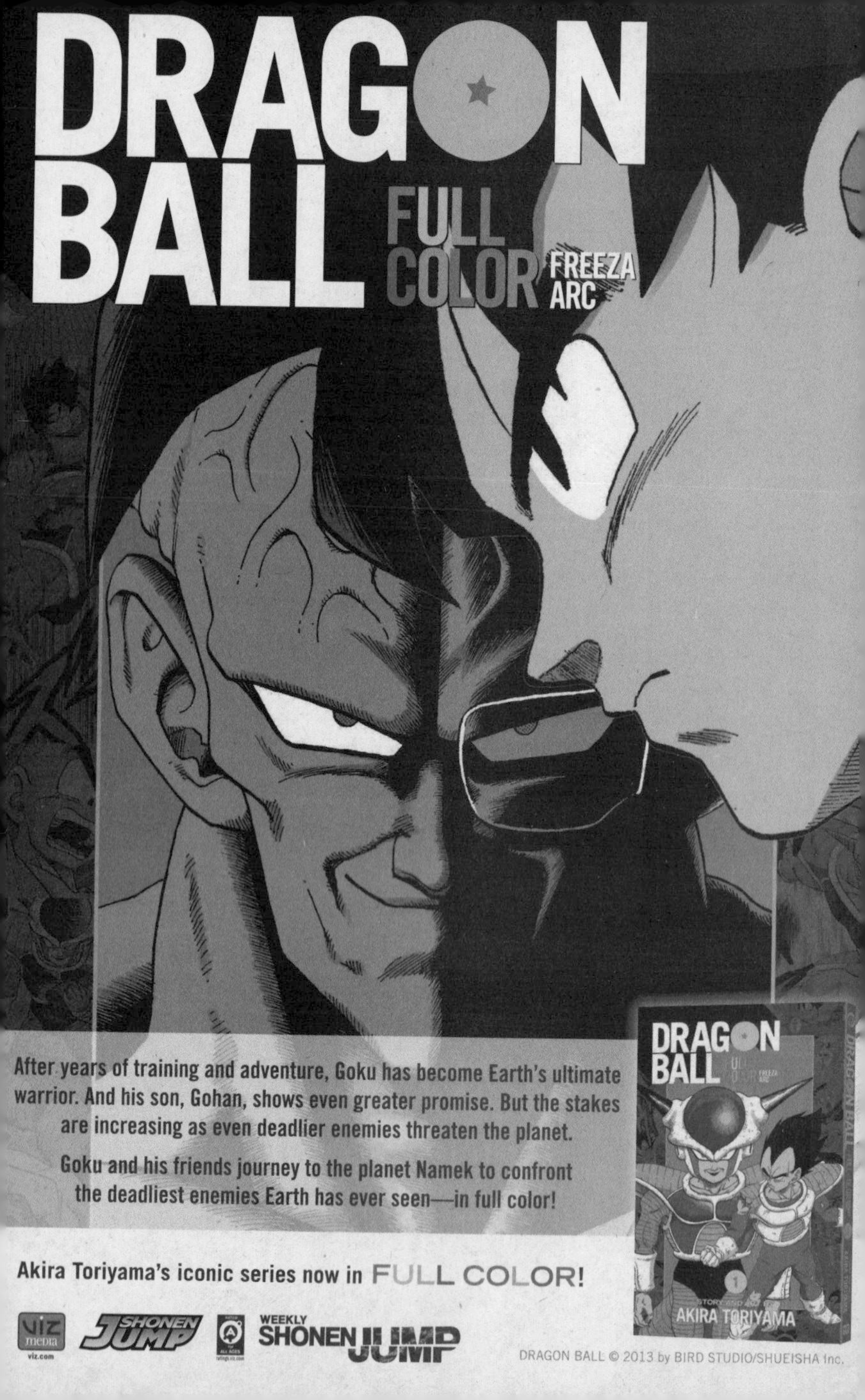
DRAGON BALL
FULL COLOR
FREEZA ARC
After years of training and adventure, Goku has become Earth's ultimate warrior. And his son, Gohan, shows even greater promise. But the stakes are increasing as even deadlier enemies threaten the planet.
Goku and his friends journey to the planet Namek to confront the deadliest enemies Earth has ever seen—in full color!
Akira Toriyama's iconic series now in FULL COLOR!
DRAGON BALL
FREEZA ARC
AKIRA TORIYAMA
viz media
viz.com
SHONEN JUMP
WEEKLY SHONEN JUMP
DRAGON BALL © 2013 by BIRD STUDIO/SHUEISHA Inc.

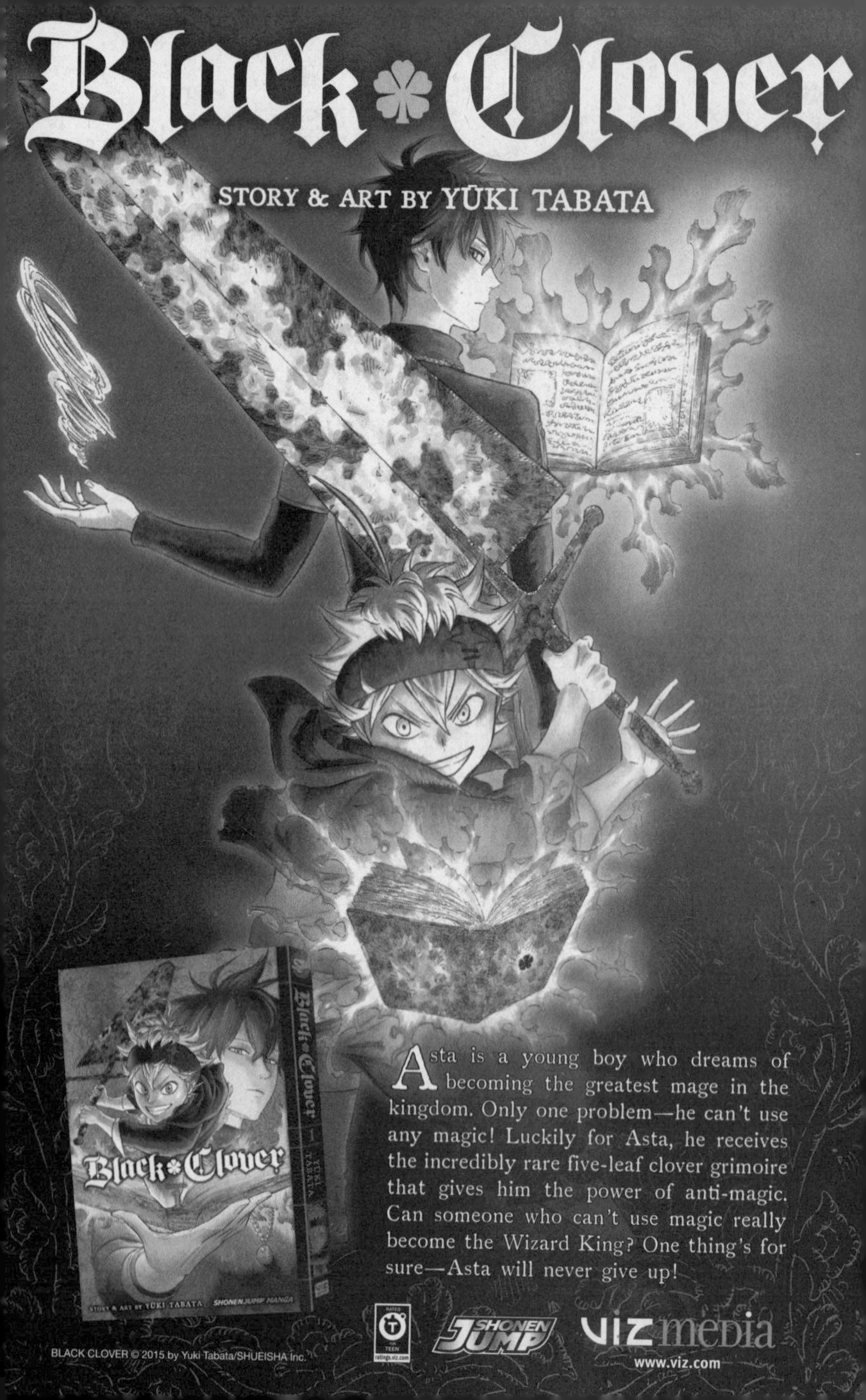
Black*Clover
STORY & ART BY YŪKI TABATA
Black*Clover
STORY & ART BY YUKI TABATA
SHONEN JUMP MANGA
Asta is a young boy who dreams of becoming the greatest mage in the kingdom. Only one problem—he can't use any magic! Luckily for Asta, he receives the incredibly rare five-leaf clover grimoire that gives him the power of anti-magic. Can someone who can't use magic really become the Wizard King? One thing's for sure—Asta will never give up!
RATED T FOR TEEN
ratings.viz.com
SHONEN JUMP
VIZ media
www.viz.com
BLACK CLOVER © 2015 by Yuki Tabata/SHUEISHA Inc.

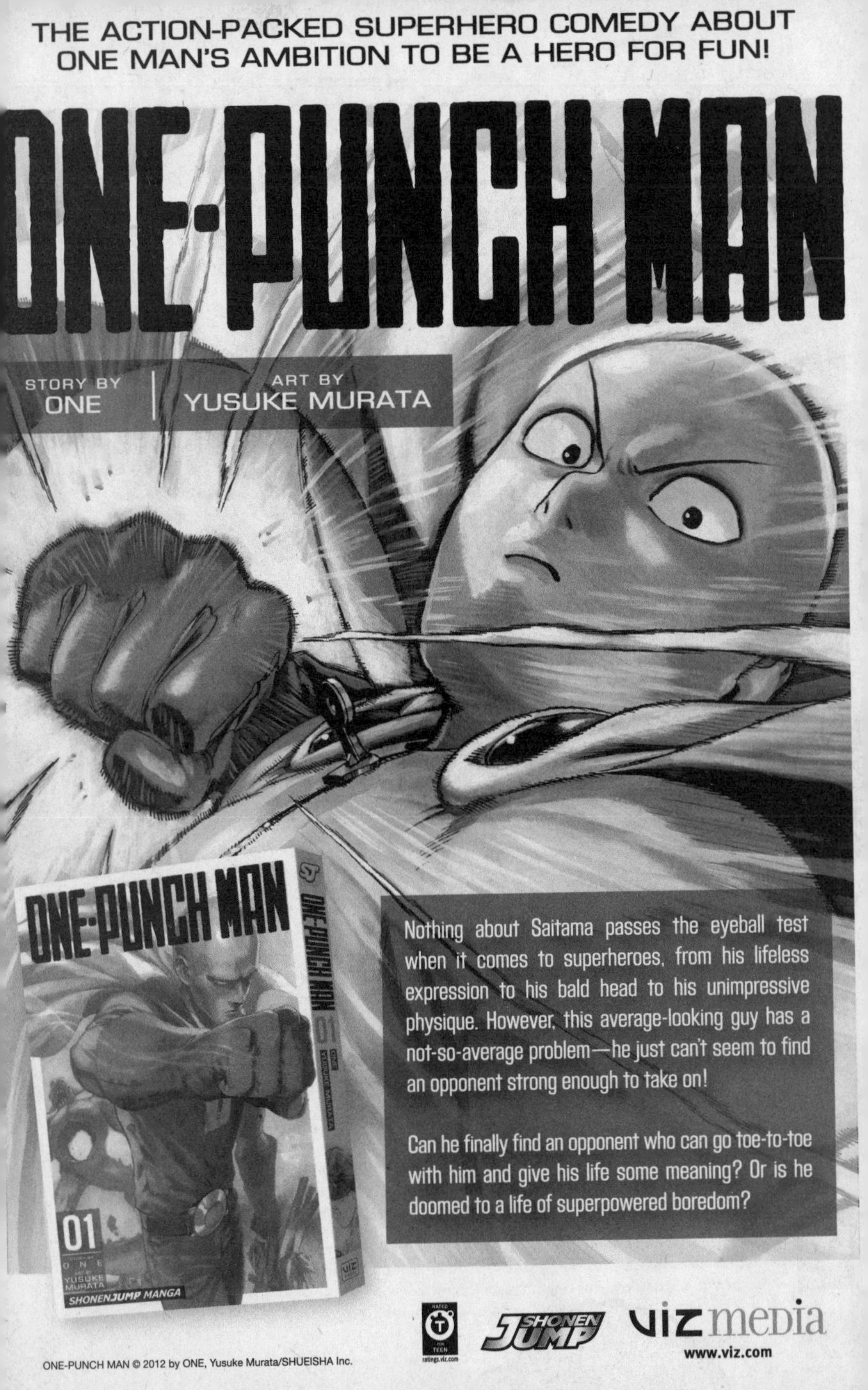
THE ACTION-PACKED SUPERHERO COMEDY ABOUT ONE MAN'S AMBITION TO BE A HERO FOR FUN!
ONE-PUNCH MAN
STORY BY ONE
ART BY YUSUKE MURATA
ONE-PUNCH MAN
01
ONE
YUSUKE MURATA
SHONENJUMP MANGA
Nothing about Saitama passes the eyeball test when it comes to superheroes, from his lifeless expression to his bald head to his unimpressive physique. However, this average-looking guy has a not-so-average problem—he just can't seem to find an opponent strong enough to take on!
Can he finally find an opponent who can go toe-to-toe with him and give his life some meaning? Or is he doomed to a life of superpowered boredom?
RATED T FOR TEEN
ratings.viz.com
SHONEN JUMP
viz media
www.viz.com
ONE-PUNCH MAN © 2012 by ONE, Yusuke Murata/SHUEISHA Inc.

Rurouni Kenshin

Story & Art by
Nobuhiro Watsuki

Slash your way through 3 volumes in one of the epic samurai classic!

Himura Battōsai was once an assassin of ferocious power during the violent upheaval of the Bakumatsu era. But as the Meiji Restoration heals the wounds of civil war, Battōsai takes up a new name and a new calling. As Himura Kenshin, he fights only to protect the honor of those in need.

WORLD TRIGGER

Story and Art by
DAISUKE ASHIHARA

DESTROY THY NEIGHBOR!

A gate to another dimension has burst
open, and invincible monsters called
Neighbors invade Earth. Osamu Mikumo
may not be the best among the elite
warriors who co-opt other-dimensional
technology to fight back, but along with his
Neighbor friend Yuma, he'll do whatever it
takes to defend life on Earth as we know it.

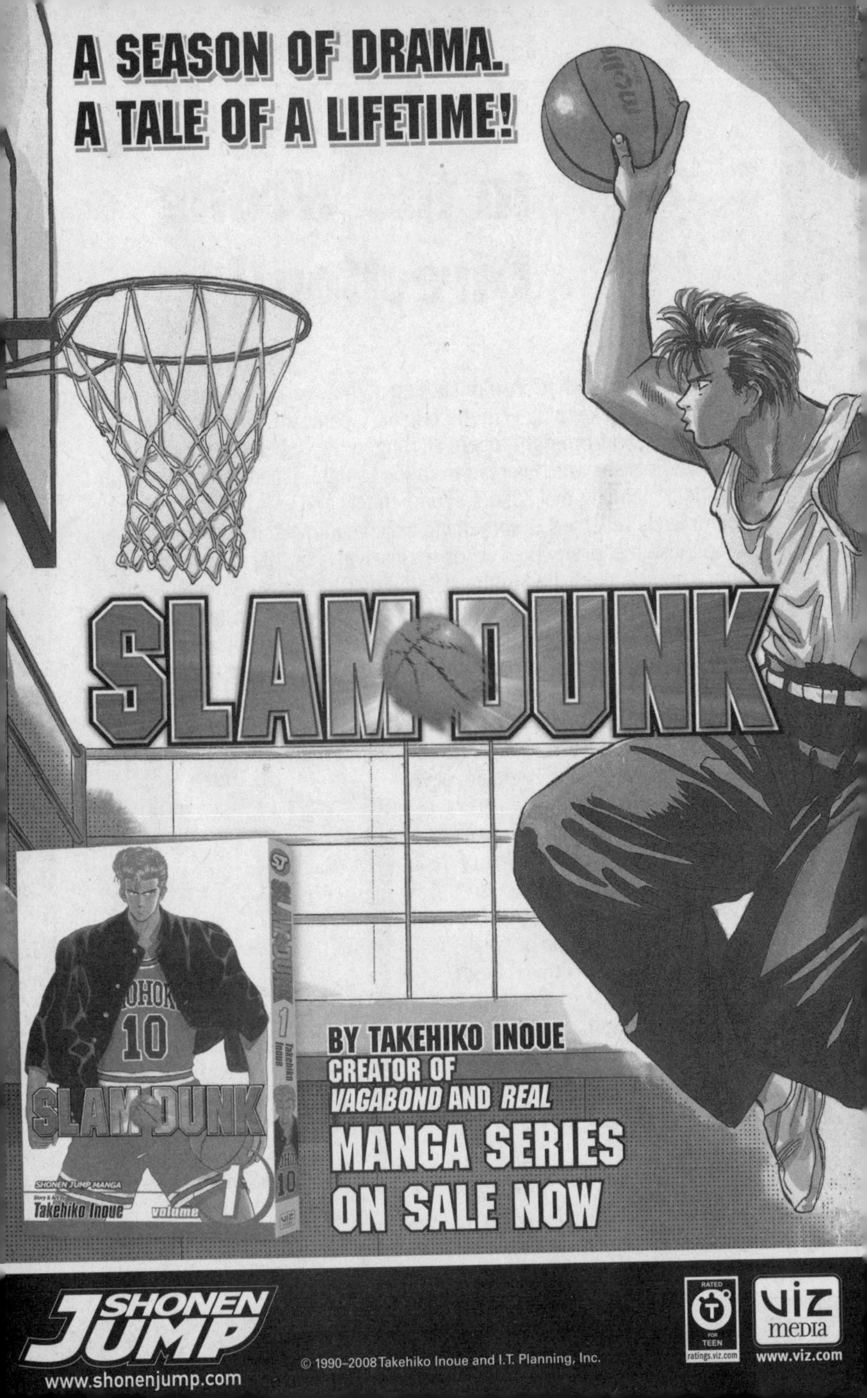
A SEASON OF DRAMA.
A TALE OF A LIFETIME!
SLAM DUNK
SLAM DUNK
SHONEN JUMP MANGA
Story & Art by
Takehiko Inoue
volume 1
BY TAKEHIKO INOUE
CREATOR OF
VAGABOND AND REAL
MANGA SERIES
ON SALE NOW
SHONEN JUMP
www.shonenjump.com
© 1990–2008 Takehiko Inoue and I.T. Planning, Inc.
RATED T FOR TEEN
ratings.viz.com
VIZ media
www.viz.com

You're Reading in the Wrong Direction!!

Whoops! Guess what? You're starting at the wrong end of the comic!

...It's true! In keeping with the original Japanese format, **Naruto** is meant to be read from right to left, starting in the upper-right corner.

Unlike English, which is read from left to right, Japanese is read from right to left, meaning that action, sound effects and word-balloon order are completely reversed... something which can make readers unfamiliar with Japanese feel pretty backwards themselves. For this reason, manga or Japanese comics published in the U.S. in English have sometimes been published "flopped"—that is, printed in exact reverse order, as though seen from the other side of a mirror.

By flopping pages, U.S. publishers can avoid confusing readers, but the compromise is not without its downside. For one thing, a character in a flopped manga series who once wore in the original Japanese version a T-shirt emblazoned with "M A Y" (as in "the merry month of") now wears one which reads "Y A M"! Additionally, many manga creators in Japan are themselves unhappy with the process, as some feel the mirror-imaging of their art alters their original intentions.

We are proud to bring you Masashi Kishimoto's **Naruto** in the original unflopped format. For now, though, turn to the other side of the book and let the ninjutsu begin...!

—Editor

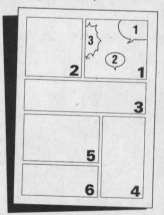